Practical Microcontroller
Engineering with
ARM® Technology

T0219364

IEEE Press
445 Hoes Lane
Piscataway, NJ 08854

IEEE Press Editorial Board
Tariq Samad, *Editor in Chief*

George W. Arnold	Vladimir Lumelsky	Linda Shafer
Dmitry Goldgof	Pui-In Mak	Zidong Wang
Ekram Hossain	Jeffrey Nanzer	MengChu Zhou
Mary Lanzerotti	Ray Perez	George Zobrist

Kenneth Moore, *Director of IEEE Book and Information Services (BIS)*

Practical Microcontroller Engineering with ARM® Technology

Ying Bai

Department of Computer Science and Engineering
Johnson C. Smith University
Charlotte, North Carolina

IEEE PRESS

WILEY

Copyright © 2016 by The Institute of Electrical and Electronics Engineers, Inc.

Published by John Wiley & Sons, Inc., Hoboken, New Jersey. All rights reserved
Published simultaneously in Canada

No part of this publication may be reproduced, stored in a retrieval system, or transmitted in any form or by
any means, electronic, mechanical, photocopying, recording, scanning, or otherwise, except as permitted
under Section 107 or 108 of the 1976 United States Copyright Act, without either the prior written permission
of the Publisher, or authorization through payment of the appropriate per-copy fee to the Copyright
Clearance Center, Inc., 222 Rosewood Drive, Danvers, MA 01923, (978) 750-8400, fax (978) 750-4470, or on
the web at www.copyright.com. Requests to the Publisher for permission should be addressed to the
Permissions Department, John Wiley & Sons, Inc., 111 River Street, Hoboken, NJ 07030, (201) 748-6011,
fax (201) 748-6008, or online at http://www.wiley.com/go/permission.

Limit of Liability/Disclaimer of Warranty: While the publisher and author have used their best efforts in
preparing this book, they make no representations or warranties with respect to the accuracy or completeness
of the contents of this book and specifically disclaim any implied warranties of merchantability or fitness for a
particular purpose. No warranty may be created or extended by sales representatives or written sales materials.
The advice and strategies contained herein may not be suitable for your situation. You should consult with a
professional where appropriate. Neither the publisher nor author shall be liable for any loss of profit or any
other commercial damages, including but not limited to special, incidental, consequential, or other damages.

For general information on our other products and services or for technical support, please contact our
Customer Care Department within the United States at (800) 762-2974, outside the United States
at (317) 572-3993 or fax (317) 572-4002.

Wiley also publishes its books in a variety of electronic formats. Some content that appears in print may
not be available in electronic formats. For more information about Wiley products, visit our web site at
www.wiley.com.

Library of Congress Cataloging-in-Publication Data is available.

ISBN: 978-1-119-05237-1

Printed in the United States of America

10 9 8 7 6 5 4 3 2 1

This book is dedicated to my wife, Yan Wang,
and to my daughter, Susan (Xue) Bai.

Contents

Preface   xxix

Acknowledgments   xxxi

Trademarks and Copyrights   xxxiii

Copyright Permissions   xxxv

About the Companion Website   xxxix

Chapter 1 Introduction to Microcontrollers and This Book   **1**

1.1   Microcontroller Configuration and Structure   2
1.2   The ARM® Cortex®M4 Microcontroller System   3
1.3   The TM4C123GH6PM Microcontroller Development Tools and Kits   4
1.4   Outstanding Features About This Book   5
1.5   Who This Book Is For   5
1.6   What This Book Covers   6
1.7   How This Book Is Organized and How to Use This Book   8
1.8   How to Use the Source Code and Sample Projects   9
1.9   Instructors and Customers Supports   11

Chapter 2 ARM® Microcontroller Architectures   **13**

2.1   Overview and Introduction   13
2.2   Introduction to ARM® Cortex®-M4 MCU   15
    2.2.1   The Architecture of ARM® Cortex®-M4 MCU   17
        2.2.1.1   The ARM® MCU Architecture   17
        2.2.1.2   The Architecture of the ARM® Cortex®-M4 Core (CPU)   20
            2.2.1.2.1   The Register Bank in the Cortex®-M4 Core   21
            2.2.1.2.2   The Special Registers in the Cortex®-M4 Core   22
        2.2.1.3   The Architecture of the Floating-Point Registers   25
2.3   The Memory Architecture   27
    2.3.1   The Memory Map   28
    2.3.2   The Stack Memory   29
    2.3.3   The Program Models and States   32
    2.3.4   The Memory Protection Unit (MPU)   33
2.4   The Nested Vectored Interrupt Controller (NVIC) Architecture   34
    2.4.1   The Nested Vectored Interrupt Controller (NVIC) Features   35
    2.4.2   Exception and Interrupt Sources   35
    2.4.3   Exception Priority Levels and Mask Registers   35

2.4.4   Respond and Process Exceptions and Interrupts   36
2.4.5   Exception and Interrupt Vector Table   37
2.5   The Debug Architecture   37
2.6   Introduction to Tiva™ C Series ARM® Cortex®-M4 MCU-TM4C123GH6PM   38
   2.6.1   TM4C123GH6PM Microcontroller Overview   39
   2.6.2   TM4C123GH6PM Microcontroller On-Chip Memory Map   40
      2.6.2.1   The System Peripherals   42
      2.6.2.2   The On-Chip Peripherals   42
      2.6.2.3   Interfaces to External Parallel Peripherals   44
      2.6.2.4   Interfaces to External Serial Peripherals   44
   2.6.3   TM4C123GH6PM Microcontroller General-Purpose Input–Output (GPIO) Module   44
      2.6.3.1   The System Clock   45
      2.6.3.2   The General Configuration Procedures for GPIO Peripherals   47
      2.6.3.3   Tiva™ TM4C123GH6PM GPIO Architecture   47
         2.6.3.3.1   The Port Control Register (GPIOPCTL)   49
         2.6.3.3.2   The Data Control Registers   49
         2.6.3.3.3   The Mode Control Registers   49
         2.6.3.3.4   The Commit Control Registers   51
         2.6.3.3.5   The Interrupt Control Registers   51
         2.6.3.3.6   The Pad Control Registers   52
         2.6.3.3.7   The Identification Registers   55
      2.6.3.4   The Initialization and Configuration of TM4C123GH6PM GPIO Ports   55
   2.6.4   TM4C123GH6PM Microcontroller System Controls   57
      2.6.4.1   Device Identification   58
      2.6.4.2   Reset Control   59
         2.6.4.2.1   The Power-On Reset   60
         2.6.4.2.2   The External Reset   61
         2.6.4.2.3   The Brown-Out Reset (BOR)   61
         2.6.4.2.4   The Software Reset   61
         2.6.4.2.5   The Watchdog Timer Reset   62
      2.6.4.3   Non-Maskable Interrupt Control   63
      2.6.4.4   Clock Control   64
      2.6.4.5   Other System Controls   67
         2.6.4.5.1   The Run Mode   67
         2.6.4.5.2   The Sleep Mode   68
         2.6.4.5.3   The Deep-Sleep Mode   68
         2.6.4.5.4   The Hibernate Mode   68
         2.6.4.5.5   The System Timer (SysTick)   69
         2.6.4.5.6   System Control Block (SCB)   70
      2.6.4.6   System Clock Initialization and Configuration   71
2.7   Introduction to Tiva™ C Series LaunchPad™ TM4C123GXL Evaluation Board   72
2.8   Introduction to EduBASE ARM® Trainer   77
2.9   Chapter Summary   77
Homework   79

Chapter 3 ARM® Microcontroller Development Kits   **83**

3.1   Overview and Introduction   83
3.2   The Entire Tiva™ TM4C123G-based Development System   84
3.3   Download and Install Development Suite and Specified Firmware   86
3.4   Introduction to the Integrated Development Environment—Keil® MDK
      µVersion5   87
    3.4.1   The Keil® MDK-ARM® for the MDK-Cortex-M Family   88
    3.4.2   General Development Flow with MDK-ARM®   89
    3.4.3   Warming Up Keil® MDK Cortex-M Kit with Example Projects   91
    3.4.4   The Functions of the Keil® MDK-ARM® µVersion®5 GUI   95
        3.4.4.1   The File Menu   97
        3.4.4.2   The Edit Menu   98
        3.4.4.3   The Project Menu   101
        3.4.4.4   The Flash Menu   121
        3.4.4.5   The Debug Menu   121
        3.4.4.6   The Peripherals Menu   123
        3.4.4.7   The Tools Menu   124
        3.4.4.8   The SVCS Menu   125
        3.4.4.9   The Window Menu   126
        3.4.4.10   The Help Menu   126
3.5   Embedded Software Development Procedure   127
3.6   The Keil® ARM®-MDK µVision5 Debugger and Debug Process   128
    3.6.1   The ARM® µVision5 Debug Architecture   129
    3.6.2   The ARM® Debug Adaptor and Debug Adaptor Driver   130
    3.6.3   Tiva™ C Series LaunchPad™ Debug Adaptor and Debug Adaptor Driver   132
    3.6.4   The ARM® µVersion5 Debug Process   133
    3.6.5   The ARM® Trace Feature   134
        3.6.5.1   Some Useful Trace Features Provided by Cortex®-M4 MCU   135
    3.6.6   The ARM® Instruction Set Simulator   136
    3.6.7   The ARM® Programs Running from SRAM   137
    3.6.8   ARM® Optimizations   139
3.7   The TivaWare™ for C Series Software Suite   140
    3.7.1   The TivaWare™ C Series Software Package   142
        3.7.1.1   The Peripheral Driver Library (DriverLib)   143
        3.7.1.2   The Boot Loader   144
        3.7.1.3   The Utilities   144
    3.7.2   TivaWare™ C Series for TM4C123G LaunchPad™ Evaluation Kit   145
        3.7.2.1   TivaWare™ C Series LaunchPad™ Evaluation Software
                Package   145
3.8   The TivaWare™ for C Series Utilities and Other Supports   147
    3.8.1   Additional Utilities Provided by TivaWare™ for C Series   148
        3.8.1.1   The LMFlash Programmer   148
        3.8.1.2   The UniFlash   149
        3.8.1.3   The FTDI Drivers   149
        3.8.1.4   The IQMath Library   149
        3.8.1.5   TivaWare™ for C Series CMSIS Support   150

3.9   Program Examples   151
3.10   Chapter Summary   152
Homework   152

Chapter 4 ARM® Microcontroller Software and Instruction Set   **155**

4.1   Overview and Introduction   155
4.2   Introduction to ARM® Cortex®-M4 Software Development Structure   156
4.3   Introduction to ARM® Cortex®-M4 Assembly Instruction Set   157
  4.3.1   The ARM® Cortex®-M4 Assembly Language Syntax   158
  4.3.2   The ARM® Cortex®-M4 Pseudo Instructions   160
  4.3.3   The ARM® Cortex®-M4 Addressing Modes   161
    4.3.3.1   The Immediate Offset Addressing Mode   162
      4.3.3.1.1   Regular Immediate Offset Addressing Mode   162
      4.3.3.1.2   Pre-Indexed Immediate Offset Addressing Mode   163
      4.3.3.1.3   Post-Indexed Immediate Offset Addressing Mode   163
      4.3.3.1.4   Regular Immediate Offset Addressing Mode with Unprivileged
                  Access   163
    4.3.3.2   The Register Offset Addressing Mode   164
    4.3.3.3   The PC-Relative Addressing Mode   165
    4.3.3.4   Load and Store Multiple Registers Addressing Mode   167
    4.3.3.5   PUSH and POP Register Addressing Mode   170
    4.3.3.6   Load and Store Register Exclusive Addressing Mode   170
    4.3.3.7   Inherent Addressing Mode   171
    4.3.3.8   Addressing Mode Summary   171
  4.3.4   The ARM® Cortex®-M4 Instruction Set Categories   172
    4.3.4.1   Data Moving Instructions   172
    4.3.4.2   Arithmetic Instructions   174
    4.3.4.3   Logic Instructions   176
    4.3.4.4   Shift and Rotate Instructions   178
    4.3.4.5   Data Conversion Instructions   179
    4.3.4.6   Bit-Field Processing Instructions   182
    4.3.4.7   Compare and Test Instructions   186
    4.3.4.8   Program Flow Control Instructions   187
    4.3.4.9   Saturation Instructions   191
    4.3.4.10   Exception-Related Instructions   193
    4.3.4.11   Sleep Mode Instructions   194
    4.3.4.12   Memory Barrier Instructions   194
    4.3.4.13   Miscellaneous Instructions   195
    4.3.4.14   Unsupported Instructions   196
4.4   ARM® Cortex®-M4 Software Development Procedures   196
4.5   Using C Language to Develop ARM® Cortex®-M4 Microcontroller
      Applications   197
  4.5.1   The Standard Data Types Used in Intrinsic Functions   198
  4.5.2   The CMSIS-Core-Specific Intrinsic Functions   200
  4.5.3   The Keil® ARM® Compiler-Specific Intrinsic Functions   202
  4.5.4   Inline Assembler   204

4.5.5   Idiom Recognition   205
4.5.6   C Programming Development Guideline and Procedure   206
    4.5.6.1   Organization of the C Program Files   207
    4.5.6.2   The Header Files   208
    4.5.6.3   The Implementation Files   209
    4.5.6.4   The Application Files   211
    4.5.6.5   Naming Convention and Definition   211
4.5.7   The TivaWare™ Peripheral Driver Library   213
    4.5.7.1   The Programming Models   213
    4.5.7.2   The Direct Register Access Model   214
        4.5.7.2.1   The Hardware Architecture of the Example Project   214
        4.5.7.2.2   The Structure and Bit Function of System Control and GPIO Registers   215
        4.5.7.2.3   The Symbolic Definitions and Macros   218
        4.5.7.2.4   The Programming Operations for Symbolic Definitions   219
        4.5.7.2.5   Develop a Sample Project Using the DRA Model   220
    4.5.7.3   The Peripheral Driver Library and API Functions   224
        4.5.7.3.1   System Control API Functions   225
        4.5.7.3.2   GPIO API Functions   229
        4.5.7.3.3   Develop a Sample Project Using the SD Model   232
    4.5.7.4   A Comparison Between Two Programming Models   238
    4.5.7.5   A Combined Programming Model Example   238
        4.5.7.5.1   Create the Header File   239
        4.5.7.5.2   Create the C Source File   240
        4.5.7.5.3   Include System Header Files and Add Static Library into the Project   241
        4.5.7.5.4   Compile and Link Project to Create the Image or Executable File   242
4.6   Chapter Summary   243
Homework   244

Chapter 5 ARM® Microcontroller Interrupts and Exceptions   **261**

5.1   Overview and Introduction   261
5.2   Exceptions and Interrupts in the ARM® Cortex®-M4 MCU System   263
    5.2.1   Exception and Interrupt Types   265
    5.2.2   Exceptions and Interrupts Management   265
    5.2.3   Exception and Interrupt Processing   268
        5.2.3.1   Exception and Interrupt Inputs and Pending Status   269
        5.2.3.2   Exception and Interrupt Vector Table   270
        5.2.3.3   Definitions of the Priority Levels   271
5.3   Exceptions and Interrupts in the TM4C123GH6PM Microcontroller System   273
    5.3.1   Local Interrupt Configurations and Controls for GPIO Pins   273
        5.3.1.1   Initialize and Configure GPIO Interrupt Control Registers   274
    5.3.2   Local Interrupt Configurations and Controls for GPIO Ports   276
        5.3.2.1   The NVIC Interrupt Priority-Level Registers   276
        5.3.2.2   The NVIC Interrupt Set Enable Registers   280

5.3.3   Global Interrupt Configurations and Controls   281

5.3.4   The Vector Table and Vectors Used in the TM4C123GH6PM MCU   282

5.3.5   The GPIO Interrupt Handling and Processing Procedure   284

5.4   Developing GPIO Port Interrupt Projects to Handle GPIO Interrupts   285

5.4.1   Two Software Packages Used in the TM4C123GH6PM MCU System   286

5.4.1.1   The TivaWare™ Software Package (TWSP)   286

5.4.1.1.1   Two Header Files Used in the TM4C123GH6PM MCU System   288

5.4.1.1.2   The Register Driver Definition Header File in the TivaWare™ Software Package   289

5.4.1.1.3   The CMSIS Cortex-M4 Peripheral Layer Header File for TM4C123GH6PM   289

5.4.1.2   The CMSIS Core Software Package (CMSISCSP)   290

5.4.2   Using DRA Programming Model to Handle GPIO Interrupts   290

5.4.2.1   Create a New Project GPIOInt and the Header File   291

5.4.2.2   Create a New C Code File GPIOInt and Add It into the Project   292

5.4.2.3   Set Up the Environment to Compile and Link the Project   294

5.4.3   Using CMSIS Core Macros for NVIC Registers to Handle GPIO Interrupts   294

5.4.3.1   Popular Data Structures Defined in the CMSIS Core Header File   295

5.4.3.2   IRQ Numbers Defined in the TivaWare™ System Header File   297

5.4.3.3   The NVIC Macros Defined in the TivaWare™ System Header Files   299

5.4.3.4   The NVIC Structure Defined in the CMSIS Core Header File   300

5.4.3.5   Building Sample Project to Use CMSIS Core Macros for NVIC to Handle Interrupts   302

5.4.3.6   Create a New Project NVICInt and Add the C Code File   303

5.4.4   Using TivaWare™ Peripheral Driver Library API Functions to Handle GPIO Interrupts   306

5.4.4.1   NVIC API Functions Defined in the TivaWare™ Peripheral Driver Library   306

5.4.4.2   GPIO Interrupt-Related API Functions in the TivaWare™ Peripheral Driver Library   308

5.4.4.3   Building Sample Project to Use Peripheral Driver Library to Handle Interrupts   309

5.4.4.4   Create a New Project SDInt and Add the C Code File   310

5.4.4.5   Configuring the Environments and Run the Project   312

5.4.5   Using CMSIS Core Access Functions to Handle GPIO Interrupts   313

5.4.5.1   Building Sample Project to Use CMSIS Core Functions to Handle Interrupts   314

5.4.5.2   Create a New Project CMSISInt and Add the C Code File   314

5.4.5.3   Configure the Environments and Run the Project   316

5.5   Comparison Among Four Interrupt Programming Methods   317

5.6   Chapter Summary   318

Homework   319

Chapter 6 ARM® Microcontroller Memory System **333**

6.1   Overview and Introduction   333
6.2   Memory Architecture in the TM4C123GH6PM MCU System   334
   6.2.1   Static Random Access Memory (SRAM)   336
   6.2.2   Flash Memory   336
      6.2.2.1   Basic Operations of the Flash Memory   337
      6.2.2.2   The 32-Word Flash Memory Write Buffer   338
      6.2.2.3   Flash Control Registers   339
      6.2.2.4   Boot Configuration Register (BOOTCFG)   339
      6.2.2.5   Flash Memory Address Register (FMA)   341
      6.2.2.6   Flash Memory Data Register (FMD)   342
      6.2.2.7   Flash Memory Control Register (FMC)   342
      6.2.2.8   Flash Memory Control 2 Register (FMC2)   342
      6.2.2.9   The Flash Write Buffer Valid Register (FWBVAL)   343
      6.2.2.10   Flash Controller Raw Interrupt Status Register (FCRIS)   344
      6.2.2.11   Flash Controller Interrupt Mask Register (FCIM)   346
      6.2.2.12   Flash Controller Masked Interrupt Status and Clear Register (FCMISC)   346
      6.2.2.13   Other Control Registers Related to Flash Memory Control   349
   6.2.3   Flash Memory Protection Control   349
   6.2.4   Internal Read-Only Memory (ROM)   351
      6.2.4.1   The Boot Loader   352
      6.2.4.2   The TivaWare™ Peripheral Driver Library   352
      6.2.4.3   The ROM Control Register (RMCTL)   354
      6.2.4.4   The ROM Software Map Register (ROMSWMAP)   354
   6.2.5   Electrical Erased Programmable Read-Only Memory (EEPROM)   354
      6.2.5.1   EEPROM Initialization and Configuration   356
      6.2.5.2   Most Important Control Registers Used in the EEPROM Module   357
         6.2.5.2.1   The EEPROM Current Block Register (EEBLOCK)   357
         6.2.5.2.2   The EEPROM Current Offset Register (EEOFFSET)   357
         6.2.5.2.3   EEPROM Done Status Register (EEDONE)   357
         6.2.5.2.4   EEPROM Support Control and Status Register (EESUPP)   359
         6.2.5.2.5   EEPROM Protection Register (EEPROT)   359
      6.2.5.3   Other Important Control Registers Used in the EEPROM Module   360
6.3   Memory Map in TM4C123GH6PM MCU System   361
6.4   Bit-Band Operations   362
   6.4.1   The Mapping Relationship Between the Bit-Band Region and the Bit-Band Alias Region   365
   6.4.2   The Advantages of Using the Bit-Band Operations   365
   6.4.3   An Illustration Example of Using Bit-Band Alias Addresses   367
   6.4.4   Bit-Band Operations for Different Data Sizes   369
   6.4.5   Bit-Band Operations Built in C Programs   369
6.5   Memory Requirements and Memory Properties   370
   6.5.1   Memory Requirements   371
   6.5.2   Memory Access Attributes   372

6.5.3   Memory Endianness   373
   6.5.3.1   The Little Endian Format   374
   6.5.3.2   The Big Endian Format   374
6.6   Memory System Programming Methods   375
  6.6.1   The API Functions Used for Flash Memory Programming   376
  6.6.2   The API Functions Used for EEPROM Programming   378
6.7   Memory System Programming Projects   380
  6.7.1   Flash Memory Programming   380
   6.7.1.1   Programming Flash Memory for Multiple Words with DRA
       Method (Polled)   380
    6.7.1.1.1   The Operational Sequence of the Programming Flash
         Memory   380
    6.7.1.1.2   The Programming Macros for Flash Memory Registers and
         Parameters   381
    6.7.1.1.3   Build the Project to Program Multiple Words for Flash
         Memory   382
    6.7.1.1.4   Build and Run the Project to Perform Erase and Write
         Operations   386
   6.7.1.2   Programming Flash Memory for Multiple Words with the DRA
       Method (Interrupt Driven)   388
    6.7.1.2.1   The Erase and Write Interrupts Processing Procedure   389
    6.7.1.2.2   Special Features Utilized in the Project   390
    6.7.1.2.3   Build the Project to Program Multiple Words for Flash Memory
         with Interrupts   390
    6.7.1.2.4   Set Up the Environment to Build and Run the
         Project   396
   6.7.1.3   Programming Flash Memory for Buffered Words with the DRA
       Method   397
    6.7.1.3.1   The Buffer Words Programming Procedure   397
    6.7.1.3.2   Develop the Buffer Words Programming Project
         DRAFlashBuffer   398
    6.7.1.3.3   Build and Set Up the Environment to Run the Project   400
  6.7.2   EEPROM Programming   401
   6.7.2.1   Special Features in the EEPROM Programming Process   401
   6.7.2.2   EEPROM Programming Operational Sequence   402
    6.7.2.2.1   Configure and Set Up EEBLOCK and EEOFFSET
         Registers   403
    6.7.2.2.2   Implement and Update the EEBLOCK and EEOFFSET
         Registers   404
  6.7.3   Three Kinds of System Header Files in the TM4C123GH6PM MCU
     System   405
   6.7.3.1   The Register Driver Definitions Header File TM4C123GH6PM.h   405
   6.7.3.2   The CMSIS Cortex®-M4 Peripheral Hardware Layer Header File
       TM4C123GH6PM.h   406
   6.7.3.3   System Header Files for All Internal Peripherals and System Control
       Devices   406
   6.7.3.4   Enable the EEPROM Module in Run Mode and Reset EEPROM   407

6.7.4   Build Example EEPROM Programming Projects   408
    6.7.4.1   Programming EEPROM with the DRA Method (Polling-Driven)   408
       6.7.4.1.1   Create the Header File DRAEEPROMPoll.h   408
       6.7.4.1.2   Create the Source File DRAEEPROMPoll.c   409
       6.7.4.1.3   Set Up the Environment to Build and Run the Project   413
    6.7.4.2   Programming EEPROM with the DRA Method (Interrupt-Driven)   414
       6.7.4.2.1   Modify the Header File DRAEEPROMInt.h   416
       6.7.4.2.2   Modify the Source File DRAEEPROMInt.c   417
       6.7.4.2.3   Set Up the Environment to Build and Run the Project   419
6.8   Chapter Summary   420
Homework   421

Chapter 7 ARM® Cortex®-M4 Parallel I/O Ports Programming   433

7.1   Overview and Introduction   433
7.2   GPIO Module Architecture and GPIO Port Configuration   434
7.3   GPIO Port Control Registers   437
   7.3.1   GPIO Port Initialization and Configuration   438
7.4   On-Board Keypad Interface Programming Project   440
   7.4.1   The Keypad Interfacing Programming Structure   441
   7.4.2   Create the Keypad Interfacing Programming Project (Polling-Driven)   442
     7.4.2.1   Create the C Source File DRAKeyPadPoll.c   443
   7.4.3   Set Up the Environment to Build and Run the Project   446
7.5   Analog-to-Digital Converter Programming Project   446
   7.5.1   ADC Modules in the TM4C123GH6PM MCU System   446
   7.5.2   ADC Module Architecture and Functional Block Diagram   447
   7.5.3   ADC Module Components and Signal Descriptions   448
     7.5.3.1   Analog Input Signals and GPIO Analog Control Registers   449
       7.5.3.1.1   GPIO Alternate Function Select (GPIOAFSEL) Register   450
       7.5.3.1.2   GPIO Digital Enable (GPIODEN) Register   450
       7.5.3.1.3   GPIO Analog Mode Select (GPIOAMSEL) Register   451
     7.5.3.2   Sample Sequencer Controls and Their Control Registers   451
       7.5.3.2.1   ADC Sample Sequencer Input Multiplexer Select (ADCSSMUXn) Register   452
       7.5.3.2.2   ADC Sample Sequencer Control (ADCSSCTLn) Register   454
       7.5.3.2.3   ADC Active Sample Sequencer (ADCACTSS) Register   458
       7.5.3.2.4   ADC Processor Sample Sequencer Initiate (ADCPSSI) Register   459
       7.5.3.2.5   ADC Sample Sequencer Result FIFO (ADCSSFIFOn) Register   460
     7.5.3.3   ADC Module Control Functions and Related Registers   461
       7.5.3.3.1   ADC Module Clocking   461
       7.5.3.3.2   ADC Interrupt Request and Handling   463
       7.5.3.3.3   Sampling Events and Trigger Sources   467
       7.5.3.3.4   DMA Operations   470
   7.5.4   Analog-to-Digital Converter   470

7.5.4.1   Voltage Reference and Resolutions   471
7.5.4.2   Differential Input Mode   471
7.5.4.3   Internal Temperature Sensor   472
7.5.5   Initialization and Configuration   473
7.5.5.1   ADC-Related GPIO Ports Initialization   473
7.5.5.2   ADC Module Initialization   474
7.5.5.3   Sample Sequencers Initialization   474
7.5.6   Build the Analog-to-Digital Converter Programming Project   475
7.5.6.1   ADC Module in EduBASE ARM® Trainer   475
7.5.6.2   Create the ADC Programming Project (Polling-Driven)   476
7.5.6.3   Create the Source File DRAADCPoll.c   476
7.5.6.4   Set Up the Environment to Build and Run the Project   479
7.5.7   ADC Module API Functions Provided in the TivaWare™ Peripheral Driver
          Library   480
7.5.7.1   Configuring and Handling the Sample Sequencers API Functions   481
7.5.7.2   Configuring and Controlling the Processor Trigger API Functions   481
7.5.7.3   Configuring and Processing the ADC Interrupt API Functions   483
7.5.7.4   Build an Example ADC Project Using API Functions   484
7.6   PWM-Controlled DC and Step Motors Programming Project   486
7.6.1   The PWM Principle and Implementations   487
7.6.2   PWM Modules in the TM4C123GH6PM MCU System   487
7.6.2.1   The PWM Generator Block   488
7.6.2.1.1   The PWM Counter (Timer)   488
7.6.2.1.2   The PWM Comparators   488
7.6.2.1.3   The PWM Output Signals Generator   489
7.6.2.1.4   The Dead-Band Generator   490
7.6.3   PWM Generator Functional Block Diagram   490
7.6.3.1   PWM Generator Block Control Register (PWMnCTL)   491
7.6.3.2   PWM Generator Block Load Register (PWMnLOAD)   493
7.6.3.3   PWM Generator Block Count Register (PWMnCOUNT)   493
7.6.3.4   PWM Generator Block Comparator A Register (PWMnCMPA)   493
7.6.3.5   PWM Generator Block Comparator B Register (PWMnCMPB)   494
7.6.3.6   PWM Generator A Register (PWMnGENA)   494
7.6.3.7   PWM Generator B Register (PWMnGENB)   495
7.6.3.8   PWM Generator Dead-Band Control Register (PWMnDBCTL)   496
7.6.3.9   PWM Generator Dead-Band Rising-Edge Delay Register
            (PWMnDBRISE)   497
7.6.3.10   PWM Generator Dead-Band Falling-Edge Delay Register
            (PWMnDBFALL)   497
7.6.3.11   PWM Interrupt and Trigger Enable Register (PWMnINTEN)   498
7.6.3.12   PWM Raw Interrupt Status Register (PWMnRIS)   498
7.6.3.13   PWM Interrupt Status and Clear Register (PWMnISC)   499
7.6.3.14   PWM Fault Source n Register (PWMFLTSRCn)   501
7.6.4   PWM Module Architecture and Functional Block Diagram   502
7.6.4.1   The Control and Status Block   503
7.6.4.1.1   The Run-Mode Clock Configuration Register (RCC)   504
7.6.4.1.2   The PWM Master Control Register (PWMCTL)   504

7.6.4.1.3   The PWM Timer Base Synchronous Register (PWMSYNC)   504
7.6.4.1.4   The PWM Status Register (PWMSTATUS)   505
7.6.4.1.5   The PWM Peripheral Properties Register (PWMPP)   505
7.6.4.2   The Output Control Block   505
7.6.4.2.1   The PWM Output Enable Register (PWMENABLE)   505
7.6.4.2.2   The PWM Output Inversion Register (PWMINVERT)   506
7.6.4.2.3   The PWM Output Fault Register (PWMFAULT)   506
7.6.4.2.4   The PWM Fault Condition Value Register (PWMFAULTVAL)
              507
7.6.4.2.5   The PWM Enable Update Register (PWMENUPD)   507
7.6.4.3   The Interrupt Control Block   507
7.6.4.3.1   The PWM Interrupt Enable Register (PWMINTEN)   508
7.6.4.3.2   The PWM Raw Interrupt Status Register (PWMRIS)   509
7.6.4.3.3   The PWM Interrupt Status and Clear Register (PWMISC)   509
7.6.5   PWM Module Components and Signal Descriptions   509
7.6.5.1   PWM Signal Description   510
7.6.5.2   Synchronization Methods   511
7.6.5.3   Fault Conditions   512
7.6.6   PWM Module Initialization and Configuration   513
7.6.6.1   Initialize and Configure the Clock Source for PWM Module and GPIO
              Ports   513
7.6.6.2   Initialize and Configure GPIO Ports and Pins Related to PWM
              Modules   513
7.6.6.3   Initialize and Configure the PWM Module and Generators   514
7.6.7   PWM Module Architecture in the EduBASE ARM® Trainer   515
7.6.8   Build an Example PWM Programming Project   516
7.6.8.1   Create a PWM Application Project DRAPWM   517
7.6.8.2   Set Up the Environment to Build and Run the Project   520
7.7   The PWM API Functions in the TivaWare™ Peripheral Driver Library   521
7.7.1   PWM Modules and Generators Configuration and Set Up Control
              Functions   521
7.7.2   PWM Output Control Functions   523
7.7.3   PWM Interrupt and Fault Control Functions   523
7.8   Chapter Summary   525
Homework   527

Chapter 8 ARM® Cortex®-M4 Serial I/O Ports Programming   **547**

8.1   Overview and Introduction   547
8.2   GPIO Module Architecture and GPIO Port Configuration   548
8.3   Synchronous Serial Interface (SSI)   551
8.3.1   Asynchronous and Synchronous Communication Protocols and Data
              Framing   552
8.3.2   Synchronous Serial Interface Architecture and Functional Block Diagram   555
8.3.3   The Synchronous Data Transmission Format and Frame   556
8.3.3.1   Texas Instruments™ Synchronous Serial Frame   558
8.3.3.2   Freescale SPI Frame   558

8.3.3.3   MICROWIRE Frame   559

8.3.4   SSI Module Components and Signal Descriptions   560

8.3.4.1   SSI Control Signals and GPIO SSI Control Registers   560

8.3.4.2   SSI Module Bit Rate Generation and Clock Control   562

8.3.4.3   SSI Module Control/Status and FIFO Control   564

8.3.4.3.1   SSI Control 1 Register (SSICR1)   564

8.3.4.3.2   SSI Status Register (SSISR)   565

8.3.4.3.3   SSI Data Register (SSIDR)   565

8.3.4.3.4   FIFO Operations   566

8.3.4.4   SSI Module Interrupt and DMA Control   567

8.3.4.4.1   SSI Interrupt Mask Register (SSIIM)   568

8.3.4.4.2   SSI Raw Interrupt Status Register (SSIRIS)   569

8.3.4.4.3   SSI DMA Control Register (SSIDMACTL)   569

8.3.4.5   SSI Module Transmit/Receive Logic Control   570

8.3.4.6   SSI Modules Initialization and Configurations   570

8.3.4.6.1   SSI-Module-Related GPIO Ports Initialization   570

8.3.4.6.2   SSI Module Initialization and Configuration   571

8.3.4.6.3   SSI Module Clock Source and Bit Rate Initialization and Configuration   571

8.3.5   Build the On-Board LCD Interface Programming Project   572

8.3.5.1   SSI Module Interface for the LCD in EduBASE ARM® Trainer   572

8.3.5.2   The Serial Shift Register 74VHCT595   573

8.3.5.3   The LCD Module TC1602A and LCD Controller SPLC780   574

8.3.5.3.1   Interfacing Control Signals Between the MCU and the SPLC780   576

8.3.5.3.2   Control and Interface Programming for SPLC780   578

8.3.5.3.3   LCD Programming Instruction Structure and Sequence   580

8.3.5.4   Build the Example LCD Interfacing Project   583

8.3.5.4.1   Create a Direct Register Access LCD Project DRALCD   584

8.3.5.4.2   Create the Header File DRALCD.h   584

8.3.5.4.3   Create the C Source File DRALCD.c   585

8.3.5.4.4   Set Up the Environment to Build and Run the Project   589

8.3.6   Build On-Board 7-Segment LED Interface Programming Project   589

8.3.6.1   Structure of 7-Segment LEDs   589

8.3.6.2   SSI Module Interface for the 7-Segment LED in the EduBASE ARM® Trainer   590

8.3.6.3   Build the Example LED Interfacing Project   592

8.3.6.3.1   Create a Direct Register Access LED Project DRALED   593

8.3.6.3.2   Create the C Source File DRALED.c   593

8.3.6.3.3   Set Up the Environment to Build and Run the Project   595

8.3.7   Build Digital-to-Analog Converter Programming Project   595

8.3.7.1   SSI Module Interface for the DAC-MCP4922 in the EduBASE ARM® Trainer   595

8.3.7.2   The Operations and Programming for MCP4922 DAC   596

8.3.7.3   The Analog-to-Digital Converter TLC-548   598

8.3.7.4   Build the Example DAC Interfacing Project   599

8.3.7.4.1   Create a Direct Register Access DAC Project DRADAC   600

8.3.7.4.2   Create the Header File DRADAC.h   600
8.3.7.4.3   Create the C Source File DRADAC.c   600
8.3.7.4.4   Set Up the Environment to Build and Run the Project   603
8.3.8   SSI API Functions Provided by TivaWare™ Peripheral Driver Library   604
8.3.8.1   The SSI Module Initialization and Configuration Functions   604
8.3.8.2   The SSI Module Control and Status Functions   605
8.3.8.3   The SSI Module Data Processing Functions   606
8.3.8.4   The SSI Module Interrupt Source and Processing Functions   607
8.3.8.5   Build an Example Project to Interface Serial Peripherals Using the SSI Module   608
8.3.8.5.1   Create a New Software Driver Model Project SDLCD   608
8.3.8.5.2   Create the Header File SDLCD.h   608
8.3.8.5.3   Create the C Source File SDLCD.c   608
8.4   Inter-Integrated Circuit (I2C) Interface   611
8.4.1   I2C Module Bus Configuration and Operational Status   612
8.4.2   I2C Module Architecture and Functional Block Diagram   613
8.4.3   I2C Module Data Transfer Format and Frame   614
8.4.4   I2C Module Operational Sequence   614
8.4.4.1   I2C Module Works in the Master Transmit Mode   614
8.4.4.2   I2C Module Works in the Master Receive Mode   616
8.4.4.3   I2C Module Works in the Slave Transmit and Receive Modes   616
8.4.5   I2C Module Major Operational Components and Control Signals   618
8.4.6   I2C Module Running Speeds (Clock Rates) and Interrupts   620
8.4.6.1   I2C Module High-Speed Mode   621
8.4.6.2   I2C Module Interrupts Generation and Processing   621
8.4.6.2.1   I2C Master Interrupts   622
8.4.6.2.2   I2C Slave Interrupts   622
8.4.7   I2C Interface Control Signals and GPIO I2C Control Registers   622
8.4.8   I2C Module Control Registers and Their Functions   623
8.4.8.1   I2C Module Master Control Registers   623
8.4.8.1.1   I2C Master Slave Address Register (I2CMSA)   623
8.4.8.1.2   I2C Master Control/Status Register (I2CMCS)   624
8.4.8.1.3   I2C Master Data Register (I2CMDR)   624
8.4.8.1.4   I2C Master Timer Period Register (I2CMTPR)   624
8.4.8.1.5   I2C Master Configuration Register (I2CMCR)   625
8.4.8.1.6   I2C Master Clock Low Timeout Count Register (I2CMCLKOCNT)   625
8.4.8.1.7   I2C Master Bus Monitor Register (I2CMBMON)   626
8.4.8.1.8   I2C Master Interrupt Mask Register (I2CMIMR)   626
8.4.8.1.9   I2C Master Raw Interrupt Status Register (I2CMRIS)   626
8.4.8.1.10   I2C Master Masked Interrupt Status Register (I2CMMIS)   626
8.4.8.1.11   I2C Master Interrupt Clear Register (I2CMICR)   627
8.4.8.2   I2C Module Slave Control Registers   627
8.4.8.2.1   I2C Slave Own Address Register (I2CSOAR)   627
8.4.8.2.2   I2C Slave Control Status Register (I2CSCSR)   627
8.4.8.2.3   I2C Slave Data Register (I2CSDR)   628
8.4.8.2.4   I2C Slave Own Address 2 Register (I2CSOAR2)   628

8.4.8.2.5   I2C Slave ACK Control Register (I2CSACKCTL)   628
8.4.8.2.6   I2C Slave Interrupt Mask Register (I2CSIMR)   629
8.4.8.2.7   I2C Slave Raw Interrupt Status Register (I2CSRIS)   629
8.4.8.2.8   I2C Slave Masked Interrupt Status Register (I2CSMIS)   629
8.4.8.2.9   I2C Slave Interrupt Clear Register (I2CSICR)   629
8.4.9   I2C Module Initializations and Configurations   630
8.4.9.1   Initializations and Configurations for the I2C-Related GPIO Pins   630
8.4.9.2   Initializations and Configurations for the I2C Module   630
8.4.10   Build an Example I2C Module Project   631
8.4.10.1   The BQ32000 Real Time Clock (RTC)   631
8.4.10.2   The Interface Between the BQ32000 and EduBASE ARM®
Trainer   633
8.4.10.3   Create a DRA Model I2C Project DRAI2C   634
8.4.10.4   Create the Source File DRAI2C   634
8.4.10.5   Set Up the Environment to Build and Run the Project   638
8.4.11   I2C API Functions Provided by TivaWare™ Peripheral Driver Library   639
8.4.11.1   Master Operations   639
8.4.11.2   I2C Module Status and Initialization API Functions   640
8.4.11.3   I2C Module Sending and Receiving Data API Functions   641
8.5   Universal Asynchronous Receivers/Transmitters (UARTs)   642
8.5.1   Asynchronous Serial Communication Protocols and Data Framing   642
8.5.2   Asynchronous Serial Interface Architecture and Functional Block
Diagram   643
8.5.3   UART Module Operations and Control Registers   645
8.5.3.1   Transmit/Receive Logic and Data Transmission and Receiving   645
8.5.3.2   UART Modem Handshake Support   645
8.5.3.3   UART FIFO Operations   647
8.5.3.4   UART Interrupts and DMA Control   648
8.5.3.5   UART Serial IR (SIR) Support   649
8.5.3.6   9-Bit UART Mode   649
8.5.3.7   UART Module Clock Control and Baud Rate Generation
Registers   650
8.5.3.8   UART Module Control/Status and FIFO Control Registers   651
8.5.3.8.1   UART Control Register (UARTCTL)   651
8.5.3.8.2   UART Line Control Register (UARTLCRH)   653
8.5.3.8.3   UART Receive Status/Error Clear Register
(UARTRSR/UARTECR)   653
8.5.3.8.4   UART Data Register (UARTDR)   654
8.5.3.8.5   UART Flag Register (UARTFR)   655
8.5.3.9   UART Module Interrupt and DMA Control Registers   655
8.5.3.9.1   UART Interrupt FIFO Level Select (UARTIFLS) Register   656
8.5.3.9.2   UART Raw Interrupt Status (UARTRIS) Register   656
8.5.3.9.3   UART Interrupt Mask (UARTIM) Register   656
8.5.3.9.4   UART Masked Interrupt Status (UARTMIS) Register   657
8.5.3.9.5   UART Interrupt Clear Register (UARTICR)   657
8.5.3.9.6   UART DMA Control (UARTDMACTL) Register   657
8.5.4   UART Module Control Signals and Related GPIO Pins   658

8.5.5   UART Module Initializations and Configurations   659
   8.5.5.1   Initialize and Configure the UART-Related GPIO Ports and Pins   659
   8.5.5.2   Initialize and Configure Clock Source and Baud Rate for the UART Module   659
   8.5.5.3   Initialize and Configure the UART Module   660
8.5.6   Build an Example UART Module Project   660
   8.5.6.1   Create a New UART Module Project DRAUART   661
   8.5.6.2   Create a New C Source File   661
   8.5.6.3   Set Up the Environment to Build and Run the Project   664
8.5.7   The UART API Functions Provided by the TivaWare™ Peripheral Driver Library   664
   8.5.7.1   Clock Source for the Baud Rate Generator API Functions   665
   8.5.7.2   Configure and Control the UART Modules API Functions   666
   8.5.7.3   UART Send and Receive Data API Functions   667
   8.5.7.4   UART Interrupt Handling API Functions   667
8.6   Chapter Summary   668
Homework   669

Chapter 9 ARM® Cortex®-M4 Timer and USB Programming   691

9.1   Overview and Introduction   691
9.2   General-Purpose Timers   692
9.2.1   The GPTM Architecture and Functional Block Diagram   693
9.2.2   The General-Purpose Timer Module Components   694
   9.2.2.1   Prescaler Registers   695
   9.2.2.2   Match Registers   695
   9.2.2.3   Shadow Registers   695
9.2.3   The General-Purpose Timer Module Operational Modes   695
   9.2.3.1   One-Shot and Periodic Timer Mode   696
   9.2.3.2   Periodic Snapshot Timer Mode   698
   9.2.3.3   Wait-for-Trigger Mode   699
   9.2.3.4   Real-Time Clock Timer Mode   699
   9.2.3.5   Input Edge-Count Mode   699
   9.2.3.6   Input Edge-Time Mode   700
   9.2.3.7   PWM Mode   702
   9.2.3.8   DMA Mode   703
   9.2.3.9   Synchronizing GP Timer Blocks   703
   9.2.3.10   Concatenated Modes   703
9.2.4   The General-Purpose Timer Module Registers   704
   9.2.4.1   Timer A Control Register Group   704
      9.2.4.1.1   GPTM Configuration Register (GPTMCFG)   705
      9.2.4.1.2   GPTM Control Register (GPTMCTL)   705
      9.2.4.1.3   GPTM Timer A Mode Register (GPTMTAMR)   705
      9.2.4.1.4   GPTM Timer A Interval Load Register (GPTMTAILR)   705
      9.2.4.1.5   GPTM Timer A Match Register (GPTMTAMATCHR)   706
      9.2.4.1.6   GPTM Timer A Prescale Register (GPTMTAPR)   707

9.2.4.1.7   GPTM Timer A Prescale Match Register (GPTMTAPMR)   708
9.2.4.1.8   GPTM Timer A Prescale Snapshot Register (GPTMTAPS)   708
9.2.4.2   Timer A Status Register Group   708
9.2.4.2.1   GPTM Timer A Register (GPTMTAR)   708
9.2.4.2.2   GPTM Timer A Value Register (GPTMTAV)   709
9.2.4.2.3   GPTM Timer A Prescale Value Register (GPTMTAPV)   709
9.2.4.3   Timers A and B Interrupt and Configuration Register Group   709
9.2.4.3.1   GPTM Interrupt Mask Register (GPTMIMR)   710
9.2.4.3.2   GPTM Raw Interrupt Status Register (GPTMRIS)   711
9.2.4.3.3   GPTM Masked Interrupt Status Register (GPTMMIS)   711
9.2.4.3.4   GPTM Interrupt Clear Register (GPTMICR)   711
9.2.4.3.5   GPTM Synchronize Register (GPTMSYNC)   711
9.2.4.3.6   GPTM Peripheral Properties Register (GPTMPP)   711
9.2.5   The General-Purpose Timer Module GPIO-Related Control Signals   712
9.2.6   The General-Purpose Timer Module Initializations and Configurations   713
9.2.6.1   Initialization and Configuration for One-Shot/Periodic Timer Mode   714
9.2.6.2   Initialization and Configuration for Input Edge-Count Mode   714
9.2.6.3   Initialization and Configuration for Input Edge-Time Mode   715
9.2.6.4   Initialization and Configuration for Real-Time Clock (RTC) Mode   716
9.2.6.5   Initialization and Configuration for PWM Mode   716
9.2.7   Build an Example General Purpose Timer Project   717
9.2.8   Popular Implementations on GPTM Modules   718
9.2.8.1   Input Edge-Count Implementations   719
9.2.8.2   Input Edge-Time Implementations   721
9.2.8.3   PWM Implementations   723
9.2.9   The API Functions Used for General-Purpose Timer Module   727
9.2.9.1   The API Functions Used for GPTM Module Configurations and Controls   727
9.2.9.2   The API Functions Used for GPTM Module Contents and Related Operations   727
9.2.9.3   The API Functions Used for GPTM Module Interrupt Handling   730
9.2.9.4   An Implementation of Using Timer API Functions to Measure PWM Pulses   731
9.3   Watchdog Timers   732
9.3.1   The Watchdog Timer Architecture and Functional Block Diagram   734
9.3.2   The Watchdog Timer Operational Sequence and Timing Access   735
9.3.3   The Watchdog Timer Registers   735
9.3.3.1   The Watchdog Module Control and Content Registers   735
9.3.3.1.1   Watchdog Timer Control Register (WDTCTL)   736
9.3.3.1.2   Watchdog Timer Load Register (WDTLOAD)   736
9.3.3.1.3   Watchdog Timer Value Register (WDTVALUE)   736
9.3.3.1.4   Watchdog Timer Lock Register (WDTLOCK)   736
9.3.3.1.5   Watchdog Timer Test Register (WDTTEST)   737
9.3.3.2   The Watchdog Module Interrupt Handling Registers   737
9.3.3.2.1   Watchdog Raw Interrupt Status Register (WDTRIS)   737

9.3.3.2.2   Watchdog Masked Interrupt Status Register (WDTMIS)   737

9.3.3.2.3   Watchdog Interrupt Clear Register (WDTICR)   737

9.3.3.2.4   Watchdog Timer Software Reset Register (SRWD)   738

9.3.4   The Watchdog Timer Module Initializations and Configurations   738

9.3.5   Build an Example Watchdog Timer Project   739

9.3.6   The API Functions Used for Watchdog Timer Modules   739

9.3.6.1   The API Functions Used to Configure and Control the Watchdog Timers   740

9.3.6.2   The API Functions Used to Handle Interrupts of the Watchdog Timers   742

9.3.6.3   An Implementation Example of Using API Functions to Control the Watchdog Timer   743

9.4   Universal Serial Bus (USB) Controller   743

9.4.1   The Hardware Configuration of the USB Devices   744

9.4.2   The USB Components and Operational Sequence   745

9.4.3   The Serial Interface Protocol of the USB Communications   747

9.4.4   The USB Interface Used in the Embedded System   748

9.4.5   The USB in the TM4C123GH6PM MCU System   749

9.4.5.1   USB Working as a Device   749

9.4.5.1.1   IN Transactions as a Device   750

9.4.5.1.2   OUT Transactions as a Device   751

9.4.5.1.3   Other Device Functions   752

9.4.5.2   USB Working as a Host   754

9.4.5.2.1   IN Transactions as a Host   755

9.4.5.2.2   OUT Transactions as a Host   755

9.4.5.2.3   Transactions Scheduling   756

9.4.5.2.4   Other Host Functions   756

9.4.5.3   The OTG Mode   757

9.4.5.3.1   Using OTG to Start a Session   758

9.4.5.3.2   Using OTG to Perform Detecting Activity   759

9.4.5.3.3   Using OTG to Perform Host Negotiation   759

9.4.5.4   The USB Module Functional Block Diagram   759

9.4.5.5   The USB Module Control Signals   760

9.4.6   The USB Registers   761

9.4.6.1   USB Host-Related Registers   762

9.4.6.2   USB Device-Related Registers   763

9.4.6.3   USB Host/Device-Related Registers   764

9.4.6.4   USB FIFO-Related Registers   765

9.4.6.5   USB-Interrupt-Related Registers   771

9.4.7   The USB Initializations and Configurations   774

9.4.7.1   Enable and Clock the USB Controller and Related GPIO Ports and Pins   774

9.4.7.2   USB Control Pins Configurations   774

9.4.7.3   Endpoint Configurations   775

9.4.8   A USB Implementation Example Project   775

9.4.9   The USB API Functions Provided by the TivaWare™ Peripheral Driver Library   780

9.4.9.1 The USBClock and USBMode API Functions 781
9.4.9.2 The USBDev API Functions 781
9.4.9.3 The USBHost API Functions 783
9.4.9.4 The USBEndpoint API Functions 784
9.4.9.5 The USBFIFO API Functions 786
9.4.9.6 The USBInterrupt API Functions 786
9.4.9.7 The USBOTG API Functions 788
9.4.10 Build a USB Implementation Example Project Using the API Functions 788
9.5 Chapter Summary 788
Homework 790

Chapter 10 ARM® Cortex®-M4 Other Peripherals Programming 805

10.1 Overview and Introduction 805
10.2 The Controller Area Network (CAN) 805
10.2.1 CAN Standard Frame 806
10.2.2 CAN Extended Frame 807
10.2.3 Detecting and Signaling Errors 808
10.2.4 The CAN Functional Block Diagram in the TM4C123GH6PM System 809
10.2.5 The CAN Components and Operational Procedures 810
10.2.5.1 CAN Initialization and Configuration Process 811
10.2.5.2 Transmit Message Objects 812
10.2.5.3 Receive Message Objects 815
10.2.5.4 Handle CAN Module Interrupts 817
10.2.5.5 CAN Module Operational Modes 818
10.2.5.6 CAN Clock and Baud Rate Configuration 819
10.2.5.6.1 Calculate the Bit Time Parameters and Configure the CANBIT Register 821
10.2.6 The CAN Module Registers 823
10.2.6.1 The CAN Global Control and Status Registers 823
10.2.6.1.1 The CAN Global Control Register (CANCTL) 823
10.2.6.1.2 The CAN Global Status Register (CANSTS) 824
10.2.6.1.3 The CAN Error Counter Register (CANERR) 825
10.2.6.1.4 The CAN Bit Timing Register (CANBIT) 825
10.2.6.1.5 The CAN Test Register (CANTST) 826
10.2.6.1.6 The CAN Baud Rate Prescaler Extension Register (CANBRPE) 826
10.2.6.1.7 The CAN Interrupt Register (CANINT) 827
10.2.6.2 The CAN Interface 1 Registers 828
10.2.6.2.1 CAN IF1 Command Request Register (CANIF1CRQ) 828
10.2.6.2.2 CAN IF1 Command Mask Register (CANIF1CMSK) 828
10.2.6.2.3 CAN IF1 Message Control Register (CANIF1MCTL) 830
10.2.6.2.4 CAN IF1 Mask 1 Register (CANIF1MSK1) 831
10.2.6.2.5 CAN IF1 Mask 2 Register (CANIF1MSK2) 831
10.2.6.2.6 CAN IF1 Arbitration 1 Register (CANIF1ARB1) 831
10.2.6.2.7 CAN IF1 Arbitration 2 Register (CANIF1ARB2) 832

          10.2.6.2.8   CAN IF1 Data A1, CAN IF1 Data A2, CAN IF1 Data B1,
                      CAN IF1 Data B2 (CANIF1DA1–CANIF1DA2,
                      CANIF1DB1~CANIF1DB2) Registers   832

10.2.6.3   The CAN Message Object Registers   833
10.2.7   The CAN Module Interfacing and External Control Signals   833
10.2.8   The CAN API Functions Provided by TivaWare™ Peripheral Driver
      Library   834
     10.2.8.1   Special Data Structures and Enumerations Used in the CAN
              Programming   834
     10.2.8.2   CAN Module Initialization and Configuration Functions   835
     10.2.8.3   CAN Module Message Setting and Processing Functions   836
     10.2.8.4   CAN Module Interrupt Configuration and Handle Functions   838
10.2.9   A CAN Module Implementation Example Project   838
     10.2.9.1   Build a Simple CAN Self-Test Project   839
     10.2.9.2   Build the Header File for the CAN Project CANLoopBack   840
     10.2.9.3   Build the Source File for the CAN Project CANLoopBack   841
     10.2.9.4   Set Up the Environment to Build and Run the Project   846
10.3   The Quadrature Encoder Interface (QEI)   847
   10.3.1   Introduction to Quadrature Encoder   847
   10.3.2   The Working Principle of the Increment Rotary Encoder   849
   10.3.3   The Increment Rotary Encoder Applied in the Closed-Loop Control
      System   850
   10.3.4   The Increment Rotary Encoder Applied in the TM4C123GH6PM MCU
      System   851
   10.3.5   The QEI Module Registers   852
     10.3.5.1   QEI Control and Status Registers   852
     10.3.5.2   QEI Position Control Registers   854
     10.3.5.3   QEI Velocity Control Registers   855
     10.3.5.4   QEI Interrupt Processing Registers   855
   10.3.6   The QEI Interfacing Signals and Related GPIO Pins   856
   10.3.7   The QEI Initialization and Configuration Process   856
   10.3.8   QEI API Functions Provided by the TivaWare™ Peripheral Driver
      Library   857
     10.3.8.1   QEI Configuration and Enable API Functions   858
     10.3.8.2   QEI Position Capture API Functions   858
     10.3.8.3   QEI Velocity Capture API Functions   859
     10.3.8.4   QEI Interrupt Handling API Functions   859
   10.3.9   An Implementation of Using Rotary Encoder for a Closed-Loop Control
      System   860
     10.3.9.1   Calibration of the Rotary Encoder   861
     10.3.9.2   Build the Floating Chart for the Motor Closed-Loop Control
              System   867
     10.3.9.3   Build the Closed-Loop Control Program Based on the Floating
              Chart   869
10.4   The Continuous and Discrete PID Closed-Loop Control System   871
   10.4.1   Identify the Dynamic Model for the Motor Plant   873
     10.4.1.1   Format the Input and Output Data for the DC Motor   874

10.4.1.2   Identify the DC Motor Dynamic Model with Identification Toolbox™   876

10.4.2   Design the PID Controller Using the MATLAB® Control System Toolbox™   878

10.4.3   Simulate the PID Control System Using the MATLAB® SIMULINK®   881

10.4.4   Build the Control Software to Implement the PID Controller   883

10.5   The Fuzzy Logic Closed-Loop Control System   887

10.5.1   The Fuzzification Process   887

10.5.2   Design of Control Rules   889

10.5.3   The Defuzzification Process   889

10.5.4   Apply the Fuzzy Logic Controller to the DC Motor Control System   891

10.5.5   Build the Fuzzy Logic Control Project Fuzzy-Control   894

10.5.5.1   Create the Header File Fuzzy-Control.h   894

10.5.5.2   Create the C Source File Fuzzy-Control.c   895

10.5.5.3   Set Up Environments to Build and Run the Project   898

10.6   The Analog Comparators   899

10.6.1   The Analog Comparator Architecture and Functional Block Diagram   899

10.6.2   The Control Registers Used in the Analog Comparator Modules   899

10.6.3   The Voltage Reference Registers Used in the Analog Comparator Modules   900

10.6.4   The Interrupt Processing Registers Used in the Analog Comparator Modules   903

10.6.5   The Input and Output Control Signals Used in the Analog Comparators   903

10.6.6   The Initialization and Configuration Process for the Analog Comparator   904

10.6.7   Build a Project to Test the Functions of the Analog Comparator Module   904

10.6.8   Set Up the Environments to Build and Run the Project   907

10.7   Chapter Summary   908

Homework   909

Chapter 11 ARM® Floating Point Unit (FPU)   **927**

11.1   Overview and Introduction   927

11.2   Three Types of the Floating-Point Data   928

11.2.1   The Half-Precision Floating-Point Data   928

11.2.2   The Single-Precision Floating-Point Data   930

11.2.3   The Double-Precision Floating-Point Data   932

11.3   The FPU in the Cortex®-M4 MCU   934

11.3.1   The Architecture of the Floating-Point Registers   934

11.3.2   The FPU Operational Modes   937

11.4   Implementing the Floating-Point Unit   938

11.4.1   Floating-Point Support in CMSIS-Core   938

11.4.2   Floating-Point Programming in the TM4C123GH6PM MCU System   939

11.4.2.1   FPU in the Direct Register Access Model   940

11.4.2.2   FPU in the Software Driver Model   942

11.4.3   An FPU Example Project Using the Direct Register Access Model   942

11.5   Chapter Summary   946

Homework   946

Chapter 12 ARM® Memory Protection Unit (MPU) **951**

12.1   Overview and Introduction   951
12.2   Implementation of the MPU   952
   12.2.1   Memory Regions, Types, and Attributes   953
   12.2.2   MPU Configuration and Control Registers   953
      12.2.2.1   The MPU Type Register (MPUTYPE)   954
      12.2.2.2   The MPU Control Register (MPUCTRL)   954
      12.2.2.3   The MPU Region Number Register (MPUNUMBER)   956
      12.2.2.4   MPU Region Base Address Register (MPUBASE)   956
      12.2.2.5   The MPU Region Attribute and Size Register (MPUATTR)   957
12.3   Initialization and Configuration of the MPU   959
12.4   Building A Practical Example MPU Project   960
   12.4.1   Create a New DRA Model MPU Project DRAMPU   960
   12.4.2   Set Up the Environment to Build and Run the Project   963
12.5   The API Functions Provided by the TivaWare™ Peripheral Driver Library   964
   12.5.1   The MPU Set Up and Status API Functions   965
      12.5.1.1   The API Function MPURegionSet()   966
   12.5.2   The MPU Enable and Disable API Functions   967
   12.5.3   The MPU Interrupt Handler Control API Functions   968
12.6   Chapter Summary   969
Homework   970

Index   **975**

About the Author   **987**

Preface

The ARM® Cortex®-M4 MCU is one of the most popular and updated micro-controllers widely implemented in education, industrial, and manufacturing fields in recent years. Because of their relatively simple structure and powerful functions, the ARM® Cortex®-M4 MCU systems have been applied in more and more applications in our real world, including automatic controls, intelligent controls, industrial controls, and academic implementations.

The advantages of using an ARM® Cortex®-M4 microcontroller include but are not limited to the following:

- The ARM® Cortex®-M4 MCU is a 32-bit microcontroller, and it can work independently as a single controller to provide real-time and multifunction controls to effectively and easily control most real objectives in our world.

- The internal bus system used in Cortex®-M4 MCU is 32-bit, and it is based on the so-called Advanced Microcontroller Bus Architecture (AMBA) standard. The AMBA standard provides efficient operations and low power cost on the hardware.

- The main bus interface between the MCU and external components is the Advanced High-performance Bus (AHB), which provide interfaces for memory and system bus, as well as peripheral devices.

- A Nested Vectored Interrupt Controller (NVIC) is used to provide all supports and managements to the interrupt responses and processing to all components in the system.

- The Cortex®-M4 MCU also provides standard and extensive debug features and helps to enable users to easily check and trace their program with breakpoints and steps.

- The TM4C123GXL EVB provides fundamental and basic peripherals and interfaces to enable users to conveniently communicate to other parallel or serial peripherals via GPIO Ports to perform specific control tasks and functions.

- The EduBASE ARM® Trainer provides the most popular I/O devices, such as 4-LED, a 4-bit DIP switch, four 7-segment LEDs, a 4 × 4 keypad working as an input keyboard, a 16 × 2 LCD connected to the LCD Controller HD44780 to work as an output displaying device, two H-Bridge motor drivers, three analog input sensors, a CAN protocol and other peripheral interfaces. All of these I/O devices and interfaces provide great flexibility to enable users to design and build advanced and professional control units applied in our real world.

- The integrated development environment Keil® ARM-MDK μVersion®5 provides an inte-grated development environment to enable users to easily create, compile, build, and run professional application projects to control and coordinate the entire control system to perform a desired task in short period of time.

The author of this book tries to provide a complete package to cover all components and materials related to ARM® Cortex®-M4 microcontroller systems, including hardware and software as well as practical application notes with real examples. All example projects in the book have been compiled, built, and tested. To help students to master the main techniques and ideas, five appendices are provided to facilitate the students to overcome some possible learning curves.

Any questions or comments regarding this book are welcome.

Charlotte, North Carolina   YING BAI

Acknowledgments

The first and most special thanks go to my wife, Yan Wang; I could not finish this book without her sincere encouragements and supports.

Many thanks should be given to the editor Mary Hatcher, who made this book available to the public. You could not find this book on the market without her deep perspective and hard work. The same thanks are extended to the editing team for this book. Without their contributions, it would have been impossible for this book to have been published.

Acknowledgments should also be extended to the following book reviewers for their valuable opinions to the book:

- Dr. Jiang (Linda) Xie, Professor, Department of Electrical and Computer Engineering, University of North Carolina at Charlotte
- Dr. Xiaohong Yuan, Associate Professor, Department of Computer Science, North Carolina A&T State University
- Dr. Daoxi Xiu, Application Analyst Programmer, North Carolina Administrative Office of the Courts
- Dr. Dali Wang, Associate Professor, Department of Physics and Computer Science, Christopher Newport University

Last but not least, thanks should be given to all the people who have supported me while writing this book.

YING BAI

Trademarks and Copyrights

- ARM®, Cortex®, Keil® and μVision® are registered trademarks of ARM Limited (or its subsidiaries) in the EU and/or elsewhere.
- ARM7™, ARM9™ and ULINK™ are trademarks of ARM Limited (or its subsidiaries) in the EU and/or elsewhere. All rights reserved.
- MATLAB® is a trademark and product of The MathWorks, Inc.
- MATLAB Simulink® is a trademark and product of The MathWorks, Inc.
- MATLAB System Identification Toolbox™ is a trademark and product of The MathWorks, Inc.
- MATLAB System Control Toolbox™ is a trademark and product of The MathWorks, Inc.
- MATLAB Fuzzy Logic Toolbox™ is a trademark and product of The MathWorks, Inc.
- Texas Instruments™ is a trade mark of the Texas Instruments Incorporated.
- Tiva™ is a trademark and product of the Texas Instruments Incorporated.
- TivaWare™ is a trademark and product of the Texas Instruments Incorporated.
- LaunchPad™ is a trademark and product of the Texas Instruments Incorporated.
- Code Composer Studio™ is a trademark and product of the Texas Instruments Incorporated.
- Stellaris® is a trademark and product of the Texas Instruments Incorporated.

Copyright Permissions

All copyright permitted Figures and Tables used in this book are listed below based on the different venders and companies.

Table I lists the copyright permitted Figures and Tables originated by the Texas Instruments Incorporated and used in this book. All those Figures and Tables have been permitted to be re-printed in this book under the copyright permissions of the Texas Instruments Incorporated.

Table I. Copyright Permitted Figures and Tables by Texas Instruments Incorporated.

Chapter	Figures and Tables	Page
Chapter 2	Figure 2.14: Block diagram of TM4C123GH6PM MCU.	39
	Figure 2.17: Function block diagram of Analog/Digital GPIO control.	48
	Figure 2.20: The TM4C123GXL evaluation board.	73
	Figure 2.21: The functional block diagram of the LaunchPad board.	76
	Table 2.3: Exception and interrupt types and priority numbers.	36
	Table 2.8: GPIO Pins with special considerations.	58
Chapter 4	Figure 4.34: An example of using mask byte to do data reading and writing.	230
Chapter 5	Figure 5.6: An example of the NVIC Priority Level Register PRI0.	276
Chapter 6	Figure 6.3: Bit field and function on BOOTCFG Register.	339
	Figure 6.4: Bit field and function on FMA Register.	341
	Figure 6.5: Bit field and function on the FMC Register.	342
	Figure 6.6: Bit field and function on the FMC2 Register.	343
	Figure 6.7: Bit field and function on FCRIS Register.	344
	Figure 6.8: Bit field and function on FCIM Register.	346
	Figure 6.9: Bit field and function on FCMISC Register.	347
	Figure 6.11: The functional block diagram of the EEPROM.	355
	Figure 6.12: The bit field values and related functions in the EEDONE register.	358
	Figure 6.13: The bit field values and related functions in the EEPROT register.	360
Chapter 7	Figure 7.12: The bit fields for the ADCSSMUX0 register.	452
	Figure 7.13: The bit fields for the ADCSSMUX1, 2 registers.	453
	Figure 7.14: The bit fields for the ADCSSMUX3 register.	454
	Figure 7.15: The bit fields for the ADCSSCTL0 register.	455
	Figure 7.16: The bit fields for the ADCSSCTL1, 2 registers.	456
	Figure 7.17: The bit fields for the ADCSSCTL3 register.	458
	Figure 7.32: PWM Count-Down and Count Up/Down modes.	488
	Figure 7.33: An example of using the count-up/down mode to generate PWM outputs.	489
	Figure 7.34: The output PWM signals generated by Dead-Band generator.	490

Table I   (*Continued*)

Chapter	Figures and Tables	Page
	Figure 7.35: The detailed block diagram for the PWM Generator block.	491
	Figure 7.36: Bit fields in the PWM generator control register.	492
	Figure 7.37: Bit fields in the PWM generator A register.	494
	Figure 7.41: Architecture and functional block diagram of PWM module.	503
	Figure 7.42: Bit fields in the Run-Mode Clock Configuration (RCC) register.	504
Chapter 8	Figure 8.4: Functional block diagram of the SSI module.	556
	Figure 8.5: Operational timing sequence of the TI synchronous serial frame.	558
	Figure 8.6: The operational sequence for Freescale SPI frame (SPO = SPH = 0).	559
	Figure 8.7: The operational sequence for Freescale SPI frame (SPO = 0, SPH = 1).	559
	Figure 8.8: The operational sequence for MACROWIRE frame.	560
	Figure 8.11: The bit field and functions of the SSICR0 Register.	563
	Figure 8.42: The I2C bus configuration and status.	612
	Figure 8.43: The definition of START and STOP conditions.	612
	Figure 8.44: The functional block diagram of each I2C module.	613
	Figure 8.45: The I2C data transfer format and frame.	614
	Figure 8.46: The operational sequence of the master working in the transmit mode.	615
	Figure 8.47: The operational sequence of the master working in the receive mode.	617
	Figure 8.48: The operational sequence of the I2C module working in the slave mode.	618
	Figure 8.62: The functional block diagram for one UART module.	644
	Figure 8.65: Bit configurations of the UARTCTL register.	652
Chapter 9	Figure 9.1: The architecture and block diagram of one GPTM block.	693
	Figure 9.3: An example of using a count-down timer to detect input edge events.	700
	Figure 9.4: An example of using the count-down mode timer to detect the edge time.	701
	Figure 9.5: An example of using Timer A to generate a PWM signal.	703
	Figure 9.20: The functional block diagram of the watchdog modules.	734
	Figure 9.27: Functional block diagram of the USB module.	760
Chapter 10	Figure 10.2: A typical standard CAN frame format.	807
	Figure 10.3: Functional block diagram of the CAN modules.	809
	Figure 10.5: A normal CAN bit time configuration.	820
	Figure 10.25: Functional block diagram of the QEI Modules.	851
	Figure 10.26: The inversion and swapping logic circuit.	852
	Figure 10.63: Architecture and functional block diagram of the Analog Comparator modules.	900

Table II lists the copyright permitted Figures and Tables originated by the ARM Limited and used in this book. All those Figures and Tables have been reproduced with permission from ARM Limited. Copyright © ARM Limited.

Table II. Copyright Permitted Figures and Tables by ARM Limited.

Chapter	Figures and Tables	Page
Chapter 3	Figure 3.4: The components included in the MDK Core.	
	Figure 3.5: Components in the Software Packs.	
	Figure 3.9: The opened Keil® MDK-ARM µVersion® 5.1 suite.	87
	Figure 3.11: The opened Hello World project.	88
	Figure 3.12: The opened source file hello.c.	92
	Figure 3.13: Rebuild the hello project.	93
	Figure 3.14: The building result of the hello project.	94
	Figure 3.15: The debugging result of the hello world project.	95
	Figure 3.16: The opened MDK-ARM IDE.	95
	Figure 3.17: The opened Device Database wizard.	96
	Figure 3.18: The detailed information for the device TM4C123GH6PM.	97
	Figure 3.19: The License Management wizard.	98
	Figure 3.20: An example of the Configuration submenu.	99
	Figure 3.22: The Select Device for Target wizard.	99
	Figure 3.23: The Manage Run-Time Environment wizard.	100
	Figure 3.24: The selected components in the Manage Run-Time Environment wizard.	103 103
	Figure 3.25: The new project wizard.	
	Figure 3.26: The Add New Item to Group wizard.	104
	Figure 3.28: The finished codes for the source file MyProject.c.	105
	Figure 3.29: Add a header file MyProject.h into the project.	106
	Figure 3.31: The finished header file MyProject.h.	108
	Figure 3.32: The project building process.	108
	Figure 3.33: The finished debugger checking wizard.	109
	Figure 3.34: The download process for our project.	110
	Figure 3.35: The debug process for our project.	111
	Figure 3.36: The Components, Environment, Books wizard.	111
	Figure 3.37: The Manage Run-Time Environment wizard for our sample project.	112 114
	Figure 3.38: Functions provided by the Options for Target Project wizard.	
	Figure 3.39: The Target option for the sample project MyProject.	114
	Figure 3.40: The Output option for the sample project MyProject.	116
	Figure 3.41: The Listing option for the sample project MyProject.	116
	Figure 3.42: The Debug option for the sample project MyProject.	117
	Figure 3.43: The Utilities option for the sample project MyProject.	117
	Figure 3.44: The opened Settings wizard.	119
	Figure 3.45: An example of using System Viewer for TIMER0 device.	119
	Figure 3.46: The Nested Vectored Interrupt Controller configuration dialog.	120 123
	Figure 3.50: A debug example for our sample project MyProject.	125
	Figure 3.51: The optimization wizard for our sample project.	134
	Figure 3.52: An example of using the code optimization under the Target tab.	139 141
Chapter 4	Figure 4.38: The finished Options wizard.	236
Chapter 6	Figure 6.26: The running result of the project DRAFlash.	387
	Figure 6.27: The 1-KB erased flash memory block (0x1000~0x13FF).	388

Table II (*Continued*)

Chapter	Figures and Tables	Page
	Figure 6.32: The running result of the DRAFlashInt project.	397
	Figure 6.34: The running result of the project DRAFlashBuffer.	400
	Figure 6.38: The 18 read-out data stored in the data array prData[].	414
	Figure 6.42: The read back data stored in the prData[] array.	420
Chapter 8	Figure 8.74: Running result of the project DRAUART.	664
	Figure 8.75: Running result of the project Lab8_5.	685
	Figure 8.76: Running result of the project Lab8_6.	689
Chapter 11	Figure 11.6: The FPU is automatically used in MDK-ARM μ Version 5 IDE.	939
	Figure 11.11: The running result of the project DRAFPU.	945

Table III list the copyright permitted Figures and Tables originated by the Math-Works, Inc. and used in this book. All those Figures and Tables have been permitted to be re-printed in this book under the copyright permissions of the MathWorks, Inc.

Chapter	Figures and Tables	Page
Chapter 10	Figure 10.38: The MATLAB Script file getMData.m.	875
	Figure 10.39: Load the data array mdata.dat into the MATLAB Workspace.	876
		876
	Figure 10.40: The opened Identification Toolbox and Import data wizard.	877
	Figure 10.41: The modified data array mdatad in the identification Toolbox.	878
		879
	Figure 10.42: The opened Process Models wizard.	
	Figure 10.43: The identified model responses and analysis.	880
	Figure 10.44: Commands used to set transfer function of the DC motor and start PID tuner.	880
	Figure 10.45: The opened PID Tuner and the tuning result.	881
	Figure 10.46: The opened SIMULINK window.	882
	Figure 10.47: The finished SIMULINK bock connections.	883
	Figure 10.48: The simulated step response result.	
	Figure 10.51: The step response of the actual closed-loop motor control system.	886
		890
	Figure 10.55: Graphic representation of the control rules.	890
	Figure 10.56: The fuzzy output surface or envelope.	898
	Figure 10.62: The step response of the fuzzy logic control system.	
Chapter 11	Figure 11.12: The plotting result for the data array gSData[].	945

About the Companion Website

This book is accompanied by a companion website: http://www.wiley.com/go/armbai
The website includes:

- Class Projects
- Appendix A
- Appendix B
- Appendix C
- Appendix D
- Appendix E

If you are an instructor and adopted this book for your course, please email
ieeeproposals@wiley.com to get access to the instructor files for this book.

Chapter 1

Introduction to Microcontrollers and This Book

As the development of Very Large Scale Integrated Circuits (VLSI) in recent years, more and more advanced semiconductor devices and equipments have been built with very high intensity and density. Millions of MOSFETs can be integrated in a very small semiconductor chip to generate multifunction processors, called `Microprocessors`. Microprocessors can be considered as a very large scale integrated circuit device that can be programmed to perform specific functions or tasks.

One of the most popular and important microprocessors is the Center Processing Unit, or CPU, which is the center of a computer and used to process and coordinate all operations on a computer. Some other popular microprocessors can be categorized into the different groups based on their functions. Some popular microprocessors are:

1. CPU—Including the Intel family such as 8080/8085/8086/80286/80386/80486/80586 and Pentium, the Motorola family such as M6800, M68000, M68HC11, and M68HC12, and the Apple family such as 6502.

2. Parallel 8-bit I/O ports—Including the Intel family such as 8255 and the Motorola family such as M68230 Parallel Interface and Timer (PIT).

3. Parallel-to-Serial Converter—Including the Intel family such as 8251 and the Motorola family such as M68681 dual UART.

4. Timer and Counter—Including the Intel family such as 8253 and the Motorola family such as MC1555U timer.

5. Interrupt Control Unit—Including the Intel family such as 8259 and the Motorola family such as MC6828 Priority Interrupt Controller.

6. Random Access Memory (RAM) Chips—Including the Intel family 28C256 (32 K × 8), 62512 (64 K × 8), and 62158 (1024 K × 8).

7. Erasable Programmable Read-Only Memory (EPROM) Chips—Including the Intel family such as 27128 (128 K×8), 27256 (256 K × 8), and 27512 (512 K × 8).

By combining microprocessors with memory units and I/O ports, a `Microcontroller` system can be built. Sometimes a microcontroller is also called a microcomputer. In fact, a microcontroller is made by embedding processors, a memory unit, and I/O ports into a single semiconductor chip, and this is the current module of a modern

Practical Microcontroller Engineering with ARM® Technology, First Edition. Ying Bai.
© 2016 by The Institute of Electrical and Electronics Engineers, Inc. Published 2016 by John Wiley & Sons, Inc.
Companion Website: www.wiley.com/go/armbai

microcontroller unit (MCU) used in all aspects in our present-day society. The latest MCU module is the ARM® Cortex®-M4 family.

Let's have a closer look at the structure and configuration of a microcontroller or a microcomputer system.

1.1   MICROCONTROLLER CONFIGURATION AND STRUCTURE

As we mentioned, by combining some microprocessors with memory units and I/O ports, a microcontroller can be built. In fact, a microcontroller can be built by combining three basic components with three system buses as shown in Figure 1.1.

Three components are CPU, Memory, and I/O Ports. These three components are connected with three system buses, Address Bus (A.B.), Data Bus (D.B.) and Control Bus (C.B.), to provide the following functions:

- The CPU works as headquarters for the microcontroller to provide all controls to other components and coordinate them to fulfill the desired tasks assigned to the microcontroller.
- The memory unit works as a storage unit to store the user's program, including the user's instructions and data. Some system programs and data are also stored in special memory units such as PROM, EPROM, EEPROM, or flash memory.
- The I/O Ports work as an interface and provide the communications between the CPU and the peripheral devices.

The communications between these three components are performed via three system buses. The Address Bus provides a valid address to the memory to enable the CPU to select and pick up the desired instruction or data from the selected memory space. The Data Bus is used to transfer a valid data item between components. The Control Bus provides valid operational signals to coordinate the information transfer between components. Some popular control signals are Read/Write (R/W) signal used to read from or write into the memory, Chip Select (CS) signal used to decode the address to select the desired microprocessor chip, and Enable signal E that is similar to the CS signal.

Three components are connected together via three buses in tri-state mode, which means that the connection between any two components is disconnected or high

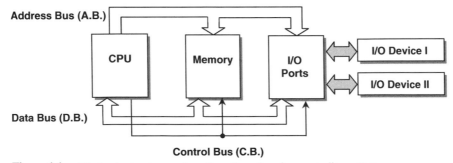

Figure 1.1.   The basic structure and configuration of a microcontroller system.

impedance until a valid address is applied and decoded to enable the selected tri-state gates to turn on.

Regularly, a CPU contains three components: (1) a group of registers made of flip-flops, (2) Arithmetic and Logic Unit (ALU), and (3) control signal generator. The registers are used to assist the instruction's decoding and data operations since most operations between the CPU and memory are performed inside registers in the CPU because of the high execution speed of registers. The ALU is used to perform arithmetic and logic operations, and the control unit provides all timing and control signals required to perform all related operations of the CPU.

Generally the memory space is divided into two separate areas: One is the system memory space that is used to store instructions and data related to the normal operations of the microcontroller, and the other one is the users' memory space that is used to store the users' instructions and data.

The memory spaces also can be divided into the catch and heap areas based on the materials used to build the memory; the former is made of high-speed static RAM (SRAM), and the latter is made of dynamic RAM (DRAM) with relatively slower accessing speeds. The advantage of using the SRAM is that a higher memory accessing speed can be obtained, but much more MOSFETs are utilized for each SRAM unit and therefore makes the memory structure complicated with higher cost. The advantage of using DRAM is that higher memory densities or integration intensities can be obtained with mush simpler MOSFET structure and lower cost for each DRAM unit, but the working speed is relatively slower because of an additional refresh circuit applied on the DRAM. Because of the cost issue, usually the size of SRAM or the catch memory is small but the size of the heap or DRAM is huge.

The memory can also be categorized to the Random Access Memory (RAM), the Read Only Memory (ROM), the Erasable Programmable ROM (EPROM), or Electrically Erased Programmable ROM (EEPROM). Generally, the system instructions and data are stored in the ROM, EPROM, or EEPROM spaces. The users' instructions and data are stored in the RAM space. Based on the functions, the memory can be divided into either volatile memory or nonvolatile memory. The RAM belongs to the volatile memory since all information stored in this kind of memory would be gone when the power is off. However, the ROM, EPROM, and EEPROM belong to the nonvolatile memory since the information stored in this kind of memory would be still in there even the power is off.

Based on the structure, the RAM can be categorized to static RAM (SRAM) or dynamic RAM (DRAM). We will provide more detailed discussion about the static and dynamic RAM in Chapter 6.

The I/O Ports can be divided into two categories: the parallel and the serial I/O ports. Each I/O port can be mapped to a memory address, or each of them can have special I/O address that is different with a normal memory address. The former is called the I/O memory mapping addressing and the latter is called the direct I/O addressing.

1.2 THE ARM® CORTEX®M4 MICROCONTROLLER SYSTEM

Different embedded systems or MCUs have been developed and built by different vendors in recent years. One of the popular MCUs is the ARM® Cortex®-M MCU family. This kind of MCU provides multifunctions and control abilities, low-power consumptions, high-efficiency signal processing functionality, and low-cost and easy to use advantages. The latest product of the ARM® Cortex®-M family is Cortex®-M4 MCU.

The ARM® Cortex-M is a group of 32-bit Reduced Instruction Set Computing (RISC) ARM® processor cores licensed by ARM® Holdings. The cores are intended for microcontroller use and consist of the Cortex®-M0, Cortex®-M0+, Cortex®-M1, Cortex®-M3, and Cortex®-M4.

The ARM® Cortex®-M4 processor is the latest embedded processor by ARM® specifically developed to address digital signal control markets that demand an efficient, easy-to-use blend of control and signal processing capabilities. The combination of high-efficiency signal processing functionality with the low-power, low-cost, and ease-of-use benefits of the Cortex-M family of processors is designed to satisfy the emerging category of flexible solutions specifically targeting the motor control, automotive, power management, embedded audio, and industrial automation markets.

The ARM® Cortex®-M4 MCU provides the following specific functions:

- Although the Cortex-M4 processor is a 32-bit MCU, it can also handle 8-bit, 16-bit, and 32-bit data efficiently.
- The Cortex®-M4 MCU itself does not include any memory, but it provides different memory interfaces to the external Flash ROMs and SRAMs.
- Due to its 32-bit data length, the maximum searchable memory space is 4 GB.
- In order to effectively manage and access this huge memory space, different regions are created to store system instructions and data, users' instructions, data, and mapped peripheral device registers and related interfaces.
- The internal bus system used in Cortex-M4 MCU is 32-bit, and it is based on the so-called Advanced Microcontroller Bus Architecture (AMBA) standard. The AMBA standard provides efficient operations and low power cost on the hardware.
- The main bus interface between the MCU and external components is the Advanced High-performance Bus (AHB), which provides interfaces for memory and system bus, as well as for peripheral devices.
- A Nested Vectored Interrupt Controller (NVIC) is used to provide all supports and managements to the interrupt responses and processing to all components in the system.
- The Cortex-M4 MCU also provides standard and extensive debug features and supports to enable users to easily check and trace their program with breakpoints and steps.

To assist users to build professional microcontroller application projects, some useful development tools and kits are involved in this book to enable users to develop specific implementations easier and faster.

1.3   THE TM4C123GH6PM MICROCONTROLLER DEVELOPMENT TOOLS AND KITS

In this book, we concentrate on a typical and popular ARM® Cortex®-M4 MCU system built by Texas Instruments™ called TM4C123GXL, in which two ARM® Cortex®-M4 MCUs, TM4C123GH6PM, are utilized. The related development tools and kits can be categorized into two parts: the hardware part and the software part.

The hardware part includes:

- Tiva™ LaunchPad TM4C123GXL Evaluation Board (EVB).
- EduBASE ARM® Trainer (contains most popular peripherals and interfaces).
- Some other related peripherals, such as DC Motors, CAN interfaces, and D/A converters.

The software part includes:

- Integrated Development Environment Keil® ARM®-MDK μVersion®5 (IDE).
- TivaWare™ SW-EK-TM4C123GXL Software Driver Package.
- Stellaris In-Circuit Debug Interface (ICDI).

Appendices A~D, available from the website www.wiley.com, provide detailed information and directions for downloading and installing these software tools in your host computers.

1.4 OUTSTANDING FEATURES ABOUT THIS BOOK

1. Both ARM® assembly and C codes are provided in this book to assist users to develop professional projects with any language easily and faster.

2. More than 70 real example projects are provided in this book with detailed and line-by-line explanations and illustrations to enable users to understand and learn the programming skills easily and faster. These example projects covered most popular peripherals, such as Flash Memory and EEPROM, ADC, 4×4 Keypad, 7-Segment LEDs, LCD, DAC, I2C, UART, PWM, USB, Timers, Watchdog Timers, QEI, Analog Comparator, PID Controller, Fuzzy Logic Controller, FPU, and MPU, in different chapters.

3. Both the Direct Register Access (DRA) model and the Software Driver (SD) model programming techniques are introduced and discussed with a set of complete real example projects to cover all peripherals in the book.

4. A complete set of home works, including the true/false, multi-choice questions, comprehensive questions, and lab projects, is attached after each chapter. This enables students to understand what they learned better by doing something themselves.

5. A complete set of answers to all home works is provided for the instructors.

6. A complete set of MS Power Point teaching slides are provided for the instructors to make them teaching this book easily and conveniently.

7. Appendices A~E, available from the website www.wiley.com, provide a complete set of instructions and directions to enable users to download and install development tools and kits easily and faster.

8. Good textbook for college students and a good reference book for programmers, software engineers, and academic researchers.

1.5 WHO THIS BOOK IS FOR

This book is designed for college students and software programmers who want to develop practical and commercial control programming with ARM® Cortex®-M4 MCU and related development tools. Fundamental knowledge and understanding on C language programming is assumed.

1.6 WHAT THIS BOOK COVERS

This book is composed of 12 chapters with an easy study way to enable students to learn the ARM® Cortex®-M4 microcontroller technology and interface implementations easily. Each chapter contains homework and exercises as well as lab projects to enable students to perform necessary exercises to improve their learning and understanding for the related materials and technologies.

Chapter 1: Provides an overview and introduction about the microcontrollers and a global review for the book with highlights on outstanding features and organizations of the book.

Chapter 2: Provides detailed discussion and analysis about the ARM® Cortex®-M4 MCU hardware, which includes the architecture of the Cortex®-M4 Core and processor, memory (flash memory, SRAM, and EEPROM), GPIO Parallel and serial ports, Nested Vectored Interrupt Controller (NVIC), Private Peripheral Bus (PPB) and Advanced High-performance Bus (AHB), System Timer SysTick, system control block (SCB), floating point unit (FPU) and memory protection unit (MPU). The detailed discussions and introductions to the special MCU used in this book, TM4C123GH6PM, are also given in this chapter.

Chapter 3: Provides detailed discussion and analysis about the development tools and kits for the Cortex-M4 MCU. These tools and kits are discussed separately based on the hardware and software sections. The TM4C123GXL EVB and EduBASE ARM® Trainer are discussed as the hardware kits and tools. The Keil® ARM®-MDK μVersion®5 that works as an IDE and the TivaWare™ SW-EK-TM4C123GXL Software Driver Package that works as a software suite and driver library are introduced as software tools and kits. The Stellaris® ICDI driver that works as a debugger for the TM4C123GXL EVB is also discussed in this chapter.

Chapter 4: Provides detailed and complete discussion about the ARM® Cortex®-M4 microcontroller software and instruction set. These discussions include the ARM® Cortex®-M4 software development structure, a complete Cortex®-M4 assembly instruction set, the Keil® CMSIS Core specific intrinsic functions, inline assembler, C programming procedure for the Cortex®-M4 MCU, and two programming models applied by the TivaWare™ Peripheral Driver Library. The detailed procedure of building and developing an example ARM® Cortex®-M4 MCU project with C codes is discussed step by step at the end of this chapter.

Chapter 5: Provides detailed discussions about the ARM® Cortex®-M4 interrupts and exceptions. These discussions covered the interrupt and exception sources, interrupt handlers, and interrupt and exception vector tables. Most popular control registers involved in the Nested Vectored Interrupt Controller (NVIC) are introduced in details with related examples. The NVIC macros and NVIC API functions supported by the CMSIS Core software package are also introduced in this chapter. The GPIO interrupts handled by some API functions provided by the TivaWare™ Peripheral Driver Library are discussed at the end of this chapter.

Chapter 6: Provides detailed discussion about ARM® Cortex®-M4 memory system. In particular, the memory system used in the TM4C123GH6PM MCU is discussed in extensive detail. These discussions include the memory architecture, the entire memory map with accurate addresses for each component, SRAM, Flash Memory, internal ROM, and EEPROM. Most popular control registers applied on these memory models are introduced and discussed in detail with related example projects. The API functions used for flash memory and EEPROM are also discussed in this chapter. Some special memory implementation techniques, such as bit-band alias, flash memory programming, and EEPROM programming, are introduced with actual example projects.

Chapter 7: Provides detailed discussions about the ARM® Cortex®-M4 Parallel I/O Ports programming. The major parallel peripherals discussed in this chapter include the on-board keypads, analog-to-digital converter, and PWM. All peripherals in the Cortex-M4 MCU system, including the parallel and serial, are interfaced to the processor via a group of General-Purpose Input–Output ports, also called GPIO Ports. All GPIO Ports and control registers related to these parallel peripherals are introduced with some real example projects in details. Those peripheral-related API functions provided by the TivaWare™ Peripheral Driver Library are also discussed in this chapter with actual example projects.

Chapter 8: Provides detailed discussions about the ARM® Cortex®-M4 Serial I/O Ports programming. The major serial peripherals discussed in this chapter include the Synchronous Serial Interface (SSI), Inter-Integrated Circuit (I2C) Interface, and Universal Asynchronous Receivers/Transmitters (UARTs). Several real example projects related to these serial peripherals include: on-board LCD Interface project, on-board 7-segment LED project, digital-to-analog converter project, I2C interfacing project, and UART project. The related API functions provided by the TivaWare™ Peripheral Driver Library are also discussed with some real example projects in this chapter.

Chapter 9: Provides detailed discussions about the ARM® Cortex®-M4 Timer system and the USB system as well as their applications. These discussions include the General-Purpose Timers Module (GPTM), Watchdog Timers Module (WDTM), and USB Controllers. All timer-related control registers, including the GPTM, WDTM, and USB, are introduced and discussed in detail with several real example projects. The 64-bit Wide-Purpose Timers Module (WGPTM) is also discussed. Different implementations of using GPTM, WGPTM, and WDTM are analyzed and discussed with some real example projects. These implementations include the one-shot/periodic timer, input edge-count mode, input edge-time mode, real-time clock (RTC) mode, and PWM mode. The related API functions supporting those modes and provided by the TivaWare™ Peripheral Driver Library are also introduced with example projects.

Chapter 10: Provides detailed discussion about the ARM® Cortex®-M4 other peripheral programming. These peripherals include the Controller Area Network (CAN), Quadrature Encoder Interface (QEI), and Analog Comparators (ACMP). The fundamental architectures of the CAN, QEI, and ACMP are introduced first. Then all control registers related to these peripherals are introduced with several example projects. Some advanced and updated control strategies, such as PID control and fuzzy logic control, are applied in those projects to attract the students' interests with regard to learning these peripherals. Some professional techniques, such as motor model identification and PID controller design with MATLAB® simulation, are also involved in these projects. The related API functions for these peripherals are introduced in this chapter.

`Chapter 11`: Provides detailed discussion about the ARM® Cortex®-M4 Floating Point Unit (FPU). First the single-precision and double-precision floating point numbers and protocols are introduced. Then the FTP architecture applied in the Cortex-M4 MCU is discussed in details. All control registers used for the FPU are discussed and illustrated in detail. The FPU-related API functions provided by the TivaWare™ Peripheral Driver Library are also discussed. Finally a real example project is provided to illustrate how to use the FPU to perform some sophisticated floating point data operations.

`Chapter 12`: Provides detailed discussion about the ARM® Cortex®-M4 Memory Protection Unit (MPU). An overview about the MPU is provided first in this chapter. All control registers used for the MPU are discussed and illustrated in details. The MPU-related API functions provided by the TivaWare™ Peripheral Driver Library are also discussed. Finally a real example project is provided to illustrate how to use the MPU to perform desired protection functions for the selected memory regions.

- `Appendix A`—Provides instructions about downloading and installing the Keil® MDK-ARM® 5.1 IDE.
- `Appendix B`—Provides instructions about downloading and installing the TivaWare™ SW-EK-TM4C123GXL Software Package.
- `Appendix C`—Provides instructions about downloading and installing the Stellaris ICDI and Virtual COM Port.
- `Appendix D`—Provides the Tiva™ C Series TM4C123G Based EVB Hardware Setup.
- `Appendix E`—Provides a set of CMSIS Core-Specific Intrinsic Functions.

1.7 HOW THIS BOOK IS ORGANIZED AND HOW TO USE THIS BOOK

This book is designed for both college students who are new to ARM® Cortex®-M4 microcontroller system and professional application programmers who have professional experience on this topic.

Chapters 2~9 provide fundamental and professional introductions and discussions about the most popular ARM® Cortex®-M4 MCU applications with the most widely used peripherals, such as flash memory and EEPROM, ADC, DAC, PWM, UART, USB, I2C, SSI, LCD, and GPTM. Some other peripherals, including the CAN, ACMP, and QEI, are discussed in Chapter 10. Two optional components, FPU and MPU, are discussed in Chapters 11 and 12.

Based on the organization of this book we described above, this book can be used as two categories such as Level I and Level II, which is shown in Figure 1.2.

For undergraduate or graduate college students or beginning software programmers, it is highly recommended to learn and understand the contents of Chapters 2~9 since those are fundamental knowledge and techniques used in the ARM® Cortex®-M4 microcontroller programming and implementations (Level I). For the material in Chapters 10~12, they are only related to the additional and optional peripherals and components used in the ARM® Cortex®-M4 microcontroller programming, and it is optional to instructors and it depends on the time and schedule (Level II).

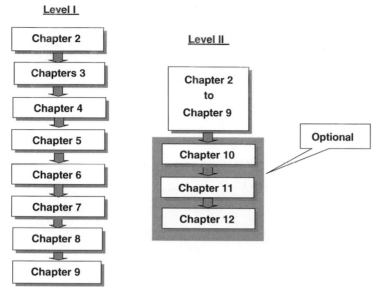

Figure 1.2.   Two study levels in the book.

1.8   HOW TO USE THE SOURCE CODE AND SAMPLE PROJECTS

All projects in the book can be divided into two parts: the class projects and the lab projects. All source codes for those projects are available in the book. However, all class projects are available to both instructors and students, but the lab projects are only available to instructors since students need to build these lab projects themselves. All sources codes for these projects have been debugged and tested, and they are ready to be executed in any TM4C123GXL EVB.

All class projects are categorized into the associated chapters that are located at the folder ARM Class Projects that is located at the site http://booksupport.wiley.com. You need to use either the book ISBN, the book Title, or the Author name to access and download these projects into your computer and run each project as you like. To successfully run those projects on your computer, the following conditions must be met:

1. The Keil™ MDK-ARM® 5.1 and above IDE must be installed in your computer.
2. The TivaWare™ SW-EK-TM4C123GXL Software Package should be installed in your computer, and this package must be installed if you want to use any API function provided by TivaWare™ Peripheral Driver Library.
3. The Stellaris ICDI and Virtual COM Port driver must be installed in your computer.
4. The TM4C123GXL EVB and EduBASE ARM® Trainer must be installed and connected to your host computer.

Refer to Appendices A~C to complete steps 1~3, and refer to Appendix D for step 4.

All book-related teaching and learning materials, including the class projects, lab projects, appendices, faculty teaching slides, and home work solutions, can be found from the associated folders located at the Wiley Book Support site, as shown in Figure 1.3.

These materials are categorized and stored at different folders in two different sites based on the teaching purpose (for instructors) and learning purpose (for students).

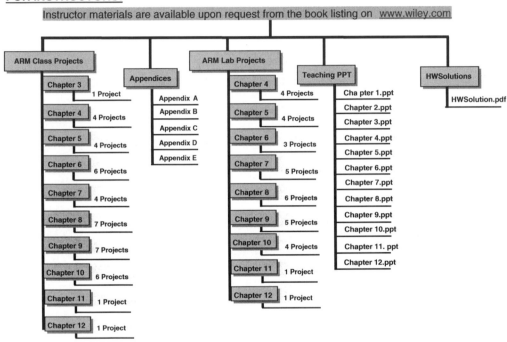

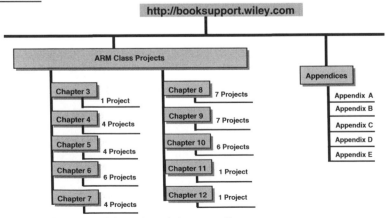

Figure 1.3.   Book-related materials on the website www.wiley.com.

FOR INSTRUCTORS

1. ARM Class Projects Folder: Contains all class projects for different chapters.
2. ARM Lab Projects Folder: Contains all lab projects included in the home work sections in different chapters. Students need to follow the directions provided in each homework lab section to build and develop these lab projects themselves.
3. Appendices Folder: Contains all Appendices (Appendices A~E) that provide useful references and practical instructions to download and install the ARM® Cortex®-M4-related development tools and kits.
4. TeachingPPT Folder: Contains all MS-PPT teaching slides for each chapter.
5. HWSolutions Folder: Contains a set of complete solutions for the homework developed and used in the book. The solutions are categorized and stored at the different chapter subfolder based on the book chapter sequence.

FOR STUDENTS

1. ARM Class Projects Folder: Contains all class projects in different chapters. Students can download and run these class projects in their host computers after a suitable environment has been set up (refer to conditions listed above).
2. Appendices Folder: Contains all Appendices (Appendices A~E) that provide useful references and practical instructions to download and install the ARM® Cortex®-M4 related development tools and kits.

1.9 INSTRUCTORS AND CUSTOMERS SUPPORTS

The teaching materials for all chapters have been extracted and represented by a sequence of Microsoft Power Point files, each file for one chapter. The interested instructors can find those teaching materials from the folder TeachingPPT that is located at the site www. wiley.com, and those instructor materials are available upon request from the book listing on www.wiley.com.

A set of complete homework solution is also available upon request from the book listing on www.wiley.com.

E-mail support is available to readers of this book. When you send e-mail to us, please provide the following information:

- The detailed description about your problems, including the error message and debug message as well as the error or debug number if it is provided.
- Your name, job title, and company name.

Please send all questions to the e-mail address: ybai@ieee.org.

Detailed structure and distribution of all book-related material in the Wiley site, including the teaching materials for instructors and learning materials for students, are shown in Figure 1.3.

Chapter 2

ARM® Microcontroller Architectures

The main topics to be discussed in this chapter are about the architectures and organizations of most popular embedded systems, including the most updated microcontroller ARM® Cortex®-M4, Tiva™ TM4C123GH6PM MCU, Tiva for C Series LaunchPad™ TM4C123GXL evaluation board, and EduBASE ARM® Trainer. All of these components will be used in this book to make our project development process easier and simpler.

2.1 OVERVIEW AND INTRODUCTION

A so-called embedded system is generally composed of a group of programmable devices with some memory devices and a set of peripheral device I/O ports. In fact, an embedded system can be considered as an integrated system by embedding some Central Processing Units (CPUs) with some Memory subsystems, I/O Ports, and maybe several Peripheral Devices together into a single semiconductor chip to get an intelligent control unit, called a Microcontroller Unit (MCU). Therefore a typical embedded system can be thought of as an MCU. An illustration block diagram for a general MCU is shown in Figure 2.1.

Most important components involved in this MCU include:

- ARM® CPU or Processor
- Memory (SRAM and Flash Memory)
- Parallel Input and Output (PIO) Ports
- Some internal devices (Timer/Counters) or peripheral devices (ADC and USB)

Different embedded systems or MCUs have been developed and built by different vendors in recent years. One of the most popular MCUs is the ARM® Cortex®-M MCU family. This kind of MCU provides multifunctions and control abilities, low power consumptions, high-efficiency signal processing functionality, low cost, and easy-to-use advantages. The latest product of the ARM® Cortex®-M family is Cortex®-M4 MCU.

This chapter is organized into the following sections:

- The architecture of the ARM® Cortex®-M4 MCU is discussed first. This includes the architecture of the Cortex®-M4 MCU and the architecture of the ARM® Cortex®-M4 Core processor (CPU).

Practical Microcontroller Engineering with ARM® Technology, First Edition. Ying Bai.
© 2016 by The Institute of Electrical and Electronics Engineers, Inc. Published 2016 by John Wiley & Sons, Inc.
Companion Website: www.wiley.com/go/armbai

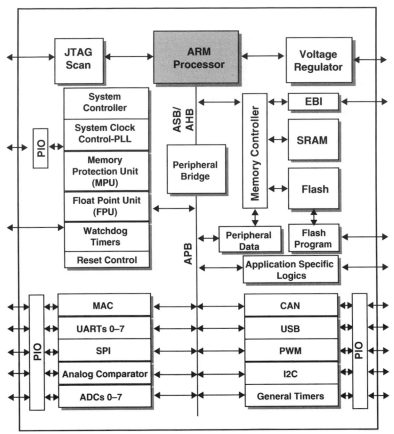

Figure 2.1.   The block diagram for a general MCU.

- Then the external memory architecture is discussed with the interfaces between the Cortex®-M4 MCU and memory (Flash Memory and SRAM) because the Cortex®-M4 is a special MCU and it does not contain any internal memory. Since a memory mapping technique is adopted in the ARM® Cortex®-M4 MCU, which means that all related registers in peripheral devices are mapped to certain memory addresses, the peripheral architecture can be involved in this section.

- The Nested Vectored Interrupt Controller (NVIC) architecture is introduced since this unit is integrated into the MCU chip.

- The debug architecture, which is an important feature and plays a key role in the development of the user programs, is introduced here.

- The programmer's model, including the operation modes and states, are discussed after the architectures have been discussed.

Because the ARM® Cortex®-M4 is the latest version of a microcontroller unit involving a lot of new and advanced techniques, its architecture definitely becomes very complicated if one wants to get a very detailed picture about this product. Fortunately, as a software developer or software engineer, you do not need to understand each detail of the architecture; namely, what you need to learn is the basic functions of most popular or required components, their block diagrams and interfaces in this MCU. Following this style, we try to avoid some details for those optional components in this MCU to reduce the learning curves and to save the reader's precious time.

2.2 INTRODUCTION TO ARM® CORTEX®-M4 MCU

The ARM® Cortex®-M is a group of 32-bit Reduced Instruction Set Computing (RISC) ARM® processor cores licensed by ARM® Holdings. The cores arc intended for microcontroller use, and they consist of the Cortex®-M0, Cortex®-M0+, Cortex®-M1, Cortex®-M3, and Cortex®-M4. Table 2.1 shows a development history for ARM® MCUs family.

Table 2.1. Development history of the ARM® MCUs family.

Architecture	Bit Width	Cores Designed by ARM Holdings	Cores Designed by Third Parties	Cortex Profile
ARMv1	32/26	ARM1		
ARMv2	32/26	ARM2, ARM3	Amber, STORM Open Soft Core	
ARMv3	32	ARM6, ARM7		
ARMv4	32	ARM8	StrongARM, FA526	
ARMv4T	32	ARM7TDMI, ARM9TDMI		
ARMv5	32	ARM7EJ, ARM9E, ARM10E	XScale, FA626TE, Feroceon, PJ1/Mohawk	
ARMv6	32	ARM11		
ARMv6-M	32	ARM Cortex-M0, ARM Cortex-M0+, ARM Cortex-M1		Microcontroller
ARMv7-M	32	ARM Cortex-M3		Microcontroller
ARMv7E-M	32	ARM Cortex-M4		Microcontroller
ARMv7-R	32	ARM Cortex-R4, ARM Cortex-R5, ARM Cortex-R7		Real-time
ARMv7-A	32	ARM Cortex-A5, ARM Cortex-A7, ARM Cortex-A8, ARM Cortex-A9, ARM Cortex-A12, ARM Cortex-A15, ARM Cortex-A17	Krait, Scorpion, PJ4/Sheeva, Apple A6/A6X	Application
ARMv8-A	64/32	ARM Cortex-A53, ARM Cortex-A57	X-Gene, Denver, Apple A7 (Cyclone), K12	Application
ARMv8-R	32	No announcements yet		Real-time

It can be found from Table 2.1 that the ARM® Cortex®-M3 and Cortex®-M4 MCUs belong to the ARMv7 family, and they are 32-bit microcontroller units. However, the early ARM® Cortex®-M MCUs, such as Cortex®-M0–Cortex®-M1, belong to the ARMv6-M family.

The ARM® Cortex®-M4 processor is the latest embedded processor by ARM® specifically developed to address digital signal control markets that demand an efficient, easy-to-use blend of control and signal processing capabilities. The combination of high-efficiency signal processing functionality with the low-power, low cost, and ease-of-use benefits of the Cortex®-M family of processors is designed to satisfy the emerging category of flexible solutions specifically targeting the motor control, automotive, power management, embedded audio, and industrial automation markets.

The ARM® Cortex®-M4 MCU provides the following specific functions:

- Although the Cortex®-M4 processor is a 32-bit MCU, it can also handle 8-bit, 16-bit, and 32-bit data efficiently.
- The Cortex®-M4 MCU itself does not include any memory, but it provides different memory interfaces to the external Flash Memory and SRAMs.
- Because of its 32-bit data length, the maximum searchable memory space is up to 4 GB.
- In order to effectively manage and access this huge memory space, different regions are created to store system instructions and data, users' instructions, data, and mapped peripheral device registers and related interfaces.
- The internal bus system used in Cortex®-M4 MCU is 32-bit and is based on the so-called Advanced Microcontroller Bus Architecture (AMBA) standard. The AMBA standard provides efficient operations and low power cost on the hardware.
- The main bus interface between the MCU and external components is the Advanced High-performance Bus (AHB), which provides interfaces for memory and system bus as well as for peripheral devices.
- A Nested Vectored Interrupt Controller (NVIC) is used to provide all supports and managements to the interrupt responses and processing to all components in the system.
- The Cortex®-M4 MCU also provides standard and extensive debug features and supports to enable users to easily check and trace their program with breakpoints and steps.

Overall, the Cortex®-M4 MCU processor incorporates:

- A Processor Core or CPU.
- A Nested Vectored Interrupt Controller (NVIC) closely integrated with the processor core to achieve low-latency interrupt processing.
- Multiple high-performance bus interfaces, including Code Interface and SRAM and Peripheral Interface.
- A System Timer unit SysTick.
- A low-cost debug solution with the optional ability, such as Debug Access Port (DAP) and Data Watchpoint.
- An optional Memory Protection Unit (MPU).
- An optional Floating Point Unit (FPU).
- Embedded Trace Macrocell (ETM) interface.
- Instrumentation Trace Macrocell (ITM) interface.
- The debug and Serial Wire Viewer (SWV) interface.

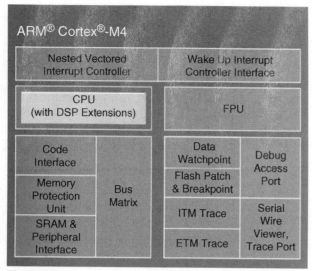

Figure 2.2.   The structure block diagram for ARM® Cortex®-M4 MCU. (Reproduced with permission from ARM® Limited. Copyright © ARM Limited.)

A structure block diagram for ARM® Cortex®-M4 MCU is shown in Figure 2.2.

2.2.1 The Architecture of ARM® Cortex®-M4 MCU

Generally, an ARM® Cortex®-M4 MCU is related to the following four architectures:

- ARM® architecture.
- Memory architecture.
- Nested Vectored Interrupt Control (NVIC) architecture.
- Debug architecture.

Let's discuss these architectures one by one in the following sections.

2.2.1.1 The ARM® MCU Architecture

First let's introduce the ARM® architecture. Figure 2.3 shows a functional block diagram for the ARM® Cortex®-M4 MCU.

The Cortex®-M4 Core or Center Processing Unit (CPU)   This is a center control unit for the entire Cortex®-M4 MCU. All instructions are fetched into, decoded, and executed inside this CPU. This CPU or processor consists of three key components, namely, Register Bank, Internal Data Path, and control unit. This is the core for the normal operations of the entire MCU.

Floating Point Unit (FPU)   One of the important differences between the Cortex®-M4 MCU and Cortex®-M3 MCU is that an optional Floating Point Unit (FPU) is added into the Cortex®-M4 Core to enhance the floating point data operations. The Cortex®-M4 FPU

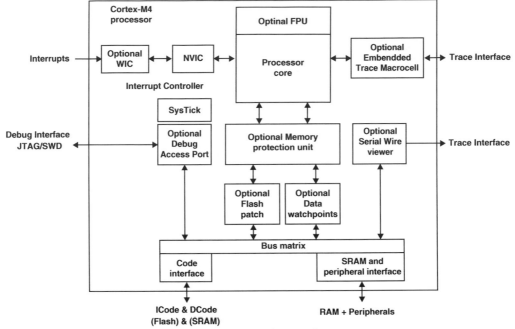

Figure 2.3. The functional block diagram for the ARM® Cortex®-M4 MCU. (Reproduced with permission from ARM® Limited. Copyright © ARM Limited.)

implements ARMv7E-M architecture with FPv4-SP extensions. It provides floating-point computation functionality that is compliant with the *ANSI/IEEE Std 754-2008, IEEE Standard for Binary Floating-Point Arithmetic*.

A System Timer SysTick The ARM® Cortex®-M4 MCU provides an integrated system timer, SysTick (System Tick), which includes a 24-bit counter with clear-on-writing, decrementing, and reloading-on-zero control mechanism. The main purpose of using this timer is to provide a periodic interrupt to ensure that the OS kernel can invoke regularly.

If you do not need to use any embedded OS in your application, the SysTick timer can work as a simple timer peripheral for periodic interrupt generator, delay generator, or timing measurement device. The reason for installing this timer inside the MCU is to make software portable, and any program built with a Cortex®-M processor can run any OS written for Cortex®-M4 MCU. More detailed discussion about this timer can be found in Section 2.6.4.

Nested Vectored Interrupt Controller (NVIC) The Nested Vectored Interrupt Controller (NVIC) is closely integrated with the processor core to achieve low latency interrupt processing. These features include the following:

- Monitor and pre-process any exception or interrupt occurred during the normal running of the processor. All exceptions and interrupts are categorized into different emergency levels based on their priority levels, from 1 to 15 for exceptions and from 16 to 240 for interrupts.

- Identify the exception or interrupt source if an exception/interrupt occurred, and direct the main control to the entry point (address) of the related exception/interrupt Interrupt Service Routine (ISR) to process the exception/interrupt.
- Dynamically manage all exceptions and interrupts based on their priority levels.
- Automatically store the processor states on interrupt entry, and restore it on interrupt exit, with no instruction overhead.
- Optional *Wake-up Interrupt Controller* (WIC) supports the ultra-low-power sleep mode.

Bus Matrix and Bus Interfaces   The Bus Matrix and Bus Interfaces provide:

- Three Advanced High-Performance Bus-Lite (AHB-Lite) interfaces: ICode interface to flash ROM, DCode interface to SRAM and peripheral interfaces, as well as System bus interfaces, including the internal control bus and debug components.
- Private Peripheral Bus (PPB) based on Advanced Peripheral Bus (APB) interface.
- Bit-Band support that includes atomic bit-band writing and reading operations.
- Memory access alignment and Write buffer for buffering of write data.
- Exclusive access transfers for multiprocessor systems.

Memory Protection Unit (MPU)   This is an optional MPU used for memory protection purpose and it includes:

- Eight memory regions.
- Sub-Region Disable (SRD), enabling efficient use of memory regions.
- The ability to enable a background region that implements the default memory map attributes.

System Control Block (SCB)   This block is located in the System Control Space (SCS) in the memory map, and it is integrated with the NVIC unit together to provide the following features:

- Monitor and control the processor configurations, such as low power modes.
- Provide fault detection information via fault status register.
- Relocate the Vector Table in the memory map by adjusting the content of the Vector Table Offset Register (VTOR).

Debug Access Port (DAP)   The DAP is an optional unit and it provides the following features:

- Debug access to all memory and registers in the system, including access to memory mapped devices, access to internal core registers when the core is halted, and access to debug control registers even while SYSRESETn is asserted.
- Serial Wire Debug Port (SW-DP)/Serial Wire JTAG Debug Port (SWJ-DP) debug access.
- Optional Flash Patch and Breakpoint (FPB) unit for implementing breakpoints and code patches.
- Optional Data Watchpoint and Trace (DWT) unit for implementing watchpoints, data tracing, and system profiling.
- Optional Instrumentation Trace Macrocell (ITM) for support of printf() style debugging.

- Optional Trace Port Interface Unit (TPIU) for bridging to a Trace Port Analyzer (TPA), including Single Wire Output (SWO) mode.
- Optional Embedded Trace Macrocell (ETM) for instruction trace.

2.2.1.2 The Architecture of the ARM® Cortex®-M4 Core (CPU)

Figure 2.4 shows an architecture block diagram for the ARM® Cortex®-M4 Core or CPU.

The ARM® Cortex®-M4 Core is a 32-bit RISC CPU and it provides the following components:

- Twenty-one 32-bit Registers
- 32-bit Internal Data Path
- 32-bit Bus Interface

Similar to most other microcontrollers' core or CPU, a Cortex®-M4 Core is composed of three important components:

- Register bank.
- Control unit.
- Internal Data Path (IDP) or Arithmetic and Logic Unit (ALU).

The ARM® Cortex®-M4 Core provides a group of registers, and all registers are 32 bits long. These registers can be combined together to form a register group or a register bank.

For each instruction, the Cortex®-M4 Core utilized a three-stage pipeline operation, which is a popular instruction operational style. This operation allows the CPU to get, decode, and execute multiple instructions simultaneously.

The data processing mode in the Cortex®-M4 used a so-called Load-Store Architecture, which means, in order to process data, the following three steps must be performed:

1. Load data from the memory and write them into registers in the register bank.
2. Process data inside the core.
3. Write the processed result back to the memory

Let's have a closer look at these registers in the register bank first.

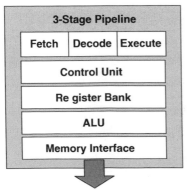

Figure 2.4. The architecture of the ARM® Cortex®-M4 CPU.

2.2.1.2.1 The Register Bank in the Cortex®-M4 Core Totally there are 21 32-bit registers located inside the Cortex®-M4 core. These registers can be divided into two groups:

1. Sixteen registers located in the register bank.

2. Five special registers located outside of the register bank.

A structure block diagram of these registers is shown in Figure 2.5. First let's take a look at those 16 registers in the register bank.

Inside the register bank, 13 registers R0~R12, belong to general-purpose registers and the other three registers R13~R15 are special registers with different specific functions. As we mentioned, all of these registers are 32-bit.

All 13 general-purpose registers can be used to store instructions, data, and addresses. These registers can also be further divided into two subgroups. The first eight registers, R0~R7, can be categorized to the Low Register group, and the R8~R12 can be grouped to a High Register set. Most 16-bit data operations should be performed in the Low Register group, and most 32-bit data operations should be processed in the High Register group.

The remaining three registers in the register bank belong to special registers with specific functions. The register R13 is a `Stack Pointer Register` (SPR) used to store the current stack address. In Cortex®-M4 core, there are two kinds of stack pointers: the `Main Stack Pointer` (MSP) and the `Process Stack Pointer` (PSP). The MSP is used for the system program working in the `Handler` Mode and the PSP is used for the user's program working in the `Thread` Mode. Only one stack pointer is active at a time. The default Stack Pointer is the MSP after the system is reset. But this stack pointer can be selected by programming of the CONTROL Register to be discussed later.

The register R14 is a `Link Register` (LR) and this register provides some linking functions to set up a connection between the main program and the calling functions or subroutines. When a function or subroutine is called, the returning address should be entered into the R14. After the function or subroutine is done, the content of the Link

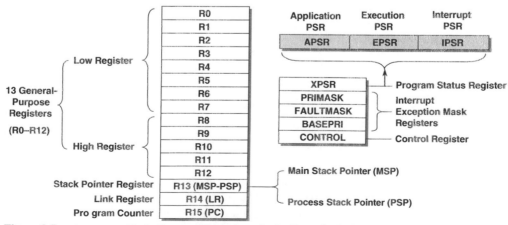

Figure 2.5. A structure block diagram of 21 registers in the Cortex®-M4 Core.

Register R14, which is the returning address to the main program, is fed into the Program Counter (PC) to enable the processor to continue the work from the address stored in the PC.

A similar situation occurred with the interrupts or exceptions. If some exception or interrupt happened, the returning address to the main program (or the next instruction's address in the main program) should be stored into the Link Register before the control can be transferred to the `Interrupt Service Routine` (ISR). As the ISR is done, the control can be returned to the main program by popping up the returning address to the PC.

The register R15 is the `Program Counter` (PC). This register keeps the sequence running of the program by automatically updating its content to point to the next instruction's address in the memory. Since the address line is 32 bits wide, each address needs 4 bytes space. Therefore the interval between the neighboring and the adjacent addresses is always 4 (bytes). In other words, the increment of an address is 4. This makes the LSB of an address always 0.

During the programming process, one can use R0~R12 (or r0~r12) to access general-purpose registers in the register bank. For three special registers used in the register bank, one can use different names to access them, such as: R13, r13, SP, or sp for the stack pointer register; R14, r14, LR, or lr for the link register, and R15, r15, PC, or pc for the program counter.

2.2.1.2.2 The Special Registers in the Cortex®-M4 Core
In additional to those registers in the register bank, the Cortex®-M4 core also includes five special registers located in the outside of the register bank, as shown in Figure 2.5. The purposes of these registers are used to monitor the running status of the CPU, system working states, and interrupt/exception masking. These special registers have the following properties:

- They are not memory mapped, which means that you cannot access them by using any memory mapped addresses, instead, you must use special register access instructions such as MSR or MRS.
- They are mainly used for the low-level language programming, such as Assembly, and not for the high-level programming such as C. However, you can access these special registers by using some C functions provided by CMSIS-Core.

Now let's discuss these special registers one by one.

The Program Status Register This register can be divided into three different status registers to show the running status of different units:

- Application Program Status Register (APSR)
- Execution Program Status Register (EPSR)
- Interrupt Program Status Register (IPSR)

These three registers can be accessed individually, such as APSR, EPSR, and IPSR, or in combination as one combined register PSR in your program. Different status is presented or reflected by using different bit on these registers. The meaning and purpose of each bit in these registers are shown in Figure 2.6 and Table 2.2.

Bits	31 30 29 28 27	26:25	24	23:20	19:16	15:10	9	8 7 6 5 4 3 2 1 0
APSR	N Z C V Q				GE˙			Reserved
IPSR	Reserved							Exception Number
EPSR	Reserved	ICI/IT	T	Reserved		ICI/IT		Reserved

(a) Three individual register –APSR, IPSR and EPSR.

Bits	31 30 29 28 27	26:25	24	23:20	19:16	15:10	9	8 7 6 5 4 3 2 1 0
PSR	N Z C V Q	ICI/IT	T		GE˙	ICI/IT		Exception Number

(b) The combined register PSR.

Figure 2.6.   Structure and bit functions in special registers.

Figure 2.6a shows the bit functions on three different status registers, APSR, IPSR, and EPSR, respectively. Figure 2.6b shows the bit functions on a combined status register PSR. The following important points must be in mind when trying to use these special registers:

- The running status, N, Z, V, and C bits provide information about the execution result of the previous DataPath or ALU operations. The associated bit should be set if a running result is matched. For example, bit Z is set to 1 if the execution result is zero.
- The Q bit is used to indicate whether a sticky saturation occurred. It is set by the SSAT and USAT instructions.
- The GE bits are used to indicate whether a Greater Than or Equal result happened when comparing two operands. These bits do not work for a Cortex®-M3 processor.
- The EPSR cannot be accessed by user's software codes directly using MRS or MSR instructions.
- The IPSR is a read-only register and can be read with the combined PSR.

Next let's take care of the Interrupt Exception Mask Registers.

The Interrupt Exception Mask Registers Three special registers, Primary Mask (PRIMASK) register, Fault Mask (FAULTMASK) register, and Base Priority (BASEPRI) register, are mainly used for interrupt or exception masking purpose.

Table 2.2.   Bit functions in the program status register (PSR).

Bit	Function
N	Negative Flag
Z	Zero Flag
C	Carry Flag
V	Overflow Flag
Q	Sticky Saturation Flag
GE[19:16]	Greater Than or Equal Flag for each byte lane
ICI/IT	Interrupt-Continuable-Instruction (ICI) bits/IF-THEN (IT) instruction status bit for conditional exception
T	Thumb State (Always 1)
Exception Number	Indicates which Exception occurred and is underprocessed by CPU

In the Cortex®-M4 system, the interrupts and exceptions have the following properties:

- All interrupts and exceptions are categorized into two major groups: Maskable or Non-Maskable, which means that those maskable interrupts/exceptions can be masked or disabled by the CPU, but those non-maskable interrupts/exceptions cannot be masked or disabled by the CPU.
- Both maskable and non-maskable interrupts/exceptions are further divided into the different priority levels based on their importance or emergency levels. The smaller the number on the priority level, the higher priority the interrupt/exception has.
- Generally a single bit in a mask register is used to mask (disable) or unmask (enable) certain interrupt/exception to be occurred. A 1 in that bit is to mask (disable) the selected interrupt/exception, and a 0 is to unmask (enable) the associated interrupt/exception.

The PRIMASK register is a Primary Interrupt Mask register, and it uses one bit (bit 0) to (a) mask or disable all maskable interrupts/exceptions when this bit is set to 1 and (b) unmask or enable all maskable interrupts/exceptions when this bit is reset to 0.

Similarly, the FAULTMASK register also uses its bit 0 to enable or disable all maskable interrupts/exceptions. However, one significant difference between the PRIMASK and the FAULTMASK registers is that the latter can be used to block the HardFault exception that belongs to the non-maskable exceptions. By using this register, we can block any further fault by inhibiting the triggering of further faults during fault processing. Another difference is that the FAULTMASK register can be reset to 0 automatically as the exception returns.

The BASEPRI register provides more flexible interrupt masking strategies. Unlike the PRIMASK register, the BASEPRI register can perform masking or unmasking functions based on the priority levels of related interrupts/exceptions. In this way, if a higher-level interrupt/exception is being executed or handled, any other lower-level interrupt/exception will not get a response until the current interrupt/exception has been processed.

Unlike the PRIMASK and the FAULTMASK registers, the BASEPRI uses more than one bit to handle different level interrupts and exceptions. The number of bits is determined by the total number of priority levels defined in a microcontroller system. For instance, in most Cortex®-M4 system, either 8 or 16 priority levels are adopted, and therefore this makes the BASEPRI register use either 3 bits or 4 bits to handle those 8 or 16 priority level interrupts.

After resetting, the BASEPRI register is reset to 0, and this disables the operation of the BASEPRI register. A nonzero number, which is equivalent to certain priority level, in the BASEPRI register will enable all interrupts/exceptions that have higher priority levels and will block or disable all other interrupts/exceptions that have the same or lower priority levels compared with the current level.

Generally one should use Assembly language codes to access these interrupt mask registers. However, the CMSIS-Core also provides some functions to access these registers with the C codes. More detailed discussion about these registers can be found in Section 4.5.2 in Chapter 4.

The CONTROL Register The CONTROL Register provides the following controllabilities:

- Select the stack pointer to use either a Main Stack Pointer or a Process Stack Pointer.
- Determine the access level in the Thread mode to use either the Privileged or Unprivileged level.

Bits	31 ~ 3	2	1	0
Cortex-M4 CONTROL			SPSEL	TMPL
Cortex-M4 with FPU CONTROL		FPCA	SPSEL	TMPL

Figure 2.7. Bit functions and structures of the CONTROL Register.

- Indicate whether the current executed codes use the Floating Point Unit (FPU) or not if the Cortex®-M4 contained a FPU.

Figure 2.7 shows the bit functions and structures for Cortex®-M4 MCU with and without FPU. The function of each bit (bits 0~2) on this CONTROL register is:

- TMPL (Bit 0): Thread Mode Privilege Level. This bit is used to define the privileged level in the Thread mode. Under the Thread mode, it is the privileged level when this bit is 0 (default). It is unprivileged level when this bit is 1. The processor is always in the privileged level when it works in the Handler Mode.

- SPSEL (Bit 1): Select the Stack Pointer. Under the Thread mode, it uses a Main Stack Pointer (MSP) when this bit is 0 (default). Otherwise, it uses a Process Stack Pointer (PSP) when this bit is 1. When it works in the Handler mode, this bit is always 0. This means that the Handler mode always uses a Main Stack Pointer (MSP).

- FPCA (Bit 2): Floating-Point Context Active bit. This bit is only available in the Cortex®-M4 with a FPU involved. The exception handler uses this bit to determine whether registers in the FPU need to be saved when an exception occurred. When this bit is 0 (default), it indicates that no any FPU has been used and therefore there is no need to save any register in FPU. However, if this bit is set to 1, an FPU has been used and related registers in the FPU need to be saved. The FPCA bit is automatically set when a floating point instruction is executed. This bit can be cleared by hardware on exception entry.

Bits 3~31 in this register are reserved for the future usage. More detailed discussion about the CONTROL register can be found in Sections 4.5.2 and 4.5.3 in Chapter 4.

2.2.1.3 *The Architecture of the Floating-Point Registers*

The Cortex®-M4 MCU provides an optional Floating-Point Unit (FPU). Additional registers are needed to support floating data operations if this FPU is used. These registers include Floating-Point Data Processing Registers (FPDPR) and Floating-Point Status and Control Register (FPSCR).

The FPDPR are composed of 32 single-precision registers, S0~S31, or 16 double-precision registers, D0~D15, respectively. Each of the 32-bit single-precision registers S0 to S31 can be accessed using floating-point instructions. These registers can also be accessed as a pair or double-precision registers D0 to D15 (64-bit). The configuration of these registers is shown in Figure 2.8.

One point to be noted is that the FPU in the Cortex®-M4 does not support double-precision floating-point calculations, but you can still use floating point instructions to transfer double-precision data.

All floating-point data calculations are under the control of the Floating-Point Status and Control Register (FPSCR). This register provides the following control functions:

- Define the floating-point operation behaviors.
- Provide status information about the floating-point operation results.

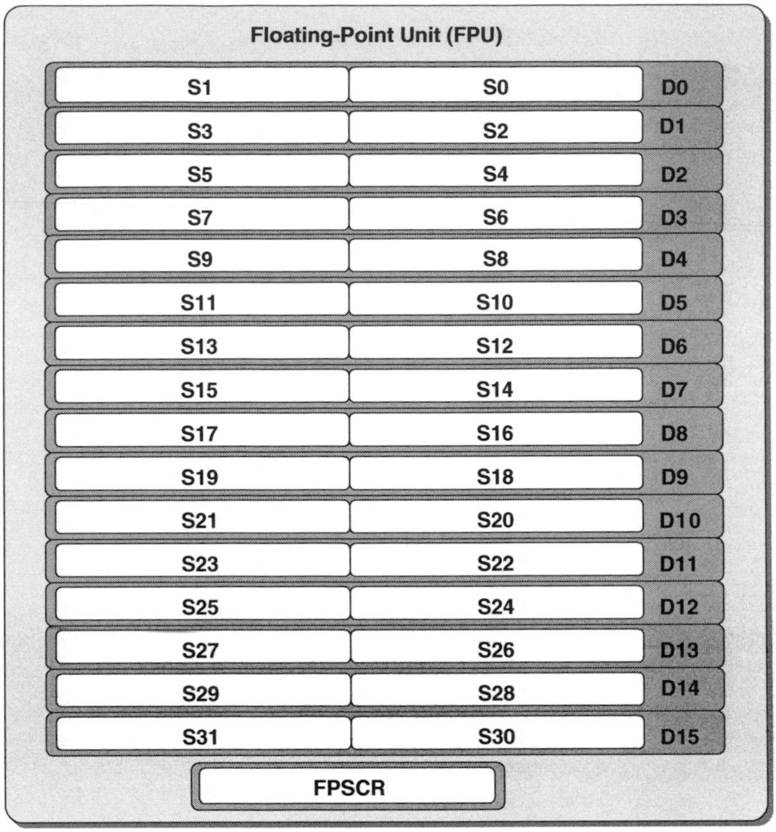

Figure 2.8. The configuration of the floating-point registers.

Bit functions on the FPSCR are shown in Figure 2.9.

The functions of bits N, Z, C, and V are identical to those in the PSR. The function of each other bit in the FPSCR is as follows (bits 5~6, 8~21, and 27 are reserved):

- AHP (Bit 26): The value on this bit defines the Alternative Half-Precision format for the floating-point operations. A 0, which is the default value on this bit, is used to define the IEEE half-precision format. A 1 is to define an alternative half-precision format.

- DN (Bit 25): The value on this bit is used to define the default Not a Number (NaN) mode. A 0 means that the NaN operands propagate through to the output of a floating-point operation, and this is the default value. A 1 indicates that any operation including one or more NaNs returns the default NaN.

- FZ (Bit 24): The value on this bit indicates whether the Flush-to-Zero model is enabled or disabled. A value of 0, which is the default value, on this bit means that the FZ model is disabled; otherwise if this bit value is 1, this means that the FZ model is enabled.

Bits	31 30 29 28	27	26	25	24	23:22	21:8	7	6:5	4	3	2	1	0
FPSCR	N Z C V		AHP	DN	FZ	RMode		IDC		IXC	UFC	OFC	DZC	IOC

Figure 2.9. Bit function and structure on FPSCR.

- RMode (Bits 23 and 22): These two bits are used to set up the specified rounding mode that is used by all floating-point operational instructions. The values of these bits are:
  - 00—Round to Nearest (RN) mode (default).
  - 01—Round to Plus Infinity (RP) mode.
  - 10—Round to Minus Infinity (RM) mode.
  - 11—Round to Zero (RZ) mode.
- IDC (Bit 7): This bit is used to monitor whether a floating-point exception has occurred or not. A 1 indicated that a floating-point exception has happened, and the result is not within the normalized value range. A 0 means that no floating point exception occurred. This bit can be cleared by writing 0 to it.
- IXC (Bit 4): This bit is used to detect whether an Inexact Cumulative exception occurred or not. A 1 in this bit indicated that a floating exception has occurred; otherwise a 0 means that no floating-point exception occurred. This bit can be cleared by writing 0 to it.
- UFC (Bit 3): This bit is the Underflow Cumulative exception status bit. A 1 in this bit indicated that an Underflow Cumulative exception has occurred. Otherwise if this bit is 0, it means that no Underflow Cumulative exception has occurred. This bit can be cleared by writing 0 to it.
- OFC (Bit 2): This bit is the Overflow Cumulative exception status bit. A 1 in this bit indicated that an Overflow Cumulative exception has occurred. Otherwise if this bit is 0, it means that no Overflow Cumulative exception has occurred. This bit can be cleared by writing 0 to it.
- DZC (Bit 1): This bit is the Divided by Zero cumulative exception status bit. A 1 in this bit indicated that a Divided by Zero Cumulative exception has occurred. Otherwise if this bit is 0, it means that no Divided by Zero Cumulative exception has occurred. This bit can be cleared by writing 0 to it.
- IOC (Bit 0): This bit is the Invalid Operation cumulative exception status bit. A 1 in this bit indicated that an Invalid Operation Cumulative exception has occurred. Otherwise if this bit is 0, it means that no Invalid Operation Cumulative exception has occurred. This bit can be cleared by writing 0 to it.

Next let's take a look at the memory architecture in Cortex®-M4 system.

2.3   THE MEMORY ARCHITECTURE

As we discussed in Section 2.2, the Cortex®-M4 MCU utilizes a 32-bit data bus and an address bus. These bus systems greatly improved the performances and the operation efficiency of the MCU as well as the entire microcontroller system. With these advantages in mind, the Cortex®-M4 memory system provides the following special features:

- With the 32-bit address bus, the maximum searchable memory capacity in the Cortex®-M4 system can be up to 4 GB. The bus interface between the MCU and external memory is the Advanced High-performance Bus (AHB), which provides interfaces and connections to various 32/16/8-bit memory devices.
- In order to access and control a 4 GB memory space effectively and easily, the entire 4 GB memory space in the Cortex®-M4 system is divided into the different regions for various predefined memory and peripheral devices uses. With the help of the multiple bus interfaces provided by the Cortex®-M4, the Cortex®-M4 processor can access different memory regions, such as from the CODE region stored program codes to DATA region in the SRAM or

peripheral regions, simultaneously or at the same time. The following buses can be used to access memory or peripheral devices in parallel:

- ICode Bus: Fetch Opcode from the flash ROM.
- DCode Bus: Read constant data from flash ROM.
- System Bus: Read/Write data from SRAM or I/O, fetch opcode from SRAM.
- Private Peripheral Bus (PPB): Read/Write data from internal peripheral devices like NVIC.
- Advanced High-performance Bus (AHB): Read/Write data from high-speed I/O and parallel ports.

- The Cortex®-M4 processors can work with either little endian or big endian memory systems. Generally, the Cortex®-M4 is designed with just one endian configuration.

- The ARM® Cortex®-M4 provides a bit-band feature to enable read/write access to individual bits in one 1-MB SRAM region (from 0x22000000 to 0x220FFFFF) and one 256-MB I/O Port region (from 0x42000000 to 0x43FFFFFF) in the memory devices used in the Texas Instruments Tiva™ for C Series LaunchPad™ MCU-TM4C123GH6PM. To use this bit-band feature, two parameters are needed: the target memory address and the target bit number to be accessed. An example of using this bit-band feature will be discussed in the next section.

- In the ARM® Cortex®-M4 MCU, an optional unit, Memory Protection Unit (MPU), is provided to enable users to access different memory regions with certain permissions. The MPU is a programmable unit that defines access permissions for different regions. The MPU supports eight programmable regions.

- In Cortex®-M4 memory systems, the unaligned transfer operations are supported to perform unaligned data transfers.

- The bus interfaces on the ARM® Cortex®-M4 MCU are generic bus interfaces, which means that these kinds of interfaces enable the processors to connect and interface to different types and sizes of memory with various memory controllers. Generally, two types of memories—flash ROM memory for program codes and static RAM (SRAM) for program data—are widely adopted in most Cortex®-M microcontroller systems. However, in some applications, the Electrically Erasable Programmable ROM (EEPROM) is also used in the memory devices.

2.3.1 The Memory Map

The memory architectures in the ARM® Cortex®-M4 MCU system provide great flexibilities by dividing the entire memory space into different regions for different usages. This flexibility enables users to use different memory architectures to meet the needs of their special applications. Because different microcontroller vendors developed various memory architectures with different memory sizes and peripheral address locations, in this section we will use a typical memory architecture produced and used in the Texas Instruments Tiva™ for the C Series MCU, TM4C123G family, since we will use this MCU through in this book.

The memory map used in the TM4C123G MCU family is shown in Figure 2.10.

It can be found from this memory map shown in Figure 2.10 that the default memory capacity for the flash ROM is 4 MB with an address range of 0x00000000~0x0003FFFF. Currently only a 256 KB flash memory is used for user's program codes and exception vector table. Similarly, the default memory capacity for the SRAM is 512 KB, but only a 32 KB space is available to the users in this map. Additional flash memory and SRAM can be added if more memory spaces are needed for special applications. The memory space used for peripherals has the same situations.

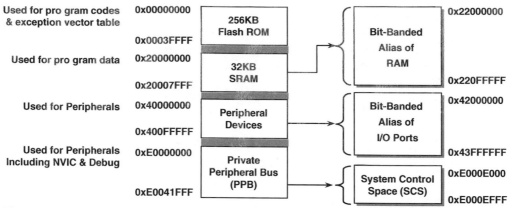

Figure 2.10.   The memory map for TM4C123G MCU.

One point to be noted is the bit-band feature used in this memory map. By using this bit-band technique, the following advantages can be achieved:

- The number of read–modify–write operations can be reduced.
- Both SRAM and Peripheral space used address aliases to access individual bits in a single, atomic operation.
- The SRAM starts at the base address 0x20000000; equivalently the Bit-banded SRAM can be mapped to start at the base address 0x2200000.
- The Peripheral space starts at the base address 0x40000000; equivalently the Bit-banded peripheral space is mapped to start at the base address 0x42000000.

The relationship between the actual memory address and the bit-band alias can be described by the following equation:

$$\text{Bit-band alias} = \text{bit-band base} + (\text{byte offset} \times 0x20) + (\text{bit number} \times 4).$$

This means that the bit-band alias can be calculated by using this equation. For example, bit-7 at address 0x20002000 is

$$\text{Bit-band alias} = 0x20002000 + (0x2000 \times 0x20) + (7 \times 4) = 0x2204001C$$

2.3.2 The Stack Memory

A stack can be considered as a plate rack used in some restaurants. When the restaurant starts, the bus boys push some cleaning plates into this rack, one by one. The first plate is pushed to the bottom and the last plate is pushed to the top, as shown in Figure 2.11a. When the first customer comes, he picks up the top plate by pulling it from the top. When the first plate has been picked up, the second plate goes up and becomes the top one (Figure 2.11b).

The second customer does the same pulling from the top to get the second plate. This operational sequence or procedure is called First-In-Last-Out (FILO). The conclusion is: The last plate put into the rack is the first plate removed from the rack. Therefore, the rack is called a first-in-last-out device.

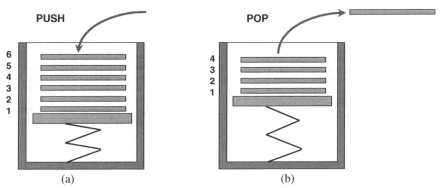

Figure 2.11.   An illustration of the operational sequence of a stack.

Similar to this rack, the stack in a microcontroller system has the same function and operational procedure. Therefore a stack is also a first-in-last-out device. A stack can be considered as a block of special memory space with first-in-last-out property. The specialty is that this piece of memory space performs a first-in-last-out function.

In the ARM® Cortex®-M4 system, the stack always operates on 32-bit data. A PUSH instruction is used to save a 32-bit data or an instruction from a register into the stack, and a POP instruction is used to retrieve a 32-bit data or instruction from the stack to a register. The current stack address is stored in the Stack Pointer register SP, and this address can be automatically adjusted by executing each PUSH and POP instruction.

In the Cortex®-M4 memory system, the stack uses a full-descending operation mode. This means that the stack pointer SP points to the bottom or the largest address of the stack area at the beginning or after the system is reset. For each PUSH operation, the processor first decrements the SP by 4, and then it stores the data (32-bit) in the memory location pointed by SP. In a POP operation, the data of the memory location pointed by SP is read, and then the SP is incremented by 4.

Figure 2.12 shows an example of pushing and popping a 32-bit data item into/from the stack space.

Referring to Figure 2.12a, the operational procedure to PUSH a data or an instruction from a register to the stack is as follows:

1. Initially the Stack Pointer register SP is initialized to point to the bottom of the stack by assigning 0x20007FFF to the SP.

2. After some pushing and popping operations, some data items are pushed into the stack space and the SP now points to the current address 0x20007000 where some data are stored.

3. Before performing the PUSH operation, the content on the SP will be first decreased by 4 to adjust the SP to point to a new address 0x20006FFC to reserve 4 contiguous bytes to store a 32-bit data or instruction.

4. Then the PUSH instruction is executed to push 4 bytes, MSB, MS, LS, and LSB, into the stack area starting from the lower address 0x20006FFC which is pointed by the SP.

5. When the PUSH operation is done, the SP points to the Most Significant Byte (MSB) with the lower address 0x20006FFC. When the next PUSH operation is executed, first the SP performs another −4 operation, and it follows the same operational procedure as above to push another data or instruction into the stack space.

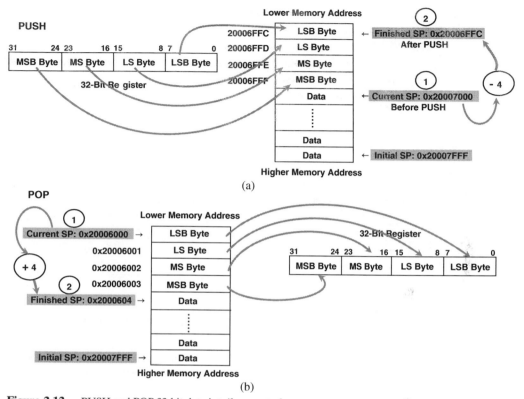

Figure 2.12.   PUSH and POP 32-bit data into/from a stack.

Referring to Figure 2.12b, the operational procedure to POP a data or an instruction from the stack to a register is the following:

1. Similarly the Stack Pointer register SP is initialized to point to the bottom of the stack by assigning 0x20007FFF to the SP.

2. After some pushing and popping operations, some data items are pushed into the stack space and the SP now points to the current address 0x20006000 where the current data item are stored.

3. Now perform the POP operation to retrieve the current data item, which is a 32-bit or 4-byte data stored at the addresses 0x20006000~0x20006003, in a sequence of MSB, MS, LS, and LSB Bytes, from the stack and assign them to a 32-bit register.

4. When the POP operation is done, the SP will perform an increment-by-4 operation to adjust the SP to point to the MSB Byte of the next valid data in the stack space. The finished SP contains an address 0x20006004.

The most common use for the stack is to call a function or a subroutine. Before entering a function or subroutine, some intermediate data items stored in some registers in the register bank need to be reserved for the future usage, such as when the control is retuned back to the main body when the function or subroutine is done. Those data stored in the registers can be reserved by pushing them into the stack and popping them back when the function is done.

Another important stack usage is for the interrupts or exceptions processing. Similarly to functions or subroutines, before entering the Interrupt Service Routine (ISR) as an interrupt occurred, all contents in most registers inside the CPU should be reserved by pushing them into the stack. Those registers can be easily recovered by popping them back from the stack when the interrupt has been handled.

Before we can discuss the memory protection unit, let's first take a look at the program models and states as well as the privilege levels applied in the Cortex®-M4 MCU.

2.3.3 The Program Models and States

The ARM® Cortex®-M4 processor provides various operation modes, privilege levels, and running states to improve and strengthen the reliability and efficiency of the executions of the different programs, including the system programs and the user programs.

Generally the Cortex®-M4 provides the following privilege levels, modes, and states:

1. Privilege Levels:
- `Privileged`: Software can use all the instructions and has access to all resources.
- `Unprivileged`: Software has
  - Limited access to the Priority Mask register.
  - No access to the system Timer, NVIC, or system control block.
  - Possibly restricted access to memory or peripherals (FPU, MPU, etc.).

  The ARM® Cortex®-M4 provides two privilege levels, `Privileged` and `Unprivileged`. The only differences between the privileged access level and the unprivileged access level are the memory access permission and access to some special instructions in the Cortex®-M4 system. However, almost all NVIC registers are privileged access only.

  In fact, the privilege levels offer additional protection for software, particularly for embedded operating systems.

  Two important points to be noted are:
- When the program is running in the `Handler` Mode, the processor always has privileged access level.
- When the program is running in the `Thread` Mode, the processor can be either in privileged access level or in the unprivileged access level, and this access level can be controlled by bit 0 in a special register, CONTROL register.

2. Operation Modes:
- `Thread` Mode: The processor is running normal application programs.
- `Handler` Mode: The processor is running the exception or interrupt programs, such as Interrupt Service Routine (ISR).

  When the program is running in the Thread Mode, the bit 0 in the CONTROL register, which is called the `Thread Mode Privilege Level` (TMPL) bit, can be used to control the running mode for the processor as below (refer to Figure 2.7):
- TMPL = 1: The processor is running in the privileged thread mode.
- TMPL = 0: The processor is running in the unprivileged thread mode.

  Two important points to be noted are:
- The processor can be switched from the privileged level to the unprivileged level by adjusting bit 0 (TMPL) in the CONTROL register when it works in the thread mode. However, it cannot switch itself back from the unprivileged level to the privileged level.

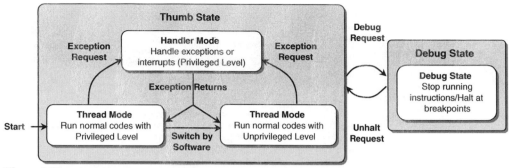

Figure 2.13.   Switching between Thread and Debug modes.

- If you do need to switch the processor from the unprivileged thread mode to the privileged thread mode, you may use some exception mechanisms to handle this switching.

    As for switching between the thread mode and the handler mode, this switching can be done automatically by the system since the processor knows whether the system is running in the thread mode or in the handler mode.

3. Operation States
    - Thumb State: When the processor is running the normal application codes, it is in the Thumb State.
    - Debug State: When the processor is running in the debug process, including the step and breakpoint halt or stop, it is in the Debug State since it stops the instructions' executions.

The Debug State is generally used by debugger to perform debugging operations only. This state can be entered by a halt request from the debugger or by debug events. Under this state, the debugger can access and change the processor register values. The system memory can also be accessed by the debugger in either Thumb state or Debug state.

As we mentioned in Section 2.2.1.2.2, the bit 1 in the CONTROL register, SPSEL, can be used to select the stack pointer. Under the Thread mode, it uses Main Stack Pointer (MSP) when this bit is 0 (default). Otherwise, it uses Process Stack Pointer (PSP) when this bit is 1. When working in the Handler mode, this bit is always 0. This means that the Handler mode always uses Main Stack Pointer (MSP). Figure 2.13 shows an illustration block diagram for switching between the Thread Mode and the Handler Mode with two different states.

In summary, the Cortex®-M4 processors always start in the privileged Thread Mode and in the Thumb state by default. In fact, there is no need to use the unprivileged Thread Mode at all for many simple applications.

2.3.4 The Memory Protection Unit (MPU)

The Memory Protection Unit (MPU) is an optional component in the ARM® Cortex®-M4 MCU. This component is not used in most applications and can be ignored. The main purpose of using this MCU is to protect memory regions by defining different access permissions in privileged and unprivileged access levels for some embedded operating systems (OS).

The MPU is a programmable unit and can be programmed up to eight regions. In some simple applications, the MPU can be programmed to protect certain memory regions only, for example, to make some memory regions read only.

In Tiva™ for C Series LaunchPad™ evaluation board, TM4C123GXL, the MPU has been defined with the following protection functions:

- Defines eight separate memory regions plus a background region accessible only from privileged mode.
- Regions of 256 bytes or more are divided into eight equal-sized subregions.
- MPU definitions for all regions include:
  - Location
  - Size
  - Access permissions
  - Memory attributes
- Accessing a prohibited region causes a memory management fault.

More detailed information about the MPU can be found in Chapter 12.

2.4 THE NESTED VECTORED INTERRUPT CONTROLLER (NVIC) ARCHITECTURE

The Nested Vectored Interrupt Controller (NVIC) is a control unit that is embedded inside the Cortex®-M4 MCU, and it is used to handle and pre-process all exceptions and interrupts, including maskable and unmaskable interrupts, that occurred during the normal running of application codes in the ARM® Cortex®-M4 system.

Like any other Interrupt Processing Unit (IPU), the NVIC processes any exception or interrupt in the following sequence:

1. An exception or interrupt is first created by an interrupt source, and an interrupt-service-request is sent to the Cortex®-M4 CPU.
2. Based on the mask register's content and the interrupt priority level, CPU will determine whether to response or process the interrupt request.
3. If the interrupt request is accepted, the associated hardware will provide interrupt-related information, such as the interrupt source and related Interrupt Service Routine (ISR) entry point, in a Vector Table format.
4. Before the control can be transferred to the ISR, all related registers, including R0–R3, R12, LR, PSR, and PC, are pushed into the stack to reserve their contents. During this protection process, all other interrupts or exceptions are masked or disabled to avoid any data to be lost.
5. Then the control will be directed to the entry point (entry address of the ISR) to run the ISR to perform the required interrupt service. During this process, all other interrupts and exceptions are unmasked or enabled to allow higher-level-priority interrupts or exceptions to be requested and responded.
6. After the ISR is done and before the control can be transferred back to the main program, (a) all other interrupts or exceptions are masked or disabled to avoid any data to be lost and (b) all related registers protected in step 4, including the PC, will be recovered by popping them back to the related registers.

7. Then the control can be directed to the main program to continue executing the normal application codes based on the old PC content. At this time, all interrupts and exceptions are unmasked or enabled to allow any interrupt or exception to be requested and responded.

Now let's take a closer look at the corresponding procedures performed by the NVIC in the Cortex®-M4 system.

2.4.1 The Nested Vectored Interrupt Controller (NVIC) Features

The NVIC is a programmable unit, and its registers are located in the System Control Space (SCS) of the memory map shown in Figure 2.10. Overall, the NVIC provides the following exception or interrupt processing functions:

- Flexible exception and interrupt managements
- Nested exception and interrupt support
- Vectored exception and interrupt identifications and entry
- Interrupt masking

2.4.2 Exception and Interrupt Sources

The NIVC in the Cortex®-M4 system can handle up to 240 interrupt inputs and exceptions. However, in most real applications, they do not have so many interrupt or exception sources available.

In the Cortex®-M4 system, the exception and interrupt are considered as two different kinds of Fault Sources with two different Interrupt Requests (IRQs). There are 15 exceptions in the Cortex®-M4 system, and their exception numbers are ranged from 1 to 15. The exceptions with number greater than 15 and above (until up to 240) are considered as interrupts. The smaller the number, the higher level the exception or interrupt has, and this is true for both exceptions and interrupts.

The exceptions and interrupts in the Cortex®-M4 system have the following properties:

- The exception and interrupt can be categorized to hardware-related exceptions/interrupts or software-related exceptions/interrupts. For example, the watchdog timer and voltage monitor belong to hardware-related interrupts, but the divided-by-zero is a software-related exception.

- The interrupt requests can be divided into two categories: Maskable IRQs and Non-Maskable Interrupt (NMI) request.

- If a mapping relationship between the exception numbers and interrupt request numbers IRQs is made, all exception numbers would be negative (−1 to 14) since the interrupt request number (IRQs) starts from 0.

Table 2.3 shows all exception types and priority numbers, which includes all interrupts.

2.4.3 Exception Priority Levels and Mask Registers

All exceptions and interrupts in the Cortex®-M4 system have certain priority levels, either maskable or unmaskable sources. Most maskable interrupts have programmable priority levels, but all Non-Maskable Interrupt (NMI) have fixed priority levels. When an exception or interrupt occurs, the NVIC performs a comparison between the priority

Table 2.3.   Exception and interrupt types and priority numbers. (Reprinted with the permission of the Texas Instruments Incorporated.)

Vector Number	Exception Type	Priority	Vector Address	Descriptions
1	Reset	−3	0x04	Reset
2	NMI	−2	0x08	Non-Maskable Interrupt
3	Hard Fault	−1	0x0C	Error during exception processing
4	Memory Management Fault	Programmable	0x10	MPU violation
5	Bus Fault	Programmable	0x14	Bus error (Prefetch or data abort)
6	Usage Fault	Programmable	0x18	Exception due to program errors
7–10	Reserved	—	0x1C–0x28	
11	SVCall	Programmable	0x2C	SVC instruction
12	Debug Monitor	Programmable	0x30	Exception for debug
13	Reserved	—	0x34	
14	PendSV	Programmable	0x38	
15	SysTick	Programmable	0x3C	System Tick Timer
16 and above	Interrupts	Programmable	0x40	External interrupts (Peripherals)

level of current exception or interrupt and the priority level of the new coming exception/interrupt. The current running task will be suspended and the control will be transferred to the service routine of the new coming exception/interrupt if the priority level of the new coming exception/interrupt is higher.

After the control is transferred to the Interrupt Service Routine (ISR) to handle the interrupt request, all other exceptions/interrupts that have lower priority levels will be masked or disabled by setting the related mask registers, such as PRIMASK, FAULTMASK and BASEPRI we discussed in Section 2.2.1.2.2. These masks will be kept valid until the current exception/interrupt has been processed.

By setting mask to the PRIMASK register, one can mask or disable all maskable exceptions/interrupts. However, all non-maskable-interrupt (NMI) and HardFault cannot be masked by this setting. By setting the BASEPRI register, one can use different priority levels to process different exception/interrupt requests.

2.4.4 Respond and Process Exceptions and Interrupts

After an exception/interrupt request has been accepted, the NVIC will help the CPU to identify the exact exception/interrupt source and determine the entry address of the related Interrupt Service Routine (ISR) to further process this exception/interrupt. In the early ARM® Cortex®-M MCUs, these jobs are handled by using software that is low in efficiency and slow in processing speed. Starting from Cortex®-M3, these jobs can be handled by hardware with the help of the NVIC. The entry address of the related ISR for the identified exception/interrupt can be easily and quickly located from a so-called Interrupt Vector Table, in which all exception and interrupt sources are located according to their priority levels in order.

One of the most important advantages of using the Tiva™ C Series NVIC is that a new technique called `tail-chained` is used to greatly simplify and speed up a nested exception/interrupt response. Multiple intermediate PUSH and POP operations used in the nested exceptions and interrupts can be removed to speed up the exception/interrupt processing time and simplify the related processing procedures.

More detailed discussions about the exceptions and interrupts handling with Tiva™ C Series NVIC are provided in Chapter 6.

Next let's take a look at the interrupt vector table.

2.4.5 Exception and Interrupt Vector Table

The Vector Table is exactly a word collection of all exception and interrupt sources used in the ARM® Cortex®-M4 system. This collection is distributed in a block of memory with a table format and is on the order of the priority levels of all exception and interrupt sources. Each source in this collection, which takes 4 bytes or one word, represents the starting address of the related exception or interrupt. Since the address bus used in the Cortex®-M4 is 32 bits wide and the width of each byte in the memory is 8 bits, a 4-byte memory is needed to store one starting address.

This Vector Table can be located at any area of the system memory. However, the default location for this Table is the bottom of the memory. The exact location of the Vector Table is determined by a programmable register in the NVIC, the `Vector Table Offset Register` (VTOR). The content of this register is 0 when a reset operation is performed. Therefore the Vector Table is located at address 0x00000000 after a system reset.

The starting address of each related exception or interrupt can also be called a Vector since it provides not only a direction to the related ISR but also a detailed entry address of the ISR. As we mentioned, each Vector takes 4-byte space in the memory. To access the desired Vector, the selected Exception Number or Vector Number in the Vector Table must be multiplied by 4, and then go to that resulted address to pick up the desired Vector for the selected exception/interrupt. For example, the system reset is considered as an exception and its Exception Number is 1 (the highest priority level). To get its Vector or the starting address of its ISR, the target address for this Vector in the Vector Table is: $1 \times 4 = 0x00000004$. Inside this address following with 4 continuous bytes, or from 0x00000004 ~ 0x00000007, a 32-bit starting address of the ISR related to the reset is stored.

The LSB of each vector indicates if the exception is to be processed in the Thumb state. Because all Cortex®-M processors support only Thumb instructions, the LSB of all exception and interrupt vectors should be 1.

More detailed discussions about the exceptions and interrupts handling with Tiva™ C Series NVIC are provided in Chapter 6.

2.5 THE DEBUG ARCHITECTURE

The debug is a process or a tool used to find and identify a bug or problem existing in the user's application codes. Generally two components are needed to perform any debug functions:

Table 2.4. Two types of trace interfaces.

Trace Interface	Description
Serial Wire Viewer (SWV)	Is a low-cost simple-structure trace interface. The trace data bandwidth is limited.
Trace Port (TP)	Supports higher trace data bandwidth with 5 pins, 4 data pins and 1 clock pin. Needs Embedded Trace Macrocell (ETM) support.

- Debug Adapter (a piece of hardware)
- Debug Adapter Driver or Debug Interface (a piece of software)

In the ARM® Cortex®-M4 system, two types of interfaces are provided: (1) Debug, (2) Trace.

The debug interface provides a software driver and an interface to enable debug adapter to be connected to a Cortex®-M4 MCU to perform the debug functions, including:

- Run Control of the processor allowing you to start and stop programs
- Single Step one source or assembler line
- Set breakpoints while the processor is running
- Read/write memory contents and peripheral registers on-the-fly
- Program internal and external Flash memory

The trace interface can be sued to collect dynamic information from the CPU as the system is running, which includes the data, event, profiling or complete details of a user's application program.

The Cortex®-M4 supports conventional JTAG debug interface protocol and updated Serial Wire Debug (SWD) protocol. The debug adapter used in the Tiva™ C Series LaunchPad™ EVB TM4C123GXL is a built-in In-Circuit Debug Interface (ICDI) interface that is compatible with the JTAG protocol.

Table 2.4 lists two important trace interfaces, a single pin protocol Serial Wire Viewer (SWV) and a multi-pin protocol Trace Port.

More discussions about the Debug functions and Trace features are coved in Section 3.6 in Chapter 3.

2.6 INTRODUCTION TO TIVA™ C SERIES ARM® CORTEX®-M4 MCU - TM4C123GH6PM

Texas Instrument's Tiva™ C Series ARM® Cortex®-M4 microcontrollers provide developers a high-performance ARM® Cortex®™-M-based architecture with a broad set of integration capabilities and a strong ecosystem of software and development tools. Targeting performance and flexibility, the Tiva™ C Series ARM® Cortex®-M4 architecture offers an 80 MHz Cortex®-M4F with FPU, a variety of integrated on-chip memories and multiple programmable GPIO. Tiva™ C Series devices offer consumers compelling cost-effective solutions by integrating application-specific peripherals and providing a comprehensive library of software tools that minimize board costs and design-cycle time.

Offering quicker time-to-market and cost savings, the Tiva™ C Series ARM® Cortex®-M4 microcontrollers are the leading choice in high-performance 32-bit applications.

This section contains an overview and details about one of the Tiva™ C Series ARM® Cortex®-M4 microcontrollers, TM4C123GH6PM.

2.6.1 TM4C123GH6PM Microcontroller Overview

The TM4C123GH6PM Microcontroller Unit (MCU) is a high-performance embedded controller with multiple functions and advanced features. Unlike ARM® Cortex®-M4, this MCU contains quite a few components, such as on-chip memory and some on-chip peripherals as well as various peripheral device interfaces, and integrates them into this chip. The main components embedded in this MCU include (Figure 2.14):

- A 32-bit ARM® Cortex®-M4F Processor Core with a Floating Point Unit (FPU). The CPU speed is 80 MHz with 100 DMIPS performance.
- On-Chip Memory Devices include:
  - 256-KB single-cycle Flash memory
  - 32-KB single-cycle SRAM

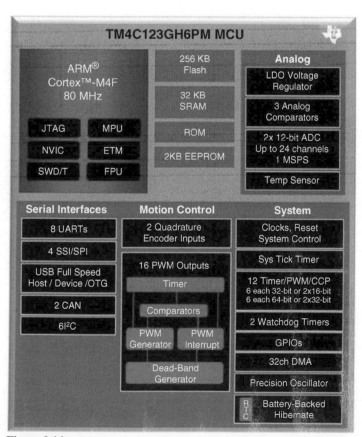

Figure 2.14.   Block diagram of TM4C123GH6PM MCU. (Reprinted with the permission of the Texas Instruments Incorporated.)

- 2-KB EEPROM
  - Internal ROM loaded with TivaWare™ for C Series software
- A System Timer (SysTick).
- Six physical General-Purpose Input–Output (GPIO) blocks.
- Two high-speed 12-bit Analog-to-Digital Converters (ADCs) up to 1 MSPS.
- Three independent Integrated Analog Comparators (IACs) and 16 Digital Comparators.
- Two Control Area Network (CAN) 2.0 A/B controllers.
- Optional full-speed USB 2.0 OTG/Host/Device.
- Six 16/32-bit General-Purpose Timer (GPTM) and six 32/64-bit Wide GPTM blocks.
- Two PWM modules with each having four PWM generator blocks and a control block, and this makes a total of 16 Pulse Width Modulation (PWM) outputs.
- Two Watchdog Timers (WDTs).
- Serial communication with eight UARTs, six I²Cs, four Serial Peripheral Interface (SPI) or Synchronous Serial Interface (SSI).
- Two Quadrature Encoder Interface (QEI) modules.
- Intelligent low-power design power consumption as low as 1.6 μA.

A block diagram of the TM4C123GH6PM MCU is shown in Figure 2.14.

Let's have a closer look at some useful components since we need these components to develop our application programs later. First let's take care of the on-chip memory map.

2.6.2 TM4C123GH6PM Microcontroller On-Chip Memory Map

The TM4C123GH6PM MCU contains the following memory devices on this chip:

- 256-KB Flash ROM memory
- 32-KB SRAM
- 2-KB EEPROM
- A internal ROM

A detailed memory map for TM4C123GH6PM MCU is shown in Figure 2.15.

All on-chip memory devices are controlled by the related control registers, such as Flash Control registers, ROM Control registers, SRAM Control registers, and EEPROM Control registers. These registers are located at the associated memory spaces.

The 256-KB Flash Memory is used to store the user's program codes and exception vector tables. The exception and interrupt vector tables are located at the lower memory space starting from 0x0000.0000. To perform any programming for this flash memory, the Tiva™ C Series devices provide a user-friendly interface with three registers. All erase or program operations are handled via these three registers: Flash Memory Address (FMA), Flash Memory Data (FMD), and Flash Memory Control (FMC).

The 2-KB EEPROM module provides a well-defined register interface to support accesses to the EEPROM with both a random access style of read and write as well as a rolling or sequential access scheme.

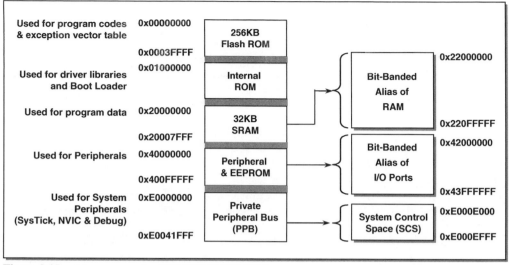

Figure 2.15. Memory map for TM4C123GH6PM MCU.

The `Internal` ROM is a new memory device in TM4C123GH6PM MCU, and this unit can be preprogrammed with the following software and programs:

- TivaWare™ Driver Libraries, including the Peripheral Devices Library, USB Library, Graphical Library and Sensor Hub Library.
- TivaWare™ Boot Loader
- Advanced Encryption Standard (AES) cryptography tables.
- Cyclic Redundancy Check (CRC) error-detection functionality.

The TivaWare™ Boot Loader is used to download code to the Flash memory of a device without the use of a debug interface. When the core is reset, the user has the opportunity to direct the core to execute the ROM Boot Loader or the application in Flash memory by using any GPIO signal in Ports A~H as configured in the `Boot Configuration` (BOOTCFG) register. More detailed information about the Boot Loader can be found in Section 3.7.1.2 in Chapter 3.

AES is ideal for applications that can use prearranged keys, such as setup during manufacturing or configuration.

The CRC technique can be used to validate correct receipt of messages (nothing lost or modified in transit), to validate data after decompression, to validate that Flash memory contents have not been changed, and for other cases where the data needs to be validated.

The `Peripheral` area is used to map all on-chip I/O devices and interfaces to external I/O devices to be used in the system. The main on-chip peripheral devices include:

- Watchdog Timers
- Six 16/32-bit Timers and six 32/64 Timers
- Two Analog-to-Digital Converters (ADCs)
- Analog Comparators

The main peripheral interfaces used for the external I/O devices include:

- General-Purpose Input–Output (GPIO) Ports A~F.
- Synchronous Serial Interfaces (SSI), SSI0~SSI3.
- UART0~URAT7
- CAN0~CAN1
- USB

One point to be noted is that each GPIO Port can be accessed through one of two bus apertures: (1) the Advanced Peripheral Bus (APB), which is backwards-compatible with previous devices, and (2) the Advanced High-Performance Bus (AHB). The AHB offers the same register map but provides better back-to-back access performance than the APB bus. Note that each GPIO module clock must be enabled before the registers can be programmed. There must be a delay of three system clocks after the GPIO module clock is enabled before any GPIO registers are accessed.

A more detailed memory map for TM4C123GH6PM MCU is shown in Table 2.5.

Basically all peripherals in the TM4C123GH6PM can be divided into the following groups:

1. System Peripherals
2. On-Chip Peripherals
3. Interfaces to External Parallel Peripherals
4. Interfaces to External Serial Peripherals

For the interfaces to external serial peripherals, they can be further categorized into another two subgroups: synchronous and asynchronous communication mode.

2.6.2.1 *The System Peripherals*

The System Peripherals are related controls to the system peripherals, and the most popular system peripherals involved in this MCU are:

- System Timer (SysTick)
- Two Watchdog Timers
- Six 16/32-bit and Six 32/64 Timers
- Instrumentation Trace Macrocell (ITM)
- Data Watchpoint and Trace (DWT)
- Flash Patch and Breakpoint (FPB)
- Trace Port Interface Unit (TPIU)

2.6.2.2 *The On-Chip Peripherals*

The On-Chip Peripherals are controls or components integrated on the TM4C123GH6PM chip, which include:

- Two 12-bit Analog-to-Digital Converters (ADCs)
- Three Analog Comparators
- One Voltage Regulator

Table 2.5. Memory map for TM4C123GH6PM MCU.

Start Address	End Address	Descriptions
256-KB On-Chip Flash ROM		
0x0000.0000	0x0000.003C	Exceptions Vector Table
0x0000.0040	0x0000.00A8	Interrupts Vector Table
0x0000.00B0	0x0000.0268	System Controls
0x0002.0000	0x0003.FFFF	User Codes
Internal ROM		
0x0100.0000	0x01FF.FFFF	Tiva Driver Libraries, Boot Loader, AES & CRC
32-KB SRAM		
0x2000.0000	0x2000.7FFF	User Data
0x2200.0000	0x23FF.FFFF	Bit-band alias of bit-banded on-chip SRAM starting at 0x2000.0000
Peripherals		
0x4000.0000	0x4000.0FFF	Watchdog Timer 0
0x4000.1000	0x4000.1FFF	Watchdog Timer 1
0x4000.4000	0x4000.4FFF	GPIO Port A (APB Aperture)
0x4000.5000	0x4000.5FFF	GPIO Port B (APB Aperture)
0x4000.6000	0x4000.6FFF	GPIO Port C (APB Aperture)
0x4000.7000	0x4000.7FFF	GPIO Port D (APB Aperture)
0x4000.8000	0x4000.BFFF	SSI0–SSI3
0x4000.C000	0x4001.3FFF	UART0–UART7
0x4002.0000	0x4002.3FFF	I^2C0–I^2C3
0x4002.4000	0x4002.4FFF	GPIO Port E (APB Aperture)
0x4002.5000	0x4002.5FFF	GPIO Port F (APB Aperture)
0x4002.8000	0x4002.9FFF	PWM0–PWM1
0x4002.C000	0x4002.DFFF	QEI0–QEI1
0x4003.0000	0x4003.5FFF	16/32-Bit Timer 0–16/32-Bit Timer 5
0x4003.6000	0x4003.7FFF	32/64-Bit Timer 0–32/64-Bit Timer 1
0x4003.8000	0x4003.8FFF	ADC0
0x4003.9000	0x4003.9FFF	ADC1
0x4003.C000	0x4003.CFFF	Analog Comparators
0x4004.0000	0x4004.1FFF	CAN0–CAN1 Controllers
0x4004.C000	0x4003.FFFF	32/64-Bit Timer 2–32/64-Bit Timer 5
0x4005.0000	0x4005.0FFF	USB
0x4005.8000	0x4005.DFFF	GPIO Port A–Port F (AHB Aperture)
0x400A.F000	0x400A.FFFF	2-KB EEPROM and Key locker
0x400F.9000	0x400F.9FFF	System Exception Module
0x400F.C000	0x400F.CFFF	Hibernation Module
0x400F.D000	0x400F.DFFF	Flash Memory Control
0x400F.E000	0x400F.EFFF	System Control
0x400F.F000	0x400F.FFFF	µDMA
0x4200.0000	0x43FF.FFFF	Bit-banded alias of 0x4000.0000 through 0x400F.FFFF
Private Peripheral Bus		
0xE000.0000	0xE000.0FFF	Instrumentation Trace Macrocell (ITM)
0xE000.1000	0xE000.1FFF	Data Watchpoint and Trace (DWT)
0xE000.2000	0xE000.2FFF	Flash Patch and Breakpoint (FPB)
0xE000.E000	0xE000.EFFF	Cortex-M4F System Peripherals (SysTick, NVIC, MPU, FPU, and SCB)
0xE004.0000	0xE004.0FFF	Trace Port Interface Unit (TPIU)
0xE004.1000	0xE004.1FFF	Embedded Trace Macrocell (ETM)

- One Temperature Sensor
- Two PWM Modules (PWM0 and PWM1) with total of 16 PWM Outputs
- Two QEI Modules (QEI0 and QEI1) providing control of two motors at the same time

2.6.2.3 Interfaces to External Parallel Peripherals

The TM4C123GH6PM MCU provides a General-Purpose Input–Output (GPIO) module. This module contains six GPIO blocks, and each block is related to an individual GPIO Port. Each GPIO Port is programmable or configurable to provide multiple functions to enable the port to handle different tasks. For example, each port can work as either input or output port, either parallel or serial port. Furthermore, each bit or pin on each port can be programmed separately to perform desired functions, such as an input bit, an output bit, a parallel bit, or a serial bit. Also each bit or pin on each GPIO Port can be configured as an interrupt source to create an associate interrupt request to the Cortex®-M4 core. These interrupt requests can be configured to be triggered by either a rising or falling edge, or by voltage levels.

Six GPIO blocks range from Port A through Port F with 8 pins for each port. Two kinds of accessing modes can be used to access each GPIO Port in the TM4C123GH6PM MCU: via the Advanced Peripheral Bus (APB) or via the Advanced High-Performance Bus (AHB). The latter provides better performances than the former.

2.6.2.4 Interfaces to External Serial Peripherals

The TM4C123GH6PM MCU supports both asynchronous and synchronous serial communications with:

- Two CAN 2.0 A/B controllers
- One USB 2.0 OTG/Host/Device
- Eight UARTs with IrDA, 9 bits and ISO 7816 support
- Four I²C modules with four transmission speeds including high-speed mode
- Four Synchronous Serial Interface modules (SSI)

In fact, all interfaces to external peripherals, including to the external parallel or serial interfaces, are physically executed via the GPIO ports in the TM4C123GH6PM MCU. There is no extra interface to perform either parallel or serial peripheral jobs separately.

Because the GPIO plays such a vital role in the interfaces to all peripheral devices, now let's take a closer look at these ports and related interfaces.

2.6.3 TM4C123GH6PM Microcontroller General-Purpose Input–Output (GPIO) Module

As we mentioned, the GPIO module is composed of six physical GPIO blocks, and each block is corresponding to an individual GPIO port (Port A~Port F). Each GPIO port can be configured to perform a special function, such as input or output with interrupt property. Also even each pin on the selected GPIO port can be configured to work as an input or output pin. However, not all 48 pins (6 GPIO Ports with each port having 8 pins) are configurable or programmable since some pins are not available. Therefore totally the GPIO module supports up to 43 programmable input/output pins, depending on the peripherals being used.

One very important point is that each GPIO module performs its works based on an independent clock source, which is a timing base to make each GPIO works properly. In order to make GPIO to work, the related registers in the GPIO module must be initialized or programmed. The prerequisite for programming any GPIO module is that each GPIO module clock must be enabled before the registers can be programmed. There must be a delay of three system clocks after the GPIO module clock is enabled before any GPIO registers are accessed.

Before we can continue to discuss the GPIO programming process, let's first take a look at the system clock and GPIO module clock.

2.6.3.1 The System Clock

As we know, the clock is a timing base and it provides an operational timing standard or criterion to enable computers to perform their jobs step by step based on each clock cycle. Similarly, in order to enable microcontrollers to execute their instructions in a definite sequence, a clock source is definitely needed. Without a clock source, no any microcontroller or computer can run their instructions properly.

In TM4C123GH6PM MCU, four different clock sources are provided (Figure 2.16):

- Precision Internal Oscillator (PIOSC): 16 MHz.
- Main Oscillator (MOSC): It can use an external clock source or an external crystal.
- Low-Frequency Internal Oscillator (LFIOSC): An on-chip internal 30-kHz Oscillator used for Deep-Sleep power-saving modes.
- Hibernate RTC Oscillator (RTCOSC) Clock Source: It can be configured to be the 32.768-KHz external oscillator source from the Hibernation (HIB) module or the HIB Low-Frequency clock source (HIB LFIOSC), which is intended to provide the system with a real-time clock source.

The ARM® Cortex®-M4 Core or processor can be driven by:

1. Any clock source shown above. The CPU can also use a 4-MHz clock that is the internal 16-MHz oscillator divided-by-4 (Figure 2.16).
2. Phase-Locked Loop (PLL) clock generator.

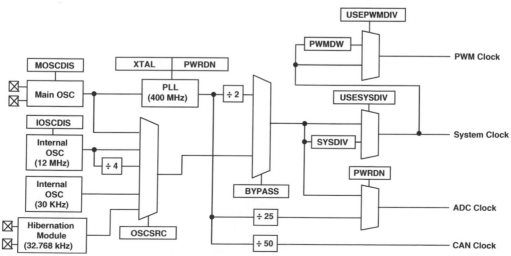

Figure 2.16.   Four clock sources and system clock.

Refer to Figure 2.16: Two multiplexers (MUXs) are used to select different clock sources, and two ways can be used to create a system clock to be used by the CPU.

One way is to use the Phase-Locked Loop (PLL) clock generator that needs a clock source as the input source to create this system clock. It can be found from Figure 2.16 that two clock sources, Main OSC and Precision Internal OSC (16 MHz), can work as a clock source for the PLL, and this source can be selected via the MUX in the top path.

Another way is to directly use any one of four clock sources, and this can be selected via a MUX in the bottom path. An easy way is to use Precision Internal OSC (16 MHz) divided by 4 to get a 4-MHz system clock.

Now let's have a closer look at Figure 2.16 to get more details about the system clock generation process.

- In the top path, the system clock is generated by a PLL that can be driven by any crystals or oscillators running between 5 and 25 MHz. The output frequency of the PLL is always 400 MHz, and it is independent on the input clock sources. In Figure 2.16, a 16-MHz crystal on the Main Oscillator (MOSC) is selected to drive the PLL (dark line). After a default divided-by-2 divider, the system clock should be 200 MHz.
- In the bottom path, the system clock can be generated by any clock source we discussed above. The selected clock source can avoid the SYSDIV and USESYSDIV dividing operations via BYPASS for both MUXs and can be directly sent out as the system clock.

When using the PLL, the output frequency of 400 MHz is pre-divided by 2 (becomes 200 MHz) before the other user's divisor is applied. The users can modify this 200-MHz system clock by adding different dividing factors in the SYSCTL_SYSDIV_X (SYSDIV) in their program to use a lower-frequency system clock. The X is an integer for the desired factor. For example, if a SYSCTL_SYSDIV_5 is used, the system clock would be 400 MHz/2/5 = 400 MHz/10 = 40 MHz.

Two registers, Run-Mode Clock Configuration (RCC) register and Run-Mode Clock Configuration 2 (RCC2) register, provide controls for the system clock. The RCC2 register is used to provide additional control parameters that offer additional encodings over the RCC register. When used, the RCC2 register field values are used by the logic over the corresponding field in the RCC register. In particular, RCC2 provides a larger assortment of clock configuration options. These registers control the following clock functionality:

- Source of clocks in sleep and deep-sleep modes
- System clock derived from PLL or other clock source
- Enable or disable the oscillators and PLL
- Clock divisors
- Crystal input selection

A point to be noted is that during the clock configuration process, always write the RCC register prior to writing the RCC2 register.

In the RCC register, the SYSDIV field specifies which divisor is used to generate the system clock from either the PLL output or the oscillator source. When using the PLL, the VCO frequency of 400 MHz is pre-divided by 2 before the divisor is applied.

For detailed information about the system clock API functions and related programming procedures, refer to Section 4.5.7.3.1 in Chapter 4.

2.6.3.2 *The General Configuration Procedures for GPIO Peripherals*

Because the GPIO module provides various interface supports to meet the needs of multiple different peripheral functions, including the parallels and serials, inputs and outputs, synchronous and asynchronous, and even bit-band input/output operations, the configuration of this module should be very complicated compared with other simple peripheral interfaces. The more functions the device provided, the more complicated the device configurations, which is also true to GPIO.

Regularly, to enable GPIO in the Cortex®-M4 system to work properly, the following initialization processes are needed:

1. Enable the system clock to be connected to the selected GPIO peripheral, exactly to connect the clock signal source to the corresponding peripheral device I/O pins. Typically the clock signal is disconnected to any peripheral after the system is reset by default. You need to enable this clock connection before you can program the desired peripheral. You also need to enable the clock to the peripheral bus system.

2. Configure the operational mode of the selected peripheral I/O pins, such as input/output, parallel/serial, or special function. As we mentioned, the GPIO in the Cortex®-M4 system provides various modes with multiplexed I/O pins. For example, one I/O pin on Port A (PA0) provides either parallel or serial, either input or output functions. Therefore you need to program related configuration registers to set up and configure each pin to meet your requirement.

3. Configure the interrupt control registers on NVIC to enable the interrupt and define the priority level for the desired interrupt if the interrupt function is used for the peripheral.

4. Include and use the related peripheral driver library in your program to make your program development process easier. Most vendors provide device driver library code to facilitate the developers coding jobs.

For the GPIO module used in the Cortex®-M4 MCU, the similar configuration procedures should be used to initialize all ports and pins before they can be used.

Now let's have a clear picture about the architecture and organization of the GPIO used in the TM4C123GH6PM MCU.

2.6.3.3 *Tiva™ TM4C123GH6PM GPIO Architecture*

Figure 2.17 shows an analog/digital functional block diagram of the GPIO module used in the TM4C123GH6PM MCU. It can be found that the GPIO module is controlled by seven controls with several control registers involved in each control.

Six GPIO blocks, each can be mapped to a GPIO Port, provide six GPIO Ports, from Port A to Port F, with 8 bits mapping to 8 I/O pins for each port. The 8-pin mode is used to try to compatible with the old I/O interface configurations.

Although each control register is 32-bit, only the lowest 8-bit is used to provide a control byte function. Depending on two different I/O buses accessing modes, APB or AHB, six GPIO Ports are available and can be accessed by these two different accessing buses. Because of these two different accessing buses, these six GPIO Ports have different memory map addresses. Refer to Table 2.5 to get detailed address ranges for these six GPIO Ports.

All GPIO Ports can be configured by programming their related registers, and each port has several registers used to initialize, configure, and control the functions of each port and each pin. Each register has a unique address, even each pin or bit has an aliased address (like bit-band), in the GPIO memory map.

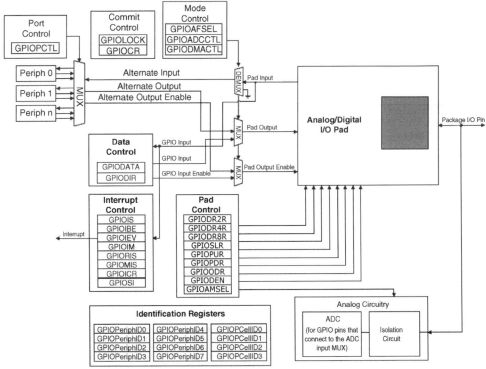

Figure 2.17.   Function block diagram of Analog/Digital GPIO control. (Reprinted with the permission of the Texas Instruments Incorporated.)

Refer to Figure 2.17: Seven controls in all GPIO blocks are:

1. `Port Control`: Used to select the operational mode for the selected GPIO port, either GPIO mode or Peripheral mode, via a multiplexing selector MUX.

2. `Commit Control`: Used to enable or disable the other four registers' operational bits. In other words, the GPIOCR register is to control the transferring ability of each bit on the other four registers. The GPIOLOCK register is used to lock (disable) or unlock (enable) the GPIOCR register.

3. `Mode Control`: The GPIOAFSEL register works together with GPIOPCTL to determine the selected GPIO port mode. Another two registers are used to set up either the ADC mode or DMA mode for the selected GPIO port.

4. `Data Control`: Used to control the data modification ability and data transfer direction.

5. `Interrupt Control`: Determine all interrupt properties for the selected GPIO port or bits, such as the interrupt triggering method, edges or levels, interrupt enabled or disabled, interrupt masking, interrupt status, and interrupt clear function.

6. `Pad Control`: Enable software to configure the GPIO pads based on the application requirements. The pad control includes nine registers. These registers control drive strength, open-drain configuration, pull-up and pull-down resistors, slew-rate control, and digital input enable for each GPIO.

7. `Identification Registers`: These registers configured at reset enable software to detect and identify the module as a GPIO block. The identification registers include 12 related registers.

Although there are over 30 control registers available for each port, basically the following control registers are most popular and widely utilized for programming of GPIO Ports:

2.6.3.3.1 The Port Control Register (GPIOPCTL) This register is used to work together with the GPIOAFSEL register to select the specific peripheral signal for each GPIO pin when using the alternate function mode. Most bits in the GPIOAFSEL register are 0 on reset; therefore most GPIO pins are initialized to GPIOs mode by default. Unlike other control registers, the GPIOPCTL uses all 32 bits to define peripherals for all 8 pins. This 32-bit code is divided into 8 segments; each segment is 4 bits and contains a Port Mux Control (PMC) code, from PMC0 to PMC7, and each 4-bit PMC code selects peripherals for each pin. Refer to Table 2.6 to get detailed information about the PMC values in the GPIOPCTL register and related peripheral functions.

Bit Value   If a GPIOAFSEL bit = 0: The corresponding GPIO pin works in GPIO mode.
              If a GPIOAFSEL bit = 1: The corresponding GPIO pin is controlled by certain
                 peripherals. The GPIOPCTL register selects one peripheral function for
                 each GPIO.

2.6.3.3.2 The Data Control Registers Two registers, Data Control Register (GPIODATA) and Data Direction Register (GPIODIR), are included in this group. These registers are used to configure the operational modes of the GPIOs, which include:

- Data Control Register (GPIODATA): The GPIO ports allow for the modification of individual bits in the GPIODATA register by using bits [9:2] of the address bus as a mask. In this manner, software drivers can modify individual GPIO pins in a single instruction without affecting the state of the other pins.
- Data Direction Register (GPIODIR): Configure each port or each individual pin as an input or output. If a bit = 0, the associated bit in the GPIODATA is an input bit. If a bit = 1, the associated bit in the GPIODATA is an output bit.

2.6.3.3.3 The Mode Control Registers Three registers are involved in this group: GPIO Alternate Function Select Register (GPIOAFSEL), GPIO ADC Control Register (GPIOADCCTL), and GPIO DMA Control Register (GPIOD-MACTL). These registers provide a protection layer against accidental programming of critical hardware peripherals, which include:

- GPIO Alternate Function Select Register (GPIOAFSEL): This register is the mode control selection register. If a bit = 0, the corresponding pin is used as a GPIO and is controlled by the GPIO registers (software). If a bit = 1, the corresponding pin is controlled by an associated peripheral (hardware). This register can work together with the GPIOPCTL register to enable users to select one of several peripheral functions for each GPIO when a bit in this register is set to 1. The reset value for this register is 0x0000.0000 for ports.
- GPIO ADC Control Register (GPIOADCCTL): Configure a GPIO pin as a source for the ADC input. If the GPIOADCCTL Register in Port B is cleared, PB4 can still be used as an external trigger for the ADC.

    Bit Value   0: The corresponding pin is not used to trigger the ADC.
                   1: The corresponding pin is used to trigger the ADC.

Table 2.6.   GPIO pins and alternate functions.

I/O	Pin	Analog Function	Digital Functions (GPIOPCTL PMCx Bit Field Encoding)									
			1	2	3	4	5	6	7	8	9	14
PA0	17	—	U0RX	—	—	—	—	—	—	CAN1RX	—	—
PA1	18	—	U0TX	—	—	—	—	—	—	CAN1TX	—	—
PA2	19	—	—	SSI0CLK	—	—	—	—	—	—	—	—
PA3	20	—	—	SSI0FSS	—	—	—	—	—	—	—	—
PA4	21	—	—	SSI0RX	—	—	—	—	—	—	—	—
PA5	22	—	—	SSI0TX	—	—	—	—	—	—	—	—
PA6	23	—	—	—	I2C1SCL	—	M1PWM2	—	—	—	—	—
PA7	24	—	—	—	I2C1SDC	—	M1PWM3	—	—	—	—	—
PB0	45	USB0ID	U1RX	—	—	—	—	—	T2CCP0	—	—	—
PB1	46	USB0VBUS	U1TX	—	—	—	—	—	T2CCP1	—	—	—
PB2	47	—	—	—	I2C0SCL	—	—	—	T3CCP0	—	—	—
PB3	48	—	—	—	I2C0SDC	—	—	—	T3CCP1	—	—	—
PB4	58	AIN10	—	SSI2CLK	—	M0PWM2	—	—	T1CCP0	CAN0RX	—	—
PB5	57	AIN11	—	SSI2FSS	—	M0PWM3	—	—	T1CCP1	CAN0TX	—	—
PB6	1	—	—	SSI2RX	—	M0PWM0	—	—	T0CCP0	—	—	—
PB7	4	—	—	SSI2TX	—	M0PWM1	—	—	T0CCP1	—	—	—
PC0	52	—	TCK SWCLK	—	—	—	—	—	T4CCP0	—	—	—
PC1	51	—	TMS SWDIO	—	—	—	—	—	T4CCP1	—	—	—
PC2	50	—	TDI	—	—	—	—	—	T5CCP0	—	—	—
PC3	49	—	TDO SWO	—	—	—	—	—	T5CCP1	—	—	—
PC4	16	C1−	U4RX	U1RX	—	M0PWM6	—	IDX1	WT0CCP0	U1RTS	—	—
PC5	15	C1+	U4TX	U1TX	—	M0PWM7	—	PHA1	WT0CCP1	U1CTS	—	—
PC6	14	C0+	U3RX	—	—	—	—	PHB1	WT1CCP0	USB0EPEN	—	—
PC7	13	C0−	U3TX	—	—	—	—	—	WT1CCP1	USB0PFLT	—	—
PD0	61	AIN7	SSI3CLK	SSI1CLK	I2C3SCL	M0PWM6	M1PWM0	—	WT2CCP0	—	—	—
PD1	62	AIN6	SSI3FSS	SSI1FSS	I2C3SDC	M0PWM7	M1PWM1	—	WT2CCP1	—	—	—
PD2	63	AIN5	SSI3RX	SSI1RX	—	M0FAULT0	—	—	WT3CCP0	USB0EPEN	—	—
PD3	64	AIN4	SSI3TX	SSI1TX	—	—	—	IDX0	WT3CCP1	USB0PFLT	—	—
PD4	43	USB0DM	U6RX	—	—	—	—	—	WT4CCP0	—	—	—
PD5	44	USB0DP	U6TX	—	—	—	—	—	WT4CCP1	—	—	—
PD6	53	—	U2RX	—	—	M0FAULT0	—	PHA0	WT5CCP0	—	—	—
PD7	10	—	U2TX	—	—	—	—	PHB0	WT5CCP1	NMI	—	—
PE0	9	AIN3	U7RX	—	—	—	—	—	—	—	—	—
PE1	8	AIN2	U7TX	—	—	—	—	—	—	—	—	—
PE2	7	AIN1	—	—	—	—	—	—	—	—	—	—
PE3	6	AIN0	—	—	—	—	—	—	—	—	—	—
PE4	59	AIN9	U5RX	—	I2C2SCL	M0PWM4	M1PWM2	—	—	CAN0RX	—	—
PE5	60	AIN8	U5TX	—	I2C2SDC	M0PWM5	M1PWM3	—	—	CAN0TX	—	—
PF0	28	—	U1RTS	SSI1RX	CAN0RX	—	M1PWM4	PHA0	T0CCP0	NMI	C0O	—
PF1	29	—	U1CTS	SSI1TX	—	—	M1PWM5	PHB0	T0CCP1	—	C1O	TRD1
PF2	30	—	—	SSI1CLK	—	M0FAULT0	M1PWM6	—	T1CCP0	—	—	TRD0
PF3	31	—	—	SSI1FSS	CAN0TX	—	M1PWM7	—	T1CCP1	—	—	TRCLK
PF4	5	—	—	—	—	M1FAULT0	IDX0	T2CCP0	USB0EPEN	—	—

- GPIO DMA Control Register (GPIODMACTL): Configure a GPIO pin as a source for the µDMA trigger.

    Bit Value   0: The corresponding pin is not used to trigger the µDMA.
                       1: The corresponding pin is used to trigger the µDMA.

2.6.3.3.4 The Commit Control Registers These two registers, GPIO Lock Register (GPIOLOCK) and GPIO Commit Register (GPIOCR), are used to provide commit controls to each bit for other four registers.

- GPIO Lock Register (GPIOLOCK): Control writes access to the GPIOCR register. If the GPIOLOCK is unlocked (writing 0x4C4F434B to GPIOLOCK), the contents on GPIOCR can be modified by writing. Otherwise if this register is locked (writing any other number to GPIOLOCK), any writing to the GPIOCR is ignored and its contents cannot be changed.
- GPIO Commit Register (GPIOCR): Control (enable or disable) each bit on the other 4 registers: GPIOAFSEL, GPIOPUR, GPIOPDR and GPIODEN. The value of the GPIOCR register determines which bits of those four registers are committed when a write to these registers is performed.
  - If a bit in the GPIOCR = 0, the data being written to the corresponding bit in those registers cannot be committed or disabled and retains its previous value.
  - If a bit in the GPIOCR = 1, the data being written to the corresponding bit of those registers is committed or enabled to the register and reflects the new value.

The contents of the GPIOCR register can only be modified if the status in the GPIOLOCK register is unlocked.

2.6.3.3.5 The Interrupt Control Registers This group contains seven related registers and used to provide interrupt controllability for each GPIO Port. The control function for each register is:

- GPIO Interrupt Sense Register (GPIOIS): Determine the triggering mode of an interrupt source. All bits are cleared by a reset.

  Bit Value   0: The corresponding pin in the selected GPIO port will detect edges.
                   1: The corresponding pin in the selected GPIO port will detect levels.

- GPIO Interrupt Both Edges Register (GPIOIBE): Allows both edges to cause interrupts. When a bit in the GPIOIS equals 0, if the corresponding bit in the GPIOIBE equals 1, the corresponding pin in the selected port detects both rising and falling edges, regardless of the corresponding bit in the GPIOIEV register. If the corresponding bit in the GPIOIBE equals 0, the corresponding pin in the selected port will be controlled by the GPIOIEV register. All bits are cleared by a reset.

- GPIO Interrupt Event Register (GPIOIEV): If a bit equals 1, the corresponding pin in the selected port detects rising edge (when the corresponding bit in the GPIOIS equals 0) or high levels (when the corresponding bit in the GPIOIS equals 1). If a bit equals 0, the corresponding pin in the selected port detects falling edge (when the corresponding bit in the GPIOIS equals 0) or low levels (when the corresponding bit in the GPIOIS equals 1). All bits are cleared by a reset.

- GPIO Interrupt Mask Register (GPIOIM): Mask (disable) or unmask (enable) an interrupt generated by the corresponding pin to be transferred to the interrupt controller NVIC. All bits are cleared by a reset.

  Bit Value   0: Disable an interrupt generated by the corresponding pin to be sent
                      to the interrupt controller NVIC.
                   1: Enable an interrupt generated by the corresponding pin to be sent
                      to the interrupt controller NVIC.

- GPIO Raw Interrupt Status Register (GPIORIS): Indicate the raw interrupt status for a specified bit. When an interrupt condition occurs on a GPIO pin, the corresponding bit in this register is set to 1. If the corresponding bit in the GPIOIM equals 1, the interrupt is sent to the interrupt controller. Bits read as zero indicate that corresponding input pins have not initiated an interrupt. For edge-detect interrupts, this bit is cleared by writing a 1 to the corresponding bit in the GPIOICR register. For a GPIO level-detect interrupt, the bit is cleared when the level is deasserted.

- GPIO Masked Interrupt Status Register (GPIOMIS): Indicate the state of the interrupt after masking. If a bit in this register equals 1, the corresponding interrupt has triggered an interrupt to the interrupt controller. If a bit in this register equals 0, either no interrupt has been generated or the interrupt is masked.

- GPIO Interrupt Clear Register (GPIOICR): For edge-detect interrupts, writing a 1 to the IC bit in the GPIOICR register clears the corresponding bit in the GPIORIS and GPIOMIS registers. If the interrupt is a level-detect, the IC bit in this register has no effect. In addition, writing a 0 to any of the bits in the GPIOICR register has no effect.

2.6.3.3.6 The Pad Control Registers Nine control registers are involved in the Pad Control group. These registers control drive strength, open-drain configuration, pull-up and pull-down resistors, slew-rate control, and digital input enable for each GPIO. The function of each register is:

- GPIO 2-mA Drive Select Register (GPIODR2R)
- GPIO 4-mA Drive Select Register (GPIODR4R)
- GPIO 8-mA Drive Select Register (GPIODR8R)

These three registers are used to select the drive strength (2, 4, and 8 mA) for selected pin on the GPIO port. The GPIODR2R is for 2-mA, GPIODR4R is for 4-mA, and GPIODR8R is for 8-mA drive current.

Each GPIO pin in the port can be configured individually without affecting the other pads. As we mentioned, although all control registers are 32-bit, only the lowest 8-bit (1-byte) is used to provide the control function. When setting the DRV2 byte, which is the lowest 8-bit in the GPIODR2R register, the corresponding DRV4 byte in the GPIODR4R register and DRV8 byte in the GPIODR8R register are automatically cleared by hardware. The same thing will happen to GPIODR4R and GPIODR8R, which means that only one drive strength can be selected for all of these three registers at a time. If a drive strength is selected in one register, the other two registers will be reset to 0 to disable other drive strength selections.

By default, all GPIO pins have 2-mA drive.

- GPIO Open-Drain Select Register (GPIOODR): This register is used to configure the open-drain mode for each bit in the selected GPIO port. The lowest 8 bits, with each bit to each pin, called an Open-Drain Enable (ODE) byte in this register, can be used to configure whether a bit or a pin for the GPIO port works in the open-drain mode or not. The open-drain mode enables the selected bit to output in a high-impendence status to drive more loads. When the open-drain mode is set, the corresponding bit should also be set in the GPIO Digital Enable Register (GPIODEN).

  Bit Value   0: Disable the corresponding pin to work in the open drain mode.
  1: Enable the corresponding pin to work in the open drain mode.

- GPIO Pull-Up Select Register (GPIOPUR)
- GPIO Pull-Down Select Register (GPIOPDR)

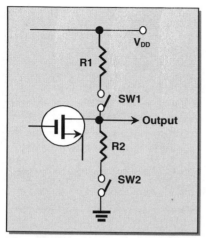

Figure 2.18.   Pull-Up and Pull-Down mode.

These two registers are used to select either Pull-Up or Pull-Down resistor on the output of a pin. Figure 2.18 shows an illustration for pull-up and pull-down connections. These modes only work for output pins and have no effect if a pin works as an input one.

The resistor R1 is called a pull-up resistor, and R2 is a pull-down resistor. When a bit in the GPIOPUR is set to 1 (a Pull-Up is selected), the SW1 is closed but the SW2 is open to connect R1 to the voltage source V_{DD} to enable the output of the corresponding pin is HIGH when no load is applied. Otherwise if a bit in the GPIOPDR is set to 1 (a Pull-Down is selected), the SW2 is closed but the SW1 is open to connect R2 to the output to enable the output of the corresponding pin is LOW when no load is applied.

The real control bits are the lowest 8 bits for both registers, `Pull-Up Enable` (PUE) byte and `Pull-Down Enable` (PDE) byte. Setting a bit to 1 in the GPIOPUR register clears the corresponding bit in the GPIOPDR register, and vice versa. *Both registers are reset to 0 after the reset*, which means that both resistors are not connected to any output pin after a reset operation. This means that after a system reset, most GPIO pins are in high-impendence (HZ) or a tri-state status.

- `GPIO Slew Rate Control Select Register` (GPIOSLR): The GPIOSLR register is the slew rate control register. Slew rate control is only available when using the 8-mA drive strength option setup in the GPIODR8R register. The real control bits are the lowest 8 bits on the 32-bit GPIOSLR register, which is called SLR byte.

  Bit Value   0: Disable the slew rate control for the corresponding pin.
                   1: Enable the slew rate control for the corresponding pin.

- `GPIO Digital Enable Register` (GPIODEN): The GPIODEN register is the digital enable register. By default, most GPIO pins are configured to work as the GPIO mode with tri-state or undriven status. In the tri-state, the digital functions are disabled, which means that they do not output a logic value on the pin and they do not allow the pin to receive any voltage signal into the GPIO receiver. The actual control bits are the lowest 8 bits, called DEN byte. However, some special consideration pins may be programmed to a non-GPIO function or may have special commit controls after a reset. All the lowest 8 bits or DEN byte are cleared to 0 after a system reset, which means that the digital functions for all GPIO pins are disabled.

Bit Value   0: The digital functions for the corresponding pin are disabled.
                 1: Enable a corresponding pin to work as a digital input or output.

- GPIO Analog Mode Select Register (GPIOAMSEL): This register is used to enable or disable the analog input isolation status for the selected GPIO bits/pins. This register is only valid for ports and pins that can be used as ADC AINx inputs. Since the GPIOs may be driven by a 5-V source and affect analog operation, analog circuitry requires isolation from the pins when they are not used in their analog function. If any pin is to be used as an ADC input, the related bit in GPIOAMSEL must be set to 1 to disable the analog isolation circuit and enable the analog input function. Otherwise if a bit in the GPIOAMSEL is 0, the analog isolation circuit is enabled and the analog input function is disabled for the corresponding pin.

Bit Value   0: Enable the analog isolation circuit and disable the analog input function
                    when a pin is not used for ADC.
                 1: Disable the analog isolation circuit and enable the analog input function
                    when a pin is used for ADC.

Since the GPIO Alternate Function Select Register (GPIOAFSEL) needs to work with the GPIO Port Control Register (GPIOPCTL) together to determine the operational mode and related peripheral functions for the selected GPIO pins, we need to take a closer look at these two registers with Table 2.6 to provide a clear picture about the working principle of these three components. Figure 2.19 shows the relationship between these components.

If a bit in the lowest 8-bit in the GPIOAFSEL is 0, this means that the GPIO mode has been selected for the corresponding pin, and the pin will be controlled by the GPIO registers to perform the default GPIO functions. This mode has nothing to do with the GPIOPCTL register.

However, if a bit in the lowest 8 bits in the GPIOAFSEL is set to 1, such as bit 0 and bit 6 shown in Figure 2.19, the control for these two pins will be determined by the PMCx encoding bits value in Table 2.6. Since the GPIOPCTL is a 32-bit register and it has been divided into 8 PMCx nibbles, each nibble has four bits and used to control one pin selected by the bit in the GPIOAFSEL register. These nibbles have a one-to-one mapping

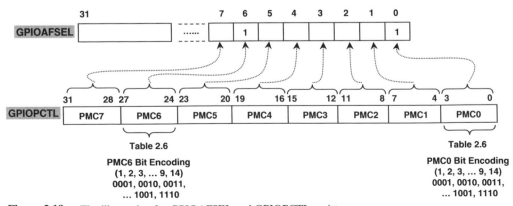

Figure 2.19.   The illustration for GPIOAFSEL and GPIOPCTL registers.

relationship between the PMCx in the GPIOPCTL and bits in the GPIOAFSEL register. For example, PMC0 is for bit 0, PMC1 is for bit 1, and PMC7 is for bit 7 in the GPIOAFSEL register. Since bit 0 in the GPIOAFSEL is set to 1, if the nibble PMC0 or bits 3~0 in the GPIOPCTL are 1 (0x0001), pin PA0 in GPIO Port A works as UART0 Receiver (U0RX). Similarly if bit 6 in the GPIOAFSEL is set to 1 and the PMC6 nibble is 5 (0x0101), then pin 6 in the Port A (PA6) works as a PWM generator (M1PWM2) to output a sequence of PWM signal.

2.6.3.3.7 The Identification Registers There are eight peripheral identification registers and four primeCell identification registers used for GPIO Ports. The eight peripheral identification registers and four primeCell identification registers are:

- GPIO Peripheral Identification 0 (GPIOPeriphID0)~GPIO Peripheral Identification 7 (GPIOPeriphID7).
- GPIO PrimeCell Identification 0 (GPIOPCellID0)~GPIO PrimeCell Identification 3 (GPIOPCellID3).

The main purpose of using eight peripheral identification registers is to identify the used peripherals by software. These eight registers can be divided into two groups:

- The GPIOPeriphID0, GPIOPeriphID1, GPIOPeriphID2, and GPIOPeriphID3 registers can conceptually be treated as one 32-bit register; each register contains eight bits of the 32-bit register.
- The GPIOPeriphID4, GPIOPeriphID5, GPIOPeriphID6, and GPIOPeriphID7 registers can conceptually be treated as one 32-bit register; each register contains eight bits of the 32-bit register.

All registers use their lowest 8 bits, from PID0 to PID7, to reserve the related peripheral identification code used to match the desired peripheral device.

Four PrimeCell identification registers are used as standard cross-peripheral identification systems. All these registers are four 8-bit-wide registers that can conceptually be treated as one 32-bit register.

2.6.3.4 The Initialization and Configuration of TM4C123GH6PM GPIO Ports

To access a GPIO Port or a pin, most of the time the full address of a GPIO port is divided into a combination of a Base address and an Offset. The Base address is the starting address of a port and the Offset is a distance or an interval of the related pin from the starting address.

The base addresses for six GPIO Ports or blocks are (APB and AHB apertures):

GPIO Port A (APB): 0x4000.4000   GPIO Port A (AHB): 0x4005.8000
GPIO Port B (APB): 0x4000.5000   GPIO Port B (AHB): 0x4005.9000
GPIO Port C (APB): 0x4000.6000   GPIO Port C (AHB): 0x4005.A000
GPIO Port D (APB): 0x4000.7000   GPIO Port D (AHB): 0x4005.B000
GPIO Port E (APB): 0x4002.4000   GPIO Port E (AHB): 0x4005.C000
GPIO Port F (APB): 0x4002.5000   GPIO Port F (AHB): 0x4005.D000

Each GPIO Port (Ports A~F) contains a set of all GPIO Registers discussed above, and each register can be accessed by using an offset address combining (plus) with a base address.

Table 2.7. Some popular GPIO port a registers in APB bus aperture.

GPIO Register	Base Address	Offset	Full Address	SW Symbolic Definition
GPIO Port A Data Register	0x4000.4000	0x000	0x4000.4000	GPIO_PORTA_DATA_R
GPIO Port A Direction Register	0x4000.4000	0x400	0x4000.4400	GPIO_PORTA_DIR_R
GPIO Port A AFSEL Register	0x4000.4000	0x420	0x4000.4420	GPIO_PORTA_AFSEL_R
GPIO Port A IS Register	0x4000.4000	0x404	0x4000.4404	GPIO_PORTA_IS_R
GPIO Port A ODR Register	0x4000.4000	0x50C	0x4000.450C	GPIO_PORTA_ODR_R
GPIO Port A PUR Register	0x4000.4000	0x510	0x4000.4510	GPIO_PORTA_PUR_R
GPIO Port A PDR Register	0x4000.4000	0x514	0x4000.4514	GPIO_PORTA_PDR_R
GPIO Port A DEN Register	0x4000.4000	0x51C	0x4000.451C	GPIO_PORTA_DEN_R
GPIO Port A LOCK Register	0x4000.4000	0x520	0x4000.4520	GPIO_PORTA_LOCK_R
GPIO Port A CR Register	0x4000.4000	0x524	0x4000.4524	GPIO_PORTA_CR_R

For example, the Port A in the APB bus aperture has a base address 0x4000.4000. Its corresponding registers have different associate offset addresses. Table 2.7 shows a relationship between the base address, offset address and full address for some Port A registers.

In Table 2.7, the symbolic definition of each related register in the last column is used for programming purpose. Users can use these definitions in their program to access each register.

To initialize and configure a specific GPIO Port, the following additional system control registers should be used:

- GPIO High-Performance Bus Control (GPIOHBCTL) Register. As we mentioned, GPIO can be accessed by two kinds of bus apertures, APB or AHB. These two bus apertures are mutually exclusive, which means that at any time, only one bus aperture can be used to access the desired GPIO port. The bus aperture used for each GPIO Port is under the control of the associate bit in the GPIO High-Performance Bus Control (GPIOHBCTL) Register, which is a 32-bit register. In the lowest six bits, bits 5~0, of this register, each bit is used to control one GPIO Port, Ports A~F, with the following accessed bus aperture:

  Bit Value 0: The Advanced Peripheral Bus (APB) is used for the mapped GPIO Port.
  1: The Advanced High-Performance Bus (AHB) is used for the GPIO Port.

  After a system reset, all these six bits are reset to 0, which means that all ports use an APB bus aperture after a system reset. Optionally you can configure and set up the associate bits in the GPIOHBCTL register to select the accessing bus aperture for the specific GPIO port. This step is optional since all ports use the APB bus aperture after a system reset.

- GPIO Run Mode Clock Gating Control (RCGCGPIO) Register. This register is used to control the connection between the system clock and the desired GPIO Port. All GPIO Ports must have a clock as a timing base to work properly. Similarly to the GPIOHBCTL register, each bit of the lowest six bits in this register is mapped to one of six GPIO Ports, from A to F.

  Bit Value 0: The mapped GPIO Port is disabled and no clock is provided.
  1: The mapped GPIO Port is enabled and a clock is provided.

  After a system reset, all these six bits are reset to 0, which means that all ports are disabled and no clock is connected after a system reset.

Refer to Section 4.5.7.2.2.1 in Chapter 4 to get more details about these registers.

Now let's start the initialization and configuration process for a specific GPIO Port. Perform the following operations to initialize and configure a specific GPIO Port:

1. Set up a connection between the system clock and the specific GPIO Port to enable the clock to drive the port by setting the appropriate bits in the GPIO Run Mode Clock Gating Control (RCGCGPIO) Register.

2. Set up the direction for each pin on the GPIO port by programming the GPIODIR register.

   Bit Value   0: The pin works as an Input pin.
                    1: The pin works as an Output pin.

3. Optionally you can configure the GPIOAFSEL register to program each bit as a GPIO Mode or Alternate Mode. This step is optional since most ports work in the GPIO Mode after a system reset. If an alternate pin is chosen for a bit, then the PMCx field must be programmed in the GPIOPCTL register for the specific peripheral function. There are also two registers, GPIOADCCTL and GPIODMACTL, which can be used to program a GPIO pin as an ADC or μDMA trigger, respectively.

4. Enable GPIO pins as digital I/Os by setting the appropriate DEN bit in the GPIODEN register. Since all GPIO pins are tri-state status after a reset, this step is necessary. To enable GPIO pins to their analog function, set the GPIOAMSEL bit in the GPIOAMSEL register.

5. Optionally, you can setup the drive strength for each pin through the GPIODR2R, GPIODR4R, or GPIODR8R registers. This step is optional since the default drive strength is 2 mA.

6. Optionally, you can configure each pad in the port to have pull-up, pull-down, or open drain function through the GPIOPUR, GPIOPDR, or GPIOODR register. Slew rate may also be configured, if needed, through the GPIOSLR register.

7. Optionally, you can configure the GPIOIS, GPIOIBE, GPIOEV, and GPIOIM registers to set up the type, event, and mask of the interrupts for each port if interrupts are used for the port. This step is optional and unnecessary until interrupts are utilized for a specific GPIO port.

8. Optionally, you can lock the configurations of the NMI and JTAG/SWD pins on the GPIO port pins by setting the LOCK bits in the GPIOLOCK register.

It can be found from the initialization and configuration process for a specific GPIO Port shown above that only three steps, steps 1, 2, and 4, are necessary to be done to configure a GPIO Port by the user, and all other steps are optional.

After a system reset, all GPIO pins are configured to be undriven or tri-state with the following values in four registers: GPIOAFSEL = 0, GPIODEN = 0, GPIOPDR = 0, and GPIOPUR = 0, except for the pins shown in Table 2.8. This table shows special consideration GPIO pins, and these pins may be programmed to a non-GPIO function or may have special commit controls out of reset.

Since some GPIO Ports controls are related to several system controls, let's take a closer look at these controls in the next section.

2.6.4 TM4C123GH6PM Microcontroller System Controls

The TM4C123GH6PM MCU provides a system control used to configure and manage the overall operation of the devices and provides necessary control information about the device.

Table 2.8. GPIO pins with special considerations. (Reprinted with the permission of the Texas Instruments Incorporated.)

GPIO Pins	Default Reset State	GPIOAFSEL	GPIODEN	GPIOPDR	GPIOPUR	GPIOPCTL	GPIOCR
PA[1:0]	UART0	0	0	0	0	0x1	1
PA[5:2]	SSI0	0	0	0	0	0x2	1
PB[3:2]	I2C0	0	0	0	0	0x3	1
PC[3:0]	JTAG/ SWD	1	1	0	1	0x1	0
PD[7]	GPIO[a]	0	0	0	0	0x0	0
PF[0]	GPIO[a]	0	0	0	0	0x0	0

[a] This pin is configured as a GPIO by default but is locked and can only be reprogrammed by unlocking the pin in the GPIOLOCK register and uncommitting it by setting the GPIOCR register.

These system controls and configurations include the device identification, reset control, Non-Maskable Interrupts (NMI) operations, power control, clock control, and other controls.

The system control is composed of a group of control registers and most of these registers are read-only registers. Their mapping addresses are located in the Internal ROM space in the on-chip memory. To access these registers in the internal ROM space, a set of special API functions (located in the Tiva™ Peripheral Drive Library and Boot Loader) are defined and used in the TM4C123GH6PM MCU system.

The main system control functions included in the TM4C123GH6PM MCU are:

- Device Identification
- Reset Control
- Non-Maskable Interrupt Control
- Clock Control
- Other System Controls
- System Initialization and Configuration

Let's discuss these functions one by one in the following sections.

2.6.4.1 Device Identification

Two 32-bit read-only registers, Device Identification 0 (DID0) and Device Identification 1 (DID1), are used to provide identification information for the MCU chip used in the system. The information includes the version, part number, package, and temperature range of the used MCU.

The DID0 register is used to identify the version of the microcontroller (MCU). Each MCU can be uniquely identified by the combined values of the CLASS field in the DID0 register and the PARTNO field in the DID1 register. The DID1 register is used to identify the device family, part number, temperature range, pin count, and package type.

Some other system information including the EEPROM memory and peripherals used in the MCU can be identified by using EEPROM Peripheral Present (PPEEPROM) Register and some Peripheral Present Registers, such as General-Purpose Input/Output Peripheral Present (PPGPIO) Register, Watchdog Timer Peripheral Present (PPWD) Register, and GPTM Peripheral Properties (GPTMPP) Register.

The identification process is to check the associate bit on each register related to a certain peripheral device. A value of 1 in that bit indicated that the related peripheral is presented in the system. Otherwise the selected peripheral is not presented in the system if a 0 is appeared in that bit in the register.

The mapping addresses of all these registers are located in the Internal ROM memory space starting at 0x400F.E000.

When implementing these registers to perform the identification process for MCU and peripherals with software, some predefined API functions can be called to access or read these registers. These API functions are packaged or integrated in the TivaWare™ Peripheral Driver Library. For example, to identify or check whether a specified peripheral is presented or used in the system, the following API function can be used:

```
ROM_SysCtlPeripheralPresent (uint32_t ui32Peripheral)
```

All of these functions should be prefixed with a keyword ROM since this function will access a mapped register in the internal ROM space. Note that the running speed of this instruction can also be faster by using this prefix. The unique argument `ui32Peripheral` is the desired peripheral to be identified in the system. All peripherals used in the TM4C123GH6PM MCU have been predefined by using a set of symbolic names. Some popular peripherals' names are:

```
SYSCTL_PERIPH_GPIOA
SYSCTL_PERIPH_MPU
SYSCTL_PERIPH_ADC0
SYSCTL_PERIPH_CAN1
SYSCTL_PERIPH_PWM
SYSCTL_PERIPH_UART0
```

The returned value of calling this function is a Boolean value. A `True` indicated that the desired peripheral is presented in the system. Otherwise a returned `False` means that the desired peripheral is not used in the system.

Similarly, you can check if the identified peripheral is ready to work or you can power-on, or even enable, the peripheral using the following API functions:

```
ROM_SysCtlPeripheralReady (uint32_t ui32Peripheral)
ROM_SysCtlPeripheralPowerOn (uint32_t ui32Peripheral)
ROM_SysCtlPeripheralEnable (uint32_t ui32Peripheral)
```

There is a table at the beginning of the Internal ROM space, which points to the entry point of each API function that is provided in the Peripheral Driver Library. The main table is located at 0x0100.0010, which is just right after the User Codes area in the flash ROM space.

2.6.4.2 Reset Control

TM4C123GH6PM MCU provides six reset sources and most of them belong to internal reset operations. These reset sources include:

1. The Power-On Reset (POR)
2. The External Reset via pin $\overline{\text{RST}}$

Table 2.9.   Reset source and bit number in RESC.

Bit Number	Reset Source	Bit Value
16	MOSC Failure (MOSCFAIL)	1—Occurred, 0—Inactive
5	Watchdog Timer 1 (WDT1)	1—Occurred, 0—Inactive
4	Software Reset (SW)	1—Occurred, 0—Inactive
3	Watchdog Timer 0 (WDT0)	1—Occurred, 0—Inactive
2	Brown-Out Detection Reset (BOR)	1—Occurred, 0—Inactive
1	Power-On Reset (POR)	1—Occurred, 0—Inactive
0	External Reset (EXT)	1—Occurred, 0—Inactive

3. The Brown-Out Detection Reset (BOR)

4. The Software Reset

5. The Watchdog Timer Reset

6. The MOSC Failure Reset

Except for the power-on reset, all other resets belong to error-triggered resets because of something wrong in the system, including the microcontroller core or other devices. If an error-triggering reset occurred, the reset source can be identified and recorded in the `Reset Cause` (RESC) Register. Although the RESC is a 32-bit register, only seven bits are used in that register to record the reset source, one bit for one reset source. Table 2.9 shows the relationship between each bit and each related reset source. A value of 1 in a certain bit indicated that the corresponding reset has occurred.

After a reset occurred, the user can direct the microcontroller core to execute the Boot Loader stored in the Internal ROM space or the user's application in the Flash ROM memory by using any GPIO signal as configured in the `Boot Configuration` (BOOTCFG) Register.

Almost all resets will trigger the microcontroller core to perform similar jobs in the following sequence:

1. Waiting for the reset to be exited or released.

2. Load PC and SP registers with the initial programmer count and initial stack pointer, and begin to execute the instruction starting from the current PC's content.

2.6.4.2.1 The Power-On Reset   After the system is power-on, a system Power-On Reset (POR) is generated. An internal POR circuit will monitor the power supply voltage (V_{DD}) and generates a reset signal to all of the internal logic including JTAG when the power supply ramp reaches a threshold value (V_{VDD_POK}). The POK means Power-OK (POK). The internal POR is only active on the initial power-up of the microcontroller or when the microcontroller wakes from hibernation mode.

Regularly, the microcontroller must be operating within the specified operating voltage ranges, such as 2.7~2.9 V, when the on-chip power-on reset pulse is complete. For applications that require the use of an external reset signal to hold the microcontroller in reset longer than the internal POR, the external reset source, $\overline{RST}$ input, can be used.

The internal POR monitor circuit is used to keep the analog circuitry in reset until the voltage supply for analog circuits (V_{DDA}) has reached the correct range for the analog circuitry to begin operating. The POK monitor is used to keep the digital circuitry in reset until the V_{DDA} power supply is at an acceptable operational level.

2.6.4.2.2 The External Reset An external reset can be triggered by the $\overline{RST}$ pin via external circuits or reset sources. This pin should be connected to the power supply via a pull-up resistor if it is not used. The external reset source resets the microcontroller including the core and all on-chip peripherals.

In general, the external reset pin should be connected to several important and high-level priority peripheral circuits. The main purpose of using this external reset is to force the entire system to reset as soon as some error or bug occurred in those high-level peripheral circuits in an application. The emergency level is higher compared with those internal reset sources.

In order to reduce noise effects, a low-pass R-C filter could be connected to the $\overline{RST}$ pin to make external reset sources more reliable.

2.6.4.2.3 The Brown-Out Reset (BOR) In the TM4C123GH6PM MCU system, a Brown-Out detection circuit is provided to monitor and check the operational power supply voltage levels. A Brown-Out reset can be triggered if the voltage level is below the threshold values, either V_{BOR0TH} (2.93 V) or V_{BOR1TH} (2.83 V).

The application can identify a BOR source by checking the Reset Cause (RESC) register, exactly the value on bit 2 in the RESC register (Table 2.9). The BOR sources can also be programmed to generate an interrupt by clearing the BOR0 or BOR1 bit in the Power-On and Brown-Out Reset Control (PBORCTL) Register.

Although PBORCTL is a 32-bit register, only two bits, bit 2 and bit 1, are used for checking the BRO sources in this register. Table 2.10 shows the functions of these two bits and their source to trigger either an interrupt or a reset action.

2.6.4.2.4 The Software Reset Similar to those internal and external reset sources, the software can also trigger a reset action to a microcontroller core, each individual peripheral or even entire system. One needs to use two bits in the Application Interrupt and Reset Control (APINT) register and specific peripheral reset registers to perform the related resetting jobs via software:

- To reset the microcontroller core only, one needs to set the VECTRESET bit (bit 0) to 1 in the APINT Register. This register can only be accessed from the privileged mode.
- To reset the entire microcontroller system including the core via software, one needs to set the SYSRESREQ bit (bit 2) to 1 in the APINT Register.

Table 2.10. Two bits on the PBORCTL register.

Bit Number	Reset Source	Bit Value
2	BOR0	0: The BOR0 source creates an interrupt to be generated in the interrupt controller NVIC
		1: The BOR0 source creates a reset to the MCU
1	BOR1	0: The BOR1 source creates an interrupt to be generated in the interrupt controller NVIC
		1: The BOR1 source creates a reset to the MCU

Table 2.11. Mapping bits in SRGPIO register.

Bit Number	GPIO Port	Bit Value
5	GPIO Port F	0: GPIO Port F is not reset
		1: GPIO Port F is reset
4	GPIO Port E	0: GPIO Port E is not reset
		1: GPIO Port E is reset
3	GPIO Port D	0: GPIO Port D is not reset
		1: GPIO Port D is reset
2	GPIO Port C	0: GPIO Port C is not reset
		1: GPIO Port C is reset
1	GPIO Port B	0: GPIO Port B is not reset
		1: GPIO Port B is reset
0	GPIO Port A	0: GPIO Port A is not reset
		1: GPIO Port A is reset

- Peripherals can be individually reset by software via peripheral-specific reset registers, and these registers are mapped to the System Control space starting with an offset of 0x500. If the bit position corresponding to a peripheral is set and then cleared, the peripheral is reset.

For example, if you want to reset GPIO Port F via software, you need to use the `General-Purpose Input/Output Software Reset (SRGPIO)` register to do this job. This register has the same capability as the `Software Reset Control n (SRCRn)` registers for the GPIO modules and has the same bit polarity as the corresponding SRCRn bits.

Although the SRGPIO is a 32-bit register, only six bits, bits 5~0, are used. Each bit is for one GPIO Port arranging from Ports F to A, respectively.

If a bit on SRGPIO is 0, the corresponding port is not reset. However, if a bit is 1, the corresponding port is reset. Table 2.11 shows the bit map for those six GPIO ports in the SRGPIO register and the relationship between each bit and each port.

2.6.4.2.5 The Watchdog Timer Reset The TM4C123GH6PM MCU provides two watchdog timer modules, WDT0 and WDT1. The main purpose of using these watchdog timers is to monitor and check the processor's running status to make sure that the entire system works fine. The reason for using two watchdog timers is to make sure that the system is still being monitored by at least one watchdog timer even one of them is failed.

In fact, each watchdog timer is a 32-bit counting-down counter. After a system reset, an initial value is loaded into either watchdog timer and the timer begins its counting down operation. When the counter gets to zero, a time-up tick is generated and this time-up tick can be used to generate three different signals:

1. A normal maskable interrupt to the Interrupt Controller NVIC.
2. A Non-Maskable Interrupt (NMI) to the system.
3. A Reset signal to the CPU.

Both watchdog timers are controlled by their `Watchdog Timer Controllers` (WDTCTL) with two different clock sources. The first Watchdog Timer WDT0 is clocked by the system clock and the second Watchdog Timer WDT1 is clocked by the `Precision Internal Oscillator` (PIOSC). Each WDT module operates in the same manner except that because the PIOSC watchdog timer module is in a different clock domain, register accesses must have a time delay between them.

The working procedure of a watchdog timer can be described as follows:

- When the watchdog timer gets its time up in the first time, a maskable or a non-maskable interrupt should be generated.
- After the watchdog's first time-out event, the 32-bit watchdog counter is reloaded with the value of the `Watchdog Timer Load` (WDTLOAD) register and resumes counting down from that value.
- When the watchdog timer gets its time up in the second time but before the first time-out interrupt is cleared, a reset signal should be created by the timer.

All signals generated by each watchdog timer, including the interrupts and reset, can be controlled via the software by programming-related WDT control registers.

2.6.4.3 Non-Maskable Interrupt Control

In TM4C123GH6PM MCU system, four NMI sources exist:

1. The NMI signal coming from the NMI pin.
2. The Main Oscillator Verification Circuit Error.
3. The NMISET bit in the `Interrupt Control and State` (INTCTRL) register.
4. The Watchdog Timer time-out interrupt.

The NMI signal is an Alternate Function for either GPIO port pin PD7 or PF0. To enable the NMI source for these pins, the alternate function must be enabled in the GPIOAFSEL register and the PMCx encoding bits must be set correctly in the GPIOPCTL register for the NMI signal to be used as an interrupt. Refer to Table 2.6 to get more details about these settings. Also, the Commit Control Register GPIOCR must be correctly configured to enable the related bits in the GPIOAFSEL register to take effect.

A main oscillator verification circuit is used to monitor and detect any possible failure caused by the `Main Oscillator` (MOSC). An error signal would be generated and sent to the system if the running frequency of the oscillator is beyond the normal operational range. If this error signal is detected, two possible actions take place:

- A Power-On Reset (POR) is created and it will be processed by a NMI Interrupt Service Routine (ISR).
- An interrupt is generated.

The `Main Oscillator Control` (MOSCCTL) Register is used to provide control to the features of the main oscillator, which include:

1. The ability to enable the MOSC clock verification circuit.
2. What action to take when the MOSC fails.
3. Whether or not a crystal is connected.

Table 2.12. The bits map and functions in the MOSCCTL register.

Bit Number	Bit Name	Bit Function
0	CVAL	0: The MOSC monitor circuit is disabled
		1: The MOSC monitor circuit is enabled
1	MOSCIM	0: If the MOSC fails, a MOSC failure reset is generated and reboots to the NMI handler
		1: If the MOSC fails, an interrupt is generated as indicated by the MOFRIS bit in the **RIS** register
2	NOXTAL	0: When a crystal or oscillator is connected to the OSC0 and OSC1 inputs
		1: When a crystal or external oscillator is not connected to the OSC0 and OSC1 inputs to reduce power consumption

Although the MOSCCTL is a 32-bit register, only three bits are used and two bits are related to the MOSC failure. Table 2.12 shows these bits' map and functions.

Depending on reading or writing operations, the value in the NMISET bit in the Interrupt Control and State (INTCTRL) register has different functions. Table 2.13 shows the bit values and related functions.

For the Watchdog Timer time-out interrupt, refer to Section 2.6.4.2.5. An interrupt would be generated when the Watchdog Timer gets its time-out if the INTEN bit (bit 0) in the Watchdog Timer Control (WDTCTL) register is set to 1.

2.6.4.4 Clock Control

We have provided some discussions about the system clock control in Section 2.6.3.1.

Basically the system clock is controlled by two registers: the Run-Mode Clock Configuration (RCC) and Run-Mode Clock Configuration 2 (RCC2). When used, the field values in the RCC2 register are used by the logic over the corresponding field in the RCC register. In particular, RCC2 register provides a larger assortment of clock configuration options. These registers provide the following clock control functions:

- Clock sources in sleep or deep-sleep modes
- System clock derived from PLL or from other clock source
- Enable or disable oscillators and PLL

Table 2.13. The bit values and functions in the INTCTRL register.

Bit Number	Bit Name	Bit Function
31	NMISET	0: On reading, indicates an NMI exception is not pending. On writing, no effect
		1: On reading, indicates an NMI exception is pending. On writing, changes the NMI exception state to pending
22	ISRPEND	0: No interrupt is pending
		1: An interrupt is pending

- Clock divisors
- Crystal input selection

A point to be noted is that during the EEPROM operation process, no any configuration of the system clock can be changed. This can be identified by checking the WORKING bit in the EEPROM Done Status (EEDONE) Register, and any modification for the configuration of the system clock cannot be performed until this bit is reset to 0.

Some useful control bits used for system clock in the RCC register is shown in Table 2.14.

Most bits and their functions are straightforward and easy to be understood. But the bits 26~23 need more attention since the different combinations of these bits provide various divisors. Table 2.15 shows these combinations and related divisors.

Table 2.14. Some useful control bits used in the RCC register.

Bit Number	Bit Name	Bit Function
27	ACG	0: The Run-Mode Clock Gating Control (RCGCn) registers are used when the microcontroller enters a sleep mode
		1: The **SCGCn** or **DCGCn** registers are used to control the clocks distributed to the peripherals when the microcontroller is in a sleep mode
26–23	SYSDIV	System Clock Divisor Specifies which divisor is used to generate the system clock from either the PLL output or from the oscillator source, depending on how the BYPASS bit in this register is configured (refer to Table 2.15 for bit encoding)
22	USESYSDIV	0: The system clock is used undivided
		1: The system clock divider is used for the system clock. The system clock divider is forced to be used when the PLL is selected as the source
13	PWRDN	0: The PLL is operating normally
		1: The PLL is powered down. Make sure that another clock source is functioning and that the BYPASS bit is set before setting this bit
11	BYPASS	0: The system clock uses the **PLL** output clock divided by the divisor specified by SYSDIV (bits 26–23 in this register)
		1: The system clock uses the **OSC** source and divided by the divisor specified by SYSDIV (bits 26–23 in this register)
5–4	OSCSRC	Oscillator Source Selection: 0x0: Main Oscillator (MOSC) 0x1: Precision Internal Oscillator (PIOSC)—Default 0x2: Precision Internal Oscillator/4 (PIOSC/4) 0x3: Low-Frequency Internal Oscillator (LFIOSC)
0	MOSCDIS	0: The main oscillator is enabled
		1: The main oscillator is disabled—Default

Table 2.15. System clock frequencies for different SYSDIV values.

SYSDIV	DIVISOR	Frequency (BYPASS = 0)	Frequency (BYPASS = 1)	Symbolic Definition
0x0	÷1	Reserved	Clock source frequency/1	SYSCTL_SYSDIV_1
0x1	÷2	Reserved	Clock source frequency/2	SYSCTL_SYSDIV_2
0x2	÷3	66.67 MHz	Clock source frequency/3	SYSCTL_SYSDIV_3
0x3	÷4	50 MHz	Clock source frequency/4	SYSCTL_SYSDIV_4
0x4	÷5	40 MHz	Clock source frequency/5	SYSCTL_SYSDIV_5
0x5	÷6	33.33 MHz	Clock source frequency/6	SYSCTL_SYSDIV_6
0x6	÷7	28.57 MHz	Clock source frequency/7	SYSCTL_SYSDIV_7
0x7	÷8	25 MHz	Clock source frequency/8	SYSCTL_SYSDIV_8
0x8	÷9	22.22 MHz	Clock source frequency/9	SYSCTL_SYSDIV_9
0x9	÷10	20 MHz	Clock source frequency/10	SYSCTL_SYSDIV_10
0xA	÷11	18.18 MHz	Clock source frequency/11	SYSCTL_SYSDIV_11
0xB	÷12	16.67 MHz	Clock source frequency/12	SYSCTL_SYSDIV_12
0xC	÷13	15.38 MHz	Clock source frequency/13	SYSCTL_SYSDIV_13
0xD	÷14	14.29 MHz	Clock source frequency/14	SYSCTL_SYSDIV_14
0xE	÷15	13.33 MHz	Clock source frequency/15	SYSCTL_SYSDIV_15
0xF	÷16	12.5 MHz— Default	Clock source frequency/16	SYSCTL_SYSDIV_16

The RCC2 provides extend fields and functions compared with the RCC register. The SYSDIV2 field in the RCC2 register is 2 bits wider than the SYSDIV field in the RCC register so that additional larger divisors up to 64 are available to allow a lower system clock frequency to be used to improve the system Deep Sleep power consumption. Table 2.16 shows how the SYSDIV2 encoding affects the system clock frequency, depending on whether the PLL is used (BYPASS2=0) or another clock source is used (BYPASS2=1).

When the RCC2 is used, it will override the functions provided by the RCC register.

Table 2.16. System clock frequencies using SYSDIV2 field.

SYSDIV2	DIVISOR	Frequency (BYPASS2 = 0)	Frequency (BYPASS2 = 1)	Symbolic Definition
0x0	÷1	Reserved	Clock source frequency/1	SYSCTL_SYSDIV_1
0x1	÷2	Reserved	Clock source frequency/2	SYSCTL_SYSDIV_2
0x2	÷3	66.67 MHz	Clock source frequency/3	SYSCTL_SYSDIV_3
0x3	÷4	50 MHz	Clock source frequency/4	SYSCTL_SYSDIV_4
0x4	÷5	40 MHz	Clock source frequency/5	SYSCTL_SYSDIV_5
. . . . . .	. . . . . .	. . . . . .	. . . . . .	. . . . . .
0x9	÷10	20 MHz	Clock source frequency/10	SYSCTL_SYSDIV_10
. . . . . .	. . . . . .	. . . . . .	. . . . . .	. . . . . .
0x3F	÷64	3.125 MHz	Clock source frequency/64	SYSCTL_SYSDIV_64

2.6.4.5 Other System Controls

Some additional system controls include the System Power Controls, System Timer (SysTick) Controls, and System Control Block (SCB).

In order to save the power consumptions, four different operational modes are available in the TM4C123GH6PM MCU system; they are:

1. Run mode
2. Sleep mode
3. Deep-Sleep mode
4. Hibernate mode

In order to save or reduce the power consumptions in the entire system, three set of registers are used to control and distribute the driving clocks for the different system components, such as processor, memory, or peripherals implemented in the MCU system. In the TM4C123GH6PM system, these registers are categorized as three groups:

- Run-Mode Clock Gating Control (RCGCx) Registers
- Sleep-Mode Clock Gating Control (SCGCx) Registers
- Deep-Sleep Clock Gating Control (DCGCx) Registers

The **x** attached with each register group represents the specified device or peripheral. Each register group is used to control the same set of devices or peripherals with different driving clocks to enable them to work at different modes. For example, in the normal running mode, the clock gating control registers used for that group devices and peripherals are:

- RCGCGPIO: Run-Mode Clock Gating Control register for GPIO peripherals
- RCGCUART: Run-Mode Clock Gating Control register for UART
- RCGCDMA: Run-Mode Clock Gating Control register for μDMA
- RCGCCAN: Run-Mode Clock Gating Control register for CAN
- RCGCWD: Run-Mode Clock Gating Control register for Watchdog Timer
- RCGCSSI: Run-Mode Clock Gating Control register for SSI
- RCGCPWM: Run-Mode Clock Gating Control register for PWM

Similar definitions are used for SCGCx and DCGCx registers.

These registers are used to control the driving clocks for the same devices or peripherals when they are working in the different modes. These registers are located in the System Control register map starting at offsets 0x600, 0x700, and 0x800, respectively. The offset listed is a hexadecimal increment to the register's address, relative to the System Control base address of 0x400F.E000. There must be a delay of three system clocks after a peripheral module clock is enabled in the RCGC register before any module registers can be accessed.

Now let's have a closer look at these modes one by one.

2.6.4.5.1 The Run Mode   Under this mode, the processor, memory, and peripherals are operated in the normal running mode to execute the instructions in a normal sequence with the full power. All used peripherals are specified by the related bits in the RCGC registers. The system clock can be any clock source including the PLL.

2.6.4.5.2 The Sleep Mode A Wait For Interrupt (WFI) instruction can force the Cortex®-M4 microcontroller core to enter this sleep mode. As soon as entering this mode, the clocks driving the core and memory are disabled, and therefore both the processor and the memory system stop their operations with no instruction being executed. The processor and memory are working in the sleep mode. But both of them can be woken up to return to the normal run-mode when an interrupt occurred.

In the sleep mode, the peripherals can still work with the normal driving clock inputs. The driving clock control can be determined by the value on the bit ACG (Auto Clock Gating) in the Run-Mode Clock Configuration (RCC) register. Refer to Table 2.14 to get more details about the possible values and functions for this bit.

2.6.4.5.3 The Deep-Sleep Mode To enter the deep-sleep mode, the following two operations are needed:

1. The SLEEPDEEP bit (bit 2) in the System Control (SYSCTRL) Register must be set.
2. A Wait For Interrupt (WFI) instruction is executed.

There is no significant difference between the sleep mode and deep-sleep mode. The only difference between them is that the frequency of the driving clock used for peripherals may be reduced in the deep-sleep mode, and this lower running frequency on peripherals can further reduce the power dissipations in the system. The driving clock can be controlled by the value on the bit ACG (Auto Clock Gating) in the Run-Mode Clock Configuration (RCC) register.

The processor and memory can be woken up to return to the normal run mode when an interrupt occurred. A Clock Control Register is provided to assist the users to select the PIOSC as the clock source to enable a smooth transferring from the deep-sleep mode to the normal run mode.

In addition to the Sleep mode and Deep-Sleep mode as well as the clock gating for the on-chip modules, there are several additional power mode options that allow the LDO, Flash memory, and SRAM into different levels of power savings while in Sleep mode or Deep-Sleep mode. Note that these features may not be available on all devices; the System Properties (SYSPROP) register provides information on whether a mode is supported on a given MCU.

2.6.4.5.4 The Hibernate Mode In addition to the normal system, TM4C123GH6PM provides an additional Hibernation module to support the Hibernate Mode or module.

The Hibernate Module manages removal and restoration of power to provide a better way to reduce the system power consumption. When the processor and peripherals are idle, power can be completely removed with only the Hibernation module remaining powered. Power can be restored based on an external signal or at a certain time using the built-in Real-Time Clock (RTC). The Hibernation module can be independently supplied from an external battery or an auxiliary power supply.

The Hibernation module provides two ways for power control:

- Use internal switches to control power to the Cortex®-M4F as well as to most analog and digital functions while retaining I/O pin power (VDD3ON mode).
- Control the power to the microcontroller with a control signal (HIB) that signals an external voltage regulator to turn on or off.

2.6.4.5.5 The System Timer (SysTick) The ARM® Cortex®-M4 MCU provides an integrated system timer, SysTick, which includes a 24-bit counter with clear-on-writing, decrementing, and reloading-on-zero control mechanism. The counter can work as:

- A RTOS tick timer that works at a programmable rate (for example, 100 Hz) and invokes a SysTick routine.
- A high-speed alarm timer using the system clock.
- A variable rate alarm or signal timer, the duration is range-dependent on the reference clock used, and the dynamic range of the counter.
- A simple counter used to measure time to completion and time used.
- An internal clock source control based on missing/meeting durations. The COUNT bit in the SysTick Control and Status (STCTRL) register can be used to determine whether an action is completed within a set duration, as part of a dynamic clock management control loop.

The system timer consists of three registers:

- SysTick Control and Status (STCTRL) Register: This is a control and status register used to configure its clock, enable the counter, enable the SysTick interrupt, and determine the counter status.
- SysTick Reload Value (STRELOAD) Register: This register is used to reload a new value for the counter.
- SysTick Current Value (STCURRENT) Register: This register provides the current value of the counter.

When enabled, the timer counts down on each clock from the reload value to zero, and then it reloads to the value in the STRELOAD register on the next clock edge. Then the counter performs decrements on subsequent clock inputs. Clearing the STRELOAD register will disable the counter on the next reloading operation. When the counter reaches zero, the COUNT status bit is set to 1. The COUNT bit is cleared on reads.

Writing to the STCURRENT register clears the register and the COUNT status bit. The write does not trigger the SysTick exception logic. On a read, the returned value is the current value of the register at the time the register is accessed.

The SysTick counter runs on either the system clock or the Precision Internal Oscillator (PIOSC) divided by 4. If this clock signal is stopped for low power mode, the SysTick counter stops. The SysTick can be kept running during Deep-sleep mode by setting the CLK_SRC bit in the SysTick Control and Status Register (STCTRL) and ensuring that the PIOSCPD bit in the Deep Sleep Clock Configuration (DSLPCLKCFG) register is clear. Ensure software uses aligned word accesses to access the SysTick registers.

The SysTick counter reloading and current value are undefined at reset; the correct initialization sequence for the SysTick counter should be:

1. Program the value in the STRELOAD register.
2. Clear the STCURRENT register by writing to it with any value.
3. Configure the STCTRL register for the required operation.

One point to be noted is: When the ARM® processor is halted for debugging, the counter does not decrement.

2.6.4.5.6 System Control Block (SCB) The System Control Block (SCB) provides system controls and implementation information, including configuration, control, and reporting of the system exceptions.

These controls and implementations are performed via 15 control registers, which are shown in Table 2.17. The base address for these registers is 0xE000.E000 in the memory map, which is the System Control Space (SCS) in the PPB area on the On-Chip memory. The offset address shown in Table 2.17 is the offset or a distance to the base address.

The registers and their control functions can be categorized into the following groups:

1. System Controls: The following registers are used for system controls.

    a. Auxiliary Control Register (ACTLR)—Provides the disabling functions for IT-folding, automatic update, write buffer, and multiple-cycle interrupts.

    b. CPU ID Register (CPUID)—Provides the ARM® Cortex®-M4 processor part number, version and other implementation information.

    c. System Control Register (SYSCTRL)—Controls the features of entry to and exit from the low-power working modes, such as sleep mode or deep-sleep mode. Three bits on this register are used to control: (1) What kinds interrupts or events can wake up the processor (bit 4), (2) Whether to use the sleep-mode or deep-sleep mode as the low-power mode (bit 2), (3) Whether to use sleep-mode or not when return from the Handler mode to the Thread mode.

    d. Configuration and Control Register (CFGCTRL)—Controls entry to Thread Mode and enables the handlers for NMI, hard fault, and faults escalated by the FAULTMASK register to ignore bus faults; trapping of divide by zero and unaligned accesses; and access to the SWTRIG register by unprivileged software.

2. System Running Status: The following registers are used for system status:

    a. System Handler Control and State Register (SYSHNDCTRL)—Enables the system handlers, and indicate the pending status of the usage fault, bus fault, memory management fault, and SVC exceptions as well as the active status of the system handlers.

Table 2.17. Control registers used for system control block.

Offset	Register Name	Functions
0x008	ACTLR	Auxiliary Control Register
0xD00	CPUID	CPU ID Register
0xD04	INTCTRL	Interrupt Control Register
0xD08	VTABLE	Vector Table Offset Register
0xD0C	APINT	Application Interrupt and Reset Control Register
0xD10	SYSCTRL	System Control Register
0xD14	CFGCTRL	Configuration and Control Register
0xD18	SYSPRI1	System Handler Priority 1 Register
0xD1C	SYSPRI2	System Handler Priority 2 Register
0xD20	SYSPRI3	System Handler Priority 3 Register
0xD24	SYSHNDCTRL	System Handler Control and State Register
0xD28	FAULTSTAT	Configurable Fault Status Register
0xD2C	HFAULTSTAT	Hard Fault Status Register
0xD34	MMADDR	Memory Management Fault Address Register
0xD38	FAULTADDR	Bus Fault Address Register

    b. `Configurable Fault Status Register` (FAULTSTAT)—Indicates the cause of a memory management fault, bus fault, or usage fault.

    c. `Hard Fault Status Register` (HFAULTSTAT)—Provides information about events that activate the hard fault handler.

    d. `Memory Management Fault Address Register` (MMADDR)—Provides the address of the location that generated a memory management fault. When an unaligned access faults, the address in this register is the actual address that faulted.

    e. `Bus Fault Address Register` (FAULTADDR)—Provides the address of the location that generated a bus fault. When an unaligned access faults, the address in this register is the one requested by the instruction, even if it is not the address of the fault.

3. System Interrupts and Priority Controls: The following registers are used for interrupts and priority controls:

    a. `Interrupt Control and State Register` (INTCTRL)—Provides a set-pending bit for the NMI exception, and set-pending and clear-pending bits for the PendSV and SysTick exceptions.

    b. `Vector Table Offset Register` (VTABLE)—Provides the offset address of the vector table relative to the base address 0x0000.0000.

    c. `Application Interrupt and Reset Control Register` (APINT)—Provides priority grouping control for the exception model, endian status for data accesses, and reset control of the system. To write to this register, 0x05FA must be written to the VECTKEY field, otherwise the write is ignored.

    d. `System Handler Priority 1 Register` (SYSPRI1)—Configures the priority level, 0 to 7 of the usage fault, bus fault, and memory management fault exception handlers. This register is byte-accessible.

    e. `System Handler Priority 2 Register` (SYSPRI2)—Configures the priority level, 0 to 7 of the SVCall handler. This register is byte-accessible. The SVCall is a supervisor call (SVC) that is an exception triggered by the SVC instruction. In an OS environment, applications can use SVC instructions to access OS kernel functions and device drivers.

    f. `System Handler Priority 3 Register` (SYSPRI3)—Configures the priority level, 0 to 7 of the SysTick exception and PendSV handlers. This register is byte-accessible. The PendSV is a pendable, interrupt-driven request for system-level service. In an OS environment, use PendSV for context switching when no other exception is active. A PendSV can be triggered by the Interrupt Control and State (INTCTRL) register.

There are some system controls related to Cortex®-M4 processor and TM4C123GH6PM MCU, such as Nested Vectored Interrupt Controller (NVIC), Memory Protection Unit (MPU), and Floating-Point Unit (FPU) controls. We have provided some introductions about these controls in Sections 2.2.1.3 (FPU), 2.3.4 (MPU), and 2.4.1 (NVIC). More detailed discussions about these controls can be found in the following each related section.

Now let's take a look at the system initialization and configuration procedure after a system reset operation, especially for the system clock source selection process.

2.6.4.6 *System Clock Initialization and Configuration*

The system clock can be any clock sources as we discussed in Section 2.6.3.1, such as Precision Internal Oscillator (PIOSC), Main Oscillator (MOSC), Low-Frequency Internal Oscillator (LFIOSC), Hibernate RTC Oscillator (RTCOSC), and the Phase-Locked Loop (PLL) clock generator. The popular way is to use the PLL as the system clock generator.

Generally the PLL is configured using direct register writes to the RCC/RCC2 register. If the RCC2 register is being used, the USERCC2 bit must be set and the appropriate RCC2 bit/field is used. The steps required to successfully set the PLL-based system clock are as follows:

1. Bypass the PLL and system clock divider by setting the BYPASS bit and clearing the USESYS bit in the RCC register, thereby configuring the microcontroller to run off a "raw" clock source and allowing for the new PLL configuration to be validated before switching the system clock to the PLL.

2. Select the crystal value (XTAL) and oscillator source (OSCSRC), and clear the PWRDN bit in RCC/RCC2. Setting the XTAL field automatically pulls valid PLL configuration data for the appropriate crystal, and clearing the PWRDN bit powers and enables the PLL and its output.

3. Select the desired system divider (SYSDIV) in RCC/RCC2 and set the USESYS bit in RCC. The SYSDIV field determines the system frequency for the microcontroller.

4. Wait for the PLL to lock by polling the PLLLRIS bit in the Raw Interrupt Status (RIS) register.

5. Enable use of the PLL by clearing the BYPASS bit in RCC/RCC2.

2.7 INTRODUCTION TO TIVA™ C SERIES LAUNCHPAD™ TM4C123GXL EVALUATION BOARD

The Tiva™ C Series TM4C123G LaunchPad™ Evaluation Board (EVB) EK-TM4C123GXL is a low-cost and multiple-function evaluation platform specially designed based on ARM® Cortex®-M4F microcontrollers. Two TM4C123GH6PM microcontrollers are included in this EVB to enable the board to provide various control functions, such as TM4C123GH6PM USB 2.0 device interface, on-board ICDI interface, hibernate module, and motion control PWM module.

The TM4C123GXL EVB is specially designed for applying the Tiva™ for C Series Software, including the Tiva™ C Series TivaWare™ libraries, such as Peripheral Driver Library, USB library, Sensor Hub library, Graphical library, and Tiva™ Boot Loader.

Figure 2.20 shows an illustration photo for the TM4C123GXL evaluation board. The following components and their functions are involved in this board:

- Two TM4C123GH6PM microcontrollers, MCU-1 and MCU-2, are included in this EVB. The former is used as a program loading/debugging controller, and the latter works as a real microcontroller for this board.

- Two USB connectors are provided to support the program development. The ICDI/Debug USB Connector is used for programming/debugging purpose, and the USB Micro-A/-B Connector can be used as an interface to enable this EVB to work as an USB Device.

- The Power Select Switch is used to select the power for the board. When the board works as an evaluation board, the switch should be in the Debug position to enable the program to be downloaded and debugged in the board. Otherwise the switch should be in the Device position when it works as a USB Device.

- Two user buttons, SW1 and SW2, are provided to support the users' multi-application functions. Both user buttons can be used in the preloaded application program to adjust the light spectrum of the RGB LED as well as going into and returning from the hibernation

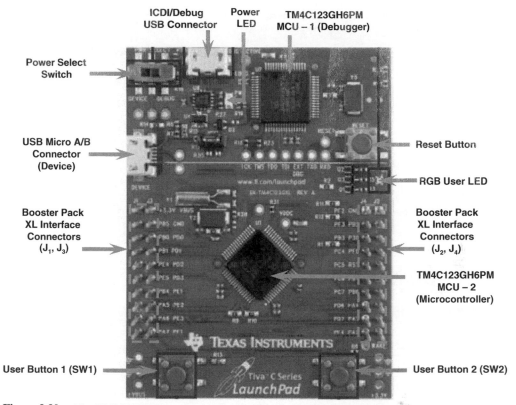

Figure 2.20.   The TM4C123GXL evaluation board. (Reprinted with the permission of the Texas Instruments Incorporated.)

mode. The user button SW2 can be used to wake the processor up from the hibernation mode since it is connected to the $\overline{WAKE}$ pin in the MCU. The user buttons can also be used for other purposes in the user's custom application.

- One RGB User LED is provided in the board to enable users to use this LED to develop and build different application programs.

- The Reset Button enables users to perform a reset operation for the processor and the entire system.

- There are two double rows of stackable headers that connected to most GPIO pins of the TM4C123GH6PM MCU located at both sides of the board. These rows are labeled as connectors J1, J2, J3, and J4, respectively. All of these headers are connected to related GPIO pins in the MCU and can be connected to other peripheral devices. Tables 2.18~2.21 show these connections. Among them, all five pins in the Port F, PF0~PF4, have been connected to five on-board devices, which is shown in Table 2.22.

In addition to components listed above, the TM4C123GXL EVB contains the following components with the related functions:

1. Power Supply: The EVB can be powered by (1) On-Board ICDI USB cable (Debug — default, and (2) USB Device cable (Device).

Table 2.18. Pin distributions and functions in J1 connector.

J1 Pin	GPIO	Analog Function	On-Board Function	1	2	3	4	5	6	7	8	9	14
				Digital Functions (GPIOPCTL PMCx Bit Field Encoding)									
1	Power Supply 3.3 V												
2	PB5	AIN11	—	—	SSI2Fss	—	M0PWM3	—	—	T1CCP1	CAN0Tx	—	—
3	PB0	USB0ID	—	U1Rx	—	—	—	—	—	T2CCP0	—	—	—
4	PB1	USB0VBUS	—	U1Tx	—	—	—	—	—	T2CCP1	—	—	—
5	PE4	AIN9	—	U5Rx	—	I2C2SCL	M0PWM4	M1PWM2	—	—	CAN0Rx	—	—
6	PE5	AIN8	—	U5Tx	—	I2C2SDA	M0PWM5	M1PWM3	—	—	CAN0Tx	—	—
7	PB4	AIN10	—	—	SSI2Clk	—	M0PWM2	—	—	T1CCP0	CAN0Rx	—	—
8	PA5	—	—	—	SSI0Tx	—	—	—	—	—	—	—	—
9	PA6	—	—	—	—	I2C1SCL	—	M1PWM2	—	—	—	—	—
10	PA7	—	—	—	—	I2C1SDA	—	M1PWM3	—	—	—	—	—

Table 2.19. Pin distributions and functions in J2 connector.

J2 Pin	GPIO	Analog Function	On-Board Function	1	2	3	4	5	6	7	8	9	14
				Digital Functions (GPIOPCTL PMCx Bit Field Encoding)									
1	GROUND												
2	PB2	—	—	—	—	I2C0SCL	—	—	—	T3CCP0	—	—	—
3	PE0	AIN3	—	U7Rx	—	—	—	—	—	—	—	—	—
4	PF0	—	USR_SW2/WAKE (R1)	U1RTS	SSI1Rx	CAN0Rx	—	M1PWM4	PhA0	T0CCP0	NMI	C0o	—
5	RESET												
6	PB7	—	—	—	SSI2Tx	—	M0PWM1	—	—	T0CCP1	—	—	—
6	PD1	AIN6	Compatible MSP430	SSI3Fss	SSI1Fss	I2C3SDA	M0PWM7	M1PWM1	—	WT2CCP1	—	—	—
7	PB6	—	—	—	SSI2Rx	—	M0PWM0	—	—	T0CCP0	—	—	—
7	PD0	AIN7	Compatible MSP430	SSI3Clk	SSI1Clk	I2C3SCL	M0PWM6	M1PWM0	—	WT2CCP0	—	—	—
8	PA4	—	—	—	SSI0Rx	—	—	—	—	—	—	—	—
9	PA3	—	—	—	SSI0Fss	—	—	—	—	—	—	—	—
10	PA2	—	—	—	SSI0Clk	—	—	—	—	—	—	—	—

Table 2.20. Pin distributions and functions in a J3 connector.

J3 Pin	GPIO	Analog Function	On-Board Function	1	2	3	4	5	6	7	8	9	14
				Digital Functions (GPIOPCTL PMCx Bit Field Encoding)									
1	Power Supply 5.0 V												
2	GROUND												
3	PD0	AIN7	—	SSI3Clk	SSI1Clk	I2C3SCL	M0PWM6	M1PWM0	—	WT2CCP0	—	—	—
	PB6	—	Compatible MSP430 -R9	—	SSI2Rx	—	M0PWM0	—	—	T0CCP0	—	—	—
4	PD1	AIN6	—	SSI3Fss	SSI1Fss	I2C3SDA	M0PWM7	M1PWM1	—	WT2CCP1	—	—	—
	PB7	—	Compatible MSP430-R10	—	SSI2Tx	—	M0PWM1	—	—	T0CCP1	—	—	—
5	PD2	AIN5	—	SSI3Rx	SSI1Rx	—	M0FAULT0	—	—	WT3CCP0	USB0EPEN	—	—
6	PD3	AIN4	—	SSI3Tx	SSI1Tx	—	—	—	—	WT3CCP1	USB0PFLT	—	—
7	PE1	AIN2	—	U7Tx	—	—	—	—	—	—	—	—	—
8	PE2	AIN1		—	—	—	—	—	—	—	—	—	—
9	PE3	AIN0	—	—	—	—	—	—	—	—	—	—	—
10	PF1	—	—	U1CTS	SSI1Tx	—	—	M1PWM5	—	T0CCP1	—	C1o	TRD1

Table 2.21. Pin distributions and functions in a J4 connector.

| J4 Pin | GPIO | Analog Function | On-Board Function | Digital Functions (GPIOPCTL PMCx Bit Field Encoding) | | | | | | | | | |
				1	2	3	4	5	6	7	8	9	15
1	PF2	—	Blue LED (R11)	—	SSI1Clk	—	M0FAULT0	M1PWM6	—	T1CCP0	—		TRD0
2	PF3	—	Green LED (R12)	—	SSI1Fss	CAN0Tx	—	M1PWM7	—	T1CCP1	—	—	TRCLK
3	PB3	—	—	—	—	I2C0SDA	—	—	—	T3CCP1	—	—	
4	PC4	C1−	—	U4Rx	U1Rx	—	M0PWM6	—	IDX1	WT0CCP0	U1RTS	—	—
5	PC5	C1+	—	U4Tx	U1Tx	—	M0PWM7	—	PhA1	WT0CCP1	U1CTS	—	—
6	PC6	C0+	—	U3Rx	—	—	—	—	PhB1	WT1CCP0	USB0EPEN	—	—
7	PC7	C0−	—	U3Tx	—	—	—	—	—	WT1CCP1	USB0PFLT	—	—
8	PD6	—	—	U2Rx	—	—	—	—	PhA0	WT5CCP0	—	—	—
9	PD7	—	—	U2Tx	—	—	—	—	PhB0	WT5CCP1	NMI	—	—
10	PF4	—	USR_SW1 (R13)	—	—	—	—	M1FAULT0	IDX0	T2CCP0	USB0EPEN	—	—

2. Clocking: The EVB used the main internal clock circuit driven by a 16-MHz crystal (Y2) by default. This clock can be modified by software to program a PLL clock generator to get higher clock frequency.

3. In-Circuit Debug Interface (ICDI): The EVB provides an on-board In-Circuit Debug Interface (ICDI) to enable users to download their program to the flash ROM space in the TM4C123GH6PM MCU and perform the debugging functions for that program. This ICDI only supports the JTAG protocol.

4. Virtual COM Ports: When plugged in to a PC, the device enumerates as a debugger and a virtual COM port. Table 2.23 shows the connections of the COM port and the pins on the MCU.

5. Hibernate Mode: The EVB provides an external 32.768-kHz crystal (Y1) as the clock source for the TM4C123GH6PM Hibernation module clock source to enable to MCU to work in the hibernate mode to save power consumptions. The user button 2 (SW2) can be used as a wake signal to wake up the processor to return to the normal run mode.

The Tiva™ C Series LaunchPad™ provides an easy and inexpensive way to develop applications with the TM4C123GH6PM microcontroller. Tiva™ C Series BoosterPacks and

Table 2.22. GPIO Port F pins and on-board devices.

GPIO Pin	Pin Function	On-Board Devices
PF4	GPIO	User Button 1 (SW1)
PF0	GPIO	User Button 2 (SW2)
PF1	GPIO	RGB LED—Red
PF2	GPIO	RGB LED—Blue
PF3	GPIO	RGB LED—Green

Table 2.23. Virtual COM port signals.

GPIO Pin	Pin Function
PA0	U0Rx
PA1	U0Tx

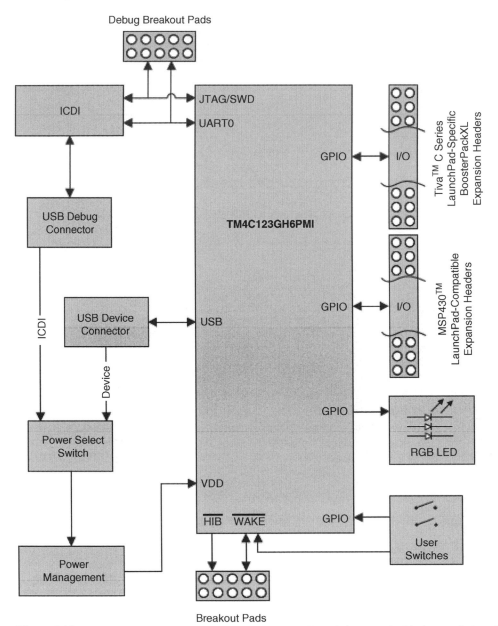

Figure 2.21. The functional block diagram of the LaunchPad board. (Reprinted with the permission of the Texas Instruments Incorporated.)

MSP430 BoosterPacks expand the available peripherals and potential applications of the Tiva™ C Series LaunchPad™. BoosterPacks can be used with the Tiva™ C Series Launch-Pad™ or you can simply use the on-board TM4C123GH6PM microcontroller as its processor.

Figure 2.21 shows a functional block diagram for this TM4C123GXL evaluation board.

Two USB connectors, USB Debug and USB Device, enable the TM4C123GXL evaluation board to connect to either a host computer to download the user's program into the flash memory in this EVB and debug it or some other controllers to allow this EVB to work as a USB device.

Two user buttons, SW1 and SW2, are used to control the RGB LED intensity and wake the processor up from the hibernation mode via the GPIO Port F (PF4 and PF0).

One of the most important components in this EVB is the 40-pin BoosterPack XL expansion headers (J1~J4). These headers allow users to connect other desired peripherals with this EVB to perform multiple control functions for their actual applications. These headers are also compatible with MSP430 MCU.

2.8   INTRODUCTION TO EDUBASE ARM® TRAINER

The EduBASE ARM® Trainer is specially designed for Tiva™ for C Series LaunchPad™ microcontroller evaluation board EK-TM4C123GXL. Multiple peripheral devices and components are provided by this trainer.

Figure 2.22 shows the photo of this trainer.

The main peripherals and components by this board include:

- 16×2 LCD display module with LED backlight.
- 4-digit, 7-segment display module for learning multiplexing technique
- 4 × 4 keypad
- Four data LEDs
- A 4-position DIP switch
- Four pushbutton switches
- Speaker
- Light sensor for home automation applications
- Potentiometer for analog input
- X-Y-Z accelerometer module interface header
- Three analog sensor inputs
- Four servo or relay outputs
- SPI-based dual 12-bit DAC for generating analog waveforms
- I^2C-based Real-Time Clock with a capacitor backup
- High-efficiency dual H-Bridge for controlling two DC motors or one stepper motor

An interface is provided to allow the TM4C123GXL EVB to be inserted into this Trainer. Two dashed lines in Figure 2.22 show these two connectors. The complete connection between the TM4C123GXL EVB and the EduBASE ARM® Trainer is shown in Figure D.1 in Appendix D.

2.9   CHAPTER SUMMARY

The main topics discussed in this chapter include the architectures and organizations of most popular embedded systems, including the most updated microcontroller ARM® Cortex®-M4, Tiva™ TM4C123GH6PM MCU, TivaWare™ for C Series LaunchPad™ TM4C123GXL

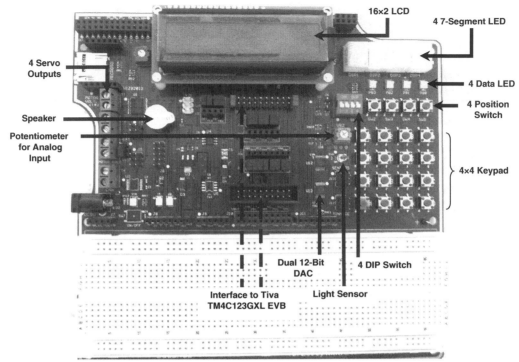

Figure 2.22.   The EduBASE ARM® Trainer.

evaluation board, and EduBASE ARM® Trainer. All of these components will be used in this book to make our project development process easier and simpler.

Starting with an overview of the organizations and architectures of most popular embedded systems and microcontrollers, one of the most popular and powerful microcontrollers, ARM® Cortex®-M4, is introduced and discussed in details with the following components:

- An ARM® Cortex®-M4 Processor Core or CPU.
- A Nested Vectored Interrupt Controller (NVIC) closely integrated with the processor core to achieve low-latency interrupt processing.
- Multiple high-performance bus interfaces, including Code Interface and SRAM and Peripheral Interface.
- A System Timer unit SysTick.
- A low-cost debug solution with the optional ability, such as Debug Access Port (DAP) and Data Watchpoint.
- An optional Memory Protection Unit (MPU).
- An optional Floating Point Unit (FPU).
- Embedded Trace Macrocell (ETM) interface.
- Instrumentation Trace Macrocell (ITM) interface
- The debug and Serial Wire Viewer (SWV) interface.

Then each main component's architectures are discussed in the following sequence:

- ARM® Cortex®-M4 CPU or processor
- Floating Point Unit (FPU)
- External Memory Map
- Memory Protection Unit (MPU)
- Nested Vectored Interrupt Controller (NVIC)
- System Debug

The Tiva™ LaunchPad™ for C Series microcontroller, TM4C123GH6PM, is then discussed in details, including:

- On-Chip Memory Map
- System Clock
- GPIO Ports Architectures
- System Controls

Then the TM4C123GXL evaluation board is discussed with detailed introductions to all components and their functions. The EduBASE ARM® Trainer is also introduced in the last part of this chapter to enable users to have a global picture about the entire development system used in this book.

HOMEWORK

I. True/False Selections

_____**1.** The ARM® Cortex®-M4 processor contains CPU, on-chip memory and I/O Ports.

_____**2.** The only difference between the ARM® Cortex®-M3 and Cortex®-M4 is that the latter has an optional Floating Point Unit (FPU).

_____**3.** The Nested Vectored Interrupt Controller (NVIC) is integrated inside the ARM® Cortex®-M4 MCU chip.

_____**4.** Although the Cortex®-M4 processor is a 32-bit MCU, it can also handle 8-bit, 16-bit, and 32-bit data efficiently.

_____**5.** In Cortex®-M4 system, only one peripheral bus system is used and it is called Advanced Peripheral Bus (APB).

_____**6.** In Cortex®-M4 CPU, there are totally 21 registers in the register bank. Registers 0–15 are general purpose registers.

_____**7.** The operation mode of the Cortex®-M4 can be divided into Thread Mode and Handler Mode. The former is used to run the normal user's program and the latter is used to run the exception or interrupt service routines.

_____**8.** The TM4C123GH6PM MCU contains six General-Purpose Input/Output (GPIO) blocks or Ports, and each Port has a set of related control registers.

_____**9.** The Port Control Register (GPIOPCTL) is used to select the specific peripheral signal for each GPIO pin when using the alternate function mode.

_____**10.** TM4C123GH6PM MCU provides six reset sources and most of them belong to internal reset operations.

II. Multiple Choices

1. All embedded systems or microcontrollers contain the _____ components.

    a. CPU

    b. Memory device

    c. I/O Ports

    d. All of the above

2. The ARM® Cortex®-M4 MCU contains _____.

    a. No memory

    b. 32-KB RAM

    c. 256-KB Flash Memory

    d. 2-KB EEPROM

3. Two bus interfaces between the TM4C123GH6PM MCU and external components are _____.

    a. Advanced Peripheral Bus (APB) and General Peripheral Bus (GPB)

    b. Advanced High-performance Bus (AHB) and Advanced Microcontroller Bus (AMB)

    c. Advanced Peripheral Bus (APB) and Advanced High-performance Bus (PHB)

    d. Advanced High-performance Bus (AHB) and General Peripheral Bus (GPB)

4. The TM4C123GH6PM MCU memory map system includes _____.

    a. 256-KB Flash Memory

    b. 32-KB SRAM

    c. 2-KB EEPROM and Internal ROM

    d. All of the above

5. The Internal ROM includes _____.

    a. Peripheral device driver library and Graphical library

    b. USB library and Sensor Hub library

    c. TivaWare™ Boot Loader

    d. All of the above

6. Any of the following clock sources can work as the system clock except ___.

    a. Precision Internal Oscillator (PIOSC)

    b. Main Oscillator (MOSC)

    c. Hibernate RTC Oscillator (RTCOSC)

    d. Phase-Locked Loop (PLL)

7. One prerequisite job of using any GPIO Port is to _____.

    a. Configure the operational mode of the GPIO Port

    b. Configure the interrupt control registers on NVIC

    c. Enable the system clock to be connected to the selected GPIO Port

    d. Include and use the related peripheral driver library

8. Although each GPIO control register is 32 bits, only the ____ is used to provide a control byte function.

    a. Lowest 8 bits

    b. Highest 8 bits

    c. Lower 16 bits

    d. Highest 16 bits

9. Because of the APB and AHB accessing mode, each GPIO Port can be accessed by using ___ of address(es).

    a. 1 set

    b. 2 sets

    c. 3 sets

    d. 4 sets

10. To save power, the TM4C123GH6PM MCU can run in ___ mode(s), it is (they are) _____.

    a. 1, Run-Mode

    b. 2, Run-Mode and Sleep Mode

    c. 3, Run-Mode, Sleep-Mode, and Deep Sleep-Mode

    d. 4, Run-Mode, Sleep-Mode, Deep Sleep-Mode, and Hibernate Mode

III. Exercises

1. Provide a brief description about basic components used in an embedded system or a micro-controller system.

2. Provide a brief description about basic components used in an ARM® Cortex®-M4 MCU.

3. Explain the functions of 13 general purpose registers and 3 special registers in the register bank inside an ARM® Cortex®-M4 CPU.

4. Explain the operational procedure of stack memory used in TM4C123GH6PM MCU.

5. Provide a description about general procedure to configure the GPIO Ports.

6. Explain the initialization and configuration process for TM4C123GH6PM GPIO Port with desired registers.

Chapter 3

ARM® Microcontroller Development Kits

This chapter provides general information on software development tools and platforms used for Tiva™ TM4C123GXL evaluation board.

3.1 OVERVIEW AND INTRODUCTION

Texas Instruments' Tiva™ C Series MCUs offer the industry's most popular ARM® Cortex®-M4 core with scalable memory and package options, unparalleled connectivity peripherals, and advanced analog integration. From Ethernet connectivity to basic UARTs, the Tiva™ C Series MCUs offer a variety of solutions for networking, displays, sensor hubs, industrial automation, and much more.

One of the most popular Tiva™ C Series microcontroller evaluation boards is the Tiva™ C Series TM4C123G LaunchPad evaluation platform from Texas Instruments. These low-cost kits provide developers with everything you need to start designing new applications. The award-winning Tiva™ C Series LaunchPad™ and the newly released Tiva™ C Series Connected LaunchPad™ are an ideal introduction to the world of ARM® Cortex®-M4 microcontrollers.

Many commercial development tools, including the Integrated Development Environment (IDE), debug adapters, compilers, loaders, and runners, are available for the ARM® Cortex®-M4 microcontrollers. Generally, there are different layers of software used for each different microcontroller system. Figure 3.1 shows an example configuration of using a Tiva™ TM4C123G LaunchPad™ evaluation board platform.

Basically the whole development kit can be divided into two layers: (1) the Keil® MDK-ARM® Suite that provides a graphic user interface (GUI) with all general required development tools and (2) the TivaWare™ for C Series LaunchPad™ firmware that provides specified software and libraries for Tiva™ C Series TM4C123G evaluation board.

It can be found from Figure 3.1 that two dashed lines are pointed to the Debug Adaptor. This means that both Keil® MDK and TivaWare™ provide a related device driver for the debug adaptor that is connected between the host computer and the evaluation board: the ULINK2 and the Tiva™ In-Circuit Debug Interface (ICDI). The former is a device driver for the Debug Adaptor developed by the Kei® MDK,

Practical Microcontroller Engineering with ARM® Technology, First Edition. Ying Bai.
© 2016 by The Institute of Electrical and Electronics Engineers, Inc. Published 2016 by John Wiley & Sons, Inc.
Companion Website: www.wiley.com/go/armbai

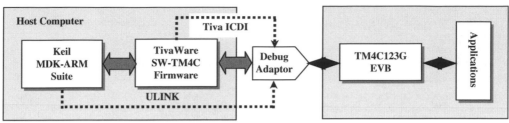

Figure 3.1. Configuration of a Tiva TM4C123G-based EVB.

and the latter is a device driver built by the Texas Instruments. This debug adaptor is used to perform some necessary communications between the software development tools and the microcontroller hardware—in this case, TM4C123G EVB. These communications include the debugging user's programs and downloading the compiled programs to the EVB, either to RAM or to Flash memory.

3.2 THE ENTIRE TIVA™ TM4C123G-BASED DEVELOPMENT SYSTEM

As we mentioned, we will use a Tiva™ TM4C123G-based evaluation trainer, EduBASE ARM® Trainer, which is composed of a Tiva™ TM4C123GXL EVB and some other useful peripheral devices, to get a powerful trainer. The hardware setup and connection for the whole evaluation system is shown in Figure 3.2.

It can be found from Figure 3.2 that the entire Tiva™ TM4C123G-based development system, EduBASE ARM® Trainer, is composed of two pieces of important hardware components: the host computer (PC) that works as a control unit and the EduBASE ARM® Trainer Evaluation Board. The components and functions of these two pieces of hardware are as follows:

- The host computer works as an interface to enable users to create, assembly, debug, and test the user's program in the EduBASE ARM® Trainer using the Keil® IDE and TivaWare™

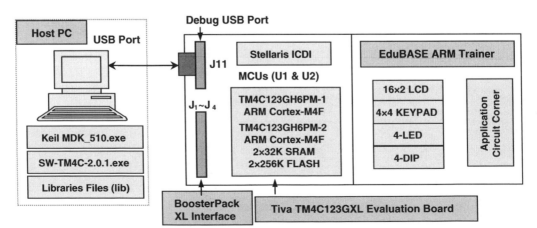

Figure 3.2. The setup and connection of entire Tiva TM4C123G-based development system.

firmware installed in the host computer. All these functions are performed by accessing various libraries and tools provided by the TivaWare™ firmware and Keil® IDE installed in the host computer.

- The EduBASE ARM® Trainer provides all hardware and software interfacing abilities to facilitate the above operations performed in the host computer.

The commands and data communications between the host computer and the EduBASE ARM® Trainer are made through the USB ports, USB Port in the host computer, and the Debug USB Port in the Tiva™ TM4C123GXL EVB, via a USB cable.

For the Tiva™ TM4C123GXL microcontroller evaluation board, more than 15 development platforms are available and they are provided by the different vendors. However, the following platforms and tools are relatively popular:

- Keil MDK-ARM Microcontroller Development Kit (MDK)
- Texas Instruments' Code Composer Studio™ IDE (CCS)
- ARM® DS-5 Development Studio 5
- IAR Embedded Workbench for ARM®
- Mentor Graphics Sourcery CodeBench
- GNU Compiler Collection (GCC)

Among those tools and platforms, one of the popular choices is the Keil® Microcontroller Development Kit for ARM®, or MDK-ARM®. This MDK contains all required components and tools to develop application programs for ARM®-related microcontrollers.

The MDK-ARM® is a complete software development environment for Cortex™-M, Cortex-R4, ARM7™, and ARM9™ processor-based devices. MDK-ARM® is specifically designed for microcontroller applications; it is easy to learn and use and is powerful enough for the most demanding embedded applications.

MDK-ARM® is available in four editions: MDK-Lite, MDK-Cortex-M, MDK-Standard, and MDK-Professional. All editions provide a complete C/C++ development environment, and MDK-Professional includes extensive middleware libraries. Since we are using ARM® Cortex®-M4 MCU, we will concentrate our discussion on the MDK-Cortex-M development system.

As we discussed in Chapter 2, the hardware configuration of the entire Tiva™ TM4C123G development system is composed of the following components:

- ARM® Cortex®-M4F MCUs
- Tiva™ TM4C123GH6PM MCUs
- Tiva™ C Series TM4C123GXL EVB
- EduBASE ARM® Trainer
- Host Computer

This configuration can be presented in Figure 3.3.

Based on the discussion above, the entire development system for ARM® microcontroller can be composed of the following components or tools:

1. Development Kits or Suites
2. Debug Adaptor and Drivers
3. Specified MCU-related Firmware

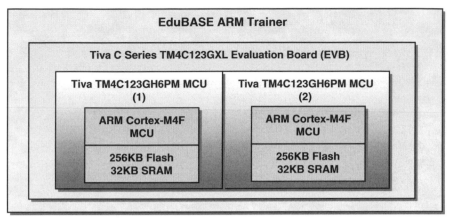

Figure 3.3. The configuration of the EduBASE ARM Trainer hardware.

4. Program Examples

5. Development or Evaluation Boards

Since the development evaluation board has been discussed in the last chapter, now let's discuss the top four components in the following section one by one. However, before we can continue our discussions for these components, we need first to download and install them in the host computer.

3.3 DOWNLOAD AND INSTALL DEVELOPMENT SUITE AND SPECIFIED FIRMWARE

The first three components—development kits, specified firmware, and debug adaptor drivers—are three different components and can be downloaded and installed separately. The program examples are MCU-related and they can be installed with the specified firmware together.

Refer to Appendix A to download and install Keil® MDK-ARM® 5.1. This installation process not only installs the MDK Core, but also installs some Software Packs. An icon of installed Keil® MDK, **Keil µVersion5**, will be added into your desktop when the installation is complete. The default installation location of this development suite on your host PC is `C:/Keil_v5`.

Refer to Appendix B to download and install Tiva™ C Series specified firmware-`TivaWare SW-EK-TM4C123GXL` Package. The default installation location of this firmware in your host computer is `C:/ti/TivaWare_C_Series-2.0.1.11577`.

Refer to Appendix C to download and install Stellaris® In-Circuit Debug Interface (ICDI) and Virtual COM Port. The installation location for this ICDI device driver is in the folder `Stellaris® In-Circuit Debug Interface`, which is under the **Device Manager** in the **Control Panel** in your host computer.

Now let's discuss these four components in the following section one by one. Since the MDK Core contains the Debugger, we will discuss these two components together.

3.4   INTRODUCTION TO THE INTEGRATED DEVELOPMENT ENVIRONMENT—KEIL® MDK µVERSION5

The Keil® MDK is the most comprehensive software development environment for ARM®-based microcontrollers. MDK Version 5 is now split into the MDK Core and Software Packs which makes new device support and middleware updates independent from the toolchain.

The entire Keil® MDK development system can be divided into the following key components:

- The MDK Core
  - µVersion® IDE with Source Editor and GUI
  - Pack Installer
  - ARM® C/C++ Compiler
  - µVersion® Debugger with Trace Function
- Software Packs
  - Device Drivers for Serial Peripheral Interface (SPI), USB and Ethernet
  - The Cortex Microcontroller Software Interface Standard (CMSIS) support, including the CMSIS-CORE, CMSIS-DSP, and CMSIS-RTOS
  - MDK Middleware support
  - Example programs

MDK Core

The MDK Core contains all development tools including µVersion IDE, Compiler, and Debugger. By using the MDK Core, you can create, build, and debug an embedded application for Cortex-M processor-based microcontroller devices. The new Pack Installer adds and updates Software Packs for devices, CMSIS, and middleware. The purpose of the new added Pack Installer is to manage Software Packs that can be added any time to the MDK Core. This makes new device support and middleware updates independent from the toolchain. Software Packs that add support for a complete microcontroller family are called Device Family Packs.

An illustration block diagram of the MDK Core and its components is shown in Figure 3.4.

Software Packs

Software Packs contain device support, CMSIS libraries, middleware, board support, code templates, and example projects. Among all components included in the Software Packs, two components, CMSIS and Middleware, need to be explained in more detail.

Figure 3.4.   The components included in the MDK Core. (Reproduced with permission from ARM® Limited. Copyright © ARM Limited.)

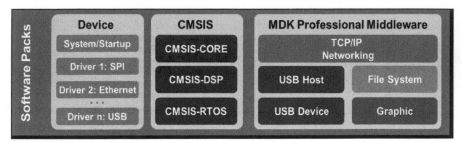

Figure 3.5.   Components in the Software Packs. (Reproduced with permission from ARM® Limited. Copyright © ARM Limited.)

The CMSIS provides a ground-up software framework for embedded applications that run on Cortex-M-based microcontrollers. The CMSIS enables consistent and simple software interfaces to the processor and the peripherals, simplifying software reuse and reducing the learning curve for microcontroller developers.

The CMSIS application software components include:

- CMSIS-CORE: Defines the API for the Cortex-M processor core and peripherals and includes a consistent system startup code. The software components CMSIS:CORE and Device: Startup are all you need to create and run applications on the native processor that uses exceptions, interrupts, and device peripherals.

- CMSIS-RTOS: Provides standard real-time operating systems and therefore enables software templates, middleware, libraries, and other components that can work across supported RTOS systems.

- CMSIS-DSP: Is a library collection for digital signal processing (DSP) with over 60 functions for various data types: fixed point (fractional q7, q15, q31) and single precision floating point (32 bits).

The MDK Professional Middleware offers a wide range of communication peripherals to meet many embedded design requirements, and it is essential to make efficient use of these complex on-chip peripherals. The MDK Professional Middleware provides a Software Pack that includes royalty-free middleware with components for TCP/IP networking, USB Host and USB Device communication, file system for data storage, and a Graphical User Interface.

A complete block diagram including all Software Packs components is shown in Figure 3.5.

Because the MDK is a powerful development suite with great amount of components, we will divide our discussions for these components in different chapters. In this chapter, we will concentrate our discussions on the MDK Core, especially on the MDK-Cortex-M family. Two components, µVersion IDE and Debugger, are main topics to be discussed in this chapter.

First let's have a closer look at the Keil® MDK-ARM® working for the Tiva™ C Series LaunchPad™ evaluation board.

3.4.1 The Keil® MDK-ARM® for the MDK-Cortex-M Family

Similar to Keil® MDK-ARM®, the MDK-Cortex-M family contains the following components:

1. µVision5 Integrated Development Environment (IDE): Provides a GUI with all general required development tools, such as debugger and simulation environment.

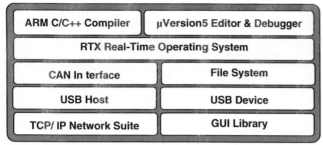

Figure 3.6.   The complete structure of the MDK-Cortex-M development system.

2. ARM Compilation Tools: These tools include C/C++ Compiler, ARM® Assembler, Linker, and other utilities.

3. Debugger: Provides debug functions for ARM® microcontroller programs.

4. Simulator: Provides simulation environment to enable users to build and run program without any real hardware.

5. Keil RTX Real-Time Operating System Kernel: Provides a real operating system kernel.

6. TCP/IP Networking Suite: Offers multiple protocols and various applications.

7. USB Device and USB Host stacks: These are provided with standard driver classes.

8. ULINK*pro*: This enables on-the-fly analysis of running applications and records every executed Cortex-M instruction.

9. Complete Code Coverage: Information about your program's execution.

10. Execution Profiler and Performance Analyzer: These enable program optimization.

11. CMSIS Cortex Microcontroller Software Interface Standard: Compliant.

12. Reference start-up codes: These are for about 1000 microcontrollers.

13. Flash Programming Algorithms.

14. Program examples.

A complete configuration of the MDK-ARM® for the Cortex®-M family is shown in Figure 3.6.

To better understand the program development process with Keil® MDK, first let's have a detailed discussion about the general development flow of a user project by using the MDK-Cortex®-M development system.

3.4.2 General Development Flow with MDK-ARM®

Figure 3.7 shows a general development process of a user project in the Keil® MDK. Generally, a user project in Keil® MDK can be developed in the following steps:

- A new project is created using the Keil® MDK.
- The user's source files with source codes, either C or ARM Assembly codes, are added into the project.

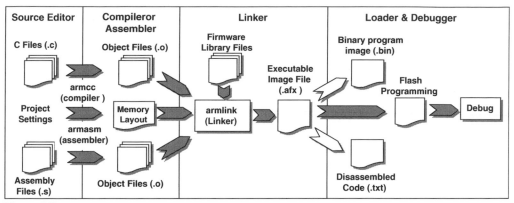

Figure 3.7.   Development structure of a user project with MDK.

- Depending on your source codes, the armcc (ARM® Compiler) or the armasm (ARM® Assembler) is called and executed to translate the user's source codes to the object codes and stored in the host computer. The start-up codes with Project Settings will be involved into this compiling or assembling process.

- The object code files will be linked with all other system library files or MCU-related library files and converted to the executable files, or image file in the ARM® terminology, and downloaded into flash memory or RAM in the EVB.

- Finally the executable codes can be sent to the debugger to perform the debugging or executing operations. In fact, the compiler, linker and loader are integrated into one unit, the Builder in the ARM® μVersion® IDE.

- Alternatively, the executable file can also be converted to the binary file or text file for the users' reference.

To successfully build a basic user project with Keil® MDK, one needs to use the following two key components:

1. Keil® MDK Core

2. CMSIS Core

The MDK Core provides all development tools including μVersion IDE, Compiler, and Debugger. The CMSIS-CORE defines the API for the Cortex-M processor core and peripherals and includes a consistent system startup code. The software components CMSIS:CORE and Device:Startup are all you need to create, build, and run applications on the native processor that uses exceptions, interrupts, and device peripherals.

All user source codes can be written in C; however, the startup codes that are provided by MCU vendors and generally included in the Keil® MDK installation process are ARM® assembly codes. The users also need to use some library files provided by the MCU vendor—in our case, the firmware TivaWare™ SW-EK-TM4C123GXL Package provided by Texas Instruments. This situation is shown in Figure 3.8.

As shown in Figure 3.8, to build and develop an ARM® application project, a native Cortex-M Core with CMSIS Core should be used. In fact, one CMSIS Core component CMSIS:CORE, which should be used together with the software component

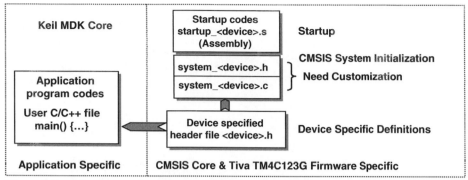

Figure 3.8.   The program development with MDK Core and CMSIS Core.

`Device:Startup`, is used to build a successful project. These components provide the following central files:

- The `startup_<device>.s` file with reset handler and exception vectors.
- The `system_<device>.c` configuration file for basic device setup (clock and memory bus).
- The `system_<device>.h`, which includes a file for user code accessing to the micro-controller device.

The device specified `<device>.h` header file is included in C source files and defines:

- Peripheral Access with standardized register layout.
- Access to Interrupts and Exceptions and the Nested Interrupt Vector Controller (NVIC).
- Intrinsic Functions to generate special instructions, for example to activate sleep mode.
- Systick Timer (SYSTICK) functions to configure and start a periodic timer interrupt.
- Debug Access for printf-style I/O and ITM communication via on-chip CoreSight.

One point to be noted is that in an actual application file, the `<device>`, is the name of the microcontroller device used in the real user project. For example, in our case, this device name should be `<tm4c123gh6pm>`. Also, not all these four files can be found at the development stage; and some files, `system_<device>.h` and device-specified `<device>.h`, cannot be found until the program has been built successfully.

Now that we have a basic understanding about the Keil® MDK-Cortex-M development kit, let's make our feet a little wet with an example project to familiarize us with this kit.

3.4.3 Warming Up Keil® MDK Cortex-M Kit with Example Projects

Before opening the Keil® MDK-ARM® μVersion 5.1 Suite, make sure that the following two important components have been set up with your host computer:

- The Tiva™ TM4C123G based EVB has been connected to your host PC with the USB cable. Refer to Appendix D to complete this hardware setup if you have not.
- All development tools have been downloaded and installed as we did in Section 3.3.

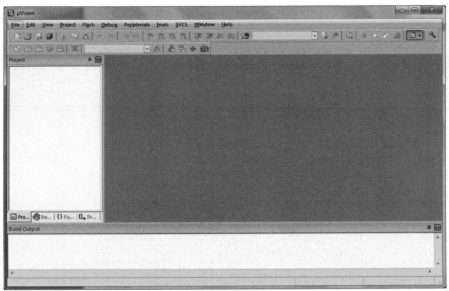

Figure 3.9. The opened Keil® MDK-ARM µVersion® 5.1 suite. (Reproduced with permission from ARM® Limited. Copyright © ARM Limited.)

Perform the following operations to launch Keil® MDK-ARM® µVersion® 5.1 IDE, and load and run an example project Hello World.

1. Double click on the icon Keil µVersion5, which is located on your PC's desktop, to launch and open this kit, which is shown in Figure 3.9.

2. From the Project menu, select Open Project menu to open the Select Project File wizard.

3. Use this wizard to browse to the **Hello World** project, which should be located in the ti folder when we installed this TivaWare™ package. The actual location of this project is: C:/ti/TivaWare_C_Series-2.0.1.11577/examples/boards/ek-tm4c123gxl/hello. Browse to that folder and select the project file hello.uvproj, and click on the **Open** button to load and open this project (Figure 3.10).

4. The opened project Hello World is shown in Figure 3.11.

5. You can view any file in the Project Workspace Pane in the left by double clicking on the desired file. For example, to view the source file, hello.c, just double click on this file. The opened source file is shown in Figure 3.12.

6. You can build the project Hello World by clicking on the Project|Rebuild all target files, as shown in Figure 3.13. All of the source files are compiled and linked. The activity can be seen in the Build window at the bottom of the µVision IDE. The process completes with an application named hello.axf built with no errors and no warnings, which can be shown in Figure 3.14.

7. Now let's load the Hello Program into the flash memory in the Tiva™ C Series LaunchPad™ EVB, TM4C123G. You can debug with either the on-board ICDI or you can use the Keil® ULINK™ debug probe. We did install the Keil® MDK Debugger driver, ULINK2, when we installed the Keil® MDK. However, we did not have this debug adaptor or the debug hardware. Therefore we have to use the Tiva C Series on board ICDI since the TI has a built-in debug adaptor installed in the TM4C123G EVB.

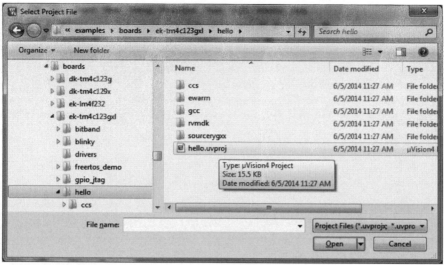

Figure 3.10.　The Hello World project. (Reproduced with permission from ARM® Limited. Copyright © ARM Limited.)

8. To begin this loading process, select the Download menu item from the Flash menu, or click the Download button (icon). The process takes a few seconds. A progress bar will show at the bottom of the IDE window as the device is programmed. When it is finished, the Build window will show that the device was erased, programmed, and verified OK. The Hello application is now programmed into the flash memory of the Stellaris® microcontroller on the Evaluation Board.

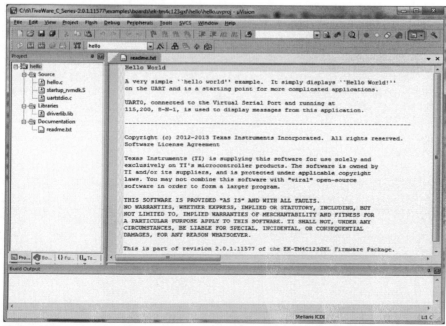

Figure 3.11.　The opened Hello World project. (Reproduced with permission from ARM® Limited. Copyright © ARM Limited.)

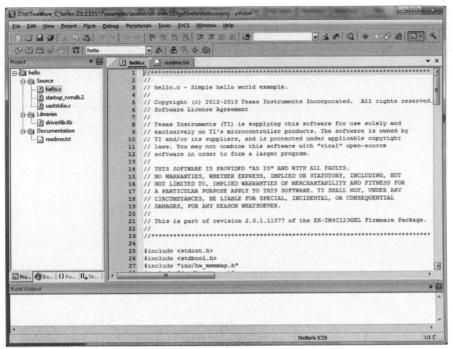

Figure 3.12. The opened source file hello.c. (Reproduced with permission from ARM® Limited. Copyright © ARM Limited.)

9. Now let's debug and run the Hello World project. Select the Start/Stop Debug Session from the Debug menu or click the Debug button. The IDE switches to debugging mode. A warning message is displayed to indicate that the board using the evaluation mode with a space limitation of 32 KB. Click on the OK button to continue. The processor registers show in a window on the left, the debugger command window is visible at the bottom, and the main window shows the source code being debugged. The debugger automatically stops at main, as shown in Figure 3.15.

10. To run this project, select the Run from the Debug menu, or click on the Run button (icon). The application runs and the text Hello World! should be displayed on an UART related device. Since we do not connect to any UART with our PC, the only visible running result is that the RGB User LED (D1) on the TM4C123G EVB is flashing with the blue color periodically. This flashing function is related to the codes written in the hello.c file, exactly the codes between lines 145 and 166 in a while() loop.

Now you can stop the project by clicking on the Stop menu item from the Debug menu. You also need to go to Flash|Erase menu item to erase your download program from the Flash memory in the EVB. Otherwise your program will continue to run forever. Select the Close Project item from the Project menu to close this Hello World project.

After finishing this example project, you should have some basic idea and feeling about the Keil® MDK μVersion IDE. Next let's have a closer look at all functions of this IDE.

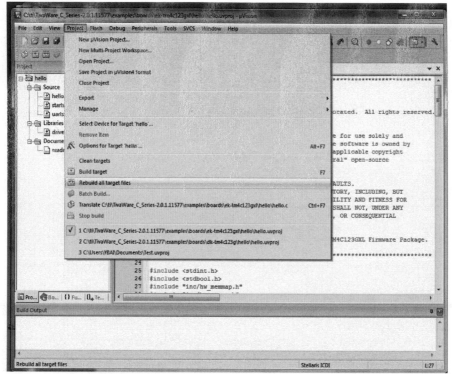

Figure 3.13. Rebuild the hello project. (Reproduced with permission from ARM® Limited. Copyright © ARM Limited.)

3.4.4 The Functions of the Keil® MDK-ARM® μVersion®5 GUI

In this section, we will have a detailed discussion about this MDK-ARM® μVision®5 GUI.

The μVision5 is an updated window-based software development platform that combines a robust and modern editor with a project manager and make facility tool. It integrates all the tools needed to develop embedded applications including a C/C++ compiler, macro assembler, linker/locator, and a HEX file generator. The μVision5 helps expedite the development process of embedded applications by providing the following:

- Full-featured source code editor.
- Device Database® for configuring the development tool.

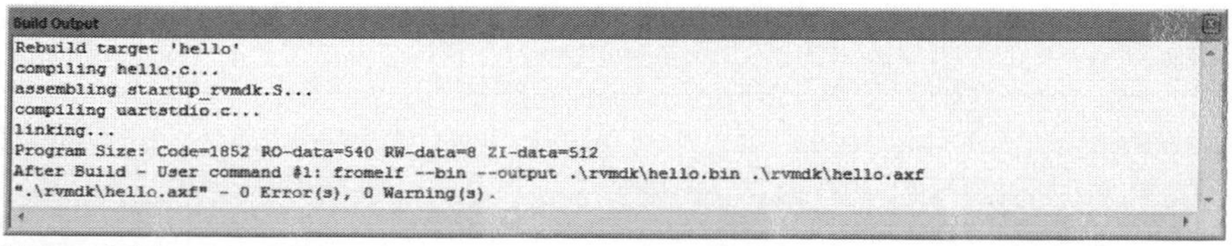

```
Build Output
Rebuild target 'hello'
compiling hello.c...
assembling startup_rvmdk.S...
compiling uartstdio.c...
linking...
Program Size: Code=1852 RO-data=540 RW-data=8 ZI-data=512
After Build - User command #1: fromelf --bin --output .\rvmdk\hello.bin .\rvmdk\hello.axf
".\rvmdk\hello.axf" - 0 Error(s), 0 Warning(s).
```

Figure 3.14. The building result of the hello project. (Reproduced with permission from ARM® Limited. Copyright © ARM Limited.)

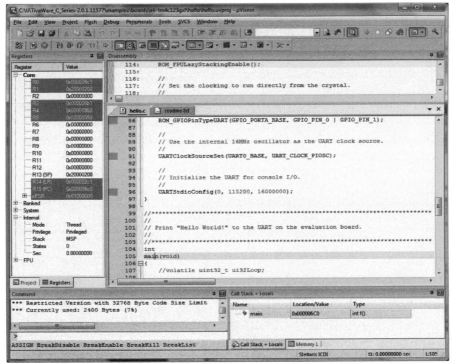

Figure 3.15.   The debugging result of the hello world project. (Reproduced with permission from ARM® Limited. Copyright © ARM Limited.)

- Project Manager for creating and maintaining your projects.
- Integrated Make Utility functionality for assembling, compiling, and linking your embedded applications.
- Dialogs for all development environment settings.
- True integrated source-level and assembler-level Debugger with high-speed CPU and peripheral Simulator.
- Advanced GDI interface for software debugging on target hardware and for connecting to a Keil® ULINK™ Debug Adapter.
- Flash programming utility for downloading the application program into Flash ROM.
- Links to manuals, on-line help, device datasheets, and user guides.

The µVision5 IDE and Debugger are the central part of the Keil® development toolchain and have numerous features that help the programmer to develop embedded applications quickly and successfully. The Keil® tools are easy to use and are guaranteed to help you achieve your design goals in a timely manner.

The µVision5 offers a Build Mode for creating applications and a Debug Mode for debugging applications. Applications can be debugged with the integrated µVision5 Simulator or directly on hardware, for example with adapters of the Keil® ULINK™ USB-JTAG family. Developers can also use other AGDI adapters or external third-party tools for analyzing applications.

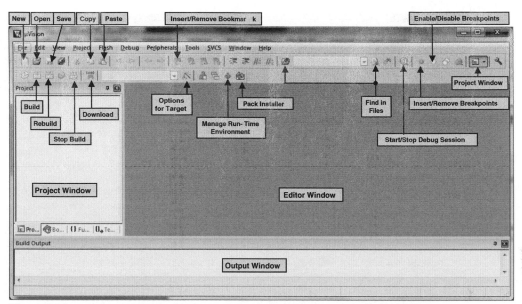

Figure 3.16.   The opened MDK-ARM IDE. (Reproduced with permission from ARM® Limited. Copyright © ARM Limited.)

The μVision5 GUI provides Menus for selecting commands and Toolbars with command buttons. The Status Bar, at the bottom of the window, displays information and messages about the current μVision5 command. Windows can be relocated and even docked to another physical screen. The window layout is saved for each project automatically and restored the next time the project is used. You can restore the default layout using the menu Window|Reset View to Defaults.

Now open the MDK μVersion5 IDE by double clicking on the icon Keil uVision5 from the desktop. The opened IDE is shown in Figure 3.16. Some important tools in the Toolbar have been highlighted. We will discuss all important menu items one by one in the next section.

3.4.4.1 The File Menu

Under the File menu, there are 12 menu items or submenus, but only two items, Device Database and License Management are new and important to us.

File:

- Device Database
- License Management

The Device Database lists all available devices offered by different vendors and provides download access to the related Software Packs. You can also confirm or check the installed device by using this menu item. For example, in our case, we are using a Tiva™ M4C123GH6PM MCU. To check this device, click on Device

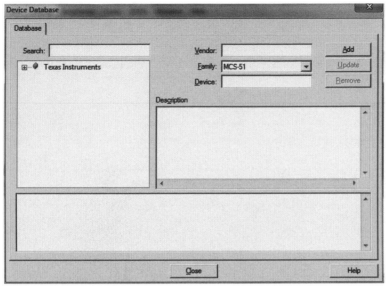

Figure 3.17.   The opened Device Database wizard. (Reproduced with permission from ARM® Limited. Copyright © ARM Limited.)

`Database` item from the `File` menu. The Device Database wizard is displayed, as shown in Figure 3.17.

The vendor's name, `Texas Instruments` (TI), is displayed in the device textbox since the device (Tiva™ TM4C123GH6PM MCU) we are using is made by Texas Instruments. Expand the folders, `Texas Instruments`, `Tiva C Series`, and finally `TM4C123x Series`. Then you can find our target device, TM4C123GH6PM, in the list. Click on this device and you can find all related information, as shown in Figure 3.18, about this device.

The `License Management` is used to manage the license version for the MDK you are using. The following license types are available in the current MDK µVersion5:

- `Single-User License` (Node-Locked) grants the right to use the product by one developer on two computers at the same time.
- `Floating-User License` or `FlexLM License` grants the right to use the product on several computers by a number of developers at the same time.

If you select the License Management item from the File menu, the License Management wizard will be displayed, as shown in Figure 3.19. By clicking on the Single-User License tab, you can find the detailed information for the single user. However, when clicking on the `Floating License` and `FlexLM License` tabs, the similar information will be displayed, but some controls would be disabled. This means that those controls are not available to the single-user.

3.4.4.2 The Edit Menu

There are 18 menu items or submenus under the `Edit` menu, but only three items, `Outlining`, `Advanced` and `Configuration`, are new and important to us.

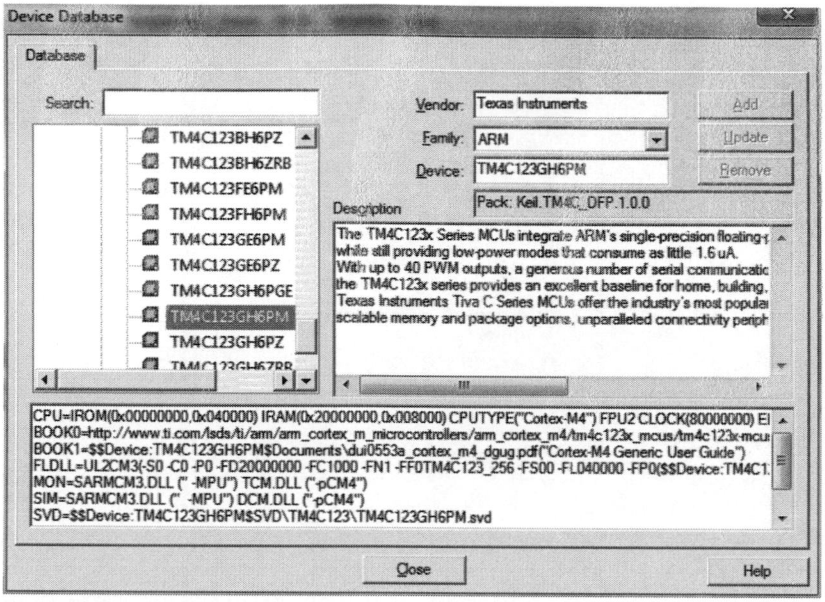

Figure 3.18. The detailed information for the device TM4C123GH6PM. (Reproduced with permission from ARM® Limited. Copyright © ARM Limited.)

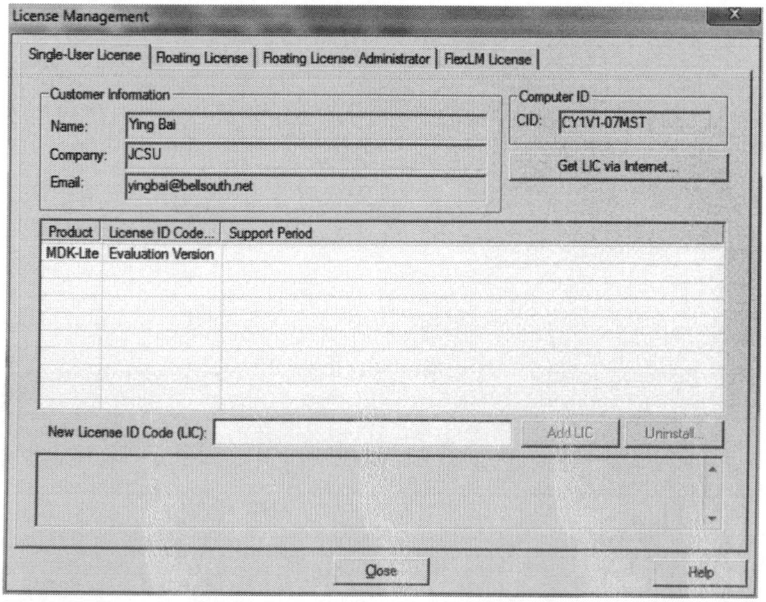

Figure 3.19. The License Management wizard. (Reproduced with permission from ARM® Limited. Copyright © ARM Limited.)

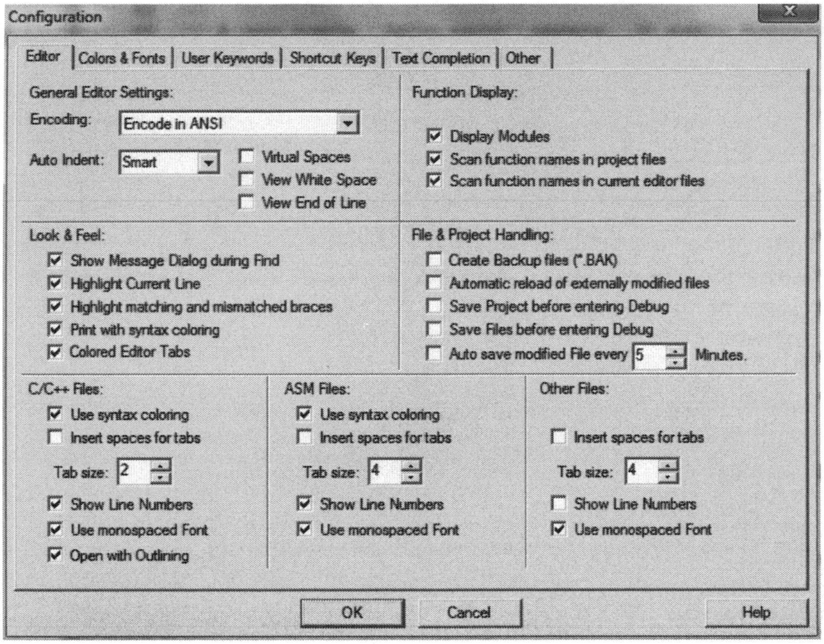

Figure 3.20. An example of the Configuration submenu. (Reproduced with permission from ARM® Limited. Copyright © ARM Limited.)

Edit:

- Outlining
- Advanced
- Configuration

The Outlining is a MDK-ARM® Plug-in for Eclipse and it lists the structural elements of a C/C++ file that is currently open in the editor. Developers can sort the list, set filters, and group elements for viewing. With this menu, you can Show or Hide All Outlining for your source codes. Also you can expand and collapse all Definitions, Current Block, or Current Procedure by selecting the related item in this menu.

The Advanced is used to assist the editing and formatting of the source codes. These assistants include converting the codes to upper or lower cases, or to comments, increasing or decreasing the line indentation for the selected code line, cutting or deleting the selected lines. When this item is selected, it opens a submenu with extended editor features. The commands are also accessible through the context menu.

The Configuration is another editor assistant and it is used to set up and configure the general settings for the MDK Editor. An example of a Configuration wizard is shown in Figure 3.20.

These configuration tools include:

- Encoding mode
- Color and fonts for the specified editor
- User keywords

- Shortcut keys
- Text completion
- Other settings

The user can define and select desired format and style from this menu for the MDK Editor to get specific codes editing and displaying format.

The View menu provides 10 items to enable users to select the desired windows and tools on the Toolbar. These windows and tools include:

- Status Bar
- Toolbars
- Project Window
- Books Window
- Functions Window
- Templates Window
- Source Browser Window
- Build Output Window
- Error List Window
- Find In File Window

There are two submenu items under the Toolbars, File Toolbar and Build Toolbar. The former provides all tools used to manage user's files development, and the latter provides all support tools to build the user's projects. You can open or close any of these tools or windows by clicking the selected item from this menu.

3.4.4.3 The Project Menu

The Project is a very important menu in the MDK-ARM® μVersion5 IDE. It includes commands to create, open, save, and close project files, Export the project to a previous version, μVision4, Manage project components, or set Options for the target, group, and file, or Build the project. Multiple projects can be managed through the menu Project|Manage|Multi-Project Workspace. 16 commands are included in this Project menu:

Project:

- New μVersion Project
- New Multi-Project Workspace
- Open Project
- Save Project in μVersion4 Format
- Close Project
- Export
- Manage
- Select Device for Target Project
- Options for File
- Clean Target

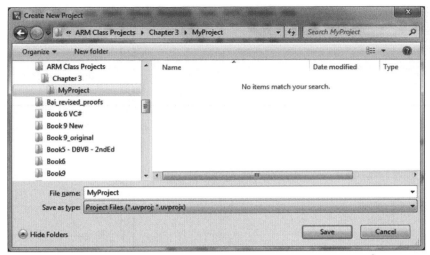

Figure 3.21. Save the new project. (Reproduced with permission from ARM® Limited. Copyright © ARM Limited.)

- `Build Target`
- `Rebuild All Target Files`
- `Translate`
- `Stop Build`

Let's discuss these menu items one by one with a real new user project `MyProject`. The `New µVersion Project` menu item enables users to create a new project in the following sequence:

1. Open the Windows Explorer to create a new folder named MyProject under the C:\ARM Class Projects\Chapter 3 folder.

2. Open the Keil® ARM®-MDK µVersion5 IDE and click on the New µVersion Project item. On the opened Create New Project wizard, browse to our new folder MyProject created above, enter the project name, MyProject (Figure 3.21). The file extension is *.uvproj for MDK µVersion4, or *.uvprojx for µVersion5. Click on the Save button to save this new project. It is good practice to use a separate folder for each project.

3. The `Select Device for Target` 'Target1' wizard is displayed after this new project is saved, as shown in Figure 3.22. Expand the folders, `Texas Instruments—Tiva C Series—TM4C123x Series`, and select our device, TM4C123GH6PM, from the list, as shown in Figure 3.22. This selection defines essential tool settings such as compiler controls, the memory layout for the linker, and the Flash programming algorithms. Click on the **OK** button to continue.

4. Immediately the `Manage Run-Time Environment` wizard is shown, as shown in Figure 3.23, after a new project is created and saved. The `Manage Run-Time Environment` (RTE) wizard allows you to manage Software Components of this new project. Software Components can be added, deleted, disabled, or updated during the software development process at any time.

5. MDK µVersion5 offers Software Components for creating applications with a framework called `Manage Run-Time Environment` (RTE). Software Components are delivered

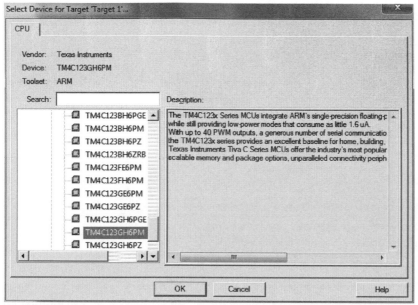

Figure 3.22.   The Select Device for Target wizard. (Reproduced with permission from ARM® Limited. Copyright © ARM Limited.)

in Software Packs that get installed independently from the MDK Core. Third-party Software Packs can also be installed to add other middleware libraries.

When a new project is created, the RTE window opens automatically after you have selected a device. You can open this wizard by going to the menu `Project|Manage|Run-Time Environment`. The `Manage Run-Time Environment` wizard provides the following functionality:

a. Lists pre-built Software Components that are installed and available for the selected MCU. Software Components can exist in different variants and versions.

Software Component	Sel.	Variant	Version	Description
⊞ ◈ CMSIS				Cortex Microcontroller Software Interface Components
⊞ ◈ Device				Startup, System Setup
⊞ ◈ Drivers				Unified Device Drivers
⊞ ◈ File System		MDK-Pro	5.0.5	File Access on various storage devices
⊞ ◈ Graphics		MDK-Pro	5.22.1	User Interface on graphical LCD displays
⊞ ◈ Network		MDK-Pro	5.0.4	IP Networking using Ethernet or Serial protocols
⊞ ◈ USB		MDK-Pro	5.0.4	USB Communication with various device classes

Validation Output	Description

Figure 3.23.   The Manage Run-Time Environment wizard. (Reproduced with permission from ARM® Limited. Copyright © ARM Limited.)

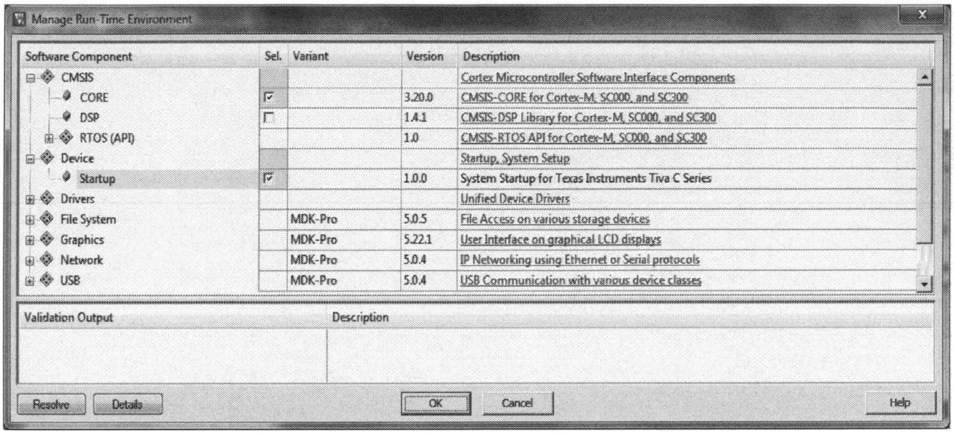

Figure 3.24. The selected components in the Manage Run-Time Environment wizard. (Reproduced with permission from ARM® Limited. Copyright © ARM Limited.)

b. Manages Software Components of a project. Only configurable files are copied to the project folder. Header files, source code, or libraries that need no modification are included directly from the folder structure of the Software Pack. This simplifies maintenance of different component versions or variants.

c. Handles Software Component versions and variants in a project. Various project targets can use different microcontrollers and/or different versions/variants of a Software Component. The RTE manager replaces the relevant files of the selected Software Components automatically.

d. Identifies conflicts between Software Components. For example, it is not possible to select multiple LCD interfaces for the Graphic component.

e. Identifies other required Software Components. For example, the RTOS kernel or a driver for a device peripheral. The button **Resolve** selects other components in case of unambiguous requirements.

f. Provides access to the documentation of a Software Component.

Now let's expand the following nodes since we need to use some components and need to set up some of them in this `Manage Run-Time Environment` wizard:

- CMSIS
- Device

For a basic user application, we only need the MDK Core and CMSIS Core. Select and set up the following components by checking the related checkbox in the `Sel` column:

- `CMSIS:CORE`
- `Device:Startup`

Your finished setup and selection for this `Manage Run-Time Environment` wizard should match one that is shown in Figure 3.24.

One point to be noted is that different colors may be displayed for the different selected components when you do this setup and selection. Also the detailed information will be displayed in the Validation Output window in the bottom of this wizard to indicate some missed or required components you need to get to complete these setups and selections.

- **Green color:** The Software Component has been resolved or a Software Component allowing multiple instances has been resolved. Nothing has been displayed in the Validation Output window.

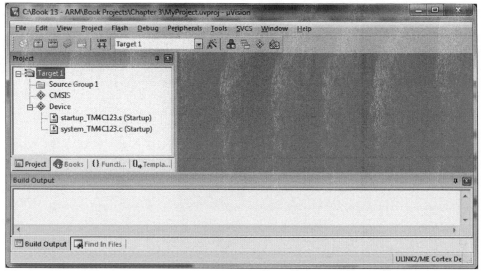

Figure 3.25.   The new project wizard. (Reproduced with permission from ARM® Limited.)
Copyright © ARM Limited.)

- **Yellow color:** This Software Component is unresolved. Other components are required for correct operation and are listed in the Validation Output window.
- **Red color:** The Software Component conflicts with other components or is not installed on the computer. Detailed information is listed in the `Validation Output` window.

Click on the **OK** button to close this wizard when the setup and selection process is done. If you encountered either yellow or red colors, you may need to use the `Pack Installer` to install those missed components.

6. Now our new project `MyProject` has been created, and necessary environments have been set up using the Manage Run-Time Environment as we did above. The MDK µVersion5 GUI looks like the one shown in Figure 3.25.

As we discussed in Section 3.4.2 (Figure 3.8), to make a user project in the MDK environment, the following four files are needed:

- Startup code file, `startup_TM4C123.s` (Assembly file provided by the MDK)
- System source file, `system_TM4C123.c` (C file provided by the CMSIS:CORE)
- System header file, `system_TM4C123.h` (Header file provided by the CMSIS:CORE)
- Device specified definition file, `TM4C123GH6PM.h` (Header file provided by the Texas Instruments for Tiva™ C Series TM4C123GH6PM)

However, right now we can only find the first two code files, `startup_TM4C123.s` and `system_TM4C123.c`, from the **Project** pane in the left in Figure 3.25. Do not worry about this and you will see all of these four files later as we begin to build our project.

7. In MDK µVersion5, the projects are organized in a special format, called `Target→Source Group→Source Files`. All related projects can be collected together to form a group and put into one special group. The default group is `Source Group 1`. You can add additional source files into a source group by double clicking on the selected source group and then use the file browser to add the source file. Different source groups can also be collected together to form a Target, the default target is `Target 1`. You can also add any additional source groups into the Target by right clicking on `Target 1`, and select `Add Group`.

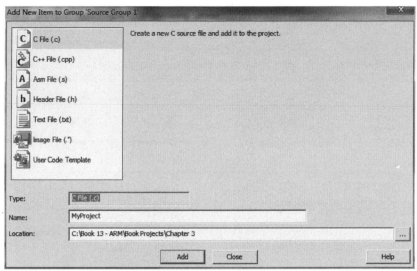

Figure 3.26.   The Add New Item to Group wizard. (Reproduced with permission from ARM® Limited. Copyright © ARM Limited.)

8. Refer to Figure 3.25, you can find that the default group, Source Group 1, has been added into the Target 1 under the Project pane in the left. To add our project source file, MyProject.c, into this default source group, perform the following operations:

   a. Right click on the Source Group 1 and select Add New Item to Group 'Source Group 1' to open the Add New Item to Group wizard, as shown in Figure 3.26.
   b. Select C File (.c) as the template and enter MyProject into the **Name** box. Click on the **Add** button to add this source file into our new project.
   c. Add the following codes into this source file, as shown in Figure 3.27.
   d. Go to File|Save menu item to save this source file. The function of this piece of codes is to setup and enable the GPIO port used for the User LED on the TM4C123G EVB. Then send commands as digital outputs to turn on and off the LED with some time delay. A while() loop is used to make this project run in an infinitive loop. You do not need to know all of these codes now and we will discuss these later in the following chapters. Your finished source file MyProject.c is shown in Figure 3.28.

9. Next we need to create our header file, MyProject.h, to define all GPIO and system SYSCTL registers used in our source file MyProject.c. Do the same steps as we did in step 1, right click on the Source Group 1, and select Add New Item to Group 'Source Group 1' to open the Add New Item to Group wizard. Then select Header File (.h) as the template and enter MyProject into the **Name** box, as shown in Figure 3.29. Click on the **Add** button to add this header file into our new project.

10. Enter the codes shown in Figure 3.30 into this header file. Your finished header file should match the one that is shown in Figure 3.31. Go to File|Save menu item to save this header file into our project. The codes in the header file are used to define all registers used in this project, include the GPIO and system control SYSCTRL registers. The SYSCTRL_ RCGC2_R is a control register and the SYSCTRL_RCGC2_GPIOF is a port F register used to connect and control the on-board user LED. The GPIO-related registers are data direction (DIR), digital output (DEN), and data (DATA) registers.

```c
//**********************************************************************
// Blink the on-board LED in TM4C123G.
//**********************************************************************
#include <stdint.h>
#include "MyProject.h"

Int main(void)
{
    volatile uint32_t ui32Loop;

    // Enable the GPIO port that is used for the on-board LED.
    SYSCTL_RCGC2_R = SYSCTL_RCGC2_GPIOF;

    // Do a dummy read to insert a few cycles after enabling the peripheral.
    ui32Loop = SYSCTL_RCGC2_R;

    // Enable the GPIO pin for the LED (PF3).  Set the direction as output, and
    // enable the GPIO pin for digital function.
    GPIO_PORTF_DIR_R = 0x08;
    GPIO_PORTF_DEN_R = 0x08;

    // Loop forever.
    while(1)
    {
        // Turn on the LED.
        GPIO_PORTF_DATA_R |= 0x08;

        // Delay for a bit.
        for(ui32Loop = 0; ui32Loop < 200000; ui32Loop++)
        {
        }

        // Turn off the LED.
        GPIO_PORTF_DATA_R &= ~(0x08);

        // Delay for a bit.
        for(ui32Loop = 0; ui32Loop < 200000; ui32Loop++)
        {
        }
    }
}
```

Figure 3.27.   The source codes in the MyProject.c file.

11. Now let's build our project by going to Project|Rebuild all target files menu item. The building process begins and the detailed building steps are shown in the Build Output window in the bottom, as shown in Figure 3.32.

12. Now if you expand our project source file, MyProject.c, and the system specified startup file, system_TM4C123.c (Startup) from the Project pane in the left, you can find all four code files as we mentioned in Section 3.4.2 (Figure 3.8), which are:

   a. Startup code file, startup_TM4C123.s (Assembly file provided by the MDK)
   b. System source file, system_TM4C123.c (C file provided by the CMSIS:CORE)
   c. System header file, system_TM4C123.h (Header file provided by the CMSIS: CORE), which is located under System source file, system_TM4C123.c
   d. Device specified definition file, TM4C123GH6PM.h (Header file provided by the Texas Instruments for Tiva™ C Series TM4C123GH6PM), which is also located under System source file, system_TM4C123.c

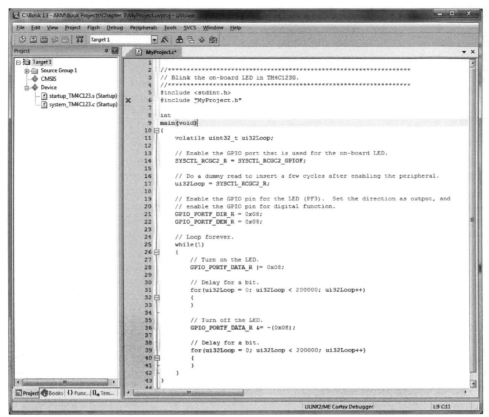

Figure 3.28. The finished codes for the source file MyProject.c. (Reproduced with permission from ARM® Limited. Copyright © ARM Limited.)

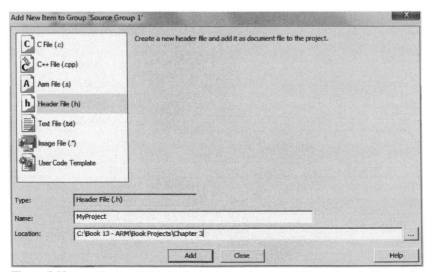

Figure 3.29. Add a header file MyProject.h into the project. (Reproduced with permission from ARM® Limited. Copyright © ARM Limited.)

```
//***********************************************************
// MyProject.h
// Header file for the project MyProject.c
//***********************************************************

//***********************************************************
// System Control registers (SYSCTL)
//***********************************************************

#define SYSCTL_RCGC2_R        (*((volatile uint32_t *)0x400FE108))
#define SYSCTL_RCGC2_GPIOF    0x00000020  // Port F Clock Gating Control

//***********************************************************
// GPIO registers (PORTF)
//***********************************************************

#define GPIO_PORTF_DIR_R       (*((volatile uint32_t *)0x40025400))
#define GPIO_PORTF_DEN_R       (*((volatile uint32_t *)0x4002551C))
#define GPIO_PORTF_DATA_R      (*((volatile uint32_t *)0x400253FC))
```

Figure 3.30.   The project header file MyProject.h.

This means that some code files will not be available until the project has been built successfully.

13. Now let's load our project into the flash memory in the Tiva™ C Series LaunchPad EVB, TM4C123G. This download process needs a debug adaptor and related driver. Before you can do this, you need to double check the debug driver used for the debugger provided by the MDK. The MDK provides the ULINK2 debug adaptor and related driver. However, a

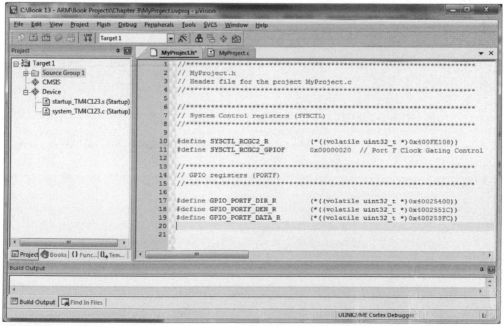

Figure 3.31.   The finished header file MyProject.h. (Reproduced with permission from ARM® Limited. Copyright © ARM Limited.)

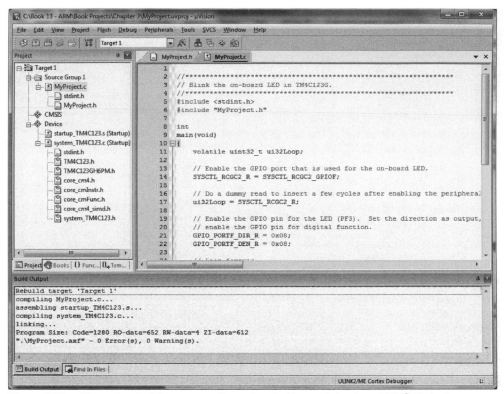

Figure 3.32. The project building process. (Reproduced with permission from ARM® Limited. Copyright © ARM Limited.)

similar debug adaptor has been built in the Tiva™ C Series LaunchPad™ board, TM4C123G. Also a related debug driver called ICDI has also been installed in our host computer in Section 3.3. Therefore, we can use this debug driver to save our cost. Otherwise, you have to spend costs to get ULINK2 debug adaptor.

14. Perform the following operations to finish this debug driver checking:
- Go to `Project|Options for Target 'Target 1'` item to open this wizard.
- Click on the `Debug` tab to open its settings.
- On the upper right of this wizard, click on the dropdown arrow for the `Use` combobox, and select `Stellaris ICDI` from the list.

  Your finished wizard should match one that is shown in Figure 3.33. Click on the **OK** button to close this wizard.

15. Select the `Download` item from the `Flash` menu, or click the `Download` button (icon). The process takes a few seconds. A progress bar will show at the bottom of the IDE window as the device is programmed. When it is finished, the `Build` window will show that the device was erased, programmed, and `Verified` OK, as shown in Figure 3.34. Our project application, `MyProject.axf`, which is an image file, is now programmed and downloaded into the flash memory on the Evaluation Board.

16. We can now start to debug our project by going to `Debug|Start/Stop Debug Session` menu item. Click on the **OK** button for the popup memory limitation message for the evaluation version to begin this debug process. Your finished debug process for our project is shown in Figure 3.35.

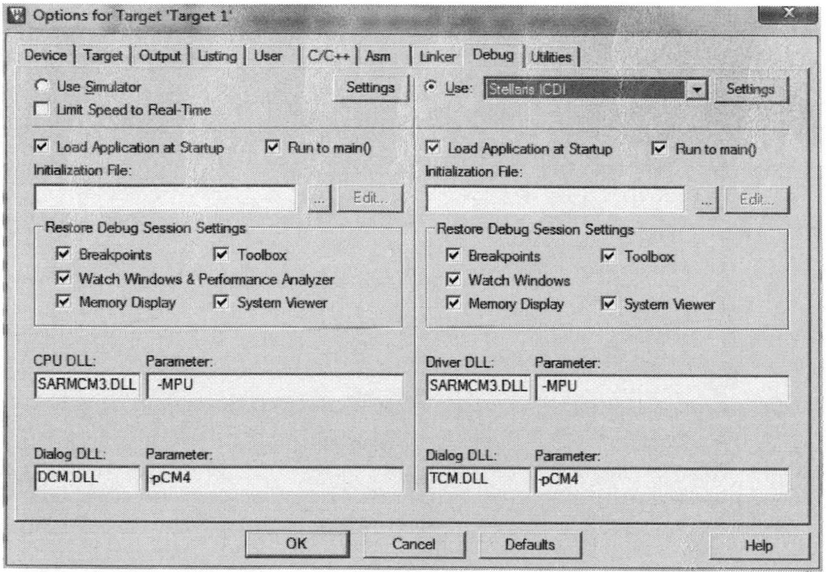

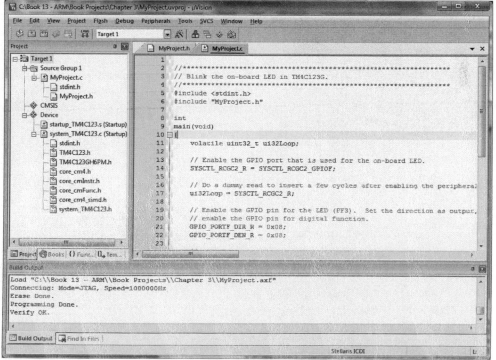

Figure 3.33. The finished debugger checking wizard. (Reproduced with permission from ARM® Limited. Copyright © ARM Limited.)

Figure 3.34. The download process for our project. (Reproduced with permission from ARM® Limited. Copyright © ARM Limited.)

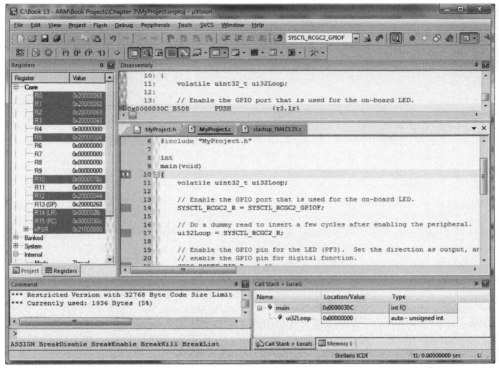

Figure 3.35. The debug process for our project. (Reproduced with permission from ARM® Limited. Copyright © ARM Limited.)

17. To run our project, go to Debug|Run menu item to run it. The user LED in the TM4C123G EVB will be flashed periodically. Click on the Stop item from the Debug menu to stop our project.
18. Click on the Erase item from the Flash menu to erase our project from the flash memory in the TM4C123G EVB.

Now let's continue to discuss the following menu items under the Project menu, the New Multi-Project Workspace and Open Project.

Project:

- New Multi-Project Workspace
- Open Project

The New Multi-Project Workspace menu item is used to create multiple projects in the µVision project environment Multiple Projects is a simple-to-use feature for managing more than one project in a single µVision project environment. Often, system designs are targeting different devices. In such cases, it is comfortable to manage the system design using one project environment. Create a µVision5 project for each device and include them into a multiple project.

Multiple project files have the extension .UVMPW. You can use Project|Open Project menu item to open a single project or a multiple projects file.

The rest menu items under the Project menu are:

Project:

- Save Project in µVersion4 Format
- Close Project
- Export
- Manage
- Select Device for Target Project
- Options for Target Project
- Clean Targets
- Build Target
- Rebuild All Target Files
- Translate
- Stop Build

Save Project in µVersion4 Format is used to save the project created in µVersion5 or later to the µVersion format. The condition is: When no RTE is used, you can save projects in µVision4 format (extension *.uvproj). Software Components must be removed using Project|Manage|Run-Time Environment before you do this saving operation.

Close Project is to close the current project.

Export is used to export the active project, or the current multi-project, to the µVision3 format. Options specific to later µVision versions, such as µVersion5, are not converted. The original project file will still exist untouched.

Under the Manage menu item, five submenu items are existed:

Manage

- Components, Environment, Books
- Multi-Project Workspace
- Run-Time Environment
- Reload Software Packs
- Pack Installer

Components, Environment, Books can be used to configure Targets, Groups, and Files. Set file extensions and tool paths, and select development tools. Configure your books and manuals. Figure 3.36 shows an example of using this item to manage target, group, and files in the sample project, MyProject, we built above in this section. You can add additional files from any location in your host computer by using the **Add Files** button.

Multi-Project Workspace is used to add, delete, or rearrange the µVision Project Files in a Multi-Project file.

The Run-Time Environment (RTE) wizard allows you to manage Software Components of a project. Software Components can be added, deleted, disabled, or

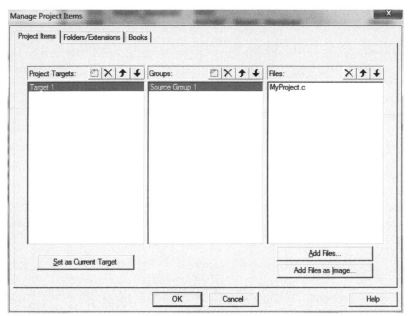

Figure 3.36.   The Components, Environment, Books wizard. (Reproduced with permission from ARM® Limited. Copyright © ARM Limited.)

updated during the software development process at any time. When a new project is started, the RTE window opens automatically after you have selected a device. The menu `Project|Manage|Run-Time Environment` opens the wizard.

We have provided a very detailed discussion about the Manage Run-Time Environment wizard when we created our sample project `MyProject` using New µVersion `Project`; refer to that part for this tool. For your convenience, an example of using this tool to manage our sample project is redisplayed in Figure 3.37.

The `Reload Software Packs` can be used to refresh Software Pack information in the Pack Installer window.

Software Component	Sel.	Variant	Version	Description
⊟ ◈ CMSIS				Cortex Microcontroller Software Interface Components
● CORE	☑		3.20.0	CMSIS-CORE for Cortex-M, SC000, and SC300
● DSP	☐		1.4.1	CMSIS-DSP Library for Cortex-M, SC000, and SC300
⊞ ◈ RTOS (API)			1.0	CMSIS-RTOS API for Cortex-M, SC000, and SC300
⊟ ◈ Device				Startup, System Setup
● Startup	☑		1.0.0	System Startup for Texas Instruments Tiva C Series
⊞ ◈ Drivers				Unified Device Drivers
⊞ ◈ File System		MDK-Pro	5.0.5	File Access on various storage devices
⊞ ◈ Graphics		MDK-Pro	5.22.1	User Interface on graphical LCD displays
⊞ ◈ Network		MDK-Pro	5.0.4	IP Networking using Ethernet or Serial protocols
⊞ ◈ USB		MDK-Pro	5.0.4	USB Communication with various device classes

Figure 3.37.   The Manage Run-Time Environment wizard for our sample project. (Reproduced with permission from ARM® Limited. Copyright © ARM Limited.)

The `Pack Installer` is a utility program and it allows users to install, update, and remove Software Packs and can be launched from within µVision or standalone, outside of µVision. The Pack Installer window offers the following functionality:

- Installs, updates, or removes Software Packs and thus, Software Components.
- Lists installed Software Packs and checks for updates on the Internet. A brief release history might be displayed before updating a Software Pack.
- Lists example projects available from installed Software Packs.
- Offers filters to narrow the list of Software Packs or example projects.
- Displays the progress of the executed function in the status bar at the bottom of the window.

When a new project is created and saved, the Pack Installer wizard is opened automatically. You can also open this wizard by going to `Project|Manage|Pack Installer`.

The `Select Device for Target Project` allows users to select the target device (MCU) for the current project. Depending on the evaluation board and MCU used in your project, you can find and select desired MCU/CPU for your project via this tool. We have provided a very detailed discussion about this wizard when we created our sample project `MyProject` using `New µVersion Project` menu item (Figure 3.22); refer to that part for this tool and its applications.

The `Options for Target Project` is a very important tool to support the project development process with multiple functions. We will pay more attention to this tool and provide more detailed discussions about it.

This tool contains 10 functions or options, each function is presented with a tab, as shown in Figure 3.38.

1. The `Device` option allows users to select the desired device (MCU) for the current project. This is similar to the function of the `Select Device for Target Project` wizard. When a device is selected, all related settings, including the complier, memory map, and flash algorithms, are configured for the device. If the MCU that you are using is not listed in the list, you can still select Cortex-M4 under the ARM® section and manually set the configuration options. An example of `Device` option selection wizard for our sample project `MyProject` we built above is shown in Figure 3.38.

2. The `Target` option enables users to define the memory map of the device, such as the address ranges of the ROM and the RAM used in the EVB, options to use the Floating Point Unit (FPU) on the Cortex-M4 MCU if installed on your device, options to utilize the RTX Kernel, and a real-time operating system (RTOS) that comes with CMSIS-RTOS. The memory map setup is generally created automatically when you selected the desired device (MCU). An example of `Target` option selection wizard for our sample project `MyProject` we built above is shown in Figure 3.39.

    It can be found from Figure 3.39 that no any operating system (RTOS) is used for this target project. The memory ROM and RAM are configured from addresses 0x0 and 0x2000000 with a size of 0x40000 (256 KB) and 0x8000 (32 KB), respectively.

3. The `Output` option allows users to select a different location to save the project output file, either an executable image file or a library file. Object and listing files are created in subfolders of the project folder by default. However, the output can be redirected to other folders. Thus, each project target can have its own output folder. To do this, you can use the `Select Folder for Objects` wizard to set the output directory to a folder you

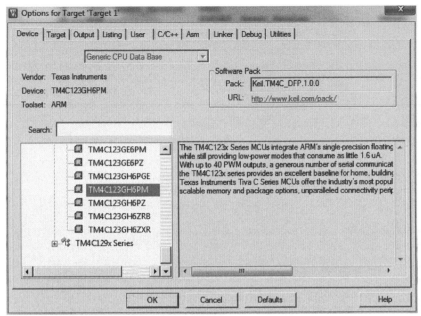

Figure 3.38. Functions provided by the Options for Target Project wizard. (Reproduced with permission from ARM® Limited. Copyright © ARM Limited.)

created in your desired folder. Furthermore, object and listing files from previous build processes can be preserved. An example of using the `Output` option wizard for our sample project `MyProject` is shown in Figure 3.40.

4. The `Listing` option, similar to the Output option, also allows users to select a different folder to store the output listing files by using the `Select Folder for Listing`

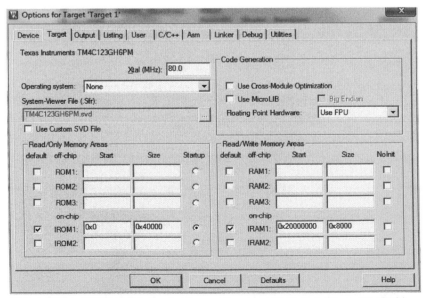

Figure 3.39. The Target option for the sample project MyProject. (Reproduced with permission from ARM® Limited. Copyright © ARM Limited.)

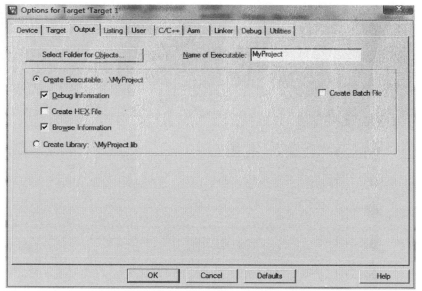

Figure 3.40.   The Output option for the sample project MyProject. (Reproduced with permission from ARM® Limited. Copyright © ARM Limited.)

wizard. This option also allows users to enable or disable assembly listing files. The C Compiler listing file is turned off by default. You can turn this option on during the debug process to monitor the generating sequence of the assembly instructions. An example of using the `Listing` option wizard for our sample project `MyProject` is shown in Figure 3.41.

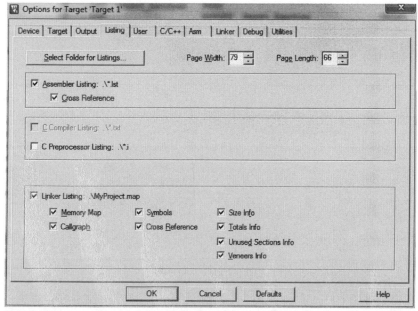

Figure 3.41.   The Listing option for the sample project MyProject. (Reproduced with permission from ARM® Limited. Copyright © ARM Limited.)

5. The User option enables users to use some external tools during the process of an application. This option allows users to execute external programs in three ways:

- Before compiling a C or C++ file (checking for MISRA compliance).
- Before building an application (invoking a data management utility).
- After building an application (invoking data converters or debuggers).

You need to enter the desired external tools or commands into one of three boxes, which is related to one of three ways shown above.

- The C/C++ option allows users to define optimization options (including path) and misc controls for the C/C++ Compiler. By default, some file directories are automatically included in the project compiler string list. You can check No Auto Includes checkbox if you do not want to these files to be included automatically.

- The Asm option, or Assembler option, enables users to define preprocessing directives (including paths) and additional assembler command switches.

- The Linker option allows users to use Memory Layout from the Target wizard. When enabled, μVision creates a linker scatter file from the memory information supplied in the Target wizard. When disabled, the X/O Base, R/O Base, R/W Base, and Scatter File can be set manually. The scatter file defines the memory layout and allows assigning modules to specific memory areas.

- The Debug option defines options that apply when a debugging session is started. The screen is split into options for the Simulator and for the target driver. This means that the Debug option provides two selections for the user: either using an Instruction Simulator or using an actual hardware device with a debug adaptor. This option also provides the following functions:

  - The type of debug adaptor
  - The type of debug driver
  - Breakpoint setup
  - Watch windows and performance analyzer
  - Memory display
  - System Viewer & Toolbox

An example of using the Debug option wizard for our sample project MyProject is shown in Figure 3.42. One point to be noted is that the debug driver selection tool, which is located at the Use part at the upper-right corner on this wizard, is very important. Since we are using the Stellaris ICDI as out driver, you need to select this driver from the Use list. Otherwise you may encounter some link and download error if the default driver, ULINK Pro Cortex Debugger, is selected and used.

- The Utilities option enables users to select the target debug adaptor for flash programming. μVision5 supports several Flash programming utilities, for example:

  - Adapters of the Keil® ULINK USB-JTAG family that also offers debugging and tracing capabilities.
  - Third-party adapters that can be selected from the configuration dialog.
  - External, command-line-driven utilities that are provided by chip vendors.

  Using this Utilities wizard, applications can be downloaded to flash ROM:

  - Manually—through the menu Flash|Download.
  - Automatically—by enabling the checkbox Utilities|Update Target before Debugging.

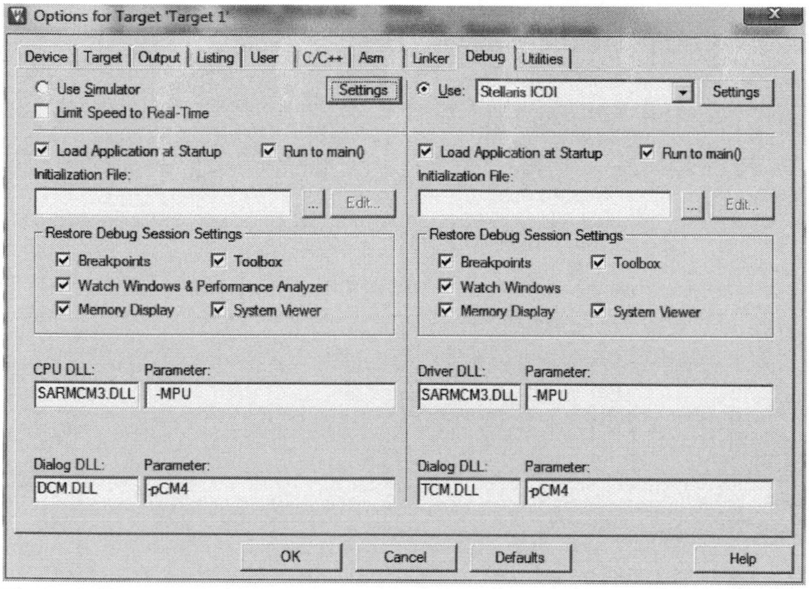

Figure 3.42. The Debug option for the sample project MyProject. (Reproduced with permission from ARM® Limited. Copyright © ARM Limited.)

An example of using the `Utilities` option wizard for our sample project `MyProject` is shown in Figure 3.43. The following utilities options have been selected for our project:

- Use Target Driver for Flash Programming
- Use Debug Driver
- Update Target before Debugging

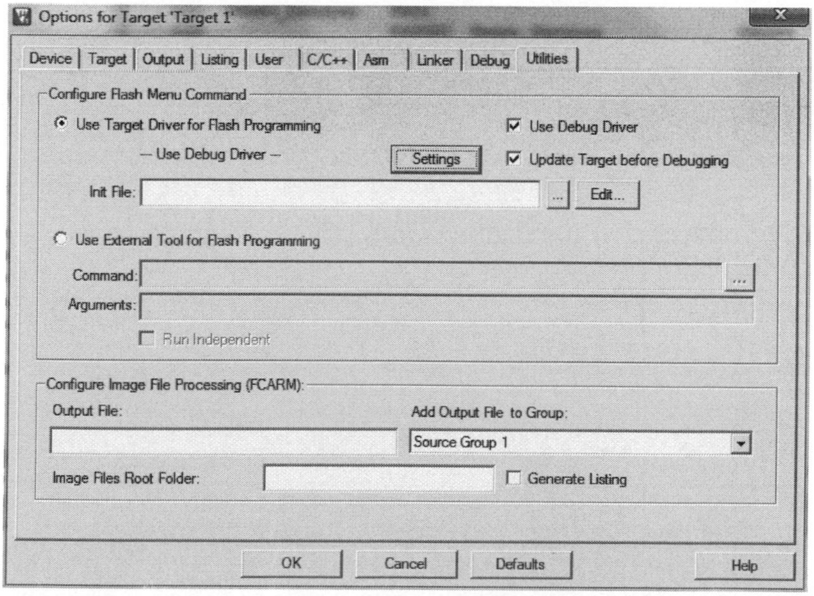

Figure 3.43. The Utilities option for the sample project MyProject. (Reproduced with permission from ARM® Limited. Copyright © ARM Limited.)

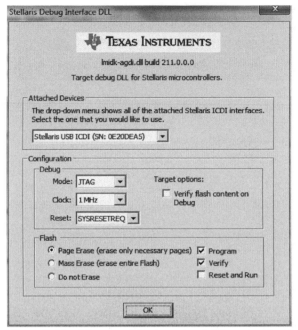

Figure 3.44. The opened Settings wizard. (Reproduced with permission from ARM® Limited. Copyright © ARM Limited.)

Because the Update Target before Debugging checkbox is checked, our program will be automatically downloaded into the flash memory as the debug process starts.

If you click on the Settings button, more details about this debug configuration are displayed, as shown in Figure 3.44. The debug adaptor is Stellaris USB ICDI, which is displayed under the Attached Devices group combobox on the top. The debug mode, clock, and reset information are shown under theConfiguration group combobox in the middle.

At this point, we complete the introduction to all tabs under the Options for Target Project menu item in the Project menu. The rest menu items under the Project are relatively simple. Let's take a closer look at these items.

Project:

- Clean Targets
- Build Target
- Rebuild All Target Files
- Translate
- Stop Build

The Clean Targets is used to delete the intermediate files of the project target. These intermediate files include all source files with the extension .obj, .o, ._ii, ._ia, ._i, .map and .list.

The Build Target is used to build the project, includes the compile and link processes.

The Rebuild All Target Files is similar to Build Target. It will re-translate all source files and build the application.

The Translate is used to translate all active files in the project.

The Stop Build is to stop the building process.

3.4.4.4 The Flash Menu

This menu is used to download the user's executable program into the flash memory. Three submenu items are under this menu:

Flash:

- Download
- Erase
- Configure Flash Tools

The Download and Erase items are simple, and the functions of these menus just download the user's executable program to the flash memory in the EVB, or delete it from the flash memory in the EVB. The function of the Configure Flash Tools is exactly identical with the Utilities option under the Options for Target Project in the Project menu, which we have discussed above.

Some useful functions can be executed after these flash tools are configured:

- Enable Use Debug Driver when using the Debugger adapter as a debug and Flash programming unit.
- Enable Update target before Debugging to download the application to flash whenever a new debugging session is started.
- Enter a Pre-Download Script into the field Init File to specify commands which prepare the device for Flash programming—for example, to configure the bus.
- Enable Use External Tool for Flash Programming to enter options for third-party command-line-based utilities that are not in the list of target drivers. You can use Key Sequences.
- Enter options to Configure Image File Processing (FCARM) by invoking FCARM during the build process. This converts image files into C-source code. Refer to Using FCARM with µVision.

3.4.4.5 The Debug Menu

This menu is used to perform debugging and running functions for the user program. Most submenu items are used to debug the program, including Step, Step Over, Step Out, Insert/Remove Breakpoint. We will concentrate on some new and important commands for this menu; in particular, we will provide our discussions for the following items:

Debug:

- Start/Stop Debug Session
- Reset CPU
- Run
- Stop
- OS Support
- Execution Profiling
- Memory Map
- Inline Assembly
- Function Editor
- Target Settings

The Start/Stop Debug Session command enables users to start or stop the debug process.

The Reset CPU command sets the CPU to the RESET state.

The Run item starts to run the user's program until hits a breakpoint.

The Stop command is used to stop the running of the user's program.

The OS Support command is used to access kernel-aware debug information. Define an RTOS in the field Options for Target Project|Target|Operating System to activate the menu items. Two submenu items are under this command,

- System and Thread Viewer: Open the dialog RTX Tasks and System
- Event Viewer: Opens the dialog Event Viewer

The first command is used to monitor all system and thread related tasks running with the user program, and the second is to watch all related events.

The menu Execution Profiling enables the Execution Profiler to record and display execution statistics for each instruction in the user program. Users can view the instruction time and calls in the Disassembly Window and in the Editor. The values are cumulative numbers. The Execution Profiler records timing and execution statistics about instructions for the complete program code. To view the values in the Editor or Disassembly Window, you need to useShow Time or Show Calls from this menu.

The Memory Map provides some functions to enable the user to

- Display the currently mapped memory ranges.
- Remove the selected mapped range from the list.
- Read or Write memory ranges.
- Identify the specified memory range asvon Neumann memory. When specified, μVision5 overlaps the external data memory (XDATA) range and code memory (0xFFxxxx). Write access to external data memory also change code memory.

These operations can be performed via a Memory Map configuration dialog.

The Inline Assembly command can be used to modify instructions while debugging to allow correcting the code or making temporary changes.

The Function Editor is used to create, modify, and compile debug functions using the built-in debug function editor.

The `Target Settings` provides a function similar to that of `Settings` button under the `Utilities` option in the `Options for Target Project` in the `Project` menu. We have already provided detailed discussions about this function at the end of the Section 3.4.4.3.

3.4.4.6 The Peripherals Menu

The `Peripherals` menu includes dialogs to view and change on-chip peripheral settings. The content of this menu is tailored to show specific peripherals of the CPU selected for the application. This menu is active only inDebug Mode.

Two submenu items are under this menu, which are:

- `System Viewer`
- `Core Peripherals`

The `System Viewer` can be used to open the related monitor window for all peripheral devices connected to the MCU evaluation board. The real-time running status of selected peripheral devices can be traced or inspected in these monitor windows. You can select any desired device by checking on it from the System Viewer submenu. An example of System Viewer, `TIMER0`, is shown in Figure 3.45. Table 3.1 shows some typical dialogs provided by this menu.

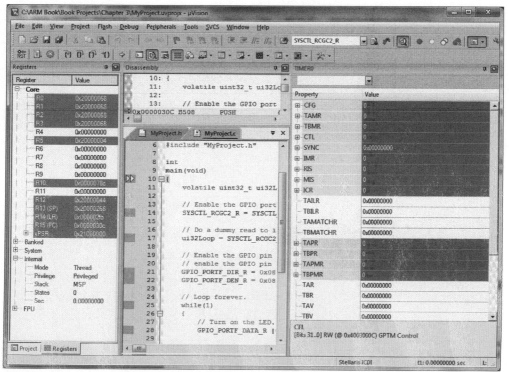

Figure 3.45. An example of using System Viewer for TIMER0 device. (Reproduced with permission from ARM® Limited. Copyright © ARM Limited.)

Table 3.1. Typical system viewers.

Menu Items	Descriptions
WATCHDOG	Watchdog Timer
GPIO	GPIO Interface
UART	UART Controller
PWM	PWM Controller
TIMER	Timers/Counters
ADC	Analog to Digital Converter
CAN	Control Area Network Controller
USB0	USB Controller
EEPROM	EEPROM Device
SYSCTL	System Control Registers

Under the Core Peripherals menu, there are five submenu items. Each of them is used to open a related window to display the running status of selected device. You can also set or change the related configuration for the selected device.

- Nested Vectored Interrupt Controller
- System Control and Configurations
- System Tick Timer
- Fault Reports
- Memory Protection Unit

One point to be noted is that all of these five items can be available only when the program has been debugged. An example of using the Core Peripherals for the Nested Vectored Interrupt Controller is shown in Figure 3.46.

3.4.4.7 The Tools Menu

The Tools menu allows you to configure and run Gimpel PC-Lint and other custom programs. Four submenu items are under this menu; they are:

Tools:

- Set-up PC-Lint
- Lint
- Lint All C-Source Files
- Customize Tools Menu

The Set-up PC-Lint is used to configure PC-Lint from Gimpel Software.

The Lint is to run PC-Lint on the current editor file. PC-Lint from Gimpel Software checks the syntax and semantics of C codes; and it reports possible bugs

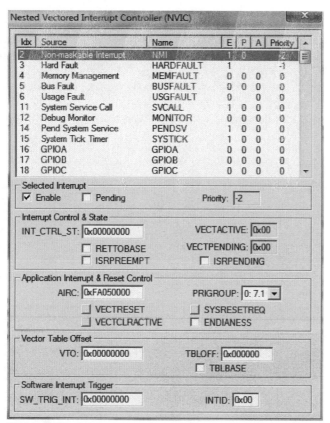

Figure 3.46. The Nested Vectored Interrupt Controller configuration dialog.
(Reproduced with permission from ARM® Limited. Copyright © ARM Limited.)

and inconsistencies and locates unclear, erroneous, or invalid C codes. PC-Lint could reduce debugging efforts considerably. Configuration templates are provided for each toolset and various device types, including a PC-LINT configuration file for ARM7™, ARM9™, and Cortex®-Mx devices (..\ARM\BIN\CO-RV.LNT). The files have the extension *.LNT. It is strongly recommended to use the template configuration files, because they contain options required by various compilers.

The Lint All C-Source Files item can be used to run PC-Lint on all C source files in your project.

The Customize Tools Menu is used to add user programs to the Tools menu. External programs can be integrated into and run from the Tools menu. To do this, you need to add menu items for running external programs through the Tools|Customize Tools Menu.

3.4.4.8 The SVCS Menu

The SVCS menu is used to configure the Software Version Control System (SVCS). In fact, The SVCS menu allows you to configure and add commands for a Software Version Control System. Commands that steer the SVCS can be added to and executed from the menu. The command output is shown in the µVision5 windowBuild Output after the command finished executing.

Template files are provided for: Intersolv PVCS, Microsoft SourceSafe, MKS Source Integrity, and Rational Clear Case. The files have the extension *.SVCS and are located in the folder C:\Keil_v5\UV4. Adapt the templates to your needs.

3.4.4.9 The Window Menu

The Window menu includes commands to control text editor files and windows format. Three submenu items are:

Window:

- Reset View to Defaults
- Split
- Close All

The Reset View to Defaults is to reset the window layout to the µVision5 default look and feel.

The Split is used to divide the active editor file into two horizontal or vertical panes.

The Close All item can be used to close all open editor files. A dialog box is displayed for files that have been changed but not saved yet.

In the bottom of this Window menu, all user projects that had been opened before are listed in the order they are opened. This provides a good record for all projects you opened and built.

3.4.4.10 The Help Menu

The Help menu includes commands to start the on-line help system, to list information about on-chip peripherals, to access the knowledge base, to contact the Technical Support team, to check for product updates, and to display product version information.

Six submenu items are listed under this menu:

Help:

- µVision Help
- Open Books Window
- Simulated Peripherals for Specified MCU
- Contact Support
- Check for Update
- About µVision

The functions for all of these menu items are simple and easy to be understood, except the Simulated Peripherals for Specified MCU, which provides information about the simulated peripherals of the selected device.

The µVision5 Debugger can simulate the behavior of the target application. This enables developers to test applications prior to having the hardware.

The logic behavior of communication peripherals is reflected through virtual registers that can be listed with the command DIR VTREG. Thus, debug functions that stimulate complex peripherals can be written easily. The µVision5 Simulator mimes the timing and logical behavior of serial communication protocols like UART, I²C, SPI, and CAN, but does not simulate the I/O port toggling of the physical communication pins on the I/O port.

To perform the simulation task using the simulator, you need to select the Use Simulator checkbox in the Debug tab under the Options for Target Project submenu in the Project menu. We will provide more detailed discussions about using the Simulator in the following section.

At this point, we finished introductions to all menu items for MDK µVersion5. Now let's have a summarization about topics we discussed in those sections.

3.5 EMBEDDED SOFTWARE DEVELOPMENT PROCEDURE

Generally, to successfully develop and build an embedded software project, one needs the following components:

1. Development Kits or Suites
2. Debug Adaptor and Debug Drivers
3. Development Boards or Evaluation Boards
4. Specified Software Device Drivers

Specially, to successfully develop and build a user project with MDK µVersion5 IDE, the following operational sequence is needed:

1. Create a new user project using the New µVersion Project menu item.
2. Select the target device (MCU) installed in your evaluation board using the Select Device for Target 'Target1' wizard.
3. Configure and set up the required software components you will use in your project using the Manage Run-Time Environment wizard, such as CMSIS:CORE and Device:Startup. The MDK:CORE is automatically setup and involved in your project.
4. Add the user's source files, either Assembly or C codes files, into the project using the Add New Item to Group 'Source Group 1' wizard. If you prefer to use only C codes, you also need to add some header files.
5. Build your project using the Project|Rebuild all target files menu item.
6. Download your executable or image file to the flash memory in your evaluation board using the Download item from the Flash menu. If the checkbox Update Target before Debugging under the Utilities menu has been checked, your image file will be automatically downloaded into the flash ROM when the debug process starts.
7. Debug your project by going to Debug|Start/Stop Debug Session menu item.
8. Run your project using the Debug|Run menu item.
9. Stop your project using Debug|Stop or click the Start/Stop Debug Session menu item again.
10. Erase your project from the flash memory using the Erase item from the Flash menu.

Figure 3.47 shows an illustration block diagram for this project development, building, debugging, and running steps.

Next let's have a closer look at the debug process in Cortex-M microcontrollers, including the debug adaptor, debug driver, and debug process.

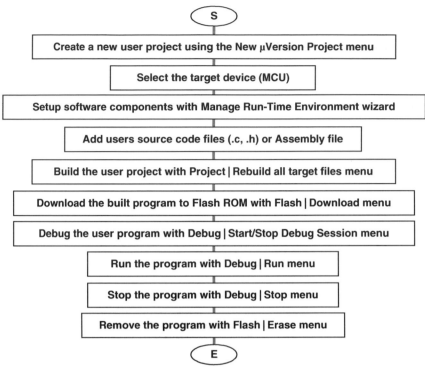

Figure 3.47. The project development steps.

3.6 THE KEIL® ARM®-MDK µVISION5 DEBUGGER AND DEBUG PROCESS

We have discussed and implemented quite a few debug functions while we developed and built our sample project MyProject in the previous section; however, because of the importance of this component, we will introduce this component in more details in this part.

The basic functions of a debugger are to find, locate, identify, and trace any possible bugs or errors existing in your project. Different strategies and technologies are implemented in different debuggers.

The ARM® CoreSight™ technology integrated into the ARM® Cortex®-M processor-based devices provides powerful debug and trace capabilities. It enables run control to start and stop programs, breakpoints, memory access, and Flash programming. Features like PC sampling, data trace, exceptions including interrupts, and instrumentation trace are available in most devices. Devices integrate instruction trace using Embedded Trace Macrocell (ETM), Embedded Trace Buffer (ETB), or Micro Trace Buffer (MTB) to enable analysis of the program execution.

The processor implementation determines the debug configuration, including whether debug is implemented. If the processor does not implement debug, no ROM table is present and the halt, breakpoint, and watchpoint functionality is not present.

Basic debug functionality includes processor halt, single-step, processor core register access, Vector Catch, unlimited software breakpoints, and full system memory access.

The debug option might include:

- A breakpoint unit supporting two literal comparators and six instruction comparators, or only two instruction comparators
- A watchpoint unit supporting one or four watchpoints

For processors that implement debug, ARM® recommends that a debugger identify and connect to the debug components using the CoreSight debug infrastructure.

3.6.1 The ARM® μVision5 Debug Architecture

The μVision5 Debugger from Keil® supports simulation using only your PC or laptop, as well as debugging using your target system and a debugger interface. The μVision5 includes traditional features like simple and complex breakpoints, watch windows, and execution control as well as sophisticated features like trace capture, execution profiler, code coverage, and logic analyzer.

Most popular debug features involved in the μVision5 Debugger include:

- Run Control of the processor allowing you to start and stop programs
- Single Step one source or assembler line
- Set breakpoints while the processor is running
- Read/write memory contents and peripheral registers on-the-fly
- Program internal and external Flash memory

The MDK contains the μVision5 Debugger that can be connected to various Debug/Trace adapters and allows you to program the Flash memory. It supports traditional features like simple and complex breakpoints, watch windows, and execution control. Using trace, additional features like event/exception viewers, logic analyzer, execution profiler, and code coverage are supported.

The ARM® debugger is composed of two elements: the hardware (Debug Adapter) and the software (Debug Adapter Driver). These two elements make up a complete debug system. Different interface protocols are developed to meet the needs of different debug processes. Most popular debug interfaces include: JTAG, SWD, and SWV.

Let's first have a clear picture about these terminologies used in the debug adaptor interfaces.

- JTAG (Join Test Action Group). JTAG is the industry-standard interface used to download and debug programs on a target processor, as well as many other functions. It offers a convenient and easy way to connect to devices and is available on all ARM® processor-based devices. The JTAG interface can be used with Cortex-M devices to access the CoreSight debug capabilities.
- SWD (Serial Wire Debug). The Serial Wire Debug mode is an alternative to the standard JTAG interface. SWD uses 2 pins to provide the same debug functionality as JTAG with no performance penalty, and it introduces data trace capabilities with the Serial Wire Viewer (SWV). The SWD interface pins can be overlayed with the JTAG signals, allowing the standard target connectors to be used.
  - TCLK−SWCLK (Serial Wire Clock)
  - TMS−SWDIO (Serial Wire debug Data Input/Output)
  - TDO−SWO (output pin for Serial Wire Viewer)

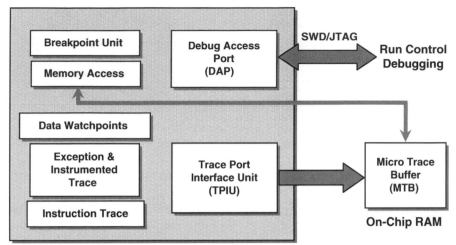

Figure 3.48. An illustration block diagram of the μVision5 Debugger.

JTAG and SWD modes are fully supported by ULINK2, ULINK-ME, and ULINK*Pro*.

- SWV (Serial Wire Viewer). Cortex®-M3 and Cortex-M4 based devices are able to provide high-speed data trace information in a number of ways depending on the type of information or analysis you require. The SWV provides real-time data trace information from various sources within the Cortex®-M3/M4 device. This is output via the single SWO pin while your system processor continues running at full speed. Information is available from the ITM (Instrumentation Trace Macrocell) and DWT (Data Watchpoint and Trace) units, providing:
  - PC (Program Counter) sampling
  - Event counters that show CPU cycle statistics
  - Exception and Interrupt execution with timing statistics
  - Trace data—data reads and writes used for timing analysis
  - ITM trace information used for simple *printf*-style debugging
  - SWV Data trace is available via the SWO pin in two output formats:
  - UART style (1Mb/s)—supported by ULINK2 and ULINK-ME
  - Manchester Encoded (100 Mb/s)—supported by ULINK*Pro*

Figure 3.48 shows an illustration block diagram of the μVision5 Debugger used for ARM® Cortex-M3/M4 microcontrollers.

All debug components, including the Breakpoint unit, memory access, and data watchpoints, are embedded into this debugger. Two trace components, exception and instrumented trace, and instruction trace, also included in this debugger. Two different interfaces, Debug Access Port (DAP) and Trace Port Interface Unit (TPIU), are used to interface to the run-time debugging control via a JTAG or SWD debug adaptor interfaces and the Micro Trace Buffer (MTB). The former is to perform run-time debug processes and the later is used to perform trace operations.

3.6.2 The ARM® Debug Adaptor and Debug Adaptor Driver

The Debug Adapter is a piece of hardware or a hardware interface connected from your host computer to your microcontroller evaluation board. The debug adapter needs to work with a `Debug Adapter Driver`, a piece of software installed in your host computer, to perform all debug functions, including downloading your program to the flash in the EVB, debugging any possible bugs in your program, and tracing the performances of related components in your system.

The µVision5 Debugger can be configured as a `Simulator` or as a `Target Debugger`. Go to the `Debug` tab of the `Options for Target project` dialog to switch between the two debug modes and to configure each mode.

The `Simulator` is a software-only product that simulates most features of a microcontroller without the need for target hardware. By using the Simulator, you can test and debug your embedded application before any target hardware or evaluation board is available. µVision also simulates a wide variety of peripherals including the serial port, external I/O, timers, and interrupts. Peripheral simulation capabilities vary depending on the device you have selected.

The `Target Debugger` is a hybrid product that combines µVision5 with a hardware debugger interfacing to your target system. The following debug devices are supported:

- `JTAG/OCDS Adapters` that connect to on-chip debugging systems like the ARM® Embedded ICE
- `Target Monitors` that are integrated with user hardware and that are available on many evaluation boards
- `Emulators` that connect to the MCU pins of the target hardware
- `In-System Debuggers` that are part of the user application program and provide basic test functions

Third-party tool developers may use the Keil® Advanced GDI to interface µVision5 to their own hardware debuggers.

No matter whether you choose to debug with the Simulator or with a target debugger, the µVision5 IDE implements a single user interface that is easy to learn and master.

The Keil® ULINK™ Debug Adapters family provides three types of debug adapters:

- ULINK2 (ULINK2 USB-JTAG Adapter)
- ULINKpro
- ULINK-ME

All of these adapters provide supports to ARM7™, ARM9™, and Cortex®-M microcontroller devices, to perform the following:

- Download programs to your target hardware.
- Examine memory and registers.
- Single step through programs and insert multiple breakpoints.
- Run programs in real time.
- Program Flash Memory.
- Connect using JTAG or Serial Wire modes.
- On-the-fly debug of ARM® Cortex®-M-based devices.
- Examine Trace information from ARM® Cortex®-M3 and Cortex®-M4 devices.

The following debug adaptor interfaces are popular and compatible with the µVision5 Debugger:

- The ULINK2 and ULINK-ME Debug adapters interface to JTAG/SWD debug connectors and support trace with the Serial Wire Output (SWO). The ULINK*pro* Debug/Trace adapter also interfaces to Embedded Trace Macrocell (ETM) trace connectors and uses streaming trace technology to capture the complete instruction trace for code coverage and execution profiling.
- The CMSIS-DAP-based USB JTAG/SWD debug interfaces are typically part of an evaluation board or starter kit and offer integrated debug features. In addition, several proprietary interfaces that offer a similar technology are supported.
- The MDK supports third-party debug solutions such as Segger J-Link or J-Trace. Some starter kit boards provide the J-Link Lite technology as an on-board solution.

The ULINK2 may be also used for:

- On-chip Debugging (using on-chip JTAG, SWD, or SWV).
- Flash Memory Programming (using user-configurable Flash programming algorithms).

Using the ULINK2 adapter together with the Keil® µVision5 IDE/Debugger, you can easily create, download, and test embedded applications on target hardware.

3.6.3 Tiva™ C Series LaunchPad™ Debug Adaptor and Debug Adaptor Driver

Since we use the Tiva™ C Series LaunchPad evaluation board TM4C123G with this book, we need to emphasize the specified debugger used in this system.

The Tiva™ C Series LaunchPad evaluation board comes with an on-board In-Circuit Debug Interface (ICDI). This interface is mainly composed of a TM4C123GH6PM microcontroller unit (MCU), and it can be considered as a debug controller with a debug adapter. Therefore, we do not need to use any other debug adapter since it has been built on this evaluation board.

As you know, there are two pieces of MCU units, TM4C123GH6PM, on the Tiva™ C Series LaunchPad evaluation board TM4C123G. The one located at the top of this EVB works as a debug controller/adapter. This debugger, combined with other related debug elements in this EVB, is called an ICDI interface.

The ICDI allows for the programming and debug of the TM4C123GH6PM using the LM Flash Programmer and/or any of the supported tool chains. Note that the ICDI supports only JTAG debugging. An external debug interface can be connected for Serial Wire Debug (SWD) and SWO (trace).

To access the on-board ICDI, a debug adapter driver is needed. A good choice is the Stellaris® ICDI Driver. Depends on the different operating systems the user used, different debug drivers are provided by Stellaris®. Refer to Appendix C to download and install this debug driver on your host computer if you have not done it.

One point to be noted is that the Stellaris® ICDI driver can only work for the JTAG interface.

An illustration block diagram of using the Keil® ULINK2 and Stellaris® ICDI debug interfaces and adapters for the different MCU boards are shown in Figure 3.49.

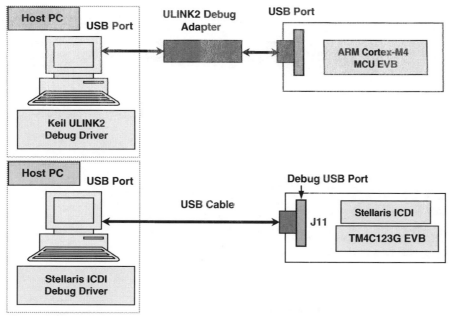

Figure 3.49. The debug system connections for ULINK2 and Stellaris®.

Next let's discuss the detailed debug process.

3.6.4 The ARM® μVersion5 Debug Process

Based on discussions above, now we can start to do some debug jobs for our project. We will use our sample project MyProject built in the last section as an example to illustrate this debug process.

Go to the Debug menu and click on the Start/Stop Debug Session item to start the debug process for this sample project. The debug result is shown in Figure 3.50.

From this debug window, you can perform the following debug functions:

- Examine and modify memory via Memory Window.
- Program variables and processor registers via Register Window.
- Set breakpoints via Debug|Insert/Remove Breakpoint menu item.
- Single step through a program using Debug|Step menu item.
- Perform other typical debugging activities.

Since we did not set up any break point and watch point in this project, the debug automatically stopped at the main() body, as a blue and a yellow arrow pointed to in the Source Editor.

The contents for all registers inside the ARM® Cortex®-M4 MCU are displayed in the Register Window on the left. In the Command Window, the limitation of the used memory size for this evaluation board, which is 32 KB, is displayed. The current used memory size for this sample project is also shown in this window.

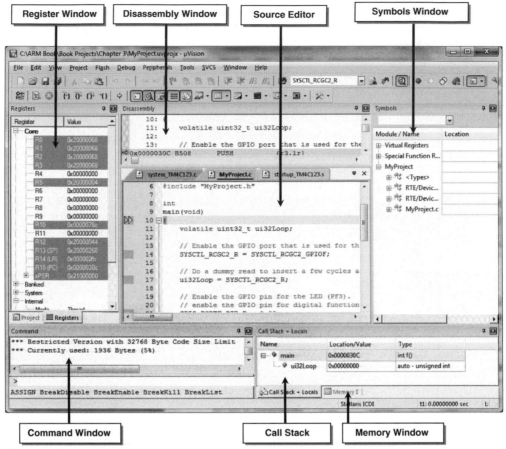

Register Window   Disassembly Window   Source Editor   Symbols Window

Command Window   Call Stack   Memory Window

Figure 3.50. A debug example for our sample project MyProject. (Reproduced with permission from ARM® Limited. Copyright © ARM Limited.)

The Call Stack window shows the function nesting and variables of the current program location. The addresses for all modules and names of variables used in this project are shown in the Symbols Window. Go to the Debug|Stop menu to stop this debug process.

Because we did not use any debug function, some debug-related windows and functions, such as Memory Window and Peripheral Window, did not show up in our debug process.

3.6.5 The ARM® Trace Feature

The Keil® μVision5 IDE and Debugger supports Cortex-M devices with dedicated windows which display debug information, trace records, state changes, and instruction trace.

The Run-Stop Debugging, as described in the last section, has some limitations that become apparent when testing time-critical programs, such as motor control or communication applications. As an example, breakpoints and single stepping commands change

Table 3.2. Trace features for different debug adapters.

Feature	ULINK*pro*	ULINK*pro*-D	ULINK2	ST-Link v2
Thread Management	✓	✓	✓	✓
Maximum SWO clock frequency	200 MHz	200 MHz	3.75 MHz	2 MHz
4-Pin Trace Output for Streaming	✓	×	×	×
Embedded Trace Buffer (ETB)	✓	✓	✓	×
Micro Trace Buffer (MTB)	✓	✓	✓	×

the dynamic behavior of the system. As an alternative, a more powerful tool is to use the trace features explained in this section to analyze running systems.

Cortex-M processors integrate CoreSight logic that is able to generate the following trace information using the following:

- Data Watchpoints can record memory accesses with data value and program address and, optionally, stop program execution.
- Exception-Trace outputs details about interrupts and exceptions.
- Instrumented Trace communicates program events and enables printf-style debug messages and the RTOS Event Viewer.
- Instruction Trace streams the complete program execution for recording and analysis.

The Trace Port Interface Unit (TPIU) is available on most Cortex-M4 based microcontrollers and outputs above trace information via:

- Serial Wire Trace Output (SWO) works only in combination with the Serial Wire Debug mode (not with JTAG) and does not support Instruction Trace.
- 4-Pin Trace Output is available on high-end microcontrollers and has the high bandwidth required for Instruction Trace.

On some microcontrollers, the trace information can be stored on an on-chip Trace Buffer that can be read using the standard debug interface. The Cortex-M4 has an optional Embedded Trace Buffer (ETB) that stores all trace data described above. The required trace interface needs to be supported by both the microcontroller and the debug adapter. Table 3.2 shows supported trace methods of various debug adapters.

Generally, different IDEs and additional components are needed to perform some trace functions. For example, Texas Instruments XDS560 Trace tooling only supports the Code Composer Studio™ (CCS) debug environment via JTAG. Since the TM4C123G EVB does not provide related supports for SWO and related trace functions, in this section we only provide a quick introduction about those functions.

3.6.5.1 Some Useful Trace Features Provided by Cortex®-M4 MCU

The CoreSight features are available via JTAG and new Serial Wire interfaces using standard low-cost target connectors.

The Data Watchpoints and Trace (DWT) is an optional debug unit that provides watchpoints, data tracing, and system profiling for the processor. A full DWT contains four comparators that you can configure as:

- A hardware watchpoint.
- An ETM trigger.
- A PC sampler event trigger.
- A data address sampler event trigger.

The first comparator, DWT_COMP0, can also compare against the clock cycle counter, CYCCNT. You can also use the second comparator, DWT_COMP1, as a data comparator. A reduced DWT contains one comparator that you can use as a watchpoint or as a trigger. It does not support data matching. The DWT, if present, contains counters for:

- Clock cycles (CYCCNT).
- Folded instructions.
- Load Store Unit (LSU) Operations.
- Sleep Cycles.
- CPI that is all instruction cycles except for the first cycle.
- Interrupt overhead.

An event is generated each time a counter overflows.

You can configure the DWT to generate PC samples at defined intervals and to generate interrupt event information. The DWT provides periodic requests for protocol synchronization to the ITM and the TPIU, if your implementation includes the Cortex-M4 TPIU.

The `Instrumentation Trace Macrocell` (ITM) is a an optional application-driven trace source that supports printf style debugging to trace operating system and application events and generates diagnostic system information.

The ITM generates trace information as packets. There are four sources that can generate packets. If multiple sources generate packets at the same time, the ITM arbitrates the order in which packets are output. The four sources in decreasing order of priority are:

- Software trace. Software can write directly to ITM stimulus registers to generate packets.
- Hardware trace. The DWT generates these packets, and the ITM outputs them.
- Time stamping. Timestamps are generated relative to packets. The ITM contains a 21-bit counter to generate the timestamp. The Cortex-M4 clock or the bitclock rate of the `Serial Wire Viewer` (SWV) output clocks the counter.
- Global system time stamping. Timestamps can optionally be generated using a system-wide 48-bit count value. The same count value can be used to insert timestamps in the ETM trace stream, permitting coarse-grain correlation.

3.6.6 The ARM® Instruction Set Simulator

The μVision5 Debugger can be configured as a Simulator or as a Target Debugger. To switch between these two modes, one needs to go to the `Debug` tab of the `Options for Target Project` submenu under the `Project` menu.

However, there is only a Cortex-M Simulator as a target within Code Composer Studio™ (CCS) IDE, and the Tiva™ C Series of ARM® Cortex®-M4 microcontrollers do not provide any support to this kind of simulator function in the Keil® µVision5 IDE. Therefore we only provide a short introduction to this Simulator with some MCUs in this part.

The `Simulator` is a software-only product that simulates most features of a microcontroller without the need for target hardware. By using the Simulator, you can test and debug your embedded application before any target hardware or evaluation board is available. The µVision5 also simulates a wide variety of peripherals including the serial port, external I/O, timers, and interrupts. Peripheral simulation capabilities vary depending on the device you have selected.

The µVision5 simulates up to 4 GB of memory from which specific areas can be mapped for reading, writing, executing, or a combination of these. In most cases, the µVision5 can deduce the correct memory map from the program object module. Any illegal memory access is automatically trapped and reported. A number of device-specific simulation capabilities are possible with the µVision5.

When you select a microcontroller from the Device Database, the µVision5 configures the Simulator accordingly and selects the appropriate instruction set, timing, and peripherals.

The µVision5 Simulator has the following capabilities:

- Runs programs using the ARM7™, ARM9™, Thumb, Thumb2, 8051, C166/XE166/XC2000 instruction sets.

- Is cycle-accurate and correctly simulates instructions and on-chip peripheral timing, where possible.

- Simulates on-chip peripherals of many 8051, C166/XE166/XC2000, ARM7™, ARM9™, and Cortex®-Mx devices.

- Can provide external stimulus using the debugger C script language.

The µVision5 Debugger provides complete instruction set simulation for all ARM7™, ARM9™, Cortex-M3, XC16x, C16x, ST10, 251, and 8051 devices.

When debugging your program, op-codes are interpreted and executed as their corresponding instructions would be. You may view program disassembly in mixed mode or in assembly code.

All registers and flags are updated as each instruction executes. Results display in the Register Tab of the Project Workspace. As you step through your program, affected registers are highlighted. Instruction timings are accurately simulated so you can easily determine how long a function or module takes to execute. Timing is cycle-accurate for deterministic parts.

3.6.7 The ARM® Programs Running from SRAM

One of the important properties of Cortex-M4 microcontrollers is that the user program codes can be run in the SRAM area in some evaluation boards, not in the flash ROM. This property becomes more important, even critical, for some non-ARM® MCU architectures since those microcontrollers do not have internal flash ROMs and must use external memory devices.

The good news is that for Tiva™ C Series LaunchPad evaluation board, such as TM4C123GXL, some users codes can be run in the SRAM area in that EVB. However, the bad news is that all SRAM areas in that EVB have been predefined and only recommended staff should be stored or located at those related areas.

In Tiva™ C Series LaunchPad EVB, the memory map and the programming of the MPU split the memory map into different regions. Each region has a defined memory type, and some regions have additional memory attributes. The memory type and attributes determine the behavior of accesses to the region.

The memory types can be defined as:

- Normal: The processor can reorder transactions for efficiency and perform speculative reads.
- Device: The processor preserves transaction order relative to other transactions to Device or Strongly Ordered memory.
- Strongly Ordered: The processor preserves transaction order relative to all other transactions.

The different ordering requirements for Device and Strongly Ordered memory mean that the memory system can buffer a write to Device memory but must not buffer a write to Strongly Ordered memory. An additional memory attribute is Execute Never (XN), which means the processor prevents instruction accesses. A fault exception is generated only on execution of an instruction executed from an XN region.

Table 3.3 shows the behavior of accesses to each region in the memory map. Tiva™ C Series devices may have reserved memory areas within the address ranges.

Table 3.3. The memory access behavior for Tiva™ C series LaunchPad EVB.

Address Range	Memory Region	Memory Type	Execute Never (XN)	Description
0x0000.0000–0x1FFF.FFFF	Code/ Interrupt Table	Normal	—	This executable region is for program code. Data can also be stored here.
0x2000.0000–0x3FFF.FFFF	SRAM	Normal	—	This executable region is for data. Code can also be stored here. This region includes bit band and bit band alias areas.
0x4000.0000–0x5FFF.FFFF	Peripheral	Device	XN	This region includes bit band and bit band alias areas.
0x6000.0000–0x9FFF.FFFF	External RAM	Normal	—	This executable region is for data.
0xA000.0000–0xDFFF.FFFF	External Device	Device	XN	This region is for external device memory.
0xE000.0000–0xE00F.FFFF	Private Peripheral Bus	Strongly Ordered	XN	This region includes the NVIC, system timer, and system control block.
0xE010.0000–0xFFFF.FFFF	Reserved	—	—	—

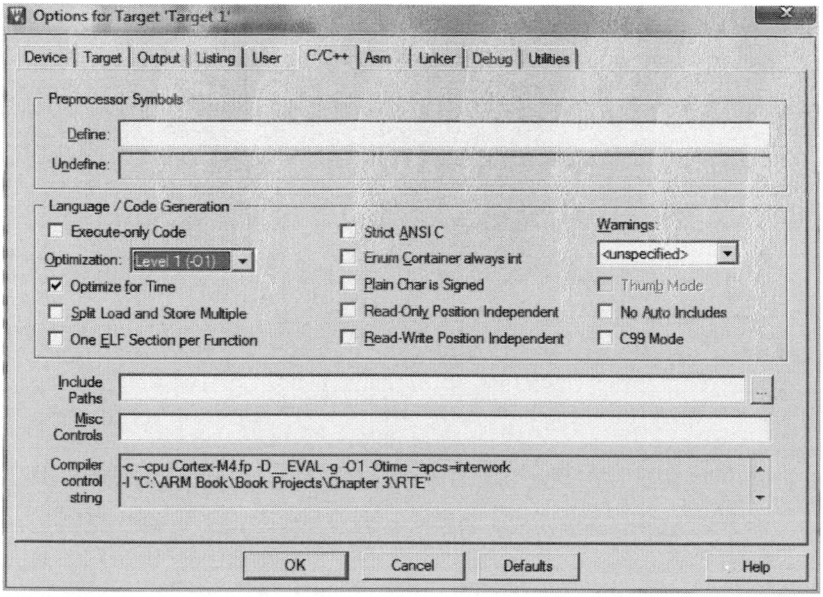

Figure 3.51.   The optimization wizard for our sample project. (Reproduced with permission from ARM® Limited. Copyright © ARM Limited.)

The Code, SRAM, and external RAM regions can hold programs. However, it is recommended that programs always use the Code region because the Cortex-M4F has separate buses that can perform instruction fetches and data accesses simultaneously.

The MPU can override the default memory access behavior described in this section. The Cortex-M4F prefetches instructions ahead of execution and speculatively prefetches from branch target addresses.

3.6.8 ARM® Optimizations

In the Keil® µVersion5 IDE, exactly in the ARM® Compiler, `armcc` can be used to optimize your codes for small code size and high performance.

The compiler provides two options for optimizing for code size and performance:

`Ospace`: Causes the compiler to optimize mainly for code size. This is the default option.

`Otime`: Causes the compiler to optimize mainly for speed.

An example of using the Optimization function for our sample project `MyProject` is shown in Figure 3.51. To open this wizard, go to `Project|Options for Target Project` and select the C/C++ tab.

The actual optimizations performed by the compiler depend both on the level of the optimization chosen by the users, and whether the user is optimizing for the program performance or the program's code size.

The MDK µVersion5 compiler supports the following optimization levels:

- **O0:** Minimum optimization. This level turns off most optimizations. When debugging is enabled, this option gives the best possible debug view because the structure of the generated code directly corresponds to the source code.

- **O1:** Restricted optimization. The compiler only performs optimizations that can be described by debug information. Removes unused inline functions and unused static functions. The compiler also turns off optimizations that seriously degrade the debug view. If used with --debug in the command line, this option gives a generally satisfactory debug view with good code density.

- **O2:** High optimization. If used with --debug, the debug view might be less satisfactory because the mapping of object codes to source codes is not always clear. The compiler may perform optimizations that cannot be described by debug information and inline functions automatically.

- **O3:** Maximum optimization. When debugging is enabled, this option typically gives a poor debug view. ARM® recommends debugging at lower optimization levels.

It can be found from Figure 3.51 that the compiler is selected to perform an O1 level optimization with the Optimize for Time checkbox selected for our sample project MyProject. This means that our project will have a restricted optimization with speed as the optimization target.

If you use **O3** and Optimize for Time together, the compiler performs extra optimizations that are more aggressive, such as:

- High-level scalar optimizations, including loop unrolling. This can give significant performance benefits at a small code size cost, but at the risk of a longer build time.

A point to be noted is: Do not rely on the implementation details of these optimizations, because they might change in future releases.

By default, the compiler optimizes to reduce image size at the expense of a possible increase in execution time. That is, Ospace is the default, rather than Otime. Note that Ospace is not affected by the optimization level O*num*. That is, O3 Ospace enables more optimizations than O2 Ospace, but does not perform more aggressive size reduction.

Another optimization function can be found from the Target tab under the Options for Target Project menu item. An example of using this optimization for our sample project MyProject is shown in Figure 3.52.

In the Code Generation group, the user can select the code optimization mode, either the Cross-Module Optimization or the Micro LIB.

- The Cross-Module Optimization can help users to reduce the code size by placing unused functions into separate sections in the ELF file, and therefore these sections can be omitted if they are not referenced during the linking stage.

- The Micro LIB can be used to optimize devices with small memory foot-prints. If this option is not selected, the standard C library, which is optimized mostly for performance, is selected. The Micro LIB run-time library is much smaller in program size compared with that of the C standard library, but it is slower with some limitations in the optimization functions.

The Floating Point Hardware selection enables users to use different library for this code optimization. You can select to use either the Floating Point Unit, a standard C library or the Micro LIB as the optimization library.

3.7 THE TIVAWARE™ FOR C SERIES SOFTWARE SUITE

Texas Instruments TivaWare™ software for C Series is an extensive suite of software tools designed to simplify and speed development of Tiva™ C Series-based MCU applications.

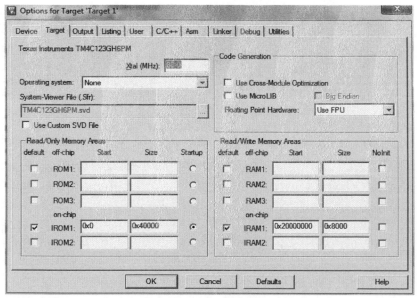

Figure 3.52. An example of using the code optimization under the Target tab. (Reproduced with permission from ARM® Limited. Copyright © ARM Limited.)

All TivaWare™ for C Series software has a free license and allows royalty-free use so users can create and build full-function, easy-to-maintain code. TivaWare™ for C Series software is written entirely in C to make development and deployment efficient and easy.

The complete TivaWare™ for C Series software suite includes:

- Royalty-free libraries (Peripheral, USB, Graphics, Sensor)
- Powerful utilities
- Kit- and peripheral-specific code examples for different devices
- Release notes and related documentation
- Speeds design and development
- Written entirely in C
- Everything you need to use your Tiva™ C Series kits or boards

The Tiva™ C Series software supports different development tools and IDEs, and the following development tools and IDEs are involved:

- TivaWare™ C Series for Code Composer Studio™ (CCS)
- TivaWare™ C Series for IAR Embedded Workbench
- TivaWare™ C Series for Keil® ARM®-MDK μVersion®
- TivaWare™ C Series for Mentor Sourcery CodeBench

All of these IDEs and development suites support Tiva™ C Series software with a limitation (32 KB) on SRAM in the related EVB. The Stellaris® ICDI provides a built-in debug interface with a debugger to work with these IDEs via the JTAG/OCDS interface protocol.

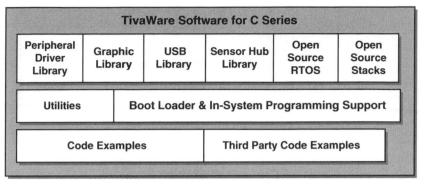

Figure 3.53.   Tools included in the TivaWare for C Series suite.

3.7.1 The TivaWare™ C Series Software Package

Texas Instruments' Tiva™ C Series software provides supports to most popular MCUs, such as ARM® Cortex™-M4 core, with scalable memory and package options, unparalleled connectivity peripherals, and advanced analog integration.

The TivaWare™ for C Series suite contains and integrates all user-required source-code functions and object libraries, which include:

- Peripheral Driver Library (DriverLib)
- Graphic Library
- USB Library
- Sensor Hub Library
- Open Source RTOS
- Open Source Stacks
- Utilities
- Boot Loader and In-System Programming Support
- Example Codes
- Third-Party Examples

Figure 3.53 shows an illustration block diagram for these source-code functions and libraries included in the TivaWare™ for C Series suite. TivaWare™ for C Series libraries offer users the flexibility of working with sample applications or the freedom to create their own projects.

Different source-code functions and libraries are provided by this suite, which include:

- The `Peripheral Driver Library` offers an extensive set of functions for controlling the peripherals found on various TM4C devices.
- The `Graphic Library` includes a set of graphics primitives and a widget set for creating graphical user interfaces on Tiva™ C Series-based microcontroller boards that have a graphical display.
- The `USB Library` provides a TivaWare™ royalty-free USB stack to enable efficient USB host, device, and on-the-go operations.
- The `Sensor Hub Library` offers an advanced sensor fusion algorithm and a broad range of sensor support.

- The Utilities provide all required developing tools and user-friendly functions to make the user-program development easier and simpler.
- The Boot Loader & In-System Programming support users to build the startup codes, install them at the beginning of the flash ROM in the EVB, and run them when the user program starts.
- The Open Source RTOS is a Free RTOS that is a popular real-time operating system for most popular embedded devices. This RTOS accelerates development schedules by eliminating the need to create basic system software functions from scratch. It also scales from a real-time multitasking kernel, the TI-RTOS Kernel to a complete RTOS solution including additional middleware components and device drivers. By providing essential system software components pre-tested and pre-integrated, the RTOS enables developers to focus on differentiating their application.
- The Open Source Stacks offers different stacks for most popular host and peripheral devices.
- The Code Examples offer some useful coding guides to help users to start and speed up their coding developments.
- The Third Party Code Examples provide some codes developed by different venders.

Among those code functions and object libraries, some of them are very important and useful in the user's program development. We need to highlight those functions and libraries.

3.7.1.1 *The Peripheral Driver Library (DriverLib)*

Basically this library provides a collection of source code (.c) files and related header (.h) files, and those files should be installed on or integrated with the related development IDE to facilitate the user's program development.

All of these source and header files should be located at the related folders when the TivaWare™ for C Series software is installed in your host computer. These folders are:

- C:/ti/TivaWare_C_Series-<version>/inc: Contains all hardware or device related specified header files. These files include:
  - Peripheral specific definitions
  - Required Type definitions
  - Macros
- C:/ti/TivaWare_C_Series-<version>/driverlib: Contains all project library files and compiler output directory, which include:
  - C source and header files peripheral specific functionality
  - Compiler specific project file for building the driver library 'libraries'
  - Compiler specific output directories and files for the used compiler. It should be: C:/ti/TivaWare_C_Series-<version>/driverlib/rvmdk for the ARM®-MDK μVersion5

A point to be noted is that the TivaWare™ for C Series peripheral driver library is also preprogrammed into the internal ROM space on all Tiva™ C Series MCUs.

A set of high-level API interfaces is provided by this library to enable users to access and select all related peripheral devices during the program building process. This library is compatible with most popular IDEs, such as CCS, ARM®/Keil® MDK, IAR, and GNU.

3.7.1.2 The Boot Loader

The Texas Instruments™ Tiva™ boot loader is a small piece of code that can be programmed at the beginning of flash to act as an application loader as well as an update mechanism for applications running on a Tiva™ ARM® Cortex®-M4-based microcontroller. The boot loader can be built to use the UART0, SSI0, I2C0, CAN, Ethernet, or USB ports to update the code on the microcontroller. The boot loader is customizable via source code modifications, or simply deciding at compile time which routines to include. Since full source code is provided, the boot loader can be completely customized.

Three update protocols are utilized. On UART0, SSI0, I2C0, and CAN, a custom protocol is used to communicate with the download utility to transfer the firmware image and program it into flash. When using Ethernet or USB Device Firmware Upgrade (DFU), however, different protocols are employed. On Ethernet the standard bootstrap protocol (BOOTP) is used and for USB DFU, updates are performed via the standard DFU class.

When configured to use UART0, Ethernet, or USB, the LM Flash Programmer GUI can be used to download an application via the boot loader.

Some other functions provided by the Boot Loader are as follows:

- Download codes to the flash memory for firmware updates.
- Interface options include USB, UART, CAN, I2C, and SPI.

After the TivaWare™ for C Series software package is installed in your host computer, all Boot Loader related codes, including the source code files, header files and assembly code files, are located at: `C:/ti/TivaWare_C_Series-<version>/boot_loader`.

3.7.1.3 The Utilities

The TivaWare™ for C Series Utilities make it easier to work with your applications and designs. The Utilities contain some useful tools and functions to facilitate the user to develop their projects. One of them is the checksum security function that provides some optimized commonly used functions such as CRC checking and AES table. Another powerful utility function is provided by the Tiva™ C Series PinMux Utility.

The Tiva™ C Series PinMux Utility provides a quick and easy-to-use tool for configuring the GPIOs on Tiva™ C Series MCUs. Whether you are an experienced firmware engineer, hobbyist, or student, the combination of graphical configuration and code generation tools ensures that you can build your project in an easy and simple way.

The Tiva™ C Series PinMux Utility allows a Tiva™ C Series MCU developer to graphically configure the device peripherals intuitively and rapidly. This tool provides an easy-to-use interface that makes setting up alternate functions for GPIOs easy and error-free.

The TM4C PinMux Utility helps users generate custom schematics symbols for Tiva™ C Series MCUs for customized applications. The LMFlash Programmer enables users to load software to TM4C development and evaluation boards more easily. Use the TM4C ICDI Drivers to program and debug the TM4C microcontroller on a Tiva™ C Series evaluation board.

Additional utilities are also available and these utilities include:

- The PinMux Utility
- The LMFlash Programmer
- The Uniflash
- The ICDI Drivers
- The FTDI Drivers
- The IQMath Library
- The Windows-Side USB Code Examples

In order to use the onboard FTDI-based ICDI interface, Stellaris® FTDI drivers must be first installed on the host computer.

The TivaWare™ for C Series suite is developed and built to meet the needs of different microcontrollers, mostly based on ARM® Cortex®-M4 MCUs and related evaluation boards. Currently, one of the most updated MCU families, Tiva™ C Series LaunchPad, is fully supported by the specified TivaWare™ for C Series software package.

Two major evaluation kits families, Tiva™ C Series Connected LaunchPad: EK-TM4C129x, and Tiva™ C Series LaunchPad: EK-TM4C123x, are more popular and widely implemented in both industrial and commercial applications. Since we are using the kit, Tiva™ C Series TM4C123G, in this book, we will concentrate on this evaluation kit.

3.7.2 TivaWare™ C Series for TM4C123G LaunchPad™ Evaluation Kit

The Tiva™ C Series TM4C123G LaunchPad Evaluation Kit is a low-cost evaluation platform for ARM® Cortex™-M4F-based microcontrollers from Texas Instruments. The design of the TM4C123G LaunchPad highlights the TM4C123GH6PM microcontroller with a USB 2.0 device interface and hibernation module. This kit is mainly composed of two parts: The TM4C123G Evaluation Board (hardware) and SW-EK-TM4C123GXL package (software).

Since we have provided a detailed discussion about the TM4C123G Evaluation Board, EK-TM4C123GXL, in Chapter 2, we will concentrate on the software package in this part.

3.7.2.1 TivaWare™ C Series LaunchPad™ Evaluation Software Package

The SW-EK-TM4C123GXL package contains the TivaWare™ for C Series release for the Tiva™ C Series TM4C123G LaunchPad. This package includes the latest version of the TivaWare™ for C Series Peripheral Driver Library, USB Library, Sensor Hub Library, and Graphics Library. The package also contains some Utilities supports and Boot Loader as well as In-System Programming functions. It also includes several complete example applications for the Tiva™ C Series LaunchPad. Refer to Appendix B to download and install this package on your host computer system if you have not done it.

The four separate EK-TM4C123GXL packages each contain the SW-EK-TM4C123GXL software as well as installation files for each respective IDE (CCS, Keil®/ARM®-MDK, IRA and GNU) and the Microsoft® Windows® drivers for the debug interface. These packages also contain several documents to help you get started with using the Tiva™ C Series

LaunchPad. Each of the four files is single package with everything you need to program and debug the Tiva™ C Series LaunchPad using the respective toolset.

Use one of these packages if you need to install a different IDE on your host computer:

- EK-TM4C123GXL-CCS: TivaWare™ for C Series and Code Composer Studio™ (CCS) for the Tiva™ C Series TM4C123G LaunchPad™.

- EK-TM4C123GXL-IAR: TivaWare for C Series and IAR Embedded Workbench for the Tiva C Series TM4C123G LaunchPad.

- EK-TM4C123GXL-KEIL: TivaWare™ for C Series and Keil® ARM®-MDK for the Tiva C Series TM4C123G LaunchPad™.

- EK-TM4C123GXL-CB: TivaWare™ for C Series and Mentor Sourcery CodeBench for the Tiva C Series TM4C123G LaunchPad™.

- SW-EK-TM4C123GXL: TivaWare™ for the Tiva™ C Series TM4C123G LaunchPad Evaluation Board Software.

One point to be noted is that no matter which IDE you selected and have installed in your host computer, you must download and install the software package SW-EK-TM4C123GXL if you used a Tiva™ C Series TM4C123G LaunchPad Evaluation Board since you need this package to provide all required supporting code functions and object libraries to help you develop your desired projects in your selected IDE. As we mentioned, this package contains four different versions of software SW-EK-TM4C123GXL, and each one works for one related IDE.

For our discussions and implementations in this book, we used Keil® ARM®-MDK as the IDE (Keil® μVersion5 IDE) and Tiva™ for C Series TM4C123G evaluation board, therefore we need to download and install EK-TM4C123GXL-KEIL and SW-EK-TM4C123GXL package on our host computer. In fact, the package EK-TM4C123GXL-KEIL only includes all libraries and functions supporting to Keil® ARM-MDK IDE. Instead of installing that package, we can download and install the Keil® ARM-MDK μVersion5 IDE, MDK.510.exe, and a TivaWare™ general-purpose software package, SW-TM4C-2.0.1.11557.exe, which contains libraries and functions supporting to all four IDEs. Refer to Appendices A and B to download and install these software if you have not done so.

In fact, the Tiva™ C Series TM4C123G LaunchPad Evaluation Kit is composed of the following components:

- Tiva™ C Series TM4C123G LaunchPad Evaluation Board (TM4C123GXL)
- On-board In-Circuit Debug Interface (ICDI)
- USB Micro-B plug to USB-A plug cable
- README First document
- Free SW-EK-TM4C123GXL TivaWare™ for C Series software package

The software package provided with the SW-EK-TM4C123GXL provides access to all of the peripheral devices supplied in the design. The TivaWare™ for C Series Peripheral Driver Library is used to operate the on-chip peripherals.

The software includes a set of example applications that use the TivaWare™ Peripheral Driver Library. These applications demonstrate the capabilities of the TM4C123GH6PM microcontroller, as well as provide a starting point for the development of the applications for use on the TM4C123GXL development board.

After the TivaWare™ C Series LaunchPad Evaluation Software Package SW-EK-TM4C123GXL has been installed in your host computer, all related code functions and object libraries files are located at the following folders by default:

- Hardware/device-related specified header files: `C:/ti/TivaWare_C_Series-<version>/inc`
- Peripheral driver library files: `C:/ti/TivaWare_C_Series-<version>/driverlib/rvmdk`
- Graphic library files: `C:/ti/TivaWare_C_Series-<version>/grlib/rvmdk`
- Sensor hub library files: `C:/ti/TivaWare_C_Series-<version>/sensorlib/rvmdk`
- USB library files: `C:/ti/TivaWare_C_Series-<version>/usblib/rvmdk`
- All Utilities function files: `C:/ti/TivaWare_C_Series-<version>/utils`
- Compiler specific output directories: `C:/ti/TivaWare_C_Series-<version>/driverlib/rvmdk`
- Loader related codes, include source code and header files: `C:/ti/TivaWare _ C_ Series-<version>/boot_loader`
- All example program files: `C:/ti/TivaWare_C_Series-<version>/examples/boards/ek-tm4c123gxl`
- All related documents or user guide files: `C:/ti/TivaWare_C_Series-<version>/docs`
- All related tools files: `C:/ti/TivaWare_C_Series-<version>/tools`

The `<version>` tab used in these folders is the actual version of the software package installed in your host computer. In our case, it is `2.0.1.11577`, which means that the `<version>` should be replaced by `2.0.1.11577`.

An example of the documents and user guide folder `docs` is shown in Figure 3.54.

An illustration block diagram that contains complete components, including hardware and software, for our project development system is shown in Figure 3.55.

Next let's discuss one of the most important properties applied on the TivaWare™ for C Series LaunchPad™ system, TivaWare™ for C Series CMSIS support.

3.8 THE TIVAWARE™ FOR C SERIES UTILITIES AND OTHER SUPPORTS

Texas Instruments, with the C Series of ARM® Cortex®-M microcontrollers (MCUs), provides various supports to most different embedded devices developments. Most of these supports are either involved in the TivaWare™ for C Series Utilities or included in different tools. The major Utilities included in the TivaWare™ for C Series are:

- The PinMux Utility
- The LMFlash Programmer
- The UniFlash
- The ICDI Drivers
- The FTDI Drivers
- The IQMath Library

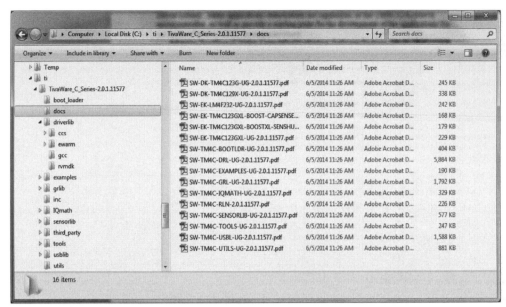

Figurer 3.54. An example folder docs.

The most popular support tools involved with the TivaWare™ for C Series are:

- TivaWare™ for C Series CMSIS Support

We have provided some discussions about related Utilities, such as PinMux and ICDI Drivers in the previous sections. In this section we will concentrate on some other Utilities.

3.8.1 Additional Utilities Provided by TivaWare™ for C Series

In this section, we will provide a quick introduction to additional Utilities provided by TivaWare™ for C Series software, which include: the LMFlash Programmer, the UniFlash, the FTDI Drivers, and the IQMath Library.

3.8.1.1 The LMFlash Programmer

LM Flash Programmer is a free flash programming utility intended to be used with Texas Instruments Tiva™ C Series and Stellaris® microcontrollers, development boards, or evaluation boards.

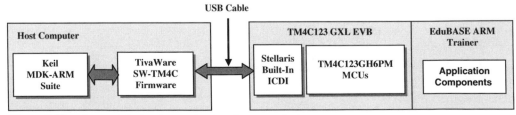

Figure 3.55. A complete development system for our project.

LM Flash Programmer is also compatible with a Stellaris® microcontroller custom board if the board has a serial (UART) interface, Ethernet interface, USB interface, or a standard JTAG connector. For the JTAG connector, a Stellaris® evaluation board can be used as an In-Circuit Debug Interface.

3.8.1.2 The UniFlash

The UniFlash provides a graphic interface for users to program their Flash targets, as well as to perform Flash Operations. Not only does the GUI provide a graphical way to interact with the UniFlash application, it also provides extra functionality like automatic session saving, providing the most recently used list, the ability to view the installed versions of each component, and, in the future, the ability to update the application using the provided dialog.

Once you have downloaded the UniFlash installer from the Download site, you can install the UniFlash application using the provided executable. During installation, on top of choosing where you would like to install the application, you will also be able to choose to install the `Complete Feature Set`, or choose specific product family of devices and communication interface support to meet your needs. The final disk usage is determined by the number of device and communication interface support you choice.

After successfully installing, there are three main ways to interact with the application:

1. Graphical User Interface (GUI)—Provides a graphic interface for users to program their Flash targets, as well as to perform Flash Operations.
2. Scripting—Provides JavaScript based scripting support for Flash Programming or Operations.
3. Command Line—Single line interface for quick access to Flash Programming/Operations.

3.8.1.3 The FTDI Drivers

The FTDI provides application-specific integrated circuit (ASIC) design services. They also provide consultancy services for product design, specifically in the realm of electronic devices. The hardware related to the FTDI is an FTDI Chip, an integrated circuit which is a common component on electronic devices using microcontrollers, such as the Arduino physical computing platform (up to before Arduino Uno).

Stellaris® evaluation kits such as the DK-LM3S9D96 come with an integrated Stellaris® In-Circuit Debug Interface (ICDI) which allows for the programming and debugging of the onboard (target) LM3S microcontroller, using the LM Flash Programmer and/or any of the supported tool chains such as TI's Code Composer Studio™. Both JTAG and Serial Wire Debug (SWD) are supported. In order to use the onboard FTDI-based ICDI interface, Stellaris® FTDI drivers must be first installed on the host computer.

3.8.1.4 The IQMath Library

The Texas Instruments™ Stellaris® IQmath Library is a collection of highly optimized and highprecision mathematical functions for C/C++ programmers to seamlessly port a floating-point algorithm into fixed-point code on Stellaris® devices. These routines are typically used in computationally intensive real-time applications where optimal execution speed and high accuracy is critical. By using the IQmath library, it is possible to achieve execution speeds considerably faster than equivalent code written using floating-point math.

The following tool chains and IDEs are supported:

- Keil® RealView® Microcontroller Development Kit
- CodeSourcery Sourcery G++ for Stellaris® EABI
- IAR Embedded Workbench®
- Code Red Technologies tools
- Texas Instruments Code Composer Studio™

The following functions are provided by this library:

- IQmath Data Type
- Calling IQmath Functions From C
- Calling IQmath Functions From C++
- Selecting the GLOBAL_Q Format
- Converting An IQmath Application To Floating-Point
- IQmath Function Groups

3.8.1.5 TivaWare™ for C Series CMSIS Support

Texas Instruments, with the C Series of ARM® Cortex®-M microcontrollers (MCUs), supports the ARM® Cortex® Microcontroller Software Interface Standard (CMSIS), a standardized hardware abstraction layer for the Cortex-M processor series. The CMSIS enables consistent and simple software interfaces to the processor core and simple basic MCU peripherals for silicon vendors and middleware providers, simplifying software reuse, reducing the learning curve for new microcontroller developers, and reducing the time to market for new devices.

The CMSIS DSP library includes source code and example applications, and saves time by including common DSP algorithms such as complex arithmetic, vector operations, and filters and control functions. The ARM® Cortex®-M4 core uses the DSP SIMD instruction set and floating-point hardware that enhances the Tiva™ C Series microcontroller algorithm capabilities for digital signal control applications.

A standardized software interface allows developers to make the switch from a competitive MCU to TI's Tiva™ C Series microcontrollers and more easily migrates the existing software to any C Series microcontroller

Many microcontroller-based applications can benefit from the use of an efficient digital signal processing (DSP) library. To that end, ARM® has developed a set of functions called the CMSIS DSP library that is compatible with all Cortex®-M3 and -M4 processors and that is specifically designed to use ARM® assembly instructions to quickly and easily handle various complex DSP functions. Currently, ARM® supplies example projects for use in their Keil® μVision IDE that are meant to show how to build their CMSIS DSP libraries and run them on an M3 or M4.

The basic idea of using this TivaWare™ for C Series support to CMSIS is to develop a set of interface functions to access the CMSIS DSP Library files developed by the ARM® in the Keil® ARM-MDK environment from the TivaWare™ for C Series evaluation boards.

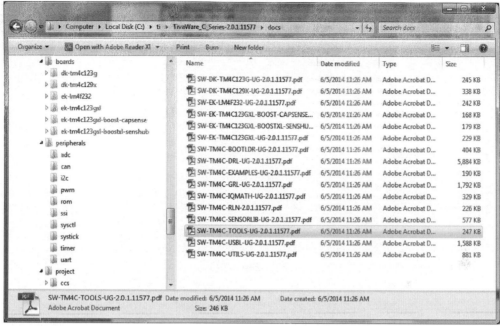

Figure 3.56. The example programs.

A complete CMSIS DSP Library is under development by the TI, and some application examples can be found in the CCS IDE for TivaWare™ for C Series evaluation boards.

3.9 PROGRAM EXAMPLES

When you finished downloading and installing TivaWare™ for C Series software package, SW-EK-TM4C123GXL, a group of example programs is also installed in your host computer. These example programs are categorized into three subfolders:

- Boards
- Peripherals
- Project

Depends on different evaluation boards and peripheral devices used in your project, the example programs are located at different folders, as shown in Figure 3.56.

Under the `boards` folder, four kinds of evaluation boards, DK-4M123G, DK-4M129X, EK-TM4C1232, and EK-TM4C123GXL, related to four different example programs are stored in those folders.

Under the `peripherals` folder, different example programs related to those devices are located at different subfolders.

Currently only some example programs are provided for the CCS IDE, therefore only one subfolder, `ccs`, is located under the `project` folder.

3.10 CHAPTER SUMMARY

The main topics in this chapter are about the microcontroller device development environments and kits.

To successfully develop and build your embedded application software for specified microcontroller unit (MCU), you need the following kits or tools:

- Microcontroller Development Kits (MDK)
- Application specified development kits
- Software examples

Since we used the Keil® ARM® Microcontroller Development Kits (MDK) and TivaWare™ for C Series evaluation kits in this book, we concentrated our discussions on these two components.

The contents on this chapter include:

1. An overview and introduction to the MDK and related kits.
2. The entire Tiva TM4C123G based development kits.
3. The related development suite and specified firmware.
4. An introduction to the Integrated Development Environment - Keil® MDK μVersion5.
5. Embedded software development procedure.
6. The ARM-MDK μVision5 debugger and debug process.
7. The TivaWare™ for C Series software suite.
8. The TivaWare™ for C Series Utilities and other supports.
9. Program examples

In Section 3.4, detailed introductions and discussions about the Keil® ARM-MDK μVersion5 are given since this kit is a key to build our user projects. These discussions include:

- A step-to-step introduction to each menu and menu items in the Keil® ARM-MDK μVersion5 IDE.
- A real sample project MyProject, which is used to facilitate the introductions to those menus.

In Section 3.7, a detailed discussion about the TivaWare™ for C Series software development package and related firmware is provided with the TM4C123GXL Evaluation Board used in this book.

HOMEWORK

I. True/False Selections

_____**1.** To successfully develop a microcontroller project, one needs the general –purpose development kits and the specified EVB related development kits.

_____**2.** The ICDI built-in debugger in the TM4C123GXL EVB is not compatible with the JTAG interface.

_____**3.** The Keil MDK μVersion5 kit includes an Integrated Development Environment (IDE) and a debug driver.

_____**4.** The debug driver is a piece of software used to perform the debug functions only.

_____**5.** One needs to use both debug adapter and debug driver to perform debug related functions.

_____**6.** In TivaWare for C Series LaunchPad EVB, the debug adapter is built-in unit on the EVB.

_____**7.** Starting Keil MDK μVersion5, the kit is split into MDK Core and Software Packs. The MDK Core includes a μVersion IDE with editor, a C/C++ compiler and a debugger.

_____**8.** One needs to use MDK Core, CMSIS Core and Device Startup to successfully build a basic ARM-MDK project.

_____**9.** JTAG is the industry-standard interface used to download and debug programs on a target processor, as well as many other functions.

_____**10.** The TivaWare for C Series software package includes two libraries, Peripheral Driver Library and USB Library.

II. Multiple Choices

1. The Tiva™ C Series TM4C123G evaluation board is composed of _____ TM4C123GH6PM MCU(s).

    a. 1

    b. 2

    c. 3

    d. 4

2. To build a basic microcontroller project, one needs _____.

    a. Development Kits

    b. Debug Adaptor and Drivers

    c. Specified MCU-related Firmware

    d. Development or Evaluation Boards

    e. All of the above

3. The Keil MDK Core contains _____.

    a. μVersion IDE with Source Editor and GUI

    b. ARM® C/C++ Compiler and Pack Installer

    c. μVersion Debugger

    d. All of the above

4. Two important components in the MDK Software Packs are _____.

    a. Device Supports and Middleware

    b. CMSIS libraries and Middleware

    c. Board support and Code Templates

    d. CMSIS and Device Supports

5. The CMSIS application software components include _____.

    a. CMSIS:CORE, CMSIS:RTOS

    b. CMSIS:CORE, CMSIS:DSP

    c. Device:Startup, CMSIS:CORE

    d. CMSIS:CORE, CMSIS:RTOS, CMSIS:DSP

6. The μVersion debugger in the Keil MDK Core can _____.

    a. Perform the debugging functions for the user's program

    b. Download the user's image files into the flash ROM in the EVB

    c. Both a and b

    d. None of the above

7. The μVision5 offers a _____ for creating applications and a _____ for debugging applications.

    a. Debug Mode and Running Mode

    b. Debug Mode and Download Mode

    c. Build Mode and Debug Mode

    d. Build Mode and Running Mode

8. When the `Load Application at Startup` checkbox in the `Debug` tab under the `Options for Target Project` menu is selected, your image file will be automatically download to the flash ROM as the _____.

    a. Flash|Download menu item is selected

    b. Debug process begins

    c. Debug process is done

    d. Debug|Run menu item is selected

9. The TivaWare C Series Software Package includes _____.

    a. Code functions and object libraries

    b. Utilities and RTOS

    c. Boot Loader and In-System Programming

    d. All of the above

10. Tiva™ C Series TM4C123G LaunchPad Evaluation Kit is composed of the following components: _____.

    a. SW-EK-TM4C123GXL TivaWare for C Series software package

    b. EK-TM4C123GXL TivaWare for C Series Evaluation Board

    c. On-board In-Circuit Debug Interface (ICDI) and USB Cable

    d. All of the above

III. Exercises

1. Provide a brief description about components to be used to develop a basic microcontroller project.

2. Provide a brief description about components used to build a microcontroller project with Keil® MDK μVersion IDE and running in the TivaWare™ for C Series Evaluation Board EK-TM4C123GXL.

3. Explain the debug components used in Keil® μVersion5 debugger and TivaWare™ built-in ICDI in the TM4C123G Evaluation Board.

4. Explain the relationship between the general-purpose development kit (Keil® MDK) and specified TivaWare™ for C Series LaunchPad™ software package.

5. Explain the development steps used to build a basic microcontroller project with Keil® MDK μVersion5 IDE.

Chapter 4

ARM® Microcontroller Software and Instruction Set

This chapter provides general information about the ARM® Cortex®-M4 microcontroller software and instruction set. The discussion is divided into two major parts: First the ARM® Cortex®-M4 Assembly instruction set is introduced, and then the related C codes are discussed with some necessary peripheral device driver libraries provided by the vendor.

4.1 OVERVIEW AND INTRODUCTION

To make any microcontroller or computer work, some directions should be provided to enable the microcontroller to follow those directions to perform certain tasks as the user desired. In fact, those directions can be represented as a sequence of instructions that can be integrated into a group called program. Furthermore, in order to enable a microcontroller to understand the users' directions represented as programs, a programming language is necessary to perform a valid communication between the users and the microcontroller. Like human beings, different languages have been used for their communications. In the computer world, the computing languages can be categorized into two levels:

- *High-Level Language:* This kind of language is very similar to English language, and it is easy to be understood by the human beings. However, it cannot be understood by the microcontrollers or computers. Some popular high-level languages are C/C++, Visual C++, Visual Basic.NET, Visual C#, and Java. The high-level language is computer- or machine-independent, which means that this kind of language can be understood by any computer with any operating system. A translator or interpreter is needed to convert the high-level language instructions into the low-level instructions to enable microcontrollers to understand and execute them.
- *Low-Level Language:* This kind of language is composed of binary code or machine code sequence, like 01101110. The low-level language is a computer- or machine-dependent language, which means that different microcontrollers have their own language and cannot be recognized by other microcontrollers or computers.

Practical Microcontroller Engineering with ARM® Technology, First Edition. Ying Bai.
© 2016 by The Institute of Electrical and Electronics Engineers, Inc. Published 2016 by John Wiley & Sons, Inc.
Companion Website: www.wiley.com/go/armbai

In order to enable human beings to use certain language to communicate for each other, only a language is not enough. A word set written by that language is needed to allow people to use those words to represent their meaning to communicate for each other. Similarly, in order to use certain high-level programming language to develop the user's application program, an instruction set written by that language is also needed. Unlike other 8-bit or 16-bit microcontrollers, the ARM® defines its instruction set as architecture; it is called Instruction Set Architecture (ISA).

In the early days, most ARM® processors can only handle 32-bit instructions. However, as the development of new mobile and microcontroller technologies, more and more devices only need 8-bit or 16-bit instruction sets. The advantage of using short bit size is that both the size and capacity of the applications in most modern devices become small and the running speed is also faster compared with those 32-bit instruction set. Therefore a contradiction arises between the instruction lengths.

To solve this problem, ARM® developed two different instruction set architectures: (1) a traditional 32-bit instruction set that is called an ARM® instruction set and (2) a 16-bit instruction set that is called a Thumb instruction set.

However, these two instruction sets are not compatible at all. To make them compatible, ARM® developed Thumb-2 technology in 2003. This technology enables a mixture of 16-bit and 32-bit instructions to be executed within one operating state. All the ARM® Cortex®-M processors are based on Thumb-2 technology.

The advantage of using this Thumb-2 instruction set is that during the operation, the ARM® processor can switch between the ARM® state (ARM® instruction set) and the Thumb state (Thumb-2 instruction set) under the software control. Therefore some codes are compiled with ARM® instruction set for better performance, and some other codes are compiled as Thumb instructions to make the program size smaller.

Both ARM® Cortex®-M3 and Cortex®-M4 processors are based on Thumb-2 technology, however, they can only support Thumb instruction set.

All ARM® Cortex®-M4 instructions are developed by using the ARM® Cortex®-M4 assembly language, which is a low-level and processor-dependent language. There are large numbers of assembly instructions used by the ARM® Cortex®-M4 processors, but you do not need to learn all of them in details because a C compiler is available to enable users to develop their codes in the C language and translate them to the assembly and machine codes. It is easy to develop a user application with the C codes if you have some knowledge on the C language.

4.2 INTRODUCTION TO ARM® CORTEX®-M4 SOFTWARE DEVELOPMENT STRUCTURE

We have provided some discussions about the software development process under Keil® ARM® MDK environment in Chapter 3. Since we will use the Keil® ARM® MDK as our application development IDE, we just copy and re-display Figure 3.7 in this chapter to illustrate the software development process under this environment.

Figure 4.1 shows a general software development process for ARM® Cortex®-M4 processor.

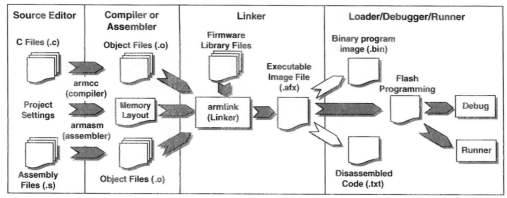

Figure 4.1. The ARM Cortex-M4 software development procedure.

Generally, a user ARM® Cortex®-M4 application program can be developed and built with the following five steps:

1. Source Editor: Create user's source code files, either C codes (.c) or assembly codes (.s).
2. Compiler or Assembler: Translate the user's codes to the machine object codes (.o).
3. Linker: Connect the system library files with the user's object files to create the final executable file (image files .afx).
4. Loader and Debugger: Load or download the user's executable or image files to the flash memory in the development board and perform debugging functions.
5. Runner: Run the user's program in the flash memory.

The Keil® ARM® MDK μVersion5 provides all of these five components. The compiler and assembler are armcc and armasm. The linker is armlink. The user's executable or image file (.afx) can be downloaded into the 256-KB flash memory space. Then two options can be selected by the users. A debugging function is available in the MDK μVersion5 IDE, which can be used to debug and test the users program. The users can also run the program in the flash memory space.

As we mentioned, over hundreds of assembly instructions are provided by ARM® Cortex®-M4 processor. However, you do not need to know them in detail because all of these instructions can be replaced by the related C codes. You can easily develop your program using the C language and convert it to the object file with the help of the ARM® Compiler armcc.

In the following sections, we will provide a brief introduction and illustration about the ARM® Cortex®-M4 instruction set. The main purpose of introducing these assembly instructions is to enable users to have a basic idea about them and use some of them during the debugging process if it is necessary.

4.3 INTRODUCTION TO ARM® CORTEX®-M4 ASSEMBLY INSTRUCTION SET

There are about 203 instructions in the ARM® Cortex®-M4 instruction set excluding the FPU related instructions. All of these instructions can be categorized into 14 groups based on the functions of those instructions. These groups include:

1. Data Moving Instructions
2. Arithmetic Instructions
3. Logic Instructions
4. Shift and Rotate Instructions
5. Data Conversion Instructions
6. Bit-Field Processing Instructions
7. Compare and Test Instructions
8. Program Flow Control Instructions
9. Saturation Instructions
10. Exception Related Instructions
11. Sleep Mode Instructions
12. Memory Barrier Instructions
13. Miscellaneous Instructions
14. Unsupported Instructions

There are about 65 FPU-related instructions if the FPU is available and enabled in the Cortex-M4 microcontroller system. All these instructions are Cortex-M4 assembly instructions with certain format or syntax. To enable the ARM® Cortex®-M4 processor to execute these instructions, an Assembler is used to convert the assembly codes into the binary codes. In order for the Assembler to do this conversion job correctly, all of these assembly instructions must follow a rule or syntax to enable the Assembler to recognize them. So first let's take a look at the format or syntax of these assembly instructions.

4.3.1 The ARM® Cortex®-M4 Assembly Language Syntax

As we mentioned in the last section, the user's source codes developed by assembly language must follow certain rules and meet some requirements to enable the assembler to recognize and understand those source codes and, furthermore, to enable the assembler to correctly convert them to the target or object codes.

Generally each user's instruction in the user's source code file is composed of four fields:

1. Label field
2. Operation field
3. Operands field
4. Comment field

Each field can be considered as a column and each column is separated with the Tab key in the user's source code file, as shown in Figure 4.2.

Let's have a closer look at these fields by discussing them one by one.

- Label Field: A label is an identifier to mark a line in the user's program. It is optional but when used it can provide a symbolic memory reference, such as a branch instruction's address or a symbol for a constant.

  A label must be located at the first column and started in the first character position in the instruction line. The length of each label is limited to 15 characters, which include upper- or

Label Field	Operation Field	Operands Field	Comment Field
NVIC_IRQ_SETEN	EQU	0xE000E100	;define NVIC SETEN
NVIC_IRQ_ENABLE	EQU	0x1	;define the NVIC Enable
START:	MOVS	R0, #0x56	; set R0 = 0x56
	MOVS	R1, #NVIC_IRQ_ENABLE	; set R1 = 0x1
	STR	R1, [R0]	; set 0x1 => 0x56

Figure 4.2.   The syntax of the ARM Cortex-M4 assembly instructions.

lowercase letters (a~z), digits 0~9, a period, a dollar sign, and an underscore. The first character must be alphabetic, a period, or an underscore. A label may end with a colon. Refer to Figure 4.2 for an example of using the label START.

- Operation Field: This field is also called Mnemonic Field. Two types of instructions may appear in this field: the opcode and the pseudo-instruction, which we will discuss in the next section. The opcode is the mnemonic form of a Cortex-M4 instruction and it tells the microprocessor what kind of operation should be performed, such as MOV, STR, and so on. The pseudo instruction tells the assembler what to do. An example of using this pseudo instruction is EQU. Refer to Figure 4.2 for an example of using the operation EQU.

- Operands Field: The operands field contains the data or an address for its corresponding instruction to be operated or performed. Both opcodes and pseudo codes can have operands. The number of operands depends on the type of instructions. Some instructions do not necessarily need any operand, such as NOP, SEV, and WFI instructions. However, some other instructions may need one, two, or three operands, such as SADD8 R0, R1, and R5. The operands must follow the opcode.

- Comment Field: This field enables users to place some comments for each instruction to illustrate the function or purpose of the related instruction line. All comments must start with the semi-colon (;) to tell the assembler that this is a comment, and the assembler will not convert any comment to the object codes. Refer to Figure 4.2 for an example of using the comments.

Since the Operands field may contain multiple operands and the following rules are useful to define the related operand:

- For data processing instructions written for the ARM® assembler, the first operand is the destination of the operation.
- For a memory read instruction, excluding multiple load instructions, the first operand is the destination register that data is to be loaded into.
- For a memory write instruction, excluding multiple store instructions, the first operand is the source register that holds the data to be written into the memory.
- For a multiple load instruction, the register list which is the third operand is the destination operand that the data will be loaded into.
- For a multiple store instruction, the register list which is the third operand is the source operand that the stored data will be written into the memory.

When using ARM® Cortex®-M4 assembly instructions to build the user's applications, the following points must be paid attention to:

1. For each instruction, the Label and Comment fields are optional. However, the Operation and Operands fields are necessary parts.

2. An instruction operand can be an ARM® register, a constant, or another instruction-specific parameter. When there is a destination register in the instruction, it is usually specified before the operands. Operands in some instructions are flexible and they can either be a register or a constant.

3. Bit 0 of any address written to the PC with a BX, BLX, LDM, LDR, or POP instruction must be 1 for correct execution, because this bit indicates the required instruction set, and the Cortex-M4 processor only supports thumb instructions

In order to enable the assembler to successfully convert the user's source codes into the object codes, the user's program must provide a full description about the user's source codes to enable the assembler to recognize and understand each instruction in the user's program, and furthermore to transfer it to the target or object codes.

To meet this requirement, we need to introduce the pseudo assembly instructions provided by the ARM® Cortex®-M4 Assembler. The so-called pseudo assembly instructions mean that these codes are not real Cortex-M4 program assembly instructions. Instead, they are a set of assembler-helping codes to assist the assembler to assign and define memory spaces for user's variables, constants, and program. These pseudo assembly instructions will not be converted to the object codes when the assembler is executed.

4.3.2 The ARM® Cortex®-M4 Pseudo Instructions

Generally, the function of the pseudo assembly instructions is to help and assist the ARM® Cortex®-M4 assembler to convert and build the user's object code file. These assistants include the final real flash memory addresses in which the user's target program, data, constants, and labels should be located and stored, the memory spaces reserved, and the ending point for the user's object code program to be determined. Table 4.1 shows a list of most popular pseudo assembly instructions used by ARM® Cortex®-M4 Assembler working for Keil® MDK-ARM®. Different IDE vendors may provide different assemblers with different pseudo instruction sets.

In ARM® Cortex®-M4 system, all data are categorized into the following data types:

- A 64-bit data item is called a Double-Word and its length is 8 bytes.
- A 32-bit data item is called a Word and its length is 4 bytes.
- A 16-bit data item is called a Half-Word and its length is 2 bytes.
- An 8-bit data item is called a Byte and its length is 1 byte.

One point to be noted for these pseudo instructions is the different roles played by THUMB and CODE16. Both instructions are used to ask the assembler to treat the following codes as Thumb (16-bit) codes. However, the THUMB indicates to the assembler that the following codes should be Thumb codes in a Unified Assembly Language (UAL) format, but the CODE16 asks the assembler to treat the following codes as Thumb codes with a pre-UAL format. The difference between the UAL and pre-UAL format is:

- The pre-UAL is an early Thumb syntax and only suitable to the Thumb instruction set.
- The UAL is a new Thumb-2 syntax and it is more powerful in cross-platform or cross-architecture applications.

Table 4.1. Popular pseudo instructions used in Cortex-M4 MCU.

Pseudo Instruction	Function	Example
DCB n	Reserve 1 byte space (8-bit) for data	DCB 1, DCB 0x25
DCW n	Reserve half-word space (16-bit) for data	DCW 2, DCW 0x1234
DCD n	Reserve 1 word space (32-bit) for data	DCD 0x12345678
DCQ n	Reserve 2 words space (64-bit) for data	DCQ 0x0123456789ABCDEF
DCFS n	Define a single precision floating point data	DCFS 1E3
DCFD n	Define a single precision floating point data	DCFD 3.141593
DCB s	Reserve a space for a String	DCB "Hello World\n" 0
DCI n	Reserve a space for an instruction	DCI 0xBE00
ALIGN n	Align the current location to a specified boundary by padding with 0 or NOP instructions. The following number **n** is the number of bytes to be aligned	ALIGN 4: align the next data or instruction to 4 bytes or a word boundary
AREA section_name	Ask assembler to assemble a new code or data section	
CODE16	Specify assembly codes as Thumb codes (16-bit)	
EXPORT symbol	Declare a symbol that can be used by the linker to resolve symbol references in separate object or library files	
FILL num_of_bytes	Reserve a block of memory and fill it with the specific value	
IMPORT symbol	Declare a symbol reference in separate object or library files that is to be resolved by linker	
LTORG	Ask assembler to assemble the current literal pool immediately	
THUMB	Specify assembly codes as Thumb codes in UAL format	

The pre-UAL syntax is still accepted by most IEDs, including the Keil® MDK-ARM®. But it is highly recommended to use the UAL syntax for new projects.

Pseudo instructions are very useful to help users to build and develop their application programs by providing more controls and managements to the memory space, variables, and constants used in the program.

Before we can start our discussion about the detailed instruction set, first let's have a clear picture about the addressing modes used in the Cortex-M4 assembler system.

4.3.3 The ARM® Cortex®-M4 Addressing Modes

Generally there are seven addressing modes used in the ARM® Cortex®-M4 assembly language system, and they are:

1. Immediate Offset Addressing Mode
2. Register Offset Addressing Mode
3. PC-Relative Addressing Mode
4. Load and Store Multiple Registers Addressing Mode
5. PUSH and POP Register Addressing Mode
6. Load and Store Register Exclusive Addressing Mode
7. Inherent Addressing Mode

Let's take a closer look at each of these addressing modes one by one.

4.3.3.1 The Immediate Offset Addressing Mode

To access a memory space to load or store a data item, a valid target memory address is needed to do this loading and storing operation. In Cortex-M4 system, this target address is obtained by adding an offset to a base address that is stored in a register. The offset value can be positive or negative, and the register used to store a base address can be any general-purpose register R0~R12. Depending on the different ways to calculate the target memory address, four different Immediate Offset Addressing Modes are available:

1. Regular Immediate Offset Addressing Mode
2. Pre-Indexed Immediate Offset Addressing Mode
3. Post-Indexed Immediate Offset Addressing Mode
4. Regular Immediate Offset Addressing Mode with Unprivileged Access

4.3.3.1.1 Regular Immediate Offset Addressing Mode   The syntax of this addressing mode is:

LDR{type} Rd, [Rn, {#Offset}];	for example,	LDRB R0, [R2, #0x5];
STR{type} Rt, [Rn, {#Offset}];	for example,	STRSB R0, [R2, #0x10];

where the {type} is one of the following:

- B: Unsigned byte, zero extends to 32 bits on loads
- SB: Signed byte, sign extends to 32 bits (LDR only)
- H: Unsigned halfword, zero extends to 32 bits on loads
- SH: Signed halfword, sign extends to 32 bits (LDR only)
- -: Omit, for word

The Rd is the destination register for the Load Data from the memory into the Register (LDR), but the Rt is the source register for the Store data from the Register into the memory (STR). The Rn is the register that contains a base memory address. The Offset must be prefixed with a # sign to indicate that it is an immediate number or offset.

The square bracket [] covering the Rn and an Offset indicates that the combination of the content of the Rn and the Offset is a valid memory address. In general, the square bracket sign [] means the content of the operand inside the [], not the operand itself. For instance, if the register R2 stores a hexadecimal number 0x01234567, the [R2] means the content of the R2, which is equivalent to a memory address 0x1234567, not R2 itself.

The running result of executing the LDRB R0, [R2, #0x5] is to load an unsigned byte located at a memory address that is equal to the sum of the content of the R2 and 0x5, 0x1234567 + 0x5 = 0x123456C, into the register R0. In this mode, the offset is an immediate number and the content of the register R2 keeps unchanged after the execution of this instruction.

The range of the offset depends on the operation mode used in the instruction. For the regular Immediate Offset mode, the offset is ranged −255~4095.

4.3.3.1.2 Pre-Indexed Immediate Offset Addressing Mode

Similarly to the Immediate Offset Addressing mode we discussed above, the operation procedure for this mode is:

1. The target memory address is first calculated by summing the content of the register Rn and the Offset (Pre-Indexed).
2. Then the data item stored in that target address will be loaded into the destination register Rt (for LDR instructions). For the STR operations, the data item stored in the source register Rt will be written into the target memory address.

The only difference between this mode and the regular Immediate Offset mode is that the content of the register Rn will be modified after running this instruction. For example, after the instruction LDRB R0, [R2, #0x5] is executed, the content of the register R2 will be changed to 0x123456C. However, the content of this register will be kept unchanged after running the regular Immediate Offset mode instructions.

4.3.3.1.3 Post-Indexed Immediate Offset Addressing Mode

The only difference between this mode and the previous modes is that the target memory address is directly obtained from the register Rn without using the Offset value. Then either the loading or storing instructions use this address as the target memory address to access the memory to perform either loading or storing operations. After the instruction is executed, a combination of the content of the register Rn and the offset is performed, and this sum is sent back to the register Rn. This means that the content of the register Rn is modified or changed *after* (*post*) this mode's instruction is executed. The difference between this mode and the Pre-Indexed Immediate Offset mode is that the target address is first calculated based on the Rn and the Offset before accessing the memory in the pre-Indexed mode, however, this mode directly uses the content of the register Rn as the target memory address to access the memory without using the Offset value.

For example, to run LDRB R0, [R2, #0x5] instruction in this mode, the target memory address is the content of the register R2, which is 0x1234567. The data item located at this address will be loaded into the register R0. Then the content of the register R2 is added with the offset 0x5 to get the target address 0x123456C, and this target address is sent to the R2. After running this instruction, the content of the register R2 is changed to 0x123456C, not 0x1234567.

4.3.3.1.4 Regular Immediate Offset Addressing Mode with Unprivileged Access

The syntax of this addressing mode is:

LDR{type}T Rd, [Rn, {#Offset}];	for example,	LDRBT R0, [R2, #0x5];
STR{type}T Rt, [Rn, {#Offset}];	for example,	STRSBTR0, [R2, #0x10];

Table 4.2. The offset range for different addressing modes.

Instruction Type	Immediate Offset	Pre-Indexed	Post-Indexed
Word, halfword, Signed halfword, Byte, Signed Byte	$-255 \sim 4095$	$-255 \sim 255$	$-255 \sim 255$
Double Words	$4 \times (-1020 \sim 1020)$	$4 \times (-1020 \sim 1020)$	$4 \times (-1020 \sim 1020)$

where the {type} is one of the following:

- B: Unsigned byte, zero extends to 32 bits on loads
- SB: Signed byte, sign extends to 32 bits (LDR only)
- H: Unsigned halfword, zero extends to 32 bits on loads
- SH: Signed halfword, sign extends to 32 bits (LDR only)

These load and store instructions perform the same function as the Regular Immediate Offset Addressing Mode did. The difference is that these instructions have only unprivileged access even when used in the privileged software. When used in the unprivileged software, these instructions perform exactly the same function as regular memory access instructions with immediate offset.

Table 4.2 shows the ranges of the Offset values used for the different operation modes. It can be found that the regular immediate offset addressing mode has a larger offset range.

4.3.3.2 The Register Offset Addressing Mode

The operation of this addressing mode is similar to that of the Immediate Offset Addressing Mode. The only difference between this mode and the Immediate Offset mode is that this mode uses a register to replace the immediate offset. In other words, the content of one register works as an offset for the target memory address.

The syntax of this kind of instruction is:

```
LDR{type} Rd, [Rn, Rm, {LSL #n}];    for example,   LDRB R0, [R2, R5];
STR{type} Rt, [Rn, Rm, {LSL #n}];    for example,   STRSB R0, [R2, R5, LSL #2];
```

where the {type} is one of the following:

- B: Unsigned byte, zero extends to 32 bits on loads
- SB: Signed byte, sign extends to 32 bits (LDR only)
- H: Unsigned halfword, zero extends to 32 bits on loads
- SH: Signed halfword, sign extends to 32 bits (LDR only)
- -: Omit, for word

Four registers Rt, Rd, Rn, and Rm are used in this mode and a LSL (Logic Shift Left) instruction with the number of shift bits is an optional operation. The function of this mode is as follows:

For loading data from the memory and putting it into the destination register, the Rd is the destination register. The register Rn stores a base address and the register Rm stores an offset. Before performing the sum operation to combine the Rn (base address) and the Rm (offset) to get the target memory address, an LSL #n instruction could be used to shift Rm left up to 3 bits, which is equivalent to multiple Rm by 8. The range of the shifting bit n is 0~3. Since the LSL #n shift instruction is an optional, it is covered by a brace sign {}.

The target memory address can be obtained by using

$$\text{Target Memory Address} = \underset{\text{(Base address)}}{\text{The content of Rn [Rn]}} +$$
$$\underset{\text{(Offset)}}{\text{The content of Rm [Rm]}} \times 2^n, n = 0\text{~}3.$$

Then the instruction goes to the target memory address to pick the data item stored in that address and load it into the register Rt.

For storing data from the register to the memory, calculate the target memory address as above. Then write the data item stored in the source register Rt into the target memory address.

For instance, the instruction LDRSB R0, [R5, R1, LSL #1]; is to read a byte value from a target address that is equal to sum of R5 and two times R1, and sign-extend it to a word value and put it into the register R0. If the R5 contains a hexadecimal value: 0x12345678 and the R1 contains another hexadecimal value: 0x00000002, then the target address is $0x12345678 + 2 \times 0x00000002 = 0x1234567C$. The data byte stored in the address 0x1234567C is loaded, and the sign is extended to 32 bits and put into the register R0.

Another example is the instruction STR R0, [R5, R1]; This instruction is to store the content of R0 into an address that is equal to the sum of R5 and R1. Still using the contents of R5 and R1 in the above example, the target address is $0x12345678 + 0x00000002 = 0x1234567A$. The content of the source register R0 will be stored into the target memory address 0x1234567A.

One condition of using this mode is that the registers Rn and Rm must not be PC or SP.

4.3.3.3 The PC-Relative Addressing Mode

This mode is similar with the Immediate Offset Addressing Mode, and the only difference for this mode is that the current PC value is used to replace the content of the base address register Rn. In other words, the current PC value works a base address for the target memory address. The final target memory address is a sum of the PC value and an offset. The offset can be considered as a relative index to the current PC value.

The syntax of this kind of instruction is

LDR{type} Rd, [PC, #Offset];	for example, LDRB R0, [PC, #0x30];
LDRD{type} Rd, Rd2, [PC, #Offset];	for example, LDRD R0, R1, [PC, #0x200];

where the {type} is one of the following:

- B: Unsigned byte, zero extends to 32 bits on loads
- SB: Signed byte, sign extends to 32 bits

Table 4.3.   The PC relative offset range for different instruction types.

Instruction Type	Offset Range
Word, halfword, Signed halfword, Byte, Signed Byte	$-4095 \sim 4095$
Double Words	$-1020 \sim 1020$

- H: Unsigned halfword, zero extends to 32 bits on loads
- SH: Signed halfword, sign extends to 32 bits
- -: Omit, for word

The LDR instruction loads the destination register Rd with a data item whose address is a sum of the current PC value and the offset. The loaded byte and halfword will be extended to 32-bit.

The LDRD instruction loads the destination registers Rd and Rd2 with double words whose address is a sum of the current PC value and the offset. The lower word is loaded into the Rd and the higher word is loaded into the Rd2.

The value to be loaded can be a byte, halfword, or word. The loaded bytes and halfwords can either be signed or unsigned, but both loaded byte and halfword must be extended to 32-bit.

Three points must be noted when using this addressing mode:

1. The current PC value should be exactly equal to the current PC value plus 4.
2. The offset must be within a limited range relative to the current PC value. An error may be generated by the Assembler if the offset is beyond this limitation. Table 4.3 shows some offset limitations used for the different instructions.
3. The bit 1 or bit[1] of the target address must be cleared to 0 to make it word-aligned.

The reason why the current PC value is $PC+4$ is because the so-called current PC value exactly should be the address of the next instruction, not the current instruction. This is due to the calculation process used by the Assembler. When the Assembler calculates the target address, the PC value used by the Assembler is the address of the next instruction ($PC+4$), not the address of the current instruction (PC) since this instruction takes 4 bytes space itself. To correctly calculate the relative interval or offset between the current instruction's address and the target address, the starting address should not be the current instruction's address since it already takes 4 bytes space. Therefore the correct starting address should be the next instruction's address, which is $PC+4$, since each instruction takes 32-bit or 4 bytes space.

The reason why the bit 1 or bit[1] in the result target address must be 0 is because each instruction takes 4 bytes space in ARM® Cortex®-M4 system. To align each 8-bit or 16-bit instruction to a word (32-bit) instruction, the bit 1 should be 0 since the last two bits (bit 1 and bit 0) on each instruction should be a sequence of $00 \rightarrow 01 \rightarrow 10 \rightarrow 11$. The next instruction should repeat this sequence to get another 4 bytes space, $00 \rightarrow 01 \rightarrow 10 \rightarrow 11$. In this way, the starting address of each instruction on the last two bits, bit 1 and bit 0, is always 00. Therefore bit 1 should always be 0 to make sure that each instruction is a word (32-bit).

Some restrictions may be applied when using these instructions:

- Rd2 must be neither SP nor PC
- Rd must be different from Rd2
- Rd can be SP or PC only for word loads

4.3.3.4 Load and Store Multiple Registers Addressing Mode

The LDM and STM instructions enable users to load and store multiple data items that are contiguous in the memory space. These instructions only support 32-bit data.

The syntax of these kinds of instructions is

LDM{mode} Rn{!}, {reglist};	for example,	LDM R0!, {R1, R2, R3};
STM{mode} Rn{!}, {reglist};	for example,	STMDB R1!, {R3–R6, R11, R12};

where the {mode} is one of the following:

- IA: **I**ncrement the target address **A**fter the Load or Store operation
- DB: **D**ecrement the target address **B**efore the Load or Store operation

The Rn is the address register used to store a valid memory address. The instructions can use this address to load from or store into any data items starting from that address.

The exclamation sign ! is an optional writeback suffix. If it is present, the target address that is loaded from or stored to is written back into the address register Rn.

The `reglist` is a list of multiple registers to be loaded, or stored, and it should be comma-separated if more than one register is used or multiple ranges are used. The reglist can contain a register range, such as R0~R3.

The LDM instructions load the registers in reglist with word values from memory addresses stored in the Rn. The STM instructions store the word values in the registers in the reglist to memory addresses stored in the Rn.

For the LDM, LDMIA, STM, and STMIA instructions, the memory addresses to be accessed are at 4-byte intervals ranging from Rn to $Rn + 4 \times (n-1)$, where n is the order number of registers in `reglist`. The accesses happen in an order of increasing register numbers, with the lowest numbered register using the lowest memory address and the highest number register using the highest memory address. If the exclamation sign ! is present, the final address $Rn + 4 \times n$ is written back to Rn.

For example, the instruction LDMIA R0!, {R1, R2, R3}; is to load 3 words of data starting from the memory address indicated in the register R0 and put them into three registers R1, R2, and R3. Three registers, R1, R2, and R3, in the `reglist` are numbered as 1, 2, and 3. If the address in the R0 is 0x12345678, the following operational sequence will be executed to fulfill this instruction:

- For the first register located in the reglist R1, which is numbered 1. The first word located in the starting address $R0 + 4 \times (n-1) = 0x12345678 + 4 \times (1-1) = 0x12345678$ is loaded into the register R1. This word takes 4 bytes with a range of 0x12345678~0x1234567B.

- For the second register located in the reglist R2, which is numbered 2. The second word located in the starting address $R0 + 4 \times (n-1) = 0x12345678 + 4 \times (2-1) = 0x12345678 + 0x4 = 0x1234567C$ is loaded into the register R2. This word takes 4 bytes with a range of 0x1234567C ~ 0x1234567F.

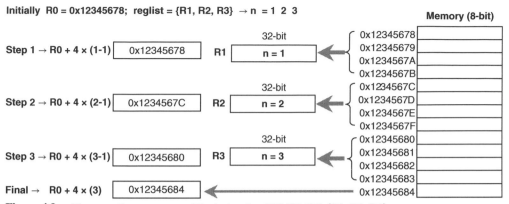

Figure 4.3. The operation sequence of the instruction LDMIA R0!, {R1, R2, R3}.

- For the third register located in the reglist R3, which is numbered 3. The third word located in the starting address $R0 + 4 \times (n-1) = 0x12345678 + 4 \times (3-1) = 0x12345678 + 0x8 = 0x12345680$ is loaded into the register R3. This word takes 4 bytes with a range of $0x12345680 \sim 0x12345683$.

- Finally the final address $R0 + 4 \times n = 0x12345678 + 4 \times 3 = 0x12345678 + 12D = 0x12345678 + 0x0C = 0x12345684$ is written back into the R0 since an exclamation sign ! is present following the register R0 in this instruction.

Figure 4.3 shows the operation sequence for this instruction.

For the LDMDB and STMDB instructions, the memory addresses to be accessed are at 4-byte intervals ranging from Rn to Rn − 4 * n, where n is the order number of registers in reglist. The accesses happen in an order of decreasing register numbers, with the lowest numbered register using the highest memory address and the highest number register using the lowest memory address. If the exclamation sign ! is present, the value Rn − 4 × n is written back to Rn.

Another example is the instruction STMDB R1!, {R3−R6, R11, R12};. This instruction is to store 6 registers' contents, including R3, R4, R5, R6, R11, and R12 (6 words), into the memory address starting at R1 − 4 × n. The order numbers for these six registers are: R3 → 1, R4 → 2, R5 → 3, R6 → 4, R11 → 5, R12 → 6. Assume that the R1 contains a hexadecimal value 0x00008000, the following sequence will be executed to fulfill this instruction:

- For the first register R3 whose order number is 1, its content is stored into the memory address starting at R1 − 4×n = 0x8000 - 4×1 = 0x7FFC. This word takes 4 bytes with a range of 0x7FFC ~ 0x8000. Since the mode is DB, therefore a decrement is performed first before the data storing.

- For the second register R4 whose order number is 2, its content is stored into the memory address starting at R1 − 4 × n = 0x8000 - 4 × 2 = 0x8000 − 0x8 = 0x7FF8. This word takes 4 bytes with a range of 0x7FF8~0x7FFB.

- For the third register R5 whose order number is 3, its content is stored into the memory address starting at R1 − 4 × n = 0x8000 − 4 × 3 = 0x8000 − 12D = 0x8000 − 0x0C = 0x7FF4. This word takes 4 bytes with a range of 0x7FF4~0x7FF7.

- For the fourth register R6 whose order number is 4, its content is stored into the memory address starting at R1 − 4 × n = 0x8000 − 4 × 4 = 0x8000 − 0x10 = 0x7FF0. This word takes 4 bytes with a range of 0x7FF0~0x7FF3.

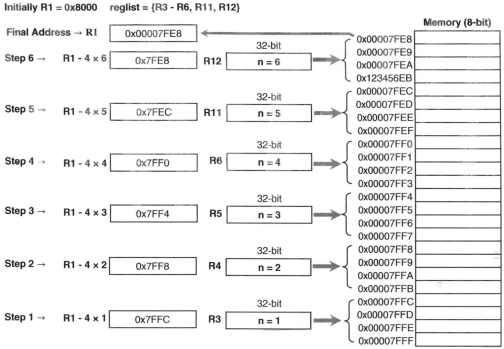

Figure 4.4.   The running sequence of the instruction STMDB R1!,{R3–R6, R11, R12}.

- For the fifth register R11 whose order number is 5, its content is stored into the memory address starting at R1 − 4×n = 0x8000 − 4×5 = 0x8000 − 0x14 = 0x7FEC. This word takes 4 bytes with a range of 0x7FEC~0x7FEF.
- For the sixth register R12 whose order number is 6, its content is stored into the memory address starting at R1 − 4×n = 0x8000 − 4×6 = 0x8000 − 24D = 0x8000 − 0x18 = 0x7FE8. This word takes 4 bytes with a range of 0x7FE8~0x7FEB.
- The final address R1 − 4×n = 0x8000 − 4×6 = 0x8000 − 24D = 0x8000 − 0x18 = 0x7FE8 is written back to the R1 since a ! sign is present after the register R1.

Figure 4.4 shows the operation sequence for this instruction.
Some restrictions are applied when using these instructions:

- The register Rn cannot be PC.
- The reglist cannot contain SP.
- In any STM instruction, the reglist cannot contain PC.
- In any LDM instruction, the reglist cannot contain PC if it contains LR.
- The reglist must not contain Rn if you specify the writeback suffix when PC is in the reglist in an LDM instruction:
  - Bit[0] of the value loaded to the PC must be 1 for correct execution, and a branch occurs to this halfword-aligned address.
  - If the instruction is conditional, it must be the last instruction in the IT block.

Next let's take care of the PUSH and POP Register Addressing Mode.

4.3.3.5 PUSH and POP Register Addressing Mode

The PUSH instruction is used to store registers into the memory space and the POP instruction performs an opposite operation, which is to load the data items into the registers from the memory space.

The function of the PUSH instruction is similar to that of the STMDB instruction discussed in the last section, and the function of the POP instruction is similar to that of the LDM (or LDMIA) instruction discussed in the last section. The syntaxes of these instructions are:

PUSH {reglist};	for example,	PUSH {R0, R3–R5, R9};
POP {reglist};	for example,	POP {R2, R3};

The definition for the reglist is same as those used for the LDM and STM instructions. Multiple registers can be used in the reglist with each register being separated with comma, and the register ranges can also be used.

Some restrictions are applied when using these instructions, they are as follows:

- The reglist cannot contain **SP**.
- For the PUSH instruction, the reglist cannot contain **PC**.
- For the POP instruction, the reglist cannot contain **PC** if it contains **LR**.

We have provided very detailed discussions about the PUSH and POP instructions in Section 2.3.2 in Chapter 2. Refer to that section for more details about these instructions.

4.3.3.6 Load and Store Register Exclusive Addressing Mode

Both the Load Register Exclusive mode and the Store Register Exclusive mode are a special group of memory accessing instructions. Normally they are used for a system or environment that contains multiple sources to access the memory devices, and those sources can share a common memory space. In that case, a control strategy is used to select and enable only one source to access the memory device at a time. Different control strategies have been developed to do this kind of selection, such as Semaphores or Mutex (Mutual Exclusive).

In Load Register Exclusive and Store Register Exclusive modes, a destination register Rd is used to perform this kind of control and selection.

The syntaxes of these instructions are:

LDREX Rt, [Rn, #Offset];	for example,	LDREX R0, [R1, #0x12];
STREX Rd, Rt, [Rn, #Offset];	for example,	SREX R0, R1, [R2, #0x0B];
LDREXB Rt, [Rn];	for example,	LDREXB R0, [R1];
STREXB Rd, Rt, [Rn];	for example,	STREXB R0, R5, [R1];
LDREXH Rt, [Rn];	for example,	LDREXH R0, [R1];
STREXH Rd, Rt, [Rn];	for example,	STREXH R0, R1, [R2];

where

- Rd: The destination register for returned status.
- Rt: The register to load or store.
- Rn: The register stored the memory address to be accessed to load or store.
- Offset: Is an optional value to be applied with the address in Rn to get the target address.

The LDREX, LDREXB, and LDREXH can be used to load a word, byte, and halfword respectively from a memory address and put them into the register Rt.

The STREX, STREXB, and STREXH instructions are used to store a word, byte, and halfword respectively from the register Rt to a memory address.

The address used in any Store-Exclusive instruction must be the same as the address in the most recently executed Load-Exclusive instruction. The value stored by the Store-Exclusive instruction must also have the same data size as the value loaded by the preceding Load-Exclusive instruction. This means that both LDRXX and STRXX instructions must be used in pair with the LDRXX instruction being first and the STRXX instruction being second.

The destination register Rd is used to store the current memory-accessing status. When it is reset to 0 by a STRXX instruction, it indicated that no other source is accessing the memory device between the current Load-exclusive and Store-Exclusive instructions.

Some restrictions are applied when using these instructions:

- Do not use **PC** for any register.
- Do not use **SP** for Rd and Rt.
- For the STREX instruction, Rd should be different from both Rt and Rn.
- The value of the Offset must be in the range $4 \times (0\text{--}1020)$.

Finally let's take a look at the Inherent Addressing Mode.

4.3.3.7 Inherent Addressing Mode

The so-called Inherent Addressing Mode means that both operands are registers and all operational data are located inside registers without needing to access the memory space.

Most Arithmetic and Logic as well as Shift and Rotate instructions use this addressing mode, such as the instructions ADD Rd, Rn, Rm; SBC Rd, Rn, Rm; AND Rd, Rn; ASR Rd, Rn. Some other instructions using this mode include:

Compare Instruction: CMP.

Compare Negative Instruction: CMN.

Signed and Unsigned Extension Instructions: SXTB, SXTH, UXTB.

Reversing Data Instructions: REV, REVSH.

Test Instruction: TST.

Now let's give a quick summary about these addressing modes.

4.3.3.8 Addressing Mode Summary

Figure 4.5 provides a graphic summary presentation of most memory accessing addressing modes we discussed. The PUSH, POP, and Load and Store Register Exclusive Addressing Modes are similar to STMDB, LDM, and Immediate Offset Addressing Modes. The Inherent Addressing Mode is very easy since this mode only uses registers without memory accessing.

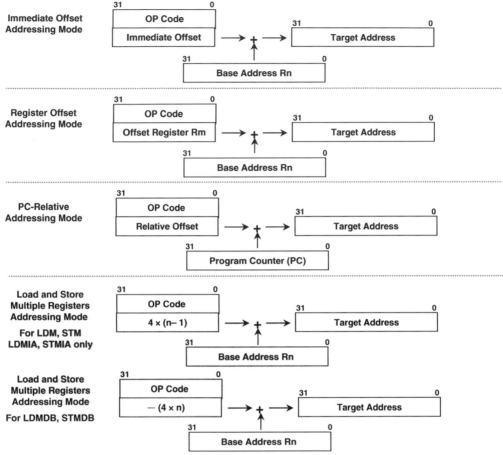

Figure 4.5. A summary of different addressing modes.

4.3.4 The ARM® Cortex®-M4 Instruction Set Categories

As we mentioned, the ARM® Cortex®-M4 assembly language instructions can be divided into 14 groups based on their functions. We will provide a quick review for all of these instructions in the following sections one by one.

4.3.4.1 Data Moving Instructions

The data moving operation is one of the most popular operations used in any micro-controller programming. In Cortex-M4 instruction set, the data moving instructions include:

1. Move data from one register to another register.
2. Move data between a general-purpose register and a special register.
3. Move an immediate data into a register.

4. Move data from registers to memory space.

5. Move data from memory space to registers.

The syntax for the first three (1~3) data moving instructions are:

- MOV Rd, Operand2
- MOVS Rd, Operand2
- MOVT Rd, Operand2
- MOV Rd, #imm16
- MOVW Rd, #imm16
- MRS Rd, Rs
- MSR Rs, Rt
- MVN Rd, Operand2
- MVNS Rd, Operand2

Basically these instructions have the syntax of MOV Destination, Source. The function of these instructions is to move a data value from the source to the destination register. The second operand, Operand2, is a flexible operand and it can be an immediate number or a source register with a shifting operation. The #imm16 is a halfword or a 16-bit data. The registers Rd and Rt represent the destination and the source registers. The Rs means a special register.

The suffix S and W are used to indicate that these instructions will affect the flag bits after it is executed. The suffix T indicates that a 16-bit data item is sent to the upper 16-bit of the destination register. Table 4.4 shows these data moving instructions and their functions.

The syntaxes for the last two (4~5) data moving instructions are those syntaxes of top 6 addressing modes instructions we discussed in the previous sections. Table 4.5 shows these data moving instructions and their functions.

Figure 4.6 shows an example of using these data moving instructions. The exclamation sign ! means that the execution of the related instruction affects the flag bits, NZVC. If all flag bits are 0, this means that the execution of the related instruction has no effect on any flag.

Table 4.4. The data moving instructions with no memory access.

Instruction	Function	Flags
MOV Rd, Rt	Rd ← Rt	—
MOVS Rd, Rt	Rd ← Rt & Update APSR flag	N, Z, C
MOV Rd, #Offset	Rd ← #Offset	—
MOVS Rd, #Offset	Rd ← #Offset & Update APSR flag	N, Z, C
MOVW Rd, #Imm16	Rd ← #Imm16 & Update APSR flag	N, Z, C
MOVT Rd, #Imm16	Upper 16-bit of Rd ← #Imm16	—
MRS Rd, Rs	Rd ← A special register Rs	—
MSR Rs, Rt	A special register Rs ← Rt	N, Z, C
MVN Rd, Rt	Rd ← Negative value of Rt	N, Z, C

Table 4.5. The data moving instructions with memory access.

Instruction	Function	Flags
LDR Rd, [Rn, #Offset]	$Rd \leftarrow [Rn + \#Offset]$	—
LDRB Rd, [Rn, #Offset]	$Rd \leftarrow$ Extended to 32-bit of $[Rn + \#Offset]$	—
LDRH Rd, [Rn, #Offset]	$Rd \leftarrow$ Extended to 32-bit of $[Rn + \#Offset]$	—
LDREX Rd, [Rn, #Offset]	$Rd \leftarrow [Rn + \#Offset]$	—
STR Rt, [Rn, #Offset]	$[Rn + \#Offset] \leftarrow Rt$	—
STRD Rt, Rt2, [Rn, #Offset]	$[Rn + \#Offset] \leftarrow Rt, [Rn + \#Offset + 4] \leftarrow Rt2$	—
LDM Rn! {Reglist}	$Reglist \leftarrow [Rn + 4 \times (n - 1)]$	—
LDMDB Rn! {Reglist}	$Reglist \leftarrow [Rn - 4 \times n]$	—
STM Rn! {Reglist}	$[Rn + 4 \times (n - 1)] \leftarrow Reglist$	—
STMDB Rn! {Reglist}	$[Rn - 4 \times n] \leftarrow Reglist$	—

4.3.4.2 Arithmetic Instructions

The Cortex-M4 processor provides many different arithmetic operation instructions, including the addition, subtraction, multiplication, and division. The addition instruction group contains addition with carry bit, and the subtraction instruction group includes subtraction with borrow bit.

The ARM® Cortex®-M4 arithmetic instructions include the following popular operations:

- Addition (ADD, ADC)
- Subtraction (SUB, SBC)

```
 1                MovingDataExample.s
 2   ; DEMO PROGRAM TO USE DATA MOVING INSTRUCTIONS
 3   ───────────────     No Memory Access Modes     ───────────────
 4
 5   START:      MOV    R3, R0            ;R3 ← R0                    NZVC = 000-
 6               MOVS   R4, R0            ;R4 ← R0 & update APSR      NZVC = !!!!-
 7               MOV    R0, #0x25         ;R0 ← #0x25                 NZVC = 000-
 8               MRS    R6, PRIMASK       ;R6 ← PRIMASK               NZVC = !!!!-
 9
10   ───────────   Immediate Offset Addressing Mode   ───────────
11   PLOOP:      LDR    R5, [R0, #0x20]   ;R5 ← [R0 + #0x20]          NZVC = 000-
12               STR    R0, [R5, #0x0C]   ;[R5 + #0x0C] ← R0          NZVC = 000-
13
14   ───────────   Register Offset Addressing Mode   ───────────
15   SLOOP:      LDR    R3, [R0, R2]      ; R3 ← [R0 + R2]            NZVC = 000-
16               STR    R5, [R0, R7]      ;[R0 + R7] ← R5             NZVC = 000-
17               LDREX  R0, [R2, #0x10]   ;R0 ← [R2 + #0x10]          NZVC = 000-
18
19   ──────── Load & Store Multiple Register Addressing Mode ────────
20   LOOP:       LDM    R1!, {R3-R5}          ; R3,R4,R5 ← [R1+4×(n-1)]  NZVC = 000-
21               STM    R0, {R1, R6}          ; [R0+4×(n-1)] ← R1 & R6   NZVC = 000-
22               STMDB  R0!, {R5, R8}         ;[R0-4×n] ← R5 & R8        NZVC = 000-
23               LDRH   R1, {R2, R5, LSL #2}  ;R1 ← [R2 + R5 × 4]        NZVC = 0000-
24               STR    R0, {R1, R2, LSL #1}  ;R0 ← [R1 + R2 × 2]        NZVC = 0000-
25               LDMDB  R7, {R1-R2, R5}       ;(R1, R2, R5) ← [R7 − 4 × n] NZVC = 0000-
```

Figure 4.6. Some example codes for the data moving instructions.

Table 4.6. The syntaxes for most popular arithmetic instructions.

Instruction	Function	Flags
ADD{S} {Rd}, Rn, Operand2;	Rd ← Rn + Operand2 (if Rd omits, Rn ← Rn + Operand2)	N, Z, V, C
ADD{S} {Rd}, Rn, Imm12;	Rd ← Rn + Imm12 (if Rd omits, Rn ← Rn + Imm12)	N, Z, V, C
ADC{S} {Rd}, Rn, Operand2;	Rd ← Rn + Operand2 + Carry (if Rd omits, result → Rn)	N, Z, V, C
SUB{S} {Rd}, Rn, Operand2;	Rd ← Rn − Operand2 (if Rd omits, Rn ← Rn − Operand2)	N, Z, V, C
SUB{S} {Rd}, Rn, Imm12;	Rd ← Rn − Imm12 (if Rd omits, Rn ← Rn - Imm12)	N, Z, V, C
SBC{S} {Rd}, Rn, Operand2;	Rd ← Rn − Operand2 - Carry (if Rd omits, Rn ← Rn − Operand2 − Carry)	N, Z, V, C
RSB{S} {Rd}, Rn, Operand2;	Rd ← Operand2 − Rn (if Rd omits, Rn ← Operand2 − Rn)	N, Z, V, C
RSB{S} {Rd}, Rn, Rm;	Rd ← Rm − Rn (if Rd omits, Rn ← Rm − Rn)	N, Z, V, C
MUL{S} {Rd}, Rn, Rm;	Rd ← Rn × Rm (if Rd omits, Rn ← Rn × Rm)	N, Z, V, C
MLA Rd, Rn, Rm, Ra;	Rd ← Rn × Rm + Ra	—
MLS Rd, Rn, Rm, Ra;	Rd ← Ra − Rn × Rm	—
SDIV {Rd}, Rn, Rm;	Rd ← Rn/Rm (if Rd omits, Rn ← Rn/Rm) Signed Division	—
UDIV {Rd}, Rn, Rm;	Rd ← Rn/Rm (if Rd omits, Rn ← Rn/Rm) Unsigned Division	—

- Reverse Subtraction (RSB)
- Multiplication (MUL)
- Division (SDIV, UDIV)
- Multiplication with Accumulation (MLA)
- Multiplication with Subtraction (MLS)

The syntaxes and functions of the most popular arithmetic instructions are shown in Table 4.6.

The following points should be noted when using Table 4.6:

- The S is an optional suffix and if the S is specified, the condition codes on the related flag bits are updated when this instruction is done.
- The Rd is an optional destination register and if this register is omitted, the Rn will work as a destination register. The {} means that the variable inside is an optional one.
- The Rm is any other register that can be used to store some operating data.
- The Imm12 is a 12-bit offset constant with a range of $0 \sim 4095$.
- The Operand2 is a flexible operand and it can be a register or an offset.
- The running results of most of these arithmetic instructions affect the condition codes in the flag register, such as Negative, Zero, overflow, and Carry (NZVC) bits.

Some other addition and subtraction instructions are available in the Cortex-M4 assembly instruction set, which include signed addition, unsigned addition, 8-bit or 16-bit additions, signed subtraction, unsigned subtraction, 8-bit and 16-bit subtractions. Table 4.7 shows these additional arithmetic instructions.

Figure 4.7 shows an example of using some popular arithmetic instructions to perform Addition, Subtraction, Multiplication, and Division operations.

All data items used for this example program are first defined, and related memory spaces are reserved. Then all data items are assigned to the different registers based on

Table 4.7. Some other additional arithmetic instructions.

Instruction	Function	Flags
SADD8 {Rd}, Rn, Rm;	Rd ← Rn + Rm; Perform four 8-bit signed additions	N, Z, V, C
SADD16 {Rd}, Rn, Rm;	Rd ← Rn + Rm; Perform two 16-bit signed additions	N, Z, V, C
UADD8 {Rd}, Rn, Rm;	Rd ← Rn + Rm; Perform four 8-bit unsigned additions	N, Z, V, C
UADD16 {Rd}, Rn, Rm;	Rd ← Rn + Rm; Perform two 16-bit unsigned additions	N, Z, V, C
SSUB8 {Rd}, Rn, Rm;	Rd ← Rn − Rm; Perform four 8-bit signed integer subtractions	N, Z, V, C
SSUB16 {Rd}, Rn, Rm;	Rd ← Rn − Rm; Perform two 16-bit signed integer subtractions	N, Z, V, C
USUB8 {Rd}, Rn, Rm;	Rd ← Rn − Rm; Perform four 8-bit unsigned subtractions	N, Z, V, C
USUB16 {Rd}, Rn, Rm;	Rd ← Rn + Rm; Perform two 16-bit unsigned subtractions	N, Z, V, C

their assigned addresses. Four different arithmetic operations are executed using related arithmetic instructions, such as Addition, Subtraction with carry, multiplication, and division. The running results are assigned to the related assigned memory space.

4.3.4.3 Logic Instructions

The ARM® Cortex®-M4 logic instructions include the following popular operations:

- AND (Bitwise AND operations)
- ORR (Bitwise OR operations)

```
                          ARITHMETIC.s
1
    ; DEMO PROGRAM TO USE ARITHMETIC INSTRUCTIONS TO PERFORM SOME OPERATIONS
2
3   ═══════════════ Define and Reserve Memory Spaces for Source Data ═══════════════
4   DATA1       DCD     1            ;Reserve 1-word memory space for data source 1
5   DATA2       DCD     1            ;Reserve 1-word memory space for data source 2
6   SUM         DCD     1            ;Reserve 1-word memory space for sum
7   MINUS       DCD     1            ;Reserve 1-word memory space for minus
8   PRODUCT     DCQ     1            ;Reserve 2-word memory spaces for product
9   QUOTIENT    DCD     1            ;Reserve 1-word memory spaces for quotient
10
11  ═══════════════ Perform Data Assignment Operations ═══════════════
12              LDR     R0, = DATA1      ;R0 ← [DATA1], Set R0 = Address of DATA1
13              LDR     R1, = DATA2      ;R1 ← [DATA2], Set R1 = Address of DATA2
14              LDR     R2, = SUM        ;R2 ← [SUM], Set R2 = Address of SUM
15              LDR     R3, = MINUS      ;R3 ← [MINUS], Set R3 = Address of MINUS
16              LDR     R4, = PRODUCT    ;R4 ← [PRODUCT], Set R4 = Address of PRODUCT
17              LDR     R5, = QUOTIENT   ;R5 ← [QUOTIENT], Set R5 = Address of QUOTIENT
18  ═══════════════ Perform Data Arithmetic  Operations ═══════════════
19
20              ADD     R0, R0, R1       ;R0 ← DATA1 + DATA2, Get the SUM
21              STR     R0, [R2, #0]     ;SUM ← R0, Save the SUM
22              SBC     R0, R0, R1       ;R0 ← (DATA1 + DATA2) − DATA2, Get the MINUS
23              STR     R0, [R3, #0]     ;MINUS ← R0, Save the MINUS
24              MUL     R0, R0, R1       ;R0 ← DATA1 × DATA2, Get the PRODUCT
25              STR     R0, [R4, #0]     ; PRODUCT← R0, Save the PRODUCT
26              UDIV    R0, R0, R1       ;R0 ← (DATA1 × DATA2) / DATA2, Get the QUOTIENT
27              STR     R0, [R5, #0]     ;QUOTIENT← R0, Save the QUOTIENT
```

Figure 4.7.   An example of using some instructions to do arithmetic operations.

Table 4.8.   The syntaxes for most popular logic instructions.

Instruction	Function	Flags
AND{S} {Rd}, Rn, Operand2;	Rd ← Rn & Operand2 (if Rd omits, Rn ← Rn & Operand2)	N, Z, C
AND{S} {Rd}, Rn, #Immed;	Rd ← Rn & Immed (if Rd omits, Rn ← Rn & Immed)	N, Z, C
ORR{S} {Rd}, Rn, Operand2;	Rd ← Rn | Operand2 (if Rd omits, Rn ← Rn | Operand2)	N, Z, C
ORR{S} {Rd}, Rn, #Immed;	Rd ← Rn | Immed (if Rd omits, Rn ← Rn | Immed)	N, Z, C
ORN{S} {Rd}, Rn, Operand2;	Rd ← Rn | ~ Operand2 (if Rd omits, Rn ← Rn | ~ Operand2)	N, Z, C
ORN{S} {Rd}, Rn, #Immed;	Rd ← Rn | ~ Immed (if Rd omits, Rn ← Rn | ~ Immed)	N, Z, C
EOR{S} {Rd}, Rn, Operand2;	Rd ← Rn ⊕ Operand2 (if Rd omits, Rn ← Rn ⊕ Operand2)	N, Z, C
EOR{S} {Rd}, Rn, #Immed;	Rd ← Rn ⊕ Immed (if Rd omits, Rn ← Rn ⊕ Immed)	N, Z, C
BIC{S} {Rd}, Rn, #Immed;	Rd ← Rn & (~Immed), (if Rd omits, Rn ← Rn & (~Immed))	N, Z, C
BIC{S} {Rd}, Rn, Rm;	Rd ← Rn & (~Rm), (if Rd omits, Rn ← Rn & (~Rm))	N, Z, C
BIC{S} {Rd}, Rn, Operand2;	Rd ← Rn & (~Operand2), (if Rd omits, Rn ← Rn & (~Operand2))	N, Z, C

- ORN (Bitwise OR NOT operations)
- EOR (Bitwise Exclusive OR operations)
- BIC (Logic AND NOT or Bit clear operations)

The syntaxes and functions of the most popular logic instructions are shown in Table 4.8.

The following points should be noted when using Table 4.8:

- The S is an optional suffix and if the S is specified, the condition codes on the related flag bits are updated when this instruction is done.
- The Rd is an optional destination register and if this register is omitted, the Rn will work as a destination register. The {} means that the variable inside is an optional one.
- The Rm is any other register that can be used to store some operating data.
- The Immed is a 32-bit immediate constant.
- The Operand2 is a flexible operand and it can be a register or an offset.
- The running results of most of these arithmetic instructions affect the condition codes in the flag register, such as Negative, Zero, and Carry (NZC) bits.
- The AND instruction is to perform a bitwise (bit-by-bit) AND operation between two registers or between one register and an Operand2 or an immediate constant.
- The ORR instruction is to perform a bitwise (bit-by-bit) OR operation between two registers or between one register and an Operand2 or an immediate constant.
- The ORN instruction is to perform a bitwise (bit-by-bit) OR operation in the register Rn with the complementary of the corresponding bits in the value of Operand2 or the complementary of an immediate constant. The sign ~ means a complementary or an inverse of the bits in a variable. For example, if Rn = 0x1110111000110010, the complementary or inverse of the Rn is: 0x0001000111001101. Each bit's value gets its inverse value, from 1 to 0, and from 0 to 1.
- The EOR instruction is to perform a bitwise (bit-by-bit) Exclusive OR (⊕) between the registers or between one register and an Operand2 or an immediate constant.
- The BIC instruction is to perform a bitwise (bit-by-bit) AND operation on the bits in the Rn with the complements of the corresponding bits in the value of Operand2 or a register. For

```
1                          LOGIC.s
2   ; DEMO PROGRAM TO USE LOGIC INSTRUCTIONS TO PERFORM SOME OPERATIONS
3   ───────────     Define and Reserve Memory Spaces for Source Data   ───────────
4   DATA1        DCD    1          ;Reserve 1-word memory space for data source 1
5   DATA2        DCD    1          ;Reserve 1-word memory space for data source 2
6   ARESULT      DCD    1          ;Reserve 1-word memory space for AND Result
7   ORESULT      DCD    1          ;Reserve 1-word memory space for ORR Result
8   NRESULT      DCD    1          ;Reserve 1-word memory space for ORN Result
9   ERESULT      DCD    1          ;Reserve 1-word memory spaces for EOR Result
10  BRESULT      DCD    1          ;Reserve 1-word memory spaces for BIC Result
11
12  ───────────────     Perform Data Assignment Operations   ───────────────
13              LDR    R0, = DATA1    ;R0 ← [DATA1], Set R0 = Address of DATA1
14              LDR    R1, = DATA2    ;R1 ← [DATA2], Set R1 = Address of DATA2
15              LDR    R2, = ARESULT  ;R2 ← [ARESULT], Set R2 = Address of ARESULT
16              LDR    R3, = ORESULT  ;R3 ← [ORESULT], Set R3 = Address of ORESULT
17              LDR    R4, = NRESULT  ;R4 ← [NRESULT], Set R4 = Address of NRESULT
18              LDR    R5, = ERESULT  ;R5 ← [ERESULT], Set R5 = Address of ERESULT
19              LDR    R6, = BRESULT  ;R5 ← [BRESULT], Set R5 = Address of BRESULT
20  ───────────────     Perform Data Logic  Operations   ───────────────
21
22              AND    R0, R0, R1     ;R0 ← DATA1 & DATA2, Get the AND Result
23              STR    R0, [R2, #0]   ;ARESULT← R0, Save the AND Result
24              ORR    R0, R0, R1     ;R0 ← (DATA1 & DATA2) I DATA2, Get the ORR Result
25              STR    R0, [R3, #0]   ;ORESULT← R0, Save the ORR Result
26              ORN    R0, R0, R1     ;R0 ← ((DATA1 & DATA2) I DATA2) I (~ DATA2), Get the ORN
27              STR    R0, [R4, #0]   ;NRESULT← R0, Save the ORN Result
28              EOR    R0, R0, R1     ;R0 ← (R0 ⊕ R1), Get the EOR Result
29              STR    R0, [R5, #0]   ;ERESULT← R0, Save the EOR Result
30              BIC    R0, R0, R1     ;R0 ← R0 & ( ~ R1), Get the BIC Result
31              STR    R0, [R6, #0]   ;BRESULT← R0, Save the BIC Result
```

Figure 4.8. An example of using some popular logic instructions.

example, if $Rn = 0x1110111000110010$, instruction BIC Rn, Rn will make $Rn = 0x00000000$ since the complements of Rn or $\sim Rn = 0x0001000111001101$, which is just inverse of the original value in the Rn. 0 AND 1 must be 0, and this is equivalent to clear Rn bit-by-bit.

Figure 4.8 shows an example of using some popular logic instructions to perform AND, ORR, EOR, ORN, and BIC operations.

Next let's take care of the shift and rotation instructions.

4.3.4.4 Shift and Rotate Instructions

The Cortex-M4 processor provides five different shift and rotation operation instructions, including the arithmetic shift right, logic shift left, logic shift right, rotate right, and rotate right with extended.

The ARM® Cortex®-M4 instructions contain the following five popular operations:

- Arithmetic Shift Right (ASR)
- Logic Shift Left (LSL)
- Logic Shift Right (LSR)
- Rotate Right (ROR)
- Rotate Right with Extended (RRX)

Table 4.9. The syntaxes for shift and rotate instructions.

Instruction	Function	Flags
ASR{S} Rd, Rn, Rs;	Rd ← Rn ≫ Rs; Rn is shifted right by number of bits stored in Rs	N, Z, C
ASR{S} Rd, Rn, #n;	Rd ← Rn ≫ n; Rn is shifted right by n bits. The range of n is 1 ~ 32	N, Z, C
ASR{S} Rd, Rn;	Rd ← Rn ≫ Rn; Rn is shifted right by number of bits stored in Rn.	N, Z, C
LSL{S} Rd, Rn, Rs;	Rd ← Rn ≪ Rs; Rn is shifted left by number of bits stored in Rs	N, Z, C
LSL{S} Rd, Rn, #n;	Rd ← Rn ≪ n; Rn is shifted left by n bits. The range of n is 0 ~ 31	N, Z, C
LSL{S} Rd, Rn;	Rd ← Rn ≪ Rn; Rn is shifted left by number of bits stored in Rn	N, Z, C
LSR{S} Rd, Rn, Rs;	Rd ← Rn ≫ Rs; Rn is shifted right by number of bits stored in Rs	N, Z, C
LSR{S} Rd, Rn, #n;	Rd ← Rn ≫ n; Rn is shifted right by n bits. The range of n is 1 ~ 32	N, Z, C
LSR{S} Rd, Rn;	Rd ← Rn ≫ Rn; Rn is shifted right by number of bits stored in Rn	N, Z, C
ROR{S} Rd, Rn, Rs;	Rd ← Rn rotate right by Rs	N, Z, C
ROR{S} Rd, Rn, #n;	Rd ← Rn rotate right by n bits. The range of n is 1 ~ 31	N, Z, C
ROR{S} Rd, Rn;	Rd ← Rn rotate right by Rn	N, Z, C
RRX{S} Rd, Rn;	{C, Rd} = {Rn, C}; Rn is shifted right with Carry bit by 1 bit	N, Z, C

The syntaxes and functions of these shift and rotate instructions are shown in Table 4.9. The following points should be noted when using Table 4.9:

- The S is an optional suffix and if the S is specified, the condition codes on the related flag bits are updated when this instruction is done.
- The Rd is a destination register used to store the shifting result.
- The Rn is any other register that contains the value to be shifted.
- The Rs is a register holding the shift length to be applied to the value in the register Rn. Only the least significant byte is used and its value can be in the range 0~255.
- The n is a constant representing the shift length, and its range depends on the instruction.
- The running results of most of these arithmetic instructions affect the condition codes in the flag register, such as Negative, Zero, and Carry (NZC) bits.
- In all of these instructions, the shifting result is written into the destination register Rd, but the content of the register Rn remains unchanged.
- To use 16-bit version of these instructions, all registers used must be low registers (R0~R7). The RRX instruction is not available in 16-bit version.
- For arithmetic shift and rotate instructions, only shift right instructions are available. The reason for that is (1) The Logic Shift Left (LSL) instruction is equivalent to Arithmetic Shift left (ASL) instruction and both of them perform the same function, and (2) The Rotate Right (ROR) instruction can work as a Rotate Left (ROL) instruction since a rotate right is equivalent to rotate to left since this rotate is a cycle or a closed-loop operation.

Figure 4.9 shows a function description of using these shift and rotate instructions to perform related operations. Figure 4.10 shows an example of using the shift and rotate instructions to perform related operations.

4.3.4.5 Data Conversion Instructions

The Cortex-M4 processor provides some data conversion and reversion instructions to help users to convert and reverse some data items during the program development to

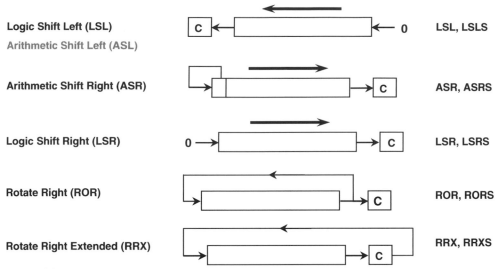

Figure 4.9. Function description of shift and rotate instructions.

facilitate the coding process. Generally these instructions enable users to convert 8-bit and 16-bit data items to 32-bit data in either signed or unsigned format. Some instructions provide a pre-rotate function to enable the data items to be rotated before the data conversion. For the data reversion instructions, these instructions allow users to get inverse versions of bytes, halfwords, or words.

The ARM® Cortex®-M4 instructions contain the following popular conversion and reversion operations:

- Signed Extended Byte to Word (SXTB)
- Signed Extended Half-Word to Word (SXTH)
- Unsigned Extended Byte to Word (UXTB)
- Unsigned Extended Half-Word to Word (UXTH)

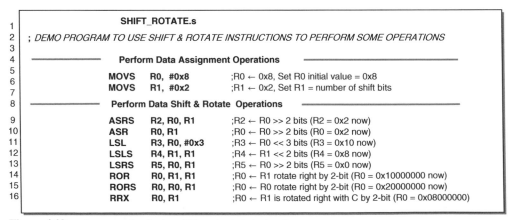

Figure 4.10. An example of using shift and rotate instructions.

Table 4.10. The syntaxes for data conversion and reversion instructions.

Instruction	Function	Flags
SXTB {Rd}, Rn, {ROR #n};	Rd ← Signed_Extend (Rn[7:0]) to32-bit. ROR #n for Rn. Rd = Rn if Rd missed	N, Z, C
SXTH {Rd}, Rn, {ROR #n};	Rd ← Signed_Extend (Rn[15:0]) to32-bit. ROR #n for Rn. Rd = Rn if Rd missed	N, Z, C
SXTB16 {Rd}, Rn, {ROR #n};	Rd[15:0] ← Signed_Extend (Rn[7:0]); ROR #n for Rn. Rd = Rn if Rd omits Rd[31:16] ← Signed_Extend (Rn[23:16])	N, Z, C
UXTB {Rd}, Rn, {ROR #n};	Rd ← Unsigned_Extend (Rn[7:0]) to32-bit. ROR #n for Rn. Rd = Rn if Rd omits	N, Z, C
UXTH {Rd}, Rn, {ROR #n};	Rd ← Unsigned_Extend (Rn[15:0]) to32-bit. ROR #n for Rn. Rd = Rn if Rd omits	N, Z, C
UXTB16 {Rd}, Rn, {ROR #n};	Rd[15:0] ← Unsigned_Extend (Rn[7:0]); ROR #n for Rn. Rd = Rn if Rd omits Rd[31:16] ← Unsigned_Extend (Rn[23:16])	N, Z, C
REV Rd, Rn;	Rd ← REV (Rn); Reverse byte order in Word	N, Z, C
REV16 Rd, Rn;	Rd ← REV16 (Rn); Reverse byte order in each Half-Word independently	N, Z, C
REVSH Rd, Rn;	Rd ← REVSH (Rn); Reverse byte order in lower Half-Word and sign extend result	N, Z, C
RBIT Rd, Rn;	Rd ← RBIT (Rn); Reverse the bit order in a 32-bit Word in Rn	N, Z, C

- Reverse Bytes in Word (REV)
- Reverse Bytes in Each Half-Word (REV16)
- Reverse Bytes in Lower Half-Word and Sign Extend the Result (REVSH)
- Reverse Bit Order in a 32-bit Word (RBIT)

The syntaxes and functions of these shift and rotate instructions are shown in Table 4.10. The following points should be noted when using Table 4.10:

- The Rd is an optional destination register. If it is omitted, the Rn replaces the Rd and works as the destination register.
- The ROR #n is an optional operation to perform a ROR #n function before the Rn can be converted. The available value for the rotation number n is: 8, 16, and 24, which means that you can rotate Rn right with 8, 16, or 24 bits before the conversion.
- The SXTB instruction extracts the lowest 8-bit value of Rn, Rn [7:0], and sign extends to a 32-bit value. The so-called sign-extended means that when extending an 8-bit data to a 32-bit data, copy the bit value on the MSB of the 8-bit data, bit[7] on Rn, and paste this value to the upper 24 bits. For example, if Rn = 0x23456789, after the execution of the instruction SXTB Rd, Rn; the Rd = 0xFFFFFF89 since the MSB of the Rn, bit[7] is 1.
- The SXTH instruction extracts the lower 16-bit value of Rn, Rn [15:0], and sign extends to a 32-bit value. The so-called sign-extended means that when extending a 16-bit data to a 32-bit data, copy the bit value on the MSB of the 16-bit data, bit[15] on Rn, and paste this value to the upper 16 bits. Still using the above example in SXTB, after the execution of the instruction SXTH Rd, Rn; the Rd = 0x00006789 since the MSB of the 16-bit data on Rn, bit[15] is 0 (6 → 0110).
- The UXTB instruction extracts the lowest 8-bit value of Rn, Rn [7:0], and zero extends to a 32-bit value. The so-called zero-extended means that when zero extends an 8-bit data to a 32-bit data, put 24 zeros to the upper 24 bits. Still using the above example in SXTB, after the execution of the instruction UXTB Rd, Rn; the Rd = 0x00000089 since 24 zeros are put in the upper 24 bits in the Rd even the MSB of the lowest 8-bit on the Rn is 1.
- The UXTH instruction extracts the lower 16-bit value of Rn, Rn [15:0], and zero extends to a 32-bit value. The so-called zero-extend means that when zero extends a 16-bit data to a 32-bit data, put 16 zeros to the upper 16 bits. If we are still using the above example in SXTB, we have Rn = 0x23456789. After executing: UXTH Rd, Rn; the Rd = 0x00006789.

- The SXTB16 instruction extracts bits[7:0] on Rn and sign extends to 16 bits (Rd[15:0]), and extracts bits [23:16] on Rn and sign extends to 16 bits (Rd[31:16]).
- The UXTB16 instruction extracts bits[7:0] on Rn and zero extends to 16 bits (Rd[15:0]), and it extracts bits [23:16] and zero extends to 16 bits (Rd[31:16]).
- The REV instruction reverses the byte order in a Word stored in the register Rn. For example, if Rn = 0x11223344, which is a word, after the execution REV Rd, Rn; the Rd = 0x44332211. Only the order of each byte, 11, 22, 33, 44, is reversed to: 44, 33, 22,11.
- The REV16 instruction only reverses the byte order in each half-word stored in the register Rn independently. For example, if Rn = 0x12345678, after executing the instruction: REV16 Rd, Rn; the Rd = 0x34127856. It only reverses two bytes in each half-word.
- The REVSH instruction reverses byte order in the lower half-word, and it sign extends to 32 bits. For example, if Rn = 0x23456789, after the instruction: REVSH Rd, Rn; is executed, the Rd = 0xFFFF8967. First the lower half-word in Rn, 6789, is reversed in the byte order to: 8967. Then it is sign extended to 32-bit word by putting 16 '1' into the upper 16-bit since the MSB value of the lower half-word in Rn, bit[15], is 1 (8 → 0x1000).
- The RBIT instruction reverses the bit order in a 32-bit word. For example, if Rn = 0x00000001. After the execution of the instruction: RBIT Rd, Rn; the Rd = 0x80000000.

Figure 4.11 shows a function description of using these conversion instructions to perform related operations.

Figure 4.12 shows a function description about these reverse instructions. Figure 4.13 shows an example of using the shift and rotate instructions to perform related operations.

4.3.4.6 Bit-Field Processing Instructions

The Cortex-M4 processor provides five different bit-field operation instructions. These instructions are used to help users to manipulate and control a single bit or a range of bits in

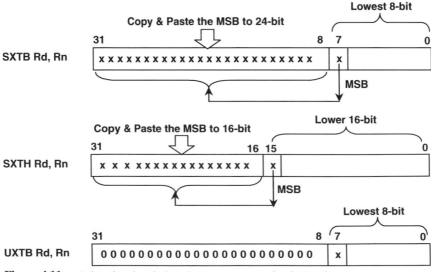

Figure 4.11. A function description about some conversion instructions.

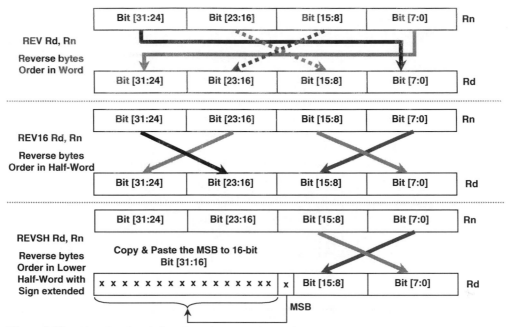

Figure 4.12.   Function description about the reverse instructions.

a register. The bit-field operation is a brand new technology in the Cortex-M4 microcontroller.

The ARM® Cortex®-M4 processor contains the following five popular bit-field instructions:

- Bit-Field Clear (BFC)
- Bit-Field Insert (BFI)
- Count Leading Zero (CLZ)

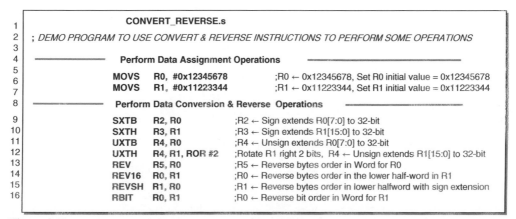

Figure 4.13.   An example of using some Reversion instructions.

Table 4.11. The syntaxes for bit field processing instructions.

Instruction	Function	Flags
BFC Rd, #1stb, #width;	Clears **width** bits in Rd, starting at the low bit position **lstb** (1st bit) to the (*1stb + width* -1) bit. Other bits in Rd are unchanged.	–
BFI Rd, Rn, #1stb, #width;	Replaces **width** bits in Rd starting at the low bit position **lstb** (1st bit), with **width** bits from Rn starting at bit[0]. Other bits in Rd keep unchanged	–
CLZ Rd, Rn;	Count the number of leading zeros in Rn and return result to Rd. If all bits in Rn are 0, it returns 32. If bit [31] in Rn is 1, it returns 0.	–
SBFX Rd, Rn; #1stb, #width;	Rd ← Extract a bit-field from Rn and sign extends it to 32 bits.	–
UBFX Rd, Rn; #1stb, #width;	Rd ← Extract a bit-field from Rn and zero extends it to 32 bits.	–

- Signed Bit-Field Extract (SBFX)
- Unsigned Bit-Field Extract (UBFX)

The syntaxes and functions of these shift and rotate instructions are shown in Table 4.11. The following points should be noted when using Table 4.11:

- The Rd is the destination register.
- The Rn is the operand register.
- The 1stb is the first-bit or starting-bit position of the least significant bit of the bit field. For example, if a 1stb is 5 and a width is 3, which means that the starting position in the Rd should be bit [5] and the ending bit should be bit [7] (1stb + width − 1 = 5 + 3 − 1 = 7). All bits in this field (bit [5]~bit [7]) belong to the selected or target bit field. The 1stb must be in the range 0 to 31, and the width must be in the range 1~32.
- The BFC instruction is used to clear a bit field in the register Rd. The range of selected bit field starts from the 1stb bit and ends at 1stb + width − 1 bit. Refer to Figure 4.14 to get more details about this instruction.
- The BFI instruction is used to replace a bit field in the Rd with the content of a bit field in the Rn starting at bit [0]. The range of the bit field is from 1stb to 1stb + width − 1.
- The CLZ instruction is used to count the leading zeros before the first bit whose value is 1 in the operand register Rn and return the result to the destination register Rd.
- The SBFX instruction is used to extract a bit field from the register Rn, sign extends it to 32 bits, and writes the result to the destination register Rd.
- The UBFX instruction is to extract a bit field from the register Rn, zero extends it to 32 bits, and writes the result to the destination register Rd.

For example, the following instructions perform the related clear and insert functions:

1. BFC R4, #8, #12; Clear bit 8 to bit 19 (12 bits) of R4 to 0.
2. BFI R9, R2, #5, #14; Replace bit 5 to bit 18 (14 bits) of R9 with bit 0 to bit 13 from R2.

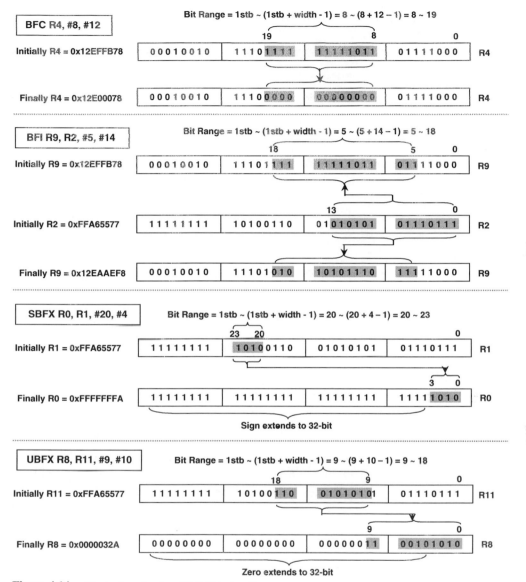

Figure 4.14. Illustrations for four bit-field instructions.

3. SBFX R0, R1, #20, #4; Extract bit 20 to bit 23 (4 bits) from R1 and sign extend to 32 bits and then write the result to R0.

4. UBFX R8, R11, #9, #10; Extract bit 9 to bit 18 (10 bits) from R11 and zero extend to 32 bits and then write the result to R8.

It can be found from the above examples that the range of the bit field is always starting from bit 1stb and ending at bit 1stb + width − 1. The reason to minus 1 is because the least significant bit starts at 0, not 1. Figure 4.14 shows the execution process for these four instructions.

4.3.4.7 Compare and Test Instructions

The Cortex-M4 processor provides some compare and bit testing instructions. These instructions arc used to help users to make comparisons between registers and between register and immediate data. The comparison result is used to update the condition codes in the flag bits, but the result is not reserved. The bit testing instructions are used to perform bit-by-bit checking.

The ARM® Cortex®-M4 processor contains the following two compare instructions and two bit testing instructions:

- Compare (CMP)
- Compare Negative (CMN)
- Bitwise and Test (TST)
- Bitwise XOR Test (TEQ)

The syntaxes and functions of these compare and bit testing instructions are shown in Table 4.12. The following points should be noted when using Table 4.12:

- The Rn is the operand register.
- The Operand2 is a flexible operand and it can be a register or an immediate constant.
- The CMP instruction subtracts the value of Operand2 from the value in the Rn. This is the same as a SUBS instruction, except that the result is discarded.
- The CMN instruction compares the negative number with the Rn by adding the value of Operand2 to the value in the Rn. This is the same as an ADDS instruction, except that the result is discarded. If this addition result is negative, the flag bit N is set to 1.
- The TST instruction performs a bitwise AND operation on the value of Rn and the value of Operand2. This is the same as the ANDS instruction, except that it discards the result.

Table 4.12. The syntaxes for compare and bit testing instructions.

Instruction	Function	Flags
CMP Rn, Operand2;	Compare the value in the Rn with Operand2. They update the condition flags on the result, but do not write the result to the Rn.	N, Z, C, V
CMN Rn, Operand2;	Compare the value in the Rn with Operand2 by adding the value of Operand2 to the value in Rn. The result updates the flag bits but does not write to the Rn.	N, Z, C, V
TST Rn, Operand2;	Perform a bitwise AND operation on the value in Rn and the value of the Operand2. The result do not write to Rn.	N, Z, C, V
TEQ Rn, Operand2;	Perform a bitwise exclusive OR operation on the value in Rn and the value of the Operand2. The result does not write to Rn.	N, Z, C, V

- The TEQ instruction performs a bitwise exclusive OR operation on the value in the Rn and the value of the Operand2. This is the same as the EORS instruction, except that it discards the result. This instruction can be used to test if two values are equal without affecting the V or C flags.

The following example instructions perform related compare and bit test functions:

1. CMP R0, R1;

2. CMN R2, #1;

3. TST R0, 0x101;

4. TEQ R1, 0x80;

The first instruction CMP R0, R1 is to compare the content of R0 with the content of R1. The related flag bit will be set if $R0 > R1$ ($N = 0$), if $R0 < R1$ ($N = 1$), and if $R0 = R1$ ($Z = 1$).

The second instruction CMN R2, #1 is to compare if the R2 equal to −1. In fact, the so-called compare with negative is to subtract the NOT value of the Operand2 from the Rn. Here it is to subtract ~1 from the R2, or $R2 - (NOT\ 1) = R2 - (-1) = R2 + 1$.

The third instruction TST R0, 0x101 is to test whether bit [0] and bit [8] in the R0 is zeros since an AND operation is performed between these two bits in the R0 and the immediate constant $0x101 = 000100000001B$. If the running result of this instruction is 0, which means that both bit[0] and bit[8] in the R0 is 0. The flag bit Z is set to 1. But the content of the R0 keeps unchanged.

The fourth instruction TEQ R1, 0x80 is to test whether the content of the R1 is equal to 0x80. The flag bits Z and N will be affected based on the running result. Still the content of the R1 keeps unchanged.

4.3.4.8 Program Flow Control Instructions

The Cortex-M4 processor provides 10 program branch and control instructions. These instructions are used to control the program flows and executions with certain conditions or without any conditions. So these instructions provide intelligent control ability for the microcontrollers. These instructions can be divided into five groups based on their functions:

1. Unconditional Branches

2. Conditional Branches

3. Compare and Branches

4. Table Branches (TBB, TBH)

5. Conditional Executions (If-Then or IT)

The unconditional branch instructions include:

- Branch to Label (B <label>)
- Branch with Link (BL <label>)
- Branch Indirect (BX Rn)
- Branch Indirect with Link (BLX Rn)
- Branch Wider (B.W <label>)

The conditional branch instructions are same with those unconditional branch instructions, and the only difference is that a condition <cond> is attached with each related instruction for the conditional branch instructions.

In fact, all B, BL, BLX, BX, and B.W can be either unconditional or conditional branch instructions depending on whether the optional condition <cond> item is attached with each branch instruction.

The compare and branch instructions include:

- Compare and Branch if Zero (CBZ)
- Compare and Branch if Nonzero (CBNZ)

The Table Branch instructions include:

- Table Branch Byte (TBB)
- Table Branch Half-Word (TBH)

The conditional execution has only one instruction, If-Then or IT block instruction. By using the IT block instruction, up to four subsequent instructions can be conditionally executed based on the condition provided by the IT instruction and the Application Program Status Register (APSR) value.

The syntaxes and functions of these branch instructions are shown in Table 4.13. The following points should be noted when using Table 4.13:

- The Label is a PC-Relative address and it can be expressed as an address label. Different branch instructions have different ranges for this address label. Refer to Table 4.13 to get more details about the range for each branch instruction.
- The {cond} is one of the 14 possible condition suffixes shown in Table 4.14. All branch instructions use these suffixes to compare with the current condition values in the Application Program Status Register (APSR), exactly the values on four flag bits: N, Z, C and V. If the comparison result is True, the branch occurs. Otherwise if the comparison result is False, the branch has not happened and the program continues running the next instruction.
- For branch instructions, the Rn is a register that contains the target address to be branched to. For CBZ and CBNZ instructions, the Rn is an operand register holding an operand. For TBB and TBH instructions, the Rn contains the address of the table and the Rm contains an index into the table.
- Both BL and BLX instructions perform a Branch and a Link function, which means that before branching the program to an address label (directly) or an address stored in a register Rn (indirect), write the address of the next instruction to the Link Register (LR), or register R14, to reserve the returning point for this branch operation. These two instructions are mostly used for calling functions or subroutines since they execute the branch and save the return address (next instruction's address) to the Link Register (LR) at the same time, so the processor can branch back to the original program after the function or subroutine call is finished.
- Both BX and BLX are indirect branch instructions, which means that the program is branched to an address that is stored in the register Rn, not a direct address label.
- For the IT instruction, the<X><Y><Z> indicates the number of possible executable subsequent instructions included in this IT block. Each of <X>, <Y>, and <Z> can either be T (true) or E (else) for the condition (cond). The number of T or E appeared in an IT instruction block determined the number of subsequent instructions involved in this IT block.

Table 4.13. The syntaxes for branch instructions.

Instruction	Function	Flags
B Label;	Branch program to Label unconditionally. Branch range: −16 MB ~ 16 MB	—
B {cond}, Label	Branch program to Label if the {cond} is True. Branch range: −16 MB ~ 16 MB (inside IT block); −1 MB ~ 1 MB (outside IT block)	—
B.W {cond}, Label	Branch program widely to Label if the {cond} is True. The W indicates that a 32-bit version of branch instruction is used for wider range	—
BL {cond} Label;	Branch and Link program to Label either conditionally (with {cond} item) or unconditionally (without {cond} item). Branch range: −16 MB ~ 16 MB	—
BX {cond} Rn;	Branch (indirect) program to the address indicated in the Rn if the {cond} is True. This instruction also creates a UsageFault exception if bit[0] of the Rn is 0	—
BLX {cond} Rn;	Branch (indirect) and Link program to the address indicated in the Rn if the {cond} is True. This instruction also creates a UsageFault exception if bit[0] of the Rn is 0	—
CBZ Rn, Label	Compare the content of the Rn with 0, branch the program to Label if the Rn is 0. Rn must be lower registers (R0 ~ R7)	—
CBNZ Rn, Label	Compare the content of the Rn with 0, branch the program to Label if the Rn is not 0. Rn must be lower registers (R0 ~ R7)	—
TBB [Rn, Rm];	Branch program to [Rn + Rm]. The Rn contains the address of the table and the Rm contains an index into the table. The offset in the Rm is a single byte.	—
TBH [Rn, Rm, LSL #n]	Branch program to [Rn + Rm]. The Rn contains the address of the table and the Rm contains an index into the table. The offset in the Rm is a half-word	—
IT <X><Y><Z> cond	IT block instruction allows up to four subsequent instructions to be executed or not based on the condition (cond) provided by the IT instruction	—

The <X> indicates the execution condition for the second instruction in the IT block, and the <Y> indicates the execution condition for the third instruction in the IT block, and the <Z> indicates the execution condition for the fourth instruction in the IT block.

- The IT block instruction can have up to four subsequent instructions, and even a branch instruction can be involved into an IT block. However, the B {cond}, Label is the only conditional instruction that can be either inside or outside an IT block. All other branch instructions must be conditional inside an IT block, and must be unconditional outside the IT block.

Figure 4.15 shows some branch and compare-branch instruction examples.

The TBB instruction is used to branch the program to a location inside a branch table and all entries in that table are arranged as a byte array. The maximum offset relative to the base address is $2 \times 2^8 = 512$ B, which is stored in the Rm. The TBH instruction is used to branch a program to a location inside the branch table, and all entries in that table are

Table 4.14. The condition suffixes for conditional branch (execution) instructions.

Suffix	Branch Condition	Flags (APSR)
EQ	Equal	$Z = 1$ if equal
NE	Not equal	$Z = 0$ if not equal
CS/HS	Carry Set/Unsigned Higher or same	$C = 1$ if unsigned higher or same
CC/LO	Carry Clear/Unsigned lower	$C = 0$ if unsigned lower
MI	Minus/Negative	$N = 1$ if minus
PL	Plus/Positive or Zero	$N = 0$ if positive or zero
VS	Overflow	$V = 1$ if overflow
VC	No Overflow	$V = 0$ if no overflow
HI	Unsigned higher	$C = 1$ & $Z = 0$
LS	Unsigned lower or same	$C = 0$ & $Z = 1$
GE	Signed greater than or equal	$N = 0$ & $V = 0$
LT	Signed less than	$N = 1$ & $V = 0$
GT	Signed greater than	$Z = 0, N = V$
LE	Signed less than or equal	$Z = 1, N \mathrel{!=} V$

arranged as a half-word (16-bit) array. The maximum offset from the base address is $2 \times 2^{16} = 128$ KB, which is stored in the Rm.

The base table address stored in the Rn could be the current PC value; in other words, the Rn could be PC, or an address stored in some other register. Since all instructions in the Cortex-M4 must be aligned to a word, the current PC value should be PC + 4 if the PC value works as a base address of the branch table.

Figure 4.16 provides a functional illustration for execution of two Table Branch instructions, namely, TBB [Rn, Rm] ; and TBH [Rn, Rm, LSL #1] ;. These two examples suppose that the Table base address is the current PC value (Rn = PC), and the Branch Table starts immediately after these instructions.

```
                    BRANCH.s
1
2  ; DEMO PROGRAM TO USE BRANCH & COMPARE BRANCH INSTRUCTIONS TO PERFORM SOME OPERATIONS
3
4  ──────────    Perform Branch & Compare and Branch  Operations   ──────────
5
6       B        LOOP           ;Branch program to a label address LOOP
7       BLE      DONE           ;Branch & Link program to DONE if the result is Signed Less Than or Equal.
                                ;The next instruction's address is written into the register Link Register (LR).
8       B.W      TARGET         ;Branch program to TARGET within 16MB range.
9       BEQ      EXIT           ;Branch program to EXIT if the last operation result is equal.
10      BL       FUNC           ;Branch with Link (Call) to a function FUNC, the return address (next
11                              ;instruction's address) is written into the Link Register (LR).
12      BX       LR             ;Return from the function call.
13      BXNE     R0             ;Branch program to an address stored in the R0 if the last operation result is
                                ;not equal.
14      BLX      R0             ;Branch with Link program to an address stored in the R0.
15      CBZ      R2, TARGET     ;Compare R2 with 0. If R2 = 0, branch program to TARGET.
16      CBNZ     R0, EXIT       ;Compare R0 with 0, If R0 ≠ 0, branch program to EXIT.
17
```

Figure 4.15. Some coding examples of using branch and compare-branch instructions.

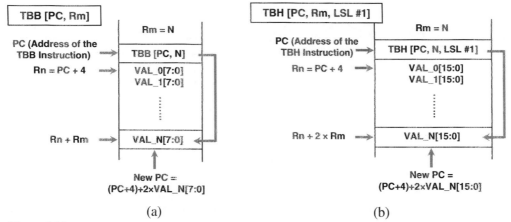

Figure 4.16.   Illustrations for two Table Branch instructions.

For the first instruction (Figure 4.16a), The $Rn = PC$ and the $Rm = N$, where N is an offset or an index. The offset value is located in the memory unit $[Rn + Rm]$, or VAL_N $[7:0]$. Since the TBB branch offset is twice the unsigned value of the byte returned from the table (align to word), the target table address is $PC + 4 + 2 \times VAL\_N[7:0]$. The program is branched to that location.

Similarly, the second instruction TBH performs a similar table branch operation with half-word data arrangement (Figure 4.16b). A similar result can be obtained.

Figure 4.17 shows an example of using an IT instruction block to control two subsequent instructions to be executed conditionally.

4.3.4.9 Saturation Instructions

As we experienced in most analog amplifier circuits, sometimes the gain of an amplifier is so large, such as an ideal Operational Amplifier (OP), to make the output of the amplifier either too small in negative or too large in positive. This is called saturations. This means that the positive peak value of the output is beyond the positive voltage V^+, and the negative peak value of the output is below the negative voltage V^-.

```
1                          IF_THEN _BLOCK.s
2    ; DEMO PROGRAM TO USE IF-THEN INSTRUCTIONS TO PERFORM SOME OPERATIONS
3
4         ─────────────  Perform IT Block Instruction  Operations  ─────────────
5
6         CMP    R0, #0         ;Compare R0 with 0.
7         ITTE   EQ             ;ITTE means: The 1st T means that if cond is True (Equal to 0), the 1st
8                               ;instruction executes. The 2nd T means that if cond is True (Equal to 0),
9                               ;the 2nd instruction executes. The 3rd E means that if cond is Else (Not
10                              ;Equal to 0), the 3rd instruction executes.
11        MOVEQ  R3, #5         ;The 1st instruction is executed (R3 ← 0x5) if R0 = 0.
12        MOVEQ  R5, #8         ;The 2nd instruction is executed (R5 ← 0x8) if R0 = 0.
13        MOVNE  R5, #2         ;The 3rd instruction is executed (R5 ← 0x2) if R0 ≠ 0.
```

Figure 4.17.   An example of using IF-THEN branch instructions.

Table 4.15. The syntaxes for saturation instructions.

Instruction	Function	Flags
SSAT Rd, #n, Rn, {shift #s};	Rd ← Apply the specified shift, then saturates data to the signed range $-2^{n-1} \leq x \leq 2^{n-1} - 1$.	—
USAT Rd, #n, Rn, {shift #s};	Rd ← Apply the specified shift, then saturates data to the unsigned range $0 \leq x \leq 2^{n} - 1$.	—

Similarly, in Cortex-M4 and other microcontrollers, the situations also existed and also happened in some situations. They are similar to overflows for arithmetic operations. To reduce any possible saturation, Cortex-M4 provides some instructions, such as SSAT to handle the Signed Saturations, USAT to handle Unsigned Saturations, QADD to handle saturating addition, QSUB to handle saturating subtraction, and so on. In order to save space, we only introduce the SSAT and USAT instructions since they are popular in the signal processing.

The syntaxes and functions of these saturation instructions are shown in Table 4.15. The following points should be noted when using Table 4.15:

- The Rd is the destination register.
- The n specifies the bit position to saturate to
  - For SSAT, $n = 1 \sim 32$
  - For USAT, $n = 0 \sim 31$
- The Rn is the register containing the value to be saturated.
- The shift #s is an optional shift applied to Rn before saturating. It must be one of the following:
  - ASR #s (where s is in the range $1 \sim 31$).
  - LSL #s (where s is in the range $0 \sim 31$).

Generally the SSAT and USAT perform the following operations to reduce any possible occurrence of saturation:

SSAT (for signed n-bit saturation):

1. If the value to be saturated is less than -2^{n-1}, the result returned is -2^{n-1}.
2. If the value to be saturated is greater than $2^{n-1} - 1$, the result returned is $2^{n-1} - 1$.
3. Otherwise, the result returned is the same as the value to be saturated.

USAT (for unsigned n-bit saturation):

1. If the value to be saturated is less than 0, the result returned is 0.
2. If the value to be saturated is greater than 2^{n-1}, the result returned is 2^{n-1}.
3. Otherwise, the result returned is the same as the value to be saturated.

If the returned result is different from the original value to be saturated, it is called saturation. If saturation occurs, the Q flag bit is set to 1 in the APSR by the instruction. Otherwise, it leaves the Q flag unchanged. To clear the Q flag to 0, one must use the MSR instruction. To access the Q flag bit, you need to use the MRS instruction to read the state of the Q flag.

Two examples of using SSAT and USAT instructions to process the saturations are:

SSAT R1, #16, R7, LSL #2;	Logical shift left value in R7 by 2, then saturate it as a signed 16-bit value and write it back to R1.
USATNE R0, #8, R5;	Conditionally saturate value in R5 as an unsigned 8-bit value and write it to R0.

When processing saturation with SSAT and USAT, each bit on the original register should be checked and adjusted if any of them is beyond the required ranges.

4.3.4.10 Exception-Related Instructions

The Cortex-M4 processor provides quite a few of instructions related to system exceptions, such as Change Processor State (CPS), Send Event (SEV), Supervisor Call (SVC), Wait For Event (WFE), and Wait For Interrupt (WFI). Among them, two instructions, CPS and SVC, are more important and popular in most implementations. We will introduce these instructions with more details in this section.

The CPS instruction is used to change the processor state, especially to change the state or value of some interrupt masking registers, such as PRIMASK and FAULTMASK. These registers can also be accessed by using the MSR and MRS instructions.

The syntaxes and functions of the CPS instruction are shown in Table 4.16. The following points should be noted when using Table 4.16:

- The CPS can only be used for privileged software, and it has no effect if used in unprivileged software.
- The CPS cannot be used in any conditional block, including the IT block.

The SVC instruction is used to create a SVC exception. Mostly this instruction is used for a real-operating system or embedded operating system (RTOS or Embedded OS) environment. In particular, when an application is running in the unprivileged level, it can send a request to ask some services that are running in the privileged state from the OS.

The SVC also enables applications to access various system services without knowing the actual program memory address of the service. The only information an application needs to know is the SVC service number, the input parameters, and the returned results.

Table 4.16. The syntaxes and functions for CPS instruction.

Instruction	Function	Flags
CPSIE I;	Clear the PRIMASK register to enable interrupts (same as _enable_irq(); function)	—
CPSID I;	Set the PRIMASK register to disable interrupts (same as _disable_irq(); function). The NMI and HardFault are not affected.	—
CPSIE F;	Clear the FAULTMASK register to enable fault interrupt (same as _enable_fault_irq();)	—
CPSID F;	Set the FAULTMASK register to disable fault interrupt (same as _disable_fault_irq(); function). The NMI is not affected.	—

The syntax of the SVC instruction is simple; it looks like

SVC #immed;

The immed is an 8-bit-value parameter to be evaluated to an integer with the range 0~255. This parameter is regularly ignored by the processor. If required, it can be retrieved by the exception handler to determine what service is being requested.

No flag bit would be affected by running this instruction.

An example of using this SVC instruction is

SVC 0x32; SVC handler can extract the immediate value by locating it via the stacked PC.

Next let's take a look at the sleep mode instructions.

4.3.4.11 Sleep Mode Instructions

The ARM® Cortex®-M4 processor provides two major sleep mode instructions to allow the processor to enter the sleep mode: Wait For Event (WFE) and Wait For Interrupt (WFI). The syntaxes for these two instructions are very simple as shown below:

WFE;	Wait for Events
WFI;	Wait for Interrupts

Depending on the value in the single bit event register, the processor can enter the sleep mode or not when a WFE instruction is executed:

- If the single bit event register is reset to 0, the processor enters the sleep mode and will be woken up by the next event.
- If the single bit event register is set to 1, the processor will not enter the sleep mode and continue executing the next instruction.

Unlike the WFE instruction, the WFI instruction causes the processor to enter the sleep mode immediately. The processor will be woken up by next interrupt or reset.

The CMSIS-Compliant device driver provides similar C functions for these two instructions: _WFE(); and _WFI();. By using these functions, users can perform the same functionalities in C codes as the assembly codes did.

4.3.4.12 Memory Barrier Instructions

The ARM® architecture provides some parallel data processing abilities, which means that the memory accessing can occur at the same time as other non-memory-accessing instructions are executed. In order to coordinate these parallel data processes and protect memory transfer, three memory barrier instructions are provided in the Cortex-M4 system:

- Data Memory Barrier (DMB)
- Data Synchronization Barrier (DSB)
- Instruction Synchronization Barrier (ISB)

The function of the DMB is to ensure that all memory accesses that appear before the DMB instruction are completed before any new memory access that appears after the

DMB instruction. The DMB instructions do not affect the ordering or execution of instructions that do not access memory.

The function of the DSB is to ensure that all memory accesses are completed before next instruction is executed. In other words, all instructions that come after DSB (in program order) do not execute until the DSB instruction completes.

The function of the ISB is to ensure that all previous instructions are completed before executing any new instruction. In other words, all instructions following the ISB instruction are fetched from the cache or memory, but cannot be executed until the ISB is completed.

The CMSIS-Compliant device driver provides similar C functions for these three instructions:

1. void_DMB(void);

2. void_DSB(void);

3. void_ISB(void);

By using these functions, users can perform the same functionalities in C codes as the assembly codes did.

4.3.4.13 Miscellaneous Instructions

In addition to instruction set we discussed above, the Cortex-M4 processor also provides some other useful instructions, such as Breakpoint (BKPT), No Operation (NOP), and Send Event (SEV). These instructions cannot be clearly categorized into certain related instruction groups. Therefore they can be considered as miscellaneous instructions.

The syntaxes for these miscellaneous instructions are shown in Table 4.17.

The CMSIS-Compliant device driver provides similar C functions for these three instructions:

1. _BKPT (immed);

2. _NOP ();

3. _SEV();

By using these functions, users can perform the same functionalities in C codes as the assembly codes did.

Table 4.17. The syntaxes and functions for miscellaneous instruction.

Instruction	Function	Flags
BKPT #immed;	Set a breakpoint for a program to enable program to enter debug mode. The immed is an expression evaluating to an integer in the range 0~255. Generally the immed indicates the address line in which the instruction is stopped and debugged.	—
NOP;	No any operation and just do nothing. The time delay caused by the NOP instruction is not guaranteed and the processor may remove it from the pipeline before it can be executed.	—
SEV;	Send an event to all processors, and set the single bit event register to 1.	—

4.3.4.14 Unsupported Instructions

The entire Thumb instruction set, including 32-bit instructions covered by the Thumb-2 Technology, is designed to support a wide range of microprocessors. However, some instructions defined in that set cannot be used in the Cortex-M4 processor, such as BLX <Label> and SETEND.

Some CPS instructions defined in the Thumb instruction set are also not available in the Cortex-M4 processor because of the different definition on the Program Status Register (PSR) between the Cortex-M and Cortex-A/R processors.

In addition to those unsupported instructions, the Cortex-M4 processor does not support co-processors; therefore all co-processor-related instructions cannot be used in the Cortex-M4 processor system. A fault exception may be generated when these unsupported instructions were used in the Cortex-M4 system.

At this point, we have finished our discussion about the instruction set for Cortex-M4 processor. Next let's begin our journey to the program development process for the ARM® Cortex®-M4 processor and TM4C123GXL microcontroller.

First let's have a quick review about the software development procedure for the ARM® Cortex®-M4 system.

4.4 ARM® CORTEX®-M4 SOFTWARE DEVELOPMENT PROCEDURES

In Chapter 3, we have provided detailed introductions about the software development tools and kits for the ARM® Cortex®-M4 MCU. The Keil® ARM®-MDK provides a full set of development kits and tools, including the source code editor, assembler, compiler, linker, loader, debugger, and runner, to enable users to design and build their applications easily and quickly in an integrated development environment (IDE) with various GUIs.

To successfully develop the user applications, it is not enough by using only those IDE and GUIs. Some peripheral device drivers included in certain related driver libraries are needed to enable users to combine their application object codes with those drivers located in the peripheral libraries provided by the vendors to build a complete executable file. When we use the Tiva™ for C Series LaunchPad evaluation board, TM4C123GXL, these libraries are located in the Internal ROM space in the on-chip memory map discussed in Section 2.6.2 in Chapter 2. These libraries and system files include:

- TivaWare™ Driver Libraries, including the Peripheral Devices Library, USB Library, Graphical Library, and Sensor Hub Library.
- TivaWare™ Boot Loader.
- Advanced Encryption Standard (AES) cryptography tables.
- Cyclic Redundancy Check (CRC) error-detection functionality.

In fact, each library is a collection of interfacing functions written by C and different library provides different control and interfacing functions. One of the most popular libraries is the Driver Library, which provides all control and interfacing functions for peripheral devices in the TM4C123GXL EVB.

As we discussed in Section 3.4 in Chapter 3, to successfully design and build users application programs, the following software and tools are needed:

1. The Keil ARM-MDK Core (including μVersion5 IDE, Compiler and Debugger)
2. CMSIS:CORE (including the API for the Cortex-M processor core and peripherals, and a consistent system startup code - Device:Startup)
3. TivaWare for C Series Software, which includes:
   a. TivaWare™ Driver Libraries, including the Peripheral Devices Library, USB Library, Graphical Library and Sensor Hub Library.
   b. TivaWare™ Boot Loader.
   c. Advanced Encryption Standard (AES) cryptography tables.
   d. Cyclic Redundancy Check (CRC) error-detection functionality.

For all of these software and tools, refer to Section 3.3 in Chapter 3 to download and install these development tools and software.

To successfully develop and build users application programs, the following hardware and components are needed (since we are using Tiva™ for C Series LaunchPad TM4C123GXL EVB and EduBASE Trainer):

1. A Tiva™ for C Series LaunchPad Evaluation Board – TM4C123GXL.
2. A USB with Micro-A/-B Cable.
3. An EduBASE Trainer.
4. A Host Computer.

One important point to be noted for the TivaWare™ for C Series software is:

1. TivaWare™ for C Series Software, which contains all Driver Libraries and will be downloaded and installed by the users to their host computer.
2. However, the same libraries are also installed in an Internal ROM space in the On-Chip memory in the TM4C123GH6PM MCU.

The first libraries are located at the user's host computer and will be used by the users when they build and develop their application program.

The second libraries are located at the Internal ROM space in the On-Chip memory unit in the TM4C123GH6PM MCU, which is included in the TM4C123GXL Evaluation Board. All interfacing functions in these libraries can also be used or called by the users as Read-Only functions from the users' application program. A prefix ROM_ must be added before each function to distinguish them from those same functions included in the libraries installed in the users' host computer.

In order to make our application development process easy and simple, we will use C language to replace assembly codes to build our application program in this book. This will significantly reduce the learning curves for assembly language and greatly simplify our project building and developing process.

4.5 USING C LANGUAGE TO DEVELOP ARM® CORTEX®-M4 MICROCONTROLLER APPLICATIONS

Today most software program developers prefer to use high-level language, such as C or C++, not low-level language, such as ARM® Assembly, to build and develop their applications. The reason for that is obvious since the high-level language is easy to learn and understand, and the most important point is that the programmers do not require to have very detailed knowledge about the hardware and components they are using in their development system. Of course, it would be much better if the developers can have some solid and deep understanding and knowledge about the hardware components they used, and in this way they can develop and build more professional and high efficient applications to be implemented in our real world.

One possible barrier or problem when using high-level language, such as C or C++, to build and develop users' applications is:

1. How to use C or C++ codes to directly access hardware components, such as general and special registers in the register bank in the Cortex-M4 Core.
2. How to use high-level language to access all special registers.
3. How to use C/C++ codes to replace and simulate the assembly instructions to perform the same functions.

The answers to these questions are:

1. Use the Intrinsic Functions provided by C/C++ Compiler related to the vendor-dependent IDE, such as Keil® ARM® C/C++ Compiler Specific Intrinsic Functions.
2. Use special software packages, such as Keil® CMSIS Core Specific Intrinsic Functions.
3. Use inline assembler, such as embedded assembler in Keil® ARM® toolchains, to insert the required assembly instructions in the C/C++ codes.
4. Use compiler specific feature such as keywords or idiom recognitions.

For most applications, the two top answers are most widely adopted: The Keil® ARM® C/C++ Compiler Specific Intrinsic Functions and the Keil® CMSIS Core Intrinsic Functions.

Before we can go too deep on these two sources, first let's have a clear picture about the standard data-type definitions about data items used in these two source systems.

4.5.1 The Standard Data Types Used in Intrinsic Functions

Different standard data types are defined for data items to be used for those intrinsic functions. Table 4.18 shows an example of some standard data type definitions for intrinsic functions provided by the Keil® ARM® C/C++ Compiler (`stdint.h`), and Table 4.19

Table 4.18.   The standard data types used in Keil® ARM® C/C++ Compiler.

Data Type	Description
int8_t	Signed Char (8-bit)
int16_t	Signed short integer (16-bit)
int32_t	Signed integer (32-bit)
uint8_t	Unsigned Char (8-bit)
uint16_t	Unsigned short integer (16-bit)
uint32_t	Unsigned integer (32-bit)
INT8_MIN	−128
INT8_MAX	127

Table 4.19.   The standard data types used in Keil® CMSIS Core.

Data Type	Description
int8_t	Signed 8-bit integer
int16_t	Signed 16-bit integer
int32_t	Signed 32-bit integer
uint8_t	Unsigned 8-bit integer
uint16_t	Unsigned 16-bit integer
uint32_t	Unsigned 32-bit integer

shows another example of standard data-type definitions for intrinsic functions provided by the CMSIS Core (stdint.h).

It can be found from these two tables that there are tiny differences between these two kinds of standard data-type definitions. However, in some applications, there is no difference between a signed char and signed integer.

Like Object-Oriented Programming (OOP) style, in order to organize data types better and make them to an integrated format or a collection format, some data structures are used in most intrinsic functions. A data structure, or struct, is exactly a data collection with different data items and related data types integrated into this collection to make data well-organized.

For example, to use a union type APSR_TYPE to access the Application Program Status Register (APSR), a data structure shown in Figure 4.18 is used.

To use this APSR_TYPE structure to access each item defined in this structure, one needs to create a variable apsr based on this structure, such as

struct APSR_TYPE apsr;

apsr.Q = 0;

apsr.Z = 0;

apsr.C = 1;

Another example is the CONTROL_TYPE data structure shown in Figure 4.19.

```
typedef union
{
    struct
    {
        uint32_t    _reserved0:26;          /* bit: 0..26 Reserved */
        uint32_t    Q:1;                    /* bit: 27 Saturation condition flag  */
        uint32_t    V:1;                    /* bit: 28 Overflow condition code flag */
        uint32_t    C:1;                    /* bit: 29 Carry condition code flag */
        uint32_t    Z:1;                    /* bit: 30 Zero condition code flag */
        uint32_t    N:1;                    /* bit: 31 Negative condition code flag */
    } b;                                    /* Structure used for bit access. */
    uint32_t  w;                            /* Type used for word access. */
} APSR_TYPE;
```

Figure 4.18.   The APSR_TYPE data structure.

```
typedef union
{
   struct
   {
      uint32_t nPRIV:1;              /* bit:0  Execution privilege in Thread mode */
      uint32_t SPSEL:1;             /* bit: 1  Stack to be used  */
      uint32_t FPCA:1;              /* bit: 2  FP extension active flag */
      uint32_t _reserved0:29;       /* bit: 3..31  Reserved */
   } b;                             /* Structure used for bit access. */
   uint32_t  w;                     /* Type used for word access. */
} CONTROL_TYPE;
```

Figure 4.19. The CONTROL_TYPE data structure.

4.5.2 The CMSIS-Core-Specific Intrinsic Functions

As we discussed in Chapter 3, the CMSIS-Core provides a basic run-time system for the Cortex-M4 device and enables the user to access the Cortex-M4 processor and the related device peripherals. The system includes:

1. Hardware Abstraction Layer (HAL) for Cortex-M4 processor registers with standardized definitions for the SysTick, NVIC, System Control Block registers, MPU registers, FPU registers, and processor access functions.

2. System Exception Names to interface to system exceptions without having compatibility issues.

3. Methods to Organize Header Files. These methods make it easy to learn new Cortex-M4 microcontroller products and improve software portability. This includes naming conventions for device-specific interrupts.

4. Methods for System Initialization to be used by each MCU vendor. For example, the standardized SystemInit() function is essential for configuring the clock system of the device.

5. Intrinsic Functions used to generate CPU and memory access instructions that are not supported by some standard C functions. These intrinsic functions also contain a group of Core peripheral access functions.

6. A variable is used to determine the system clock frequency which simplifies the setup of the SysTick timer.

All of these features are included in related intrinsic functions, and these intrinsic functions and core peripheral access functions are defined in the following C/C++ header files:

- core_cm4.h - CMSIS Cortex-M4 Core Peripheral Access Layer Header File.
- core_cmInstr.h - CMSIS Cortex-M Core Instruction Access Header File.
- core_cmFunc.h - CMSIS Cortex-M Core Function Access Header File.
- core_cm4_simd.h - CMSIS Cortex-M4 Single Instruction Multi-Data (SIMD) Header File.

Table 4.20. The header files and related intrinsic functions.

Header File	Description
core_cm4.h	This is the HAL definition file for Cortex-M4 processor registers with standardized definitions for the SysTick, NVIC, System Control Block registers, MPU registers, FPU registers, and processor access functions
core_cmInstr.h	This is the definition file for all intrinsic functions used to simulate most ARM assembly instructions, including data moving, memory access, arithmetic, logic, shift and rotate, exception related and miscellaneous instructions.
core_cmFunc.h	This is the definition file for all intrinsic functions used to access all special registers in the Cortex-M4 Core, such as CONTROL, APSR, IPSR, PSP, MSP, PRIMASK, FAULTMASK. These intrinsic functions allow users to get and set related registers, enable and disable interrupts.
core_cm4_simd.h	This is the definition file for intrinsic functions used to simulate most ARM assembly arithmetic instructions, including SADD8, SADD16, SSUB8, USUB8, SSAX, and SEL. These intrinsic functions allow users to perform similar arithmetic operations as those assembly instructions did.

Table 4.20 shows these header files and related intrinsic functions involved in these header files. These intrinsic functions can be further divided into the following eight groups based on their functions:

1. Peripheral Access: Define all I/O naming conventions, requirements and optional features to access peripherals. These definitions include the I/O data type, peripheral device name, constants or arguments.

2. System and Clock Configuration: Two intrinsic functions and one variable are included in this group. SystemInit(), SystemCoreClockUpdate(), and SystemCoreClock. Two functions are used to initialize a microcontroller system and update a device-specific system clock. The SystemCoreClock is a global variable used to store the system clock frequency.

3. Interrupts and Exceptions: Define the conventions and features of all interrupts and exceptions used in the MCU system. These include the interrupt numbers, priority levels, and IRQ types. These intrinsic functions allow users to access related interrupt registers to enable or disable any interrupt, set or clear pending for selected interrupt source, and even perform a system Reset function via NVIC mechanism.

4. Core Register Access: Provides all intrinsic functions to simulate related assembly instructions to access special registers used in the Cortex-M4 processor. Most popular registers include CONTROL, PRIMASK, APSR, IPSR, PSP, MSP, BASEPRI, and FAULTMASK. Four functions can be used to enable or disable general IRQs and FAULT_IRQs interrupts.

5. Intrinsic Functions for CPU Instructions: These intrinsic functions generate specific Cortex-M4 instructions that cannot be directly accessed by using the ARM® C/C++ Compiler. The related functions can be used to perform the same function as the assembly instructions did, such as NOP, WFI, WFE, SEV, BKPT, ISB, DSB, REV, and CLZ.

6. Intrinsic Functions for SIMD Instructions: This is the definition file for intrinsic functions used to simulate most ARM® assembly arithmetic instructions, including

Table 4.21.   Some popular intrinsic functions provided by CMSIS Core.

Instructions	CMSIS Core Intrinsic Function	Functions
NOP	void __NOP (void);	No operation
SEV	void __SEV(void);	Send event
WFI	void __WFI(void);	Wait for interrupt (enter sleep mode)
WFE	void __WFE(void);	Wait for event
BKPT	void __BKPT(uint8_t value);	Set a software breakpoint
LDREXB	uint8_t __LDREXB (volatile uint8_t addr*);	Exclusive load byte
LDREX	uint32_t __LDREXW (volatile uint32_t addr*);	Exclusive load word
STREXB	uint32_t __STREXB (uint8_t value, volatile uint8_t addr*);	Exclusive store byte
CLZ	uint8_t __CLZ (unsigned int val);	Count leading zeros
RBIT	uint32_t __RBIT (uint32_t val);	Reverse bits order in word
ROR	unit32_t __ROR (uint32_t value, uint32_t shift);	Rotate shift right by n bits
SADD8	uint32_t __SADD8 (uint32_t val1, uint32_t val2);	Perform four 8-bit signed addition
SSUB8	uint32_t __SSUB8 (uint32_t val1, uint32_t val2);	Perform four 8-bit signed subtraction
MRS	uint32_t __get_CONTROL (void);	Read the CONTROL register
MSR	uint32_t __set_CONTROL (uint32_t control);	Set the CONTROL register
MRS	uint32_t __get_APSR (void);	Read the APSR register
MSR	uint32_t __set_PRIMASK (uint32_t priMask);	Set the PRIMASK register
CPSIE I	void __enable_irq (void);	Globally enable the IRQ interrupts
CPSID I	void __disable_irq (void);	Globally disable the IRQ interrupts

SADD8, SADD16, SSUB8, USUB8, SSAX, and SEL. These intrinsic functions allow users to perform similar arithmetic operations as those assembly instructions did.

7. SysTick Timer: One intrinsic function, SysTick_Config(uint32_t tick), is defined in this group and it is used to initialize and start the SysTick timer.

8. Debug Access: Three intrinsic functions and one external variable are defined in this group to enable users to enter the debug mode to perform debugging function.

Table 4.21 shows some popular intrinsic functions included in the CMSIS Core. Refer to Appendix E to get a complete list of CMSIS Core specific intrinsic functions.

4.5.3 The Keil® ARM® Compiler-Specific Intrinsic Functions

The intrinsic functions provided by the Keil® C/C++ Compiler are very similar to those defined in the CMSIS Core discussed above. Although the functions are very similar, some parameters and arguments may be differently defined in two systems. These intrinsic functions are included with the compiler itself, and therefore they are platform or vendor dependent. This means that different microcontrollers developed and built by the various vendors may have different compilers with different intrinsic functions. In other words, these intrinsic functions cannot be portable across platforms or tools.

Table 4.22 shows some example intrinsic functions provided by the Keil® C/C++ Compiler (c55x.h and dspfns.h).

Compare Table 4.22 with the CMSIS Core intrinsic functions shown in Table 4.21; it can be found that there are some small differences between the intrinsic functions provided

Table 4.22. Some example intrinsic functions provided by Keil® C/C++ Compiler.

Instructions	C/C++ Compiler Intrinsic Function	Functions
NOP	void __nop(void);	No operation
SEV	void __sev(void);	Send event
WFI	void __wfi(void);	Wait for interrupt (enter sleep mode)
WFE	void __wfe(void);	Wait for event
BKPT	void __breakpoint(int value);	Set a software breakpoint
LDREXB	unsigned int __ldrex (volatile void *ptr);	Exclusive load byte
LDREXH	unsigned int __ldrex (volatile void *ptr);	Exclusive load half-word (16-bit)
LDREX	unsigned int __ldrex (volatile void *ptr);	Exclusive load word
STREXB	int __strex (unsigned int value, volatile void *ptr);	Exclusive store byte
STREXH	int __strex (unsigned int value, volatile void *ptr);	Exclusive store half-word (16-bit)
STREX	int __strex (unsigned int value, volatile void *ptr);	Exclusive store word
CLZ	unsigned char __clz (unsigned int val);	Count leading zeros
RBIT	unsigned int __rbit (unsigned int val);	Reverse bits order in word
ROR	unsigned int __ror (unsigned int val, unsigned int shift);	Rotate shift right by n bits
SADD16	_ARM_INTRINSIC int16_t _sadd(int16_t src1, int16_t src2);	Perform four 16-bit signed addition
SSUB8	_ARM_INTRINSIC int16_t _ssub(int16_t src1, int16_t src2);	Perform four 16-bit signed subtraction
ADD	__ARM_INTRINSIC int16_t add(int16_t x, int16_t y);	Add two signed 16-bit data
SUB	__ARM_INTRINSIC int16_t sub(int16_t x, int16_t y);	Subtract two signed 16-bit data
ADC	__ARM_INTRINSIC int32_t L_add_c(int32_t x, int32_t y);	Add two 32-bit signed data with carry
SBC	__ARM_INTRINSIC int32_t L_sub_c(int32_t x, int32_t y);	Subtract two 32-bit signed data with carry
SDIV	__ARM_INTRINSIC int16_t div_s(int16_t x, int16_t y);	Divide two 16-bit signed data
MUL	__ARM_INTRINSIC int32_t L_mult(int16_t x, int16_t y);	Multiply two 16-bit data to get 32-bit result
ASR (LSL)	__ARM_INTRINSIC int32_t L_shr(int32_t x, int16_t shift);	Shift 32-bit data to right (to left if shift <0)
CLREX	void __clrex(void);	Clear exclusive
CPSID I	void __disable_irq(void);	Disable IRQ interrupts & fault handlers
CPSIE I	void __enable_irq(void);	Enable IRQ interrupts & fault handlers
CPSID F	void __disable_fiq(void);	Disable fault interrupts
CPSIE F	void __enable_fiq(void);	Enable fault interrupts
USAT	int __usat(unsigned int val, unsigned int sat);	Unsigned saturation
SSAT	int __ssat(int val, unsigned int sal);	Signed saturation

by the CMSIS Core and the Keil® C/C++ Compiler, especially for the data types and arguments used for these two systems. In some microcontroller development kits or toolchains, the CMSIS Core intrinsic functions are fully supported by the compilers. However, in Keil® ARM-MDK μVersion5, these intrinsic functions are different and cannot be supported for each other.

The Keil® ARM®-MDK C/C++ Compiler, `armcc`, also provides a method called Named Register Variables to enable users to access special registers in the Cortex-M4 processor. To use this method to access any special register, you need first to declare the special register as a variable.

The Named Register Variables are declared by combining the `register` keyword with the __asm keyword. The __asm keyword takes one parameter, a character string, which is the name of the special register. The syntax is

```
register intregname_asm("regname");
```

```
typedef union
{
    struct
    {
            uint32_t    _reserved0:26;          /* bit: 0..26 Reserved */
            uint32_t    Q:1;                    /* bit: 27 Saturation condition flag */
            uint32_t    V:1;                    /* bit: 28 Overflow condition code flag */
            uint32_t    C:1;                    /* bit: 29 Carry condition code flag */
            uint32_t    Z:1;                    /* bit: 30 Zero condition code flag */
            uint32_t    N:1;                    /* bit: 31 Negative condition code flag */
    } b;                                        /* structure used for bit access. */
        uint32_t  w;                            /* type used for word access. */
} APSR_TYPE;

register  APSR_TYPE apsr _asm("apsr");          /* declare apsr as a named register variable */

void  set_Q(void)                               /* the set_Q() method */
{
    apsr.b.Q = 1;                               /* access bit Q to set it to 1  */
}
```

Figure 4.20. An example of using named register variables to access a bit in the APSR.

where the `regname` is the name of the special register to be accessed in the Cortex-M4 processor. For example, to declare the general register R0 as a named register variable, use

```
register intR0 _asm("r0");
```

A typical use of named register variables is to access bits in the Application Program Status

Register (APSR). Recall that we introduced a data structure, struct APSR_- TYPE, in Section 4.5.1 and used that structure as the data type for the APSR register. Figure 4.20 shows an example of using that structure and the named register variables to set the saturation flag Q in the APSR.

Table 4.23 lists most often used special registers in the Cortex-M4 processor and their related reference names. You can use these names to generate associate named register variables to access each of these registers.

4.5.4 Inline Assembler

Another way to access the Cortex-M4 processor registers from the C/C++ codes is to use the inline assembler method. This means that you can insert some assembly instructions in your C/C++ programs to execute them when your program runs. The Keil® ARM® C/C++ Compiler supports the inline assembler feature with Thumb-2 technology. However, some instructions are not supported and cannot be executed in the inline assembler way:

- The instructions TBB, TBH, CBZ, and CBNZ.
- The instruction SETEND.

Table 4.23. The most often used special registers in the Cortex-M4 processor.

Register	Named Register String Name in __asm()
APSR	"apsr"
BASEPRI	"basepri"
BASEPRI_MAX	"basepri_max"
CONTROL	"control"
EAPSR (EPSR + APSR)	"eapsr"
EPSR	"epsr"
FAULTMASK	"faultmask"
IAPSR (IPSR + APSR)	"iapsr"
IEPSR (IPSR + EPSR)	"iepsr"
IPSR	"ipsr"
MSP	"msp"
PRIMASK	"primask"
PSP	"psp"
PSR	"psr"
R0 ~ R12	"r0" ~ "r12"
R13	"r13" or "sp"
R14	"r14" or "lr"
R15	"r15" or "pc"
XPSR	"xpsr"

However, for these limitations the inline assembler is still a powerful tool to facilitate programmers to build their mix-code applications easily and quickly. The inline assembler provides great flexibility for users to access the low-level components from their high-level code program. In addition to the inline assembler, the Keil® ARM® C/C++ Compiler also supports a feature called embedded assembler, and that feature enables user to create some assembly functions in a C/C++ program.

Figure 4.21 shows some examples of using the inline assembler to call assembly instructions to perform special functions from the C code program.

Similar to inline assembler, the opposite way is also working. This means that you can call a C function from assembly codes. You can use IMPORT instruction to select and import your C function into the assembly codes and use BL to call this C function.

Figure 4.22 shows an example of using these instructions to call a C function from assembly codes to perform some addition function, and return result to the assembly codes.

4.5.5 Idiom Recognition

The so-called idiom recognition means that when some C codes are constructed in a special way, the C/C++ Compiler can automatically recognize and convert those codes into a special instruction sequence that can be executed by the microcontroller system. The Keil®

```
/* call inline assembler to perform addition with s1 and s2, returned result is in res   */
int ADD32(int s1, int s2)                    /* C code function header */
{
   int res;                                  /* C code returned variable */
    __asm                                    /* call inline assembler */
  {
      ADD res, s1, s2                         /* { assembly instruction } */
  }
   return res;                               /* C code */
}

/* call inline assembler to enable the CPU to enter the sleep mode   */
void CPUSleep(void)                          /* C code function header */
{
    __asm (" WFI\n");                         /* call inline assembler */
   return;                                   /* C code */
}
```

Figure 4.21.   Some examples of using inline assembler from C codes.

ARM® C/C++ Compiler supports a limited number of idiom recognition forms, as shown in Table 4.24.

4.5.6 C Programming Development Guideline and Procedure

Now we have a clear picture about the ARM® Cortex®-M4 Microcontroller assembly instruction set and related intrinsic functions provided by the Keil® ARM® C/C++ Compiler and CMSIS Core. It looks like we are ready to use C codes to develop and build our applications to access Cortex-M4 MCU and peripherals to fulfill our desired tasks. However, before we can do that, we need to get some detailed knowledge about C program development guidelines and procedures, as well as special definitions used by the C codes for the Cortex-M4 processor and actual registers and peripherals.

```
/* call C function from assembly codes  to perform a ddition with s1 and s2, retu rned result is in res */
/* definition of the C function ADD_C

int ADD_C(int s1, int s2)                    /* C code function header */
{
   int res;                                  /* C code returned variable */
   res = s1 + s2;                            /* perform addition in C code */
   return res;                               /* C code*/
}
; call C function ADD_C to perform addition and get result from R0 = res

MOVS    R0, #0x3                             ; assembly codes, R0 = 0x3
MOVS    R1, #0x2                             ; assembly codes, R1 = 0x2
IMPORT ADD_C                                 ; import C function ADD_C()
BL      ADD_C                                ; call C function ADD_C to do the addition
```

Figure 4.22.   An example of calling a C function from the assembly codes.

Table 4.24. Some idiom recognition forms in Keil® ARM® C/C++ Compiler.

Instruction	C code can be recognized by C/C++ Compiler
BFC	x.b = 0;
BFI	x.b = n;
MLA	x += y × z;
MLS	c = c − a × b;
PKHBT	(a & 0xFFFF0000) | (b & 0x0000FFFF);
PKHTB	(a & 0xFFFF0000) | ((b ≫ 1) & 0x0000FFFF);
SMLABB	x16 × y16 + z32;
SMLABT	x × (y ≫ 16) + z32;
SMMUL	((int)(((long long) I × j) ≫ 32));
SMULBB	x16 × y16;
SMULBT	(x16 ≫ 16) × y16;
SMULTB	x16 × (y16 ≫ 16);
SMULTT	(x16 ≫ 16) × (y16 ≫ 16);
SMULWB	(((long long) x × y) ≫ 16);
SMULWT	(((long long) x × (y ≫ 16)) ≫ 16);
SSAT	(x < −8) ? −8: (x > 7 ? 7: x);
SXTAB	((a ≪ 24) ≫ 24) + i;
SXTAH	((a ≪ 16) ≫ 16) + i;
UMLAL	u64 a; a += ((u64) x × y);
UXTAB	((unsigned)(a ≪ 24) ≫ 24) = i;
UXTAH	((a ≪ 16) ≫ 16) + i;

First let's have a closer look at the organization of a C programming project.

4.5.6.1 Organization of the C Program Files

A complete C/C++ project contains multiple files and it is composed of the following files:

- The header files
- The implementation files
- The application files

The purpose of the header files is to define all variables, constants, and functions used in this project. In other words, the header files provide the abstract definitions for all variables, constants, and functions without concrete descriptions.

For example, the variables and constants can be defined by their names or data types, with or without actual initial values. The functions may be defined by their names, returning data types (void if no returning data), and passed arguments (including the arguments' nominal names and data types) without a detailed function body.

The implementation files contain the detailed definitions and descriptions about all functions, including the function body, which are defined in the header files. In some simple applications, the implementation files can be combined with the application files to be discussed below.

The application files are the main program bodies, and they contain everything the developers need to build and run their project successfully. The user's codes should be included in this application file. The application files are needed to be compiled and linked with the system and other external files together to get the final executable file. In most systems, the linker is included inside the compiler.

4.5.6.2 The Header Files

There are two kinds of header files, the system header files and user header files. The system header files are generated by the vendors and the software manufactures, and these header files generally come with the system software together.

Users need to include these system header files in their user header files or application files to access those system variables and functions by using the system including style, such as #include <stdio.h>, where the stdio.h is a system header file and a pair of arrow brackets is needed to enclose it to indicate that this is a system header file.

The user header files are generated by the users based on their actual applications. To include a user header file, you need to use the user including style, such as #include "myheader.h", where the myheader.h is a user generated header file and a pair of double quotation marks must be used to enclose it to indicate that this is a user header file.

In recent years, some new software protocols are developed. If you are using some namespaces, you can omit the .h extension for the system header file. For example, if you used using namespace std; in your header or application files, you can use #include <stdio> to include the stdio.h system header file.

The following components are regularly included in a header file:

- The #include statements used to include all other necessary system or user header files. These should be located at the top of a header file.
- The #define statements used to announce and define all variables, constants and functions to be used in the project.
- The struct union or enum statements used to define some data types as structures or enums to be used in the project. Recall that we defined the APSR_TYPE as a structure to save space and integrate all data bits in the APSR register into a struct body. The structure union enables users to make their projects more portable and object oriented.
- The global variables and constants to be used in the project. All global and constants should be declared in the header files.
- The protocols of all functions to be used in the project. The protocol of a function includes the function name, returning data type, the nominal names of the arguments and data types. The protocol of a function should not contain any details, including the function body, in the header file.

When using the #define statement to define variables or functions, one key point to be noted is how to avoid multiple and repeated definitions for the same variable, function, or other header files. One useful way to avoid this is to use the #ifndef with #endif statement to cover the variables or functions you do not want to define for

```
//*********************************************************************************
// MyProject.h
// Header file for the project MyProject.c
//*********************************************************************************

//*********************************************************************************
// System Control registers (SYSCTL)
//*********************************************************************************

#define SYSCTL_RCGC2_R        (*((volatile uint32_t *)0x400FE108))

#ifndef  SYSCTL_RCGC2_GPIOF
#define SYSCTL_RCGC2_GPIOF      0x00000020  // Port F Clock Gating Control
#endif

//*********************************************************************************
// GPIO registers (PORTF)
//*********************************************************************************

#define GPIO_PORTF_DIR_R       (*((volatile uint32_t *)0x40025400))
#define GPIO_PORTF_DEN_R       (*((volatile uint32_t *)0x4002551C))
#define GPIO_PORTF_DATA_R      (*((volatile uint32_t *)0x400253FC))
```

Figure 4.23.   Using #ifndef to avoid multiple definitions.

multiple times. For example, the #ifndef statement is used in the header file MyPro-
ject.h shown in Figure 4.23 to avoid the multiple definitions for the constant
SYSCTL_RCGC2_GPIO.

Figure 4.24 shows an example header file, Sample.h, which contains all popular items
that should be located in a header file. Depending on the actual applications, not all items
must be included in a header file.

4.5.6.3 The Implementation Files

The implementation file can belong to either the header file or the C code file. You
must include this implementation file in your application file to make your project
work.

The purpose of using an implementation file is to provide detailed descriptions
about all variables, constants, and functions. Some required header files should also be
included in this file. The detailed function body should be given in this file. According
to the Object-Oriented Programming (OOP) terminology, the header files only
provide the data or attributes for the application, but the implementation files contain
the methods or behaviors of the application. The application itself can be considered as
an object.

The following items are recommended to be appeared in a header, an implementation
or application file:

- The file name
- The function of the file
- The input and output of the file

Figure 4.25 shows an example of an implementation file Sample.c.

```
//*********************************************************************************************
// Sample.h

/* include other header files */

#include <stdio.h>          // system header file
#include <gpio.h>           // system header file
#include "MyProject.h"      // user header file

/ *define all variables, constants used in the project  */
#define SYSCTL_RCGC_GPIO      0x00000010
#ifndef  SYSCTL_RCGC2_GPIOF
#define SYSCTL_RCGC2_GPIOF      0x00000020  // Port F Clock Gating Control
#endif

/* structure definitions   */
typedef  union{
    struct
   {
       uint32_t  PF0;                        /* bit0- Port F */
       uint32_t   PF1;                       /* bit1-Port F */
    } b;                                     /* structure used for bit access. */
       uint32_t  w;                          /* type used for word access. */
} PORTF;

/*  global variables and constants   */
uint32   GPIO_PORTA_DATA_R;
uint32   GPIO_PORTA_DIR_R;
uint32   GPIO_PORTA_DEN_R;

/*   protocols of all functions     */
uint32   get_gpio_port(uint32 *ptr);
void      set_gpio_port(uint32 *ptr);
unsigned int  read_gpio_date(uint32 *ptr);
```

Figure 4.24.   An example header file Sample.h.

```
//*********************************************************************************************
// Sample.c

/* include required header files  */
#include <gpio.h>            /* the getPort(), setPort() and readPort() are defined in this gpio.h file.

/* assign values to global variables and constants   */

uint32   GPIO_PORTA_DATA_R = 0x40004000;
uint32   GPIO_PORTA_DIR_R  = 0x40004400;
uint32   GPIO_PORTA_DEN_R  = 0x4000451C;

/*   details of all functions     */
uint32   get_gpio_port(uint32 *ptr)
{
    uint32  res;
    res = getPort(uint32 *ptr);
    return  res;
}

void      set_gpio_port(uint32 *ptr)
{
    setPort(uint32  *ptr);
}

unsigned int  read_gpio_date(uint32 *ptr)
{
    unsigned int  result;
    result = readPort(uint21  *ptr);
    return  result;
}
```

Figure 4.25.   An example implementation file Sample.c.

Both variables and constants used in this project are initialized by assigned certain values. The detailed function bodies are also provided in this file.

The point to be noted is that three functions, `getPort()`, `setPort()`, and `readPort()` are system functions and they have been defined in the system header file `<gpio.h>`. In order to use them, you need to include this system header file in this implementation file.

4.5.6.4 The Application Files

The application file is the core or main body of your project. It should integrate all files together to make your project as one target application.

Similar with header and implementation files, the application file should contain the following items:

- Other necessary header files used in the project
- External variables, constants, and functions defined in other files
- #define statements used to define other useful variables and constants to be used in the project
- Struct union or enum statements used to define other useful structures and enums
- Global variable and constants used in the project

In some cases, one C code file (either implementation file or an application file) is not enough in some complex project, and multiple C code files may be involved in a project. In that case, different variables and constants, and even functions, may be declared and defined in different files. You need to use the `extern` statement in your main application file to indicate to the compiler to enable it to find and locate them in the compiling time. These variables, constants, and functions can be considered as global items.

Regularly, the global items are not recommended and should be avoided in a project. The following points should be considered as you use any variable, constant, or function:

- Using a different accessing mode, such as public, private, and protected, to limit the scopes for variables, constants and functions used in the project.
- Using a `static` keyword to limit variables, constants, and functions to be used in the current file only even it is a global one.
- Using the keyword `const` to make any constant store in the ROM space, not RAM space.

Figure 4.26 shows an example application file `MyProject.c`.

4.5.6.5 Naming Convention and Definition

From the sample application file shown in Figure 4.26, you may be confused by some variables and constants definitions. These definitions are closely related to the peripherals or I/O devices used in the TM4C123GH6PM MCU. In Section 2.6.3.4 in Chapter 2, we have discussed most GPIO Ports used in this MCU and their addresses.

In order to use those ports, you need to access related registers located at those ports. To facilitate users to use these peripherals to develop their software in C codes, the following rules have been built to help developers to build their program easily and quickly:

1. Each GPIO Port contains a group of related registers with unique addresses. To access each register in C code, a symbolic definition is applied to each register based on its address. Refer

```
//*********************************************************************************************
// MyProject.c
/* include other header files */

#include <stdio.h>          // system header file
#include <gpio.h>           // system header file
#include "MyProject.h"      // user header file

/* other external variables or constants */

extern  intResult;          // global variable in other file
extern  analogInput;        // glob al variable in other file

/ *define other variables & constants used in the project */

#define GPIO_PORTF_DIR_R     (*((volatile uint32_t *)0x40025400))
#define GPIO_PORTF_DEN_R     (*((volatile uint32_t *)0x4002551C))
#define GPIO_PORTF_DATA_R    (*((volatile uint32_t *)0x400253FC))

int main(void)             // Main body of the project
{
   volatile uint32_t ui32Loop;                          // Volatile variable is a temporary local variable.

   SYSCTL_RCGC2_R = SYSCTL_RCGC2_GPIOF;                 // Enable the GPIO PORTF  connected to on-board LED.

   ui32Loop = SYSCTL_RCGC2_R;                           // Do a dummy read to insert a few cycles.

   // Enable the GPIO pin for the LED (PF3).  Set the direction as output, and enable the GPIO pin for digital function.
   GPIO_PORTF_DIR_R = 0x08;
   GPIO_PORTF_DEN_R = 0x08;

   while(1)                                             // Loop forever.
   {
     GPIO_PORTF_DATA_R |= 0x08;                         // Turn on the LED.

     for(ui32Loop = 0;  ui32Loop < 200000;  ui32Loop++)
     {                                                  // Delay for a bit.
     }
     GPIO_PORTF_DATA_R &= ~(0x08);                      // Turn off the LED.

     for(ui32Loop = 0; ui32Loop < 200000; ui32Loop++)  // Delay for a bit.
     {
     }
   }
}
```

Figure 4.26.   An example application file MyProject.c.

to Table 2.7 in Section 2.6.3.4 to get more details about these GPIO Ports and related addresses. Most often-used registers for each GPIO Port are: Data register (GPIO_POR-TA_DATA_R), Direction register (GPIO_PORTA_DIR_R), Digital Enable register (GPIO_PORTA_DEN_R), and Alternate Function Selection register (GPIO_PORTA_AF-SEL_R). In your C program, you need to use these symbolic definitions as the related registers' names to access them.

2. To use these registers, you should first declare them by using the #define statement. In fact, you need to define each register in your C codes based on its address. Since the address in C code can be mapped a pointer, you can define each register by using a pointer points to this register. One easy way to do this definition is to use #define statement to define each register one by one. A better way is to define a structure for a port that contains all registers. An example of this definition for Port A Data register is

```
#define GPIO_PORTA_DATA_R    (* ((volatile uint32_t *) 0x40004000))
```

It looks like that this is a double pointer definition. The (volatile uint32_t *) indicates that this is a pointer or address with the volatile uint32_t data type, and the keyword `volatile` means that the data written into this address can be modified, which is opposite to the keyword `const`. The whole address is defined as (`*((volatile uint32_t *) 0x40004000)`), and the first * points to the starting bit on this address (totally 32-bit on this register). Only the lowest 8 bits in GPIO PORTA are used even if it has 32 bits. The first * is pointed to the entire 8 bits of GPIO PORTA, exactly pointing to the starting bit. This register can be considered as a 2D array, such as DATA_R = {{bit31}, {bit30}, ..., {bit1}, {bit0}}; since each single bit (pin) of this port may be accessed during the programming stage.

3. Similarly, you need to use the #define statement to define and declare all port registers, interrupt numbers, and bit fields used for GPIO-related components. Two examples of these kind of definitions are

---

```
#define GPIO_PORTA_DATA_BITS_R  ((volatile uint32_t *) 0x40004000)
#define INT_GPIOA               16
```

The first code line is to define specific bits on the PORTA; therefore only one * is used. The second line is to define the interrupt number for the PORTA.

Later on during your program development process, you can directly use these symbolic definitions to access all registers on related ports. You can use these registers to do inputs, outputs, and other functions by using logic AND or logic OR operations.

4.5.7 The TivaWare™ Peripheral Driver Library

The Tiva™ for C Series LaunchPad software, TivaWare™ for C Series, provides a set of complete software development tools and libraries to support the users to build their applications.

4.5.7.1 The Programming Models

In TivaWare™ for C Series software driver library, two programming models are provided to support for the user's program development: the `Direct Register Access` (DRA) model and the `Software Driver` (SD) model. Each model can be used independently or combined, based on the users' needs for their applications or the programming environment desired by the developer.

The advantage of using the DRA model is that the target program can be developed in smaller size with higher efficiency. But the developers need to get very detailed knowledge about the processor and peripheral hardware architectures and interfacing configurations as well as detailed interfacing parameters. By using the SD model, the users do not need to know too much about the peripheral hardware architecture and interfacing configurations and can easily build their interfacing functions with the help of the driver library to control and interface to peripherals to get the desired objectives.

In the SD model, a related Application Program Interface (API) is provided by the peripheral driver library and the API enables users to access and control the peripherals via a set of interfacing functions involved in that API. Because these drivers provide complete control of the peripherals in their normal mode of operation, it is possible to write an entire application without direct access to the hardware. This method provides for rapid development of the application without requiring detailed knowledge of how to program the peripherals. Because we have provided very detailed introductions and discussions about the Cortex-M4 MCU and related architecture as well as about the assembly instruction set, we can handle either a DRA or an SD programming model with our applications without any problem.

In the following sections and chapters, we will use a combining model to build and develop our application projects. In other words, we will combine the DRA model and SD model together to build our applications. In part of our programs, we can use the DRA model to directly access the hardware, including the MCU-related registers, memory, and peripherals. In some other parts, we can call the API functions provided by the Driver Library to indirectly access and control the hardware and peripherals to realize our objectives.

First let's take a look at Direct Register Access model by using an example project.

4.5.7.2 The Direct Register Access Model

In the Direct Register Access (DRA) model, the users can access and control peripherals by writing values directly into the peripheral's registers. The users need to use a set of register macros or register symbolic definitions provided by the Peripheral Driver Library to simplify their coding process. These register symbolic definitions are stored in MCU-Specific header files contained in the `inc` directory. The name of the header file matches the MCU number. For example, the header file for the TM4C123GH6PM MCU is in the `inc/tm4c123gh6pm.h` directory under the `C:\ti\TivaWare_C_Series-2.0.1.11577` in your host computer. By including this header file that matches the MCU used, macros or symbolic definitions are available for accessing all registers on that MCU, as well as all bit fields within those registers.

Before we can continue our discussion about how to use the DRA model to build our sample project, first let's have a closer look at the hardware architecture used for this example.

4.5.7.2.1 The Hardware Architecture of the Example Project
We try to use an example project named `MyProject` to illustrate how to use the DRA model to build a simple project. The TM4C123GXL Evaluation Board is used as the hardware base to support our project development. In fact, we will use one LED that is connected to the GPIO PORTF in that EVB to test our project. The hardware configuration for this connection is shown in Figure 4.27.

As shown in Figure 4.27, the pins PF4 and PF0 on PORTF are connected to two user switches or user buttons, SW1 and SW2, respectively. The remaining three pins, PF1, PF2, and PF3, are connected to three different colors LEDs. In fact, these three LEDs are integrated into one three-color LED in this TM4C123GXL Evaluation Board and can be driven by three pins in the Port F.

In this example, we use PF3 which is connected to the green color LED as an output pin to drive that LED to turn it on and off to make a flashing action.

As we discussed in Section 2.6.3.4 in Chapter 2, to enable a GPIO Port to work properly, you need firstly to initialize and configure the GPIO Port in the following sequence:

1. Enable the system clock to drive the port by setting the appropriate bits in the GPIO Run Mode Clock Gating Control (RCGCGPIO) Register.

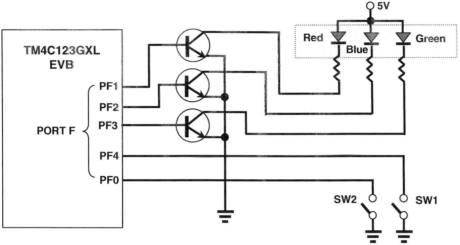

Figure 4.27. The PORT F configuration in TM4C123GXL EVB.

2. Set up the direction for each pin on the GPIO port by programming the GPIODIR register.
3. Enable GPIO pins as digital I/Os by setting the appropriate DEN bit in the GPIODEN register.
4. Optionally you can configure the GPIOAFSEL register to program each bit as a GPIO Mode or Alternate Mode. This step is optional since most ports work in the GPIO Mode after a system reset.

4.5.7.2.2 The Structure and Bit Function of System Control and GPIO Registers In order to effectively using symbolic definitions to define and use those registers to successfully initialize and control the GPIO PORTF, let's have a closer look at the structure and bit function for these registers used by the Port F.

These registers include:

- The General-Purpose Run Mode Clock Gating Control Register (RCGCGPIO)
- The GPIO PORTF Direction Register (GPIOPORTFDIR)
- The GPIO PORTF Digital Enable Register (GPIOPORTFDEN)
- The GPIO PORTF Data Register (GPIOPORTFDATA)

Since the GPIO Alternate Mode Selection Register (GPIOAFSEL) will be set to work in the GPIO mode after a system reset, and the GPIO High-Performance Bus Control (GPIOHBCTL) Register is set to use the Advanced Peripheral Bus (APB) after a system reset, therefore we can temporarily skip these two registers setting up in this example.

4.5.7.2.2.1 The General-Purpose Run Mode Clock Gating Control Register (RCGCGPIO) As we discussed in Section 2.6.3.4 in Chapter 2, to initialize a GPIO Port and provide a system clock for the port, the GPIO Run Mode Clock Gating Control (RCGCGPIO) register should be used. This register provides software the capability to enable and disable GPIO modules in the Run mode. When enabled, a Port is provided with a clock and accesses to Port registers are allowed. When disabled, the clock is disabled to save power and accesses to port registers generate a bus fault. This register

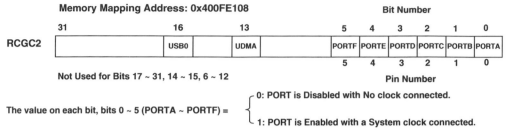

Figure 4.28. The bit number and bit function of the RCGC2 register.

provides the same capability as the Run Mode Clock Gating Control Register 2 (RCGC2) register did.

Because of the similar functionality between the RCGCGPIO and RCGC2 registers, we used the latter in this example to initialize the GPIO Port F. Figure 4.28 shows an illustration for the bit number and bit function of this register. The memory mapping address of this register in the On-Chip memory map is 0x400FE108.

Recall that in Section 2.6.2 in Chapter 2, we discussed the On-Chip memory map for the microcontroller TM4C123GH6PM. It can be found from Table 2.5 that the memory addresses ranging from 0x400F.E000 to 0x400F.EFFF are used to store System Control related registers. All System Control registers, including the RCGC0~RCGC2 clock gating control registers, are located in this space range.

Each bit on this register, including bits 16, 13, and 5~0, controls one peripheral device. If the associate bit is set to 1, the related peripheral connected to the corresponding pin is enabled and a system clock is connected or gated. Otherwise if a bit is reset to 0, the peripheral connected to the corresponding pin is disabled and no clock can be setting.

It can be found from Figure 4.28 that a binary sequence, 00100000B, or a hexadecimal number of 0x20, can be used to enable the PORTF (bit 5 in the RCGC2) and set a clock connection to that port.

4.5.7.2.2.2 The GPIO Ports and Port Control Registers Recall that in Section 2.6.3.3 in Chapter 2, we introduced the GPIO module used in TM4C123GH6PM MCU. Each GPIO Port contains more than 30 32-bit control registers. However, most of the time we only need to use several of them to perform our peripheral control functions. In this example project, we only need to use three registers related to the GPIO PORTF:

1. PORTF Data Register (GPIO_PORTF_DATA_R).
2. PORTF Direction Register (GPIO_PORTF_DIR_R).
3. PORTF Digital Enable Register (GPIO_PORTF_DEN_R).

Although the registers used in each GPIO Port are 32-bit, only the lowest 8 bits are used, in which each bit is corresponding to each pin, as shown in Figure 4.29.

When working in the Advanced Peripheral Bus (APB) aperture, the memory mapping addresses for these registers are

- PORT F DATA Register (GPIO_PORTF_DATA_R): 0x400253FC
- PORTF Direction register (GPIO_PORTF_DIR_R): 0x40025400
- PORTF Digital Enable register (GPIO_PORTF_DEN_R): 0x4002551C

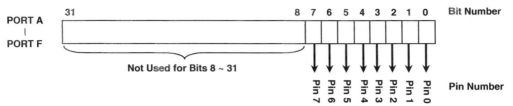

Figure 4.29.   The structure of GPIO Port registers.

Figure 4.30 shows the bit number and bit function for these three registers.

The functions of three registers are as follows: The DATA Register is used to transfer data between the processor and the Port F; the Direction Register is used to define the transferring direction, either input or output, for the data to be transferred in the DATA Register; and the Digital Enable Register is used to enable desired bits in the DATA Register to be transferred.

When using these registers, the following points should be noted:

- The GPIO DATA Register is used to store an 8-bit input or an output data. Although this is a 32-bit register, only the lowest 8 bits are used with one bit matching to one pin as shown in Figure 4.30. Each bit (pin) in this register can be operated separately; in other words, each bit

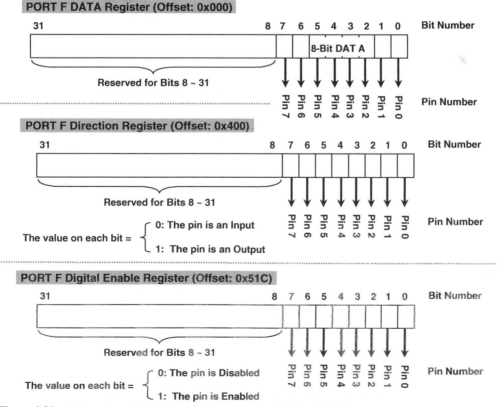

Figure 4.30.   Bit number and function of three registers related to PORTF.

can be read out or written in and can be set up as an input or output bit (pin) separately by configuring the GPIO Direction Register

- The GPIO Direction Register is used to define the data transferring direction, either input or output, for each bit in the DATA Register. A 0 in a bit in this register indicates that the corresponding pin in the DATA Register is an input pin, and a 1 in a bit in this register means that the corresponding pin in the DATA Register is an output pin.

- The GPIO Digital Enable Register is to enable digital input/output function for each bit in the DATA Register. Generally after a system reset, most GPIO pins are configured as GPIO pins and all of them are set to tri-state or disabled. This means that most GPIO pins cannot perform either input or output functions after a reset. In order to enable desired pins to work as input or output pins, the corresponding bits on this Digital Enable Register must be set to 1 as shown in Figure 4.30. However, in some special cases, some GPIO pins can be configured to work for special external peripherals, such as UART0, SSI0, and I²C0, after a system reset, and this is determined by the special setup by some registers, such as GPIO Port Control Register (GPIOPCTL) and GPIO Commit Register (GPIOCR). More details about these functions can be found in Section 2.6.3.4 in Chapter 2.

Now that we have a clear picture about these registers, let's start to define these registers in our software to use them to run our sample project.

4.5.7.2.3 The Symbolic Definitions and Macros
The #define statements used by the Direct Register Access model follow a naming convention that makes it easier to know how to use a particular symbolic definition. The rules are as follows:

- Symbolic definitions that end in _R are used to access the value of a register. For example, GPIO_PORTF_DATA_R is used to access the DATA register in the GPIO PORTF.
- Symbolic definitions that end in _M represent the mask for a multi-bit field in a register.
- Symbolic definitions that end in _S represent the number of bits to shift a value in order to align it with a multi-bit field. These values match the macro with the same base name but ending with _M.
- All other symbolic definitions represent the value of a bit field.
- All register name symbolic definitions start with the module (port) name and instance number. For example, the GPIO is for the GPIO module, and it is followed by the name of the register as it appears in the data sheet, such as the PORTF DATA register in the data sheet resulting in GPIO_PORTF_DATA_R.
- All register bit fields start with the module name, followed by the register name, and is then followed by the bit field name as it appears in the data sheet. For example, the SCR bit field in the CR0 register in the SSI module is identified by SSI_CR0_SCR. In the case where the bit field is a single bit, there is nothing further. For example, SSI_CR0_SPH is a single bit in the CR0 register. If the bit field is more than one bit, there is a mask value _M and either (a) a shift _S if the bit field contains a number or (b) a set of enumerations if not.

The GPIO modules have many registers that do not have bit field definitions. For those registers, the register bits represent the individual GPIO pins. Therefore the bit 0 in these registers corresponds to the Px0 pin on the port, where x represents a GPIO module letter, such as A for PORTA and B for PORTB, and bit 1 corresponds to the Px1 pin, and so on.

A complete register symbolic definitions or macros for the TM4C123GH6PM MCU can be found in the related system header file provided by the TivaWare™ for C Series

Table 4.25. The RGCG2 and GPIO Port F related registers in APB bus aperture.

SYSCTL/GPIO Register	Base Address	Offset	Full Address	SW Symbolic Definition
RCGC2 Register	0x400F.E000	0x108	0x400F.E108	SYSCTL_RCGC2_R
GPIO Port F Direction Register	0x4002.5000	0x400	0x4002.5400	GPIO_PORTF_DIR_R
GPIO Port F DEN Register	0x4002.5000	0x51C	0x4002.551C	GPIO_PORTF_DEN_R
GPIO Port F DATA Register	0x4002.5000	0x3FC	0x4002.53FC	GPIO_PORTF_DATA_R

software package. In most applications, it should be located in the folder `inc/tm4c123gh6pm.h` that is under the folder `C:\ti\TivaWare_C_Series-2.0.1.11577` in your host computer.

Table 4.25 shows all registers, including their names, base address, offset, and software symbolic definitions or macros, to be used in this sample project.

Figure 4.31 shows a header file that contains all symbolic definitions for these registers used in our sample project based on defined items listed in Table 4.25.

As we mentioned in Section 4.5.6.2.2.1, the Run Mode Clock Gating Control Register 2 (RCGC2), whose memory mapping address is `0x400FE108`, can be used to setup the clock for the GPIO Port F and enable this port by setting a 1 to the bit 5 in this register (refer to Figure 4.28). This is equivalent to writing `0x20` to this register.

The coding line 6 in Figure 4.31 is used to define the RCGC2 register as a symbolic register, SYSCTL_RCGC2_R, and assign its mapping address `0x400FE108` to it. Line 7 is to define a constant SYSCTL_RCGC2_GPIOF whose value is `0x20`, and the bit 5 (PORTF) in the register RCGC2 would be set to 1 if this constant is assigned to the RCGC2 register to connect the system clock and enable the GPIO PORTF.

Similarly, in the coding lines 9, 10, and 11, three GPIO PORTF-related registers are defined with GPIO_PORTF_DIR_R (PORTF Direction Register), GPIO_PORTF_-DEN_R (PORTF Digital Enable Register), and GPIO_PORTF_DATA_R (PORTF Data Register), with related memory mapping addresses based on the addresses and symbolic definitions listed in Table 4.25.

4.5.7.2.4 The Programming Operations for Symbolic Definitions To use those symbolic definitions to access each register and perform some data assignment operations

```
1   //*******************************************************************************
2   // MyProject.h -- Header file for the sample project MyProject.c
3   //*******************************************************************************
4
5   // System Control registers (SYSCTL)
6   #define SYSCTL_RCGC2_R          (*((volatile uint32_t *)0x400FE108))
7   #define SYSCTL_RCGC2_GPIOF      0x00000020  // Port F Clock Gating Control
8   // GPIO registers (PORTF)
9   #define GPIO_PORTF_DIR_R        (*((volatile uint32_t *)0x40025400))
10  #define GPIO_PORTF_DEN_R        (*((volatile uint32_t *)0x4002551C))
11  #define GPIO_PORTF_DATA_R       (*((volatile uint32_t *)0x400253FC))
```

Figure 4.31. The symbolic definitions or macros for registers used in the sample project.

in our program, we need to introduce some popular programming operations for the symbolic definitions in the C codes. Most popular operations include:

- Set or reset a bit to 1 or 0: Using direct assignments to assign a 1 (HIGH) or a 0 (LOW) to a specified bit or pin. For example, using the following assignments to set and reset bit 3 (pin 3 – PF3) in the Port F Direction Register (DIR):

GPIO_PORTF_DIR_R = 0x08;	Set PF3 (pin 3) to 1 to make this pin output.
GPIO_PORTF_DIR_R = 0x0;	Reset PF3 (pin 3) to 0 to make this pin input.

- Set a bit to 1 (HIGH): Using a logic OR operation to set a bit to 1 (HIGH). For example, using the following logic OR operation, one can set bit 5 in the Port F Data register:

GPIO_PORTF_DATA_R |= 0x20;	→ GPIO_PORTF_DATA_R = GPIO_PORTF_DATA_R|0x20

Regardless of the original value on bit 5 (either 0 or 1) in Port F, the bit 5 would be definitely set to 1 after this OR operation.

- Reset a bit to 0 (LOW): Using logic AND Complement operation to reset a bit to 0. For example, using the following logic AND Complement operation, one can reset bit 5 in the Port F Data register to 0:

GPIO_PORTF_DATA_R &= ~0x20;	→ GPIO_PORTF_DATA_R = GPIO_PORTF_DATA_R &~0x20

Regardless of the original value on bit 5 (either 0 or 1) in Port F, the bit 5 would be definitely reset to 0 after this AND Complement operation.

- Toggle a bit value from 0 to 1 or from 1 to 0: Using logic Exclusive OR (EOR) operation to toggle a bit value. The following EOR operation can toggle bit 5 on GPIO PORTF Data register:

GPIO_PORTF_DATA_R ∧ = 0x20;	→ PF5_PORTF_DATA_R = ~ PF5_PORTF_DATA_R

- Get a bit value by shifting operation: By using shift left or right operations, one can get desired value for a data bit. For example, the following shift operations enable users to get desired bit result:

#define	PF0	(1<<0)	→ PF0 = 0x00000001 (1 in bit 0 is shifted left 0 bit)
#define	PF1	(1<<1)	→ PF1 = 0x00000002 (1 in bit 0 is shifted left 1 bit)
#define	PF2	(1<<2)	→ PF2 = 0x00000004 (1 in bit 0 is shifted left 2 bit)
#define	PF3	(1<<3)	→ PF3 = 0x00000008 (1 in bit 0 is shifted left 3 bit)

The instruction return (GPIO_PORTF_DATA_R >> 4); is equivalent to shift right all 32-bit data in Port F Data register by 4 bits to move PF7 ~ PF4 to bits 3~0 in Port F register.

Now we have everything done and we are ready to go to build our sample project.

4.5.7.2.5 Develop a Sample Project Using the DRA Model In this sample project, we use PF3 which is connected to the green color LED as an output pin to drive that LED to turn it on and off to make a flashing action (Figure 4.27).

Since this project is very simple, we only use a header file and an application file with the names of "DRAModel.h" and "DRAModel.c".

The general steps to develop a microcontroller application with Keil® ARM®-MDK include:

1. Create a new µVersion5 project with selecting of the MCU and MDK Core/CMSIS Core.
2. Create the user's header files and add them into the project.
3. Create the user's C source files and add them into the project.
4. Include the system header files and other header files into the project by either adding them into the project or using the `Include Paths` function in the ARM®-MDK µVersion5.
5. Include the external functions, variables and other C source files into the project by placing them under the current project folder.
6. Link the library (static or dynamic library) provided by the vendor with the project by adding it as a project file into the project.
7. Compile and link project to create the image or executable file.
8. Download the image file into the flash memory by using `Flash|Download` menu item.
9. Run the project by using the `Debug|Run` menu item.

Now let's follow these nine steps to build our first sample project DRAModel.

4.5.7.2.5.1 Create a New µVersion5 Project DRAModel Perform the following operations to create this new project DRAModel:

1. Open the Windows Explorer window to create a new folder named DRAModel under the C: \ARM Class Projects\Chapter 4 folder.
2. Open the Keil® ARM®-MDK µVersion5 and go to `Project|New µVersion Project` menu item to create a new µVersion Project. On the opened wizard, browse to our new folder DRAModel that is created in step 1 above. Enter DRAModel into the `File` name box and click on the `Save` button to create this project.
3. On the next wizard, you need to select the device (MCU) for this project. Expand three icons, `Texas Instruments`, `Tiva C Series` and `TM4C123x Series`, and select the target device TM4C123GH6PM from the list by clicking on it. Click on the OK to close this wizard.
4. Next the Software Components wizard is opened, and you need to setup the software development environment for your project with this wizard. Expand two icons, `CMSIS` and `Device`, and check the CORE and `Startup` checkboxes in the `Sel.` column, and click on the OK button since we need these two components to build our project.

4.5.7.2.5.2 Create the User's Header Files Perform the following operations to create this new header file DRAModel.h:

1. In the `Project` pane, expand the `Target` folder and right click on the `Source Group 1` folder and select the `Add New Item to Group 'Source Group 1'`.
2. Select the `Header File (.h)` and enter DRAModel into the `Name:` box, and click on the Add button to add this file into the project.
3. Enter the codes shown in Figure 4.32 into this header file, and click on the `File|Save` menu item to save this file. The function for each code line in this header file has been explained in Section 4.5.6.2.3.

```
1    //********************************************************************************
2    // DRAModel.h -- Header file for the sample project DRAModel.c
3    //********************************************************************************
4
5    // System Control registers (SYSCTL)
6    #define SYSCTL_RCGC2_R          (*((volatile uint32_t *)0x400FE108))
7    #define SYSCTL_RCGC2_GPIOF      0x00000020  // Port F Clock Gating Control
8    // GPIO registers (PORTF)
9    #define GPIO_PORTF_DIR_R        (*((volatile uint32_t *)0x40025400))
10   #define GPIO_PORTF_DEN_R        (*((volatile uint32_t *)0x4002551C))
11   #define GPIO_PORTF_DATA_R       (*((volatile uint32_t *)0x400253FC))
```

Figure 4.32. The header file DRAModel.h.

4.5.7.2.5.3 Create the User's Source Files Perform the following operations to create this new source file DRAModel.c:

1. In the Project pane, expand the Target folder and right click on the Source Group 1 folder and select the Add New Item to Group 'Source Group 1'.

2. Select the C File (.c) and enter DRAModel into the Name: box, and click on the Add button to add this source file into the project.

3. Enter the codes shown in Figure 4.33 into this source file, and click on the File|Save menu item to save this file.

```
1    //********************************************************************************
2    // DRAModel.c – Main Application File for the Sample Project
3    //********************************************************************************
4    #include <stdint.h>
5    #include "DRAModel.h"
6    int main(void)
7    {
8      volatile uint32_t  ui32Loop;
9      SYSCTL_RCGC2_R = SYSCTL_RCGC2_GPIOF;      // Enable PORTF in RCGC2
       // Do a dummy read to insert a few cycles after enabling the peripheral.
10     ui32Loop = SYSCTL_RCGC2_R;
11     GPIO_PORTF_DIR_R = 0x08;                  // Set PF3 pin as output pin
12     GPIO_PORTF_DEN_R = 0x08;                  // Enable PF3 pin for digital function
13     while(1)                                  // Loop forever.
14     {
15       GPIO_PORTF_DATA_R |= 0x08;              // Set PF3 pin to turn on LED.
16       for(ui32Loop = 0; ui32Loop < 200000; ui32Loop++)      // Delay for a bit.
17       {
18       }
19       GPIO_PORTF_DATA_R &= ~(0x08);           // Reset PF3 pin to turn off LED.
20       for(ui32Loop = 0; ui32Loop < 200000; ui32Loop++)      // Delay for a bit.
21       {
22       }
       }
     }
```

Figure 4.33. The application file for the sample project DRAModel.

Let's have a closer look at this piece of codes to see how it works.

- The coding lines 4 and 5 are used to include all related header files, including the system header and user header files, <stdint.h> and "DRAModel.h". The system header file <stdint.h> provides all integer data type definitions, including int8, int16 and int32 types, and you need to add this header file into the project later.

- The program entry point starts at line 6. A local unsigned integer 32-bit variable ui32Loop is declared in line 8 and this variable will work as a loop counter in a for loop later.

- A hexadecimal number 0x20 that is defined as a symbolic constant SYSCTL_RCGC2_G-PIOF in the header file is assigned to the RCGC2 register in line 9. This step is used to enable the GPIO Port F and setup a system clock for this port. In fact, the 0x20 is equivalent to 00100000B, which sets bit 5 in the RCGC2 (PORTF) to 1 to enable the port.

- In line 10, the symbolic constant SYSCTL_RCGC2_GPIOF (0x20) defined in the header file is assigned to local variable ui32Loop. This step has nothing to do with the program process except delaying some cycle times to stabilize the enabling process for the GPIO Port F registers.

- A hexadecimal number 0x08 (00001000B) is assigned to the PORTF Direction register (GPIO_PORTF_DIR_R) and Digital Enable register (GPIO_PORTF_DEN_R) to set bit 3 or PF3 pin to 1 to configure PF3 pin as an output pin and enable its digital function in lines 11 and 12.

- Starting from line 13, an infinitive loop is used to perform a turning on and off action to the green color LED connected to PF3 pin. Line 15 is to set PF3 to HIGH to turn the LED on by assigning 0x08 (00001000B) to Port F Data register (GPIO_PORTF_DATA_R).

- In the coding lines 16 and 20, two for loops are used to delay some times to enable the LED to keep on and off at certain period of time.

- After delay certain period of time, the PF3 pin is reset to 0 by ANDing a complement of 0x08 (~0x08 = 11110111B) with the original content of the Port F Data register in line 19. Note that the bit 3 (PF3) for the complement of 0x08 is 0. We have discussed this kind of programming operation to reset a bit in the last section.

4.5.7.2.5.4 Include the System Header Files and Other Header Files into the Project Perform the following operations to add the system header file <stdint.h> into the project:

1. This header file is a Keil® ARM®-MDK C/C++ Compiler system header file used to define all integer data types used in the C/C++ files. This file is located at a folder in which the MDK µVersion5 is installed: C:\Keil_v5\ARM\ARMCC\include.

2. In the Project pane, expand the Target folder and right click on the Source Group 1 folder and select the Add Existing Files to Group 'Source Group 1'. In the opened wizard, browse to the location of this file located, C:\Keil_v5\ARM\ARMCC\include, and select this header file by clicking on it. Then click on the Add button to add it into our project.

4.5.7.2.5.5 Include the External Functions and Other C Source Files into the Project Because we did not use any other C source file and external function in this sample project, we need to do nothing in this step. However, in some other complicated projects, you must do this step otherwise your project cannot work properly.

4.5.7.2.5.6 Link the Static or Dynamic Library with the Project In this sample project, we do not use any static or dynamic link library since we used Direct Register Access model for this project. Therefore we need to do nothing with this step. However, in some other projects where either a static or dynamic link library, such as TivaWare™ Peripheral Driver Library, is used, you must do this step. Otherwise you cannot run your project at all.

4.5.7.2.5.7 Compile and Link Project to Create the Image or Executable File Go to `Project|Build Target` menu item to compile and link this sample project with system files to make our project image or executable file. A message displaying 0 `Error (s)` with 0 `Warning(s)` should be displayed in the `Build Output` window at the bottom if nothing wrong with this sample project.

4.5.7.2.5.8 Download the Image File into the Flash Memory and Run the Project By using `Flash|Download` menu item, you can download the project image file into the flash memory. Now you can run this program by going to the `Debug|Run` menu item. As the program is running, you can find that the green color LED will be flashing forever. Make sure that the debugger you are using is the `Stellaris ICDI`, which can be checked from the `Debug` tab in the `Options for Target` 'Target 1' item under the `Project` menu.

Next let's discuss how to use the Software Driver (SD) model to call the driver library functions to perform this LED flashing function.

4.5.7.3 The Peripheral Driver Library and API Functions

The Driver Library is installed in the internal ROM space in the On-Chip memory, and it also is included in the TivaWare™ for the C Series software package and can be downloaded and installed in the user's host computer.

This library contains more than 35 drivers for related peripherals. The most popular drivers included in this library are:

1. GPIO Ports
2. Analog Comparators
3. Analog To Digital Converters (ADC)
4. Advanced Encryption Standard (AES)
5. Controller Area Network (CAN)
6. EEPROM
7. External Peripheral Interface (EPI)
8. Fan Controller
9. Flash Memory
10. Floating Point Unit (FPU)
11. Interrupt Controller (NVIC)
12. LCD Controller (LCD)
13. Pulse-Width Modulator (PWM)
14. Quadrature Encoder (QEI)
15. Synchronous Serial Interface (SSI)
16. System Control

17. System Tick (SysTick)

18. Timer

19. UART

20. USB Controller

21. Watchdog Timer

We will discuss most these peripherals in the following chapters. However, in this section we want to use the GPIO and System Control libraries as an example to illustrate how to use these library functions to access the GPIO Ports to develop our sample project.

As we know, in order to enable GPIO Ports to work properly, each port must be initialized by connecting the system clock to clock and enable the port to work normally. Therefore before we can go to discuss the details about the API functions for GPIO Ports, we should have a clear picture about the system clock control and GPIO clock gating control API functions provided by this library. These API functions belong to the System Control library functions.

As we discussed in Section 2.6.2.3 in Chapter 2, the TM4C123GH6PM MCU provides a General-Purpose Input and Output (GPIO) module. This module contains six GPIO blocks, and each block is related to an individual GPIO Port (Port A~Port F). Each GPIO Port is programmable or configurable to provide multiple functions to enable the port to handle different tasks. Not all 48 pins (6 GPIO Ports with each port having 8 pins) are configurable or programmable since some pins are not available. Therefore totally the GPIO module supports up to 43 programmable input/output pins, depending on the peripherals being used. Each GPIO pin provides the following capabilities:

- Can be configured as an input or an output. On reset, they default to be an input.
- In the input mode, each pin can generate interrupts on high level, low level, rising edge, falling edge, or both edges.
- In the output mode, each pin can be configured to output 2-mA, 4-mA, or 8-mA drive strength. The 8-mA drive strength configuration has optional slew rate control to limit the rise and fall times of the signal. On reset, they default to 2-mA drive strength.
- Optional weak pull-up or pull-down resistors. On reset, they default to a weak pull-up on Sandstorm-class devices, and they default to disabled on all other devices.
- Optional open-drain operation. On reset, they default to standard push/pull operation.
- Can be configured to be a GPIO or a peripheral pin. On reset, they default to GPIOs.
- All pins on all parts have peripheral functions, in which case the pin is only useful as a GPIO pin. In other words, when it is configured for special peripheral function the pin will not do anything useful.

First let's have a closer look at the API functions for System Control drivers.

4.5.7.3.1 System Control API Functions The System Control API functions determine the overall operation of the device. They control the clocking of the device, the set of peripherals that are enabled, and the configuration of the device and its resets, and they provide information about the device.

In Sections 2.6.3.1 and 2.6.4.4 in Chapter 2, we have provided detailed discussions about the system clock architecture and its control programming. Generally there are five clock sources that can be used as the system clock source:

1. Precision Internal Oscillator (PIOSC): 16 MHz.
2. Main Oscillator (MOSC): It can use an external clock source or an external crystal.
3. Low-Frequency Internal Oscillator (LFIOSC): An on-chip internal 30-kHz Oscillator used for Deep-Sleep power-saving modes.
4. Hibernate RTC Oscillator (RTCOSC) Clock Source: It can be configured to be the 32.768-kHz external oscillator source from the Hibernation (HIB) module.
5. Phase-Locked Loop (PLL) clock generator.

However, in the Tiva™ for C Series LaunchPad microcontrollers, only the MOSC, LFIOSC, RTCOSC, and PLL are available for the TM4C123G MCU family.

When the PLL is used as the system clock generator, a fixed 400 MHz is produced by this generator. However, the system clock that is the output of the PLL can be divided by a pre-divided-by-2 divisor and some divider parameters that can be controlled by the software in the user's program. The output range of the PLL is 5~25 MHz. Refer to Tables 2.15 and 2.16 in Chapter 2 to get more details for these parameters.

This driver is contained in a C file `sysctl.c` with a header file `sysctl.h` that contains the API declarations for use by applications. Both files are at the folder: `C:\ti\TivaWare_C_Series-2.0.1.11577\driverlib` in your host computer.

The most popular API functions used for system clock controls are:

- SysCtlClockSet()
- SysCtlPeripheralEnable()
- SysCtlPeripheralReady()
- SysCtlDelay()

4.5.7.3.1.1 The SysCtlClockSet() API Function The purpose of this function is to set up and configure the system clock for the selected peripheral device. The protocol of this function is

```
void SysCtlClockSet(uint32_t ui32Config);
```

The argument `ui32Config` is the required setup parameter of the device to be configured in an appropriate clocking source. This argument can be used as logic OR combinations of different parameters used to configure the clock for a device. Most popular parameters used to configure a device include:

1. The input crystal frequency
2. The oscillator to be used
3. Whether use of the PLL
4. The system clock divider

Table 4.26 shows most popular parameters to be used in the configuration argument for this function. Some crystal frequencies are not listed in this table, such as

Table 4.26. The popular parameters used in system clock configuration argument.

System Clock Divider	PLL Use	Crystal Frequency	Oscillator Source
SYSCTL_SYSDIV_2 SYSCTL_SYSDIV_3 SYSCTL_SYSDIV_4 SYSCTL_SYSDIV_5 ... ... SYSCTL_SYSDIV_64	SYSCTL_USE_PLL SYSCTL_USE_OSC	SYSCTL_XTAL_5_12MHZ SYSCTL_XTAL_6MHZ SYSCTL_XTAL_8MHZ SYSCTL_XTAL_10MHZ SYSCTL_XTAL_12MHZ SYSCTL_XTAL_16MHZ SYSCTL_XTAL_16_3MHZ SYSCTL_XTAL_18MHZ SYSCTL_XTAL_20MHZ SYSCTL_XTAL_24MHZ SYSCTL_XTAL_25MHz	SYSCTL_OSC_MAIN SYSCTL_OSC_INT SYSCTL_OSC_INT4 SYSCTL_OSC_INT30 SYSCTL_OSC_EXT32

SYSCTL_XTAL_5_12MHZ, SYSCTL_XTAL_7_37MHZ, SYSCTL_XTAL_8_19MHZ, and SYSCTL_XTAL_14_3MHZ.

When using these arguments to configure the selected devices, the following points need to be noted:

- Crystal frequency below SYSCTL_XTAL_5MHZ is not valid when the PLL is used.
- The SYSCTL_OSC_EXT32 is an only available parameter on devices with the hibernate module, and then only when the hibernate module has been enabled.
- The internal and main oscillators are disabled with the SYSCTL_INT_OSC_DIS and
- SYSCTL_MAIN_OSC_DIS flags. The external oscillator must be enabled in order to use an external clock source. Note that attempts to disable the oscillator used to clock the device is prevented by the hardware.
- To clock the system from an external source, such as an external crystal oscillator, use SYSCTL_USE_OSC | SYSCTL_OSC_MAIN.
- To clock the system from the main oscillator, use SYSCTL_USE_OSC | SYSCTL_OSC_MAIN.
- To clock the system from the PLL, use SYSCTL_USE_PLL | SYSCTL_OSC_MAIN, and select the appropriate crystal with one of the crystal frequency shown in Table 4.26.

For example, to configure the GPIO PORTF by using a 16-MHz crystal on the main oscillator with using the PLL whose output is 400 MHz. With a default pre-divided-by-2 divisor in the clock path (Figure 2.16), you can select another divided-by-5 divisor in software, which is totally divided by 10, and then you can get a 400-MHz/10 = 40-MHz system clock applied on the PORTF. The following API function can be used to do this configuration:

```
SysCtlClockSet(SYSCTL_SYSDIV_5|SYSCTL_USE_PLL|SYSCTL_XTAL_16MHZ| SYSCTL_OSC_MAIN);
```

The multiple parameters are ORed together to form this input argument to configure the port.

4.5.7.3.1.2 The SysCtlPeripheralEnable() API Function   This function is used to enable a peripheral device. After a system reset, all peripherals are disabled. Any peripheral must be enabled by executing this function before they can operate or respond to register reads/ writes operation.

Table 4.27. The popular peripherals and their parameter names.

Peripheral Device	ui32Peripheral Parameter
Analog-To-Digital Converter0 (ADC0) Analog-To-Digital Converter1 (ADC1)	SYSCTL_PERIPH_ADC0 SYSCTL_PERIPH_ADC1
Control Area Network0 (CAN0) Control Area Network1 (CAN1) Control Area Network2 (CAN2)	SYSCTL_PERIPH_CAN0 SYSCTL_PERIPH_CAN1 SYSCTL_PERIPH_CAN2
Analog Comparator0 (COMP0) Analog Comparator1 (COMP1) Analog Comparator2 (COMP2)	SYSCTL_PERIPH_COMP0 SYSCTL_PERIPH_COMP1 SYSCTL_PERIPH_COMP2
Fan Controller0 (FAN0) Fan Controller1 (FAN1)	SYSCTL_PERIPH_FAN0 SYSCTL_PERIPH_FAN1
GPIO PORTA (GPIOA) GPIO PORTB (GPIOB) GPIO PORTC (GPIOC) GPIO PORTD (GPIOD) GPIO PORTE (GPIOE) GPIO PORTF (GPIOF)	SYSCTL_PERIPH_GPIOA SYSCTL_PERIPH_GPIOB SYSCTL_PERIPH_GPIOC SYSCTL_PERIPH_GPIOD SYSCTL_PERIPH_GPIOE SYSCTL_PERIPH_GPIOF
I^2C Controller0(I2C0) I^2C Controller1(I2C1) I^2C Controller2(I2C2) I^2C Controller3(I2C3) I^2C Controller4(I2C4) I^2C Controller5(I2C5)	SYSCTL_PERIPH_I2C0 SYSCTL_PERIPH_I2C1 SYSCTL_PERIPH_I2C2 SYSCTL_PERIPH_I2C3 SYSCTL_PERIPH_I2C4 SYSCTL_PERIPH_I2C5
Pulse Width Modulator0 (PWM0) Pulse Width Modulator1 (PWM1)	SYSCTL_PERIPH_PWM0 SYSCTL_PERIPH_PWM1
Quadrature Encoder Interface0 (QEI0) Quadrature Encoder Interface1 (QEI1)	SYSCTL_PERIPH_QEI0 SYSCTL_PERIPH_QEI1
Synchronous Serial Interface0 (SSI0) Synchronous Serial Interface1 (SSI1)	SYSCTL_PERIPH_SSI0 SYSCTL_PERIPH_SSI1
System Timer0 (TIMER0) Universal Asynchronous Receiver/Transmitter0 (UART0) Universal Serial Bus0 (USB0) Watchdog Timer0 (WDOG0) Watch Timer0 (WTIMER0)	SYSCTL_PERIPH_TIMER0 SYSCTL_PERIPH_UART0 SYSCTL_PERIPH_USB0 SYSCTL_PERIPH_WDOG0 SYSCTL_PERIPH_WTIMER0

The protocol of this function is

```
void SysCtlPeripheralEnable(uint32_t ui32Peripheral);
```

The argument `ui32Peripheral` is the peripheral to be enabled. Table 4.27 shows some popular peripherals and their symbolic definitions or macros to be used as the argument `ui32Peripheral`.

For example, to enable the GPIO PORTA, the following function can be used:

```
SysCtlPeripheralEnable(SYSCTL_PERIPH_GPIOA);
```

One point to be noted when using this function is that it will take about five clock cycles after this function is executed to enable a peripheral before that peripheral is actually enabled. During this time, attempts to access the peripheral result in a bus fault. Therefore a time delay subroutine is recommended and should be inserted into the user's program to wait for this enabling function complete, and the peripheral device is stable and ready to be accessed.

4.5.7.3.1.3 The SysCtlPeripheralReady() API Function This function is used to determine whether a particular peripheral is ready to be accessed. The peripheral may be in a disable state if it is not enabled, is being held in reset, or is in the process of becoming ready after being enabled or taken out of reset.

The protocol of this function is

```
bool SysCtlPeripheralReady(uint32_t ui32Peripheral);
```

The argument `ui32Peripheral` is the selected peripheral device to be tested, and the symbolic definition or macro for this argument can be found from Table 4.27. This function returns a Boolean value. A True means that the tested peripheral is ready to be accessed, and a False indicates that the device is not ready.

4.5.7.3.1.4 The SysCtlDelay() API Function This function is used to provide a small time delay with 3 clock cycles for each loop delay time. The protocol of this function is

```
void SysCtlDelay(uint32_t ui32Count);
```

The argument `ui32Count` is the number of delay loop iterations to be performed.

For example, if a 40-MHz system clock is used (one cycle $= 0.025 \,\mu s$) to delay $500 \,\mu s$, this `ui32Count` is $500/0.025 = 20,000$. Use this parameter to delay $500 \,\mu s$ with the following line:

```
SysCtlDelay(20000);
```

This function only performs a time delay without returning any value.

Now we have completed the discussions about the system control API functions and we are ready to take a closer look at the GPIO API functions.

4.5.7.3.2 GPIO API Functions Most of the GPIO API functions in this library can operate on more than one pin at a time. The argument parameter `ucPins` in these functions is used to specify the pins that are affected; only the pins corresponding to the related bits in this parameter that are set are affected. There is a one-to-one relationship between each bit and the corresponding pin on each Port, where bit 0 is pin 0, bit 1 is pin 1, and so on. For example, if `ucPins` is 0x09 (00001001B), then only pins 0 and 3 are affected by the function.

This operation model is most useful for the `GPIOPinRead()` and `GPIOPinWrite ()` functions. A `GPIOPinRead()` returns only the values of the requested pins that have been indicated by the masking bits or `ucPins` parameter with the other pin values masked out, and a `GPIOPinWrite()` only affects the requested pins simultaneously. This data masking for the GPIO pin state occurs in the hardware.

Some functions can operate only a single pin. For those functions that have a parameter `ucPin`, only a single pin is affected by executing the function. In this case, the value of `ucPin` specifies the pin number, which is 0 through 7.

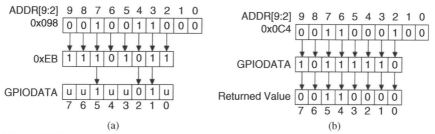

Figure 4.34. An example of using mask byte to do data reading and writing. (Reprinted with the permission of the Texas Instruments Incorporated.)

There are about 49 API functions provided by the GPIO library, and these functions are used to control all GPIO-related peripherals in TM4C123GH6PM MCU system. We will select some functions as an example to illustrate how to create our sample application program to access GPIO Port F to control a LED via these functions.

4.5.7.3.2.1 The GPIOPinRead() and GPIOPinWrite() Functions In order to perform a reading or writing operation to GPIO DATA register for any port by using the GPIOPin-Read() and GPIOPinWrite() functions, a masking byte must be provided with this reading or writing function. The corresponding bits in the mask, resulting from the address bus bits [9:2], must be set to enable the selected bits to be read out or written in. Otherwise, the bit values remain unchanged by the write or the returned bit values are zero by the read. Figure 4.34 shows an example of using this mask byte to perform a reading and a writing operation as well as the results.

A writing operation is shown in Figure 4.34a, and a reading operation is shown in Figure 4.34b. Most times the mask byte is used with the API reading and writing functions.

When writing (Figure 4.34a), the mask byte is 0x098 = 000010011000B. However, a mask must be a byte (8-bit); therefore only the bits 2~9 on this 12-bit mask data is used to make this mask byte as 00100110B = 0x26. When applying this mask to perform a writing 0xEB to the Data Register, only bits 1, 2, and 5 in the written data 0xEB are selected by the mask byte and written into the Data Register since those bits are set to 1 in the mask byte. All other bits in the Data Register keep unchanged and indicated by a letter u.

When reading (Figure 4.34b), the data value in the Data Register is 10111110B = 0xBE, and this value should be read out and returned. However, the mask data applied to this reading is 0x0C4, but after converting this to the mask byte, it becomes 00110001B = 0x31 since we only need the bits 2~9 for this mask data (or address bits 2~9). Therefore only bits 0, 4, and 5 on the Data Register's content, 0xBE, are read out since those bits are set to 1 in the mask byte. All other bits are read out as 0.

The protocol of the function GPIOPinWrite() is

```
void GPIOPinWrite(uint32_t ui32Port, uint8_t ui8Pins, uint8_t ui8Val);
```

Three arguments are used in this function and the meanings for these arguments are as follows:

1. The first argument ui32Port is the base address of the GPIO Port.

2. The second argument ui8Pins is the masking byte used to select the bits to be written.

3. The third argument ui8Val is the data value to be written into this port.

This function returns nothing.

Using Figure 4.34a as an example, when we write data 0xEB with the making byte as 0x098 into the GPIO Port A Data register, two forms of this function can be used:

1. GPIOPinWrite(GPIO_PORTA_BASE, 0x098, 0xEB);

2. GPIOPinWrite(GPIO_PORTA_BASE,   (GPIO_PIN_1|GPIO_PIN_2|GPIO_-PIN_5), 0xEB);

The masking byte 0x098 is equivalent to selecting bits 1, 2, and 5 in the 8-bit data 0xEB (11101011). Therefore only these three bits' values can be written into the Port A Data register with all other bits unchanged. The second form uses the symbolic definitions or macros for each pin as the masking byte to perform this writing operation.

Note that the macro GPIO_PORTA_BASE is defined in the gpio.c system C file, and the symbolic definition GPIO_PIN_X is defined in the gpio.h system header file. Both files are located at the folder driverlib directory in your host computer. You need to include these files in your application if you want to use these symbolic definitions or macros.

The protocol of the function GPIOPinRead() is

int32_t GPIOPinRead(uint32_t ui32Port, uint8_t ui8Pins);

Two arguments are used in this function, and the meanings for these arguments are:

1. The first argument ui32Port is the base address of the GPIO Port.

2. The second argument ui8Pins is the masking byte used to select the bits to be read out.

The function returns a 32-bit reading result. However, as we mentioned, bits 31~8 on this reading result are reserved with no actual values for this reading. Only the lowest 8 bits contain the data reading result. Only those bits that have been masked by the masking byte contain the reading result, and any bit that is not specified or selected by the masking byte is returned as 0.

Using Figure 4.34b as an example, the data value in the Data Register is 10111110B = 0xBE. The making byte is 0x0C4, but after converting this to the mask byte, it becomes 00110001B = 0x31. Therefore only bits 0, 4, and 5 on the Port A Data Register's content, 0xBE, are read out since those bits are set to 1 in the mask byte. All other bits are read out as 0. When using this function to read the GPIO Port A Data register, two forms of this function can be used:

1. i32Val = GPIOPinRead(GPIO_PORTA_BASE, 0x0C4);

2. i32Val = GPIOPinRead(GPIO_PORTA_BASE, (GPIO_PIN_0|GPIO_PIN_4|GPIO_PIN_5));

The masking byte 0x0C4 is equivalent to 0x31 and only bits 0, 4, and 5 in the 8-bit data 0xBE (10111110) are selected. Therefore only these three bits' values can be read out from the Port A Data register with all other bits as 0. This result is returned to the variable i32Val. The second form uses the symbolic definitions or macros for each pin as the masking byte to perform this reading operation.

4.5.7.3.2.2 The GPIOPinTypeGPIOInput() Function This function allows users to configure the GPIO Pins as Input pins. The protocol of this function is

void GPIOPinTypeGPIOInput(uint32_t ui32Port, uint8_t ui8Pins);

Two arguments are used in this function and the meanings for these arguments are:

1. The first argument `ui32Port` is the base address of the GPIO Port.

2. The second argument `ui8Pins` is the masking byte used to select the pins to be input pins.

For example, the following two functions perform the same function, that is, to configure pins 2, 4, and 5 on the GPIO PORTA as input pins:

```
GPIOPinTypeGPIOInput(GPIO_PORTA_BASE, GPIO_PIN_2 | GPIO_PIN_4 |
  GPIO_PIN_5);
GPIOPinTypeGPIOInput(GPIO_PORTA_BASE, 0x0D0);
```

In the second function, the masking byte is `0x0D0`, which is equivalent to `0x34` (`00110100B`). This masking byte will reset bits 2, 4, and 5 in the GPIO PORTA Direction register to 0 to enable these bits (pins) in the Port A to work as input bits (pins).

4.5.7.3.2.3 The GPIOPinTypeGPIOOutput() Function This function allows users to configure the GPIO Pins as Output pins. The protocol of this function is

```
void GPIOPinTypeGPIOOutput(uint32_t ui32Port, uint8_t ui8Pins);
```

Two arguments are used in this function and the meanings for these arguments are as follows:

1. The first argument `ui32Port` is the base address of the GPIO Port.

2. The second argument `ui8Pins` is the masking byte used to select the pins to be output pins.

For example, the following two functions perform the same function, that is, to configure pins 0 and 3 on the GPIO PORTA as output pins:

```
GPIOPinTypeGPIOOutput(GPIO_PORTA_BASE, GPIO_PIN_0 | GPIO_PIN_3);
GPIOPinTypeGPIOOutput(GPIO_PORTA_BASE, 0x024);
```

In the second function, the masking byte is `0x024` that is equivalent to `0x09` (`00001001B`). This masking byte will set bits 0 and 3 in the GPIO PORTA Direction register to 1 to enable these bits (pins) in the Port A to work as output bits (pins).

The above API functions provided us with the fundamental interfacing functions to the GPIO Ports in the TM4C123GXL EVB, and they are good enough for our sample project development. Other driver library API functions will be discussed in the following related chapters when more peripherals are introduced.

Now let's use the GPIO PORT F as our target GPIO Port to illustrate how to call these related GPIO API functions provided by the GPIO library to initialize, configure, access, and control this port to perform a LED flashing function on the TM4C123GXL Evaluation Board.

4.5.7.3.3 Develop a Sample Project Using the SD Model Refer to Figure 4.27 to get details about the hardware configuration of the GPIO Port F in the TM4C123GXL Evaluation Board.

In this sample project, we still use PF3, which is connected to the green color LED as an output pin to drive that LED to turn it on and off to make a LED flashing action.

Since this project is very simple, we only use a header file and an application file with the names of "BLSDModel.h" and "BLSDModel.c". The prefix BL means that a binary static library is used in the sample project. Another project that uses a C file static library is named CLSDModel is also developed and stored in the Chapter 4 folder for the user's reference. In this part, we only take care of the project BLSDModel.

Perform the following steps to build our sample project BLSDModel.

4.5.7.3.3.1 Create a New μVersion5 Project BLSDModel Perform the following operations to create this new project BLSDModel:

1. Open the Windows Explorer window to create a new folder named BLSDModel under the C:\ARM Class Projects\Chapter 4 folder.
2. Open the Keil® ARM®-MDK μVersion5 and go to Project|New μVersion Project menu item to create a new μVersion Project. On the opened wizard, browse to our new folder BLSDModel that is created in step 1 above. Enter BLSDModel into the File name box and click on theSave button to create this project.
3. On the next wizard, you need to select the device (MCU) for this project. Expand three icons, Texas Instruments, Tiva C Series, and TM4C123x Series, and select the target device TM4C123GH6PM from the list by clicking on it. Click on the OK to close this wizard.
4. Next the Software Components wizard is opened, and you need to set up the software development environment for your project with this wizard. Expand two icons, CMSIS and Device, and check the CORE and Startup checkboxes in the Sel. column, and click on the OK button since we need these two components to build our project.

4.5.7.3.3.2 Create the User's Header Files Perform the following operations to create this new header file BLSDModel.h:

1. In the Project pane, expand the Target folder and right click on the Source Group 1 folder and select the Add New Item to Group 'Source Group 1'.
2. Select the Header File (.h) and enter BLSDModel into the Name: box, and click on the Add button to add this file into the project.
3. Enter the codes shown in Figure 4.35 into this header file, and click on the File|Save menu item to save this file. The function for each code line is:
   • The code lines 4 and 5 are used to include two system header files, <stdint.h> and <stdbool.h>. These two header files defined most standard integer data types and Boolean data types used in C/C++ programs. Two files are located at the default folder of installing the Keil® ARM®-MDK μVersion5 IDE, exactly in the folder C:\Keil_v5\ARM\ARMCC\include.

```
1   //********************************************************************************
2   // BLSDModel.h  (Header file for the project BLSDModel.c)
3   //********************************************************************************
4
5   #include <stdint.h>                        // for uint32, uint16, ....
6   #include <stdbool.h>                       // for bool
7   #define SYSCTL_RCGC2_GPIOF     0x00000020 // Port F Clock Gating Control
```

Figure 4.35. The header file BLSDModel.h.

```
1   //********************************************************************************
2   // BLDSModel.c -- Main source file for sample project BLSDModel
3   //********************************************************************************
4   #include "BLSDModel.h"
5   #include <inc/hw_memmap.h>
6   #include <inc/hw_types.h>
7   #include <driverlib/sysctl.h>
8   #include <driverlib/gpio.h>
9   int main(void)
10  {
11    bool  res = false;
12    SysCtlClockSet(SYSCTL_SYSDIV_10|SYSCTL_USE_PLL|SYSCTL_XTAL_16MHZ|SYSCTL_OSC_MAIN);
13    SysCtlPeripheralEnable(SYSCTL_PERIPH_GPIOF);                 // enable PORT F
14    GPIOPinTypeGPIOOutput(GPIO_PORTF_BASE, GPIO_PIN_3);          // enable PF3 as output pin
15    res = SysCtlPeripheralReady(SYSCTL_PERIPH_GPIOF);
16    if (res == true)
17    {
18      while(1)
19       {
20         GPIOPinWrite(GPIO_PORTF_BASE, GPIO_PIN_3, 0x8);         // set PF3 to HIGH
21         SysCtlDelay(500000);                                    // Delay for a bit.
22         GPIOPinWrite(GPIO_PORTF_BASE, GPIO_PIN_3, 0x0);         // reset PF3 to LOW
23         SysCtlDelay(500000);                                    // Delay for a bit.
       }
     }
  }
```

Figure 4.36. The C source codes for the application file BLSDModel.c.

- The code line 7 is used to define a constant 0x00000020 that is to set bit 5 in the RCGC2 to 1 to enable Port F clock gating. This line is not used in this program.

Now let's take care of the C source file BLSDModel.c.

4.5.7.3.3.3 Create the User's Source Files Perform the following operations to create this new source file BLSDModel.c:

1. In the Project pane, expand the Target folder and right click on the Source Group 1 folder and select the Add New Item to Group 'Source Group 1'.

2. Select the C File (.c) and enter BLSDModel into the Name: box, and click on the Add button to add this source file into the project.

3. Enter the codes shown in Figure 4.36 into this source file, and click on the File|Save menu item to save this file.

Let's have a closer look at this piece of codes to see how it works.

- The coding lines 4 and 8 are used to include all related header files, including the user header files and system header files. The system header file <inc/hw_memmap.h> provides all symbolic definitions for GPIO Ports, and the <inc/hw_types.h> provides all macros for hardware access. The <driverlib/sysctl.h> and <driverlib/gpio.h> provide all symbolic definitions for system control registers and GPIO-related registers. The point to be noted is that all of these header files are located at different locations and we need to provide include paths to enable the compiler to know where to find them later.

- The program entry point starts from the main() function in line 9.

- In line 11, a local Boolean variable res is declared since we need to use it to receive the returning value for calling the function SysCtlPeripheralready() later.

- The API function `SysCtlClockSet()` is called to set up and use our system clock in line 12. A software divider, SYSCTL_SYSDIV_10, is used to divide the clock generated by the PLL by 20 to get a 20-MHz system clock for this project.
- The API function `SysCtlPeripheralEnable()` is called in line 13 to enable the GPIO Port F. After this function executing, the Port F is enabled to be accessed by users to perform input or output functions.
- The GPIO API function `GPIOPinTypeGPIOOutput()` is called in line 14 to configure PF3 to work as an output pin. The masking byte used in this function is replaced by a symbolic definition GPIO_PIN_3, and the base address is the macro GPIO_PORTF_BASE. This function should be called after the selected GPIO Port is enabled.
- The system control API function `SysCtlPeripheralReady()` is called and executed in line 15. The purpose of this function is to detect whether the GPIO Port F has been ready to work or not. A returned value of `True` means that the port is ready to work.
- In line 16, an `if` decision-making instruction is used to check whether the Port F is ready. If it is (`res = True`), an infinitive `while()` loop is used to continuously output a HIGH and a LOW to the PF3 to turn on and off the LED that is connected to the PF3.
- Inside the `while()` loop, the GPIO API function `GPIOPinWrite()` is called to set PF3 to HIGH to turn on the LED in line 20. The data argument is `0x8` (00001000B), which points to the bit 3 in the PORTF Data register.
- In line 21, a system control API function `SysCtlDelay(500000)` is executed to delay a small period of time to keep the LED in the ON state for a while.
- Another GPIO API function `GPIOPinWrite()` is called to reset the bit 3 in the Port F to 0 to turn the LED off in line 22. The argument data is `0x0` (00000000B), which makes bit 3 0.
- Another `SysCtlDelay()` function is called to delay a small period of time to keep the LED in the off state for a while in line 23.

4.5.7.3.3.4 Include the System Header Files and Other Header Files   We used four system header files in our application C source file, `<inc/hw_memmap.h>`, `<inc/hw_types.h>`, `<driverlib/sysctl.h>`, and `<driverlib/gpio.h>`. There are two ways to include or add these header files into our project.

- Use the `Include Paths` function provided by the Keil® ARM®-MDK C/C++ Compiler to include a path for those header files to enable the compiler to know where to find these header file when the project is compiled.
- Add all of these header files into the project.

The advantage of using the first method is that it is very easy for the users to include these header files with one path. However, the shortcoming is that the project developed in this way cannot be portable since all header files may not be in the same paths in another computer. In other words, those header files are not included into your project and may be in some other locations in other computers.

The advantage of using the second way is that these header files are included into your project and the project can be portable to anywhere you want. The bad thing is that you need to spend your time to add those header files one by one into your project.

To save time, in this project we used the first way. Perform the following operations to include these system header files into the project:

1. When the project is open, go to the `Project|Options for Target 'Target 1'` menu item to open the Options wizard.

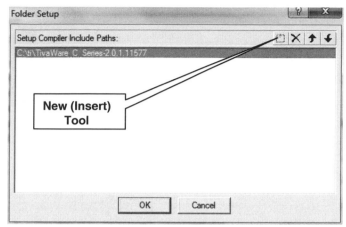

Figure 4.37.   The finished Folder Setup wizard.

2. Then click on the C/C++ tab and go to the Include Paths box.

3. Click on the three-dot button on the right of this box to open the Folder Setup wizard, as shown in Figure 4.37. Click on the New (Insert) tool to open a new textbox. Click on the three-dot button on the right of this textbox to browse to the location where these header files are located, which is C:\ti\TivaWare_C_Series-2.0.1.11577. Then click on the OK button to select this location. Your finished Folder Setup wizard should look like one that is shown in Figurer 4.37. Click on the OK button to close this wizard.

4. Your finished Options wizard is shown in Figure 4.38. Click the OK to close this wizard.

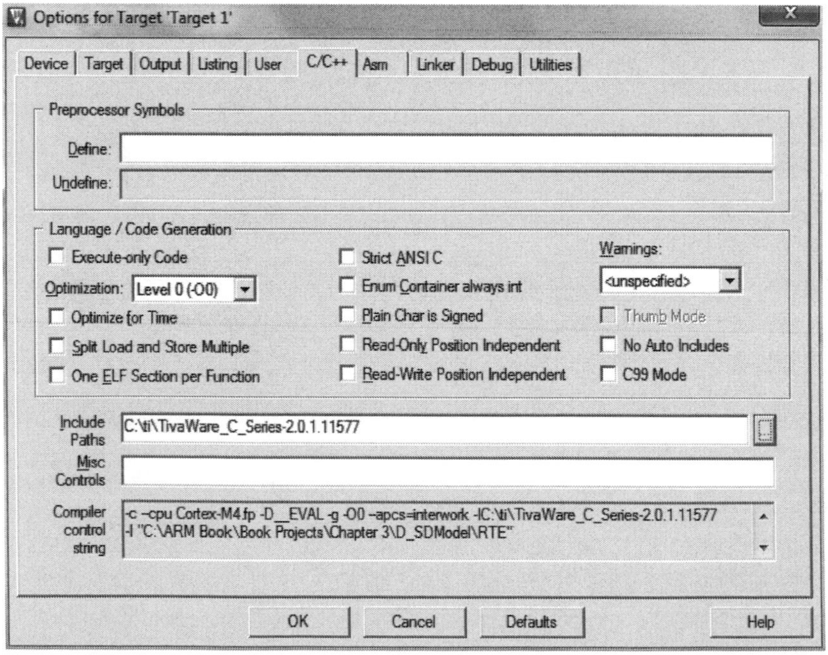

Figure 4.38.   The finished Options wizard. (Reproduced with permission from ARM® Limited. Copyright © ARM Limited.)

4.5.7.3.3.5 Include the External Functions and Other C Source Files   Because we did not use any other C source file and external function in this sample project, we need to do nothing in this step. However, in some other complicated projects, you must do this step; otherwise your project cannot work properly.

4.5.7.3.3.6 Link the Static or Dynamic Library with the Project   Generally there are two kinds of libraries you can link to the user's project: the static library (.lib) and dynamic link library (.dll).

The dynamic link library means that you will not add this library into your project until your project runs, which means that the library is dynamically added or linked with your project when the project is running. In this way, compiler will not consider that this library is a part of your project and will not link it until your project runs. Therefore the size of your target file is much smaller since it does not contain the library but only links the library when it runs.

The static library is composed of a collection of files with related header files. Depending on the type of the files included in a static library, a static library can be further divided into two categories: (1) The library is composed of a collection of C code files with related header files, and (2) the library is made up of a binary file that is the compiling result of those C code files with the related header files. The difference between these two static libraries is that the first one is only a group of C files with related header files, but the second is the compiling result of the first one and it is a binary file.

To link the first kind of static library, you need to add all of those C files and header files into your project. This method is a little time-consuming since you need time to do those files addition. To link the second kind of static library, you only need to add a single binary library file with related header files. We will use the second way since it is simple and easy.

The compiler considered that this library is with your project together and compiles this library with your project together to get the target file. Because the library is added into your project before your project runs, it is called a static link or a static library.

In this sample project, we need to use the TivaWare™ Peripheral Driver Library, which is a static binary library, to access GPIO Port F. Therefore we need to link that library with our project. Perform the following operations to link this library with our project:

- In the `Project` pane, expand the `Target` folder and right click on the `Source Group 1` folder and select the `Add Existing Files to Group 'Source Group 1'`.
- Browse to find the library, the TivaWare™ Peripheral Driver Library, which is located at `C:\ti\TivaWare_C_Series-2.0.1.11577\driverlib\rvmdk` in your host computer and the library is `driverlib.lib`.
- Select this library by clicking on it and click on the `Add` button to add it into our project.

4.5.7.3.3.7 Compile and Link Project to Create the Image or Executable File   Before you can build the project, make sure that the debugger you are using is `Stellaris ICDI`. You can do this checking as follows:

- Go to `Project|Options for Target 'Target 1'` menu item to open the Options wizard.

- On the opened Options wizard, click on the Debug tab.
- Make sure that the debugger shown in the Use: box is Stellaris ICDI. Otherwise you can click on the dropdown arrow to select this debugger from the list.

Go to Project|Build Target menu item to compile and link this sample project with system files to make our project image or executable file. A message displaying 0 Error(s) with 0 Warning(s) should be displayed in the Build Output window at the bottom if nothing wrong with this sample project.

4.5.7.3.3.8 Download the Image File into the Flash Memory and Run the Project By using Flash|Download menu item, you can download the project image file into the flash memory. Now you can begin to debug this project by going to Debug|Start/Stop Debug Session. Click on the OK button for the memory limitation for the evaluation version message, and run this program by going to Debug|Run menu item. As the program running, you can find that the green color LED will be flashing forever.

Go to Debug|Stop menu item to stop the project running.

4.5.7.4 A Comparison Between Two Programming Models

Comparing for these sample projects with two programming models, we can get the following conclusions:

1. The sample project developed with the Direct Register Access (DRA) model has small size and less program coding lines. But good and solid knowledge and understanding about the microcontroller hardware is a necessary requirement to build the project in this model.
2. The sample project developed with the Software Driver (SD) model has relatively large size and more program coding lines. More system header files and a static link library are needed to build this kind of projects. But the developers do not need to have deep and detailed understanding about the microcontroller hardware to build this kind of project.

An interesting question is, How can we develop a project by combining these two programming models together? The following section is an answer to this question.

4.5.7.5 A Combined Programming Model Example

In this section, we try to use the Wayne EduBASE Trainer and a combined programming model to build a project with the following functions:

- Use GPIO Port D bit 3 (PD3) as an input pin to receive the state of a position switch SW2 installed on the EduBASE Trainer since the pins PD3~PD0 are connected to SW2~SW5 position switches in the EduBASE Trainer (refer to Figure 2.22 in Chapter 2).
- Use GPIO Port F bit 2 (PF2) as an output pin to turn on or off the blue color LED.
- When the position switch SW2 is pressed, the blue color LED is ON.
- When the position switch SW2 is released, the blue color LED is OFF.

First let's have a closer look at the hardware configuration on the EduBASE Trainer and the interfacing connection between the EduBASE Trainer and TM4C123GXL Evaluation Board. Figure 4.39 shows this configuration and connection.

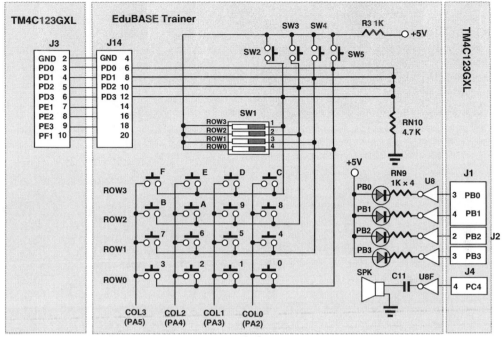

Figure 4.39.   Some hardware configurations for EduBASE Trainer.

The interfacing jack J3 in the TM4C123GXL EVB is connected to the interfacing jack J14 in the EduBASE Trainer. Four bits or pins in the Port D, PD0~PD3, are connected to four position switches, SW5~SW2, in the EduBASE Trainer respectively. These four pins are also connected to a DIP switch SW1 and four rows, ROW0~ROW3, in a 4×4 keypad.

A logic LOW is applied to a pin on the Port D if no associate position switch is pressed since a 4.7K resistor that is connected to the ground is connected to these pins. A logic HIGH would appear on a pin if the related position switch is pressed since a voltage divider applied on the resistors R3 and RN10 generates a HIGH ($V_{pin} = 4.7/(4.7+1) \times 5\,V = 4.1$ V). One point to be noted is that all switches on the DIP switch SW1 should be in the OFF position when using these position switches SW2~SW5 to interface to Port D to do the related program controls.

Four pins on GPIO Port B, PB0–PB3, in the TM4C123GXL EVB are connected to 4 LEDs (PB0~PB3) in the EduBASE Trainer via pins 3 and 4 in the J1, pin 2 in the J2, and pin 3 in the J4 in the TM4C123GXL EVB. Also the PC4 is connected to a speaker via pin 4 in the J4.

Based on this hardware configuration, now let's build our combining model project CPModel.

4.5.7.5.1 Create the Header File   Refer to Section 4.5.6.3.3 to create a new folder named CPModel under the folder C:\ARM Class Projects\Chapter 4 in the Windows Explorer. Then create a new µVersion5 project named CPModel in the Keil® ARM®-MDK µVersion5 IDE and add it into the folder CPModel.

Create a new header file named CPModel.h and add it into the project CPModel. Enter the codes shown in Figure 4.40 into this header file.

```
1   //*********************************************************************************************
2   // CPDModel.h  -  Header file for the sample project CPDModel.c
3   //*********************************************************************************************
4   #include <stdint.h>                    // for uint32, uint16, ....
5   #include <stdbool.h>                   // for bool
6   #define SYSCTL_RCGC2_R          (*((volatile uint32_t *)0x400FE108))
7   #define GPIO_PORTD_DATA_R       (*((volatile uint32_t *)0x400073FC))
8   #define SYSCTL_RCGC2_GPIOF      0x00000020               // Port F Clock Gating Control
9   #define SYSCTL_RCGC2_GPIOD      0x00000008               // Port D Clock Gating Control
```

Figure 4.40. The header file CPModel.h.

Two system header files, <stdint.h> and <stdbool.h>, are included since these files contain definitions for all integer data types and Boolean data types in the ARM® C/C++ compiler system. The system clock gating control register RCGC2 is defined in line 6, and the GPIO PORTD DATA Register is defined in line 7. Two constants defined in lines 8 and 9 are used to set bit 5 (PORTF) and bit 3 (PORTD) in the RCGC2 to enable these two registers. Save this header file by going to File|Save menu item.

4.5.7.5.2 Create the C Source File Now create a new C code file CPModel.c and add it into the project. Enter the codes shown in Figure 4.41 into this source file.

Let's have a closer look at this piece of codes to see how it works.

- The code lines 4~8 include all system header files to be used in this project. For the portable reason, we will add all of these header files into our project in the next section. Therefore we do not need to use any path before any of these header file.
- The program starts at main() entry point at line 9.
- Two local variables, res and ui32Input, are declared here since we need to use them to receive and hold the returned values by calling the API function SysCtlPeripheral-Ready() and getting the input data from pin 3 on the Port D, PD3 later.
- In line 13, the system control API function SysCtlClockSet() is called to set up the system clock and its running frequency. The main oscillator crystal with 16-MHz frequency and PLL is used, and a software divider coefficient (divided by 10) is adopted to make the system clock frequency become (400 MHz/2/10 = 400 MHz/20) 20 MHz.
- A Direct Register Access model instruction is used to set bit 3 and bit 5 in the RCGC2 register to enable GPIO PORTD and PORTF in line 14. An OR logic operator is used to combine these two symbolic definitions or macros together to save space.
- Two GPIO API functions, GPIOPinTypeGPIOOutput() and GPIOPinTypeG-PIOInput(), are called to set PF2 as an output pin and PD3 as an input pin, respectively, in lines 15 and 16.
- A system control API function SysCtlPeripheralReady() is called two times to check whether Port F and Port D are ready to be accessed in line 17. These two function calls are ORed together to save the coding space. This function returns a Boolean value to indicate whether the enabled port is ready or not. A True means that the port is ready.
- If the returned value is True, an infinitive while() loop is executed to continuously check the input pin PD3 and send either HIGH or LOW to the pin PF2 to turn on or off the blue LED in the TM4C123GXL EVB to test our project.
- In line 22, a Direct Register Access model instruction is used to get the input from PD3 to check the state of the position switch SW2.

```
1    //**********************************************************************************************
2    // CPSModel.c – Main source file for sample project CPDModel
3    //**********************************************************************************************
4    #include "CPModel.h"
5    #include "hw_memmap.h"
6    #include "hw_types.h"
7    #include "sysctl.h"
8    #include "gpio.h"
9    int main(void)
10   {
11       bool res = false;
12       volatile uint32_t ui32Input;
13       SysCtlClockSet(SYSCTL_SYSDIV_10|SYSCTL_USE_PLL|SYSCTL_XTAL_16MHZ|SYSCTL_OSC_MAIN);
14       SYSCTL_RCGC2_R = SYSCTL_RCGC2_GPIOF|SYSCTL_RCGC2_GPIOD ; // Enable PORTs F & D in RCGC2
15       GPIOPinTypeGPIOOutput(GPIO _PORTF_BASE, GPIO_PIN_2);           // set PF2 as output pin
16       GPIOPinTypeGPIOInput(GPIO_PORTD_BASE, GPIO_PIN_3);           // set PD3 as input pin
17       res = SysCtlPeripheralReady(SYSCTL_PERIPH_GPIOF)|SysCtlPeripheralReady(SYSCTL_PERIPH_GPIOD);
18       if (res == true)
19       {
20          while(1)                                    // loop forever......
21          {
22             ui32Input = GPIO_PORTD_DATA_R;           // get input from PD3 (SW2 on EduBASE Trainer)
23             if ((ui32Input & 0x8)== 0x8)             // if SW2 is pressed
24             {
25                GPIOPinWrite(GPIO_PORTF_BASE, GPIO_PIN_2, 0x4);    // set PF2 to HIGH
26                SysCtlDelay(500000);                               // Delay for a bit
27                GPIOPinWrite(GPIO_PORTF_BASE, GPIO_PIN_2, 0x0);    // reset PF2 to LOW
28                SysCtlDelay(500000);                               // Delay for a bit
             }
          }
       }
   }
```

Figure 4.41.   The C source codes for the project CPModel.

- The returned input value is ANDed with 0x8 (00001000B) to inspect whether the bit 3 or PD3 pin is HIGH or not in line 23. This logic AND operation is necessary since we do not want any other bits or pins in the Port D to be involved in this checking.

- If the returned value is 1 in PD3 (0x8), which means that the position switch SW2 in the EduBASE Trainer is pressed, the GPIOPinWrite() API function is executed to set PF2 to HIGH to turn on the blue color LED in the TM4C123GXL EVB in line 25.

- In code line 26, the system control API function SysCtlDelay() is called to delay the program for about 12.5 ms (0.025 µs × 500000) to stabilize the ON state of the LED.

- The GPIO API function GPIOPinWrite() is called again to turn off the blue color LED connected to the PF2 in the TM4C123GXL EVB in line 27.

- Finally the program is delayed again for about 12.5 ms by calling the system control API function SysCtlDelay() in line 28.

Go to File|Save menu item to save this source file and add it into our project.

4.5.7.5.3 Include System Header Files and Add Static Library into the Project   As we mentioned in the last section, in this project we want to add all system header files into our project to make it portable. The system header files we need to use and add into this project are

- hw_memmap.h
- hw_types.h
- sysctl.h
- gpio.h

The top two header files are located at the folder `C:\ti\TivaWare_C_Series-2.0.1.11577\inc` and the lower two header files are at the folder `C:\ti\TivaWare_C_Series-2.0.1.11577\driverlib`. Perform the following operations to add these header files into our project:

1. Open the Windows Explorer and browse to our project folder, which is `C:\ARM Class Projects\Chapter 4\CPModel`.

2. Go to those two folders listed above to find and copy those four header files, and paste them into our project folder listed in step 1.

It would not work if you want to add these header files directly in the Keil® ARM®-MDK μVersion5 IDE.

The Driver Library is at the folder `C:\ti\TivaWare_C_Series-2.0.1.11577\driverlib\rvmdk`. To add this library into our project, perform the following operations:

1. In the `Project` pane, expand the `Target` folder and right click on the `Source Group 1` folder and select the `Add Existing Files to Group 'Source Group 1'`.

2. Browse to find the library, the TivaWare™ Peripheral Driver Library, which is located at `C:\ti\TivaWare_C_Series-2.0.1.11577\driverlib\rvmdk` in your host computer and the library is `driverlib.lib`.

3. Select this library by clicking on it and click on the Add button to add it into our project.

Now we are almost ready to compile, build, and run our project. Before you can do that, make sure that the debugger you are using is the `Stellaris ICDI`. You can do this checking by:

- Going to `Project|Options for Target 'Target 1'` menu item to open the Options wizard.
- On the opened Options wizard, click on the `Debug` tab.
- Make sure that the debugger shown in the `Use:` box is `Stellaris ICDI`. Otherwise you can click on the dropdown arrow to select this debugger from the list.

Now we are ready to compile, load, and run our project.

4.5.7.5.4 Compile and Link Project to Create the Image or Executable File   Go to `Project|Build Target` menu item to compile and link this sample project with system files to make our project image or executable file. A message displaying `0 Error(s)` with `0 Warning(s)` should be displayed in the `Build Output` window at the bottom if nothing is wrong with this sample project.

By using the `Flash|Download` menu item, you can download the project image file into the flash memory. Now you can begin to debug this project by going to `Debug|-Start/Stop Debug Session`. Click on the OK button for the memory limitation for the evaluation version message, and run this program by going to the `Debug|Run` menu item. As the program running, you can find that the blue color LED will be flashing as soon as you pressed the `SW2` position switch in the EduBASE Trainer. Otherwise, no LED can be flashing at all.

Go to the `Debug|Stop` menu item to stop the project running.

At this point, we have finished introductions and discussions about the software, instruction set, and C code programming for this TM4C123GXL Evaluation Board with the EduBASE Trainer.

One more step you can do is: can you use some position switches in the EduBASE Trainer to control the flashing of some LEDs in the EduBASE Trainer, not in the TM4C123GXL EVB? This may be considered as one of your homework assignments or labs in this chapter.

4.6 CHAPTER SUMMARY

This chapter is mainly about the introduction and discussion about the software development and application of using Tive for C Series LaunchPad™ ARM® Microcontroller and evaluation board TM4C123GXL. The EduBASE Trainer is also a useful tool and development emulator to be used in these software implementations.

Following the overview section, the development architecture and procedure of using the ARM® Cortex®-M4 MCU to build a microcontroller system is introduced. This chapter is basically divided into the following three parts:

1. Introductions and discussions about the ARM® Cortex®-M4 Assembly instruction set, including 14 groups of instructions that are categorized based on their functions and implementations. The instruction set includes

   - ARM® Cortex®-M4 assembly instruction structure and syntax
   - ARM® Cortex®-M4 pseudo assembly instructions
   - ARM® Cortex®-M4 complete assembly instruction set
   - ARM® Cortex®-M4 assembly instruction addressing modes
   - ARM® Cortex®-M4 unsupported assembly instructions

2. Discussions and introductions to ARM® Cortex®-M4 software development procedure, including the Keil® ARM®-MDK μVersion5 Integrated Development Environment (IDE), CMSIS Core, Devices drivers, and TivaWare™ Software for C Series LaunchPad TM4C123GH6PM MCU and TM4C123GXL Evaluation Board. The TivaWare™ Driver Library, including the peripheral driver library, graphical library, sensor hub library, USB library, and boot loader, which are provided by the TivaWare™ software package, is also introduced in this part. An introduction to intrinsic instructions is also included in this part, which contains

   - The Standard data types used in intrinsic instructions program
   - The CMSIS Core-Specific Intrinsic Functions
   - The Keil® ARM® Compiler-Specific Intrinsic Functions
   - Inline Assembler
   - Idiom recognition

3. Using the C codes to build and develop ARM® Cortex®-M4 MCU application programs. This part includes

   - An introduction to C programming development guideline and procedure, which including the organization of the C code programming, such as the header files, the implementation files, and the application files.
   - Introduction to the TivaWare™ Driver Library, mainly about the peripheral driver library and GPIO API functions.
   - Introduction to two popular application programming models used in the TivaWare™ driver library, the Direct Register Access (DRA) model, and the Software Driver (SD) model.
   - Introduction to use the TivaWare™ driver library to build a sample project DRAModel, in which only the DRA method is used.

- Introduction to use the TivaWare™ peripheral driver library to build a sample project BLSDModel, in which the static library is used.
- Introduction to use a combining model method to build a sample project CPModel, in which both the TivaWare™ driver library API functions and the DRA method are used.
- Introduction to the EduBASE Trainer, including the interface and connection between the Jacks, J1~J4, in the TM4C123GXL EVB and some peripheral devices provided in the EduBASE Trainer.

When finished with this chapter, users can develop and build the most simple ARM® Cortex®-M4 MCU application projects by using any models or methods discussed in this chapter.

HOMEWORK

I. True/False Selections

_1. The *Low-Level Language* codes are composed of programming codes similar to English and are easily understood by the human being.

_2. The Thumb-2 technology enables a mixture of 16-bit and 32-bit instructions to be executed within one operating state.

_3. The different addressing modes used in ARM® Cortex®-M4 instructions are to access the memory using the different methods to calculate the target memory address.

_4. The instruction SXTB extracts the lowest 8-bit value of Rn, Rn [7:0], and sign extends to a 32-bit value.

_5. The CMP instruction performs a subtraction between two operands, and it modifies the contents of two operands when the instruction is done.

_6. The Keil® ARM-MDK Core includes a μVersion5 IDE, a Compiler, and a Debugger.

_7. To access some ARM® Cortex®-M4 CPU registers, one can use intrinsic functions provided by CMSIS Core and Keil® ARM® C/C++ Compiler.

_8. To develop a standard C application project, one needs to create two files, the header file and application file.

_9. Two programming models are used in the TivaWare™ Driver Library, the Direct Register Access (DRA) model, and Sequence Development (SD) model.

_10. Although all GPIO Port registers are 32-bit registers, only lowest 8 bits in those registers are used.

II. Multiple Choices

1. The following instruction(s), ____, is (are) ARM® Cortex®-M4 assembly instructions.
   - a. ui32int uiLoop;
   - b. $a = b + c$;
   - c. void __WFI(void);
   - d. WFI

2. The ARM® Cortex®-M4 assembly instructions contain _____.
   - a. Label field
   - b. Operation field and operands field
   - c. Operation field, operands field and comment field
   - d. Both a and c

3. The pseudo instruction DCW 2 is to _____.

    a. Reserve 2-byte space for a data item in the program

    b. Reserve 2 half-word space for a data item in the program

    c. Reserve 4-byte space for a data item in the program

    d. Reserve 2-word space for a data item in the program

4. The LDRB R0, [R2, #0x5] is to load an unsigned byte located at ____ into the register R0 if the R2 contains 0x40004000.

    a. 0x40000005

    b. 0x40004000

    c. 0x40004005

    d. 0x40000000

5. The instruction BFC R4, #8, #12; is to _____.

    a. Set bits 8–12 in the register R4 to 1

    b. Reset bits 8–12 in the register R4 to 0

    c. Set bits 8–19 in the register R4 to 1

    d. Reset bits 8–19 in the register R4 to 0

6. The TivaWare™ Driver Libraries include ___.

    a. Peripheral driver library

    b. Graphical library

    c. Sensor hub library and USB library

    d. All of the above

7. Two sets of popular intrinsic functions are provided by _____.

    a. Keil® ARM C/C++ Compiler and CMSIS Core

    b. TivaWare™ driver library and Keil® ARM-MDK µVersion5 IDE

    c. Keil® ARM® C/C++ Compiler and TivaWare™ driver library

    d. TivaWare™ driver library and Keil® ARM® C/C++ Compiler

8. To build a C code project, usually one needs to develop _____ file(s).

    a. The implementation and application

    b. The header and application

    c. The header and implementation

    d. The application

9. To use macros or symbolic definitions to define the GPIO PORTA DATA Register, one can use ___ macro.

    a. GPIO_PORTA_DATA

    b. GPIO_PORTA_DATA_REG

    c. GPIO_PORTA_DATA_R

    d. PORTA_DATA_R

10. To use RCGC2 register to set the system clock and enable the GPIO Ports A and C, one needs to set the RCGC2 register with a hexadecimal data item _____.

    a. 0x3

    b. 0x4

c. 0x5

d. 0x6

III. Exercises

1. Provide a brief description about the ARM® Cortex®-M4 assembly instruction syntax.

2. Provide a brief description about seven addressing modes used in the ARM® Cortex®-M4 assembly instructions.

3. Explain the difference between the data conversion instructions SXTB and UXTB.

4. Provide a description about the software and tools to be used to build an ARM® Cortex®-M4 MCU application project with Tiva™ for C Series LaunchPad TM4C123GXL EVB.

5. Provide a brief description about two programming models used in the TivaWare™ Peripheral Driver Library.

IV. Practical Laboratory

Laboratory 4: ARM® Cortex®-M4 Software and C Programming

4.0 Goals   This laboratory exercise allows students to practice ARM® Cortex®-M4 instructions and C programming through developing four labs.

> **1.** Program Lab4_1 lets you practice several ARM® Cortex®-M4 assembly instructions such as **LDR**, **STR**, and **MOV** with inline assembler.
> **2.** Program Lab4_2 enables you to build a C code program to access and control a single LED with a DIP switch in the EduBASE Trainer.
> **3.** Program Lab4_3 allows you to control a single LED with one position switch combined with a sound output driven by the speaker in the EduBASE Trainer.
> **4.** Program Lab4_4 provides you a chance to control four LEDs with four position switches in the EduBASE Trainer.

After completion of these programs, you should understand some popular ARM® Cortex®-M4 assembly instructions and the architecture of the inline assembler, as well as architectures and configurations of some popular peripherals installed in the EduBASE Trainer. You should be able to code some interfacing and controlling programs to access those peripherals to perform some closed-loop control functions.

4.1 Lab4_1

4.1.1 Goal   The Lab4_1 project builds a C code program with inline assembler to use some popular ARM® Cortex®-M4 assembly instructions to perform a simulated PUSH and POP operation (Keil® C/C++ compiler does not allow to directly use PUSH and POP instructions in the inline assembler). The tasks of the program are as follows:

- Push 10 data 0, 1, 2, . . . , 9 into the stack in the order from 0x0 to 0x9.
- Pop them back to another memory space in the same order.

4.1.2 Data Assignment   The 10 data items should be first written into a memory space 0x20002000 and read back from another memory space 0x20003000. This memory space change is made by the PUSH and POP instructions. These two memory spaces can be defined by using the #define macro:

- #define   WADDRESS   0x20002000
- #define   RADDRESS   0x20003000

4.1.3 Development of the Source Code   Following the steps below to develop this C source code. Only a C code file is used in this project since it is a simple application without needing any header file.

1. Refer to Section 4.5.6.3.3 to create a new folder named Lab4_1 under the folder C:\ARM Lab Projects\Chapter 4 in the Windows Explorer.

2. Open the Keil® ARM-MDK μVersion5 and go to Project|New μVersion Project menu item to create a new μVersion Project. On the opened wizard, browse to our new folder Lab4_1 that is created in step 1 above. Enter Lab4_1 into the File name box and click on the Save button to create this project in the folder Lab4_1 created in step 1.

3. On the next wizard, you need to select the device (MCU) for this project. Expand three icons, Texas Instruments, Tiva C Series, and TM4C123x Series, and select the target device TM4C123GH6PM from the list by clicking on it. Click on the OK to close this wizard.

4. Next the Software Components wizard is opened, and you need to set up the software development environment for your project with this wizard. Expand two icons, CMSIS and Device, and check the CORE and Startup checkboxes in the Sel. column, and click on the OK button since we need these two components to build our project.

5. In the Project pane, expand the Target folder and right click on the Source Group 1 folder and select the Add New Item to Group 'Source Group 1'.

6. Select the C File (.c) and enter Lab4_1 into the Name: box, and click on the Add button to add this source file into the project.

7. On the top of this C source file, include two system header files, <stdint.h> and <stdbool.h>.

8. Use the #define macro to define two memory addresses, WADDRESS 0x20002000 and RADDRESS 0x20003000.

9. Since we need to use inline assembler to include some ARM® Cortex®-M4 assembly instructions to perform PUSH and POP operations, we need to create two functions to cover these inline assemblers since all inline assemblers must be included inside functions in the Keil® ARM-MDK C/C++ Compiler.

10. Create the first C function named pushdata() with one argument int uidata and returning a void value.

11. Inside the function pushdata(), create three local integer variables, R0, R2, and SP, which are three pseudo registers representing three real corresponding registers in the ARM® CPU. You have to use those pseudo registers, not real registers, to perform any data operation and the compiler can perform data transferring between those pseudo and real registers later.

12. Put an inline assembler sign, __asm, to tell the compiler that the following codes are assembly codes, not C codes. The point to be noted is that the underscore before the asm keyword is a double underscore, not a single one.

13. Put a starting brace under the __asm inline assembler sign to start this assembler block.

14. Use the MOV instruction to move the WADDRESS into the register R0 (#WADDRESS).

15. Use the MOV instruction to move the R0 into the SP to set up the SP to point to the written address **WADDRESS**.

16. Use the MOV instruction to move the argument `#uidata` to the register R2.

17. Use the STR instruction to store the data stored in the R2 into the SP with an immediate offset `#uidata` multiplied by 4. The reason to multiply by 4 is to align each data to a word (4 bytes). If you do not do this alignment, each data item would be a byte to be stored in each memory address.

18. Put an ending brace to finish this inline assembler block.

19. Put another ending brace to finish the first function.

20. Create the second C function named `popdata()` with one argument `int uidata` and returning a `void` value

21. Inside the function `popdata()`, create four local integer variables, R0, R1, R3, and SP.

22. Put an inline assembler sign, `__asm`, to tell the compiler that the following codes are assembly codes, not C codes.

23. Put a starting brace under the `__asm` inline assembler sign to start this assembler block.

24. Use the MOV instruction to move the WADDRESS into the register R0 (#WADDRESS).

25. Use the MOV instruction to move the RADDRESS into the register R1 (#RADDRESS).

26. Use the MOV instruction to move the R0 into the SP to setup the SP to point to the written address **WADDRESS**.

27. Use the LDR instruction to load data from the SP with an immediate offset `#uidata` multiplied by 4 into the register R3.

28. Use the STR instruction to store the data in the R3 into the R1 with an immediate offset `#uidata` multiplied by 4.

29. Put an ending brace to finish this inline assembler block. Put another ending brace to finish the second function.

30. Put `int main(void)` to start our main program and put a starting brace under this main function to begin our main program.

31. Declare a `uint32_t` local variable `uiData`.

32. Use a `for` loop with `uiData` as the loop counter, starting at 0 and ending at less than `10`. Put a starting brace under this for loop to start this loop.

33. Call `pushdata()` function to perform the data pushing operation with the argument `uiData`.

34. Put an ending brace to finish this for loop block.

35. Use another for loop with the same argument `uiData` to call `popdata()` function to perform data popping operation.

36. Put another ending brace to finish the main program.

4.1.4 Demonstrate Your Program by Testing the Running Result Now you can compile your program by going to `Project|Build target` menu item. However, before you can download your program into the flash memory in the EVB, make sure that the debugger you are using is the `Stellaris ICDI`. You can do this checking as follows:

- Go to `Project|Options for Target 'Target 1'` menu item to open the Options wizard.
- On the opened Options wizard, click on the `Debug` tab.
- Make sure that the debugger shown in the `Use:` box is `Stellaris ICDI`. Otherwise you can click on the dropdown arrow to select this debugger from the list.

Perform the following operations to run your program and check the running results:

- Go to the Flash|Download menu item to download your program into the flash ROM.
- Go to the Debug|Start/Stop Debug Session to begin debugging your program. Click on the OK button on the 32-KB memory size limitation message box to continue.
- Then go to Debug|Run menu item to run your program.
- To check your running result, do the following checks:
  - Click on the Memory 1 tab on the Memory 1 window located at the lower-right corner of your screen.
  - Enter the address 0x20002000 into the Address: box and press the Enter key.
  - You can find that all 10 data items, from 0 to 9, have been stored in this piece of memory space (00 00 00 00 01 00 00 00 02 00 00 00 03 00 00 00 04 00 00 00 . . .).
  - Enter another address 0x20003000 into the Address: box and press the Enter key again, and you would find the same result in that piece of memory space.
  - Go to Debug|Start/Stop Debug Session again to stop your program.

Based on these results, try to answer the following questions:

- Can you tell me whether these results are correct or not? If they are right, why are these data items arranged in this way?
- Can you modify your codes to remove all multiplied by 4 for each immediate offset? What is the result of your program after this modification?
- What did you learn from this project?

4.2 Lab4_2

4.2.1 Goal   This project is to build a C code program to access and control a single LED with a DIP switch in the EduBASE Trainer. Refer to Figure 4.39 to get more details about the hardware configuration for some popular peripherals installed in the EduBASE Trainer. In this lab, we try to use DIP switch 1 to control the LED PB0 with a combined programming model.

4.2.2 Data Assignment   It can be found from Figure 4.39 that the DIP switch 1 is connected to the PD3 pin and the LED PB0 is connected to the PB0 pin of the GPIO Ports in the TM4C123GXL EVB. To enable and set the clock for these two GPIO Ports, the following data and registers should be used:

- Bits 1 and 3 in the RCGC2 register should be set to 1 to enable Port B and Port D (refer to Figure 4.28).
- Bit 3 in the Port D Direction register should be reset to 0 to enable PD3 to work as an input pin, and bit 0 in the Port B Direction register should be set to 1 to enable PB0 to work as an output pin.

4.2.3 Development of the Project and the Header File   Following the steps below to develop this project. Both the header and C source files are used in this project since this project is a little more complicated. Create the project and develop the header file with the following steps:

1. Create a new folder Lab4_2 under the folder C:\ARM Lab Projects\Chapter 4 in the Windows Explorer.
2. Open the Keil® ARM-MDK μVersion5 and go to Project|New μVersion Project menu item to create a new μVersion Project. On the opened wizard, browse to our new folder

Lab4_2 that is created in step 1 above. Enter Lab4_2 into the File name box and click on the Save button to create this project in the folder Lab4_2 created in step 1.

3. On the next wizard, you need to select the device (MCU) for this project. Expand three icons, Texas Instruments, Tiva C Series and TM4C123x Series, and select the target device TM4C123GH6PM from the list by clicking on it. Click on the OK to close this wizard.

4. Next the Software Components wizard is opened, and you need to set up the software development environment for your project with this wizard. Expand two icons, CMSIS and Device, and check the CORE and Startup checkboxes in the Sel. column, and click on the OK button since we need these two components to build our project.

5. In the Project pane, expand the Target folder and right click on the Source Group 1 folder and select the Add New Item to Group 'Source Group 1'.

6. Select the Header File (.h) and enter Lab4_2 into the Name: box, and click on the Add button to add this header file into the project.

7. On the top of this header file, first let's include two system header files, <stdint.h> and <stdbool.h>.

8. Using the #define macros to define the following constants to be used in this project:

■ #define SYSCTL_RCGC2_R	(*((volatile uint32_t *)0x400FE108))
■ #define GPIO_PORTD_DATA_R	(*((volatile uint32_t *)0x400073FC))
■ #define GPIO_PORTB_DATA_R	(*((volatile uint32_t *)0x400053FC))
■ #define SYSCTL_RCGC2_GPIOB	0x00000002//Port B Clock Gating Control
■ #define SYSCTL_RCGC2_GPIOD	0x00000008//Port D Clock Gating Control

The top three macros can be found from the system header file tm4c123gh6pm.h that is located at the folder C:\ti\TivaWare_C_Series-2.0.1.11577\inc in your host computer.

4.2.4 Development of the C Source File

1. In the Project pane, expand the Target folder and right click on the Source Group 1 folder and select the Add New Item to Group 'Source Group 1'.

2. Select the C File (.c) and enter Lab4_2 into the Name: box, and click on the Add button to add this source file into the project.

3. Include the following header files into this source file first:
   • "Lab4_2.h"
   • "inc/hw_memmap.h"
   • "inc/hw_types.h"
   • "driverlib/gpio.h"
   • "driverlib/sysctl.h"

4. Place the int main(void) to start our main program and put a starting brace under this main function to begin our main program.

5. Declare a uint32_t local variable ui32Input and a bool variable res to receive and hold the returning values for calling some GPIO API functions later.

6. Use the system control API function SysCtlClockSet() to setup the clock for our project with the following arguments:
   • SYSCTL_SYSDIV_10|SYSCTL_USE_PLL|SYSCTL_XTAL_16MHZ|SYSCTL_OSC_MAIN

7. Use the Direct Register Access model instruction to setup the RCGC2 to enable the GPIO PORTB and PORTD:
   - SYSCTL_RCGC2_R = SYSCTL_RCGC2_GPIOB|SYSCTL_RCGC2_GPIOD;

8. Use Software Driver model API function GPIOPinTypeGPIOOutput() with arguments GPIO_PORTB_BASE, GPIO_PIN_0 to set PB0 as an output pin.

9. Use Software Driver model API function GPIOPinTypeGPIOInput() with arguments GPIO_PORTD_BASE, GPIO_PIN_3 to set PD3 as an input pin.

10. Use the system control API functions SysCtlPeripheralReady(SYSCTL_PERIPH_GPIOB) and SysCtlPeripheralReady(SYSCTL_PERIPH_GPIOD) to check whether both ports are ready to be accessed. These two functions can be ORed together and the returned value should be assigned to the Boolean variable res.

11. Use an if () statement to check whether the returning value res is True or False.

12. If the returned res is True, which means that both Port B and Port D are ready, an infinitive while(1) loop will be used to continuously send HIGH or LOW to turn LED PB0 ON or OFF in the EduBASE Trainer.

13. Inside the while() loop, get the input value from the PD3 pin that is connected to the DIP switch SW1 by using the instruction ui32Input = GPIO_PORTD_DATA_R;. In fact, this instruction is used to get all 8 bits (pins) values in the PORTD.

14. In order to check whether the PD3 pin is HIGH, which means that the DIP-SW1 is pressed, an if () statement is used with a condition (ui32Input & 0x8)== 0x8. Bit 3 in the PORTD (PD3) is 00001000B = 0x8, therefore a 0x8 is ANDed with the ui32Input to check if the PD3 is 1 (HGIH).

15. If the PD3 is 1, a GPIO API function GPIOPinWrite(GPIO_PORTB_BASE, GPIO_PIN_0, 0x1); is called to set PB0 to HIGH to turn ON the LED PB0 in the EduBASE Trainer.

16. A system control API function SysCtlDelay(500000); is called to delay the program about 12.5 ms to keep the LED PB0 ON for a while.

17. Then the same GPIO API function GPIOPinWrite(GPIO_PORTB_BASE, GPIO_PIN_0, 0x0); is called again to reset PB0 to LOW to turn OFF the LED PB0.

18. A system control API function SysCtlDelay(500000); is called to delay the program about 12.5 ms to keep the LED PB0 OFF for a while.

19. Some necessary ending braces should be added to finish the while() loop, the if () statement and the main program.

4.2.5 Setup of the Include Path and Linking of the Static Library Now you need to include the system header files by adding the include path and link the static TiveWare Peripheral Driver Library by adding that library into the project.

Refer to Section 4.5.7.3.3.4 to add this include path into the project. Perform the following operations to link this library with our project:

- In the Project pane, expand the Target folder and right click on the Source Group 1 folder and select the Add Existing Files to Group 'Source Group 1'.
- Browse to find the library, the TivaWare™ Peripheral Driver Library, which is located at: C:\ti\TivaWare_C_Series-2.0.1.11577\driverlib\rvmdk in your host computer and the library is driverlib.lib.
- Select this library by clicking on it and click on the Add button to add it into our project.

Now you can compile your program by going to `Project|Build target` menu item. However, before you can download your program into the flash ROM in the EVB, make sure that the debugger you are using is the `Stellaris ICDI`. You can do this checking as follows:

- Go to `Project|Options for Target 'Target 1'` menu item to open the Options wizard.
- On the opened Options wizard, click on the `Debug` tab.
- Make sure that the debugger shown in the `Use:` box is `Stellaris ICDI`. Otherwise you can click on the dropdown arrow to select this debugger from the list.

4.2.6 Demonstrate Your Program   Perform the following operations to run your program and check the running results:

- Go to `Flash|Download` menu item to download your program into the flash ROM.
- Go to `Debug|Start/Stop Debug Session` to begin debugging your program. Click on the OK button on the 32-KB memory size limitation message box to continue.
- Then go to `Debug|Run` menu item to run your program.

As the project runs, the LED PB0 will be flashing when you slide the DIP-SW1 to the ON position, and stop flashing when you slide the DIP-SW1 back to OFF position. Based on these results, try to answer the following questions:

- Can you modify your codes to control any other LED, such as PB1 – PB3, by checking the other DIP switches, such as DIP-SW2 – DIP-SW4 in the EduBASE Trainer?
- What did you learn from this project?

4.3 Lab4_3

4.3.1 Goal   This project is to build a C code program to access and control a single LED with one position or a DIP switch combined with a sound output driven by the speaker in the EduBASE Trainer. Refer to Figure 4.39 to get more details about the hardware configuration for some popular peripherals installed in the EduBASE Trainer. In this lab, we try to use the position switch SW2 or switch 1 in the DIP-SW1 switch to control the LED PB0 and send the speaker in the EduBASE Trainer with a 400-Hz frequency with a combined programming model.

4.3.2 Data Assignment   It can be found from Figure 4.39 that the DIP switch 1 is connected to the PD3 pin and the LED PB0 is connected to the PB0 pin of the GPIO Ports in the TM4C123GXL EVB. Also the PC4 pin is connected to a speaker via pin 4 in the J4 in the TM4C123GXL EVB. To enable and set the clock for these three GPIO Ports (Ports B~D), the following data and registers should be used:

- Bits 1, 2, and 3 in the RCGC2 register should be set to 1 to enable Port B, Port C, and Port D (refer to Figure 4.28).
- Bit 3 in the Port D Direction register should be reset to 0 to enable PD3 to work as an input pin, and bit 0 in the Port B Direction register should be set to 1 to enable PB0 to work as an output pin.
- Bit 4 in the Port C Direction register should be set to 1 to enable PC4 to work as an output pin.

4.3.3 Development of the Project and the Header File   Use steps below to develop this project. Both the header and C source files are used in this project since this project is a little more complicated. Create the project and develop the header file with the following steps:

1. Create a new folder `Lab4_3` under the folder `C:\ARM Lab Projects\`Chapter 4 in the Windows Explorer.

2. Open the Keil® ARM-MDK µVersion5 and go to the `Project|New µVersion Project` menu item to create a new µVersion Project. On the opened wizard, browse to our new folder `Lab4_3` that is created in step 1 above. Enter `Lab4_3` into the `File` name box and click on the `Save` button to create and save this project in the folder `Lab4_3` created in step 1.

3. On the next wizard, you need to select the device (MCU) for this project. Expand three icons, `Texas Instruments`, `Tiva C Series`, and `TM4C123x Series`, and select the target device `TM4C123GH6PM` from the list by clicking on it. Click on the `OK` to close this wizard.

4. Next the Software Components wizard is opened, and you need to setup the software development environment for your project with this wizard. Expand two icons, `CMSIS` and `Device`, and check the CORE and `Startup` checkboxes in the `Sel.` column, and click on the OK button since we need these two components to build our project.

5. In the `Project` pane, expand the `Target` folder and right click on the `Source Group 1` folder and select the `Add New Item to Group 'Source Group 1'`.

6. Select the `Header File (.h)` and enter `Lab4_3` into the `Name:` box, and click on the Add button to add this header file into the project.

7. On the top of this header file, first let's include two system header files, `<stdint.h>` and `<stdbool.h>`.

8. Using the `#define` macros to define the following constants to be used in this project:

■ #define SYSCTL_RCGC2_R	`(*((volatile uint32_t *)0x400FE108))`
■ #define GPIO_PORTD_DATA_R	`(*((volatile uint32_t *)0x400073FC))`
■ #define GPIO_PORTC_DATA_R	`(*((volatile uint32_t *)0x400063FC))`
■ #define GPIO_PORTB_DATA_R	`(*((volatile uint32_t *)0x400053FC))`
■ #define SYSCTL_RCGC2_GPIOB	`0x00000002//Port B Clock Gating Control`
■ #define SYSCTL_RCGC2_GPIOC	`0x00000004//Port C Clock Gating Control`
■ #define SYSCTL_RCGC2_GPIOD	`0x00000008//Port D Clock Gating Control`

The top three macros can be found from the system header file `tm4c123gh6pm.h`, which is located at the folder `C:\ti\TivaWare_C_Series-2.0.1.11577\inc` in your host computer.

4.3.4 Development of the C Source File

1. In the `Project` pane, expand the `Target` folder and right click on the `Source Group 1` folder and select the `Add New Item to Group 'Source Group 1'`.

2. Select the `C File (.c)` and enter `Lab4_3` into the `Name:` box, and click on the Add button to add this source file into the project.

3. Include the following header files into this source file first:
   - "`Lab4_3.h`"
   - "`inc/hw_memmap.h`"
   - "`inc/hw_types.h`"
   - "`driverlib/gpio.h`"
   - "`driverlib/sysctl.h`"

4. Place the `int main(void)` to start our main program and put a starting brace under this main function to begin our main program.

5. Declare a `uint32_t` local variable `ui32Input` and a `bool` variable `res` to receive and hold the returning values for calling some GPIO API functions later.

6. Use the system control API function `SysCtlClockSet()` to setup the clock for our project with the following arguments:
   - SYSCTL_SYSDIV_10|SYSCTL_USE_PLL|SYSCTL_XTAL_16MHZ|SYSCTL_ OSC_MAIN

7. Use the Direct Register Access model instruction to setup the RCGC2 to enable the GPIO PORTB, PORTC and PORTD:
   - SYSCTL_RCGC2_R = SYSCTL_RCGC2_GPIOB|SYSCTL_RCGC2_GPIOC|SYSCTL_ RCGC2_GPIOD;

8. Use Software Driver model API function `GPIOPinTypeGPIOOutput()` with arguments GPIO_PORTB_BASE, GPIO_PIN_0 to set PB0 as an output pin.

9. Use Software Driver model API function `GPIOPinTypeGPIOOutput()` with arguments GPIO_PORTC_BASE, GPIO_PIN_4 to set PC4 as an output pin.

10. Use Software Driver model API function `GPIOPinTypeGPIOInput()` with arguments GPIO_PORTD_BASE, GPIO_PIN_3 to set PD3 as an input pin.

11. Use the system control API functions `SysCtlPeripheralReady(SYSCTL_PER-IPH_GPIOB)`, `SysCtlPeripheralReady(SYSCTL_PERIPH_GPIOC)`,`SysCtl-PeripheralReady(SYSCTL_PERIPH_GPIOD)` to check whether three ports are ready to be accessed. These three functions can be ORed together and the returned value should be assigned to the Boolean variable `res`.

12. Use an `if ()` statement to check whether the returning value `res` is True or False.

13. If the returned `res` is True, which means that Port B, Port C and Port D are ready, an infinitive `while(1)` loop will be used to continuously send HIGH or LOW to turn LED PB0 ON or OFF in the EduBASE Trainer via PB0. Also a 400-Hz signal is sent to the speaker in the EduBASE Trainer via PC4.

14. Inside the `while()` loop, get the input value from the PD3 pin that is connected to the DIP switch SW1 by using the instruction `ui32Input = GPIO_PORTD_DATA_R;`. In fact, this instruction is used to get all 8 bits (pins) values in the PORTD.

15. In order to check whether the PD3 pin is HIGH, which means that the DIP-SW1 is pressed, an `if ()` statement is used with a condition `(ui32Input & 0x8)== 0x8`. Bit 3 in the PORTD (PD3) is 00001000B = 0x8; therefore a 0x8 is ANDed with the `ui32Input` to check if the PD3 is 1 (HGIH).

16. If the PD3 is 1, a GPIO API function `GPIOPinWrite(GPIO_PORTB_BASE, GPIO_-PIN_0, 0x1);` is called to set PB0 to 1 to turn ON the LED PB0 in the EduBASE Trainer.

17. Also another GPIO function `GPIOPinWrite(GPIO_PORTC_BASE, GPIO_PIN_4, 0x10);` is called to set PC4 to 1 to send a HIGH during the first half-cycle of 400-Hz signal to the speaker in the EduBASE Trainer.

18. A system control API function `SysCtlDelay(50000);` is called to delay the program about 1.25 ms to keep the LED PB0 ON for a while and provides a half-cycle time (1.25 ms) for a 400-Hz signal sent to the speaker.

19. Then the same GPIO API function `GPIOPinWrite(GPIO_PORTB_BASE, GPIO_-PIN_0, 0x0);` is called again to reset PB0 to 0 to turn OFF the LED PB0.

20. Also another GPIO function `GPIOPinWrite(GPIO_PORTC_BASE, GPIO_PIN_4,` `0x0);` is called to reset PC4 to 0 to send a LOW during the first half-cycle of 400 Hz signal to the speaker in the EduBASE Trainer.

21. A system control API function `SysCtlDelay(50000);` is called to delay the program about 1.25 ms to keep the LED PB0 OFF for a while and provides another half-cycle time (1.25 ms) for a 400-Hz signal sent to the speaker.

22. Some necessary ending braces should be added to finish the `while()` loop, the `if ()` statement, and the main program.

4.3.5 Setup of the Include Path and Linking of the Static Library   Now you need to include the system header files by adding the include path and link the static TiveWare Peripheral Driver Library by adding that library into the project.

Refer to Section 4.5.7.3.3.4 to add this include path into the project. Perform the following operations to link this library with our project:

- In the`Project` pane, expand the `Target` folder and right click on the `Source Group 1` folder and select the `Add Existing Files to Group 'Source Group 1'`.
- Browse to find the library, the TivaWare™ Peripheral Driver Library, which is located at `C: \ti\TivaWare_C_Series-2.0.1.11577\driverlib\rvmdk` in your host computer and the library is `driverlib.lib`.
- Select this library by clicking on it and click on the Add button to add it into our project.

Now you can compile your program by going to `Project|Build target` menu item. However, before you can download your program into the flash memory in the EVB, make sure that the debugger you are using is the `Stellaris ICDI`. You can do this checking as follows:

- Go to the `Project|Options for Target 'Target 1'` menu item to open the Options wizard.
- On the opened Options wizard, click on the `Debug` tab.
- Make sure that the debugger shown in the `Use:` box is `Stellaris ICDI`. Otherwise you can click on the dropdown arrow to select this debugger from the list.

4.3.6 Demonstrate Your Program   Perform the following operations to run your program and check the running results:

- Go to the `Flash|Download` menu item to download your program into the flash ROM.
- Go to the `Debug|Start/Stop Debug Session` to begin debugging your program. Click on the `OK` button on the 32KB memory size limitation message box to continue.
- Then go to `Debug|Run` menu item to run your program.

As the project runs, the LED PB0 will be ON when you slide the DIP-SW1 to the ON position or press the SW2 position switch. Also a 400-Hz signal is sent to the speaker during the SW2 switch is pressed or DIP-SW1 is kept in the ON position. The LED PB0 will stop flashing when you slide the DIP-SW1 back to OFF position, and no signal is sent to the speaker.

Based on these results, try to answer the following questions:

- Can you modify your codes to control any other LED, such as PB1~PB3, by checking the other DIP switches, such as DIP-SW2~DIP-SW4 in the EduBASE Trainer?
- Can you modify your codes to send the speaker with other frequency?
- What did you learn from this project?

4.4 Lab4_4

4.4.1 Goal   This project is to build a C code program to access and control all four LEDs with all DIP switches combined with different sound outputs driven by the speaker in the EduBASE Trainer. Refer to Figure 4.39 to get more details about the hardware configuration for some popular peripherals installed in the EduBASE Trainer. In this lab, we try to build this project with the Direct Register Access (DRA) programming model.

4.4.2 Data Assignment   It can be found from Figure 4.39 that four DIP switches, sw1 ~ sw4, are connected to four pins in the Port D, PD3 ~ PD0 and four LEDs, PB0 ~ PB3, are connected to four pins in the Port B, PB0 ~ PB3 in the GPIO Ports in the TM4C123GXL EVB. Also the PC4 pin is connected to a speaker via pin 4 in the J4 in the TM4C123GXL EVB. To enable and set the clock for these three GPIO Ports (Ports B~D), the following data and registers should be used:

- Bits 1, 2, and 3 in the RCGC2 register should be set to 1 to enable Port B, Port C, and Port D (refer to Figure 4.28).
- Four bits, bits 0~3, in the Port D Direction register should be reset to 0 to enable PD0 ~ PD3 to work as input pins, and four bits, bits 0–3, in the Port B Direction register should be set to 1 to enable PB0 ~ PB3 to work as output pins.
- Bit 4 in the Port C Direction register should be set to 1 to enable PC4 to work as an output pin.

The project is designed to perform the following functions:

1. The main oscillator crystal of 16 MHz is used as the clock source to input the PLL clock generator to create a 400 MHz output. Then a software divider 10 is used to get a 40 MHz system clock from the output of the PLL with a default divided-by-2 divisor. Therefore the clock cycle for this 40 MHz clock is 0.025 μs.

2. When the different DIP switch is pressed, the related LED will be ON and a related sound with certain frequency is sent to the speaker in the EduBASE Trainer. The relationship between each switch and related sound is:

- If DIP-SW1 is pressed: A 400 Hz signal is sent to the speaker.
- If DIP-SW1 and SW2 are pressed: A 600 Hz signal is sent to the speaker.
- If DIP-SW1, SW2, and SW3 are pressed: An 800 Hz signal is sent to the speaker.
- If all four DIP-switches are pressed: A 1000 Hz signal is sent to the speaker.
- If DIP-SW2, SW3, and SW4 are pressed: A 1200 Hz signal is sent to the speaker.
- If DIP-SW2 and SW3 are pressed: A 1400 Hz signal is sent to the speaker.
- For all other combinations of the DIP switches, a 200 Hz signal is sent to the speaker.

The sound signal is sent out with a square waveform, half-cycle is HIGH, and another half-cycle is LOW. Therefore we need to send a HIGH signal with half-cycle time and send a LOW with another half-cycle to the speaker. The half-cycle time of the sound signal for each frequency can be calculated in this way:

1. Determine the whole cycle time by dividing the desired frequency by 1.
2. Divide the half cycle time by the system clock cycle time to get the delay time count.
3. Use this delay time count to call related subroutine to send that signal with that frequency.

Table 4.28. The half-cycle delay time for different frequency signals.

Desired Frequency	Half-Cycle Time (µs)	Delay Time Count
400 Hz	1250	25,000
600 Hz	833	17,000
800 Hz	625	12,500
1000 Hz	500	10,000
1200 Hz	417	7,500
1400 Hz	357	7,142
200 Hz	2500	50,000

For example, for a 400 Hz signal, the calculation steps are:

1. The whole-cycle time for 400 Hz is $1/400 = 0.0025\,s = 2.5\,ms = 2500\,\mu s$.
2. The half-cycle time is 1250 µs, which is divided by the system clock cycle time $1/20\,MHz = 0.05\,\mu s$, the result is 25,000.
3. Use this 25,000 to call the related subroutine to send this signal to the speaker to get a 400 Hz frequency sound signal.

Table 4.28 shows this relationship between each frequency signal, related half-cycle time, and delay time counts used in this project.

4.4.3 Development of the Project and the Header File Using steps below to develop this project. Both the header and C source files are used in this project since this project is a little more complicated. Create the project and develop the header file with the following steps:

1. Create a new folder Lab4_4 under the folder C:\ARM Lab Projects\Chapter 4 in the Windows Explorer.
2. Open the Keil® ARM-MDK µVersion5 and go to Project|New µVersion Project menu item to create a new µVersion Project. On the opened wizard, browse to our new folder Lab4_4 that is created in step 1 above. Enter Lab4_4 into the File name box and click on the Save button to create and save this project in the folder Lab4_4 created in step 1.
3. On the next wizard, you need to select the device (MCU) for this project. Expand three icons, Texas Instruments, Tiva C Series and TM4C123x Series, and select the target device TM4C123GH6PM from the list by clicking on it. Click on the OK to close this wizard.
4. Next the Software Components wizard is opened, and you need to set up the software development environment for your project with this wizard. Expand two icons, CMSIS and Device, and check the CORE and Startup checkboxes in the Sel. column, and click on the OK button since we need these two components to build our project.
5. In the Project pane, expand the Target folder and right click on the Source Group 1 folder and select the Add New Item to Group 'Source Group 1'.
6. Select the Header File (.h) and enter Lab4_4 into the Name: box, and click on the Add button to add this header file into the project.
7. On the top of this header file, first let's include two system header files, <stdint.h> and <stdbool.h>.

8. Using the `#define` macros to define the following constants to be used in this project:

■ `#define SYSCTL_RCGC2_R`	`(*((volatile uint32_t *)0x400FE108))`
■ `#define GPIO_PORTB_DATA_R`	`(*((volatile uint32_t *)0x400053FC))`
■ `#define GPIO_PORTB_DIR_R`	`(*((volatile uint32_t *)0x40005400))`
■ `#define GPIO_PORTB_DEN_R`	`(*((volatile uint32_t *)0x4000551C))`
■ `#define GPIO_PORTC_DATA_R`	`(*((volatile uint32_t *)0x400063FC))`
■ `#define GPIO_PORTC_DIR_R`	`(*((volatile uint32_t *)0x40006400))`
■ `#define GPIO_PORTC_DEN_R`	`(*((volatile uint32_t *)0x4000651C))`
■ `#define GPIO_PORTD_DATA_R`	`(*((volatile uint32_t *)0x400073FC))`
■ `#define GPIO_PORTD_DIR_R`	`(*((volatile uint32_t *)0x40007400))`
■ `#define GPIO_PORTD_DEN_R`	`(*((volatile uint32_t *)0x4000751C))`
■ `#define SYSCTL_RCC_R`	`(*((volatile uint32_t *)0x400FE060))`
■ `#define SYSCTL_RCC_XTAL_16MHZ`	`0x00000540//use 16 MHz crystal`
■ `#define SYSCTL_RCC_USESYSDIV`	`0x00400000//enable System Clock Divider`
■ `#define SYSCTL_SYSDIV_10`	`0x04C00000//system clock is osc-pll/10`
■ `#define SYSCTL_RCGC2_GPIOB`	`0x00000002//Port B Clock Gating Control`
■ `#define SYSCTL_RCGC2_GPIOC`	`0x00000004//Port C Clock Gating Control`
■ `#define SYSCTL_RCGC2_GPIOD`	`0x00000008//Port D Clock Gating Control`

All of these macros, except the macro SYSCTL_SYSDIV_10, can be found from the system header file `tm4c123gh6pm.h` that is located at the folder `C:\ti\TivaWare_C_Series-2.0.1.11577\inc` in your host computer. The macro SYSCTL_SYSDIV_10 is defined in the system header file `sysctl.h` that is located at the folder `C:\ti\TivaWare_C_Series-2.0.1.11577\driverlib` in your host computer. If you do not like to define these macros in this user header file, you can include them into the project and add the include path to enable the compiler to refer to these definitions.

4.4.4 Development of the C Source File

1. In the `Project` pane, expand the `Target` folder and right click on the `Source Group 1` folder and select the `Add New Item to Group 'Source Group 1'`.

2. Select the `C File (.c)` and enter `Lab4_4` into the `Name:` box, and click on the `Add` button to add this source file into the project.

3. Include the following header files into this source file first:

• "`Lab4_4.h`"

4. Define the first user function `Delay()` with an integer variable `time` as the argument for this function. This function returns a `void`. The function body includes a local integer variable i that works as a loop counter and a for() loop. The lower bound of the for loop counter i is 0, and the upper bound is the `time`.

5. Define the second user function `SetSound()` with an integer variable `period` as the argument for this function. This function returns a `void`. The function body includes:

• Assign logic HIGH (0x10) to the PC4 (GPIO_PORTC_DATA_R) to send a HIGH to the speaker.

• Call the `Delay()` function we defined in step 4 to delay a `period` of time to keep PC4 as HIGH for half-cycle.

• Assign logic LOW (0x0) to the PC4 (GPIO_PORTC_DATA_R) to send a LOW to the speaker.

• Call the `Delay()` function we defined in step 4 to delay a `period` of time to keep PC4 as LOW for half-cycle.

6. Place the `int main(void)` to start our main program and put a starting brace under this main function to begin our main program.

7. Declare two `uint32_t` local variables, `ui32Input` and RCC, to receive and hold the returning values for calling some DRA model functions later.

8. Use the system macros to setup the clock for our project with the following code:

   RCC = (SYSCTL_RCC_XTAL_16MHZ|SYSCTL_RCC_USESYSDIV|SYSCTL_SYSDIV_10);

   The first macro is to select the oscillator crystal is 16 MHz. The second macro is to select the PLL and the user divider is used. The third macro is to select the user's divider to be 10. Therefore the system clock used for this project is 400 MHz (PLL output)/2/10 = 400 MHz/ 20 = 20 MHz.

9. Use the Direct Register Access model instruction to assign this clock setup to the RCC register:

   SYSCTL_RCC_R = RCC;

10. Use the Direct Register Access model instruction to enable Ports B, C, and D in the RCGC2 register:

    SYSCTL_RCGC2_R = SYSCTL_RCGC2_GPIOB|SYSCTL_RCGC2_GPIOC|SYSCTL_RCGC2_GPIOD;

11. Use 0x0F to set PB0~PB3 as output pins by using the macro of GPIO Port B Direction Register GPIO_PORTB_DIR_R.

12. Use 0x0F to enable PB0~PB3 as digital function pins by using the macro of GPIO Port B Digital Enable Register GPIO_PORTB_DEN_R.

13. Use 0xF0 to set PD0~PD3 as input pins by using the macro of GPIO Port D Direction Register GPIO_PORTD_DIR_R.

14. Use 0x0F to enable PD0~PD3 as digital function pins by using the macro of GPIO Port D Digital Enable Register GPIO_PORTD_DEN_R.

15. Use 0x10 to set PC4 as an output pin by using the macro of GPIO Port C Direction Register GPIO_PORTC_DIR_R.

16. Use 0x10 to enable PC4 as a digital function pin by using the macro of GPIO Port C Digital Enable Register GPIO_PORTC_DEN_R.

17. Place an infinitive `while()` loop. Inside the `while()` loop, get four input values from the PD0~PD3 pins that are connected to the DIP switches SW1~SW4 by using the instruction `ui32Input = GPIO_PORTD_DATA_R;`. In fact, this instruction is used to get all 8 bits (pins) values in the Port D. However, only the lower 4 bits (pins) are valid since the upper 4-bit are defined as output pins and four 0 will be read out for those upper 4 pins.

18. Assign the read out values from Port D to the Port B to turn ON or OFF corresponding LEDs in the EduBASE Trainer by using `GPIO_PORTB_DATA_R = ui32Input;`.

19. In the following codes, use seven if () statements to check which DIP switch is pressed.

20. If the DIP-SW1 is pressed (`ui32Input == 0x8`), a 400 Hz signal is sent to the speaker in the EduBASE Trainer by calling the user function `SetSound(25000)`.

21. Else if the DIP-SW1 and SW2 are pressed (`ui32Input == 0x0C`), a 600 Hz signal is sent to the speaker in the EduBASE Trainer by calling the user function `SetSound(17000)`.

22. Else if the DIP-SW1, SW2, and SW3 are pressed (ui32Input == 0x0E), an 800 Hz signal is sent to the speaker in the EduBASE Trainer by calling the user function SetSound(12500).

23. Else if all DIP switches are pressed (ui32Input == 0x0F), a 1000 Hz signal is sent to the speaker in the EduBASE Trainer by calling the user function SetSound(10000).

24. Else if the DIP-SW2–SW4 are pressed (ui32Input == 0x07), a 1200 Hz signal is sent to the speaker in the EduBASE Trainer by calling the user function SetSound(7500).

25. Else if the DIP-SW2 and SW3 are pressed (ui32Input == 0x06), a 1400 Hz signal is sent to the speaker in the EduBASE Trainer by calling the user function SetSound(7142).

26. Else for all other combinations of the DIP switches, a 200 Hz signal is sent to the speaker in the EduBASE Trainer by calling the user function SetSound(50000).

27. Some necessary ending braces should be added to finish the while() loop, the if () statement and the main program.

4.4.5 Setup of the Include Path and Linking of the Static Library Now you need to include the system header files by adding the include path and link the static TiveWare Peripheral Driver Library by adding that library into the project.

Refer to Section 4.5.7.3.3.4 to add this include path into the project. Perform the following operations to link this library with our project:

Since we did not use any system header files and static library in this project, we do not need to include any header file and link any library.

Now you can compile your program by going to Project|Build target menu item. However, before you can download your program into the flash ROM in the EVB, make sure that the debugger you are using is the Stellaris ICDI. You can do this checking as follows:

- Go to Project|Options for Target 'Target 1' menu item to open the Options wizard.
- On the opened Options wizard, click on the Debug tab.
- Make sure that the debugger shown in the Use: box is Stellaris ICDI. Otherwise you can click on the dropdown arrow to select this debugger from the list.

4.4.6 Demonstrate Your Program Perform the following operations to run your program and check the running results:

- Go to Flash|Download menu item to download your program into the flash ROM.
- Go to Debug|Start/Stop Debug Session to begin debugging your program. Click on the OK button on the 32-KB memory size limitation message box to continue.
- Then go to Debug|Run menu item to run your program.

As the project runs, the corresponding LEDs will be ON when you slide the DIP switches to the ON position or press any the position switch. Also different sound signal with different frequency is sent to the speaker during the DIP switches are kept in the ON position.

Based on these results, try to answer the following questions:

- Can you modify your codes to control any other combinations of the DIP switches, such as only DIP-SW2, DIP-SW3, or DIP-SW4 is in the ON position in the EduBASE Trainer?
- What did you learn from this project?

Chapter 5

ARM® Microcontroller Interrupts and Exceptions

This chapter provides general information about exceptions and interrupts occurred and handled in the Tiva™ ARM® Cortex®-M4 microcontrollers. The discussion is divided into several parts, which includes: the exception and interrupt sources, the priority levels of different exceptions and interrupts, and the interrupt vector table used to direct the processor to response and handle the accepted exceptions and interrupts, the interrupt service routines used to process the exception and interrupt requests. Two programming models in the TivaWare™ Peripheral Driver Library (TWPDL) are covered in these discussions. Both CMSIS Core and TWPDL API functions used to access NVIC registers to process exceptions and interrupts are also introduced.

5.1 OVERVIEW AND INTRODUCTION

Generally a user's application program is composed of a sequence of assembly or high-level instructions stored in the user memory space in most microcontroller systems. The CPU in a microcontroller sequentially executes the user's program by fetching them one by one from the memory to the Instructor Register (IR) in the CPU and then decoding each of instructions in the CPU and running them in that sequence. However, in many applications, it is necessary to stop the execution of the current instructions and execute sets of instructions in response to requests from various events or peripheral devices during the user's program running. These requests, called exceptions or interrupts, are often asynchronous to the execution of the user's program, called the main program. Exceptions and interrupts provide a way to temporarily suspend the user's program execution so the CPU can be freed to service these exceptions or interrupts requests. After an exception/interrupt has been serviced, the main program resumes as if there had been no interruption. Generally, an exception/interrupt processing system contains three components:

- Exception/Interrupt Request coming from exceptions or interrupts sources.
- Exception/Interrupt Monitor and Masking installed in the CPU to monitor, enable or disable any exception or interrupt request. This includes both global and local masking systems.

Practical Microcontroller Engineering with ARM® Technology, First Edition. Ying Bai.
© 2016 by The Institute of Electrical and Electronics Engineers, Inc. Published 2016 by John Wiley & Sons, Inc.
Companion Website: www.wiley.com/go/armbai

- `Exception/Interrupt Response` allowing the CPU to response and handle accepted exception or interrupt request.

The exception/interrupt source works as an exception/interrupt request, and it is provided by an internal or an external device that needs the interrupting service with an interrupt request sending to the CPU. This exception/interrupt request is sent to the CPU with an interrupt flag signal and waits for the CPU's response. When CPU finished the current instruction, exactly at the end of the third clock cycle of the execution of the current instruction, it checks whether there is any exception or interrupt request by inspecting all interrupt flags. If an interrupt has occurred and the interrupt flag has been set with no other higher-priority interrupt occurring, CPU will transfer the control to the interrupt service routine (ISR) to execute the service subroutine to process the request sent by the associated exception or interrupt source.

To successfully identify, accept, and respond to an exception or interrupt request sent by either an internal or an external device, the following working units are necessary:

- A *global exception/interrupt control register*, which is under the control of the CPU, is needed. By resetting or setting certain bits in this global interrupt control register, CPU can unmask (enable) or mask (disable) all maskable interrupt requests. In the ARM® Cortex®-M4 system, the Primary Interrupt Mask (`PRIMASK`) register is equivalent to this register.

- A *local exception/interrupt control register* is related to some associated events or devices. Certain bits on this register can be accessed and controlled by the programmer by setting (enabling) or resetting (disabling) the interrupt created by the associated device by programming. In the ARM® Cortex®-M4 system, the Base Priority (`BASEPRI`) register is equivalent to this register and provides this priority control function.

- An *exception or interrupt vector table* or a collection of the entry addresses of the interrupt service routines is needed. This vector table is device-dependent or interrupt-source-dependent, which means that each different exception or interrupt source has a different unique vector. In the ARM® Cortex®-M4 system, a vector table is provided to collect and store entry addresses for all exceptions and interrupts to be occurred.

Figure 5.1 provides an illustration for exceptions and interrupts processing structure in most microcontroller systems.

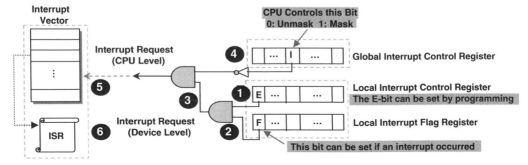

Figure 5.1.   An illustration for exception/interrupt processing.

5.2 EXCEPTIONS AND INTERRUPTS IN THE ARM® CORTEX®-M4 MCU SYSTEM

As we discussed in Section 2.4 in Chapter 2, all exceptions and interrupts are controlled and managed by a Nested Vectored Interrupt Controller (NVIC) in the ARM® Cortex®-M4 system. The NVIC is a control unit that is embedded inside the Cortex-M4 MCU, and it is used to handle and pre-process all exceptions and interrupts, including maskable and unmaskable interrupts, occurring during the normal running of application codes in the ARM® Cortex®-M4 system.

Like any other Interrupt Processing Unit (IPU), the NVIC processes any exception or interrupt in the following sequence:

1. An exception or interrupt is first created by an exception/interrupt source and an interrupt-service-request is sent to the Cortex-M4 CPU.

2. Based on the mask register's content (PRIMASK) and the interrupt priority level (BASE–PRI), CPU will determine whether to response or process the interrupt request.

3. If the interrupt request is accepted, the associated hardware will provide interrupt-related information, such as the interrupt source number and related Interrupt Service Routine (ISR) entry point, in a Vector Table.

4. Before the control can be transferred to the ISR, all related registers, including R0~R3, R12, LR, PSR, and PC, are pushed into the stack to reserve their contents. During this protection process, all other interrupts or exceptions are masked or disabled to avoid any data to be lost.

5. Then the control will be directed to the entry point (entry address of the ISR) stored in the Vector Table to run the ISR to perform the required interrupt service. During this process, all other interrupts and exceptions are unmasked or enabled to allow higher-level-priority interrupts or exceptions to be requested and responded.

6. After the ISR is done and before the control can be transferred back to the main program, (a) all other interrupts or exceptions are masked or disabled to avoid any data to be lost and, (b) all related registers protected in step 4, including the PC, will be recovered by popping them back to the related registers.

7. Then the control can be directed to the main program to continue executing the normal application codes based on the old PC content. At this time, all interrupts and exceptions are unmasked or enabled to allow any interrupt or exception to be requested and responded.

In fact, there is no significant difference between an exception and an interrupt in the ARM® Cortex®-M4 system. Regularly an exception is generated by the ARM® processor or the CPU, and it has a higher-priority level compared with other interrupts. An exception is often generated by an event, such as the system fault event and other system mis-operation event. An interrupt is generally created by an internal or an external peripheral with lower priority level. Figure 5.2 shows an illustration for all exceptions and interrupts used in the ARM® Cortex®-M4 microcontroller system.

It can be found from Figure 5.2 that all exceptions, except the SysTick Time exception and NMI, are related to the ARM® processor and generated by the related event in this CPU. All Interrupt Requests (IRQs), including one Non-Maskable Interrupt (NMI) that can be considered as an exception, are generated either by internal

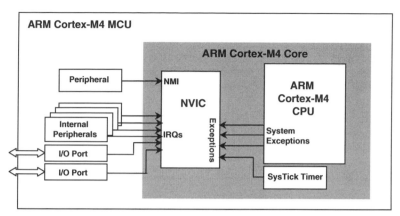

Figure 5.2. An illustration for all exceptions and interrupts in the ARM® NVIC.

peripherals located in the ARM® Cortex®-M4 Evaluation Board or by external peripherals via some I/O Ports.

Table 5.1 lists most popular used exceptions and interrupts, including the exception types, numbers, and priority levels. Three exceptions, Reset, NMI and Hard Fault, have the fixed priority levels and cannot be modified by programming.

Table 5.1. The exception and interrupt types in the cortex-M4 system.

Exception Number	Exception Type	Priority Level	Description
1	Reset	−3 (Highest)	Reset
2	NMI	−2	Non-Maskable Interrupt
3	Hard Fault	−1	Hardware Related Fault
4	Memory Manage Fault	Programmable	Memory Management Fault. MPU violations or program address faults
5	Bus Fault	Programmable	Bus Error
6	Usage Fault	Programmable	Program Error
7–10	Reserved	N/A	—
11	SVC	Programmable	SuperVisor Call
12	Debug Monitor	Programmable	Debug related exceptions, such as brealpoints
13	Reserved	N/A	—
14	PendSV	Programmable	Pendable Service Call
15	SYSTICK	Programmable	System Tick Timer
16	Interrupt 0	Programmable	These interrupts can be generated by on-chip internal peripherals or external peripherals
17	Interrupt 1	Programmable	
18	Interrupt 3	Programmable	
. . .	. . .	. . .	
240	Interrupt 239	Programmable	

5.2.1 Exception and Interrupt Types

It can be found from Table 5.1 that the NIVC in the Cortex-M4 system can handle up to 240 exceptions and interrupt inputs. However, in most real applications, they do not have so many interrupt or exception sources available.

There are 15 system exceptions in the Cortex-M4 system, and their exception numbers range from 1 to 15. The exceptions with number greater than 15 and above (until up to 240) are considered as interrupts. The smaller the number, the higher the priority level the exception or interrupt has, and this is true for both exceptions and interrupts.

The top three exceptions, Reset, NMI, and Hard Fault, have fixed priority levels with minus numbers to indicate that these exceptions cannot be masked or disabled by using PRIMASK register, and they have the highest priority level and must be handled first if they are coming. Starting from exception 4, the priority levels for all the following exceptions and interrupts can be programmed to the different priority levels based on those exceptions and peripherals applied in your applications. Also these exceptions and interrupts can be masked or disabled by using PRIMASK register in your application programs.

To respond to an exception or an interrupt, a related exception handler (EXH) or a related interrupt service subroutine (ISR) is developed and they are composed of a piece of program codes to process the exception or interrupt.

5.2.2 Exceptions and Interrupts Management

All exceptions and interrupts in the Cortex-M4 MCU are handled by the NVIC. In order to manage and control all of those exceptions and interrupts, the NVIC provides a group of programmable registers. Most of these registers are located inside the NVIC and the System Control Block (SCB), and the SCB can be considered as an assistant to the NVIC to help it to control and manage exceptions and interrupts in the Cortex-M4 interrupt system. The special registers inside the ARM® Cortex®-M4 processor, such as PRIMASK, FAULTMASK, and BASEPRI, also provide mask, unmask, and priority level selections for most exceptions and interrupts to support their processing.

Besides NVIC and SCB, the Keil® CMSIS Core also provides a set of registers, definitions, and functions to support the handling and processing of exceptions and interrupts. The CMSIS Core defines a set of different priority levels called enumeration values for exceptions and interrupts with a set of macros or symbolic definitions for related handlers. Table 5.2 lists most popular macros for these exceptions and interrupts. Table 5.3 lists the most popular CMSIS Core functions used to access related special registers to mask, unmask, and set priority levels for selected exceptions and interrupts.

It can be found from Table 5.2 that both exceptions and interrupts are all considered as IRQn, and each IRQ has a different priority levels. The Enumeration (IRQn) and Exception Handler columns defined macros for these IRQn names and handler names, and the users can use these macros to define related exceptions and call related handlers in their program.

The exception numbers and exception handlers for all interrupts are device-dependent and are defined in related device-specified header files in a typedef structure called IRQn, which are provided by the different microcontroller vendors.

Table 5.2.   The CMSIS core exception definitions in the cortex-M4 system.

Exception Number	Exception Type	CMSIS Core Enumeration (IRQn)	Enumeration Value	Exception Handler
1	Reset	–	–	Reset_Handler
2	NMI	NonMaskableInt_IRQn	−14	NMI_Handler
3	Hard Fault	HardFault_IRQ	−13	HardFault_Handler
4	Memory Manage Fault	MemoryManagement_IRQn	−12	MemManage_Handler
5	Bus Fault	BusFault_IRQn	−11	BusFault_Handler
6	Usage Fault	UsageFault_IRQn	−10	UsageFault_Handler
11	SVC	SVCall_IRQn	−5	SVC_Handler
12	Debug Monitor	DebugMonitor_IRQn	−4	DebugMon_Handler
14	PendSV	PendSV_IRQn	−2	PendSV_Handler
15	SYSTICK	SysTick_IRQn	−1	SysTick_Handler
16	Interrupt 0	(device-specified)	0	(device-specified)
17	Interrupt 1~239	(device-specified)	1~239	(device-specified)

Table 5.3 shows some exceptions and interrupts accessing functions defined in the CMSIS Core. The users can use and call these functions to access related registers to configure exception and interrupt in their program. Of course, the users can also directly access those registers in NVIC and SCB in their program to configure related interrupts. However, a limitation of using this method is the portable issue, which means that if the porting codes are defined based on different processors, the users' codes may not be compatible with another Cortex-M processor.

For the TM4C123GH6PM MCU, most definitions for related exceptions and interrupts are defined in the system header files, such as hw_ints.h, hw_nvic.h and tm4c123gh6pm.h.

The TivaWare™ Peripheral Driver Library also provides a group of interrupt controller API functions to facilitate users to directly access related NVIC registers to configure and control selected exceptions and interrupts. Table 5.4 shows all of these NVIC API functions. When using these NVIC API functions, the following points should be noted:

- If two interrupts with the same priority are asserted at the same time, the one with the lower interrupt number is processed first. The NVIC keeps track of the nesting of interrupt handlers,

Table 5.3.   The CMSIS core functions for interrupt controls.

CMSIS Core Function	Description
void NVIC_EnableIRQ(IRQn_Type IRQn)	Enable an external interrupt
void NVIC_DisableIRQ(IRQn_Type IRQn)	Disable an external interrupt
void NVIC_SetPriority(IRQn_Type IRQn, uint32_t priority)	Set the priority for an interrupt
void __enable_irq(void)	Clear PRIMASK to enable all interrupts
void __disable_irq(void)	Set PRIMASK to disable all interrupts
void NVIC_SetPriorityGrouping(uint32_t PriorityGroup)	Set priority grouping structure

Table 5.4. The NVIC API functions in the TivaWare peripheral driver library.

API Function	Description
void IntEnable(uint32_t ui32Interrupt)	Enable an interrupt
void IntDisable(uint32_t ui32Interrupt)	Disable an interrupt
uint32_t IntIsEnabled(uint32_t ui32Interrupt)	Check if an interrupt has been enabled. Returning a non-zero indicates that the interrupt is enabled
bool IntMasterEnable(uint32_t ui32Interrupt)	Enable processor to receive any interrupt. Returning a True means that all interrupts are enabled
bool IntMasterDisable(uint32_t ui32Interrupt)	Prevent processor from receiving any interrupt. Returning a True means that all interrupts are disabled
void IntPendClear(uint32_t ui32Interrupt)	Clear a specified pending interrupt
void IntPendSet(uint32_t ui32Interrupt)	Set a specified interrupt to be pending status
int32_t IntPriorityGet(uint32_t ui32Interrupt)	Get the priority level for a specified interrupt
void IntPrioritySet(uint32_t ui32Interrupt, uint8_t ui8Priority)	Set the priority level for a specified interrupt
uint32_t IntPriorityGroupingGet(void)	Get the priority grouping configuration
void IntPriorityGroupingSet(uint32_t ui32Bits)	Set the priority grouping configuration
uint32_t IntPriorityMaskGet(void)	Get the current priority masking bits
void IntPriorityMaskSet(uint32_t ui32PriorityMask)	Set the current priority masking level
void IntRegister(uint32_t ui32Interrupt, void (*pfnHandler)(void))	Register an interrupt handler
void IntTrigger(uint32_t ui32Interrupt)	Trigger a specified interrupt
void IntUnregister(uint32_t ui32PriorityMask)	Unregister a specified interrupt

allowing the processor to return from interrupt context only once all nested and pending interrupts have been handled.

- Interrupt Service Routine (ISR) can be configured in two ways: statically at compile time or dynamically at run time. Static configuration of an ISR is accomplished by editing the interrupt vector table in the application's startup code. When statically configured, the interrupts must be explicitly enabled in the NVIC via the API function `IntEnable()` before the processor can respond to the interrupt. Statically configuring the interrupt vector table provides the fastest interrupt response time.

- Alternatively, interrupts can be configured at runtime using another NVIC API function `IntRegister()`. When using `IntRegister()`, the interrupt must also be enabled as before. Runtime configuration of interrupts adds a small latency to the interrupt response time because the stacking operation (a write to SRAM) and the interrupt handler table fetch (a read from SRAM) must be performed sequentially.

For most general applications and implementations, the users can use the NVIC API functions provided by the TivaWare™ Peripheral Driver Library to handle any exception and interrupt implemented in their applications. The users can also select to use the CMSIS Core accessing functions shown in Table 5.3 to access related registers in the NVIC to process those exceptions and interrupts. The point to be noted is that you must select the CMSIS Core tool when you create your new µVersion5 project with the Keil® ARM®-MDK IDE if you want to use the CMSIS Core access functions to handle the exceptions and interrupts in applications.

As we discussed in Section 2.3.1 in Chapter 2, the NVIC and SCB are located in the System Control Space (SCS) at the on-chip memory map with a memory range of 0xE000E000~0xE000EFFF.

5.2.3 Exception and Interrupt Processing

After a system reset, all maskable exceptions and interrupts are disabled with a priority level of zero. In order to use any exception or interrupt, you need to:

1. Set up the priority level for the required exception or interrupt.
2. Enable the exception or interrupt generation mechanism in the processor or the peripheral.
3. Enable the interrupt in the related register in the NVIC.

When these preparations jobs have been done, the processor will run the user's program in a normal sequence and will wait for an exception or interrupt to come. The ARM® Cortex®-M4 NVIC provides the following registers to support to access, configure, and response to all different exceptions and interrupts:

- Interrupt Priority-Level Register (0xE000E400~0xE000E4EF)
- Interrupt Set Enable Register (0xE000E100~0xE000E11C)
- Interrupt Clear Enable Register (0xE000E180~0xE000E19C)
- Interrupt Set Pending Register (0xE000E200~0xE000E21C)
- Interrupt Clear Pending Register (0xE000E280~0xE000E29C)
- Interrupt Active Status Register (0xE000E300~0xE000E31C)
- Interrupt Controller Type Register (0xE000E004)
- Software Trigger Interrupt Register (0xE000EF00)

Table 5.5 shows the most popular NVIC registers, CMSIS Core macros and functions used for exceptions and interrupts in the ARM® Cortex®-M4 system.

Each register takes 32 bits or 4 bytes. For example, the Interrupt Set Enable Register NVIC→ISER[0] is a 32-bit register and has an address range of 0xE000E100~0xE000E103; and another Interrupt Set Enable Register, NVIC→ISER[1], is also a 32-bit register and has an address range of 0xE000E104~0xE000E107. Since the register NVIC→ISER[0] is a 32-bit register, it can enable 32 interrupts, and each bit is for one interrupt source. This means that bit 0 is for Interrupt 0, bit 1 is for Interrupt 1, and so on. Therefore this register can be used to enable the first 32 interrupts, from Interrupt 0 through to Interrupt 31. Similarly, the NVIC→ISER[1] can be used to enable Interrupt 32~Interrupt 63. For example, if you want to enable the Interrupt 12 using this register, just set bit 12 in the NVIC→ISER[0] to 1. You can write the code as follows: NVIC→ISER[0] = 0x00001000 or NVIC→ISER[0] = 1 << 12.

Table 5.5. The most popular NVIC registers used for interrupt controls.

NVIC Register	CMSIS Core Macros	CMSIS Core Function	Function
Interrupt Set Enable Registers	NVIC→ISER[0] to NVIC→ISER[7]	void NVIC_EnableIRQ(IRQn)	1 → enable
Interrupt Clear Enable Registers	NVIC→ICER[0] to NVIC→ICER[7]	void NVIC_DisableIRQ(IRQn)	1 → clear enable
Interrupt Set Pending Registers	NVIC→ISPR[0] to NVIC→ISPR[7]	void NVIC_SetPendingIRQ(IRQn)	1 → set pending
Interrupt Clear Pending Registers	NVIC→ICPR[0] to NVIC→ICPR[7]	void NVIC_ClearPendingIRQ (IRQn)	1 → clear pending
Interrupt Active Bits Registers	NVIC→IABR[0] to NVIC→IABR[7]	uint32_t NVIC_GetActive(IRQn)	Get active bits
Interrupt Priority Registers	NVIC→IP[0] to NVIC→IP[239]	void NVIC_SetPriority(IRQn, Pri) uint32_t NVIC_GetPriority(IRQn)	Priority level (8 bits wide) for each INT
Software Trigger Interrupt Register	NVIC→STIR	Write an interrupt number to set its pending status	Write an interrupt number to set its pending status

5.2.3.1 Exception and Interrupt Inputs and Pending Status

As any exception or interrupt occurs, the processor will response to the exception or interrupt source in one of the following possible ways:

- The interrupt can be masked (disabled) or unmasked (enabled).
- The interrupt can be pending or not pending.
- The interrupt can be in an active or inactive state.

All of these functions can be achieved by using several NVIC programmable registers, such as Interrupt Set (Clear) Enable Register, Interrupt Set (Clear) Pending Register, and read-only Interrupt Active Status Register,listed in Table 5.5.

An exception or an interrupt request can be accepted by the processor if:

- The processor is in the normal running status (not reset or halt state).
- The exception or interrupt is enabled or in pending status (exclude Reset, NMI, and Hard Fault).
- The exception or interrupt has higher priority level compared with the current running program or handler.

After an exception/interrupt request has been accepted, the NVIC will help the CPU to identify the exact exception/interrupt source and determine the entry address of the related Interrupt Service Routine (ISR) to further process this exception/interrupt. In the early ARM® Cortex®-M MCUs, these jobs are handled by using software, which is low in efficiency and slow in processing speed. Starting from Cortex-M3, these jobs can be handled by hardware with the help of the NVIC. The entry address of the related ISR for the identified exception/interrupt can be easily and quickly located from a so-called Interrupt Vector Table, in which all exception and interrupt sources are located according to their priority levels in order.

5.2.3.2 Exception and Interrupt Vector Table

The Vector Table is a word collection of all exception and interrupt sources used in the ARM® Cortex®-M4 system. This collection is distributed in a block of memory with a table format, and it is in the order of the priority levels of all exception and interrupt sources. Each source in this collection, which takes 4 bytes or one word, represents the starting address of an exception handler or an ISR for related exception or interrupt. Since the address bus used in the Cortex-M4 is 32 bits wide and the width of each byte in the memory is 8 bits, 4 bytes are needed to store one starting address for the handler or ISR.

This Vector Table can be located at any area of the system memory. However, the default location for this Table is the bottom of the memory. The exact location of the Vector Table can be determined by a programmable register in the NVIC, the `Vector Table Offset Register` (VTOR). The content of this register is 0 when a reset operation is performed. Therefore the Vector Table is located at address 0x00000000 after a system reset.

The starting address of each related exception handler or interrupt ISR can also be called a Vector since it provides not only a direction to the related handler or ISR but also a detailed entry address of the handler or ISR. As we mentioned, each Vector takes 4-byte space in the memory. To access the desired Vector, the selected Exception Number or Vector Number in the Vector Table must be multiplied by 4, and then go to that resulted address to pick up the desired Vector for the selected exception/interrupt. For example, the system reset is considered to be an exception, and its Exception Number is 1 (the highest priority level). To get its Vector or the starting address of its ISR, the target address for this Vector in the Vector Table is 1 × 4 = 0x00000004. Inside this address following with 4 continuous bytes, or from 0x00000004~0x00000007, a 32-bit starting address of the ISR related to the reset is stored.

The LSB of each vector indicates if the exception is to be processed in the Thumb state. Because all Cortex-M processors support only Thumb instructions, the LSB of all exception and interrupt vectors should be 1.

Based on this analysis, the starting memory address used to store a Vector or starting address for each related exception handler or interrupt ISR can be calculated as

Starting memory address = Exception Number × 4

The memory address 0x00000000 is used to store the Main Stack Pointer (MSP) after a system reset operation.

Table 5.6 shows a typical Vector Table with related starting addresses for most popular exception handlers and interrupt ISRs.

Since the actual vector for each exception handler or interrupt ISR can be modified either statically or dynamically by programming via the Vector Table Offset Register (VTOR), therefore the real value for each vector cannot be indicated at this moment. For detailed default vector table and interrupt related vectors, refer to the `startup_TM4C123.s` file; this file contains the definitions for all exceptions and interrupts used in the TM4C123GH6PM microcontroller system. This file should be loaded into your project when you selected the `Device|Startup` tool as you created your new project. The LSB for each vector must be 1 to indicate that this is compatible for the Thumb instructions.

Table 5.6. The vector table used in the cortex-M4 microcontroller.

Exception Number	Memory Address	Related Vector	LSB
· · · · · · ·	· · · · · · ·	· · · · · · ·	
19	0x0000004C	Interrupt 3 Vector	[1]
18	0x00000048	Interrupt 2 Vector	[1]
17	0x00000044	Interrupt 1 Vector	[1]
16	0x00000040	Interrupt 0 Vector	[1]
15	0x0000003C	SysTick Vector	[1]
14	0x00000038	PendSV Vector	[1]
13	0x00000034	Not Used	
12	0x00000030	Debug Monitor Vector	[1]
11	0x0000002C	SVC Vector	[1]
10	0x00000028	Not Used	
9	0x00000024	Not Used	
8	0x00000020	Not Used	
7	0x0000001C	Not Used	
6	0x00000018	Usage Fault Vector	[1]
5	0x00000014	Bus Fault Vector	[1]
4	0x00000010	MemManage Vector	[1]
3	0x0000000C	HardFault Vector	[1]
2	0x00000008	NMI Vector	[1]
1	0x00000004	Reset Vector	[1]
0	0x00000000	MSP Initial Value	

5.2.3.3 Definitions of the Priority Levels

All exceptions and interrupts in the Cortex-M4 system have certain priority levels, either maskable or unmaskable sources. Most maskable interrupts have programmable priority levels, but all Non-Maskable Interrupts (NMIs) have fixed priority levels. When an exception or interrupt occurs, the NVIC performs a comparison between the priority level of current exception or interrupt and the priority level of the new coming exception/interrupt. The current running task will be suspended and the control will be transferred to the service routine of the new coming exception/interrupt if the priority level of the new coming exception/interrupt is higher.

In the ARM® Cortex®-M4 system, the interrupt priority levels are controlled by the Interrupt Priority Registers, as shown in Table 5.5. Each priority register can use 3 bits, 4 bits, or 8 bits to cover all priority levels used in the priority control system. A total of 8 priority levels can be used if 3 bits are used in this register, and 16 priority levels can be obtained if 4 bits are used in this register. Devices within the Tiva™ family support up to 154 interrupt sources and 8 priority levels, which means that 3 bits are used in the priority register in the TM4C123GH6PM MCU.

Figure 5.3 shows an illustration of using 3 bits and 4 bits in the priority level configuration register. A total of 8 and 16 priority levels are generated and available to the NVIC unit.

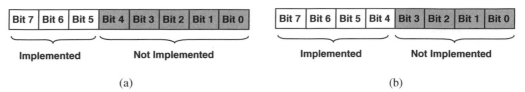

Figure 5.3.   Priority levels used in the Priority Register.

In Figure 5.3a, 3 bits (bits 7~4) are used in the Priority Register to provide 8 priority levels. Since bits 4~0 are not used, they always read out as zero. Therefore the 8 priority levels are 0x00, 0x20, 0x40, 0x60, 0x80, 0xA0, 0xC0, and 0xE0.

Similarly, 4 bits are used in the Priority Register in Figure 5.3b. Therefore 16 priority levels are provided by this kind of bits setting. The reason of using only the MSB, not LSB, in the Priority Register is that a 4-bit priority configuration can run on devices with 3-bit priority configuration register.

In some more complex applications, the `group priority` and `sub-priority` configuration may be used to extend the functions of the priority levels. For example, for an 8-bit priority configuration register, the upper 4 bits are defined as the group priority and the lower 4 bits are considered to be the sub-priority. Of course, it is unnecessary to divide the group and sub-priority in this even way; any combinations, such as 7 bits for group and 1 bit for sub-priority for an 8-bit priority register configuration, and 2 bits for group and 1 bit for sub-priority for a 3-bit priority configuration, are acceptable and work.

Table 5.7 shows an example of bit fields and their values for the different combinations of group priority and sub-priority. In TM4C123GH6PM MCU system, only the last 4 groups, from group priority 4 to group priority 7, are available since only 3 bits (bits 7~5) are used for the priority levels definitions in this system.

The reason for using the group priority level is to determine whether an interrupt that has the same priority level as one that is currently being processed by the processor can be accepted. If this happened, the processor will further check the sub-priority levels for both interrupts to determine whether the new coming interrupt should be accepted or not. Generally, the sub-priority that has a higher level (lower value) should be accepted and processed. Tables 5.3 and 5.4 provide some popular functions, either CMSIS Core supported functions or The TivaWare™ Peripheral Driver Library supported API functions, to facilitate to set up and access these group priority level configurations.

Table 5.7.   Definitions of group priority and sub-priority fields.

Priority Group	Group Priority Field	Sub-priority Field
0 (default)	Bits 7~1	Bit 0
1	Bits 7~2	Bits 1~0
2	Bits 7~3	Bits 2~0
3	Bits 7~4	Bits 3~0
4	Bits 7~5	Bits 4~0
5	Bits 7~6	Bits 5~0
6	Bit 7	Bits 6~0
7	None	Bits 7~0

Refer to Table 5.1 to get a detailed description about the priority levels for most exceptions and interrupts used in the ARM® Cortex®-M4 microcontroller system.

Next let's concentrate on the exceptions and interrupts used in the TM4C123GH6PM MCU system.

5.3 EXCEPTIONS AND INTERRUPTS IN THE TM4C123GH6PM MICROCONTROLLER SYSTEM

In TM4C123GH6PM MCU system, all exceptions and interrupts are handled by the different handlers or Interrupt Service Routines (ISR) based on the exception and interrupt sources. This can be summarized as follows:

1. All maskable Interrupt Requests (IRQs) are handled by the related ISRs.
2. All faults, including the hard fault, memory management fault, usage fault, and bus fault, are handled by the fault handlers.
3. All other exceptions, including NMI, PendSV, SVCall, SysTick, and the fault exceptions, belong to system exceptions and are handled by system handlers.

Generally both the second and the third handlers are developed and controlled by the microcontroller vendors. Therefore in this section we only pay our attention to the first one.

The interrupts are widely applied in all events and peripherals in the TM4C123GH6PM MCU system, but one of the most popular peripherals is the GPIO. In this section we try to introduce the interrupts used by the GPIO Ports to illustrate how to use a GPIO-related interrupt mechanism to handle different interrupts in this system since all other peripherals in this MCU system used the similar interrupt handling configurations and procedures. In this way, we do not need to discuss the interrupt configurations and procedures for all other peripherals one by one. So we will concentrate on the interrupts used in the GPIO Ports at this part.

In TM4C123GH6PM MCU system, the GPIO-related interrupts are controlled by three layers or three levels with different control components:

1. Local interrupt configurations and controls for each GPIO pin (seven interrupt control registers).
2. Local interrupt configurations and controls for each GPIO Port (NVIC interrupt control registers).
3. Global interrupt configurations and controls for all peripherals by the processor (PRIMASK and BASEPRI registers).

These interrupt controls and configurations are performed by the different registers that belong to the various components. Let's discuss these one by one in details in the following sections.

5.3.1 Local Interrupt Configurations and Controls for GPIO Pins

As we discussed in Section 2.6.3.3.5 in Chapter 2, seven interrupt control registers are used to process interrupts that occurred in each GPIO Port. These registers include:

- GPIO Interrupt Both Edges Register (GPIOIBE): Allows both edges to cause interrupts.

Table 5.8. The bit values and functions for GPIO interrupt controls.

GPIO Register	Each Bit Value (Lowest 8-Bit) and Each Pin Function
GPIOIS	0: Detect an edge (edge-sensitive) on the pin, 1: Detect a level (level-sensitive) on the pin.
GPIOIBE	0: Interrupt is controlled by GPIOIEV, 1: Both edges on the corresponding pin trigger an interrupt
GPIOIEV	0: A falling edge or a LOW level, 1: A rising edge or a HIGH level triggers an interrupt
GPIOIM	0: Interrupt is masked (disabled), 1: Interrupt is unmasked (enabled).
GPIORIS	0: No interrupt occurred on the pin, 1: An interrupt is occurred on the pin. For the edge-triggered interrupts, writ a 1 to the pin to clear that interrupt. For level-triggered interrupt, no action is needed.
GPIOMIS	0: No interrupt occurred or the pin has been masked, 1: An interrupt has been occurred.
GPIOICR	0: No action, 1: The corresponded edge-triggered interrupt is cleared.

- GPIO Interrupt Event Register (GPIOIEV): Determines the detecting edges or levels.
- GPIO Interrupt Mask Register (GPIOIM): Masks (disables) or unmask (enable) an interrupt.
- GPIO Raw Interrupt Status Register (GPIORIS): Indicates the raw interrupt status for a pin.
- GPIO Masked Interrupt Status Register (GPIOMIS): Indicates the state of the interrupt.
- GPIO Interrupt Clear Register (GPIOICR): Clears an edge-triggered interrupt.

All of these registers are 32-bit, but only lowest 8 bits are used and each bit corresponds to each pin in the selected GPIO Port: bit 0 is for pin 0, bit 1 is for pin 1, and so on. Table 5.8 shows the bit values and their functions for these registers.

Before any exception or interrupt can be applied to any pin on any GPIO Port, all GPIO pins on selected GPIO Port should be initialized and configured via related GPIO registers.

5.3.1.1 Initialize and Configure GPIO Interrupt Control Registers

To initialize and configure GPIO interrupt controls, one needs to program the GPIOIS, GPIOIBE, GPIOEV, and GPIOIM registers to configure the type, event, and mask of the interrupts for each port. The following steps should be used to do this initialization and configuration process:

- Configure the GPIOIM register to disable (mask) the undesired pins.
- Configure the GPIOIS register to indicate the interrupt-triggering type, edge, or level.
- Configure the GPIOIBE register to indicate if this interrupt is triggered by both edges.
- Reset the GPIORIS register to 0 to make it ready to set a flag if any interrupt occurred.
- Configure the GPIOIM register to enable (unmask) the desired pins.

```
#define GPIO_PORTF_IS_R      (*((volatile uint32_t *)0x40025404))    GPIOIS for PORTF
#define GPIO_PORTF_IBE_R     (*((volatile uint32_t *)0x40025408))    GPIOIBE for PORTF
#define GPIO_PORTF_IEV_R     (*((volatile uint32_t *)0x4002540C))    GPIOIEV for PORTF
#define GPIO_PORTF_IM_R      (*((volatile uint32_t *)0x40025410))    GPIOIM for PORTF
#define GPIO_PORTF_RIS_R     (*((volatile uint32_t *)0x40025414))    GPIORIS for PORTF
#define GPIO_PORTF_MIS_R     (*((volatile uint32_t *)0x40025418))    GPIOMIS for PORTF
#define GPIO_PORTF_ICR_R     (*((volatile uint32_t *)0x4002541C))    GPIOICR for PORTF
```

Figure 5.4.   Seven interrupt control registers for GPIO Port F.

One point to be noted is that each GPIO Port has seven interrupt control registers, and these seven interrupt control registers only control the interrupts for this Port. Figure 5.4 shows the macros of all seven interrupt control registers used only for GPIO Port F.

For example, we try to initialize and configure pin 4 in the GPIO Port F (PF4) as an interrupt-driven pin with the following configurations:

- Triggered by a HIGH-level voltage, not an edge.
- The pin is interrupt-enabled.

Table 5.9 shows the bit values for related interrupt control registers (x = don't care).

As shown in Table 5.9, the value on each bit of different registers determined the interrupt functions on the PF4 pin as follows (see Figure 5.4):

- Bit 4 on GPIO_PORTF_IS_R = 1 indicates that an interrupt on this pin is triggered by levels.
- Bit 4 on GPIO_PORTF_IBE_R = 0 means that the interrupt is controlled by the GPIOIEV register.
- Bit 4 on GPIO_PORTF_IEV_R = 1 indicates that the interrupt on this pin is driven by a HIGH-level voltage.
- Bit 4 on GPIO_PORTF_IM_R = 1 means that the interrupt on this pin is enabled.

All of these GPIO interrupt control registers are 32-bit, but only the least significant 8 bits or the lowest 8 bits in these registers are used to provide various control signals. Figure 5.5 shows the GPIO Interrupt Sense Register as an example for the configurations of these registers.

Table 5.9.   Most popular priority registers used in the TM4C123GH6PM NVIC.

Register	Interrupt Trigger	GPIO PORTF Interrupt Control Registers							
		7	6	5	4	3	2	1	0
GPIOIS	0: Edge 1: Level	x	x	x	1	x	x	x	x
GPIOIBE	0: Single Edge 1: Double Edges	x	x	x	0	x	x	x	x
GPIOIEV	0: LOW Level or Falling Edge 1: HIGH Level or Rising Edge	x	x	x	1	x	x	x	x
GPIOIM	0: Masked (Disabled) 1: Unmasked (Enabled)	x	x	x	1	x	x	x	x

31
7
0
GPIOIS
Reserved
0: An edge is detected on that pin.
Each bit on bits 7:0 =
1: A level is detected on that pin.

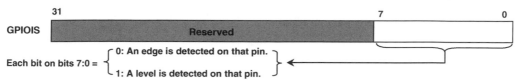

Figure 5.5. The GPIO Interrupt Sense Register.

5.3.2 Local Interrupt Configurations and Controls for GPIO Ports

In addition to configuring and initializing each GPIO pin, one also needs to configure the priority levels and enable the related interrupts for the selected GPIO Ports. These jobs are handled by using some NVIC Interrupt Control Registers. In fact, two registers are necessary to be configured and initialized to make GPIO Ports to correctly generate interrupt requests to be responded by the processor.

In Section 5.2.3, we have provided a brief review about most popular NVIC Interrupt Control Registers. Among them, two register groups are very useful and they are:

- Interrupt Priority-Level Registers (`0xE000E400~0xE000E4EF`)
- Interrupt Set Enable Registers (`0xE000E100~0xE000E11C`)

These two register groups are used to set the priority levels for all peripherals and enable selected peripherals.

5.3.2.1 The NVIC Interrupt Priority-Level Registers

The NVIC Interrupt Control Unit provides 35 Interrupt Priority Level Registers as a group used to configure and set up all peripheral, including both internal and external peripherals, interrupt priority levels. These registers are arranged from `NVIC PRI0~ NVIC PRI34`, and each register can be considered to be a group `PRIn` ($n = 0 \sim 34$ is the group number) and is a 32-bit register taking 4 bytes memory space starting from `0xE000E400` to `0xE000e4EF`.

Each of these 32-bit priority register group can be ordered from 0 to 34, and it is divided into 4 segments with each segment having 8 bits. Each 8-bit segment only used the upper 3 bits as the priority level bits for each different peripheral. Therefore a total of $35 \times 4 = 140$ different priority levels can be defined and used for 140 peripherals. Figure 5.6 shows an example of this kind of priority level register, group 0 or `NVIC PRI0`.

31 30 29 28 27 26 25 24 23 22 21 20 19 18 17 16
INTD
reserved
INTC
reserved
Type RW RW RW RO RO RO RO RO RW RW RW RO RO RO RO RO
Reset 0 0 0 0 0 0 0 0 0 0 0 0 0 0 0 0
15 14 13 12 11 10 9 8 7 6 5 4 3 2 1 0
INTB
reserved
INTA
reserved
Type RW RW RW RO RO RO RO RO RW RW RW RO RO RO RO RO
Reset 0 0 0 0 0 0 0 0 0 0 0 0 0 0 0 0

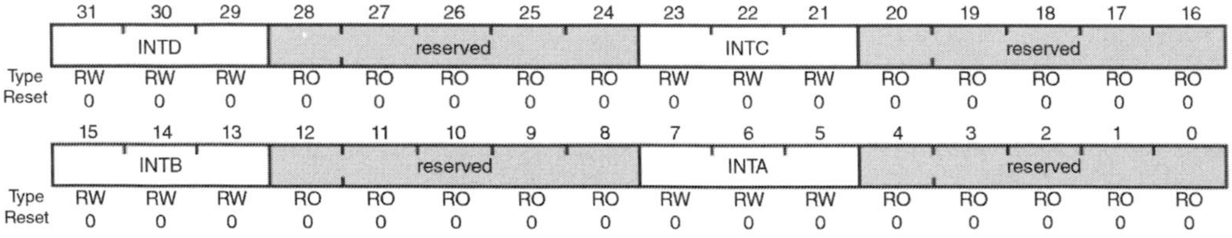

Figure 5.6. An example of the NVIC Priority Level Register PRI0. (Reprinted with the permission of the Texas Instruments Incorporated.)

It can be found from Figure 5.6 that PRIO is a group 0 priority register with four segments:

1. Segment 1—Bits 7~5:   GPIO Port A interrupt priority level control.
2. Segment 2—Bits 15~13:   GPIO Port B interrupts priority level control.
3. Segment 3—Bits 23~21:   GPIO Port C interrupts priority level control.
4. Segment 4—Bits 31~29:   GPIO Port D interrupts priority level control.

Table 5.10 shows the relationship between each interrupt, its handler, and its priority bits.

When using Table 5.10 to build the user's program to access NVIC registers directly to configure and set up related exceptions and interrupts, the following points should be noted:

1. The third column in Table 5.10 lists the interrupt numbers or IRQ numbers for all interrupts. Note that the interrupts that have IRQ numbers 0~3 (GPIO Ports A~D) are controlled by the same priority level register (group **0**) NVIC_PRIO, and this means that each group **n** register NVIC_PRIn can control up to 4 peripherals (priority levels) with the interrupt numbers from $4n$ to $(4n+3)$. This relationship is shown in Table 5.11. The related priority bits filed for each PRIn are shown in column 6 on Table 5.10. These IRQ numbers are closely related to the associated peripherals to be enabled by using five NVIC Interrupt Enable Registers, NVIC_EN0_R~NVIC_EN4_R. These registers are similar to those Interrupt Set Enable Registers NVIC→ISER[] defined in the CMSIS Core macros in Table 5.5. Table 5.13 shows the relationship between each bit on these five registers and each related peripheral to be enabled.

2. The fifth column lists the macro or symbolic definition for each NVIC Priority Register for the related interrupt that is associated with each interrupt handler in column 4. Each NVIC Priority Register (NVIC_PRIn_R) is a 32-bit register. Table 5.12 shows most popular Priority Registers used in the TM4C123GH6PM system. For example, the Priority Register NVIC_PRIO_R corresponds to the peripherals that have interrupt number from $4 \times \mathbf{0} \sim [4 \times \mathbf{0} + 3] = 0 \sim 3$. It can be found from Table 5.10 that 4 peripherals, 4 GPIO Ports, Port A~Port D, have these interrupt numbers. Therefore the priority levels of these 4 peripherals should be configured by using the same priority level register, NVIC_PRIO_R, which is: bits 31~29 define the priority levels for the GPIO Port D, and bits 23~21 define the priority levels for the GPIO Port C, and so on. Do not be confused about the address shown in the first column in Table 5.10, which is only for the handler's vector address, not for the Priority Register's address.

3. The first column lists the vector locations for related interrupts in the Vector Table. Each vector is a 32-bit entry address of the related interrupt handler and takes 4 bytes in the on-chip memory space.

4. Corresponding to each vector location in column 1, the related interrupt handler's name defined in the Startup_TM4C123.s file is shown in column 4. The users are highly recommended to use these handler's names defined in this startup file in their program without any modifications. Of course, you can change these handlers' names (statically or dynamically) to meet the needs of your special applications. However, the name you changed in this startup file must be identical to the name you used in your program.

Table 5.11 shows the relationship for each group number (**n**) on priority register, the related priority bit-field, and IRQ number. The macro NVIC_PRn_R is defined by the

Table 5.10. The relationship between vectors and NVIC definitions.

Vector Address	Exception Number	IRQ Number	ISR Name in Startup_TM4C123.s	NVIC Macros for Priority Register	Priority Bits
0x00000038	14	−2	PendSV_Handler	NVIC_SYS_PRI3_R	23–21
0x0000003C	15	−1	SysTick_Handler	NVIC_SYS_PRI3_R	31–29
0x00000040	16	0	GPIOA_Handler	NVIC_PRI0_R	7–5
0x00000044	17	1	GPIOB_Handler	NVIC_PRI0_R	15–13
0x00000048	18	2	GPIOC_Handler	NVIC_PRI0_R	23–21
0x0000004C	19	3	GPIOD_Handler	NVIC_PRI0_R	31–29
0x00000050	20	4	GPIOE_Handler	NVIC_PRI1_R	7–5
0x00000054	21	5	UART0_Handler	NVIC_PRI1_R	15–13
0x00000058	22	6	UART1_Handler	NVIC_PRI1_R	23–21
0x0000005C	23	7	SSI0_Handler	NVIC_PRI1_R	31–29
0x00000060	24	8	I2C0_Handler	NVIC_PRI2_R	7–5
0x00000064	25	9	PWM0_Fault_Handler	NVIC_PRI2_R	15–13
0x00000068	26	10	PWM0_0_Handler	NVIC_PRI2_R	23–21
0x0000006C	27	11	PWM0_1_Handler	NVIC_PRI2_R	31–29
0x00000070	28	12	PWM0_2_Handler	NVIC_PRI3_R	7–5
0x00000074	29	13	QEI0_Handler	NVIC_PRI3_R	15–13
0x00000078	30	14	ADC0SS0_Handler	NVIC_PRI3_R	23–21
0x0000007C	31	15	ADC0SS1_Handler	NVIC_PRI3_R	31–29
0x00000080	32	16	ADC0SS2_Handler	NVIC_PRI4_R	7–5
0x00000084	33	17	ADC0SS3_Handler	NVIC_PRI4_R	15–13
0x00000088	34	18	WDT0_Handler	NVIC_PRI4_R	23–21
0x0000008C	35	19	TIMER0A_Handler	NVIC_PRI4_R	31–29
0x00000090	36	20	TIMER0B_Handler	NVIC_PRI5_R	7–5
0x00000094	37	21	TIMER1A_Handler	NVIC_PRI5_R	15–13
0x00000098	38	22	TIMER1B_Handler	NVIC_PRI5_R	23–21
0x0000009C	39	23	TIMER2A_Handler	NVIC_PRI5_R	31–29
0x000000A0	40	24	TIMER2B_Handler	NVIC_PRI6_R	7–5
0x000000A4	41	25	COMP0_Handler	NVIC_PRI6_R	15–13
0x000000A8	42	26	COMP1_Handler	NVIC_PRI6_R	23–21
0x000000AC	43	27	COMP2_Handler	NVIC_PRI6_R	31–29
0x000000B0	44	28	SYSCTL_Handler	NVIC_PRI7_R	7–5
0x000000B4	45	29	FLASH_Handler	NVIC_PRI7_R	15–13
0x000000B8	46	30	GPIOF_Handler	NVIC_PRI7_R	23–21
0x000000BC	47	31	GPIOG_Handler	NVIC_PRI7_R	31–29
0x000000C0	48	32	GPIOH_Handler	NVIC_PRI8_R	7–5
0x000000C4	49	33	UART2_Handler	NVIC_PRI8_R	15–13
0x000000C8	50	34	SSI1_Handler	NVIC_PRI8_R	23–21
0x000000CC	51	35	TIMER3A_Handler	NVIC_PRI8_R	31–29
0x000000D0	52	36	TIMER3B_Handler	NVIC_PRI9_R	7–5
0x000000D4	53	37	I2C1_Handler	NVIC_PRI9_R	15–13
0x000000D8	54	38	QEI1_Handler	NVIC_PRI9_R	23–21
0x000000DC	55	39	CAN0_Handler	NVIC_PRI9_R	31–29
0x000000E0	56	40	CAN1_Handler	NVIC_PRI10_R	7–5
0x000000E4	57	41	CAN2_Handler	NVIC_PRI10_R	15–13
0x000000E8	58	42	0 (Reserved)	NVIC_PRI10_R	23–21
0x000000EC	59	43	HIB_Handler	NVIC_PRI10_R	31–29
0x000000F0	60	44	USB0_Handler	NVIC_PRI11_R	7–5
0x000000F4	61	45	PWM0_3_Handler	NVIC_PRI11_R	15–13
0x000000F8	62	46	UDMA_Handler	NVIC_PRI11_R	23–21
0x000000FC	63	47	UDMAERR_Handler	NVIC_PRI11_R	31–29

Table 5.11. The bit filed of priority levels and related interrupt priority group.

PRIn Register Bit Field	Interrupt Source	Priority Register Macros
Bits 31:29	Interrupt[IRQ] = Interrupt[4n + 3]	
Bits 23:21	Interrupt[IRQ] = Interrupt[4n + 2]	NVIC_PRI**n**_R
Bits 15:13	Interrupt[IRQ] = Interrupt[4n + 1]	NVIC→IP[4**n**] – NVIC→IP[4**n** + 3]
Bits 7:5	Interrupt[IRQ] = Interrupt[4n]	

TivaWare™ software system, but the NVIC→IP[ ] is defined by the CMSIS Core system. Figure 5.11 shows some of the most popular NVIC Priority Level Registers and bit fields used for each different peripheral in the TM4C123GH6PM MCU system.

In fact, Tables 5.10, 5.11, and 5.12 can be used together to get a clear picture about the peripheral devices, their interrupt numbers, their interrupt vectors, their interrupt handlers, and their related priority registers and bit fields.

For example, the ADC2_Handler corresponds to the Analog-to-Digital Converter 2 peripheral in Table 5.10, and the IRQ number for this peripheral is 16. From Table 5.11, it can be found that in order to make the equation Interrupt[4**n**] = 16 hold, the group number of the priority register, **n**, equals **4**. Therefore the corresponded Priority Level Register should be NVIC_PRI4_R and it can configure priority levels for 4**n** ~ 4**n** + 3 peripherals whose IRQ numbers range from $4 \times 4 \sim 4 \times 4 + 3 = 16 \sim 19$. It can be found from Table 5.10 that the peripherals whose IRQ numbers are 16~19 are: ADC2_Handler, ADC3_ Handler, WDT0_Handler and TIMER0A_Handler, respectively. Take a look at Table 5.12, the Priority Level Register NVIC_PRI4_R that is located at row 5 can exactly handle the priority levels for these four peripherals in 4 segments: bits 7~5, bits 15~13, bits 23~21, and bits 31~29.

Table 5.12. Most popular priority registers used in the TM4C123GH6PM NVIC.

Priority Register	Priority Bits				Address
	31–29	23–21	15–13	7–5	
NVIC_PRI0_R	GPIO Port D	GPIO Port C	GPIO Port B	GPIO Port A	0xE000E400
NVIC_PRI1_R	SSI0, Rx Tx	UART1, Rx Tx	UART0, Rx Tx	GPIO Port E	0xE000E404
NVIC_PRI2_R	PWM Gen 1	PWM Gen 0	PWM Fault	I2C0	0xE000E408
NVIC_PRI3_R	ADC Seq 1	ADC Seq 0	Quad Encoder	PWM Gen 2	0xE000E40C
NVIC_PRI4_R	Timer 0A	Watchdog	ADC Seq 3	ADC Seq 2	0xE000E410
NVIC_PRI5_R	Timer 2A	Timer 1B	Timer 1A	Timer 0B	0xE000E414
NVIC_PRI6_R	Comp 2	Comp 1	Comp 0	Timer 2B	0xE000E418
NVIC_PRI7_R	GPIO Port G	GPIO Port F	Flash Control	System Control	0xE000E41C
NVIC_PRI8_R	Timer 3A	SSI1, Rx Tx	UART2, Rx Tx	GPIO Port H	0xE000E420
NVIC_PRI9_R	CAN0	Quad Encoder 1	I2C1	Timer 3B	0xE000E424
NVIC_PRI10_R	Hibernate	Ethernet	CAN2	CAN1	0xE000E428
NVIC_PRI11_R	uDMA Error	uDMA Soft Tfr	PWM Gen 3	USB0	0xE000E42C
NVIC_SYS_PRI3_R	SysTick	PendSV	–	Debug	0xE000ED20

Since only the upper 3 bits is used for each segment, the available priority levels for group 0 priority register NVIC_PRI0_R are:

- 0x00, 0x20, 0x40, 0x60, 0x80, 0xA0, 0xC0 and 0xE0 for segment 1 (GPIO Port A).
- 0x0000, 0x2000, 0x4000, 0x6000, 0x8000, 0xA000, 0xC000 and 0xE000 for segment 2 (GPIO Port B).
- 0x000000, 0x200000, 0x400000, 0x600000, 0x800000, 0xA00000, 0xC00000 and 0xE00000 for segment 3 (GPIO Port C).
- 0x00000000, 0x20000000, 0x40000000, 0x60000000, 0x80000000, 0xA0000000, 0xC0000000 and 0xE0000000 for segment 4 (GPIO Port D).

During the programming process, users can directly use various macros defined for all Priority Level Registers, NVIC_PRI0_R~NVCI_PRI34_R, in their program to access them to perform priority level configurations for selected peripherals.

5.3.2.2 The NVIC Interrupt Set Enable Registers

All NVIC registers can be fully accessed from privileged mode, but interrupts can be pended while they are in the unprivileged mode by enabling the Configuration and Control (CFGCTRL) register. Any other unprivileged mode access may cause a bus fault.

In TM4C123GH6PM MCU system, the NVIC provides five Interrupt Set Enable Registers, EN0~EN4. The symbolic definitions or macros for these registers are NVIC_EN0_R~NVIC_EN4_R.

All these five Set Enable Registers are 32-bit registers. Except for EN4, all other Set Enable Registers use the full length, 32 bits, to enable related peripherals. These registers, EN0~EN4, use single bit, or bit by bit, to enable related peripheral with the following functions:

- NVIC_EN0_R: Provides 32 bit-by-bit enable control ability to 32 peripherals whose IRQ numbers are 0~31 (see Table 5.10 for IRQ numbers). This means that bit 0 controls the peripheral whose IRQ number is 0 (GPIO Port A), bit 1 controls the peripheral whose IRQ number is 1 (GPIO Port B), and bit 31 controls the peripheral whose IRQ number is 31 (GPIO Port G).
- NVIC_EN1_R: Provides 32 bit-by-bit enable control ability to 32 peripherals whose IRQ numbers are 32~63.
- NVIC_EN2_R: Provides 32 bit-by-bit enable control ability to 32 peripherals whose IRQ numbers are 64~95.
- NVIC_EN3_R: Provides 32 bit-by-bit enable control ability to 32 peripherals whose IRQ numbers are 96~127.
- NVIC_EN4_R: Provides 11 bit-by-bit enable control ability to 10 peripherals whose IRQ numbers are 128~138.

These registers are only used to set enables to related peripherals by writing 1 to the related bits. Writing zeros to any bits has no effects. To disable any peripherals, one needs to use the corresponding bits in the NVIC Clear Enable Registers, NVIC_DIS0_R through NVIC_DIS4_R.

Each bit on the Set Enable Register is to enable one peripheral, and the bit number is equal to the IRQ number of the peripheral to be enabled. For example, to enable the

Table 5.13. Relationship between each bit on interrupt enable register and related peripheral.

Enable Register	32 Enable Bits									Address
	0	1	2	3	4	5	6–29	30	31	
NVIC_EN0_R	PORTA	PORTB	PORTC	PORTD	PORTE	UART0	......	PORTF	PORTG	0xE000E100
NVIC_EN1_R	PORTH	UART2	SSI1	Timer3A	Timer3B	I2C1	......	UART6	UART7	0xE000E104
NVIC_EN2_R	...	...	...	...	I2C2	I2C3	......	WTimer0A	WTimer0B	0xE000E108
NVIC_EN3_R	WT1A	WT1B	WT2A	WT2B	WT3A	WT3B	......	GPIOQ2	GPIOQ3	0xE000E10C

GPIO Port F whose IRQ number is 30 (Table 5.10), the bit 30 on the NVIC_EN0_R should be set to 1. To enable UART2 whose IRQ number is 33, the bit 1 on the NVIC_EN1_R should be set to 1. Since each NVIC_ENn_R register can only handle 32 peripherals (0~31), if the IRQ number is greater than 31, the target bit number should be calculated as

$$\textbf{Target bit number} = \textbf{IRQ number} - \textbf{32} \times (\textbf{n} - \textbf{1}). \textbf{ n} = \textbf{1} \text{ if IRQ} < 31,$$
$$\textbf{n} = \textbf{2} \text{ if } (64 > \text{IRQ} > 31),$$
$$\textbf{n} = \textbf{3} \text{ if } (96 > \text{IRQ} > 63), \textbf{ n} = \textbf{4} \text{ if } (128 > \text{IRQ} > 95).$$

Table 5.13 lists the most popular used peripherals and their bit numbers in the NVIC Set Enable Registers. Each bit is associated with a peripheral, and a setting to a bit enables the selected peripheral. Each 32-bit Set Enable Register can be used to enable 32 peripherals.

During the programming process, users can directly use various macros defined for all Set Enable Registers, NVIC_EN0_R~NVCI_EN4_R, in their program to access them to perform the enable configurations for selected peripherals.

Now let's take care of the last interrupt configuration process.

5.3.3 Global Interrupt Configurations and Controls

To enable the ARM® Cortex®-M4 processor to globally control all interrupts for all peripherals used in the system, two special registers, Primary Mask (PRIMASK) and Base Priority (BASEPRI), are provided inside the Cortex-M4 CPU to support this control function. We have discussed these two registers in detail in Section 2.2.1.2.2 in Chapter 2.

The PRIMASK register is a Primary Interrupt Mask register, and it uses one bit (bit 0) to mask or disable all maskable interrupts/exceptions in the Cortex-M4 MCU system. When this bit is set to 1, it masks or disables all maskable interrupts. When this bit is reset to 0, it will unmask or enable all maskable interrupts used in the system. This function provides the global interrupt control ability for the Cortex-M4 processor.

The BASEPRI register provides more flexible interrupt masking strategies, and it can perform masking or unmasking functions based on the priority levels of related interrupts/exceptions. In this way, if a higher-level interrupt/exception is being executed or handled, any other lower-level interrupt/exception will not receive a response until the current interrupt/exception has been processed. As we mentioned, although this register is a 32-bit register, only three bits (bits 7~5), are used to configure eight different priority levels for peripherals.

The BASEPRI can be considered to be a global priority control register, and its contents on bits 7~5 should be compared with the contents of all local priority registers, such as NVIC_PRIn_R, to determine whether the peripherals whose priority levels are configured by the NVIC_PRIn_R can be accepted or not by the processor. If the NVIC_PRIn_R includes higher priority (smaller number) than that of the BASEPRI, the interrupt requested by the peripheral can be accepted. Otherwise the interrupt may be pending until the current task is done.

As we discussed in Chapter 2, these two special registers can only be accessed by using ARM® Assembly instructions MSR or MRS. Fortunately some intrinsic functions are provided by the ARM® MDK C/C++ Compiler and the CMSIS Core to help users to avoid using the assembly instructions to fulfill these control abilities. Three options can be adopted by the users when they build their applications to access these special registers:

1. Use inline assembler.
2. Use intrinsic function __enable_irq() provided by the ARM® MDK C/C++ Compiler.
3. Use intrinsic function __enable_irq() provided by CMSIS Core.

Although it looks like that both intrinsic functions provided by two different sources are the same, they are different in definitions and in codes, but perform the same function. Refer to Sections 4.5.2 and 4.5.3 in Chapter 4 to get more details for these intrinsic functions.

Now we have completed the interrupts initialization and configuration process. However, before we can accept and respond any interrupt, we need to know how to direct the accepted interrupt to the correct interrupt handler or ISR to process that interrupt. The vector table is used for this purpose. Let's have a clear picture about the vector table and vectors located in that table.

5.3.4 The Vector Table and Vectors Used in the TM4C123GH6PM MCU

When an interrupt is accepted by the processor, the related hardware provides a way to direct the software control to the vector table to transfer the control to the entry address of the accepted interrupt service routine (ISR) to respond and process that interrupt.

We have provided a brief discussion about the vector table used in the TM4C123GH6PM MCU system in Section 5.2.3.2. In this part, we will concentrate on the software control aspect to see how to define and complete this control transfer.

A complete vector table is defined in the startup file Startup_TM4C123.s, which should be added into your project when you select the program environment, such as COMSIS Core and Device, when you create a new project.

For the TM4C123GH6PM MCU system, there are 138 interrupt vectors defined in this vector table. Figure 5.7 shows some of the most popular and used vectors in this table.

The top 15 vectors (vectors 1~15) in this vector table are exceptions with system defined exception handlers. Starting from exception 16, all of the following vectors are interrupt vectors.

__Vectors	DCD	__initial_sp	; **Top of Stack**
	DCD	Reset_Handler	; Reset Handler
	DCD	NMI_Handler	; NMI Handler
	DCD	HardFault_Handler	; Hard Fault Handler
	DCD	MemManage_Handler	; MPU Fault Handler
	DCD	BusFault_Handler	; Bus Fault Handler
	DCD	UsageFault_Handler	; Usage Fault Handler
	DCD	0	; Reserved
	DCD	0	; Reserved
	DCD	0	; Reserved
	DCD	0	; Reserved
	DCD	SVC_Handler	; SVCall Handler
	DCD	DebugMon _Handler	; Debug Monitor Handler
	DCD	0	; Reserved
	DCD	PendSV_Handler	; PendSV Handler
	DCD	SysTick_Handler	; SysTick Handler

; **External Interrupts**		**Vector or Handler**	; **IRQ#**	**Peripheral**
	DCD	GPIOA_Handler	; 0:	GPIO Port A
	DCD	GPIOB_Handler	; 1:	GPIO Port B
	DCD	GPIOC_Handler	; 2:	GPIO Port C
	DCD	GPIOD_Handler	; 3:	GPIO Port D
	DCD	GPIOE_Handler	; 4:	GPIO Port E
	DCD	UART0_Handler	; 5:	UART0 Rx and Tx
	DCD	UART1_Handler	; 6:	UART1 Rx and Tx
	DCD	SSI0_Handler	; 7:	SSI0 Rx and Tx
	DCD	I2C0_Handler	; 8:	I2C0 Master and Slave
	DCD	PMW0_FAULT_Handler	; 9:	PWM Fault
	DCD	PWM0_0_Handler	; 10:	PWM Generator 0
	DCD	PWM0_1_Handler	; 11:	PWM Generator 1
	DCD	PWM0_2_Handler	; 12:	PWM Generator 2
	DCD	QEI0_Handler	; 13:	Quadrature Encoder 0
	DCD	ADC0SS0_Handler	; 14:	ADC Sequence 0
	DCD	ADC0SS1_Handler	; 15:	ADC Sequence 1
	DCD	ADC0SS2_Handler	; 16:	ADC Sequence 2
	DCD	ADC0SS3_Handler	; 17:	ADC Sequence 3
	DCD	WDT0_Handler	; 18:	Watchdog timer
	DCD	TIMER0A_Handler	; 19:	Timer 0 subtimer A
	DCD	TIMER0B_Handler	; 20:	Timer 0 subtimer B
	DCD	TIMER1A_Handler	; 21:	Timer 1 subtimer A
	DCD	TIMER1B_Handler	; 22:	Timer 1 subtimer B
	DCD	TIMER2A_Handler	; 23:	Timer 2 subtimer A
	DCD	TIMER2B_Handler	; 24:	Timer 2 subtimer B
	DCD	COMP0_Handler	; 25:	Analog Comparator 0
	DCD	COMP1_Handler	; 26:	Analog Comparator 1
	DCD	COMP2_Handler	; 27:	Analog Comparator 2
	DCD	SYSCTL_Handler	; 28:	System Control (PLL, OSC, BO)
	DCD	FLASH_Handler	; 29:	FLASH Control
	DCD	GPIOF_Handler	; 30:	GPIO Port F
	DCD	GPIOG_Handler	; 31:	GPIO Port G
	DCD	GPIOH_Handler	; 32:	GPIO Port H
	DCD	UART2_Handler	; 33:	UART2 Rx and Tx
	DCD	SSI1_Handler	; 34:	SSI1 Rx and Tx
	DCD	TIMER3A_Handler	; 35:	Timer 3 subtimer A
	DCD	TIMER3B_Handler	; 36:	Timer 3 subtimer B
	DCD	I2C1_Handler	; 37:	I2C1 Master and Slave
	DCD	QEI1_Handler	; 38:	Quadrature Encoder 1
	DCD	CAN0_Handler	; 39:	CAN0
	DCD	CAN1_Handler	; 40:	CAN1
	DCD	CAN2_Handler	; 41:	CAN2
	DCD	0	; 42:	Reserved
	DCD	HIB_Handler	; 43:	Hibernate
	DCD	USB0_Handler	; 44:	USB0

Figure 5.7.   The vector definitions in the Cortex-M4 microcontroller.

Four column elements are used in this vector table starting from interrupt 0 (exception 16):

- The first column is the Cortex-M4 pseudo assembly instruction, DCD, which is used to define a 32-bit or a word constant. This constant is a 32-bit entry address of the ISR for the corresponding interrupt.

- The second column is the 32-bit constants or entry addresses of the ISR for matched interrupts. These constants or vectors are default handlers for interrupts defined for the TM4C123GH6PM MCU system. Generally one can use these default handlers as the names of ISRs in the user's program to access related ISRs to respond to the related interrupts. Of course, one can change these handlers' names to meet the needs of the real applications. However, the names of the handlers in this startup file must be identical to those names of the ISRs used in the user's program.

- The third column lists all IRQ numbers for interrupts. The IRQ numbers start from 0. These IRQ numbers are very important since one needs to use them to find the bit locations for the related interrupts in the NVIC Priority Register NVIC_PRIn_R and in the NVIC Set Enable Register NVIC_ENn_R as discussed in the last section.

- The fourth column lists all peripherals related to the vectors.

Now let's provide an example to illustrate how to configure and set up an interrupt and its handler based on Tables 5.10~5.13 and Figure 5.7.

For example, we want to set up and configure an interrupt for GPIO Port D. Perform the following operations to complete this job:

1. Find the IRQ number for this interrupt from Table 5.10. The IRQ number for the GPIO Port D is 3.

2. Based on Table 5.11, obtain the group number of the priority register (**n**). The IRQ number is 3. In order to make the equation $3 = \texttt{interrupt[4n + 3]}$ hold, **n** must be 0. This means that we need to use group 0 priority register NVIC_PRI0_R with bits 31~29 to configure the priority level for the GPIO Port D. Since the IRQ number of this port is 3, we can set the priority level for this port as 3, or 0x3 (011B), in bits 31~29 on the NVIC_PRI0_R. This setup can be written as NVIC_PRI0_R = 0x600000000 in the user's program.

3. Based on Table 5.13, obtain the bit field in the NVIC Set Enable Register to enable this port. Since the IRQ number of the Port D is 3, the bit 3 in the NVIC_EN0_R register should be set to 1 to enable this port. This setup can be written as NVIC_EN0_R = 0x8 in the user program (0x8 = 00001000B).

4. Based on Figure 5.7, locate the name of the ISR or the handler for the GPIO Port D interrupt. It can be found from Figure 5.7 that the handler for this interrupt is GPIOD_Handler. You can directly copy this handler into your program as the ISR to respond the interrupt triggered by the GPIO Port D.

Now we are ready to develop our interrupt projects to handle various interrupt requests coming from the different sources. Let's have a global picture about the interrupts and related components used in various interrupts again to refresh our brain.

5.3.5 The GPIO Interrupt Handling and Processing Procedure

When all related Interrupt Control Registers for a GPIO Port and pins have been initialized and configured, the system is ready to accept and response to any interrupt.

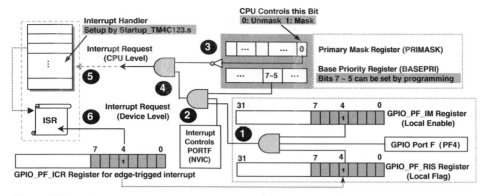

Figure 5.8. The interrupt handling and processing procedure.

Figure 5.8 shows a functional block diagram for responding to a level-triggered interrupt occurred on PF4 pin.

- First, seven GPIO Port F Interrupt Control Registers should be initialized and configured to setup pin PF4 to generate an appropriate interrupt request when a level-triggered interrupt is applied on PF4 pin.

- Then the NVIC Priority Register NVIC_PRI7_R and the NVIC Set Enable Register NVIC_EN0_R should be configured to set up the priority level and set to enable the Port F. Refer to Tables 5.10~5.13, bits 23~21 in the NVIC_RPI7_R should be configured to set up a priority level 3 to this port and bit 30 on the NVIC_EN0_R should be set to enable this port (NVIC_PRI7_R = 0x00600000, NVIC_EN0_R = 0x1E).

- Two CPU-controlled special registers, PRIMASK and BASEPRI, should be programmed to globally enable all interrupts and set up the appropriate priority level to enable CPU to accept and respond to any interrupts whose priority level is higher than that setting in the BASEPRI. Generally the BASEPRI is reset to 0 after a system is reset to enable the processor to accept any level's interrupt.

- When the PF4 is triggered by a level, an interrupt request is sent to the NVIC interrupt controller and directed to the ISR entry address via the vector (GPIOF_Handler) in the Vector Table. The users can build their codes to process this interrupt request inside this handler in their program.

- If the interrupt is triggered by an edge or both edges, the user needs to reset the related bit on the Interrupt Clear Register (GPIO Port F ICR) to clear that interrupt request in the ISR. Write 1 to this bit (PF4) is to clear this edge-triggered interrupt. For a level-triggered interrupt, no any action is needed since this bit will be reset automatically after the interrupt deasserts.

Since the GPIO Port F IM register is set to 1 on pin 4, the bit 4 on the GPIO Port F RIS register (local interrupt flag) will be set to 1 if a level-triggered interrupt is applied on PF4 pin.

5.4 DEVELOPING GPIO PORT INTERRUPT PROJECTS TO HANDLE GPIO INTERRUPTS

Generally there are four ways to build GPIO-related interrupt programs to configure and respond to all GPIO-related interrupts:

1. Use the Direct Register Access (DRA) model to configure GPIO Port and pins, as we discussed in Sections 5.3.1 and 5.3.2, to accept and handle related interrupts that occurred on the desired pins with the selected GPIO Port.

2. Use CMSIS Core macros defined for NVIC Interrupt Control Registers, as we discussed in Section 5.2.3, to configure and handle interrupts that occurred on the desired pins with the selected GPIO Ports.

3. Use TivaWare™ Peripheral Driver Library API functions discussed in Section 5.2.2 to configure and handle interrupts that occurred on the desired pins on the selected GPIO Ports.

4. Use CMSIS Core functions, as we discussed in Section 5.2.2, to configure and handle interrupts that occurred on the desired pins with the selected GPIO Ports.

Basically the first two ways belong to the Direct Register Access (DRA) programming model, and the third and fourth ways belong to the Software Driver (SD) programming model. We will introduce and discuss all of these four ways to build our interrupt applications in this chapter. The point to be noted is that the first method works only for GPIO Port interrupts, but the remaining three methods work for all peripheral interrupts. We may combine the first two methods together as the DRA model to handle the GPIO-related interrupts in this chapter.

Before we can start our sample project development process, one crystal issue we need to clarify is that there are two software packages used in the TM4C123GH6PM MCU system:

1. The TivaWare™ Software Package (TWSP) that provides various libraries with related header files to support users to build their projects.

2. The CMSIS Core Software Package (CMSISCSP) that provides a set of API functions for Cortex-M4 MCU and related header files.

Basically both packages provide different definitions for all system components used in the TM4C123GH6PM MCU system. The TivaWare™ Software Package provides a group of libraries, including the Peripheral Driver Library, Graphical Library, Sensor Hub Library, and UART Library, with related header files to support the building and development of projects of using the TM4C123GH6PM MCU. The CMSIS Core Package provides a set of API functions and related header files to help build projects involving the use of the ARM® Cortex®-M4 MCU. You can use either package to develop and build your project. However, in order to use these packages correctly and efficiently, you need to get a clear picture about these packages and related header files before you can use them.

First let's have a brief discussion about these two packages.

5.4.1 Two Software Packages Used in the TM4C123GH6PM MCU System

To assist users to develop their projects, two packages, the TivaWare™ Software package and the CMSIS Core Package, are provided by two vendors. In order to use these packages correctly, we need to have a solid understanding about the header files provided by these packages.

5.4.1.1 The TivaWare™ Software Package (TWSP)

The TivaWare™ Software Package (TWSP) contains a whole set of configuration and definition files for all components, including the processor, memory, MPU, FPU, and all peripherals used in this system. This package includes a set of header files and various libraries, including the Peripheral Driver Library, Graphical Library, USB Library, Sensor Hub Library, and Boot Loader file. The protocols of these library functions are defined in a set of header files. These header files are located at different folders under the installation location of this package, which should be in your host computer at: C:\ti\TivaWare_ C_Series-2.0.1.11577. Two kinds of popular header files are located at the folders:

1. C:\ti\TivaWare_C_Series-2.0.1.11577\driverlib

2. C:\ti\TivaWare_C_Series-2.0.1.11577\inc

Some popular header files related to the TivaWare™ libraries are shown in Table 5.14, and these header files are located at the folder 1 above. Some other popular header files related to the TM4C123GH6PM MCU system are shown in Table 5.15, and these header files are located at the folder 2 above.

Figure 5.9 shows an illustration block diagram to describe the relationship between the users program codes, the header files used for device drivers, and the hardware abstract layers as well as the actual hardware used in this microcontroller system.

It can be found from Figure 5.9 that the header files defined for the drivers, such as adc.h, can.h and gpio.h, can be mapped to the system definition macros (1). The header files defined for the hardware layers, such as hw_adc.h, hw_can.h and hw_gpio.h, can be mapped to the memory mapping addresses where the corresponding peripheral registers are located (2). The real hardware, such as the GPIO PortB, is mapped to the actual GPIO PORTB (3).

Among these header files, we are more interested in the header file, tm4c123gh6pm. h, since this file provides a set of complete definitions for the components and peripherals used in the TM4C123GH6PM MCU system. In fact, the TivaWare™ Software Package also provides another header file, TM4C123GH6PM.h. It looks like both header files are the

Table 5.14. Popular header files used in TivaWare libraries.

Header Files	Function
adc.h	Definitions for ADC-related drivers
can.h	Definitions for CAN-related drivers
comp.h	Definitions for Analog Comparator related drivers
fpu.h	Definitions for FPU-related drivers
gpio.h	Definitions for GPIO-related drivers
i2c.h	Definitions for I2C-related drivers
interrupt.h	Definitions for Interrupt-related drivers
lcd.h	Definitions for LCD-related drivers
pwm.h	Definitions for PWM-related drivers
sysctl.h	Definitions for System Control-related drivers
timer.h	Definitions for Timer-related drivers
uart.h	Definitions for UART-related drivers
usb.h	Definitions for USB-related drivers
watchdog.h	Definitions for Watchdog-related drivers

Table 5.15.   Popular header files used in TM4C123GH6PM MCU.

Header Files	Function
hw_adc.h	Definitions for ADC-related hardware layer
hw_can.h	Definitions for CAN-related hardware layer
hw_comp.h	Definitions for Analog Comparator-related hardware layer
hw_fan.h	Definitions for FAN-related hardware layer
hw_gpio.h	Definitions for GPIO-related hardware layer
hw_i2c.h	Definitions for I2C-related hardware layer
hw_ints.h	Definitions for Interrupt-related hardware layer
hw_lcd.h	Definitions for LCD-related hardware layer
hw_memmap.h	Definitions of memory maps for peripheral hardware layer
hw_nvic.h	Definitions for NVIC related registers
hw_ssi	Definitions for Synchronous Serial Interface hardware layer
hw_pwm.h	Definitions for PWM-related hardware layer
hw_ sysctl.h	Definitions for System Control-related hardware layer
hw_timer.h	Definitions for Timer-related hardware layer
hw_types.h	Definitions for peripheral types
hw_uart.h	Definitions for UART-related hardware layer
hw_usb.h	Definitions for USB-related hardware layer
hw_watchdog.h	Definitions for Watchdog-related hardware layer
tm4c123gh6pm.h	Definitions for all registers used in TM4C123GH6PM MCU

same, but they provide different definitions with different purposes for peripherals and interrupt sources. Therefore let's first have a look at these two header files.

5.4.1.1.1 Two Header Files Used in the TM4C123GH6PM MCU System   The Tiva-Ware™ Software package provides two kinds of header files to support the TM4C123GH6PM MCU system:

1. The Register Driver Definitions Header File for TM4C123GH6PM. This header file is named `tm4c123gh6pm.h`.

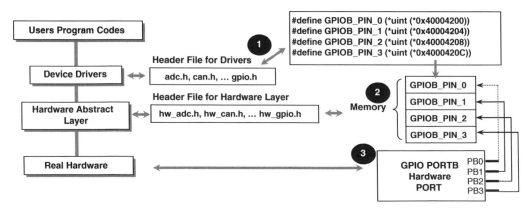

Figure 5.9.   Relationship among software and hardware components.

2. The CMSIS Cortex-M4 Peripheral Hardware Layer Header File for TM4C123GH6PM. This header file is named TM4C123GH6PM.h.

Basically, both header files provide different definitions for all system components used in the TM4C123GH6PM MCU system. The Register Driver Definitions header file defined a set of macros for all registers used in this system with their corresponding memory mappings. The Peripheral Hardware Layer header file defined a set of structures for all peripherals and a set of interrupt type (IRQn_Type) structure.

First let's have a brief discussion about these two header files.

5.4.1.1.2 The Register Driver Definition Header File in the TivaWare™ Software Package The Register Driver Definitions header file tm4c123gh6pm.h provides a complete set of definitions for all registers used in this system. This definition is achieved by mapping each register to its memory map address in the TM4C123GH6PM MCU on-chip memory system.

After these definitions, the users can directly use these macros in their program to access and configure each register. A set of interrupt numbers is also defined for all peripherals used in the system. Figure 5.10 shows a piece of definitions for the GPIO Port A in the tm4c123gh6pm.h header file.

5.4.1.1.3 The CMSIS Cortex-M4 Peripheral Layer Header File for TM4C123GH6PM The TivaWare™ for C Series Software also provides a CMSIS Cortex-M4 Peripheral Layer header file for the TM4C123GH6PM MCU system to support users to develop their applications in the CMSIS Core environment. This header file defined each peripheral as a

```
#define GPIO_PORTA_DATA_BITS_R  ((volatile uint32_t *)0x40004000)
#define GPIO_PORTA_DATA_R       (*((volatile uint32_t *)0x400043FC))
#define GPIO_PORTA_DIR_R        (*((volatile uint32_t *)0x40004400))
#define GPIO_PORTA_IS_R         (*((volatile uint32_t *)0x40004404))
#define GPIO_PORTA_IBE_R        (*((volatile uint32_t *)0x40004408))
#define GPIO_PORTA_IEV_R        (*((volatile uint32_t *)0x4000440C))
#define GPIO_PORTA_IM_R         (*((volatile uint32_t *)0x40004410))
#define GPIO_PORTA_RIS_R        (*((volatile uint32_t *)0x40004414))
#define GPIO_PORTA_MIS_R        (*((volatile uint32_t *)0x40004418))
#define GPIO_PORTA_ICR_R        (*((volatile uint32_t *)0x4000441C))
#define GPIO_PORTA_AFSEL_R      (*((volatile uint32_t *)0x40004420))
#define GPIO_PORTA_DR2R_R       (*((volatile uint32_t *)0x40004500))
#define GPIO_PORTA_DR4R_R       (*((volatile uint32_t *)0x40004504))
#define GPIO_PORTA_DR8R_R       (*((volatile uint32_t *)0x40004508))
#define GPIO_PORTA_ODR_R        (*((volatile uint32_t *)0x4000450C))
#define GPIO_PORTA_PUR_R        (*((volatile uint32_t *)0x40004510))
#define GPIO_PORTA_PDR_R        (*((volatile uint32_t *)0x40004514))
#define GPIO_PORTA_SLR_R        (*((volatile uint32_t *)0x40004518))
#define GPIO_PORTA_DEN_R        (*((volatile uint32_t *)0x4000451C))
#define GPIO_PORTA_LOCK_R       (*((volatile uint32_t *)0x40004520))
#define GPIO_PORTA_CR_R         (*((volatile uint32_t *)0x40004524))
#define GPIO_PORTA_AMSEL_R      (*((volatile uint32_t *)0x40004528))
#define GPIO_PORTA_PCTL_R       (*((volatile uint32_t *)0x4000452C))
#define GPIO_PORTA_ADCCTL_R     (*((volatile uint32_t *)0x40004530))
#define GPIO_PORTA_DMACTL_R     (*((volatile uint32_t *)0x40004534))
```

Figure 5.10. The definitions for the GPIO Port A in the Register Definition header file.

structure type and furthermore defined all similar peripherals as the structure pointers. All popular peripherals used in the TM4C123GH6PM MCU system, including the Watchdog, GPIO Ports, CAN, and UART, are defined as different structure pointers. More important, all exceptions and interrupts used in the TM4C123GH6PM MCU system are defined as an IRQn_Type, and each interrupt source can be considered as a member of this IRQn_Type.

Some significant differences between this header file and the Register Driver Definition header file tm4c123gh6pm.h are:

- The TM4C123GH6PM.h header file defined a structure enum definition for all Cortex-M4 exception and interrupt sources used in the TM4C123GH6PM system. All exceptions and interrupts are numbered and covered by an IRQn_Type structure. Each interrupt is defined as an IRQn Type, such as GPIOA_IRQn, UART0_IRQn, CAN0_IRQn, and TIMER0A_IRQn. A complete definition for the IRQn Type can be found in Figure 5.16 in Section 5.4.3.2.
- The TM4C123GH6PM.h header file defined each peripheral with a structure type and structure pointer. After this definition, the users can easily access each register by using the pointer operator to simplify the coding process.

Most times, we will use the Register Driver Definitions header files tm4c123gh6pm.h to build our sample projects. However, we will use the CMSIS Cortex-M4 Peripheral Layer header file TM4C123GH6PM.h when we build our sample project CMSISInt to illustrate how to use the CMSIS Core functions to configure and handle a GPIO interrupt in Section 5.4.5.

5.4.1.2 *The CMSIS Core Software Package (CMSISCSP)*

The CMSIS Core Software Package also provides a set of NVIC macros and NVIC API functions to support users to build and develop projects based on Cortex-M4 MCU since the TM4C123GH6PM MCU used a Cortex-M4 MCU as its core. Most of these macros and functions are defined to access and configure the NVIC-related registers to assist the interrupt handling and processing in the system. These header files include:

- The core_cm4.h defined all CMSIS Core functions used to access related NVIC registers to perform interrupt configurations.
- The system_TM4C123.h defined the system initialization function SystemInit() to initialize the TM4C123GH6PM MCU.
- The startup file Startup_TM4C123.s defined all interrupt handlers used in the microcontroller TM4C123GH6PM MCU system.

Refer to Sections 5.4.3.1 and 5.4.3.3 to get more details about these header files and their implementations in our sample projects to be developed in the following sections.

Now let's start to build our sample project using the Direct Register Access (DRA) method.

5.4.2 Using DRA Programming Model to Handle GPIO Interrupts

Similar to all other interrupt and exception processing procedure, to accept and handle an interrupt in the TM4C123GH6PM MCU system using the DRA model, the following operations should be performed:

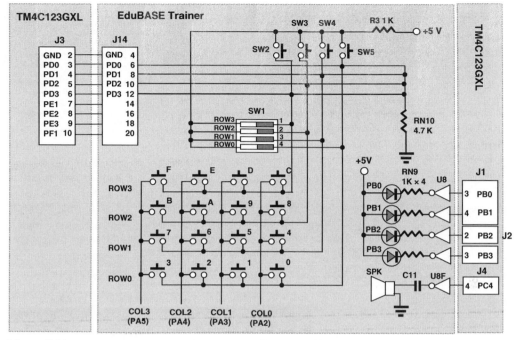

Figure 5.11.   Some hardware configurations for EduBASE ARM® Trainer.

1. Set up and configure the interrupt for GPIO pins using seven Interrupt Control Registers.
2. Configure the priority level and enable the GPIO Port using NVIC-related registers.
3. Set up the global interrupt control using two special registers in the processor.
4. Connect the interrupt handler with the users' project.
5. Respond and process to the interrupt as it occurred, and reset the active bit for the RIS if the interrupt is triggered by an edge.

In this section we will use an example project GPIOInt to illustrate how to build a GPIO related interrupt project to access, respond, and process a interrupt triggered by a GPIO pin.

The hardware we will use is the EduBASE ARM® Trainer, and some configurations for this trainer were shown in Figure 4.39. For your convenience, we redraw this configuration in this section as shown in Figure 5.11. We will use the header file tm4c123gh6pm.h in this project.

In this project, we try to use PD3 that is connected to a position switch SW2 in the EduBASE Trainer as a level-triggered interrupt as this switch is pressed. It can be found from Figure 5.11 that the PD3 gets a LOW level as the SW2 is opened and a HIGH level if the SW2 is pressed. As this interrupt is occurred, an ISR is executed to turn on the LED PB0 installed in the EduBASE Trainer via PB0 pin in the GPIO Port B.

5.4.2.1 Create a New Project GPIOInt and the Header File

Refer to Sections 4.5.7.2.5.1 and 4.5.7.2.5.2 in Chapter 4 to create a new μVersion5 project named GPIOInt and add a new header file named GPIOInt.h into this project. Enter the codes shown in Figure 5.12 into this header file.

```
1  // GPIOInt.h  -  Header file for the sample project GPIOInt.c
2  #include <stdint.h>                                    // for uint32, uint16, ....
3  #include <stdbool.h>                                   // for bool
4  #define  SYSCTL_RCC_XTAL_16MHZ       0x00000540        // use 16 MHz crystal
5  #define  SYSCTL_RCC_USESYSDIV        0x00400000        // enable System Clock Divider
6  #define  SYSCTL_SYSDIV_10            0x04C00000        // system clock is osc-pll/10
7  #define  SYSCTL_RCGC2_GPIOB          0x00000002        // Port B Clock Gating Control
8  #define  SYSCTL_RCGC2_GPIOD          0x00000008        // Port D Clock Gating Control
```

Figure 5.12. The project header file GPIOInt.h.

Two system header files, <stdint.h> and <stdbool.h>, are declared first to enable the compiler to know most integer and Boolean data types used in this project. Then some constants related to the system controls, such as RCGC2, RCC, and SYSDIV, are declared since we need to use them to initialize and configure system clock and enable GPIO Ports B and D.

5.4.2.2 Create a New C Code File GPIOInt and Add It into the Project

Refer to Section 4.5.7.2.5.3 in Chapter 4 to create a new C File named GPIOInt.c and add it into the project GPIOInt. Enter the codes shown in Figure 5.13 into this file.

```
1  //************************************************************************************************
2  // GPIOInt.c – Main Application File for the GPIO Interrupt Sample Project
3  //************************************************************************************************
4  #include "GPIOInt.h"
5  #include "tm4c123gh6pm.h"
6  void Enable_IRQ(void)
7  {
8     int R2;
9     __asm { MOV  R2, 0x0;  MSR  BASEPRI, R2;  CPSIE I }
10 }
11 int main(void)
12 {
13    volatile uint32_t RCC;
14    RCC = (SYSCTL_RCC_XTAL_16MHZ|SYS  CTL_RCC_USESYSDIV|SYSCTL_SYSDIV_10);  // setup clock
15    SYSCTL_RCC_R = RCC;
16    SYSCTL_RCGC2_R = SYSCTL_RCGC2_GPIOB|SYSCTL_RCGC2_GPIOD;  // Enable PORT B & D in RCGC2
17    GPIO_PORTB_DIR_R = 0x01;                          // set PB0 as out put pin
18    GPIO_PORTB_DEN_R = 0x01;                          // enable PB0 as digital function
19    GPIO_PORTD_DIR_R = ~0x8;                          // set PD3 as input pin
20    GPIO_PORTD_DEN_R = 0x08;                          // enable PD3 as digital function
21    GPIO_PORTD_IS_R = 0x8;                            // enable PD3 is level-triggered interrupt
22    GPIO_PORTD_IBE_R = 0x0;                           // disable PD3 IBE function
23    GPIO_PORTD_IEV_R = 0x8;                           // enable PD3 HIGH level/Rising edge
24    GPIO_PORTD_ICR_R = 0x8;                           // clear PD3 for any previous interrupt
25    GPIO_PORTD_IM_R = 0x8;                            // enable (unmask) PD3 interrupt
26    NVIC_PRI0_R = 0x60000000;              // NVIC->IP[3] = 0x60; or NVIC->IP[3] = 6 << 28; priority = 3
27    NVIC_EN0_R = 0x8;                      // NVIC->ISER[0] |= 0x00000008;  enable IRQ3
28    Enable_IRQ();                          // __enable_irq();  global enable IRQs
29    while(1) { GPIO_PORTB_DATA_R = 0x0; }  // wait for PD3 interrupt/set PB0 to LOW to turn off LED
30 }
31 void GPIOD_Handler(void)                  // ISR for PD3 interrupt
32 {
33    GPIO_PORTB_DATA_R = 0x1;               // set PB0 to HIGH to turn on LED PB0
34 }
```

Figure 5.13. The codes for the C file GPIOInt.c.

Let's have a closer look at this piece of codes to see how it works.

- In lines 4 and 5, two header files, GPIOInt.h and tm4c123gh6pm.h, are included into this file. The first is the user header file that contains all symbolic definitions for bit field values used to initialize system clock, and the second is a system header file that contains all macros or symbolic definitions for GPIO-related registers and NVIC-related registers to handle the interrupt request.

- A C-function Enable_IRQ() is defined in lines 6 and 10. An inline assembler is used to insert some ARM® Cortex®-M4 assembly instructions to configure the PRIMASK and the BASEPRI registers to globally enable interrupts and reset the global priority register BASEPRI to 0 allow any interrupt to be accepted by the processor. The MSR instruction is used to configure BASEPRI register and the CPSIE is to configure PRIMASK to unmask all interrupts. In fact, the BASEPRI is reset to 0 after a system reset operation.

- Inside the main() program, a local unint32_t integer variable RCC is declared and it is used to receive and hold the returned value from calling of the clock setup operation.

- The system clock is generated and assigned to the RCC register in lines 14 and 15.

- In line 16, the system clock is passed to the GPIO Ports B and D to enable both ports to be driven by this clock. An OR operation is performed to enable both ports.

- Between lines 17 and 20, the GPIO Ports B and D are initialized and configured to make pin PB0 (0x01) as an output pin and pin PD3 (0x08) as an input pin. In line 19, an inverse of 0x8,~0x8 = 11110111B, is used to make sure that the PD3 bit is 0.

- In lines 21 through to 25, five GPIO Interrupt Registers are used to initialize and configure pin PD3 as a HIGH-level triggered interrupt pin. Refer to Section 5.3.1 to get more details about these registers and their settings.

- In lines 26 and 27, both NVIC registers, NVIC Priority Register (NVIC_PRI0_R) and NVIC Set Enable Register (NVIC_EN0_R), are used to set the priority level and enable the entire GPIO Port D. Since the IRQ number of the GPIO Port D is 3 (refer to Table 5.10), a level 3 (0x3 = 011B) priority level is selected for this port. Because only 3 bits, bits 31~29, are used in the NVIC_PRI0_R (refer to Table 5.12), therefore the correct priority bits value should be 0110.0000.0000.0000.0000.0000.0000B = 0x60000000. All other bits are not used for this priority setting and therefore can be considered as 0. If you use the CMSIS Core macros defined for these NVIC registers in your codes (see Table 5.5), you can use the code: NVIC→IP[3] = 0x60 or NVIC→IP[3] = 6 << 28 to replace that lone code line above. The reason for that is because in CMSIS Core definitions, you can access each 8-bit segment on NVIC_PRI0_R register individually without considering other 24 bits. Bits 31~29 belong to the 4th segment, and it can be considered as an individual 8-bit segment without any relationship with other 24 bits in this register. The expression 6 << 28 means that a number 6 (0x6 = 0110B) is shifted left by 28 bits to make it become 0110B and locating it at bits 31~28. A similar idea is used for the NVIC_EN0_R register to enable PD3.

- In line 28, a user-defined C-function Enable_IRQ() is called to use an inline assembler to execute some Cortex-M4 assembly instructions to globally enable all interrupts and set priority level to 0 to enable all interrupts to be accepted. An option is that you can call an intrinsic function, __enable_irq(), which is defined by either Keil® ARM® MDK C/C++ Compiler or CMSIS Core, to perform this global-interrupt-enable function.

- An infinitive while() loop is executed to wait for the PD3 interrupt to occur. During the waiting period, the pin PB0 in the GPIO Port B is reset to 0 to turn off the PB0 LED in the EduBASE Trainer in line 29.

- The code lines 31~34 contain the PD3 interrupt handler and the interrupt processing codes. The name of this handler, GPIOD_Handler, is defined in the system startup file,

Startup_TM4C123.s, which has been added into this project. When using this handler, you must make sure that the name of this handler used in your program must be identical to that defined in the startup file. Otherwise you may encounter some compiling errors if you used a different name for this handler. It is highly recommended to use the default handler name defined in this startup file. Refer to this startup file to get the handler name you want to use in your program. The processing code for this interrupt is simple, just turn on the PB0 LED in the EduBASE Trainer via pin PB0 in the GPIO Port B.

Now we are ready to compile, link, download, and run this project to test the interrupt function via pin PD3 in the GPIO Port D. Wait a moment! Before you can do these jobs, make sure that the environment used by your project meets the requirements of the compiler, linker, download ICDI, and runner.

5.4.2.3 Set Up the Environment to Compile and Link the Project

To set up the correct environment for this project, you need to:

1. Include the necessary path for all header files used in the project. There are two ways to do this job. The first way is to include the system header file via C/C++ tab in the Project| Options for Target 'Target 1' menu. Since we used the tm4c123gh6pm.h header file, you need to browse to the folder: C:\ti\TivaWare_C_Series-2.0.1.11577\inc and select this header file and add it into the **Include Paths** box under the C/C++ tab. The second way is to copy this header file and paste it into the project folder C:\ARM Class Projects\Chapter 5\GPIOInt in the Windows Explorer. The second way is better since this header file has been added into your project to make it portable.

2. Open the Debug tab in the Project|Options for Target 'Target 1' menu to make sure that the debugger you are using is Stellaris ICDI in the **Use** box. If not, select it from the list and click on the **OK** button.

Now it is time to compile, download, and run the project. During the project runs, press the position switch SW2 in the EduBASE Trainer, and a PD3 HIGH-level triggered interrupt occurs and is directed to the related handler, GPIOD_Handler. Inside the handler, the PB0 LED in the EduBASE Trainer is turned on. When you release the SW2 switch, the LED is off since it is turned off in the while(1) loop in your codes.

5.4.3 Using CMSIS Core Macros for NVIC Registers to Handle GPIO Interrupts

In this section we will use the CMSIS Core macros defined for the NVIC Interrupt Control Registers to set up and configure some GPIO Ports and pins to perform interrupt generations, priority level detections, interrupt enables, and the interrupt processing process.

We have provided a brief discussion and introduction about the CMSIS Core macros defined for NVIC Interrupt Control Registers in Section 5.2.3. Refer to Table 5.5 to get more details about these macro definitions.

As we discussed in Section 5.4.1, two software packages are provided to support users to build an application project with the TM4C123GH6PM MCU system. Two system header files are provided by the TivaWare™ Software Package; tm4c123gh6pm.h and TM4C123GH6PM.h. In this section, we will use the header files TM4C123GH6PM.h and

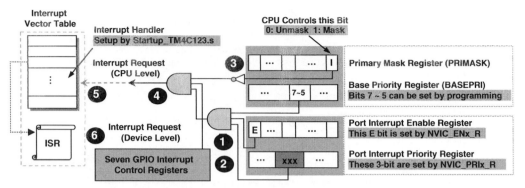

Figure 5.14. The block diagram demonstrating the use of NVIC macros to handle GPIO interrupts.

core_cm4.h that are provided by the CMSIS Core package since the former provides all structure definitions for GPIO Ports and the latter provides all structure definitions for the NVIC registers.

5.4.3.1 Popular Data Structures Defined in the CMSIS Core Header File

Figure 5.14 shows a block diagram demonstrating the use of the CMSIS Core macros for NVIC Interrupt Control Registers to handle GPIO interrupts.

Two important registers, NVIC_PRIn_R and NVIC_ENn_R, are used to control those related GPIO interrupt registers to configure the priority level for the interrupt and enable the selected GPIO Port to generate an interrupt request to the processor.

In order to facilitate and help users to build and develop their application programs, the TivaWare™ Software package provides another system header file TM4C123GH6PM.h to define a set of special structures for all peripheral registers and IRQ numbers to make the users' program neat and simple.

These structures are defined based on all peripherals (both internal and external peripherals), NVIC registers, and system control registers, used in the TM4C123GH6PM MCU system with one by one relationship. This means that each peripheral has a corresponding structure and is defined in the following way:

- First the structure type for each peripheral is defined with the peripheral name and all registers and constants used by that peripheral.
- Then the peripheral is defined as a pointer of the structure type of the peripheral.

Some examples of structure types for the peripheral WatchDog0 and GPIOA are shown in Figures 5.15 and 5.16.

After the structure type for the peripheral is defined, each peripheral can be further defined as a pointer of the defined structure type of the peripheral. Figure 5.17 shows an example of using the peripheral GPIOA structure-type GPIOA_Type to define the GPIOA~GPIOF as a pointer of the GPIOA_Type with the base address of each port. Using the WatchDog0_Type structure type to define the WATCHDOG0 as a pointer of that type is also shown here.

The advantage of using the peripheral structure type to define the peripheral as a pointer of that type is that the users' program codes can be significantly shortened and

```
typedef struct {                                /*!< WATCHDOG0 Structure    */
  __IO uint32_t LOAD;                           /*!< Watchdog Load    */
  __IO uint32_t VALUE;                          /*!< Watchdog Value    */
  __IO uint32_t CTL;                            /*!< Watchdog Control    */
  __O  uint32_t ICR;                            /*!< Watchdog Interrupt Clear    */
  __IO uint32_t RIS;                            /*!< Watchdog Raw Interrupt Status      */
  __IO uint32_t MIS;                            /*!< Watchdog Masked Interrupt Status     */
  __I  uint32_t RESERVED0[256];
  __IO uint32_t TEST;                           /*!< Watchdog Test    */
  __I  uint32_t RESERVED1[505];
  __IO uint32_t LOCK;                           /*!< Watchdog Lock    */
} WATCHDOG0_Type;
```

Figure 5.15. A structure type example — WATCHDOG0_Type.

simplified, and therefore make them easy to be coded and understood. For example, by using this definition, to access each register inside a peripheral, such as GPIOA, the pointer format can be used and the following code line is a valid one:

- GPIOA->DEN = 0x1;
- GPIOA->DIR = 0x2;
- GPIOA->DATA = 0x3;

```
typedef struct {                                /*!< GPIOA Structure    */
  __I  uint32_t RESERVED0[255];
  __IO uint32_t DATA;                           /*!< GPIO Data    */
  __IO uint32_t DIR;                            /*!< GPIO Direction    */
  __IO uint32_t IS;                             /*!< GPIO Interrupt Sense    */
  __IO uint32_t IBE;                            /*!< GPIO Interrupt Both Edges    */
  __IO uint32_t IEV;                            /*!< GPIO Interrupt Event    */
  __IO uint32_t IM;                             /*!< GPIO Interrupt Mask     */
  __IO uint32_t RIS;                            /*!< GPIO Raw Interrupt Status */
  __IO uint32_t MIS;                            /*!< GPIO Masked Interrupt Status    */
  __O  uint32_t ICR;                            /*!< GPIO Interrupt Clear    */
  __IO uint32_t AFSEL;                          /*!< GPIO Alternate Function Select */
  __I  uint32_t RESERVED1[55];
  __IO uint32_t DR2R;                           /*!< GPIO 2-mA Drive Select    */
  __IO uint32_t DR4R;                           /*!< GPIO 4-mA Drive Select    */
  __IO uint32_t DR8R;                           /*!< GPIO 8-mA Drive Select    */
  __IO uint32_t ODR;                            /*!< GPIO Open Drain Select    */
  __IO uint32_t PUR;                            /*!< GPIO Pull-Up Select    */
  __IO uint32_t PDR;                            /*!< GPIO Pull-Down Select    */
  __IO uint32_t SLR;                            /*!< GPIO Slew Rate Control Select    */
  __IO uint32_t DEN;                            /*!< GPIO Digital Enable    */
  __IO uint32_t LOCK;                           /*!< GPIO Lock    */
  __I  uint32_t CR;                             /*!< GPIO Commit    */
  __IO uint32_t AMSEL;                          /*!< GPIO Analog Mode Select    */
  __IO uint32_t PCTL;                           /*!< GPIO Port Control    */
  __IO uint32_t ADCCTL;                         /*!< GPIO ADC Control    */
  __IO uint32_t DMACTL;                         /*!< GPIO DMA Control    */
} GPIOA_Type;
```

Figure 5.16. A structure-type example — GPIOA_Type.

```
#define  WATCHDOG0              ((WATCHDOG0_Type *) WATCHDOG0_BASE)
#define  WATCHDOG1              ((WATCHDOG0_Type *) WATCHDOG1_BASE)
#define  GPIOA                  ((GPIOA_Type     *) GPIOA_BASE)
#define  GPIOB                  ((GPIOA_Type     *) GPIOB_BASE)
#define  GPIOC                  ((GPIOA_Type     *) GPIOC_BASE)
#define  GPIOD                  ((GPIOA_Type     *) GPIOD_BASE)
#define  GPIOE                  ((GPIOA_Type     *) GPIOE_BASE)
#define  GPIOF                  ((GPIOA_Type     *) GPIOF_BASE)
```

Figure 5.17.   Some examples of using structure type to define the peripheral.

The meaning of each definition, such as #define GPIOB ((GPIOA_Type *) GPIOB_BASE), is to define the peripheral GPIOB as a pointer of the GPIOA_Type structure with the starting address as GPIOB_BASE. In this way, the peripheral macro GPIOB now is a structure (not a constant) and it contains all registers involved in this peripheral. To access each register in this peripheral, a pointer format → should be used. The starting address of this structure is GPIOB_BASE, which is also defined in this header file.

Similarly, all peripherals' registers can be accessed and initialized in this way by using this kind of pointer definition.

Table 5.16 shows a comparison between the register accessing with normal peripheral register macros and peripheral macros defined with the pointer of the peripheral structure type. It can be found that the pointer of structure-type definition has a shorter code line and is easy to remember and program.

In the TM4C123GH6PM MCU system, all peripherals have been defined with this structure-type pointer format. Table 5.17 shows the most popular peripheral structure-type definitions. All of these structure definitions can be found from the CMSIS Cortex-M4 Peripheral Layer header file TM4C123GH6PM.h provided by the TivaWare™ Software package.

5.4.3.2 IRQ Numbers Defined in the TivaWare™ System Header File

Besides all peripherals and related registers, the system header file TM4C123GH6PM.h also contains the macro definitions for all exceptions and interrupts, especially for the IRQ number definitions for all exceptions and interrupts used in the TM4C123GH6PM system.

Table 5.16.   Comparison between normal and structure definitions for register accessing.

Normal Definition Accessing	Structure-Type Definition Accessing
GPIO_PORTA_DATA_R = 0x01	GPIOA→DATA = 0x1
GPIO_PORTB_DATA_R = 0x01	GPIOB→DATA = 0x1
GPIO_PORTA_DIR_R = 0x01	GPIOA→DIR = 0x1
GPIO_PORTB_DEN_R = 0x01	GPIOB→DEN = 0x1
GPIO_PORTA_IS_R = 0x01	GPIOA→IS = 0x1
GPIO_PORTF_IEV_R = 0x01	GPIOF→IEV = 0x1
GPIO_PORTE_ICR_R = 0x01	GPIOE→ICR = 0x1

Table 5.17.   Popular peripherals structure type definitions.

Peripheral	Structure Type Definition
Watch Dog0	WATCHDOG0_Type
GPIO PORTA	GPIOA_Type
GPIO PORTB	GPIOA_Type
GPIO PORTC	GPIOA_Type
GPIO PORTD	GPIOA_Type
GPIO PORTE	GPIOA_Type
GPIO PORTF	GPIOA_Type
SSI0	SSI0_Type
UART0	UART0_Type
I2C0	I2C0_Type
PWM0	PWM0_Type
QEI0	QEI0_Type
TIMER0	TIMER0_Type
WTIMER0	WTIMER0_Type
ADC0	ADC0_Type
COMP	COMP_Type
CAN0	CAN0_Type
USB0	USB0_Type
EEPROM	EEPROM_Type
SYSCTL	SYSCTL_Type
SYSEXC	SYSEXC_Type

Figure 5.18 shows an example of structure definitions (IRQn_Type) for all exceptions involved in this header file and used in the TM4C123GH6PM MCU system.

Figure 5.19 shows an example of structure definitions (IRQn_Type) for all interrupts involved in this header file and used in the TM4C123GH6PM MCU system.

```
typedef  enum {
/* -------------------- Cortex-M4 Processor Exceptions Numbers -------------------- */
   Reset_IRQn               = -15,       /*!<  1  Reset Vector, invoked on Power up and warm reset */
   NonMaskableInt_IRQn      = -14,       /*!<  2  Non maskable Interrupt, cannot be stopped     */
   HardFault_IRQn           = -13,       /*!<  3  Hard Fault, all classes of Fault  */
   MemoryManagement_IRQn    = -12,       /*!<  4  Memory Management, MPU mismatch */
   BusFault_IRQn            = -11,       /*!<  5  Bus Fault, Pre-Fetch-, Memory Access Fault */
   UsageFault_IRQn          = -10,       /*!<  6  Usage Fault, i.e. Undef Instruction, Illegal State */
   SVCall_IRQn              = -5,        /*!< 11  System Service Call via SVC instruction */
   DebugMonitor_IRQn        = -4,        /*!< 12  Debug Monitor  */
   PendSV_IRQn              = -2,        /*!< 14  Pendable request for system service  */
   SysTick_IRQn             = -1,        /*!< 15  System Tick Timer  */
   ......                     ......            ......
} IRQn_Type;
```

Figure 5.18.   Structure definitions for exceptions.

```
typedef  enum {
/* ------------------ TM4C123GH6PM Specific Interrupt Numbers ------------------ */
  GPIOA_IRQn              = 0,           /*!<  0  GPIOA            */
  GPIOB_IRQn              = 1,           /*!<  1  GPIOB            */
  GPIOC_IRQn              = 2,           /*!<  2  GPIOC            */
  GPIOD_IRQn              = 3,           /*!<  3  GPIOD            */
  GPIOE_IRQn              = 4,           /*!<  4  GPIOE            */
  UART0_IRQn              = 5,           /*!<  5  UART0            */
  UART1_IRQn              = 6,           /*!<  6  UART1            */
  SSI0_IRQn               = 7,           /*!<  7  SSI0             */
  I2C0_IRQn               = 8,           /*!<  8  I2C0             */
  PWM0_FAULT_IRQn         = 9,           /*!<  9  PWM0_FAULT       */
  PWM0_0_IRQn             = 10,          /*!<  10  PWM0_0          */
  PWM0_1_IRQn             = 11,          /*!<  11  PWM0_1          */
  PWM0_2_IRQn             = 12,          /*!<  12  PWM0_2          */
  QEI0_IRQn               = 13,          /*!<  13  QEI0            */
  ADC0SS0_IRQn            = 14,          /*!<  14  ADC0SS0         */
  ADC0SS1_IRQn            = 15,          /*!<  15  ADC0SS1         */
  ADC0SS2_IRQn            = 16,          /*!<  16  ADC0SS2         */
  ADC0SS3_IRQn            = 17,          /*!<  17  ADC0SS3         */
  WATCHDOG0_IRQn          = 18,          /*!<  18  WATCHDOG0       */
  TIMER0A_IRQn            = 19,          /*!<  19  TIMER0A         */
  TIMER0B_IRQn            = 20,          /*!<  20  TIMER0B         */
  TIMER1A_IRQn            = 21,          /*!<  21  TIMER1A         */
  TIMER1B_IRQn            = 22,          /*!<  22  TIMER1B         */
  TIMER2A_IRQn            = 23,          /*!<  23  TIMER2A         */
  TIMER2B_IRQn            = 24,          /*!<  24  TIMER2B         */
  COMP0_IRQn              = 25,          /*!<  25  COMP0           */
  COMP1_IRQn              = 26,          /*!<  26  COMP1           */
  SYSCTL_IRQn             = 28,          /*!<  28  SYSCTL          */
  FLASH_CTRL_IRQn         = 29,          /*!<  29  FLASH_CTRL      */
  GPIOF_IRQn              = 30,          /*!<  30  GPIOF           */
  ......                   ......         ......
} IRQn_Type;
```

Figure 5.19.   Structure definitions for interrupts.

In some other version of this header file, the IRQ numbers are defined with direct mapping method, such as

```
    #define INT_GPIOA              16                //GPIO Port A IRQ number = 16
```

Now we are ready to build our sample interrupt project using the CMSIS Core macros for NVIC Interrupt Registers to handle GPIO related interrupts.

5.4.3.3 The NVIC Macros Defined in the TivaWare™ System Header Files

In addition to data structures and IRQ numbers, the TM4C123GH6PM MCU system also defined a set of macros used for the NVIC interrupt control register accessing and configuration. These macros are defined based on the actual addresses of each NVIC register, and the users can directly access these registers and assign values to them.

```
//****************************************************************************************************
// NVIC registers (NVIC)
//****************************************************************************************************
#define NVIC_EN0_R          (*((volatile uint32_t *)0xE000E100))
#define NVIC_EN1_R          (*((volatile uint32_t *)0xE000E104))
#define NVIC_EN2_R          (*((volatile uint32_t *)0xE000E108))
#define NVIC_EN3_R          (*((volatile uint32_t *)0xE000E10C))
#define NVIC_EN4_R          (*((volatile uint32_t *)0xE000E110))
#define NVIC_DIS0_R         (*((volatile uint32_t *)0xE000E180))
#define NVIC_DIS1_R         (*((volatile uint32_t *)0xE000E184))
#define NVIC_DIS2_R         (*((volatile uint32_t *)0xE000E188))
#define NVIC_DIS3_R         (*((volatile uint32_t *)0xE000E18C))
#define NVIC_DIS4_R         (*((volatile uint32_t *)0xE000E190))
#define NVIC_PRI0_R         (*((volatile uint32_t *)0xE000E400))
#define NVIC_PRI1_R         (*((volatile uint32_t *)0xE000E404))
#define NVIC_PRI2_R         (*((volatile uint32_t *)0xE000E408))
#define NVIC_PRI3_R         (*((volatile uint32_t *)0xE000E40C))
#define NVIC_PRI4_R         (*((volatile uint32_t *)0xE000E410))
#define NVIC_PRI5_R         (*((volatile uint32_t *)0xE000E414))
#define NVIC_PRI6_R         (*((volatile uint32_t *)0xE000E418))
#define NVIC_PRI7_R         (*((volatile uint32_t *)0xE000E41C))
#define NVIC_PRI8_R         (*((volatile uint32_t *)0xE000E420))
#define NVIC_PRI9_R         (*((volatile uint32_t *)0xE000E424))
#define NVIC_PRI10_R        (*((volatile uint32_t *)0xE000E428))
#define NVIC_PRI11_R        (*((volatile uint32_t *)0xE000E42C))
#define NVIC_PRI12_R        (*((volatile uint32_t *)0xE000E430))
#define NVIC_PRI13_R        (*((volatile uint32_t *)0xE000E434))
#define NVIC_PRI14_R        (*((volatile uint32_t *)0xE000E438))
```

Figure 5.20.   NVIC register macros defined by TM4C123GH6PM MCU system.

For example, to enable GPIO Port B and GPIO Port F, the NVIC_EN0_R should be initialized with the following code line (bits 30 and 1 are set to 1):

NVIC_EN0_R = 0100.0000.0000.0000.0000.0000.0000.0010B = 0x40000002

To set the priority for the GPIO Port F to level 3, the NVIC_PRI7_R should be coded:

NVIC_PRI7_R = 0000.0000.0110.0000.0000.0000.0000.0000B = 0x00600000

Figure 5.20 shows some popular NVIC registers defined in the header file tm4c123gh6pm.h.

5.4.3.4 The NVIC Structure Defined in the CMSIS Core Header File

As we discussed in Section 5.4.1.2, to help users to develop the interrupt application programs, the CMSIS Core provides a set of structure-type definitions for the System Control and NVIC Interrupt Control Registers as well as some NVIC interfacing functions. These definitions and functions include:

- Structure-type definitions for system special control and status registers, including ASPR, ISPR, CONTROL, SysTick, and SCB.

```
typedef struct
{
   __IO uint32_t ISER[1];            /*!< Offset: 0x000 (R/W)  Interrupt Set Enable Register       */
      uint32_t RESERVED0[31];
   __IO uint32_t ICER[1];            /*!< Offset: 0x080 (R/W)  Interrupt Clear Enable Register     */
      uint32_t RSERVED1[31];
   __IO uint32_t ISPR[1];            /*!< Offset: 0x100 (R/W)  Interrupt Set Pending Register      */
      uint32_t RESERVED2[31];
   __IO uint32_t ICPR[1];            /*!< Offset: 0x180 (R/W)  Interrupt Clear Pending Register    */
      uint32_t RESERVED3[31];
      uint32_t RESERVED4[64];
   __IO uint32_t IP[8];              /*!< Offset: 0x300 (R/W)  Interrupt Priority Register         */
} NVIC_Type;

#define SCS_BASE      (0xE000E000UL)              /* System Control Space Base Address */
#define NVIC_BASE     (SCS_BASE + 0x0100UL)       /* NVIC Base Address  */
#define NVIC  ((NVIC_Type *) NVIC_BASE )          /* NVIC configuration struct */
```

Figure 5.21.   The structure type definition for the NVIC.

- Structure-type definition for the NVIC.
- NVIC interface functions, such as NVIC_EnableIRQ(), NVIC_DisableIRQ(), NVIC_GetPriority(), and NVIC_SetPriority().

These structure-type macros and NVIC functions are defined in a CMSIS Core system header file core_cm0.h. Figure 5.21 shows an example of the structure-type definition NVIC_Type and the pointer structure definition for NVIC.

It can be found from Figure 5.21 that the NVIC_Type is first defined as a structure, and this structure contains all registers used in the NVIC, including the Interrupt Set Enable (ISER[]), Interrupt Priority (IP[]), and Interrupt Clear Enable (ICER[]) registers. Then the NVIC variable is defined as a pointer of the NVIC_Type structure with its base address 0xE000E100UL (UL means Unsigned Long). If you need to access any NVIC register by using this pointer structure definition in your program, you must use the pointer operator ($\rightarrow$). For example, you want to configure the NVIC Interrupt Set Enable Register ISER[0] to enable an interrupt source in your program, then you need to use NVIC$\rightarrow$ISER[0] to do this job. With a similar way, you can access any other register in this NVIC structure.

Recall that in Section 5.2.3 we discussed the CMSIS Core macros for NVIC registers and CMSIS Core functions to interface these NVIC registers. The point to be noted is that each Interrupt Set Enable Register, from ISER[0] to ISER[7], is a 32-bit register and can be used to enable 32 interrupts bit by bit. For example, the ISER[0] is a 32-bit register and it can enables 32 interrupt sources with one bit for one interrupt source. Each ISER[] can be used to enable different 32 interrupt sources. Table 5.18 shows that the range of interrupts can be enabled by the different ISER[] registers. The bit order is equivalent to the IRQ order of the interrupt. Bit 0 is for the interrupt whose IRQ number is 0, bit 1 is for the interrupt whose IRQ number is 1, . . . , and so on.

To enable one interrupt, the corresponding bit in the ISER[] should be set to 1. If ISER[0] = 0x00000001, it enabled the interrupt whose IRQ number is 0; and if ISER[0] = 0x00000008, it enabled the interrupt whose IRQ number is 3, and so on. The ISER[0] is

Table 5.18. The NVIC registers used for enable and priority controls.

CMSIS Core Macros	Enabled Interrupt Source	TM4C123GH6PM Macros
NVIC→ISER[0]	Interrupt sources 0–31	NVIC_EN0_R
NVIC→ISER[1]	Interrupt sources 32–63	NVIC_EN1_R
NVIC→ISER[2]	Interrupt sources 64–95	NVIC_EN2_R
NVIC→ISER[3]	Interrupt sources 96–127	NVIC_EN3_R
CMSIS Core Macros	**Set Interrupt Priority Level**	**TM4C123GH6PM Macros**
NVIC→IP[0]–NVIC→IP[3]	Interrupt sources with IRQ0–IRQ3	NVIC_PRI0_R
NVIC→IP[4]–NVIC→IP[7]	Interrupt sources with IRQ4–IRQ7	NVIC_PRI1_R
NVIC→IP[8]–NVIC→IP[11]	Interrupt sources with IRQ8–IRQ11	NVIC_PRI2_R
NVIC→IP[12]–NVIC→IP[15]	Interrupt sources with IRQ12–IRQ15	NVIC_PRI3_R
NVIC→IP[16]–NVIC→IP[19]	Interrupt sources with IRQ16–IRQ19	NVIC_PRI4_R
NVIC→IP[20]–NVIC→IP[23]	Interrupt sources with IRQ20–IRQ23	NVIC_PRI5_R
NVIC→IP[24]–NVIC→IP[27]	Interrupt sources with IRQ24–IRQ27	NVIC_PRI6_R
NVIC→IP[28]–NVIC→IP[31]	Interrupt sources with IRQ28–IRQ31	NVIC_PRI7_R
NVIC→IP[32]–NVIC→IP[35]	Interrupt sources with IRQ32–IRQ35	NVIC_PRI8_R
NVIC→IP[36]–NVIC→IP[39]	Interrupt sources with IRQ36–IRQ39	NVIC_PRI9_R
NVIC→IP[40]–NVIC→IP[43]	Interrupt sources with IRQ40–IRQ43	NVIC_PRI10_R
NVIC→IP[44]–NVIC→IP[47]	Interrupt sources with IRQ44–IRQ47	NVIC_PRI11_R
NVIC→IP[48]–NVIC→IP[51]	Interrupt sources with IRQ48–IRQ51	NVIC_PRI12_R

equivalent to NVIC_EN0_R shown in Table 5.13. The NVIC_ENn_R and NVIC_PRIn_R macros are defined by the TM4C123GH6PM MCU system. Refer to Table 5.13 to get more details for this register.

However, the Interrupt Priority Register IP[], which can be considered to be an 8-bit register, is used to set up the priority level for one interrupt source. In fact, only 3 bits on each segment are used to set up the priority level for one interrupt source. The IP[0], which is equivalent to 7~5 bits in the register NVIC_PRI0_R shown in Table 5.12, is an 8-bit register and it is used to set up a priority level for the interrupt whose IRQ number is 0. Figure 5.22 shows a mapping relationship between each IP[] register and each NVIC_PRI0_R register. In this mapping way, the NVIC_PRI1_R includes IP[4]~IP[7], NVIC_PRI2_R contains IP[8]~IP[11], and NVIC_PRI3_R includes IP[12]~IP[15], as shown in Table 5.18.

5.4.3.5 Building Sample Project to Use CMSIS Core Macros for NVIC to Handle Interrupts

In this section we want to use an example project named NVICInt to use CMSIS Core macros for NVIC Interrupt Registers to handle a rising edge detected interrupt at pin

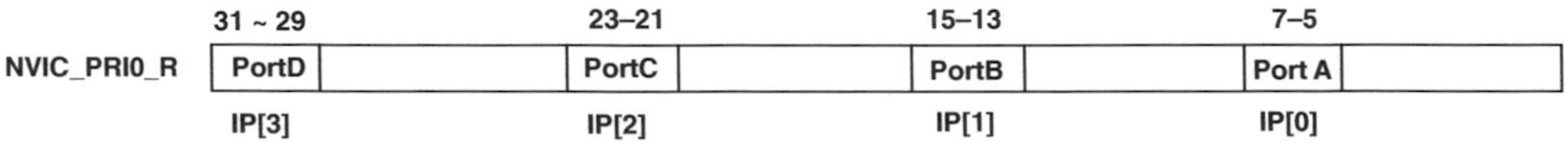

Figure 5.22. Mapping relationship between NVIC_PRI0_R and IP[].

Table 5.19. The interrupt setup parameters for pin PD3 on GPIO Port D.

Register	Interrupt Trigger	GPIO PORTD Interrupt Control Registers							
		7	6	5	4	3	2	1	0
GPIOIS	0: Edge 1: Level	x	x	x	x	**0**	x	x	x
GPIOIBE	0: Single Edge 1: Double Edges	x	x	x	x	**0**	x	x	x
GPIOICR	0: No action 1: Clear the interrupt flag bit	x	x	x	x	**1**	x	x	x
GPIOIEV	0: LOW Level or Falling Edge 1: HIGH Level or Rising Edge	x	x	x	x	**1**	x	x	x
GPIOIM	0: Masked (Disabled) 1: Unmasked (Enabled)	x	x	x	x	**1**	x	x	x

Table 5.20. The NVIC macros for GPIO Port D.

NVIC Register	CMSIS Core Macros	Function
Interrupt Set Enable Registers	NVIC→ISER[0] = 0x00000008	Write 1 to enable the interrupt
Interrupt Priority Registers	NVIC→IP[3] = 0x60	Priority level 3 (8-bit wide) for the PORTD

PD3 at the GPIO Port D since this pin is connected to a position switch SW2 in the EduBASE Trainer. Refer to Figure 5.11 to get details about the hardware configuration for this connection. As the SW2 switch is pressed, an interrupt is occurred at PD3, and four LEDs installed in the EduBASE Trainer will be toggled in this interrupt handler.

Still we need to perform three steps to establish and configure the interrupt on pin PD3 at GPIO Port D:

1. Use seven GPIO Interrupt Control Registers to initialize and configure pin 3 at the GPIO Port D, PD3 to detect a rising edge interrupt request signal.
2. Use two NVIC Interrupt Control Registers to configure priority for the GPIO Port D and enable this port.
3. Use an intrinsic function __enable_irq() to globally enable all interrupts.

Table 5.19 shows a set of interrupt parameters for the pin PD3 at the GPIO Port D to enable this pin to perform the interrupt functions listed in step 1.

Table 5.20 lists NVIC macro configuration parameters for the GPIO Port D to set up the priority level and enable this port to perform the interrupt functions shown in step 2 above.

Now we are ready to develop our sample interrupt project NVICInt.

5.4.3.6 Create a New Project NVICInt and Add the C Code File

Refer to Sections 4.5.7.2.5.1 and 4.5.7.2.5.2 in Chapter 4 to create a new μVersion5 project named NVICInt. Because this project is simple, no header file is needed.

```
1  //*************************************************************************************************
2  // NVICInt.c – Main Application File for the NVIC Interrupt Sample Project
3  //*************************************************************************************************
4  #include <stdint.h>
5  #include <stdbool.h>
6  #include "TM4C123GH6PM.h"

7  int main(void)
8  {
9      SYSCTL->RCGCGPIO |= 0x08;              // enable clock to PORTD
10     SYSCTL->RCGCGPIO |= 0x02;              // enable clock to PORTB

11     // configure PORTB for LED output
12     GPIOB->DIR |= 0x0F;                    // set PB0 ~ PB3 as output pins
13     GPIOB->DEN |= 0x0F;                    // enable PB0 ~ PB3 as digital functions

14     // configure PORTD3 for rising edge trigger interrupt
15     GPIOD->DIR &= ~0x8;                    // make PD3 input pin
16     GPIOD->DEN |= 0x8;                     // make PD3 digital pin
17     GPIOD->IS  &= ~0x8;                    // make   PD3 as an edge sensitive
18     GPIOD->IBE &= ~0x8;                    // trigger is controlled by IEV
19     GPIOD->IEV &= 0x8;                     // rising edge trigger
20     GPIOD->ICR |= 0x8;                     // clear any prior interrupt on PD3
21     GPIOD->IM  |= 0x8;                     // unmask interrupt PD3

22     // enable interrupt PD3 in NVIC and set priority to 3
23     NVIC->IP[3] = 6 << 5;                  // set interrupt priority to 3
24     NVIC->ISER[0] |= 0x00000008;           // enable IRQ3

25     __enable_irq();                        // global enable all IRQs

26     while(1)                               // wait for interrupts
27     {
28     }
29  }

30 void  GPIOD_Handler(void)                  // ISR for PD3 interrupt
31 {
32     GPIOD->ICR |= 0x8;                     // clear PD3 interrupt flag
33     GPIOB->DATA ^= 15;                     // toggle 4 LEDs PB0 ~ PB3 in Trainer
34 }
```

Figure 5.23. The C code file for the NVICInt project.

Refer to Section 4.5.7.2.5.3 in Chapter 4 to create a new C File named NVICInt.c and add it into the project NVICInt. Enter the codes shown in Figure 5.23 into this file. Let's have a closer look at this file to see how it works.

- Three system header files, <stdint.h>, <stdbool.h> and "TM4C123GH6PM.h," are declared first to enable the compiler to know most integer and Boolean data types used in this project. All GPIO Ports and all CMSIS Core macros of the NVIC Interrupt Control Registers are defined in the third header file and we need to use them to initialize and configure system clock and enable GPIO Ports B and D.

- In lines 9 and 10, the system RCGCGPIO clock gating control register used for the GPIO Ports is assigned with two constants, 0x08 and 0x02, which means that bits 3 and 1 in this register are set to 1. We have provided detailed introductions for The GPIO Run-mode Clock Gating Control (RCGCGPIO) register in Section 4.5.7.2.2.1 in Chapter 4. In fact, this clock gating control register performs the same control functions as the Run-mode Clock Gating Control 2 (RCGC2) register did, and both registers have the same bit field and bit control function. Refer to Figure 4.28 in Section 4.5.7.2.2.1 in Chapter 4 to get a bit configuration and function for this register. Each bit on the lowest 6 bits, bits 5~0, on this RCGCGPIO register is corresponding to each GPIO Port, Ports F~A, respectively. This means that bit 0 is for Port A, bit 1 is for Port B, . . . , and bit 5 is for Port F. Any of these five bits is set to 1, and the corresponding Port is enabled. A 0 on a bit means that the corresponding port is disabled. Therefore 0x08 → Port D and 0x02 → Port B. The SYSCTL is defined as a structure type in the TM4C123GH6PM.h header file as we discussed in the last section, and the → is a pointer point to the RCGCGPIO that is a member of the structure type SYSCTL.

- In lines 12 and 13, the pins 3–0 on the GPIO Port B are defined as output pins with digital functions enabled. Similarly, the GPIOB is also defined as a structure type in the TM4C123GH6PM.h header file. However, this structure definition is indirectly defined via a GPIOA_Type structure in that header file. Therefore, to access its members, DIR and DEN, which are two registers in the Port B, the pointer operator, →, is used again. Of course, if you do not want to use this pointer operator and prefer to use the register names directly, you can use GPIO_PORTB_DIR_R and GPIO_PORTB_DEN_R to replace these two code lines as GPIO_PORTB_DIR_R | = 0x0F and GPIO_PORTB_DEN_R | = 0x0F, respectively.

- In lines 15 and 16, the pin PD3 in the Port D is configured as an input pin with digital function enabled. An inverse sign ~ is used in front of the 0x08 (~ 0x08 = 0xF7) and it is assigned to the GPIO Port D Direction register to make PD3 as an input pin. This inverting number is to make sure that the bit 3 or PD3 in the DIR register is 0 (0xF7).

- The code lines between 17 and 21 are used to initialize and configure the pin PD3 on the GPIO Port D to set up the GPIO Interrupt Control Registers to enable PD3 to detect and accept a rising edge interrupt signal when the position switch SW2 in the EduBASE Trainer is pressed. The Interrupt Clear Register (ICR) on this pin should be set to 1 to clear any previous possible interrupt occurred to this pin.

- The NVIC Interrupt Priority register NVIC → IP[3] is used to set up the priority level for the GPIO Port D. Refer to Tables 5.5 and 5.18 to get more details about using the IP[] register to setup the priority level for the interrupt source.

- In line 24, the NVIC Set Enable Register is used to set the enable bit (bit 3) for the PD3. The CMSIS Core macro, NVIC→ISER[0], is used to do this enabling job.

- An intrinsic function __enable_irq() is called in line 25 to perform the global interrupt enable job.

- Then an infinitive while() loop is executed to wait for the PD3 interrupt to be occurred.

- The code lines between 30 and 31 are the codes for the PD3 ISR or the GPIO Port D interrupt handler. First the bit 3 on the GPIO Port D Interrupt Clear Register (ICR) is set to 1 to clear the rising-edge triggered interrupt on PD3 pin, and then the four LEDs on the EduBASE Trainer are toggled with a number 15. The purpose of using this toggle action is to turn on four LEDs when the interrupt is accepted and handled in the odd time, and turn off four LEDs when the interrupt is accepted and handled in the even time. One point is that you have to use the decimal number (15) to replace the hexadecimal number (0xF) to do this toggle action, otherwise your program may not work properly.

Now you can compile, download, and run the program to test the interrupt function as the project runs. Make sure that the debugger in the Debug tab under the Project| Options for Target 'Target 1' is Stellaris ICDI before you compile your project.

As the project runs, press the position switch SW2, and all four LEDs on the EduBASE Trainer should be ON, and they should be OFF when you pressed that position switch SW2 again in the second time.

5.4.4 Using TivaWare™ Peripheral Driver Library API Functions to Handle GPIO Interrupts

In the TM4C123GH6PM MCU system, the TivaWare™ Peripheral Driver Library provides all API interfacing control functions for all peripherals used in the system. However, for the GPIO system, it provides two sets of Interrupt Controller API functions; The NVIC Interrupt Control API functions and the GPIO Interrupt Control API functions to support users to access most NVIC control and GPIO port registers to perform configuration, setup, and control functions to all interrupts used in the GPIO Ports system.

The TivaWare™ Peripheral Driver Library provides all API functions for the most popular and the most often used peripherals, including the internal and external peripherals, as we discussed in Section 4.5.7.3 in Chapter 4. In this section we try to use the GPIO interrupt mechanism as an example to illustrate how to call these API functions to perform and handle GPIO-related interrupts.

We have also provided detailed discussions about the System Control and GPIO API functions in Sections 4.5.7.3.1 and 4.5.7.3.2 in Chapter 4. In the following sections, we will concentrate on the NVIC and GPIO interrupt-related API functions in details since we need to use these API functions to develop a sample project to illustrate how to access related registers to initialize and configure them to perform our desired interrupt control functions.

Since both NVIC and GPIO interrupt-related API functions will be used in our project, we need to discuss both of them. First let's take a look at the NVIC API functions.

5.4.4.1 NVIC API Functions Defined in the TivaWare™ Peripheral Driver Library

As we mentioned, the TivaWare™ software package supports up to 154 interrupt sources with 8 priority levels. Each maskable interrupt can be masked or disabled, enabled, or pending for the further being processed. The NVIC integrated in the TM4C123GH6PM MCU also supports the group priority and sub-priority configurations.

Table 5.4 in Section 5.2.2 shows a complete set of NVIC API functions provided by the Peripheral Driver Library and used in the TM4C123GH6PM MCU system. Table 5.21 shows most popular NVIC API functions to be used in general interrupt control functions.

The NVIC is closely coupled with the Cortex-M4 microprocessor. When the processor accepts and responds to an interrupt, the NVIC provides the address of the Interrupt Service Routine (ISR) to handle the interrupt directly to the processor. This action eliminates the need for a global interrupt handler that queries the interrupt controller to determine the source of the interrupt and branch to the appropriate handler, reducing interrupt response time.

As we mentioned in Section 5.2.2, the interrupt handler or the entry address of the ISR can be configured or modified in two ways, either statically or dynamically. The API function `IntEnable()` must be used to enable the processor to know the existence of

Table 5.21. The most popular NVIC API functions used in the TM4C123GH6PM MCU system.

API Function	Description
void IntEnable(uint32_t ui32Interrupt)	Enable an interrupt
void IntDisable(uint32_t ui32Interrupt)	Disable an interrupt
uint32_t IntIsEnabled(uint32_t ui32Interrupt)	Check if an interrupt has been enabled. Returning a nonzero indicates that the interrupt is enabled
bool IntMasterEnable(uint32_t ui32Interrupt)	Enable processor to receive any interrupt. Returning a True means that all interrupts are enabled
bool IntMasterDisable(uint32_t ui32Interrupt)	Prevent processor from receiving any interrupt. Returning a True means that all interrupts are disabled
void IntPendClear(uint32_t ui32Interrupt)	Clear a specified pending interrupt
void IntPendSet(uint32_t ui32Interrupt)	Set a specified interrupt to be pending status
int32_t IntPriorityGet(uint32_t ui32Interrupt)	Get the priority level for a specified interrupt
void IntPrioritySet(uint32_t ui32Interrupt, uint8_t ui8Priority)	Set the priority level for a specified interrupt
void IntPriorityMaskSet(uint32_t ui32PriorityMask)	Set the current priority masking level
void IntRegister(uint32_t ui32Interrupt, void (*pfnHandler)(void))	Register an interrupt handler
void IntTrigger(uint32_t ui32Interrupt)	Trigger a specified interrupt

the interrupt handler when an interrupt handler is statically configured. Similarly, the API function `IntRegister()` must be applied to enable the processor to response to the interrupt when the interrupt is dynamically configured.

The so-called static configuration is to modify the handler's name before the project can be compiled. This modification includes the editing or changing of the interrupt handler's name in both the system startup file, such as `Startup_TM4C123.s`, and the user's program, and both names must be identical.

The so-called dynamic configuration is to change the handler's name after the user's project runs. The API function `IntRegister()` is used to enable this changing to be acknowledged by the processor, and furthermore it can be accepted and responded.

Each interrupt can be locally enabled or disabled by using the `IntEnable()` and `IntDisable()` API function. However, to allow the processor to know and respond to each interrupt, two special registers, PRIMASK and BASEPRI, must be globally configured by using another pair of API functions, `IntMasterEnable()` and `IntMasterDisable()`, to enable or disable the CPU to respond to each interrupt.

Let's have a closer look at these NVIC API functions.

- The enable state of each interrupt source can be checked by using the API function `IntIsEnabled()`. This function returns a nonzero value if the tested interrupt source has been enabled.

- Each interrupt source can be set up with a certain priority level with an `IntPrioritySet()` API function. In TM4C123GH6PM MCU system, only the upper 3 bits for each 8-bit segment is used to configure the priority levels for all interrupts. The smaller the priority number, the higher the priority level is. Priority 0 is the highest and priority 7 is the lowest level.

- The priority level setup for each interrupt source can be retrieved back by using the API function `IntPriorityGet()`. A -1 would be returned if the checked interrupt is not existed.

- Each interrupt source can be dynamically configured via the API function `IntRegister()`. This means that an interrupt handler can be modified when the project runs. The function of the `IntRegister()` is to move the vector table from the flash memory to the SRAM space to enable this modification to be occurred. A point to be noted is that you need to make sure that the vector table is moved and located at the beginning of the SRAM space when linking your project with other system libraries and files.

- The API function `IntTrigger()` is used to create and trigger a Software Interrupt to the system. This function is similar to generating a hardware interrupt.

Next we need to build a sample project to illustrate how to use these functions to configure, generate, and process a GPIO interrupt.

5.4.4.2 GPIO Interrupt-Related API Functions in the TivaWare™ Peripheral Driver Library

In this section we will introduce and discuss some GPIO Interrupt-related API functions. These functions are very important and useful for processing of the GPIO-related interrupts. Because these API functions are specially used for the GPIO interrupts, they are not included in those GPIO API functions we discussed in Section 4.5.7.3.2 in Chapter 4.

Table 5.22 lists the most popular and the most often used GPIO interrupt-related API functions.

For all of these functions, the meanings of used arguments are:

- `uint32_t ui32Port`: Indicate the GPIO Port to be accessed. Generally this is the base address of the port and can be expressed by using the macro GPIO_PORTA_BASE (for GPIO Port A) in the program.
- `uint32_t ui32IntFlag(s)`: Indicate the bit mask or the pin number(s) to be accessed. For multiple pins, the OR operator can be used to make them work. Generally this or these bit masks can be expressed by using the macro GPIO_PIN_0 (GPIO_INT_PIN_0), GPIO_PIN_1 (GPIO_INT_PIN_1), or GPIO_PIN_7 (GPIO_INT_PIN_7).

Table 5.22. The most popular GPIO interrupt-related API functions.

GPIO Interrupt Related API Function	Description
void GPIOIntEnable(uint32_t ui32Port, uint32_t ui32IntFlag)	Enable an interrupt. ui32Port is the port to be enabled, and ui32IntFlag is the bit-mask, such as GPIO_PIN_0.
void GPIOIntDisable(uint32_t ui32Port, uint32_t ui32IntFlag)	Disable an interrupt. ui32Port is the port to be disabled, and ui32IntFlag is the bit-mask, such as GPIO_PIN_0.
void GPIOIntClear(uint32_t ui32Port, uint32_t ui32IntFlags)	Clear an interrupt source. ui32Port is the port to be cleared and ui32IntFlag is the bit-mask or the pin to be cleared, such as GPIO_PIN_3.
void GPIOIntRegister(uint32_t ui32Port, void (*pfnIntHandler)(void))	Register an interrupt with its handler. ui32Port is the port to be registered and pFnIntHandler is the name of the interrupt handler.
uint32_t GPIOIntStatus(uint32_t ui32Port, bool bMasked)	Get the interrupt status for a port. The bMasked is used to specify whether the masked (true) or raw (false) interrupt status is returned.
uint32_t GPIOIntTypeGet(uint32_t ui32Port, uint8_t ui8Pin)	Get the interrupt type for a pin. The ui8Pin is the pin number. Interrupt types are: levels or edges triggered.
void GPIOIntTypeSet(uint32_t ui32Port, uint8_t ui8Pins, uint32_t ui32IntType)	Set the interrupt type for a pin. The ui32IntType includes: GPIO_FALLING_EDGE, GPIO_RISING_EDGE, GPIO_BOTH_EDGES, GPIO_LOW_LEVEL, GPIO_HIGH_LEVEL
void GPIOIntUnregister(uint32_t ui32Port)	Removes an interrupt handler for a GPIO port

- `uint8_t ui8Pin`: Indicate the pin number. The same macros used for the ui32IntFlag can also be used for this argument.

Some points should be noted when using these GPIO interrupt-related API functions to handle GPIO-related interrupts in your program:

1. The `GPIOIntRegister()` function is a very important function and must be used in your program to enable the processor to know the interrupt and its handler. By default, the processor should know the interrupt and its handler if you used the default vector located in the vector table in the startup file. However, you must explicitly indicate this by using this function in your program when you are using the API functions provided by the Tiva™ Peripheral Driver Library. Otherwise your program may not work properly.

2. Two types of GPIO interrupt-related API functions, Interrupt Master Enable and Interrupt Priority Setup, are not provided by these GPIO interrupt-related API functions. Therefore you must use two NVIC API functions, `IntMasterEnable()` and `IntPrioritySet()`, to perform these configuration jobs in your program.

3. One of the key functions, to set up the interrupt type for a GPIO pin, has no any mapping function available in the NVIC API function set. You have to use the `GPIOIntTypeSet()` function to do this job in your program.

After finishing these API functions introduction and discussion, now we are ready to develop and build our sample project to use API functions to handle some GPIO-related interrupts.

5.4.4.3 Building Sample Project to Use Peripheral Driver Library to Handle Interrupts

In this section, we still use a sample project to illustrate how to use the API functions provided by the TivaWare™ Peripheral Driver Library to handle a GPIO interrupt.

We want to develop an example project named `SDInt` to use GPIO and NVIC API functions provided by the TivaWare™ Peripheral Driver Library to handle a falling edge detected interrupt at pin PD0 at the GPIO Port D since this pin is connected to a position switch SW5 in the EduBASE Trainer.

Refer to Figure 5.11 to get details about the hardware configuration for this connection. As the SW5 switch is pressed as the project is running, a falling edge interrupt occurs at PD0, and four LEDs (PB0~PB3) installed in the EduBASE Trainer and a three-color LED installed in the Tiva™ LaunchPad™ TM4C123GXL EVB (see Figure 4.27) will be toggled in this interrupt handler.

The coding for this project is divided into eight parts:

1. Using System Control API function `SysCtlPeripheralEnable()` to clock and enable GPIO Ports B, D, and F.

2. Using GPIO API functions to configure and initialize GPIO Port B to enable the lower 4 bits on Port B (PB3~PB0) as output pins since they are connected to 4 LEDs PB0~PB3 in the ARM® EduBASE Trainer.

3. Using GPIO API functions to configure and initialize GPIO Port F to enable bits 3, 2, and 1 (PF3, PF2, and PF1) on Port F as output pins since they are connected to a three-color LED on the TM4C123GXL EVB (see Figure 4.27).

4. Using GPIO API functions to configure and initialize GPIO Ports D to enable PD0 on Port D as an input pin since it is connected to a position switch SW5 in the Trainer.

5. Using GPIO API functions to initialize pin PD0 on the GPIO Port D as a falling-edge-detected interrupt source. This initialization process includes the priority level setup using the NVIC API function and port enable functions.

6. Using GPIO Interrupt-related API function `GPIOIntRegister()` to register the interrupt handler to enable the processor to know this handler.

7. Using NVIC API functions to globally enable all interrupts in the system.

8. Developing the codes for the interrupt handler to respond to the PD0 interrupt to toggle 4 LEDs in the Trainer and a three-color LED in the TM4C123GXL EVB. The PD0 interrupt flag should also be cleared in this interrupt handler.

Now let's start our sample project developing process.

5.4.4.4 *Create a New Project SDInt and Add the C Code File*

Refer to Sections 4.5.7.2.5.1 and 4.5.7.2.5.2 in Chapter 4 to create a new µVersion5 project named SDInt. Because this project is simple, no header file is needed.

Refer to Section 4.5.7.2.5.3 in Chapter 4 to create a new C File named SDInt.c and add it into the project SDInt. Enter the codes shown in Figure 5.24 into this file.

Let's have a closer look at this file to see how it works.

- Some system header files, such as `<stdint.h>`, `<stdbool.h>` and "tm4c123gh6pm.h," are declared first to enable the compiler to know most integer and Boolean data types used in this project. All GPIO Ports and all CMSIS Core macros of the NVIC Interrupt Control Registers are defined in the eighth header file, and we need to use them to initialize and configure system clock and enable GPIO Ports B, D, and F. The header files between lines 6 and 10 include all definitions for memory mapping addresses for peripherals, system control macros, GPIO macros, and GPIO interrupt-related macros.

- In line 12, the interrupt handler for Port D is declared. This declaration is necessary since we need to use `GPIOIntRegister()` to register this handler in line 22. Therefore we need to enable the compiler to know this handler before we can register it.

- The main program starts at line 13.

- The system clock is generated in line 15 with the clock setting parameters as follows: the PLL is used with a user divider of 10, and the main oscillator is adopted with the 16 MHz crystal as the clock source. The system clock used for this project is 400 MHz/10/2 = 20 MHz.

- The code lines between 16 and 18 are used to set up the clock for three GPIO Ports, Ports B, D, and F, and enable these ports. Refer to Section 4.5.7.3.1 in Chapter 4 to get more details about this System Control API function.

- Two GPIO API functions, `GPIOPinTypeGPIOOutput()` and `GPIOPinTypeG-PIOInput()`, are used in lines 19~21 to configure PF3, PF2, and PF1 as output pins, PB3–PB0 as output pins, and PD0 as an input pin. Since PF3~PF1 are connected to a three-color LED in the TM4C123GXL EVB and PB3~PB0 are connected to four LEDs in the EduBASE Trainer, PD0 is connected to a position switch SW5 in the EduBASE Trainer.

- In line 22, a GPIO interrupt-related API function `GPIOIntRegister()` is called to register the interrupt handler used for the GPIO PD0 falling-edge-detected interrupt, and

```
1    //*********************************************************************************************************
2    // SDInt.c - Application file
3    //*********************************************************************************************************
4    #include <stdint.h>
5    #include <stdbool.h>
6    #include "inc/hw_memmap.h"
7    #include "inc/hw_types.h"
8    #include "driverlib/sysctl.h"
9    #include "driverlib/gpio.h"
10   #include "driverlib/interrupt.h"
11   #include "inc/tm4c123gh6pm.h"
12   void GPIOD_Handler(void);
13   int main(void)
14   {
15       SysCtlClockSet(SYSCTL_SYSDIV_10|SYSCTL_USE_PLL|SYSCTL_OSC_MAIN|SYSCTL_XTAL_16MHZ);
16       SysCtlPeripheralEnable(SYSCTL_PERIPH_GPIOB);
17       SysCtlPeripheralEnable(SYSCTL_PERIPH_GPIOD);
18       SysCtlPeripheralEnable(SYSCTL_PERIPH_GPIOF);
19       GPIOPinTypeGPIOOutput(GPIO_PORTF_BASE, GPIO_PIN_3|GPIO_PIN_2|GPIO_PIN_1);
20       GPIOPinTypeGPIOOutput(GPIO_PORTB_BAS  E, GPIO_PIN_3|GPIO_PIN_2|GPIO_PIN_1|GPIO_PIN_0);
21       GPIOPinTypeGPIOInput(GPIO_PORTD_BASE, GPIO_PIN_0);
22       GPIOIntRegister(GPIO_PORTD_BASE, GPIOD_Handler);
23       IntPrioritySet(INT_GPIOD, 0x60);
24       GPIOIntTypeSet(GPIO_PORTD_BASE, GPIO_PIN_0, GPIO_FALLING_EDGE);
25       GPIOIntEnable(GPIO_PORTD_BASE, GPIO_INT_PIN_0);
26       IntMasterEnable();
27       while(1)                                           // wait for interrupt
28       {
29           __wfi();
30       }
31   }
32   void GPIOD_Handler(void)                               // interrupt handler
33   {
34       GPIOIntClear(GPIO_PORTD_BASE, GPIO_INT_PIN_0);
35       if(GPIOPinRead(GPIO_PORTF_BASE, GPIO_PIN_1))       // toggle LEDs
36       {
37           GPIOPinWrite(GPIO_PORTF_BASE, GPIO_PIN_3|GPIO_PIN_2|GPIO_PIN_1, 0);
38           GPIOPinWrite(GPIO_PORTB_BASE, GPIO_PIN_3|GPIO_PIN_2|GPIO_PIN_1|GPIO_PIN_0, 0);
39       }
40       else
41       {
42           GPIOPinWrite(GPIO_PORTF_BASE, GPIO_PIN_3|GPIO_PIN_2|GPIO_PIN_1, 0xE);
43           GPIOPinWrite(GPIO_PORTB_BASE, GPIO_PIN_3|GPIO_PIN_2|GPIO_PIN_1|GPIO_PIN_0, 0xF);
44       }
     }
```

Figure 5.24.   The detailed codes for the SDInt.c file.

this interrupt occurs as the position switch SW5 is released (a falling edge is detected). This step is very important, and your program may not work if you missed it.

- A NVIC API function `IntPrioritySet()` is executed to set up the priority level for the Port D to 6. As you know, the priority levels in the TM4C123GH6PM system have a range of 0~7 for each port.

- In line 24, a GPIO interrupt-related API function `GPIOIntTypeSet()` is executed to configure the interrupt type for PD0.

- The falling-edge-detective interrupt at PD0 is also enabled in line 25 by calling a GPIO-interrupt related API function `GPIOIntEnable()`. The point to be noted is that the macro GPIO_INT_PIN_0 is identical to the macro GPIO_PIN_0, both indicate the pin0.

- The processor interrupt is globally enabled in line 26 by calling a NVIC API function `IntMasterEnable()`.
- The code lines between 27 and 30 include an infinitive `while()` loop and an intrinsic function `__wfi()` – wait `for` interrupt to wait for any interrupt to occur.
- The interrupt handler is coded between lines 32 and 44.
- First, a GPIO interrupt-related API function `GPIOIntClear()` is called in line 34 to clear any previous interrupt that occurred at PD0 to enable the future interrupt to occur at this pin. This clear operation is very important and your program may not work properly if you missed this operation because the future interrupt cannot occur if you did not clear this flag, and this would block any future interrupt to occur.
- The code lines between 35 and 43 are used to perform a toggle operation for all LEDs installed in both TM4C123GXL EVB and EduBASE Trainer. An `if` statement is used to check one LED status (PF1), either ON or OFF, during the last entry to this handler. If it is ON (`GPIOPinRead()` ≠0), turn off all LEDs via a GPIO API function `GPIOPinWrite()` by assigning all pins to 0. Otherwise turn on all LEDs via the same API function by assigning `0xE` (1110B) to Port F and `0xF` (1111B) to Port B, respectively.

Now we can compile, link, download, and run this project to test the interrupt function. However, before we can do that, we need to configure the environments to enable our project to be compiled and linked correctly. Two jobs are related to these configurations: (1) Set up the include path for all system header files used in the project, and (2) select the correct debugger to download and run the project.

5.4.4.5 *Configuring the Environments and Run the Project*

Perform the following operations to include all system header files into our project:

1. When the project is open, go to `Project| Options for Target 'Target 1'` menu item to open the Options wizard.
2. Then click on the `C/C++` tab and go to the `Include Paths` box.
3. Click on the three-dot button on the right of this box to open the **Folder Setup** wizard.
4. Click on the `New (Insert)` tool to open a new textbox. Click on the three-dot button on the right to browse to the location where these header files are located, which is `C:\ti\Tiva-Ware_C_Series-2.0.1.11577`. Then click on the **OK** button to select this location.
5. Click on the **OK** button to close this wizard.

Refer to Section 4.5.7.3.3.4 in Chapter 4 to get more details for this operation. Perform the following operation to select the correct debugger for this project:

1. Go to `Project|Options for Target 'Target 1'` menu item to open the Options wizard.
2. On the opened Options wizard, click on the `Debug` tab.
3. Make sure that the debugger shown in the `Use:` box is `Stellaris ICDI`. Otherwise you can click on the dropdown arrow to select this debugger from the list.

Now you can compile, download, and run the project to test the interrupt function.

As the project runs, press the position switch SW5, and you can find that all LEDs in the EduBASE Trainer and one three-color LED in the TM4C123GXL EVB are on. But they are all off when pressing SW5 in the second time. Again and again pressing this switch, you can find that our project responded to each interrupt with no problem.

Next let's take care of the interrupt response with the CMSIS Core functions.

5.4.5 Using CMSIS Core Access Functions to Handle GPIO Interrupts

Like the TivaWare™ Peripheral Driver Library, the CMSIS Core also provides a set of interrupt API functions to map to the related NVIC registers to perform interrupt configurations and controls for peripherals used in the TM4C123GH6PM MCU system. In the previous section we introduced the interrupt API functions provided by the TivaWare™ Peripheral Driver Library. In this section we will discuss another set of interrupt API functions provided by the CMSIS Core.

We have provided a detailed discussion about the CMSIS Core functions used to access NVIC Interrupt Control Registers to perform interrupt configurations and controls for peripherals in Section 5.2.2. Table 5.23 lists the most popular and the most often used CMSIS Core functions used for interrupt controls and configurations in the TM4C123GH6PM MCU system.

It can be found from Table 5.23 that only a limited number of functions are provided by the CMSIS Core, and some other useful functions, such as setting up the priority for a specified pin, clearing an interrupt for a pin and configuring the interrupt type for a pin, are not provided by this Core package. Therefore we cannot use these pure CMSIS Core functions to build our sample interrupt control project; instead, we need to use a combined set of functions, which include both CMSIS Core functions for NVIC registers and GPIO macros defined for GPIO registers, to develop our sample project to illustrate how to use the CMSIS Core functions defined for NVIC registers to process and handle a GPIO interrupt.

In order to use these CMSIS Core functions for NVIC registers and GPIO structures to access and configure related NVIC and GPIO registers, we first need to have a clear picture about header files we should use in this project.

- To use CMSIS Core functions for NVIC registers, we need to use the header file, core_cm4.h, since this header file contains all definitions for NVIC interrupt API functions listed in Table 5.23. This header file is provided by the CMSIS Core Software Package.

- To use System Control and GPIO registers with their structure definitions, we need to use the header file, TM4C123GH6PM.h, since this header file provides all structure definitions for System Controls (SYSCTL_Type) and GPIO Ports (GPIOA_Type). This header file is provided by the TivaWare™ Software Package.

Table 5.23. The most popular CMSIS Core functions used for interrupt controls.

NVIC Register	CMSIS Core Function	Description
Interrupt Set Enable Registers	void **NVIC_EnableIRQ**(IRQn_Type IRQn)	Enable an external interrupt
Interrupt Clear Enable Registers	void **NVIC_DisableIRQ**(IRQn_Type IRQn)	Disable an external interrupt
Interrupt Set Pending Registers	void **NVIC_SetPendingIRQ**(IRQn_Type IRQn)	Set the pending status for an interrupt
Interrupt Clear Pending Registers	void **NVIC_ClearPendingIRQ**(IRQn_Type IRQn)	Clear pending status for an interrupt
Interrupt Active Bits Registers	uint32_t **NVIC_GetActive**(IRQn_Type IRQn)	Get the active status for an interrupt
Interrupt Set Priority Register	void **NVIC_SetPriority**(IRQn_Type IRQn, uint32_t Priority)	Set the priority for an interrupt
Interrupt Get Priority Register	uint32_t **NVIC_GetPriority**(IRQn_Type IRQn)	Get the priority for an interrupt
Global enable an interrupt	void **__enable_irq**(void)	Clear PRIMASK to enable all interrupts
Global disable an interrupt	void **__disable_irq**(void)	Set PRIMASK to disable all interrupts

As we discussed in Section 5.4.1.1.1, the TivaWare™ Software Package provides two kinds of header files to support the TM4C123GH6PM MCU system: (1) the Register Driver Definitions header file tm4c123gh6pm.h and (2) the CMSIS Cortex-M4 Peripheral Hardware Layer header file TM4C123GH6PM.h. To make it clear, we will use the second header file TM4C123GH6PM.h in this section to build our project.

5.4.5.1 Building Sample Project to Use CMSIS Core Functions to Handle Interrupts

In this section we will use a sample project to illustrate how to use the CMSIS Core NVIC functions provided by the CMSIS Core Software Package to handle a GPIO interrupt.

We want to develop an example project named CMSISInt to use GPIO and NVIC API functions to handle a rising edge detected interrupt at pin PD0 at the GPIO Port D since this pin is connected to a position switch SW5 in the EduBASE Trainer.

Refer to Figure 5.11 to get details about the hardware configuration for this connection. As the SW5 switch is pressed as the project is running, a rising edge interrupt occurs at PD0, and four LEDs (PB0~PB3) installed in the EduBASE Trainer and a three-color LED installed in the Tiva™ LaunchPad™ TM4C123GXL EVB (see Figure 4.27) will be toggled in this interrupt handler.

The coding for this project is divided into seven steps:

1. Use System Control structure pointer to clock and enable GPIO Ports B, D and F.
2. Use a GPIO structure pointer to configure and initialize GPIO Port B to enable the lower 4 bits on Port B (PB3~PB0) as output pins since they are connected to four LEDs, PB0~PB3, in the ARM® EduBASE Trainer.
3. Use a GPIO structure pointer to configure and initialize GPIO Port F to enable bits 3, 2, and 1 (PF3, PF2, and PF1) on Port F as output pins since they are connected to a three-color LED on the TM4C123GXL EVB (see Figure 4.27).
4. Use a GPIO structure pointer to configure and initialize GPIO Ports D to enable PD0 on Port D as an input pin since it is connected to a position switch SW5 in the Trainer.
5. Use a GPIO structure pointer to initialize pin PD0 on the GPIO Port D as a rising-edge-detected interrupt source.
6. Use a CMSIS Core functions for NVIC to set up the priority level (3) for GPIO Port D and enable its interrupt source.
7. Develop the codes for the interrupt handler to respod to the PD0 interrupt to toggle four LEDs in the Trainer and a three-color LED in the TM4C123GXL EVB. The PD0 interrupt flag should also be cleared in this interrupt handler.

Now let's start our sample project developing process.

5.4.5.2 Create a New Project CMSISInt and Add the C Code File

Refer to Sections 4.5.7.2.5.1 and 4.5.7.2.5.2 in Chapter 4 to create a new µVersion5 project named CMSISInt. Because this project is simple, no header file is needed.

Refer to Section 4.5.7.2.5.3 in Chapter 4 to create a new C File named CMSISInt.c and add it into the project CMSISInt. Enter the codes shown in Figure 5.25 into this file.

```
1   //*************************************************************************************************
2   // CMSISInt.c - Application file
3   //*************************************************************************************************
4   #include <stdint.h>
5   #include <stdbool.h>
6   #include "TM4C123GH6PM.h"
7   int main(void)
8   {
9     SYSCTL->RCGCGPIO |= 0x08;                    // enable clock to PORTD
10    SYSCTL->RCGCGPIO |= 0x02;                    // enable clock to PORTB
11    SYSCTL->RCGCGPIO |= 0x20;                    // enable clock to PORTF
12    GPIOB->DIR |= 0x0F;                          // set PB0 ~ PB3 as out put pins
13    GPIOB->DEN |= 0x0F;                          // enable PB0 ~ PB3 as digital function
14    GPIOF->DIR |= 0xE;                           // set PF3 ~ PF1 as output pins
15    GPIOF->DEN |= 0xF;                           // enable PF3 ~ PF0 as digital function
16    GPIOD->DIR |= 0x0;                           // set PD0 as an input pin
17    GPIOD->DEN |= 0x1;                           // enable PD0 as digital function
18    GPIOD->IS  &= ~0x1;                          // make bit PD0 as an edge sensitive
19    GPIOD->IBE &= ~0x1;                          // trigger is controlled by IEV
20    GPIOD->IEV |= 0x1;                           // rising edge trigger
21    GPIOD->ICR |= 0x1;                           // clear any prior interrupt
22    GPIOD->IM  |= 0x1;                           // unmask interrupt
23    NVIC_SetPriority(GPIOD_IRQn, 0x60);          // set PORTD priority level as 3
24    NVIC_EnableIRQ(GPIOD_IRQn);                  // enable PORTD to generate interrupt
25    __enable_irq();                             // globally enable interrupt
26    while(1)                                     // wait for interrupt
27    {
28    }
29  }
30  void GPIOD_Handler(void)                       // PD0 interrupt handler
31  {
32    if ((NVIC_GetActive(GPIOD_IRQn)) == 1)      // check whether PD0 interrupt flag is set
33    {
34        GPIOD->ICR |= 0x01;                      // if it is, clear any interrupt flag
35    }
36    GPIOB->DATA ^= 15;                           // toggle 4 LEDs PB0 ~ PB3 in Trainer
37    GPIOF->DATA ^= 14;                           // toggle a 3-color LED in TM4C123GXL EVB
    }
```

Figure 5.25.   The detailed codes for the CMSISInt.c file.

Let's have a closer look at this file to see how it works.

- Some system header files, such as <stdint.h>, <stdbool.h> and "TM4C123GH6PM.h," are declared first to enable the compiler to know most integer and Boolean data types used in this project. All System Controls and GPIO Port structure pointers are defined in the third header file, and we need to use them to initialize and configure the system clock and enable GPIO Ports B, D, and F. The header file core_cm4.h that contains all definitions for CMSIS Core functions for NVIC is provided by the CMSIS Core Software Package, and it has been included in this project as the CMSIS Core tool is selected when you create this project CMSISInt.

- The main program starts at line 7.

- The code lines between 9 and 11 are used to set up the clock for three GPIO Ports, Ports B, D, and F, and enable these ports. Since the System Control structure pointer defined in the header file TM4C123GH6PM.h is used, the pointer operator → is applied to assign the related port's value to each bit in the RCGCGPIO register.

- Three GPIO Ports, B, D, and F, are initialized and configured in lines 12~17 to set up PF3~PF1 as output pins, PB3~PB0 as output pins, and PD0 as an input pin. PF3~PF1 are connected to a three-color LED in the TM4C123GXL EVB, PB3~PB0 are connected to four LEDs in the EduBASE Trainer, and PD0 is connected to a position switch SW5 in the EduBASE Trainer.

- The code lines between 18 and 22 are used to configure PD0 as a rising-edge-detective interrupt pin. Any previous interrupt flag is cleared by setting ICR to 1. Since the GPIO Port structure pointer is used, a pointer operator → is applied to all related bits in the GPIO interrupt-related registers.

- A CMSIS Core function NVIC_SetPriority() is executed in line 23 to set up the priority level for the Port D to 3. As you know, the priority levels in the TM4C123GH6PM system are in the range 0~7 for each port. The passed argument of this function is the IRQn_Type, GPIOD_IRQn.

- In line 24, another CMSIS Core function NVIC_EnableIRQ() is called to enable a rising-edge-detective interrupt for the PortD.

- The processor interrupt is globally enabled in line 25 by calling an intrinsic function __enable_irq().

- The code lines between 25 and 28 include an infinitive while() loop to wait for any interrupt to occur.

- The interrupt handler is coded between lines 30 and 37.

- First, a CMSIS Core for NVIC function NVIC_GetActive() is called in line 32 to check whether an interrupt has occurred and an interrupt flag has been set. If this function call returns 1, which means that an interrupt flag has been set, the Interrupt Clear Register (ICR) on the Port D is set to 1 to clear this flag to enable any further interrupt to occur in line 34.

- The code lines between 36 and 37 are used to perform a toggle operation for all LEDs installed in both TM4C123GXL EVB and EduBASE Trainer.

Now we can compile, link, download, and run this project to test the interrupt function. However, before we can do that, we need to configure the environments to enable our project to be compiled and linked correctly. Two jobs are related to these configurations: (1) Set up the include path for all system header files used in the project, and (2) select the correct debugger to download and run the project.

5.4.5.3 Configure the Environments and Run the Project

Since we used the header file TM4C123GH6PM.h, we need to include it into our project. This file is in the folder: C:\Keil_v5\ARM\Pack\Keil\TM4C_DFP\1.0.0 \Device\Include\TM4C123 in your host computer. Although this header file belongs to the TivaWare™ Software Package, it is installed in the Keil_v5\ARM \Pack folder since it is related to the CMSIS Core package.

Perform the following operations to include this header file into our project:

1. When the project is open, go to the Project|Options for Target 'Target 1' menu item to open the Options wizard.

2. Then click on the C/C++ tab and go to the Include Paths box.

3. Click on the three-dot button on the right of this box to open the **Folder Setup** wizard.

4. Click on the New (Insert) tool to open a new textbox. Click on the three-dot button on the right to browse to the folder where the header file TM4C123GH6PM.h is located, which is

`C:\Keil_v5\ARM\Pack\Keil\TM4C_DFP\1.0.0\Device\Include\TM4C123.`
Then click on the **OK** button to select this location.

5. Click on the **OK** button to close this wizard.

Refer to Section 4.5.7.3.3.4 in Chapter 4 to get more details for this operation. Perform the following operation to select the correct debugger for this project:

1. Go to `Project|Options for Target` 'Target 1' menu item to open the Options wizard.

2. On the opened Options wizard, click on the `Debug` tab.

3. Make sure that the debugger shown in the `Use:` box is `Stellaris ICDI`. Otherwise you can click on the dropdown arrow to select this debugger from the list.

Now you can compile, download, and run the project to test the interrupt function.

As the project runs, press the position switch SW5, and you can find that all LEDs in the EduBASE Trainer and one three-color LED in the TM4C123GXL EVB are on. But they are all off when pressing SW5 in the second time. Again and again pressing this switch, you can find that our project responded to each interrupt with no problem.

5.5 COMPARISON AMONG FOUR INTERRUPT PROGRAMMING METHODS

By developing and building our sample interrupt projects with four different methods as we did in the last sections, we can compare these methods to get some conclusions as listed below:

1. Comparably speaking, the Direct Register Access (DRA) methods look better in the coding process and interrupt configuration and handling process. Relatively speaking, the project `NVICInt` developed by using the CMSIS Core functions for the NVIC method is a little better than the project `GPIOInt` built by using the GPIO Interrupt-related registers method since the NVIC and GPIO structure pointers are used in the first method.

2. Another two projects, `SDInt` and `CMSISInt`, developed by using the Software Driver method, have a little longer codes with more coding process. In particular the project SDInt that is built by using the API functions provided by TivaWare™ Peripheral Driver Library involves a lot of function calls and make the project codes much longer compared with the coding process in the other three methods.

3. Summarily, the advantage of using the DRA method to develop interrupt projects is that the project coding process is easier with less code lines. However, the developers must have good understanding and knowledge about the details of the Cortex-M4 MCU and peripheral devices as well as all related registers and the NVIC interrupt mechanism.

4. The advantage of using the SD method to build interrupt projects is that most API functions in the TivaWare™ Peripheral Driver Library and in the CMSIS Core package provide a good path and an easy way to facilitate the coding and development process for the users, and the users do not need solid understanding about the microcontroller hardware and interrupt processing mechanism to build a professional interrupt application.

Developers can use any method to build their interrupt-related project, and this depends on the requirements of real applications and developing environments.

5.6 CHAPTER SUMMARY

This chapter concentrates mainly on exceptions and interrupts that belong to the ARM® Cortex®-M4 MCU system. All exceptions and interrupts related to the ARM® Cortex®-M4 processor are introduced, but only interrupts are discussed in detail in this chapter since most exceptions belong to system faults or errors, and they should be processed and handled by the system itself.

First an overview and introduction about the general interrupts are given with a function block diagram of a most popular interrupt processing procedure. Then the exceptions and interrupts involved in the ARM® Cortex®-M4 MCU system is introduced. These discussions include the following basic interrupt elements:

- Interrupt sources
- Interrupt masks
- Interrupt priorities
- Interrupt vector table
- Interrupt handler or ISR

Then the fundamental interrupt processing procedure for the ARM® Cortex®-M4 processor is provided, which includes the following:

- Interrupt request is established
- Interrupt is accepted or pended
- Interrupt is responded
- Interrupt is processed

Popular interrupt processing API functions provided by two software packages, the TivaWare™ Software Package and the CMSIS Core Software Package, are introduced and discussed in detail. These discussions include the API function protocols, syntax, operational principle, and possible running results. The main interrupt control unit, Nested Vectored Interrupt Controller (NVIC), is also introduced in detail.

Following these basic introductions and discussions, all exceptions and interrupts related to the TM4C123GH6PM MCU system is provided. The peripheral GPIO is used as an example to illustrate how to generate, respond, and process interrupts coming from any GPIO Port.

Two major interrupt processing modes and functions provided by the TivaWare™ Peripheral Driver Library and the CMSIS Core package, are discussed and analyzed with some examples. Both the TivaWare™ library and the CMSIS Core package provide a set of API functions to map NVIC-related registers to facilitate the interrupt configuration and processing.

Four types of interrupt processing methods are introduced with that four actual example projects, and these methods include the following:

1. Use the Direct Register Access (DRA) model to configure GPIO Port and pins to accept and handle a related interrupt that occurred on the desired pins with the selected GPIO Port.
2. Use CMSIS Core macros defined for NVIC Interrupt Control Registers to configure and handle interrupts that occurred on the desired pins with the selected GPIO Ports.
3. Use the TivaWare™ Peripheral Driver Library API functions to configure and handle interrupts that occurred on desired pins on the selected GPIO Ports.

4. Use CMSIS Core functions to configure and handle interrupts that occurred on the desired pins with the selected GPIO Ports.

The detailed discussions, line-by-line explanations, and illustrations for each project are given to help readers to understand the purpose and function of each coding line. When finishing this chapter, the readers should be able to develop and build general interrupt projects to handle most GPIO-related interrupts with different methods.

HOMEWORK

I. *True/False Selections*

_____**1.** An exception is often generated by an event, such as the system fault event and other system mis-operation event. An interrupt is generally created by an internal or an external peripheral with lower priority level.

_____**2.** The Reset belongs to an exception and has the highest priority level in the ARM® Cortex®-M4 MCU system.

_____**3.** In the Cortex-M4 system, about 240 interrupts can be handled by this MCU system. Each interrupt has an interrupt number ranging from 0 to 240.

_____**4.** The top three exceptions, Reset, NMI and Hard Fault, have fixed priority levels with minus numbers to indicate that these exceptions cannot be masked or disabled by using PRIMASK register and they have the highest priority levels.

_____**5.** Two software packages, the TivaWare™ Software Package and the CMSIS Core package, provide different interrupt processing API functions to access, configure, and handle all interrupts via NVIC.

_____**6.** The CMSIS Core macro NVIC→ISER[1] is an 8-bit register and can be used to enable 8 interrupts, from Interrupt 0 to Interrupt 7.

_____**7.** The starting address of each interrupt ISR can be called a Vector since it provides not only a direction to the related handler but also an entry address of the ISR.

_____**8.** In the TM4C123GH6PM MCU system, an 8-bit segment is used to define the priority levels for each related interrupt. Therefore, totally 256 priority levels can be used by each interrupt source.

_____**9.** The GPIO Interrupt Sense Register (GPIOIS) is used to determine the triggering mode of an interrupt source, either an edge or a level. All bits are cleared by a reset.

_____**10.** The PRIMASK and BASEPRI registers are used to globally enable or disable all interrupts in the TM4C123GH6PM MCU system.

II. *Multiple Choices*

1. Each vector in the vector table takes ____ bytes to make a starting address of the ISR.

    a. 1

    b. 2

    c. 3

    d. 4

2. All GPIO Interrupt related registers are __bits, but only _____ are used.

    a. 32, 16

    b. 32, the highest 8-bit

    c. 32, the lowest 8-bit

    d. 8, 3

3. Each NVIC Priority Register NVIC_PRIn_R is a 32-bit register and it can configure __ priority levels for ____ related interrupt sources.

    a. 1, 1

    b. 2, 2

    c. 3, 3

    d. 4, 4

4. In order to configure an interrupt coming from the GPIO Port A as a priority level of 5, which of the following codes is correct?

    a. NVIC_PRI0 = 0x000000A0

    b. NVIC_PRI0 = 0x0000A000

    c. NVIC_PRI0 = 0x00A00000

    d. NVIC_PRI0 = 0xA0000000

5. To use the NVIC PRIn_R register to configure the priority level for an interrupt coming from the GPIO Port F, which NVIC_PRIn_ R register with which 3 bits should be used?

    a. NVIC_PRI4_R, 23 – 21

    b. NVIC_PRI5_R, 31 – 29

    c. NVIC_PRI6_R, 7 – 5

    d. NVIC_PRI7, 23 – 21

6. To use NVIC Set Enable Register NVIC_EN0_R to enable a GPIO Port E interrupt, which bit in this register should be set to 1?

    a. Bit 1

    b. Bit 2

    c. Bit 3

    d. Bit 4

7. To configure the priority level for an interrupt coming from the CAN1 whose IRQ number is 40, which NVIC Priority Register group (n) should be used with which 3 bits?

    a. NVIC_PRI9_R, 7 – 5

    b. NVIC_PRI10_R, 7 – 5

    c. NVIC_PRI11_R, 7 – 5

    d. NVIC_PRI12_R, 7 – 5

8. The difference between two header files, tm4c123gh6pm.h and TM4C123GH6PM.h, is _____.

    a. The first header file defined most peripheral register addresses, and the second header file defined most peripheral structures.

    b. The first header file defined most peripheral structures, and the second header file defined most registers addresses.

    c. The first header file defined most NVIC registers, and the second header file defined most GPIO Port structures.

    d. The first header file defined the NVIC structure pointer, and the second header file defined most GPIO Port structures.

9. The intrinsic function _____enable_irq() is defined by the _____ and it can be used to _____.

    a. CMSIS Core Software Package, enable all interrupts

    b. TivaWare™ Software Package, enable all interrupts

    c. TivaWare™ and CMSIS Core Software Packages, enable all interrupts

    d. ARM® MDK µVersion5, enable all interrupts

10. To dynamically register an interrupt handler, one can use _____ API function.

    a. NVIC_IntRegister()

    b. IntRegister()

    c. GPIOIntRegister()

    d. Both b and c

III.   *Exercises*

1. Provide a brief description about three components used in the general exceptions and interrupts processing system.

2. Provide a brief description about interrupts processing configuration and procedure in the ARM® Cortex®-M4 MCU system.

3. Explain three layers used in the configurations and responses for the GPIO interrupts in the TM4C123GH6PM MCU system.

4. Provide a description about four methods used to configure and response GPIO related interrupts in the TM4C123GH6PM MCU system.

5. Provide a brief explanation for two header files provided by the TivaWare™ Software package, tm4c123gh6pm.h and TM4C123GH6PM.h.

IV.   *Practical Laboratory*

Laboratory 5: ARM® Cortex®-M4 Exceptions and Interrupts

5.0 Goals   This laboratory exercise allows students to learn and practice ARM® Cortex®-M4 interrupts handling and processing for GPIO-related interrupts by developing four labs.

    1. Program Lab5_1 let you build an interrupt processing project to handle a level-triggered interrupt on GPIO PD1 pin by using the DRA programming model.

    2. Program Lab5_2 enables students to build a high-level-triggered interrupt on GPIO PD2 pin by using the CMSIS Core macros defined for NVIC Interrupt Control Registers to access and control a single LED PB0 with a DIP switch in the EduBASE Trainer. A 400 Hz signal is also sent to the speaker to make a sound for this interrupt.

    3. Program Lab5_3 allows students to use both PD0 and PF4 pins to handle two level-triggered interrupts to control two different sets of LEDs, PB0 and PB3, PB1 and PB2, in the EduBASE Trainer. This lab enables students to learn and practice how to set up priority levels for two interrupts coming from two different ports based on their real priority levels and how to control and respond to these two interrupts asynchronously and synchronously. Any programming model can be used in this project.

    4. Program Lab5_4 provides you another way to use both PD0 and PF4 pins to handle two level-triggered interrupts to control two different sets of LEDs, PB0 and PB3, PB1 and PB2, in the EduBASE Trainer. In this project, students need to use the NVIC Set Priority Grouping and the NVIC Encoder Priority functions to configure two interrupts coming from GPIO Ports D and F to replace the CMSIS NVIC→IP[] macros to set up the priority levels for these two interrupts.

After completion of these programs, you should understand most popular interrupts applied in the GPIO Ports, and these interrupt architectures and configurations as well as interrupt handling methods. You should be able to code some interrupt controlling programs to access the NVIC registers to control and respond to related interrupt requests sent by the peripherals to perform desired interrupt control functions.

5.1 Lab5_1

5.1.1 Goal   In this project, students need to use the PD1 pin that is connected to a position switch SW4 in the EduBASE Trainer to handle a level-triggered interrupt as this switch is pressed. It can be found from Figure 5.11 that the PD1 gets a LOW level as the SW4 is released and a HIGH level if the SW4 is pressed. As this interrupt is occurred, an ISR is executed to turn on a three-color LED in the TM4C123GXL EVB via PF3~PF1 pins in the GPIO Port F.

The Direct Register Access (DRA) model is required to use to build this project.

5.1.2 Data Assignment and Hardware Configuration   It can be found from Figure 5.11 that the position switch SW4 is connected to the PD1 pin and the three-color LED is connected to PF3~PF1 pins of the GPIO Ports in the TM4C123GXL EVB (refer to Figure 4.27). To enable and set the clock for these two GPIO Ports, Ports D and F, the following data and registers should be used:

- Bits 3 and 5 in the RCGC2 register should be set to 1 to enable Port D and Port F (refer to Figure 4.28).
- Bit 1 in the Port D Direction register should be reset to 0 to enable PD1 pin to work as an input pin.

5.1.3 Development of the Source Code   Refer to Figure 5.11 and follow the steps below to develop this C source code. Only a C code file is used in this project since it is a simple application without needing any header file.

1. Create a new folder named `Lab5_1` under the folder `C:\ARM Lab Projects\Chapter 5` in the Windows Explorer.
2. Create a new µVersion5 project named `Lab5_1` and save this project to the folder `Lab5_1` that is created in step 1 above.
3. On the next wizard, you need to select the device (MCU) for this project. Expand three icons, `Texas Instruments`, `Tiva C Series`, and `TM4C123x Series`, and select the target device `TM4C123GH6PM` from the list by clicking on it. Click on the **OK** to close this wizard.
4. Next the Software Components wizard is opened, and you need to set up the software development environment for your project with this wizard. Expand two icons, `CMSIS` and `Device`, and check the `CORE` and `Startup` checkboxes in the **Sel.** column, and click on the **OK** button since we need these two components to build our project.
5. In the **Project** pane, expand the `Target` folder and right click on the `Source Group 1` folder and select the `Add New Item to Group 'Source Group 1'`.
6. Select the `C File (.c)` and enter `Lab5_1` into the **Name:** box, and click on the **Add** button to add this source file into the project.
7. On the top of this C source file, you need first to include three system header files, `<stdint.h>`, `<stdbool.h>`, and "`tm4c123gh6pm.h`," since we need to use them in this project.
8. Start the main program with the code `int main(void)`.

9. Enable and set up a clock source for GPIO Ports D and F using an OR operation via the code SYSCTL_RCGC2_R = SYSCTL_RCGC2_GPIOD|SYSCTL_RCGC2_GPIOF;.

10. Set up three pins, PF3~PF1 on the GPIO Port F, to output pins using the code line GPIO_PORTF_DIR_R = 0xE;.

11. Enable three pins, PF3~PF1, to work as digital function pins via the code line GPIO_PORTF_DEN_R = 0xF;.

12. Use the similar codes to configure the pin PD1 as an input pin and enable this pin to perform digital function. A 0 should be assigned to the pin to configure that pin as an input pin.

13. Use five GPIO interrupt-related registers, GPIO_PORTD_IS_R, GPIO_PORTD_IBE_R, GPIO_PORTD_IEV_R, GPIO_PORTD_ICR_R, and GPIO_PORTD_IM_R, to configure PD1 as a HIGH-Level triggered interrupt, clearing the previous interrupt on this pin and unmasking this pin. All of these registers should be set to 0x2 except for the IBE register that should be reset to 0. The pin PD1 is corresponding to bit 2 (0x2) in the Port D data register.

14. Use NVIC Priority Register NVIC_PRI0_R to set up the priority level for the GPIO Port D as 3. The code could be NVIC_PRI0_R = 0x60000000;.

15. Use NVIC Set Enable Register NVIC_EN0_R to enable the GPIO Port D to be triggered by an interrupt source. The GPIO Port D is located at bit 3 in the NVIC_EN0_R register, and this bit should be set to 1 (0x8).

16. Use an intrinsic function __enable_irq(); to globally enable all interrupts.

17. Use an infinitive while() loop to wait for any interrupt to occur. During the waiting time, the three-color LED connected to PF3~PF1 in the TM4C123GXL EVB should be turned off, and therefore the GPIO_PORTF_DATA_R should be reset to 0 (0x0).

18. Now you need to develop the codes for the interrupt handler, GPIOD_Handler(). Use the code void GPIOD_Handler(void) to start this handler.

19. Inside this handler, you need to turn on the three-color LED via PF3~PF1 pins. In fact, you need to set these three bits to 1 to turn on this LED. Equivalently, sending 0xE to the GPIO_PORTF_DATA_R can complete this job.

5.1.4 Demonstrate Your Program by Testing the Running Result   Now you can compile your program by going to Project|Build target menu item. However, before you can compile your project, you need to set the correct path for all header files you used in the project to enable the compiler to know where these files are located. Perform the following operations to include this header file path in your project:

- Go to the Project|Options for Target 'Target 1' menu item.
- Then click on the C/C++ tab.
- Go to the Include Paths box and browse to the folder where our header file tm4c123gh6pm.h is located, which is C:\ti\TivaWare_C_Series-2.0.1.11577 \inc. Select this folder and click on the **OK** button.

Before you can download your program into the flash ROM in the EVB, make sure that the debugger you are using is the Stellaris ICDI. You can do this checking as follows:

- Go to Project|Options for Target 'Target 1' menu item to open the Options wizard.
- On the opened Options wizard, click on the Debug tab.

- Make sure that the debugger shown in the Use: box is Stellaris ICDI. Otherwise you can click on the dropdown arrow to select this debugger from the list.

Perform the following operations to run your program and check the running results:

- Go to Flash|Download menu item to download your program into the flash ROM.
- Go to Debug|Start/Stop Debug Session to begin debugging your program. Click on the **OK** button on the 32-KB memory size limitation message box to continue.
- Then go to Debug|Run menu item to run your program.
- As the project runs, you can press the SW4 position switch and the three-color LED on the TM4C123GXL EVB will be on, and it will be off as you release the SW4 switch.
- Go to Debug|Start/Stop Debug Session to stop your program.

Based on these results, try to answer the following questions:

- Can you tell me what color is displayed on this three-color LED? Why?
- Why are there no codes used to initialize and set up the system clock for this project? What is the default system clock?
- What did you learn from this project?

5.2 Lab5_2

5.2.1 Goal This project enables students to build a high-level-triggered interrupt on GPIO PD2 pin by using the CMSIS Core macros defined for NVIC Interrupt Control Registers to access and control a single LED PB0 with a DIP switch 2 in the EduBASE Trainer. A 400 Hz signal is also sent to the speaker to make a sound for this interrupt.

5.2.2 Data Assignment and Hardware Configuration It can be found from Figure 5.11 that the DIP switch 2 is connected to the PD2 pin, the LED PB0 is connected to the PB0 pin, and the speaker is connected to the PC4 pin of the GPIO Ports in the TM4C123GXL EVB. To enable and set the clock for these three GPIO Ports, the following data and registers should be used:

- Bits 1, 2, and 3 in the RCGC2 register should be set to 1 to enable Ports B, C, and D (refer to Figure 4.28).
- Bit 2 in the Port D Direction register should be reset to 0 to enable PD2 to work as an input pin, bit 4 in the Port C Direction register should be set to 1 to enable PC4 pin to work as an output pin, and bit 0 in the Port B Direction register should be set to 1 to enable PB0 pin to work as an output pin.

5.2.3 Development of the Project Follow the steps below to develop this project. Only a C code source file is used in this project since this project is simple. Create the project and develop the C source file with the following steps:

1. Create a new folder Lab5_2 under the folder C:\ARM Lab Projects\Chapter 5 in the Windows Explorer.
2. Open the Keil® ARM®-MDK μVersion5, create a new project named Lab5_2, and save this project into the folder Lab5_2 created in step 1.

3. On the next wizard, you need to select the device (MCU) for this project. Expand three icons, Texas Instruments, Tiva C Series, and TM4C123x Series, and select the target device TM4C123GH6PM from the list by clicking on it. Click on the **OK** to close this wizard.

4. Next the Software Components wizard is opened, and you need to set up the software development environment for your project with this wizard. Expand two icons, CMSIS and Device, and check the CORE and Startup checkboxes in the **Sel.** column, and click on the **OK** button since we need these two components to build our project.

5.2.4 Development of the C Source File

1. In the **Project** pane, expand the Target folder and right click on the Source Group 1 folder and select the Add New Item to Group 'Source Group 1'.

2. Select the C File (.c) and enter Lab5_2 into the **Name:** box, and click on the **Add** button to add this source file into the project.

3. Include the following header files into this source file first:
- <stdint.h>
- <stdbool.h>
- "tm4c123gh6pm.h"

4. Create two user-defined functions, void Delay(int time) and void SetSound (int period), since we need to use these functions to generate a 400 Hz signal.

5. Inside the function Delay(), declare an integer local variable i that works as a loop count, and use for() loop to delay a period of time. The starting value for the loop count is 0, and the ending value is the input argument time.

6. Inside the function SetSound(), set PC4 to 1 to generate the first half-cycle of the 400 Hz signal by using the GPIO structure pointer (GPIOC→DATA = 0x10;). Then call the function Delay() to delay a period. Reset the PC4 to 0 to generate the second half-cycle of the 400 Hz signal by using another GPIO structure pointer (GPIOC→DATA = 0x0;). Call the function Delay() to delay another period.

7. Place the int main(void) to start the main program and put a starting brace under this main function to begin the main program.

8. Use the System Control structure pointer to set up the RCGCGPIO register to enable the GPIO Ports B, C, and D:
- SYSCTL→RCGCGPIO = 0x08|0x04|0x02;

9. Use the GPIO Port B structure pointer to set PB0 as an output pin (GPIOB→DIR) and enable its digital function (GPIOB→DEN). PB0 should be located at 0x1.

10. Use the GPIO Port C structure pointer to set PC4 as an output pin (GPIOC→DIR) and enable its digital function (GPIOC→DEN). PC4 should be located at 0x10.

11. Use the GPIO Port D structure pointer to set PD2 as an input pin (GPIOD→DIR) and enable its digital function (GPIOD→DEN). PD2 should be located at 0x4.

12. Use the GPIO Port D structure pointer to configure PD2 as a HIGH-level-triggered interrupt pin. Five interrupt control registers should be used, including GPIOD→IS, GPIOD→IBE, GPIOD→IEV, GPIOD→ICR, and GPIOD→IM. PD2 should be located at 0x4.

13. Use the NVIC structure pointer (NVIC→IP[3]) to set up the priority level for the Port D as priority level 3. Refer to Tables 5.5, 5.11 and 5.12 to get more details about this setting.

14. Use the NVIC structure pointer (NVIC→ISER[0]) to enable the Port D interrupt. Refer to Tables 5.5, 5.11, and 5.12 to get more details about this setting.

15. Use an intrinsic function `__enable_irq()` to globally enable all interrupts.

16. Use an infinitive `while(1)` loop to wait for any possible interrupt to occur. During this waiting period, turn off the LED PB0 by using the GPIO Port B structure pointer (GPIOB→DATA).

17. Generate the interrupt handler `void GPIOD_Handler(void)` to handle interrupts coming from PD2.

18. Inside the handler, turn on the LED PB0 by using the GPIO Port B structure pointer (GPIOB→DATA). Then call the user-defined function `SetSound()` with an argument 25000 to send out a 400 Hz signal to the speaker.

19. Some necessary ending braces should be added to finish the `while()` loop and the main program.

5.2.5 Setup of the Include Path and Check the Debugger   Now you need to include the system header files by adding the include path and check the debugger used in the project. Perform the following operations to include this header file path in your project:

- Go to `Project|Options for Target 'Target 1'` menu item.
- Then click on the C/C++ tab.
- Go to `Include Paths` box and browse to the folder where our header file `tm4c123gh6pm.h` is located, which is `C:\ti\TivaWare_C_Series-2.0.1.11577\inc`. Select this folder and click on the **OK** button.

Perform the following operations to make sure that the debugger you are using is the `Stellaris ICDI`. You can do this checking as follows:

- Go to the `Project|Options for Target 'Target 1'` menu item to open the Options wizard.
- On the opened Options wizard, click on the `Debug` tab.
- Make sure that the debugger shown in the `Use:` box is `Stellaris ICDI`. Otherwise you can click on the dropdown arrow to select this debugger from the list.

5.2.6 Demonstrate Your Program   Perform the following operations to run your program and check the running results:

- Go to the `Flash|Download` menu item to download your program into the flash ROM.
- Go to the `Debug|Start/Stop Debug Session` to begin debugging your program. Click on the **OK** button on the 32-KB memory size limitation message box to continue.
- Then go to `Debug|Run` menu item to run your program.

As the project runs, the LED PB0 will be ON when you slide the DIP-SW2 to the ON position (or press the position switch SW3 since both are connected together), and a 400 Hz signal is sent to the speaker. The LED PB0 is OFF when you slide the DIP-SW2 back to the OFF position.

Based on these results, try to answer the following questions:

- Can you modify your codes to make any other LED, such as PB1~PB3, ON or OFF controlled by different interrupts coming from any other pins on the Port D, which are connected to the other DIP switches, such as DIP-SW2~DIP-SW4 in the EduBASE Trainer?
- What did you learn from this project?

5.3 Lab5_3

5.3.1 Goal   This project allows students to use both PD0 and PF4 pins to handle two level-triggered interrupts to control two different sets of LEDs, PB0 and PB3, PB1 and PB2, in the EduBASE Trainer. This lab enables students to learn and practice how to set up priority levels for two interrupts coming from two different ports based their real priority levels and how to control and respond to these two interrupts asynchronously and synchronously. Any programming model can be used in this project.

5.3.2 Data Assignment and Hardware Configuration   In this project, two interrupts, one coming from PD0 and the other one coming from the PF4, are developed with two interrupt handlers, `GPIOD_Handler()` and `GPIOF_Handler()`. The PD0 has a higher priority level (3) and the PF4) has a lower priority level (5). When the PD0 interrupt occurs, two LEDs (PB0 and PB3 are turned ON and a 400 Hz signal is sent to the speaker. As the PF4 interrupt happened, two LEDs PB1 and PB2 are turned ON and an 800 Hz signal is sent to the speaker.

It can be found from Figure 5.11 that the PD0 pin is connected to the position switch SW5 in the EduBASE Trainer and the PF4 pin is connected to the user switch SW1 in the TM4C123GXL EVB. The LEDs PB0~PB3 are connected to the PB0~PB3 pins on the GPIO Port B in the TM4C123GXL EVB. The PC4 pin is connected to the speaker controller in the EduBASE Trainer. To enable and set the clock for these four GPIO Ports (Ports B, C, D, and F), the following data and registers should be used:

- Bits 1~3 and 5 in the RCGC2 register should be set to 1 to enable Ports B, C, D, and F (refer to Figure 4.28).
- Bit 0 in the Port D Direction register and bit 4 in the Port F Direction register should be reset to 0 to enable PD0 and PF4 to work as input pins, and bits 0 through 3 in the Port B Direction register should be set to 1 to enable PB0~PB3 to work as output pins. Bit 4 in the Port C Direction register should be set to 1 to enable this pin to work as an output pin.

5.3.3 Development of the Project   Use the steps below to develop this project. Only the C source file is used in this project since this project is not complicated. Create a new project with the following steps:

1. Create a new folder `Lab5_3` under the folder `C:\ARM Lab Projects\Chapter 5` in the Windows Explorer.
2. Open the Keil® ARM®-MDK μVersion5, create a new project named `Lab5_3`, and save this project in the folder `Lab5_3`, created in step 1.
3. On the next wizard, you need to select the device (MCU) for this project. Expand three icons, `Texas Instruments`, `Tiva C Series`, and `TM4C123x Series`, and select the target device `TM4C123GH6PM` from the list by clicking on it. Click on the **OK** to close this wizard.
4. Next the Software Components wizard is opened, and you need to set up the software development environment for your project with this wizard. Expand two icons, `CMSIS` and `Device`, and check the CORE and `Startup` checkboxes in the **Sel.** column, and click on the **OK** button since we need these two components to build our project.

The top three macros can be found from the system header file `tm4c123gh6pm.h` that is located at the folder `C:\ti\TivaWare_C_Series-2.0.1.11577\inc` in your host computer.

5.3.4 Development of the C Source File

1. In the **Project** pane, expand the `Target` folder and right click on the `Source Group 1` folder and select the `Add New Item to Group 'Source Group 1'`.

2. Select the `C File (.c)` and enter `Lab5_3` into the **Name:** box, and click on the **Add** button to add this source file into the project.

3. Include the following header files into this source file first:
- `#include <stdint.h>`
- `#include <stdbool.h>`
- `#include "TM4C123GH6PM.h"`

   The `TM4C123GH6PM.h` is the CMSIS Cortex-M4 Peripheral Access Layer header file located at the folder `C:\Keil_v5\ARM\Pack\Keil\TM4C_DFP\1.0.0\Device\Include\TM4C123` in your host computer. All GPIO and NVIC structure and structure pointers are defined in this file since we will use these structure pointers in this project.

4. In this project we need to use three user-defined functions, `Ports_Init()`, `Delay()`, and `SetSound()`, to initialize the GPIO Ports, B, C, D, and F, delay a period of time, and send two sound signals with two different frequencies, 400 and 800 Hz, to the speaker controller in the EduBASE Trainer. First we need to declare these three functions as:

```
void Ports_Init(void);
void Delay(int time);
void SetSound(int period);
```

5. Place the `int main(void)` to start our main program and put a starting brace under this main function to begin our main program.

6. Use the system control structure pointer `SYSCTL` to access the `RCGCGPIO` register to set up the clock and enable the GPIO PORTB, PORTC, PORTD, and PORTF: `SYSCTL→RCGCGPIO = 0x20|0x08|0x04|0x02;` (what these hexadecimal numbers mean?). Since the RCGCGPIO register performs the same function as the RCGC2 register, refer to Figure 4.28 to get more details about the bit field of this register.

7. Call the `Ports_Init()` function to initialize and configure GPIO Ports B, C, D, and F.

8. Use the GPIO Port D structure pointer to configure the PD0 pin as a high-level-triggered interrupt pin. Five Port D interrupt-related registers, GPIOD→IS, GPIOD→IBE, GPIOD→IEV, GPIOD→ICR, and GPIOD→IM, will be configured. Refer to Table 5.18 to get details about the bit-field values to be set up for these registers. The point is that PD0 is located at bit 0 at Port D Data register and can be expressed as `0x1`.

9. Use the GPIO Port F structure pointer to configure the PF4 pin as a low-level-triggered interrupt pin. Five Port F interrupt-related registers, GPIOF→IS, GPIOF→IBE, GPIOF→IEV, GPIOF→ICR, and GPIOF→IM, will be configured. Refer to Table 5.18 to get details about the bit-field values to be set up for these registers. The point is that PF4 is located at bit 4 at the Port F Data register and can be expressed as `0x10`.

10. Use the NVIC structure pointer to set up the interrupt priority level of PD0 pin as 3, and enable this pin based on its IRQ number with the following codes:

   ■ NVIC→IP[3] = 0x60;   //set interrupt priority to 3
   ■ NVIC→ISER[0] |= 0x00000008;   //enable IRQ3

   Refer to Tables 5.5 and 5.9–5.12 to get more details about these bits values.

11. Use the NVIC structure pointer to setup the interrupt priority level of PF4 pin as 5, and enable this pin based on its IRQ number with the following codes:

    ◼ NVIC→IP[30] = 0xA0 ;   //set interrupt priority to 5
    ◼ NVIC→ISER[0] |= 0x40000000;   //enable IRQ30

Refer to Tables 5.5 and 5.9–5.12 to get more details about these bit values.

12. Call the intrinsic function __enable_irq() to globally enable all interrupts.

13. Use an infinitive while() loop to wait for any interrupt to occur. During this waiting period, all four LEDs, PB0~PB3, at the EduBASE Trainer should be turned off by sending 0x0 to the GPIO Port B Data Register (GPIOB→DATA).

14. Now let's develop the codes for our first user-defined function Ports_Init(). The purpose of this function is to:

    a. Configure four lower pins, PB3~PB0, on the GPIO Port B as output pins and enable the digital function for those pins. Those pins are numbered as 0xF.

    b. Configure one pin, PC4, on the GPIO Port C as an output pin and enable the digital function for that pin. This pin is numbered as 0x10.

    c. Configure one pin, PD0, on the GPIO Port D as an input pin and enable the digital function for that pin. This pin is numbered as 0x1.

    d. Configure one pin, PF4, on the GPIO Port F as an input pin and enable the digital function for that pin. This pin is numbered as 0x10.

    e. Configure pin PF4 to work as a pull-up mode to enable the SW1 to connect to a pull-up resister to work properly to provide either HIGH or LOW input signals.

    The point to be noted is in step (e) above: When using the PF4 pin that is connected to a user switch SW1 in the TM4C123GXL EVB as an input pin to receive any interrupt, the PF4 pin by default is connected to the SW1 in an open-collector mode, which means that the PF4 is in the tri-state and the SW1 must be configured by software to either in the pull-up or the pull-down connection mode to enable the SW1 to work as a normal switch to generate a HIGH or a LOW voltage output signal to the PF4 pin. To do this, program the GPIO Port F with its PUR register as GPIOF→PUR |= 0x10;. This coding is very important and the SW1 may not work if you missed this code line.

15. The codes for the second function Delay() are:

```
void Delay(int time)
{
  int i;
  for(i = 0; i < time; i++) {}
}
```

16. The codes for the third function SetSound() are:

```
void SetSound(int period)
{
  GPIOC->DATA = 0x10;        //send high half-cycle
  Delay(period);
  GPIOC->DATA = 0x0;         //send low half-cycle
  Delay(period);
}
```

17. The codes for the GPIO Port D handler are:

```
void GPIOD_Handler(void)
```

```
{
    GPIOB->DATA = 0x6;          //turn on LED PB1 & PB2 in Trainer
    SetSound(25000);            //send 400 Hz signal to speaker
}
```

18. The codes for the GPIO Port F handler are:

```
void GPIOF_Handler(void)
{
    GPIOB->DATA = 0x9;          //turn LED PB0 & PB3 in Trainer
    SetSound(12500);            //send 800 Hz signal to speaker
}
```

5.3.5 Set Up the Include Path Now you need to include the system header files by adding the include path. Perform the following operations to include the header file TM4C123GH6PM.h in your project:

- Go to the Project|Options for Target 'Target 1' menu item.
- Then click on the C/C++ tab.
- Go to the Include Paths box and browse to the folder where our header file TM4C123GH6PM.h is located, which is C:\Keil_v5\ARM\Pack\Keil\TM4C_DFP \1.0.0\Device\Include\TM4C123. Select this folder and click on the **OK** button.

Now you can compile your program by going to the Project|Build target menu item. However, before you can download your program into the flash ROM in the EVB, make sure that the debugger you are using is the Stellaris ICDI. You can do this checking as follows:

- Go to Project|Options for Target 'Target 1' menu item to open the Options wizard.
- On the opened Options wizard, click on the Debug tab.
- Make sure that the debugger shown in the Use: box is Stellaris ICDI. Otherwise you can click on the dropdown arrow to select this debugger from the list.

5.3.6 Demonstrate Your Program Perform the following operations to run your program and check the running results:

- Go to the Flash|Download menu item to download your program into the flash ROM.
- Go to the Debug|Start/Stop Debug Session to begin debugging your program. Click on the **OK** button on the 32-KB memory size limitation message box to continue.
- Then go to the Debug|Run menu item to run your program.

As the project runs, the LEDs PB1 and PB2 will be ON and a 400 Hz signal is sent to the speaker when you press and hold down the position switch SW5 in the EduBASE Trainer. But both LEDs will be OFF when you release SW5. This means that a high-level-triggered interrupt occurs when the SW5 is pressed. The LEDs PB0 and PB3 will be ON and an 800 Hz signal is sent to the speaker when you press and hold down the user switch SW1 in the TM4C123GXL EVB. This means that a low-level-triggered interrupt occurs when the SW1 is pressed. Based on these results, try to answer the following questions:

- Now try to press and hold down the switch SW1 first, and then press and hold SW5. What happened? Why?

- Now try to press and hold down the switch SW5 first, and then press and hold SW1. What happened? Why?
- What did you learn from this project?

5.4 Lab5_4

5.4.1 Goal This project is similar to Lab5_3 but it provides students with another way to use both PD0 and PF4 pins to handle two level-triggered interrupts to control two different sets of LEDs, PB0 and PB3, PB1 and PB2, in the EduBASE Trainer. In this project, students need to use the NVIC Set Priority Grouping and NVIC Encoder Priority functions to configure two interrupts coming from GPIO Ports D and F to replace the CMSIS NVIC→IP[] macros to set up the priority levels for these two interrupts.

5.4.2 Data Assignment and Hardware Configuration Refer to project Lab5_3 above to get details about the hardware configurations for this project.

In this project, students need to use two NVIC API functions to configure and set up the priority levels for PD0 and PF4. These functions are as follows:

1. void NVIC_SetPriorityGrouping(uint32 PriorityGroup). This function can be used to split the three-priority bit used in the TM4C123GH6PM MCU system into two regions: the group priority and the sub-priority. Only four possible group levels (PriorityGroup) are available in the TM4C123GH6PM MCU system (refer to Table 5.7), which are:
   - Group 4: Bits 7~5 work as group bits, no bit (0 bit) works as the sub-priority bit.
   - Group 5: Bits 7~6 work as group bits, bit 5 (1 bit) works as the sub-priority bit.
   - Group 6: Bit 7 works as group bit, bits 6~5 (2 bits) work as the sub-priority bits.
   - Group 7: No bit works as group bit, bits 7~5 (3 bits) work as the sub-priority bits.

   In this project, students are recommended to use group 5 to make 2 bits, bits 7~6, as group bits (4 group options) and 1 bit, bit 5, as a sub-priority bit (1 sub-priority option).

2. uint32_t NVIC_EncodePriority(uint32_t PriorityGroup, uint32_t GroupPriority, uint32_t SubPriority). This function is used to generate encoded priority levels for GroupPriority and SubPriority under the same group. The smaller the number, the higher the priority level. In this project, students are recommended to use 2 as the group priority level for PD0 and 3 as the group priority level for PF4, but both have the same sub-priority level of 1. Then students can change these priority levels to make both pins have the same group priority level but different sub-priority levels.

5.4.3 Development of the Project Refer to 5.3.3 and 5.3.4 in Lab5_3 part to create a new project Lab5_4 and add a new C code file Lab5_4.c into this project. Copy all codes in the file Lab5_3.c and paste them into the Lab5_4.c file. Perform the following modifications to this file:

1. Before the code lines to set priority and enable PD0, use the NVIC_SetPriority-Grouping() function to set the priority group as 5 for both PD0 and PF4 interrupt sources.
2. Replace the code line NVIC→IP[3] = 0x60; with

   NVIC_SetPriority(GPIOD_IRQn, NVIC_EncodePriority(5, 2, 1));
3. Replace the code line NVIC→IP[30] = 0xA0; with

   NVIC_SetPriority(GPIOF_IRQn, NVIC_EncodePriority(5, 3, 1));

4. Try to understand the meanings of these two new code lines and their functions, especially for three arguments in two functions.

5.4.4 Setup of the Include Path and Linking of the Static Library Now you need to include the system header files by adding the include path into the project.

Refer to Section 5.3.3 in Lab5_3 part to add this include path into the project.

Now you can compile your program by going to the `Project|Build target` menu item. However, before you can download your program into the flash memory in the EVB, make sure that the debugger you are using is the `Stellaris ICDI`. You can do this checking as follows:

- Go to `Project|Options for Target 'Target 1'` menu item to open the Options wizard.
- On the opened Options wizard, click on the `Debug` tab.
- Make sure that the debugger shown in the `Use:` box is `Stellaris ICDI`. Otherwise you can click on the dropdown arrow to select this debugger from the list.

5.4.5 Demonstrate Your Program Perform the following operations to run your program and check the running results:

- Go to the `Flash|Download` menu item to download your program into the flash ROM.
- Go to the `Debug|Start/Stop Debug Session` to begin debugging your program. Click on the **OK** button on the 32-KB memory size limitation message box to continue.
- Then go to the `Debug|Run` menu item to run your program.

As the project runs, what will happen if you press the user switch SW1 in the TM4C123GXL EVB? What will occur if you press and hold down the SW1 and press the position switch SW5 in the EduBASE Trainer? What will happen if you change the order of pressing these two switches?

Based on these results, try to answer the following questions:

- If you change the second argument's value in two NVIC_EncodePriority() functions above to make both equal, what will happen if you press two switches?
- What did you learn from this project?

Chapter 6

ARM® Microcontroller Memory System

This chapter provides general information about the ARM® Cortex®-M4 microcontroller memory system. The discussion is mainly concentrated on the memory system used in the TM4C123GH6PM MCU system. This discussion includes the system memory map specially designed for the TM4C123GH6PM MCU, connections between the processor and memory, and the connection between the memory and peripherals, memory architecture and requirements, bit-band principle and operations, memory access attributes, memory endianness, memory access behaviors, and memory programming applications in TM4C123GH6PM MCU system.

6.1 OVERVIEW AND INTRODUCTION

The ARM® Cortex®-M4 processor provides an internal bus matrix to enable the processor to access external memory system via two interfaces: the Code Interface and SRAM/Peripheral interface. The address buses used in both inside and outside of the Cortex®-M4 processor are 32 bits to make the maximum searchable space up to 4 GB. The bus interface between the processor and external memory is the Advanced High-performance Bus (AHB), which provide interfaces and connections to various 32/16/8-bit memory devices.

In order to access and control 4-GB memory space effectively and easily, the entire 4-GB memory space in the Cortex®-M4 system is divided into the different regions for various predefined memory and peripheral devices uses. With the help of the multiple bus interfaces provided by the Cortex®-M4, the Cortex®-M4 processor can access different memory regions, such as from the CODE region stored program codes to DATA region in the SRAM or peripheral regions, simultaneously or at the same time. The following buses can be used to access memory or peripheral devices in parallel:

- ICode Bus: Fetch Opcode from the flash memory
- DCode Bus: Read constant data from flash memory
- System Bus: Read/Write data from SRAM or I/O, fetch opcode from SRAM
- Private Peripheral Bus (PPB): Read/Write data from internal peripheral devices like NVIC

Practical Microcontroller Engineering with ARM® Technology, First Edition. Ying Bai.
© 2016 by The Institute of Electrical and Electronics Engineers, Inc. Published 2016 by John Wiley & Sons, Inc.
Companion Website: www.wiley.com/go/armbai

- Advanced High-performance Bus (AHB): Read/Write data from high-speed I/O and parallel ports

In summary, the ARM® Cortex®-M4 memory system provides the following specifications and advantages:

- The Cortex®-M4 processors can work with either little endian or big endian memory systems. Generally, the Cortex®-M4 is designed with just one endian configuration.
- The ARM® Cortex®-M4 provides a bit-band feature to enable read/write access to individual bits in one 1-MB SRAM region (from 0x22000000 to 0x220FFFFF) and one 256 MB I/O Port region (from 0x42000000 to 0x43FFFFFF) in the memory devices used in the Texas Instruments™ Tiva™ for C Series LaunchPad™ MCU-TM4C123GH6PM. To use this bit-band feature, two parameters are needed: the target memory address and the target bit number to be accessed. An example of using this bit-band feature will be discussed in the next section.
- In the ARM® Cortex®-M4 MCU, an optional unit, Memory Protection Unit (MPU) is provided to enable users to access different memory regions with certain permissions. The MPU is a programmable unit that defines access permissions for different regions. The MPU supports eight programmable regions.
- In Cortex®-M4 memory systems, the unaligned transfer operations are supported to perform unaligned data transfers.
- To assist to access different memory regions, memory attributes and access permissions are provided to facilitate these accessing.
- The bus interfaces on the ARM® Cortex®-M4 MCU are generic bus interfaces, which mean that these kinds of interfaces enable the processors to connect and interface to different types and sizes of memory with various memory controllers. Generally, two types of memories—flash ROM memory for program codes and static RAM (SRAM) for program data—are widely adopted in most Cortex®-M microcontroller systems. However, in some applications, the Electrically Erasable Programmable ROM (EEPROM) is also used in the memory devices.

In Sections 2.3 and 2.6.2 in Chapter 2, we have provided brief discussions about the memory system used for ARM® Cortex®-M4 and about the memory map system used for TM4C123GH6PM MCU. In this chapter we will focus our discussions on the memory system used in the TM4C123GH6PM MCU system.

First let's take a closer look at the memory architecture in TM4C123GH6PM MCU.

6.2 MEMORY ARCHITECTURE IN THE TM4C123GH6PM MCU SYSTEM

Figure 6.1 shows an architecture block diagram for the TM4C123GH6PM MCU memory system.

It can be found from Figure 6.1 that the following components or devices exist in the TM4C123GH6PM MCU memory system:

- SRAM (32 KB)
- Flash Memory (256 KB)
- Internal ROM

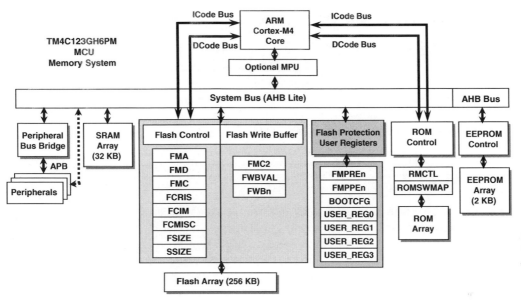

Figure 6.1.   Memory system in the TM4C123GH6PM MCU system.

- EEPROM (2 KB)
- Flash Protection Unit
- Optional MPU

Most components or devices inside the memory system are connected to the ARM® Cortex®-M4 processor via a system bus, such as SRAM, Peripheral Bus Bridge, Flash Control, and EEPROM. However, the Internal ROM and Flash Memory spaces are connected to the Cortex®-M4 processor via two bus interfaces, ICode and DCode. In simple designs, these two buses can be combined together by using a bus multiplexer to get a simple bus system.

The advantages of using ICode and DCode bus interfaces are as follows:

- The Cortex®-M4 processor can perform data access and fetch the next instruction at the same time, just like a pipeline operation.
- During the interrupt processing period, the processor can access the stack space to reserve or recover all used registers and read the vector table simultaneously.
- Different microcontroller vendors can use these two interfaces to speed up the accessing to the internal ROM space to execute some built-in library functions, such as TivaWare™ Peripheral Driver Library, Boot Loader program, Graphical Library, Sensor Hub Library, USA Library, and so on.

The general connection between the Cortex®-M4 processor and peripherals is by the Advanced Peripheral Bus (APB) protocol via the Peripheral Bus Bridge that is connected to the system bus. However, the peripherals can also be accessed via the Advanced High-Performance Bus (AHB) protocol directly by the processor using the different macros based on memory mappings in the TM4C123GH6PM MCU system. The APB is the default accessing protocol used by the Tiva™ TM4C123GH6PM MCU.

Now let's take a look at these components or devices one by one.

6.2.1 Static Random Access Memory (SRAM)

The 32-KB SRAM is used to store users' program data and provides system stack and user stack spaces. To reduce the time required for read-modify-write (RMW) operations, the ARM® Cortex®-M4 provides bit-banding technology in the processor. With a bit-band-enabled processor, certain regions in the memory map (SRAM and peripheral space) can use address aliases to access individual bits in a single and atomic operation. This 32-KB SRAM space can be extended up to 500 MB.

6.2.2 Flash Memory

The 256-KB Flash Memory is used to store the user's program codes, exceptions, and interrupts vector tables. The exception and interrupt vector tables are located at the lower memory space starting from 0x0000.0000. To perform any programming for this flash memory, the Tiva™ C Series devices provide a user-friendly interface with three registers. Most erase or program operations are handled via these three registers: Flash Memory Address (FMA), Flash Memory Data (FMD), and Flash Memory Control (FMC).

Generally the Flash Memory is composed of the following units:

1. Flash Controls
2. 32-Word Flash Write Buffer
3. Flash Protection Unit
4. 256-KB Flash Memory Array

The 256-KB Flash memory array is controlled and managed by three units listed in 1~3.

When the system clock frequency is 40 MHz or below, each Flash memory unit is read in a single cycle. As the system clock is above 40 MHz, the prefetch buffer fetches two 32-bit words on each cycle. No wait states for sequential code. The Flash memory is organized as 256 sets of 1-KB blocks that can be individually erased. An individual 32-bit word can also be programmed to change bits from 1 to 0. In addition, a 32-word flash memory write buffer provides the ability to program or write 32 continuous words in Flash memory in half the time of programming the words individually. Erasing a 1-KB block causes the entire contents of the block to be set to all 1s. The 256 1-KB blocks can be paired into 128 sets of 2-KB blocks that can be individually protected by the Flash Protection Unit.

The Flash Control unit is used to control the flash memory programming process, including the reading, writing (programming), or erasing operations. When performing writing or erasing operations, the following points need to be noted:

- Only an erasing operation can change bits' values from 0 to 1.
- A writing operation can only change bits from 1 to 0. If the write attempts to change a 0 to a 1, the write fails and no bits are changed.
- A flash operation can be started before entering the Sleep or Deep-Sleep mode (by using instruction WFI). It can also be completed while in a Sleep or Deep-Sleep period. If the Flash program/erase event comes in succession to EEPROM access, the Flash event gets completed after waking from Sleep/Deep-Sleep and is started after the wake-up.

During a Flash memory operation (writing, page erasing, or mass erasing), any access to the Flash memory is inhibited. As a result, instruction and literal fetches are held off until the Flash memory operation is done. If an instruction execution is required during a Flash memory operation, that instruction must be placed in the SRAM space and executed from there while the flash operation is in progress.

The basic operations of a flash memory include the reading, writing (programming), and erasing. Since the reading operation is very simple, we will pay more attention to the flash memory writing (programming) and erasing, and these belong to the flash control.

6.2.2.1 Basic Operations of the Flash Memory

The basic operations for a flash memory include the flash memory writing and erasing. The flash memory writing and erasing can be divided into two categories:

- Perform the flash memory normal writing and erasing operations under the control of the Flash Control.
- Perform flash memory blocks writing and erasing operations under the controls of the Flash Control and Flash Write Buffer.

The flash memory normal writing (programming) and erasing operations can be performed for either a 32-bit word or a 1-KB page in the flash memory space.

Program or Write a 32-bit Word:
Perform the following operations to write (program) a 32-bit word in the flash memory:

1. Write source data to the FMD register.

2. Write the target address to the FMA register.

3. Write the Flash memory write key and the WRITE bit to the FMC register. Depending on the value of the KEY bit in the BOOTCFG register, the value 0xA442 or 0x71D5 must be written into the WRKEY field for a Flash memory write to occur.

4. Poll the FMC register until the WRITE bit is cleared.

Erase a 1-KB Page:
Perform the following operations to erase a 1-KB page in the flash memory:

1. Write the page address to the FMA register.

2. Write the Flash memory write key and the ERASE bit to the FMC register. Depending on the value of the KEY bit in the BOOTCFG register, the value 0xA442 or 0x71D5 must be written into the WRKEY field for a Flash memory write to occur.

3. Poll the FMC register until the ERASE bit is cleared or, alternatively, to enable the programming interrupt using the PMASK bit in the FCIM register.

Erase a Mass Block:
Perform the following operations to erase a mass the flash memory:

1. Write the Flash memory write key and the MERASE bit to the FMC register. Depending on the value of the KEY bit in the BOOTCFG register, the value 0xA442 or 0x71D5 must be written into the WRKEY field for a Flash memory write to occur.

2. Poll the FMC register until the MERASE bit is cleared or, alternatively, to enable the programming interrupt using the PMASK bit in the FCIM register.

To perform flash memory blocks writing and erasing operations under the controls of the Flash Control and Flash Write Buffer, let's take a look at the 32-word flash memory write buffer.

6.2.2.2 The 32-Word Flash Memory Write Buffer

A 32-word write buffer provides the capability to perform faster write accesses to the Flash memory by programming two 32-bit words at a time, allowing 32 words to be programmed in the same time as 16-word would take. The data for the buffered write is written to 32 Flash Write Buffers (FWBn) registers (n = 0~31).

These flash buffer registers (FWB0~FWB31) are 32-words aligned with Flash memory. The so-called 32-word aligned address means that each register's address is an aligned offset address that is determined by bits [6:0] in the flash memory address register FMA. The values on bits [6:0] in the FMA must be 0 to provide a continuous $2^7 = 128$-byte (32-word) space in the flash memory array where the 32-word can be written into. Therefore the register FWB0 corresponds to the address in bits [6:0] in the FMA, which is 0x00. The FWB1 corresponds to the address that equals (bits [6:0] of FMA) + 0x4 = (0x04) and so on. Only the FWBn registers that have been updated since the previous buffered Flash memory write operation can be written into the related flash array. The Flash Write Buffer Valid (FWBVAL) register shows which registers have been written since the last buffered Flash memory writing operation. This register is a 32-bit register, and each bit is for each of the 32 FWBn registers, where bit-n of FWBVAL corresponds to FWBn. The FWBn register has been updated if the corresponding bit in the FWBVAL register is set to 1.

To program 32-words with a single buffered Flash memory write operation, perform the following operations:

1. Write the 32 source data into the 32 FWBn registers.
2. Write the target address to the FMA register. This address must be a 32-word aligned address, which is, bits [6:0] in FMA must be 0s.
3. Write the Flash memory write key and the WRBUF bit to the FMC2 register. Depending on the value of the KEY bit in the BOOTCFG register, the value 0xA442 or 0x71D5 must be written into the WRKEY field for a Flash memory write to occur.
4. Poll the FMC2 register until the WRBUF bit is cleared or waited for the PMIS interrupt to be signaled.

Figure 6.2 shows a functional block diagram to illustrate how to write a 32-bit data into the flash memory and how to program 32-word data into the flash array using the FWBn.

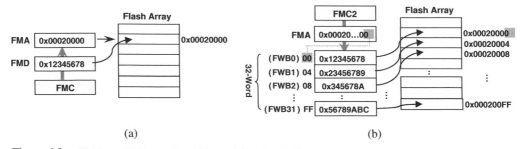

(a)   (b)

Figure 6.2.   Writing a 32-bit word and 32-word data into flash memory.

6.2.2.3 Flash Control Registers

As we mentioned, all erase or write (program) operations are handled via three registers: FlashMemoryAddress (FMA), FlashMemoryData (FMD), and FlashMemory Control (FMC).

However, all of these registers and associated writing or erasing operations are closely related to some other registers, such as BOOTCFG (exactly related to a single bit, bit-4 or the bit KEY in the BOOTCFG register), FMC2, FWBVAL, FWBn, FCIM, FCRIS, FSIZE, and SSIZE registers.

In order to have a clear picture about these registers and related operations, first let's have a closer look at these registers.

6.2.2.4 Boot Configuration Register (BOOTCFG)

The Boot Configuration Register belongs to the System Control space in the memory map and its mapping address is 0x400FE1D0. The base address of the System Control is 0x400FE000 and the offset address for the BOOTCFG is 0x1D0.

This register cannot be written directly, but instead using the FMD register one can modify some contents on this register. This register provides configuration of a GPIO pin to enable the internal ROM Boot Loader as well as a write-once mechanism to disable the external debugger to access the device. At reset, the user has the opportunity to direct the core to execute the internal ROM Boot Loader or an application in Flash memory by using any GPIO signal from Ports A~Q as configured by the bits in this register. At reset, the following sequence is performed:

1. First the BOOTCFG register is read. If the EN bit is clear, the internal ROM Boot Loader is executed.
2. In the internal ROM Boot Loader, the status of the specified GPIO pin is compared with the specified polarity. If the status matches the specified polarity, the ROM is mapped to address 0x0000.0000 and execution continues from the ROM Boot Loader.
3. If the EN bit is set or the status doesn't match the specified polarity, the data at address 0x0000.0004 is read, and if the data at this address is 0xFFFF.FFFF, the ROM is mapped to the address 0x0000.0000 and execution continues from the ROM Boot Loader.
4. If the data at address 0x0000.0004 is not 0xFFFF.FFFF, the stack pointer SP is loaded from Flash memory at address 0x0000.0000 and the program counter PC is loaded from address 0x0000.0004. The user application begins executing.

Figure 6.3 shows a function block diagram and bits field values of the BOOTCFG register. The bit field value and related function of this register is shown in Table 6.1.

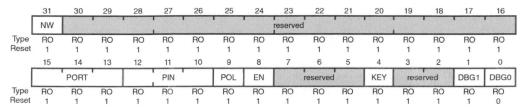

Figure 6.3. Bit field and function on BOOTCFG Register. (Reprinted with the permission of the Texas Instruments Incorporated.)

Table 6.1. Bit value and its function for BOOTCFG register.

Bit	Name	Reset	Function
31	NW (Not Written)	0x1	0: the content of this register cannot be changed. 1: the content of this register can be changed from 1 to 0.
30:16	Reserved	0xFFFF	
15:13	PORT	0x7	Indicate which Port to enable ROM Boot Loader at Reset: 0x0: Port A; 0x1: Port B; 0x2: Port C; 0x3: Port D; 0x4: Port E; 0x5: Port F; 0x6: Port G; 0x7: Port H
12:10	PIN	0x7	Indicate which Port Pin to enable ROM Boot Loader at Reset: 0x0: Pin 0; 0x1: Pin 1; 0x2: Pin 2; 0x3: Pin 3; 0x4: Pin 4; 0x5: Pin 5; 0x6: Pin 6; 0x7: Pin 7
9	POL (Boot GPIO Polarity)	0x1	0: A LOW level is selected for the GPIO Pin to enable ROM Boot Loader at Reset. 1: A HIGH level is selected for the GPIO Pin to enable ROM Boot Loader at Reset.
8	EN (Boot GPIO Enable)	0x1	0: Enable the use of a GPIO pin to enable the ROM Boot Loader at reset. 1: The contents of address 0x0000.0004 are checked to see if the Flash memory has been programmed. If the contents are not 0xFFFF.FFFF, the core executes from Flash memory. If the Flash has not been programmed, the core executes from ROM.
7:5	Reserved	0x7	
4	KEY (Key Select)	0x1	Chooses between using the value 0xA442 or 0x71D5 as the WRKEY value in the FMC/FMC2 register. 0: The value 0x71D5 is used as the WRKEY in the FMC/FMC2 register. Write to the FMC/FMC2 register with a 0xA442 key is ignored. 1: The 0xA442 is used as the WRKEY in the FMC/FMC2 register. Write to the FMC/FMC2 register with a 0x71D5 key is ignored
3:2	Reserved	0x3	
1	DBG1 (Debug Control 1)	0x1	The DBG1 bit must be 1 and DBG0 must be 0 for debug to be available.
0	DBG0 (Debug Control 0)	0x0	The DBG1 bit must be 1 and DBG0 must be 0 for debug to be available

It can be found from Table 6.1 that bit 31, Not Written (NW) is used to control whether the content of this register can be changed or not. If this bit is set to 1, the content of this register can be changed from 1 to 0 only. Generally we do not need to modify this register for our most general applications.

Bits [15:13] (PORT), [12:10] (PIN), 9 (POL), and 8 (EN) are used to indicate if a GPIO Port has been used to enable the internal ROM Boot Loader at a system reset. Bits [15:13] and [12:10] are used to determine which GPIO Port and which GPIO Pin has been selected to enable the ROM Boot Loader after a reset, and bit 9 is used to select the GPIO Pin polarity, either LOW or HIGH, to trigger or enable the ROM Boot Loader. Bit 8 is used to enable to use a GPIO Pin to enable the ROM Boot Loader at reset.

The bit 4 (KEY) is used to choose between using the value 0xA442 or 0x71D5 as the WRKEY value in the FMC register when performing a programming (writing) operation to the Flash memory.

Regularly this register is a read-only register and all bits are set to 1 after a system reset.

6.2.2.5 Flash Memory Address Register (FMA)

This register stores an address where the data should be written into on the flash memory. The memory mapping address of this register is 0x400FD000, which is located at the peripheral devices memory mapping addresses range.

Depending on different writing and erasing operations, this register contains different addresses:

- For a single word (32-bit) data writing: This register contains a 4-byte-aligned address and specifies where the data is written. The so-called 4-byte-aligned address means that only 18 bits, bits [17:0], in this FMA register are used to provide a $2^{18} = 256$-KB space for the flash array to perform programming or erasing operations.
- For a data writing operation that uses the write buffer, this register contains an aligned starting address (0x00) in bits [6:0] for 128-byte (32-word) block to be written. Bits [6:0] on the FMA register provides totally seven bits, or $2^7 = 128$ bytes or 32-word addresses for 32 Flash Write Buffer registers (FWB0~FWB31).
- For the erasing operations, this register contains a 1-KB-aligned CPU byte address and specifies which block is erased. Note that the alignment requirements must be met by software; otherwise the results of the operation are unpredictable.

The point to be noted is that for the 32-word buffer writing operation. This register contains a 128-byte aligned address; but this does not mean that this register contains a 128-byte address, instead it only contains an aligned address in the bits [6:0] on this register to cover 128 bytes. All 7 bits, bits [6:0], in this register must be 0 to provide a continuous 128-byte or 32-word space in the flash array to enable the 32-word to be written into this space.

Figure 6.4 shows a function block diagram and bits field values of the FMA register.

It can be found from Figure 6.4 that the upper 14 bits, bits [31:18], on this FMA register are reserved, and only the lower 18 bits, bits [17:0] are used to provide a 4-byte-aligned address for the flash array. This 18-bit address provides a 256-KB searchable space on flash array.

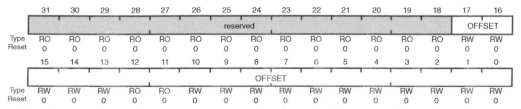

Figure 6.4. Bit field and function on FMA Register. (Reprinted with the permission of the Texas Instruments Incorporated.)

31	30	29	28	27	26	25	24	23	22	21	20	19	18	17	16
							WRKEY								
WO	WO	WO	WO	WO	WO	WO	WO	WO	WO	WO	WO	WO	WO	WO	WO
0	0	0	0	0	0	0	0	0	0	0	0	0	0	0	0

15	14	13	12	11	10	9	8	7	6	5	4	3	2	1	0
							reserved					COMT	MERASE	ERASE	WRITE
RO	RO	RO	RO	RO	RO	RO	RO	RO	RO	RO	RO	RW	RW	RW	RW
0	0	0	0	0	0	0	0	0	0	0	0	0	0	0	0

Type / Reset labels apply to the two rows below each bit-number row.

Figure 6.5. Bit field and function on the FMC Register. (Reprinted with the permission of the Texas Instruments Incorporated.)

6.2.2.6 Flash Memory Data Register (FMD)

This is a 32-bit register and it is used to store the data to be written into the flash array during the writing or programming cycle. This register is not used during erase cycles.

The memory mapping address for this register is 0x400FD004.

6.2.2.7 Flash Memory Control Register (FMC)

This is a 32-bit register and it is used to control the programming and writing operations for the flash array during the writing or programming cycle. The memory mapping address for this register is 0x400FD008.

This register must be the last register to be programmed since it initiates the memory operation. The four control bits in the lower byte of this register are used to initiate memory operations.

Figure 6.5 shows the bit-field values and related functions of this FMC register. The detailed bit field value and related function of this register is shown in Table 6.2.

6.2.2.8 Flash Memory Control 2 Register (FMC2)

This register is used to control a 32-word buffer writing or programming operation. The memory mapping address for this register is 0x400FD020.

When this register is written, the Flash memory controller initiates the appropriate access cycle for the location specified by the FMA register. If the access is a write access, the data contained in the FWBn registers are written into the related flash memory array.

This register must be the last register to be programmed as it initiates the memory operation.

Figure 6.6 shows an illustration for bit fields in this register. Table 6.3 lists bit fields and related functions of this register.

It can be found from Table 6.3 that bits 31:16 in this register contains a Write Key (WRKEY) that is used to reduce the conflict writing or accessing to the flash memory array. Two possible keys can be chosen based on the KEY value in the BOOTCFG register:

- If the KEY value is 0, the value 0x71D5 is written into this WRKEY field.
- If the KEY value is 1, the value 0xA442 is written into this WRKEY field.

The bit 0 is a buffered-write control bit (WRBUF) that is used to control a 32-word buffer programming or writing operation. If this bit is set to 1, the 128-byte data stored in the FWB0~FWB31 are written into the flash memory array based on the 32-word aligned address in FMA.

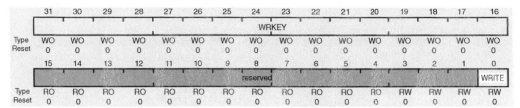

Figure 6.6.   Bit field and function on the FMC2 Register. (Reprinted with the permission of the Texas Instruments Incorporated.)

6.2.2.9 The Flash Write Buffer Valid Register (FWBVAL)

This register is used to monitor the writing status for all 32 FWBn registers. The memory mapping address for this register is 0x400FD030.

This register is a 32-bit register and each bit is for each related FWBn register. For example, bit 0 is for FWB0, bit 1 is for FWB1, and so on. Each bit value and its function is:

> 0: The corresponding FWBn register has no new data to be written.

> 1: The corresponding FWBn register has been updated since the last buffer write operation and is ready to be written into the Flash memory array.

Table 6.2.   Bit value and its function for FMC register.

Bit	Name	Reset	Function
31:16	WRKEY (Write Key)	0x0000	This write key is to minimize the incidence of accidental Flash memory writes. Depending on the value of the KEY bit in the BOOTCFG register, two different values must be written into this field for a Flash memory write to occur. If KEY = 0: 0x71D5 is written into this WRKEY field. If KEY = 1: 0xA442 is written into this WRKEY field. Writes to the FMC register without this WRKEY value are ignored. A read of this field returns the value 0.
15:4	Reserved	0x00	
3	COMT (Commit Register Value)	0	This bit is to commit writes to Flash-memory-resident registers and to monitor the progress of that process. When read, a 1 indicates that the previous commit access is not complete 0: No effect. 1: Commit (write) the register value to a Flash-memory-resident register.
2	MERASE (Mass Erase)	0	0 : No effect. 1 : Mass erase the Flash main memory. When read, a 0 indicates that the previous mass erase operation is complete.
1	ERASE (Erase a Page)	0	0: No effect. 1: Erase the Flash memory page specified by the contents of the FMA register. When read, a 0 indicates that the previous page erase operation is complete.
0	WRITE (Write a Word)	0	0: No effect. 1: Write the data stored in the FMD register into the Flash memory location specified by the contents of FMA register. When read, a 0 indicates that the write update operation is complete

Table 6.3. Bit value and its function for FMC2 register.

Bit	Name	Reset	Function
31:16	WRKEY (Write Key)	0x0000	This write key is to minimize the incidence of accidental Flash memory writes. Depending on the value of the KEY bit in the BOOTCFG register, two different values must be written into this field for a Flash memory write to occur. If KEY = 0: 0x71D5 is written into this WRKEY field. If KEY = 1: 0xA442 is written into this WRKEY field. Writes to the FMC2 register without this WRKEY value are ignored.
15:1	Reserved	0x000	
0	WRBUF (Buffered Write)	0	This bit is to start a buffered write to Flash memory. 0: No effect. 1: write the data stored in the FWBn registers to the location specified by the contents of the FMA register.

This register is cleared after the write operation by hardware. A protection violation on the write operation also clears this status.

Software can program the same 32 words to various Flash memory locations by setting the FWBn bits after they are cleared by the write operation. The next write operation then uses the same data as the previous one. In addition, if you do not want an FWBn register change to be written into the Flash memory array, software can clear the corresponding FWBn bit to preserve the existing data when the next write operation occurs.

6.2.2.10 Flash Controller Raw Interrupt Status Register (FCRIS)

This register is to monitor whether a flash memory controller has generated an interrupt request. However, this interrupt request cannot be sent to the MCU interrupt controller until the corresponding bit in the Flash Controller Interrupt Mask (FCIM) Register is set to 1. The memory mapping address for this register is 0x400FD00C.

Figure 6.7 shows an illustration for bit fields in this register. Table 6.4 lists bit fields and related functions of this register.

It can be found from Table 6.4 that all used bits in this register work like indicators to indicate whether a related operation has generated a pending interrupt or not. The PROGRIS and ERRIS bits are used to monitor whether the verification for a programming (writing) operation or an erasing operation has been failed. The INVDRIS and VOLTRIS

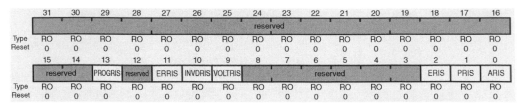

Figure 6.7. Bit field and function on FCRIS Register. (Reprinted with the permission of the Texas Instruments Incorporated.)

Table 6.4. Bit value and its function for FCRIS register.

Bit	Name	Reset	Function
31:14	Reserved	0	
13	PROGRIS (Program Verify Error Raw Interrupt Status)	0	0: An interrupt has not occurred. 1: An interrupt is pending because the verify of a PROGRAM operation failed. If this error occurs when using the Flash write buffer, software must inspect the affected words to determine where the error occurred. This bit is cleared by writing a 1 to the PROGMISC bit in the FCMISC register.
12	Reserved	0	
11	ERRIS (Erase Verify Error Raw Interrupt Status)	0	0: An interrupt has not occurred. 1: An interrupt is pending because the verify of an ERASE operation failed. If this error occurs when using the Flash write buffer, software must inspect the affected words to determine where the error occurred. This bit is cleared by writing a 1 to the ERMISC bit in the FCMISC register
10	INVDRIS (Invalid Data Raw Interrupt Status)	0	0: An interrupt has not occurred. 1: An interrupt is pending because a bit that was previously programmed as a 0 is now being requested to be programmed as a 1. This bit is cleared by writing a 1 to the INVMISC bit in the FCMISC register.
9	VOLTRIS (Pump Voltage Raw Interrupt Status)	0	0: An interrupt has not occurred. 1: An interrupt is pending because the regulated voltage of the pump went out of spec during the Flash operation and the operation was terminated. This bit is cleared by writing a 1 to the VOLTMISC bit in the FCMISC register.
8:3	Reserved	0	
2	ERIS (EEPROM Raw Interrupt Status)	0	0: An EEPROM interrupt has not occurred. 1: An EEPROM interrupt has occurred. This bit is cleared by writing a 1 to the EMISC bit in the FCMISC register
1	PRIS (Programming Raw Interrupt Status)	0	0: The programming or erase cycle has not completed. 1: The programming or erase cycle has completed. This status is sent to the interrupt controller when the PMASK bit in the FCIM register is set. This bit is cleared by writing a 1 to the PMISC bit in the FCMISC register
0	ARIS (Access Raw Interrupt Status)	0	0: No access has tried to improperly program or erase the Flash memory. 1: A program or erase action was attempted on a block of Flash memory that contradicts the protection policy for that block as set in the FMPPEn registers. This status is sent to the interrupt controller when the AMASK bit in the FCIM register is set. This bit is cleared by writing a 1 to the AMISC bit in the FCMISC register.

bits are used to monitor whether an illegal programming operation (try to change the bit value from 0 to 1) or an out-of-range of the pumped regulated voltage has occurred.

The bit ERIS is used to monitor whether an EEPROM interrupt has occurred or not. The bit PRIS is to indicate whether a program or an erase cycle has been completed. The bit ARIS is used to monitor whether any program or erase operation is against the flash memory protection policy.

Most of these bits can be cleared by setting related bits in the Flash Controller Masked Interrupt Status and Clear Register (FCMISC). Another point is that this register must be

31	30	29	28	27	26	25	24	23	22	21	20	19	18	17	16
							reserved								
RO	RO	RO	RO	RO	RO	RO	RO	RO	RO	RO	RO	RO	RO	RW	RW
0	0	0	0	0	0	0	0	0	0	0	0	0	0	0	0

15	14	13	12	11	10	9	8	7	6	5	4	3	2	1	0
reserved		PROGMASK	reserved	ERMASK	INVDMASK	VOLTMASK			reserved				EMASK	PMASK	AMASK
RO	RO	RW	RW	RW	RW	RW	RO	RO	RO	RO	RO	RO	RW	RW	RW
0	0	0	0	0	0	0	0	0	0	0	0	0	0	0	0

Figure 6.8. Bit field and function on FCIM Register. (Reprinted with the permission of the Texas Instruments Incorporated.)

used with the Flash Controller Interrupt Mask (FCIM) Register together to allow any flash memory-related interrupt to be sent to the MCU interrupt controller or NVIC.

6.2.2.11 Flash Controller Interrupt Mask Register (FCIM)

This register is used to mask (disable) or unmask (enable) the related Flash memory interrupt generated and pended in the FCRIS register. In other words, this register controls each Flash-related interrupt reported in the FCRIS and enables or disables each of these interrupts to be sent to the MCU interrupt controller NVIC or not.

The memory mapping address for this register is 0x400FD010.

Figure 6.8 shows an illustration for bit fields in this register. Table 6.5 lists bit fields and related functions of this register.

It can be found from Table 6.5 that each bit on the FCIM register can be mapped to a corresponding bit on the FCRIS register, and these bits have a one-to-one relationship between them. For example, the bit PROGMASK in the FCIM register works with the bit PROGRIS in the FCRIS register together to determine whether a program verify error interrupt can be sent to the MCU interrupt controller NVIC or not. Only both bits are set to 1, this interrupt can be sent to the NVIC to request that this interrupt to be processed by the NVIC.

A similar relationship and bit value also work for all other bits in both registers. The bit ERMASK in the FCIM register works with bit ERRIS in the FCRIS register, the bit INVDMASK in the FCIM register works with the bit INVDRIS in the FCRIS register, and so on.

All bit values in the FCIM register can be set to 1 or cleared to 0 by writing 1 or 0 to this register. However, to clear bits in the FCRIS register, you need to write 1 to the related bits in the Flash Controller Masked Interrupt Status and Clear Register (FCMISC).

6.2.2.12 Flash Controller Masked Interrupt Status and Clear Register (FCMISC)

This register provides two functions for any interrupt related to the Flash memory operations. First, it monitors and reports whether one or multiple interrupts have occurred by indicating the related interrupt source or sources that have been signaled. Second, it provides a method to clear the interrupt reporting.

The memory mapping address for this register is 0x400FD014.

Figure 6.9 shows an illustration for bit fields in this register. Table 6.6 lists bit fields and related functions of this register.

Table 6.5. Bit value and its function for FCIM register.

Bit	Name	Reset	Function
31:14	Reserved	0	
13	PROGMASK (PROGVER Interrupt Mask)	0	0: The PROGRIS interrupt is suppressed and not sent to the interrupt controller. 1: An interrupt is sent to the interrupt controller when the PROGRIS bit is set.
12	Reserved	0	
11	ERMASK (ERVER Interrupt Mask)	0	0: The ERRIS interrupt is suppressed and not sent to the interrupt controller. 1: An interrupt is sent to the interrupt controller when the ERRIS bit is set.
10	INVDMASK (Invalid Data Interrupt Mask)	0	0: The INVDRIS interrupt is suppressed and not sent to the interrupt controller. 1: An interrupt is sent to the interrupt controller when the INVDRIS bit is set.
9	VOLTMASK (VOLT Interrupt Mask)	0	0: The VOLTRIS interrupt is suppressed and not sent to the interrupt controller. 1: An interrupt is sent to the interrupt controller when the VOLTRIS bit is set.
8:3	Reserved	0	
2	EMASK (EEPROM Interrupt Mask)	0	0: The ERIS interrupt is suppressed and not sent to the interrupt controller. 1: An interrupt is sent to the interrupt controller when the ERIS bit is set.
1	PMASK (Programming Interrupt Mask)	0	0: The PRIS interrupt is suppressed and not sent to the interrupt controller. 1: An interrupt is sent to the interrupt controller when the PRIS bit is set.
0	AMASK (Access Interrupt Mask)	0	0: The ARIS interrupt is suppressed and not sent to the interrupt controller. 1: An interrupt is sent to the interrupt controller when the ARIS bit is set.

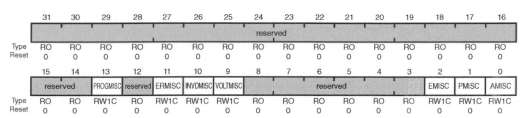

Figure 6.9. Bit field and function on FCMISC Register. (Reprinted with the permission of the Texas Instruments Incorporated.)

Table 6.6. Bit value and its function for FCMISC register.

Bit	Name	Reset	Function
31:14	Reserved	0	
13	PROGMISC (PROGVER Masked Interrupt Status & Clear)	0	0: When reading, a PROGRIS interrupt has not been occurred. 1: When reading, an unmasked PROGRIS interrupt has been occurred. Write a 1 to this bit clears PROGMISC and PROGRIS bit in the FCRIS register.
12	Reserved	0	
11	ERMISC (ERVER Masked Interrupt Status & Clear)	0	0: When reading, an ERRIS interrupt has not been occurred. 1: When reading, an ERRIS interrupt has been occurred. Write a 1 to this bit clears ERMISC and ERRIS bit in the FCRIS register.
10	INVDMISC (Invalid Data Masked Interrupt Status & Clear)	0	0: When reading, an INVDRIS interrupt has not been occurred. 1: When reading, an INVDRIS interrupt has been occurred. Write a 1 to this bit clears INVDMISC and INVDRIS bit in the FCRIS register.
9	VOLTMISC (VOLT Masked Interrupt Status & Clear)	0	0: When reading, a VOLTRIS interrupt has not been occurred. 1: When reading, a VOLTRIS interrupt has been occurred. Write a 1 to this bit clears VOLTMISC and VOLTRIS bit in the FCRIS register.
8:3	Reserved	0	
2	EMISC (EEPROM Masked Interrupt Status & Clear)	0	0: When reading, an ERIS interrupt has not been occurred. 1: When reading, an ERIS interrupt has been occurred. Write a 1 to this bit clears EMISC and ERIS bit in the FCRIS register.
1	PMISC (Programming Masked Interrupt Status & Clear)	0	0: When reading, a PRIS interrupt has not been occurred. 1: When reading, a PRIS has been occurred. Write a 1 to this bit clears PMISC and PRIS bit in the FCRIS register.
0	AMISC (Access Interrupt Mask)	0	0: When reading, a 0 indicates that no improper accesses have occurred. 1: When reading, a 1 indicates that an AMISC interrupt was signaled because a program or erase action was attempted on a block of Flash memory that contradicts the protection policy for that block as set in the FMPPEn registers. Write a 1 to this bit clears AMISC and ARIS bit in the FCRIS register.

It can be found from Table 6.6 that any attempt to try to write a 0 to any of these bits has no effect to these bits. This means that the normal operations to these bits are either a reading or a writing a 1 to these bits to clear these bits on this register and the corresponding bits on the FCRIS register.

6.2.2.13 *Other Control Registers Related to Flash Memory Control*

Some other control registers related to the Flash memory controls and operations are:

- Flash Write Buffer n Registers (FWBn) with memory mapping addresses 0x400FD100 ~ 0x400FD17C.
- Flash Size Register (FSIZE) with memory mapping address 0x400FDFC0.
- SRAM Size Register (SSIZE) with memory mapping address 0x400FDFC4.

The 32 FWBn registers (FWB0~FWB31) are 32-bit registers used to store the contents to be written into the related Flash memory when a Flash Write Buffer Writing operation is executed. The address of each of these registers is determined by the bits [6:0] in the FMA register. The values on bits [6:0] in the FMA must be 0 to provide a continuous $2^7 = 128$-byte (32-word) space in the flash memory array where the 32-word can be written into. Therefore the register FWB0 corresponds to the address in bits [6:0] in the FMA, which is 0x00. The FWB1 corresponds to the address that equals (bits [6:0] of FMA) + 0x4 = (0x04) and so on. Only the FWBn registers that have been updated since the previous buffered Flash memory write operation can be written into the related flash array. The Flash Write Buffer Valid (FWBVAL) register shows which registers have been written since the last buffered Flash memory writing operation.

The FSIZE register can be used to indicate the size of the Flash memory implemented on the current microcontroller. However, to support legacy software, the Device Capabilities 0 (DC0) register is available. A read of the DC0 register (bits 15~0) correctly identifies legacy memory sizes. Software must use the FSIZE register to determine the memory sizes that are not listed in the DC0 register description.

The SSIZE register is used to determine the size of the SRAM implemented on the current microcontroller. However, similar to FSIZE register, to support legacy software, the DC0 register is available. A read of the DC0 register (bits 31~16) correctly identifies legacy memory sizes. Software must use the SSIZE register for memory sizes that are not listed in the DC0 register.

6.2.3 Flash Memory Protection Control

As shown in Figure 6.1, besides the Flash Memory Controller and Flash Array, there is a Flash Protection Control unit with several control registers, such as Flash Memory Protection Program Enable (FMPPEn) registers, Flash Memory Protection Read Enable (FMPREn) registers, BOOTCFG register, and four USER_REGn registers (n = 0~3).

All four USER_REGn registers are 32-bit registers and each of them is used to provide 32-bit user-defined data that are nonvolatile, and the values on these 32-bit can only be changed from 1 to 0.

The Flash Memory Protection Control unit provides some ways to protect the Flash memory array from being programmed, erased, or read when some operations are executed on the flash memory array. These protections are mainly performed by using two kinds of registers: the FMPPEn and FMPREn.

The FMPPEn registers provide protection abilities to protect the flash memory from programming or writing operations inexpertly, and the FMPREn registers provide abilities to protect the flash memory from reading operation incidentally.

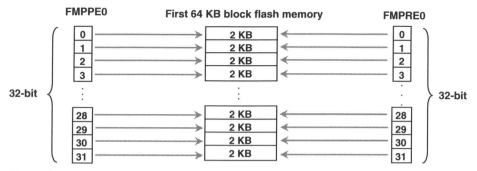

Figure 6.10.   The protection functions provided by the FMPPE0 and FMPRE0 registers.

The FMPPEn (n=0~3) registers include four registers, FMPPE0 ~ FMPPE3. Each register is a 32-bit register and each bit can be used to control one 2-KB block flash memory space. Therefore each 32-bit register FMPPEn can provide protection control for $32 \times 2\,KB = 64\,KB$ flash memory space. Four FMPPEn (n=0~3) registers can control $4 \times 64\,KB = 256\,KB$ flash memory space.

Similar to these four FMPPEn registers, there are four 32-bit FMPREn (n=0~3) registers, FMPRE0~FMPRE3. Each of these registers is a 32-bit register and each bit can control a 2-KB block flash memory space. They can control 256 KB flash memory space.

Figure 6.10 provides an example functional block diagram for FMPPE0 and FMPRE0 registers to provide the writing and reading protections for the first 64-KB block flash memory array.

The protection or control abilities provided by these two kinds of registers are:

- Flash Memory Protection Program Enable Register (FMPPEn): If a bit in this register is set to 1, the corresponding 2-KB block flash memory space may be programmed (written) or erased. If a bit is cleared, the corresponding block may not be changed.

- Flash Memory Protection Read Enable Register (FMPREn): If a bit in this register is set, the corresponding 2-KB block may be executed or read by software or debuggers. If a bit is cleared, the corresponding block may only be executed, and contents of the memory block are prohibited from being read as data.

These protection or control abilities can be summarized in Table 6.7.

A Flash memory access that attempts to read a read-protected block (FMPREn bit is 0) is prohibited and generates a bus fault. A Flash memory access that attempts to program or

Table 6.7.   Flash memory protection policy combinations.

FMPPEn	FMPREn	Protection Function
0	0	Execute-Only Protection. The block may only be executed and cannot be written or erased. This mode is used to protect code.
0	1	Read-Only Protection. The block may be read or executed but cannot be written or erased. This mode locks the block from further modification while allowing any read or execute access.
1	0	The block may be written, erased, or executed, but not read.
1	1	No protection. The block may be written, erased, executed, or read.

erase a program-protected block (FMPPEn bit is 0) is prohibited and can optionally generate an interrupt if the AMASK bit in the `Flash Controller Interrupt Mask` (FCIM) register is set to 1 to alert software developers of poorly behaving software during the development and debug process.

The default settings for the FMPREn and FMPPEn registers are all 1s for all implemented flash memory 2-KB banks. These settings create a policy of open access and programmability. The register bits may be changed by clearing the specific register bits. The changes are effective immediately, but are not permanent until the register is committed (saved), at which point the bit change is permanent. If a bit is changed from a 1 to a 0 and not committed, it may be restored by executing a power-on reset sequence.

In fact, for all possible protection situations listed in Table 6.7, only two protection policies are often used in the flash memory protection controls: the `Execution-Only Protection` and the `Read-Only Protection` policies.

- `Execution-Only Protection`: Provides the protection ability to prevent the flash memory from being written (programmed) and read access. This mode provides a situation where a device needs the debug process, yet portions of the application space must be protected from external access.
- `Read-Only Protection`: Prevents the contents of the flash block from being re-programmed, while still allowing the content to be read by processor or the debug interface. Note that if a FMPREn bit is cleared, all read accesses to the Flash memory block are disabled, which includes any data accesses. Care must be taken not to store required data in a Flash memory block that has the associated FMPREn bit cleared. The read-only mode does not prevent read access to the stored program, but it does provide protection against accidental erasure or programming.

Next let's take care of the internal ROM installed in the 4M4C123GH6PM MCU.

6.2.4 Internal Read-Only Memory (ROM)

As we discussed in Section 2.6.2 in Chapter 2, the Internal ROM is a new memory device in TM4C123GH6PM MCU and this device contains the following software and programs:

- TivaWare™ Driver Libraries, including the Peripheral Devices Library, USB Library, Graphical Library, and Sensor Hub Library
- TivaWare™ Boot Loader
- Advanced Encryption Standard (AES) cryptography tables
- Cyclic Redundancy Check (CRC) error-detection functionality

The TivaWare™ Boot Loader is used to download code to the Flash memory of a device without the use of a debug interface. When the core is reset, the user has the opportunity to direct the core to execute the ROM Boot Loader or the application in Flash memory by using any GPIO signal in Ports A~H as configured in the `Boot Configuration` (BOOTCFG) register. More detailed information about the Boot Loader can be found in Section 3.7.1.2 in Chapter 3. For detailed information about the BOOTCFG register, refer to Section 6.2.2.4 in this chapter.

AES is ideal for applications that can use prearranged keys, such as setup during manufacturing or configuration.

The CRC technique can be used to validate correct receipt of messages (nothing lost or modified in transit), to validate data after decompression, to validate that Flash memory contents have not been changed, and for other cases where the data needs to be validated.

6.2.4.1 The Boot Loader

The Texas Instruments™ Tiva™ boot loader is a small piece of code that can be programmed at the beginning of flash to act as an application loader as well as an update mechanism for applications running on a Tiva™ ARM® Cortex®-M4-based microcontroller. The boot loader can be built to use the UART0, SSI0, I2C0, CAN, Ethernet, or USB ports to update the code on the microcontroller. The boot loader is customizable via source code modifications, or simply by deciding at compile time which routines to include. Since a full source code is provided, the boot loader can be completely customized.

Three update protocols are utilized. On UART0, SSI0, I2C0, and CAN, a custom protocol is used to communicate with the download utility to transfer the firmware image and program it into flash. When using Ethernet or USB Device Firmware Upgrade (DFU), however, different protocols are employed. On Ethernet the standard bootstrap protocol (BOOTP) is used and for USB DFU, updates are performed via the standard DFU class.

When configured to use UART0, Ethernet, or USB, the LM Flash Programmer GUI can be used to download an application via the boot loader.

Some other functions provided by the Boot Loader are as follows:

- Download codes to the flash memory for firmware updates.
- Interface options include USB, UART, CAN, I2C, and SPI.

After the TivaWare™ for C Series software package is installed in your host computer, all Boot Loader-related codes, including the source code files, header files and assembly code files, are located at `C:/ti/TivaWare_C_Series-<version>/ boot_loader`.

6.2.4.2 The TivaWare™ Peripheral Driver Library

The TivaWare™ for the C Series suite contains and integrates all user-required source-code functions and object libraries, which include the following:

- The `Peripheral Driver Library` offers an extensive set of API functions for controlling the peripherals found on various TM4C devices.
- The `Graphic Library` includes a set of graphics primitives and a widget set for creating graphical user interfaces on Tiva™ C Series-based microcontroller boards that have a graphical display.
- The `USB Library` provides a TivaWare™ royalty-free USB stack to enable efficient USB host, device, and on-the-go operations.
- The `Sensor Hub Library` offers an advanced sensor fusion algorithm and a broad range of sensor support.
- The `Utilities` provide all required developing tools and user-friendly functions to make the user-program development easier and simpler.

- The `Boot Loader & In-System Programming` support users to build the startup codes, install them at the beginning of the flash ROM in the EVB, and run them when the user program starts.
- The `Open Source RTOS` is a Free RTOS that is a popular real-time operating system for most popular embedded devices. This RTOS accelerates development schedules by eliminating the need to create basic system software functions from scratch. It also scales from a real-time multitasking kernel, the TI-RTOS Kernel, to a complete RTOS solution including additional middleware components and device drivers. By providing essential system software components pre-tested and pre-integrated, the RTOS enables developers to focus on differentiating their application.
- The `Open Source Stacks` offer different stacks for most popular host and peripheral devices.
- The `Code Examples` offer some useful coding guides to help users to start and speed up their coding developments.
- The `Third-Party Code Examples` provide some codes developed by different venders.

In this section we only pay attention to the Peripheral Driver Library.

Basically the Peripheral Driver Library provides a set of high-level API interfaces to enable users to access and interface all related peripheral devices to build their applications. This set of API interfaces is a collection of source code (`.c`) files and related header (`.h`) files used to support users to develop and build their application projects by calling those API interface functions. This library is compatible with most popular IDEs, such as CCS, ARM®/Keil® MDK, IAR, and GNU.

This library should be installed on or integrated with the related development IDE to facilitate the user's program development. All source and header files in the library are located at the related folders when the TivaWare™ for C Series software is installed in your host computer. These folders are:

- `C:/ti/TivaWare_C_Series-<version>/inc`: Contains all hardware or device related specified header files. These files include:
  - Peripheral specific definitions
  - Required Type definitions
  - Macros
- `C:/ti/TivaWare_C_Series-<version>/driverlib`: Contains all project library files (object codes) and compiler output directory, which include:
  - C source and header files peripheral specific functionality
  - Compiler specific project file for building the driver library 'libraries'
  - Compiler specific output directories and files for the used compiler. It should be: `C:/ti/TivaWare_C_Series-<version>/driverlib/rvmdk` for the ARM-MDK μVersion5

A point to be noted is that this TivaWare™ for C Series Peripheral Driver Library is also installed in the internal ROM space on all Tiva™ C Series MCUs. Two header files, `rom.h` and `rom_map.h`, provide assistants to the user to access and use these API functions in the library. These two header files are located at the folder: `C:\ti\TivaWare_C_Series-<version>/driverlib` in your host computer.

Several tables at the beginning of the internal ROM point to the entry points for the API functions that are provided in the ROM. Accessing the API functions through these tables provides scalability; while the API locations may be changed in future versions of the ROM, the API tables will not. The tables are split into two levels: The main table contains one pointer per peripheral which points to a secondary table that contains one pointer per API function that is associated with that peripheral. This means that one peripheral can have multiple API functions. The main table is located at 0x0100.0010, right after the Cortex®-M4F vector table in the ROM.

To access or use these API functions, a prefix ROM_ must be added before each function to distinguish them from those same functions included in the library that is installed in the users' host computer. For example, to access or use the API function, GPIOPinWrite(), you must use ROM_GPIOPinWrite() to distinguish the same function in the Peripheral Driver Library installed in your host computer.

6.2.4.3 The ROM Control Register (RMCTL)

This register provides control of the ROM controller state. The memory mapping address for this register is 0x400F.E0F0.

Although this is a 32-bit register, however, only 1 bit, bit 0 or called Boot Alias (BA), is used to indicate which memory device is located at the memory mapping address 0x0:

- If BA = 0, the flash memory is at address 0x0. This means that the program starts from the flash memory.
- If BA = 1, the internal ROM is at the address 0x0. This means that the program starts from the internal ROM.

This bit is cleared by writing a 1 to this bit position.

6.2.4.4 The ROM Software Map Register (ROMSWMAP)

The ROM Software Map Register (ROMSWMAP) is used to determine the presence of third-party software in the on-chip ROM on the current microcontroller. The memory mapping address for this register is 0x400FDFCC.

However, in order to support legacy software, the Non-Volatile Memory Information (NVMSTAT) register is available. A read of the TPSW bit in the NVMSTAT register can correctly identify the presence of legacy third-party software. Software should use the ROMSWMAP register for software that is not on legacy devices.

6.2.5 Electrical Erased Programmable Read-Only Memory (EEPROM)

In the TM4C123GH6PM MCU system, a 2-KB EEPROM is installed and used to support the users' software development. This 2-KB EEPROM array can be considered and accessed in the following two different formats:

- 512 32-bit words (512×4 Bytes = 2048 Bytes = 2 KB).
- 32 blocks of 16-word with each block containing 16 words ($32 \times 16 \times 4$ Bytes = 2 KB).

The EEPROM Size Information (EESIZE) register provides the number of 16-word blocks and 32-bit word in the current EEPROM.

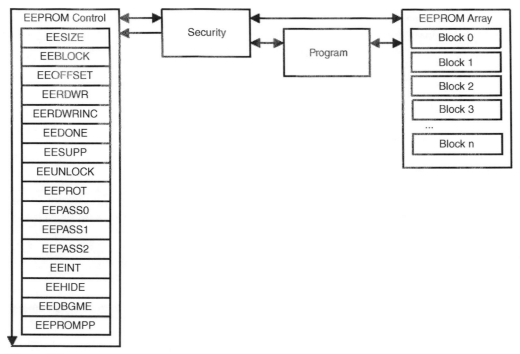

Figure 6.11. The functional block diagram of the EEPROM. (Reprinted with the permission of the Texas Instruments Incorporated.)

Figure 6.11 shows a functional block diagram of this EEPROM module.

All these 32 blocks are controlled and managed by 16 EEPROM Control Registers. Under the controls of these registers, the EEPROM can perform the following functions:

- The whole EEPROM body, including 32 blocks, can be protected in accessing, reading, and writing operations by EEPROM Protection (EEPROT) register.
- Each block can be individually protected in accessing, reading, and writing operations.
- The password model allows the application to lock one or more EEPROM blocks to control access on 16-word boundaries by EEPROM Password (EEPASS0~EEPASS2) registers.
- Each block is addressable as an offset within the EEPROM, using a block select register. Each word is offset addressable within the selected block. The EEPROM Read–Write (EERDWR) register is used to read or write the EEPROM word at the address pointed to by the EEPROM Current Block (EEBLOCK) and EEPROM Current Offset (EEOFFSET) registers.
- After enabling or resetting the EEPROM module, software must wait until the WORKING bit in the EEPROM Done Status (EEDONE) register is clear before accessing any EEPROM registers.
- The current block is selected by the EEBLOCK register. The current offset is selected by the EEOFFSET register. The application may write the EEOFFSET register any time, and it is also automatically incremented when the EEPROM Read–Write with Increment (EERDWRINC) register is accessed.
- Blocks are individually protected and any attempt to read from a block for which the application does not have permission returns 0xFFFF.FFFF. Attempts to write into a block for which the application does not have permission results in an error in the EEDONE register.

- All password-protected blocks are locked at reset. To unlock a block, the correct password value must be written to the EEPROM Unlock (EEUNLOCK) register by writing to it one to three times to form the 32-bit, 64-bit, or 96-bit password registered using the EEPASSn (n = 0~2) registers. The value used to configure the EEPASS0 register must always be written last. For example, for a 96-bit password, the value used to configure the EEPASS2 register is written first, followed by the EEPASS1 and the EEPASS0 register values. A block or the module may be re-locked by writing 0xFFFF.FFFF to the EEUNLOCK register because 0xFFFF.FFFF is not a valid password.
- EEPROM operations must be completed before entering Sleep or Deep-Sleep mode. Ensure the EEPROM operations have completed by checking the EEDONE register before issuing a WFI instruction to enter Sleep or Deep-Sleep.
- Interrupt support for writing completion to avoid the polling by EEPROM Interrupt (EEINT) register. An interrupt is generated at any time when the EEDONE register goes from working to done (WORKING bit from 1 to 0), because of either an error or the successful completion of a program or erase operation.
- This interrupt mechanism works for data writes, writes to password and protection registers, forced erase by the EEPROM Support Control and Status (EESUPP) register, and mass erase using the EEPROM Debug Mass Erase (EEDGBME) register. The EEPROM interrupt is signaled to the core using the Flash memory interrupt vector. Software can determine that the source of the interrupt was the EEPROM by examining bit 2 of the Flash Controller Masked Interrupt Status and Clear (FCMISC) register.
- The EEPROM Block Hide (EEHIDE) register provides a temporary form of protection for the EEPROM array. Every block except block 0 can be hidden, which prevents all accesses until the next reset.
- The EEPROM Peripheral Properties (EEPROMPP) register indicates the size of the EEPROM array installed in the current system.

Before the EEPROM array can be accessed to perform either reading or writing operations, it must be initialized and configured to enable the users to use and implement this array.

6.2.5.1 EEPROM Initialization and Configuration

Before writing to any EEPROM registers to enable and set up the EEPROM control functions, the following initializations and configurations must be performed:

1. The system clock to the EEPROM module must be enabled through the EEPROM Run Mode Clock Gating Control (RCGCEEPROM) register.
2. Delay 6 clock cycles to stabilize the system clock applied on the EEPROM module.
3. Check the WORKING bit in the EEPROM Done Status (EEDONE) register until it is clear, indicating that the EEPROM has completed its power-on initialization.
4. Read the PRETRY and ERETRY bits in the EEPROM Support Control and Status (EESUPP) register. If both bits are 0, which means that both programming and erasing operations are fine, continue to the next step. If either of the bits is set to 1, return an error.
5. Reset the EEPROM module using the EEPROM Software Reset (SREEPROM) register at offset 0x558 in the System Control register space.
6. Delay 6 clock cycles to stabilize this software reset action.

7. Check the WORKING bit in the EEDONE register to determine whether this reset is done. When WORKING bit = 0, this means that it is done and continue to the next step.

8. Read the PRETRY and ERETRY bits in the EESUPP register. If both bits are 0, this means that the EEPROM initialization is complete and software may use the peripheral as normal. If either of the bits are set, this means that something is wrong and an error is returned.

In order to understand the operations of the EEPROM module better, we need to have more detailed knowledge about some registers used in the EEPROM module controls. Since there are 16 control registers used in this module, we can only select some important and key registers to discuss in the following section.

6.2.5.2 Most Important Control Registers Used in the EEPROM Module

These registers include:

- EEPROM Current Block Register (EEBLOCK).
- EEPROM Current Offset Register (EEOFFSET).
- EEPROM Done Status Register (EEDONE).
- EEPROM Support Control and Status Register (EESUPP).
- EEPROM Protection Register (EEPROT).

Let's discuss these registers one by one in more details in the following sections.

6.2.5.2.1 The EEPROM Current Block Register (EEBLOCK) This is a 32-bit register used to select the EEPROM block for reading, writing, and protection control. The memory mapping address for this register is 0x400A.F004.

Only the lower 16 bits, bits [15:0], in this register are used to provide the block offset values. The value is exactly a block offset into the EEPROM, such that the first block is 0, then second block is 1, etc. Each block contains 16 words. Attempts to set an invalid block causes the 16-bit BLOCK field to be configured to 0. To verify that the intended block is being accessed, software can read the lower 16-bit BLOCK field after it has been written. Totally there are 32 blocks in this EEPROM module and each block contains 16 words.

6.2.5.2.2 The EEPROM Current Offset Register (EEOFFSET) This is a 32-bit register used to select the EEPROM word to read or write within the block selected by the EEBLOCK register. The memory mapping address for this register is 0x400A.F008.

Only the lowest 4 bits, bits [3:0], in this register are used to provide the word offset values. The value is a word offset into the block. Because accesses to the EERDWRINC register change the offset, software can read the contents of this register to determine the current offset.

When perform writing or reading operation, The EEPROM Read-Write (EERDWR) register is used to read or write the EEPROM word at the address pointed to by the EEPROM Current Block (EEBLOCK) and EEPROM Current Offset (EEOFFSET) registers.

6.2.5.2.3 EEPROM Done Status Register (EEDONE) This is a 32-bit register used to provide the current running status of the EEPROM module. The memory mapping address for this register is 0x400A.F018.

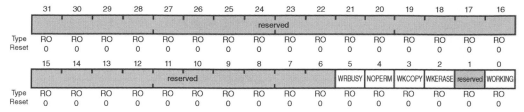

Figure 6.12. The bit field values and related functions in the EEDONE register. (Reprinted with the permission of the Texas Instruments Incorporated.)

The EEDONE register indicates the following running status for the EEPROM module:

- Successful or failed completion of a writing using the EERDWR or EERDWRINC register.
- Protection set using the EEPROT register.
- Password registered using the EEPASS register.
- Copy buffer erasing or programming retry using the EESUPP register.
- Debug mass erase using the EEDBGME register.

Figure 6.12 shows the bit-field values and related functions for this register. Table 6.8 lists all bit field values and functions for each bit.

The EEDONE register can also be used with the EEINT register to generate an interrupt to report the status. The normal usage is to poll and check the EEDONE register or read the register after an interrupt is triggered. When the EEDONE bit 0 (WORKING bit) is set, the operation is still in progress. When the EEDONE bit 0 is clear, the value of EEDONE indicates the completion status. If all bits on the EEDONE register are equal to 0, then the write completed successfully. If some bits on the EEDONE not equal to 0, then an error occurred and the source of the error is given by the set bit(s).

Table 6.8. Bit value and its function for EEDONE register.

Bit	Name	Reset	Function
31:6	Reserved	0	
5	WRBUSY (Write Busy)	0	0: No error and a writing is allowed. 1: A write is in progress and the EEPROM is busy.
4	NOPERM (Write Without Permission)	0	0: No error. 1: An attempt was made to write without permission. This error can result for the block being locked, the write violates the programmed access protection, or an attempt is made to write a password when the password has already been written.
3	WKCOPY (Working on a Copy)	0	0: The EEPROM is not copying. 1: A write is in progress and is waiting for the EEPROM to copy to or from the copy buffer.
2	WKERASE (Working on an Erase)	0	0: The EEPROM is not erasing. 1: A write is in progress and the original block is being erased after being copied.
1	Reserved	0	
0	WORKING (EEPROM is Working)	0	0: The EEPROM is not working. 1: The EEPROM is working.

6.2.5.2.4 EEPROM Support Control and Status Register (EESUPP)
This is a 32-bit register used to provide the additional support and current running status of the EEPROM module. The memory mapping address for this register is 0x400A.F01C.

Only the lowest 4 bits, bits [3:0], are used for this register to provide additional support and running status of the EEPROM module. Table 6.9 lists all bit-field values and related functions for each bit.

The bit field values and related functions for the EESUPP register are as follows:

- The EREQ bit is set if the internal copy buffer must be erased before the next time it is used because it is full. To avoid the delay of waiting for the copy buffer to be erased on the next write, it can be erased manually using this register by setting the START bit.

- If either PRETRY or ERETRY is set, this indicates that an operation is failed and it must be restarted. Setting the START bit causes the operation to be performed again.

- The PRETRY and ERETRY bits are cleared automatically after the failed operation has been successfully completed.

- These bits are not changed by reset, so any condition that occurred before a reset is still indicated after a reset.

6.2.5.2.5 EEPROM Protection Register (EEPROT)
This is a 32-bit register used to set or read the protection level for the current block, as selected by the EEBLOCK register. The memory mapping address for this register is 0x400A.F030.

Only the lowest 4 bits, bits [3:0], are used in this register to provide the protection levels and access levels for this EEPROM module and all blocks. Figure 6.13 shows the bit

Table 6.9. Bit value and its function for EESUPP register.

Bit	Name	Reset	Function
31:4	Reserved	0	
3	PRETRY (Programming Must Be Restarted)	—	0: Programming has not failed. 1: Programming is failed and must be restarted by setting the START bit.
2	ERETRY (Erase Must Be Restarted)	—	0: Erasing has not failed. 1: Erasing is failed and must be restarted by setting the START bit.
1	EREQ (Erase Required)	—	0: The copy buffer has available space. 1: An erase of the copy buffer is required.
0	START (Start an Erase)	0	Setting this bit starts error recovery if the PRETRY or ERETRY bit is set. If both the PRETRY and the ERETRY bits are clear, setting this bit starts erasing the copy buffer if EREQ is set. If none of the other bits in this register are set, setting this bit is ignored. After this bit is set, the WORKING bit in the EEDONE register is set and is cleared when the operation is complete. In addition, the EEINT register can be used to generate an interrupt on completion. If this bit is set while an operation is in progress, the write is ignored. The START bit is automatically cleared when the operation completes.

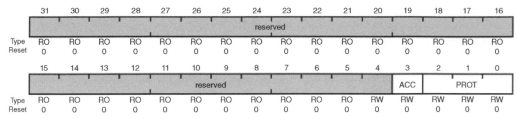

Figure 6.13. The bit field values and related functions in the EEPROT register. (Reprinted with the permission of the Texas Instruments Incorporated.)

field values and functions for each bit on this register. Table 6.10 lists all bit field values and functions for each bit.

Protection and access control is used to determine when a block's contents can be read or written. The protection level for block 0 sets the minimum protection level for the entire EEPROM. Any other blocks must use an equal or a higher protection level compared with the level set for the block 0. For example, if the PROT field is configured to 0x1 for block 0, then block 1 could be configured with the PROT field to be 0x1, 0x2, or 0x3, but not 0x0.

6.2.5.3 Other Important Control Registers Used in the EEPROM Module

The other important control registers used in the EEPROM array include:

- EEPROM Read-Write Register (EERDWR). The memory mapping address for this register is 0x400A.F010. This is a 32-bit register used to read or write the EEPROM word at the address pointed to by the EEBLOCK and EEOFFSET registers.
- EEPROM Read-Write with Increment Register (EERDWRINC). The memory mapping address for this register is 0x400A.F014. This 32-bit register provides the similar function as the EERDWR register did, but the only difference is that an increment in the

Table 6.10. Bit value and its function for EEPROT register.

Bit	Name	Reset	Function
31:4	Reserved	0	
3	ACC (Access Control)	—	0: Both user and supervisor code may access this block of the EEPROM. 1: Only supervisor code may access this block of the EEPROM. If this bit is set for block 0, then the whole EEPROM may only be accessed by supervisor code.
2:0	PORT (Protection Control)	—	0x0: This setting is the default. If there is no password, the block is not protected and is readable and writable. If there is a password, the block is readable, but only writable when unlocked. 0x1: If there is a password, the block is readable or writable only when unlocked. This value has no meaning when there is no password. 0x2: If there is no password, the block is readable, not writable. If there is a password, the block is readable only when unlocked, but is not writable under any conditions. 0x3: Reserved

OFFSET field in the EEOFFSET register is executed after the execution of reading or writing operations.

- EEPROM Unlock Register (EEUNLOCK). The memory mapping address for this register is 0x400A.F020. This 32-bit register is used to unlock the whole EEPROM or a single block using a password. Unlocking is only required if a password is registered using the EEPASSn registers for the block that is selected by the EEBLOCK register.

- EEPROM Interrupt Register (EEINT). The memory mapping address for this register is 0x400A.F040. This is a 32-bit register but only one bit, named INT or bit[0], in this register is used to control whether an interrupt can be generated when a writing to the EEPROM completes, which is indicated by the WORKING bit in the EEDONE register changing from 0x1 to 0x0. If the INT bit in this register is set, which means that any writing–done interrupt is enabled, the ERIS bit in the Flash Controller Raw Interrupt Status (FCRIS) register is also set whenever the WORKING bit in the EEDONE register changes from 0x1 to 0x0 since the Flash memory and the EEPROM share the same interrupt vector.

- EEPROM Block Hide Register (EEHIDE). The memory mapping address for this register is 0x400A.F050. This 32-bit register is used to hide one or more blocks other than block 0. Once hidden, the block is not accessible until the next reset.

- EEPROM Debug Mass Erase Register (EEDBGME). The memory mapping address for this register is 0x400A.F080. This 32-bit register is used to mass erase the EEPROM block back to its default state from the factory. This register is intended to be used only for debug and test purposes, not in production environments.

6.3 MEMORY MAP IN TM4C123GH6PM MCU SYSTEM

We have provided detailed discussions about the memory map used in the TM4C123GH6PM MCU system in Sections 2.3.1 and 2.6.2 in Chapter 2. Therefore in this section we just highlight some important sections in this map and devices mapped to this system.

Figure 6.14 shows a system memory map for the TM4C123GH6PM MCU system.

It can be found from this memory map that the default memory capacity for the Flash Memory is 16 MB with an address range of 0x0000.0000~0x00FF.FFFF. Currently only a 256-KB Flash memory space (0x0000.0000~0x0003.FFFF) is used for user's program codes and exception/interrupt vector tables. Similarly, the default memory capacity for the SRAM is 512-KB, but currently only a 32-KB space is available to the users in this map. Additional flash ROM and SRAM can be added if more memory spaces are needed for special applications. The memory space used for peripherals has the similar situations.

Regularly the users should use Flash memory to store their program codes and use SRAM to save their program data since the Cortex®-M4 processor uses the different system buses to fetch instructions and data synchronously. In this way, the application programs can be executed fast and effectively.

The 16-MB Internal ROM is used to store the TivaWare™ Peripheral Driver Library and Boot Loader, AES and CRC. The microcontroller can use this Boot Loader as an initial program loader to load and run the user's program if the Flash memory is empty.

Both 32-KB SRAM and 1-MB Peripheral memory spaces include bit-band regions. Bit-banding provides atomic operations to bit data. A bit-band region maps each word in a bit-band alias region to a single bit in the bit-band region. The bit-band regions occupy the lowest 1 MB of the SRAM and peripheral memory regions. More detailed discussions about the bit-band operations can be found in Section 6.4.

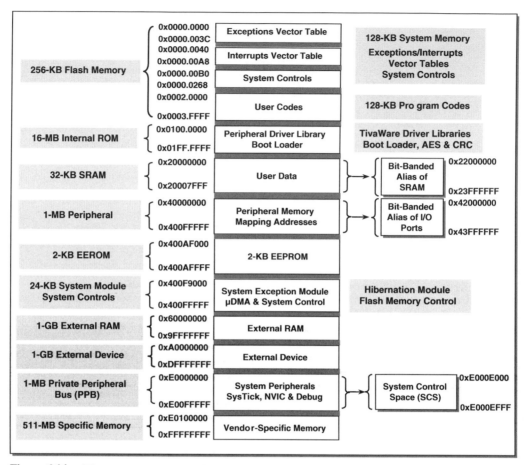

Figure 6.14.   The system memory map for TM4C123GH6PM MCU.

Most system control related registers are located at the memory space ranging from 0x400F.9000 to 0xE00F.FFFF in this memory map. The last 511-MB space is reserved for the vendor-specific memory usage.

Table 6.11 provides a more detailed memory map for this TM4C1233GH6PM MCU system.

6.4 BIT-BAND OPERATIONS

It can be found from Figure 6.14 and Table 6.11 that both the 32-KB SRAM and the Peripheral memory spaces in the memory map can be mapped to two bit-band alias regions, bit-banded alias of SRAM and bit-banded alias of I/O Ports, respectively.

The first 1-MB memory space for SRAM, 0x2000.0000~0x200F.FFFF, and the first 1-MB space for the Peripheral, 0x400.0000~0x400F.FFFF, in the memory map are called bit-band regions and they can be accessed in two different ways. This

Table 6.11. Memory map for TM4C123GH6PM MCU.

Start Address	End Address	Descriptions
256 KB On-Chip Flash Memory		
0x0000.0000	0x0000.003C	Exceptions Vector Table
0x0000.0040	0x0000.00A8	Interrupts Vector Table
0x0000.00B0	0x0000.0268	System Controls
0x0002.0000	0x0003.FFFF	User Codes
Internal ROM		
0x0100.0000	0x01FF.FFFF	Tiva Driver Libraries, Boot Loader, AES & CRC
32 KB of SRAM		
0x2000.0000	0x2000.7FFF	User Data
0x2200.0000	0x23FF.FFFF	Bit-band alias of bit-banded on-chip SRAM starting at 0x2000.0000
Peripherals		
0x4000.0000	0x4000.0FFF	Watchdog Timer 0
0x4000.1000	0x4000.1FFF	Watchdog Timer 1
0x4000.4000	0x4000.4FFF	GPIO Port A (APB Aperture)
0x4000.5000	0x4000.5FFF	GPIO Port B (APB Aperture)
0x4000.6000	0x4000.6FFF	GPIO Port C (APB Aperture)
0x4000.7000	0x4000.7FFF	GPIO Port D (APB Aperture)
0x4000.8000	0x4000.BFFF	SSI0 ~ SSI3
0x4000.C000	0x4001.3FFF	UART0 ~ UART7
0x4002.0000	0x4002.3FFF	I^2C0–I^2C3
0x4002.4000	0x4002.4FFF	GPIO Port E (APB Aperture)
0x4002.5000	0x4002.5FFF	GPIO Port F (APB Aperture)
0x4002.8000	0x4002.9FFF	PWM0–PWM1
0x4002.C000	0x4002.DFFF	QEI0–QEI1
0x4003.0000	0x4003.5FFF	16/32-Bit Timer 0–16/32-Bit Timer 5
0x4003.6000	0x4003.7FFF	32/64-Bit Timer 0–32/64-Bit Timer 1
0x4003.8000	0x4003.8FFF	ADC0
0x4003.9000	0x4003.9FFF	ADC1
0x4003.C000	0x4003.CFFF	Analog Comparators
0x4004.0000	0x4004.1FFF	CAN0–CAN1 Controllers
0x4004.C000	0x4003.FFFF	32/64-Bit Timer 2–32/64-Bit Timer 5
0x4005.0000	0x4005.0FFF	USB
0x4005.8000	0x4005.DFFF	GPIO Port A–Port F (AHB Aperture)
0x400A.F000	0x400A.FFFF	2KB EEPROM and Key locker
0x400F.9000	0x400F.9FFF	System Exception Module
0x400F.C000	0x400F.CFFF	Hibernation Module
0x400F.D000	0x400F.DFFF	Flash Memory Control
0x400F.E000	0x400F.EFFF	System Control
0x400F.F000	0x400F.FFFF	µDMA
0x4200.0000	0x43FF.FFFF	Bit-banded alias of 0x4000.0000 through 0x400F.FFFF
External RAM		
0x6000.0000	0x9FFF.FFFF	1 GB External RAM (Reserved)
External Device		
0xA000.0000	0xDFFF.FFFF	1 GB External Device (Reserved)
Private Peripheral Bus		
0xE000.0000	0xE000.0FFF	Instrumentation Trace Macrocell (ITM)
0xE000.1000	0xE000.1FFF	Data Watchpoint and Trace (DWT)
0xE000.2000	0xE000.2FFF	Flash Patch and Breakpoint (FPB)
0xE000.E000	0xE000.EFFF	Cortex-M4F System Peripherals (SysTick, NVIC, MPU, FPU, and SCB)
0xE004.0000	0xE004.0FFF	Trace Port Interface Unit (TPIU)
0xE004.1000	0xE004.1FFF	Embedded Trace Macrocell (ETM)
511 MB of Vendor-Specific Memory		

Table 6.12. Bit-banding regions in SRAM and Peripheral.

Address Range	Memory Region	Instruction and Data Accesses
0x20000000~0x200FFFFF	SRAM Bit-Band Region (1 MB)	This SRAM memory space can be accessed as normal SRAM, but this region can also be accessed via bit-band alias region.
0x22000000~0x23FFFFFF	SRAM Bit-Band Alias Region (32 MB)	Data accesses to this region are remapped to the SRAM bit band region. A write operation is performed as read–modify–write. Instruction accesses are not remapped.
0x40000000~0x400FFFFF	Peripheral Bit-Band Region (1 MB)	This peripheral memory range can be accessed as normal peripheral space, but this region can also be accessed via bit-band alias region.
0x42000000~0x43FFFFFF	Peripheral Bit-Band Alias Region (32 MB)	Data accesses to this region are remapped to the peripheral bit-band region. A write operation is performed as read–modify–write. Instruction accesses are not permitted.

means that this first 1 MB can be accessed as normal SRAM or Peripheral memory mapping spaces, but they can also be accessed via different memory regions called the bit-band alias regions.

A bit-band region maps each word in a bit-band alias region to a single bit or the Least Significant Bit (LSB) in the bit-band region. Since each word contains 32 bits, the 1 MB bit-band region can be mapped to 32-MB bit-band alias regions. The memory map has two 32-MB alias regions that map to two 1-MB bit-band regions:

- Accesses to the 32-MB SRAM alias region map to the 1-MB SRAM bit-band region.
- Accesses to the 32-MB peripheral alias region map to the 1-MB peripheral bit-band region.

The mapping relationships between the bit-band regions and the bit-band alias regions for the SRAM and the peripheral are shown in Table 6.12.

Within the 1-MB bit-band region, each bit is mapped to a 32-bit word in the bit-band alias region, and each bit in the bit-band region can be mapped to the Least Significant Bit (LSB) of a 32-bit word in the bit-band alias region. In this way, each word in the bit-band region can be mapped to an LSB of 32 words in the bit-band alias region. When using the bit-band alias regions, the following points should be noted:

- When the bit-band alias address is accessed, this address is remapped into a bit-band address. For reading operations, the word is read and the desired bit location is shifted to the LSB of the returned data. For writing operations, the written bit data is shifted to the required bit location, and a Read–Modify–Write operation is executed.

- For the Cortex®-M4 processor, there is no special instruction to access the bit-band alias addresses. However, when data accesses to these regions that are defined as the bit-band alias address ranges, the addresses can be automatically converted to the bit-band regions.
- The SRAM starts at the base address 0x20000000, and equivalently the Bit-banded SRAM can be mapped to start at the base address 0x2200000.
- The Peripheral space starts at the base address 0x40000000, and equivalently the Bit-banded peripheral space is mapped to start at the base address 0x42000000.

Let's take a closer look at the mapping relationship between the bit-band region and bit-band alias region for SRAM and the peripheral memory space.

6.4.1 The Mapping Relationship Between the Bit-Band Region and the Bit-Band Alias Region

The relationship between the bit-band region address and the bit-band alias address can be described by the following equation:

$$\text{Bit-band alias} = \text{bit-band-base} + (\text{byte\_offset} \times 32) + (\text{bit\_number} \times 4)$$

This means that the bit-band alias address can be calculated by using this equation, where:

- The bit-band-base is the starting address of the bit-band alias regions. For the SRAM, it is 0x22000000, and for the peripheral it is 0x42000000.
- The byte_offset is the number of the bytes in the bit-band region that contains the targeted bit.
- The bit_number is the bit position, 0~7, of the targeted bit.

For example, bit-7 (bit_number) at the address 0x22002000 (bit-band-base) is

$$\text{Bit-band alias} = 0x22002000 + (0x2000 \times 32) + (7 \times 4) = 0x2204201C$$

Based on this equation, some remapping bit-band addresses in the SRAM alias region are shown in Table 6.13. The remapping bit-band addresses in the peripheral alias region are shown in Table 6.14.

It can be found from these tables that both the bit-band region of the SRAM and the bit-band region of the peripheral memory space can be accessed via bit-band aliased addresses, which means that as long as an access to the bit-band alias address is created, it can be automatically converted or remapped to the associated bit-band address in either SRAM or the peripheral memory space. In fact, both bit-band region and the bit-band alias region are physically the same memory region but they can be accessed in two different ways.

6.4.2 The Advantages of Using the Bit-Band Operations

The advantages of using the bit-band alias to access the memory space include the following:

- Allows a single load/store operation to access to a single data bit to simplify the data writing operations.

Table 6.13. Remapping of bit-band addresses in the SRAM alias region.

Bit-Band Range	Bit-Band Alias Region
0x20000000 bit[0]	0x22000000 bit[0]
0x20000000 bit[1]	0x22000004 bit[0]
0x20000000 bit[2]	0x22000008 bit[0]
0x20000000 bit[3]	0x2200000C bit[0]
0x20000000 bit[4]	0x22000010 bit[0]
0x20000000 bit[5]	0x22000014 bit[0]
0x20000000 bit[6]	0x22000018 bit[0]
0x20000000 bit[7]	0x2200001C bit[0]
. . . . . .	. . . . . .
0x20000000 bit[31]	0x2200007C bit[0]
0x20000004 bit[0]	0x22000080 bit[0]
0x20000004 bit[1]	0x22000084 bit[0]
. . . . . .	. . . . . .
0x20000004 bit[31]	0x220000FC bit[0]
. . . . . .	. . . . . .
0x200FFFFC bit[31]	0x23FFFFFC bit[0]

Table 6.14. Remapping of bit-band addresses in the peripheral alias region.

Bit-Band Range	Bit-Band Alias Region
0x40000000 bit[0]	0x42000000 bit[0]
0x40000000 bit[1]	0x42000004 bit[0]
0x40000000 bit[2]	0x42000008 bit[0]
0x40000000 bit[3]	0x4200000C bit[0]
0x40000000 bit[4]	0x42000010 bit[0]
0x40000000 bit[5]	0x42000014 bit[0]
0x40000000 bit[6]	0x42000018 bit[0]
0x40000000 bit[7]	0x4200001C bit[0]
. . . . . .	. . . . . .
0x40000000 bit[31]	0x4200007C bit[0]
0x40000004 bit[0]	0x42000080 bit[0]
0x40000004 bit[1]	0x42000084 bit[0]
. . . . . .	. . . . . .
0x40000004 bit[31]	0x420000FC bit[0]
. . . . . .	. . . . . .
0x400FFFFC bit[31]	0x43FFFFFC bit[0]

	Without Bit-Band	—— **Write Operation**	——	**With Bit-Band**	
LDR	R1, = 0x20000004;	*Set address*	LDR	R1, =0x22000080;	*Set address*
LDR	R0, [R1];	*Read*	MOV	R0, #1;	*Set data*
ORR.W	R0, #0x1;	*Modify bit value*	STR	R0, [R1];	*Write data*
STR	R0, [R1];	*Write back data*			
	Without Bit-Band	—— **Read Operation**	——	**With Bit-Band**	
LDR	R1, = 0x20000004;	*Set address*	LDR	R1, = 0x22000080;	*Set address*
LDR	R0, [R1];	*Read data*	LDR	R0, R1;	*Read data*
UBFX.W	R0, R0, #0, #1;	*Extract bit[0]*			

Figure 6.15.   Bit data writing and reading with and without a bit-band.

- Allows a single load/store operation to access to a single data bit to simplify the data reading operations.

Figure 6.15 shows an example of performing data bit writing and reading operations with and without bit-band method.

It can be found from Figure 6.15 that four assembly instructions are used to perform a data bit writing operations without the bit-band support, but only three instructions are used to do the same job with the bit-band alias method. A situation similar to that of the reading operations occurred.

Regularly, to modify a data bit value in the ARM® Cortex®-M4 system, a three-step operation, read–modify–write, should be performed. This means that at least three instructions are needed to complete this modification. However, with the bit-band region support, this modification only needs two steps, modify and write (without read), which means that only two instructions are needed to complete this modification.

To get a clearer picture about the bit-band technology, we try to use the following example to illustrate the mapping relationships between the bit-band region and the bit-band alias region with SRAM. Similar ideas can be obtained for the peripheral memory regions.

6.4.3 An Illustration Example of Using Bit-Band Alias Addresses

Figure 6.16 shows an example to illustrate how to map a 32-bit-band alias word to a related 1-MB bit-band region for SRAM.

Based on the mapping equation shown in Section 6.4.1, the following bit-band alias words, namely the LSB or bit[0] of the following bit-band alias words, can be mapped to related bits on the bit-band region:

1. The bit[0] of the alias word at 0x22000000 maps to bit[0] of the bit-band byte at $0x20000000 \rightarrow 0x22000000 = 0x22000000 + (0*32) + (0*4)$. In this mapping, the bit-band base is 0x22000000, the byte offset is 0, and the bit number is 0.
2. The bit[0] of the alias word at 0x2200001C maps to bit[7] of the bit-band byte at $0x20000000 \rightarrow 0x2200001C = 0x22000000 + (0*32) + (7*4)$. In this mapping, the bit-band base is 0x22000000, the byte offset is 0 and the bit number is 7.
3. The bit[0] of the alias word at 0x23FFFFE0 maps to bit[0] of the bit-band byte at $0x200FFFFF \rightarrow 0x23FFFFE0 = 0x22000000 + (0xFFFFF*32) + (0*4)$. In this

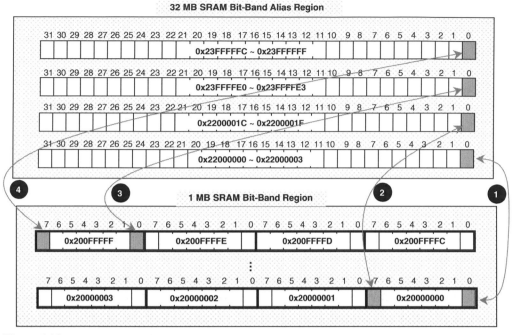

Figure 6.16. Bit-Band mapping for SRAM.

mapping, the bit-band base is 0x22000000, the byte offset is 0xFFFFF and the bit number is 0.

4. The bit[0] of the alias word at 0x23FFFFFC maps to bit[7] of the bit-band byte at 0x200FFFFF → 0x23FFFFFC = 0x22000000 + (0xFFFFF*32) + (7*4). In this mapping, the bit-band base is 0x22000000, the byte offset is 0xFFFFF and the bit number is 7.

Some points to be noted when do this mapping calculation are:

• When performing the bit_number × 4 calculation, the product should be converted to the hexadecimal number before adding it to the sum. For example, the product of 7 × 4 = 28 should be converted to 0x1C before it can be added into the sum to get the alias address.

• When performing the byte_offset × 32 operation, first convert the byte_offset from the hexadecimal number to the binary number, and then attach five 0s at the end of this binary number, which is equivalent to multiply by 32. Finally convert that binary number back to the hexadecimal number and add it into the sum to get the alias address.

• Each bit[0] on the related bit-band alias word has four bytes or 32 bits. Therefore the calculated address for the alias word is the address of the first byte of that word. For example, in the first mapping in Figure 6.16, the bit[0] of the alias word 0x22000000 maps to bit[0] of the bit-band byte at 0x20000000. This means that the 0x22000000 is the address of the first byte that is included in the word who takes four bytes with addresses ranged from 0x22000000~0x22000003.

Now we can determine some bit-band alias addresses easily with the equation

$$\text{Bit-band alias} = \text{bit-band-base} + (\text{byte\_offset} \times 32) + (\text{bit\_number} \times 4)$$

For example, determine the bit-band alias addresses for the following bits at the bit-band regions: (1) bit[2] of the bit-band region at 0x20000FFD, (2) bit[5] of the bit-band region at 0x20002222, and (3) bit[3] of the bit-band region at 0x20007890.

1. Bit-band alias $= 0\text{x}22000000 + (0\text{xFFD} \times 32) + (2 \times 4) = 0\text{x}2201\text{FFA8}$.
2. Bit-band alias $= 0\text{x}22000000 + (0\text{x}2222 \times 32) + (5 \times 4) = 0\text{x}22044454$.
3. Bit-band alias $= 0\text{x}22000000 + (0\text{x}7890 \times 32) + (3 \times 4) = 0\text{x}220\text{F}120\text{C}$.

Based on these results, the bit[0] of the alias word at 0x2201FFA8 maps to bit[2] of the bit-band region at 0x20000FFD, the bit[0] of the alias word at 0x22044454 maps to bit[5] of the bit-band region at 0x20002222, and the bit[0] of the alias word at 0x220F120C maps to bit[3] of the bit-band region at 0x20007890.

6.4.4 Bit-Band Operations for Different Data Sizes

The bit-band operations are not only limited to map each bit in the bit-band region to a word in the bit-band alias region, but are also available to map bits in the bit-band region to bytes and half-words in the bit-band alias region. For example, when a byte or a half-word access instruction, such as LDRB/STRB or LDRH/STRH, is used to access a bit-band alias region, the accesses generated to the bit-band region will be in byte size or in half-word size.

Refer to the bit mapping example shown in Figure 6.16. For the first mapping, the bit [0] of the alias word at 0x22000000 maps to bit[0] of the bit-band byte at 0x20000000. In fact, this can be considered as the bit[0] of the alias *byte* at 0x22000000 maps to bit[0] of the bit-band region at 0x20000000. You can also consider that the bit[0] of the alias *half-word* at 0x22000000 ~ 0x22000001 maps to bit[0] of the bit-band region at 0x20000000.

6.4.5 Bit-Band Operations Built in C Programs

Since the bit-band operations belong to special features used in the assembly instructions in the Cortex®-M4 MCU system, this feature cannot be recognized by any high-level language, such as C/C++. The C/C++ compiler does not know that the same memory space can be accessed by using two different mapping regions, the bit-band region and the bit-band alias region. Also, the compiler cannot convert from a bit-band region to the related bit-band alias region. In order to use the bit-band feature in C/C++, the easiest way is to declare the memory addresses related to the bit-band region and bit-band alias region separately.

For example, you can declare the SRAM bit-band region and bit-band alias region as two separate base addresses as shown in Figure 6.17.

The first declaration is to define a normal SRAM memory address starting at 0x20000000. The data type is a volatile 32-bit pointer. The volatile property is used to inform the compiler that the data value in this memory address can be changed and that each time a variable is accessed, the memory location is accessed instead of a copy of the data inside the processor.

The second through the fourth declarations define bit-band alias addresses. The first two assignments are for normal memory operations, but the last two assignments used the bit-band alias addresses to set the bits values.

```
Define SRAM Bit-Band Address ──────────────────────────────────────

#define   MEM_REG0        *((volatile  unsigned  long *) (0x20000000)       // bit-band region
#define   MEM_REG0_BIT0   *((volatile  unsigned  long *) (0x22000000)       // bit-band alias region
#define   MEM_REG0_BIT1   *((volatile  unsigned  long *) (0x22000004)       // bit-band alias region
#define   MEM_REG0_BIT2   *((volatile  unsigned  long *) (0x22000008)       // bit-band alias region
......
MEM_REG0 = 0x18;                      // access the memory register by normal address
MEM_REG0 = MEM_REG0|0x2;              // set bit without using bit-band feature
MEM_REG0_BIT2 = 0x1;                  // set bit using the bit-band feature via bit-band alias address
MEM_REG0_BIT1 = 0x1;                  // set bit using the bit-band feature via bit-band alias address
```

Figure 6.17.   Declare bit-band and bit-band alias regions in C.

You can also develop some C macros to define useful bit-band-related operations and addresses, and this makes the bit-band operations easier in the C programs. For example, the macros defined in Figure 6.18 are used to convert the bit-band address and the bit number into the bit-band alias address, which is the converting equation shown in Section 6.4.1, and access the memory bit-band region to set data bit value.

In Figure 6.18, the macro used to define the SRAM Bit-Band Conversion Equation is to convert the bit-band region with the bit number to the associated bit-band alias address. The bit-band-base address for SRAM is 0x22000000. The (addr & 0xFFFFF) is used to AND the input bit-band address with 0xFFFFF to get the byte_offset (the SRAM bit-band region is 0x20000000~0x200FFFFF). Then the byte_offset is shifted left by 5 bits (<< 5), which is equivalent to multiplying the byte_offset by 32. The (bitnum << 2) is to shift bitnum left by 2 bits, which is equivalent to multiplying the bitnum by 4. Finally, all of these items are added together to get the bit-band alias address.

The last assignment MEM_ADDR(BIT_BAND(MEM_REG0, 1)) = 0x1; is to set the LSB of the bit-band alias word at 0x22000004 to 1, which is equivalent to setting the bit[1] in the bit-band region at 0x20000000 to 1. The BIT_BAND(MEM_REG0, 1) is used to getting the bit-band alias address 0x22000004. The MEM_ADDR(addr) is used to define an address pointer.

6.5   MEMORY REQUIREMENTS AND MEMORY PROPERTIES

The memory map and the programming of the TM4C123GH6PM MPU split the memory map into different regions, as shown in Figure 6.14 and Table 6.11. Each region has a

```
Define SRAM Bit-Band Conversion Equation ─────────────────────────────
#define   BIT_BAND (addr, bitnum)  ((0x22000000 + ((addr & 0xFFFFF) << 5) + (bitnum << 2))

Convert the Address to a Pointer ─────────────────────────────────────
#define   MEM_ADDR (addr)   *((volatile  unsigned  long *) (addr))

Define SRAM Bit-Band  Address ────────────────────────────────────────
#define   MEM_REG0          *((volatile  unsigned  long *) (0x20000000)      // bit-band region

Data Assignments without and wit Bit-Band Operations ─────────────────
MEM_ADDR (MEM_REG0) = 0x18;                            // access the memory register by normal address
MEM_ADDR (MEM_REG0) = MEM_ADDR (MEM_REG0) | 0x2;      // set bit without using bit-band feature
MEM_ADDR (BIT_BAND(MEM_REG0, 1)) = 0x1;              // set bit using the bit-band feature via bit-band
                                                      // alias address
```

Figure 6.18.   C macros used to convert bit-band alias and bit-band operations.

defined memory type, and some regions have additional memory attributes. The memory type and attributes determine the behavior of accesses to the region.

In order to correctly and effectively access the desired memory region to perform the selected operations, we need to have a clear and fully picture about the memory requirements and some important memory properties.

There are so many different memory properties applied on memory systems in most popular microcontroller systems. However, in this section we only limit our discussions on some most important properties, such as memory endianness, memory access attributes, and behavior of memory accesses. For some memory properties listed below, we will not cover them in this part since they are not very important from the point of view of applications:

- Memory data alignment and unaligned data access
- Memory exclusive accesses
- Memory barriers
- Memory access permissions

First let's take care of the memory requirements.

6.5.1 Memory Requirements

In Section 6.2, we provided a detailed discussion about the memory architecture used in the TM4C123GH6PM MCU system. From Figure 6.1, it can be found that different types of memories can be connected to the processor and peripherals via different buses. Although the bus size is 32 bits in the Cortex®-M4 MCU, the memories can also be connected with other width in the bus, such as 8 bits, 16 bits, 64 bits, and 128 bits, and so on, if related conversion hardware exists.

In the TM4C123GH6PM MCU system, the used memories are categorized as SRAM (Static RAM), EEPROM, Flash Memory, and ROM, as shown in Figure 6.1. However, there is no real limitation on what kind of memories can be used in this system. For instance, the SRAM can be replaced by DRAM (Dynamic RAM), SDRAM (Synchronous DRAM), DDR SDRAM (Double Data Rate SDRAM), and so on. Also, the program codes could be in the Flash memory, RAM, EPROM, EEPROM, and even ROM.

The memory size used in a microcontroller system is also flexible. Some low-cost Cortex®-M MCUs have only 8 KB of Flash memory and 4 KB of on-chip SRAM. In the TM4C123GH6PM MCU system, the default memory capacity for the SRAM is 512 MB, but only 32 KB of SRAM is used for this system. Similarly, the default size for the Flash memory is 512 MB, however, only 256 KB has been used by the TM4C123GH6PM MCU system.

The only requirement for the data memory, such as SRAM, is that the memory must be byte addressable and the memory interface needs to support byte, half-word, and word conversions.

For the memory spaces used for external RAM and external device, as shown in Figure 6.14, the user needs to refer to the specifications of the memory chips and peripherals connected to those spaces.

The most popular memory types include:

- Normal: The processor can change the order of transactions to improve the efficiency or to perform speculative reads.
- Device: The processor keeps transaction order relative to other transactions to Device or Strongly ordered memory.
- Strongly Ordered: The processor preserves transaction order relative to all other transactions.

The different ordering requirements for Device and Strongly ordered memory mean that the memory system can buffer a write to Device memory, but must not buffer a write to Strongly ordered memory.

The additional memory attribute is the Execute Never (XN). This means that the processor prevents instruction accesses. Any attempt to fetch an instruction from an XN region causes a memory management fault exception.

Table 6.15 shows the different requirements for the different memory regions used in the TM4C123GH6PM MCU memory system.

The Code, SRAM, and external RAM regions can hold user's programs and data. These regions can be accessed by instructions. However, it is recommended that programs always use the Code region. This is because the processor has separate buses that enable instruction fetches and data accesses to be occurred simultaneously.

6.5.2 Memory Access Attributes

In the last section we discussed the memory requirements, and different memory regions can be accessed with various methods. Besides these requirements, the memory map also

Table 6.15. Requirements to use different memory regions.

Address Range	Memory Region	Memory Type	XN	Description
0x00000000~0x1FFFFFFF	Code	Normal	—	Executable region for program code. Can also put data here.
0x20000000~0x3FFFFFFF	SRAM	Normal	—	Executable region for data. Can also put code here. This region includes bit band and bit band alias areas.
0x40000000~0x5FFFFFFF	Peripheral	Device	XN	This region includes peripheral registers mapping & bit band and bit band alias areas.
0x60000000~0x9FFFFFFF	External RAM	Normal	—	Executable region for data.
0xA0000000~0xDFFFFFFF	External Device	Device	XN	External device memory
0xE0000000~0xE00FFFFF	Private Peripheral Bus	Strongly-Ordered	XN	This region includes the NVIC, System timer, and system control block.
0xE0100000~0xFFFFFFFF	Vendor-Specific Memory	Device	XN	This region include vendor-specific memory space.

defines the memory attributes of the access. The most popular memory attributes used in the Cortex®-M4 processor system are:

- **Bufferable**: The instructions or data written to the memory can be carried out by a writing buffer, and the processor can continue execute the next instruction.
- **Cacheable**: The data read out from the memory can be copied to a memory cache, and it can be used then next time it is accessed. In this way, the data processing can be speeded up to improve the execution efficiency of instructions.
- **Executable**: The processor can fetch and execute instructions from this memory region.
- **Sharable**: Data in this memory space can be shared by multiple bus systems. The memory system needs to ensure coherency of data among different bus systems in the sharable memory space.

The processor bus interfaces send out the memory access attributes information to the memory controller for each instruction and data processing. If the MPU is present and the MPU region configurations are re-programmed, the default memory attributes can be overridden.

Only the Executable and Bufferable attributes affect the operations of the most applications in Cortex®-M4 microcontroller systems. The Cacheable and Sharable attributes are generally used by a cache controller, as shown in Table 6.16.

However, the Sharable attribute is often needed and used in systems where multiple cores or processors and multiple cache units with cache coherency control. The cache controller needs to make sure that the value is coherent with other cache units when a sharable data is used.

Usually, there is no any cache memory or cache controller available for the Cortex®-M4 microcontroller. However, a cache unit can be added into the microcontroller to improve the memory accessing performances and behaviors.

6.5.3 Memory Endianness

The so-called memory endianness is to define how to store or arrange data bytes into words in the memory system and registers. As you know, each data word is composed of four data bytes. In Cortex®-M4 microcontroller system, there are two memory endian formats; the little endian and the big endian.

Table 6.16. Memory attributes related to different memory types.

Bufferable	Cacheable	Memory Type
0	0	Strongly ordered. The processor must wait until the current instruction is complete before the next instruction can be executed.
1	0	Device. The processor can use the write buffer to execute the current instruction while continuing to the next instructions unless the next instruction is also needs a memory access.
0	1	Normal memory access with Write Through (WT) cache.
1	1	Normal memory access with Write Back (WB) cache.

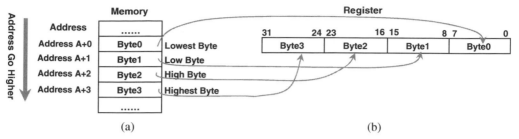

Figure 6.19. Memory little endian format.

6.5.3.1 The Little Endian Format

In general, the Cortex®-M4 processor views memory as a linear collection of bytes numbered in ascending order starting from zero. For example, bytes 0~3 hold the first stored word, and bytes 4~7 hold the second stored word. In other words, the lowest byte should be located on the top of the memory space, and the highest byte should be in the bottom of the memory space, just as shown in Figure 6.19a.

However, when each word is loaded from the memory and stored into a register, the lowest byte should be loaded to the lowest byte in a register, and the higher byte should be loaded into the higher byte in the register, as shown in Figure 6.19b.

It can be found from Figure 6.19a that the lowest byte (byte0) is located at the top or lowest memory address (A + 0), the low byte (byte1) is in the low address (A + 1), the high byte (byte2) is in the high address (A + 2), and the highest byte (byte3) is located at the bottom memory address (A + 3). These four bytes make up a single 32-bit word and are stored in the memory in this way, which is called memory little endian format.

When loading this word into a register, each byte is loaded into the corresponding byte location shown in Figure 6.19b.

In summary, in the little-endian format, the processor stores the Least Significant Byte (LSB) of a word at the lowest-numbered byte, and the Most Significant Byte (MSB) at the highest-numbered byte.

For most microcontroller systems, including the Cortex®-M4, the little endian format is used.

6.5.3.2 The Big Endian Format

Optionally the data can be stored in the memory in the big endian format, which means that the bytes 4~7 hold the first stored word, and bytes 0~3 hold the second stored word. In other words, the highest byte is located on the top of the memory space (lowest address) and the lowest byte is in the bottom of the memory space (highest address), just as shown in Figure 6.20a.

However, when each word is loaded from the memory and stored into a register, the highest byte should be loaded to the highest byte in a register, and the lower byte should be loaded into the lower byte in the register, as shown in Figure 6.20b.

It can be found from Figure 6.20a that the highest byte (byte3) is located at the top or lowest memory address (A + 0), the high byte (byte2) is in the high address (A + 1), the low byte (byte1) is in the high address (A + 2), and the lowest byte (byte0) is located at

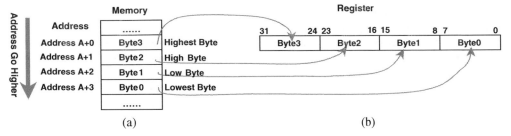

Figure 6.20. Memory big endian format.

the highest memory address (A + 3). These four bytes make up a single 32-bit word and are stored in the memory in this way, which is called memory big endian format.

When loading this word into a register, each byte is loaded into the corresponding byte location shown in Figure 6.20b.

In summary, in the big-endian format the processor stores the Most Significant Byte (MSB) of a word at the lowest-numbered address and stores the Least Significant Byte (LSB) at the highest-numbered address.

6.6 MEMORY SYSTEM PROGRAMMING METHODS

As we discussed in Section 6.2 in this chapter, the TM4C123GH6PM MCU memory system contains following memory components or devices:

- SRAM (32 KB)
- Flash Memory (256 KB)
- Internal ROM
- EEPROM (2 KB)
- Flash Protection Unit
- Optional MPU

Because the internal ROM is used by the vendor to store necessary peripheral driver library and boot loader, we cannot and do not need to touch that component. The optional MPU will be discussed in Chapter 12. Therefore, in this section we will focus our discussions on the following three components:

1. Flash Memory Programming
2. EEPROM Programming
3. SRAM Bit-Band Operation Programming

There are different ways to program the flash memory with C programming language. Three popular ways are:

- Programming flash memory with Direct Register Access (DRA).
- Programming flash memory with Software Driver (SD) library provided by TivaWare™ Peripheral Driver Library.
- Programming flash memory with ARM® flash library provided by ARM® Flash Utility API Functions.

Because of the similarity between the SD library and the ARM® Flash API Library Functions, we only discuss the top two ways in the following sections.

For the EEPROM programming, we can also use two ways to access internal EEPROM to perform desired reading and writing operations: using the DRA method and the SD method provided by the TivaWare™ Peripheral Driver Library.

For the bit-band operations, there are no library and API functions available, and therefore we need to build some accessing API functions ourselves to implement this kind of technology.

In the previous sections we have provided detailed discussions about all registers used for flash memory and EEPROM programming in the memory architecture and memory map parts. These provided good bases for programming the flash memory and EEPROM with the Direct Register Access (DRA) method. In the following sections we will concentrate on the TivaWare™ Peripheral Driver Library since it provides all API functions to enable us to program flash memory and EEPROM with the Software Driver (SD) method.

6.6.1 The API Functions Used for Flash Memory Programming

To facilitate developers to build and develop flash memory projects to program and erase flash memory blocks, the TivaWare™ for C Series package provides a set of API functions. These APIs provide 14 functions for dealing with the on-chip flash. Functions are provided to program and erase the flash, configure the flash protection, and handle the flash interrupts.

The flash memory block can be erased based on a 1-KB block space interval. When erasing, the entire 1-KB block flash memory spaces are reset or changed from all 0s to all 1s. Each block can be protected or marked as read-only or execute-only. The read-only blocks cannot be erased or programmed, protecting the contents of those blocks from being modified. Execute-only blocks cannot be erased or programmed and can only be read by the processor.

The flash memory block can be programmed on a word-by-word basis. The programming process can only make a bit from 1 to 0 (not from 0 to 1). With a flash buffer written function, 32-word can be programmed or written in a flash memory block at one operation.

The timing for the flash is automatically handled by the flash memory controller.

The flash controller has the ability to generate an interrupt when an invalid access is attempted, such as reading from execute-only flash. This capability can be used to validate the operation of a program. The flash memory controller can also generate an interrupt when an erase or programming operation has completed.

All of these API functions are located in the TivaWare™ Peripheral Driver Library and contained at the file flash.c that is located at C:\ti\TivaWare_C_Series-2.0.1.11577\driverlib, with the header file flash.h containing the API declarations for those functions.

In this section we only discuss some of the most popular and important flash API functions. These functions include FlashErase(), FlashProgram(), FlashInt-Enable(), FlashIntRegister(), and FlashIntClear(). For some flash memory protecting functions, we will discuss them in Chapter 12.

Table 6.17 lists some most popular and useful flash memory API functions. The point to be noted is that the two API functions listed on the bottom on this list do not belong to

Table 6.17.   Some popular flash API functions provided by TivaWare Driver Library.

API Function	Parameter	Description
int32_t FlashErase(uint32_t ui32Address)	ui32Address is the starting address of the flash block to be erased.	Erases a 1-KB block of the flash. After erasing, the block is filled with 0xFF bytes. This function does not return until the block has been erased. Returns 0 on success, or -1 if an invalid block address was specified or the block is write protected.
int32_t FlashProgram(uint32_t *pui32Data, uint32_t ui32Address, uint32_t ui32Count)	pui32Data is a pointer to the data to be programmed. ui32Address is the starting address in flash to be programmed. Must be a multiple of four. ui32Count is the number of bytes to be programmed. Must be a multiple of four.	Programs a sequence of words into the on-chip flash. The starting address and byte count must both be multiples of four. This function does not return until the data has been programmed. Returns 0 on success, or −1 if a programming error is encountered.
void FlashIntRegister(void (*pfnHandler)(void))	pfnHandler is a pointer to the function to be called when the flash interrupt occurs	This function sets the handler to be called when the flash interrupt occurs. This function has no returned value.
void FlashIntEnable(uint32_t ui32IntFlag)	ui32IntFlag is a bit mask of the interrupt sources to be enabled. Can be any of the FLASH_INT_PROGRAM or FLASH_INT_ACCESS values.	This function enables the indicated flash controller interrupt sources. Only the sources that are enabled can be reflected to the processor interrupt; disabled sources have no effect on the processor. This function has no returned value.
void FlashIntClear(uint32_t ui32IntFlag)	ui32IntFlag is the bit mask of the interrupt sources to be cleared. Can be any of the FLASH_INT_PROGRAM or FLASH_INT_AMISC values.	The specified interrupt sources are cleared, so that they no longer assert. This function must be called in the interrupt handler to keep the interrupt from being triggered again immediately upon exit. This function has no returned value.
void IntRegister(uint32_t ui32Int, void (*pfnHandler)(void))	ui32Int is the interrupt in question. pfnHandler is a pointer to the function to be called.	This function is used to specify the handler function to be called when the given interrupt is generated to the processor. The interrupt must have been enabled. This function has no returned value.
void IntEnable(uint32_t ui32Int)	ui32Int specifies the interrupt to be enabled.	The specified interrupt is enabled in the interrupt controller. This function has no returned value.

the API functions related to the flash memory operations. Instead they belong to general API functions and can be used for all other interrupt sources. Since we need to use these two functions in our projects, they are also listed in this table.

When using these API functions, including the interrupt-driven functions, to perform flash memory block programming and erasing operations, the following operational sequence should be followed:

1. The flash memory interrupt sources, either program-complete-interrupt or erase-complete interrupt, should be registered first with the flash memory interrupt handler by using the API function IntRegister(). The handler can be built by the user in any name and declared in the project file.

2. The flash memory interrupt sources must be then enabled by using the API function `IntEnable()` to allow the processor to unmask that interrupt source and to respond it.

3. The TivaWare™ Peripheral Driver Library file, `driverlib.lib`, must be added into the user's project to enable the compiler to know it and to connect all API functions contained in that library with the user's project.

4. The related header files including the declarations for those API functions should also be included in the project source file.

Next let's take a look at the API functions used for the EEPROM programming operations.

6.6.2 The API Functions Used for EEPROM Programming

The TivaWare™ Peripheral Driver Library provides 18 EEPROM-related API functions to assist users to access and program the on-chip EEPROM. These API functions can be divided into the following groups based on their functions:

- EEPROM Reading: This reading operation is managed by one function, `EEPROMRead()`. This function performs a reading operation from a given EEPROM address.
- EEPROM Programming: The program operation is managed by three API functions, the `EEPROMMassErase()`, `EEPROMProgram()`, and `EEPROMProgramNonBlocking()`.
- EEPROM Protection: The EEPROM protection is managed with six API functions, `EEPROMBlockProtectGet()`, `EEPROMBlockProtectSet()`, `EEPROMBlock-PasswordSet()`, `EEPROMBlockLock()`, `EEPROMBlockUnlock()`, and `EEPROM-BlockHide()`.
- EEPROM Interrupt Handling: This is managed with four API functions, `EEPROMIntEnable()`, `EEPROMIntDisable()`, `EEPROMIntStatus()`, and `EEPROMIntClear()`.
- An additional function, `EEPROMSizeGet()`: This is provided to allow an application to query the size of the device storage and the number of blocks the EEPROM contained.

These API functions can be used to interact with the on-chip EEPROM to provide easy-to-use nonvolatile data storage. Functions are provided to program and erase the EEPROM, configure the EEPROM protection, and handle the EEPROM interrupt.

The EEPROM can be programmed on a word-by-word basis. However, unlike flash, the applications need not explicitly erase a word or page before writing a new value to it.

The EEPROM controller has the ability to generate an interrupt when an invalid access is attempted, such as reading from a protected block. An interrupt can also be generated when an erase or programming operation has completed.

All of these API functions are located in the TivaWare™ Peripheral Driver Library and contained at the file `eeprom.c` that is located at `C:\ti\TivaWare_C_Series-2.0.1.11577\driverlib`, with the header file `eeprom.h` containing the API declarations for those functions.

We will discuss the EEPROM protection functions in Chapter 10. Therefore in this section we concentrate our discussions on some popular and important EEPROM API functions. These functions are shown in Table 6.18.

Table 6.18. Some popular EEPROM API functions provided by TivaWare Driver Library.

API Function	Parameter	Description
uint32_t EEPROMBlockCountGet (void)	No input parameter.	Determines the number of blocks in the EEPROM. Returns the total number of blocks in the device EEPROM
uint32_t EEPROMInit(void)	No input parameter. Returns EEPROM_INIT_OK if no errors were detected. If the EEPROM peripheral cannot currently recover from an interrupted write or erase operation, EEPROM_INIT_ERROR is returned.	Performs necessary recovery in case of power failures during write. It must be called after SysCtlPeripheralEnable() and before the EEPROM is accessed.
void EEPROMIntClear (uint32_tui32IntFlag)	ui32IntFlag indicates the interrupt source to clear. The only valid value is EEPROM_INT_PROGRAM	Clears the EEPROM interrupt.
void EEPROMIntDisable (uint32_tui32IntFlag)	ui32IntFlag indicates which EEPROM interrupt source to disable. This is EEPROM_INT_PROGRAM.	Disables the EEPROM interrupt.
void EEPROMIntEnable (uint32_tui32IntFlag)	ui32IntFlag indicates the interrupt source to enable. The only valid value is EEPROM_INT_PROGRAM	Enable the EEPROM interrupt.
uint32_t EEPROMIntStatus(bool bMasked)	bMasked determines whether the masked or unmasked state of the interrupt is to be returned. If bMasked is true, the masked state is returned, otherwise the unmasked state is returned.	Reports the state of the EEPROM interrupt. Returns EEPROM_INT_PROGRAM if an interrupt is being signaled or 0 otherwise.
uint32_t EEPROMMassErase (void)	Returns 0 on success or non-0 values on failure. Failure codes are logical OR combinations of EEPROM_RC_WRBUSY, EEPROM_RC_NOPERM, EEPROM_RC_WKCOPY, EEPROM_RC_WKERASE, and EEPROM_RC_WORKING	Erases the EEPROM and returns it to the factory default condition.
uint32_t EEPROMProgram(uint32_t *pui32Data, uint32_t ui32Address, uint32_t ui32Count)	pui32Data points to the first word of data to write to the EEPROM. ui32Address defines the byte address within the EEPROM that the data is to be written to. This value must be a multiple of 4. ui32Count defines the number of bytes of data to be written. This value must be a multiple of 4.	Writes data to the EEPROM.
uint32_t EEPROMProgramNon Blocking(uint32_t ui32Data, uint32_t ui32Address)	ui32Data is the word to write to the EEPROM. ui32Address defines the byte address within the EEPROM to which the data is to be written. This value must be a multiple of 4.	This function is intended to allow EEPROM programming under interrupt control. It may be called to start the process of writing a single word of data into the EEPROM at a given word-aligned address.
void EEPROMRead(uint32_t *pui32Data, uint32_t ui32Address, uint32_t ui32Count)	pui32Data is a pointer to storage for the data read from the EEPROM. This pointer must point to at least ui32Count bytes of available memory. ui32Address is the byte address in the EEPROM from which data is read. This value must be a multiple of 4. ui32Count is the number of bytes of data to read from the EEPROM. This value must be a multiple of 4.	This function may be called to read a number of words of data from a word-aligned address within the EEPROM. Data read is copied into the buffer pointed to by the pui32Data parameter.
uint32_t EEPROMSizeGet(void)	No input parameter.	This function returns the size of the EEPROM in bytes.
uint32_t EEPROMStatusGet (void)	No input parameter. Returns 0 if the last program or erase completed without any error.	This function returns the current status of the last program or erase operation performed by the EEPROM.

The most popular EEPROM API functions are

- `EEPROMInit()`
- `EEPROMProgram()`
- `EEPROMIntEnable()`
- `EEPROMIntClear()`
- `EEPROMRead()`

We will leave these API functions for users to perform EEPROM accessing, erasing, reading, and programming operations in the homework EEPROM programming sections.

Now let's develop and build some memory programming projects to illustrate how to use the DRA programming model to access, erase, and program memory space with the TM4C123GH6PM MCU system.

6.7 MEMORY SYSTEM PROGRAMMING PROJECTS

In the following sections we will develop and build two kinds of memory programming projects; Flash memory and EEPROM programming projects. Only the DRA programming model will be used to build these projects since this model is more difficult compared with the SD model. We will leave the latter as homework projects. Let's start with the flash memory.

6.7.1 Flash Memory Programming

In this section we will use the DRA model to access the flash memory and perform erasing and programming operations. Three projects will be developed to perform the programming and erasing operations for multiple words data and buffered word data with polling and interrupting driven ability. First let's take care of the first project with the DRA method.

6.7.1.1 Programming Flash Memory for Multiple Words with DRA Method (Polled)

Usually, before writing any data into the flash memory, an erasing operation should be performed to make all flash memory units from 0s to 1s. The result of writing data into the flash memory units is to change 1s to 0s. A write from 0 to 1 for the flash memory units is ignored.

6.7.1.1.1 The Operational Sequence of the Programming Flash Memory
As we discussed in Section 6.2.2.1, to perform an erasing operation, a 1-KB block flash memory space must be erased with the following operational steps:

1. Write the page or starting address into the Flash Memory Address (FMA) register.
2. Write the Flash memory write key and set the ERASE bit to the Flash Memory Control (FMC) register. Depending on the value of the KEY bit in the BOOTCFG register, the value 0xA442 or 0x71D5 must be written into the WRKEY field to make a Flash memory write effective. The value 0xA442 should be written into the WRKEY field on the FMC register since the KEY

bit in the BOOTCFG register is set to 1 after a system reset (refer to Figure 6.3). Also, the ERASE bit (bit[1]) in the FMC should be set to 1 to enable the erasing operation to work effectively (refer to Figure 6.5).

3. Poll the FMC register until the ERASE bit is cleared. Alternatively, you can enable the programming interrupt using the PMASK bit in the FCIM register to generate an interrupt when an erasing operation is completed.

Perform the following operations to write (program) a 32-bit word into the flash memory:

1. Write the source data to the FMD register.
2. Write the target address to the FMA register.
3. Write the Flash memory write key and the WRITE bit to the FMC register. Depending on the value of the KEY bit in the BOOTCFG register, the value 0xA442 or 0x71D5 must be written into the WRKEY field for a Flash memory write to occur. The value 0xA442 should be written into the WRKEY field on the FMC register since the KEY bit in the BOOTCFG register is set to 1 after a system reset (refer to Figure 6.3). Also, the WRITE bit (bit[0]) in the FMC should be set to 1 to enable the writing operation to take effect immediately (refer to Figure 6.5).
4. Poll the FMC register until the WRITE bit is cleared.

In TivaWare™ for C Series Software, all flash-memory-related registers and parameters have been defined with different macros to facilitate the users to build their applications. Let's have a closer look at these macros and parameters.

6.7.1.1.2 The Programming Macros for Flash Memory Registers and Parameters   All flash-memory-related registers and parameters are defined with different macros in the TivaWare™ for C Series Software package. All these macros and parameters are defined in the system header files, tm4c123gh6pm.h. Table 6.19 shows some definitions for these registers.

Table 6.19. Flash memory registers and their macros.

Register	Macro
Flash Memory Address Register (FMA)	FLASH_FMA_R
Flash Memory Data Register (FMD)	FLASH_FMD_R
Flash Memory Control Register (FMC)	FLASH_FMC_R
Flash Controller Raw Interrupt Status Register (FCRIS)	FLASH_FCRIS_R
Flash Controller Interrupt Mask Register (FCIM)	FLASH_FCIM_R
Flash Controller Masked Interrupt Status and Clear Register (FCMISC)	FLASH_FCMISC_R
Flash Memory Control 2 Register (FMC2)	FLASH_FMC2_R
Flash Write Buffer Valid Register (FWBVAL)	FLASH_FWBVAL_R
Flash Write Buffer N Register (FWBN)	FLASH_FWBN_R
Flash Size Register (FSIZE)	FLASH_FSIZE_R
SRAM Size Register (SSIZE)	FLASH_SSIZE_R
ROM Software Map Register (ROMSWMAP)	FLASH_ROMSWMAP_R
ROM Control Register (RMCTL)	FLASH_RMCTL_R
Boot Configuration Register (BOOTCFG)	FLASH_BOOTCFG_R

```
//*****************************************************************************
// FLASH registers (FLASH CTRL)
//*****************************************************************************
#define FLASH_FMA_R              (*(( volatile uint32_t *)0x400FD000))
#define FLASH_FMD_R              (*(( volatile uint32_t *)0x400FD004))
#define FLASH_FMC_R              (*(( volatile uint32_t *)0x400FD008))
#define FLASH_FCRIS_R            (*(( volatile uint32_t *)0x400FD00C))
#define FLASH_FCIM_R             (*(( volatile uint32_t *)0x400FD010))
#define FLASH_FCMISC_R           (*(( volatile uint32_t *)0x400FD014))
#define FLASH_FMC2_R             (*(( volatile uint32_t *)0x400FD020))
#define FLASH_FWBVAL_R           (*(( volatile uint32_t *)0x400FD030))
#define FLASH_FWBN_R             (*(( volatile uint32_t *)0x400FD100))
#define FLASH_FSIZE_R            (*(( volatile uint32_t *)0x400FDFC0))
#define FLASH_SSIZE_R            (*(( volatile uint32_t *)0x400FDFC4))
#define FLASH_ROMSWMAP_R         (*(( volatile uint32_t *)0x400FDFCC))
#define FLASH_RMCTL_R            (*(( volatile uint32_t *)0x400FE0F0))
#define FLASH_BOOTCFG_R          (*(( volatile uint32_t *)0x400FE1D0))
#define FLASH_USERREG0_R         (*(( volatile uint32_t *)0x400FE1E0))
#define FLASH_USERREG1_R         (*(( volatile uint32_t *)0x400FE1E4))
#define FLASH_USERREG2_R         (*(( volatile uint32_t *)0x400FE1E8))
#define FLASH_USERREG3_R         (*(( volatile uint32_t *)0x400FE1EC))
#define FLASH_FMPRE0_R           (*(( volatile uint32_t *)0x400FE200))
#define FLASH_FMPRE1_R           (*(( volatile uint32_t *)0x400FE204))
#define FLASH_FMPRE2_R           (*(( volatile uint32_t *)0x400FE208))
#define FLASH_FMPRE3_R           (*(( volatile uint32_t *)0x400FE20C))
#define FLASH_FMPPE0_R           (*(( volatile uint32_t *)0x400FE400))
#define FLASH_FMPPE1_R           (*(( volatile uint32_t *)0x400FE404))
#define FLASH_FMPPE2_R           (*(( volatile uint32_t *)0x400FE408))
#define FLASH_FMPPE3_R           (*(( volatile uint32_t *)0x400FE40C))
```

Figure 6.21. Macros for the most popular flash memory registers.

Figure 6.21 shows the most popular macros defined for flash-memory-related registers. The macros for most popular parameters used for flash memory are shown in Figure 6.22.

With these macros defined for flash memory registers and parameters combined with the operational sequence we discussed in Section 6.6.1.1.1, we can start to build our first project to erase and program some flash memory spaces with multiple words.

6.7.1.1.3 Build the Project to Program Multiple Words for Flash Memory Perform the following operations to create this new project DRAFlash:

1. Open the Windows Explorer window to create a new folder named DRAFlash under the C: \ARM Class Projects\Chapter 6 folder.

2. Open the Keil® ARM-MDK μVersion5 and go to the Project|New μVersion Project menu item to create a new μVersion Project. On the opened wizard, browse to our new folder DRAFlash that is created in step 1 above. Enter DRAFlash into the File name box and click on the Save button to create this project.

3. On the next wizard, you need to select the device (MCU) for this project. Expand three icons, Texas Instruments, Tiva C Series, and TM4C123x Series, and select the target device TM4C123GH6PM from the list by clicking on it. Click on the OK to close this wizard.

```
//************************************************************************
// FLASH Bit Field Macros
//************************************************************************
#define   FLASH_FMC_WRKEY          0xA4420000     // FLASH write key
#define   FLASH_FMC_COMT           0x00000008     // Commit Register Value
#define   FLASH_FMC_MERASE         0x00000004     // Mass Erase Flash Memory
#define   FLASH_FMC_ERASE          0x00000002     // Erase a Page of Flash Memory
#define   FLASH_FMC_WRITE          0x00000001     // Write a Word into Flash Memory
#define   FLASH_FCRIS_PROGRIS      0x00002000     // PROGVER Raw Interrupt Status
#define   FLASH_FCRIS_PRIS         0x00000002     // Programming Raw Interrupt Status
#define   FLASH_FCRIS_ARIS         0x00000001     // Access Raw Interrupt Status
#define   FLASH_FCIM_PMASK         0x00000002     // Programming Interrupt Mask
#define   FLASH_FCIM_AMASK         0x00000001     // Access Interrupt Mask
#define   FLASH_FCMISC_PMISC       0x00000002     // Program Masked Interrupt Status & Clear
#define   FLASH_FCMISC_AMISC       0x00000001     // Access Masked Interrupt Status & Clear
#define   FLASH_FMC2_WRBUF         0x00000001     // Buffered Flash Memory Write
#define   FLASH_FWBVAL_FWB_M       0xFFFFFFFF     // Flash Memory Write Buffer
#define   FLASH_FWBN_DATA_M        0xFFFFFFFF     // Data
```

Figure 6.22. Macros for the most popular flash memory parameters.

4. Next the Software Components wizard is opened, and you need to set up the software development environment for your project with this wizard. Expand two icons, CMSIS and Device, and check the CORE and Startup checkboxes in the Sel. column, and click on the OK button since we need these two components to build our project.

Perform the following operations to create a new source file DRAFlash.c:

1. In the Project pane, expand the Target folder and right click on the Source Group 1 folder and select the Add New Item to Group 'Source Group 1'.

2. Select the C File (.c) and enter DRAFlash into the Name: box, and click on the Add button to add this source file into the project.

3. Enter the codes shown in Figure 6.23 into this source file.

4. Now go to the Project|Build target menu item to build the project to get the project map file, DRAFlash.map. The reason we need this map file is to determine the starting address for erasing and writing data in the flash memory block. Because in order to run our project, our project image file will also be downloaded into this flash memory later. Therefore we must make sure that the flash memory block we try to erase and write is not the same block in which our project image file will be downloaded.

```
//************************************************************************
// DRAFlash.c - Main Application File
//************************************************************************
#include <stdint.h>
#include <stdbool.h>
#include "tm4c123gh6pm.h"

int main(void)
{

}
```

Figure 6.23. The initial codes of the source file DRAFlash.c.

```
===============================================================================
Memory Map of the image

  Image Entry point : 0x00000311

  Load Region LR_1 (Base: 0x00000000,Size: 0x00000714, Max: 0xffffffff, ABSOLUTE)

    Execution Region ER_RO (Base: 0x00000000Size: 0x00000710, Max: 0xffffffff, ABSOLUTE)
    ......
```

Figure 6.24. The opened DRAFlash.map file.

5. Open the Windows Explorer and browse to the project folder, which is C:/ARM Class Projects/Chapter 6/DRAFlash, and open the DRAFlash.map file that is under this folder.

6. Scroll down this map file until you find the memory map for our image file, which is indicated by the Memory Map of the image line, as shown in Figure 6.24. It can be found from this map file that the download starting address of our project image file is 0x00000311, the loading and the running regions of our project image file start from base address 0x0 with the sizes of 0x0714 and 0x0710. Therefore it should not have any conflict if we select the 0x1000 as the starting address of the flash memory block to perform the erasing or writing operations since it is greater than 0x714, which is the ending address of our stored project image file in the flash memory.

7. Now enter the codes shown in Figure 6.25 into this source file to complete the erasing and writing operations to the flash memory block starting at 0x1000.

Let's have a closer look at these codes to see how they work.

- The codes in lines 9~10 are used to define and declare local data variables to be used in this project. The ui32Loop works as a loop counter in a for() loop later to delay a period of time to keep the PF3 LED on. The ulCount and ulAddress are two unsigned long variables. The former is used to contain the number of words to be erased and written onto the flash memory block, and the latter is used to contain the starting address from where the data will be erased and written onto the flash memory block. The *proData is an unsigned long pointer variable used to store the data to be written into the flash memory.

- Three data words that will be written into the flash memory are defined with an array Data [3] and initialized with three words in line 11.

- In line 12, the starting address of the Data[] array is assigned to the pointer proData.

- The ulAddress and ulCount are initialized in line 13.

- The codes in lines 14~16 are used to configure the GPIO Port F and setup PF3~PF1 as output pins and enable them to perform digital functions. Two LEDs, Green color and Blue color LEDs, are connected to PF3 and PF2 pins in the TM4C123GXL Evaluation Board (refer to Figure 4.27 in Chapter 4). We will use PF3 (Green LED) to indicate the finishing of the erasing operation and PF2 (Blue LED) to indicate the completion of the programming process.

- The codes in lines 18~20 are used to configure some flash memory related registers to prepare and begin the erasing operation. First the Flash Controller Masked Interrupt Status and Clear Register (FCMISC), whose macro is FLASH_FCMISC_R (Figure 6.21), is configured. The bit [0] of the FCMISC register (refer to Figure 6.9), whose macro is FLASH_FCMISC_AMISC (Figure 6.22), is set to 1 to clear any previous possible interrupt request caused by the improperly accessing the flash block in line 18.

```
1    //----------------------------------------------------------------------------------
2    // DRAFlash.c - Main Application for programming Flash Memory with DRA Method
3    //----------------------------------------------------------------------------------
4    #include <stdint.h>
5    #include <stdbool.h>
6    #include "tm4c123gh6pm.h"
7    int main(void)
8    {
9       volatile uint32_t  ui32Loop;
10      unsigned long ulCount, ulAddress, *proData;
11      unsigned long Data[3] = {0x78563412, 0x8B674523, 0xA3456789};
12      proData = Data;
13      ulAddress = 0x1000; ulCount = 3;                          // Starting address and number of words to be written
14      SYSCTL_RCGC2_R = SYSCTL_RCGC2_GPIOF;          // Enable PORTF in RCGC2
15      GPIO_PORTF_DIR_R = 0x0E;                              // Set PF1 ~ PF3 pins as output pins
16      GPIO_PORTF_DEN_R = 0x0E;                              // Enable PF1 ~ PF3 pins for digital function
17      // Erase flash memory 1 KB block starting 0x1000
18      FLASH_FCMISC_R = FL ASH_FCMISC_AMISC;          // Clear the flash access interrupt
19      FLASH_FMA_R = ulAddress;                              // Erase the block
20      FLASH_FMC_R = FLASH_FMC_WRKEY | FLASH_FMC_ERASE;
21      // Wait for the erase complete...
22      while(FLASH_FMC_R & FLASH_FMC_ERASE)
23      {
24      }
25      GPIO_PORTF_DATA_R = 0x08;                          // Set PF3 to HIGH to indicate erasing done
26      for(ui32Loop = 0; ui32Loop < 2000000; ui32Loop++)
27      {
28      }                                                    // Delay a period to keep PF3 on
29      // Loop to perform words programming
30      while(ulCount)
31      {
32         FLASH_FMA_R = ulAddress;
33         FLASH_FMD_R = *proData;
34         FLASH_FMC_R = FLAS H_FMC_WRKEY | FLASH_FMC_WRITE;
35         // Wait until the word has been programmed.
36         while(FLASH_FMC_R & FLASH_FMC_WRITE)
37         {
38         }
39         // Increment to the next word.
40         proData++;
41         ulAddress += 4;
42         ulCount--;
43      }
44      GPIO_PORTF_DATA_R = 0x04;                          // Set PF2 to HIGH to indicate writing done
     }
```

Figure 6.25. The codes for the source file DRAFlash.c.

- Then the Flash Memory Address Register (FMA), whose macro is FLASH_FMA_R defined in Figure 6.21, is assigned with the starting address of the flash memory block to be erased and stored in the local variable ulAddress in line 19.

- Finally the Flash Memory Control Register (FMC), whose macro is FLASH_FMC_R defined in Figure 6.21, is configured and initialized. The bits [31:16] of the FMC (Figure 6.5) are assigned with the Write Key (0xA442), whose macro is FLASH_FMC_WRKEY defined in Figure 6.22. Also, the bit[1] of the FMC, whose macro is FLASH_FMC_ERASE (Figure 6.22), is set to 1 to enable the FMC to begin to perform the erase operation in line 20.

- Starting from coding line 22, a while() loop is executed to poll or wait for the erasing operation to be completed. As we learned from Section 6.2.2.7, especially in Table 6.2, the value of the bit[1] of the FMC register, ERASE whose macro is FLASH_FMC_ERASE, can be used to monitor whether an erase operation is completed or not. If this bit is reset to 0, it means that the current erase operation is complete. Otherwise if this bit is 1, it means that the current erase operation is not done. In this while() loop, two macros, FLASH_FMC_R and FLASH_FMC_ERASE, are ANDed together as the loop condition for the while() loop, and this loop will be terminated if the bit[1] of the FMC is reset to 0, or if macro FLASH_FMC_ERASE = 0, which means that the erase operation is complete.

- As soon as the erase operation is complete, a 0x8 is sent to the pin 3 of the GPIO Port F (PF3) to turn on the Green color LED in line 25.

- Then a for() loop with the loop counter ui32Loop is used to delay a period of time to keep the Green color LED on in code lines 26~28.

- The codes between lines 30 and 43 are used to perform three data words writing operation starting from flash memory block at 0x1000. A while() loop is used in line 30 with the ulCount as the loop condition to perform a three-word writing operation until three words are completely written into the flash memory block.

- In code line 32, the Flash Memory Address Register (FMA) is initialized by assigning the starting address ulAddress (0x1000) to it. Then the first word *proData is assigned to the Flash Memory Data Register (FMD), whose macro is FLASH_FMD_R in line 33.

- The programming or writing operation is initiated in line 34 by configuring the FMC. The bits [31:16] of the FMC (Figure 6.5) are assigned with the Write Key (0xA442), whose macro is FLASH_FMC_WRKEY defined in Figure 6.22. Also, the bit[0] of the FMC (WRITE), whose macro is FLASH_FMC_WRITE (Figure 6.22), is set to 1 to enable the FMC to begin to perform the write operation in line 34. These two configurations are ORed together to make them take effect.

- A while() loop is executed to poll or wait for this writing operation to be completed. As we learned from Section 6.2.2.7, especially in Table 6.2, the value of the bit[0] of the FMC register, WRITE whose macro is FLASH_FMC_WRITE, can be used to monitor whether a programming operation is completed or not. If this bit is reset to 0, it means that the current write operation is complete. Otherwise if this bit is 1, it means that the current write operation is not done. In this while() loop, two macros, FLASH_FMC_R and FLASH_FMC_WRITE, are ANDed together as the loop condition for the while() loop, and this loop is terminated if the bit[0] of the FMC is reset to 0, or the macro FLASH_FMC_WRITE = 0, which means that the current programming operation is complete.

- After the first word is written into the flash memory block, the next word is prepared to be written into the flash memory. This preparation includes updating the next word address (proData++) and the next flash memory location (ulAddress += 4) as well as reducing the word count (ulCount--).

- As soon as all three words are written into the flash memory and the writing operation is complete, a 0x04 is sent to the pin 2 of the GPIO Port F (PF2) to turn on the Blue color LED to indicate that the write operation is complete in line 44.

Now let's build and run the project to perform the erasing and programming operations to the flash memory block starting at 0x1000.

6.7.1.1.4 Build and Run the Project to Perform Erase and Write Operations Before you can build and run the project, make sure that the following two issues have been setup correctly:

- The path of the system header file tm4c123gh6pm.h has been included into the project Include Paths, which is in the C/C++ tab under the menu item Project|Options for Target 'Target 1'. The path is C:\ti\TivaWare_C_Series-2.0.1.11577\inc.

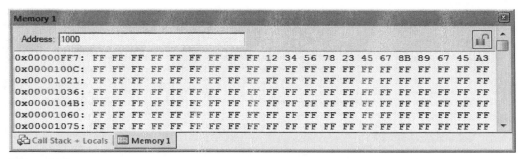

Figure 6.26. The running result of the project DRAFlash. (Reproduced with permission from ARM® Limited. Copyright © ARM Limited.)

- The debug adapter used for this project is `Stellaris ICDI`. This adapter can be configured in the `Debug` tab under the menu item `Project|Options for Target 'Target 1'`.

Now go to the `Project|Build target` menu item to build the project. Then go to the menu item `Flash|Download` to download the project image file into the flash memory starting at `0x00000311` (refer to Figure 6.24).

Run the project by going to the `Debug|Start/Stop Debug Session` menu item, then click on the `OK` button on the pop-up MessageBox and also click on the `Run` menu item.

As the project running, watch the LED on the TM4C123GXL Evaluation Board. The LED first comes on with Green color and then changes to the Blue color. The Green color LED means that the erasing operation is done, and the Blue color LED indicates that the programming process is complete.

Now open the `Memory 1` window located at the lower-right corner to check and confirm the running result of this project. On the opened `Memory 1` window, enter `1000` into the `Address` box and scroll down to the address `0x00000FF7`, as shown in Figure 6.26.

As you can see from Figure 6.26, starting with the address `0x1000`, three data words, `12345678`, `2345678B`, and `896745A3`, have been written into this flash memory block successfully. Compare the original three words in our project source file `DRAFlash.c`, especially the order of these three words in our source file and the order in the flash memory block. What conclusion you can obtain? One hint to answer this question is that the little endian format is used in the memory system in the TM4C123GH6PM MCU. In this way, the order of the words written into the flash memory block should be opposite to the original order.

Another point to be checked is the size of the flash memory block to be erased. As we supposed, the 1-KB flash memory block should be erased starting the address `0x1000`. Therefore the address range for this 1 KB (1024 bytes) should be `0x1000~0x13FF`. Scroll down the memory addresses until you find the address `0x13FC`, as shown in Figure 6.27.

It can be seen from Figure 6.27 that until the address `0x13FF`, all flash memory bytes are erased to `FF`, and this is identical to the ideal erasing operation result, all memory units are erased from 0s to 1s. After the address `0x13FF`, the flash memory contents are random numbers.

Next let's take care of using the interrupt-driven method to program the flash memory block for multiple words with the DRA method.

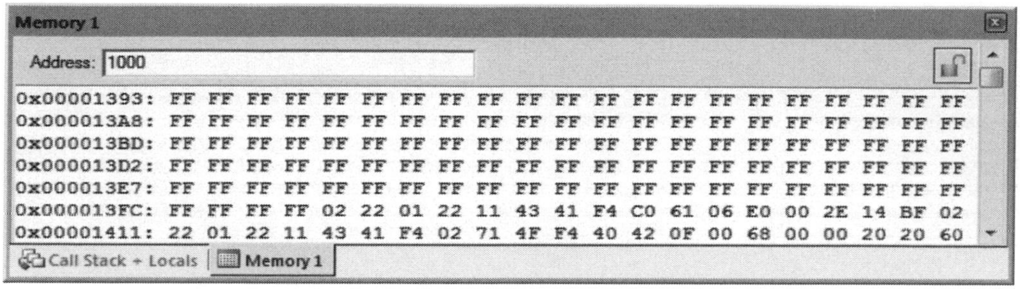

Figure 6.27.   The 1-KB erased flash memory block (0x1000~0x13FF). (Reproduced with permission from ARM® Limited. Copyright © ARM Limited.)

6.7.1.2 Programming Flash Memory for Multiple Words with the DRA Method (Interrupt Driven)

As we discussed in Sections 6.2.2.10~6.2.2.12, three control registers are used to control and manage the Flash controller to implement the interrupt strategy in flash memory:

1. Flash Controller Raw Interrupt Status Register (FCRIS). The macro for this register is FLASH_FCRIS_R (Figure 6.21). This register contains the raw interrupt status. The related bit is set whenever a flash-operation-related interrupt is generated if the associated bits on the FCIM register are set. Among bits, only two bits, bit[1] and bit[0], in this register are closely related to the data erasing and writing operations.

   • Bit[1] is the Programming Raw Interrupt Status (PRIS) bit. The value on this bit indicates the running status of the programming or erasing process. If this bit is 0, it means that the current writing or erasing operation is not complete. If this bit is set to 1, it indicates that the current writing or erasing operation is complete. This status is sent to the interrupt controller when the PMASK bit in the FCIM register is set. This bit is cleared by writing a 1 to the PMISC bit in the FCMISC register. The macro of the this bit is FLASH_FCRIS_PRIS (Figure 6.22).

   • Bit[0] is the Access Raw Interrupt Status (ARIS) bit. The value on this bit indicates the running status of the access to the flash memory block. If this bit is 0, it means that no any improperly access to flash memory block has been occurred. If this bit is set to 1, it indicates that an attempt to access a protected flash block has occurred. The macro of this bit is FLASH_FCRIS_ARIS (Figure 6.22). This status is sent to the interrupt controller when the AMASK bit in the FCIM register is set. This bit is cleared by writing a 1 to the AMISC bit in the FCMISC register

2. Flash Controller Interrupt Mask Register (FCIM). The macro for this register is defined as FLASH_FCIM_R (Figure 6.21). This register contains bits that control whether a raw interrupt condition is promoted to an interrupt sent to the processor. If a mask bit is set to 1, the related raw interrupt is sent to the NVIC; otherwise, if a mask bit is clear to 0, the raw interrupt is blocked and cannot be sent to the NVIC. Among bits, only two bits, bit[1] and bit[0], in this register are used to mask or unmask interrupts related to flash memory data erase or write operations.

   • Bit[1] is the Programming Interrupt Mask (PMASK) bit. If this bit is set to 1, it enables the PRIS in the FCRIS register to be sent to the NVIC to generate an interrupt request to the processor. Otherwise if it is 0, it masks the PRIS and disables it to be sent out. The macro for this bit is FLASH_FCIM_PMASK (Figure 6.22).

   • Bit[0] is the Access Interrupt Mask (AMASK) bit. If this bit is set to 1, it enables the ARIS in the FCRIS register to be sent to the NVIC to generate an interrupt request to the processor. Otherwise if it is 0, it masks the ARIS and disables it to be sent out. The macro for this bit is FLASH_FCIM_AMASK (Figure 6.22).

3. Flash Controller Masked Interrupt Status and Clear Register (FCMISC). The symbolic definition for this register is FLASH_FCMISC_R (Figure 6.21). This register contains bits that have a dual purpose. If the register is read, the bits indicate that an interrupt has been generated and sent to the processor. When written, an interrupt can be cleared. Writing a 1 to a bit in this register clears the related interrupt. Writing a 0 to a bit does not affect the state of the bit. Among bits, only two bits, bit[1] and bit[0], in this register are used to read and clear interrupts related to flash memory data erase or write operations.

- Bit[1] is the Programming Masked Interrupt Status and Clear (PMISC) bit. When read, a 0 in this bit means that no erase or write complete interrupt occurred. However, when read, a 1 in this bit indicates that an erasing or writing complete interrupt has occurred. Writing a 1 to this bit clears PMISC and also the PRIS bit in the FCRIS register. The macro for this bit is FLASH_FCMISC_PMISC (Figure 6.22).
- Bit[0] is the Access Masked Interrupt Status and Clear (AMISC) bit. When read, a 0 in this bit means that no improper access has occurred. However, when read, a 1 in this bit indicates that an improper access has been occurred. Writing a 1 to this bit clears AMISC and also the ARIS bit in the FCRIS register. The macro for this bit is FLASH_FCMISC_AMISC (Figure 6.22).

6.7.1.2.1 The Erase and Write Interrupts Processing Procedure   In summary, these three registers performed the traditional interrupt control functions:

1. The FCRIS works as a local interrupt flag register to set up the interrupt flags if the related interrupt condition is met. But this flag belongs to the local interrupt flag and can only be used to indicate that a local interrupt has occurred. Whether this local interrupt can be sent to the processor is determined by the interrupt mask register FCIM.

2. The FCIM works as an interrupt enable register to enable whether an interrupt flagged in the FCRIS can be sent to the NVIC. If a bit is set to 1, it enables the related interrupt flagged in the FCRIS register to be sent to the processor.

3. The FCMISC works as an interrupt status and reset register. Once an interrupt flagged in the FCRIS register has been sent out, the related bit on this register is set to 1 to indicate this situation. After an interrupt has been handled and processed, the related bit should be cleared to reset that interrupt to enable the same interrupt to occur in the future.

Since both the erase and write operation to the flash memory block use the same bit, bit[1], in three registers to provide interrupt-related operations, we need to treat this bit in different time with different functions. This bit provides the following functions:

- If an erasing or a writing operation is complete with the interrupt mechanism activated, the bit [1] in the FCRIS register, PRIS (FLASH_FCRIS_PRIS), is set to 1 to indicate this case.
- If the bit[1] in the FCIM register, PMASK (FLASH_FCIM_PMASK), is set to 1 to enable this PRIS interrupt, the PRIS interrupt is sent to the processor as an interrupt request to inform the CPU that the current erasing or writing operation is complete.
- When this interrupt request is responded by the processor, the program is directed to the related interrupt handler to be processed. By checking the bit[1] in the FCMISC register, PMISC (FLASH_FCMISC_PMISC), this interrupt can be identified if it is set to 1. After the interrupt is processed, this bit should be reset to 0 to clear this interrupt by writing a 1 to this bit. When this happened, the PRIS bit in the FCRIS register is also cleared.

From the above operational procedure, it can be found that both erase and write uses the same interrupt flag and enable mechanism. In order to distinguish these two different operations, we need to respond and handle them in a timing sequence. Since we know that we need to do an erasing first, therefore the first interrupt must be for erasing complete interrupt, and the following interrupts should be the writing complete interrupts.

Based on these discussions, we can build our second project to erase and program multiple words to a flash memory block with the DRA method combined with two API functions in the TivaWare™ Peripheral Driver Library via an interrupt-driven mechanism. First let's take a look at some special features used in this project.

6.7.1.2.2 Special Features Utilized in the Project
In this project, we want to build a C source file with the following features:

- Use a combined strategy to build this project. In other words, we will use the Direct Register Access (DRA) method combined with two API functions, IntRegister() and IntEnable(), in the TivaWare™ Peripheral Driver Library to build this flash memory programming and erasing project with interrupt-driven ability. The reason we need to use these two API functions in this project is that when accessing the flash memory to perform erase or program operations, the interrupt vector table will be relocated and aligned to the beginning on the SRAM space. It would be very complicated if you use the DRA method to perform these functions directly. Therefore we use these two API functions to reduce our coding job and make the project short and simple.
- Integrate the erase and write operations into two user's defined functions, DRAFlashErase() and DRAFlashWrite().
- Use four LEDs, PB0~PB3, installed on the EduBASE ARM® Trainer as indicators to indicate the completion of the erasing operation (PB0 is ON) and the completion of the three-word programming operations (PB0~PB3 are ON).

6.7.1.2.3 Build the Project to Program Multiple Words for Flash Memory with Interrupts
Perform the following operations to create a new project DRAFlashInt:

1. Open the Windows Explorer window to create a new folder named DRAFlashInt under the C:\ARM Class Projects\Chapter 6 folder.
2. Open the Keil® ARM-MDK µVersion5 and go to the Project|New µVersion Project menu item to create a new µVersion Project. On the opened wizard, browse to our new folder DRAFlashInt that is created in step 1 above. Enter DRAFlashInt into the File name box and click on the Save button to create this project.
3. On the next wizard, you need to select the device (MCU) for this project. Expand three icons, Texas Instruments, Tiva C Series, and TM4C123x Series, and select the target device TM4C123GH6PM from the list by clicking on it. Click on the OK to close this wizard.
4. Next the Software Components wizard is opened, and you need to set up the software development environment for your project with this wizard. Expand two icons, CMSIS and Device, and check the CORE and Startup checkboxes in the Sel. column, and click on the OK button since we need these two components to build our project.

Since this project is a little more complex, we need to create both a header file and a source file for this project. Perform the following operations to create a new header file DRAFlashInt.h:

```
1   //********************************************************************************************************
2   // DRAFlashInt.h - Header File for Main Application File
3   //********************************************************************************************************
4   #include <stdint.h>
5   #include <stdbool.h>
6   #include "inc/tm4c123gh6pm.h"
7   #include "driverlib/interrupt.h"
8   #define INT_FLASH    45              // Flash Memory Control and EEPROM
9   void FLASHM_Handler(void);
10  void Delay(void);
11  uint32_t DRAFlashErase(uint32_t  uiAddr);
12  uint32_t DRAFlashWrite(uint32_t *pData, uint32_t uiAddr, uint32_t uiCount);
13  uint32_t eraseFlag = 0, writeFlag = 0;
14  uint32_t  ui32Loop,  intCount = 0;
```

Figure 6.28.   The codes of the header file DRAFlashInt.h.

1. In the `Project` pane, expand the `Target` folder and right click on the `Source Group 1` folder and select the `Add New Item to Group 'Source Group 1'`.

2. Select the `Header File (.h)` and enter `DRAFlashInt` into the `Name:` box, and click on the `Add` button to add this header file into the project.

3. Enter the codes shown in Figure 6.28 into this header file.

Let's have a closer look at this header file to see how it works.

- The code lines in 4~7 are used to include all system header files to be implemented in this project. The system header file `interrupt.h` defined the protocols of all interrupt-related API functions, including the `IntRegister()` and `IntEnable()`.

- The `INT_FLASH` is defined in line 8 as the interrupt number. In fact, you can use any other number to define this flash interrupt source.

- The flash interrupt handler `FLASHM_Handler()` and a user's defined function `Delay()` is declared in lines 9 and 10. The former is used to response and process any generated interrupt related to the flash memory operations, and the latter is used to delay a period of time in the project.

- Two user's defined functions, `DRAFlashErase()` and `DRAFlashWrite()`, are declared in lines 11 and 12, respectively. These two functions are used to perform flash erasing and programming operations later.

- Four global variables, `eraseFlag`, `writeFlag`, `ui32Loop`, and `intCount`, are declared and initialized in lines 13 and 14. The first two variables are used to hold and stop two `while()` loops inside `DRAFlashErase()` and `DRALashWrite()` functions are used to wait for two interrupts to occur; erase-complete and write-complete interrupts. The `ui32Loop` is used for a `for()` loop to delay a period of time in the project. The `intCount` is used to identify whether an erase-complete interrupt or a write-complete interrupt is generated inside the interrupt handler.

Perform the following operations to create a new source file `DRAFlashInt.c`:

1. In the `Project` pane, expand the `Target` folder and right click on the `Source Group 1` folder and select the `Add New Item to Group 'Source Group 1'`.

2. Select the `C File (.c)` and enter `DRAFlashInt` into the `Name:` box, and click on the `Add` button to add this source file into the project.

3. Enter the initial codes shown in Figure 6.29 into this source file.

```
//****************************************************************************************
// DRAFlashInt.c - Main Application File
//****************************************************************************************
#include "DRAFlashInt.h"

int main(void)
{


}
```

Figure 6.29. The initial codes of the source file DRAFlashInt.c.

4. Now go to `Project|Build target` menu item to build the project to get the project map file, `DRAFlashInt.map`. The reason we need this map file is to determine the starting address for erasing and writing data in the flash memory block, because in order to run our project, our project image file will also be downloaded into this flash memory later. Therefore we must make sure that the flash memory block we try to erase and write is not the same block in which our project image file will be downloaded.

5. Similarly as we did in steps 5 and 6 in Section 6.6.1.1.3, we can open this map file to identify the starting address of the flash memory block to be erased and written is `0x2000`.

Now let's develop the full source codes for this `DRAFlashInt.c` file. First add the first part of the codes shown in Figure 6.30 into this file.

Then enter the second part codes shown in Figure 6.31 into this source file. Now let's have a closer look at the entire codes to see how they work.

- The user header file `DRAFlashInt.h` is included in line 4 since this header file contains most declarations for flash memory control registers, operation parameters, and macros.
- The code in line 7 is used to declare all used local variables. The variables `uiCount` and `uiAddress` are unsigned integer variables used to define the number of words to be written into the flash memory block starting at the address stored in `uiAddress` variable. The `proData` is a pointer variable pointing to the first data to be written.
- In line 8, a new data array `Data[]` with three data words is created and initialized with three 32-bit data values.
- The codes in lines 9~10 are used to initialize these variables, including the `uiCount`, `uiAddress`, and pointer `proData`.
- The code lines between 11 and 13 are used to configure GPIO Port B to connect the system clock to it and make PB0~PB3 as output pins. We need these pins to drive 4 LEDs on the EduBase Trainer to indicate the erase and write completion states.
- In line 14, the bit PMISC in the FCMISC register and the bit PRIS in the FCRIS register are reset to 0 by writing a 1 to bit PMISC to enable any future interrupt to be occur as an erasing or writing operation is complete.
- The bit PMASK in the FCIM register is set to 1 to enable or unmask the PRIS interrupt to be sent to the interrupt controller NVIC when an erase or a write operation complete interrupt is signaled in line 15.
- The code lines 16 and 17 are used to call two API functions, `IntRegister()` and `IntEnable()`, to register the flash memory interrupt handler `FLASHM_Handler()` and to enable this interrupt.

```
1    //*********************************************************************************
2    // DRAFlashInt.c - Main Application File (The First Part Codes)
3    //*********************************************************************************
4    #include "DRAFlashInt.h"
5    int main(void)
6    {
7        uint32_t ret, uiC  ount, uiAddress, *proData;
8        uint32_t Data[3] = {0x78563412, 0x8B674523, 0xA3456789};
9        uiAddress = 0x2000;  uiCount = 3;
10       proData = Data;

11       SYSCTL_RCGCGPIO_R = 0x02;                          // enable clock to Port B
12       GPIO_PORTB_DIR_R |= 0xF;                           // set PB0 ~ PB3 as output pins
13       GPIO_PORTB_DEN_R |= 0xF;                           // enable PB0 ~ PB3 as digital function

14       FLASH_FCMISC_R = FLASH_FCMISC_PMISC;               // reset PMISC & PRIS bit in FCRIS to clear interrupt
15       FLASH_FCIM_R = FLASH_FCIM_PMASK;                   // unmask bit[1] (PMASK) in the FCIM register
16       IntRegister(INT_FL   ASH, FLASHM_Handler);         // register the interrupt handler
17       IntEnable(INT_FLASH);                              // enable the flash interrupt

18       ret = DRAFlashErase(uiAddress);
19       if (ret != 0) { return 1; }                        // if erase operation is wrong, return 1
20       ret = DRAFlashWrite(proData, uiAddress, uiCount);
21       if (ret != 0) { return 1; }                        // if program operation is wrong, return 1
22       return 0;
23   }

24   uint32_t DRAFlashErase(uint32_t uiAddr)
25   {
26       eraseFlag++;
27       // erase flash memory 1 KB block starting 0x2000
28       FLASH_FCMISC_R = FLASH_FCMISC_AMISC;                       // clear any flash access interrupt
29       FLASH_FMA_R = uiAddr;                                      // assign the starting address to FMA
30       FLASH_FMC_R = FLASH_FMC_WRKEY|FLASH_FMC_ERASE;             // perform the erase operation...

31       while(eraseFlag)        // wait for erase-complete interrupt...
32       {
33       }
34       return 0;
35   }

36   uint32_t DRAFlashWrite(uint32_t *pData, uint32_t uiAddr, uint32_t uiCount)
37   {
38       FLASH_FCMISC_R = FLASH_FCMISC_AMISC;                       // clear any flash access interrupt

39       while(uiCount)                                             // wait for all 3 words to be written
40       {
41           writeFlag++;
42           FLASH_FMA_R = uiAddr;                                  // assign the starting address to FMA
43           FLASH_FMD_R = *pData;
44           FLASH_FMC_R =  FLASH_FMC_WRKEY|FLASH_FMC_WRITE;

45           while(writeFlag)        // Wait for write-complete interrupt...
46           {
47           }
48           pData++;                                               // Increment to the next word
49           uiAddr += 4;
50           uiCount--;
51       }

52       if(FLASH_FCRIS_R & FLASH_FCRIS_ARIS)                       // if FCRIS_ARIS is 1, an error occurred
53       {
54           return 1;
55       }
56       return 0;
     }
```

Figure 6.30.   The first part codes for the source file DRAFlashInt.c.

```
57  //*************************************************************************************
58  // DRAFlashInt.c - Main Application File (The Second Part Codes)
59  //*************************************************************************************
60  void FLASHM_Handler(void)                              // flash memory interrupt handler
61  {
62      intCount++;
63      if (FLASH_FCMISC_R & FLASH_FCMISC_PMISC)           // an erase/write comple te interrupt occurred
64      {
65          switch(intCount)                               // check which interrupt occurred...
66          {
67              case 1:                                    // an erase-complete interrupt occurred
68              GPIO_PORTB_DATA_R = 0x1;                    // set PB0 to HIGH to indicate erasing done
69              eraseFlag--;                               // stop while(eraseFlag) loop in DRAFlashErase()
70              break;
71              case 2:                                    // first-word write-complete interrupt occurred
72              GPIO_PORTB_DATA_R = 0x3;                    // turn on LEDs PB0 & PB1
73              writeFlag--;                               // stop the while(writeFlag) loop in DRAFlashWrite()
74              break;
75              case 3:                                    // second-word write-complete interrupt occurred
76              GPIO_PORTB_DATA_R = 0x7;                    // turn on LEDs PB0 & PB1 & PB2
77              writeFlag--;                               // stop the while(writeFlag) loop in DRAFlashWrite()
78              break;
79              case 4:                                    // third-word write-complete interrupt occurred
80              GPIO_PORTB_DATA_R = 0xF;                    // turn on LEDs PB0 ~ PB3
81              writeFlag--;                               // stop the while(writeFlag) loop in DRAFlashWrite()
82              break;
83          }
84          Delay();
85          FLASH_FCMISC_R = FLASH_FCMISC_PMISC;           // clear PMISC and PRIS bits to clear interrupt
86      }
87  }
88  void Delay(void)
89  {
90      for (ui32Loop = 0; ui32Loop < 600000; ui32Loop++) {}
    }
```

Figure 6.31. The second part codes for the source file DRAFlashInt.c.

- Then the DRAFlashErase() function is called to perform 1-KB flash memory block erasing operation starting at the address uiAddress in line 18. A zero is returned if this function is executed successfully. Otherwise a nonzero is returned.

- In line 20, another user defined function DRAFlashWrite() is executed to write three words into the flash memory block starting at the address uiAddress. The first word is pointed by the pointer variable proData and the total number of words is indicated by the uiCount. A 0 is returned if this function is executed successfully. Otherwise a nonzero is returned.

- The user defined function DRAFlashErase() starts at line 24.

- In line 26, first the global variable eraseFlag is increased by 1 to make it equal to 1 since we need to use this variable as the loop condition for a while() loop in line 31 to wait for an erasing-completion interrupt to occur.

- Before the erase operation can be performed, the bit AMISC in the FCMISC register should be set to 1 to clear any previous interrupt caused by any improper accessing to the flash memory in line 28.

- In line 29, the address uiAddr is assigned to the flash memory address register FMA to enable the erase operation to start from this address.

- The control parameters WRKEY (0xA442) and FLASH_FMC_ERASE are assigned to the flash memory control register FMC to begin this erasing operation in line 30.

- In lines 31~33, a while() loop with a loop condition eraseFlag is executed to wait for the erasing-complete interrupt to occur. This loop will be terminated if the loop condition eraseFlag becomes 0. Later you can find that this loop condition will be reset to 0 in the flash memory interrupt handler FLASHM_Handler().
- This function returns a zero if nothing is wrong in line 34.
- Another user defined function DRAFlashWrite() starts at line 36.
- Before the write operation can be performed, the bit AMISC in the FCMISC register should be set to 1 to clear any previous interrupt caused by any improper accessing to the flash memory in line 38.
- The writing operation starts at line 39 with a while() loop. This while() loop will not be terminated until all three words are written into the flash memory starting at the address uiAddr. The loop condition uiCount contains the number of words to be written.
- First the global flag variable writeFlag is incremented to make it equal to 1 in line 41 since we need to use this variable as the loop condition for a while() loop in line 45 to wait for a writing-completion interrupt to be occurred.
- In line 42, the address uiAddr is assigned to the flash memory address register FMA to enable the write operation to start from this address.
- The first data word *pData is assigned to the flash memory data register FMD in line 43.
- The control parameters WRKEY (0xA442) and FLASH_FMC_WRITE are assigned to the flash memory control register FMC to begin this writing operation in line 44.
- In lines 45~47, a while() loop with a loop condition writeFlag is executed to wait for the writing-complete interrupt to be occurred. This loop will be terminated if the loop condition writeFlag becomes 0. Later you can find that this loop condition will be reset to 0 in the flash memory interrupt handler FLASHM_Handler().
- The code lines between 48 and 50 are used to update the address, the data word, and the number of the data words to be written into the flash memory block when a word has been written into the flash memory.
- During the writing operation process, if an improper accessing to the flash memory occurs, the bit ARIS in the FCRIS register is set to 1. In this case, a nonzero value is returned to indicate this situation. The code lines in 52~55 perform this function.
- Otherwise this function returns a zero to indicate that nothing is wrong for the execution of this function in line 56.
- The second-part codes include the flash memory interrupt handler FLASHM_Handler() and a Delay() function.
- The flash memory interrupt handler FLASHM_Handler() starts at line 60.
- First the global variable intCount is increased by 1 to make it equal to 1. We need to use this variable to identify whether this interrupt is triggered by either an erasing-completion or a writing-completion operation. This variable is initialized to 0 at the beginning of this file.
- As we know, either an erasing-completion or a writing-completion action triggers the same interrupt by setting the PMISC bit to 1 in the FCMISC register. In line 63, this bit is checked to confirm that the interrupt is triggered by these two actions.
- In order to distinguish these two possible interrupt sources, a switch-case instruction structure is used with the global variable intCount as the case condition. If the intCount = 1, this means that this interrupt is triggered by an erasing-completion action. Then the LED PB0 in the EduBASE Trainer is turned on to indicate this, and the global flag variable eraseFlag

is decreased by 1 to make it 0 to terminate the while() loop inside the function DRA-FlashErase() to enable the program to continue executing. The code lines between 67 and 70 perform these functions.

- Otherwise the variable intCount equals 2, 3, or 4, which means that this interrupt is triggered by the word-writing-completion action (2 → word 1 writing-completion, 3 → word 2 writing-completion, 4 → word 3 writing-completion). The related LED PB$_i$ will be turned on and the global flag variable writeFlag is decreased to terminate the while() loop inside the function DRAFlashWrite() to enable the program to continue executing. The code lines between 71 and 82 perform these functions.
- In line 84, the user-defined function Delay() is called to delay a period of the time to enable the LEDs to be on a certain period to enable them to be seen.
- The PMISC bit in the FCMISC register is set to 1 to clear any interrupt triggered by the PRIS (programming-completion or erasing-completion) to enable future same interrupt to be occurred in line 85.
- The codes for the Delay() function are shown in lines 88~90.

Now let's build and run the project to test its function. Before we can do this, we need first to set up the project running environment. These include the system header file path including and TivaWare™ Peripheral Driver Library adding since we used two API functions in that library.

6.7.1.2.4 Set Up the Environment to Build and Run the Project   Perform the following operations to set up the running environment for this project:

- Include the system header file path C:\ti\TivaWare_C_Series-2.0.1.11577 in the C/C++ tab under the Project|Options for Target 'Target 1' menu item.
- Select the debug adapter Stellaris ICDI in the Dubeg tab under the Project-|Options for Target 'Target 1' menu item.
- Add the TivaWare™ Peripheral Driver Library file driverlib.lib into the project. To do this, right click on the Source Group 1 folder in the Project pane and select the Add Existing Files to Group 'Source Group 1' item. The library file is located at C:\ti\TivaWare_C_Series-2.0.1.11577\driverlib\rvmdk.

Now build the project by going to Project|Build target menu item. If everything is fine, go to Flash|Download item to download the image file of the project into the flash memory. Then go to Debug|Start/Stop Debug Session and Debug|Run item to run the project.

After the project running, you can find that four LEDs, PB0~PB3, on the EduBASE Trainer will be on in a sequence starting from PB0. This means that if the erasing-completion triggered the interrupt, the first LED, PB0, is on. Then after each word is written into the flash memory, each word-writing-completion triggered an interrupt to enable the related LEDs, PB1, PB2, and PB3, to be on, respectively.

In order to confirm these operations, open the Memory 1 window and enter 2000 into the Address box. Scroll down the address until the 0x00001FEE. You can find that three words, 0x78563412, 0x8B674523, and 0xA3456789, have been successfully written into the flash memory block starting at 0x2000, as shown in Figure 6.32. Since the little endian format is used in the ARM® Cortex®-M4 MCU, the data bytes are stored in an opposite way. All other spaces are written as 0xFF, and this means that they have been all

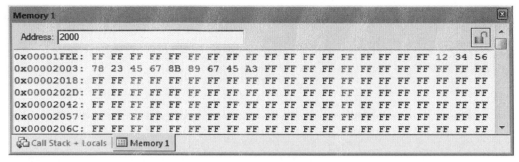

Figure 6.32.   The running result of the DRAFlashInt project. (Reproduced with permission from ARM® Limited. Copyright © ARM Limited.)

erased from 0s to 1s. Since 1 KB of bytes should be erased starting from 0x2000 when performing this erase operation, a 1-KB block starting from 0x2000 to 0x23FF should be erased to 0xFF. You can confirm this by scrolling down to the address 0x23FF in the Memory 1 window if you like.

Our project is successful. Click on the Start/Stop Debug Session item to stop the project.

Now let's take care of programming the flash memory block in the buffered words with the DRA method. In this method, 32-word will be written into 32 Flash Write Buffer n Registers (FWBn) and then written into the desired flash memory block.

6.7.1.3 *Programming Flash Memory for Buffered Words with the DRA Method*

As we discussed in Section 6.2.2.2, the 32 FWBn registers (FWB0~FWB31) are 32-bit registers used to store the contents to be written into the related Flash memory when a Flash Write Buffer Writing operation is executed. The address of each of these registers is determined by the bits [6:0] in the FMA register. The values on bits [6:0] in the FMA must be 0 to provide a continuous $2^7 = 128$-byte (32-word) space in the flash memory array where the 32-word can be written into. Therefore the register FWB0 corresponds to the address in bits [6:0] in the FMA, which is 0x00. The FWB1 corresponds to the address that equals (bits [6:0] of FMA) + 0x4 = (0x04) and so on. Only the FWBn registers that have been updated since the previous buffered Flash memory write operation can be written into the related flash array. The Flash Write Buffer Valid (FWBVAL) register shows which registers have been written since the last buffered Flash memory writing operation.

6.7.1.3.1 The Buffer Words Programming Procedure   To program 32 words with a single buffered Flash memory write operation, perform the following operations:

1. Write the 32 source data into the 32 FWBn registers.
2. Write the target address to the FMA register. This address must be a 32-word aligned address, which is, bits [6:0] in FMA must be 0s.
3. Write the Flash memory write key and the WRBUF bit to the FMC2 register. Depending on the value of the KEY bit in the BOOTCFG register, the value 0xA442 or 0x71D5 must be written into the WRKEY field for a Flash memory write to occur.

4. Poll the FMC2 register until the WRBUF bit is cleared or else waited for the PMIS interrupt to be signaled.

Now let's build this project to program 32 words with the buffer word programming method.

6.7.1.3.2 Develop the Buffer Words Programming Project DRAFlashBuffer Perform the following operations to create a new project DRAFlashBuffer:

1. Open the Windows Explorer window to create a new folder named DRAFlashBuffer under the C:\ARM Class Projects\Chapter 6 folder.

2. Open the Keil® ARM-MDK μVersion5 and go to the Project|New μVersion Project menu item to create a new μVersion Project. On the opened wizard, browse to our new folder DRAFlashBuffer that is created in step 1 above. Enter DRAFlashBuffer into the File name box and click on the Save button to create this project.

3. On the next wizard, you need to select the device (MCU) for this project. Expand three icons, Texas Instruments, Tiva C Series, and TM4C123x Series, and select the target device TM4C123GH6PM from the list by clicking on it. Click on the OK to close this wizard.

4. Next the Software Components wizard is opened, and you need to set up the software development environment for your project with this wizard. Expand two icons, CMSIS and Device, and check the CORE and Startup checkboxes in the Sel. column, and click on the OK button since we need these two components to build our project.

Since this project is very simple, we only need a source file. Perform the following operations to create a new C source file DRAFlashBuffer.c:

1. In the Project pane, expand the Target folder and right click on the Source Group 1 folder and select the Add New Item to Group 'Source Group 1'.

2. Select the C File (.c) and enter DRAFlashBuffer into the Name: box, and click on the Add button to add this header file into the project.

3. Enter the codes shown in Figure 6.33 into this source file.

Let's have a closer look at this header file to see how it works.

- The codes in lines 4~6 are used to include three system header files that will be used in this project.
- The flash write buffer register FWBN is defined as a macro with its base address 0x400FD100 in line 7. In fact, this is the address of the register FWB0. This macro is defined in a system header file hw_flash.h. We can use this address as a base to expand to all other 31 FWBN (N = 1~31) registers by adding an offset of 0x4 × N. To save space, we defined this macro in this file instead of including that system header file.
- The macro HWREG(x) is defined in line 8. With this macro, we can easily convert the base address of the FWBN that is defined as a constant 0x400FD100 in line 7 to an address and add the related offset to that base address to get all 32 buffer registers.
- In line 9, the user-defined function InitFWBN() is declared and this function is used to initialize and configure 32 FWBN registers by assigning 32 words to 32 FWBN registers to make them ready for this buffer write operation.
- The main program starts from line 10.
- The starting address 0x1000 from which the buffered data should be written into the flash memory block is declared in line 12.

```
1    //********************************************************************************
2    // DRAFlashBuffer.c - Mian Application File
3    //********************************************************************************
4    #include <stdint.h>
5    #include <stdbool.h>
6    #include "tm4c123gh6pm.h"

7    #define  FLASH_FWBN      0x400FD100
8    #define  HWREG(x)           (*((volatile  uint32_t *)(x)))
9    void  InitFWBN(void);

10   int main(void)
11   {
12      uint32_t uiAddress = 0x1000;

13      // erase flash memory 1 KB block starting 0x1000
14      FLASH_FCMISC_R = FLASH_FCMISC_AMISC;                    // Clear the flash access interrupt
15      FLASH_FMA_R = uiAddress;                                // Erase the block
16      FLASH_FMC_R = FLASH_FMC_WR KEY | FLASH_FMC_ERASE;

17      // wait for the erase complete...
18      while(FLASH_FMC_R & FLASH_FMC_ERASE) {}
19      FLASH_FWBVAL_R = 0xFFFFFFFF;
20      FLASH_FMA_R = uiAddress;
21      InitFWBN();
22      FLASH_FMC2_R = FLASH_FMC_WRKEY | FLASH_FMC2_WRBUF;

23      // wait for the buffer writing complete...
24      while(FLASH_FMC2_R & FLASH_FMC2_WRBUF) {}
25      return 0;
26   }

27   void InitFWBN(void)                                        // Initialize 32 words to FWBN
28   {
29      uint32_t uiLoop, wData = 0x78563412;

30      for(uiLoop = 0; uiLoop < 32; uiLoop++)
31      {
32         HWREG(FLASH_FWBN + 4 * uiLoop) = wData + 4 * uiLoop;
33      }
   }
```

Figure 6.33. The codes for the source file DRAFlashBuffer.c.

- The codes in lines 14~18 are used to erase a 1-KB block from the flash memory space starting from 0x1000.

- In line 19, the Flash Write Buffer Valid register (FWBVAL) is initialized with a value of 0xFFFFFFFF to indicate that each FWBN has been updated since the last programming operation and is ready to be programmed into the flash memory. In fact, this 0xFFFFFFFF can be replaced by −1 and assigned to the FWBVAL register since both of them are equal.

- The starting address uiAddress, which is 0x1000, is assigned to the Flash Memory Address register (FMA) to enable this buffer writing operation to start from this address in line 20.

- The user-defined function InitFWBN() is called to initialize and configure 32 FWBN registers to make them ready to perform this buffer writing operation in line 21.

- In line 22, the Flash Memory Control 2 register (FMC2) is configured with the WRKEY (0xA442) and WRBUF macro (bit[0] on FMC2 is set to 1) to enable the buffer writing operation to start.

- Then in line 24 a while() loop is executed to wait for the completion of this buffer writing operation. The loop condition is a combination of the FMC2 and WRBUF bit, or bit[0] on the

FMC2 register. When the buffer writing is complete, the WRBUF bit is cleared to 0, and this will terminate this `while()` loop to indicate the completion of this buffer writing.

- A zero is returned to the operating system to indicate that the main program is done with no any error in line 25.
- The user-defined function `InitFWBN()` starts at line 27. This function is used to initialize and configure 32 buffer registers with 32 data words.
- First a local loop counter variable `uiLoop` and a base word `wData` is declared, and the latter is initialized with the initial value `0x78563412` in line 29.
- The codes in lines 30~33 are used to initialize 32 FWBN registers. This job is done by using a `for()` loop to access each FWBN register by adding an offset 4 × `uiLoop` to the base address `FLASH_FWBN` (`0x400FD100`) and assign a word value to each FWBN register by adding the base data word `wData` with an offset 4 × `uiLoop`, too.

One point to be noted is that when we perform this adding offset to the base address process, the base address must be a real address (`0x400FD100`), not an address pointer, like `FLASH_FWBN_R`. The latter is a pointer (`*((volatile uint32_t *) 0x400FD100))`, not a real address.

6.7.1.3.3 Build and Set Up the Environment to Run the Project   Perform the following operations to set up the running environment for this project:

- Include the system header file path `C:\ti\TivaWare_C_Series-2.0.1.11577\inc` in the C/C++ tab under the `Project|Options for Target 'Target 1'` menu item.
- Select the debug adapter `Stellaris ICDI` in the Dubeg tab under the `Project-|Options for Target 'Target 1'` menu item.

Now build the project by going to the `Project|Build target` menu item. If everything is fine, go to the `Flash|Download` item to download the image file of the project into the flash memory. Then go to `Debug|Start/Stop Debug Session` and `Debug|Run` item to run the project.

To confirm this buffer writing operation, open the `Memory 1` window and enter `1000` into the `Address` box. Scroll down the address until the `0x00000FF7`. You can find that 32 words have been successfully written into the flash memory block starting at `0x1000`, as shown in Figure 6.34. The 32 words take 32 × 4 = 128 bytes, and this is equivalent to an address range from `0x1000` to `0x107F`, as shown in Figure 6.34.

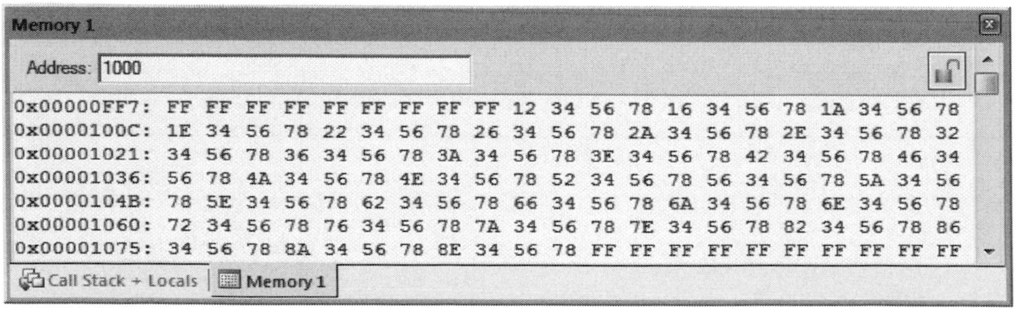

Figure 6.34.   The running result of the project DRAFlashBuffer. (Reproduced with permission from ARM® Limited. Copyright © ARM Limited.)

Since the little endian format is used in the ARM® Cortex®-M4 MCU, the data bytes are stored in an opposite way. All other spaces are written as 0xFF, and this means that they have been all erased from 0s to 1s. Since 1-KB bytes should be erased starting from 0x1000 when performing the erase operation, a 1-KB block starting from 0x1000 to 0x13FF should be erased to 0xFF. You can confirm this by scrolling down to the address 0x13FF in the Memory 1 window if you like. Our project is successful. Click on the Start/Stop Debug Session item to stop the project.

Next let's take care of programming the EEPROM in the 4M4C123GH6PM MCU system.

6.7.2 EEPROM Programming

In TM4C123GH6PM MCU system, the EEPROM programming process is similar to the flash memory programming process, but it has some important different features with the flash memory programming and erasing operations. The similar parts are both devices use a set of registers to control the programming process, including the reading, writing, and erasing. But the different parts involve the programming configurations and operations. First let's take a look at these differences.

6.7.2.1 Special Features in the EEPROM Programming Process

Some special features used in the EEPROM programming are listed below:

1. In order to perform any EEPROM programming process, including the reading, writing, and erasing operation, the EEPROM module clock must be enabled before the EEPROM registers can be programmed.

2. Unlike the flash memory programming, the EEPROM programming does not need to perform any erasing operation before its programming process.

3. The EEPROM programming process needs an initialization process to make sure that the EEPROM is ready to be accessed to perform any operation.

4. Unlike the flash memory, the EEPROM does not directly use any address to access the EEPROM to perform any reading or writing operation, instead it uses two registers, EEPROM Current Block (EEBLOCK) and EEPROM Current Offset (EEOFFSET), to store the target address to access the EEPROM to perform any desired operation.

5. Unlike the flash memory, the EEPROM uses a register, EEPROM Read-Write Register (EERDWR), to perform reading from and writing into the EEPROM space operation. This is a 32-bit register used to read or write the EEPROM word at the address pointed to by the EEBLOCK and EEOFFSET registers. When writing, the word to be written into the EEPROM is stored in this register. When reading, the reading result from the EEPROM is also stored in this register.

6. The EEPROM uses the same interrupt vector as the flash memory did to generate an interrupt when a write to EEPROM completes as indicated by the bit[0] (WORKING bit) in the EEDONE register. When this bit's value is changed from 1 to 0, it means that a word has been successfully written into the EEPROM. The EEDONE register can work together with the EEPROM Interrupt (EEINT) register to generate an interrupt. If the INT bit (bit[0]) in the EEINT register is set, the ERIS bit (bit[2]) in the Flash Controller Raw Interrupt Status (FCRIS) register is also set whenever the WORKING bit (bit[0])

in the EEDONE register's value changes from 1 to 0 since the Flash memory and the EEPROM share an interrupt vector. You need to distinguish these two different interrupt sources by checking the bit[2] in the FCRIS inside the interrupt handler when this interrupt vector is triggered.

Now let's take a closer look at the operational sequence of the EEPROM programming.

6.7.2.2 EEPROM Programming Operational Sequence

As we discussed in Section 6.2.5, in the TM4C123GH6PM MCU system, a 2-KB EEPROM is installed and used to support the users' software development. This 2-KB EEPROM array can be considered and accessed in the following two different formats:

- 512 32-bit words (512×4 Bytes = 2048 Bytes = 2 KB).
- 32 blocks of 16-word with each block containing 16 words ($32 \times 16 \times 4$ Bytes = 2 KB).

The popular way to access the EEPROM is to use the second format; the 2-KB space can be divided into 32 blocks with each block containing 16 words.

To successfully perform any programming operation to an EEPROM space, the following operational sequence should be followed:

1. Initialize and configure the EEPROM based on the following initialization steps:
    a. The system clock to the EEPROM module must be enabled through the EEPROM Run Mode Clock Gating Control (RCGCEEPROM) register.
    b. Delay 6 clock cycles to stabilize the system clock applied on the EEPROM module.
    c. Check the WORKING bit (bit[0]) in the EEPROM Done Status (EEDONE) register until it is clear, indicating that the EEPROM has completed its power-on initialization.
    d. Read the PRETRY and ERETRY bits in the EEPROM Support Control and Status (EESUPP) register. If both bits are 0, which means that both programming and erasing operations are fine, continue to the next step. If either of the bits is set to 1, return an error.
    e. Reset the EEPROM module using the EEPROM Software Reset (SREEPROM) register at offset 0x558 in the System Control register space.
    f. Delay 6 clock cycles to stabilize this software reset action.
    g. Check the WORKING bit (bit[0]) in the EEDONE register to determine whether this reset is done. When WORKING bit = 0, this means that it is done and continue to the next step.
    h. Read the PRETRY and ERETRY bits in the EESUPP register. If both bits are 0, this means that the EEPROM initialization is complete and software may use the peripheral as normal. If either of the bits are set, this means that something is wrong and an error is returned.
2. Configure the EEPROM Current Block (EEBLOCK) register and EEPROM Current Offset (EEOFFSET) register based on the actual address to which the data to be read from or written into the EEPROM space. The result of this configuration is to assign the correct block number and the correct word offset number to the EEBLOCK and EEOFFSET registers to enable the EEPROM controller to access the correct address to do the desired operations.
3. For a poll reading operation, the EEPROM Read-Write Register (EERDWR) contains the read-out data value at the word pointed to by EEOFFSET. Pick up that data from the EERDWR and assign it to a user buffer or a variable to store it.
4. For a poll writing operation, first check the WORKING bit in the EEDONE register to make sure that it is 0 (idle), and then put the writing data into the EERDWR register to begin this

data-writing operation. Check or poll the WORKING bit in the EEDONE register until it is clear to 0. This means that the data has been successfully written into the EEPROM.

5. For an interrupt data writing operation, it is similar to perform a poll data writing to the EEPROM. The difference is that you do not need to check the WORKING bit in the EEDONE register, instead you need to enable the EEPROM Interrupt register (EEINT) by setting the INT bit (bit[0]) to 1. A writing-completion interrupt is generated when the WORKING bit in the EEDONE is changed from 1 to 0. You need to check the ERIS bit (bit[2]) in the Flash Controller Raw Interrupt Status (FCRIS) register inside the interrupt handler, FLASH_Handler(), to confirm that this interrupt is triggered by this EEPROM writing completion action since both flash memory and the EEPROM use the same interrupt vector in the TM4C123GH6PM MCU system.

Since step 2 is very important in the EEPROM programming process, we need to have a closer look at this configuration operation to confirm that the address is correct and valid.

6.7.2.2.1 Configure and Set Up EEBLOCK and EEOFFSET Registers
Unlike other internal devices, the EEPROM does not use an absolute addressing mode to perform any programming operations in the TM4C123GH6PM MCU system. Instead, it uses a byte relative or offset addressing mode to access the EEPROM. This byte offset address is then converted to the block number and the offset number, and these numbers are stored into two registers, EEBLOCK and EEOFFSET, to provide the actual target address for the EEPROM to be accessed.

Suppose the 2-KB EEPROM has an address range of 0x400AF400~0x400AFC00. If the starting address 0x400AF400 is considered as the base address uiBaseAddr, a real address uiRealAddr can be obtained based on the following equation:

$$uiReadAddr = uiBaseAddr + Block\_Number \times 16 \times 4 + Offset\_Number \times 4$$

In total there are 32 blocks and each block has 16 words, and each word has 4 bytes. Each offset contains 1 word that has 4 bytes.

For a given real address uiRealAddr, the byte offset address ui32Addr can be calculated based on the following equation:

$$ui32Addr = uiReadAddr - uiBaseAddr$$

In fact, for all real projects related to EEPROM operations, you do not need to use any actual or real address to access to the EEPROM. Instead, you should use the byte offset address to access EEPROM to perform any data writing or reading operations. The byte offset addresses range from 0x0 to 0x7FC in the TM4C123GH6PM MCU system. The address range 0x0~0x7FF is 2 KB space. However, for the alignment reason, the last two bits on the address 0x7FF must be 00, and this changes the upper bound of this address to 0x7FC.

To assist users to convert from the byte offset addresses to the correct block number and the offset number and store them into the EEBLOCK and the EEOFFSET registers, the TivaWare™ software package provides two macros for this purpose; EEPROMBlock-FromAddr(ui32Addr) and OFFSET_FROM_ADDR(x). The first macro is defined in the system header file eeprom.h and the second macro can be found from the source file eeprom.c. Both files are located at the folder: C:\ti\TivaWare_C_Series-2.0.1.11577\driverlib in your host computer.

The first macro defined in the header file `eeprom.h` is

define EEPROMBlockFromAddr(ui32Addr) ((ui32Addr)≫6)

The argument of this macro, `ui32Addr`, is a byte offset address, and it is a byte relative or byte offset address from the base address of the EEPROM. Each block contains 16 words or $16 \times 4 = 64$ bytes. Therefore if this byte offset address `ui32Addr` is divided by 64, we can get the block number for this byte offset address. As you know, shifting this address right by 6 bits (>>6) is equivalent to dividing it by 64 ($2^6 = 64$).

The second macro defined in the source file `eeprom.c` is

define OFFSET_FROM_ADDR(x) (((x)≫2) & 0x0F)

The argument of this macro x is also a byte offset address. Since each offset contains a word that has 4 bytes, dividing this address by 4 is to get the number of the offset. Also, only the last 4 bits are related to this offset ($2^4 = 16$); therefore the 0x0F is ANDed with this shifting result because there are 16 offsets (words) available for each block.

6.7.2.2.2 Implement and Update the EEBLOCK and EEOFFSET Registers
When using these two registers, EEBLOCK and EEOFFSET, to perform the EEPROM programming operations, these two registers have the following operational features:

- Both registers must be initialized by users with two macros discussed above to enable the EEPROM read or write operations to start.
- When performing the normal reading or writing operation with the EERDWR, the EERDWR register is used to read or write the EEPROM word at the address pointed to by the EEBLOCK and EEOFFSET registers. The contents of the EEBLOCK and the EEOFFSET must be updated manually by users with software after each word is read out or written into the EEPROM. If these operations are within one block, only the EEOFFSET should be updated.
- When using the EEPROM Read-Write with Increment (EERDWRINC) register to perform read or write operations, the EERDWRINC register is used to read or write the EEPROM word at the address pointed to by the EEBLOCK and EEOFFSET registers. After each word is read out or written in the EEPROM, the content or the OFFSET field (bits [3:0]) of the EEOFFSET register can be automatically incremented by 1 to point to the next word. If the last value is reached, OFFSET wraps around to 0 and points to the next first word.
- If more than 1 block words (16 words) are needed to be read out or write into the EEPROM, the OFFSET field in the EEOFFSET register should be checked after each word is read or written. If this field is 0, it means that the reading or writing total 16 words have been completed, and the number in the EEBLOCK register should be incremented by 1 to point to the next block.

Table 6.20 shows some byte offset addresses and related block numbers as well as offset numbers for the EEPROM device used in the TM4C123GH6PM MCU system. The byte offset address range for this EEPROM is 0x0~0x7FC.

Before we can build our example projects to perform EEPROM programming, we need first to have a closer look at three kinds of different header files used in the TM4C123GH6PM MCU system.

Table 6.20.   Some byte offset addresses and block-offset numbers.

Byte Offset Address	Block Number in EEBLOCK	Offset Number in EEOFFSET
0x000~0x03F	0	0~15
0x040~0x07F	1	0~15
0x080~0x0BF	2	0~15
0x0C0~0x0FF	3	0~15
0x100~0x13F	4	0~15
0x140~0x17F	5	0~15
0x180~0x1BF	6	0~15
0x1C0~0x1FF	7	0~15
0x200~0x23F	8	0~15
0x240~0x27F	9	0~15
0x280~0x2BF	10	0~15
. . . . . .	. . . . . .	. . . . . .
0x7C0~0x7FC	31	0~15

6.7.3 Three Kinds of System Header Files in TM4C123GH6PM MCU System

Generally there are three kinds of different system header files widely used for TM4C123GH6PM MCU programming development. They can be divided into different categories based on their functions and implementations:

- The Register Driver Definitions Header File tm4c123gh6pm.h.
- The CMSIS Cortex®-M4 Peripheral Hardware Layer Header File TM4C123GH6PM.h.
- System header files for all internal peripherals and system control devices, such as gpio.h for GPIO Ports, flash.h for flash memory, eeprom.h for the EEPROM, and timer.h for the system timers.

These header files defined different macros for registers, interfaces, and control parameters used for all peripheral devices and system controls. Let's have a clear picture about these files by taking a closer look at them one by one.

6.7.3.1 The Register Driver Definitions Header File TM4C123GH6PM.h

The header file tm4c123gh6pm.h provides a complete set of definitions for all registers used in this system. This definition is achieved by mapping each register to its memory map address in the TM4C123GH6PM MCU on-chip memory system. As we discussed in Section 5.4.1.1.2 in Chapter 5, this header file defined all registers and control parameters used in all peripheral and system control devices. All macros defined for registers in this file are directly addresses-mapped, which means that each register is defined as an address or a pointer. Then each register can be assigned with certain value directly by using the assignment symbol (=) in the user's programs. For example, the DATA register of the GPIO Port F can be defined as: #define GPIO_PORTF_DATA_R (*((volatile uint32_t *)0x400253FC)). In this way, the DATA register in the Port F is defined as a macro GPIO_PORTF_DATA_R and the user can directly assign any valid value to this register with assignment symbol, like GPIO_PORTF_DATA_R = 0x8. This assignment assigns a value of 0x8 to the DATA register of GPIO Port F.

6.7.3.2 The CMSIS Cortex®-M4 Peripheral Hardware Layer Header File TM4C123GH6PM.h

As we discussed in Section 5.4.1.1.3 in Chapter 5, this header file defined all registers and control parameters as structure and structure pointers. This means that all registers are grouped into different structures based on their functions and their categories. For example, all GPIO control registers, including registers used by each GPIO Port (Ports A~F), are integrated into a structure GPIOA_Type. Then each GPIO Port is further defined as a pointer based on this GPIO_Type structure. The user can directly access each register for the selected GPIO Port by using the structure pointer to point to the selected register inside the structure. For example, to access the GPIO Port F Direction register, one can use GPIOF->DIR to do this accessing. When using this header file, one can access each register by using this pointer operator only. Also, one can assign any valid value directly to each register with the assignment symbol (=). To assign the GPIO Port B Digital Enable register with a value of 0xF, one can use GPIOB->DEN = 0xF.

6.7.3.3 System Header Files for All Internal Peripherals and System Control Devices

Unlike the above two system header files, these header fills are categorized into different files based on the peripherals they belong to. Generally, each peripheral or a group of peripherals that have the similar control functions have its own header files, and these header files can be divided into two header files. One is the direct definitions for all registers used for that peripheral, and another one is the hardware mapping definitions for each register used for that device. For example, all definitions related to GPIO Ports are defined in the gpio.h and the hw_gpio.h header files. All definitions related to EEPROM control registers are defined in the eeprom.h and the hw_eeprom.h header files. Each register is defined as a constant in these files, and the user cannot directly assign any valid value to these registers with these header files since they are defined as constants, not addresses. In order to assign any valid value to these registers, one must use a macro HWREG(x), which is defined in the system header file hw_types.h, to redefine these registers as addresses or pointers. Then one can directly assign valid values to those register macros. The macro HWREG(x) is defined as

```
define HWREG(x) (*((volatile uint32_t*)(x)))
```

For example, the EEPROM Read Write Register (EERDWR) is defined as a constant in the header file hw_eeprom.h as:

```
define EEPROM_EERDWR 0x400AF010
```

In order to assign any valid value to this register, one must use the HWREG(x) macro to convert this constant to an address or a pointer, and then assign a value of 0x3F, like

```
HWREG(EEPROM_EERDWR)=0x3F
```

Regularly these header files are used to support the single peripheral involved in the TivaWare™ Peripheral Driver Library.

When using these header files to build the users' projects, the following points must be noted:

1. All these three header files are exclusive, which means that you can only use one of them but you cannot use any two of them together in a project at the same time since all macros for registers are defined in different ways in each header file. The compiler would be confused if you use any two of these header files for a same project at the same time since each register has been defined in different ways in these files, and the compiler does not know which macro it should use.

2. Both `tm4c123gh6pm.h` and `TM4C123GH6PM.h` header files defined all registers used for all peripherals and system control devices in the TM4C123GH6PM MCU system. You cannot use these two header files together in a project because they provided different definitions for all registers. Also, the compiler cannot distinguish these two header files since they have the same name with different cases. When using normal register mapping, one can use the first header file to access each register based on its address. When using the structure pointer to access register, one should use the second header file.

3. When accessing a single peripheral, it is recommended to use the third kind of header files to make the volume of the project small. Generally one should use two header files; one is the normal header file and the other one is the hardware-mapping header file with the hw_ prefixed for that peripheral.

Next let's take a look at how to enable the EEPROM module in the Run mode and how to reset the EEPROM module to enable it to recover from some error status.

6.7.3.4 Enable the EEPROM Module in Run Mode and Reset EEPROM

To enable the EEPROM to perform its role in the proper way, the EEPROM module must be configured or enabled to work in the Run mode. When enabled, the module is provided a clock and accesses to module registers are allowed. When disabled, the clock is disabled to save power and accesses to module registers generate a bus fault.

The EEPROM Run Mode Clock Gating Control (RCGCEEPROM) register, whose memory mapping address is 0x400FE658, provides this enable function for the EEPROM. This is a 32-bit register; however, only bit[0], or bit R0, on this register is used. The EEPROM module is enabled when this bit is set to 1. Otherwise the EEPROM is disabled if this bit is cleared to 0. The macros for this register, SYSCTL_RCGCEEPROM, and the bit R0, SYSCTL_RCGCEEPROM_R0, are defined in the system header file hw_sysctl.h.

If the EEPROM experienced some wrong operations, some bits on the EEPROM Support Control and Status (EESUPP) register, such as PRETYR and ERETRY, will be set to indicate this situation and ask the processor to retry the previous operations. In order to recover from these possible error processes, a reset operation is necessary to make the EEPROM to return to the original status.

The EEPROM Software Reset (SREEPROM) register, whose memory mapping address is 0x400FE558, provides this EEPROM software reset function. This is a 32-bit register; however, only bit[0], or bit R0, on this register is used. To reset the EEPROM via software, a two-step operation is needed:

1. First the bit R0 on the SREEPROM register needs to be set to 1.
2. Then the bit R0 on the SREEPROM register needs to be cleared to 0.

The macros for this register, SYSCTL_SREEPROM, and the bit R0, SYSCTL_ SREEPROM_R0, are defined in the system header file hw_sysctl.h.

Based on the discussions above, now we are ready to build our example projects to perform EEPROM programming, reading, and writing operations.

6.7.4 Build Example EEPROM Programming Projects

Now let's start to build some example projects to perform EEPROM programming operations. We will develop two projects to illustrate how to use the DRA model to access EEPROM to perform reading and writing operations:

- Use the DRA method to perform EEPROM reading and writing with the polling or checking the WORKING bit in the EEDONE register.
- Use the DRA method to read from and write into the EEPROM with the interrupt driven.

We will leave the EEPROM programming with the SD method as the homework to allow students to handle this issue since it is relatively simple.

First let's use the DRA method to access the EEPROM to perform reading and writing operations with the polling strategy.

6.7.4.1 Programming EEPROM with the DRA Method (Polling-Driven)

Perform the following operations to create a new project DRAEEPROMPoll:

1. Open the Windows Explorer window to create a new folder named DRAEEPROMPoll under the C:\ARM Class Projects\Chapter 6 folder.
2. Open the Keil® ARM-MDK μVersion5 and go to the Project|New μVersion Project menu item to create a new μVersion Project. On the opened wizard, browse to our new folder DRAEEPROMPoll that is created in step 1 above. Enter DRAEEPROMPoll into the File name box and click on the Save button to create this project.
3. On the next wizard, you need to select the device (MCU) for this project. Expand three icons, Texas Instruments, Tiva C Series, and TM4C123x Series, and select the target device TM4C123GH6PM from the list by clicking on it. Click on the OK to close this wizard.
4. Next the Software Components wizard is opened, and you need to set up the software development environment for your project with this wizard. Expand two icons, CMSIS and Device, and check the CORE and Startup checkboxes in the Sel. column, and click on the OK button since we need these two components to build our project.

6.7.4.1.1 Create the Header File DRAEEPROMPoll.h
Refer to Section 6.7.2.2, we can build this project by following that sequence. We need to build a header file and a source file for this project. Perform the following operations to create a new header file DRAEE-PROMPoll.h:

1. In the Project pane, expand the Target folder and right click on the Source Group 1 folder and select the Add New Item to Group 'Source Group 1'.
2. Select the Header File (.h) and enter DRAEEPROMPoll into the Name: box, and click on the Add button to add this header file into the project.
3. Enter the codes shown in Figure 6.35 into this header file.

```
1   //**************************************************************************
2   // DRAEEPROMPoll.h - Heade File for DRAEEPROMPoll.c
3   //**************************************************************************
4   #include <stdint.h>
5   #include <stdbool.h>
6   #include "inc\hw_eeprom.h"
7   #include "inc\hw_sysctl.h"
8   #include "driverlib\eeprom.h"

9   #define SREEPROM   0x400FE558
10  #define HWREG(x)    (*((volatile uint32_t *)(x)))
11  #define OFFSET_FROM_ADDR(x) (((x) >> 2) & 0x0F)

12  uint32_t EEPROMInit(void);
13  uint32_t EEPROMWrite(uint32_t *puiData, uint32_t uiAddr, uint32_t uiCount);
14  void EEPROMRead(uint32_t *puiData, uint32_t uiAddr, uint32_t uiCount);

15  uint32_t pwData[] = {0x12345678,  0x23456789, 0x3456789A, 0x456789AB,  0x56789ABC,
                         0x6789ABCD, 0x789ABCDE, 0xDEBC9A78, 0xEFCDAB89, 0x78563412,
                         0x89674523,  0x9A785634,  0xAB896745,  0xBC9A7856,  0x00112233,
                         0xABABABAB,  0x11223344,  0x22334455 };
```

Figure 6.35. The header file DRAEEPROMPoll.h.

Let's have a closer look at this header file to see how it works.

- The codes in lines 4~7 are used to declare some useful system header files that will be used in this project.
- Starting from code line 9, some system control registers macros are defined. First the EEPROM Software Reset (SREEPROM) register is defined as a constant 0x400FE558. Then the macro HWREG(x) is defined in line 10, and this macro is used to convert a constant to an address or a pointer. The macro OFFSET_FROM_ADDR() is defined in line 11, and this macro is used to get the word offset address from a given byte offset address.
- Three user-defined EEPROM operational functions, EEPROMInit(), EEPROMWrite(), and EEPROMRead(), are declared in lines 12~14. With these three functions, one can perform, initialize, write data into, and read data from the EEPROM in the source file.
- In line 15, a data array pwData[] is created and initialized with 18 words. This data array will be sent to the EEPROMWrite() function later to write them into the EEPROM block in the source file.

6.7.4.1.2 Create the Source File DRAEEPROMPoll.c
Perform the following operations to create a new C source file DRAEEPROMPoll.c:

1. In the Project pane, expand the Target folder and right click on the Source Group 1 folder and select the Add New Item to Group 'Source Group 1'.
2. Select the C File (.c) and enter DRAEEPROMPoll into the Name: box, and click on the Add button to add this source file into the project.
3. Enter the first part codes shown in Figure 6.36 into this source file.

Let's have a closer look at this first part source file to see how it works.

- The user-defined header file DRAEEPROMPoll.h is included in line 4 since we need to use all macros and user-defined functions in that header file in this source file.
- The codes in lines 7 and 8 are used to declare some local variables and data array. The variable uiStatus is used to receive the running status of a function to check whether the function is executed successfully or not. The data array prData[] is used to retrieve and hold the data

```
1    //*********************************************************************
2    // DRAEEPROMPoll.c - Main Application File
3    //*********************************************************************
4    #include "DRAEEPROMPoll.h"
5    int main(void)
6    {
7      uint32_t uiStatus, prData[18];
8      uint32_t uiAddress = 0x100, uiCount = 18;
9      HWREG(SYSCTL_RCGCEEPROM) = SYSCTL_RCGCEEPROM_R0;           // enable clock to EEPROM
10     uiStatus = EEPROMInit();                                    // initialize EEPROM
11     if (uiStatus) { return 1; }
12     uiStatus = EEPROMWrite(pwData, uiAddress, uiCount);         // writing data into EEPROM
13     if (uiStatus) { return 1; }
14     EEPROMRead(prData, uiAddress, uiCount);                     // reading data from EEPROM
15     while(1) {}
16   }
17   uint32_t EEPROMInit(void)
18   {
19     uint32_t  uiStatus;
20     volatile  uint_fast8_t  ui8Delay;
21     // wait for WORKING bit is cleared to 0...
22     while(EEPROM_EEDONE & EEPROM_EEDONE_WORKING){}   // wait for WORKING bit clear...
23     uiStatus = HWREG(EEPROM_EESUPP);                          // check the PRETRY & ERETRY bits values
24     if(uiStatus & (EEPROM_EESUPP_PRETRY|EEPROM_EESUPP_ERETRY))
25     {   // reset the EEPROM by setting and clearing SREEPROM register
26       HWREG(SREEPROM) = 0x1;
27       for (ui8Delay = 0; ui8Delay < 16; ui8Delay++){}
28       HWREG(SREEPROM) = 0x0;
29       while(EEPROM_EEDONE & EEPROM_EEDONE_WORKING){}    // wait for WORKING bit is cleared to 0...
30       uiStatus = HWREG(EEPROM_EESUPP);                        // check the PRETRY & ERETRY bits values again
31       if(uiStatus & (EEPROM_EESUPP_PRETRY|EEPROM_EESUPP_ERETRY))
32         { return(EEPROM_INIT_ERROR); }
33       else { return  (EEPROM_INIT_RETRY); }
34     }
35     return( EEPROM_INIT_OK);
36   }
37   uint32_t EEPROMWrite(uint32_t *puiData, uint32_t uiAddr, uint32_t uiCount)
38   {
39     uint32_t  uiStatus;
40     // wait for WORKING bit clear...
41     do { uiStatus = HWREG(EEPROM_EEDONE); }while(uiStatus & EEPROM_EEDONE_WORKING);
42     // configure & setup EEBLOCK & EEOFFSET
43     HWREG(EEPROM_EEBLOCK) = EEPROMBlockFromAddr(uiAddr);
44     HWREG(EEPROM_EEOFFSET) = OFFSET_FROM_ADDR(uiAddr);
45     while(uiCount)
46     {
47       HWREG(EEPROM_EERDWR) = *puiData;              // write the data into the EEPROM
48       do                                            // wait for data-writing to be done
49       { uiStatus = HWREG(EEPROM_EEDONE); }while(uiStatus & EEPROM_EEDONE_WORKING);
50       puiData++;                                    // update data pointer to next data
51       uiCount--;                                    // update the data count
52       HWREG(EEPROM_EEOFFSET)++;                      // increment EEOFFSET to point to the next word
53       if(HWREG(EEPROM_EEOFFSET) == 0)
54       { HWREG(EEPROM_EEBLOCK) += 1;    }             // increment block number to point to next block
55     }
56     return(HWREG(EEPROM_EEDONE));
     }
```

Figure 6.36.   The first part codes for the source file DRAEEPROMPoll.c.

written into the EEPROM block to confirm the correctness of the data writing function. The starting byte offset address uiAddress is 0x100, which is the fourth block in the EEPROM space (refer to Table 6.20), and the uiCount is initialized to 18 since we want to write 18 words into the EEPROM starting at 0x100.

- In line 9, the EEPROM Run Mode Clock Gating Control (RCGCEEPROM) register is initialized by setting its bit R0 to 1 to enable the EEPROM module in the Run mode and set up a clock to allow the EEPROM to begin to work properly. The HWREG() macro must be used to convert the constant SYSCTL_RCGCEEPROM defined in the system header file hw_sysctl.h to an address and assign the SYSCTL_RCGCEEPROM_R0 (0x1) to it.

- The user-defined function EEPROMInit() is called to initialize the EEPROM block to make it ready for data writing and reading operations in line 10.

- Return 1 if this function is failed.

- In line 12, another user-defined function EEPROMWrite() is executed to write 18 data words into the block 4 in the EEPROM space. The starting address of the data array pwData [] is passed into this function as the data source to be written into the EEPROM space. The starting byte offset address uiAddress and the number of words uiCount are also passed into this function along with the data source.

- Return 1 if this function is failed.

- Finally the user-defined function EEPROMRead() is called in line 14 to try to read back the data written into the EEPROM to confirm the correctness of that data writing function. Three passed arguments are similar to those passed into the EEPROMWrite() function. But the first argument, the starting address of the data array prData[], is passed into this function, and this array works as a receiving holder to receive and keep the data read back from the EEPROM.

- In line 15, an infinitive while() loop is used here to hold the program and keep it running. In this way, we can dynamically check the running result of this program by checking the user-defined array prData[] to confirm whether our project runs successfully or not. Without this while() loop, all data stored in any user-defined array or variables would be gone after the program is terminated.

- The user-defined function EEPROMInit() starts at line 17.

- Two local variables are defined in lines 19 and 20.

- In line 22, a while() loop is executed to wait for the WORKING bit in the EEDONE register to be clear. If this bit is 1, it means that the previous operation on the EEPROM is still going on. When this bit is cleared to 0, it means that the previous operation is done. We cannot perform any operation on EEPROM until the previous operation has been done.

- Then in line 23 we need to check the bits PRETRY and ERETRY in the EESUPP register to make sure the previous operation is executed successfully. If any of these bits is set to 1, it means that the previous operation needs to be either re-programmed or re-erased. To do this check, the macro HWREG() is used to convert the constant EEPROM_EESUPP defined in the header file hw_eeprom.h to an address and assign its contents to the local variable uiStatus.

- If either bit PRETRY or bit ERETRY is set to 1, we need to reset the EEPROM via software to recover the EEPROM in line 24. This reset operation is achieved by using the codes in lines 26~28. First the bit[0] (bit R0) in the EEPROM Software Reset (SREEPROM) register is set to 1 in line 26. Then a for() loop is used to perform a time delay in line 27. Finally this bit is cleared to 0 to fulfill this reset function in line 28. The macro HWREG() must be used to convert the constant SREEPROM defined in our header file to an address and assign a valid value to it.

- Then a while() loop is used in line 30 to wait for the WORKING bit in the EEDONE register to be cleared, which means that this reset operation is finished.

- The codes in lines 30 and 31 are used to re-check the bits PRETRY and ERETRY in the EESUPP register to make sure the reset operation is executed successfully and the EEPROM is in error-free status. If either bit PRETRY or bit ERETRY is still 1, an error is returned to the main program in line 32 to indicate that this initialization process has failed.

- Otherwise a retry message is returned to the main program in line 33 to ask to redo this initialization process.

- If nothing is wrong for this initialization process, the EEPROM_INIT_OK (0) is returned to the main program in line 35.

- The user-defined function EEPROMWrite() starts at line 37. A local variable uiStatus is declared in line 39.

- A do-while() loop is used in line 41 to wait for the WORKING bit in the EEDONE register to be cleared to make sure that the EEPROM is in the idle status.

- Two macros, EEPROMBlockFromAddr() and OFFSET_FROM_ADDR(), are used to configure and set up the block register EEBLOCK and the offset register EEOFFSET based on the byte offset address in lines 43 and 44. The macro HWREG() must be used to convert two constants, EEPROM_EEBLOCK and EEPROM_EEOFFSET, which are defined in the system header file hw_eeprom.h, to two addresses and assign the block and the offset numbers to them.

- In line 45, a while() loop with the uiCount as the loop condition to perform a 18-word writing operations.

- Each data word is written into the EEPROM by assigning the data from the data array pwData[] to the EEPROM Read-Write (EERDWR) register in line 47. The macro HWREG() must be used to convert the register constant EEPROM_EERDWR defined in the system header file hw_eeprom.h to an address and then assign each data value to it.

- Another do-while() loop is used to wait for this data writing to be completed in lines 48 and 49.

- After one data word is written, the address of the data word is updated to point to the next data word in line 50. The number of the data word is also updated in line 51. The offset number is updated in line 52 to enable the EEPROM to pick up the next word.

- As we discussed in Section 6.7.2.2.2, If the last value (15) in the offset register is reached, it will wrap around to 0 and points to the next first word. This means that 16 words in a block have been picked up and no more data are available in the current block. In this case, we need to increment the block number by 1 to point to the next block. The codes in lines 53 and 54 perform this checking and incrementing function.

- Finally the current running status EEPROM_EEDONE is returned to the main program in line 56.

Now let's take a closer look at the second part codes for this source file shown in Figure 6.37, which contains the codes for the user-defined function EEPROMRead().

- As we did for the data writing operation in the function EEPROMWrite(), two macros, EEPROMBlockFromAddr() and OFFSET_FROM_ADDR(), are used to configure and set up the block register EEBLOCK and the offset register EEOFFSET based on the byte offset address in lines 4 and 5.

- The data reading operation starts from a while() loop in line 6 with a loop condition of the count of the data words to be read out.

- The data word is read out from the EEPROM Read-Write (EERDWR) register and assigned to the data array prData[] in line 8.

```
1   void EEPROMRead(uint32_t *puiData, uint32_t uiAddr, uint32_t uiCount)
2   {
3       // configure & setup EEBLOCK & EEOFFSET
4       HWREG(EEPROM_EEBLOCK) = EEPROMBlockFromAddr(uiAddr);
5       HWREG(EEPROM_EEOFFSET) = OFFSET_FROM_ADDR(uiAddr);
6
7       while(uiCount)
8       {
9           *puiData = HWREG(EEPROM_EERDWR);              // read a word from EEPROM
10          puiData++;
11          uiCount--;
12          HWREG(EEPROM_EEOFFSET)++;                     // increment EEOFFSET to point to the next word
13          if(HWREG(EEPROM_EEOFFSET) == 0)
14          { HWREG(EEPROM_EEBLOCK) += 1; }               // increment block number to point to next block
15      }
16  }
```

Figure 6.37. The second part codes for the source file DRAEEPROMPoll.c.

- Then the address of the data array and the number of data words are updated in lines 9 and 10.
- In line 11, the offset register is increased by 1 to point to the next data word to be read out from the EEPROM.
- The offset register is checked in line 12 to make sure whether the 16 words have been read out from an EEPROM block.
- If the total 16 words have been read out, the block register is increased by 1 to point to the next block in line 13. After all data words have been read out, the function is done and all read-out data are stored in the data array prData[ ].

Now we have completed the coding process for our project. Next let's set up the environment to build and run this project to test our EEPROM writing and reading operations.

6.7.4.1.3 Set Up the Environment to Build and Run the Project
Perform the following operations to setup the running environment for this project:

- Include the system header file path C:\ti\TivaWare_C_Series-2.0.1.11577 in the C/C++ tab under the Project|Options for Target 'Target 1' menu item. Since we used three system header files, hw_eeprom.h, hw_sysctl.h, and eeprom.h, in this project, we need to include the path for these header files.
- Select the debug adapter Stellaris ICDI in the Dubeg tab under the Project-|Options for Target 'Target 1' menu item.

Now build the project by going to the Project|Build target menu item. If everything is fine, go to the Flash|Download item to download the image file of the project into the flash memory. Before we can run the project to test its function, we need first to insert a breakpoint in line 15 in the main() program. The reason we do this is because we need to check the read data array prData[ ] to confirm the success of the data writing function during the project runs. All of these data would be gone after the project is terminated. Therefore we have to do this checking when the project is running. Click on line 14 in the main() program and go to the Debug|Insert/Remove Breakpoint item to insert this breakpoint in line 15.

Now go to the Debug|Start/Stop Debug Session and the Debug|Run item to run the project.

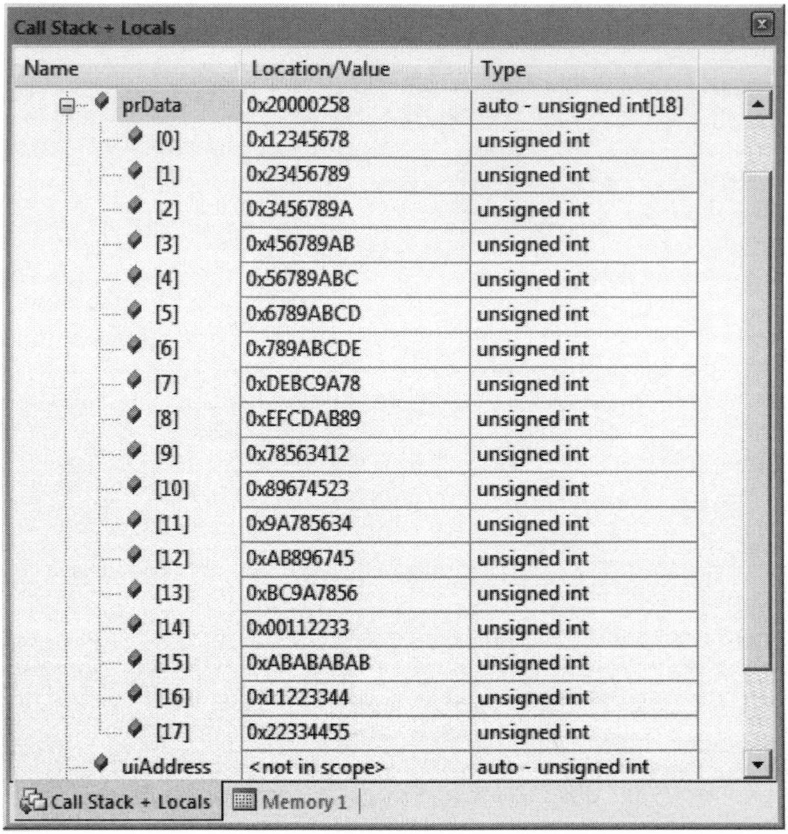

Figure 6.38. The 18 read-out data stored in the data array prData[]. (Reproduced with permission from ARM® Limited. Copyright © ARM Limited.)

When the project stops at the breakpoint, open the Call Stack + Locals window by clicking on it. Then expand the prData array by clicking the plus symbol in front of it. You can find that all 18 data words have been read out and stored in this array, as shown in Figure 6.38.

Compared with the 18 data words we initialized in the write data array pwData[] in the user header file DRAEEPROMPoll.h, you can find that all 18 data words have been written into the EEPROM space and successfully read out and stored in this read data array prData[].

Now let's handle the similar EEPROM data writing and reading operations with the interrupt-driven method.

6.7.4.2 Programming EEPROM with the DRA Method (Interrupt-Driven)

As we discussed in Section 6.7.2.2, only a data-writing completion can generate an interrupt to the NVIC controller to inform the processor that a data word has been written into the EEPROM. For an interrupt data writing operation, it is similar to perform a poll data writing to the EEPROM. The difference is that you do not need to check the WORKING bit in the EEDONE register, instead you need to enable the EEPROM Interrupt register (EEINT) by setting the INT bit (bit[0]) to 1. A writing-completion interrupt is generated when the WORKING bit in the EEDONE is changed from 1 to 0. You need to check the ERIS bit (bit[2]) in the Flash Controller Raw Interrupt Status (FCRIS) register inside the interrupt handler, FLASH_Handler(), to confirm that this interrupt is triggered by this EEPROM writing completion action since both flash memory and the EEPROM uses the same interrupt vector in the TM4C123GH6PM MCU system.

Since this project is very similar to the last one, we only need to do small modifications to the project DRAEEPROMPoll to make a new project DRAEEPROMInt.

Create a new folder DRAEEPROMInt under the C:\ARM Class Projects \Chapter 6 folder, and then create a new project DRAEEPROMInt in the Keil® ARM-MDK μVersion5 IDE. Create a header file DRAEEPROMInt.h and a source file DRAEEPROMInt.c and add them into the project DRAEEPROMInt created above.

Copy the header and source files DRAEEPROMPoll.h and DRAEEPROMPoll.c, and paste them into the DRAEEPROMInt.h and DRAEEPROMInt.c, respectively. We need to do some modifications to the header file, and the source file to enable an interrupt is generated when each data word is written into the EEPROM, and a related LED (PBn) is on in the EduBASE Trainer.

The necessary modifications include the following:

1. Add some system header files and some macros to the header file since we need these to perform the interrupt functions as a data is written into the EEPROM.

2. Register the flash interrupt handler and enable the flash memory interrupt by using two API library functions, IntRegister() and IntEnable(), to reduce our coding jobs since the EEPROM use the same interrupt vector and handler as the flash memory did.

3. Enable the GPIO Port B and set up its lower 4 bits as digital output pins since the lower 4 pins, PB3~PB0, are connected to 4 LEDs, PB3~PB0, in the EduBASE Trainer.

4. Enable the EEPROM writing completion interrupt by setting up the bit INT in the EEPROM Interrupt (EEINT) register. The macros for this register EEPROM_EEINT and its bit[0] or INT bit EEPROM_EEINT_INT are defined in the system header file hw_eeprom.h.

5. Clear any previous EEPROM interrupt by writing 1 to the EMISC bit (bit[2]) in the FCMISC register. Enable or unmask the EEPROM interrupt by writing 1 to the EMASK bit (bit[2]) in the FCIM register. These macros are defined in the system header file hw_flash.h.

6. Configure the EEPROM interrupt handler, which is the same handler as the flash memory interrupt handler FLASH_Handler(), to identify the EEPROM interrupt by checking the ERIS bit (bit[2]) in the Flash Controller Raw Interrupt Status (FCRIS) register. The macros for this register FLASH_FCRIS and ERIS bit FLASH_FCRIS_ERIS are defined in the system header file hw_flash.h.

7. Turn on the related LEDs, PB0~PB3, when the first, second, third, and fourth word is written into the EEPROM block.

8. Before leaving the interrupt handler, clear the ERIS bit in the FCRIS register to 0 to enable the following EEPROM interrupts to be generated in the future. This clearly can be done by writing 1 to the EMISC bit (bit[2]) in the FCMISC register. The macros for the FCMISC

register FLASH_FCMISC and the EMISC bit FLASH_FCMISC_EMISC are defined in the system header file hw_flash.h.

9. Disable the EEPROM interrupt by resetting the bit INT in the EEPROM Interrupt (EEINT) register when all data words have been written into the EEPROM.

Now let's do these modifications one by one. First let's start from the header file.

6.7.4.2.1 Modify the Header File DRAEEPROMInt.h Open this header file and add the codes that have been highlighted with the gray background color and shown in Figure 6.39 into this file. Let's have a closer look at these new added codes.

- Two system header files, interrupt.h and hw_flash.h, are added into this file in lines 9 and 10, respectively. The first header file contains the definitions for two API functions, IntRegister() and IntEnable(). The reason we need to use these two functions to register the flash interrupt handler and enable the Flash/EEPROM interrupt is that we try to reduce the coding jobs since it would be greatly time- and code-consuming if we directly use the DRA method to access each related register to do these jobs. The second file contains the macros for flash-memory-related control registers.

- In line 14, we defined the interrupt order number for the flash memory. In fact, you can use other numbers to define the flash. Usually, it should be larger than 15.

- Three registers related to the GPIO Port B are defined in lines 15~17. Since we do not want to include the system header file tm4c123gh6pm.h since there are some conflicted definitions between this file and some other header files, such as hw_eeprom.h and hw_flash.h, we directly define these registers in here.

```
1   //****************************************************************
2   // DRAEEPROMInt.h - Header File for DRAEEPROMInt.c
3   //****************************************************************
4   #include <stdint.h>
5   #include <stdbool.h>
6   #include "inc\hw_eeprom.h"
7   #include "inc\hw_sysctl.h"
8   #include "driverlib\eeprom.h"
9   #include "driverlib\interrupt.h"
10  #include "inc\hw_flash.h"
11  #define SREEPROM    0x400FE558
12  #define HWREG(x)    (*((volatile uint32_t *)(x)))
13  #define OFFSET_FROM_ADDR(x) (((x) >> 2) & 0x0F)
14  #define INT_FLASH      45
15  #define GPIO_PORTB_DATA 0x400053FC
16  #define GPIO_PORTB_DIR 0x40005400
17  #define GPIO_PORTB_DEN 0x4000551C
18  uint32_t EEIntFlag = 0,  wCount = 0;
19  void FLASH_Handler(void);

    uint32_t EEPROMInit(void);
    uint32_t EEPROMWrite(uint32_t *puiData, uint32_t uiAddr,  uint32_t uiCount);
    void EEPROMRead(uint32_t *puiData, uint32_t uiAddr,  uint32_t uiCount);

    uint32_t pwData[] = {0x12345678,  0x23456789, 0x3456789A,  0x456789AB,  0x56789ABC,
                        0x6789ABCD, 0x789ABCDE, 0xDEBC9A78,  0xEFCDAB89,  0x78563412,
                        0x89674523,  0x9A785634,  0xAB896745, 0xBC9A7856,  0x00112233,
                        0xABABABAB, 0x11223344,  0x22334455 };
```

Figure 6.39. Modified header file DRAEEPROMInt.h.

- Two global variables, EEIntFlag and wCount, are declared and initialized in line 18. The first variable is used as the loop condition for a while() loop inside the function EEPROM-Write() to wait for a word-writing-complete interrupt to occur. The wCount is used to identify which word has been written into the EEPROM inside the EEPROM interrupt handler to turn on the related LED.

- The interrupt handler FLASH_Handler() is declared in line 19. We will develop the codes to handle and process any EEPROM related interrupts inside this handler later.

6.7.4.2.2 Modify the Source File DRAEEPROMInt.c
Open the source file DRAEE-PROMInt.c and perform the following modifications. The modifications are only needed in three parts in this source file:

1. Change the variable uiCount in the main() body to 4 since we need to just write 4 words.
2. Modify the function EEPROMWrite() by adding some new codes.
3. Add new codes into the interrupt handler FLASH_Handler() to response the interrupt.

Open the function EEPROMWrite() and add the codes shown in Figure 6.40 into this function. The new added codes have been highlighted with the gray background color. Let's have a closer look at these new added codes to see how they work.

- Two API functions, IntRegister() and IntEnable(), are executed in lines 4 and 5 to register the flash interrupt handler FLASH_Handler() and enable the flash interrupt.

```
1   uint32_t EEPROMWrite(uint32_t *puiData, uint32_t uiAddr, uint32_t uiCount)
2   {
3     uint32_t uiStatus;
4     IntRegister(INT_FLASH, FLASH_Handler);
5     IntEnable(INT_FLASH);
6     HWREG(SYSCTL_RCGCGPIO) = 0x02;                    // enable clock to Port B
7     HWREG(GPIO_PORTB_DIR) |= 0xF;                     // set PB0 ~ PB3 as output pins
8     HWREG(GPIO_PORTB_DEN) |= 0xF;                     // enable PB0 ~ PB3 as digital function
9     // wait for WORKING bit clear...
10    do { uiStatus = HWREG(EEPROM_EEDONE); }while(uiStatus & EEPROM_EEDONE_WORKING);
11    // configure & setup EEBLOCK & EEOFFSET
12    HWREG(EEPROM_EEBLOCK) = EEPROMBlockFromAddr(uiAddr);
13    HWREG(EEPROM_EEOFFSET) = OFFSET_FROM_ADDR(uiAddr);
14    HWREG(EEPROM_EEINT) = EEPROM_EEINT_INT;           // enable the EEPROM Interrupt
15    HWREG(FLASH_FCMISC) = FLASH_FCMISC_EMISC;         // clear any previous ERIS interrupt
16    HWREG(FLASH_FCIM) = FLASH_FCIM_EMASK;             // unmask bit[2] (EMASK) in the FCIM register
17    while(uiCount)
18    {
19      EEintFlag++;                                    // increment EEIntFlag by 1
20      HWREG(EEPROM_EERDWR) = *puiData;                // write the data into the EEPROM
21      while(EEIntFlag) {}                             // wait for the word-writing-complete interrupt
22      puiData++;                                       // update data pointer to next data
23      uiCount--;                                       // update the data count
24      HWREG(EEPROM_EEOFFSET)++;                        // increment EEOFFSET to point to the next word
25      if(HWREG(EEPROM_EEOFFSET) == 0)
26      { HWREG(EEPROM_EEBLOCK) += 1;  }                // increment block number to point to next block
27    }
28    HWREG(EEPROM_EEINT) = 0x0;                         // disable the EEPROM Interrupt
29    return(HWREG(EEPROM_EEDONE));
30  }
```

Figure 6.40.   The modified function EEPROMWrite().

- The codes in lines 6~8 are to enable the GPIO Port B and configure the lower 4 pins as the digital output pins since these pins are connected to 4 LEDs in the EduBASE Trainer.
- The EEPROM Interrupt (EEINT) register is configured to enable the EEPROM interrupt to occur by setting its INT bit (bit[0]) to 1 in line 14.
- Any previous EEPROM interrupt is cleared by writing 1 to the EMISC bit (bit[2]) in the FCMISC register to be ready for the future EEPROM interrupt to be coming in line 15.
- The EEPROM interrupt is enabled or unmasked by writing 1 to the EMASK bit (bit[2]) in the FCIM register in line 16. After this unmask operation, the ERIS bit in the FCRIS register can be set to 1 when the WORKING bit in the EEDONE register is reset to 0, and an EEPROM interrupt can be generated and sent to the NVIC to be processed if the INT bit in the EEINT register is set to 1 (enabled).
- Inside the while(uiCount) loop, the data writing operation starts. First the global variable EEIntFlag is incremented by 1 (its initial value is 0 in the header file DRAEE-PROMInt.h) in line 19. This value will be as a loop condition for a while() loop in line 21 to wait for a data-writing-complete interrupt to occur.
- After a data word is written into the EEPROM, a while() loop is executed in line 21 to wait for a data-writing-complete interrupt to occur. This loop will not be terminated until the loop condition EEIntFlag becomes 0, and this will happen in the interrupt handler FLASH_Handler() later.
- After all data words have been written into the EEPROM, the EEPROM interrupt is disabled by resetting the INT bit in the EEINT register to 0 in line 28.

Now let's take care of the codes in the interrupt handler FLASH_Handler(). Just under the EEPROMWrite() function, enter the codes shown in Figure 6.41 to create this interrupt handler.

```
1   void FLASH_Handler(void)
2   {
3     uint32_t  uiLoop;

4     wCount++;                                          // increment the global variable wCount by 1
5     if (FLASH_FCRIS & FLASH_FCRIS_ERIS)                // check if an EEPROM interrupt occurred
6     {
7       switch(wCount)                                   // check which word-writing  interrupt occurred...
8       {
9         case 1:                                        // 1st word-writing-complete interrupt occurred
10        HWREG(GPIO_PORTB_DATA) = 0x1;                  // set PB0 to HIGH to indicate this
11        EEIntFlag--;                                   // stop while(EEIntFlag) loop in EEPROMWrite()
12        break;
13        case 2:                                        // 2nd-word write-complete interrupt occurred
14        HWREG(GPIO_PORTB_DATA) = 0x3;                  // turn on LEDs PB0 & PB1
15        EEIntFlag--;                                   // stop the while(EEIntFlag) loop in  EEPROMWrite()
16        break;
17        case 3:                                        // 3rd-word write-complete interrupt occurred
18        HWREG(GPIO_PORTB_DATA) = 0x7;                  // turn on LEDs PB0 & PB1 & PB2
19        EEIntFlag--;                                   // stop the while(EEIntFlag) loop in  EEPROMWrite()
20        break;
21        case 4:                                        // 4th-word write-complete interrupt occurred
22        HWREG(GPIO_PORTB_DATA) = 0xF;                  // turn on LEDs PB0 ~ PB3
23        EEIntFlag--;                                   // stop the while(EEIntFlag) loop in  EEPROMWrite()
24        break;
25      }
26      for(uiLoop = 0; uiLoop < 2000000; uiLoop++){};
27      HWREG(FLASH_FCMISC) = FLASH_FCMISC_EMISC;        // clear EMISC and ERIS bits to reset interrupt
28    }
    }
```

Figure 6.41. The codes for the interrupt handler FLASH_Handler().

Let's have a closer look at this handler to see how it works.

- A local variable `uiLoop` is declared first in line 3, and this variable works as a loop counter to delay the handler a period of the time to keep the related LED to be displayed a period when a certain word has been written into the EEPROM, and an interrupt has been triggered and transferred into this handler.
- The global variable `wCount` is incremented by 1 in line 4. As you remember, this variable is created in the header file DRAEEPROMInt.h and initialized to 0 in that file. The function of this variable is to identify which data word has been written into the EEPROM and triggered this interrupt.
- In line 5, an `if()` condition instruction is used to identify whether this interrupt is triggered by an EEPROM word-writing-complete interruption. Since both flash and EEPROM use the same interrupt vector and handler, we need to check the bit ERIS (bit [2]) in the FCRIS register to confirm this.
- If this interrupt is triggered by an EEPROM data-writing-complete action, a switch-case structure is used to check which word-writing-complete action triggered this interrupt in coding lines 7 and 25. The checking variable is the global variable `wCount`.
- When the first word-writing-complete action triggered this interrupt, the wCount should be equal to 1 since it has just been incremented by 1 in line 4 as the interrupt triggered this handler in the first time. Then the LED PB0 is set to ON to indicate this and the global variable EEIntFlag, which is incremented by 1 in the EEPROMWrite() function, is decremented by 1 here to make it 0 to terminate the `while(EEIntFlag)` loop in that function to continue writing the next data word. These codes are in lines 9~12.
- The codes in lines 13~24 are used to check the second, the third, and the fourth word-writing-complete actions, and set related LEDs ON to indicate those situations and clear the global variable EEIntFlag to enable the EEPROMWrite() function to continue to write the next word into the EEPROM.
- The code in line 26 is to use a `for()` loop to delay a period of time to keep the LEDs ON.
- In line 27, after each interrupt has been responded and handled, the EMISC bit (bit[2]) in the FCMISC register is set to 1 to clear this bit and the ERIS bit (bit[2]) in the FCRIS register to enable the future interrupt to be generated. Otherwise the future interrupt cannot be generated if these two bits are not cleared to 0.

Now we have completed the modifications to this project.

6.7.4.2.3 Set Up the Environment to Build and Run the Project   Perform the following operations to set up the running environment for this project:

- Include the system header file path C:\ti\TivaWare_C_Series-2.0.1.11577 in the C/C++ tab under the Project|Options for Target 'Target 1' menu item. Since we used five system header files, hw_eeprom.h, hw_sysctl.h, eeprom.h, interrupt.h, and hw_flash.h, in this project, we need to include the path for these header files.
- Select the debug adapter Stellaris ICDI in the Dubeg tab under the Project|Options for Target 'Target 1' menu item.
- Add the TivaWare™ Peripheral Driver Library driverlib.lib into this project since we used two API functions, IntRegister() and IntEnable(), in this project. Right click on the `Source Group 1` in the `Project` pane and select Add Existing Files to Group 'Source Group 1' item. Browse to the folder C:\ti\TivaWare_C_Series-2.0.1.11577\driverlib\rvmdk. Select the library file driverlib.lib and click on the Add button to add this file into the project.

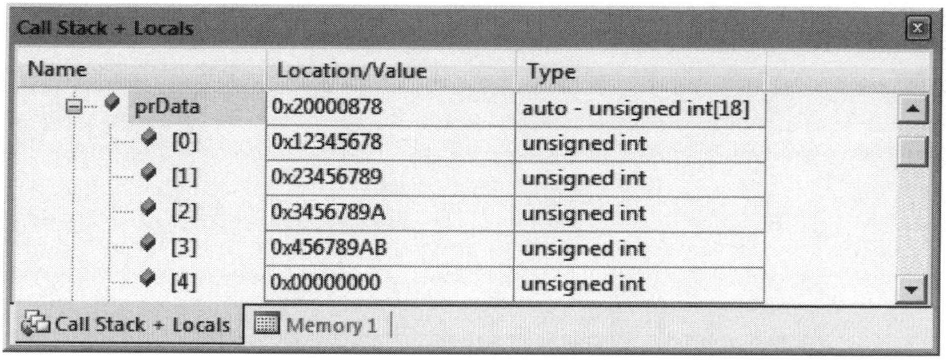

Figure 6.42. The read back data stored in the prData[] array. (Reproduced with permission from ARM® Limited. Copyright © ARM Limited.)

Now build the project by going to `Project|Build target` menu item. If everything is fine, go to the `Flash|Download` item to download the image file of the project into the flash memory. Before we can run the project to test its function, we need first to insert a breakpoint in line 15 in the `main()` program. The reason we do this is because we need to check 4 read back data from the array `prData[]` to confirm the success of the data writing function during the project runs. All of these data would be gone after the project is terminated. Therefore we have to do this checking when the project is running. Click on line 14 in the `main()` program and go to the `Debug|Insert/Remove Breakpoint` item to insert this breakpoint in line 15.

Now go to `Debug|Start/Stop Debug Session` and `Debug|Run` item to run the project.

During the project runs, four LEDs on the EduBASE Trainer will be turned ON one by one to show that each word has been written into the EEPROM and the related word-writing-complete interrupt has been generated and handled in the `FLASH_Handler()`.

When the project stops at the breakpoint, open the `Call Stack + Locals` window by clicking on it. Then expand the `prData` array by clicking the plus symbol in front of it. You can find that all 4 data words have been read out and stored in this array, as shown in Figure 6.42.

6.8 CHAPTER SUMMARY

In this chapter we discussed and analyzed all kinds of memory devices used in the TM4C123GH6PM MCU system. The memory devices we discussed include:

- SRAM (32 KB)
- Flash Memory (256 KB)
- Internal ROM
- EEPROM (2 KB)

Starting with an introduction to the memory architecture used in the 4M4C123GH6PM MCU system, each memory device is discussed and analyzed in detail with all related control registers used by those devices.

A complete and detailed system memory map is then provided in Section 6.3 to give users a clear and global picture about the address ranges and locations for all components used in this MCU system.

The bit-band operation and its principle are discussed in Section 6.4. The other memory requirements and memory properties are introduced in Section 6.5. Starting at Section 6.6, the memory system programming is discussed with related API functions provided by the TivaWare™ Peripheral Driver Library.

The memory system programming projects start at Section 6.7. Starting at Section 6.7.1, three example projects related to the flash memory programming and erasing operations are discussed and analyzed in detail in this section, which include:

- Multiple words flash memory programming and erasing with the polling method.
- Multiple words flash memory programming and erasing with the interrupt method.
- Flash memory buffer word programming.

The EEPROM programming projects are started at Section 6.7.2. This section includes some introductions and discussions about special features and functions used for EEPROM programming, which include:

- Special features in the EEPROM programming process
- EEPROM programming operational sequence
- Configure and set up EEBLOCK and EEOFFSET registers
- Three kinds of system header files in TM4C123GH6PM MCU system
- Enabling EEPROM module in Run mode and Reset EEPROM

Starting at Section 6.7.4, two example EEPROM programming projects are discussed in detail with line-by-line explanations.

HOMEWORK

I. True/False Selections

_____**1.** The Cortex®-M4 processors can only work with little endian memory system.

_____**2.** The ARM® Cortex®-M4 provides a bit-band feature to enable read/write access to individual bits in one 1-MB SRAM region.

_____**3.** The Internal ROM and Flash ROM spaces are connected to the Cortex®-M4 processor via two bus interfaces, ICode and DCode.

_____**4.** In the TM4C123GH6PM MCU system, the memory system is composed of 32-KB SRAM, 256-KB Flash memory, 2-KB EEPROM, and an internal ROM device.

_____**5.** The Flash memory is organized as 256 sets of 1-KB blocks that can be individually erased, and both erasing and writing operations can change bits' values from 0 to 1.

_____**6.** For a data writing operation that uses the flash write buffer, the flash memory address (FMA) register contains an aligned address in bits [6:0] for a 128-byte (32-word) block to be written.

_____**7.** When the WRITE bit (bit[0]) in the flash memory control (FMC) register is changed from 1 to 0, a writing operation is done and the bit PRIS in the FCRIS register is set to 1 to generate an interrupt that can be sent to the NVIC to be processed.

_____**8.** This 2-KB EEPROM array can be considered and accessed in 32 blocks of 16-word space with each block containing 16 words ($32 \times 16 \times 4$ Bytes $= 2$ KB).

_____**9.** When the WORKING bit (bit[0]) in the EEDONE register is changed from 1 to 0, an EEPROM operation is done and the ERIS bit in the FCRIS register is set to 1 to generate an interrupt that can be sent to the NVIC to be processed.

_____**10.** A bit-band region maps each word in a bit-band alias region to a single bit or the Least Significant Bit (LSB) in the bit-band region. Since each word contains 32 bits, the 1-MB bit-band region can be mapped to 32-MB bit-band alias regions.

II. *Multiple Choices*

1. Which of the following buses can be used to access memory or peripheral devices in parallel?

   a. ICode Bus, DCode Bus, System Bus, PPB

   b. DCode Bus, System Bus, PPB, AHB

   c. ICode Bus, DCode Bus, System Bus, AHB, PPB

   d. None of the above

2. Which of the following units is an optional device in the Cortex®-M4 processor?

   a. NVIC

   b. SysTick

   c. FPU

   d. MPU

3. Which of the following two memory devices can be accessed by using the ICode Bus and DCode Bus besides the system bus in the TM4C123GH6PM MCU system?

   a. Peripherals and SRAM

   b. Flash memory and internal ROM

   c. SRAM and Flash memory

   d. Flash memory and EEPROM

4. The general connection between the Cortex®-M4 processor and peripherals is by _____ protocol. However, the peripherals can also be accessed via the _____ protocol directly by the processor.

   a. Private Peripheral Bus (PPB), Advanced Peripheral Bus (APB)

   b. System Bus, Advanced Peripheral Bus (APB)

   c. Advanced Peripheral Bus (APB), Advanced High-Performance Bus (AHB)

   d. Bus Bridge, Advanced High-Performance Bus (AHB)

5. Depending on different writing and erasing operations, the FMA register contains _____.

   a. A 4-byte-aligned address when writing a single word into the flash memory

   b. An aligned starting address (0x00) in bits [6:0] of the FMA when writing 32-word

   c. A 1 KB-aligned CPU byte address when perform an erasing operation

   d. All of the above

6. Since both flash memory and EEPROM use the same interrupt vector, one needs to check bit _____ inside the interrupt handler to identify that an EEPROM interrupt has occurred.

   a. EMASK in the FCIM register

   b. ERIS in the FCRIS register

   c. INT in the EEINT register

   d. EMISC in the FCMISC register

7. Since the EEPROM cannot accept a given actual address to access the EEPROM, one needs to use two registers, _____, to get the real address to access the EEPROM.

   a. EERDWR and EEDONE

   b. EEBLOCK and EESUPP

   c. EEOFFSET and EEDONE

   d. EEBLOCK and EEOFFSET

8. Based on the Bit-Band equation in Section 6.4.1, the 0x20000000 bit[31] in the bit-band region can be mapped to _____ in the bit-band alias region.

   a. 0x2000007C bit[3]

   b. 0x2000007C bit[2]

   c. 0x2000007C bit[1]

   d. 0x2000007C bit[0]

9. To clear a flash memory interrupt, one needs to set the bit _____ in the _____ register.

   a. PMISC, FCMISC

   b. EMISC, FCMISC

   c. AMISC, FCMISC

   d. PMASK, FCIM

10. To clear an EEPROM interrupt, one needs to set the bit _____ in the _____ register.

   a. PMISC, FCMISC

   b. EMISC, FCMISC

   c. AMISC, FCMISC

   d. PMASK, FCIM

III. Exercises

1. Provide a brief description about the memory architecture implemented in the TM4C123GH6PM MCU system.

2. Provide a brief description about the flash memory used in the TM4C123GH6PM MCU system.

3. Explain the operational process of the flash memory in the TM4C123GH6PM MCU system.

4. Provide a description about the basic operations of the flash memory implemented in the TM4C123GH6PM MCU system.

5. Provide a brief explanation about the flash memory interrupt process, including how to generate a flash memory word-writing-complete interrupt and how to enable, handle, and clear that interrupt.

6. Provide a brief discussion about the initialization process of the EEPROM.

7. Explain the architecture of the EEPROM used in the TM4C123GH6PM MCU system.

8. Provide a brief explanation about the EEPROM interrupt process, including how to generate an EEPROM word-writing-complete interrupt and how to enable, handle, and clear that interrupt.

IV. Practical Laboratory

Laboratory 6: ARM® Cortex®-M4 Memory System and Device

6.0 Goals   This laboratory exercise allows students to learn and practice ARM® Cortex®-M4 memory system programming by developing three labs.

1. Program Lab6_1 lets you build a flash memory project to use API functions provided by the TivaWare™ Peripheral Driver Library to perform data words erasing and writing operations by using the Software Driver (SD) programming model.

2. Program Lab6_2 enables students to build an EEPROM project to access the desired EEPROM block and offset to perform words writing and reading operations, and control some LEDs, PB0~PB1,in the EduBASE Trainer to indicate the completion of those operations. You need to use the API functions provided by the TivaWare™ Peripheral Driver Library to build this project.

3. Program Lab6_3 allows students to become familiar with the bit-band technology by building a bit-band-related project to perform some bit-band operations.

After completion of these programs, you should understand the basic architecture and operational procedure for most popular memory devices, including the flash memory and EEPROM, installed in the TM4C123GH6PM MCU system. You should be able to code some programs to access the desired memory devices to perform popular operations, such as erasing, writing, and reading, on EEPROM and flash memory.

6.1 Lab6_1

6.1.1 Goal In this project, students need to build a flash memory project to use API functions provided by the TivaWare™ Peripheral Driver Library to perform data words erasing and writing operations by using the Software Driver (SD) programming model.

Two API functions, FlashErase() and FlashProgram(), will be used to build this project. These API functions are located at the TivaWare™ Peripheral Driver Library driverlib.lib file. Refer to Table 6.17 in Section 6.6.1 to get more details about these functions.

6.1.2 Data Assignment and Hardware Configuration No hardware configuration is needed in this project.

To use these API functions, one needs to include the related system header files, flash.h, which contains all definitions for macros and functions used in those API functions.

6.1.3 Development of the Source Code Only a C code file is used in this project since it is a simple application without needing any header file.

1. Create a new folder named Lab6_1 under the folder C:\ARM Lab Projects\ Chapter 6 in the Windows Explorer.

2. Create a new μVersion5 project named Lab6_1 and save this project to the folder Lab6_1 that is created in step 1 above.

3. On the next wizard, you need to select the device (MCU) for this project. Expand three icons, Texas Instruments, Tiva C Series, and TM4C123x Series, and select the target device TM4C123GH6PM from the list by clicking it. Click on the OK to close this wizard.

4. Next the Software Components wizard is opened, and you need to set up the software development environment for your project with this wizard. Expand two icons, CMSIS and Device, check the CORE and Startup checkboxes in the Sel. column, and click on the OK button since we need these two components to build our project.

5. In the `Project` pane, expand the `Target` folder and right click on the `Source Group 1` folder and select the `Add New Item to Group 'Source Group 1'`.

6. Select the `C File (.c)` and enter `Lab6_1` into the `Name:` box, and click on the `Add` button to add this source file into the project.

7. On the top of this C source file, you need first to include four system header files, `<stdint.h>`, `<stdbool.h>`, "`tm4c123gh6pm.h`," and "`driverlib/flash.h`" since we need to use them in this project.

8. Start the main program with the code `int main(void)`.

9. Create a new local 32-bit integer variable `ret` with the data type as `int32_t`. This variable will work as a holder to hold the returning value from executing two API functions later.

10. Create two local unsigned 32-bit integer (`uint32_t`) variables, `uiAddress` and `uiCount`, and initialize them as `0x2000` and 12, respectively. The first variable works as the starting address from which three data words will be written into the flash memory, and the second variable provides the number of bytes for three words to be written into the flash (3-word $\times$ 4 = 12 bytes since each word has 4 bytes).

11. Create an unsigned 32-bit integer pointer `*proData` and this pointer will be initialized by a data array and passed into the API function `FlashProgram()` as the address for the first data to be written into the flash memory later.

12. Create an unsigned 32-bit integer data array `Data[3]` and initialize it with three 32-bit integers, `0x78563412`, `0x8B674523`, and `0xA3456789`.

13. Assign the starting address of the data array `Data` to the integer pointer `proData`.

14. Call the API function `FlashErase()` with the starting address `uiAddress` as the argument to erase the 1-KB block flash memory space starting at `0x2000`. The function should return a feedback status, and this status should be assigned to the variable `ret`.

15. Return 1 if the returned `ret` value is nonzero. This means that the erase operation has something wrong.

16. Call the API function `FlashProgram()` with the address of the first data in the data array `proData`, the starting address `uiAddress`, and the number of bytes to be written into the flash `uiCount`, to perform writing three data in the data array into the flash memory. The function should return a feedback status, and this status should be assigned to the variable `ret`.

17. Return 1 if the returned `ret` value is nonzero. This means that the programming operation has something wrong.

18. Return 0 if nothing wrong.

6.1.4 Set Up Environment to Build and Run the Project To build and run the project, one needs to perform the following operations to set up the environments:

- Set up the path for the selected system header files in the `Include Paths` box in the C/C++ tab under the `Project|Options for Target ' Target 1'` menu item. Go to that box, and browse to the folder `C:\ti\TivaWare_C_Series-2.0.1.11577`. Then click on the OK buttons to complete this setting.

- Add the TivaWare™ Peripheral Driver Library `driverlib.lib` file into the project. Go to the `Project` pane and right click on the `Source Group 1` item, and select the `Add Existing Files to Group 'Source Group 1'` menu item. Browse to the folder where the library file is located, which is `C:\ti\TivaWare_C_Series-2.0.1.11577`

\driverlib\rvmdk. Then select that library file and click on the Add button. Click on the Close button to finish this step.

- Select the Stellaris ICDI debugger in the Debug tab under the Project| Options for Target' Target 1' menu item.
- Now let's build the project by going to Project|Build target menu item.
- Then go to Flash|Download menu item to download the image file of this project into the flash memory in the TM4C123GXL Evaluation Board.
- Now go to Debug|Start/Stop Debug Session to ready to run the project.
- Go to Debug|Run menu item to run the project.

6.1.5 Demonstrate Your Program by Checking the Running Result   After the project runs, open the Memory 1 window by clicking on it on the bottom of this screen. Type 2000 into the Address box and scroll down to the address 0x00001FEE. Then you can find that our three words, 0x12345678, 0x2345678B, and 0x896745A3, have been written into the address starting at 0x00002000. All other addresses are filled by FF, which means that all 1-KB spaces have been erased from 0s to 1s.

Go to Debug|Start/Stop Debug Session to stop your program.

Based on these results, try to answer the following questions:

- By comparing the original three words created in the data array Data[3] in our main program with the resulting three words written into the flash memory, what you can say? Why the order of each byte is opposite?
- In the flash memory space ranging between 0x2000 and 0x23FF, why have all bytes been written as FF?
- What did you learn from this project?

6.2 Lab6_2

6.2.1 Goal   This project enables students to build an EEPROM project to access the desired EEPROM block and offset to perform word-writing and word-reading operations, and control some LEDs, PB0~PB2, in the EduBASE Trainer to indicate the completion of those operations. You need to use the API functions provided by the TivaWare™ Peripheral Driver Library to build this project.

6.2.2 Data Assignment and Hardware Configuration   No hardware configurations are needed for this project. To enable and set the clock for the GPIO Port B, the following data and registers should be used:

- Bits 1 in the RCGC2 register should be set to 1 to enable Ports B (refer to Figure 4.28).
- Bits 0~2 in the Port B Direction register should be set to 1 to enable PB0~PB2 pins to work as output pins.
- Bits 0~2 in the Port B Digital Enable register should be set to 1 to enable PB0~PB2 pins to work as digital function pins.

6.2.3 Development of the Project   Following the steps below to develop this project. Only a C code source file is used in this project since this project is simple. Create the project and develop the C source file with the following steps:

1. Create a new folder `Lab6_2` under the folder `C:\ARM Lab Projects\Chapter 6` in the Windows Explorer.

2. Open the Keil® ARM-MDK μVersion5, create a new project named `Lab6_2`, and save this project into the folder `Lab6_2` created in step 1.

3. On the next wizard, you need to select the device (MCU) for this project. Expand three icons, `Texas Instruments`, `Tiva C Series` and `TM4C123x Series`, and select the target device TM4C123GH6PM from the list by clicking on it. Click on the OK to close this wizard.

4. Next the Software Components wizard is opened, and you need to set up the software development environment for your project with this wizard. Expand two icons, `CMSIS` and `Device`, and check the CORE and `Startup` checkboxes in the `Sel.` column, and click on the OK button since we need these two components to build our project.

6.2.4 Development of the C Source File

1. In the `Project` pane, expand the `Target` folder and right click on the `Source Group 1` folder and select the `Add New Item to Group 'Source Group 1'`.

2. Select the `C File (.c)` and enter `Lab6_2` into the `Name:` box, and click on the Add button to add this source file into the project.

3. Include the following system header files into this source file:
   - `#include <stdint.h>`
   - `#include <stdbool.h>`
   - `#include "inc/hw_types.h"`
   - `#include "inc/hw_memmap.h"`
   - `#include "driverlib/sysctl.h"`
   - `#include "driverlib/gpio.h"`
   - `#include "driverlib/eeprom.h"`

4. Inside the `main()` program, first create the following three local variables:
   - An unsigned 32-bit integer variable `uiAddress` and initialize it to `0x200` since we want to program the EEPROM starting at its 8th block (refer to Table 6.20).
   - An unsigned 32-bit integer array `pwData[]` and initialize it with 18 words as below:

   {0x12345678, 0x23456789, 0x3456789A, 0x456789AB, 0x56789ABC, 0x6789ABCD, 0x789ABCDE, 0xDEBC9A78, 0xEFCDAB89, 0x78563412, 0x89674523, 0x9A785634, 0xAB896745, 0xBC9A7856, 0x00112233, 0xABABABAB, 0x11223344, 0x22334455};

   - An unsigned 32-bit integer array `prData[18]`. We will use this array to store the read back data from the EEPROM after the word-writing operation is done to confirm that our EEPROM data programming is correct.

5. Use the API function `SysCtlPeripheralEnable(SYSCTL_PERIPH_GPIOB);` to enable the GPIO Port B.

6. Use the API function `GPIOPinTypeGPIOOutput()` to configure pins 0~2 (PB0~PB2) on the GPIO Port B as output pins.

7. Use the API function `SysCtlPeripheralEnable(SYSCTL_PERIPH_EEPROM0);` to enable the EEPROM device.

8. Call the API function `EEPROMInit()` to initialize the EEPROM.

9. Use the API function `GPIOPinWrite()` to set the pin 0 (PB0) of the GPIO Port B to turn it ON to indicate that the `EEPROMInit()` is done.

10. Use the API function `SysCtlDelay(4000000);` to delay a period of time to keep PB0 ON.

11. Call the API function EEPROMProgram(pwData, uiAddress, sizeof(pwData)); to write 18 words into the EEPROM starting at the byte offset address 0x200 (8th block).

12. Use the API function GPIOPinWrite() to set the pin 1 (PB1) of the GPIO Port B to turn it ON to indicate that the EEPROMProgram() is done.

13. Use the API function SysCtlDelay(4000000); to delay a period of time to keep PB1 ON.

14. Call the API function EEPROMRead(prData, uiAddress, sizeof(prData)); to read back 18 words that have been written into the EEPROM in step 11.

15. Use the API function GPIOPinWrite() to set the pin 2 (PB2) of the GPIO Port B to turn it ON to indicate that the EEPROMRead() is done.

16. Use a while(1) loop to make the program running infinitively.

6.2.5 Set Up the Environment to Build and Run the Project This setup contains the following three operations:

1. Include the system header files by adding the include path.

2. Check and configure the correct debugger used in the project.

3. Add the TivaWare™ peripheral driver library into the project since we need to use desired API functions provided by that library.

Perform the following operations to include this header file path in your project:

- Go to Project|Options for Target 'Target 1' menu item.
- Then click on the C/C++ tab.
- Go to Include Paths box and browse to the folder where our header files are located; it is C:\ti\TivaWare_C_Series-2.0.1.11577. Select this folder and click on the OK button.

Perform the following operations to make sure that the debugger you are using is the Stellaris ICDI. You can do this checking as follows:

- Go to Project|Options for Target 'Target 1' menu item to open the Options wizard.
- On the opened Options wizard, click on the Debug tab.
- Make sure that the debugger shown in the Use: box is Stellaris ICDI. Otherwise you can click on the dropdown arrow to select this debugger from the list.

Perform the below operations to add the TivaWare™ peripheral driver library into the project:

- Go to the Project pane and right click on the Source Group 1 item, and select the Add Existing Files to Group 'Source Group 1' menu item.
- Browse to the folder where the library file is located, which is C:\ti\TivaWare_C_Series-2.0.1.11577\driverlib\rvmdk. Then select the library file driverlib.lib and click on the Add button. Click on the Close button to finish this step.

6.2.6 Build and Demonstrate Your Program Perform the following operations to run your program and check the running results:

- Set up a break point at the while(1) code line from the Debug menu.
- Go to Project|Build target to build the project.

- Go to Flash|Download menu item to download your program into the flash ROM.
- Go to Debug|Start/Stop Debug Session to begin debugging your program. Click on the OK button on the 32-KB memory size limitation message box to continue.
- Then go to Debug|Run menu item to run your program.

As the project runs, the LED PB0 will be ON when the EEPROMInit() is done. Then the LED PB1 is ON when the EEPROMProgram() is complete. Finally the LED PB2 is ON when the EEPROMRead() is finished.

Now open the Call Stack + Locals window on the bottom of this screen, and expand the prData[] array from this window. You can find that all 18 words have been read back and stored in this array.

Based on these results, try to answer the following questions:

- Why we need to put a while(1) loop at the end of this main program? What will happen if we remove this loop?
- What did you learn from this project?

6.3 Lab6_3

6.3.1 Goal This project allows students to become familiar with the bit-band technology by building a bit-band-related project to perform some bit-band operations. This project enables students to write 32 bit-band values into 32 words in the bit-band alias range.

6.3.2 Data Assignment and Hardware Configuration No hardware configuration and data assignment are needed for this project.

6.3.3 Development of the Project Using steps below to develop this project. Only the C source file is used in this project since this project is not complicated. Create a new project with the following steps:

1. Create a new folder Lab6_3 under the folder C:\ARM Lab Projects\Chapter 6 in the Windows Explorer.
2. Open the Keil® ARM-MDK μVersion5, create a new project named Lab6_3 and save this project in the folder Lab6_3 created in step 1.
3. On the next wizard, you need to select the device (MCU) for this project. Expand three icons, Texas Instruments, Tiva C Series, and TM4C123x Series, and select the target device TM4C123GH6PM from the list by clicking on it. Click on the OK to close this wizard.
4. Next the Software Components wizard is opened, and you need to setup the software development environment for your project with this wizard. Expand two icons, CMSIS and Device, and check the CORE and Startup checkboxes in the Sel. column, and click on the OK button since we need these two components to build our project.

6.3.4 Development of the C Source File

1. In the Project pane, expand the Target folder and right click on the Source Group 1 folder and select the Add New Item to Group 'Source Group 1'.
2. Select the C File (.c) and enter Lab6_3 into the Name: box, and click on the Add button to add this source file into the project.

3. Include the following header files into this source file first:
- #include <stdint.h>
- #include <stdbool.h>

4. In this project, we need to use two macros:

#define MEM_REG0	0x20000000
#define HWREG(x)	(*((volatile uint32_t *)(x)))

The first macro is the starting address of the bit-band region, and the second macro is a system definition to convert a constant to an address.

5. In this project we need to use one user-defined function, Mem_Addr(), to calculate the bit-band alias address. The declaration for this function is

uint32_t Mem_Addr(uint32_t addr, uint32_t bitnum);

6. Place the int main(void) to start our main program.

7. Declare three unsigned 32-bit integer local variables, bit_alias, uiValue and uiAddr. The first variable is used to accept and hold the returned calculated bit-alias address by calling the function Mem_Addr(). The second one works as a loop number and the third variable uiAddr is the starting address of the bit-band region, which is 0x20000000. Assign this address to the variable uiAddr.

8. Declare two unsigned 32-bit integer data arrays, prData[32] and prAddr[32]. The first data array is used to hold and store 32 bit-band values into the bit-band alias range, and the second data array is to hold and store 32 bit-band alias addresses.

9. Use a for() loop to repeatedly call the function Mem_Addr() to calculate 32 bit-band alias addresses, and store those addresses into the data array prAddr[]. Assign bit-band value 0x1 to each address, and also store each value into the data array prData[].

10. Use a while(1) loop to keep the project runs forever.

11. In the function Mem_Addr(), first create a local 32-bit unsigned integer variable bit_band.

12. Then put the equation bit_band = 0x22000000 + ((addr & 0xFFFFF) << 5) + (bitnum << 2); under that local variable.

13. Return the local variable bit_band.

6.3.5 Set Up the Environment to Build and Run the Project   No environment is needed to be set up for this project.

You need to set up a breakpoint at the code line that includes a while(1) loop. Now go to Project|Build target menu item to build the project.

6.3.6 Demonstrate Your Program   Perform the following operations to run your program and check the running results:

- Go to the Flash|Download menu item to download your program into the flash ROM.
- Go to the Debug|Start/Stop Debug Session to begin debugging your program. Click on the OK button on the 32-KB memory size limitation message box to continue.
- Then go to Debug|Run menu item to run your program.

As the project runs, it will stop at the breakpoint, the while(1) loop. Now open the Call Stack + Locals window, and expand the prData[] array. You can find that all

32 bit-band alias ranges have been set up by 1, exactly in the LSB of each address. Expand the prAddr[] array, and you can find that the calculated bit-band alias addresses have been stored in this array.

Based on these results, try to answer the following questions:

- Can you find a way to change the starting address (0x20000000) on the bit-band region in this source file to allow this project to calculate any other desired bit-band alias address? If so, how?
- What did you learn from this project?

Chapter 7

ARM® Cortex®-M4 Parallel I/O Ports Programming

This chapter provides general information about ARM® Cortex®-M4 microcontroller General-Purpose Input Output (GPIO) Port programming. The discussion is mainly concentrated on the GPIO Ports-related peripherals used in TM4C123GH6PM MCU system. This discussion includes the GPIO Ports and peripherals specially designed for the TM4C123GH6PM MCU, GPIO Port architecture and configurations, general and special or alternative control functions for different GPIO Ports and pins, and GPIO Ports and peripheral programming applications in TM4C123GH6PM MCU system.

7.1 OVERVIEW AND INTRODUCTION

As we discussed in Section 2.6.2 in Chapter 2, in the TM4C123GH6PM MCU system, the GPIO module provides interfaces for multiple peripherals or I/O devices. Generally, GPIO provides six popular GPIO Ports, Ports A~F, to interface and access most system or on-chip peripherals as well as external peripherals and I/O devices to perform input/output functions. These system and on-chip peripherals can be categorized into the following groups:

- System Peripherals
    1. WDT—Two Watchdog Timers (WDT0 and WDT1)
    2. Timer—Six 16/32-bit and Six 32/64-bit Timers (Timer0 ~ Timer5)
    3. ITM—Instrumentation Trace Macrocell (ITM)
    4. DWT—Data Watchpoint and Trace (DWT)
    5. FPB—Flash Patch and Breakpoint (FPB)
    6. TPIU—Trace Port Interface Unit (TPIU)
- On-Chip Peripherals
    1. ADC—Two 12-bit Analog to Digital Converters (ADC0 ~ ADC1)
    2. AC—Three Analog Comparators (AC0 ~ AC2)
    3. VR—One Voltage Regulator
    4. TS—One Temperature Sensor
    5. PWM—Two PWM Modules with total of 16 PWM Outputs (PWM0 and PWM1)

Practical Microcontroller Engineering with ARM® Technology, First Edition. Ying Bai.
© 2016 by The Institute of Electrical and Electronics Engineers, Inc. Published 2016 by John Wiley & Sons, Inc.
Companion Website: www.wiley.com/go/armbai

6. QEI—Two Quadrature Encoder Interface modules providing control of two motors at the same time (QEI0 and QEI1)

- Interfaces to External Peripherals
  1. CAN—Two Controller Area Network 2.0 A/B controllers (CAN0 and CAN1)
  2. USB—One Universal Serial Bus 2.0 OTG/Host/Device (USB0)
  3. LCD—One LCD Controller (LCD)
  4. UART—Eight Universal Asynchronous Receiver/Transmitter (UART0 ~ URAT7)
  5. I²C—Four Inter-Integrated Circuit modules with four transmission speeds
  6. SSI—Four Synchronous Serial Interface modules (SSI0 ~ SSI3)
  7. Ethernet—High-Speed Network

As we discussed in Section 2.6.3.3 in Chapter 2, each GPIO Port can be mapped to an I/O block, and each block contains 8 bits or 8 pins. Each bit or each pin can be configured as either input or output pin. Also, with the help of the GPIO Alternate Function Selection register (GPIOAFSEL), each pin can be configured to perform multiple or different functions, which are called alternative functions.

The advantage of using this GPIOAFSEL register in the GPIO module is that multiple functions can be configured and fulfilled by using a limited number of GPIO Ports and pins. The shortcoming is that this will make the GPIO Port configurations and programming more complicated and difficult.

Most of peripherals, including system, on-chip, and interfaces to the external peripherals listed above, are connected and controlled to the GPIO Ports with related pins. We will divide these peripherals into different groups and discuss them one by one in the following different chapters. In this chapter, we will concentrate on the following peripherals since these peripherals belong to the parallel I/O peripherals:

- On-Board Keypads Interface Programming Project
- Analog to Digital Converter Programming Project
- PWM Controlled DC and Step Motors Programming Project

In Chapter 8 we will discuss SSI, UART, and I²C since these devices belong to series I/O peripherals. The following projects will be built in that chapter since these peripherals are connected to the SSI peripheral interface:

- On-Board 7 Segment LED Interface Programming Project
- On-Board LCD Interface Programming Project
- Digital-to-Analog Converter Programming Project

The timer in the TM4C123GH6PM MCU system is a big topic and we will discuss this peripheral in Chapter 9. The discussion includes six real timers and watchdog timers.

In Chapter 10 we will concentrate on our discussions on QEI, CAN, and DC motors as well as on Robotics controls.

7.2 GPIO MODULE ARCHITECTURE AND GPIO PORT CONFIGURATION

We have provided detailed discussions and introductions about the GPIO architecture and related registers in Section 2.6.3.3 in Chapter 2. In this part we will discuss more

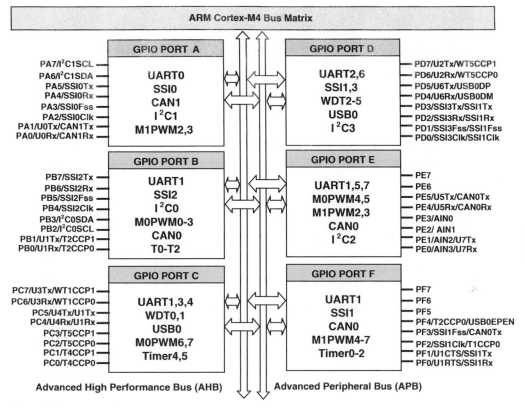

Figure 7.1.   GPIO Port and pin configuration.

about the GPIO Ports and pin configurations used in the TM4C123GH6PM MCU system.

Figure 7.1 shows a functional block diagram for GPIO Ports A~F and all related pins used in the TM4C123GH6PM MCU system.

It can be found from Figure 7.1 that each pin in each GPIO Port can provide multiple or alternative functions. The actual function for each pin is determined by the combination of the GPIO Alternate Function Select Register (GPIOAFSEL) and the GPIO Port Control Register (GPIOPCTL) together. We have provided detailed discussions about the combinations of these two registers to determine the function for each pin in Section 2.6.3.3.6 in Chapter 2. In this part we just want to emphasize some important points to make this issue clear.

The lowest 8 bits in the GPIOAFSEL register determined whether any pin in any GPIO Port works as a general GPIO pin or as an alternate function pin. For these 8 bits, each bit is mapped to each pin in a selected GPIO Port. If a bit is 0, this means that the corresponding pin works as a general GPIO pin. Otherwise if a bit is 1, the corresponding pin works as an alternate function pin. In this case, the actual function the pin supposes to perform is determined by the related 4 bits in the GPIOPCTL register.

Table 2.6 in Chapter 2 provides all alternate functions related to the bit values in the GPIOPCTL register. For your convenience, that Table is shown in this part again as Table 7.1. Figure 2.19 is also redrew here as Figure 7.2 to make this issue clear.

Refer to Figure 7.2 with Table 7.1, the alternate function for each selected pin can be uniquely determined. For example, the bits 0 and 6 in the GPIOAFSEL register in the

Table 7.1. GPIO pins and alternate functions.

I/O	Pin	Analog Function	Digital Functions (GPIOPCTL PMCx Bit Field Encoding)									
			1	2	3	4	5	6	7	8	9	14
PA0	17	—	U0RX	—	—	—	—	—	—	CAN1RX	—	—
PA1	18	—	U0TX	—	—	—	—	—	—	CAN1TX	—	—
PA2	19	—	—	SSI0CLK	—	—	—	—	—	—	—	—
PA3	20	—	—	SSI0FSS	—	—	—	—	—	—	—	—
PA4	21	—	—	SSI0RX	—	—	—	—	—	—	—	—
PA5	22	—	—	SSI0TX	—	—	—	—	—	—	—	—
PA6	23	—	—	—	I2C1SCL	—	M1PWM2	—	—	—	—	—
PA7	24	—	—	—	I2C1SDC	—	M1PWM3	—	—	—	—	—
PB0	45	USB0ID	U1RX	—	—	—	—	—	T2CCP0	—	—	—
PB1	46	USB0VBUS	U1TX	—	—	—	—	—	T2CCP1	—	—	—
PB2	47	—	—	—	I2C0SCL	—	—	—	T3CCP0	—	—	—
PB3	48	—	—	—	I2C0SDC	—	—	—	T3CCP1	—	—	—
PB4	58	AIN10	—	SSI2CLK	—	M0PWM2	—	—	T1CCP0	CAN0RX	—	—
PB5	57	AIN11	—	SSI2FSS	—	M0PWM3	—	—	T1CCP1	CAN0TX	—	—
PB6	1	—	—	SSI2RX	—	M0PWM0	—	—	T0CCP0	—	—	—
PB7	4	—	—	SSI2TX	—	M0PWM1	—	—	T0CCP1	—	—	—
PC0	52	—	TCK SWCLK	—	—	—	—	—	T4CCP0	—	—	—
PC1	51	—	TMS SWDIO	—	—	—	—	—	T4CCP1	—	—	—
PC2	50	—	TDI	—	—	—	—	—	T5CCP0	—	—	—
PC3	49	—	TDO SWO	—	—	—	—	—	T5CCP1	—	—	—
PC4	16	C1−	U4RX	U1RX	—	M0PWM6	—	IDX1	WT0CCP0	U1RTS	—	—
PC5	15	C1+	U4TX	U1TX	—	M0PWM7	—	PHA1	WT0CCP1	U1CTS	—	—
PC6	14	C0+	U3RX	—	—	—	—	PHB1	WT1CCP0	USB0EPEN	—	—
PC7	13	C0−	U3TX	—	—	—	—	—	WT1CCP1	USB0PFLT	—	—
PD0	61	AIN7	SSI3CLK	SSI1CLK	I2C3SCL	M0PWM6	M1PWM0	—	WT2CCP0	—	—	—
PD1	62	AIN6	SSI3FSS	SSI1FSS	I2C3SDC	M0PWM7	M1PWM1	—	WT2CCP1	—	—	—
PD2	63	AIN5	SSI3RX	SSI1RX	—	M0FAULT0	—	—	WT3CCP0	USB0EPEN	—	—
PD3	64	AIN4	SSI3TX	SSI1TX	—	—	—	IDX0	WT3CCP1	USB0PFLT	—	—
PD4	43	USB0DM	U6RX	—	—	—	—	—	WT4CCP0	—	—	—
PD5	44	USB0DP	U6TX	—	—	—	—	—	WT4CCP1	—	—	—
PD6	53	—	U2RX	—	—	M0FAULT0	—	PHA0	WT5CCP0	—	—	—
PD7	10	—	U2TX	—	—	—	—	PHB0	WT5CCP1	NMI	—	—
PE0	9	AIN3	U7RX	—	—	—	—	—	—	—	—	—
PE1	8	AIN0	U7TX	—	—	—	—	—	—	—	—	—
PE2	7	AIN1	—	—	—	—	—	—	—	—	—	—
PE3	6	AIN2	—	—	—	—	—	—	—	—	—	—
PE4	59	AIN9	U5RX	—	I2C2SCL	M0PWM4	M1PWM2	—	—	CAN0RX	—	—
PE5	60	AIN8	U5TX	—	I2C2SDC	M0PWM5	M1PWM3	—	—	CAN0TX	—	—
PF0	28	—	U1RTS	SSI1RX	CAN0RX	—	M1PWM4	PHA0	T0CCP0	NMI	C0O	—
PF1	29	—	U1CTS	SSI1TX	—	—	M1PWM5	PHB0	T0CCP1	—	C1O	TRD1
PF2	30	—	—	SSI1CLK	—	M0FAULT0	M1PWM6	—	T1CCP0	—	—	TRD0
PF3	31	—	—	SSI1FSS	CAN0TX	—	M1PWM7	—	T1CCP1	—	—	TRCLK
PF4	5	—	—	—	—	—	M1FAULT0	IDX0	T2CCP0	USB0EPEN	—	—

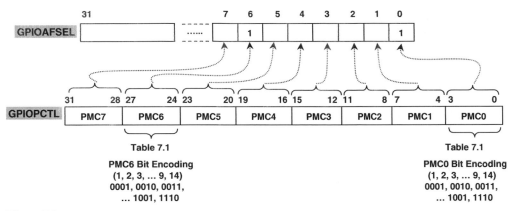

Figure 7.2. The illustration for GPIOAFSEL and GPIOPCTL registers.

GPIO Port A are set to 1. This means that both pins 0 and 6 in the GPIO Port A should work as alternate function pins to connect to the special peripherals to provide special functions. For bit 0 in the GPIOAFSEL register, the alternate function can be determined by the PMC0 (lowest 4 bits) in the GPIOPCTL register, which is shown in Table 7.1. If PMC0 in the GPIOPCTL register is 1 (0001), this means that the PA0 should work as a receiving pin for the UART0 (Table 7.1). However, for bit 6 in the GPIOAFSEL register, if the PMC6 (bits 24~27) in the GPIOPCTL register is 5 (0101), the PA6 pin should work as M1PWM2 pin to connect to that PWM peripheral to provide a pulse width modulation output.

As we discussed in Section 2.6.3.4 in Chapter 2, each GPIO Port (Ports A~F) contains a set of GPIO Registers, and each register can be accessed by using an offset address combining (plus) with a base address.

7.3 GPIO PORT CONTROL REGISTERS

Each GPIO Port or block contains a set of control registers and these registers can be categorized into seven groups as we discussed in Section 2.6.3.3 in Chapter 2. These registers include:

1. Port Control—GPIOPCTL register: Used to select the operational mode for the selected GPIO port, either GPIO mode or Peripheral mode, via a multiplexing selector MUX.
2. Commit Control—GPIOLOCK and GPIOCR registers: Used to enable or disable other four registers' operational bits. In other words, the GPIOCR register is to control the transferring ability of each bit on other four registers. The GPIOLOCK register is used to lock (disable) or unlock (enable) the GPIOCR register.
3. Mode Control: The GPIOAFSEL register works together with GPIOPCTL register to determine the selected GPIO port mode. Another two registers, GPIOADCCTL and GPIODMACTL, are used to set up either the ADC mode or DMA mode for the selected GPIO port.
4. Data Control—GPIODATA and GPIODIR registers: Used to control the data modification ability and data transfer direction.
5. Interrupt Control: Seven registers are used to determine all interrupt properties for the selected GPIO port or bits, such as interrupt triggering method, edges or levels,

interrupt enabled or disabled, interrupt masking, interrupt status, and interrupt clear function.

6. Pad Control: Enable software to configure the GPIO pads based on the application requirements. The pad control includes nine registers. These registers control drive strength, open-drain configuration, pull-up and pull-down resistors, slew-rate control, and digital input enable for each GPIO.

7. Identification Registers: These registers configured at reset enable software to detect and identify the module as a GPIO block. The identification registers include 12 related registers.

The most popular registers are those registers listed in groups 1~5 above. Most of the time, not all registers should be used and some registers may never be touched since their default setup values are good for most applications.

Table 7.2 lists some of the most often used GPIO control registers and their addresses in the memory map used in the TM4C123GH6PM MCU system. All interrupt-related registers for each GPIO Port are not shown in this table since we will discuss these registers in more detail in Chapter 5.

In Table 7.2 the system control register SYSCTL_RCGC2_R has only 6 valid bits (bits 0~5) used for 6 GPIO Ports, Ports A ~ F, with each bit corresponding to one port. Also all 8 bits for all GPIO Commit Registers, GPIO_PORTX_CR_R, are set to 1 to enable all modifications to take effect immediately for other four registers, GPIOAFSEL, GPIOPUR, GPIOPDR, and GPIODEN. Most values in this table are default values after a system reset operation.

7.3.1 GPIO Port Initialization and Configuration

We have provided detailed discussions about the GPIO Port initialization procedures in Section 2.6.3.4 in Chapter 2. Some important initialization steps include the following:

1. Set up a connection between the system clock and the specific GPIO Port to enable the clock to drive the port by setting the appropriate bits in the GPIO Run Mode Clock Gating Control (RCGCGPIO) register or RCGC2 register.

2. Set up the direction for each pin on the GPIO port by programming the GPIODIR register.

3. Optionally, you can configure the GPIOAFSEL register to program each bit as a GPIO Mode or Alternate Mode.

4. Enable GPIO pins as digital I/Os by setting the appropriate DEN bit in the GPIODEN register. Since all GPIO pins are tri-state status after a reset, this step is necessary. To enable GPIO pins to their analog function, set the GPIOAMSEL bit in the GPIOAMSEL register.

5. Optionally, you can set up the drive strength for each pin through the GPIODR2R, GPIODR4R, or GPIODR8R registers. This step is optional since the default drive strength is 2-mA.

6. Optionally, you can configure each pad in the port to have pull-up, pull-down, or open drain function through the GPIOPUR, GPIOPDR, or GPIOODR register. Slew rate may also be configured, if needed, through the GPIOSLR register.

7. Optionally, you can configure the GPIOIS, GPIOIBE, GPIOEV, and GPIOIM registers to set up the type, event, and mask of the interrupts for each port if interrupts are used for the port. This step is optional and unnecessary until interrupts are utilized for a specific GPIO port.

8. Optionally, you can lock the configurations of the NMI and JTAG/SWD pins on the GPIO port pins by setting the LOCK bits in the GPIOLOCK register.

Table 7.2. Some popular GPIO Port registers in APB bus aperture.

GPIO Register	7	6	5	4	3	2	1	0	Address
SYSCTL_RCGC2_R	–	–	GPIOF	GPIOE	GPIOD	GPIOC	GPIOB	GPIOA	$400F.E108
GPIO_PORTA_DATA_R	DATA	DATA	DATA	DATA	DATA	DATA	DATA	DATA	$4000.43FC
GPIO_PORTA_DIR_R	DIR	DIR	DIR	DIR	DIR	DIR	DIR	DIR	$4000.4400
GPIO_PORTA_AFSEL_R	SEL	SEL	SEL	SEL	SEL	SEL	SEL	SEL	$4000.4420
GPIO_PORTA_PUR_R	PUE	PUE	PUE	PUE	PUE	PUE	PUE	PUE	$4000.4510
GPIO_PORTA_DEN_R	DEN	DEN	DEN	DEN	DEN	DEN	DEN	DEN	$4000.451C
GPIO_PORTA_CR_R	1	1	1	1	1	1	1	1	$4000.4524
GPIO_PORTA_AMSEL_R	0	0	0	0	0	0	0	0	$4000.4528
GPIO_PORTB_DATA_R	DATA	DATA	DATA	DATA	DATA	DATA	DATA	DATA	$4000.53FC
GPIO_PORTB_DIR_R	DIR	DIR	DIR	DIR	DIR	DIR	DIR	DIR	$4000.5400
GPIO_PORTB_AFSEL_R	SEL	SEL	SEL	SEL	SEL	SEL	SEL	SEL	$4000.5420
GPIO_PORTB_PUR_R	PUE	PUE	PUE	PUE	PUE	PUE	PUE	PUE	$4000.5510
GPIO_PORTB_DEN_R	DEN	DEN	DEN	DEN	DEN	DEN	DEN	DEN	$4000.551C
GPIO_PORTB_CR_R	1	1	1	1	1	1	1	1	$4000.5524
GPIO_PORTB_AMSEL_R	0	0	AMSEL	AMSEL	0	0	0	0	$4000.5528
GPIO_PORTC_DATA_R	DATA	DATA	DATA	DATA	JTAG	JTAG	JTAG	JTAG	$4000.63FC
GPIO_PORTC_DIR_R	DIR	DIR	DIR	DIR	JTAG	JTAG	JTAG	JTAG	$4000.6400
GPIO_PORTC_AFSEL_R	SEL	SEL	SEL	SEL	JTAG	JTAG	JTAG	JTAG	$4000.6420
GPIO_PORTC_PUR_R	PUE	PUE	PUE	PUE	JTAG	JTAG	JTAG	JTAG	$4000.6510
GPIO_PORTC_DEN_R	DEN	DEN	DEN	DEN	JTAG	JTAG	JTAG	JTAG	$4000.651C
GPIO_PORTC_CR_R	1	1	1	1	JTAG	JTAG	JTAG	JTAG	$4000.6524
GPIO_PORTC_AMSEL_R	AMSEL	AMSEL	AMSEL	AMSEL	JTAG	JTAG	JTAG	JTAG	$4000.6528
GPIO_PORTD_DATA_R	DATA	DATA	DATA	DATA	DATA	DATA	DATA	DATA	$4000.73FC
GPIO_PORTD_DIR_R	DIR	DIR	DIR	DIR	DIR	DIR	DIR	DIR	$4000.7400
GPIO_PORTD_AFSEL_R	SEL	SEL	SEL	SEL	SEL	SEL	SEL	SEL	$4000.7420
GPIO_PORTD_PUR_R	PUE	PUE	PUE	PUE	PUE	PUE	PUE	PUE	$4000.7510
GPIO_PORTD_DEN_R	DEN	DEN	DEN	DEN	DEN	DEN	DEN	DEN	$4000.751C
GPIO_PORTD_CR_R	CR	1	1	1	1	1	1	1	$4000.7524
GPIO_PORTD_AMSEL_R	0	0	AMSEL	AMSEL	AMSEL	AMSEL	AMSEL	AMSEL	$4000.7528
GPIO_PORTE_DATA_R			DATA	DATA	DATA	DATA	DATA	DATA	$4002.43FC
GPIO_PORTE_DIR_R			DIR	DIR	DIR	DIR	DIR	DIR	$4002.4400
GPIO_PORTE_AFSEL_R			SEL	SEL	SEL	SEL	SEL	SEL	$4002.4420
GPIO_PORTE_PUR_R			PUE	PUE	PUE	PUE	PUE	PUE	$4002.4510
GPIO_PORTE_DEN_R			DEN	DEN	DEN	DEN	DEN	DEN	$4002.451C
GPIO_PORTE_CR_R			1	1	1	1	1	1	$4002.4524
GPIO_PORTE_AMSEL_R			AMSEL	AMSEL	AMSEL	AMSEL	AMSEL	AMSEL	$4002.4528
GPIO_PORTF_DATA_R				DATA	DATA	DATA	DATA	DATA	$4002.53FC
GPIO_PORTF_DIR_R				DIR	DIR	DIR	DIR	DIR	$4002.5400
GPIO_PORTF_AFSEL_R				SEL	SEL	SEL	SEL	SEL	$4002.5420
GPIO_PORTF_PUR_R				PUE	PUE	PUE	PUE	PUE	$4002.5510
GPIO_PORTF_DEN_R				DEN	DEN	DEN	DEN	DEN	$4002.551C
GPIO_PORTF_CR_R				1	1	1	1	CR	$4002.5524
GPIO_PORTF_AMSEL_R				0	0	0	0	0	$4002.5528

After a system reset, all GPIO pins are configured to be undriven or tri-state with the following values in four registers: GPIOAFSEL = 0, GPIODEN = 0, GPIOPDR = 0, and GPIOPUR = 0, except for some pins shown in Table 2.8. This table shows special consideration GPIO pins, and these pins may be programmed to a non-GPIO function or may have special commit controls out of reset.

We have discussed and reviewed the most important properties and functions for GPIO Port and related registers, and now let's use these to build and develop our projects to access and interface some parallel peripherals to perform special functions.

7.4 ON-BOARD KEYPAD INTERFACE PROGRAMMING PROJECT

In the EduBASE ARM® Trainer, there is a 4×4 keypad installed and connected to two GPIO Ports, Ports A and D. As shown in Figure 7.3, four rows (rows 0~3) are connected to four lower bits, PD3~PD0, on the Port D. Four columns (columns 3~0) are connected to four bits, PA5~PA2, on the Port A, respectively.

Since we do not need to use any special or alternate function for these GPIO Ports, therefore we do not need to take care of the initializing the GPIOAFSEL and GPIOPCTL registers for this project since by default all 8 bits on the GPIOAFSEL register are reset to 0 to enable all GPIO Ports to work as general GPIO mode.

It can be found from this keypad hardware configuration that all four pins on Ports A and D are pulled down by pull-down resistors, RN10 and RN13. Therefore all of these pins are driven as LOW if no logic signal is applied to these pins.

Generally, any keypad interface can be developed by either hardware or software. The former has higher running speed with high cost, and the latter has lower running speed with low cost. In this part, we will use software to build a keypad interfacing program to scan and identify the pressed key and display it in four LEDs, PB3~PB0, which are installed in the EduBASE ARM® Trainer.

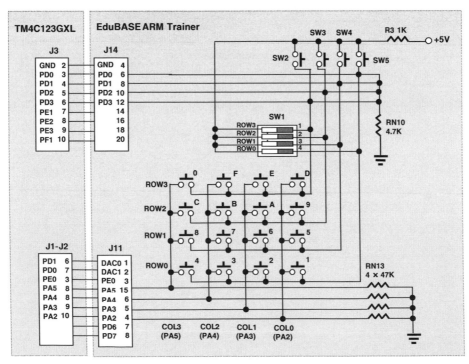

Figure 7.3. Keypad hardware configuration for EduBASE ARM Trainer.

To check and identify the pressed key, two methods can be applied on the software:

1. Using the poll-up method to repeatedly scan and check all keypad key arrays.

2. Using the interrupt method to check the pressed key.

The second method is better and more efficient than the first method. In this section we will discuss the first method and leave the second method as an experimental lab for the users.

7.4.1 The Keypad Interfacing Programming Structure

From the hardware configuration of this keypad device shown in Figure 7.3, it can be seen that four pins on the GPIO Port A, PA5~PA2, are connected to four columns, columns 0~3. These four columns are generally in the LOW status since they are pulled down by four resistors RN13.

The so-called poll-up method is to scan all four columns by outputting HIGH to each row via each pin on the GPIO Port D, PD3~PD0. If no key on any column is pressed, all four columns are still in the LOW status. These can be checked by getting them via four pins, PA5~PA2, in the GPIO Port A. If a key is pressed, this makes the corresponding column to HIGH. By checking the row number and column number, we can identify which key has been pressed.

In this way we repeatedly send HIGH to each row one by one, we and read back all columns via Port A. Then we can check if any column is HIGH to identify the pressed key.

This method is easy, but it is time-consuming with low efficiency because most of the time the program is performing scanning and reading back functions without any chance to handle other possible jobs.

The functional block diagram for this program is shown in Figure 7.4.

Two functions are involved in this project, the `InitKeypad()` and `ReadKeypad ()`, to perform the initialization process and reading key process, respectively.

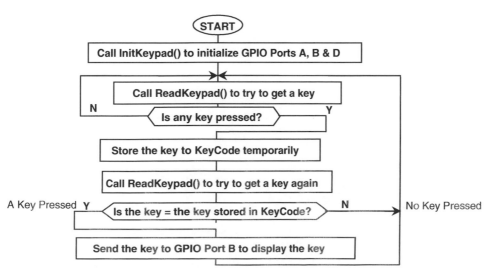

Figure 7.4. The functional block diagram of keypad scanning process.

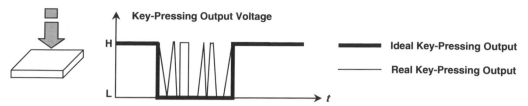

Figure 7.5.   The bouncing actions caused by pressing a key from the keypad.

In the main program, the `InitKeypad()` function is called first to initialize and configure GPIO Ports A, B, and D to make Ports B and D as output ports and Port A as input port. Then a `while(1)` loop is used to repeatedly scan the keypad to try to read a key if any of them is pressed. This scanning and reading process is performed by calling the function `ReadKey()` in two times. The first-time-reading result is saved in the `KeyCode` variable, and the second-time-reading result is compared with the first-time result to make sure that the same key is pressed. This two-time-reading process is necessary since the keypad pressing may cause some hardware vibrations and bouncing to create some wrong key-press signal. In order to avoid these possible mistakes, two-time scanning and reading is a good solution.

Figure 7.5 shows the bouncing actions caused by pressing a key from the keypad.

If both time-reading results are the same, this means that a key is pressed and the key code is sent to the GPIO Port B that connected to four LEDs to display it. Otherwise no key has been pressed and the program continues to perform loop scanning and reading for the future keys.

Another issue is the keypad connection and key number displayed in the EduBASE ARM® Trainer. The current keypad with the key numbers is only a simulation to a standard telephone keypad and numbers, as shown in Figure 7.6a. The actual connection for these keys and key numbers is shown in Figure 7.6b. Our keypad project is developed based on the actual keypad and key numbers shown in Figure 7.6b. Therefore when we test our project with this keypad later, we should use the correct keypad with their key numbers shown in Figure 7.6b.

7.4.2 Create the Keypad Interfacing Programming Project (Polling-Driven)

Now let's create our keypad project `DRAKeyPadPoll`. This project is built based on the Direct Register Access (DRA) method with the polling strategy.

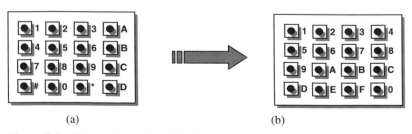

(a)   (b)

Figure 7.6.   Two configurations of the keys and key numbers in the keypad.

Perform the following operations to create a new project DRAKeyPadPoll:

1. Open the Windows Explorer window to create a new folder named DRAKeyPadPoll under the C:\ARM Class Projects\Chapter 7 folder.

2. Open the Keil® ARM®-MDK µVersion5 and go to the Project|New µVersion Project menu item to create a new µVersion Project. On the opened wizard, browse to our new folder DRAKeyPadPoll that is created in step 1 above. Enter DRAKeyPadPoll into the File name box and click on the Save button to create this project.

3. On the next wizard, you need to select the device (MCU) for this project. Expand three icons, Texas Instruments, Tiva C Series, and TM4C123x Series, and select the target device TM4C123GH6PM from the list by clicking on it. Click on the OK to close this wizard.

4. Next the Software Components wizard is opened, and you need to set up the software development environment for your project with this wizard. Expand two icons, CMSIS and Device, and check the CORE and Startup checkboxes in the Sel. column, and click on the OK button since we need these two components to build our project.

Since this project is relatively simple, only a C source file is good enough.

7.4.2.1 Create the C Source File DRAKeyPadPoll.c

Perform the following operations to create a new C source file DRAKeyPadPoll.c:

1. In the Project pane, expand the Target folder and right click on the Source Group 1 folder and select the Add New Item to Group 'Source Group 1'.

2. Select the C File (.c) and enter DRAKeyPadPoll into the Name: box, and click on the Add button to add this source file into the project.

3. Enter the first part codes shown in Figure 7.7 into this source file.

Let's have a closer look at this first part source file to see how it works.

- Three system header files, stdint.h, stdbool.h, and TM4C123GH6PM.h, are included first at lines 4–6 in this source file since we need to use them in this project. In fact, we need to use all structure pointers defined for GPIO Ports and system controls to access related pins and components in this project. All of these structure pointers are defined in the header file TM4C123GH6PM.h.

- In lines 7 and 8, two user-defined functions, InitKeypad() and ReadKeypad(), are declared since we need to use them to perform initialization and read-key processes later.

- Two local char variables, keyCode and keyNum, are created at lines 11. The first variable is used to accept and hold the returned key code by calling the ReadKeypad() function. The second variable works as a temporary storage to save the key code obtained from the first-reading process.

- In line 12, the InitKeypad() function is called to initialize and configure the GPIO Ports A, B, and D to make ports B and D as output ports and port A as input port.

- An infinitive while() loop is then executed to repeatedly scan and read the keypad to try to get the pressed key and display the key code on the four LEDs in line 13.

- In line 15, the ReadKeypad() function is called to try to get a pressed key and the returned key code is assigned to the variable keyCode.

- If the keyCode is not a 0, which means that a key has been pressed, its value is stored into the variable keyNum in line 18. This value will be compared with the next reading keycode to confirm whether the same key is pressed later.

```
1    //********************************************************************************************************
2    // DRAKeyPadPoll.c - Main Application File
3    //********************************************************************************************************
4    #include <stdint.h>
5    #include <stdbool.h>
6    #include "TM4C123GH6PM.h"
7    void  InitKeypad(void);
8    char  ReadKeypad(void);
9    int main(void)
10   {
11      char keyCode, keyNum;
12      InitKeypad();                             // initialize ports A, B & D
13      while(1)
14      {
15        keyCode = ReadKeypad();                 // try to read a key from keypad
16        if (keyCode != 0)                       // if a key is pressed...
17        {
18          keyNum = keyCode;                     // reserve the key code
19          keyCode = ReadKeypad();               // try to get the key again
20          if (keyCode == keyNum)                // is the same key?
21          { GPIOB->DATA = keyNum; }             // display key code on port B
22        }
23      }
24   }
25   void  InitKeypad(void)
26   {
27      SYSCTL->RCGC2 |= 0x1|0x2|0x8;             // enable GPIO Ports A, B & D
28      GPIOB->DIR |= 0x0F;                       // set PORTB 3-0 as output pins
29      GPIOB->DEN |= 0x0F;                       // set PORTB 3-0 as digital pins
30      GPIOA->DIR &= ~0x3C;                      // set PORTA 5-2 as input pins (rows 0-3)
31      GPIOA->DEN |= 0x3C;                       // set PORTA 5-2 as digital pins
32      GPIOD->DIR |= 0x0F;                       // set PORTD 3-0 as output pins (cols 0-3)
33      GPIOD->DEN |= 0x0F;                       // set PORTD 3-0 as digital pins
34   }
35   char  ReadKeypad(void)
36   {
37      int row = 0,  col,  rowNum = 4;
38      const  char  row_select[] = {0x01,  0x02,  0x04,  0x08};
39      while(row < rowNum)
40      {
41        GPIOD->DIR &= ~0x0F;                    // disable all rows
42        GPIOD->DIR |= row_select[row];          // enable one row
43        GPIOD->DATA |= 0x0F;                    // set the active row high
44        col = GPIOA->DATA & 0x3C;               // read all columns
45        if (col != 0) break;                    // if one of the input is high, some key is pressed.
46        row++;
47      }
48      GPIOD->DIR &= ~0x0F;                      // disable all rows
49      if (col == 0) { return  col; }            // if no key pressed, return 0
50      // get here when one of the rows has key pressed
51      if (col == 0x04)  return (row * 4 + 1);   // key in column 0
52      if (col == 0x08)  return (row * 4 + 2);   // key in column 1
53      if (col == 0x10)  return (row * 4 + 3);   // key in column 2
54      if (col == 0x20)  return (row * 4 + 4);   // key in column 3
55      return 0;
     }
```

Figure 7.7.   The codes for the source file DRAKeyPadPoll.c.

- In line 19, the `ReadKeypad()` function is called again to try to get the second pressed key.
- Now compare the second reading key-code with the first one. If both are the same, this means that a key has been really pressed and it is not a bouncing or a vibration. Then the key code is assigned to the Port B to display it in line 21.
- The `InitKeypad()` function starts at line 25.
- In line 27, the RCGC2 register is initialized and configured to enable GPIO Ports A, B, and D by setting its bits 0, 1 and 3 to 1. This setting can be done by using an OR operator to combine all of these bits together (refer to Figure 4.28 in Chapter 4 for RCGC2 register). A pointer is used since the system control register RCGC2 has been defined as an element in a `SYSCTL` structure pointer in the `TM4C123GH6PM.h` header file.
- The codes in lines 28~33 are used to configure GPIO Ports to provide different input/output functions. The ports B and D are configured as output ports, and the port A is configured to work as an input port.
- The `ReadKeypad()` function starts at line 35.
- Three local variables, `col`, `row`, and `rowNum`, are declared in line 37. These variables are used to scan the keypad to get the row and the column number for the pressed key. The variables `row` and `rowNum` represent the current row number and the maximum row number and they are initialized to 0 and 4, respectively.
- A constant char array `row_select[]` is declared in line 38. This array contains 4 rows starting from 0x1 to 0x8, which are corresponding to four pins, PD0~PD3, in the GPIO Port D. This array is used to continuously provide a row number to scan all four rows in the keypad to get the column from which the key is pressed.
- A `while()` loop is used in line 39 with the `rowNum` as the loop condition. In this way, this loop will be executed until all four rows have been scanned and the row number gets its maximum value `rowNum`.
- Inside the `while()` loop, first all rows are disabled in line 41 by assigning `0xF0` to the Port D Direction register. This step is necessary since we try to avoid any hardware vibration and bouncing caused by pressing any key. Therefore before we can start our scanning process, all rows are disabled to avoid any possible bouncing.
- In line 42, a row number in the `rwo_select[]` array is sent to the Port D Direction register to enable that row and set that row to HIGH.
- Then a `0xF` is sent to the Port D Data register to try to set all lower four pins, PD0~PD3, to HIGH in line 43. In fact, only one row (pin) is set to HIGH since only one row is selected by `rwo_select[]` array in line 42.
- In line 44, four pins at Port A, PA5~PA2, are read back and assigned to the local variable `col` to check if any column is HIGH, which means that a key is pressed.
- If one of the columns is HIGH or the `col` is nonzero, break and stop the `while()` loop in line 45.
- If the `col` equals to 0, which means that no column is HIGH and no key is pressed, the row number `row` is incremented by 1 to continue the next loop in line 46.
- In line 48, if the `col` is nonzero and a key is pressed, first all rows are disabled to avoid any vibration and bouncing caused by the hardware.
- If all four rows have been scanned and no any column is HIGH, which means that no key has been pressed, the function returns a 0 in line 49.
- For the nonzero value in the `col`, the key code or key number is calculated based on the column number `col` in lines 51~54 and returned to the main program.

- In line 55, the return 0 has nothing to do with this function and is just for the requirement of the protocol of this function.

Now let's build and run the project to test the function of this project. Before we can do this, we need first to set up the environment for this project to enable the compiler and debug to locate our software sources.

7.4.3 Set Up the Environment to Build and Run the Project

The only environment setup is to select the correct debugger adapter for this project, which is Stellaris ICDI. Go to the Project|Options for Target 'Target 1' menu item to finish this setup.

Now build the project and download the image file of this project to the flash memory. Run the project by going to Debug|Start/Stop Debug Session and then the Debug|Run menu item.

During the project runs, press any key on the keypad and you can find that the corresponding LED with the related key number should be ON. Press the 0 key to turn off all IEDs.

Go to the Debug|Stop and Debug|Start/Stop Debug Session to stop the project. Our keypad project is very successful.

We leave a similar keypad project, but one that is driven by the interrupt as a lab for the users.

7.5 ANALOG-TO-DIGITAL CONVERTER PROGRAMMING PROJECT

There are two ADC modules in the TM4C123GH6PM MCU system, ADC0 and ADC1, respectively. Each ADC module contains four sample sequencers, and these two modules can share 12 analog input channels.

In the EduBASE ARM® Trainer, the first channel (AIN0) in the module ADC0 is connected to a potentiometer VR2 and the second channel (AIN1) is connected to a photosensor Q1.

In order to have a clear picture about the ADC modules in the TM4C123GH6PM MCU system, we had better provide a detailed discussion about these modules.

7.5.1 ADC Modules in the TM4C123GH6PM MCU System

The TM4C123GH6PM microcontroller contains two identical Analog-to-Digital Converter modules. These two modules, ADC0 and ADC1, provide 12-bit conversion precision and share the same 12 analog input channels. Each ADC module operates independently and can therefore execute different sample sequences, sample any of the analog input channels at any time, and generate different interrupts and triggers.

These two ADC modules provide the following features:

- 12 shared analog input channels
- 12-bit precision ADC
- Single-ended and differential-input configurations
- On-chip internal temperature sensor

- Maximum sample rate of one million samples/second (MSPS)
- Optional phase shift in sample time programmable
- Four programmable sample conversion sequencers from one to eight entries long, with corresponding conversion result FIFOs
- Five flexible trigger controls
  - Software Trigger Controller (default)
  - Timers
  - Analog Comparators
  - PWM
  - GPIO
- Hardware averaging of up to 64 samples
- 2 Analog Comparators

Each ADC module can be composed of two major parts; the Sample Sequencers and Module Control. The core of the ADC module is the sample sequencer. Each module contains four sample sequencers. The sample sequencer controls the input signal sampling and data collecting process. The interesting issue is that each sample in a sample sequence can be programmed to have special functions. For instance, each sample sequence can be programmed to contain 1, 4, or 8 samples, and each sample can be obtained from the different input channel with different mode, either single-end or differential input. The module control contains all other necessary controls for the ADC, such as the interrupt control, ADC module clock control, input trigger control, and DMA operation control.

7.5.2 ADC Module Architecture and Functional Block Diagram

A simplified ADC module architecture and functional block diagram is shown in Figure 7.8.

As we mentioned, each ADC module contains four sample sequencers, SS0~SS3. These sample sequencers can be programmed to pre-define the way and the function for each sample via some registers in the related Sample Sequencer n block. Each sample can be obtained from different input sources in different channels. These sample sequencers are under the control of some control registers in the Control/Status block.

The operational procedure of each ADC module includes:

1. Each ADC module must be clocked by configuring the ADC Clock Configuration (ADCCC) register before it works since all ADC modules share the same clock source to facilitate the synchronization of data samples between conversion units.

2. Before the ADC can start its conversion, the sample sequencers must be configured by related registers in each sample sequencer block, such as ADC Sample Sequence Input Multiplexer Select n (ADCSSMUXn) and ADC Sample Sequence Control n (ADCSSCTLn) registers.

3. Then the sample sequencers must be enabled by configuring the ADC Active Sample Sequencer (ADCACTSS) register. If multiple triggering events were used, the ADC Sample Sequencer Priority (ADCSSPRI) register must also be configured.

4. The trigger source or trigger event must be determined by configuring the ADC Event Multiplexer Select (ADCEMUX) register, and the sampling process must be initiated by setting up the ADC Processor Sample Sequence Initiate (ADCPSSI) register.

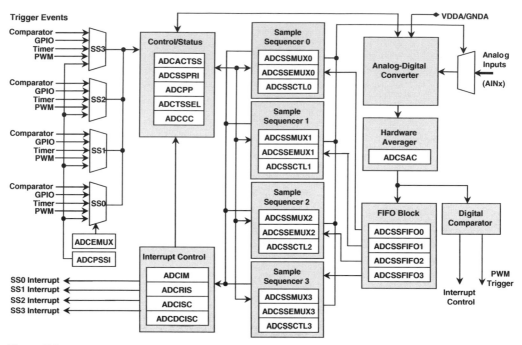

Figure 7.8.   Simplified ADC module functional block diagram.

5. Optionally, one can use the ADC Peripheral Property (ADCPP) register to set up the resolution, include the temperature sensor, and set the ADC sample rate. Generally, you do not need to touch this register and only use the default settings of this register.

6. The ADC Trigger Source Select (ADCTSSEL) register is used to select a PWM generator as the trigger source when the PWM generator is used.

7. After the analog input channel and sample property have been determined by ADCSSMUXn ADCSSCTLn registers, the ADC conversion starts. After the ADC conversion is complete, the conversion results can be obtained from the ADC Sample Sequence Result FIFO (ADCSSFIFOn) registers.

8. If interrupts are used for any ADC conversion, some registers in the Interrupt Control block should also be configured.

The Hardware Averager is used to make the ADC conversion results smoother by averaging some continuous samples. The Digital Comparator is used to compare the ADC conversion results with some pre-defined values to monitor and control the external signals.

7.5.3 ADC Module Components and Signal Descriptions

As shown in Figure 7.8, all ADC module components and their functions are globally illustrated by this block diagram. However, in order to get more details about these components and some signals, we need to discuss them one by one with more details.

Table 7.3. ADC input channels and GPIO pins distributions.

ADC Pin	GPIO Pin	Pin Type	Pin Function
AIN0	PE3	Input	ADC Analog Input Channel 0
AIN1	PE2	Input	ADC Analog Input Channel 1
AIN2	PE1	Input	ADC Analog Input Channel 2
AIN3	PE0	Input	ADC Analog Input Channel 3
AIN4	PD3	Input	ADC Analog Input Channel 4
AIN5	PD2	Input	ADC Analog Input Channel 5
AIN6	PD1	Input	ADC Analog Input Channel 6
AIN7	PD0	Input	ADC Analog Input Channel 7
AIN8	PE5	Input	ADC Analog Input Channel 8
AIN9	PE4	Input	ADC Analog Input Channel 9
AIN10	PB4	Input	ADC Analog Input Channel 10
AIN11	PB5	Input	ADC Analog Input Channel 11

7.5.3.1 *Analog Input Signals and GPIO Analog Control Registers*

As we discussed in Section 7.2, most peripheral devices in TM4C123GH6PM MCU system are related to GPIO Ports. This means that all inputs and outputs of peripherals are transferred by using some GPIO pins. This is also true for ADC modules. All ADC modules are closely related to GPIO Ports, and all ADC input channels are connected to related GPIO Port and pins.

Totally 12 ADC input channels are connected to GPIO Ports B, D, and E. Refer to Table 7.1, in column 3 (Analog Function), 12 ADC input channels, AIN0~AIN11, are connected to related GPIO Ports or pins. To make this clear, we collect those channels and GPIO pins and show their relationships in Table 7.3.

In order to enable GPIO pins to work as ADC input pins, the following configurations should be performed:

1. Enable the clock to the appropriate GPIO modules via the RCGCGPIO register.
2. The AFSEL bits (lower 8 bits) in the GPIO Alternate Function Select (GPIOAF-SEL) register must be set to 1.
3. The related bits in the GPIO Digital Enable (GPIODEN) register must be cleared to disable the digital function and enable the analog function.
4. Also, the related AMSEL bits (lower 8 bits) in the GPIO Analog Mode Select (GPIOAMSEL) register should set to 1 to disable the analog isolation circuits to enable the selected pin to work as analog input pin.

Recall that in Section 2.6.3.3.6 in Chapter 2, when we discussed the Pad Control block for the GPIO Ports module, we discussed the GPIODEN and GPIOAMSEL registers and their functions.

For the GPIOAMSEL register, since the GPIOs may be driven by a 5V source and affect analog operation, analog circuitry requires isolation from the pins when they are not used for any analog function. If any pin is to be used as an ADC input, the related bit in GPIOAMSEL register must be set to 1 to disable the analog isolation circuit and enable the

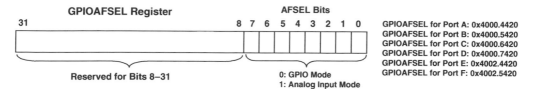

Figure 7.9. The bit fields in the GPIOAFSEL register.

analog input function. Otherwise if a bit in the GPIOAMSEL is 0, the analog isolation circuit is enabled and the analog input function is disabled for the corresponding pin.

Now let's take a closer look at these three registers since they are very important when any GPIO pin works as an analog input pin for the ADC module.

7.5.3.1.1 GPIO Alternate Function Select (GPIOAFSEL) Register
The GPIOAFSEL register is the mode control select register. If a bit in this register is clear, the pin is used as a GPIO pin and is controlled by the GPIO registers. Setting a bit in this register configures the corresponding GPIO pin to be controlled by an associated peripheral. Several possible peripheral functions are multiplexed on each GPIO pin.

A functional block diagram and bit fields of this register is shown in Figure 7.9.

Each GPIO Port has a separate GPIOAFSEL register with a different memory mapping address. All of these addresses for each GPIO Port are also shown in Figure 7.9.

Only the lowest 8 bits is used for this register, although this is a 32-bit register. Each bit is corresponded to a GPIO Port pin. If a pin is to be worked as an analog input pin to connect to an ADC input channel, the corresponding bit must be set to 1 in this register to enable that bit (pin). By default, all bits are cleared to 0 when a system reset operation is performed. This means that all GPIO pins work as GPIO mode after a system reset.

7.5.3.1.2 GPIO Digital Enable (GPIODEN) Register
The GPIODEN register is the digital enable register. By default, all GPIO pins or signals are configured to be undriven or tri-state after a system reset. Their digital function is disabled, which means that they do not drive a logic value on the pin and they do not allow the pin voltage into the GPIO receiver. To use the pin as a digital input or output, either GPIO or alternate function, the corresponding DEN bit must be set to 1.

A functional block diagram and bit fields of this register is shown in Figure 7.10.

Each GPIO Port has a separate GPIODEN register with different memory mapping address. All of these addresses for each GPIO Port are also shown in Figure 7.10.

Only the lowest 8 bits is used for this register, although this is a 32-bit register. Each bit corresponds to a GPIO Port pin. If a pin is to be worked as an analog input pin to connect

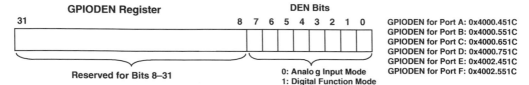

Figure 7.10. The bit fields in the GPIODEN register.

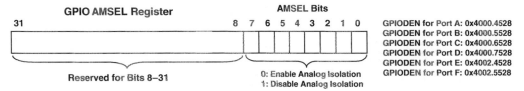

Figure 7.11. The bit fields in the GPIOAMSEL register.

to an ADC input channel, the corresponding bit in this register must be cleared to 0 to enable that bit (pin) to work as an input pin.

7.5.3.1.3 GPIO Analog Mode Select (GPIOAMSEL) Register
The GPIOAMSEL register controls isolation circuits to the analog side of a unified I/O pad. Because the GPIO Ports may be driven by a 5V voltage source and this may cause some effects to the analog operation, the analog circuitry requires isolation from the pins when they are not used in their analog function.

Each bit of this register controls the isolation circuitry for the corresponding GPIO signal. A functional block diagram and bit fields of this register are shown in Figure 7.11.

Each GPIO Port has a separate GPIOAMSEL register with a different memory mapping address. All of these addresses for each GPIO Port are also shown in Figure 7.11.

Only the lowest 8 bits (AMSEL bits) is used for this register, although this is a 32-bit register. Each bit corresponds to a GPIO Port pin. If a pin is to be worked as an analog input pin to connect to an ADC input channel, the corresponding bit in this register must be set to 1 to disable the analog isolation circuits to enable the selected pin to work as analog input pin.

7.5.3.2 Sample Sequencer Controls and Their Control Registers

As we discussed in Section 7.5.2, each ADC module contains four sample sequencers, SS0~SS3. These sample sequencers can be programmed to pre-define the way and the function for each sample via some registers in the related Sample Sequencer n block. Each sample can be obtained from different input sources in different channels.

In fact, the sampling control and data capture is handled by the sample sequencers. All of the sequencers are identical in implementation except for the number of samples that can be captured and the depth of the FIFO. Table 7.4 shows the number of samples that each sequencer can capture and its corresponding FIFO depth. Each sample that is captured is stored in the FIFO. In this implementation, each FIFO entry is a 32-bit word, with only the lower 12 bits containing the conversion result. The SS0 has the most number

Table 7.4. Samples and FIFO depth of sequencer.

Sequencer	Number of Samples	Depth of FIFO
SS3	1	1
SS2	4	4
SS1	4	4
SS0	8	8

of samples, 8 samples, but the SS3 has the smallest number of samples, only 1 sample, can be collected and stored in that sequencer.

Before each sample sequencer can be implemented to capture any sample data, it must be configured first to define the way and the function for each sample to be collected since each sample in a sample sequencer can be individually programmed to determine:

1. From which input channel or GPIO pin this sample should be collected?

2. Is this sample collected from a GPIO pin or from the ADC temperature sensor?

3. Can this sample trigger an interrupt when it is collected?

4. Is this sample the last sample in this sequence?

5. Is this sample collected in single-end mode or differential-input mode?

6. How and when should we enable and disable a sample sequencer?

7. How do we check the ADC working status? Is it busy or idle?

8. How do we initiate a sample sequencer to begin to work if all configurations are done?

9. How and from where do we get the conversion results when an ADC job is done?

In order to answer these questions, we need to have a closer look at related control registers in the `Sample Sequencer n` block and `Control/Status` block shown in Figure 7.8 since each sample sequencer is controlled and managed by these registers in those blocks.

In the following sections we will discuss these registers one by one based on the order of the questions listed above. Since the bit fields are different for each sample sequencer, we will discuss them separately.

7.5.3.2.1 ADC Sample Sequencer Input Multiplexer Select (ADCSSMUXn) Register

For all four sample sequencers, SS0~SS3, each sample sequencer has an ADCSS-MUXn (n = 0~3) register. We need to discuss them one by one separately. First let's take a look at an ADCSSMUX0 register that is working for an SS0 sample sequencer.

The memory mapping addresses are: for ADC0, 0x40038040; for ADC1, 0x40039040.

The bit-field values for this register are shown in Figure 7.12. The bit-field value and related function of this register is shown in Table 7.5.

This register defines the analog input pin configuration for each sample in a sequence executed with Sample Sequencer 0. This register is 32 bits wide and contains information for 8 possible samples.

Since 8 samples can be collected by this SS0, this 32-bit register is divided into 8 nibbles and each nibble contains 4 bits, MUXn, and it can be used to define an analog input channel from which the sample can be collected.

	31	30	29	28	27	26	25	24	23	22	21	20	19	18	17	16
		MU	X7			MU	X6			MU	X5			MU	X4	
Type	RW	RW	RW	RW	RW	RW	RW	RW	RW	RW	RW	RW	RW	RW	RW	RW
Reset	0	0	0	0	0	0	0	0	0	0	0	0	0	0	0	0
	15	14	13	12	11	10	9	8	7	6	5	4	3	2	1	0
		MU	X3			MU	X2			MU	X1			MU	X0	
Type	RW	RW	RW	RW	RW	RW	RW	RW	RW	RW	RW	RW	RW	RW	RW	RW
Reset	0	0	0	0	0	0	0	0	0	0	0	0	0	0	0	0

Figure 7.12. The bit fields for the ADCSSMUX0 register. (Reprinted with the permission of the Texas Instruments Incorporated.)

Table 7.5. Bit value and its function for ADCSSMUX0 register.

Bit	Name	Reset	Function
31:28	MUX7	0x0	The 8th sample input channel select. This nibble is used to select the input channel number for the 8th sample. For example, 0x0 is for AIN0, 0x1 for AIN1, and so on.
27:24	MUX6	0x0	The 7th sample input channel select. This nibble is used to select the input channel number for the 7th sample.
23:20	MUX5	0x0	The 6th sample input channel select. This nibble is used to select the input channel number for the 6th sample.
19:16	MUX4	0x0	The 5th sample input channel select. This nibble is used to select the input channel number for the 5th sample.
15:12	MUX3	0x0	The 4th sample input channel select. This nibble is used to select the input channel number for the 4th sample.
11:8	MUX2	0x0	The 3rd sample input channel select. This nibble is used to select the input channel number for the 3rd sample.
7:4	MUX1	0x0	The 2nd sample input channel select. This nibble is used to select the input channel number for the 2nd sample.
3:0	MUX0	0x0	The 1st sample input channel select. This nibble is used to select the input channel number for the 1st sample.

The n attached after each MUX represents the order number of samples to be collected. This definition provides a flexibility to enable each sample to be collected from the different input channels. From MUX0~MUX7, 8 samples are defined.

The ADCSSMUX1 and the ADCSSMUX2 registers are used for SS1 and SS2 sample sequencers. Since these two sample sequencers can collect up to 4 samples, both ADCSSMUX registers only use lower 16 bits to form 4 nibbles to define input channels for those 4 samples.

The memory mapping addresses for these two registers are:

- For ADC0: ADCSSMUX1 (0x40038060), ADCSSMUX2 (0x40038080).
- For ADC1: ADCSSMUX1 (0x40039060), ADCSSMUX2 (0x40039080).

The bit-field values for these two registers are shown in Figure 7.13. The bit-field value and related function of this register is shown in Table 7.6.

It can be found from Table 7.6 and Figure 7.13 that both ADCSSMUX1 and ADCSSMUX2 registers only used lower 16 bits to provide 4 nibbles to select input channels for 4 samples.

The ADCSSMUX3 register is used for the SS3 sample sequencer. Since this sample sequencer can collect up to 1 sample, this register only uses the lower 4 bits to form 1 nibble to define input channels for this single sample.

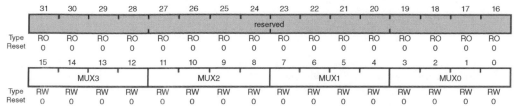

Figure 7.13. The bit fields for the ADCSSMUX1, 2 registers. (Reprinted with the permission of the Texas Instruments Incorporated.)

Table 7.6. Bit value and its function for ADCSSMUX1, 2 registers.

Bit	Name	Reset	Function
31:16	Reserved	0x0	Reserved
15:12	MUX3	0x0	The 4th sample input channel select. This nibble is used to select the input channel number for the 4th sample. For example, 0x0 is for AIN0, 0x1 for AIN1, and so on.
11:8	MUX2	0x0	The 3rd sample input channel select. This nibble is used to select the input channel number for the 3rd sample.
7:4	MUX1	0x0	The 2nd sample input channel select. This nibble is used to select the input channel number for the 2nd sample.
3:0	MUX0	0x0	The 1st sample input channel select. This nibble is used to select the input channel number for the 1st sample.

The memory mapping addresses are: for ADC0, 0x400380A0; for ADC1, 0x400390A0.

The bit-field values for this register are shown in Figure 7.14. The bit-field value and related function of this register is shown in Table 7.7.

This register defines the analog input configuration for the sample executed with Sample Sequencer 3. This register is 4 bits wide and contains information for one possible sample.

7.5.3.2.2 ADC Sample Sequencer Control (ADCSSCTLn) Register

For all 4 sample sequencers, SS0~SS3, each sample sequencer has an ADCSSCTLn (n = 0~3) register. We need to discuss them one by one separately. First let's take a look at the ADCSSCTL0 register that is working for the SS0 sample sequencer.

The memory mapping addresses are: for ADC0, 0x40038044; for ADC1, 0x40039044.

The bit-field values for this register are shown in Figure 7.15. The bit-field value and related function of the register ADCSSCTL0 is shown in Table 7.8.

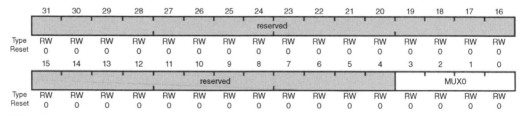

Figure 7.14. The bit fields for the ADCSSMUX3 register. (Reprinted with the permission of the Texas Instruments Incorporated.)

Table 7.7. Bit value and its function for ADCSSMUX3 register.

Bit	Name	Reset	Function
31:4	Reserved	0x0	Reserved
3:0	MUX0	0x0	The 1st sample input channel select. This nibble is used to select the input channel number for the 1st sample. For example, 0x0 is for AIN0, 0x1 for AIN1, and so on.

31	30	29	28	27	26	25	24	23	22	21	20	19	18	17	16
TS7	IE7	END7	D7	TS8	IE8	END8	D6	TS5	IE5	END5	D5	TS4	IE4	END4	D4
RW	RW	RW	RW	RW	RW	RW	RW	RW	RW	RW	RW	RW	RW	RW	RW
0	0	0	0	0	0	0	0	0	0	0	0	0	0	0	0

15	14	13	12	11	10	9	8	7	6	5	4	3	2	1	0
TS3	IE3	END3	D3	TS2	IE2	END2	D2	TS1	IE1	END1	D1	TS0	IE0	END0	D4
RW	RW	RW	RW	RW	RW	RW	RW	RW	RW	RW	RW	RW	RW	RW	RW
0	0	0	0	0	0	0	0	0	0	0	0	0	0	0	0

Type / Reset labels apply to each row above.

Figure 7.15. The bit fields for the ADCSSCTL0 register. (Reprinted with the permission of the Texas Instruments Incorporated.)

Table 7.8. Bit value and its function for the ADCSSCTL0 register.

Bit	Name	Reset	Function
31:28	TS7, IE7, END7, D7	0x0	The 8th sample control function select. TS7 = 0: Input comes from the ADCSSMUX0 MUX7, TS7 = 1: Input is temperature sensor. IE7 = 0: This sample will not create interrupt, IE7 = 1: This sample creates an ADC Interrupt. END7 = 0: This sample is not the last sample, END7 = 1: This sample is the last sample. D7 = 0: This sample is collected from a single-end mode, D7 = 1: This sample is collected from a differential-input mode.
27:24	TS6, IE6, END6, D6	0x0	The 7th sample control function select. TS6 = 0: Input comes from the ADCSSMUX0 MUX6, TS6 = 1: Input is temperature sensor. IE6 = 0: This sample will not create interrupt, IE6 = 1: This sample creates an ADC Interrupt. END6 = 0: This sample is not the last sample, END6 = 1: This sample is the last sample. D6 = 0: This sample is collected from a single-end mode, D6 = 1: This sample is collected from a differential-input mode.
23:20	TS5, IE5, END5, D5	0x0	The 6th sample control function select. TS5 = 0: Input comes from the ADCSSMUX0 MUX5, TS5 = 1: Input is temperature sensor. IE5 = 0: This sample will not create interrupt, IE5 = 1: This sample creates an ADC Interrupt. END5 = 0: This sample is not the last sample, END5 = 1: This sample is the last sample. D5 = 0: This sample is collected from a single-end mode, D5 = 1: This sample is collected from a differential-input mode.
19:16	TS4, IE4, END4, D4	0x0	The 5th sample control function select. TS4 = 0: Input comes from the ADCSSMUX0 MUX4, TS4 = 1: Input is temperature sensor. IE4 = 0: This sample will not create interrupt, IE4 = 1: This sample creates an ADC Interrupt. END4 = 0: This sample is not the last sample, END4 = 1: This sample is the last sample. D4 = 0: This sample is collected from a single-end mode, D4 = 1: This sample is collected from a differential-input mode.
15:12	TS3, IE3, END3, D3	0x0	The 4th sample control function select. TS3 = 0: Input comes from the ADCSSMUX0 MUX3, TS3 = 1: Input is temperature sensor. IE3 = 0: This sample will not create interrupt, IE3 = 1: This sample creates an ADC Interrupt. END3 = 0: This sample is not the last sample, END3 = 1: This sample is the last sample. D3 = 0: This sample is collected from a single-end mode, D3 = 1: This sample is collected from a differential-input mode.
11:8	TS2, IE2, END2, D2	0x0	The 3rd sample control function select. TS2 = 0: Input comes from the ADCSSMUX0 MUX2, TS2 = 1: Input is temperature sensor. IE2 = 0: This sample will not create interrupt, IE2 = 1: This sample creates an ADC Interrupt. END2 = 0: This sample is not the last sample, END2 = 1: This sample is the last sample. D2 = 0: This sample is collected from a single-end mode, D2 = 1: This sample is collected from a differential-input mode.
7:4	TS1, IE1, END1, D1	0x0	The 2nd sample control function select. TS1 = 0: Input comes from the ADCSSMUX0 MUX1, TS1 = 1: Input is temperature sensor. IE1 = 0: This sample will not create interrupt, IE1 = 1: This sample creates an ADC Interrupt. END1 = 0: This sample is not the last sample, END1 = 1: This sample is the last sample. D1 = 0: This sample is collected from a single-end mode, D1 = 1: This sample is collected from a differential-input mode.
3:0	TS0, IE0, END0, D0	0x0	The 1st sample control function select. TS0 = 0: Input comes from the ADCSSMUX0 MUX0, TS0 = 1: Input is temperature sensor. IE0 = 0: This sample will not create interrupt, IE0 = 1: This sample creates an ADC Interrupt. END0 = 0: This sample is not the last sample, END0 = 1: This sample is the last sample. D0 = 0: This sample is collected from a single-end mode, D0 = 1: This sample is collected from a differential-input mode.

This register contains the configuration information for each sample in a sequence executed with Sample Sequencer 0. This register is 32 bits wide and contains information for 8 possible samples. Since 8 samples can be collected by this SS0, this 32-bit register is divided into 8 nibbles and each nibble contains 4 bits, and each bit can be used to define a control property for a sample that is collected. Each 4 bits in a nibble includes (refer to Figure 7.15):

- TSn: Is this sample collected from a GPIO pin or from the ADC temperature sensor?
  - 0: This sample is collected from the input channel defined by ADCSSMUX0 register.
  - 1: This sample is collected from the internal temperature sensor.
- IEn: Can this sample trigger an interrupt when it is collected?
  - 0: This sample cannot trigger any interrupt when it is collected.
  - 1: This sample can trigger an ADC interrupt when it is collected.
- ENDn: Is this sample the last sample in this sequence?
  - 0: This sample is not the last sample in this sample sequence.
  - 1: This sample is the last sample in this sample sequence.
- Dn: Is this sample is collected in single-end mode or differential-input mode?
  - 0: This sample is collected from a single-end analog input.
  - 1: This sample is collected from a differential input mode.

In the case of Dn = 1, the corresponding ADCSSMUXn nibble must be set to the pair number i, where the paired inputs are 2i and 2i+1. Because the temperature sensor does not have a differential option, this bit must not be set when the TSn bit is set.

The n (=0~7) attached with each bit indicates the order number of the samples. Nibble7 includes 4 bits, TS7, IE7, END7, and D7, for the 7th sample. Nibble0 contains 4 bits, TS0, IE0, END0, and D0, for the first sample.

For example, if we want to use this register to collect 8 samples in SS0, with the 8th sample as the last sample and single-end mode, without using the temperature sensor and any interrupt, the bit-field values should be 0x2000.0000.

Similar to ADCSSMUXn register, the ADCSSCTL1 and the ADCSSCTL2 registers are used for SS1 and SS2 sample sequencers. Since these two sample sequencers can collect up to 4 samples, both ADCSSCTL registers only use the lower 16 bits to form 4 nibbles to define sample control functions for those 4 samples.

The memory mapping addresses for these two registers are:

- For ADC0: ADCSSCTL1 (0x40038064), ADCSSCTL2 (0x40038084).
- For ADC1: ADCSSCTL1 (0x40039064), ADCSSCTL2 (0x40039084).

The bit-field values for these two registers are shown in Figure 7.16. The bit-field value and related function of this register is shown in Table 7.9.

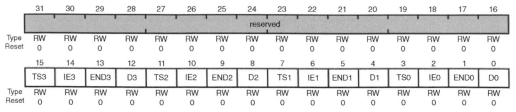

Figure 7.16. The bit fields for the ADCSSCTL1, 2 registers. (Reprinted with the permission of the Texas Instruments Incorporated.)

Table 7.9. Bit value and its function for ADCSSCTL1 and 2 registers.

Bit	Name	Reset	Function
31:16	Reserved	0x0	Reserved
15:12	TS3, IE3, END3, D3	0x0	The 4th sample control function select. TS3 = 0: Input comes from the ADCSSMUX0 MUX3, TS3 = 1: Input is temperature sensor. IE3 = 0: This sample will not create interrupt, IE3 = 1: This sample creates an ADC Interrupt. END3 = 0: This sample is not the last sample, END3 = 1: This sample is the last sample. D3 = 0: This sample is collected from a single-end mode, D3 = 1: This sample is collected from a differential-input mode.
11:8	TS2, IE2, END2, D2	0x0	The 3rd sample control function select. TS2 = 0: Input comes from the ADCSSMUX0 MUX2, TS2 = 1: Input is temperature sensor. IE2 = 0: This sample will not create interrupt, IE2 = 1: This sample creates an ADC Interrupt. END2 = 0: This sample is not the last sample, END2 = 1: This sample is the last sample. D2 = 0: This sample is collected from a single-end mode, D2 = 1: This sample is collected from a differential-input mode.
7:4	TS1, IE1, END1, D1	0x0	The 2nd sample control function select. TS1 = 0: Input comes from the ADCSSMUX0 MUX1, TS1 = 1: Input is temperature sensor. IE1 = 0: This sample will not create interrupt, IE1 = 1: This sample creates an ADC Interrupt. END1 = 0: This sample is not the last sample, END1 = 1: This sample is the last sample. D1 = 0: This sample is collected from a single-end mode, D1 = 1: This sample is collected from a differential-input mode.
3:0	TS0, IE0, END0, D0	0x0	The 1st sample control function select. TS0 = 0: Input comes from the ADCSSMUX0 MUX0, TS0 = 1: Input is temperature sensor. IE0 = 0: This sample will not create interrupt, IE0 = 1: This sample creates an ADC Interrupt. END0 = 0: This sample is not the last sample, END0 = 1: This sample is the last sample. D0 = 0: This sample is collected from a single-end mode, D0 = 1: This sample is collected from a differential-input mode.

These two registers contain the configuration information for each sample in a sequence executed with Sample Sequencers 1 and 2. These two registers are 32 bits wide and contain information for 4 possible samples. Since 4 samples can be collected by SS1 and SS2, these 32-bit registers are divided into 4 nibbles and each nibble contains 4 bits, and each bit can be used to define a control property for a sample that is collected.

The ADCSSCTL3 register is used for SS3 sample sequencer. Since this sample sequencer can collect up to 1 sample, this register only uses lower 4 bits to form 1 nibble to define the control function for this single sample.

The memory mapping addresses are: for ADC0, 0x400380A4; for ADC1, 0x400390A4.

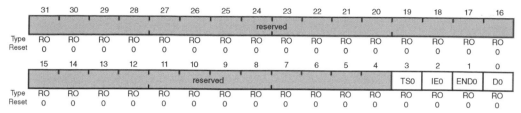

Figure 7.17. The bit fields for the ADCSSCTL3 register. (Reprinted with the permission of the Texas Instruments Incorporated.)

The bit-field values for this register are shown in Figure 7.17. The bit-field value and related function of this register is shown in Table 7.10.

This register defines the analog input configuration for the sample executed with Sample Sequencer 3. This register is 4 bits wide and contains information for one possible sample.

At this point, we finished discussions for all control registers used for all four sample sequencers, SS0~SS3, in the `Sample Sequencer n` blocks shown in Figure 7.8. However, these sample sequencers are also controlled by some registers in the `Control/Status` block, therefore we need also to discuss these registers one by one. These registers include:

- ADC `Active Sample Sequencer (ADCACTSS)` Register
- ADC `Processor Sample Sequencer Initiate (ADCPSSI)` Register
- ADC `Sample Sequencer Result FIFO (ADCSSFIFOn)` Register

First let's concentrate on the ADCACTSS register.

7.5.3.2.3 ADC Active Sample Sequencer (ADCACTSS) Register This register provides two functions; first the bit 16 (BUSY bit) on this register provides the current running status of the ADC. A 0 on this bit means that the ADC is idle, and a 1 means that the ADC is currently working on some conversion jobs. Secondly, the lowest 4 bits in this register are used to enable and disable any sample sequencer, SS0~SS3, with one bit for one sample sequencer.

The memory mapping addresses are: for ADC0, 0x40038000, for ADC1, 0x40039000.

The bit-field values for this register are shown in Figure 7.18.

Table 7.10. Bit value and its function for the ADCSSCTL3 register.

Bit	Name	Reset	Function
31:4	Reserved	0x0	Reserved
3:0	TS0, IE0, END0, D0	0x0	The 1st sample control function select. TS0 = 0: Input comes from the ADCSSMUX0 MUX0, TS0 = 1: Input is temperature sensor. IE0 = 0: This sample will not create interrupt, IE0 = 1: This sample creates an ADC Interrupt. END0 = 0: This sample is not the last sample, END0 = 1: This sample is the last sample. D0 = 0: This sample is collected from a single-end mode, D0 = 1: This sample is collected from a differential-input mode.

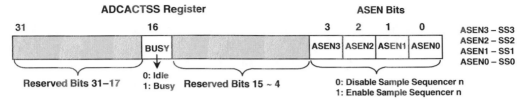

Figure 7.18. The bit fields for the ADCACTSS register.

When using this register to enable or disable the sample sequencers, the following points must be noted:

1. The BUSY bit (bit 16) on this register must be 0 before any configurations can be performed for any sample sequencers, SS0~SS3.

2. Before writing to the `Analog-to-Digital Converter Run Mode Clock Gating Control` (RCGCADC) register to enable the ADC clock, the BUSY bit on this register must be 0.

3. Before performing any configuration or programming to any sample sequencer, make sure that the sample sequencer is disabled by clearing the corresponding ASENn bit in this ADCACTSS register. One cannot do any configuration or programming to any sample sequencer until it is disabled. Programming of the sample sequencers is allowed without having them enabled.

Now let's take care of the ADC `Processor Sample Sequencer Initiate` (ADCPSSI) register.

7.5.3.2.4 ADC Processor Sample Sequencer Initiate (ADCPSSI) Register

This 32-bit register is used to initiate a sample sequencer or all sample sequencers to begin the sampling jobs after the sample sequencers are enabled by using the ADCACTSS register discussed in the last section. When multiple sequencers are initiated simultaneously, the priority encodings in the `ADC Sample Sequencer Priority` (ADCSSPRI) register indicates the execution order.

The memory mapping addresses are: for ADC0, 0x40038028; for ADC1, 0x40039028.

The bit-field values for this register are shown in Figure 7.19. The bit-field value and related function of this register are shown in Table 7.11.

This register also provides a method to configure and then initiate concurrent sampling on all ADC modules. To do this, the first ADC module should be configured. The ADCPSSI register for that module should then be written. The appropriate SS bits should

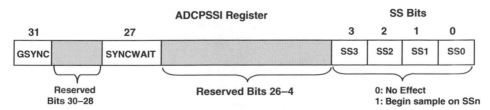

Figure 7.19. The bit fields for the ADCPSSI register.

Table 7.11. Bit value and its function for the ADCPSSI register.

Bit	Name	Reset	Function

31	GSYNC	0x0	Global Synchronization
			0: The sampling has been initiated.
			1: Initiates sampling in multiple ADC modules at the same time.
			   Any ADC module that has been initialized by setting an SSn bit and
			   the SYNCWAIT bit starts sampling once this bit is set to 1.

30:28	Reserved	0x0	Reserved

27	SYNCWAIT	0x0	Synchronization Wait
			0: Sampling begins when a sample sequence has been initiated
			   (no waiting).
			1: Allows the sample sequences to be initiated, but delays sampling until
			   the GSYNC bit is set.

26:4	Reserved	0x0	Reserved
3	SS3	0x0	SS3 Initiate. 0: No effect. 1: Begin sampling on SS3, if the sequencer is enabled in the ADCACTSS register.
2	SS2	0x0	SS2 Initiate. 0: No effect. 1: Begin sampling on SS2, if the sequencer is enabled in the ADCACTSS register.
1	SS1	0x0	SS1 Initiate. 0: No effect. 1: Begin sampling on SS1, if the sequencer is enabled in the ADCACTSS register.
0	SS0	0x0	SS0 Initiate. 0: No effect. 1: Begin sampling on SS0, if the sequencer is enabled in the ADCACTSS register.

be set along with the SYNCWAIT bit. Additional ADC modules should then be configured following the same procedure. Once the final ADC module is configured, its ADCPSSI register should be written with the appropriate SS bits set along with the GSYNC bit. All of the ADC modules then begin concurrent sampling according to their configuration.

It can be found from Table 7.11 that the bits GSYNC (bit 31) and SYNCWAIT (bit 27) in this register take effects only when the multiple sample sequencers are initiated synchronously. If only single sample sequencer or multiple sample sequencers are initiated at different times or nonsynchronously, you do not need to touch these two bits at all. To initiate any sample sequencer SSn, just set the associated SSn bit to 1 and leave the bits GSYNC and SYNCWAIT as 0.

7.5.3.2.5 ADC Sample Sequencer Result FIFO (ADCSSFIFOn) Register   There are four ADCSSFIFOn registers (n = 0 ~ 3) available in the ADC FIFO block shown in Figure 7.8. Each ADCSSFIFO register is a 32-bit register and matched to a sample sequencer, ADCSSFIFO0 is for SS0, ADCSSFIFO1 is for SS1, and so on. These ADCSSFIFO registers are used to store the ADC conversion results, and reads of these registers return conversion result data in the order sample 0, sample 1, and so on, until the FIFO is empty. Because the ADC module contains a 12-bit Analog-To-Digital converter,

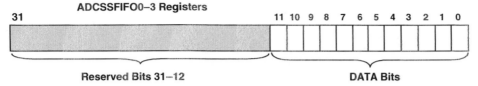

Figure 7.20.   The bit fields for four ADCSSFIFOn registers.

the conversion result is 12-bit, and therefore only the lower 12-bit are used for these four 32-bit FIFO registers.

The memory mapping addresses for these four FIFO registers are:

• For ADC0 –	ADCSSFIFO0: 0x40038048, ADCSSFIFO1: 0x40038068
	ADCSSFIFO2: 0x40038088, ADCSSFIFO3: 0x400380A8
• For ADC1 –	ADCSSFIFO0: 0x40039048, ADCSSFIFO1: 0x40039068
	ADCSSFIFO2: 0x40039088, ADCSSFIFO3: 0x400390A8

The bit-field values for these four registers are shown in Figure 7.20.

The upper 20 bits on these registers are reserved and the lower 12 bits, bits 11~0, are used to store the conversion results.

7.5.3.3 ADC Module Control Functions and Related Registers

In addition to sample sequencer controls, another important component in the ADC module is the module controls. This component contains the following controls except the Analog-to-Digital converter:

- ADC Module Clocking
- ADC Interrupt Request and Handling
- Sampling Events and Trigger Sources
- DMA Operations
- Sequence prioritization

Now let's discuss these issues one by one in the following sections.

7.5.3.3.1 ADC Module Clocking   Most of the ADC control logics run at the ADC clock rate of 16 MHz. The internal ADC divider is configured for 16-MHz operation automatically by hardware when the system XTAL is selected with the PLL.

The ADC module is generally clocked by a 16-MHz clock that can be sourced by a divided version of the PLL output, the PIOSC or an external source connected to MOSC with the PLL in bypass mode. When we select these different sources as the clock source to the ADC module, the following operations should be performed:

1. When the PLL is selected as the clock source, the ADC clock is derived from the PLL $\div 25$ (400 MHz $\div 25 = 16$ MHz) by default.
2. When the PIOSC is selected as the clock source, the ADC Clock Configuration (ADCCC) register should be used to configure this kind of source. To use the PIOSC to clock the ADC, first power up the PLL and then enable the PIOSC in the CS bit field in the ADCCC register, and then disable the PLL.

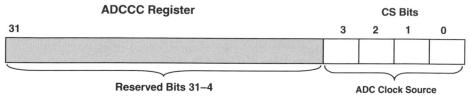

Figure 7.21. The bit fields for the ADCCC register.

3. When the PLL is bypassed, the module clock source attached to the MOSC must be 16 MHz unless the PIOSC is used for the clock source. To use the MOSC to clock the ADC, first power up the PLL and then enable the clock to the ADC module, and then disable the PLL and switch to the MOSC for the system clock. The ADC module can continue to operate in Deep-Sleep mode if the PIOSC is the ADC module clock source.

The system clock must be at the same frequency or higher than the ADC clock. Two ADC modules (ADC0 and ADC1) share the same clock source to facilitate (a) the synchronization of data samples between conversion units, (b) the selection, and (c) the programming. The clock source is basically selected and determined by the ADC0 module's ADCCC register. Both ADC modules always run at the same conversion rate.

The ADC Clock Configuration (ADCCC) register controls the clock source for the ADC module.

The memory mapping addresses for this register are: for ADC0, 0x40038FC8; for ADC1, 0x40039FC8.

The bit-field values for this register are shown in Figure 7.21. The bit-field value and related function of this register are shown in Table 7.12.

It can be found from Table 7.12 that only the lowest 4 bits are used in the ADCCC register to determine the clock source for the ADC modules. When these 4 bits are 0x0000, either the 16-MHz system clock or a 16-MHz clock driven by the PLL/25 can be used as the clock source for both ADC modules. As these 4 bits become 0x0001, the PIOSC can be used as a clock source but the frequency of this PIOSC must be 16 MHz.

Table 7.12. Bit-field value and its function for the ADCCC register.

Bit	Name	Reset	Function
31:4	Reserved	0x0	Reserved
3:0	CS	0x0	ADC Clock Source. 0x0 : Either the 16-MHz system clock (if the PLL bypass is in effect) or the 16-MHz clock derived from PLL ÷ 25 (default). Note that when the PLL is bypassed, the system clock must be at least 16 MHz. 0x1 : PIOSC The PIOSC provides a 16-MHz clock source for the ADC. If the PIOSC is used as the clock source, the ADC module can continue to operate in Deep-Sleep mode. 0x2 – 0xF Reserved

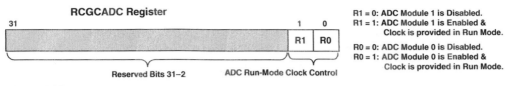

Figure 7.22. The bit fields for the RCGCADC register.

After a system reset, the default value for these 4 bits are 0x0000, which means that either the 16-MHz system clock or a 16-MHz clock driven by the PLL/25 can be used as the clock source for both ADC modules.

In addition to using the ADCCC register to initialize and configure the clock source for the ADC modules, another popular way is to use the ADC Run Mode Clock Gating Control (RCGCADC) register.

The RCGCADC register provides software the ability to enable and disable the ADC modules in Run mode. When enabled, an ADC module is provided a clock and accessing to all module registers is allowed. When disabled, the clock is disabled to save power and accessing to any module register generates a bus fault. This register provides the same capability as the legacy Run Mode Clock Gating Control Register n (RCGCn) registers specifically for the watchdog modules and has the same bit polarity as the corresponding RCGCn bits.

The memory mapping address for this register is 0x400FE638. The bit-field values for this register are shown in Figure 7.22.

As shown in Figure 7.22, the two lowest bits, R1 and R0, are used to enable or disable two ADC modules (R1 → Module1, R0 → Module 0) with the clocks provided.

7.5.3.3.2 ADC Interrupt Request and Handling
There are two types of interrupts can be generated and handled in the ADC modules: One is generated by the sample sequencers and the other is created by the digital comparators. The first one is called the sequencer interrupt and the second is called the digital comparator interrupt.

In the TM4C123GH6PM MCU system, six control registers can be used to control and monitor those two types of interrupts, they are

- ADC Sample Sequencer Control (ADCSSCTLn) Registers
- ADC Raw Interrupt Status (ADCRIS) Register
- ADC Interrupt Mask (ADCIM) Register
- ADC Interrupt Status and Clear (ADCISC) Register
- ADC Digital Comparator Control (ADCDCCTLn) Registers
- ADC Digital Comparator Interrupt Status and Clear (ADCDCISC) Register

The top four registers are used to control and monitor the sample sequencer interrupts and the lower two registers are used to control the digital comparators interrupts.

The procedure of generating and handling a sample sequencer interrupt is as follows:

1. The selected sample that will create an interrupt is determined by setting the related IEn bit in the ADCSSCTLn register. In this way, the selected sample is enabled to generate an interrupt when it finished its ADC conversion.

2. As the selected sample is converted to a digital value, the corresponding INRn bit in the ADCRIS register will be set to 1 to generate a raw interrupt for the SSn.

3. If the corresponding MASKn bit in the ADCIM register is set to 1 (unmask), the INRn bit in the ADCRIS register will generate an SSn interrupt and sent to the NVIC to be processed.

4. After an SSn interrupt is generated and sent to the NVIC, the corresponding INn bit in the ADCISC register is set to 1 to indicate this situation. This interrupt can be cleared by writing 1 to the corresponding INn bit in this ADCISC register. The corresponding INRn bit in the ADCRIS register is also cleared when performing this writing 1 action.

5. When an SSn interrupt is sent to the NVIC and responded, the program control will be transferred to the corresponding interrupt handler ADCnSSn_Handler() to process this interrupt. The users need to develop the codes for this handler to response the interrupt.

The procedure of generating and handling a digital comparator interrupt is similar to the procedure of generating and handling a sample sequencer interrupt except the handler's name.

Now let's have a closer look at these control registers to see how they work.

The ADCSSCTLn registers have been discussed in Section 7.5.3.2.2 and therefore we can start our discussion from ADCRIS register.

7.5.3.3.2.1 ADC Raw Interrupt Status (ADCRIS) Register This register is used to show the status of the raw interrupt signal of each sample sequencer. The related INRn bit is set to 1 if a selected sample finished its ADC conversion and it has been enabled by configuring the IEn bit in the ADCSSCTLn register. These bits may be polled by software to look for interrupt conditions without sending the interrupts to the interrupt controller.

The memory mapping address for this register is: for ADC0, 0x40038004; for ADC1, 0x40039004. The bit-field values for this register are shown in Figure 7.23. The bit-field value and related function of this register are shown in Table 7.13.

It can be found from Figure 7.23 and Table 7.13 that the 32-bit ADCRIS register only used the bit 16 and the lowest 4 bits to indicate the raw interrupt status for digital comparator and four sample sequencers. Each of the lowest 4 bits, INR3~INR0, represents the raw interrupt status of a sample sequencer, SS3~SS0, respectively. If one of these four bits is set to 1, this means that a sample in the corresponding sample sequencer has completed its ADC conversion and a raw interrupt has been established in this bit.

This raw interrupt cannot be sent to the NVIC to be further processed until the corresponding MASKn bit in the ADCIM register has been set to 1 to enable this interrupt to be sent to the NVIC.

To clear this raw interrupt status and this interrupt, one needs to perform writing 1 to the corresponding INn bit in the ADCISC register.

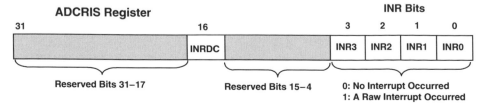

Figure 7.23. The bit fields for the ADCRIS register.

Table 7.13. Bit field value and its function for ADCRIS register.

Bit	Name	Reset	Function
31:17	Reserved	0x0	Reserved
16	INRDC	0x0	Digital Comparator Raw Interrupt Status. 0 : No digital comparator interrupt occurred. 1 : A digital comparator interrupt has occurred.
15:4	Reserved	0x0	Reserved
3	INR3	0x0	SS3 Raw Interrupt Status. 0 : No Interrupt Occurred. 1 : A SS3 raw interrupt has occurred. This bit is cleared by writing a 1 to the IN3 bit in the ADCISC register.
2	INR2	0x0	SS2 Raw Interrupt Status. 0 : No Interrupt Occurred. 1 : A SS2 raw interrupt has occurred. This bit is cleared by writing a 1 to the IN2 bit in the ADCISC register.
1	INR1	0x0	SS1 Raw Interrupt Status. 0 : No Interrupt Occurred. 1 : A SS1 raw interrupt has occurred. This bit is cleared by writing a 1 to the IN1 bit in the ADCISC register.
0	INR0	0x0	SS0 Raw Interrupt Status. 0 : No Interrupt Occurred. 1 : A SS0 raw interrupt has occurred. This bit is cleared by writing a 1 to the IN0 bit in the ADCISC register.

7.5.3.3.2.2 ADC Interrupt Mask (ADCIM) Register This register is used to control whether a sample sequencer or a digital comparator raw interrupt in the ADCRIS register can be sent to the interrupt controller to be further processed. Each raw interrupt can be masked (disabled) or unmasked (enabled) independently by the corresponding bits in this ADCIM register.

The memory mapping address for this register is: for ADC0, 0x40038008; for ADC1, 0x40039008. The bit-field values for this register are shown in Figure 7.24. The bit-field value and related function of this register is shown in Table 7.14.

As shown in Figure 7.24 and Table 7.14, four bits, bits 19~16, are used to unmask or mask four digital comparator interrupts. Four lowest bits, bits 3~0, are used to control four sample sequencers' interrupts. Whether any raw interrupt can be sent to the NVIC is determined by the corresponding mask bit's value in this register. Only the corresponding mask bit is set to 1; the raw interrupt, either from the digital comparator or from the sample sequencer, can be sent to the interrupt controller to be further processed.

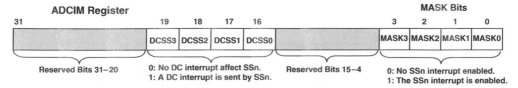

Figure 7.24. The bit fields for the ADCIM register.

Table 7.14. Bit field value and its function for ADCIM register.

Bit	Name	Reset	Function
31:20	Reserved	0x0	Reserved
19	DCSS3	0x0	Digital Comparator Interrupt on SS3. 0: No digital comparator interrupt affected SS3. 1: A digital comparator interrupt is enabled to be sent to NVIC via SS3 interrupt line.
18	DCSS2	0x0	Digital Comparator Interrupt on SS2. 0: No digital comparator interrupt affected SS2. 1: A digital comparator interrupt is enabled to be sent to NVIC via SS2 interrupt line.
17	DCSS1	0x0	Digital Comparator Interrupt on SS1. 0: No digital comparator interrupt affected SS1. 1: A digital comparator interrupt is enabled to be sent to NVIC via SS1 interrupt line.
16	DCSS0	0x0	Digital Comparator Interrupt on SS0. 0: No digital comparator interrupt affected SS0. 1: A digital comparator interrupt is enabled to be sent to NVIC via SS0 interrupt line.
15:4	Reserved	0x0	Reserved
3	MASK3	0x0	SS3 Interrupt Mask. 0: The sample sequencer 3 does not affect the SS3 interrupt status. 1: A SS3 raw interrupt is enabled to be sent to the NVIC.
2	MASK2	0x0	SS2 Interrupt Mask. 0: The sample sequencer 2 does not affect the SS2 interrupt status. 1: A SS2 raw interrupt is enabled to be sent to the NVIC.
1	MASK1	0x0	SS1 Interrupt Mask. 0: The sample sequencer 1 does not affect the SS1 interrupt status. 1: A SS1 raw interrupt is enabled to be sent to the NVIC.
0	MASK0	0x0	SS0 Interrupt Mask. 0: The sample sequencer 0 does not affect the SS0 interrupt status. 1: A SS0 raw interrupt is enabled to be sent to the NVIC.

This register should be used together with the ADCRIS register to enable the raw interrupt to be sent to the interrupt controller to be further processed.

7.5.3.3.2.3 ADC Interrupt Status and Clear (ADCISC) Register This register provides two functions to the interrupts generated by sample sequencers or digital comparators:

1. Show the status of interrupts generated by the sample sequencers and the digital comparators that have been sent to the interrupt controller. When read, each bit field is the logical AND of the respective INRn bit in the ADCRIS register and MASKn bit in the ADCIM register.
2. Clear the sample sequencer interrupts by writing a 1 to the corresponding bit in this register. Also the related INRn bit in the ADCRIS register is also cleared when writing a 1 to this ADCISC register.

Digital comparator interrupts are cleared by writing a 1 to the corresponding bits in the ADCDCISC register. If software is polling the ADCRIS instead of generating interrupts,

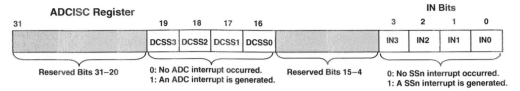

Figure 7.25. The bit fields for the ADCISC register.

the sample sequence INRn bits are still cleared via the ADCISC register, even if the INn bit is not set.

The memory mapping address for this register is: for ADC0, 0x4003800C; for ADC1, 0x4003900C. The bit-field values for this register are shown in Figure 7.25. The bit-field value and related function of this register are shown in Table 7.15.

As shown in Figure 7.25 and Table 7.15, this register can be used to monitor the interrupt status, either the digital comparator interrupt or the sample sequencer interrupt status. If a corresponding bit is set to 1, this means that the related interrupt has occurred and was sent to the NVIC. To clear an interrupt, just write a 1 to the related bit in this register. When an interrupt in this register is cleared, the related bit INRn in the ADCRIS register is also cleared.

As for ADC Digital Comparator Control (ADCDCCTLn) and ADC Digital Comparator Interrupt Status and Clear (ADCDCISC) registers, refer to TM4C123GH6PM MCU Data Sheet to get more details.

7.5.3.3.3 Sampling Events and Trigger Sources As shown in Figure 7.8 for the ADC architecture and control block diagram, each sample sequencer has four sampling events or trigger sources. One of these trigger events can be selected by the ADC Event Multiplexer Select (ADCEMUX) register as a sampling source and input to the sample sequencer.

In fact, more trigger events exist and can be used for each sample sequencer in the TM4C123GH6PM MCU system. These trigger events include:

- Microprocessor Cortex®-M4 (Default Trigger Event)
- Analog Comparators (Analog Comparator0 and Analog Comparator1)
- An External Signal Controlled by the GPIO ADC Control (GPIOADCCTL) Register
- A General Timer
- A PWM Generator (PWM0~PWM3)
- Continuous Sampling

Once the trigger event or source has been selected by the ADCEMUX register, the related sample sequencer can be initiated to perform the sampling job by setting the SSn bits in the ADC Processor Sequencer Initiate (ADCPSSI) register we discussed in Section 7.5.3.2.4.

Now let's have a closer look at two registers, ADCEMUX and GPIOADCCTL.

7.5.3.3.3.1 ADC Event Multiplexer Select (ADCEMUX) Register This register is used to select the trigger event that initiates sampling for each sample sequencer. Each sample sequencer can be configured with a unique trigger source. When using a PWM generator as

Table 7.15.   Bit field value and its function for ADCISC register.

Bit	Name	Reset	Function
31:20	Reserved	0x0	Reserved
19	DCSS3	0x0	Digital Comparator Interrupt Status on SS3. 0: No digital comparator interrupt occurred or the interrupt is masked. 1: A digital comparator interrupt is generated and sent to NVIC via SS3 interrupt line. This bit is cleared by writing a 1 to it. Clearing this bit also clears the INRDC bit in the ADCRIS register.
18	DCSS2	0x0	Digital Comparator Interrupt Status on SS2. 0: No digital comparator interrupt occurred or the interrupt is masked. 1: A digital comparator interrupt is generated and sent to NVIC via SS2 interrupt line. This bit is cleared by writing a 1 to it. Clearing this bit also clears the INRDC bit in the ADCRIS register.
17	DCSS1	0x0	Digital Comparator Interrupt Status on SS1. 0: No digital comparator interrupt occurred or the interrupt is masked. 1: A digital comparator interrupt is generated and sent to NVIC via SS1 interrupt line. This bit is cleared by writing a 1 to it. Clearing this bit also clears the INRDC bit in the ADCRIS register.
16	DCSS0	0x0	Digital Comparator Interrupt Status on SS0. 0: No digital comparator interrupt occurred or the interrupt is masked. 1: A digital comparator interrupt is generated and sent to NVIC via SS0 interrupt line. This bit is cleared by writing a 1 to it. Clearing this bit also clears the INRDC bit in the ADCRIS register.
15:4	Reserved	0x0	Reserved
3	IN3	0x0	SS3 Interrupt Status and Clear. 0: No interrupt is occurred or the interrupt is masked. 1: A SS3 interrupt is generated and sent to the NVIC. This bit is cleared by writing a 1. Clearing this bit also clears the INR3 bit in the ADCRIS register.
2	IN2	0x0	SS2 Interrupt Status and Clear. 0: No interrupt is occurred or the interrupt is masked. 1: A SS2 interrupt is generated and sent to the NVIC. This bit is cleared by writing a 1. Clearing this bit also clears the INR2 bit in the ADCRIS register.
1	IN1	0x0	SS1 Interrupt Status and Clear. 0: No interrupt is occurred or the interrupt is masked. 1: A SS1 interrupt is generated and sent to the NVIC. This bit is cleared by writing a 1. Clearing this bit also clears the INR1 bit in the ADCRIS register.
0	IN0	0x0	SS0 Interrupt Status and Clear. 0: No interrupt is occurred or the interrupt is masked. 1: A SS0 interrupt is generated and sent to the NVIC. This bit is cleared by writing a 1. Clearing this bit also clears the INR0 bit in the ADCRIS register.

the trigger source, this register selects which generator within a PWM module is used as a trigger, and the PSn field in the ADC Trigger Source Select (ADCTSSEL) register specifies the PWM module instance in which the generator is located.

This is a 32-bit register, but only the lower 16 bits are used to select a trigger event. The 16 bits are grouped into 4 nibbles, EM3~EM0, and each nibble is used to select one of six possible trigger sources for each related sample sequencer, SS3~SS0. The memory mapping address for this register is: for ADC0, 0x40038014; for ADC1, 0x40039014.

The bit-field values for this register are shown in Figure 7.26. The bit-field value and related function of this register is shown in Table 7.16.

It can be found from Figure 7.26 and Table 7.16 that each nibble, EM3~EM0, provides 16 possible trigger sources for the corresponding sample sequencer, SS3~SS0, respectively. In

ADCEMUX Register

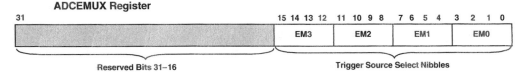

Figure 7.26. The bit fields for the ADCEMUX register.

fact, only 10 trigger sources can be selected for each sample sequencer since all other six statuses are reserved for the future use. The default trigger source is the Cortex®-M4 processor.

All four nibbles have the same values for the trigger sources to be selected.

7.5.3.3.3.2 GPIO ADC Control (GPIOADCCTL) Register This register is used to configure a GPIO pin as a source for the ADC trigger.

Each GPIO Port has an independent GPIOADCCTL register to control and configure its 8-pin to work as an ADC source pin. If the GPIO Port B GPIOADCCTL register is cleared, the PB4 pin can still be used as an external trigger for the ADC. This is a legacy mode that allows a code written for previous devices to operate on this microcontroller.

Table 7.16. Bit field value and its function for the ADCEMUX register.

Bit	Name	Reset	Function
31:16	Reserved	0x0	Reserved
15:12	EM3	0x0	SS3 Trigger Select. 0x0: Processor (default). The trigger is initiated by setting SSn bit in the ADCPSSI register. 0x1: Analog Comparator 0. This trigger is configured by the ACCTL0 register. 0x2: Analog Comparator 1. This trigger is configured by the ACCTL1 register. 0x3: Reserved. 0x4: External (GPIO Pins). This trigger is connected to the GPIO interrupt for a GPIO pin. 0x5: Timer. The trigger must be enabled with the TnOTE bit in the GPTMCTL register. 0x6: PWM Generator 0. The PWM0 trigger is configured by the PWM0INTEN register. 0x7: PWM Generator 1. The PWM1 trigger is configured by the PWM1INTEN register. 0x8: PWM Generator 2. The PWM2 trigger is configured by the PWM2INTEN register. 0x9: PWM Generator 3. The PWM3 trigger is configured by the PWM3INTEN register. 0xF: Always (Continuous Sample). 0xA – 0xE: Reserved.
11:8	EM2	0x0	SS2 Trigger Select. 0x0 – 0xF: Identical with SS3 Trigger Select.
7:4	EM1	0x0	SS1 Trigger Select. 0x0 – 0xF: Identical with SS3 Trigger Select.
3:0	EM0	0x0	SS0 Trigger Select. 0x0 – 0xF: Identical with SS3 Trigger Select.

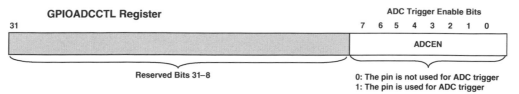

Figure 7.27. The bit fields for the GPIOADCCTL register.

This is a 32-bit register, but only the lowest 8 bits are used to provide control for each pin on the selected port. The memory mapping offset address for this register is 0x530. The bit-field values for this register are shown in Figure 7.27.

As shown in Figure 7.27, each bit corresponds to a pin in the selected GPIO Port. If a bit is 0, this means that the corresponding pin is not used to trigger the ADC. But if a bit is 1, this means that the corresponding pin is used to trigger the ADC.

Now let's take a look at other module control functions.

7.5.3.3.4 DMA Operations The Direct Memory Access (DMA) technique may be used to increase the transferring efficiency of samples by enabling each sample sequencer to operate independently and transfer data without using the microprocessor intervention or reconfiguration. The ADC module provides a request signal from each sample sequencer to the associated dedicated channel of the μDMA controller. The ADC does not support single transfer requests. A burst transfer request is generated when the interrupt bit for the sample sequence is set, or the IE bit in the ADCSSCTLn register is set.

The arbitration size of the μDMA transfer must be a power of 2, and the associated IE bits in the ADCSSCTLn register must be set. For example, if the μDMA channel of SS0 has an arbitration size of four, the IE3 bit or the 4th sample and the IE7 bit or the 8th sample must be set. Thus the μDMA request occurs every time 4 samples have been acquired. No other special steps are needed to enable the ADC module for μDMA operation.

Next let's concentrate on the ADC itself and its related properties.

7.5.4 Analog-to-Digital Converter

In the TM4C123GH6PM MCU system, the Analog-to-Digital Converter (ADC) module uses a Successive Approximation Register (SAR) architecture to deliver 12-bit, low-power, high-precision conversion values. The successive approximation uses a switched capacitor array to perform the dual functions of sampling and holding the signal as well as providing the 12-bit DAC operation.

The ADC can operate from both the 3.3V analog and 1.2V digital power supplies. The ADC clock can be configured to reduce power consumption when ADC conversions are not required. The analog inputs are connected to the ADC through specially balanced input paths to minimize the distortion and cross-talk on the inputs.

Two ADC modules share 12 analog input channels via different GPIO pins. Since GPIO pins can be configured to be connected to different peripherals to perform multiple functions, the GPIOAFSEL register must be configured to enable GPIO pins to do these alternate jobs or functions. The voltage range of the power supply and the reference voltage determines the resolution of the ADC.

7.5.4.1 *Voltage Reference and Resolutions*

In the TM4C123GH6PM MCU system, the ADC uses internal signals Voltage Reference Positive (VREFP) and Voltage Reference Negative (VREFN) as references to produce a conversion value from the selected analog input. The VREFP is connected to the analog power supply VDDA, and VREFN is connected to the analog ground GNDA.

The range of the ADC conversion value is from 0x000 to 0xFFF. When working in the single-ended-input mode, the 0x000 value corresponds to the voltage level on VREFN; the 0xFFF value corresponds to the voltage level on VREFP. This configuration results in a resolution that can be calculated using the following equation:

ADC Conversion Resolution $=$ (VREFP-VREFN)/4096

While the analog input pads can handle voltages beyond this range, the analog input voltages must remain 0~VDDA for the single-ended-input mode, and –VDDA ~ VDDA for the differential-input mode.

7.5.4.2 *Differential Input Mode*

Besides the traditional single-ended input mode, the ADC module supports the differential-input mode for two analog input channels. To enable the ADC to work in the differential-input mode, software must set the Dn bit in the ADCSSCTL0n register in a step's configuration nibble.

When a sequence step is configured for differential sampling, the input pair to sample must be configured in the ADCSSMUXn register. Differential pair 0 samples analog input channels 0 and 1; differential pair 1 samples analog input channels 2 and 3; and so on. Table 7.17 lists the relationship between each of the differential pair inputs and related input channels. The ADC does not support other differential pairings such as analog input 0 with analog input 3.

The voltage sampled in differential mode is the difference between the odd and even channels since they are paired:

- Input Positive Voltage: $V_{IN+} = V_{IN\_EVEN}$ (even channel)
- Input Negative Voltage: $V_{IN-} = V_{IN\_ODD}$ (odd channel)

The input differential voltage is then defined as $V_{IND} = V_{IN+} - V_{IN-}$; therefore:

- If $V_{IND} = 0$, then the conversion result equals 0x800
- If $V_{IND} > 0$, then the conversion result is greater than 0x800 (range is 0x800~0xFFF)
- If $V_{IND} < 0$, then the conversion result is less than 0x800 (range is 0x000~0x800)

Table 7.17. Differential input pair channels.

Differential Input Pair	Analog Input Channels
0	0 and 1
1	2 and 3
2	4 and 5
3	6 and 7
4	8 and 9
5	10 and 11

The maximum possible differential input swing, or the maximum differential range, is from −VREFD to +VREFD, so the maximum peak-to-peak input differential signal is [+VREFD − (−VREFD)] = 2 ∗ VREFD = 2 ∗ (VREFP − VREFN).

Because the maximum peak-to-peak differential signal voltage is 2 ∗ (VREFP − VREFN), the ADC resolution under the differential-input mode is

ADC Conversion Resolution = (2∗(VREFP − VREFN))/4096

When using a differential-input mode, the following conditions are important:

1. The Input Common Mode Voltage: $V_{INCM} = (V_{IN+} + V_{IN-})/2$.
2. The Reference Positive Voltage: VREFP.
3. The Reference Negative Voltage: VREFN.
4. The Reference Differential Voltage: VREFD = VREFP − VREFN.
5. The Reference Common Mode Voltage: VREFCM = (VREFP + VREFN)/2.

The following conditions can provide the optimal results in differential mode:

1. Both VIN_EVEN and VIN_ODD must be in the range of (VREFP to VREFN) for a valid conversion result.
2. The maximum possible differential input swing, or the maximum differential range, is: −VREFD to +VREFD, so the maximum peak-to-peak input differential signal is

$$+VREFD − (−VREFD) = 2∗VREFD = 2∗(VREFP − VREFN)$$

3. In order to take advantage of the maximum possible differential input swing, V_{INCM} should be very close to V_{REFCM}.

If V_{INCM} is not equal to V_{REFCM}, the differential input signals may clip at either maximum or minimum voltage since the single-ended input can never be larger than VREFP or smaller than VREFN, and it is impossible to achieve full swing. Thus any difference in common mode between the input voltage and the reference voltage limits the differential dynamic range of the ADC.

7.5.4.3 Internal Temperature Sensor

There is an internal temperature sensor is provided with the ADC modules. The temperature sensor provides two primary functions: (1) It notifies the system that internal temperature is too high or too low for reliable operation of the ADC, and (2) it provides temperature measurements for calibration of the Hibernate module RTC trim value.

The temperature sensor does not have any separate enable control, because it also contains the band-gap reference and must always be enabled. The reference is also supplied to other analog modules, not just the ADC. In addition, the temperature sensor has a second power-down input in the 3.3V domain which provides control by the Hibernation module.

The internal temperature sensor converts a temperature measurement into a voltage. This voltage value, VTSENS, is given by the following equation (where TEMP is the temperature in °C):

VTSENS = 2.7 − ((TEMP + 55)/75)

The temperature sensor reading can be sampled in a sample sequencer by setting the TSn bit in the ADCSSCTLn register (refer to Section 7.5.3.2.2 for ADCSSCTLn registers). The temperature reading from the temperature sensor can also be given as a function of the ADC value. The following formula calculates temperature (TEMP in °C) based on the ADC reading that is an ADC_{CODE} given as an unsigned decimal number from 0 to 4095) and the maximum ADC voltage range (VREFP – VREFN):

$$TEMP = 147.5 - ((75*(VREFP - VREFN) \times ADC_{CODE})/4096)$$

One can use either way to get the real temperature from the temperature sensor.

At this point, we have finished all discussions about the ADC modules and most components and controls with this device. Now let's start to use this device to do some real implementations. First let's take a look at how to initialize and configure this device.

7.5.5 Initialization and Configuration

Depending on the various components and control blocks applied in the ADC modules, this initialization job can be divided into three major parts:

- Initialize the GPIO Ports and pins related to ADC modules.
- Initialize ADC module.
- Initialize sample sequencers.

Let's have a closer look at these initializations one by one in the following sections.

7.5.5.1 ADC-Related GPIO Ports Initialization

As we discussed in Section 7.5.3.1, two ADC modules in TM4C123GH6PM MCU system are related to GPIO Ports. This means that all inputs and outputs of ADC modules are transferred via some GPIO pins. Two ADC modules are closely related to GPIO Ports, and all ADC input channels are connected to related GPIO pins.

Twelve ADC input channels are connected to GPIO Ports B, D, and E. Refer to Table 7.1, column 3 (Analog Function); 12 ADC input channels, AIN0~AIN11, are connected to related GPIO Ports or pins. Refer to Table 7.3 to get a clear picture and relationship between different ADC input channels and related GPIO pins.

In order to enable GPIO pins to work as ADC input pins, the following configuration jobs should be performed:

1. Enable the clock to the appropriate GPIO modules via the RCGCGPIO or RCGC2 register.
2. The AFSEL bits (lower 8 bits) in the GPIO Alternate Function Select (GPIOAF-SEL) register must be set to 1 to enable the selected pins to work as analog inputs (refer to Section 7.5.3.1.1).
3. The related bits in the GPIO Digital Enable (GPIODEN) register must be cleared to disable the digital function and enable the analog function (refer to Section 7.5.3.1.2).
4. Also the related AMSEL bits (lower 8 bits) in the GPIO Analog Mode Select (GPIOAM-SEL) register should be set to 1 to disable the analog isolation circuits to enable the selected pin to work as analog input pin (refer to Section 7.5.3.1.3).

5. Optionally, you can use GPIO ADC Control (GPIOADCCTL) register to configure a GPIO pin as a source for the ADC trigger. By default, the processor is selected as the trigger source and the trigger is initiated by setting SSn bit in the ADCPSSI register (Section 7.5.3.3.3.2).

7.5.5.2 ADC Module Initialization

In order for the ADC module to be used as analog-to-digital converters, the PLL mode must be enabled and programmed to a supported crystal frequency in the RCC register (refer to Section 2.6.4.4 in Chapter 2 to get more details for this register). Using unsupported frequencies can cause faulty operation in the ADC module.

The initialization sequence for the ADC module is as follows:

1. Enable the ADC module clock by configuring the RCGCADC register to set bits R1 or R0 to 1 (see Section 7.5.3.3.1).
2. Optionally, you can configure the ADCCC register to select the different clock source for the ADC module. By default, the CS bits in the ADCCC register is 0x0 after a system reset, which means that either the 16-MHz system clock (if the PLL is bypassed) or the 16-MHz clock derived from PLL ÷ 25 is selected. The latter is a default setting after a system reset (refer to Section 7.5.3.3.1).
3. If required by the application, reconfigure the sample sequencer priorities in the ADCSSPRI register. The default configuration has Sample Sequencer 0 with the highest priority and Sample Sequencer 3 as the lowest priority.

Next let's take a look at the sample sequencer initialization process.

7.5.5.3 Sample Sequencers Initialization

The initialization and configuration process for the sample sequencers are more complex than the module initialization because each sample sequencer has many different control parameters for each sample and each of them can be independently programmable.

The configuration process for each sample sequencer includes the following:

1. Before any sample sequencer can be configured or programmed, all sample sequencers must be disabled by clearing the corresponding ASENn bit in the ADCACTSS register (refer to Section 7.5.3.2.3). Programming of any sample sequencers is not allowed without having them enabled. Disabling the sequencer during programming prevents erroneous execution if a trigger event occurred during the configuration process.
2. Configure and select the trigger event for the sample sequencer in the ADCEMUX register (refer to Section 7.5.3.3.3.1).
3. When using a PWM generator as the trigger source, use the ADCTSSEL register to select from which PWM module the generator is located. The default setting selects the PWM module 0 for all generators.
4. For each sample in the sample sequencer, configure the corresponding input source in the ADCSSMUXn register (refer to Section 7.5.3.2.1).
5. For each sample in the sample sequencer, configure the sample control property in the corresponding nibble in the ADCSSCTLn register (refer to Section 7.5.3.2.2). When programming the last nibble, ensure that the END bit is set. Failure to set the END bit causes unpredictable behavior.

6. If interrupts are used, set the corresponding MASKn bit in the ADCIM register and the IEn bit in the ADCSSCTLn register to enable the selected sample to generate an interrupt when it is converted to a digital value. After an interrupt is handled, the related INn bit in the ADCISC register should be set to 1 to clear that interrupt to enable the future interrupt to be occurred.

7. Enable the sample sequencer logic by setting the corresponding ASENn bit in the ADCACTSS register.

8. Initiate the selected sample sequencer by setting related SSn bits in the ADCPSSI register (refer to Section 7.5.3.2.4).

Relatively, the initialization and configuration process for the sample sequencers is more complicated since it needs eight steps to finish these operations.

Now let's start to build our projects to use ADC modules to develop interesting applications.

7.5.6 Build the Analog-to-Digital Converter Programming Project

Four of 12 analog channels are interfaced between the TM4C123GXL EVB and the EduBASE ARM® Trainer, they are AIN1~AIN3 and AIN8. In order to build some implementation applications, first let's have a closer look at these analog interfaces.

7.5.6.1 ADC Module in EduBASE ARM® Trainer

A functional block diagram for the ADC module, GPIO pins, and AIN1~AIN3, and AIN8 input channels in the EduBASE ARM® Trainer is shown in Figure 7.28.

Three analog input channels, AIN1, AIN2, and AIN8, are connected to three peripherals:

- AIN8 is connected to the output of a temperature sensor LM45 via PE5, and this channel collects an analog voltage converted by this temperature sensor.

- AIN1 is connected to a potentiometer VR2 via PE2, and this channel collects an analog input voltage from this potentiometer (0~3.3 V).

- AIN2 is connected to a photo sensor VEMT2520 via PE1, and this channel collects an analog input signal from the output of this phototransistor.

Three analog channels, AIN1, AIN2, and AIN8, are connected to the EduBASE ARM® Trainer via three GPIO Port E pins, PE2, PE1, and PE5.

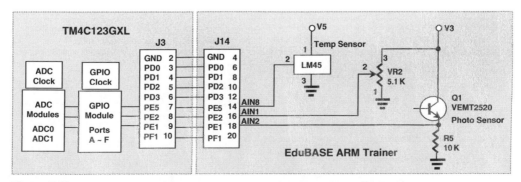

Figure 7.28. Functional block diagram of the ADC module in the EduBASE Trainer.

Although four analog input channels, AIN1~AIN3 and AIN8, are connected to the EduBASE ARM® Trainer via GPIO Port E, only three channels are connected with analog peripherals and AIN3 is not connected to any peripheral and it is open to be used for other analog source.

In the following we will create an ADC-module-related project DRAADCPoll by using the Direct Register Access method. This project contains the following features:

- The ADC module 0 or ADC0 with sample sequencer 1 (SS1) is used for this project to collect three analog signals coming from potentiometer VR2, photosensor Q1, and temperature sensor LM45 via three channels, AIN2, AIN1, and AIN8.
- The polling-driven method will be used to monitor and check the ADC conversion status.
- AIN1 collects the output voltage from the potentiometer VR2. AIN2 gets the analog voltage from the photosensor Q1, and AIN8 samples the output voltage from the LM45 temperature sensor.
- The conversion result for channel AIN1 is displayed in the three-color LED via GPIO Port F in the TM4C123GXL EVB. The conversion result for AIN2 is displayed in four LEDs, PB0– PB3, in the EduBASE ARM® Trainer, and the conversion result for AIN8 is sent to the speaker via GPIO Port C in the EduBASE ARM® Trainer.

Now let's create our ADC project DRAADCPoll.

7.5.6.2 Create the ADC Programming Project (Polling-Driven)

Perform the following operations to create a new project DRAADCPoll:

1. Open the Windows Explorer window to create a new folder named DRAADCPoll under the C:\ARM Class Projects\Chapter 7 folder.
2. Open the Keil® ARM-MDK µVersion5 and go to the Project|New µVersion Project menu item to create a new µVersion Project. On the opened wizard, browse to our new folder DRAADCPoll that is created in step 1 above. Enter DRAADCPoll into the File name box, and click on the Save button to create this project.
3. On the next wizard, you need to select the device (MCU) for this project. Expand three icons, Texas Instruments, Tiva C Series, and TM4C123x Series, and select the target device TM4C123GH6PM from the list by clicking on it. Click on the OK to close this wizard.
4. Next the Software Components wizard is opened, and you need to set up the software development environment for your project with this wizard. Expand two icons, CMSIS and Device, and check the CORE and Startup checkboxes in the Sel. column, and click on the OK button since we need these two components to build our project.

Since this project is relatively simple, only a C source file is good enough.

7.5.6.3 Create the Source File DRAADCPoll.c

Perform the following operations to create a new C source file DRAADCPoll.c:

1. In the Project pane, expand the Target folder and right click on the Source Group 1 folder and select the Add New Item to Group 'Source Group 1'.
2. Select the C File (.c) and enter DRAADCPoll into the Name: box, and click on the Add button to add this source file into the project.
3. Enter the codes shown in Figure 7.29 into this source file.

```
1   //*********************************************************************************************
2   // DRAADCPoll.c - Main Application File for ADC Module ADC0
3   //*********************************************************************************************
4   #include <stdint.h>
5   #include <stdbool.h>
6   #include "tm4c123gh6pm.h"
7   void Delay(uint32_t time);
8   int main(void)
9   {
10      int pSensor, pMeter, pTemp;
11      // initialize ADC0 related GPIO Ports. Ports B, C, E & F and ADC0 clock
12      SYSCTL_RCGC2_R =
13      SYSCTL_RCGC2_GPIOE|SYSCTL_RCGC2_GPIOB|SYSCTL_RCGC2_GPIOF|SYSCTL_RCGC2_GPIOC;
14      SYSCTL_RCGCADC_R |= 0x1;                     // enable clock to drive ADC module
15      GPIO_PORTE_AFSEL_R = 0x3F;                   // enable PE0 – PE5 work as alternate function
16      GPIO_PORTE_DEN_R = ~0x3F;                    // define PE0 – PE5 as input pins
17      GPIO_PORTE_AMSEL_R = 0x3F;                   // disable analog isolation circuit for PE0 – PE5
18      GPIO_PORTB_DEN_R = 0xF;                      // enable PB3 – PB0 as digital function pins
19      GPIO_PORTB_DIR_R = 0xF;                      // configure PB3 – PB0 as output pins
20      GPIO_PORTC_DIR_R = 0x10;                     // set PC4 as output pin
21      GPIO_PORTC_DEN_R = 0x10;                     // enable PC4 as digital function
22      GPIO_PORTF_DEN_R = 0xF;                      // enable PF3 – PF0 as digital function pins
23      GPIO_PORTF_DIR_R = 0xF;                      // configure PF3 – PF0 as output pins
24      // initialize ADC module 0 - ADC0
25      GPIO_PORTE_ADCCTL_R = 0x0;                   // use default trigger source - processor
26      // initialize ADC0 Sample Sequencer 1- SS1
27      ADC0_ACTSS_R &= ~ ADC_ACTSS_ASEN1;           // disable ADC0 SS1
28      ADC0_EMUX_R = ADC_EMUX_EM1_PROCESSOR;        // select the default trigger source
29      ADC0_SSMUX1_R |= 0x0821;                     // 1st sample AIN1, 2nd sample-AIN2, 3rd sample-AIN8
30      ADC0_SSCTL1_R |= 0x0600;                     // end at 3rd sample with interrupt
31      ADC0_ACTSS_R |= ADC_ACTSS_ASEN1;             // enable ADC0 SS1
32      while(1)
33      {
34         ADC0_PSSI_R = ADC_PSSI_SS1;               // initiate SS1
35         while((ADC0_RIS_R & 2) == 0);             // polling to wait for ADC conversion done
36         pMeter = ADC0_SSFIFO1_R;                  // read the 1st sample from AIN1
37         pSensor =ADC0_SSFIFO1_R;                  // read the 2nd sample from AIN2
38         pTemp =ADC0_SSFIFO1_R;                    // read the 3rd sample from AIN8
39         ADC0_ISC_R = ADC_ISC_IN1;                 // clear the interrupt in RIS
40         GPIO_PORTF_DATA_R = pMeter >> 8;          // send 4 MSB in the 1st sample to LEDs PF3 ~ PF1
41         GPIO_PORTB_DATA_R = pSensor >> 8;         // send 4 MSB in the 2nd sample to LEDs PB3 ~ PB0
42         GPIO_PORTC_DATA_R = pTemp << 2;           // send 3rd sample * 4 to speaker
43         Delay(50000);
44      }
45   }
46   void Delay(uint32_t time)
47   {
48      uint32_t Loop;
49      for (Loop = 0; Loop < time; Loop++) {}
50   }
```

Figure 7.29. The source codes for the DARADCPoll.c.

Let's have a closer look at this source file to see how it works.

1. Three system header files, stdint.h, stdbool.h, and tm4c123gh6pm.h, are included first at lines 4~6 in this source file since we need to use them in this project. In fact, we need to use all macros defined for GPIO Ports and ADC controls to access related registers and components in this project via different GPIO pins. All of these registers and pins are defined in the header file tm4c123gh6pm.h.

2. A user-defined function Delay() is declared here, and it is used to delay some period of time during the project runs.

3. Three local variables, pSensor, pMeter, and pTemp, are declared in the beginning of the main() program. These variables are used to receive and hold the ADC conversion results for three peripherals, potentiometer, photosensor, and temperature sensor, in line 10.

4. In line 12, four GPIO Ports, Ports B, C, E and F, are enabled with the individual clocks. Ports B, C, and F are used to drive related output devices to display the conversion results. Port B drives four LEDs, PB3~PB0, on the EduBASE Trainer, and Port C to drives a speaker, and Port F drives a three-color LED via PF3~PF1. Port E is used to interface to the ADC0 module to provide input paths or channels for ADC0.

5. The clock is enabled to drive the ADC module 0 (ADC0) via RCGCADC register in line 14. Recall in Section 7.5.3.3.1, that the bit-0 (R0) in this register is used to control the ADC0. A 1 in this bit enables the ADC0.

6. The codes in lines 15~17 are used to configure the GPIO Port E and related pins to work as an alternate function, the ADC function. These configurations include enabling PE5~PE0 to work as analog input pins and disabling the analog isolation circuit for these pins.

7. The codes in lines 18~23 are used to configure three GPIO Ports, B, C, and F, to enable them to work as output ports and pins to drive related LEDs and a speaker installed in the EduBASE Trainer and the TM4C123GXL EVB, respectively.

8. In line 25, the default trigger source, processor, is selected for the ADC0 module. Recall in Section 7.5.3.3.3.2 that the nibble EM1 (bits 7~4) in the GPIOADCCTL register is used to select the trigger source for the sample sequencer 1 (SS1). The default value is 0x0 and the related trigger source is the processor.

9. The codes in lines 27~31 are used to configure the ADC0 sample sequencer 1 (SS1). First the SS1 is disabled by resetting ASEN1 bit in the ADCACTSS register. Recall in Section 7.5.3.2.3 that the bit ASEN1 (bit 1) in this register is used to enable (set) or disable (clear) the sample sequencer 1. The macro ADC_ACTSS_ASEN1 is defined as 0x2 in the system header file tm4c123gh6pm.h. An inverse operator ~ is used to invert this value to 0x0.

10. Then the macro ADC_EMUX_EM1_PROCESSOR (0x0) is assigned to the ADCEMUX register to select the default trigger source (processor) for the SS1 in line 28. Recall in Section 7.5.3.3.3.1 that the nibble EM1 (bits 7~4) in this register is used to select the trigger event for the sample sequencer 1 (SS1).

11. In line 29, the ADCSSMUX1 register is configured to enable the SS1 to collect the first sample from AIN1 (PE2), the second sample from AIN2 (PE1), and the third sample from AIN8 (PE5) channels (pins) by assigning three nibbles 0x0821 to this register. Recall in Section 7.5.3.2.1, three nibbles MUX2 – MUX0 are used to determine the input sources for three related samples. For each sample, we have 0001 (1) → AIN1, 0010 (2) → AIN2, 1000 (8) → AIN8. Therefore 0x0821 represents four nibbles with values 0000, 1000, 0010, and 0001. These nibbles are mapped to select none for the 4th sample (0000), AIN8 for the 3rd sample (1000), AIN2 for the 2nd sample (0010), and AIN1 for the 1st sample (0001).

12. The ADCSSCTL1 register is configured to enable SS1 to stop at the 3rd sample with a raw interrupt generated in line 30. Recall in Section 7.5.3.2.2 that the lower 16-bit on this register is divided into four nibbles, and each nibble defined the control functions for each sample since only four samples can be collected by the SS1. Each nibble has four bits, TSn, IEn, ENDn, and Dn, and each bit can be used to control one function for the related sample. When the third nibble TS3-IE3-END3-D3 equals 0110 (6), which means that the 3rd

sample comes from an analog input channel (not from the internal temperature sensor), the 3rd sample generates a raw interrupt; this sample is the last sample in the sequencer, and this sample is collected from a single-end mode.

13. In line 31, the SS1 is enabled since the configurations for SS1 are done.

14. The codes in lines 32~43 are used to initiate the SS1 to start the ADC functions, as well as to collect and display the conversion results on related peripherals. An infinitive while() loop is used to repeatedly start, collect, and display the ADC results. First the SS1 is initiated by setting the SS bits in the ADCPSSI register. Recall in Section 7.5.3.2.4 that the lowest 4 bits in this register, SS3~SS0, are used to initiate the related sample sequencer. To initiate the sample sequencer 1, just set the SS1 bit in this register. The macro ADC_PSSI_SS1 has been defined as 0x2 in the head file tm4c123gh6pm.h.

15. In line 35, another while() loop is used to poll or wait for the sample conversions to be done. The related INR1 bit (bit 1) in the ADCRIS register will be set to 1 to generate a raw interrupt when the 3rd sample is complete since this has been configured in the ADCSSCTL1 register in step 12 above. Refer to Section 7.5.3.3.2.1 to get more details for this register.

16. After all three samples are collected they will be collected one by one in the order from the ADCSSFIFO1 registers in lines 36~38. The 1st sample is from AIN1 and sent to pMeter. The 2nd sample is from AIN2 and sent to pSensor. The 3rd sample is from AIN8 and sent to pTemp. Since the FIFO1 register will repeatedly collect these three samples in high frequency and store them into this queue, each of these samples includes a long sequence of samples.

17. In line 39, the IN1 bit (bit 1) in the ADCISC register is set to 1 to clear that raw interrupt to enable the following interrupts to be occurred. Refer to Section 7.5.3.3.2.3 to get more details about this register and its function.

18. The codes in lines 40~42 are used to assign the related ADC results to the appropriate peripherals. The converted results for the potentiometer are sent to the three-color LED in the TM4C123GXL EVB via Port F. The results coming from the photosensor are sent to four LEDs, PB3~PB0, in the EduBASE Trainer. The conversion results from the temperature sensor LM45 are sent to the speaker.

19. In line 43, a user-defined function Delay() is executed to delay some time for the project to keep LEDs on.

20. The codes in lines 46~50 are the function body for the function Delay().

Now let's set up the environment to build and run the project to test the related functions.

7.5.6.4 *Set Up the Environment to Build and Run the Project*

Perform the following operations to set up the running environment for this project:

- Include the system header file path C:\ti\TivaWare_C_Series-2.0.1.11577\inc in the C/C++ tab under the Project|Options for Target 'Target 1' menu item. Since we used the system header file tm4c123gh6pm.h in this project, we need to include the path for this header file.

- Select the debug adapter Stellaris ICDI in the Debug tab under the Project-|Options for Target 'Target 1' menu item.

Now build the project by going to Project|Build target menu item. If everything is fine, go to Flash|Download item to download the image file of the project into the flash memory. Now go to Debug|Start/Stop Debug Session and Debug|Run item to run the project.

During the project running, you can test it by

- Tuning the potentiometer VR2 with a small screw driver, and you can find that the intensity and color of the three-color LED on the TM4C123GXL EVB are also changed. This is because the analog input to the AIN1 on ADC0 is modified as you tune the potentiometer.
- Either covering the photo sensor by hand or exposing it under some light sources, you can find that four LEDs, PB3~PB0, on the Trainer will also be changed to ON or OFF.
- Hearing a noise coming from the speaker since the conversion result of the temperature sensor is sent to it. Because the change of the temperature needs a long time to be detected by the temperature sensor, the noise seems constant.

Now let's have a quick look at the API functions provided by TivaWare™ Peripheral Driver Library since we can use those functions to perform ADC related functions in applications.

7.5.7 ADC Module API Functions Provided in the TivaWare™ Peripheral Driver Library

As we discussed in Section 7.5.1, the Analog-to-Digital Converter (ADC) contains two ADC modules, ADC0 and ADC1. Each module includes four sample sequencers to collect and capture sampled data with 12 input channels. To assist users to build ADC-related applications, the TivaWare™ Peripheral Driver Library provides an API with a set of API functions to access and configure ADC-related registers to perform various functions to facilitate the ADC operations. The ADC related API provides a set of interfacing functions to deal with the ADC operations. Functions are provided to configure the sample sequencers, read the captured data, register a sample sequence interrupt handler, and handle interrupt process.

In the TM4C123GH6PM MCU system, the ADC supports up to 12 input channels plus an internal temperature sensor. Four sampling sequencers, each with configurable trigger events, can be captured. The first sequencer captures up to eight samples, the second and third sequencers capture up to four samples, and the fourth sequencer captures a single sample. Each sample can be the same channel, different channels, or any combination in any order.

The library provides about 40 API functions to support ADC operations, and these functions can be divided into following three groups:

1. Configure and handle the sample sequencers to collect data.
2. Configure and control the processor trigger.
3. Configure and process ADC-related interrupts.

The first group contains the following five functions:

- ADCSequenceConfigure(): Configure the trigger source/priority of a sample sequencer.
- ADCSequenceStepConfigure(): Configure a single step of a sample sequencer.
- ADCSequenceEnable(): Enable a sample sequencer.
- ADCSequenceDisable(): Disable a sample sequencer.

- ADCSequenceDataGet(): Get the sampled data from a sample sequencer.

The second group contains the following one API function:

- ADCProcessorTrigger(): Triggers a processor-initiated sample sequencer.

The third group contains the following six ADC interrupt handling functions:

- ADCIntRegister(): Register an ADC interrupt.
- ADCIntUnregister(): Unregister an ADC interrupt.
- ADCIntEnable(): Enable an ADC interrupt.
- ADCIntDisable(): Disable an ADC interrupt.
- ADCIntClear(): Clear an ADC interrupt.
- ADCIntStatus(): The current status of an ADC interrupt.

These API functions are contained in a C file driverlib/adc.c with a header file driverlib/adc.h. Both files are located at the folder C:\ti\TivaWare_C_Series_2.0.1.11577 in your host computer.

Let's discuss these API functions one by one based on their groups.

7.5.7.1 *Configuring and Handling the Sample Sequencers API Functions*

Table 7.18 shows the API functions used to configure and handle sample sequencers.

For the ADCSequenceConfigure() function, the ui32Trigger parameter indicates the trigger source for this sample sequencer, and it must be an ADC_TRIGGER_ value listed on the description part in Table 7.18 for this function.

For the ADCSequenceStepConfigure() function, this function is used to configure a single sample or a single step for a sample. As we know, each sample sequencer SSn can sample up to 8 samples, and each sample can be independently configured by using this function. The parameter ui32Config can be ORed with multiple values, such as ADC_CTL_TS, ADC_CTL_IE, ADC_CTL_END, ADC_CTL_D, and ADC_CTL_CHn ($n = 0 \sim 11$).

For the ADCSequenceDataGet() function, this function is used to get or copy the sampled or converted data from the sample sequencer FIFO registers into the buffer memory. The third parameter pui32Buffer is a pointer or a starting address of the memory buffer used to accept or store the copied data from the sample sequencer FIFO registers.

When applying these API functions to configure and control the ADC operations in an application, both functions, ADCSequenceConfigure() and ADCSequenceStepConfigure(), must be used together to configure sample sequencers. The first function is used to perform the general configurations, such as the trigger source and priority, and the second function is to perform special configurations for each individual sample in the selected sample sequencer.

7.5.7.2 *Configuring and Controlling the Processor Trigger API Functions*

Table 7.19 shows the API function used to configure and control the processor trigger.

The ADCProcessorTrigger() function is used to trigger a processor-initiated sample sequencer when the selected sample sequencer has been configured with

Table 7.18. API functions used to configure and handle sample sequencers.

API Function	Parameters	Description
void ADCSequenceConfigure(uint32_t ui32Base, uint32_t ui32SequenceNum, uint32_t ui32Trigger, uint32_t ui32Priority)	ui32Base is the base address of the ADC module. ui32SequenceNum is the sample sequencer number. ui32Trigger is the trigger source that initiates the sample sequence, it must be ADC_TRIGGER_ values. ui32Priority is the relative priority of the sample sequencer.	Configure the initiation criteria for a sample sequencer. The trigger condition and priority are set. ADC_TRIGGER_ values include: ADC_TRIGGER_PROCESSOR - A trigger generated by processor, via the ADCProcessorTrigger() function. ADC_TRIGGER_COMP0 - A trigger generated by the 1st analog comparator. ADC_TRIGGER_COMP1 - A trigger generated by the 2nd analog comparator. ADC_TRIGGER_COMP2 - A trigger generated by the 3rd analog comparator. ADC_TRIGGER_EXTERNAL - A trigger generated by an input from the Port B4 pin. ADC_TRIGGER_TIMER - A trigger generated by a timer ADC_TRIGGER_PWMn - A trigger generated by the nth PWM generator. ADC_TRIGGER_ALWAYS - A trigger is always asserted.
void ADCSequenceStepConfigure(uint32_t ui32Base, uint32_t ui32SequenceNum, uint32_t ui32Step, uint32_t ui32Config)	ui32Base is the base address of the ADC module. ui32SequenceNum is the sample sequencer number. ui32Step is the sample to be configured. ui32Config is configuration of this sample; must be a logical OR of ADC_CTL_TS, ADC_CTL_IE, ADC_CTL_END, ADC_CTL_D, (ADC_CTL_CH0 ~ADC_CTL_CH11), (ADC_CTL_CMP0~ADC_CTL_CMP7).	Configure the ADC for one sample in a sequencer. The ADC can be configured by ui32Config for: Single-ended or differential operation (ADC_CTL_D bit selects differential mode when set) The channel to be sampled can be chosen (ADC_CTL_CH0 ~ ADC_CTL_CH11 values) The internal temperature sensor can be selected (ADC_CTL_TS bit). This step can be defined as the last in the sequence (ADC_CTL_END bit) It can be configured to cause an interrupt when the step is complete (ADC_CTL_IE bit).
void ADCSequenceEnable(uint32_t ui32Base, uint32_t ui32SequenceNum)	ui32Base is the base address of the ADC module. ui32SequenceNum is the sample sequencer number.	Enable the specified sample sequencer to be captured when its trigger is detected. A sample sequencer must be configured before it is enabled.
void ADCSequenceDisable(uint32_t ui32Base, uint32_t ui32SequenceNum)	ui32Base is the base address of the ADC module. ui32SequenceNum is the sample sequencer number.	Disable a sample sequencer. A sample sequencer should be disabled before it is configured.
int32_t ADCSequenceDataGet(uint32_t ui32Base, uint32_t ui32SequenceNum, uint32_t *pui32Buffer)	ui32Base is the base address of the ADC module. ui32SequenceNum is the sample sequencer number. pui32Buffer is the address where the data is stored.	Get the captured data for a sample sequencer. This function copies data from the specified sample sequencer output FIFO to a memory resident buffer. The number of samples available in the hardware FIFO are copied into the buffer, which is assumed to be large enough to hold that many samples.

Table 7.19. API functions used to configure and control the processor trigger.

API Function	Parameters	Description
void ADCProcessorTrigger(uint32_t ui32Base, uint32_t ui32SequenceNum)	ui32Base is the base address of the ADC module. ui32SequenceNum is the sample sequencer number, with ADC_TRIGGER_WAIT or ADC_TRIGGER_SIGNAL optionally ORed into it.	Trigger a processor-initiated sample sequence if the sample sequencer trigger is configured to ADC_TRIGGER_PROCESSOR. If ADC_TRIGGER_WAIT is ORed into the sequencer number, the processor-initiated trigger is delayed until a later processor-initiated trigger to a different ADC module that specifies ADC_TRIGGER_SIGNAL, allowing multiple ADCs to start from a processor-initiated trigger in a synchronous manner.

ADC_TRIGGER_PROCESSOR. This means that the sample sequencer is triggered by the default source – processor.

If multiple trigger sources are used to trigger different sample sequencers, the parameter ADC_TRIGGER_WAIT should be used and ORed with the selected sample sequencer number (SSn) to wait until the actual trigger source ADC_TRIGGER_SIGNAL comes.

This function returns nothing.

7.5.7.3 *Configuring and Processing the ADC Interrupt API Functions*

As we discussed in Section 7.5.3.3.2, to configure and handle ADC-related interrupts, the following four registers should be used:

- ADC Sample Sequencer Control (ADCSSCTLn) Register
- ADC Raw Interrupt Status (ADCRIS) Register
- ADC Interrupt Mask (ADCIM) Register
- ADC Interrupt Status and Clear (ADCISC) Register

By setting the IEn bit in the ADCSSCTLn register, the selected sample can generate an interrupt when it is converted to a digital value. This interrupt is reflected in the related INRn bit in the ADCRIS register by setting that bit to 1 to set up an ADC raw interrupt. If the MASKn bit in the ADCIM register is set to enable this raw interrupt, this raw interrupt can be sent to the NVIC to be further processed. By setting the related INn bit in the ADCISC register, both the INn bit in the ADCISC register and the INRn bit in the ADCRIS register can be cleared to 0.

In the TivaWare™ Peripheral Driver Library, six API functions are used to match these four registers to handle any ADC-related interrupts. Table 7.20 shows these API functions.

For the ADCIntRegister() function, the third argument pfnHandler is a pointer or the entry address of the interrupt handler or interrupt service subroutine (ISR) to respond to and handle the related ADC interrupt.

For the ADCIntStatus() function, the third argument bMasked is a Boolean input variable. If this value is *False*, the status or the value in the INRn bit in the ADCRIS register is returned. This bit value only indicates that an ADC raw interrupt has been occurred, but it may not be sent to the NVIC to be processed if the MASKn bit in the ADCIM register is not set to 1 to enable this sending operation. However, if the value of the bMasked is *True*, the value on the INn bit in the ADCISC register is returned to indicate whether this ADC raw interrupt has been sent to the NVIC to be further processed or this interrupt has been disabled or masked by the ADCIM register.

When using these functions to handle any ADC-related interrupt, the following operational sequence must be followed:

- The ADCIntRegister() must be called or executed first to set up an interrupt handler to handle any ADC-related interrupt that may occur.
- The ADCIntEnable() must be called or executed secondly to enable the interrupt.
- The ADCIntClear() must be executed to clear the current interrupt to enable the next one that may occur.

Table 7.20. API functions used to configure and handle ADC interrupts.

API Function	Parameters	Description
void ADCIntRegister(uint32_t ui32Base, uint32_t ui32SequenceNum, void (*pfnHandler)(void))	ui32Base is the base address of the ADC module. ui32SequenceNum is the sample sequencer number. pfnHandler is a pointer to the function to be called when the ADC sample sequencer interrupt occurs.	Register an interrupt handler for an ADC interrupt. Set the handler to be called when a sample sequencer interrupt occurs. This function enables the global interrupt in the interrupt controller; the sequencer interrupt must be enabled with ADCIntEnable(). It is the interrupt handler's responsibility to clear the interrupt source via ADCIntClear().
void ADCIntUnregister(uint32_t ui32Base, uint32_t ui32SequenceNum)	ui32Base is the base address of the ADC module. ui32SequenceNum is the sample sequencer number	Unregister the interrupt handler for an ADC interrupt. Unregister the interrupt handler. This function disables the global interrupt in the interrupt controller; the sequencer interrupt must be disabled via ADCIntDisable().
void ADCIntEnable(uint32_t ui32Base, uint32_t ui32SequenceNum)	ui32Base is the base address of the ADC module. ui32SequenceNum is the sample sequencer number.	Enable the requested sample sequencer interrupt. Any outstanding interrupts are cleared before enabling the sample sequence interrupt.
void ADCIntDisable(uint32_t ui32Base, uint32_t ui32SequenceNum)	ui32Base is the base address of the ADC module. ui32SequenceNum is the sample sequencer number.	Disable the requested sample sequencer interrupt.
uint32_t ADCIntStatus(uint32_t ui32Base, uint32_t ui32SequenceNum, bool bMasked)	ui32Base is the base address of the ADC module. ui32SequenceNum is the sample sequence number. bMasked is false if the raw interrupt status is required and true if the masked interrupt status is required.	Gets the current interrupt status. This function returns the interrupt status for the specified sample sequencer. Either the raw interrupt status or the status of interrupts that are allowed to reflect to the processor can be returned.
void ADCIntClear(uint32_t ui32Base, uint32_t ui32SequenceNum)	ui32Base is the base address of the ADC module. ui32SequenceNum is the sample sequencer number.	Clear sample sequencer interrupt source. The specified sample sequencer interrupt is cleared, so that it no longer asserts. This function must be called in the interrupt handler to make the next interrupt to be triggered again in the future.

There are some other API functions that are available to the ADC modules. Here we only discussed the most often used functions. Refer to TM4C123GH6PM Microcontroller Data Sheet to get more details for those functions.

Next let's build an example project to use these API functions to access and control ADC0 sample sequencer 0 to collect data from channel 1 to test the functions of these API functions.

7.5.7.4 *Build an Example ADC Project Using API Functions*

Since this project is very simple and easy, we only need to create a C file to include all codes. In order to use those API functions, the following operations are needed to set up the environments to build and run this project:

- The TivaWare™ Peripheral Driver Library file, driverlib.lib, must be added into the project. This file is located at C:\ti\TivaWare_C_Series-2.0.1.11577\driverlib\rvmdk.

```
1   //********************************************************************************************************
2   // SDADCPoll.c - Main Application for ADC0 - SS0 – Channel 1
3   //********************************************************************************************************
4   #include <stdint.h>
5   #include <stdbool.h>
6   #include "driverlib\adc.h"
7   #include "inc\hw_memmap.h"
8   #include "inc\hw_types.h"
9   #include "driverlib\sysctl.h"
10  #include "driverlib\gpio.h"
11  int main(void)
12  {
13     uint32_t ui32Value,  ssn = 0,  sample = 0;
14     // Enable clocks for GPIO Ports B & F and ADC0
15     SysCtlPeripheralEnable(SYSCTL_PERIPH_GPIOB);
16     SysCtlPeripheralEnable(SYSCTL_PERIPH_GPIOF);
17     SysCtlPeripheralEnable(SYSCTL_PERIPH_ADC0);
18     // Configure GPIO Ports B & F as output ports
19     GPIOPinTypeGPIOOutput(GPIO_PORTF_BASE, GPIO_PIN_3|GPIO_PIN_2|GPIO_PIN_1);
20     GPIOPinTypeGPIOOutput(GPIO_PORTB_BASE,  GPIO_PIN_3|GPIO_PIN_2|
21                           GPIO_PIN_1|GPIO_PIN_0);
22     // Configure ADC0 - SS0 – Channel 1 & the First Sample
23     ADCSequenceDisable(ADC0_BASE,  ssn); a
24     ADCSequenceConfigure(ADC0_BASE, ssn, ADC_TRIGGER_PROCESSOR, 0);
25     ADCSequenceStepConfigure(ADC0_BASE, ssn, sample, ADC_CTL_IE|ADC_CTL_END|
26                           ADC_CTL_CH1);
27     ADCSequenceEnable(ADC0_BASE,  ssn);
28     while (1)
29     {
30        // Trigger the sample sequencer 0 – SS0.
31        ADCProcessorTrigger(ADC0_BASE, ssn);
32        // Wait until the sample sequence has completed .
33        while(!ADCIntStatus(ADC0_BASE,  ssn, false)){}
34        // Read the value from the ADC.
35        ADCSequenceDataGet(ADC0_BASE, ssn, &ui32Value);
36        GPIOPinWrite(GPIO_PORTF_BASE, GPIO_PIN_3|GPIO_PIN_2|GPIO_PIN_1, ui32Value >> 8);
37        GPIOPinWrite(GPIO_PORTB_BASE, GPIO_PIN_3|GPIO_PIN_2|GPIO_PIN_1|GPIO_PIN_0,
38                     ui32Value >> 8);
        ADCIntClear(ADC0_BASE, ssn);
     }
   }
```

Figure 7.30.   The codes for the source file SDADCPoll.c.

- Some system header files must be included, and the path to access those header files should also be added into the project by using C/C++ tab under the Project|Options for Target 'Target 1' menu item.
- The debug adaptor Stellaris ICDI must be selected by using the Debug tab under the
- Project|Options for Target 'Target 1' menu item.

Now let's create a new project SDADCPoll under the C:\ARM Class Projects \Chapter 7 folder, and add a new C file named SDADCPoll.c into this project.

Enter the codes shown in Figure 7.30 into this source file. Let's have a closer look at this piece of codes to see how it works.

1. The codes in lines 4~10 are used to include some useful system header files for this project.

2. Three local variables, `ui32Value`, `ssn`, and `sample`, are declared in line 13. The first variable is used to get and hold the converted result from the FIFO register. The second and the third variables are used to represent the sample sequencer and sample number.

3. The codes in lines 15~17 are used to enable the clocks to GPIO Ports B and F, as well as the ADC module 0–ADC0. All of these functions are also located in the library file `driverlib.lib`.

4. The codes in lines 19~21 are used to configure GPIO Ports B and F to enable them and related pins to work as output ports and pins.

5. The codes in lines 23~26 are used to initialize and configure ADC0 and sample sequencer 0 (SS0) to collect the data from channel 1 (AIN1). First the ADC0-SS0 is disabled in line 23. Then the `ADCSequenceConfigure()` API function is called to configure SS0 with the trigger source (processor) and the priority (level 0). The `ADCSequenceStepConfigure()` API function is executed to configure the first sample (sample 0) to get the analog input from channel 1 (ADC_CTL_CH1), generate an interrupt (ADC_CTL_IE), and indicate that this is the last sample (ADC_CTL_END).

6. In line 26, the sample sequencer 0 (SS0) is enabled by using `ADCSequenceEnable()` API function.

7. Starting at line 27, an infinitive `while()` loop is executed to repeatedly initiate and trigger the SS0 to collect the first sample and store it into the FIFO0 register.

8. In line 32, another `while()` loop is used to monitor and wait until the first sample to be converted and stored. The third argument of the API function `ADCIntStatus()` is *false*, which means that we only need to get the status or the value on the bit INR0 in the ADCRIS register. This bit will be set to 1 to indicate that a SS0 raw interrupt has been generated as soon as the first sample is converted to a digital value and stored in the FIFO0 register. As this bit is set to 1, the `while()` loop is done.

9. In line 34, the converted sample data is retrieved by reading it from the FIFO0 register and saved to the `ui32Value` variable via the API function `ADCSequenceDataGet()` in line 34. Since the third argument of this function should be a pointer, an address operator & is prefixed before this variable.

10. The codes in lines 35~37 are used to assign this converted sample data to the LEDs, PB3~PB0, and a three-color LED via Ports B and F, respectively. The data is first shifted right by 8 bits to enable the 4 MSB to be sent to those LEDs.

11. In line 38, the ADC SS0 interrupt is cleared by using the API function `ADCIntClear()` to enable the next interrupt to be occurred in the future.

After building the project, you can download it into the flash memory. As the project runs, you can tune the potentiometer VR2 since it is connected to channel 1 (AIN1) via PE2. As you tune the VR2, the intensity and color on the three-color LED will be changed and four LEDs on the Trainer will also be changed.

Next let's discuss the PWM and its control functions for DC or step motors.

7.6 PWM-CONTROLLED DC AND STEP MOTORS PROGRAMMING PROJECT

Pulse-Width-Modulation (PWM) is a powerful technique to enable a digital signal to be encoded to an analog signal to drive a power supply or a DC servo or step motor. This technique is widely implemented in most power supplies and motors as well as robots

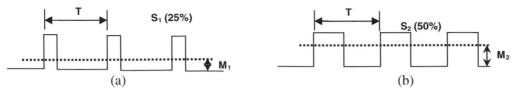

Figure 7.31. An example of PWM signals.

control applications. In order to have a fully understanding and clear picture about this technique, let's first have a closer look at the principle of the PWM technique.

7.6.1 The PWM Principle and Implementations

In all modern power supply products, most of them use the PWM idea to build power supplies. The so-called PWM is to modify or modulate a periodic rectangular digital waveform to make it with different pulse width or duty cycle, and therefore to generate different magnitude on the output analog signal.

Compare two PWM signals, S_1 and S_2, shown in Figures 7.31a and 7.31b. Both signals have the same period and frequency, but the average output magnitudes M_1 for S_1 and M_2 for S_2 are different since they have different duty cycles, 25% and 50%.

In actual circuits, this voltage average function is performed by capacitors that play an integrator role or a low-pass filter.

The PWM circuit can be easily programmed to modify the output magnitudes for their outputs. The higher the duty cycle (the wider the pulse width), the higher the output voltage. The lower the duty cycle (the narrower the pulse width), the lower the output voltage.

Now let's take a look at the PWM circuits in the TM4C123GH6PM MCU system.

7.6.2 PWM Modules in the TM4C123GH6PM MCU System

The TM4C123GH6PM MCU contains two PWM modules, PWM0 and PWM1. Each module has four PWM generator blocks and a control block, and each generator block can create two PWM output signals, therefore a total of 16 PWM output signals can be generated by these two modules. The control block determines the polarity of the PWM signals, and it also determines which signals are passed through to the output pins.

Each PWM generator block produces two PWM signals that share the same timer (counter) and frequency and can be programmed with either independent actions or as a single pair of complementary signals with dead-band delays inserted. The output signals, pwmA' and pwmB', of the PWM generation blocks are managed by the output control block before being passed to the device pins as MnPWM0 and MnPWM1 or MnPWM2 and MnPWM3, and so on.

Each TM4C123GH6PM PWM module provides a great deal of flexibility and can generate simple PWM signals, such as those required by a simple charge pump as well as paired PWM signals with dead-band delays, such as those required by a half-H bridge driver.

7.6.2.1 The PWM Generator Block

In the TM4C123GH6PM MCU system, each PWM generator block is composed of two components, one 16-bit Counter or Timer and two PWM Comparators, cmpA and cmpB.

The counter provides a timing base for two comparators, and it is mainly used to perform count-down or count-up/down functions to provide a comparison source for two comparators.

7.6.2.1.1 The PWM Counter (Timer)   The 16-bit counter or timer in each PWM generator runs in one of two modes, Count-Down mode or Count-Up/Down mode:

- In Count-Down mode, the timer counts from the LOAD value to 0, and then it goes back to the LOAD value and continues to perform the counting down.
- In Count-Up/Down mode, the timer counts from 0 up to the LOAD value and then counts down back to 0, back up to the LOAD value, and so on.

Generally, Count-Down mode is used for generating left-aligned or right-aligned PWM signals, and the Count-Up/Down mode is used to generate center-aligned PWM signals.

The timers output three signals that can be used in the PWM generation process:

1. The direction signal. This signal is always Low in Count-Down mode, but alternates between Low and High in Count-Up/Down mode.
2. A single-clock-cycle-width High pulse when the counter gets zero.
3. A single-clock-cycle-width High pulse when the counter is equal to the load value.

Note that in the Count-Down mode, the zero pulse is immediately followed by the load pulse. These signals are labeled `dir`, `zero`, and `load` in all figures in this chapter.

7.6.2.1.2 The PWM Comparators   As we mentioned, each PWM generator has two comparators that monitor the value of the counter and output a single-clock-cycle-width High when either comparator's value is equal to the counting value in the counter. These outputs are labeled `cmpA` and `cmpB` in all figures in this chapter. In the Count-Up/Down mode, these comparators match both when counting up and when counting down and thus are qualified by the counter direction signal. If either comparator match-value is greater than the counter load value, that comparator never outputs a High pulse.

Figure 7.32a shows the behavior of the counter and the relationship of these pulses when the counter is in Count-Down mode. Figure 7.32b shows the behavior of the counter and the relationship of these pulses when the counter is in Count-Up/Down mode.

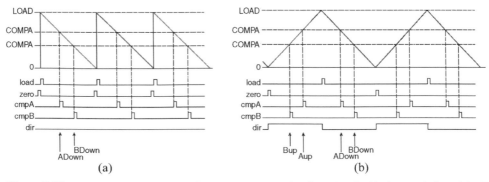

Figure 7.32.   PWM Count-Down and Count Up/Down modes. (Reprinted with the permission of the Texas Instruments Incorporated.)

The following definitions are applied for these operational modes in this figure:

- LOAD is the value stored in the PWMnLOAD register.
- COMPA is the value stored in the PWMnCMPA register.
- COMPB is the value stored in the PWMnCMPB register.
- 0 is the value zero.
- load is the internal signal that provides a single-clock-cycle-width High pulse when the counter is equal to the load value in the counter.
- zero is the internal signal that provides a single-clock-cycle-width High pulse when the counter is zero.
- cmpA is the internal signal that provides a single-clock-cycle-width High pulse when the counter is equal to COMPA.
- cmpB is the internal signal that provides a single-clock-cycle-width High pulse when the counter is equal to COMPB.
- dir is the internal signal that indicates the count direction.

Based on these elements and internal signals, now let's have a closer look at how to use them to generate PWM output signals like those shown in Figure 7.31.

7.6.2.1.3 The PWM Output Signals Generator Each PWM generator uses the load, zero, cmpA, and cmpB pulses the dir signal to generate two internal PWM signals, pwmA and pwmB, as shown in Figure 7.32.

In Count-Down mode, four events can affect these signals: zero, load, match A down, and match B down. In Count-Up/Down mode, six events can affect these signals: zero, load, match A down, match A up, match B down, and match B up. The match A or match B events are ignored when they coincide with the zero or load events. If the match A and match B events coincide, the first signal, pwmA, is generated based only on the match A event, and the second signal, pwmB, is generated based only on the match B event.

Each event can affect each output PWM signal by programming to make the output to be:

- Left alone (ignoring the event)
- Toggled
- Driven Low or High

These actions can be used to generate a pair of PWM signals of various positions and duty cycles, which do or do not overlap. Figure 7.33 shows the use of Count-Up/Down

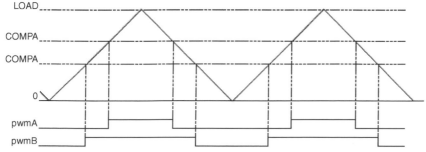

Figure 7.33. An example of using the count-up/down mode to generate PWM outputs. (Reprinted with the permission of the Texas Instruments Incorporated.)

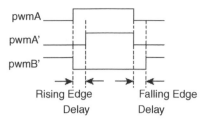

Figure 7.34.   The output PWM signals generated by Dead-Band generator. (Reprinted with the permission of the Texas Instruments Incorporated.)

mode to generate a pair of center-aligned, overlapped PWM signals that have different duty cycles. The pwmA and pwmB signals shown in this figure are before they have passed through the dead-band generator.

In Figure 7.33, the first PWM generator is set to output High on match A up (COMPA), output Low on match A down (COMPA), and ignore the other four events. The second PWM generator is set to output High on match B up (COMPB), output Low on match B down (COMPB), and ignore the other four events. Changing the value of comparator A (COMPA) changes the duty cycle of the pwmA signal, and changing the value of comparator B (COMPB) changes the duty cycle of the pwmB signal.

In addition to normal PWM outputs, these two PWM output signals can be combined together to form a so-called Dead-Band output to drive a half-H bridge circuit for some motors.

7.6.2.1.4 The Dead-Band Generator   The pwmA and pwmB signals generated by each PWM generator can be passed to the dead-band generator. If the dead-band generator is disabled, these PWM signals can be passed through to the pwmA' and pwmB' signals without any modification. If the dead-band generator is enabled, the pwmB signal is ignored and only the pwmA signal is used to generate two PWM signals, pwmA' and pwmB'.

The first output PWM signal, pwmA', is the pwmA signal with the rising edge delayed by a programmable amount. The second output PWM signal, pwmB', is just the inversion of the pwmA signal with a programmable delay added between the falling edge of the pwmA signal and the rising edge of the pwmB' signal, as shown in Figure 7.34.

The resulting signals are therefore suitable for driving a half-H bridge, with the dead-band delays preventing shoot-through current from damaging the power electronics. These resulting pwmA' and pwmB' signals will be transmitted to the output control block.

Now let's have a closer look at the PWM module architecture and block diagram.

7.6.3 PWM Generator Functional Block Diagram

First let's have a closer look at the PWM generator block to see how this block to create two PWM output signals based on the discussion we made above.

Figure 7.35 shows a detailed structure for a PWM generator block. This block contains a 16-bit counter or timer and two comparators as we discussed above.

In fact, both the counter (timer) and two comparators are under the control of the register PWMnCTL, and each generator block contains one of these kinds of controllers to configure the setups and control the operations of each generator.

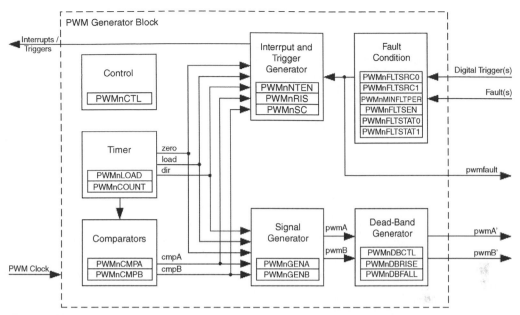

Figure 7.35.   The detailed block diagram for the PWM Generator block. (Reprinted with the permission of the Texas Instruments Incorporated.)

It can be found from Figure 7.35, five events or internal signals, `zero`, `load`, `dir`, `cmpA`, and `cmpB`, are combined and work together to generate two PWM output signals, `pwmA` and `pwmB`. Depending on the availability (enabled or disabled) of the Dead-Band Generator, these two PWM signals can be directly passed to the outputs, `pwmA'` and `pwmB'` if the Dead-Band Generator is disabled, or a dead-band signal can be generated if it is enabled.

These five events or internal signals can also be used to generate PWM-related interrupts to inform the processor that some events related to PWM have occurred.

The `Interrupt and Trigger Generator` block is used to configure and control the generating and handling of PWM-related interrupts and trigger source selections process. The `Fault Condition` block is used to configure and control any fault condition and generation process for the selected PWM generator.

Now let's take care of some useful registers in each block to see their functions.

7.6.3.1 *PWM Generator Block Control Register* (PWMnCTL)

As we mentioned, two PWM modules, PWM0 and PWM1, are installed and applied for the TM4C123GH6PM MCU system and each PWM module contains four PWM generator blocks. Each PWM generator block has an independent control register. For example, for the PWM0 module, four block control registers are: PWM0CTL~PWM0CTL3, each one controls one generator block with the same bit-field distribution.

The bit-field values for these registers are shown in Figure 7.36. The bit-field value and related function of these registers are shown in Table 7.21.

These registers are used to configure the PWM signal generation blocks. The PWM0CTL controls the PWM generator 0 block, and PWM1CTL controls the PWM

31	30	29	28	27	26	25	24	23	22	21	20	19	18	17	16
							reserved						LATCH	MNFLTPER	FITSRC

Type	RO	RO	RO	RO	RO	RO	RO	RO	RO	RO	RO	RO	RO	RW	RW	RW
Reset	0	0	0	0	0	0	0	0	0	0	0	0	0	0	0	0

15	14	13	12	11	10	9	8	7	6	5	4	3	2	1	0
DBFALLUPD		DBRISEUPD		DBCTLUPD		GENBUPD		GENAUPD		CMPBUPD	CMPAUPD	LOADUPD	DEBUG	MODE	ENABLE

RW	RW	RW	RW	RW	RW	RW	RW	RW	RW	RW	RW	RW	RW	RW	RW
0	0	0	0	0	0	0	0	0	0	0	0	0	0	0	0

Figure 7.36. Bit fields in the PWM generator control register. (Reprinted with the permission of the Texas Instruments Incorporated.)

generator 1 block and so on. The blocks produce the PWM signals that can be either (a) two independent PWM signals from the same counter or (b) a paired set of PWM signals with dead-band delays added.

Each generator block can create two PWM output signals, therefore the PWM0 block produces the MnPWM0 and MnPWM1 outputs, the PWM1 block produces the MnPWM2 and

Table 7.21. Bit field value and its function for PWMnCTL registers.

Bit	Name	Reset	Function
31:19	Reserved	0x0	Reserved
18	LATCH	0	Latch Fault Input. 0: Fault condition not latched. 1: Fault condition latched.
17	MINFLTPER	0	Minimum Fault Period. 0: The FAULT input deassertion is unaffected. 1: The PWMnMINFLTPER one-shot counter is active and extends the period of the fault condition to a minimum period.
16	FLTSRC	0	Fault Condition Source. 0: The Fault condition is determined by the Fault0 input. 1: The Fault condition is determined by the configuration of the PWMnFLTSRC0 and PWMnFLTSRC1 registers.
15:14	DBFALLUPD	0x0	PWMnDBFALL Update Mode. 0x0: Immediate. 0x1: Reserved. 0x2: Locally synchronized (update to the register is reflected to the generator the next time the counter is 0). 0x3: Globally synchronized (update to the register is delayed until the next time the counter is 0 after a synchronous update has been requested through the PWMCTL register).
13:12	DBRISEUPD	0x0	PWMnDBRISE Update Mode. Same as PWMnDBFALL Update Mode above.
11:10	DBCTLUPD	0x0	PWMnDBCTL Update Mode. Same as PWMnDBFALL Update Mode above.
9:8	GENBUPD	0x0	PWMnGENB Update Mode. Same as PWMnDBFALL Update Mode above.
7:6	GENAUPD	0x0	PWMnGENA Update Mode. Same as PWMnDBFALL Update Mode above.
5	CMPBUPD	0	Comparator B Update Mode. 0: Locally synchronized (updates to the PWMnCMPB register is reflected to the generator the next time the counter is 0). 1: Globally synchronized (update to the register is delayed until the next time the counter is 0 after a synchronous update has been requested via the PWMCTL register).
4	CMPAUPD	0	Comparator A Update Mode. Same as Comparator B Update Mode above.
3	LOADUPD	0	Load Register Update Mode. Same as Comparator B Update Mode above.
2	DEBUG	0	Debug Mode. 0: The counter stops running when it next reaches 0 & continues run again when no longer in Debug mode. 1: The counter always runs when in Debug mode.
1	MODE	0	Counter Mode. 0: Count-Down mode. 1: Count-Up/Down mode.
0	ENABLE	0	PWM Block Enable. 0: Entire block is disabled (no clock). 1: Entire block is enabled and clocked.

MnPWM3 outputs, the PWM2 block produces the MnPWM4 and MnPWM5 outputs, and the PWM3 block produces the MnPWM6 and MnPWM7 outputs.

Although there are so many parameters in this register to be configured, in fact only a few of them are important to us; they are: bits ENABLE, MODE, CMPAUPD, CMPBUPD, and LOADUPD. Some other update bits can be configured as an immediate mode to allow them to take effect immediately if no synchronized operations are needed.

7.6.3.2 *PWM Generator Block Load Register* (PWMnLOAD)

These registers are 32-bit registers, but only the lower 16 bits is used to meet the need of the 16-bit counter. Each of these registers (PWM0LOAD~PWM3LOAD) contains the load value for the PWM counter and controls the related PWM generator block. Based on the counter mode configured by the MODE bit in the PWMnCTL register, this value is either (a) loaded into the counter after it reaches zero (MODE = 0: Count-Down) or (b) the limit of up-counting after which the counter decrements back to zero (MODE = 1: Count-Up/Down). When this value matches the counter, a High pulse is output that can be configured to drive the generation of the pwmA and/or pwmB signal via the PWMnGENA or PWMnGENB register, or drive an interrupt ADC trigger via the PWMnINTEN register.

If the Load Value Update mode is locally synchronized (LOADUPD = 0 in the PWMnCTL register), the 16-bit LOAD value is used the next time the counter reaches zero. If the update mode is globally synchronized, it is used the next time the counter reaches zero after a synchronous update has been requested through the PWM Master Control (PWMCTL) register. If this register is re written before the actual update occurs, the previous value is never used and is lost.

7.6.3.3 *PWM Generator Block Count Register* (PWMnCOUNT)

These registers are 32-bit registers, but only the lower 16-bit is used to perform the counting function. Each of these registers (PWM0COUNT~PWM3COUNT) contains the current value of the PWM counter for the related PWM generator block. When this value matches zero or the value in the PWMnLOAD, PWMnCMPA, or PWMnCMPB registers, a pulse is output that can be configured to drive the generation of a PWM signal or drive an interrupt or ADC trigger.

The point to be noted is that disabling the PWM by clearing the ENABLE bit in the PWMnCTL register does not clear the COUNT field (lower 16-bit) in the PWMnCOUNT register. Before re-enabling the PWM (ENABLE = 1), the COUNT field should be cleared by resetting the PWM registers through the Pulse Width Modulator Software Reset (SRPWM) register in the System Control Module.

7.6.3.4 *PWM Generator Block Comparator A Register* (PWMnCMPA)

These registers are 32-bit registers, but only the lower 16-bit is used to store a pre-defined value to be compared with the value in the counter. Each of these registers (PWM0CMPA~ PWM3CMPA) contains a value to be compared against the counter for the related PWM generator block. When this value matches the counter, a pulse is output that can be configured to drive the generation of the pwmA and pwmB signals via the PWMnGENA and PWMnGENB registers, or drive an interrupt or ADC trigger via the PWMnINTEN register. If the value of this register is greater than the PWMnLOAD register, then no pulse is ever output.

If the Comparator A update mode is locally synchronized (CMPAUPD = 0 in the PWMnCTL register), the 16-bit COMPA value is used the next time the counter reaches zero. If the update mode is globally synchronized (CMPAUPD = 1), it is used the next time the counter reaches zero after a synchronous update has been requested through the PWM Master Control (PWMCTL) register. If this register is rewritten before the actual update occurs, the previous value is never used and is lost.

7.6.3.5 *PWM Generator Block Comparator B Register* (PWMnCMPB)

Similar to PWMnCMPA, these registers contain a value to be compared against the counter for the related PWM generator block. When this value matches the counter, a pulse is output that can be configured to drive the generation of the pwmA and pwmB signals via the PWMnGENA and PWMnGENB registers, or drive an interrupt or ADC trigger via the PWMnINTEN register. If the value of this register is greater than the PWMnLOAD register, no pulse is ever output.

If the comparator B update mode is locally synchronized (CMPBUPD = 0 in the PWMnCTL register), the 16-bit COMPB value is used the next time the counter reaches zero. If the update mode is globally synchronized, it is used the next time the counter reaches zero after a synchronous update has been requested through the PWM Master Control (PWMCTL) register.

If this register is rewritten before the actual update occurs, the previous value is never used and is lost.

7.6.3.6 *PWM Generator A Register* (PWMnGENA)

These registers are 32-bit registers but only the lower 12 bits are used to control the generation of the pwmA signal based on the load and zero output pulses from the counter, as well as the compare A and compare B pulses from the comparators. Each of these registers, PWM0GENA~PWM3GENA, controls the related PWM generator blocks. When the counter is running in Count-Down mode, only four of these events occur; when running in Count-Up/Down mode, all six occur. The lower 12 bits on this register are divided into six 2-bit segments, and each segment can be configured to take a related action when a match condition has occurred.

The bit-field values for these registers are shown in Figure 7.37. The bit-field value and related function of these registers are shown in Table 7.22.

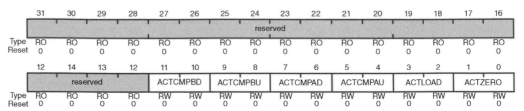

Figure 7.37.   Bit fields in the PWM generator A register. (Reprinted with the permission of the Texas Instruments Incorporated.)

Table 7.22. Bit field value and its function for PWM generator A register.

Bit	Name	Reset	Function
31:12	Reserved	0x0	Reserved
11:10	ACTCMPBD	0x0	Action for Comparator B Down. 0x0: Do nothing. 0x1: Invert pwmA. 0x2: Drive pmwA Low. 0x3: Drive pwmA High.
9:8	ACTCMPBU	0x0	Action for Comparator B Up. 0x0: Do nothing. 0x1: Invert pwmA. 0x2: Drive pmwA Low. 0x3: Drive pwmA High.
7:6	ACTCMPAD	0x0	Action for Comparator A Down. 0x0: Do nothing. 0x1: Invert pwmA. 0x2: Drive pmwA Low. 0x3: Drive pwmA High.
5:4	ACTCMPAU	0x0	Action for Comparator A Up. 0x0: Do nothing. 0x1: Invert pwmA. 0x2: Drive pmwA Low. 0x3: Drive pwmA High.
3:2	ACTLOAD	0x0	Action for Counter = LOAD. 0x0: Do nothing. 0x1: Invert pwmA. 0x2: Drive pmwA Low. 0x3: Drive pwmA High.
1:0	ACTZERO	0x0	Action for Counter = 0. 0x0: Do nothing. 0x1: Invert pwmA. 0x2: Drive pmwA Low. 0x3: Drive pwmA High.

The PWM0GENA register controls generation of the pwm0A signal, the PWM1GENA is used to control the generation of the pwm1A signal, the PWM2GENA is for the pwm2A signal, and PWM3GENA is for the pwm3A signal.

If a zero or load event coincides with a compare A or compare B event, the zero or load action is taken and the compare A or compare B action is ignored. If a compare A event coincides with a compare B event, the compare A action is taken and the compare B action is ignored.

If the Generator A update mode is immediate (the GENAUPD field = 00 in the PWMnCTL register), the ACTCMPBD, ACTCMPBU, ACTCMPAD, ACTCMPAU, ACTLOAD, and ACTZERO values are used immediately. If the update mode is locally synchronized, these values are used the next time the counter reaches zero. If the update mode is globally synchronized, these values are used the next time the counter reaches zero after a synchronous update has been requested through the PWM Master Control (PWMCTL) register. If this register is rewritten before the actual update occurs, the previous value is never used and is lost.

7.6.3.7 *PWM Generator B Register* (PWMnGENB)

Similar to the PWM Generator A register, the PWM Generator B register plays a similar function. The only difference between them is that the PWM Generator B register is used to control the generation of the pwmB signal based on the load and zero output pulses from the counter, as well as the compare A and compare B pulses from the comparators. Each of these registers, PWM0GENB~PWM3GENB, controls the related PWM generator blocks.

The PWM0GENB register controls generation of the pwm0B signal, the PWM1GENB is used to control the generation of the pwm1B signal, the PWM2GENB is for the pwm2B signal, PWM3GENB is for the pwm3B signal.

The bit-field values for these registers are identical to those shown in Figure 7.37. The bit field value and related function of these registers are shown in Table 7.23. It can be found from Table 7.23 that the bit-field values in this register are identical to those in PWM Generator A register, and the only difference is that the control target signal is pwmB.

Table 7.23. Bit-field value and its function for the PWM generator B register.

Bit	Name	Reset	Function
31:12	Reserved	0x0	Reserved
11:10	ACTCMPBD	0x0	Action for Comparator B Down. 0x0: Do nothing. 0x1: Invert pwmB. 0x2: Drive pmwB Low. 0x3: Drive pwmB High.
9:8	ACTCMPBU	0x0	Action for Comparator B Up. 0x0: Do nothing. 0x1: Invert pwmB. 0x2: Drive pmwB Low. 0x3: Drive pwmB High.
7:6	ACTCMPAD	0x0	Action for Comparator A Down. 0x0: Do nothing. 0x1: Invert pwmB. 0x2: Drive pmwB Low. 0x3: Drive pwmB High.
5:4	ACTCMPAU	0x0	Action for Comparator A Up. 0x0: Do nothing. 0x1: Invert pwmB. 0x2: Drive pmwB Low. 0x3: Drive pwmB High.
3:2	ACTLOAD	0x0	Action for Counter = LOAD. 0x0: Do nothing. 0x1: Invert pwmB. 0x2: Drive pmwB Low. 0x3: Drive pwmB High.
1:0	ACTZERO	0x0	Action for Counter = 0. 0x0: Do nothing. 0x1: Invert pwmB. 0x2: Drive pmwB Low. 0x3: Drive pwmB High.

7.6.3.8 PWM Generator Dead-Band Control Register (PWMnDBCTL)

These registers, PWM0DBCTL~PWM3DBCTL, are 32-bit registers, but only the LSB bit (bit 0 or ENABLE bit) is used to control the dead-band generator to generate MnPWMn signals based on the pwmA and pwmB signals generated by each generator block. Each of these registers controls the related PWM generator blocks.

When these registers are disabled, the pwmA signal passes through to the pwmA' signal and the pwmB signal passes through to the pwmB' signal directly. However, when the dead-band control is enabled by setting the ENABLE bit to 1, the pwmB signal is ignored, the pwmA' signal is generated by delaying the rising edge of the pwmA signal by the value in the PWMnDBRISE register (see below), and the pwmB' signal is generated by inverting the pwmA signal and delaying the falling edge of the pwmA signal by the value in the PWMnDBFALL register (see below).

The Output Control block controls the final PWM output signals MnPWMn. The relationship between each PWM Generator block and final PWM output signals via the dead-band generator is shown in Table 7.24.

If the Dead-Band Control mode is immediate (the DBCTLUPD = 0x0 in the PWMnCTL register), the ENABLE bit value is used immediately. If the update mode is

Table 7.24. The output PWM signals generated by the dead-band generators.

PWM Generator Block	Two Generated Signals	Output PWM Signals
PWM Generator 0	Pwm0A'	MnPWM0
	pwm0B'	MnPWM1
PWM Generator 1	Pwm1A'	MnPWM2
	Pwm1B'	MnPWM3
PWM Generator 2	Pwm2A'	MnPWM4
	Pwm2B'	MnPWM5
PWM Generator 3	Pwm3A'	MnPWM6
	Pwm3B'	MnPWM7

locally synchronized, this value is used the next time the counter reaches zero. If the update mode is globally synchronized, this value is used the next time the counter reaches zero after a synchronous update has been requested through the PWM Master Control (PWMCTL) register. If this register is rewritten before the actual update occurs, the previous value is never used and is lost.

The dead-band generator is disabled if the ENABLE bit (bit 0) on this register is cleared to 0.

7.6.3.9 *PWM Generator Dead-Band Rising-Edge Delay Register* (PWMnDBRISE)

These registers, PWM0DBRISE~PWM3DBRISE, are 32-bit registers, but only the lower 12 bits (bits 11~0) are used on these registers. The lower 12 bits are called RISEDELAY bits and they contain the number of clock cycles to delay the rising edge of the pwmA signal when generating the pwmA′ signal. If the dead-band generator is disabled, this register is ignored. If the value of this register is larger than the width of a High pulse on the pwmA signal, the rising-edge delay consumes the entire High time of the signal, resulting in no High output on pwmA′. Care must be taken to ensure that the pwmA High time always exceeds the rising-edge delay.

If the Dead-Band Rising-Edge Delay mode is immediate (the DBRISEUPD = 0x0 in the PWMnCTL register), the 12-bit RISEDELAY value is used immediately. If the update mode is locally synchronized, this value is used the next time the counter reaches zero. If the update mode is globally synchronized, this value is used the next time the counter reaches zero after a synchronous update has been requested through the PWM Master Control (PWMCTL) register. If this register is rewritten before the actual update occurs, the previous value is never used and is lost.

7.6.3.10 *PWM Generator Dead-Band Falling-Edge Delay Register* (PWMnDBFALL)

Similar to PWM0DBRISE~PWM3DBRISE registers, the PWM0DBFALL~PWM3DBFALL registers are used to control the delay period between the rising edge of the pwmB′ signal and the falling edge of the pwmA signal. These registers are also 32-bit registers, but only the lower 12 bits are used on these registers. The lower 12 bits are called FALLDELAY bits and they contain the number of clock cycles to delay the rising edge of the pwmB′ signal from the falling edge of the pwmA signal. If the dead-band generator is disabled, this register is ignored.

If the value of this register is larger than the width of a Low pulse on the pwmA signal, the falling-edge delay consumes the entire Low time of the signal, resulting in no Low time on the output. Care must be taken to ensure that the pwmA Low time always exceeds the falling-edge delay.

If the Dead-Band Falling-Edge-Delay mode is immediate (the DBFALLUPD = 0x0 in the PWMnCTL register), the 12-bit FALLDELAY value is used immediately. If the update mode is locally synchronized, this value is used the next time the counter reaches zero. If the update mode is globally synchronized, this value is used the next time the counter reaches zero after a synchronous update has been requested through the PWM Master Control (PWMCTL) register. If this register is rewritten before the actual update occurs, the previous value is never used and is lost.

7.6.3.11 *PWM Interrupt and Trigger Enable Register* (PWMnINTEN)

These registers, PWM0INTEN~PWM3INTEN, are used to control the interrupt and ADC trigger generation capabilities of the PWM generators. Each of these four registers controls the related PWM generator block. The events that can cause an interrupt or an ADC trigger are as follows:

- The counter is equal to the load register.
- The counter is equal to zero.
- The counter is equal to the PWMnCMPA register while counting up.
- The counter is equal to the PWMnCMPA register while counting down.
- The counter is equal to the PWMnCMPB register while counting up.
- The counter is equal to the PWMnCMPB register while counting down.

Any combination of these events can generate either an interrupt or an ADC trigger. The PWMnRIS register provides information about which events have caused raw interrupts.

The bit-field values for these registers are shown in Figure 7.38. The bit-field value and related function of these registers are shown in Table 7.25.

7.6.3.12 *PWM Raw Interrupt Status Register* (PWMnRIS)

These registers, PWM0RIS~PWM3RIS, are 32-bit registers, but only the lower 6 bits are used to provide the interrupt source information for the raw interrupts generated by the related events. When an event, such as Counter = 0 or Counter = PWMnCMPA up or down, occurred, the related bits on this register are set to 1 to indicate that some related raw interrupts or trigger events have been occurred if the related bits in the PWMnINTEN register have been set to enable these raw interrupts or triggers to occur.

Each of these registers provides the raw interrupt status for the related PWM Generator block, PWM0RIS is used for PWM Generator 0 block, PWM1RIS is for PWM Generator 1 block, and so on. Bits in this register are cleared by writing a 1 to the corresponding bit in the PWM Interrupt Status and Clear (PWMnISC) register.

The bit-field values for these registers are shown in Figure 7.39. The bit-field value and related function of these registers are shown in Table 7.26.

Unlike some interrupt control registers used for other peripherals, in the PWM module controls, there is no PWM Interrupt Mask register available. Therefore, as soon as a raw interrupt is generated and set in the PWMnRIS register, the interrupt is sent to the NVIC to be further processed and handled.

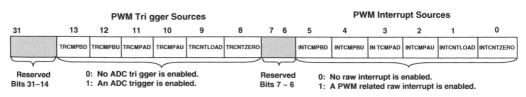

Figure 7.38. Bit fields in the PWM interrupt and trigger enable register.

Table 7.25.   Bit-field value and its function for PWM interrupt enable register.

Bit	Name	Reset	Function
31:14	Reserved	0x0	Reserved
13	TRCMPBD	0	Trigger for Counter = PWMnCMPB Down. 0: No ADC trigger is output. 1: Enable ADC trigger to output when the counter matches the value in the PWMnCMPB register value while counting down.
12	TRCMPBU	0	Trigger for Counter = PWMnCMPB Up. 0: No ADC trigger is output. 1: Enable ADC trigger to output when the counter matches the value in the PWMnCMPB register value while counting up.
11	TRCMPAD	0	Trigger for Counter = PWMnCMPA Down. 0: No ADC trigger is output. 1: Enable ADC trigger to output when the counter matches the value in the PWMnCMPA register value while counting down.
10	TRCMPAU	0	Trigger for Counter = PWMnCMPA Up. 0: No ADC trigger is output. 1: Enable ADC trigger to output when the counter matches the value in the PWMnCMPA register value while counting up.
9	TRCNTLOAD	0	Trigger for Counter = PWMnLOAD. 0: No ADC trigger is output. 1: Enable ADC trigger pulse to output when the counter matches the PWMnLOAD register.
8	TRCNTZERO	0	Trigger for Counter = 0. 0: No ADC trigger is output. 1: Enable ADC trigger pulse to output when the counter is 0.
7:6	Reserved	0x0	Reserved
5	INTCMPBD	0	Interrupt for Counter = PWMnCMPB Down. 0: Disable interrupt to occur. 1: Enable a raw interrupt to occur when the counter matches the value in the PWMnCMPB register value while counting down.
4	INTCMPBU	0	Interrupt for Counter = PWMnCMPB Up. 0: Disable interrupt to occur. 1: Enable a raw interrupt to occur when the counter matches the value in the PWMnCMPB register value while counting up.
3	INTCMPAD	0	Interrupt for Counter = PWMnCMPA Down. 0: Disable interrupt to occur. 1: Enable a raw interrupt to occur when the counter matches the value in the PWMnCMPA register value while counting down.
2	INTCMPAU	0	Interrupt for Counter = PWMnCMPA Up. 0: Disable interrupt to occur. 1: Enable a raw interrupt to occur when the counter matches the value in the PWMnCMPA register value while counting up.
1	INTCNTLOAD	0	Interrupt for Counter = PWMnLOAD. 0: Disable interrupt to occur. 1: Enable a raw interrupt to occur when the counter matches the PWMnLOAD register.
0	INTCNTZERO	0	Interrupt for Counter = 0. 0: Disable interrupt to occur. 1: Enable a raw interrupt to occur when the counter is 0.

7.6.3.13 *PWM Interrupt Status and Clear Register* (PWMnISC)

Similar to PWMnRIS register, only the lower 6 bits are used on this 32-bit register. This register has two functions. First it can be used to monitor the raw interrupt status for any PWM event. Second, this register can be used to clear a raw interrupt set in the PWMnRIS register and the related status in this register.

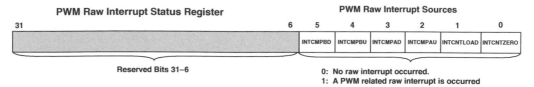

Figure 7.39. Bit fields in the PWM Raw Interrupt Status register.

Four registers, PWM0ISC~PWM3ISC, are used to monitor and clear any raw interrupt status, and each of them is used for the related PWM Generator block. The PWM0ISC is used for PWM Generator 0 block, PWM1ISC is for PWM Generator 1 block, and so on. If an event has been enabled in the PWMnINTEN register and occurred in the PWMnRIS register, the related event bit in this register is set to 1.

The bit-field values for these registers are identical to those in the PWMnRIS register shown in Figure 7.39. The bit-field value and related function of these registers are shown in Table 7.27.

When using this register to clear an interrupt, the following points must be noted:

- The interrupt status can only be cleared one PWM Clock cycle after the interrupt occurs.

Table 7.26. Bit-field value and its function for PWM raw interrupt status register.

Bit	Name	Reset	Function
31:6	Reserved	0x0	Reserved
5	INTCMPBD	0	Interrupt Status for Counter = PWMnCMPB Down. 0 : No interrupt is occurred. 1 : A raw interrupt is occurred when the counter matches the value in the PWMnCMPB register value while counting down. This bit is cleared by writing a 1 to the INTCMPBD bit in the PWMnISC register.
4	INTCMPBU	0	Interrupt Status for Counter = PWMnCMPB Up. 0 : No interrupt is occurred. 1 : A raw interrupt is occurred when the counter matches the value in the PWMnCMPB register value while counting up. This bit is cleared by writing a 1 to the INTCMPBU bit in the PWMnISC register.
3	INTCMPAD	0	Interrupt Status for Counter = PWMnCMPA Down. 0 : No interrupt is occurred. 1 : A raw interrupt is occurred when the counter matches the value in the PWMnCMPA register value while counting down. This bit is cleared by writing a 1 to the INTCMPAD bit in the PWMnISC register.
2	INTCMPAU	0	Interrupt Status for Counter = PWMnCMPA Up. 0 : No interrupt is occurred. 1 : A raw interrupt is occurred when the counter matches the value in the PWMnCMPA register value while counting up. This bit is cleared by writing a 1 to the INTCMPAU bit in the PWMnISC register.
1	INTCNTLOAD	0	Interrupt Status for Counter = PWMnLOAD. 0 : No interrupt is occurred. 1 : A raw interrupt is occurred when the counter matches the PWMnLOAD register. This bit is cleared by writing a 1 to the INTCNTLOAD bit in the PWMnISC register.
0	INTCNTZERO	0	Interrupt Status for Counter = 0. 0 : No interrupt is occurred. 1 : A raw interrupt is occurred when the counter is 0. This bit is cleared by writing a 1 to the INTCNTZERO bit in the PWMnISC register.

Table 7.27. Bit-field value and its function for PWM interrupt status and clear register.

Bit	Name	Reset	Function
31:6	Reserved	0x0	Reserved
5	INTCMPBD	0	Interrupt Status for Counter = PWMnCMPB Down. 0: No interrupt has occurred or the interrupt is masked. 1: The INTCMPBD bits in the PWMnRIS and PWMnINTEN registers are set, providing an interrupt to the interrupt controller. This bit is cleared by writing a 1 to the INTCMPBD bit in this register. Clearing this bit also clears the INTCMPBD bit in the PWMnRIS register.
4	INTCMPBU	0	Interrupt Status for Counter = PWMnCMPB Up. 0: No interrupt has occurred or the interrupt is masked. 1: The INTCMPBU bits in the PWMnRIS and PWMnINTEN registers are set, providing an interrupt to the interrupt controller. This bit is cleared by writing a 1 to the INTCMPBU bit in this register. Clearing this bit also clears the INTCMPBU bit in the PWMnRIS register.
3	INTCMPAD	0	Interrupt Status for Counter = PWMnCMPA Down. 0: No interrupt has occurred or the interrupt is masked. 1: The INTCMPAD bits in the PWMnRIS and PWMnINTEN registers are set, providing an interrupt to the interrupt controller. This bit is cleared by writing a 1 to the INTCMPAD bit in this register. Clearing this bit also clears the INTCMPAD bit in the PWMnRIS register.
2	INTCMPAU	0	Interrupt Status for Counter = PWMnCMPA Up. 0: No interrupt has occurred or the interrupt is masked. 1: The INTCMPAU bits in the PWMnRIS and PWMnINTEN registers are set, providing an interrupt to the interrupt controller. This bit is cleared by writing a 1 to the INTCMPAU bit in this register. Clearing this bit also clears the INTCMPAU bit in the PWMnRIS register.
1	INTCNTLOAD	0	Interrupt Status for Counter = PWMnLOAD. 0: No interrupt has occurred or the interrupt is masked. 1: The INTCNTLOAD bits in the PWMnRIS and PWMnINTEN registers are set, providing an interrupt to the interrupt controller. This bit is cleared by writing a 1 to the INTCNTLOAD bit in this register. Clearing this bit also clears the INTCNTLOAD bit in the PWMnRIS register.
0	INTCNTZERO	0	Interrupt Status for Counter = 0. 0: No interrupt has occurred or the interrupt is masked. 1: The INTCNTZERO bits in the PWMnRIS and PWMnINTEN registers are set, providing an interrupt to the interrupt controller. This bit is cleared by writing a 1 to the INTCNTZERO bit in this register. Clearing this bit also clears the INTCNTZERO bit in the PWMnRIS register

- The larger the PWM Clock Divider (PWMDIV) value in PWMCC register, the longer the system delay is to clear the interrupt.

Finally let's take a look at the fault source register.

7.6.3.14 *PWM Fault Source n Register* (PWMFLTSRCn)

These registers, PWM0FLTSRC0~PWM3FLTSRC0, are 32-bit registers but only the lower 2 bits (FAULT1 and FAULT0) are used. These registers specify which fault pin inputs are used to generate a fault condition. Each bit in these registers indicates whether the corresponding fault pin is included in the fault condition. All enabled fault pins are ORed together to form the PWMnFLTSRC0 portion of the fault condition.

The PWMnFLTSRC0 fault condition is then ORed with the PWMnFLTSRC1 fault condition to generate the final fault condition for the PWM generator. If the FLTSRC bit in

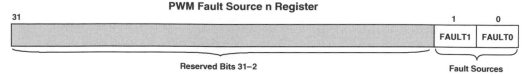

Figure 7.40.   Bit fields in the PWM Fault Source n register.

Table 7.28.   Bit-field value and its function for the PWM fault source register.

Bit	Name	Reset	Function
31:2	Reserved	0x0	Reserved
1	FAULT1	0	FAULT 1 Input. 0: The Fault1 signal is suppressed and cannot generate a fault condition. 1: The Fault1 signal value is ORed with all other fault condition generation inputs (Faultn signals and digital comparators). The FLTSRC bit in the PWMnCTL register must be set for this bit to affect fault condition generation.
0	FAULT0	0	FAULT 0 Input. 0: The Fault0 signal is suppressed and cannot generate a fault condition. 1: The Fault0 signal value is ORed with all other fault condition generation inputs (Faultn signals and digital comparators). The FLTSRC bit in the PWMnCTL register must be set for this bit to affect fault condition generation.

the PWMnCTL register is clear, only the Fault0 signal affects the fault condition generated. Otherwise, sources defined in PWMnFLTSRC0 and PWMnFLTSRC1 affect the fault condition generated.

The bit-field values for these registers are shown in Figure 7.40. The bit-field value and related function of these registers are shown in Table 7.28.

At this point, we have finished our discussion about most popular and widely used registers in PWM generators. Each PWM module contains four PWM generators or generator blocks, and each block has its own independent register ranging from PWM0 to PWM3. For example, for the PWM generator control registers, each block has its own control register, such as PWM0CTL for block 0, PWM1CTL for block 1, PWM2CTL for block 2, and PWM3CTL for block 3.

Now let's have a global picture about the PWM module with its architecture and structure.

7.6.4 PWM Module Architecture and Functional Block Diagram

Figure 7.41 shows a functional block diagram of the PWM modules used in the TM4C123GH6PM MCU system.

The entire PWM module is composed of the following components:

- Control and Status Block
- PWM Generator Blocks
- Output Control Block
- Interrupt Control Block

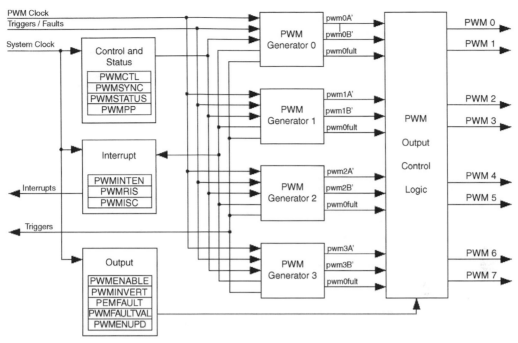

Figure 7.41. Architecture and functional block diagram of PWM module. (Reprinted with the permission of the Texas Instruments Incorporated.)

We have provided detailed discussion about the PWM generator blocks, and now let's concentrate on the rest three blocks.

7.6.4.1 The Control and Status Block

This block provides the global or master controls to all four PWM generators and monitors the running status of them. This block is driven by a system clock as the clock source. Generally, the PWM module has two kinds of clock sources to be used:

- The system clock
- A pre-divided system clock

The clock source can be selected by programming the USEPWMDIV bit in the Run-Mode Clock Configuration (RCC) register. The PWMDIV bit field specifies the divisor of the System Clock that is used to create the PWM Clock.

The control functions in this block are provided by four registers:

1. PWM Master Control Register (PWMCTL)
2. PWM Timer Base Synchronous Register (PWMSYNC)
3. PWM Status Register (PWMSTATUS)
4. PWM Peripheral Properties Register (PWMPP)

Let' take a closer look at these registers one by one. First let's have a closer look at the Run-Mode Clock Configuration (RCC) register.

31	30	29	28	27	26	25	24	23	22	21	20	19	18	17	16
reserved				ACG		SYSDIV			USESYSDIV	reserved	USEPWMDIV	PWMDIV			reserved

Type	RO	RO	RO	RO	RW	RW	RW	RW	RW	RW	RW	RW	RW	RW	RW	RW
Reset	0	0	0	0	0	1	1	1	1	0	0	0	1	1	1	0

15	14	13	12	11	10	9	8	7	6	5	4	3	2	0
reserved		PWRDN	reserved	BYPASS		XTAL				OSCSRC		reserved		MOSCDIS

Type	RO	RO	RW	RO	RW	RW	RW	RW	RW	RW	RW	RW	RO	RO	RO	RW
Reset	0	0	1	1	1	1	1	0	1	1	0	1	0	0	0	1

Figure 7.42.   Bit fields in the Run-Mode Clock Configuration (RCC) register. (Reprinted with the permission of the Texas Instruments Incorporated.)

Table 7.29.   The PWMDIV bit-field value and its function in RCC register.

Bit	Name	Reset	Function
31:28	Reserved	0x0	Reserved
19:17	PWMDIV	0x7	PWM Unit Clock Divisor. 0x0: ÷2. 0x1: ÷4. 0x2: ÷8. 0x3: ÷16. 0x4: ÷32. 0x5: ÷64. 0x6: ÷64. 0x7: ÷64 (default)

7.6.4.1.1 The Run-Mode Clock Configuration Register (RCC)

We have discussed this register in Section 2.6.4.4 in Chapter 2. In this section, we only concentrate on the bit field PWMDIV in this register.

Figure 7.42 shows the bit fields on this register. The PWMDIV bit field includes bits 19~17. Table 7.29 shows this bit field and its function. After a system reset operation, the default value for this bit field is 0x7, which means that the PWM clock source is the system clock that is divided by 64.

7.6.4.1.2 The PWM Master Control Register (PWMCTL)

This register is a master control register used to control four PWM generator blocks.

Each of the two PWM modules has an independent PWMCTL register, which is mainly used to control the updating and synchronizing of four PWM generator blocks.

Although this is a 32-bit register, only the lower 4 bits are used and each bit is used to control one PWM generator block.

The bit-field values of this register are shown in Figure 7.43.

The bit-field function for each related PWM generator is similar. When the bit is 0, it means that no updating or synchronizing action is needed for the selected PWM generator. If the bit is 1, it indicates that any updating to a load or comparator register in the related PWM generator is applied the next time the corresponding counter becomes zero.

The bit GLOBALSYNC0 is for the PWM Generator 0 block, GLOBALSYNC1 is for the PWM Generator 1 block, and so on.

7.6.4.1.3 The PWM Timer Base Synchronous Register (PWMSYNC)

Similar to the PWM Master Control register, each PWM module has an independent PWM Timer Base Synchronous (PWMSYNC) register. The lower 4 bits on this register are used to control 4 PWM generator blocks.

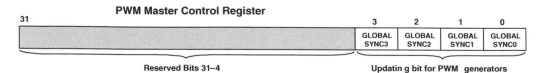

PWM Master Control Register

31				3	2	1	0
				GLOBAL SYNC3	GLOBAL SYNC2	GLOBAL SYNC1	GLOBAL SYNC0

Reserved Bits 31–4   Updating bit for PWM generators

Figure 7.43.   Bit fields in the PWM Master Control register.

This register provides a method to perform synchronization of the counters in the PWM generation blocks. Setting a bit in this register causes the specified counter to reset back to 0, while setting multiple bits resets multiple counters simultaneously. The bits are auto-cleared after the reset has occurred. Reading them back as zero indicates that the synchronization has completed.

The bit fields on this register are identical with those in the PWMCTL register shown in Figure 7.43. The difference is that the four lower bits are SYNC3~SYNC0, and each bit control the synchronization for one related PWM generator block.

7.6.4.1.4 The PWM Status Register (PWMSTATUS) Similar to PWM Fault Source register, this register provides the unlatched status of the PWM generator fault condition. The bit fields on this register are identical to those in the PWMFLTSRCn registers shown in Figure 7.40. The difference is that the bit values on this register indicate whether the fault condition is asserted or not. If a bit is 0, this means that the fault condition is not asserted. If the bit is 1, it indicates that a fault condition is asserted.

7.6.4.1.5 The PWM Peripheral Properties Register (PWMPP) The PWMPP register provides information regarding the properties of the PWM module. These properties include: extended fault, extended synchronization, fault inputs, and generators.

7.6.4.2 The Output Control Block

The output control block contains five control registers:

1. PWM Output Enable Register (PWMENABLE)
2. PWM Output Inversion Register (PWMINVERT)
3. PWM Output Fault Register (PWMFAULT)
4. PWM Fault Condition Value Register (PWMFAULTVAL)
5. PWM Enable Update Register (PWMENUPD)

Let's discuss these registers one by one in more detail.

7.6.4.2.1 The PWM Output Enable Register (PWMENABLE) Similar to the PWM Master Control register, each PWM module has an independent PWM Output Enable (PWMENABLE) register. The lower 8 bits on this register are used to control whether the pwmA′ and pwmB′ signals can be transferred to 8 PWM output pins MnPWMn.

The bit-field values of this register are shown in Figure 7.44.

This register provides a master control of which generated pwmA′ and pwmB′ signals are output to the MnPWMn pins. By disabling a PWM output, the generation process can continue without driving PWM signals to the pins. When related bits in this register are set to 1s, the corresponding pwmA′ or pwmB′ signal is passed through to the output stage.

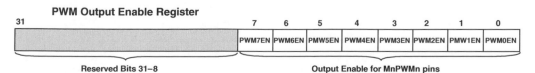

Figure 7.44. Bit fields in the PWM Output Enable (PWMENABLE) register.

Table 7.30. Bit-field value and its function for the PWM output enable register.

Bit	Name	Reset	Function
31:8	Reserved	0x0	Reserved
7	PWM7EN	0	MnPWM7 Output Enable. 0: The MnPWM7 pin has a zero value. 1: The generated pwm3B' signal is passed to the MnPWM7 pin.
6	PWM6EN	0	MnPWM6 Output Enable. 0: The MnPWM6 pin has a zero value. 1: The generated pwm3A' signal is passed to the MnPWM6 pin.
5	PWM5EN	0	MnPWM5 Output Enable. 0: The MnPWM5 pin has a zero value. 1: The generated pwm2B' signal is passed to the MnPWM5 pin.
4	PWM4EN	0	MnPWM4 Output Enable. 0: The MnPWM4 pin has a zero value. 1: The generated pwm2A' signal is passed to the MnPWM4 pin.
3	PWM3EN	0	MnPWM3 Output Enable. 0: The MnPWM3 pin has a zero value. 1: The generated pwm1B' signal is passed to the MnPWM3 pin.
2	PWM2EN	0	MnPWM2 Output Enable. 0: The MnPWM2 pin has a zero value. 1: The generated pwm1A' signal is passed to the MnPWM2 pin.
1	PWM1EN	0	MnPWM1 Output Enable. 0: The MnPWM1 pin has a zero value. 1: The generated pwm0B' signal is passed to the MnPWM1 pin.
0	PWM0EN	0	MnPWM0 Output Enable. 0: The MnPWM0 pin has a zero value. 1: The generated pwm0A' signal is passed to the MnPWM0 pin.

When bits are clear, the pwmA' or pwmB' signal is replaced by a zero value which is also passed to the output stage.

The bit-field value and related function of this register are shown in Table 7.30.

7.6.4.2.2 The PWM Output Inversion Register (PWMINVERT)   Similar to PWMEN– ABLE register, the PWM Output Inversion register also uses the lower 8 bits to enable the pwmA' and pwmB' signals transferred to the MnPWMn pins to be inverted.

The bit-field values on this register are identical with those in the PWMENABLE register shown in Figure 7.44. The only difference is that the lower 8 bits' names on this register are changed to PWMnINV, where n = 0~7 and is used for each MnPWMn pin.

If a bit on this register is 0, it means that the generated pwmA' or pwmB' can be normally transferred to the related MnPWMn pins without inversion. However, if a bit is 1, this means that the pwmA' or pwmB' signals are transferred to the related MnPWMn pins with inversion.

This register provides a master control of the polarity of the MnPWMn signals on the device pins. The pwmA' and pwmB' signals generated by the PWM generator are active High, but they can be made active Low via this register. In addition, if the PWMFAULT register enables a specific value to be placed on the MnPWMn signals during a fault condition, that value is inverted if the corresponding bit in this register is set.

7.6.4.2.3 The PWM Output Fault Register (PWMFAULT)   This register controls the behavior of the MnPWMn outputs in the presence of fault conditions. Both the fault inputs and debug events are considered fault conditions. On a fault condition, each pwmA' or pwmB' signal can be passed through unmodified or driven to the value specified by the corresponding bit in the PWMFAULTVAL register. For outputs that are configured for pass-through, the debug event handling on the corresponding PWM generator also determines if the pwmA' or pwmB' signal continues to be generated.

Fault condition control occurs before the output inverter, so PWM signals driven to a specified value on fault are inverted if the channel is configured for inversion. Therefore, the pin is driven to the logical complement of the specified value on a fault condition.

Similar to the PWMENABLE register, this register also uses the lower 8 bits to control whether the pwmA' or pwmB' signals can be normally transferred to the related MnPWMn pins or a specified value should be transferred to those MnPWMn pins if a fault condition occurred. The lower 8 bits are named FAULT7~FAULT0, and each bit is to control one MnPWMn pin. If one of these bits is 0, it means that the pwmA' or pwmB' signals can be normally transferred to the related MnPWMn pins even a fault occurred. If a bit is 1, this means that a specified value indicated in the PWMn bit in the PWMFAULTVAL register is transferred to the related MnPWMn pin if a fault occurred.

7.6.4.2.4 The PWM Fault Condition Value Register (PWMFAULTVAL) This register specifies the output value driven on the MnPWMn pins during a fault condition if enabled by the corresponding bit in the PWMFAULT register. Note that if the corresponding bit in the PWMINVERT register is set, the output value is driven to the inversion of the bit value in this register.

Similar to the PWMFAULT register, this register also uses the lower 8 bits, PWM7~PWM0, to indicate what special value should be sent to the related MnPWMn pins if a fault occurred. A Low is sent to the related MnPWMn pin if a bit on this register is 0 and if the related FAULTn bit in the PWMFAULT register is set to 1 when a fault occurred. Otherwise a High is sent to the MnPWMn pin if a bit on this register is 1 and if the related FAULTn bit in the PWMFAULT register is set to 1 when a fault condition occurred.

7.6.4.2.5 The PWM Enable Update Register (PWMENUPD) This register specifies when updates to the PWMnEN bit in the PWMENABLE register are performed. The PWMnEN bit enables the pwmA' or pwmB' output to be passed to the related MnPWMn pin. Updates can be immediate, locally or globally synchronized to the next synchronous update.

This is a 32-bit register, but the upper 16 bits are reserved and the lower 16 bits are divided into eight 2-bit segments, ENUPD7~ENUPD0, and each segment control the updating scale for a related MnPWMn pin. For a segment with 0x0, the updating is immediate. For 0x2, the updating is locally synchronized, and 0x3 is for an updating to be occurred in the globally synchronized way. The value 0x1 is reserved.

7.6.4.3 The Interrupt Control Block

Three control registers in this block are used to control and configure the PWM-related interrupts:

1. PWM Interrupt Enable Register (PWMINTEN)
2. PWM Raw Interrupt Status Register (PWMRIS)
3. PWM Interrupt Status and Clear Register (PWMISC)

Let's take a closer look at these registers.

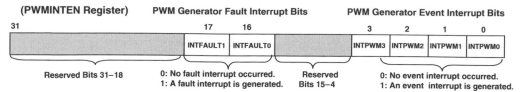

Figure 7.45.   Bit fields in the PWM Interrupt Enable (PWMINTEN) register.

7.6.4.3.1 The PWM Interrupt Enable Register (PWMINTEN) Unlike the
PWMnINTEN register, in which an interrupt is triggered by an event, this register is a global interrupt enable register and is used to enable and control the interrupts for all 4 PWM generator blocks.

In fact, this register controls the global interrupt generation capabilities of the PWM module. The events that can cause an interrupt are the fault input and the individual interrupts from the PWM generators.

The bit-field values for this register are shown in Figure 7.45. The bit-field value and related function of this register are shown in Table 7.31.

Table 7.31.   Bit field value and its function for PWM interrupt enable register.

Bit	Name	Reset	Function
31:18	Reserved	0x0	Reserved
17	INTFAULT1	0	Interrupt Fault 1. 0: The fault condition for PWM generator 1 is disabled and not sent to the interrupt controller. 1: An interrupt is sent to the interrupt controller when the fault condition for PWM generator 1 is asserted.
16	INTFAULT0	0	Interrupt Fault 0. 0: The fault condition for PWM generator 0 is disabled and not sent to the interrupt controller. 1: An interrupt is sent to the interrupt controller when the fault condition for PWM generator 0 is asserted.
15:4	Reserved	0x0	Reserved
3	INTPWM3	0	PWM3 Interrupt Enable. 0: The PWM generator 3 interrupt is disabled and not sent to the interrupt controller. 1: An interrupt is sent to the interrupt controller when the PWM generator 3 block asserts an interrupt.
2	INTPWM2	0	PWM2 Interrupt Enable. 0: The PWM generator 2 interrupt is disabled and not sent to the interrupt controller. 1: An interrupt is sent to the interrupt controller when the PWM generator 2 block asserts an interrupt.
1	INTPWM1	0	PWM1 Interrupt Enable. 0: The PWM generator 1 interrupt is disabled and not sent to the interrupt controller. 1: An interrupt is sent to the interrupt controller when the PWM generator 1 block asserts an interrupt.
0	INTPWM0	0	PWM0 Interrupt Enable. 0: The PWM generator 0 interrupt is disabled and not sent to the interrupt controller. 1: An interrupt is sent to the interrupt controller when the PWM generator 0 block asserts an interrupt.

7.6.4.3.2 The PWM Raw Interrupt Status Register (PWMRIS) This register is very similar to PWM Interrupt Enable register (PWMINTEN) with the same bit fields and similar functions. Unlike the PWMnRIS registers, in which only an event or a fault condition can trigger a raw interrupt and set in the corresponding bits in that register, this register is used to control and set raw interrupts for all 4 PWM generators by using the bits INTPWM3~INTPWM0 and bits INTFAULT1~INTFAULT0, respectively.

If a bit is 0, the related fault or PWM generator interrupt has not occurred. If a bit has 1, the related fault or PWM generator interrupt has occurred.

The fault interrupt is asserted based on the fault condition source that is specified by the PWMnCTL, PWMnFLTSRC0, and PWMnFLTSRC1 registers. The fault interrupt is latched on detection and must be cleared through the PWM Interrupt Status and Clear (PWMISC) register. The actual value of the MnFAULTn signals can be observed using the PWMSTATUS register.

7.6.4.3.3 The PWM Interrupt Status and Clear Register (PWMISC) This register provides a summary of the interrupt status of the individual PWM generator blocks. If a fault interrupt is set, the corresponding MnFAULTn input has caused an interrupt. For the fault interrupt, a write of 1 to that bit position clears the latched interrupt status. If a block interrupt bit is set, the corresponding generator block is asserting an interrupt. The individual interrupt status registers, PWMnISC, in each block must be inspected to determine the reason for the interrupt and used to clear the interrupt.

Similar to PWM Interrupt Enable (PWMINTEN) register, this register has the same bit fields. If a bit is 0, it means that the related interrupt has not been triggered. If a bit is 1, it means that the related interrupt has been triggered by a fault condition or by a PWM generator block and sent to the interrupt controller.

In order to track and find the actual interrupt triggering source, the individual or local raw interrupt status register, PWMnRIS, should be checked and it shows the source of this interrupt. This bit can be cleared by writing a 1 to the corresponding bit in the PWMnISC register.

The bit-field value and related function of this register are shown in Table 7.32.

7.6.5 PWM Module Components and Signal Descriptions

As we discussed in Section 7.6.4, each PWM module is composed of four blocks. The Control and Status block provides the global controls for four PWM generator blocks and monitors their running status. The Output Control block controls and directs related pwmA and pwmB signals to the related output MnPWMn pins via Dead-Band block. The Interrupt block provides the interrupt generations and status for PWM generators.

All PWM output pins MnPWMn can be used to drive PWM related peripherals via the related GPIO pins. In other words, any MnPWMn pin cannot be directly exposed to outside peripheral devices and must use the related GPIO pin as interface to be connected to any peripheral device.

Table 7.32. Bit-field value and its function for PWM interrupt status and clear register.

Bit	Name	Reset	Function
31:18	Reserved	0x0	Reserved
17	INTFAULT1	0	Fault 1 Interrupt Status. 0: The fault condition for PWM generator 1 is disabled and not sent to the interrupt controller. 1: An interrupt is sent to the interrupt controller when the fault condition for PWM generator 1 is asserted.
16	INTFAULT0	0	Fault 0 Interrupt Status. 0: The fault condition for PWM generator 0 is disabled and not sent to the interrupt controller. 1: An interrupt is sent to the interrupt controller when the fault condition for PWM generator 0 is asserted.
15:4	Reserved	0x0	Reserved
3	INTPWM3	0	PWM3 Interrupt Status. 0: The PWM generator 3 interrupt is disabled and not sent to the interrupt controller. 1: An interrupt is sent to the interrupt controller when the PWM generator 3 block asserts an interrupt. The PWM3RIS register shows the source of this interrupt. This bit is cleared by writing a 1 to the corresponding bit in the PWM3ISC register.
2	INTPWM2	0	PWM2 Interrupt Status. 0: The PWM generator 2 interrupt is disabled and not sent to the interrupt controller. 1: An interrupt is sent to the interrupt controller when the PWM generator 2 block asserts an interrupt. The PWM2RIS register shows the source of this interrupt. This bit is cleared by writing a 1 to the corresponding bit in the PWM2ISC register.
1	INTPWM1	0	PWM1 Interrupt Status. 0: The PWM generator 1 interrupt is disabled and not sent to the interrupt controller. 1: An interrupt is sent to the interrupt controller when the PWM generator 1 block asserts an interrupt. The PWM1RIS register shows the source of this interrupt. This bit is cleared by writing a 1 to the corresponding bit in the PWM1ISC register.
0	INTPWM0	0	PWM0 Interrupt Status. 0: The PWM generator 0 interrupt is disabled and not sent to the interrupt controller. 1: An interrupt is sent to the interrupt controller when the PWM generator 0 block asserts an interrupt. The PWM0RIS register shows the source of this interrupt. This bit is cleared by writing a 1 to the corresponding bit in the PWM0ISC register.

7.6.5.1 PWM Signal Description

In the TM4C123GH6PM MCU system, the related GPIO Ports and pins that are connected to different MnPWMn pins are shown in Table 7.33.

The PWM-related control signals are alternate functions for some GPIO Ports and default to be GPIO signals at reset. In Table 7.33, the first column lists the corresponding GPIO pins for these PWM signals. The AFSEL bit in the GPIO Alternate Function Select (GPIOAFSEL) register should be set to 1 to choose the PWM function. The number in parentheses is the PMCx encoding that must be programmed into the PMCn field in the GPIO Port Control (GPIOPCTL) register to assign the PWM signal to the specified GPIO port pin. Refer to Sections 2.6.3.3.1 and 2.6.3.3.3, Table 2.6, and Figure 2.19 in Chapter 2 to get more details about the GPIOAFSEL and GPIOPCTL registers and PMCx encoding related to the PWM control signals.

Table 7.33. GPIO pins assignment for PWM MnPWMn output pins.

GPIO Pin (PMCx)	PWM Pin	Pin Type	Description
PF2 (4) PD6 (4) PD4 (4)	M0FAULT0	Input	Module 0 PWM Fault 0.
PB6 (4)	M0PWM0	Output	Module 0 PWM 0. This signal is controlled by Module 0 PWM Generator 0.
PB7 (4)	M0PWM1	Output	Module 0 PWM 1. This signal is controlled by Module 0 PWM Generator 0.
PB4 (4)	M0PWM2	Output	Module 0 PWM 2. This signal is controlled by Module 0 PWM Generator 1.
PB5 (4)	M0PWM3	Output	Module 0 PWM 3. This signal is controlled by Module 0 PWM Generator 1.
PE4 (4)	M0PWM4	Output	Module 0 PWM 4. This signal is controlled by Module 0 PWM Generator 2.
PE5 (4)	M0PWM5	Output	Module 0 PWM 5. This signal is controlled by Module 0 PWM Generator 2.
PC4 (4) PD0 (4)	M0PWM6	Output	Module 0 PWM 6. This signal is controlled by Module 0 PWM Generator 3.
PC5 (4) PD1 (4)	M0PWM7	Output	Module 0 PWM 7. This signal is controlled by Module 0 PWM Generator 3.
PF4 (5)	M1FAULT0	Input	Module 1 PWM Fault 0.
PD0 (5)	M1PWM0	Output	Module 1 PWM 0. This signal is controlled by Module 1 PWM Generator 0.
PD1 (5)	M1PWM1	Output	Module 1 PWM 1. This signal is controlled by Module 1 PWM Generator 0.
PA6 (5) PE4 (5)	M1PWM2	Output	Module 1 PWM 2. This signal is controlled by Module 1 PWM Generator 1.
PA7 (5) PE5 (5)	M1PWM3	Output	Module 1 PWM 3. This signal is controlled by Module 1 PWM Generator 1.
PF0 (5)	M1PWM4	Output	Module 1 PWM 4. This signal is controlled by Module 1 PWM Generator 2.
PF1 (5)	M1PWM5	Output	Module 1 PWM 5. This signal is controlled by Module 1 PWM Generator 2.
PF2 (5)	M1PWM6	Output	Module 1 PWM 6. This signal is controlled by Module 1 PWM Generator 3.
PF3 (5)	M1PWM7	Output	Module 1 PWM 7. This signal is controlled by Module 1 PWM Generator 3.

Next let's discuss two important properties or functions applied in the PWM modules: the synchronization and fault conditions.

7.6.5.2 Synchronization Methods

Each PWM module provides four PWM generators, and each generator provides two PWM outputs that may be used in a wide variety of applications. Generally, the PWM module is used in one of two categories of operation:

- Unsynchronized: The PWM generator and its two output signals pwmA′ and pwmB′ are used alone, or independent of other PWM generators' outputs.
- Synchronized: The PWM generator and its two outputs signals are used in conjunction with other PWM generators using a common, unified time base. If multiple PWM generators are configured with the same counter load value, synchronization can be used to guarantee that they also have the same count value. In that case, the PWM generators must be configured before they are synchronized. With this feature, more than two MnPWMn signals can be produced with a known relationship between the edges of those signals because the counters always have the same values.

The counter in a PWM generator can be reset to zero by writing the PWM Time Base Sync (PWMSYNC) register and setting the SYNCn bit related to the generator. Multiple

PWM generators can also be synchronized together by setting all necessary SYNCn bits in one access. One of the examples is to set the SYNC0 and SYNC1 bits in the PWMSYNC register to cause the counters in PWM generators 0 and 1 to reset together.

Additional synchronization can be performed among multiple PWM generators by updating register contents in one of the following three ways:

- Immediately: The setup value has an immediate effect, and the hardware reacts immediately.
- Locally Synchronized: The setup value does not take effect until the counter reaches the value zero at the end of the PWM cycle.
- Globally Synchronized: The setup value does not affect the logic until two sequential events have occurred: (1) The Update mode for the generator function is programmed for global synchronization in the PWMnCTL register, and (2) the counter reaches zero at the end of the PWM cycle. This mode allows multiple items in multiple PWM generators to be updated simultaneously without odd effects during the update; everything runs from the old values until a point at which they all run from the new values. The Update mode of the load and comparator match values can be individually configured in each PWM generator block.

Generally, the Immediate mode is good enough to meet the requirements for most actual applications.

7.6.5.3 Fault Conditions

A fault condition is one in which the controller must be signaled to stop normal PWM function and then set the MnPWMn signals to a safe state. Two situations cause fault conditions:

- The microcontroller is stalled and cannot perform the necessary computation in the time required for motion control.
- An external error or event is detected.

Each PWM generator can use the following inputs to generate a fault condition:

- A MnFAULTn pin assertion.
- A stall of the controller generated by the debugger.
- The trigger of an ADC digital comparator.

Fault conditions are calculated based on each PWM generator. Each PWM generator configures the necessary conditions to indicate a fault condition exists. This method allows the development of applications with dependent and independent control.

Two fault input pins, MnFAULTn, are available for fault conditions. These inputs may be used with circuits that generate an active High or active Low signal to indicate an error condition.

The PWM generator's mode control, including fault condition handling, is provided in the PWMnCTL register. This register determines whether the input or a combination of MnFAULTn input signals and/or digital comparator triggers as configured by the PWMnFLTSRC0 and PWMnFLTSRC1 registers is used to generate a fault condition. The PWMnCTL register also selects whether the fault condition is maintained as long as the external condition lasts or if it is latched until the fault condition is cleared by software. Finally, this register also enables a counter that may be used to extend the period of a fault condition for external events to ensure that the duration is a minimum length. The minimum fault period count is specified in the PWMnMINFLTPER register.

At this point, we finished our discussion and introduction about the PWM modules used in the TM4C123GH6PM MCU system. Based on these discussions, now let's see how to initialize and configure a PWM module before we can use it to perform the desired PWM controls.

7.6.6 PWM Module Initialization and Configuration

Any PWM module must be initialized and configured before it can be implemented in any actual application. This initialization and configuration process can be divided into three parts:

- Initialize and Configure Clock Sources for PWM Module and GPIO Ports.
- Initialize and Configure GPIO Ports and Pins Related to PWM modules.
- Initialize and Configure PWM Module and Generators.

Now let's start this initialization and configuration process with an example. In this example, the PWM module 1 and generator 2 is configured to:

1. Generate a 25% duty cycle on the M1PWM4 pin.
2. Generate a 75% duty cycle on the M1PWM5 pin.
3. Use a divided system frequency, which is 5 KHz, as the input to the counter.
4. Use a 40-MHz system clock as the clock source.

7.6.6.1 Initialize and Configure the Clock Source for PWM Module and GPIO Ports

Perform the following operations to fulfill this initialization and configuration:

1. Configure the Run-Mode Clock Configuration (RCC) register in the System Control module:
   a. To use PLL and divisor 5 with a 16 MHz XTAL to get a 40 MHz system clock.
   b. To use the PWM, divide (USEPWMDIV) by setting this bit (bit 20) and set the divider bits PWMDIV (bits 19:17) to divide by 2 (000) to get a 20 MHz PWM clock.
2. Enable the PWM clock by writing a value of 0x0010.0000 to the RCGC0 register in the System Control module. Alternatively, use the PWM Run Mode Clock Gating Control (RCGCPWM) register to enable the PWM module 1 with a clock.
3. Enable the clock to the appropriate GPIO module via the RCGC2 register in the System Control module. Alternatively, use the GPIO Run Mode Clock Gating Control (RCGCGPIO) register to enable GPIO Ports with a clock.

7.6.6.2 Initialize and Configure GPIO Ports and Pins Related to PWM Modules

Perform the following operations to fulfill this initialization and configuration:

1. In the GPIO module, enable the appropriate pins for their alternate function using the GPIOAFSEL register. Refer to Sections 2.6.3.3.1, 2.6.3.3.3, Table 2.6 and Figure 2.19 in Chapter 2 to get more details about the GPIOAFSEL and GPIOPCTL registers and PMCx encoding related to the PWM control signals.
2. Configure the PMCx fields in the GPIOPCTL register to assign the PWM signals to the appropriate pins.
3. May need to use the GPIOLOCK and GPIOCR registers to make all modifications on GPIOAFSEL and GPIOPCTL registers above committed immediately.

7.6.6.3 Initialize and Configure the PWM Module and Generators

Perform the following operations to fulfill this initialization and configuration:

1. Configure the PWM generator for countdown mode with immediate updates to the parameters.

   a. Write the PWM1CTL register with a value of 0x0000.0000 (see Section 7.6.3.1).

   b. Write the PWM1GENA register with a value of 0x0000.008C (see Section 7.6.3.6).

   c. Write the PWM1GENB register with a value of 0x0000.080C (see Section 7.6.3.7).

2. Set the period for the counter. For a 5 kHz input frequency, the period = 1/5000, or 200 μs. The PWM clock source is 20 MHz. Thus there are 20 MHz/5 kHz = 4000 clock ticks per period.

   a. Use this value to set the PWM1LOAD register. In Count-Down mode, set the LOAD field in the PWM1LOAD register to the requested period minus one (4000 − 1 = 3999).

3. Set the pulse width of the M1PWM4 pin for a 25% duty cycle. Write the PWM1CMPA register with a value of 3000.

4. Set the pulse width of the M1PWM5 pin for a 75% duty cycle. Write the PWM1CMPB register with a value of 1000.

5. Start the counters in PWM1 generator 2. Write the PWM1CTL register with a value of 0x0000.0001.

6. Enable PWM outputs. Write the PWMENABLE register with a value of 0x0000.0003.

In the above configuration operations, steps 1, 3, and 4 are easy to be confused. Let's have a closer look at these steps.

Refer to Sections 7.6.3.6 and 7.6.3.7 for PWM1GENA and PWM1GENB registers. To generate a **pwmA** signal for the Comparator A Down mode, the bit fields ACTCMPAD (bits 7:6), ACTLOAD (bits 3:2), and ACTZERO (bits 1:0), are important and need to be configured. As shown in Figure 7.46, in order to make the **pwmA** a Low when the counter matches the value in the PWM1CMPA register when it is counting down, the bit field ACTCMPAD (bits 7:6) should be set to 0x2 (10). In order to make the **pwmA** a High when the counter matches the LOAD value in the PWM1LOAD register, the bit fields ACTLOAD (bits 3:2) should be set to 0x3 (11). For the counter equaling 0, no action should be taken, and therefore the bit fields ACTZERO (bits 1:0) should be 0x0 (00). So the PWM1GENA register should be initialized to 0x008C.

Similarly for the PWM1GENB register, in order to make the **pwmB** output a Low when the counter matches the value in the PWM1CMPB register when it is counting down, the bit

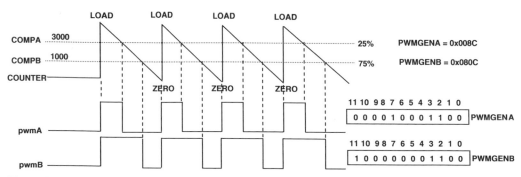

Figure 7.46. The initialization and configuration process for the PWM Module0.

field ACTCMPBD (bits 11:10) should be set to 0x2 (10). In order to make the pwmB a High when the counter matches the LOAD value in the PWM1LOAD register, the bit fields ACTLOAD (bits 3:2) should be set to 0x3 (11). For the counter equaling 0, no any action should be taken, and therefore the bit fields ACTZERO (bits 1:0) should be 0x0 (00). Thus the PWM1GENB register should be initialized to 0x080C.

For the PWM1CTL register, since we do not use any fault source and condition, any debug with local synchronization mode, and any immediate update mode with disabling this PWM generator block, all bit fields are 0. The point to be noted is that in order to initialize and configure any PWM generator, the generator must be first disabled. No any PWM generator can be configured when it is enabled.

For steps 3 and 4, a 25% duty cycle is calculated as $4000 * 0.75 = 3000$. A 75% duty cycle is $4000 * 0.25 = 1000$. Refer to Figure 7.46: The higher the duty cycle value, the lower the setup value installed in the PWM1CMPA or PWM1CMPB registers. This is just opposite to the common sense.

In step 5, after the PWM generator has been configured, the PWM1CTL is set by 0x01 to enable this generator. In step 6, the PWM Master Control register PWMENABLE register is configured with 0x03 to enable the pwm0A' signal to output to the M1PWM4 pin and enable the pwm0B' signal to output to the M1PWM5 pin, respectively.

Now let's have a look at the hardware configuration of the PWM modules in the EduBASE ARM® Trainer since we may use this trainer to connect to some motors via PWM modules.

7.6.7 PWM Module Architecture in the EduBASE ARM® Trainer

In the EduBASE ARM® Trainer, a quad half-H-bridge motor driver TB6612FNG is used to support and interface PWM modules to control and drive two servo or DC motors. A functional block diagram and hardware connection between the PWM modules and this motor driver TB6612FNG is shown in Figure 7.47. Table 7.34 shows the input and output relationship for this motor driver.

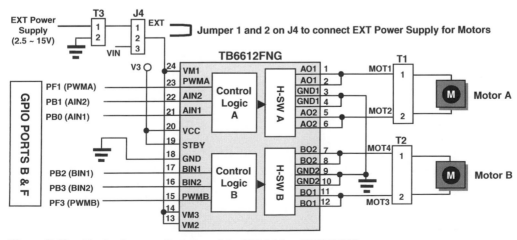

Figure 7.47.   The hardware configuration of the PWM driver TB6612FNG.

Table 7.34. Input and output of the TB6612FNG driver.

Input				Output		
IN1	IN2	PWM	STBY	OUT1	OUT2	MODE
H	H	H/L	H	L	L	Short Brake
L	H	H	H	L	H	CCW
		L	H	L	L	Short Brake
H	L	H	H	H	L	CW
		L	H	L	L	Short Brake
L	L	H	H	OFF (High Impedance)		Stop
H/L	H/L	H/L	L	OFF (High Impedance)		Standby

Each TB6612FNG driver has two control and driver blocks and each block can be used to drive one servo or DC motor. Therefore totally two motors can be driven by using this driver.

As shown in Figure 7.47 and Table 7.34, each control block in the TB6612FNG driver has three inputs and two outputs:

- Two inputs, IN1 and IN2, are used to control the rotating direction of the motor. When the input value is IN1 = L and IN2 = H (01), the motor is rotated in the counter-clockwise direction when the PWM is in High pulse. When IN1 = H and IN2 = L (10), the motor is rotated in the clockwise direction as a High pulse is obtained from the PWM input.
- The PWM input is used to control the rotating speed of the motor. The longer or the wider the High pulse, the higher of the motor rotating speed.
- Two outputs, OUT1 and OUT2, are directly connected to a motor to provide the driving power to the motor.
- The Standby signal STBY should always be High to make the driver work. If this signal is Low, it makes the driver to stand by with high output impedances on two outputs.

Now we are ready to build our example project to use PWM modules to control some DC motors to test the control and driving ability of the PWM modules.

7.6.8 Build an Example PWM Programming Project

In this example project, we need to use a DC motor fan (model number: EE80251S2-000U-999) as our target motor to drive. The hardware connection is shown in Figure 7.48.

The hardware and software configuration for this example project include:

- We use the first control and driving block, block A, in the motor driver TB6612FNG to control and drive our target 12V DC motor and fan.
- The DC motor with a fan is a 12-V DC motor with single rotating direction.
- The GPIO Ports and pins to be used include:
  - PF1 is used to provide the PWM driving signal to the motor (PWMA).

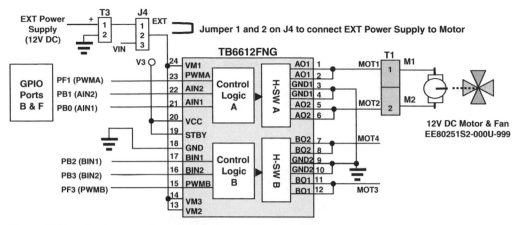

Figure 7.48.   Hardware configurations for the example project.

- PB0 (AIN1) and PB1 (AIN2) are used to provide the rotating direction signal (PB1:PB0 = 01 → CW and PB1:PB0 = 10 → CCW) for the motor. In this project, we use the first rotating direction PB1:PB0 = 01 since the motor can be rotated in a single direction.
- Connect the DC motor to two blue interfacing blocks M1 and M2 in the EduBASE ARM® Trainer with positive (red color) wire to M1 and reference (black color) wire to M2.
- Connect an external 12V DC power supply to the blue block T3 with positive wire to the + terminal on the T3.
- Change the jumper on the J4 to connect 1 and 2 pins together on the J4 to connect the external power supply to the TB6612FNG motor driver.

In this example project, we use Module 1 PWM Generator 2 (M1PWM5) to generate a duty-modified PWM signal to control this DC motor via pwm2B′ (PWM5) pin (refer to Figure 7.41) since the PF1 pin is connected to this pwm2B′ output pin for this generator in the EduBASE Trainer. The system clock we used is 40 MHz; after dividing by 2, a 20 MHz clock is applied for the PWM module 1. The input frequency to the counter is 5 kHz.

Now let's start to create this project DRAPWM.

7.6.8.1 Create a PWM Application Project DRAPWM

In this example project, we use Direct Register Access (DRA) method to implement the PWM peripheral to control a DC motor. Let's create a new MDK-ARM µVersion5 project DRAPWM under the folder C:\ARM Class Projects\Chapter 7, and add a new C file named DRAPWM.c into this project.

Enter the codes shown in Figure 7.49 into this source file. Let's have a closer look at this piece of codes to see how it works.

1. The code lines 4~7 are used to declare some useful header files used in this project.
2. In line, a user defined function Delay() is declared and this function is sued to delay some time for the project to keep the LEDs on as the project runs.
3. Two local variables, pw and RCC, are declared at the beginning of this main program.
4. The codes in lines 12~13 are used to set up the system clock to be used for this project. The SYSCTL_SYSDIV_5 is used to divide the PLL clock output by 5 to get a 40 MHz clock.

```
1   //*********************************************************************************************************
2   // DRAPWM.c - Main Application File for PWM - DC Motor
3   //*********************************************************************************************************
4   #include <stdint.h>
5   #include <stdbool.h>
6   #include "inc\tm4c123gh6pm.h"
7   #include "driverlib\sysctl.h"

8   void  Delay(uint32_t time);

9   int  main(void)
10  {
11    uint32_t  pw, RCC;

12    RCC = (SYSCTL_SYSDIV_5|SYSCTL_USE_PLL|SYSCTL_OSC_MAIN|SYSCTL_XTAL_16MHZ);
13    SYSCTL_RCC_R = RCC;                              // 40 MHz system clock source

14    SYSCTL_RCGCPWM_R |= 0x2;                         // enable PWM1 with clock
15    while((SYSCTL_PRPWM_R & 0x2) == 0) {};           // wait for PWM1 ready
16    SYSCTL_RCGCGPIO_R = 0x20 | 0x02;                 // enable Ports F & B with clocks
17    while((SYSCTL_PRGPIO_R & 0x22) == 0) {};         // wait GPIO Ports F & B ready
18    SYSCTL_RCC_R = SYSCTL_RCC_USEPWMDIV|SYSCTL_RCC_PWMDIV_2;  // 20 MHz clock
19    SYSCTL_RCGC0_R |= SYSCTL_RCGC0_PWM0;             // enable PWM1 again

20    GPIO_PORTF_LOCK_R = GPIO_LOCK_KEY;               // unlock GPTOF commit register
21    GPIO_PORTF_CR_R |= 0x2;                          // enable PF1 to be committed
22    GPIO_PORTF_LOCK_R = 0x0;                         // lock GPIOF commit register

23    // PWM1_2B - PF1 - M1PWM5 pin - Module 1 Generator 2 - pwm2B
24    PWM1_2_CTL_R = 0x0;                              // disable PWM1_2B or M1PWM5
25    PWM1_2_GENB_R = 0x0000080C;                      // high on LOAD, low on CMPB down
26    PWM1_2_LOAD_R = 3999;                            // load = 4000 - 1
27    PWM1_2_CTL_R = 0x1;                              // enable PWM1_2B or M1PWM5
28    PWM1_ENABLE_R = 0x20;                            // enable PWM1

29    GPIO_PORTF_DIR_R |= 0x02;                        // enable PF1 output pin
30    GPIO_PORTF_DEN_R |= 0x02;                        // enable PF1 digital pin
31    GPIO_PORTF_AFSEL_R |= 0x2;                       // PF1 - Alternate Function: PWM1-2B
32    GPIO_PORTF_PCTL_R |= GPIO_PCTL_PF1_M1PWM5;       // 0x00000050
33    GPIO_PORTF_AMSEL_R &= ~0x02;                     // disable analog function on PF1
34    GPIO_PORTB_DIR_R |= 0x03;                        // enable PB1, PB0 output pins
35    GPIO_PORTB_DEN_R |= 0x03;                        // enable PB1, PB0 digital function pins
36    GPIO_PORTB_DATA_R |= 0x01;                       // enable PB0 (AIN1=1) CW-rotation

37    while(1)
38    {
39      for (pw = 100; pw < 3999; pw += 20)            // increase duty cycle
40      {
41        PWM1_2_CMPB_R = pw;    Delay(50000);         // delay 15 ms
42      }
43      for (pw = 3999; pw > 100; pw -= 20)            // decrease duty cycle
44      {
45        PWM1_2_CMPB_R = pw;    Delay(50000);         // delay 15 ms
46      }
47    }
48  }

49  void Delay(uint32_t  time)                         // delay subroutine
50  {
51    uint32_t  Loop;
52    for (Loop = 0; Loop < time; Loop++) {}           // 0.3 µs at each loop for 40 MHz clock
53  }
```

Figure 7.49.   The codes for the example project DRAPWM.

5. The PWM module 1 is enabled and clocked in line 14.

6. In line 15, the PWM Peripheral Ready (PRPWM) register is used with a while() loop to wait until the PWM is fully enabled and ready to be accessed. Regularly this step is not necessary, but for the safe considerations, we used this register to temporarily hang up the program until the PWM module 1 is fully enabled. We did not discuss this register in this section since it is not always to be used in most projects.

7. The GPIO Ports B and F are enabled and clocked in line 16.

8. Similarly in line 17, the GPIO Peripheral Ready (PRGPIO) register is used with another while() loop to monitor and wait the GPIO Ports B and F are fully enabled and ready to be used. The lowest 6 bits on this register are used to check and confirm whether each GPIO Port is ready with bit 0 for Port A, bit 1 for Port B, and bit 5 for Port F. if a bit is set to 1, which means that the corresponding Port is ready. A 0x22 (00100010) mask is used to AND with this register to check both Ports B and F to make sure that they are ready.

9. The RCC register is initialized to use USEPWMDIV and PWMDIV bit fields to divide the system clock (40 MHz) by 2 to get a 20 MHz clock to drive the PWM module in line 18.

10. To make our project more robust, the PWM module 1 is re-enabled again by using the Run Mode Clock Gating Control Register 0 (RCGC0) in line 19. Setting up bit 20 (PWM0) on this register is to enable the PWM module since both PWM modules share the same clock source.

11. The codes in lines 20~22 are used to configure and set up the GPIO Commit Register (GPIOCR) to make sure that all modifications on GPIO Alternate Function Select (GPIOAFSEL) register and GPIO Port Control (GPIOPCTL) register for Port F are committed in time. In order to set up the GPIOCR, it must be unlocked first by assigning a value of 0x4C4F434B to the GPIOLOCK register since generally the GPIOCR is locked by the GPIOLOCK register, and the content of the GPIOCR cannot be modified until it is unlocked. The code in line 20 is to unlock the GPIOCR. Then the GPIOCR is updated by setting 1 to bit 2 (PF1) to enable the corresponding bits on the GPIOAFSEL and GPIOPCTL registers are committed if they are modified later. In line 22, the GPIOLOCK register is locked again to avoid any other modifications in the GPIOCR in the future. Refer to Section 2.6.3.3.4 in Chapter 2 to get more information about the GPIOCR register.

12. The codes in lines 24~28 are used to configure the PWM Module 1 Generator 2 (M1PWM5). First the PWM1 Generator 2 is disabled in line 24 by assigning a 0 to the M1PWM5 Control Register (PWM1_2_CTL_R) since any configuration can only be performed when the related PWM generator is disabled.

13. Then the PWM1 Generator 2 output pin pwm2B′ is configured to (a) output High when the counter gets the value equaling the LOAD and (b) output Low when the counter matched the value in the CMPB when the counter is counting down by assigning 0x0000080C to the PWM1_2_GENB_R in line 25.

14. The LOAD register is loaded with a value of 4000 − 1 = 3999 in line 26. Since the input frequency to the counter is 5 kHz, the PWM clock is 20 MHz; thus there are 20 MHz/ 5 kHz = 4000 clock ticks for each period. Load this number into the PWM1 Generator 2 LOAD register.

15. After these configurations, the M1PWM5 Control Register is enabled in line 27 to begin its function. When the LSB in that register, the ENABLE bit, is set to 1, the PWM1 Generator 2 is enabled and begins to work. Refer to Section 7.6.3.1 to get more details about this register.

16. The M1PWM5 output is enabled in line 28 by setting bit 5 in the PWM1 ENABLE register (PWM1_ENABLE_R) to enable pwm2B to be passed to the pwm2B′ pin.

17. The codes in lines 29~33 are used to configure Port F, pin1 or PF1, to work as an alternate function pin (PWM output pin). In lines 29~30, the PF1 is configured as an output and digital function pin. In line 31, the PF1 is configured as an alternate function pin by setting bit 2 in the GPIOAFSEL register to 1. In line 32, the GPIOPCTL register is configured to

enable PF1 pin to work as the M1PWM5 output pin by setting 0x00000050 to that register. Since the GPIOCR register has been configured in step 11 above, these settings for GPIOAFSEL and GPIOPCTL registers are committed immediately.

18. In line 33, the PF1 is disabled to work as an analog function pin. This configuration is important since the program may encounter some bug without this setup.

19. The codes in lines 34 and 35 are used to set up PB0 and PB1 as output and digital function pins to provide the rotation direction signal for the DC motor.

20. The PB0 is set to 1 to provide the motor to rotate in the CW direction in line 36.

21. The codes in lines 37~48 are used to send PWM output signals to the DC motor. These signals have different duty cycles because the comparator value stored in the CMPB register is always changed, either increased or decreased, by the codes in a while() loop.

22. The input frequency to the counter is 5 kHz with a period of 200 µs. The codes in lines 39~42 are used to increase the value in the CMPB register form 100 (100×200 µs $= 20$ ms) to 3999 (3999×200 µs $= 799.8$ ms ≈ 800 ms). Since the PWM1 Generator 2 is configured to output Low as the counter matched the CMPB value as it counts down, therefore the High pulse becomes shorter and shorter (from 779.8 ms to 0.2 ms) as this CMPB value increased. The result of this increasing is to make the duty cycle smaller and therefore make the rotation speed of the motor slower.

23. The codes in lines 43~48 are used to do the opposite job as the codes in lines 39~42. They reduce the CMPB value and therefore make the High pulse longer and longer (from 0.2 ms to 779.8 ms) and thus make the rotation speed of the motor faster and faster. Some time delay is inserted into these increment and decrement operations.

24. The codes in lines 49~53 are used to delay some time for the program to keep the motor to run at certain speed for a while.

Now let's first setup the environment to make it ready to build this project.

7.6.8.2 *Set Up the Environment to Build and Run the Project*

Perform the following operations to set up the environment for this project:

- Include the system header file path C:\ti\TivaWare_C_Series-2.0.1.11577 in the C/C++ tab under the Project|Options for Target 'Target 1' menu item. Since we used two system header files inc\tm4c123gh6pm.h and driverlib\sysctl.h in this project, we need to include the path for these header files.

- Select the debug adapter Stellaris ICDI in the Debug tab under the Project-|Options for Target 'Target 1' menu item.

Now build the project by going to Project|Build target menu item. If everything is fine, go to the Flash|Download item to download the image file of the project into the flash memory. Now go to Debug|Start/Stop Debug Session and Debug|Run item to run the project.

As the project runs, you can find that the DC motor is first rotating from a high speed to a lower speed, and then from a low speed to a high speed, and these rotations will continue in an infinitive way. Our project is successful.

Next let's have a quick discussion about the PWM API functions provided by the TivaWare™ Peripheral Driver Library.

7.7   THE PWM API FUNCTIONS IN THE TIVAWARE™ PERIPHERAL DRIVER LIBRARY

The TivaWare™ Peripheral Driver Library provides more than 35 API functions related to PWM modules operations. By using these functions, one can design some PWM-related projects in the Software Driver model, which means that the users can call these high-level built-in functions to easily and conveniently build some sophisticated projects in a short time. In this section, we only discuss some important and popular functions used for most applications. These functions can be divided into the following three groups:

1. PWM Modules and Generators Configuration and Setup Controls
2. PWM Output Controls
3. PWM Interrupt and Fault Controls

7.7.1   PWM Modules and Generators Configuration and Set Up Control Functions

The API functions involved in this group include:

- `SysCtlPWMClockSet()`: Configure and set up system clock for PWM modules.
- `PWMGenConfigure()`: Configure PWM Generators.
- `PWMGenEnable()`: Enable PWM Generators.
- `PWMGenDisable()`: Disable PWM Generators.
- `PWMGenPeriodSet()`: Set up the Cycle Time for the PWM Generator's Counter.
- `PWMPulseWidthSet()`: Set up the Pulse Width for the PWM Modules.
- `GPIOPinTypePWM()`: Configure GPIO pins for use by the PWM module.
- `GPIOPinConfigure()`: Configures the alternate function of a GPIO pin.

Table 7.35 shows the API functions used to configure and set up the PWM modules. Table 7.36 shows two GPIO API functions, `GPIOPinTypePWM()` and `GPIOPinConfigure()`.

Two API functions, `GPIOPinTypePWM()` and `GPIOPinConfigure()`, do not belong to the PWM related API functions, but they must be used to configure the related pins to work as PWM output pins. Therefore we include these two functions in this section.

For the `SysCtlPWMClockSet()` function, even this function does not belong to the PWM API function, but one must use this function to set up the PWM clock since only this function works for the TM4C123GH6PM MCU system. This function contains only one argument `ui32Config`. Its value can be ORed by any macro like SYSCTL_PWM-DIV_N (N = 1, 2, 4, 8, 16, 32, or 64). Before this function can be called, the system clock should be first configured by calling another API function `SysCtlClockSet()`.

For the `PWMGenConfigure()` function, the argument `ui32Config` can be ORed by any macros shown in Table 7.35.

For the GPIO API functions `GPIOPinTypePWM()`, the first argument is the base address of the GPIO Port that has been selected to work as an alternate function pin (PWM output pin), such as macros GPIO_PORTA_BASE ~ GPIO_PORTF_BASE that are defined in the header file **hw_memmap.h**. The second argument is the pin number to

Table 7.35.   API functions used to configure and set up PWM modules.

API Function	Parameters	Description
void SysCtlPWMClockSet(uint32_t ui32Config)	ui32Config is the configuration for the PWM clock; it must be one of SYSCTL_PWMDIV_1, SYSCTL_PWMDIV_2, SYSCTL_PWMDIV_4, SYSCTL_PWMDIV_8, SYSCTL_PWMDIV_16, SYSCTL_PWMDIV_32, or SYSCTL_PWMDIV_64.	Set the PWM clock divider as the PWM clock source. It also configures the clock frequency to the PWM module as a division of the system clock. The clocking of the PWM is dependent upon the system clock rate as configured by SysCtlClockSet(). Do not use the PWMClockSet() to set the PWM clock since that function does not work for TM4C123GH6PM MCU system.

void
PWMGenConfigure(
    uint32_t ui32Base,
    uint32_t ui32Gen,
    uint32_t ui32Config)
	ui32Base is the base address of the PWM module.
	ui32Gen is the PWM generator to configure. This parameter must be one of: PWM_GEN_0, PWM_GEN_1, PWM_GEN_2, PWM_GEN_3.
	ui32Config is the configure for the PWM generator. It is the logical OR of PWM_GEN_MODE_DOWN, PWM_GEN_MODE_UP_DOWN, PWM_GEN_MODE_GEN_NO_SYNC, PWM_GEN_MODE_GEN_SYNC_LOCAL, PWM_GEN_MODE_DB_NO_SYNC, PWM_GEN_MODE_DB_SYNC_LOCAL
		Set the mode of operation for a PWM generator. The counting mode, synchronization mode, and debug behavior are all configured. After configuration, the generator is left in the disabled state.
		A PWM generator can count in two different modes:
		
		• count down mode
		• count up/down mode.

void
PWMGenEnable(
    uint32_t ui32Base,
    uint32_t ui32Gen)
	ui32Base is the base address of the PWM module.
	ui32Gen is the PWM generator to be enabled. This parameter must be one of PWM_GEN_0, PWM_GEN_1, PWM_GEN_2, or PWM_GEN_3
		Enables the timer/counter for a PWM generator block. This function allows the PWM clock to drive the timer/counter for the specified generator block.

void
PWMGenDisable(
    uint32_t ui32Base,
    uint32_t ui32Gen)
	ui32Base is the base address of the PWM module.
	ui32Gen is the PWM generator to be enabled. This parameter must be one of PWM_GEN_0, PWM_GEN_1, PWM_GEN_2, or PWM_GEN_3
		Disables the timer/counter for a PWM generator block. This function blocks the PWM clock from driving the timer/counter for the specified generator block.

void
PWMGenPeriodSet(
    uint32_t ui32Base,
    uint32_t ui32Gen,
    uint32_t ui32Period)
	ui32Base is the base address of the PWM module.
	ui32Gen is the PWM generator to be modified. This parameter must be one of PWM_GEN_0, PWM_GEN_1, PWM_GEN_2, or PWM_GEN_3.
	ui32Period specifies the period of PWM generator output, measured in clock ticks.
		Set the period of the specified PWM generator block, where the period of the generator block is defined as the number of PWM clock ticks between pulses on the generator block zero signal.

void
PWMPulseWidthSet(
    uint32_t ui32Base,
    uint32_t ui32PWMOut,
    uint32_t ui32Width)
	ui32Base is the base address of the PWM module.
	ui32PWMOut is the PWM output to modify. This parameter must be one of PWM_OUT_0, PWM_OUT_1, PWM_OUT_2, PWM_OUT_3, PWM_OUT_4, PWM_OUT_5, PWM_OUT_6, or PWM_OUT_7.
	ui32Width specifies the width of the positive portion of the pulse.
		Set the pulse width for the specified PWM output, where the pulse width is defined as the number of PWM clock ticks.

Table 7.36. GPIO API functions used to configure and set up PWM modules.

API Function	Parameters	Description
void GPIOPinTypePWM(uint32_t ui32Port, uint8_t ui8Pins)	ui32Port is the base address of the GPIO port. ui8Pins is the bit-packed represent-ation of the pin(s).	The PWM pins must be properly configured for the PWM peripheral to function correctly. This function provides a typical configuration for those pin(s). The pin(s) are specified using a bit-packed byte, where each bit that is set identifies the pin to be accessed, and where bit 0 of the byte represents GPIO port pin 0, bit 1 represents GPIO port pin 1, and so on. This function cannot be used to turn any pin into a PWM pin; it only configures a PWM pin for proper operation. Devices wtih flexible pin muxing also require a GPIOPinConfigure() function call.
void GPIOPinConfigure(uint32_t ui32PinConfig)	ui32PinConfig is the pin configuration value, specified as only one of the following: GPIO_PB6_M0PWM0, GPIO_PB7_M0PWM1, ... GPIO_PF0_M1PWM4, or GPIO_PF1_M1PWM5 values.	Configure the pin mux that selects the peripheral function associated with a particular GPIO pin. Only one peripheral function at a time can be associated with a GPIO pin, and each peripheral function should only be associated with a single GPIO pin at a time. The available mappings are supplied on a per-device basis in pin_map.h.

be used as a PWM pin. These macros are defined in the system header file gpio.h, such as GPIO_PIN_0, GPIO_PIN_1, until GPIO_PIN_7, can be used for this argument.

7.7.2 PWM Output Control Functions

The API functions involved in this group include:

- PWMDeadBandEnable(): Enable the Dead-Band Block and its Function.
- PWMDeadBandDisable(): Disable the Dead-Band Block and its Function.
- PWMOutputInvert(): Invert the PWM Output Signal.
- PWMOutputState(): Enable or Disable the Selected PWM Outputs.
- PWMOutputUpdateMode(): Set the Update Mode or Synchronization Mode to the PWM Outputs.

Table 7.37 shows the API functions used to control the PWM outputs.

These functions are used to control the PWM output properties, such as the inversion of the outputs, synchronization of the outputs, enabling or disabling the outputs, and enabling or disabling the dead-band block functions.

7.7.3 PWM Interrupt and Fault Control Functions

The API functions involved in this group include:

- PWMGenIntRegister(): Register an Interrupt Handler for the Selected PWM Generator.
- PWMGenIntClear(): Clear a PWM Generator Interrupt.
- PWMGenIntTrigEnable(): Enable Interrupts and Triggers for Selected PWM Generators.

Table 7.37. API functions used to control the PWM outputs.

API Function	Parameters	Description
void PWMDeadBandEnable(uint32_t ui32Base, uint32_t ui32Gen, uint16_t ui16Rise, uint16_t ui16Fall)	ui32Base is the base address of the PWM module. ui32Gen is the PWM generator to modify. This parameter must be one of PWM_GEN_0, PWM_GEN_1, PWM_GEN_2, or PWM_GEN_3. ui16Rise specifies the width of delay from the rising edge. ui16Fall specifies the width of delay from the falling edge.	Enable the PWM dead band output and set the dead band delays. Set the dead bands for the specified PWM generator, where the dead bands are defined as the number of PWM clock ticks from the rising or falling edge of the generator's OutA signal. Note that this function causes the coupling of OutB to OutA.
void PWMDeadBandDisable(uint32_t ui32Base, uint32_t ui32Gen)	ui32Base is the base address of the PWM module. ui32Gen is the PWM generator to modify. This parameter must be one of PWM_GEN_0, PWM_GEN_1, PWM_GEN_2, or PWM_GEN_3.	Disable the PWM dead band output. This function disables the dead band mode for the specified PWM generator. This function decouples the OutA and OutB signals.
void PWMOutputInvert(uint32_t ui32Base, uint32_t ui32PWMOutBits, bool bInvert)	ui32Base is the base address of the PWM module. ui32PWMOutBits are the PWM outputs to be modified. This parameter must be the logical OR of any of PWM_OUT_0_BIT, PWM_OUT_1_BIT, PWM_OUT_2_BIT, PWM_OUT_3_BIT, PWM_OUT_4_BIT, PWM_OUT_5_BIT, PWM_OUT_6_BIT, or PWM_OUT_7_BIT. bInvert determines if the signal is inverted or passed through.	Select the inversion mode for PWM outputs. Select the inversion mode for the selected PWM outputs. The outputs are selected using the parameter ui32PWMOutBits. The parameter bInvert determines the inversion mode for the selected outputs. If bInvert is true, this function causes the specified PWM output signals to be inverted or made active low. If bInvert is false, the specified outputs are passed through as is or made active high.
void PWMOutputState(uint32_t ui32Base, uint32_t ui32PWMOutBits, bool bEnable)	ui32Base is the base address of the PWM module. ui32PWMOutBits are the PWM outputs to be modified. This parameter must be the logical OR of any of PWM_OUT_0_BIT, PWM_OUT_1_BIT, PWM_OUT_2_BIT, PWM_OUT_3_BIT, PWM_OUT_4_BIT, PWM_OUT_5_BIT, PWM_OUT_6_BIT, or PWM_OUT_7_BIT. bEnable determines if the signal is enabled or disabled.	Enable or disable PWM outputs. Enable or disable the selected PWM outputs. The outputs are selected using the parameter ui32PWMOutBits. The parameter bEnable determines the state of the selected outputs. If bEnable is true, then the selected PWM outputs are enabled, or placed in the active state. If bEnable is false, then the selected outputs are disabled or placed in the inactive state
void PWMOutputUpdateMode(uint32_t ui32Base, uint32_t ui32PWMOutBits, uint32_t ui32Mode)	ui32Base is the base address of the PWM module. ui32PWMOutBits are the PWM outputs to be modified. This parameter must be the logical OR of any of PWM_OUT_0_BIT, PWM_OUT_1_BIT, PWM_OUT_2_BIT, PWM_OUT_3_BIT, PWM_OUT_4_BIT, PWM_OUT_5_BIT, PWM_OUT_6_BIT, or PWM_OUT_7_BIT. ui32Mode specifies the enable update mode to use when enabling or disabling PWM outputs.	Set one of three possible update modes to enable or disable the requested PWM outputs. The ui32Mode parameter controls when changes made via calls to PWMOutputState() take effect. Possible values: PWM_OUTPUT_MODE_NO_SYNC, which enables/disables changes to take effect immediately. PWM_OUTPUT_MODE_SYNC_LOCAL, which causes changes to take effect when the local PWM generator's count next reaches 0. PWM_OUTPUT_MODE_SYNC_GLOBAL, which causes changes to take effect when the local PWM generator's count next reaches 0 following a call to PWMSyncUpdate() which specifies the same generator in its ui32GenBits parameter.

- `PWMGenIntTrigDisable()`: Disable Interrupts for the Selected PWM Generator.
- `PWMIntEnable()`: Enable Generator and Fault Interrupts for a PWM Module.
- `PWMIntDisable()`: Disable Generator and Fault Interrupts for a PWM Module.

Table 7.38 shows the API functions used to control the PWM interrupts and faults.

The API function `PWMGenIntRegister()` is used to register an interrupt handler or an interrupt service routine (ISR) for a specified interrupt to enable the responded interrupt to be transferred into this handler to be processed. The third argument of this function `pfnIntHandler` is a pointer or the entry address of the handler to be called when the interrupt occurred.

To enable or unmask an interrupt created or triggered by a PWM generator, the API function `PWMGenIntTrigEnable()` should be used by setting related bits for the selected generators to enable a related PWM generator interrupt to be generated.

To enable any interrupt related to a PWM generator to occur or be triggered, the API function `PWMIntEnable()` must be executed to first enable the related PWM module to which the PWM generator belongs.

After an interrupt or a fault has been responded to and processed by the related handler, the API function `PWMIntClear()` must be executed to clear the processed interrupt by writing 1 to the corresponding bits on the interrupt status register to enable the other interrupt to be generated in the future.

Usually the generation and processing of a PWM-related interrupt procedure includes the following:

1. Call the `PWMGenIntRegister()` function to register the related interrupt handler.
2. Call the `PWMGenIntTrigEnable()` function to enable or unmask a PWM-related interrupt to be triggered or occurred.
3. Call the `PWMIntEnable()` function to enable the PWM module containing the related PWM generator that will generate an interrupt.
4. Transfer the responded interrupt to the related handler to be processed.
5. Call the `PWMIntClear()` function to clear the processed interrupt.

In the above 5 steps, step 4 is executed by the microcontroller.

An example project that uses the API functions provided by the TivaWare™ Peripheral Driver Library to interface a PWM module 1 generator 2 to drive a DC motor is reserved for the users as a lab project `Lab7_4`.

7.8 CHAPTER SUMMARY

This chapter is mainly concentrated on the ARM® Cortex®-M4 parallel I/O interfacing programming. Three parallel I/O ports programming projects are included in this chapter; they are:

- On-Board Keypads Interface Programming Project
- Analog-to-Digital Converter Programming Project
- PWM-Controlled DC and Step Motors Programming Project

All of these parallel I/O port programming are closely related to the GPIO Ports since most GPIO Ports provide multiple functions to interface to different peripheral devices in

Table 7.38. API functions used to control the PWM interrupts and faults.

API Function	Parameters	Description
void PWMGenIntRegister(uint32_t ui32Base, uint32_t ui32Gen, void (*pfnIntHandler) (void))	ui32Base is the base address of the PWM module. ui32Gen is the PWM generator in question. This parameter must be one of PWM_GEN_0, PWM_GEN_1, PWM_GEN_2, or PWM_GEN_3. pfnIntHandler is a pointer to the function to be called when the PWM generator interrupt occurs.	Register an interrupt handler for the specified PWM generator block. Ensure that the interrupt handler pfnIntHandler is called when an interrupt is detected for the specified PWM generator block. This function also enables the corresponding PWM generator interrupt in the interrupt controller. Individual generator interrupts and interrupt sources must be enabled with PWMIntEnable() & PWMGenIntTrigEnable().
void PWMGenIntClear(uint32_t ui32Base, uint32_t ui32Gen, uint32_t ui32Ints)	ui32Base is the base address of the PWM module. ui32Gen is the PWM generator to query. This parameter must be one of PWM_GEN_0, PWM_GEN_1, PWM_GEN_2, or PWM_GEN_3. ui32Ints specifies the interrupts to be cleared.	Clear the specified interrupt for the specified PWM generator block. Clear the specified interrupt(s) by writing a 1 to the specified bits of the interrupt status register for the specified PWM generator. The ui32Ints parameter is the logical OR of PWM_INT_CNT_ZERO, PWM_INT_CNT_LOAD, PWM_INT_CNT_AU, PWM_INT_CNT_AD, PWM_INT_CNT_BU, or PWM_INT_CNT_BD.
void PWMGenIntTrigEnable(uint32_t ui32Base, uint32_t ui32Gen, uint32_t ui32IntTrig)	ui32Base is the base address of the PWM module. ui32Gen is the PWM generator to have interrupts and triggers enabled. This parameter must be one of PWM_GEN_0, PWM_GEN_1, PWM_GEN_2, or PWM_GEN_3. ui32IntTrig specifies the interrupts and triggers to be enabled.	Enable interrupts and triggers for the specified PWM generator block. Unmask the specified interrupt and trigger by setting the specified bits of the interrupt/trigger enable register for the specified PWM generator. The ui32IntTrig parameter is the logical OR of PWM_INT_CNT_ZERO, PWM_INT_CNT_LOAD, PWM_INT_CNT_AU, PWM_INT_CNT_AD, PWM_INT_CNT_BU, PWM_INT_CNT_BD, PWM_TR_CNT_ZERO, PWM_TR_CNT_LOAD, PWM_TR_CNT_AU, PWM_TR_CNT_AD, PWM_TR_CNT_BU, or PWM_TR_CNT_BD.
void PWMGenIntTrigDisable (uint32_t ui32Base, uint32_t ui32Gen, uint32_t ui32IntTrig)	ui32Base is the base address of the PWM module. ui32Gen is the PWM generator to have interrupts and triggers enabled. This parameter must be one of PWM_GEN_0, PWM_GEN_1, PWM_GEN_2, or PWM_GEN_3. ui32IntTrig specifies the interrupts and triggers to be enabled.	Disable interrupts for the specified PWM generator block. Mask the specified interrupt and trigger by clearing the specified bits of the interrupt/trigger enable register for the specified PWM generator. The ui32IntTrig parameter is the logical OR of PWM_INT_CNT_ZERO, PWM_INT_CNT_LOAD, PWM_INT_CNT_AU, PWM_INT_CNT_AD, PWM_INT_CNT_BU, PWM_INT_CNT_BD, PWM_TR_CNT_ZERO, PWM_TR_CNT_LOAD, PWM_TR_CNT_AU, PWM_TR_CNT_AD, PWM_TR_CNT_BU, or PWM_TR_CNT_BD.
void PWMIntEnable(uint32_t ui32Base, uint32_t ui32GenFault)	ui32Base is the base address of the PWM module. ui32GenFault contains the interrupts to be enabled. This parameter must be a logical OR of any of PWM_INT_GEN_0, PWM_INT_GEN_1, PWM_INT_GEN_2, PWM_INT_GEN_3, PWM_INT_FAULT0, PWM_INT_FAULT1, PWM_INT_FAULT2, PWM_INT_FAULT3.	Enable generator and fault interrupts for a PWM module. This function unmasks the specified interrupt by setting the specified bits of the interrupt enable register for the selected PWM module.
void PWMIntDisable(uint32_t ui32Base, uint32_t ui32GenFault)	ui32Base is the base address of the PWM module. ui32GenFault contains the interrupts to be enabled. This parameter must be a logical OR of any of PWM_INT_GEN_0, PWM_INT_GEN_1, PWM_INT_GEN_2, PWM_INT_GEN_3, PWM_INT_FAULT0, PWM_INT_FAULT1, PWM_INT_FAULT2, PWM_INT_FAULT3	Disable generator and fault interrupts for a PWM module. This function masks the specified interrupt by clearing the specified bits of the interrupt enable register for the selected PWM module.

the TM4C123GH6PM MCU system. All peripherals in this system are configured to be connected to the different GPIO pins to interface to the MCU and other control components. All GPIO Ports are programmable ports with a set of control registers to be programmed to perform various important and vital interfacing functions.

The on-board keypads interface programming project is directly related to GPIO ports with GPIO control. Therefore the GPIO module and its multiple function property are first discussed with its architecture. An example keypad project is built following that discussion.

As for the analog-to-digital conversion project and PWM-related project, the GPIOAFSEL and GPIOPCTL registers are introduced and discussed again since these registers provide the controllability about the alternate functions for the GPIO Ports.

Following the discussions about the GPIO module and related registers, an example project that is used to control and interface the ADC module is provided. All important registers related to ADC control registers provided by the TM4C123GH6PM MCU system are introduced and discussed in detail. The popular API functions related to the ADC module and provided by the TivaWare™ Peripheral Driver Library are also introduced and discussed in detail.

The third part of this chapter is about the PWM modules and controls implemented in the TM4C123GH6PM MCU system. A quick introduction about the operational principle of the PWM module is provided first. Then a detailed introduction about the most control and configuration registers used in the PWM modules is provided with a discussion about the architecture of the PWM generators and modules. An example project that implemented the PWM module 1 generator 2 to create a changeable duty cycle to control a DC motor is introduced and analyzed.

A quick introduction about the PWM module interfacing part in the EduBASE ARM® Trainer is given before the example project is discussed since some control and interface components in that Trainer are used in that project.

Finally some popular API functions related to PWM modules and provided by the TivaWare™ Peripheral Driver Library are introduced.

HOMEWORK

I. True/False Selections

_____**1.** With the GPIO Alternate Function Select register (GPIOAFSEL), each pin can be configured to perform multiple functions, which are called alternative functions.

_____**2.** The GPIO Port Control (GPIOPCTL) register can be used to select the operational mode for the selected GPIO port, either GPIO mode or Peripheral mode.

_____**3.** After a system reset, all GPIO pins are configured to be output state.

_____**4.** Both RCGCGPIO and RCGC2 registers can be used to configure the clock source and enable any GPIO Port and GPIO pins.

_____**5.** There are two ADC modules in the TM4C123GH6PM MCU system, ADC0 and ADC1, respectively. Each ADC module contains 2 sample sequencers, and these two modules can share 12 analog input channels.

_____**6.** Each ADC module must be clocked by configuring the ADC Clock Configuration (ADCCC) register before it works since all ADC modules share the same clock source to facilitate the synchronization of data samples between conversion units.

_____**7.** After the ADC conversion is complete, the conversion results can be obtained from the ADC `Sample Sequence Result FIFO (ADCSSFIFOn)` registers.

_____**8.** The TM4C123GH6PM MCU contains two PWM modules, PWM0 and PWM1. Each module has two PWM generator blocks and a control block, and each generator block can create two PWM output signals; therefore a total of 8 PWM output signals can be generated by these two modules.

_____**9.** Each PWM generator block produces two PWM signals that use the different timer (counter) and frequency and can either be programmed with independent actions or as a single pair of complementary signals with dead-band delays inserted.

_____**10.** Each PWM generator has two comparators that monitor the value of the counter and output a single-clock-cycle-width High when either comparator's value is equal to the counting value in the counter.

Multiple Choices

1. Which of the following initialization steps should be performed before using a GPIO Port ?

   a. Enable and clock the selected GPIO Port.

   b. Set up the direction for each pin on the GPIO port.

   c. Enable GPIO pins as digital I/O or an alternate function pins.

   d. All of the above.

2. Before each ADC module can perform normal ADC conversion, _____.

   a. Each module is clocked by configuring the ADCCC register.

   b. The sample sequencers must be configured and enabled by related registers.

   c. The trigger source must be determined by configuring the ADCEMUX register.

   d. All of the above.

3. In order to enable GPIO pins to work as ADC input pins, which one the following configurations should be performed ?

   a. Enable the clock to the appropriate GPIO modules via the RCGCGPIO register.

   b. The related bits in the GPIODEN register must be set to enable the digital function.

   c. The related AFSEL bits in the GPIOAFSEL register must be clear to 0.

   d. The related AMSEL bits in the GPIOAMSEL register should reset to 0.

4. The sample sequencer 0 (SS0) in an ADC module can capture _____ samples.

   a. 1

   b. 2

   c. 4

   d. 8

5. If we want to select AIN5 as the analog input channel for the 6th sample in SS0, the MUX5 nibble in the ADCSSMUX0 register should be set as _____.

   a. 0110

   b. 0101

   c. 0100

   d. 0011

6. If we want to configure the 4th sample to be collected from SS1 as the input is from temperature sensor and creates an interrupt, it is not the last sample and the input is from a single-end mode, bits 15:12 in the ADCSSCTL1 register should be set as _____.

   a. 1000

   b. 1100

   c. 1110

   d. 1111

7. Which of the following statement(s) is (are) true for the ADC clock ?

   a. The system clock must be at the same frequency or higher than the ADC clock.

   b. Two ADC modules (ADC0 and ADC1) share the same clock source.

   c. The clock source is basically determined by the ADC0 module's ADCCC register.

   d. All of the above.

8. An ADC-completion interrupt can be generated if _____.

   a. The corresponding IEn bit in the ADCSSCTLn register should have been set.

   b. The corresponding MASKn bit in the ADCIM register should have been set.

   c. The corresponding INRn bit in the ADCRIS register is set.

   d. All of the above.

9. The PWM Generator A Register (PWMGENA) can be triggered to output a High or Low pulse based on the following events, such as _____.

   a. The Counter = LOAD value.

   b. The Counter = 0.

   c. The Counter = PWMnCMPA or Counter = PWMnCMPB.

   d. All of the above.

10. To set the pulse width of the M1PWM4 pin to a 25% duty cycle with a 20-MHz PWM clock and a 5-kHz input to the counter, the PWM1CMPA register should be initialized with a value of _____.

    a. 1000

    b. 2000

    c. 3000

    d. 4000

Exercises

1. Provide a brief description about how to configure the GPIOAFSEL and GPIOPCTL registers to enable related GPIO pins to work as alternate functions.

2. Provide a brief description about the operational procedure of each ADC module used in the TM4C123GH6PM MCU system.

3. Provide a brief description about the configuration process to enable the selected GPIO pins to work as ADC input pins.

4. Provide a brief explanation about the procedure of generating and handling a sample sequencer interrupt.

5. Provide a brief discussion about the initialization process for each sample sequencer.

6. Provide a brief description about the PWM modules in the TM4C123GH6PM MCU system.

Practical Laboratory

Laboratory 7: ARM® Cortex®-M4 GPIO Parallel Port Programming

7.0 Goals   This laboratory exercise allows students to learn and practice ARM® Cortex®-M4 GPIO parallel ports programming by developing four labs.

1. Program Lab7_1 lets you build a 4 × 4 keypad interfacing project to use the DRA method to perform key-code scanning and key-code reading process to identify the key pressed by the user as the project runs.

2. Program Lab7_2 enables students to build an ADC project to use the ADC sample sequencer 1 (SS1) interrupt to collect analog input signals from channels 1, 2, and 8, and to display the conversion results on three different peripherals on the EduBASE ARM® Trainer.

3. Program Lab7_3 allows students to familiar with PWM modules by building a PWM project to drive a 12V DC motor in a changing-duty-cycle mode with the DRA method.

4. Program Lab7_4 enables students to build a PWM project using the Software Driver method to drive a DC motor with a modified-duty-cycle mode. In this project, some API functions provided by the TivaWare™ Peripheral Driver Library are utilized to simplify the coding process. The duty cycle is changed by pressing two switch buttons, SW2 and SW3, in the EduBASE ARM® Trainer.

After completion of these programs, you should understand the basic architecture and operational procedure for most popular GPIO-related peripheral devices, including the ADC and PWM modules installed in the TM4C123GH6PM MCU system. You should be able to code some sophisticated programs to access the desired peripheral devices to perform desired control operations via GPIO parallel ports.

7.1 Lab7_1

7.1.1 Goal   In this project, students need to build a 4 × 4 keypad interfacing project to use the DRA method to perform key-code scanning and key-code reading process to identify the key pressed by the user as the project runs. The interrupt mechanism is used to generate an interrupt via GPIO Port A when a key is pressed and handled by the interrupt handler GPIOA_Handler().

7.1.2 Data Assignment and Hardware Configuration   No hardware configuration is needed in this project. Refer to Figure 7.3 to get a detailed hardware configuration about this keypad architecture and connection in the Trainer.

7.1.3 Development of the Source Code   Only a C code file is used in this project since it is a simple application without needing any header file.

1. Create a new folder named Lab7_1 under the folder C:\ARM Lab Projects\Chapter 7 in the Windows Explorer.

2. Create a new μVersion5 project named Lab7_1 and save this project to the folder Lab7_1 that is created in step 1 above.

3. On the next wizard, you need to select the device (MCU) for this project. Expand three icons, Texas Instruments, Tiva C Series, and TM4C123x Series, and select the target device TM4C123GH6PM from the list by clicking it. Click on the **OK** to close this wizard.

4. Next the Software Components wizard is opened, and you need to set up the software development environment for your project with this wizard. Expand two icons, CMSIS and Device, and check the CORE and Startup checkboxes in the **Sel.** column, and click on the **OK** button since we need these two components to build our project.

5. In the **Project** pane, expand the Target folder and right click on the Source Group 1 folder and select the Add New Item to Group 'Source Group 1'.

6. Select the C File (.c) and enter Lab7_1 into the **Name:** box, and click on the **Add** button to add this source file into the project.

7. On the top of this C source file, you need first to include three system header files, <stdint.h>, <stdbool.h> and "TM4C123GH6PM.h" since we need to use them in this project.

8. Create three global integer variables, row, col, and rowNum, and initialize row as 0 and rowNum as 4. We will use these variables to scan and get the pressed key later.

9. Declare two user-defined functions, InitKeypad() and Delay(int n). Both functions return void. The first function is used to initialize the keypad, and the second one is used to delay the program a period of time to wait until the key-reading process is complete.

10. Start the main program with the code int main(void).

11. Call the InitKeypad() function to initialize and configure the keypad control registers.

12. Start an infinitive while() loop to repeatedly scan the keypad and read the pressed key.

13. Use another while() loop with the row < rowNum as the loop condition to perform a continuous scanning for all four rows.

14. Enable the GPIO PD3~PD0 pins as output pins by assigning 0xF to the GPIO Port D DIR register since these four pins are connected to four rows, ROW3~ROW0, on the keypad in the EduBASE Trainer (refer to Figure 7.3). You can use the structure pointer to access the DIR register in the GPIO Port D, such as GPIOD→DIR, since we are using the TM4C123GH6PM.h header file and it defined all GPIO Ports as structure pointers.

15. Set all four rows to High by assigning 0xF to the GPIO Port D DATA register.

16. Read all columns back by ANDing the GPIOA→DATA with 0x3C since only PA5~PA2 four pins are connected to four columns in the keypad, and assign this reading result to the col variable.

17. Disable all rows by ANDing and assigning (&=) an inverse of 0xF to the GPIO Port D DIR register to give all rows a release time.

18. Increment the row number to point to the next row by adding the variable row by 1 (++).

19. Outside the second while() loop, reset the row number by clearing the variable row to 0 since all 4 rows have been scanned and we need to restart this scanning from row 0.

That is for the main() program and it is always running in an infinitive loop to wait for any key-press-interrupt to be occurred and processed by the GPIOA_Handler().

Now let's do the coding for the InitKeypad() function.

1. Enable and clock the GPIO Ports A, B, and D by configuring SYSCTL→RCGC2 register.

2. Set GPIO Port B PB3~PB0 as output pins.

3. Set GPIO Port B PB3~PB0 as digital pins.

4. Configure GPIO Port A PA5~PA2 as input pins (rows 0~3).

5. Set GPIO Port A PA5~PA2 as digital pins.

6. Configure GPIO Port D PD3~PD0 as output pins (cols 0~3).

7. Set GPIO Port D PD3~PD0 as digital pins.

8. Enable PA5–PA2 are level-triggered interrupt by assigning GPIOA→IS register with 0x3C.

9. Disable PA5~PA2 IBE function by clearing the GPIOA→IBE register.

10. Enable PA5~PA2 as HIGH level/Rising edge triggered pins by configuring GPIOA→IEV register.

11. Clear any previous interrupts for PA5~PA2 pins by configuring GPIOA→ICR register.

12. Enable or unmask interrupts for PA5~PA2 pins by configuring the GPIO→IM register.

13. Set the interrupt priority level as 3 for PA5~PA2 pins by using the NVIC interrupt priority control register, NVIC→IP[0] = 0x60.

14. Enable the interrupt IRQ0 by configuring the NVIC interrupt enable register, NVIC→ISER[0] = 0x1.

15. Use the __enable_irq() function to globally enable all maskable interrupts.

Next let's code for the interrupt handler GPIOA_Handler() to respond to any key-press-interrupt.

1. Create a constant char array, const char row_select[] = {0x01, 0x02, 0x04, 0x08}, and each element in this array works as a row number for the scanning purpose.

2. A for() loop is used to scan all rows starting form row0 (row = 0) until row3 (row < 4).

3. Inside the for() loop, first all rows are disabled by ANDing and assigning (&=) an inverse of 0xF to the GPIOD→DIR register.

4. Then enable only one row by ORing and assigning (|=) GPIOD→DIR register with the select array row_select[row].

5. Set that selected row to High by ORing and assigning 0xF to the GPIOD→DATA register.

6. Call the Delay(2000) function to wait for the row and column signals stable.

7. Read all columns back by ANDing the GPIOA→DATA with 0x3C since only PA5~PA2 four pins are connected to four columns in the keypad, and assign this reading result to the col variable.

8. Use the if() block to check whether the col is 0 or not. If a key is pressed, the read back value stored in the col variable should not be 0. In that case, the for() loop is broken and a key has been pressed and we need to identify and display that key.

9. Disable all rows by ANDing and assigning (&=) an inverse of 0xF to the GPIO Port D DIR register to give all rows a release time.

10. Use if() selection structure to check which column has been affected due to a pressed key. As we know, if a key is pressed, the corresponding column is set to High. For example, if the column (col) is 0x04, a key in the column 0 is pressed and the key number is row × 4 + 1. Similarly, if the col = 0x08, a key in the column 1 is pressed and the key number should be row × 4 + 2. Assign each key number to the GPIO Port B to display each of them on the corresponding LED (GPIOB→DATA).

11. Before exiting the interrupt handler, clear the current key-pressing interrupt by writing 1 to the GPIO Port A ICR register to enable the future interrupt to be occurred. An easy and safe way to do this is to clear all GPIO Port A pins by assigning GPIOA→ICR to 0x3C.

For the time delay function Delay(int n), it is very easy. Just use a for() loop to repeat n time blank loops without doing anything.

7.1.4 Set Up the Environment to Build and Run the Project   To build and run the project, one needs to perform the following operations to set up the environments:

- Select the `Stellaris ICDI` debugger in the Debug tab under the `Project|Options for Target 'Target 1'` menu item.
- Now let's build the project by going to `Project|Build target` menu item.
- Then go to the `Flash|Download` menu item to download the image file of this project into the flash memory in the TM4C123GXL Evaluation Board.
- Now go to `Debug|Start/Stop Debug Session` to ready to run the project.
- Go to `Debug|Run` menu item to run the project.

7.1.5 Demonstrate Your Program by Checking the Running Result   After the project runs, press any key on the keypad in the EduBASE ARM® Trainer. A key-pressing interrupt is generated when a key is pressed and passed to the interrupt handler `GPIOA_Handler()` to be processed. The corresponding LED will be ON to respond to the key-pressing interrupt.

Go to `Debug|Start/Stop Debug Session` to stop your program.

Based on these results, try to answer the following questions:

- What happened when you pressed the key 0? Why?
- When you pressed two keys simultaneously, what happened? Why?
- What did you learn from this project?

7.2 Lab7_2

7.2.1 Goal   This project enables students to build an ADC project to use the ADC module 0 ADC0 sample sequencer 1 (SS1) interrupt to collect analog input signals from channels 1, 2 and 8, and to display the conversion results on three different peripherals, 3-color LED in the TM4C123GXL EVB, 4 LEDs and a speaker, on the EduBASE ARM® Trainer.

7.2.2 Data Assignment and Hardware Configuration   No hardware connections are needed for this project.

Refer to Figure 7.28 to get a clear picture about the hardware configurations for three analog input sources:

- GPIO Port E (PE2) pin is connected to a potentiometer VR2 in the EduBASE ARM® Trainer via the analog input channel 1 (AIN1).
- GPIO Port E (PE1) pin is connected to a photo sensor VEMT2520 in the EduBASE ARM® Trainer via the analog input channel 2 (AIN2).
- GPIO Port E (PE5) pin is connected to a temperature sensor LM45 in the EduBASE ARM® Trainer via the analog input channel 8 (AIN8).

To detect and check the conversion results of these three analog input signals, three peripherals have been used and configured as below:

- Three-color LED in the Tiva™ LaunchPad™ board (TM4C123GXL EVB), which is configured to receive the output of the A/D conversion for the potentiometer VR2, is connected to the GPIO Port F via PF1~PF3 pins.

- Four LEDs, PB3~PB0, on the EduBASE ARM® Trainer, which are configured to receive the output of the A/D conversion of the photo sensor VEMT2520, are connected to the GPIO Port B via PB3~PB0 pins.
- A speaker installed in the EduBASE ARM® Trainer, which is configured to receive the output of the A/D conversion of the temperature sensor LM45, is connected to the GPIO Port C via PC4 pin.

7.2.3 Development of the Project To make this project easy, we used Direct Register Access (DRA) model with two API functions, IntRegister() and IntEnable(), which are provided by the TivaWare™ Peripheral Driver Library.

Follow the steps below to develop this project. Only a C code source file is used in this project since this project is simple. Create the project and develop the C source file with the following steps:

1. Create a new folder Lab7_2 under the folder C:\ARM Lab Projects\Chapter 7 in the Windows Explorer.
2. Open the Keil® ARM-MDK µVersion5, create a new project named Lab7_2, and save this project into the folder Lab7_2 created in step 1.
3. On the next wizard, you need to select the device (MCU) for this project. Expand three icons, Texas Instruments, Tiva C Series, and TM4C123x Series, and select the target device TM4C123GH6PM from the list by clicking on it. Click on the OK to close this wizard.
4. Next the Software Components wizard is opened, and you need to set up the software development environment for your project with this wizard. Expand two icons, CMSIS and Device, and check the CORE and Startup checkboxes in the Sel. column, and click on the OK button since we need these two components to build our project.

7.2.4 Development of the C Source File

1. In the Project pane, expand the Target folder and right click on the Source Group 1 folder and select the Add New Item to Group 'Source Group 1'.
2. Select the C File (.c) and enter Lab7_2 into the Name: box, and click on the Add button to add this source file into the project.
3. Include the following system header files into this source file:
   - #include <stdint.h>
   - #include <stdbool.h>
   - #include "inc/tm4c123gh6pm.h"
   - #include "driverlib\adc.h"
   - #include "driverlib\interrupt.h"
4. Declare two user-defined functions: One is the time delay function Delay(uint32_t time), and the other one is the ADC sample sequence 1 (SS1) interrupt handler SS1Handler(void). Both functions return void.
5. Inside the main() program, first enable and clock ADC0-related GPIO Ports by using SYSCTL_RCGC2_R register. These ports include GPIO Ports B, C, E and F. You can use macros such as SYSCTL_RCGC2_GPIOB, SYSCTL_RCGC2_GPIOC, and so on. Also enable and clock the ADC0 module by using the SYSCTL_RCGCADC_R register (see Section 7.5.3.3.1).

6. Configure the GPIO Port E three pins PE1, PE2, and PE5 by using the Port E AFSEL register macro GPIO_PORTE_AFSEL_R to enable them to work as alternate functions (refer to Section 7.5.3.1.1 to get more details about this register and configuration values).

7. Configure PE1, PE2, and PE5 pins as input pins by using the Port E Digital Enable register macro GPIO_PORTE_DEN_R.

8. Disable the analog isolation circuit for PE1, PE2, and PE5 pins by using the Port E Analog Mode Select register macro GPIO_PORTE_AMSEL_R.

9. Configure GPIO Port B four pins, PB3~PB0, as digital function pins by using the Port B Digital Enable register macro GPIO_PORTB_DEN_R.

10. Configure GPIO Port B four pins, PB3~PB0, as output pins by using the Port B Direction register macro GPIO_PORTB_DIR_R.

11. Configure GPIO Port C pin PC4 as output pin by using the Port C Direction register macro GPIO_PORTC_DIR_R.

12. Enable PC4 as digital function pin by using the Port C Digital Enable register macro GPIO_PORTC_DEN_R.

13. Configure GPIO Port F pins PF3~PF0 as digital function and output pins by using the Port F Digital Enable register macro GPIO_PORTF_DEN_R and Direction register macro GPIO_PORTF_DIR_R.

14. Use the default trigger source for all three analog input signals by configuring the GPIO Port E ADCCTL register macro GPIO_PORTE_ADCCTL_R as 0x0.

The following codes are used to initialize ADC0 sample sequencer 1 (SS1).

15. First disable the ADC0 SS1 by ANDing and assign (&=) an inverse of the macro ADC_ACTSS_ASEN1 to the ADC0 Active Sample Sequencer (ADCACTSS) Register macro ADC0_ACTSS_R.

16. Select the default trigger source, processor, by assigning the ADC_EMUX_EM1_PROCES-SOR macro (0x0) to the ADC0 Event Multiplexer Select (ADCEMUX) register macro ADC0_EMUX_R (refer to Section 7.5.3.3.3).

17. Configure the ADC0 SS1 sample mode as: 1st sample, AIN1; 2nd sample, AIN2; 3rd sample, AIN8 by assigning a value of 0x0821 to the ADC0 Sample Sequencer 1 Input Multiplexer Select (ADCSSMUX1) register macro ADC0_SSMUX1_R.

18. Configure ADC0 SS1 sample mode as follows: The 3rd sample is the last sample with an interrupt being generated, by assigning a value of 0x0600 to the ADC0 Sample Sequencer 1 Control (ADCSSCTL1) register macro ADC0_SSCTL1_R.

19. Clear any previous SS1 interrupt by writing 1 to the ADC0 Interrupt Status and Clear register macro ADC0_ISC_R (refer to Section 7.5.3.3.2.3).

20. Enable the SS1 interrupt by assigning a value of 0x02 or a macro ADC_IM_MASK1 to the ADC0 Interrupt Mask register macro ADC0_IM_R.

21. Now you can enable the ADC0 SS1 register by ORing and assigning (|=) a value of 0x02 or a macro ADC_ACTSS_ASEN1 to the ADC0 Active Sample Sequencer Register macro ADC0_ACTSS_R since all configurations for ADC0 SS1 have been done.

22. Finally, you need to initiate the ADC0 SS1 by assigning a value of 0x02 or a macro ADC_PSSI_SS1 to the ADC0 Processor Sample Sequencer Initiate Register macro ADC0_PSSI_R.

The following codes are used to register and enable the ADC0 SS1 interrupt.

23. Use the API function `IntRegister()` provided by the TivaWare™ Peripheral Driver Library to register the interrupt handler `SS1Handler`. This API function has two arguments: The first one is the interrupt number and the second one is the entry address of the interrupt handler `SS1Handler()`. The interrupt number defined for the ADC0 SS1 is `INT_ADC0SS1`. The second argument is a pointer, and one can directly put the handler name SS1Handler in there.

24. Use another API function `IntEnable()` to enable this ADC0 SS1 interrupt to occur. This API function contains a single argument that is the interrupt number `INT_ADC0SS1`.

25. Use an infinitive `while()` loop to wait for any ADC0 SS1 interrupt to occur.

The following codes are used to respond to and process the ADC0 SS1 interrupt, which should be put inside the interrupt handler `SS1Handler()`.

26. Declare the interrupt handler using `void SS1Handler(void)` statement.

27. Inside the handler, first create three integer local variables, `pSensor`, `pMeter`, and `pTemp`. These variables are used to receive and hold the ADC conversion results for photosensor, potentiometer, and temperature sensor.

28. Use `if()` selection structure to confirm that an ADC0 SS1 interrupt has occurred. The condition for this structure is an `ANDing` of the content of the ADC0 Raw Interrupt Status register (`ADC0_RIS_R`) and 2. If an ADC0 SS1 interrupt occurred, the bit 1 (`INR1`) in that register will be set to 1.

29. If an ADC0 SS1 interrupt occurred, pick up all three ADC converting results from the SS1 FIFO register (`ADC0_SSFIFO1_R`) in order and assign them to those three variables we created above. The first reading from the `ADC0_SSFIFO1_R` should be assigned to the first variable `pSensor`, and the second reading from the `ADC0_SSFIFO1_R` is assigned to the variable `pMeter`, and so on.

30. Shift `pMeter` right by 8 bits (≫8) to send the 4 MSB of the conversion result of the potentiometer to the 3-color LED via PF3~PF1 pins (GPIO Port F DATA register).

31. Shift `pSensor` right by 8 bits (≫8) to send the 4 MSB of the conversion result of the photosensor to four LEDs via PB3~PB0 pins (GPIO Port B DATA register).

32. Shift `pTemp` left by 2 bits (≪2) to multiply the `pTemp` by 4 and assign the conversion result of the temperature sensor to the speaker via PC4 pin (GPIO Port C DATA register).

33. Call `Delay()` function to delay the program a period of time (50000).

34. Clear the SS1 interrupt in RIS and ICR registers by writing 1 to the ADC0 Interrupt Status and Clear register macro `ADC0_ISC_R` (refer to Section 7.5.3.3.2.3).

35. Initiate the ADC0 SS1 by assigning a value of `0x02` or a macro `ADC_PSSI_SS1` to the ADC0 Processor Sample Sequencer Initiate Register macro `ADC0_PSSI_R`. This step is important and necessary to make the program to continue to run, otherwise the SS1 cannot perform any future operation if it was not initiated.

36. For the `Delay()` function, just put a blank `for()` loop to repeat looping a certain time.

7.2.5 Set Up Environment to Build and Run the Project   This setup contains the following three operations:

1. Include the system header files by adding the include path.

2. Check and configure the correct debugger used in the project.

3. Add the TivaWare™ peripheral driver library into the project since we need to use two API functions provided by that library.

Perform the following operations to include this header file path in your project:

- Go to the `Project|Options for Target 'Target 1'` menu item. Then click on the C/C++ tab.
- Go to the `Include Paths` box and browse to the folder where our header files are located, it is `C:\ti\TivaWare_C_Series-2.0.1.11577`. Select this folder and click on the OK button.

Perform the following operations to make sure that the debugger you are using is the `Stellaris ICDI`. You can do this checking as follows:

- Go to the `Project|Options for Target 'Target 1'` menu item to open the Options wizard.
- On the opened Options wizard, click on the `Debug` tab.
- Make sure that the debugger shown in the `Use:` box is `Stellaris ICDI`. Otherwise you can click on the dropdown arrow to select this debugger from the list.

Perform the below operations to add the TivaWare™ peripheral driver library into the project:

- Go to the `Project` pane and right click on the `Source Group 1` item, and select the `Add Existing Files to Group 'Source Group 1'` menu item.
- Browse to the folder where the library file is located, which is `C:\ti\TivaWare_C_Series-2.0.1.11577\driverlib\rvmdk`. Then select the library file `driverlib.lib` and click on the Add button. Click on the `Close` button to finish this step.

7.2.6 Build and Demonstrate Your Program As the project runs, the LED PB3~PB0 will be ON or OFF based on the intensity of the light hitting on the photosensor, and you can change those LEDs by exposing or covering the photosensor by hands. Also, you can change the color of the 3-color LED by rotating the potentiometer with a small screw driver. As this is changing, the color of the LED is modified from red, blue, green and white. You can hear a low-frequency audio signal sound coming from the speaker, and this is the output of the temperature sensor LM45.

Based on these results, try to answer the following questions:

- Why the color on the three-color LED changed and why four LEDs, PB3–PB0 changed? Can you change the frequency of the audio signal sound coming from the speaker? How?
- What did you learn from this project?

7.3 Lab7_3

7.3.1 Goal This project allows students to become familiar with PWM modules by building a PWM project to drive a 12V DC motor in a changing-duty-cycle mode with the DRA method. Two switch buttons, SW2 and SW3 installed in the EduBASE ARM® Trainer, are used as two trigger sources to change the duty cycle of the PWM output via M1PWM5 pin or PWM Module 1 Generator 2.

7.3.2 Data Assignment and Hardware Configuration Refer to Section 7.6.8 and Figure 7.48 to configure and connect the hardware, including an external 12V DC power supply connected to terminal T3, a 12V DC motor with fan connected to terminals M1 and M2, and a jumper wire connected between 1 and 2 on the jumper J4. The GPIO Ports and pins to be used in this project are as follows:

- PF1 is used to provide the PWM driving signal to the motor (PWMA) via M1PWM5.
- PB0 (AIN1) and PB1 (AIN2) are used to provide the rotating direction signal (PB1:PB0 = 01 → CW and PB1:PB0 = 10 → CCW) for the motor. In this project, we use the first rotating direction PB1:PB0 = 01 since the motor can be rotated in a single direction.
- PD3 is connected to the switch button SW2, and PD2 is connected to the switch button SW3 in the EduBASE ARM® Trainer (refer to Figure 7.3). Both PD2 and PD3 pins are Low if none of these two buttons are pressed. However, a High is applied on either pin if either button is pressed.

7.3.3 Development of the Project
Use the steps below to develop this project. Both a header file and a C source file are used in this project since it is a little complicated. Create a new project with the following steps:

1. Create a new folder Lab7_3 under the folder C:\ARM Lab Projects\Chapter 7 in the Windows Explorer.
2. Open the Keil® ARM-MDK μVersion5, create a new project named Lab7_3, and save this project in the folder Lab7_3 created in step 1.
3. On the next wizard, you need to select the device (MCU) for this project. Expand three icons, Texas Instruments, Tiva C Series and TM4C123x Series, and select the target device TM4C123GH6PM from the list by clicking on it. Click on the OK to close this wizard.
4. Next the Software Components wizard is opened, and you need to setup the software development environment for your project with this wizard. Expand two icons, CMSIS and Device, and check the CORE and Startup checkboxes in the Sel. column, and click on the OK button since we need these two components to build our project.

7.3.4 Development of the Header File

1. In the Project pane, expand the Target folder and right click on the Source Group 1 folder and select the Add New Item to Group 'Source Group 1'.
2. Select the Header File (.h) and enter Lab7_3 into the Name: box, and click on the Add button to add this header file into the project.
3. Include the following system header files and macros:
   - #include <stdint.h>
   - #include <stdbool.h>
   - #include "TM4C123GH6PM.h"
   - #define GPIO_PORTF_CR_R   (*((volatile uint32_t *)0x40025524))
   - #define SYSCTL_SYSDIV_5   0x02400000
   - #define SYSCTL_USE_PLL   0x00000000
   - #define SYSCTL_OSC_MAIN   0x00000000
   - #define SYSCTL_XTAL_16MHZ   0x00000540

The reason to include the system header file "TM4C123GH6PM.h" is that we want to use structure pointers for all related registers on GPIO Ports and PWM modules. Those definitions for five macros are used to access related system constants and register.

Save this header file as Lab7_3.h.

7.3.5 Development of the C Source File

1. In the `Project` pane, expand the `Target` folder and right click on the `Source Group 1` folder and select the `Add New Item to Group 'Source Group 1'`.

2. Select the C File (`.c`) and enter `Lab7_3` into the `Name:` box, and click on the `Add` button to add this source file into the project.

3. Include the header file "`Lab7_3.h`" into this source file.

4. Declare the user-defined function `void Delay(uint32_t time);`.

5. Inside the `main(void)` program, declare two unsigned 32-bit integer local variables, `pw = 20` and RCC. The first variable is used to set up and maintain the duty cycle value. The second one works as a temporary value holder for different values.

6. Use the following macros to set up the system clock. `ORing` them together and assign this to the variable RCC.

   - SYSCTL_SYSDIV_5
   - SYSCTL_USE_PLL
   - SYSCTL_OSC_MAIN
   - SYSCTL_XTAL_16MHZ

7. Assign the resulted RCC to the Run-Mode Clock Configuration (RCC) register via the structure pointer SYSCTL→RCC.

8. Enable the PWM1 module with clock by `ORing` and assigning (`|=`) `0x2` to the Pulse-Width Modulator-Run-Mode Clock Gating Control (RCGCPWM) register using the structure pointer format (SYSCTL→RCGCPWM).

9. Use a `while()` loop to wait for this enabling and clocking configuration to be finished. The loop condition for this `while()` loop is (SYSCTL->PRPWM & 0x2) == 0. The Pulse-Width Modulator Peripheral Ready (PRPWM) register is used to monitor and indicate whether the required peripheral (PWM1) is ready or not. The bit 1 (R1) on this register is set to 1 when the PWM1 is ready.

10. Enable GPIO Ports F, D, and B with clocks by assigning appropriate values to the General-Purpose Input/Output Run-Mode Clock Gating Control (RCGCGPIO) register (refer to Figure 7.49).

11. Similarly to step 9, use another `while()` loop to wait for the GPIO Ports to be configured and enabled. The loop condition can be (SYSCTL->PRGPIO & 0x2A) == 0. The General-Purpose Input/Output Peripheral Ready (PRGPIO) register is used to monitor and indicate whether the selected GPIO Port is ready or not. Starting from bit 0 (R0) to bit 5 (R5), each bit is associated with a GPIO Port: R0, Port A; R1, Port B, . . . R5, Port F. if the selected port is ready, the corresponding bit is set to 1.

12. Configure the RCC register again to get a 20 MHz clock source for the PWM module 1 by configuring the bits USEPWMDIV and PWMDIV on this register.

13. Enable the PWM1 module again by assigning an appropriate value to the RCGC0 register.

14. Unlock the GPTO Port F Commit Register GPIOCR by assigning the unlock key 0x4C4F434B to the GPIO Port F Lock register (GPIOF→LOCK).

15. Enable PF1 to be committed by `ORing` and assign (`|=`) 0x2 to the GPIO Port F Commit Register macro (GPIO_PORTF_CR_R). This step enables the following configurations for the GPIO Port F AFSEL and PCTL registers to be committed immediately when they are set up or configured.

16. Then lock the GPIOF commit register by assigning 0x0 to the GPIO Port F Lock register macro (GPIOF→LOCK) to keep this configuration.

The following codes are used to configure and set up PWM Module 1 Generator 2 or M1PWM5 pin to enable it to output a PWM signal.

17. Disable the PWM1_2B or M1PWM5 pin by assigning 0x0 to the PWM Module 1 Generator 2 Control Register macro PWM1→_2_CTL.

18. Configure the PWM Module 1 Generator 2 register PWM1GENB by assigning a value of 0x0000080C to the PWM1GENB register macro (PWM1→_2_GENB). This configuration enables the M1PWM5 pin to output High when the counter equals the LOAD value and output Low when the counter matches the CMPB value when it is counting down.

19. Load the period value 3999 (4000–1) to the PWM1 LOAD register (PWM1→_2_LOAD).

20. Enable the PWM1_2B or M1PWM5 pin by assigning 0x1 to the PWM Module 1 Generator 2 Control Register macro PWM1→_2_CTL.

21. Enable the PWM1 module by assigning 0x20 to the PWM Master Control register macro PWM1→ENABLE (refer to Section 7.6.4.2.1 to get more details about this register).

The following codes are used to initialize and configure GPIO Ports B, D, and F.

22. Configure the PF1 pin to work as an output and digital function pin by assigning appropriate values to the Port F Direction and Digital Enable registers (GPIOF→DIR and GPIOF→DEN).

23. Configure the PF1 pin to work as an alternate function, M1PWM5 output pin, by assigning an appropriate value to the GPIO Port F AFSEL register GPIOF→AFSEL (refer to Figure 7.2 and Table 7.1 in Section 7.2 to get more details about this register).

24. Configure PF1 pin to work as a PWM output pin by assigning 0x00000050 to the Port F Port Control register macro GPIOF→PCTL.

25. Disable analog function on PF1 pin by ANDing and assigning (&=) an inverse value of 0x02 to the Port F Analog Mode Select register macro GPIOF→AMSEL.

26. Configure PD3~PD0 pins to work as input and digital function pins by assigning appropriate values to the Port D Direction and Digital Enable registers (GPIOD→DIR and GPIOD→DEN).

27. Configure PB1~PB0 pins to work as output and digital function pins by assigning appropriate values to the Port B Direction and Digital Enable registers (GPIOB→DIR and GPIOB→DEN).

28. Set PB0 to 1 to make AIN1 as HIGH to enable DC motor to rotate in the CW direction. This setup can be accomplished by assigning 0x1 to the Port B DATA register.

29. Clear the Port D by assigning 0x0 to the Port D DATA register.

The following codes are used to monitor two switch buttons SW2 and SW3 to perform related duty cycle increment or decrement operations based on these two buttons.

30. An infinitive while() loop is used to start this process.

31. First read the GPIO Port D DATA register and assign the reading value to the RCC variable.

32. Use the if() selection structure to check whether the SW2 is pressed (PD3 = 1) or the SW3 is pressed (PD2 = 1). The first checking condition is (RCC & 0x8) and the second checking condition is (RCC & 0x4).

33. If the first checking condition is true, the SW2 is pressed. The variable pw is incremented by 1. If this value is greater than 3999, adjust it to 3990. Then assign this pw value to the PWM Module 1 Generator 2 Compare B register macro PWM1→_2_CMPB.

34. If the second checking condition is true, the SW3 is pressed. The variable pw is decremented by 1. If this value is less than 100, adjust it to 100. Then assign this pw value to the PWM Module 1 Generator 2 Compare B register macro PWM1→_2_CMPB.

35. Call Delay(1000) function to delay the program a period of time.

36. For the Delay() function, just put a blank for() loop to repeat looping a certain time.

7.3.6 Set Up the Environment to Build and Run the Project   The only environment to be set is to make sure that the debugger shown in the Use: box in the Debug tab under the Project|Options for Target 'Target 1' menu item is Stellaris ICDI. Otherwise you can click on the dropdown arrow to select this debugger from the list.

7.3.7 Demonstrate Your Program   Perform the following operations to run your program and check the running results:

- Go to Flash|Download menu item to download your program into the flash ROM.
- Go to Debug|Start/Stop Debug Session to begin debugging your program. Click on the OK button on the 32KB memory size limitation message box to continue.
- Then go to Debug|Run menu item to run your program.

As the project runs, when you pressed SW2 button, the duty cycle is incremented and the rotation speed of the DC motor becomes faster. As you pressed the SW3 button, the duty cycle is decreased and the rotating speed of the DC motor is reduced.

Based on these results, try to answer the following questions:

- When either SW2 or SW3 button is pressed as the project runs, the rotation speed of the DC motor is changed, going either up or down. Why has this happened?
- What did you learn from this project?

7.4 Lab7_4

7.4.1 Goal   This project allows students to build a PWM project using the Software Driver method to drive a DC motor with a modified-duty-cycle mode. In this project, some API functions provided by the TivaWare™ Peripheral Driver Library are utilized to simplify the coding process. Two switch buttons, SW4 and SW5 installed in the EduBASE ARM® Trainer, are used as two trigger sources to change the duty cycle of the PWM output via M1PWM5 pin or PWM Module 1 Generator 2.

7.4.2 Data Assignment and Hardware Configuration   Refer to Section 7.6.8 and Figure 7.48 to configure and connect the hardware, including an external 12V DC power supply connected to terminal T3, a 12V DC motor with a fan connected to terminals M1 and M2, and a jumper wire connected between 1 and 2 on the jumper J4. The GPIO Ports and pins to be used in this project are as follows:

- PF1 is used to provide the PWM driving signal to the motor (PWMA) via M1PWM5.
- PB0 (AIN1) and PB1 (AIN2) are used to provide the rotating direction signal (PB1 : PB0 = 01 → CW and PB1 : PB0 = 10 → CCW) for the motor. In this project, we use the first rotating direction PB1 : PB0 = 01 since the motor can be rotated in a single direction.
- PD1 is connected to the switch button SW4 and PD0 is connected to the switch button SW5 in the EduBASE ARM® Trainer (refer to Figure 7.3). Both PD1 and PD0 pins are Low if no any of these two buttons are pressed. However, a High is applied on either pin if either button is pressed.

7.4.3 Development of the Project   Using steps below to develop this project. Only a C source file is used in this project since it is not complicated. Create a new project with the following steps:

1. Create a new folder Lab7_4 under the folder C:\ARM Lab Projects\Chapter 7 in the Windows Explorer.

2. Open the Keil® ARM-MDK μVersion5, create a new project named Lab7_4, and save this project in the folder Lab7_4 created in step 1.

3. On the next wizard, you need to select the device (MCU) for this project. Expand three icons, Texas Instruments, Tiva C Series, and TM4C123x Series, and select the target device TM4C123GH6PM from the list by clicking on it. Click on the OK to close this wizard.

4. Next the Software Components wizard is opened, and you need to set up the software development environment for your project with this wizard. Expand two icons, CMSIS and Device, and check the CORE and Startup checkboxes in the Sel. column, and click on the OK button since we need these two components to build our project.

7.4.4 Development of the C Source File

1. In the Project pane, expand the Target folder and right click on the Source Group 1 folder and select the Add New Item to Group 'Source Group 1'.

2. Select the C File (.c) and enter Lab7_4 into the Name: box, and click on the Add button to add this source file into the project.

3. Include the following system header files and macros:
   - #include <stdint.h>
   - #include <stdbool.h>
   - #include "inc/hw_memmap.h"
   - #include "inc/hw_types.h"
   - #include "inc/hw_gpio.h"
   - #include "driverlib/sysctl.h"
   - #include "driverlib/gpio.h"
   - #include "driverlib/pwm.h"
   - #define GPIO_PF1_M1PWM5 0x00050405

4. Inside the main(void) program, declare three unsigned 32-bit integer local variables, ui32Load, uiInput, and uiPWM. The first variable is used to set up and maintain the LOAD value. The second one works as a temporary value holder for different inputs. The third one is used as a PWM value holder for the PWM GENB register.

5. Use the following macros to set up a 40 MHz system clock. ORing them together and assign it as an argument to the API function SysCtlClockSet().
   - SYSCTL_SYSDIV_5
   - SYSCTL_USE_PLL
   - SYSCTL_OSC_MAIN
   - SYSCTL_XTAL_16MHZ

6. Use the macro SYSCTL_PWMDIV_2 as an argument to call the function SysCtlPWM-ClockSet() to select the PWMDIV field as 2 to divide the system clock by 2 to get a 20 MHz PWM clock.

7. Use the macro SYSCTL_PERIPH_PWM1 as an argument to call the API function SysCtlPeripheralEnable() to enable the PWM Module 1.

8. Use the macro SYSCTL_PERIPH_GPIOB as an argument to call the API function SysCtlPeripheralEnable() to enable the GPIO Port B.

9. Use the macro SYSCTL_PERIPH_GPIOD as an argument to call the API function SysCtlPeripheralEnable() to enable the GPIO Port D.

10. Use the macro SYSCTL_PERIPH_GPIOF as an argument to call the API function SysCtlPeripheralEnable() to enable the GPIO Port F.

11. Use macros GPIO_PORTF_BASE and GPIO_PIN_1 as arguments to call the API function GPIOPinTypePWM() to configure PF1 as a PWM pin.

12. Use macro GPIO_PF1_M1PWM5 as an argument to call the function GPIOPinConfigure() to configure PF1 as a M1PWM5 output pin.

13. Unlock the GPIO Port F Commit Register by assigning the macro GPIO_LOCK_KEY to the macro HWREG(GPIO_PORTF_BASE + GPIO_O_LOCK).

14. Enable the GPIO Port F Commit Register to commit PF1 pin by ORing and assigning (|=) 0x2 to the macro HWREG(GPIO_PORTF_BASE + GPIO_O_CR). This step enables the following configurations for the GPIO Port F AFSEL and PCTL registers to be committed immediately when they are set up or configured.

15. Assign 0x0 to the macro HWREG(GPIO_PORTF_BASE + GPIO_O_LOCK) to lock the GPIO Port F Commit Register.

16. Use macros GPIO_PORTD_BASE, GPIO_PIN_1|GPIO_PIN_0 as an argument to call the API function GPIOPinTypeGPIOInput() to define PD0 and PD1 as input pins.

17. Use macros GPIO_PORTB_BASE, PIO_PIN_3|GPIO_PIN_2|GPIO_PIN_1|GPIO_PIN_0 as an argument to call the API function GPIOPinTypeGPIOOutput() to define PB3 ~ PB0 as output pins.

The following codes are used to configure and set up PWM Module 1 Generator 2 or M1PWM5 pin to enable it to output a PWM signal.

18. Assign 4000 (clock period) to the variable ui32Load.

19. Use macros PWM1_BASE, PWM_GEN_2, PWM_GEN_MODE_DOWN as an argument to call the API function PWMGenConfigure() to configure M1PWM Generator 2 to work as the counting down mode.

20. Use macros PWM1_BASE, PWM_GEN_2, ui32Load as an argument to call the API function PWMGenPeriodSet() to set the period for the M1PWM Generator 2.

21. Use the macros PWM1_BASE, PWM_OUT_5, uiPWM as an argument to call the API function PWMPulseWidthSet() to set the initial pulse width for the M1PWM5 pin.

22. Use macros PWM1_BASE, PWM_OUT_5_BIT, true as an argument to call the API function PWMOutputState() to enable M1PWM5 signal to be transferred to pwmB' pin.

23. Use macros PWM1_BASE, PWM_GEN_2 as an argument to call the API function PWMGenEnable() to enable the M1PWM Generator 2 to begin to work.
    The following codes are used to monitor two switch buttons SW4 and SW5 to perform related duty cycle increment or decrement operations based on these two buttons.

24. Use macros GPIO_PORTB_BASE, GPIO_PIN_0, 0x1 as an argument to call the API function GPIOPinWrite() to make PB0 High to enable DC motor to rotate in the CW direction.

25. Use an infinitive while() loop to repeatedly read and check the PD0 (SW5) and PD1 (SW4) to see whether one of them is pressed.

26. Use macros GPIO_PORTD_BASE, GPIO_PIN_1|GPIO_PIN_0 as an argument to call the API function GPIOPinRead() to read PD0 and PD1 values, and assign the reading result to the variable uiInput.

27. If PD1 = 1 (uiInput & 0x2), the SW4 is pressed. First the PB3 LED should be ON to indicate this situation by calling the GPIO API function GPIOPinWrite() with the argument GPIO_PORTB_BASE, GPIO_PIN_3, 0x8. The PB2 LED should be OFF by calling the API function GPIOPinWrite() with the argument GPIO_PORTB_BASE, GPIO_PIN_2, 0x0. Then the variable uiPWM is incremented by 2. If this value is greater than 3999, adjust it to 3990. Finally assign this updated uiPWM value to the PWM Module 1 Generator 2 Compare B register by calling the API function PWMPulseWidthSet() with the argument PWM1_BASE, PWM_OUT_5, uiPWM.

28. If PD0 = 1 (uiInput & 0x1), the SW5 is pressed. First the PB2 LED should be ON to indicate this situation by calling the GPIO API function GPIOPinWrite() with the argument GPIO_PORTB_BASE, GPIO_PIN_2, 0x4. The PB3 LED should be OFF by calling the API function GPIOPinWrite() with the argument GPIO_PORTB_BASE, GPIO_PIN_3, 0x0. Then the variable uiPWM is decremented by 2. If this value is less than 100, adjust it to 100. Finally assign this updated uiPWM value to the PWM Module 1 Generator 2 Compare B register by calling the API function PWMPulseWidthSet() with the argument PWM1_BASE, PWM_OUT_5, uiPWM.

29. Call the API function SysCtlDelay(30000) to delay the program a period of time.

7.4.5 Set Up the Environment to Build and Run the Project
This setup contains the following three operations:

1. Include the system header files by adding the include path.

2. Check and configure the correct debugger driver used in the project.

3. Add the TivaWare™ Peripheral Driver Library into the project since we need to use some API functions provided by that library.

Perform the following operations to include this header file path in your project:

- Go to Project|Options for Target 'Target 1' menu item. Then click on the C/C++ tab.

- Go to Include Paths box and browse to the folder where our header files are located, it is C:\ti\TivaWare_C_Series-2.0.1.11577. Select this folder and click on the OK button.

Perform the following operations to make sure that the debugger you are using is the Stellaris ICDI. You can do this checking as follows:

- Go to Project|Options for Target 'Target 1' menu item to open the Options wizard.

- On the opened Options wizard, click on the Debug tab.

- Make sure that the debugger shown in the Use: box is Stellaris ICDI. Otherwise you can click on the dropdown arrow to select this debugger from the list.

Perform the below operations to add the TivaWare™ peripheral driver library into the project:

- Go to the Project pane and right click on the Source Group 1 item, and select the Add Existing Files to Group 'Source Group 1' menu item.

- Browse to the folder where the library file is located, which is C:\ti\TivaWare_ C_Series-2.0.1.11577\driverlib\rvmdk. Then select the library file driver-lib.lib and click on the Add button. Click on the Close button to finish this step.

7.4.6 Demonstrate Your Program   Perform the following operations to run your program and check the running results:

- Go to Flash|Download menu item to download your program into the flash ROM.
- Go to Debug|Start/Stop Debug Session to begin debugging your program. Click on the OK button on the 32-KB memory size limitation message box to continue.
- Then go to Debug|Run menu item to run your program.

As the project runs, when you pressed SW4 button, the duty cycle is incremented and the rotation speed of the DC motor becomes faster. As you pressed the SW5 button, the duty cycle is decreased and the rotating speed of the DC motor is reduced.

Based on these results, try to answer the following questions:

- Compare Lab7_3 and Lab7_4. Which one is better in coding process and control performance? Why?
- Explain advantages and disadvantages for both projects.
- What did you learn from this project?

Chapter 8

ARM® Cortex®-M4 Serial I/O Ports Programming

This chapter provides general information about ARM® Cortex®-M4 microcontroller General-Purpose Input Output (GPIO) Port programming. The discussion is mainly concentrated on the GPIO Ports related to serial peripherals used in the TM4C123GH6PM MCU system. This discussion includes the GPIO Ports and serial peripherals specially designed for the TM4C123GH6PM MCU, general and special or alternative control functions for different GPIO Ports and pins, and GPIO Ports and peripheral programming applications in the TM4C123GH6PM MCU system.

8.1 OVERVIEW AND INTRODUCTION

As we discussed in Section 2.6.2 in Chapter 2, in the TM4C123GH6PM MCU system, the GPIO module provides interfaces for multiple peripherals or I/O devices. Generally GPIO provides six popular GPIO Ports, Ports A~F, to interface and access most system or on-chip peripherals as well as external peripherals and I/O devices to perform input/output functions.

As we discussed in Section 2.6.3.3 in Chapter 2, each GPIO Port can be mapped to an I/O block, and each block contains 8 bits or 8 pins. Each bit or each pin can be configured as either input or output pin. Also with the help of the GPIO Alternate Function Selection register (GPIOAFSEL), each pin can be configured to perform multiple or different functions, which are called alternative functions.

The advantage of using this GPIOAFSEL register in the GPIO module is that multiple functions can be configured and fulfilled by using a limited number of GPIO Ports and pins. The shortcoming is that this will make the GPIO Port configurations and programming more complicated and difficult.

Most of peripherals, including system, on-chip, and interfaces to the external peripherals, are connected and controlled to the GPIO Ports with related pins. In this chapter, we

Practical Microcontroller Engineering with ARM® Technology, First Edition. Ying Bai.
© 2016 by The Institute of Electrical and Electronics Engineers, Inc. Published 2016 by John Wiley & Sons, Inc.
Companion Website: www.wiley.com/go/armbai

will concentrate on most popular serial peripherals used in the TM4C123GH6PM MCU system:

- Synchronous Serial Interface (SSI)
- Inter-Integrated Circuit (I2C) Interface
- Universal Asynchronous Receivers/Transmitters (UARTs)

Some example projects related to those serial peripherals to be developed include:

- On-Board LCD Interface Programming Project
- On-Board 7 Segment LED Interface Programming Project
- Digital-to-Analog Converter Programming Project
- I2C Interfacing Programming Project
- UART Programming Project

The first three projects are related to SSI interfacing projects.

The timer in the TM4C123GH6PM MCU system is a big topic, and we will discuss this peripheral in Chapter 9 with general-purpose timers, watchdog timers, and USB. In Chapter 10 we will concentrate on our discussions on QEI, CAN, and DC motor as well as Robotics controls, although some peripherals belong to serial devices.

8.2 GPIO MODULE ARCHITECTURE AND GPIO PORT CONFIGURATION

We have provided detailed discussions and introductions about the GPIO architecture and related registers in Section 2.6.3.3 in Chapter 2 and Section 7.2 in Chapter 7. In this part, we will provide a quick review about the GPIO Ports and pin configurations related to serial peripherals.

Figure 8.1 shows a functional block diagram for GPIO Ports A~F and all related pins used in the TM4C123GH6PM MCU system.

It can be found from Figure 8.1 that each pin in each GPIO Port can provide multiple or alternative functions. The actual function for each pin is determined by the combination of the GPIO Alternate Function Select Register (GPIOAFSEL) and the GPIO Port Control Register (GPIOPCTL) together. We have provided detailed discussions about the combinations of these two registers to determine the function for each pin in Section 2.6.3.3.6 in Chapter 2. In this part, we just want to emphasize some important points to make this issue clear.

It can also be found from Figure 8.1 that all GPIO Ports are involved in serial peripheral control and interfacing functions, such as SSI0~SSI3, I2C0~I2C3, USB0, CAN0~CAN1, and UART0~UART7. All of these serial control and interface functions for those serial peripherals are performed via related GPIO pins, and these GPIO pins can be easily defined and configured by setting up the GPIOAFSEL and GPIOPCTL registers.

The lowest 8 bits in the GPIOAFSEL register determined whether any pin in any GPIO Port works as a general GPIO pin or as an alternate function pin. For these 8 bits, each bit is mapped to each pin in a selected GPIO Port. If a bit is 0, it means that the corresponding pin works as a general GPIO pin. Otherwise if a bit is 1, the corresponding

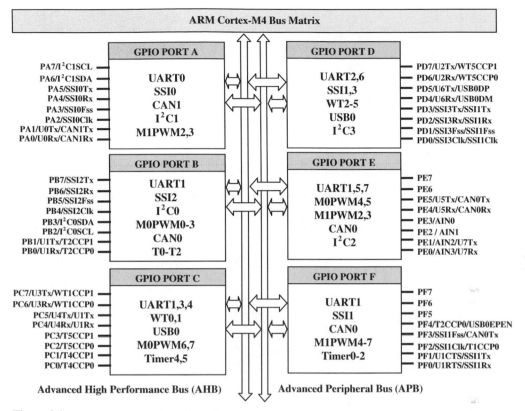

Figure 8.1.   GPIO Port and pin configuration.

pin works as an alternate function pin. In this case, the actual function the pin supposes to perform is determined by the related 4 bits in the GPIOPCTL register.

Table 8.1 is a copy of Table 2.6 in Chapter 2 and Figure 2.19 is also redrew here as Figure 8.2 to make this issue clear.

Refer to Figure 8.2 and Table 8.1: The alternate function for each selected pin can be uniquely determined. For example, the bits 0 and 6 in the GPIOAFSEL register in the GPIO Port A are set to 1. This means that both pins 0 and 6 in the GPIO Port A should work as alternate function pins to connect to the special peripherals to provide special functions. For bit 0 in the GPIOAFSEL register, the alternate function can be determined by the PMC0 (lowest 4 bits) in the GPIOPCTL register, which is shown in Table 8.1. If PMC0 in the GPIOPCTL register is 1 (0001), this means that the PA0 should work as a receiving pin for the UART0 (Table 8.1). However, for bit 6 in the GPIOAFSEL register, if the PMC6 (bits 24–27) in the GPIOPCTL register is 5 (0101), the PA6 pin should work as a M1PWM2 pin to connect to that PWM peripheral to provide a pulse width modulation output.

As we discussed in Section 2.6.3.4 in Chapter 2, each GPIO Port (Ports A~F) contains a set of GPIO Registers and each register can be accessed by using an offset address combining (plus) with a base address.

Table 8.1.   GPIO pins and alternate functions.

I/O	Pin	Analog Function	Digital Functions (GPIOPCTL PMCx Bit Field Encoding)									
			1	2	3	4	5	6	7	8	9	14
PA0	17	—	U0RX	—	—	—	—	—	—	CAN1RX	—	—
PA1	18	—	U0TX	—	—	—	—	—	—	CAN1TX	—	—
PA2	19	—	—	SSI0CLK	—	—	—	—	—	—	—	—
PA3	20	—	—	SSI0FSS	—	—	—	—	—	—	—	—
PA4	21	—	—	SSI0RX	—	—	—	—	—	—	—	—
PA5	22	—	—	SSI0TX	—	—	—	—	—	—	—	—
PA6	23	—	—	—	I2C1SCL	—	M1PWM2	—	—	—	—	—
PA7	24	—	—	—	I2C1SDC	—	M1PWM3	—	—	—	—	—
PB0	45	USB0ID	U1RX	—	—	—	—	—	T2CCP0	—	—	—
PB1	46	USB0VBUS	U1TX	—	—	—	—	—	T2CCP1	—	—	—
PB2	47	—	—	—	I2C0SCL	—	—	—	T3CCP0	—	—	—
PB3	48	—	—	—	I2C0SDC	—	—	—	T3CCP1	—	—	—
PB4	58	AIN10	—	SSI2CLK	—	M0PWM2	—	—	T1CCP0	CAN0RX	—	—
PB5	57	AIN11	—	SSI2FSS	—	M0PWM3	—	—	T1CCP1	CAN0TX	—	—
PB6	1	—	—	SSI2RX	—	M0PWM0	—	—	T0CCP0	—	—	—
PB7	4	—	—	SSI2TX	—	M0PWM1	—	—	T0CCP1	—	—	—
PC0	52	—	TCK SWCLK	—	—	—	—	—	T4CCP0	—	—	—
PC1	51	—	TMS SWDIO	—	—	—	—	—	T4CCP1	—	—	—
PC2	50	—	TDI	—	—	—	—	—	T5CCP0	—	—	—
PC3	49	—	TDO SWO	—	—	—	—	—	T5CCP1	—	—	—
PC4	16	C1-	U4RX	U1RX	—	M0PWM6	—	IDX1	WT0CCP0	U1RTS	—	—
PC5	15	C1+	U4TX	U1TX	—	M0PWM7	—	PHA1	WT0CCP1	U1CTS	—	—
PC6	14	C0+	U3RX	—	—	—	—	PHB1	WT1CCP0	USB0EPEN	—	—
PC7	13	C0-	U3TX	—	—	—	—	—	WT1CCP1	USB0PFLT	—	—
PD0	61	AIN7	SSI3CLK	SSI1CLK	I2C3SCL	M0PWM6	M1PWM0	—	WT2CCP0	—	—	—
PD1	62	AIN6	SSI3FSS	SSI1FSS	I2C3SDC	M0PWM7	M1PWM1	—	WT2CCP1	—	—	—
PD2	63	AIN5	SSI3RX	SSI1RX	—	M0FAULT0	—	—	WT3CCP0	USB0EPEN	—	—
PD3	64	AIN4	SSI3TX	SSI1TX	—	—	—	IDX0	WT3CCP1	USB0PFLT	—	—
PD4	43	USB0DM	U6RX	—	—	—	—	—	WT4CCP0	—	—	—
PD5	44	USB0DP	U6TX	—	—	—	—	—	WT4CCP1	—	—	—
PD6	53	—	U2RX	—	—	M0FAULT0	—	PHA0	WT5CCP0	—	—	—
PD7	10	—	U2TX	—	—	—	—	PHB0	WT5CCP1	NMI	—	—
PE0	9	AIN3	U7RX	—	—	—	—	—	—	—	—	—
PE1	8	AIN0	U7TX	—	—	—	—	—	—	—	—	—
PE2	7	AIN1	—	—	—	—	—	—	—	—	—	—
PE3	6	AIN2	—	—	—	—	—	—	—	—	—	—
PE4	59	AIN9	U5RX	—	I2C2SCL	M0PWM4	M1PWM2	—	—	CAN0RX	—	—
PE5	60	AIN8	U5TX	—	I2C2SDC	M0PWM5	M1PWM3	—	—	CAN0TX	—	—
PF0	28	—	U1RTS	SSI1RX	CAN0RX	—	M1PWM4	PHA0	T0CCP0	NMI	C0O	—
PF1	29	—	U1CTS	SSI1TX	—	—	M1PWM5	PHB0	T0CCP1	—	C1O	TRD1
PF2	30	—	—	SSI1CLK	—	M0FAULT0	M1PWM6	—	T1CCP0	—	—	TRD0
PF3	31	—	—	SSI1FSS	CAN0TX	—	M1PWM7	—	T1CCP1	—	—	TRCLK
PF4	5	—	—	—	—	—	M1FAULT0	IDX0	T2CCP0	USB0EPEN	—	—

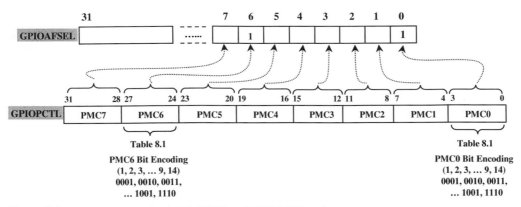

Figure 8.2. The illustration for GPIOAFSEL and GPIOPCTL registers.

In the following sections, we will discuss most popular serial peripherals used in the TM4C123GH6PM MCU system. Because of the page limitation, we move the CAN and QEI peripherals and their interfaces to Chapter 10.

8.3 SYNCHRONOUS SERIAL INTERFACE (SSI)

Two terminologies are widely implemented in the serial communication systems: (1) *Serial Communication Interface* (SCI) and (2) *Serial Peripheral Interface* (SPI). Generally, the SCI belongs to the asynchronous serial communication interface but SPI belongs to the synchronous serial communication interface. In the TM4C123GH6PM MCU system, the SPI is used to work as a synchronous serial interface.

Like any other serial communication interfaces, both SCI and SPI can use either `full-duplex` or `half-duplex` mode to perform the data transfers between terminals and peripherals.

- The full-duplex communication mode uses two data lines (input and output data lines) with one line carrying serial data from peripheral to microcontroller (input) and the other line carrying serial data from microcontroller to peripheral (output).

- The half-duplex communication mode uses only a single data line to transfer data in both directions (input and output) at the different period of the time. Obviously, the single data line cannot transfer data in both directions simultaneously. Therefore the full-duplex mode provides faster data transfer rate because it can transfer data in both directions at the same time with two separate data lines.

The TM4C123GH6PM microcontroller system includes four Synchronous Serial Interface modules (`SSI0~SSI3`). Each SSI module provides a master or a slave interface for synchronous serial communication with peripheral devices that have either Freescale SPI, MICROWIRE, or Texas Instruments™ synchronous serial interfaces.

The TM4C123GH6PM SSI modules provide the following features:

- Programmable interface operation for Freescale SPI, MICROWIRE, or Texas Instruments™ synchronous serial interfaces

- Master or slave operation

- Programmable clock bit rate and prescaler
- Separate transmit and receive FIFOs, and each FIFO contains 8 × 16-bit data
- Programmable data frame size from 4 to 16 bits
- Internal loopback test mode for diagnostic/debug testing
- Standard FIFO-based interrupts and End-of-Transmission interrupt
- Efficient transfers using Micro Direct Memory Access Controller (μDMA)

To successfully perform serial data communications, some data transmitting and receiving mode and data format should be used to make the communication more efficient. Let's first have a clear picture about these modes and formats used in the serial data communications.

8.3.1 Asynchronous and Synchronous Communication Protocols and Data Framing

Some popular asynchronous serial communication protocols are:

- *Acknowledge/Not Acknowledge* (ACK/NAK) *Flow Control*: When using this protocol to transfer data between a transmitter and a receiver, each time after a block of data is sent out by the transmitter, the transmitter will wait for an acknowledge signal from the receiver before it can send out the next block of data. After a block of data is received by the receiver, it checks and confirms whether the received data is valid. If the data is valid, the receiver sends back an acknowledgment (ACK) signal to the transmitter to inform the latter that this data transfer is successful and the transmitter can continue to send the next block of data. However, if the data is invalid, the receiver sends back a negative acknowledgment (NAK) signal to the transmitter to inform the latter that the last block of data transfer is unsuccessful, and the transmitter will resend the previous block of data.
- *XON/XOFF Flow Control*: When using this protocol to transfer data, the receiver sends an XON signal to the transmitter to inform the transmitter that the receiver is ready to receive the data from the transmitter. After receiving this XON signal, the transmitter begins to send out a sequence of block data. If for some reason the receiver cannot continue to handle and process the received data, such as the receiver's buffer being full or the receiver being busy, the receiver sends an XOFF signal back to the transmitter to tell the latter to stop data transmission. XON and XOFF are the ASCII control characters DC1 (CTRL-Q) and DC3 (CTRL-S), respectively.

The so-called data framing is the format of the data to be transmitted or received by master or slaver. This format is very important to the asynchronous interface. For asynchronous data communications, the *asynchronous* means that the data transmitter and the data receiver cannot share a common timing base, which means that the transmitter and the receiver must use different clocks as their data transfer timing bases. In order to coordinate this asynchronous serial communications, the data transmitter must send special code format or code bits before and after the serial data bits to enable the receiver to check and confirm the correctness of that data transfer based on those code bits. These code bits can be considered as the *framing bits* or *frame* to inform the receiver when the data transfer begins and when it ends. Figure 8.3 shows some popular data framing bits structures. The *synchronous* means that both transmitter and receiver use the same clock rate SClk as their data operation

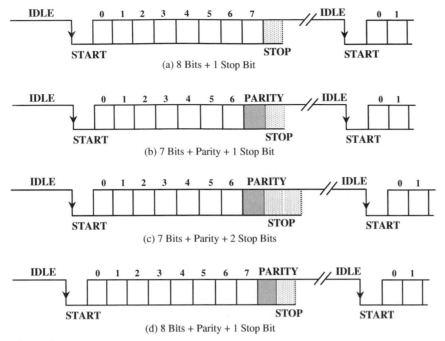

Figure 8.3. Some popular data transfer framing bits structures.

timing base. We will discuss the protocols and data framing for synchronous data communications in Section 8.3.3.

The basic data unit (group of bits) of information is the character or data frame, and normally it is a byte (8-bit) with bit by bit in a timing sequence. The transmitter can send a byte at any rate and the receiver needs to know when the byte starts and when it stops. As shown in Figure 8.3, depending on the different framing bits, the data can be transferred as an 8-bit data (1 byte) plus a stop bit (Figure 8.3a), a 7-bit data plus a parity bit with a stop bit (Figure 8.3b), 7-bit data plus parity with 2 stop bits (Figure 8.3c) or 8-bit data plus parity with a stop bit (Figure 8.3d).

Note that a constant LOW or HIGH signal is always considered as an idle status with no data being transferred. A LOW-TO-HIGH or a HIGH-TO-LOW edge is always considered as the starting signal for a block of data to be transferred. Also note that the data bits are transmitted with the MSB first, and there is no any level transition between bits of the same value. For example, if all data bits were 1, the transmitted frame would be LOW only during the start bit. This format is called non-return to zero (NRZ), which means that the voltage does not return to zero between adjacent 1 bits.

The stop bits can be either one or two. Some other systems may use 1.5 stop bits. Typically, the transmitter hardware automatically creates the framing bits and the receiver hardware automatically removes them.

The parity bit is used to check and confirm the correctness of the last data to be transferred. It refers to the quantity of 1 bits in a binary number. If that quantity is even, the number has even parity. However, if it is odd, the number has odd parity. Note that the standard ASCII code is 7-bit, therefore the eighth bit may be used as a parity bit.

The transmitter is responsible to create the parity bit and the receiver deciphers it. The parity bit's value can be either 0 or 1, depending on the following two conditions:

- The type of parity selected, even or odd.
- The quantity of 1 bits in the data byte to be transferred.

For example, the transmitter and receiver agree to use 7-bit plus odd parity with one stop bit, and an ASCII code 8 (111000) will be transferred between them. Because the 1 bits in this code is 3, which is an odd number, the parity bit will be set to 1 by the transmitter to indicate that this transferring data contains an odd number of 1's. When the receiver gets this data, it will first count the number of 1's in the received data and check the value on the received parity bit. If both agree, which means that the number of 1's in the received data is an odd number and the value on the parity bit is 1, it means that this data transfer is successful. Otherwise, if the number of 1's in the received data is an even number because of the noise or synchronization errors during that data transferring process, and the parity is 1, it means that this data transfer is wrong. The receiver will send a NAK signal back to the transmitter to ask it to resend this data.

The following items are popular used in serial data communications:

Mark and Space: In addition to the data transfer framing bits, the serial data transfer voltage levels would also be noted. The SSI drives the T_X line to 4.2V for logic 1, which is called a *Mark*, and to 0.4 V for logic 0, which is called a *Space*. The SSI recognizes 3.5~5 V on its R_X line as a mark and 0~1 V as a space.

Data Speed and Baud Rate: In serial data communications, the data speed is defined as the number of bits transmitted per second (BPS) or called Baud rate. Baud rate includes all bits involved in a serial data communication, including the start, parity, and stop bits. A 9600-baud rate means that the serial data is transmitted and received at the rate of 9600 bits per second.

The Break Signal: Sometimes it may necessary to stop or break a normal serial data communication for some unforeseen reasons. The break signal provides this function to get a device's attention to abort a data transfer in midstream. The break signal is a signal that provides a logic LOW on the data transmission line for a longer period of time than a frame time. This long logic LOW is different with any normal data frame bits. As we know, each data unit to be transferred must include at least one stop bit (HIGH) and the idle line is a constant HIGH if no any data to be transferred. A long logic LOW indicates that a break signal is being transferred to inform the device to stop any further data transferring.

Modems: A modem can be considered as an I/O port, and it is mainly used to coordinate and control the serial data communication with the following functions:

- Perform data format conversions between the microcontroller and serial data communication lines. Two typical conversions are involved: (1) Parallel-to-Serial data conversion (used to convert the parallel data sent by microcontroller to the serial data that can be accepted by the serial transmitting line) and (2) Serial-to-Parallel data conversion (used to convert the serial data received from the serial transmitting line to the parallel data that can be accepted by the microcontroller).
- Perform the voltage level conversions between the microcontroller and serial data communication lines. As we know, the typical serial data communication convention is RS-232. In this convention, the voltage level for logic HIGH is 12 V and logic LOW is −12 V. However, inside the microcontroller, it uses TTL logic with 5 V as a logic HIGH and 0.7 V as a logic LOW. Therefore a voltage level conversion is necessary for these different logic levels.

From the data communication point of view, a modem can also be considered as a modulator and demodulator. For data transmission it converts digital signals to the sound or audio signals for transmission along the telephone line, and this process is called modulation. For receiving the modem converts the audio signals back to digital signals, and this process is called demodulation. The modem also uses handshaking control to fulfill its functions.

8.3.2 Synchronous Serial Interface Architecture and Functional Block Diagram

The Synchronous Serial Interface (SSI) module provides the functionality for synchronous serial communications with peripheral devices and can be configured to use different transmission protocols, such as Freescale SPI, MICROWIRE, or the Texas Instruments™ synchronous serial interface frame formats. The size of the data frame can be configured to be between 4 and 16 bits.

The SSI module performs serial-to-parallel data conversion on the data received side and performs parallel-to-serial conversion on the data transmitted side. The T_X and R_X paths are buffered with internal FIFOs allowing up to eight 16-bit values to be stored independently.

The SSI module can be configured as either a master or a slave device. As a slave device, the SSI module can also be configured to disable its output, which allows a master device to be coupled with multiple slave devices.

The SSI module also includes a programmable bit rate clock divider and prescaler to generate the output serial clock derived from the SSI module's input clock. Some devices can use the Precision Internal Oscillator (PIOSC) as the serial bit clock. Bit rates are generated based on the input clock and the maximum bit rate supported by the connected peripheral.

For parts that include a DMA controller, the SSI module also provides a DMA interface to facilitate data transfer via DMA.

Figure 8.4 shows the architecture and functional block diagram for a single SSI module used in the TM4C123GH6PM MCU system. For all four SSI modules, each module contains an identical and independent set of these registers to control and configure each SSI module's data transmitting and receiving functions.

Each SSI module can be configured and controlled by the following groups of registers:

1. Control/Status Register Group:
   - SSI Control 0 Register (SSICR0): Set up protocol mode, clock rate, and data size.
   - SSI Control 1 Register (SSICR1): Set up master/slave mode.
   - SSI Status Register (SSISR): Provide SSI working status (busy, FIFO empty or full).
   - SSI Data Register (SSIDR): 16-bit register used to store data to be written or read.
   - Transmit FIFO (T_XFIFO): Store 8×16-bit data to be transmitted.
   - Receive FIFO (R_XFIFO): Store 8×16-bit data to be received.

2. Clock Control Group:
   - SSI Clock Configure Register (SSICC): Control and select the clock source for the SSI.
   - SSI Clock Prescale Register (SSICPSR): Determine the divisor for the system clock.

3. Interrupt and DMA Control Group:
   - SSI Interrupt Mask Register (SSIIM): Enable (unmask)/disable (mask) SSI interrupt.
   - SSI Raw Interrupt Status Register (SSIRIS): Provide SSI raw interrupt status.
   - SSI Interrupt Clear Register (SSIICR): Clear SSI interrupts.

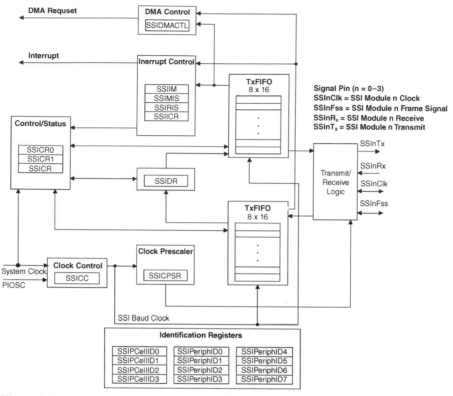

Figure 8.4. Functional block diagram of the SSI module. (Reprinted with the permission of the Texas Instruments Incorporated.)

- SSI Masked Interrupt Status Register (SSIMIS): Provide masked SSI interrupt status.
- SSI DMA Control Register (SSIDMACTL): Provide DMA control.

4. Transmit/Receive Logic: Provide four data communication control/handshaking signals:

- SSInClk: SSI Module n Clock.
- SSInFss: SSI Module n Frame.
- SSInRx: SSI Module n Receive.
- SSInTx: SSI Module n Transmit.

5. Identification Group:

- Twelve registers in this group are used to provide identification numbers for all used SSI peripherals.

We will discuss these registers and their functions one by one in the following sections. First let's have a closer look at the data transmission format or frame used in the serial data communications.

8.3.3 The Synchronous Data Transmission Format and Frame

The general transmission and receiving process for synchronous serial data are as follows:

1. Under the control and configuration of related SSI control registers, each piece of data to be transmitted is first stored into the FIFO via SSIDR.

2. When the transmission and reception process begins, each transmitted data is sent from the FIFO to the serial communication line via SSInTx pin.

3. The transmission/reception speed is controlled by the baud rate determined by the SSICC and SSICPSR registers.

4. The data transmission/reception frame is controlled by the SSInFss and the SSInClk signals together.

Each data frame is between 4 and 16 bits long, depending on the size of data programmed and is transmitted starting with the MSB. There are three basic frame types that can be selected by programming the FRF bit in the SSICR0 register:

1. Texas Instruments™ Synchronous Serial
2. Freescale SPI
3. MICROWIRE

For all three formats, the serial transmission/reception clock SSInClk is held inactive while the SSI is idle, and it becomes active and transitions at the programmed frequency only during the active transmission or reception of data. The idle state of SSInClk is used to provide a receive timeout indication that occurs when the receiving FIFO still contains data after a timeout period.

Table 8.2 lists some important properties for three data frames used in the synchronous serial interface.

Table 8.2. Three data frames used in synchronous serial interface SSI.

Frame	Mode	SSInClk Active level	SSInFss Active level	Function
TI Synchronous Serial	Full-Duplex 4 wires	LOW	One pulse at one clock period	The SSInFss is pulsed High for one SSInClk period. The value to be transmitted is transferred from the transmit FIFO to the serial shift register of the transmit logic. On the next rising edge of SSInClk, the MSB of the 4- to 16-bit data frame is shifted out on the SSInTx pin. The MSB of the received data is shifted onto the SSInRx pin by the off-chip serial slave device.
Freescale SPI	Full-Duplex 4 wires	Programmed by SPO & SPH	LOW	The Freescale SPI interface is a four-wire interface where the SSInFss signal behaves as a slave select. The main feature of the Freescale SPI format is that the inactive state and phase of the SSInClk signal are programmable through the SPO and SPH bits in the SSICR0 control register.
MICROWIRE	Half-Duplex 4 wires	Rising Edge	LOW	MICROWIRE format is very similar to SPI format, except that transmission is half-duplex instead of full-duplex and uses a master–slave message passing technique. Each serial transmission begins with an 8-bit control word that is transmitted from the SSI to the off-chip slave device. During this transmission, no incoming data is received by the SSI. After the message has been sent, the off-chip slave decodes it and, after waiting one serial clock after the last bit of the 8-bit control message has been sent, responds with the required data. The returned data is 4 to 16 bits in length, making the total frame length anywhere from 13 to 25 bits.

In summary, when transmitting/receiving data with three different data frames, the SSInFss pin is forced to LOW to provide an active signal to enable the data to be transmitted/received between master and slave devices. The SSInFss is also used to select the slave device. The differences between these three frames are:

- For the TI Synchronous Serial frame, the rising edge of the SSInClk is always an active edge used to trigger the transmitter or receiver to latch the data bit into the SSInTx or SSInRx line.

- For the Freescale SPI frame, the active level or the polarity of the SSInClk and the active triggering edge or the phase of the SSInClk can be programmed by using two bits, SPO (Serial Clock Polarity) and SPH (Serial Clock Phase) controls, in the SSICR0 register.

- For the MACROWIRE frame, it is very similar to TI Synchronous Serial format except that its transmission is half-duplex instead of full-duplex and uses a master–slave message passing technique.

Now let's have a closer look at three frames.

8.3.3.1 Texas Instruments™ Synchronous Serial Frame

Figure 8.5 shows an illustration for the data transmission/reception using the TI Synchronous Serial frame. The operational sequence for data transmitting/receiving in this frame is as follows:

1. When the SSI is idle, the transmission line SSInTx is in tri-state and the SSInClk and the SSInFss signals are forced to LOW.
2. Once the transmit FIFO contains any data, the SSInFss is pulsed High for one SSInClk period to indicate that a transmission begins. Then the SSInFss is kept in LOW for the entire data transmission/reception period. The value to be transmitted is also transferred from the transmit FIFO to the serial shift register of the transmit logic.
3. On the next rising edge of SSInClk, the MSB of the 4- to 16-bit data frame is shifted out on the SSInTx pin. Likewise, the MSB of the received data is shifted onto the SSInRx pin by the off-chip serial slave device at the same time.
4. Both the SSI and the off-chip serial slave device then clock each data bit into their serial shifter on each **falling** edge of SSInClk.
5. After the LSB has been latched, the entire received data (4~16 bits) that are located at the serial shifter is then transferred from the serial shifter to the receive FIFO on the next rising edge of SSInClk.

8.3.3.2 Freescale SPI Frame

Similar to the TI Synchronous Serial frame, the Freescale SPI interface is also a four-wire interface where the SSInFss signal works as a slave select. The special feature of the

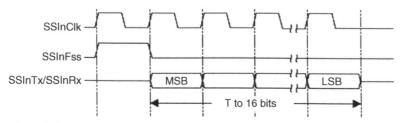

Figure 8.5.   Operational timing sequence of the TI synchronous serial frame. (Reprinted with the permission of the Texas Instruments Incorporated.)

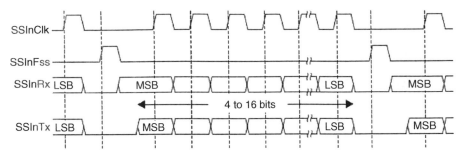

Figure 8.6. The operational sequence for Freescale SPI frame (SPO = SPH = 0). (Reprinted with the permission of the Texas Instruments Incorporated.)

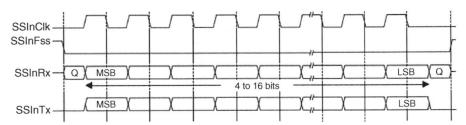

Figure 8.7. The operational sequence for Freescale SPI frame (SPO = 0, SPH = 1). (Reprinted with the permission of the Texas Instruments Incorporated.)

Freescale SPI format is that the inactive state and phase of the SSInClk signal can be programmable through the SPO and SPH bits in the SSICR0 control register.

- The SPO bit determines the inactive level of the SSInClk. When the SPO clock polarity control bit is 0, it creates Low value on the SSInClk pin. If the SPO bit is set, a steady-state High value is placed on the SSInClk pin when data is not being transferred.
- The SPH phase control bit selects the clock active edge that captures data and allows it to change state. The state of this bit has the most impact on the first bit transmitted by either allowing or not allowing a clock transition before the first data capture edge. When the SPH phase control bit is 0, data is captured on the first clock edge transition. If the SPH bit is set, data is captured on the second clock edge transition.

Figures 8.6 and 8.7 provide the operational sequence for this kind of frame. Figure 8.6 shows the timing sequence when SPO = 0 and SPH = 0, which means that the inactive level of the SSInClk is Low and the data is captured by the first clock edge transition.

Figure 8.7 shows the operational sequence when SPO = 0 and SPH = 1. This setting means that the inactive level of the SSInClk is Low and the data is captured at the second clock edge.

8.3.3.3 MICROWIRE Frame

Figure 8.8 shows an illustration of the operational sequence for MACROWIRE frame.

Each serial transmission begins with an 8-bit control word that is transmitted from the SSI to the off-chip slave device. After the message has been sent, the off-chip slave decodes it and waits one serial clock after the last bit of the 8-bit control message has been sent. Then the slave device responds with the required data. The returned data is 4 to 16 bits in length, making the total frame length anywhere from 13 to 25 bits.

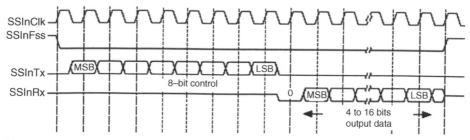

Figure 8.8.   The operational sequence for MACROWIRE frame. (Reprinted with the permission of the Texas Instruments Incorporated.)

The data transmission begins after the control byte is sent. The falling edge of SSInFss causes the value contained in the transmit FIFO to be transferred to the serial shift register of the transmit logic and the MSB of the 8-bit control frame to be shifted out onto the SSInTx pin. SSInFss remains Low for the duration of the frame transmission. The SSInRx pin remains tri-stated during this transmission.

The off-chip serial slave device latches each control bit into its serial shifter on each rising edge of SSInClk. After the last bit is latched by the slave device, the control byte is decoded during a one clock wait-state, and the slave responds by transmitting data back to the SSI. Each bit is driven onto the SSInRx line on the falling edge of SSInClk. The SSI in turn latches each bit on the rising edge of SSInClk. At the end of the frame, for single transfers, the SSInFss signal is pulled High one clock period after the last bit has been latched in the receive serial shifter, causing the data to be transferred to the receive FIFO.

For continuous transfers, data transmission begins and ends in the same manner as a single transfer. However, the SSInFss line is continuously asserted Low and transmission of data occurs back-to-back.

In most applications, the microcontroller is selected as a master device and some peripherals are selected to work as slave devices. In that case, the transmission line Master Output/Salve Input (MOSI) is connected to the SSInTx pin on the master device side, and the Master Input/Slave Output (MISO) is connected to the SSInRx pin in the slave device side.

8.3.4 SSI Module Components and Signal Descriptions

As shown in Figure 8.4, all SSI module components and their control functions are globally illustrated by this block diagram. However, in order to get more details about these components and control signals, we need to discuss them one by one with more details based on each group of registers and their functions.

8.3.4.1 SSI Control Signals and GPIO SSI Control Registers

As we discussed in the previous sections, most peripheral devices in TM4C123GH6PM MCU system are related to GPIO Ports. This means that all control signals and inputs/ outputs of peripherals are transferred by using related GPIO pins. This is also true to SSI modules. All SSI modules are closely related to GPIO Ports and all SSI control signals are connected to related GPIO Port and pins, as shown in Table 8.3.

Table 8.3. SSI control signals and GPIO pins distributions.

SSI Pin	GPIO Pin	Pin Type	Pin Function
SSI0Clk	PA2 (2)	I/O	SSI Module 0 Clock
SSI0Fss	PA3 (2)	I/O	SSI Module 0 Frame
SSI0Rx	PA4 (2)	I	SSI Module 0 Receive
SSI0Tx	PA5 (2)	O	SSI Module 0 Transmit
SSI1Clk	PF2 (2) PD0 (2)	I/O	SSI Module 1 Clock
SSI1Fss	PF3 (2) PD1 (2)	I/O	SSI Module 1 Frame
SSI1Rx	PF0 (2) PD2 (2)	I	SSI Module 1 Receive
SSI1Tx	PF1 (2) PD3 (2)	O	SSI Module 1 Transmit
SSI2Clk	PB4 (2)	I/O	SSI Module 2 Clock
SSI2Fss	PB5 (2)	I/O	SSI Module 2 Frame
SSI2Rx	PB6 (2)	I	SSI Module 2 Receive
SSI2Tx	PB7 (2)	O	SSI Module 2 Transmit
SSI3Clk	PD0 (1)	I/O	SSI Module 3 Clock
SSI3Fss	PD1 (1)	I/O	SSI Module 3 Frame
SSI3Rx	PD2 (1)	I	SSI Module 3 Receive
SSI3Tx	PD3 (1)	O	SSI Module 3 Transmit

In order to enable the corresponding GPIO pins shown in Table 8.3 to work as SSI module pins to transfer-related SSI control signals, the AFSEL bits in the GPIO Alternate Function Select (GPIOAFSEL) register should be set to 1 to choose the SSI function. The number in parentheses is the encoding that must be programmed into the PMCx field in the GPIO Port Control (GPIOPCTL) register to assign the SSI signal to the specified GPIO port pin.

In order to enable GPIO pins to work as SSI function pins, the following configurations should be performed:

1. Enable the clock to the appropriate GPIO modules via the RCGCGPIO register.
2. The related AFSEL bits (lower 8 bits) in the GPIO Alternate Function Select (GPIOAFSEL) register must be set to 1.
3. The related bits in the GPIO Digital Enable (GPIODEN) register must be set to 1 to enable the digital function and disable the analog function.
4. The related PMCx field in the GPIO Port Control (GPIOPCTL) register must be assigned with appropriate codes to enable the GPIO pins to work as desired SSI signal pins.
5. Optionally the related AMSEL bits in the GPIO Analog Mode Select (GPIOAMSEL) register should be clear to 0 to enable the analog isolation circuits to enable the selected pin to work as digital function pin.

We have provided detailed discussions about these registers in the previous chapters. Refer to Sections 2.6.3.3.1 and 2.6.3.3.3, Table 2.6, and Figure 2.19 in Chapter 2 as well as

Section 7.5.3.1 in Chapter 7 to get more details about the GPIOAFSEL and GPIOPCTL registers and PMCx encoding related to the SSI control signals.

8.3.4.2 SSI Module Bit Rate Generation and Clock Control

Two clock sources can be used as the input clock to the SSI module (SSInClk); the system clock or Precision Internal Oscillator (PIOSC). The SSI Clock Configuration (SSICC) register is used to select one of these two clock sources. The following conditions must be met to ensure that the system clock can provide suitable source to the SSInClk:

- If the PIOSC is used for the SSI baud clock, the system clock frequency must be at least 16 MHz in Run mode.
- When SSI works in the master mode, the system clock or the PIOSC must be at least two times faster than the SSInClk, but the SSInClk cannot be faster than 25 MHz.
- When SSI works in the slave mode, the system clock or the PIOSC must be at least 12 times faster than the SSInClk, but the SSInClk cannot be faster than 6.67 MHz.

The SSI includes a programmable bit rate clock divider and a prescaler to generate the serial output clock. Bit rates are supported to 2 MHz and higher, although maximum bit rate is determined by peripheral devices.

Figure 8.9 shows the bit field and functions of the SSI Clock Configuration (SSICC) Register. The lowest 4 bits or bit field CS in this register is used to select one of two clock sources. As shown in Figure 8.9, when CS = 0x0 (0000), the system clock is selected as the clock input to the SSI module. When CS = 0x5 (0101), the PIOSC is selected as the clock source for the SSI module. For all other values, they are reserved and not used for this field.

Two control registers, SSI Clock Prescale (SSICPSR) register and SSI Control 0 (SSICR0) register, are used to provide two dividers, CPSDVSR and SCR, to divide the input clock source (SysClk) to get the desired serial transmission/reception clock with appropriate frequency.

The frequency of the serial output clock SSInClk can be defined as

$$SSInClk = SysClk/(CPSDVSR \times (1 + SCR))$$

The CPSDVSR is the lowest 8 bits in the SSICPSR register. This 8-bit field must contain an even prescale value with a range of 2~254. The SCR is an 8-bit field (bits 15~8) in the SSICR0 register and it can provide a dividing value of 0~255. Therefore the denominator on the above equation is ranged $(2\sim254) \times 256 = 512\sim65024$. This means that

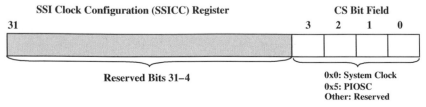

Figure 8.9. The bit field and functions of the SSICC Register.

SSI Clock Prescale (SSICPSR) Register

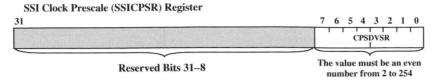

Figure 8.10.   The bit field and functions of the SSICPSR Register.

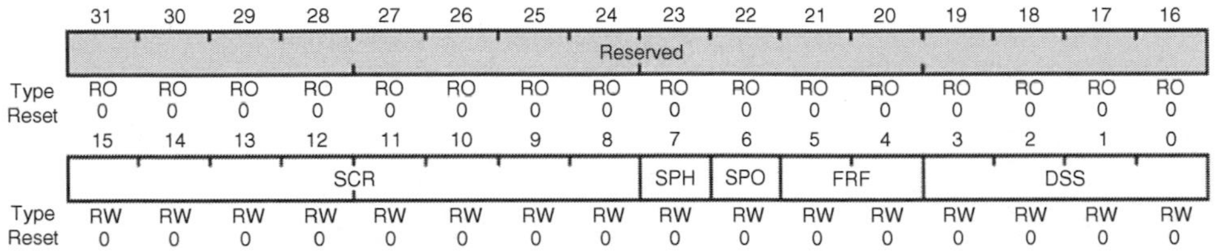

Figure 8.11.   The bit field and functions of the SSICR0 Register. (Reprinted with the permission of the Texas Instruments Incorporated.)

the frequency of the serial output clock `SSInClk` can range from `SysClk/65024` to `SysClk/512`.

Figure 8.10 shows the bit field and functions of the SSI Clock Prescale (`SSICPSR`) Register. The lowest 8 bits or bit field CPSDVSR in this register is used to provide a divider to divide the input system clock source to get the desired serial output clock with an appropriate frequency. This value must be an even number ranged from 2 to 254.

Figure 8.11 shows the bit field and functions of the SSI Control 0 (`SSICR0`) Register. Table 8.4 shows the bit value and its function for `SSICR0` register.

Table 8.4.   Bit value and its function for SSICR0 register.

Bit	Name	Reset	Function
31:16	Reserved	0x0	Reserved
15:8	SCR	0x0	SSI Serial Clock Rate. This bit field is used to generate the transmit and receive bit rate of the SSI (0–255).
7	SPH	0	SSI Serial Clock Phase (Only work for `Freescale SPI Frame`). 0: Data is captured on the `First` clock edge transition. 1: Data is captured on the `Second` clock edge transition.
6	SPO	0	SSI Serial Clock Polarity (Only work for `Freescale SPI Frame`). 0: The inactive level for the `SSInClk` pin is Low. 1: The inactive level for the `SSInClk` pin is High. If this bit is set, the software must also configure the GPIO port pin corresponding to the `SSInClk` signal as a pull-up in the `GPIO Pull-Up Select` (GPIOPUR) register.
5:4	FRF	0x0	SSI Frame Format Select. 0x0: Freescale SPI Frame Format, 0x1: Texas Instruments Synchronous Serial Frame Format 0x2: MICROWIRE Frame Format, 0x3: Reserved
3:0	DSS	0x0	SSI Data Size Select. 0x0-0x2: Reserved 0x3: 4-bit data, 0x4: 5-bit data, 0x5: 6-bit data, 0x6: 7-bit data, 0x7: 8-bit data 0x8: 9-bit data, 0x9: 10-bit data, 0xA: 11-bit data, 0xB: 12-bit data, 0xC: 13-bit data 0xD: 14-bit data, 0xE: 15-bit data, 0xF: 16-bit data

SSI Control 1 (SSICR1) Register

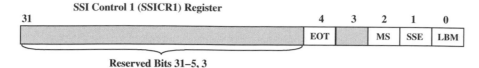

Reserved Bits 31–5, 3

Figure 8.12. The bit field and functions of the SSICR1 Register.

8.3.4.3 SSI Module Control/Status and FIFO Control

As we discussed in Section 8.3.2, the following control registers belong to SSI module control and status group:

- SSI Control 0 Register (SSICR0): Setup protocol mode, clock rate and data size.
- SSI Control 1 Register (SSICR1): Setup master/slave mode.
- SSI Status Register (SSISR): Provide SSI working status (busy, FIFO empty or full).
- SSI Data Register (SSIDR): 16-bit register used to store data to be written or read.
- Transmit FIFO (T_XFIFO): Store 8×16-bit data to be transmitted.
- Receive FIFO (R_XFIFO): Store 8×16-bit data to be received.

The SSICR0 register has been discussed in the last section. Let's start our discussion from the SSICR1 register.

8.3.4.3.1 SSI Control 1 Register (SSICR1) This register is used to provide additional control for the SSI data transmission and reception functions. Figure 8.12 shows the bit field and functions of this register. Table 8.5 shows the bit value and its function of this register.

Two points to be noted when using this register: (1) The EOT bit is only valid when the SSI works as a master device (MS = 0x0), and (2) The SSE bit must be cleared to 0 to disable the SSI when it is in the initialization or configuration process.

Table 8.5. Bit value and its function for SSICR1 register.

Bit	Name	Reset	Function
31:5	Reserved	0x0	Reserved
4	EOT	0	End Of Transmission. This bit is only valid for Master mode devices and operations (MS = 0x0). 0: The TXRIS interrupt indicates that the transmit FIFO is half-full or less. 1: The End of Transmit interrupt mode for the TXRIS interrupt is enabled.
3	Reserved	0	Reserved.
2	MS	0	SSI Master/Slave Select. Select Master or Slave mode and can be modified only when the SSI is disabled (SSE = 0). 0: The SSI is configured as a Master. 1: The SSI is configured as a Slave.
1	SSE	0	SSI Synchronous Serial Port Enable. 0: SSI operation is disabled. 1: SSI operation is enabled. This bit must be cleared before any control registers are reprogrammed.
0	LBM	0	SSI Loopback Mode. 0: Normal serial port operation enabled. 1: Output of the transmit serial shift register is connected internally to the input of the receive serial shift register.

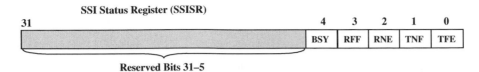

SSI Status Register (SSISR)

Figure 8.13.   The bit field and functions of the SSISR Register.

8.3.4.3.2 SSI Status Register (SSISR)   This register provides SSI working status such as busy or idle and FIFO working status such as empty or full. Figure 8.13 shows the bit field and functions of this register. Table 8.6 shows the bit value and its function of this register.

The lowest 5 bits on this register monitor and indicate the SSI running status and FIFO operational status.

8.3.4.3.3 SSI Data Register (SSIDR)   This register is used to transmit or receive data to/ from the transmit/receive FIFO. Although this is a 32-bit register, only the lower16 bits (bits 15~0) are used to store a data item to match the data width used in both FIFOs. Each FIFO can hold up to eight 16-bit data.

When the SSIDR register is read, the entry in the receive FIFO that is pointed to by the current FIFO read pointer is accessed. When a data value is moved by the SSI receive logic from the incoming data frame, it is placed into the entry in the receive FIFO pointed to by the current FIFO write pointer (Figure 8.14a).

When a data item is written to the SSIDR register by processor, the entry in the transmit FIFO that is pointed to by the write pointer is written to. Data values are moved from the transmit FIFO one value at a time by the transmit logic. Each data value is loaded into the transmit serial shifter, then serially shifted out onto the SSInTx pin at the programmed bit rate (Figure 8.14b).

Table 8.6.   Bit value and its function for SSISR register.

Bit	Name	Reset	Function
31:5	Reserved	0x0	Reserved
4	BSY	0	SSI Busy Bit. 0: The SSI is idle. 1: The SSI is busy or the transmit FIFO is not empty.
3	RFF	0	SSI Receive FIFO Full. 0: The Receive FIFO is not Full. 1: The Receive FIFO is Full.
2	RNE	0	SSI Receive FIFO Not Empty. 0: The Receive FIFO is Empty. 1: The Receive FIFO is not Empty.
1	TNF	1	SSI Transmit FIFO Not Full. 0: The Transmit FIFO is Full. 1: The Transmit FIFO is not Full.
0	TFE	1	SSI Transmit FIFO Empty. 0: The Transmit FIFO is not Empty. 1: The Transmit FIFO is Empty

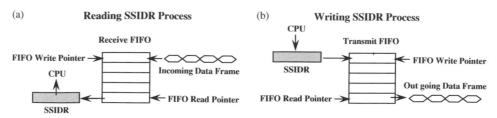

Figure 8.14. The receive FIFO and transmit FIFO operational processes.

When a data size of less than 16 bits is selected, the user must right-justify data written to the transmit FIFO. The transmit logic ignores the unused bits. Received data that are less than 16 bits are automatically right-justified in the receive buffer.

When the SSI is programmed for using the MICROWIRE data frame format, the default size for the transmit data is eight bits with the most significant byte being ignored. The receive data size is controlled by the programmer. The transmit FIFO and the receive FIFO are not cleared even when the SSE bit in the SSICR1 register is cleared to enable the software to fill the transmit FIFO before enabling the SSI.

8.3.4.3.4 FIFO Operations Both transmit FIFO and receive FIFO can hold up to eight 16-bit data items with the First In First Out operational sequence.

Both transmit FIFO (TxFIFO) and receive FIFO (RxFIFO) work as a temporary storage or buffer to store data to be transmitted to or received from the transmit/receive pins SSInTx and SSInRx. The operational sequence can be summarized as follows:

Transmit FIFO: When transmits begin, the CPU sends data to the FIFO by writing the SSI Data (SSIDR) register (Figure 8.14b), and data is stored in the FIFO until it is read out by the transmission logic. When configured as a master or a slave, parallel data is first written into the transmit FIFO and then it is serially converted and transmitted to the attached slave or master, respectively, through the SSInTx pin.

In slave mode, the SSI transmits data each time the master initiates a transaction. If the transmit FIFO is empty and the master initiates, the slave transmits the 8th most recent value in the transmit FIFO. If less than 8 values are in the transmit FIFO since the SSI module clock was enabled using the Rn bit in the Synchronous Serial Interface Run Mode Clock Gating Control (RCGCSSI) register, then 0 is transmitted. Care should be taken to ensure that valid data is in the FIFO as needed. The SSI can be configured to generate an interrupt or a μDMA request when the FIFO is empty.

Figure 8.15 shows the bit fields and related control values on the RCGCSSI register. This register is used to enable and provide clock to the desired SSI module. If the related bit Rn is 0, the corresponding SSI Module n is disabled. Otherwise if Rn is 1, the SSI module n is enabled.

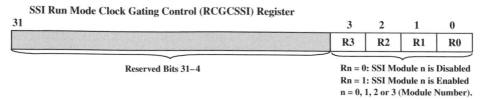

Figure 8.15. The bit field and value in RCGCSSI register.

`Receive FIFO`: Like transmit FIFO, the receive FIFO is used to store the data received from the `SSInRx` pin. The received data from the serial interface is stored in the FIFO until read out by the CPU, which accesses the read FIFO by reading the `SSIDR` register.

When configured as a master or slave, serial data received through the `SSInRx` pin is shifted and registered prior to parallel loading into the slave or master receive FIFO, respectively.

8.3.4.4 SSI Module Interrupt and DMA Control

As we discussed in Section 8.3.2, the following control registers control and monitor the SSI interrupts and DMA operations:

- SSI Interrupt Mask Register (`SSIIM`): Enable (unmask)/disable (mask) SSI interrupt.
- SSI Raw Interrupt Status Register (`SSIRIS`): Provide SSI raw interrupt status.
- SSI Interrupt Clear Register (`SSIICR`): Clear SSI interrupts.
- SSI Masked Interrupt Status Register (`SSIMIS`): Provide masked SSI interrupt status.
- SSI DMA Control Register (`SSIDMACTL`): Provide DMA control.

The SSI can generate interrupts when the following conditions are met:

- Transmit FIFO service/Receive FIFO service (when the transmit/receive FIFO is half full or less).
- Receive FIFO time out or overrun.
- End of transmission.
- Receive DMA transfer complete.
- Transmit DMA transfer complete.

All of these interrupt events can be `ORed` together before being sent to the NVIC interrupt controller, thus the SSI generates a single interrupt request to the controller regardless of the number of active interrupts.

The receive FIFO has a time out period, which is 32 clock periods of the SSI working clock `SSInClk`, whether or not it is currently active. This time out starts when the `RxFIFO` goes from EMPTY. If this time out period is less than 32 clocks, the time out period is reset. As a result, the ISR should clear the receive FIFO time out interrupt just after reading out the `RxFIFO` by writing 1 to the `RTIC` bit in the `SSI Interrupt Clear` (`SSIICR`) register. The interrupt should not be cleared so late that the ISR has been returned before the interrupt is actually cleared, otherwise the ISR may be reactivated unnecessarily.

The End-of-Transmission (EOT) interrupt indicates that the data has been transmitted completely and is only valid for Master Mode devices and operations. This interrupt can be used to indicate the time when it is safe to turn off the SSI module clock or enter sleep mode. In addition, because transmitted data and received data complete at exactly the same time, the interrupt can also indicate that the data is ready to be read immediately, without waiting for the receive FIFO time-out period to complete.

The operational sequence of the SSI interrupts and the roles of different control registers are:

1. The related interrupt sources are set up by configuring the corresponding bits in the related registers, such as `SSI Status Register` (`SSISR`), used to control the status of the FIFO, either empty or full, and `SSI Control 1` (`SSICR1`) register, used to monitor the EOT status, to allow them to work as interrupt sources.

SSI Interrupt Mask (SSIIM) Register

Figure 8.16.   The bit field and value in SSIIM register.

2. Set related bits in the SSI Interrupt Mask (SSIIM) register to enable selected SSI interrupts.

3. When interrupt events occurred, the related bits in the SSI Raw Interrupt Status (SSIRIS) register are set to 1 to indicate this situation.

4. Whether these interrupts indicated in the SSIRIS register can be sent to the NVIC interrupt controller or not, it depends on the bit values in the SSIIM register. If a bit is set to 1, which means that the related interrupt is enabled, it can be transferred to the NVIC. Otherwise if a bit is cleared to 0, it has been masked and cannot be sent out.

5. If interrupts have been accepted and handled in the ISR, the SSI Interrupt Clear Register (SSIICR) should be used to clear those interrupts, such as SSI receive timeout or overrun interrupt. Some other interrupts can be automatically cleared when the interrupt sources are recovered or modified, such as the FIFO's status being modified.

6. The SSI Masked Interrupt Status Register (SSIMIS) is used to provide the interrupt status of masked interrupt sources.

Now let's have a closer look at these control registers and their bit functions.

8.3.4.4.1 SSI Interrupt Mask Register (SSIIM)   Figure 8.16 shows the bit field and functions of the SSIIM register. Table 8.7 shows the bit value and its function of this register.

The lowest 4 bits on this register are used to control whether these 4 related interrupt sources are enabled or disabled by setting or clearing the related bits.

Table 8.7.   Bit value and its function for SSIIM register.

Bit	Name	Reset	Function
31:4	Reserved	0x0	Reserved
3	TXIM	0	SSI Transmit FIFO Interrupt Mask. 0: The transmit FIFO interrupt is masked (Disabled). 1: The transmit FIFO interrupt is not masked (Enabled).
2	RXIM	0	SSI Receive FIFO Interrupt Mask. 0: The receive FIFO interrupt is masked (Disabled). 1: The receive FIFO interrupt is not masked (Enabled).
1	RTIM	0	SSI Receive Time-Out Interrupt Mask. 0: The receive FIFO time-out interrupt is masked (Disabled). 1: The receive FIFO time-out interrupt is not masked (Enabled).
0	RORIM	0	SSI Receive Overrun Interrupt Mask. 0: The receive FIFO overrun interrupt is masked (Disabled). 1: The receive FIFO overrun interrupt is not masked (Enabled).

SSI Raw Interrupt Status (SSIRIS) Register

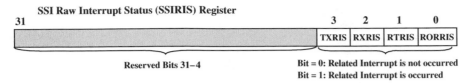

Figure 8.17. The bit field and value in SSIRIS register.

8.3.4.4.2 SSI Raw Interrupt Status Register (SSIRIS)
This register is used to monitor and indicate which raw interrupt status has been modified and generated. Similar to SSIIM register, the lowest 4 bits on this register are used to monitor 4 different interrupt sources or events.

Figure 8.17 shows the bit field and functions of the SSIRIS register. Table 8.8 shows the bit value and its function of this register.

After a raw interrupt status has been changed or a raw interrupt has been set in the register, the bit value on the corresponding bit in the SSIIM register determines whether this raw interrupt can be sent to the NVIC controller or not. A value of 1 on the related bit in the SSIIM indicates that the selected interrupt can be sent to the interrupt controller.

8.3.4.4.3 SSI DMA Control Register (SSIDMACTL)
This register is used to control the availability of the DMA for the transmit FIFO or receive FIFO. The lowest two bits, TXDMAE and RXDMAE (bits 1~0), are used to enable (1) or disable (0) the DMA as a conveyer for the transmit FIFO or the receive FIFO. The bits 31~2 in this register are reserved.

Table 8.8. Bit value and its function for SSIRIS register.

Bit	Name	Reset	Function
31:4	Reserved	0x0	Reserved
3	TXRIS	1	SSI Transmit FIFO Raw Interrupt Status. 0: No interrupt. 1: If the EOT bit in the SSICR1 register is clear, the transmit FIFO is half empty or less. If the EOT bit is set, the transmit FIFO is empty, and the last bit has been transmitted out of the serializer. This bit is cleared when the transmit FIFO is more than half full (if the EOT bit is clear) or when it has any data in it (if the EOT bit is set).
2	RXRIS	0	SSI Receive FIFO Raw Interrupt Status. 0: No interrupt. 1: The receive FIFO is half full or more. This bit is cleared when the receive FIFO is less than half full.
1	RTRIS	0	SSI Receive Time-Out Raw Interrupt Status. 0: No interrupt. 1: The receive timeout interrupt occurred. This bit is cleared by writing 1 to the RTIC bit in the SSIICR register.
0	RORRIS	0	SSI Receive Overrun Raw Interrupt Status. 0: No interrupt. 1: The receive FIFO has an overflow. This bit is cleared by writing 1 to the RORIC bit in the SSIICR register.

The DMA module should be enabled when using this mode to work with the SSI modules.

8.3.4.5 SSI Module Transmit/Receive Logic Control

The SSI transmit/receive logic control block is mainly used to assist SSI module to effectively transmit/receive data via serial communication pins/lines. The main function of this block includes the following:

- For transmit operations, perform parallel-to-serial conversion by using the transmit shift register to convert parallel data stored in the transmit FIFO to the serial format.
- Move or transmit serial data to the transmission pin and line SSInTx based on the SSInClk and SSInFss frame.
- For receive operations, perform serial-to-parallel conversion by using the receive shift register to convert serial data coming from transmission pins SSInRx to the parallel format that can be stored in the receive FIFO based on the SSInClk and SSInFss frame.
- Besides the data mode conversions, this block also performs the voltage level conversion to transfer the TTL logic level to the standard serial communication voltage levels.

At this point, we have completed our discussions about the SSI signals and components. Now let's take a look at the initialization and configuration process for the SSI modules before they can be implemented in the real applications.

8.3.4.6 SSI Modules Initialization and Configurations

Before the SSI module can be used for any peripherals, it must be initialized and configured based on the data transmission/reception requirements for the selected peripheral device. During the initialization and configuration process, the selected SSI module must not be enabled. In other words, prior to this initialization process, the SSI module must be first disabled.

This initialization and configuration process can be divided into three parts:

- Initialize and configure the GPIO Ports and pins related to SSI modules.
- Initialize and configure SSI module.
- Initialize and configure SSI clock source and bit rate.

Let's have a closer look at these initializations one by one in the following sections.

8.3.4.6.1 SSI-Module-Related GPIO Ports Initialization   As we discussed in Section 8.3.4.1, all SSI modules are interfaced to peripherals via related GPIO Ports and pins. In order to enable GPIO pins to work as SSI function pins, the following initializations and configurations should be performed:

1. Enable the clock to the appropriate GPIO modules via the RCGCGPIO register.
2. The related AFSEL bits (lower 8 bits) in the GPIO Alternate Function Select (GPIOAFSEL) register must be set to 1.
3. The related PMCx field in the GPIO Port Control (GPIOPCTL) register must be assigned with appropriate codes to enable the GPIO pins to work as desired SSI signal pins.
4. The related bits in the GPIO Digital Enable (GPIODEN) register must be set to 1 to enable the digital function and disable the analog function. In addition, the drive strength, drain select, and pull-up/pull-down functions must be configured.

5. Optionally the related AMSEL bits in the GPIO Analog Mode Select (GPIOAMSEL) register should be clear to 0 to enable the analog isolation circuits to enable the selected pin to work as digital function pin.

A point to be noted when performing step 4 above is: The pull-up mode is used here to avoid unnecessary toggles on the SSI pins since this toggle can take the slave to a wrong state. In addition, if the SSIClk signal is programmed to steady-state High through the SPO bit (SPO = 1) in the SSICR0 register, then the software must also configure the GPIO port pin corresponding to the SSInClk signal as a pull-up in the GPIO Pull-Up Select (GPIOPUR) register.

8.3.4.6.2 SSI Module Initialization and Configuration To enable and initialize the SSI module, the following steps are necessary:

1. Enable the SSI module using the RCGCSSI register (Figure 8.15 in Section 8.3.4.3.4).
2. Ensure that the SSE bit in the SSICR1 register is clear before making any initialization and configuration changes (Figure 8.12 in Section 8.3.4.3.1).
3. Select the SSI to work as a master or slave by configuring the SSICR1 register.
   - If the SSI works as a master device, set the SSICR1 register to 0x0000.0000.
   - If the SSI works as a slave device with output enabled, set the SSICR1 register as 0x0000.0004.
   - If the SSI works as a slave device with output disabled, set the SSICR1 register as 0x0000.000C.

Next let's have the SSI clock source and bit rate to be configured and initialized.

8.3.4.6.3 SSI Module Clock Source and Bit Rate Initialization and Configuration
To initialize and configure SSI module clock source and select the bit rate, the following operations are necessary:

1. Select the SSI clock source by configuring the SSICC register (Figure 8.9 in Section 8.3.4.2).
2. Define the clock prescale divisor by configuring the SSICPSR register to select the desired bit-field value CPSDVSR = [2~254] (Figure 8.10 in Section 8.3.4.2).
3. Configure the SSICR0 register with the following parameters:
   - Serial Clock Rate (SCR) = [0~255]
   - Desired Clock Phase/Polarity if using Freescale SPI mode (SPH and SPO)
   - The Protocol Mode: Freescale SPI, TI SSF, MICROWIRE (FRF)
   - The Data Size (DSS)
4. Optionally, configure the SSI module for μDMA use with the following steps:
   - Configure a μDMA for SSI use.
   - Enable the SSI Module's TxFIFO or RxFIFO by setting the TXDMAE or RXDMAE bit in the SSIDMACTL register (refer to Section 8.3.4.4.3).
5. Enable the configured SSI by setting the SSE bit in the SSICR1 register.

A SSI module 2 initialization and configuration example is illustrated below with the following assumptions:

- The system clock source is 20 MHz.
- The SSI module 2 is selected and worked as a master device.

- Use Freescale SPI frame (SPO = 0, SPH = 0).
- Use 1 MBPS bit rate and 8 data bits.

The bit rate is calculated as SSInClk = SysClk/(CPSDVSR × (1 + SCR)) or

$$1 \times 10^6 = 20 \times 10^6/(\text{CPSDVSR} \times (1 + \text{SCR}))$$

In this case, if CPSDVSR = 0x2, SCR should be 0x9. The following steps should be involved:

1. Clear the SSE bit in the SSICR1 register to disable the SSI module.
2. Write the SSICC register with 0x0000.0000 to select the system clock source.
3. Write the SSICR1 register with 0x0000.0000 to define the SSI to work as a master.
4. Write the SSICPSR register with 0x0000.0002 to define the CPSDVSR bit field as 0x2.
5. Write the SSICR0 register with 0x0000.0903 to set SCR to 0x9, SPO:SPH = 00, FRF = 00 (Freescale SPI frame) and DSS = 0x7 (8 data bits).
6. Enable the configured SSI module by setting the SSE bit in the SSICR1 register.

Based on these discussions, now let's build our example project to interface some peripherals via the SSI modules provided by TM4C123GH6PM MCU system.

8.3.5 Build the On-Board LCD Interface Programming Project

In this example project, we use the SSI Module 2 (SSI2) to interface an on-board 16×2 LCD device installed in the EduBASE ARM® Trainer to display some interesting staff. First let's have a closer look at the hardware configuration and connection for this LCD via SSI2.

8.3.5.1 SSI Module Interface for the LCD in EduBASE ARM® Trainer

A High-Speed CMOS shift register 74VHCT595 is used as an interface to the LCD from the SSI2 in the TM4C123GH6PM MCU system. A functional block diagram of this interface circuit connected to the LCD installed in the EduBASE ARM® Trainer is shown in Figure 8.18.

It can be found from Figure 8.18 that the SSI module 2 is connected to the HCOMS shift register 74VHCT595 via GPIO Ports B, exactly PB7, PB6, and PB4 pins. The functions of these pins are:

- PB7: SSI2Tx—Transmit serial signals to the peripheral 74VHCT595.
- PB4: SSI2Clk—Provide output clock signal to coordinate the serial data transmission.
- PB6: SSI2Rx—Receive serial data from the peripheral (not used in this example).
- PB5: SSI2Fss—Provide the serial data transmit frame format (not used in this example).
- PC6: CS_LCD—Provide the LCD Chip Select signal. Here it works as a trigger clock to start a serial-to-parallel data conversion to convert 8-bit serial data stored in the serial shift register to the 8-bit parallel data to be stored in the 8-bit output registers in the 74VHCT595 register.

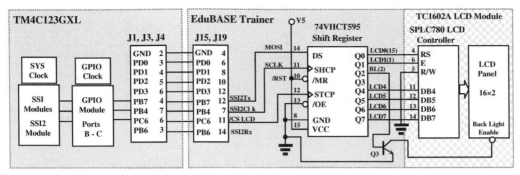

Figure 8.18.   Hardware configuration of the LCD interfacing circuit.

In this hardware configuration, the SSI2 output is connected to the LCD via a serial shift register 74VHCT595 and a LCD Controller SPLC780. The data size to be transmitted from the SSI2 to the LCD is 4 bits, not 8 bits. Therefore an 8-bit data must be broken into two sections with 4 bits for each section to be transmitted. The higher 4 bits (DB7~DB4) are LCD data and the lower 3 bits are LCD control signals, RS (Register Select), E (Enable), and BL (Back Light Enable). The R/W control signal is connected to the ground to make the LCD controller work in the writing mode.

We will discuss these components one by one in the following sections.

8.3.5.2 The Serial Shift Register 74VHCT595

74VHCT595 is an 8-bit serial-in–serial-out or serial-in–parallel-out register with output latches. In this example, we use it as a serial-in–parallel-out register to convert the serial input coming from the SSI2 to the parallel output, and the latter is fed into the LCD controller to display the result on the LCD panel.

The operational principle and sequence of this register are as follows:

- Data is shifted into the serial input pin (DS) on the positive-going edges of the shift register clock input (SHCP).
- The data in each flip-flop register is transferred to the storage register on a positive-going edge of the storage register clock input (STCP). If both clocks are connected together, the shift register will always be one clock pulse ahead of the storage register.
- The shift register has a serial input (DS) and a serial standard output (Q7S) for cascading.
- It is also provided with asynchronous master reset (MR – active LOW) for all 8 shift flip-flop registers. The storage register has 8 parallel 3-state bus driver outputs. Data in the storage register appears at the output whenever the output enable input (OE) is LOW.

Figure 8.19 shows the functional block diagram of this register.

STAGES 1 TO 6 in this figure indicate that this stage is composed of 6 shift flip-flops. All 8 parallel outputs are latched and controlled by the Output Enable (OE) signal.

In our example application, each time after SSI2 transmits 8 bits data to this shift register via DS (SSI2Tx − PB7) pin and SHCP (SSI2Clk − PB4) pin, a positive-going-edge (Low-to-High) signal should be applied on the STCP (CS_LCD − PC6) pin to transfer 8-bit serial data in the shift register into the 8-bit parallel output buffer or latches.

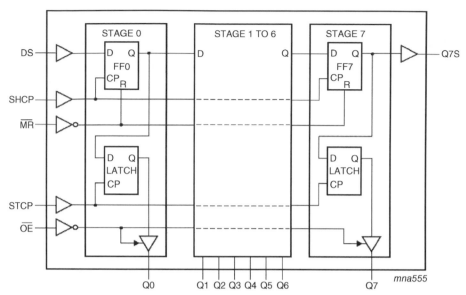

Figure 8.19. The functional block diagram of 74VHCT595 shift register.

The OE pin is connected to the ground to enable 8 latched outputs to be directly transferred to the output pins (refer to Figure 8.18).

8.3.5.3 The LCD Module TC1602A and LCD Controller SPLC780

The TC1602A LCD Module contains a LCD Controller SPLC780, which is a dot-matrix liquid crystal display (LCD) controller and driver to control and display alphanumeric characters, Japanese kana characters, and symbols in a 16×2 LCD device. It can be configured to drive a dot-matrix liquid crystal display under the control of a 4- or 8-bit microprocessor. Since all the functions such as display RAM, character generator, and liquid crystal driver, required for driving a dot-matrix liquid crystal display, are internally provided on one chip, a minimal system can be interfaced with this controller/driver.

In the TM4C123GH6PM MCU system, the SPLC780 is configured to interface with the MCU with 4-bit style; therefore we will concentrate on this style in our following discussions.

An internal structure block diagram of the SPLC780 is shown in Figure 8.20.

The SPLC780 provides a full controllability to the LCD. Some most important and popular components with the associated controlling and interfacing abilities to the LCD are listed below:

- Instruction Register (IR) and Data Register (DR). The SPLC780 has two 8-bit registers, an instruction register (IR) and a data register (DR). The IR stores instruction codes, such as display clear and cursor shift, and address information for display data RAM (DDRAM) and character generator RAM (CGRAM). The IR can only be written from the MPU. The DR temporarily stores data to be written into DDRAM or CGRAM and temporarily stores data to be read from DDRAM or CGRAM. Data written into the DR from the MPU is automatically written

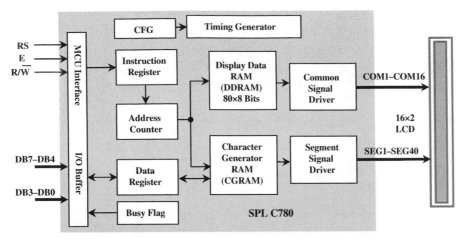

Figure 8.20. Functional block diagram of the LCD Controller SPLC780.

into DDRAM or CGRAM by an internal operation. The DR is also used for data storage when reading data from DDRAM or CGRAM. When address information is written into the IR, data is read and then stored into the DR from DDRAM or CGRAM by an internal operation. Data transfer between the MPU is then completed when the MCU reads the DR. After the read, data in DDRAM or CGRAM at the next address is sent to the DR for the next read from the MCU. By the register selector (RS) signal, these two registers can be selected as shown in Table 8.9.

- Busy Flag (BF). When the busy flag is 1, the SPLC780 is in the internal operation mode, and the next instruction will not be accepted. When RS $= 0$ and R/$\overline{W} = 1$ (Table 8.9), the busy flag is output to DB7. The next instruction must be written after ensuring that the busy flag is 0.

- Address Counter (AC). The address counter (AC) assigns addresses to both DDRAM and CGRAM. When an address of an instruction is written into the IR, the address information is sent from the IR to the AC. Selection of either DDRAM or CGRAM is also determined concurrently by the instruction. After writing into (reading from) DDRAM or CGRAM, the AC is automatically incremented by 1 (decremented by 1). The AC contents are then output to DB0 to DB6 when RS $= 0$ and R/$\overline{W} = 1$ (Table 8.9).

- Display Data RAM (DDRAM). Display data RAM (DDRAM) stores display data represented in 8-bit character codes. Its extended capacity is 80×8 dots or bits, or 80 characters. If each character is composed of 5×8 dots, each line on the LCD can display $80/5 = 16$ characters. The area in display data RAM (DDRAM) that is not used for display can be used as general data RAM. Figure 8.21 shows the relationships between DDRAM addresses and positions on the 2-line by 16 characters LCD. The DDRAM address (ADD) is set in the address counter (AC) as hexadecimal. In the TM4C123GH6PM MCU system, a 16×2 LCD is

Table 8.9. Register selection.

RS	R/W	Function
0	0	Write an instruction to the SPLC780
0	1	Read an instruction from the SPLC780
1	0	Write a data item to the SPLC780
1	1	Read a data item from the SPLC780

	1	2	3	4	5	6	7	8	9	10	11	12	13	14	15	16
Display Position	00	01	02	03	04	05	06	07	08	09	0A	0B	0C	0D	0E	0F
DDRAM Address	40	41	42	43	44	45	46	47	48	49	4A	4B	4C	4D	4E	4F

Figure 8.21. Relationship between the display positions and DDRAM addresses.

used, which means that this LCD can display 2 lines characters with 16 characters being displayed at each line.

- Character Generator ROM (CGROM). The character generator ROM generates 5×8 dots or 5×10 dots character patterns from 8-bit character codes. It can generate 208 5×8 dots character patterns and 32 5×10 dots character patterns. User-defined character patterns are also available by mask-programmed ROM.

- Character Generator RAM (CGRAM). In the character generator RAM, the user can rewrite character patterns by programming. For 5×8 dots, eight character patterns can be written, and for 5×10 dots, four character patterns can be written.

Some other components, including the timing generation circuit, LCD-driven circuit, and cursor blink control circuit, are not discussed in this section.

8.3.5.3.1 Interfacing Control Signals Between the MCU and the SPLC780
Based on the discussion and analysis in the last section, we have had a clear and global picture about the SPLC780 LCD controller. In summary, three important signals are widely used in the interfacing process between a MCU and the SPLC780:

- Register Selection RS signal: When RS = 0, it means that currently an instruction is transferred from the MCU to the SPLC780. If RS = 1, it means that currently a data item is reading from or writing into the SPLC780.

- Read/Write R/$\overline{\text{W}}$ signal: When this signal is 0, it means that a writing operation is performed from the MCU to the SPLC780. If this bit is 1, it means that a reading operation is performed by reading a data item including the Address Counter (AC) from the SPLC780 to the MCU.

- Enable E signal: When this signal is 0, it means that the SPLC780 is disabled and no matter what kind of instructions or data are read from or written into the SPLC780, no information can be obtained from the SPLC780 since it is disabled. If this bit is 1, it means that the SPLC780 is enabled and it can accept any control signal with the appropriate responses.

The SPLC780 can send data in either two 4-bit operations or one 8-bit operation, thus allowing interfacing with 4-bit or 8-bit MCUs.

- For 4-bit interface data, only four higher bits (DB4~DB7) are used for transfer. Bus lines DB0~DB3 are disabled. The data transfer between the SPLC780 and the MCU is completed after the 4-bit data has been transferred twice. As for the order of data transfer, the four high-order bits (DB4~DB7) are transferred before the four low-order bits (DB0~DB3) can be transferred. The busy flag must be checked after the 4-bit data has been transferred twice. Two more 4-bit operations then transfer the busy flag and address counter data.

- For 8-bit interface data, all eight bus lines (DB0~DB7) are used.

Since we are using TM4C123GH6PM MCU system with the EduBASE ARM® Trainer, in which a 4-bit interfacing style is used, we will concentrate on this 4-bit interfacing technique.

The operational sequence of interfacing between the MCU and the SPLC780 is as follows:

1. The LCD must be initialized first by performing a reset operation. Usually, this reset operation can be performed by the SPLC780 itself via an internal reset process when it is powered up. However, if this internal reset operation is not as good as desired, the user must perform an external reset operation by programming the SPLC780 to do that reset operation. This reset process includes the following operations:

   a. Clear the display area in the LCD.
   b. Set the display function by setting the related bit with the appropriate values:
      - DL = 0: 4-bit interface data, DL = 1: 8-bit interface data.
      - N = 0: 1-Line display, N = 1: 2-Line display.
      - F = 0: 5×8 dots character font, F = 1: 5×10 dots character font.
   c. Set the display On/Off control by setting the related bit with the appropriate values:
      - D = 0: Display Off, D = 1: Display On.
      - C = 0: Cursor Off, C = 1: Cursor On.
      - B = 0: Blinking Off, B = 1: Blinking On.
   d. Select the entry mode by setting the related bit with the appropriate values:
      - I/D = 0: Address Counter (AC) is decremented by 1 after each operation,
      - I/D = 1: Address Counter (AC) is incremented by 1 after each operation.
      - S = 0: No shift, S = 1: Shift character.
      - S/C = 0: Cursor move, S/C = 1: Display shift.
      - R/L = 0: Shift to the left, R/L = 1: Shift to the right.

2. After the reset process, perform the Instruction Writing operation to set the internal DDRAM address from which the data can be written into or read out for SPLC780.

3. To display characters in the LCD, perform the Data Writing operations to send the data to the DDRAM in the SPLC780. After each 8-bit character writing (two 4-bit writings), an Instruction Read (IR) should be performed to check the Busy Flag (BF) before the next data can be sent to the SPLC780.

All of these initialization parameters and their values are shown in Table 8.10. A block diagram of this operational sequence is shown in Figure 8.22.

Table 8.10. LCD initialization functions.

Bit	Value	Functions	Bit	Value	Functions
DL	0	4-bit interface data	C	0	Cursor Off
	1	8-bit interface data		1	Cursor On
N	0	1-Line display	B	0	Blinking Off
	1	2-Line display		1	Blinking On
F	0	5×8 dots character font	I/D	0	Decrement by 1
	1	5×10 dots character font		1	Increment by 1
D	0	Display Off	S	0	No shift
	1	Display On		1	Shift character
S/C	0	Cursor move	R/L	0	Shift to the left
	1	Display shift		1	Shift to the right

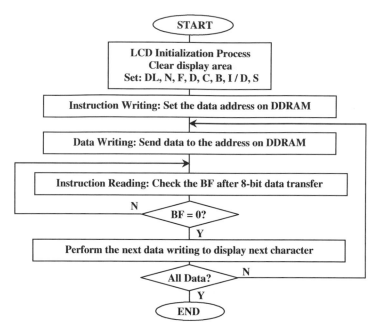

Figure 8.22. Block diagram of the operational sequence of interfacing to SPLC780.

8.3.5.3.2 Control and Interface Programming for SPLC780 Based on the introduction of the interface between the MCU and the SPLC780 in the last section, now we can begin to build the control and the interface programming to control the TC1602A LCD Module to display desired staff in the LCD panel.

All operation steps described in the operational sequence in the last section can be performed by executing a sequence of instructions. For actual reason, we only concentrate on the 4-bit data transfer since this style is used in this example project.

When the SPLC780 is connected to a MCU by using a 4-bit interface, an 8-bit instruction or data must be broken into two parts to be transferred. The higher 4-bit instruction or data is transferred first via DB7~DB4 in the SPLC780. Then the lower 4-bit is transferred via DB7~DB4 again. The relationship for the lower 4-bit in the 74VHCT595 and SPLC780 is

- $Q7 = DB7$
- $Q6 = DB6$
- $Q5 = DB5$
- $Q4 = DB4$

Tables 8.11 and 8.12 list the general LCD instructions and the actual LCD instructions specially applied in the example project for 4-bit data transfer format implemented in SPLC780 LCD Controller (X = don't care).

One important point to be noted is the operational steps 3 and 4. After the LCD initialization process, the SPLC780 uses the default data transfer format, the 8-bit data format to be set. Therefore in step 3, even the SPLC780 is configured as 4-bit mode; the SPLC780 can still be considered to be a 8-bit mode. In order to enable the SPLC780

Table 8.11. Most popular LCD Instructions for 4-bit data transfer.

	Items	Code						Description
	Instruction	RS	R/W	DB7	DB6	DB5	DB4	
1	Clear Display	0	0	0	0	0	0	Clear display area & set DDRAM address 0 in the Address Counter (AC).
		0	0	0	0	0	1	
2	Return Home	0	0	0	0	0	0	Return the display to the original position & set DDRAM address to 0.
		0	0	0	0	1	X	
3	Set Function	0	0	0	0	1	DL	Set to 4-bit operation. In this case, operation is handled as 8 bits by initialization, and only this instruction is performed with one write.
4	Set Function	0	0	0	0	1	DL	Set 4-bit operation & selects 2-line display & 5×8 dot font. 4-bit operation starts from this step and resetting is necessary. (Number of display lines and character fonts cannot be changed after this step).
		0	0	N	F	X	X	
5	Display On/Off	0	0	0	0	0	0	Turns on display (D = 1) and cursor (C = 1). Turn off blinking (B = 0). Entire display is in space mode because of initialization.
		0	0	1	D	C	B	
6	Set Entry Mode	0	0	0	0	0	0	Sets mode to increment the address by one (I/D = 1) & to shift the cursor to the right at the time of write to the DD/CGRAM. Display is not shifted (S = 0).
		0	0	0	1	I/D	S	
7	Set DDRAM Address	0	0	1	ADD	ADD	ADD	Set DDRAM address (DB7 = 1). ADD is the address bit.
		0	0	ADD	ADD	ADD	ADD	
8	Write Data to DDRAM	1	0	8-BIT WRITE-IN DATA				Write data into DDRAM & display them in the LCD.
		1	0	(ASCII CODE)				
9	Read Data from DDRAM	1	1	8-BIT READ-OUT DATA				Read data from DDRAM.
		1	1	(ASCII CODE)				

to know this 4-bit configuration, the SPLC780 needs to be reconfigured by rewriting DB7~DB4 = 0010 again in step 4. Then the lower 4-bit are written to the SPLC780 by performing the second writing operation. This rewriting is very important and necessary. Otherwise the SPLC780 may encounter some abnormal operations later.

Another point to be noted is the ENABLE signal E on the SPLC780. In the instruction sequence listed above, we did not list the ENABLE signal. In fact, this control signal is very

Table 8.12. The actual LCD Instructions for 4-bit data transfer in the example project.

	Items	Code						Description
	Instruction	RS	R/W	DB7	DB6	DB5	DB4	
1	Clear Display	0	0	0	0	0	0	Clear display area & set DDRAM address 0 in the Address Counter (AC).
		0	0	0	0	0	1	
2	Return Home	0	0	0	0	0	0	Return the display to the original position & set DDRAM address to 0.
		0	0	0	0	1	X	
3	Set Function	0	0	0	0	1	0	Set to 4-bit operation. In this case, operation is handled as 8 bits by initialization, and only this instruction is performed with one write.
4	Set Function	0	0	0	0	1	0	Set 4-bit operation & selects 2-line display & 5×8 dot font. 4-bit operation starts from this step and resetting is necessary. (Number of display lines and character fonts cannot be changed after this step).
		0	0	1	0	X	X	
5	Display On/Off	0	0	0	0	0	0	Turns on display (D = 1) and cursor (C = 1). Turn off blinking (B = 1). Entire display is in space mode because of initialization.
		0	0	1	1	1	1	
6	Set Entry Mode	0	0	0	0	0	0	Sets mode to increment the address by one (I/D = 1) & to shift the cursor to the right at the time of write to the DD/CGRAM. Display is not shifted (S = 0).
		0	0	0	1	1	0	
7	Set DDRAM Address	0	0	1	ADD	ADD	ADD	Set DDRAM address (DB7 = 1). ADD is the address bit.
		0	0	ADD	ADD	ADD	ADD	
8	Write Data to DDRAM	1	0	8-BIT WRITE-IN DATA				Write data into DDRAM & display them in the LCD.
		1	0	(ASCII CODE)				
9	Read Data from DDRAM	1	1	8-BIT READ-OUT DATA				Read data from DDRAM.
		1	1	(ASCII CODE)				

important and all operations listed in both tables need this signal to be active or HIGH when any of instruction is written and executed.

8.3.5.3.3 LCD Programming Instruction Structure and Sequence As we mentioned in Section 8.3.5.1, in this EduBASE ARM® Trainer hardware configuration, the SSI2 output is connected to the LCD via a serial shift register 74VHCT595 and a LCD Controller SPLC780. The data size to be transmitted from the SSI2 to the LCD is 4 bits, not 8 bits. Therefore an 8-bit data must be broken into two sections with 4 bits for each section to be transmitted. The higher 4 bits (DB7~DB4) are LCD data and the lower 3 bits are LCD control signals, RS (Register Select), E (Enable) and BL (Back Light Enable). The R/W control signal is connected to the ground to make the LCD controller work in the writing mode.

Each SSI2 serial data output is an 8-bit serial data sequence transmitted from the SSI2 Data Register (SSIDR) to the SSI2Tx pin via TxFIFO. Since each 8-bit data must be broken into two 4-bit sections and transmitted by two times to the serial shift register 74VHCT595, each 8-bit data should contain LCD data (upper 4-bit DB7~DB7) and LCD commands (lower 3 bits RS, E, and BL). Figure 8.23 shows an 8-bit serial data configuration that is sent to the SSI2Tx pin and transmitted to the DS serial input on the serial shift register 74VHCT595.

Refer to Table 8.12. For example, if we want to clear display on LCD panel, we need to first send DB7~DB4 = 0000 and then DB7~DB4 = 0001 as LCD data to the LCD controller in two times. In both times, we should also include the LCD command BL: E:RS = 110 with those LCD data together to send out. The resulted instruction of this 8-bit code is 00000110 (0x06) for the first 8-bit code and 00010110 (0x16) for the second 8-bit code.

In our actual project, we can build some subroutines to perform these data splitting operations, and therefore we can directly send 00000001 (0x01) to the subroutine to allow that subroutine to break this 8-bit data into two pieces of 4-bit data and send them out with the corresponding LCD command bits together.

Generally the LCD programming process includes three sections:

1. LCD Initialization (if internal initialization is not as good as desired, the programming initialization built by using the user's program is necessary).
2. LCD Function Setup and Configuration.
3. LCD Displaying Data Output and Display.

Now let's have a closer look at the LCD initialization and function setup instruction structure and sequence. First let's handle the LCD initialization process.

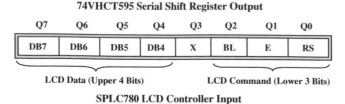

Figure 8.23. 8-bit serial data configuration to be transmitted to LCD Controller.

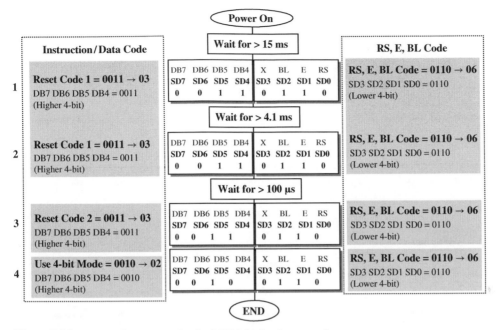

Figure 8.24.   The coding process for the LCD initialization operation.

The LCD Initialization Process   The operational sequence of the LCD manual initialization process is shown in Figure 8.24.

Since we are using 4-bit data transfer mode to interface to SPLC780 LCD Controller via serial shift register 74VHCT595, only 4 data bits DB7–DB4 are used. However, the data transfer between the 74HCT595 and the SPLC780 is 8-bit mode via Q7~Q0 (refer to Figure 8.18), which means that besides the 4 data bits transferred in DB7~DB4, three control signals, E, RS, and BL, are also transferred via Q2~Q0, respectively. Therefore we divide each instruction into two pieces: The upper 4 bits are instructions to be transferred and the lower 3 bits are RS, E, and BL commands to be transferred, as shown in Figure 8.24.

Two reset codes are used for this LCD initialization process. Reset Code 1 is sent to the SPLC780 two times (called rewritten for steps 1&2 in Figure 8.24). The combined single 8-bit code is 0x36 (DB7~DB4 = 0011, BL:E:RS = 0110). Some time delays are needed between these two reset codes to be transferred to the SPLC780. The SD7~SD0 is 8-bit data sent by SSI2.

Similarly, if we combine Reset Code 2 together to form a single reset code, it is 0x36 (step 3 in Figure 8.24). After these reset codes are sent and executed by the SPLC780, the LCD should be initialized properly and can be configured to perform our desired data display process.

Step 4 in Figure 8.24 is to set the data mode for the LCD module. The higher 4 bits are 0010 and the lower 4 bits are 0110. Combining these two pieces of nibbles together, we can get 0x26.

The reason we combine these two codes together to get a single 8-bit code is that we will use this kind of 8-bit code to do the LCD initialization in our program. With the help of some subroutines, we can decompose these combinations into two separate 4-bit codes and

```
 1  LCD_write (0x30, 0);                        // call LCD_Write () function...
 2  void LCD_write (char  data, unsigned char cmd)
 3  {
 4      data & = 0xF0;                          // clear lower nibble for data
 5      cmd & = 0x0F;                           // clear upper nibble for control
 6      SSI2_Write (data | cmd | BL);           // RS = 0, R/W = 0, E = 0  ⎤
 7      SSI2_Write (data | cmd | EN | BL);      // RS = 0, R/W = 0, E = 1  ⎬ A simulated E pulse
 8      delay ();                               //                         ⎟
 9      SSI2_Write (data | BL);                 // RS = 0, R/W = 0, E = 0  ⎦
10      SSI2_Write (BL);                        // RS = 0, R/W = 0, BL = 1
    }
```

Figure 8.25.   A piece of codes to create a simulated E pulse.

transfer them in 8-bit format with the higher 4 bits as DB7–DB4 and the lower 4 bits as RS, E and BL codes.

One point to be noted when transmitting these two-piece codes by using subroutines is that the LCD controller can only accept these instruction/data when it is enabled. Therefore in order to make the LCD controller enabled to accept these instructions/data, we need to simulate an Enable (E) pulse by using the software codes in our subroutines.

For example, to send the Reset Code 1 to the SPLC780, one needs to use the codes shown in Figure 8.25 to send 0x36 with a simulated E pulse.

The codes in lines 6~8 are used to send a combined instruction/command code 0x34 (DB7~DB4 = 0011, BL:E:RS = 100) to the LCD controller. However, in order to allow this code to be accepted by the SPLC780, the bit E must be High. The code in line 7 does this job. The codes in lines 6 and 8 are used to simulate a Low before and after the High pulse of E in line 7. The function SSI2_Write() is used to send serial data to the SPLC789 via 74VHCT595.

The LCD Function Setup and Configuration   The LCD function setup and configuration process are equivalent to performing operations in steps 1~6 shown in Table 8.12.

The operational sequence of the LCD function setup and configuration process is shown in Figure 8.26. Similar to the initialization process, each 8-bit code is broken into two pieces (higher 4 bits and lower 4 bits) and transferred to the SPLC780 in two times with the RS, E, and BL code.

For example, to transfer the Function Set Code 0x28 at step 1 in Figure 8.26, this 8-bit code 0x28 is broken into two pieces, 0x2 and 0x8, as shown in coding steps 4 and 5 in Figure 8.25. The higher 4-bit 0x2 is sent first with the RS, E, and BL code 0x7 together to form an 8-bit code 0x27. Then the lower 4-bit 0x8 is transferred with the RS, E, and BL code 0x7 to form an 8-bit code 0x87 in the second time. All of these breaking and combining jobs as well as a simulated E pulse are performed by the software codes in a subroutine similar to one shown in Figure 8.25.

Step 2 in Figure 8.26 is used to set the entry mode code, which is 0006 or 0x06. This 8-bit code is also broken to two pieces of 4-bit codes: 0000 and 0110 are sent in two times with the BL, E, and RS signal together to the SPLC780 via the 74VHCT595.

Step 3 is to set up the display mode with the code of 00001111 = 0x0F, and step 4 is to clear the display area with the code of 00000001 = 0x01. These 8-bit codes are also broken into two pieces of 4-bit codes and are sent out two times with the BL, E, and RS signal together.

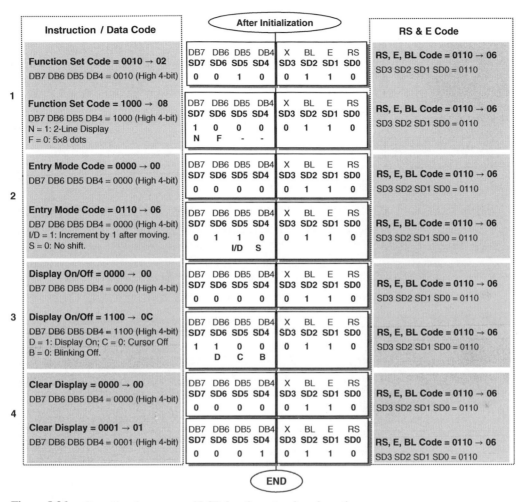

Figure 8.26. Operational sequence of LCD function set and configuration.

8.3.5.4 Build the Example LCD Interfacing Project

Now we have enough knowledge and skill to build a practical LCD interfacing project to serially transmit our desired letters or numbers to the LCD to display them on it.

The hardware configuration of this project is shown in Figure 8.18. In the EduBASE ARM® Trainer, it has been configured to use the SSI module 2 to serially transmit instructions and data to LCD Controller SPLC780 via the serial shift register 74VHTC595. The GPIO pins used in this project include:

- PB7: SSI2Tx—Transmit instructions/data to the peripheral 74VHCT595.
- PB4: SSI2Clk—Provide SSI2 with a clock to conduct the serial data transmission.
- PB6: SSI2Rx—Receive serial data from the peripheral (not used in this example).
- PB5: SSI2Fss—Provide the serial data transmit frame format (not used in this example).

- PC6: CS_LCD—Provide the LCD Chip Select signal. Here it works as a trigger clock to start a serial-to-parallel data conversion to convert 8-bit serial data stored in the serial shift register to 8-bit parallel data to be stored in the 8-bit output registers in the 74VHCT595 register.

In our example application, each time after SSI2 transmits 8 bits data to the shift register via DS (SSI2Tx–PB7) pin and clock SHCP (SSI2Clk–PB4) pin, a positive-going-edge (Low-to-High) signal should be applied on the STCP (CS_LCD–PC6) pin to transfer 8-bit serial data in the shift register into the 8-bit parallel output buffer or latches. The OE pin is connected to the ground to enable 8 latched outputs to be directly transferred to the output pins (Figure 8.18).

We try to use the Direct Register Access (DRA) model to build this project. The entire coding process includes the following four sections:

1. Initialize and configure SSI2-related GPIO Ports (Ports B and C).
2. Initialize and configure SSI2 module and related registers (SSICC, SSICPSR, SSICR0, and SSICR1).
3. Build four subroutines to break, combine, and transmit 8-bit instructions/data to the LCD controller to display desired letters and numbers on the LCD panel.
4. Build some time delay functions to delay different periods of time to make the LCD data transmissions stable and reliable.

Now let's first create a new LCD project DRALCD.

8.3.5.4.1 Create a Direct Register Access LCD Project DRALCD Perform the following operations to create a new project DRALCD:

1. Open the Windows Explorer window to create a new folder named DRALCD under the C:\ARM Class Projects\Chapter 8 folder.
2. Open the Keil® ARM-MDK μVersion5 and go to Project|New μVersion Project menu item to create a new μVersion Project. On the opened wizard, browse to our new folder DRALCD that is created in step 1 above. Enter DRALCD into the **File name** box and click on the **Save** button to create this project.
3. On the next wizard, you need to select the device (MCU) for this project. Expand three icons, Texas Instruments, Tiva C Series, and TM4C123x Series, and select the target device TM4C123GH6PM from the list by clicking on it. Click on the **OK** to close this wizard.
4. Next the Software Components wizard is opened, and you need to set up the software development environment for your project with this wizard. Expand two icons, CMSIS and Device, and check the CORE and Startup checkboxes in the **Sel.** column, and click on the **OK** button since we need these two components to build our project.

Since this project is a little complex, both a header file and a C file are needed.

8.3.5.4.2 Create the Header File DRALCD.h Create a new header file named DRALCD.h and enter the codes shown in Figure 8.27 into this header file. Let's have a closer look at this header file to see how it works.

1. In this project, we used the system header file TM4C123GH6PM.h since we want to use the structure pointers to access related register to make our codes short and simple. This header file is included in line 6.
2. The codes in lines 7~9 are used to define three LCD commands as constants. These LCD commands, RS, EN and BL are defined based on their bit values on the output of the serial

```
1   //*********************************************************************************************************
2   // DRALCD.h - Header Files for the LCD Project - DRALCD
3   //*********************************************************************************************************
4   #include <stdint.h>
5   #include <stdbool.h>
6   #include "TM4C123GH6PM.h"

7   #define  RS        1                    // 74VHCT595 Q0 bit for RS (Reg Select)
8   #define  EN        2                    // 74VHCT595 Q1 bit for E (Enable LCD)
9   #define  BL        4                    // 74VHCT595 Q2 bit for BL (Backlight)

10  void delay_ms(int  time);
11  void delay_us(int  time);
12  void LCD_cd_Write(char  data, unsigned char  control);
13  void LCD_Comd(unsigned char  cmd);
14  void LCD_Data(char  data);
15  void LCD_Init(void);
16  void SSI2_Write(unsigned char  data);
```

Figure 8.27.   The codes for the header file DRALCD.h.

shift register 74VHCT595. The RS is bit 0 (Q0) whose value is 1, the EN is bit 1 (Q1) whose value is 2, and the BL is bit 2 (Q2) whose value is 4 (Figure 8.18).

3. The codes in lines 10~16 are used to declare seven user-defined subroutines to perform different functions to be used in the project.

8.3.5.4.3 Create the C Source File DRALCD.c   Create a new C file named DRALCD.c and enter the first part codes shown in Figure 8.28 into this C file. Let's have a closer look at this first part source file to see how it works.

1. The user-defined header file DRALCD.h is first included in this source file in line 4.

2. Before we can do any writing to the LCD, first we need to reset and initialize the LCD via the LCD controller SPLC780. A user defined subroutine LCD_Init() is used for this purpose in line 7.

3. Then another user-defined subroutine LCD_Comd(1) is called to clear the LCD and set the cursor at the home position on the LCD panel in line 8.

4. The codes between lines 10 and 12 are used to write some letters, such as WELCOME TO JCSU!, to the LCD panel by calling a user defined subroutine LCD_Data().

5. The user defined subroutine LCD_Init() starts at line 14.

6. As we discussed in Section 8.3.4.6.2, to initialize the SSI module, first we need to enable the clock for that module. In line 16, the bit R2 (bit 2) in the RCGCSSI register is accessed and assigned 0x4 to enable SSI2 clock.

7. In line 17, both GPIO Ports B and C are enabled with the associated clocks.

8. The codes between lines 19 and 23 are used to configure GPIO Port B to enable it's pins PB7 and PB4 to work as alternate function. PB7 is for SSI2Tx and PB4 is for SSI2Clk. Therefore a value of 0x90 (1001) is used to configured AMSEL and AFSEL registers to make PB7 and PB4 to work as SSI2Tx and SSI2Clk pins with the alternate functions. In line 22, the PCTL register in the GPIO Port B is configured to enable PB7 and PB4 to transfer the data/control signals for SSI2Tx and SSI2Clk pins.

9. Similarly, the codes in lines 25~27 are used to configure PC6 as a digital output pin to enable it to transfer a CS_LCD control signal (a positive-going-edge) to the 74VHCT595 to enable all 8-bit serial data stored in 8 serial flip-flops to be converted to 8-bit parallel data and stored in the output latches.

```
1    //*************************************************************************************************************
2    // DRALCD.c - Main Application File for LCD Project – The First Part Codes
3    //*************************************************************************************************************
4    #include "DRALCD.H"
5    int main(void)
6    {
7      LCD_Init();                             // initialize LCD controller
8      LCD_Comd(1);                            // clear screen, move cursor to home
9      // Write "WELCOME TO JCSU!" on LCD
10     LCD_Data('W'); LCD_Data('E'); LCD_Data('L'); LCD_Data('C'); LCD_Data('O');
11     LCD_Data('M'); LCD_Data('E'); LCD_Data(' '); LCD_Data('T'); LCD_Data('O');
12     LCD_Data(' '); LCD_Data('J'); LCD_Data('C'); LCD_Data('S'); LCD_Data('U'); ;LCD_Data('!');
13   }
14   void  LCD_Init(void)                      // initialize SSI2 then initialize LCD controller
15   {
16     SYSCTL->RCGCSSI |= 0x04;                // enable clock to SSI2
17     SYSCTL->RCGCGPIO |= 0x02|0x04;          // enable clock to Port B and Port C
18     // PB7 & PB4 for SSI2Tx and SSI2Clk
19     GPIOB->AMSEL &= ~0x90;                  // turn off analog of PB7 & PB4
20     GPIOB->AFSEL |= 0x90;                   // set PB7 & PB4 for alternate functions
21     GPIOB->PCTL &= ~0xF00F0000;             // clear functions for PB7 & PB4
22     GPIOB->PCTL |= 0x20020000;              // PB7 & PB4 for SSI2 function
23     GPIOB->DEN |= 0x90;                     // PB7 & PB4 as digital function pins
24     // PC6 for SSI2 slave select and CS_LCD (STCP) clock
25     GPIOC->AMSEL &= ~0x40;                  // disable PC6 analog function
26     GPIOC->DIR |= 0x40;                     // set PC6 as output for CS_LCD signal
27     GPIOC->DEN |= 0x40;                     // set PC6 as digital pins
28     SSI2->CR1 = 0;                          // make SSI2 as master and disable SSI2
29     SSI2->CC = 0;                           // use system clock (16 MHz)
30     SSI2->CPSR = 16;                        // clock prescaler divide by 16 gets 1 MHz SSI2Clk clock
31     SSI2->CR0 = 0x0007;                     // clock rate div by 1, phase/polarity 0/0, freescale, data size 8
32     SSI2->CR1 = 2;                          // enable SSI2
33     delay_ms(20);                           // LCD controller reset sequence
34     LCD_cd_Write(0x30, 0);                  // send reset code 1 two times to SPLC780
35     delay_ms(5);
36     LCD_cd_Write(0x30, 0);
37     delay_ms(1);
38     LCD_cd_Write(0x30, 0);                  // send reset code 2 to SPLC780
39     delay_ms(1);
40     LCD_cd_Write(0x20, 0);                  // use 4-bit data mode
41     delay_ms(1);
42     LCD_Comd(0x28);                         // set 4-bit data, 2-line, 5x7 font
43     LCD_Comd(0x06);                         // move cursor right
44     LCD_Comd(0x0C);                         // turn on display, cursor off - no blinking
45     LCD_Comd(0x01);                         // clear screen, move cursor to home
46   }
47   void SSI2_Write(unsigned char  data)
48   {
49     GPIOC->DATA &= ~0x40;                   // clear STCP (CS_LCD) in 74VHCT595 to Low (PC6)
50     SSI2->DR = data;                        // write serial data into 74VHCT595
51     while (SSI2->SR & 0x10) ;               // wait for 74VHCT595 serial data shift done
52     GPIOC->DATA |= 0x40;                    // set CS_LCD (STCP) to High to simulate a positive-going-edge
53   }
```

Figure 8.28. The first part source codes for the project DRALCD.

10. The codes between lines 28 and 32 are used to configure the SSI Module 2 to enable it to transfer serial data to the serial shift register 74VHCT595 in a correct way. This includes the resetting the SSI Clock Configuration (SSICC) register to 0 to enable it to use the system clock (16 MHz), configuring the SSICPSR to divide the system clock by 16 to get a

1 MHz working clock for the SSI2Clk, setting the SSICR0 register to set up the freescale mode with SP and SO as 0, and an 8-bit data size. In line 32, the SSI2 is enabled by setting the SSE bit (bit-1) in the SSICR1 register by 1. A point to be noted is that the SSI module 2 must be disabled before it can be configured, and this is done by the codes in line 28.

11. The codes in lines 34~39 are used to reset the LCD controller by sending two reset codes, Reset Code 1 and Reset Code 2, respectively. Refer to Section 8.3.5.3.3.1 and Figure 8.24, the LCD reset process needs two Reset Codes. This reset job is fulfilled by calling a user-defined subroutine LCD_cd_Write(). This cd means that both LCD commands and Data can be processed by using this function. The first argument of this subroutine is an LCD data and the second is a LCD command. These two arguments will be broken first and then recombined together to be sent out via that subroutine.

12. In line 40, this subroutine is called again to transfer 0x20 to the LCD controller to configure LCD to use 4-bit data mode. Refer to step 4 in Figure 8.24 in Section 8.3.5.3.3.1 to get a clearer picture for this configuration.

13. The codes in lines 42~45 are used to set function mode, select display mode, set entry mode and clear the display for the LCD. Refer to Section 8.3.5.3.3.2 and Figure 8.26 to get the meaning for each coding line in this part. A user-defined subroutine LCD_Comd() is used to process and transfer these commands to the LCD controller one by one. Each command is first broken into two pieces of 4-bit commands, combined with the RS, E, and BL control bits together to form a final 8-bit command to be sent to the LCD controller via the serial shift register 74VHCT 595.

14. The codes in lines 47~53 are used to perform writing an 8-bit serial data via SSI2Tx pin to the SPLC780 via 74VHTC595. A user-defined subroutine SSI2_Write() is used to fulfill this function.

15. In line 49, an inversing code of 0x40 (10111111) is sent to the GPIO Port C or PC6 to clear STCP to make it Low via CS_LCD signal. Then the transmitted data is sent to the SSI2Tx pin via SSIDR (SSI2 → DR) register in line 50.

16. In line 51, a while() loop is used to wait for this serial data transmission to be completed. This can be done by monitoring the BSY bit (bit 4) in the SSISR register (SSI2 → SR & 0x10). When the data transmission is done, this bit is cleared to 0. As soon as this is happened, which means that all 8-bit serial data have been shifted into the 8-bit flip-flop registers in the 74VHCT595. Then in line 52, a 0x40 is sent to the PC6 to make the STCP to High to get a positive-going-edge to trigger the transferring of 8-bit data in the serial shift flip-flops into the 8-bit parallel output registers, and furthermore to output to the LCD controller SPLC780 via Q4~Q7 (DB7~DB4) and Q0~Q2 (RS, E, and BL).

Now let's take care of the second part of the source codes, which is shown in Figure 8.29.

17. The user-defined subroutine LCD_cd_Write() starts at line 57. Two arguments are involved in this subroutine: The first one is the LCD data and the second is the LCD command.

18. The codes in lines 58~59 are used to get the upper 4-bit data and the lower 4-bit control from two arguments by ANDing 0xF0 and 0x0F, for data and control respectively.

19. The codes in lines 61~64 are used to combine each piece of data with related control commands, such as RS, E and BL, to form an 8-bit serial data and then send it out via SSI2Tx pin. An OR operator is used to combine data and commands together. These codes are also used to create a simulated Low-to-High pulse for the E control signal to enable the LCD controller SPLC780 to get that serial data (see Figure 8.25).

20. Another user-defined subroutine LCD_Comd() starts at line 67. This subroutine is used to break the input command into two pieces of 4-bit command and then combine with the related control signal, RS, E, and BL, to form an 8-bit serial data to be sent out via the LCD_cd_Write() subroutine in two times.

```
54  //*********************************************************************************************************************
55  // DRALCD.c - Main Application File for LCD Project – The Second Part Codes
56  //*********************************************************************************************************************
57  void LCD_cd_Write(char  data, unsigned char  control)
58  {
59     data &= 0xF0;                                        // clear lower nibble for data
60     control &= 0x0F;                                     // clear upper nibble for control
61     SSI2_Write (data | control | BL);                   // RS = 0, R/W = 0
62     SSI2_Write (data | cont    rol | EN | BL);          // pulse E
63     delay_ms(0);
64     SSI2_Write (data | BL);
65     SSI2_Write (BL);
66  }
67  void  LCD_Comd(unsigned char  cmd)
68  {
69     LCD_cd_Write(cmd & 0xF0, 0);                        // upper nibble first
70     LCD_cd_Write(cmd << 4,  0);                         // then lower nibble
71     if (cmd < 4)
72        delay_ms(2);                                     // command 1 and 2 needs up to 1.64ms
73     else
74        delay_ms(1);                                     // all others 40 μs
75  }
76  void  LCD_Data(char  data)
77  {
78     LCD_cd_Write(data & 0xF0,  RS);                     // upper nibble first
79     LCD_cd_Write(data << 4,  RS);                       // then lower nibble
80     delay_us(40);
81  }
82  void  delay_ms(int  time)                              // delay n milliseconds (16 MHz CPU clock)
83  {
84     int i,  j;
85     for(i = 0 ; i < time; i++)
86        for(j = 0; j < 3180; j++) {}                     // do nothing for 1 ms
87  }
88  void  delay_us(int  time)                              // delay n microseconds (16 MHz CPU clock)
89  {
90     int i,  j;
91     for(i = 0 ; i < time; i++)
92        for(j = 0; j < 3; j++) {}                        // do nothing for 1 μs
93  }
```

Figure 8.29.   The second part source codes for the project DRALCD.

21. In line 72, the command is < 4, which means that if the command is 1 (Clear Display), 2 (Set Function), or 3 (Return Home), delay those commands by 2 ms. Otherwise delay 1 ms for all other commands. Refer to steps 2 and 3 in Table 8.11 to get more details for those LCD commands.

22. The codes in lines 76~81 are used to transfer the LCD data. This transmission is completed by calling a user-defined subroutine LCD_Data(). The LCD data to be transferred is first broken into two pieces of 4-bit data, the upper 4 bits and the lower 4 bits. Then each piece of data is combined with the RS command to form an 8-bit serial data to be sent via the LCD_cd_Write() subroutine. Refer to Section 8.3.5.3.1 to get more details about the RS command and its function (RS = 1 means that a LCD data is transmitted).

23. The codes in lines 86~93 are used to build two time-delay subroutines to delay certain ms and μs to make the LCD controller work properly.

Now let's set up the environment to build and run our project to test the LCD functions.

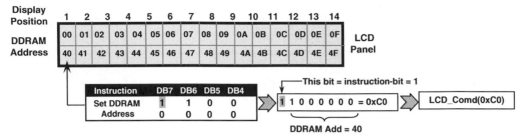

Figure 8.30. The relationship between the LCD instruction and the DDRAM address.

8.3.5.4.4 Set Up the Environment to Build and Run the Project Perform the following operations to set up the environment for this project:

- Select the debug adapter `Stellaris ICDI` in the Debug tab under the `Project-|Options for Target 'Target 1'` menu item.

Now build the project by going to `Project|Build target` menu item. If everything is fine, go to `Flash|Download` item to download the image file of the project into the flash memory. Then go to `Debug|Start/Stop Debug Session` and `Debug|Run` item to run the project.

After the project running, you can find that the letter sequence `WELCOME TO JCSU!` is displayed in the LCD panel. Our project is successful!

Can we display something on the second line in this LCD with desired starting position? Yes, but you need to refer to step 7 in Table 8.12 and Figure 8.21 to figure out the coding process. Figure 8.30 shows the relationship between the LCD instruction and the DDRAM address.

You can use the subroutine `LCD_Comd(0xC0)` to select the first position on the second line in the LCD. How about other positions? Think about it.

8.3.6 Build On-Board 7-Segment LED Interface Programming Project

In this section we illustrate how to use the SSI Module 2 (`SSI2`) to interface four on-board 7-segment LEDs installed in the EduBASE ARM® Trainer. First let's have a closer look at the hardware configuration and connection for these LEDs via `SSI2`.

In order to enable us to develop our programs to control and display our desired data on these four 7-segment LEDs, first let's have a clear picture about the hardware configuration for these four 7-segment LEDs and their control functions.

8.3.6.1 *Structure of 7-Segment LEDs*

Figure 8.31a shows a one-digit 7-segment common cathode LED and its structure.

To make any segment, such as a, b, c, etc., light up or turn ON, just apply logic HIGH to the associated input bit D_i since the cathode terminals of all of these 7-segment LEDs are connected together to the ground. In the EduBASE ARM® Trainer, these 8 input bits ($D_0 \sim D_7$) are connected to 8 latched output bits (Q0~Q7) on the 74VHCT595. Figure 8.31b shows the layout of a single bit on 7-segment LED.

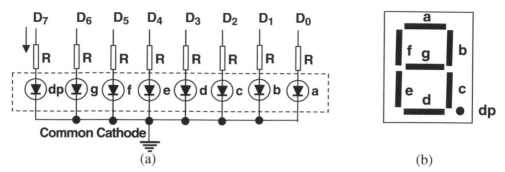

Figure 8.31. The structure of common cathode LED.

8.3.6.2 SSI Module Interface for the 7-Segment LED in the EduBASE ARM® Trainer

Similar to the LCD interface, four 7-segment LEDs are connected to the SSI2 module via two cascaded serial shift registers 74VHCT595. A functional block diagram of this interface circuit connected to the LED installed in the EduBASE ARM® Trainer is shown in Figure 8.32.

It can be found from Figure 8.32 that two serial shift registers 74VHCT595 are cascaded or serial connected together to form two 8-bit parallel outputs to perform the LED digit-selection and 7-segment selection functions. The serial input and controls to the 74VHCT595 are still from SSI module 2 control pins. The GPIO Port C pin 7 (PC7) now is used to provide the slave selection and triggering signal to convert 8-serial data into 8-parallel data in the 74VHCT595 when a positive-going-edge signal is provided by this pin.

When working this mode, the first serial 8-bit data to be transferred by SSI2 should be the 7-segment control signal used to select the required segments to display desired number on all four LEDs. The second serial 8-bit data (only the lower 4 bits are used) should be used to select the desired LED digit.

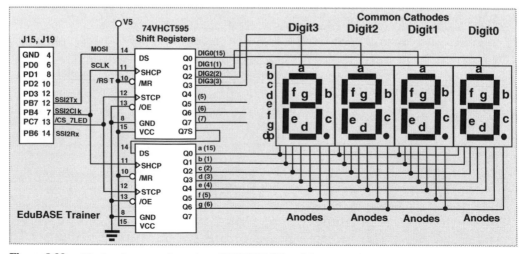

Figure 8.32. The hardware configuration of 74VHCT 595 and 7-segment LEDs.

Table 8.13. The relation between the 7-segment data code and normal code.

Number/ Letter	dp Q7	g Q6	f Q5	e Q4	d Q3	c Q2	b Q1	a Q0	7-Segment Code
0	0	0	1	1	1	1	1	1	3F
1	0	0	0	0	0	1	1	0	06
2	0	1	0	1	1	0	1	1	5B
3	0	1	0	0	1	1	1	1	4F
4	0	1	1	0	0	1	1	0	66
5	0	1	1	0	1	1	0	1	6D
6	0	1	1	1	1	1	0	1	7D
7	0	0	0	0	0	1	1	1	07
8	0	1	1	1	1	1	1	1	7F
9	0	1	1	0	1	1	1	1	6F
A	0	1	1	1	0	1	1	1	77
b	0	1	1	1	1	1	0	0	7C
C	0	0	1	1	1	0	0	1	39
d	0	1	0	1	1	1	1	0	5E
E	0	1	1	1	1	0	0	1	79
F	0	1	1	1	0	0	0	1	71
H	0	1	1	1	0	1	1	0	76
h	0	1	1	1	0	1	0	0	74
J	0	0	0	1	1	1	1	0	1E
L	0	0	1	1	1	0	0	0	38
S	0	1	1	0	1	1	0	1	6D
P	0	1	1	1	0	0	1	1	73
U	0	0	1	1	1	1	1	0	3E

In order to display desired numbers or letters on these 7-segment LEDs, a code conversion job is necessary to translate the binary or hexadecimal codes output from the 74VHCT595 to the 7-segment codes to be displayed on those LEDs. Table 8.13 shows the relationship between these code translations. In the real program, a subroutine should be developed and used to perform this coding conversion function before the number or letter can be displayed on these four 7-segment LEDs.

In addition to converting the data sent to the 74VHCT595 form binary or hexadecimal codes to 7-segment codes, a LED digit selection code should also be sent to the 74VHCT595 to select the desired LED digit. Table 8.14 shows a relationship between the codes to be sent to the 74VHCT595 and the selected LED digit.

For example, to display a number 0 in the first digit of 7-segment LED, Digit0, the following data should be created and sent to the 74VHCT595, respectively:

- A 0x3F or 00111111B should be sent to the 74VHCT595 to make Q7 ~ Q0 = 00111111 on the second 74VHCT595. This will make segments (anodes) a, b, c, d, e, and f ON, and segments g and dp OFF.

Table 8.14. The codes sent to the second 74VHCT595 and the selected LED digits.

Qn CODE LED DIGITS	Q7	Q6	Q5	Q4	Q3	Q2	Q1	Q0	HEX CODE
DIGIT0	X	X	X	X	1	1	1	0	$FE
DIGIT1	X	X	X	X	1	1	0	1	$FD
DIGIT2	X	X	X	X	1	0	1	1	$FB
DIGIT3	X	X	X	X	0	1	1	1	$F7

- A 0xFE or 11111110B should be sent to the first 74VHCT595 to make Q3~Q0 = 1110. This will make the cathode of the Digit0 to Low to select this digit (the higher 4-bit can be any values). The key is to send a Low or 0 to the cathode of the selected LED digit to enable it to be ON to display it.

Now let's build an example project to access and interface these 7-segment LEDs.

8.3.6.3 Build the Example LED Interfacing Project

Now we have enough knowledge and skill to build a practical LED interfacing project to serially transmit our desired letters or numbers to the LED to display them on it.

The hardware configuration of this project is shown in Figure 8.32. In the EduBASE ARM® Trainer, it has been configured to use the SSI module 2 to serially transmit instructions and data to LEDs via two cascaded serial shift registers 74VHTC595. The GPIO pins used in this project include:

- PB7: SSI2Tx—Transmit instructions/data to the peripheral 74VHCT595.
- PB4: SSI2Clk—Provide SSI2 with a clock to conduct the serial data transmission.
- PB6: SSI2Rx—Receive serial data from the peripheral (not used in this example).
- PB5: SSI2Fss—Provide the serial data transmit frame format (not used in this example).
- PC7: CS_7LED—Provide the LED Chip Select signal. Here it works as a trigger clock to start a serial-to-parallel data conversion to convert 8-bit serial data stored in the serial shift register to 8-bit parallel data to be stored in the 8-bit output registers in the 74VHCT595 register.

In our example application, each time after SSI2 transmits 8 bits of data to the shift register via the DS (SSI2Tx–PB7) pin and the clock SHCP (SSI2Clk–PB4) pin, a positive-going-edge (Low-to-High) signal should be applied on the STCP (CS_7LED–PC7) pin to transfer 8-bit serial data in the shift register into the 8-bit parallel output buffer or latches. The OE pin is connected to the ground to enable 8 latched outputs to be directly transferred to the output pins (Figure 8.32).

We try to use the Direct Register Access (DRA) model to build this project. The entire coding process includes the following four sections:

1. Initialize and configure SSI2-related GPIO Ports (Ports B and C).
2. Initialize and configure SSI2 module and related registers (SSICC, SSICPSR, SSICR0, and SSICR1).

3. Build one subroutine to break, combine, and transmit 8-bit instructions/data to the LED to display desired letters and numbers on the selected LEDs.

4. Build some time delay functions to delay different periods of time to make the LED data transmissions stable and reliable.

Now let's first create a new LED project DRALED.

8.3.6.3.1 Create a Direct Register Access LED Project DRALED   Perform the following operations to create a new project DRALED:

1. Open the Windows Explorer window to create a new folder named DRALED under the C: \ARM Class Projects\Chapter 8 folder.

2. Open the Keil® ARM-MDK µVersion5 and go to Project|New µVersion Project menu item to create a new µVersion Project. On the opened wizard, browse to our new folder DRALED that is created in step 1 above. Enter DRALED into the **File name** box and click on the **Save** button to create this project.

3. On the next wizard, you need to select the device (MCU) for this project. Expand three icons, Texas Instruments, Tiva C Series, and TM4C123x Series, and select the target device TM4C123GH6PM from the list by clicking on it. Click on the **OK** to close this wizard.

4. Next the Software Components wizard is opened, and you need to set up the software development environment for your project with this wizard. Expand two icons, CMSIS and Device, and check the CORE and Startup checkboxes in the **Sel.** column, and click on the **OK** button since we need these two components to build our project.

Since this project is very simple, only a C source file is good enough.

8.3.6.3.2 Create the C Source File DRALED.c   Create a new C file named DRALED.c and enter the codes shown in Figure 8.33 into this C file. Let's have a closer look at this source file to see how it works.

1. Three user-defined subroutines are declared at the top of this file at lines 4~6.

2. The LED_Init() subroutine is called to initialize and configure SSI2 registers and GPIO Ports B and C to enable PB7 and PB4 to work as SSI2Tx and SSI2Clk pins in line 12.

3. An infinitive while() loop is used to repeatedly send desired numbers to the LEDs.

4. The SSI2_Write() subroutine is called to transmit number 2 (0x5B) to the third LED (Digit3) in lines 15 and 16.

5. Similarly, the codes in lines 18~25 are used to transmit numbers 0, 1, and 5 to the 2nd, 1st, and 0th LEDs, respectively, by using the SSI2_Write() subroutine.

6. The subroutine LED_Init() starts at line 29. The codes for this subroutine are identical to those on the same subroutine we discussed in the last project. The only difference is that the GPIO Port C pin 7 or PC7 (CS_7LED) is used to replace PC6 used in the last project to provide a triggering signal for the 74VHCT595 to start the serial-to-parallel conversion.

7. The codes in lines 45~51 are built for the subroutine SSI2_Write(). In line 47, the PC7 is reset to Low to select the slave device 74VHCT595 and clear the STCP input signal.

8. The serial data is written into the SSI2 FIFO and transmitted to the SSI2Tx pin in line 48.

9. In line 49, a while() loop is used to check the BSY bit in the SSI2SR to wait for this data transmission to be done.

```
1    //*********************************************************************************************************
2    // DRALED.c - Main Application File for the LED Project
3    //*********************************************************************************************************
4    #include <stdint.h>
5    #include <stdbool.h>
6    #include "TM4C123GH6PM.h"

7    void delay_ms(int time);
8    void LED_Init(void);
9    void SSI2_Write(unsigned char data);

10   int main(void)
11   {
12     LED_Init();                              // initialize SSI2 that connects to the shift registers
13     while(1)
14     {
15       SSI2_Write(0x5B);                      // write num 2 to the seven segments
16       SSI2_Write(0xF7);                      // select digit 3
17       delay_ms(4);

18       SSI2_Write(0x3F);                      // write num 0 to the seven segments
19       SSI2_Write(0xFB);                      // select digit 2
20       delay_ms(4);

21       SSI2_Write(0x06);                      // write num 1 to the seven segments
22       SSI2_Write(0xFD);                      // select digit 1
23       delay_ms(4);

24       SSI2_Write(0x6D);                      // write num 5 to the seven segments
25       SSI2_Write(0xFE);                      // select digit 0
26       delay_ms(4);
27     }
28   }

29   void LED_Init(void)                        // enable SSI2 and associated GPIO pins
30   {
31     SYSCTL->RCGCGPIO |= 0x02|0x04;           // enable clock to GPIOB & GPIOC
32     SYSCTL->RCGCSSI = 0x04;                  // enable clock to SSI2

33     GPIOB->AFSEL |= 0x90;                    // PB7 & PB4 for alternate function
34     GPIOB->PCTL &= ~0xF00F0000;              // clear functions for PB7 & PB4
35     GPIOB->PCTL |= 0x20020000;               // PB7 & PB4 for SSI2 function - PB7 (SSI2Tx) & PB4 (SSI2Clk)
36     GPIOB->DEN |= 0x90;                      // PB7 & PB4 as digital pins
37     GPIOC->DIR |= 0x80;                      // set PC7 as output pin
38     GPIOC->DEN |= 0x80;                      // set PC7 as digital pin

39     SSI2->CR1 = 0;                           // disable SSI2 during configuration
40     SSI2->CC = 0;                            // use system clock
41     SSI2->CPSR = 16;                         // clock prescaler divide by 16 gets 1 MHz clock
42     SSI2->CR0 = 0x0007;                      // clock rate div by 1, phase/polarity 0/0, mode freescale, data size 8
43     SSI2->CR1 = 2;                           // enable SSI2 as master
44   }

45   void SSI2_Write(unsigned char data)
46   {
47     GPIOC->DATA &= ~0x80;                    // select the slave and clear STCP to Low
48     SSI2->DR = data;                         // output the serial data
49     while (SSI2->SR & 0x10) {}               // wait for transmit done by checking the BSY bit in SSISR
50     GPIOC->DATA |= 0x80;                     // set STCP to High to trigger serial-to-parallel conversion
51   }

52   void delay_ms(int time)                    // delay n milliseconds (16 MHz CPU clock)
53   {
54     int i, j;
55     for(i = 0 ; i < time; i++)
56       for(j = 0; j < 3180; j++) {}
57   }
```

Figure 8.33.   The C source file for the DRALED project.

10. As soon as that data is transmitted, the PC7 outputs a High to provide a positive-going-edge signal to convert serial data to the parallel data and output to the LEDs device via 74VHCT595 in line 50.

11. The codes in lines 52~57 are used to delay certain time to make the LED displaying stable.

8.3.6.3.3 Set Up the Environment to Build and Run the Project Perform the following operations to set up the environment for this project:

- Select the debug adapter `Stellaris ICDI` in the Debug tab under the `Project-|Options for Target 'Target 1'` menu item.

Now build the project by going to `Project|Build target` menu item. If everything is fine, go to the `Flash|Download` item to download the image file of the project into the flash memory. Then go to `Debug|Start/Stop Debug Session` and `Debug|Run` item to run the project.

After the project running, you can find that four numbers, 2015, are displayed in four LEDs. Our project is successful!

We leave a similar LED project for the readers. The function of that project is to repeatedly display each segment on each digit.

Next let's take care of the Digital-to-Analog Converter (DAC) Programming Project by using the EduBASE ARM Trainer.

8.3.7 Build Digital-to-Analog Converter Programming Project

In this section we illustrate how to use the SSI Module 2 (SSI2) to interface to a Digital-to-Analog Converter (DAC-MCP4922) installed in the EduBASE ARM® Trainer. First let's have a closer look at the hardware configuration and connection for this DAC via SSI2.

8.3.7.1 SSI Module Interface for the DAC-MCP4922 in the EduBASE ARM® Trainer

Different with the LCD and LED interfaces, the DAC-MCP4922 is directly connected to the SSI2 module without using any serial shift register. This is because the DAC-MCP4922 provides a serial data input. A functional block diagram of this interface circuit connected to the DAC-MCP4922 installed in the EduBASE ARM® Trainer is shown in Figure 8.34.

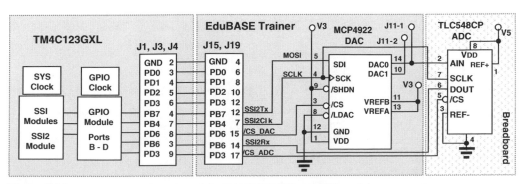

Figure 8.34. Hardware configuration of the DAC-MCP4492 and SSI2 module.

It can be found from Figure 8.34 that two SSI2 control signals, SSI2Tx and SSI2Clk, are connected to the DAC-MCP4922 to control the DAC conversions and serial data transmission. Optionally a serial ADC-TLC548 can be connected to the output of the DAC0 to receive and check the DAC transferring results. An oscilloscope can also be connected to DAC0 (J11-1) and DAC1 (J11-2) pins to monitor and check the converted analog waveform outputs.

Now let's have a closer look at these two peripherals, the Digital-to-Analog Converter (DAC MCP4922) and the Analog-to-Digital Converter (ADC-TLC548).

8.3.7.2 *The Operations and Programming for MCP4922 DAC*

The MCP4922 device is a dual 12-bit buffered voltage output Digital-to-Analog Converter (DAC). The devices operate from a single 2.7V to 5.5V supply with SPI-compatible Serial Peripheral Interface. This DAC is a programmable device and needs to be programmed to perform the desired DAC operations.

A functional block diagram of the MCP4922 DAC is shown in Figure 8.35.

The operational principle and sequence of this DAC are as follows:

- The SDI is the serial data input pin to accept serial digital data as input.
- The SCK terminal is used to accept an external clock and the DAC performs its conversions based on this clock as a timing base.

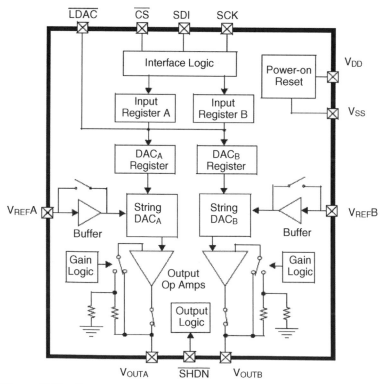

Figure 8.35. The functional block diagram of the DAC-MCP4922.

A̅/B	BUF	G̅A̅	S̅H̅D̅N̅	D11	D10	D9	D8	D7	D6	D5	D4	D3	D2	D1	D0
bit 15															bit 0

Figure 8.36.   An example of the command-data structure for the DAC-MCP4922.

- The/CS is a Chip-Select signal used to start the DAC operations. Both DAC modules use the same clock source with the same starting signal. The active level is Low.
- The/LDAC signal is used to enable both buffered conversion results to be updated in two DAC outputs. The active level of this signal is Low.
- The dual DAC can be shut down for their outputs if the/SHDN signal is Low.
- The dual DAC outputs can be obtained from V_{OUTA} and V_{OUTB} pins in serial format. Both outputs can be as high as V_{REF} ($\times 1 = 2.048$ V) or doubled V_{REF} ($\times 2 = 4.096$ V).

In the EduBASE ARM® Trainer, the/LDAC is connected to the ground, and this is equivalent to setting the/LDAC pin to Low. This connection enables both outputs to be updated as a rising edge appeared on the/CS signal (Figure 8.34).

The/SHDN pin is connected to the power supply V3, and this is equivalent to setting this pin to High. This configuration enables both DAC outputs to be available at any time.

Both reference pins, V_{REFA} and V_{REFB}, are tied to the power supply V3. This connection makes both DAC use the same reference voltage.

To configure the MCP4922 to perform any DAC operation, the DAC needs first to be programmed. Each programming instruction is 16-bit and is composed of a commands part (4 MSB bits) and a data part (following 12-bit).

The write command is initiated by driving the CS pin to Low, followed by clocking the four MSB Configuration bits and the 12 data bits into the SDI pin on the rising edge of SCK. The CS pin is then raised to High to cause the data to be latched into the selected DAC input registers. The MCP4922 utilizes a double-buffered latch structure to allow both DACA and DACB outputs to be synchronized with the LDAC pin if desired. Upon the LDAC pin achieving a Low state, the values held in the DAC input registers are transferred into the DAC output registers. The outputs will transition to the value and held in the DACA (DAC0) or DACB (DAC1) register.

All writes to the MCP4922 are 16-bit instructions. Any clocks past the 16th clock will be ignored. The Most Significant 4 bits are Configuration bits. The remaining 12 bits are data bits. No data can be transferred into the device with CS high. Figure 8.36 shows an example of the command-data structure to be written into the MCP4922 DAC.

As we mentioned, the 4 MSBs are configuration or command bits. The values for these configuration bits and related functions are shown in Table 8.15.

For example, if we want to configure the MCP4922 to transfer a 12-bit serial data with the following configurations:

- Select the DACA (DAC0) channel as the converting channel.
- Enable the buffered input and output.
- Select the output gain as 1.
- Do not shut down the DAC channel to enable it active.

The configuration bits should be: $0x7xxx = 0111xxxxxxxxxxxx$. The lower 12 data bits are x, which means that they do not matter and the real values depend on the application data.

Table 8.15. Bit value and its function for MCP4922 DAC.

Bit	Name	Function
15	$\overline{A}/B$	DACA or DACB Selection Bit 0 : Write to DACA (DAC0) 1 : Write to DACB (DAC1)
14	BUF	VREF Input Buffer Control Bit 0 : Un-Buffered 1 : Buffered
13	$\overline{GA}$	Output Gain Selection Bit 0 : 2x (VOUT = 2 * VREF * D/4096) 1 : 1x (VOUT = VREF * D/4096)
12	$\overline{SHDN}$	Output Shutdown Control Bit 0 : Shutdown the selected DAC channel. Analog output is not available at the channel that was shut down. VOUT pin is connected to 500 k 1 : Active mode operation. VOUT is available
11:0	D11:D0	DAC Input Data bits

8.3.7.3 *The Analog-to-Digital Converter TLC-548*

The TLC-548 is an 8-bit serial-in-serial-out Analog-to-Digital Converter (ADC) with 3-wire serial interface, such as SPI and SSI interfaces. The conversion results of the DAC can be fed into the TLC-548 serial ADC input via pin2 (AIN). The CS_ADC (PD3) provides a Chip-Select (/CS) signal to start the ADC conversion, and the ADC conversion process is controlled by the SSI2Clk clock signal in a timing sequence. The ADC conversion results can be received by the SSI2Rx pin (PB6) since the ADC output (DOUT) is connected to the SSI2Rx pin.

The reference pin (REF+) in the TLC-548 is connected to the power supply, and REF− is connected to the ground. With this configuration, the ADC used the internal reference to allow the output to be 4.096 V. Figure 8.37 shows the functional block diagram of the ADC-TLC548.

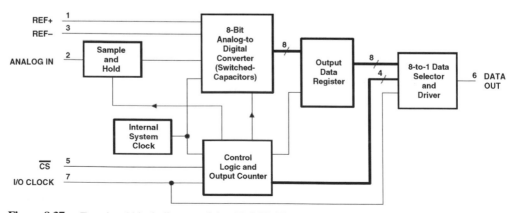

Figure 8.37. Functional block diagram of the ADC-TLC548.

The serial 8-bit output can be obtained from DOUT pin (pin 6) via the TLC548, which is controlled by the input clock sequence SCLK. The data can be shifted out bit by bit as each falling edge of the SCLK is coming.

Now let's build an example project to access and interface to the DAC-MCP4922.

8.3.7.4 *Build the Example DAC Interfacing Project*

The hardware configuration of this project is shown in Figure 8.34. In the EduBASE ARM® Trainer, it has been configured to use the SSI module 2 to serially transmit digital data to the DAC–MCP4922. You can use an oscilloscope to monitor DAC0 (J11-1) and DAC1 (J11-2) pins on the EduBASE Trainer to check the analog out results. Optionally, you build the ADC part by using the TLC548 with the breadboard provided by the EduBASE ARM® Trainer first. Refer to Figure 8.34 to finish this circuit building process. For the power supply V5 and the ground signals, you can use 5V and GND pins on the J10 connector in the EduBASE ARM® Trainer, respectively.

The GPIO pins used in this project include:

- PB7: SSI2Tx—Transmit digital data to the peripheral DAC–MCP4922.
- PB4: SSI2Clk—Provide SSI2 with a clock to conduct the serial data transmission.
- PB6: SSI2Rx—Receive serial data from the peripheral ADC-TLC548.
- PB5: SSI2Fss—Provide the serial data transmit frame format (not used in this example).
- PD6: CS_DAC—Provide the DAC Chip Select signal. Here it works as a trigger signal to start the Digital-to-Analog conversion to convert 12-bit serial digital data to 12-bit serial analog data to be sent to the serial input of the Analog-to-Digital Converter TLC548.
- PD3: CS_ADC—Provide the ADC Chip Select signal. Here it works as a trigger signal to start the Analog-to-Digital conversion to convert 12-bit serial analog data back to 8-bit serial digital data to be received by the SSI2Rx pin.

In our example application, each time after the SSI2 transmits 12 bits of digital data to the MCP4922 via an SSI2Tx (PB7) pin and a clock SSI2Clk (PB4) pin, a Low-level signal should be applied on the/CS_DAC (PD6) pin to start a DAC operation. The DAC conversion results can be obtained serially from the first conversion channel V_{OUTA} or DAC0 as each rising edge of the SSI2Clk coming (Figure 8.34). This serial analog output can be optionally sent to the serial input of the ADC-TLC548 to perform an Analog-to-Digital conversion to convert it back to the digital data. Then the digital data can be received by the SSI2Rx pin to enable us to collect and then confirm the correctness of these transmission and conversions. A point to be noted is that before this ADC can start, a Low-level signal must be applied on the/CS_ADC (PD3) to enable the TLC548 to start its conversions.

We try to use the Direct Register Access (DRA) model to build this project. The entire coding process includes the following four sections:

1. Initialize and configure SSI2-related GPIO Ports (Ports B and D).
2. Initialize and configure an SSI2 module and related registers (SSICC, SSICPSR, SSICR0, and SSICR1).
3. Build a subroutine to perform data transmission from the SSI module 2 to the DAC-MCP4922 via SSI2Tx.

4. Build a subroutine to perform data receiving from the ADC-TLC548 to the SSI module 2 via SSI2Rx.

Now let's first create a new DAC project DRADAC.

8.3.7.4.1 Create a Direct Register Access DAC Project DRADAC Perform the following operations to create a new project DRADAC:

1. Open the Windows Explorer window to create a new folder named DRADAC under the C:\ARM Class Projects\Chapter 8 folder.

2. Open the Keil® ARM-MDK μVersion5 and go to the Project|New μVersion Project menu item to create a new μVersion Project. On the opened wizard, browse to our new folder DRADAC that is created in step 1 above. Enter DRADAC into the **File name** box and click on the **Save** button to create this project.

3. On the next wizard, you need to select the device (MCU) for this project. Expand three icons, Texas Instruments, Tiva C Series, and TM4C123x Series, and select the target device TM4C123GH6PM from the list by clicking on it. Click on the **OK** to close this wizard.

4. Next the Software Components wizard is opened, and you need to set up the software development environment for your project with this wizard. Expand two icons, CMSIS and Device, and check the CORE and Startup checkboxes in the **Sel.** column, and click on the **OK** button since we need these two components to build our project.

Since this project is a little longer, a header file and a C source file are needed.

8.3.7.4.2 Create the Header File DRADAC.h Create a new header file named DRADAC.h and enter the codes shown in Figure 8.38 into this file. Since the codes are easy and straightforward, no explanation is needed.

8.3.7.4.3 Create the C Source File DRADAC.c Create a new C file named DRADAC.c and enter the codes shown in Figure 8.39 into this C file. Let's have a closer look at this source file to see how it works.

1. The main program starts at line 5.

2. Two variables, the integer variable idata and the float point variable fdata, are declared first in the main program in line 7. The idata has a data range of

```
1   //********************************************************************************************************
2   // DRADAC.h - Header File for DAC-MCP4922 (SSI2)
3   //********************************************************************************************************
4   #include <stdint.h>
5   #include <stdbool.h>
6   #include "TM4C123GH6PM.h"
7   #include <math.h>

8   void DAC_Init(void);
9   void DAC_Write(int value, int channel);
10  void ADC_Read(void);
```

Figure 8.38. The header file for the project DRADAC.

```
1    //****************************************************************************************************
2    // DRADAC.c - Main Application File for DAC-MCP4922 (SSI2)
3    //*************************************************************************************************** *
4    #include "DRADAC.h"
5    int main(void)
6    {
7       int idata = 0;  float fdata;
8       DAC_Init();
9       while(1)
10      {
11         // create a sawtooth waveform
12         DAC_Write(idata++, 0);
13         // create a sine waveform
14         fdata = sinf(0.00314159 * idata) * 0x07FF + 0x800;          // 0x800 = DC offset
15         DAC_Write((Int)fdata, 1);
16         ADC_Read();                                                 // receive the ADC result for sine wave
17      }
18   }
19   void DAC_Init(void)                              // initialize SSI2 that connects to the DAC
20   {
21      SYSCTL->RCGCGPIO |= 0x02|0x08;                // enable clock to GPIOB & GPIOD
22      SYSCTL->RCGCSSI |= 0x04;                      // enable clock to SSI2
23      GPIOB->AFSEL |= 0xD0;                         // PORTB 7, 6 & 4 for SSI2
24      GPIOB->PCTL &= ~0xFF0F0000;                   // PORTB 7, 6 & 4 for SSI2
25      GPIOB->PCTL |= 0x22020000;
26      GPIOB->DEN |= 0xDF;                           // PORTB 7, 6, 4 & 3 ~ 0 as digital pins
27      GPIOB->DIR |= 0x0F;                           // PB3 ~ PB0 as output pins
28
29      GPIOD->DIR |= 0x48;                           // use PD6 for DAC chip select
30      GPIOD->DEN |= 0x48;                           // use PD3 for ADC chip select
31      GPIOD->DATA |= 0x48;                          // set PD6 & PD3 to High to deselect DAC/ADC
32      SSI2->CR1 = 0;                                // disable SSI2 and make it master
33      SSI2->CC = 0;                                 // use system clock
34      SSI2->CPSR = 16;                              // clock prescaler divide by 16 gets 1 MHz clock
35      SSI2->CR0 = 0xF;                              // clock rate div by 1, phase/polarity 0 0, mode freescale, data size 16
36      SSI2->CR1 = 2;                                // enable SSI2
37   }
38   void DAC_Write(int value, int channel)          // write a 16-bit value to DAC through SSI2
39   {
40      Int config;
41      if (channel == 0) { config = 0x07000; }
42      else if (channel == 1) { config = 0xF000; }
43      GPIOD->DATA &= ~0x40;                         // setup chip select to Low to select DAC
44      value = (value & 0x0FFF) | config;            // configure 4 MSB with 12-bit data together
45      SSI2->DR = value;                             // send 16-bit command-data to DAC
46      while (SSI2->SR & 0x10) ;                     // wait for transmit done
47      GPIOD->DATA |= 0x40;                          // set chip select to High to deselect DAC
48   }
49   void ADC_Read(void)
50   {
51      int adc;
52      GPIOD->DATA &= ~0x08;                         // setup chip select to Low to select ADC
53      while (SSI2->SR & 0x10) ;                     // wait for SSI2 data receiving done
54      adc = SSI2->DR;                               // get the ADC data
55      GPIOB->DATA = adc;                            // display ADC result on LEDs PB3 ~ PB0
56      GPIOD->DATA |= 0x08;                          // set PD3 to High to deselect ADC
57   }
```

Figure 8.39.   The source file for the project DRADAC.

−32768∼32767 and it is used to create a sawtooth waveform later. The `fdata` is used to create a sinusoidal waveform with the `sinf()` function since that function needs to use a float point variable.

3. In line 8, the `DAC_Init()` function is called to initialize the DAC-related registers and the SSI2-related GPIO Ports and pins.

4. An infinitive `while()` loop is used to repeatedly call two user-defined functions, `DAC_Write()` and `DAC_Read()`, to create sawtooth and sinusoidal waveforms as well as to read back the data coming from the ADC-TLC548.

5. In line 12, the `DAC_Write()` function is called to create a sawtooth waveform with the `idata` as the argument. Each loop the `idata` is incremented by 1 and sent to the DAC MCP4922 via `SSI2Tx` pin to generate a sawtooth step until the `idata` gets its upper bound 32767. Then the `idata` is reset to 0 and restarts its increment action from there. The second argument is the channel number, which is 0, and it indicates that this `idata` is sent to the first DAC channel or DAC0 to create and output a sawtooth waveform.

6. In line 14, the `fdata` is calculated and it is used as an argument to be passed with the `sinf()` function to generate a sinusoidal signal. As we know, when calling the sinf() to create a sinusoidal signal in this way, the generated signal is a discrete signal. The general discrete signal can be expressed as `fdata[n] = Asinf(`$2\pi f_0 T_s n$`)`, where A = 0x7FF is the amplitude of this signal, f_0 is the signal frequency, T_s is the sampling period, and n is the sampling point number. If we let $2\pi f_0 T_s = 0.001\pi$ and if $f_0 = 31.25$ Hz, then $T_s = 16\,\mu s$. Each cycle of this sinusoidal signal should contain $T_0/T_s = 32\,ms/T_s = 2000$ samples ($T_0 = 1/f_0$). If we consider the DC offset, a `0x800` should be added into this equation, and therefore the resulting sinusoidal signal should be `fdata[idata]=0x7FF×sinf` `(0.001πxidata)+0x800`.

7. The `DAC_Write()` function is called in line 15 to write the `fdata` into the second channel of the DAC MCP4922 to generate a sinusoidal waveform on DAC1.

8. Then in line 16, the `ADC_Read()` function is called to read back the ADC result obtained from the ADC-TLC548.

9. The `DAC_Init()` function starts at line 19.

10. The related GPIO Ports B and D are enabled and clocked in line 21 since we need to use PB7 (SSI2Tx), PB4 (SSI2Clk), PB6 (SSI2Rx) to provide SSI2 controls, PD6 (CS_DAC) and PD3(CS_ADC) as chip select signals for DAC and ADC, and PB3∼PB0 to drive 4 LEDs to display the ADC results.

11. The SSI module 2 is enabled and clocked in line 22.

12. The codes in lines 23∼27 are used to configure GPIO Port B to enable three pins, PB7, PB4, and PB6, to work as an alternate function or as an SSI2 function pins to transfer SSI2-related control and data signals. Also make PB3∼PB0 as digital and output pins.

13. The codes in lines 29∼30 are used to configure GPIO Port D to enable PD6 and PD3 to work as digital and output pins.

14. In line 31, both PD6 and PD3 are set to High to deselect DAC and ADC.

15. The codes in lines 32∼36 are used to initialize and configure SSI2-related control registers to set up the correct operational mode for this module.

16. The function `DAC_Write()` starts at line 38.

17. A local integer variable `config` is declared in line 40, and this variable is used to reserve the correct configuration parameters used in MCP4922 DAC module.

18. In line 41, an `if()` selection structure is used to check which channel has been selected by the user to interface to this DAC. If the first channel DAC0 is selected, the 4 MSB configuration

parameters should be 0x7000 (see Table 8.15). If the second channel DAC1 is selected, the 4 MSB configuration parameters should be 0xF000 (Table 8.15) in line 42.

19. The PD6 is cleared to Low to select the DAC MCP4922 chip in line 43.

20. In line 44, the 12-bit transferred data value is ORed with 4 MSB configuration parameters obtained from lines 41 or 42 to get a 16-bit value since this is required by the DAC module MCP4922.

21. The code in lines 45 is used to transfer the 16-bit command-data to the MCP4922 via SSI2 Data register.

22. In line 46, a while() loop is used to wait for the BSY bit (bit 4) in the SSISR register to be clear, which means that the SSI2 has completed its current data transferring job.

23. The PD6 is set to High to deselect the MCP4922 chip in line 47 when the SSI2 completes the current data transfer processing.

24. The function ADC_Read() starts at line 49. A local integer variable adc is created in line 51 and this variable is used to hold the returned ADC result later.

25. The PD3 is reset to low in line 52 to select the ADC-TLC548 chip to begin the analog-to-digital conversion for the analog input coming from the output of the DAC-MCP4922.

26. In line 53, similarly a while() loop is used again to wait for the SSI2 data receiving done.

27. The received ADC result is sent to the local variable adc to be reserved in line 54.

28. This result is further sent to four LEDs via PB3~PB0 pins in line 55.

29. The PD7 is set to High to deselect the ADC TLC548 when this ADC is done in line 56.

Now let's set up the environment to build and run the project to test the desired functions.

8.3.7.4.4 Set Up the Environment to Build and Run the Project Perform the following operations to setup the environment for this project:

- Select the debug adapter Stellaris ICDI in the Debug tab under the Project-|Options for Target 'Target 1' menu item.

Now build the project by going to the Project|Build target menu item. If everything is fine, go to the Flash|Download item to download the image file of the project into the flash memory. Then go to the Debug|Start/Stop Debug Session and the Debug|Run item to run the project.

As the project runs, you can use an oscilloscope to monitor DAC0 and DAC1 via two pins, J11-1 and J11-2 on the J11 connector, to get two waveforms, the sawtooth and sinusoidal. The period may be different from our calculation values since this program repeatedly generates two waveforms in a while() loop and the period may be doubled. Also, you can find that the intensity and color on the three-color LED on the TM4C123GXL EVB are periodically changed based on the ADC result.

When using two probes to check two output signals with an oscilloscope, you can use channel 1 to monitor the DAC output and use channel 2 to check the ADC output. To get better results, you can comment out the sinusoidal signal to allow only the sawtooth to input to the ADC TLC548 and add a 10-ms time delay in the ADC_Read() subroutine. You cannot watch the input and output for the ADC since four LEDs cannot respond to high-frequency signals.

8.3.8 SSI API Functions Provided by TivaWare™ Peripheral Driver Library

In this section we will introduce another way to access and interface the SSI modules to perform desired synchronous serial communication tasks via SSI modules. In the TivaWare™ Peripheral Driver Library, there are more than 20 API functions used to interface to SSI modules. However, in this section, we concentrate on some most important and popular functions to illustrate how to use them to build sophisticated project to efficiently access and interface to SSI modules to fulfill desired serial data communication tasks.

These SSI API functions can be categorized into the following groups:

1. The initialization and configuration functions:
- SSIClockSourceSet()
- SSIClockSourceGet()
- SSIConfigSetExpClk()

2. The control and status functions:
- SSIEnable()
- SSIDisable()
- SSIBusy()

3. The data processing functions:
- SSIDataPut()
- SSIDataPutNonBlocking()
- SSIDataGet()

4. The interrupt source and processing functions:
- SSIIntRegister()
- SSIIntEnable()
- SSIIntDisable()
- SSIIntClear()
- SSIIntStatus()

These API functions are contained in the `driverlib/ssi.c` file and defined in the `driverlib/ssi.h` file. The `driverlib` folder is located at `C:\ti\TivaWare_C_Series-2.0.1.11577`.

Now let's have a quick introduction and discussion about these API functions based on their groups.

8.3.8.1 The SSI Module Initialization and Configuration Functions

Table 8.16 shows some popular and important SSI module initialization and configuration API functions. The API function `SSIConfigSetExpClk()` is a very important and useful function used to set up and configure the entire SSI module. Only after the SSI module is correctly configured by using this function, it can work properly to provide the normal functions. Some arguments used in this function are specified by using the system macros, such as `SSI_FRF_MOTO_MODE_0` and `SSI_MODE_MASTER`. These arguments must be used correctly to make the configurations correct.

Table 8.16. The SSI module initialization and configuration functions.

API Function	Parameter	Description
void SSIClockSourceSet(uint32_t ui32Base, uint32_t ui32Source)	ui32Base is the base address of the SSI port. ui32Source is the baud clock source for the SSI.	Select clock source for the SSI. The possible clock source are the system clock (SSI_CLOCK_SYSTEM) or the precision internal oscillator (SSI_CLOCK_PIOSC). Changing the baud clock source changes the data rate generated by the SSI. Therefore, the data rate should be reconfigured after any change to the SSI clock source.
uint32_t SSIClockSourceGet(uint32_t ui32Base)	ui32Base is the base address of the SSI port.	Return the data clock source for the specified SSI. The returned clock source is either SSI_CLOCK_SYSTEM or SSI_CLOCK_PIOSC.
void SSIConfigSetExpClk(uint32_t ui32Base, uint32_t ui32SSIClk, uint32_t ui32Protocol, uint32_t ui32Mode, uint32_t ui32BitRate, uint32_t ui32DataWidth)	ui32Base specifies the SSI module base address. ui32SSIClk is the rate of the clock supplied to the SSI. ui32Protocol specifies the data transfer protocol. ui32Mode specifies the mode of operation. ui32BitRate specifies the clock rate. ui32DataWidth specifies number of bits transferred per frame	Configure the synchronous serial interface. It sets the SSI protocol, mode of operation, bit rate, and data width. The ui32Protocol parameter can be one of the following values: SSI_FRF_MOTO_MODE_0, SSI_FRF_MOTO_MODE_1, SSI_FRF_MOTO_MODE_2, SSI_FRF_MOTO_MODE_3, SSI_FRF_TI, or SSI_FRF_NMW. The ui32Mode parameter defines the operating mode of the SSI. The SSI module can operate as a master or slave; if it is a slave, the SSI can be configured to disable output on its serial output line. The ui32Mode parameter can be one of the following values: SSI_MODE_MASTER, SSI_MODE_SLAVE, or SSI_MODE_SLAVE_OD. The ui32BitRate parameter defines the bit rate for the SSI. This bit rate must satisfy the following clock ratio criteria: FSSI >= 2 × bit rate (master mode); this speed < 25 MHz. FSSI >= 12 × bit rate or 6 × bit rate (slave modes), depending on the capability of the specific microcontroller. The ui32DataWidth parameter defines the width of the data transfers and can be a value between 4 and 16.

8.3.8.2 The SSI Module Control and Status Functions

Table 8.17 shows some popular and important SSI module control and status API functions.

Three API functions are involved in this group, SSIEnable(), SSIDisable(), and SSIBusy(). The first two functions are used to control the availability of the SSI modules, and the third function is used to check the working status of the SSI modules.

Table 8.17. The SSI module control and status functions.

API Function	Parameter	Description
void SSIEnable(uint32_t ui32Base)	ui32Base specifies the SSI module base address.	Enable operation of the synchronous serial interface. The synchronous serial interface must be configured before it is enabled.
void SSIDisable(uint32_t ui32Base)	ui32Base is the base address of the SSI port.	Disable operation of the synchronous serial interface.
bool SSIBusy(uint32_t ui32Base)	ui32Base specifies the SSI module base address.	Allow the caller to determine whether all transmitted bytes have cleared the transmitter hardware. If false is returned, then the transmit FIFO is empty and all bits of the last transmitted word have left the hardware shift register.

Table 8.18. The SSI module data processing functions.

API Function	Parameter	Description
void SSIDataPut(uint32_t ui32Base, uint32_t ui32Data)	ui32Base specifies the SSI module base address. ui32Data is the data to be transmitted over the SSI.	Place the data into the transmit FIFO of the specified SSI. If there is no space available in the transmit FIFO, this function waits until there is space available before returning. The upper 32−N bits of ui32Data are discarded by the hardware, where N is the data width as configured by SSIConfigSetExpClk(). If the SSI is configured for 8-bit data width, the upper 24 bits of ui32Data are discarded.
int32_t SSIDataPutNonBlocking(uint32_t ui32Base, uint32_t ui32Data)	ui32Base specifies the SSI module base address. ui32Data is the data to be transmitted over the SSI.	Place the data into the transmit FIFO of the specified SSI module. If there is no space in the FIFO, then this function returns a zero.
void SSIDataGet(uint32_t ui32Base, uint32_t *pui32Data)	ui32Base specifies the SSI module base address. pui32Data is a pointer to a storage location for data that was received over the SSI.	Get received data from the receive FIFO of the specified SSI and place it into the location specified by the pui32Data parameter. If there is no data available, this function waits until data is received before returning. Only the lower N bits of the value written to pui32Data contain valid data, where N is the data width as configured by SSIConfigSetExpClk().

All SSI modules must be initialized and configured to the proper working mode before they can be used to transfer and receive any serial data. However, those initializations and configurations must be performed when the SSI modules are disabled. This means that no initialization and configuration job can be performed if the SSI has been enabled.

The SSIBusy() function can return a Boolean value to indicate whether the SSI is busy or idle. A returned True means that the SSI module is busy in working, and False indicates that the SSI module is idle and any new data can be sent to it to begin a new transfer.

8.3.8.3 The SSI Module Data Processing Functions

Table 8.18 shows some popular and important SSI module data processing API functions.

The SSIDataPut() and SSIDataPutNonBlocking() functions have the similar function, and both of them is used to place the transferring data into the transmit FIFO of the specified SSI module. However, the SSIDataPut() will keep waiting and place the data until a space in the transmit FIFO is available. The SSIDataPutNon-Blocking() never wait if no space is available in the transmit FIFO and directly returns a zero.

Similar situation is true to the SSIDataGet() and SSIDataGetNonBlocking() functions.

For both SSIDataPut() and SSIDataPutNonBlocking() functions, the upper 32-N bits data are ignored and only the lower N bits data are transmitted to the transmit FIFO. This N is the data width defined in the SSIConfigSetExpClk() function. Similarly, only the lower N bits data are considered as valid data items when using the SSIDataGet() and SSIDataGetNonBlocking() functions to receive data from the specified receive FIFO.

Table 8.19. The SSI module interrupt processing functions.

API Function	Parameter	Description
void SSIIntRegister(uint32_t ui32Base, void (*pfnHandler)(void))	ui32Base specifies the SSI module base address. pfnHandler is a pointer to the function to be called when a synchronous serial interface interrupt occurs.	Register the handler to be called when an SSI interrupt occurs. This function enables the global interrupt in the interrupt controller; specific SSI interrupts must be enabled via SSIIntEnable(). It is the interrupt handler responsibility to clear the interrupt source via SSIIntClear().
void SSIIntEnable(uint32_t ui32Base, uint32_t ui32IntFlags)	ui32Base specifies the SSI module base address. ui32IntFlags is a bit mask of the interrupt sources to be enabled.	Enable the indicated SSI interrupt sources. Only the sources that are enabled can be reflected to the processor interrupt; disabled sources have no effect on the processor. The ui32IntFlags parameter can be any of the SSI_TXFF, SSI_RXFF, SSI_RXTO, or SSI_RXOR values.
void SSIIntDisable(uint32_t ui32Base, uint32_t ui32IntFlags)	ui32Base specifies the SSI module base address. ui32IntFlags is a bit mask of the interrupt sources to be disabled.	Disable the indicated SSI interrupt sources. The ui32IntFlags parameter can be any of the SSI_TXFF, SSI_RXFF, SSI_RXTO, or SSI_RXOR values.
void SSIIntClear(uint32_t ui32Base, uint32_t ui32IntFlags)	ui32Base specifies the SSI module base address. ui32IntFlags is a bit mask of the interrupt sources to be cleared.	Clear the specified SSI interrupt sources so that they no longer assert. This function must be called in the interrupt handler to keep the interrupts from being triggered again immediately upon exit. The ui32IntFlags parameter can consist of either or both the SSI_RXTO and SSI_RXOR.
uint32_t SSIIntStatus(uint32_t ui32Base, bool bMasked)	ui32Base specifies the SSI module base address. bMasked is false if the raw interrupt status is required or true if the masked interrupt status is required.	Return the interrupt status for the SSI module. Either the raw interrupt status or the status of interrupts that are allowed to reflect to the processor can be returned.

8.3.8.4 *The SSI Module Interrupt Source and Processing Functions*

Table 8.19 shows some popular and important SSI module interrupt processing API functions.

Before any interrupt can be handled and responded to by the selected SSI module, the API function SSIIntRegister() must be executed to register the related interrupt handler to respond to the interrupt if it occurs. The second argument of this function is a pointer point to the handler subroutine or an entry address of the ISR.

The argument ui32IntFlags for the SSIIntEnable(), SSIIntDisable() and SSIIntClear() API functions is a bit mask for the selected interrupt sources. A corresponding bit value of 1 indicates that the related interrupt source is selected, otherwise if a bit is 0, the related interrupt source is not included. Some system macros should be used for those interrupt sources.

For the SSIIntStatus() function, the second argument bMasked is a Boolean variable. When it is True, it indicates that the masked interrupt status is required and returned. However, if this value is False, only the raw interrupt status is needed and returned.

Now let's use an example project to illustrate how to use these API functions to build a project to access and interface some serial peripherals via the SSI modules.

8.3.8.5 *Build an Example Project to Interface Serial Peripherals Using the SSI Module*

In this section we use the SSI-related API functions to build an interfacing project to access and display desired letters and numbers on the LCD device. We can modify the project DRALCD project we built in Section 8.3.5.4 and use the related API functions to replace direct register access methods to access and interface LCD controller SPLC780 via 74VHCT595.

8.3.8.5.1 Create a New Software Driver Model Project SDLCD
Perform the following operations to create a new project SDLCD:

1. Open the Windows Explorer window to create a new folder named SDLCD under the C:\ARM Class Projects\Chapter 8 folder.

2. Open the Keil® ARM-MDK μVersion5 and go to Project|New μVersion Project menu item to create a new μVersion Project. On the opened wizard, browse to our new folder SDLCD that is created in step 1 above. Enter SDLCD into the **File name** box and click on the **Save** button to create this project.

3. On the next wizard, you need to select the device (MCU) for this project. Expand three icons, Texas Instruments, Tiva C Series, and TM4C123x Series, and select the target device TM4C123GH6PM from the list by clicking on it. Click on the **OK** to close this wizard.

4. Next the Software Components wizard is opened, and you need to set up the software development environment for your project with this wizard. Expand two icons, CMSIS and Device, and check the CORE and Startup checkboxes in the **Sel.** column, and click on the **OK** button since we need these two components to build our project.

Since this project is a little longer, therefore a header file and a C source file are needed.

8.3.8.5.2 Create the Header File SDLCD.h
Create a new header file named SDLCD.h and enter the codes shown in Figure 8.40 into this file. Since the codes are easy and straightforward, no explanation is needed. The six additional header files are system header files used to define the protocols of related API functions to be used in this project. Two macros, GPIO_PB7_SSI2TX and GPIO_PB4_SSI2CLK, are used to define two special pins PB7 and PB4 to enable them to work as SSI2 function pins, not GPIO pins.

8.3.8.5.3 Create the C Source File SDLCD.c
Create a new C file named SDLCD.c and enter the codes shown in Figure 8.41 into this C file.

In this project, we want to display "WELCOME TO JCSU" in the first line on the LCD and display "GOOD JOB" in the center of the second line on the LCD. Therefore the function LCD_Comd(0xC4) is used to select the position or address of the DDRAM for the first letter in the second line to make the second line's letters located at the center. Refer to Figure 8.30 to get more details about this start position or the address of the DDRAM and this function.

Now let's have a closer look at this piece of codes to see how it works. For those codes that are duplicated from the project DRALCD.c, we will skip them and only pay attention to those new added API functions.

1. The LCD_Init() function is called in line 7 to initialize and configure the LCD controller to make it ready to interface and control the LCD panel.

```
1    //***********************************************************************************************************
2    // SDLCD.h - Header File for the Main Application File SDLCD.c
3    //***********************************************************************************************************
4    #include <stdint.h>
5    #include <stdbool.h>
6    #include "inc/hw_memmap.h"
7    #include "inc/hw_ssi.h"
8    #include "inc/hw_types.h"
9    #include "driverlib/ssi.h"
10   #include "driverlib/gpio.h"
11   #include "driverlib/sysctl.h"

12   #define  RS 1                                    // Q0 bit for RS (Reg Select)
13   #define  EN 2                                    // Q1 bit for E (Enable LCD)
14   #define  BL 4                                    // Q2 bit for BL (Backlight)
15   #define  GPIO_PB7_SSI2TX      0x00011C02
16   #define  GPIO_PB4_SSI2CLK     0x00011002

17   void delay_ms(int  time);
18   void delay_us(int  time);
19   void LCD_cd_Write(char data, unsigned char control);
20   void LCD_Comd(unsigned char  cmd);
21   void LCD_Data(char  data);
22   void LCD_Init(void);
23   void SSI2_Write(unsigned char  data);
```

Figure 8.40.   The codes for the header file SDLCD.h.

2. In line 8, the LCD_Comd(1) is executed to clear the LCD panel and move the cursor to the home position on the LCD.

3. The codes in lines 9~15 are used to set up and send desired letters to the LCD.

4. The codes in lines 19~21 are used to enable and set the clock for the related GPIO Ports and SSI2 module. The API function SysCtlPeripheralEnable() is a popular function used to enable and set clock for any peripheral, including the GPIO and SSI.

5. In line 22, the API function GPIOPinTypeSSI() is called to set up the GPIO pins as the SSI function pins. This function only defined the operational type for the selected pins but not configure any of them. Usually, this function must be combined with another API function GPIOPinConfigure() together to configure a GPIO pin, as we did in lines 23 and 24. Both PB7 (SSI2TX) and PB4 (SSI2CLK) are defined and configured in these lines. The argument for the GPIOPinConfigure() function must be related macro, such as GPIO_PB7_SSI2TX and GPIO_PB7_SSI2TX, which are defined in the pin_map. h header file.

6. Since PC6 is used as the CS_LCD control signal to provide a positive-going-edge triggering signal for the 74VHCT595, the API function GPIOPinTypeGPIOOutput() is used to define PC6 as an output pin in line 25.

7. In line 26, the API function GPIOPinWrite() is used to set PC6 to High when it is idle.

8. The codes in lines 27~30 are used to configure SSI module 2 via related API functions. First the SSI2 is disabled by using the function SSIDisable() in line 27 since no configuration can be performed until the SSI module is disabled.

9. In line 28, the API function SSIConfigSetExpClk() is used to configure and set up operational parameters for the SSI2 module. The fifth parameter, bit rate for the SSI2Clk, is defined as 1 MHz with 1000000. The unit for this parameter is Hz.

10. After the configuration, the SSI2 module is enabled in line 30 using the SSIEnable().

```
1    //*******************************************************************************************************************
2    // SDLCD.c - Main Application File for LCD Project
3    //*******************************************************************************************************************
4    #include "SDLCD.H"
5    int main(void)
6    {
7       LCD_Init();                              // initialize LCD controller
8       LCD_Comd(1);                             // clear screen, move cursor to home
9       // Write "WELCOME TO JCSU!" on the 1st line, and "GOOD JOB" in the center of the 2nd line in LCD
10      LCD_Data('W'); LCD_Data('E'); LCD_Data('L'); LCD_Data('C'); LCD_Data('O');
11      LCD_Data('M'); LCD_Data('E'); LCD_Data(' '); LCD_Data('T'); LCD_Data('O');
12      LCD_Data(' '); LCD_Data('J'); LCD_Data('C'); LCD_Data('S'); LCD_Data('U'); ;LCD_Data('!');
13      LCD_Comd(0xC4);
14      LCD_Data('G'); LCD_Data('O'); LCD_Data('O'); LCD_Data('D'); LCD_Data(' ');
15      LCD_Data('J'); LCD_Data('O'); LCD_Data('B');
16   }
17   void LCD_Init(void)
18   {
19      SysCtlPeripheralEnable(SYSCTL_PERIPH_GPIOB);
20      SysCtlPeripheralEnable(SYSCTL_PERIPH_GPIOC);
21      SysCtlPeripheralEnable(SYSCTL_PERIPH_SSI2);

22      GPIOPinTypeSSI(GPIO_PORTB_BASE, GPIO_PIN_7|GPIO_PIN_4);
23      GPIOPinConfigure(GPIO_PB7_SSI2TX);
24      GPIOPinConfigure(GPIO_PB4_SSI2CLK);
25      GPIOPinTypeGPIOOutput(GPIO_PORTC_BASE, GPIO_PIN_6);
26      GPIOPinWrite(GPIO_PORTC_BASE, GPIO_PIN_6, 0xFF);

27      SSIDisable(SSI2_BASE);
28      SSIConfigSetExpClk(SSI2_BASE, SysCtlClockGet(), SSI_FRF_MOTO_MODE_0,
29                                      SSI_MODE_MASTER, 1000000, 8);
30      SSIEnable(SSI2_BASE);

31      delay_ms(20);                            // LCD controller reset sequence
32      LCD_cd_Write(0x30, 0);                   // send reset code 1 two times to SPLC780
33      LCD_cd_Write(0x30, 0);
34      LCD_cd_Write(0x30, 0);                   // send reset code 2 to SPLC780

35      LCD_cd_Write(0x20, 0);                   // use 4-bit data mode
36      delay_ms(1);
37      LCD_Comd(0x28);                          // set 4-bit data, 2-line, 5x7 font
38      LCD_Comd(0x06);                          // move cursor right
39      LCD_Comd(0x0C);                          // turn on display, cursor off - no blinking
40      LCD_Comd(0x01);                          // clear screen, move cursor to home
41   }
42   void LCD_cd_Write(char data, unsigned char control)
43   {
44      data &= 0xF0;                            // clear lower nibble for data
45      control &= 0x0F;                         // clear upper nibble for control
46      SSI2_Write(data | control | BL);         // RS = 0, R/W = 0
47      SSI2_Write(data | control | EN | BL);    // pulse E
48      SSI2_Write(data | BL);
49      SSI2_Write(BL);
50   }
51   void SSI2_Write(unsigned char data)
52   {
53      GPIOPinWrite(GPIO_PORTC_BASE, GPIO_PIN_6, 0xBF);   // output a Low on PC6 for STCP
54      SSIDataPut(SSI2_BASE, data);                        // transmit data into FIFO
55      while(SSIBusy(SSI2_BASE)) {};                       // wait for transmit done
56      GPIOPinWrite(GPIO_PORTC_BASE, GPIO_PIN_6, 0xFF);   // output a High on PC6 for STCP
57   }
```

Figure 8.41.   The source codes for the project SDLCD.

11. The following codes between lines 31 and 40 are duplicated with those codes in the project DRALCD. Refer to that part to get details for these codes.

12. The codes for the subroutine `LCD_cd_Write()` are also duplicated.

13. The codes for the subroutine `SSI2_Write()` are totally new. First in line 53, the API function `GPIOPinWrite()` is called to reset the CS_LCD (PC6) signal to Low to prepare a Low-to-High (positive-going-edge) signal to the STCP on the serial shift register 74VHCT595.

14. In line 54, the API function `SSIDataPut()` is used to send data item to the transmit FIFO.

15. Then a `while()` loop is used to wait for the data sent to the transmit FIFO to be transmitted in line 55. The API function `SSIBusy()` works as the loop condition for this `while()` loop, and the subroutine will not continue to execute the next instruction until this loop condition becomes `False`, which means that the SSI2 has completed this data transmission and a `False` is returned from the function `SSIBusy()`.

16. In line 56, the function `GPIOPinWrite()` is executed to set the CS_LCD (PC6) to High to create a positive-going-edge signal to trigger the 74VHCT595 to start a serial-to-parallel data conversion and output the conversion result to the LCD controller SPLC780.

The rest codes are identical with those codes in the project DRALCD.

We leave some projects as home works for the readers, and you can modify projects, such as DRAADC and DRALED, by using the API functions to rebuild those projects. These projects are included in `Lab8_3` and `Lab8_4`, respectively.

8.4 INTER-INTEGRATED CIRCUIT (I2C) INTERFACE

The Inter-Integrated Circuit (I2C) module is exactly a serial communication bus system to enable I2C devices or peripherals to perform high-speed and bi-directional data transfer via two wire designs, a serial data line SDA, and a serial clock line SCL. By using this bus system, the microcontroller and other I2C compatible devices can interface to external I2C devices such as serial memory (RAMs and ROMs), networking devices, LCDs, tone generators, external clocks, and so on. The I2C bus may also be used for system testing and diagnostic purposes in product development and manufacturing. The TM4C123GH6PM microcontrollers include and provide the ability to communicate (both transmit and receive) with other I2C devices on the bus.

In the TM4C123GH6PM MCU system, four (4) I2C modules (`I2C0~I2C3`) are provided to support the I2C-related data operations. Each I2C module can work as a master or slave to perform data transmit or receive operation via a two-wire bus.

The I2C master and slave modules provide the ability to communicate to other I2C devices over an I2C bus. The I2C bus is specified to support devices that can both transmit and receive (write and read) data. Also, devices on the I2C bus can be designated as either a master or a slave. The Tiva™ I2C modules support both sending and receiving data as either a master or a slave and also support the simultaneous operation as both a master and a slave. Finally, the Tiva™ I2C modules can operate at four speeds: Standard (100 kbps), Fast (400 kbps), Fast-Mode Plus (1 Mbps), and High-Speed (3.33 Mbps).

Both the master and slave I2C modules can generate interrupts. The I2C master module generates interrupts when a transmit or a receive operation is completed or aborted due to an error; this also occurs on some devices when a clock low timeout has occurred. The I2C slave module generates interrupts when data has been sent or requested by a master; this also occurs on some devices when a START or STOP condition is present.

8.4.1 I2C Module Bus Configuration and Operational Status

Each I2C module is composed of both master and slave units and can be identified by a unique address. A master-initiated communication generates the clock signal, SCL. For proper operation, the SDA pin must be configured as an open-drain signal. Due to the internal circuitry that supports high-speed operation, the SCL pin must not be configured as an open-drain signal. Both SDA and SCL signals must be connected to a positive power supply voltage using a pull-up resistor. When both wires are in this status, it is called that the bus is idle. A typical I2C bus configuration is shown in Figure 8.42.

As we mentioned, the I2C bus uses only two wires, SDA and SCL, named I2CSDA and I2CSCL to perform bi-directional data communications on TM4C123GH6PM microcontrollers. SDA is the bi-directional serial data line and SCL is the bi-directional serial clock line. The bus is considered idle when both lines are High.

Every transaction on the I2C bus is nine (9) bits long, consisting of eight data bits and a single acknowledge bit. The number of bytes per transfer which is defined as the time period between a valid START and STOP condition, is unrestricted, but each data byte has to be followed by an acknowledge bit, and data must be transferred MSB first.

The START and STOP are two conditions or two states defined in the protocol of the I2C module. A High-to-Low transition on the SDA line while the SCL is High is defined as a START condition, and a Low-to-High transition on the SDA line while SCL is High is defined as a STOP condition. The bus is considered busy after a START condition and free after a STOP condition. Figure 8.43 shows an illustration for both START and STOP conditions.

Usually, the data on the SDA line must be stable during the High period of the SCL line, and can only be changed during the Low period of the SCL line. In this way, the START and STOP state can be clearly distinguished with the normal data signals on the SDA line.

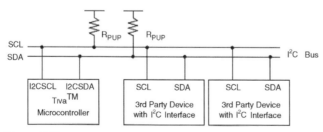

Figure 8.42. The I2C bus configuration and status. (Reprinted with the permission of the Texas Instruments Incorporated.)

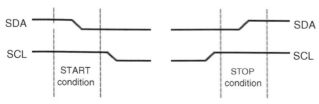

Figure 8.43. The definition of START and STOP conditions. (Reprinted with the permission of the Texas Instruments Incorporated.)

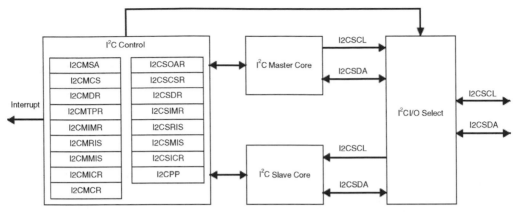

Figure 8.44. The functional block diagram of each I2C module. (Reprinted with the permission of the Texas Instruments Incorporated.)

The STOP bit determines if the cycle stops at the end of the data cycle or continues on to a repeated START condition. When a data communication operation is completed or aborted due an error, the interrupt pin becomes active and the data may be read from the I2C Master Data Register (I2CMDR).

8.4.2 I2C Module Architecture and Functional Block Diagram

A functional block diagram of each I2C module is shown in Figure 8.44.

It can be found from Figure 8.44 that each I2C module contains two cores; the I2C Master Core and the I2C Slave Core. Each core controls and coordinates the data transmit and receive operations via related registers. All I2C control registers are divided into two groups: the master and the slave group with I2CM and I2CS as prefix for each group. Some important and popular registers are listed in Table 8.20.

Each of these registers are 32-bit registers, however some registers only used limited number of bits to perform their functions.

Table 8.20. Most popular and important I2C registers.

Master Control Register		Slave Control Register	
Register Name	**Function**	**Register Name**	**Function**
I2C Master Slave Address Register (I2CMSA)	Hold the master and target slave address.	I2C Slave Own Address Register (I2CSOAR)	Hold the slave address.
I2C Master Control/Status Register (I2CMCS)	Hold the master control and status.	I2C Slave Control/Status Register (I2CSCSR)	Hold the slave control and status.
I2C Master Data Register (I2CMDR)	Hold the master data.	I2C Slave Data Register (I2CSDR)	Hold the slave data.
I2C Master Configuration Register (I2CMCR)	Configure the operational mode.	I2C Slave ACK Control Register (I2CSACKCTL)	Control the ACK or NACK signal for the slave device.

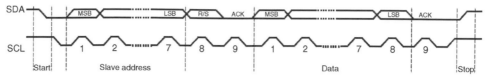

Figure 8.45.   The I2C data transfer format and frame. (Reprinted with the permission of the Texas Instruments Incorporated.)

8.4.3 I2C Module Data Transfer Format and Frame

In the I2C module, the data transfers follow the format shown in Figure 8.45. After the START condition, a slave address is first transmitted. This address is 7 bits long followed by an R/S bit, which is a data direction bit in the I2CMSA register. If the R/S bit is 0, it indicates a sending or a transmit operation. If it is 1, it indicates a receiving or a request for data.

A data transfer is always terminated by a STOP condition generated by the master, however, a master can initiate communications with another device on the bus by generating a repeated START condition and addressing another slave without first generating a STOP condition. Various combinations of receive/transmit formats are then possible within a single transfer.

The first seven bits of the first byte make up the slave address. The eighth bit determines the direction of the message. The ninth bit is the ACK bit that is generated by the master. When the I2C module operates in Master receiver mode, the ACK bit is normally set, causing the I2C bus controller to transmit an acknowledge automatically after each byte. This bit must be cleared when the I2C bus controller requires no further data to be transmitted from the slave transmitter.

Both a slave address and the following data must be transferred starting with the MSB and each piece of address or each data must be composed of nine bits.

All bus transactions have a required acknowledge clock cycle that is generated by the master. During the acknowledge (ACK) cycle, the transmitter that can be the master or slave releases the SDA line as shown in Figure 8.45. To acknowledge the transaction, the receiver must pull down SDA during the acknowledge clock cycle.

8.4.4 I2C Module Operational Sequence

The I2C module can work as either a master or a slave with data transmitting and receiving mode. The master data transmission and receiving operations are controlled by the I2C master group registers, and the slave data transmission and receiving operations are controlled by the I2C slave group registers.

The operational sequences for each different mode are listed below.

8.4.4.1 I2C Module Works in the Master Transmit Mode

1. When the I2C module works in the master transmit mode, the ACK signal is generated by the master and attached at the end of each transmitted data.

2. The target slave address is first sent after the STRAT condition by writing it into the I2CMSA. Then the transmitted data is written into the I2CMDR and the I2CMCS register is checked to wait for the ACK and the bus to be idle.

3. A 0x3 (H:ACK:STOP:START:RUN = 0X011) is written to the I2CMCS to inform the slave that a data transmission starts. The X means that either 0 or 1 is ok, the STOP is 0 means that this is a multiple bytes data transfer and cannot stop right now.

4. Check the I2CMCS status for the ACK and wait the bus to be idle.

5. Write the next data into the I2CMDR to prepare to transmit the next data.

6. Check if the last data has been transmitted. If not, write 0X001 to the I2CMCS to continue to send the next data.

7. If the last data is encountered, write 0X101 to the I2CMCS to transmit the STOP status to inform the slave that the transmission is done.

8. Check the I2CMCS for the ACK signal and wait for the bus to be idle.

9. The transfer is done and the bus goes to idle status.

From this operation sequence, it can be found that the I2CMCS register is a dual-function register; when reading, it provides the working status of the slave, when writing, it setups the operational function for the master.

Figure 8.46 shows the operational sequence for the I2C master working as a transmitter.

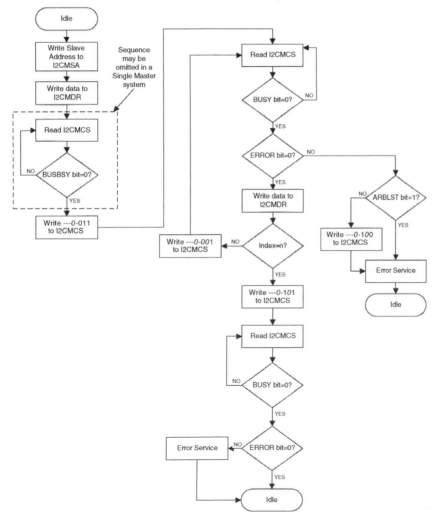

Figure 8.46.   The operational sequence of the master working in the transmit mode. (Reprinted with the permission of the Texas Instruments Incorporated.)

8.4.4.2 I2C Module Works in the Master Receive Mode

1. When the I2C module operates in Master receiver mode, the ACK bit is normally set causing the I2C bus controller to transmit an acknowledge automatically after each byte. This bit must be cleared when the I2C bus controller requires no further data to be transmitted from the slave transmitter.

2. Write the target slave address to the I2CMSA register to transmit it via the bus.

3. The I2CMCS register is checked to wait for the ACK and the bus to be idle.

4. Write 0xB (H:ACK:STOP:START:RUN = 01011) to I2CMCS register to start the data receiving.

5. Check the I2CMCS status for the ACK and wait the bus to be idle.

6. When the ACK is obtained and the data is received, read the data from the I2CMDR.

7. Check if the last data has been received. If not, write 01001 (0x9) to the I2CMCS to continue to receive the next data.

8. If the last data is coming, write 00101 (0x5) to the I2CMCS to inform the slave that the data receiving is done.

9. Check the I2CMCS for the ACK signal and wait for the bus to be idle.

10. Read the last data from the I2CMDR.

The complete operational sequence of the master working in the receiving mode is shown in Figure 8.47.

For these master transmit and receive modes, the error processing is not covered; this includes the error identification and error services.

8.4.4.3 I2C Module Works in the Slave Transmit and Receive Modes

When operating in the slave mode, the STARTRIS and STOPRIS bits in the I2C Slave Raw Interrupt Status (I2CSRIS) register indicate detection of start and stop conditions on the bus, and the I2C Slave Masked Interrupt Status (I2CSMIS) register can be configured to allow STARTRIS and STOPRIS to be promoted to controller interrupts when interrupts are enabled.

When a receiver cannot receive another complete byte, it can hold the clock line SCL Low and force the transmitter into a wait state. The data transfer continues when the receiver releases the clock SCL.

The operational sequence of the I2C module working in the slave mode is shown in Figure 8.48. The operational sequence is as follows:

1. Write the slave address into the I2CSOAR to indicate that this is a slave device.

2. Write 0x1 to the I2CSCSR to enable the I2C to work as a slave I2C device.

3. Check the I2CSCSR to identify the operational mode for this slave. If RREQ bit in this register is 1, this means that the slave is working in the receive mode and waiting for the data to be transmitted from the master.

4. Also check the FBR bit in the I2CSCSR to confirm that the first byte following the slave's own address has been received.

5. Then the received data in the I2CSDR is read out by the slave device. The slave continues for the next data receiving process until all data received and a STOP status is received from the master by checking the STOPRIS bits in the I2C Slave Raw Interrupt Status (I2CSRIS) register.

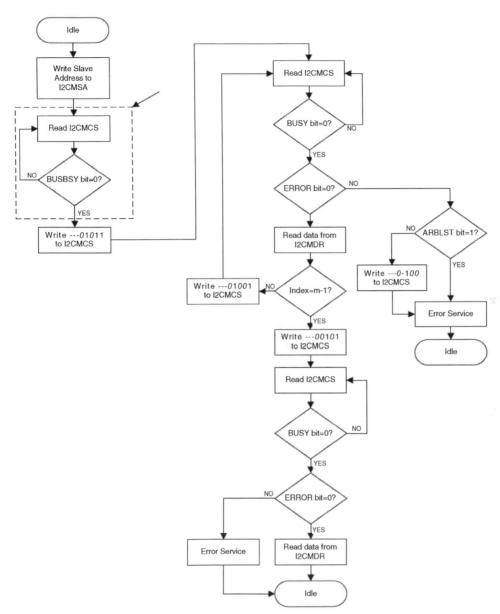

Figure 8.47. The operational sequence of the master working in the receive mode. (Reprinted with the permission of the Texas Instruments Incorporated.)

6. If the RREQ bit is 0, the slave continues to check the TREQ bit in the I2CSCSR to confirm whether the slave is working in the transmit mode. If the TREQ bit is 1, it indicates that the slave is working in the data transmit mode. The salve writes the data to be transmitted into the I2CSDR to send it out.

7. Then the slave device continues this data transmit until a STOP status is received from the master by checking the STOPRIS bits in the I2C Slave Raw Interrupt Status (I2CSRIS) register.

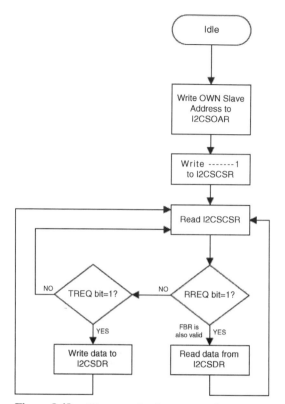

Figure 8.48. The operational sequence of the I2C module working in the slave mode. (Reprinted with the permission of the Texas Instruments Incorporated.)

Now we have a clear picture about the I2C operational sequence. Next let's have a closer look at the I2C major components.

8.4.5 I2C Module Major Operational Components and Control Signals

The following operational components are mainly implemented in the I2C module operations:

Acknowledge. All bus transactions have a required acknowledge clock cycle that is generated by the master. During the acknowledge cycle, the transmitter (either master or slave) releases the SDA line. To acknowledge the transaction, the receiver must pull down SDA during the acknowledge clock cycle.

When a slave receiver does not acknowledge the slave address, SDA must be left High by the slave so that the master can generate a STOP condition and abort the current transfer. If the master device is acting as a receiver during a transfer, it is responsible for acknowledging each transfer made by the slave. Because the master controls the number of bytes in the transfer, it signals the end of data to the slave transmitter by not generating an ACK on the last data byte. The slave transmitter must then release SDA to allow the master to generate the STOP or a repeated START condition.

If the slave is required to provide a manual ACK or NACK, the I2C Slave ACK Control (I2CSACKCTL) register allows the slave to NACK for invalid data or command or ACK for valid data or command. When this operation is enabled, the MCU slave module I2C clock is pulled low after the last data bit until this register is written with the indicated response.

Repeated Start. The I2C master module has the capability to execute a repeated START (transmit or receive) after an initial transfer has occurred. This means that after a data has been transmitted, the master does not generate a STOP condition but instead writes another slave address to the I2CMSA register and then writes 0x3 to initiate the repeated START.

Clock Low Timeout (CLTO). The I2C slave sometimes can extend the transaction by pulling the clock low periodically to create a slow bit transfer rate. The I2C module has a 12-bit programmable counter that is used to track how long the clock has been held low. The upper 8 bits of the count value are software programmable through the I2C Master Clock Low Time-out Count (I2CMCLKOCNT) register. The lower four bits are 0x0 and are not user visible. The CNTL value programmed in the I2CMCLKOCNT register has to be greater than 0x01. The application can program the eight most significant bits of the counter to reflect the acceptable cumulative low period in transaction. The count is loaded at the START condition and counts down on each falling edge of the internal bus clock of the master. Note that the internal bus clock generated for this counter keeps running at the programmed I2C speed even if SCL is held low on the bus. Upon reaching terminal count, the master forces ABORT on the bus by issuing a STOP condition at the instance of SCL and SDA release.

As an example, if an I2C module was operating at 100 kHz speed, programming the register I2CMCLKOCNT to 0xDA would translate to the value 0xDA0 since the lower four bits are 0x0. This would translate to a decimal value of 3488 clocks or a cumulative clock low period of 34.88 ms at 100 kHz.

The CLKRIS bit in the I2C Master Raw Interrupt Status (I2CMRIS) register is set when the clock timeout period is reached to allow the master to start corrective action to resolve the remote slave state. In addition, the CLKTO bit in the I2C Master Control/Status (I2CMCS) register is set; this bit is cleared when a STOP condition is sent or during the I2C master reset. The status of the raw SDA and SCL signals are readable by software through the SDA and SCL bits in the I2C Master Bus Monitor (I2CMBMON) register to help determine the state of the remote slave.

In the event of a CLTO condition, application software must choose a way to try to recover it. Most applications may attempt to manually toggle the I2C pins to force the slave to let go of the clock signal (a common solution is to attempt to force a STOP on the bus).

Dual Address. The I2C interface supports dual address capability for the slave. The additional programmable address is provided and can be matched if enabled. In dual address mode, the I2C slave provides an ACK on the bus if either the OAR field in the I2CSOAR register or the OAR2 field in the I2CSOAR2 register is matched. The enable for dual address is programmable through the OAR2EN bit in the I2CSOAR2 register and there is no disable on the legacy address.

The OAR2SEL bit in the I2CSCSR register indicates if the address that was ACKed is the alternate address or not. When this bit is clear, it indicates either legacy operation or no address match.

Arbitration. A master may start a transfer only if the bus is idle. It is possible for two or more masters to generate a START condition within minimum hold time of the START condition. In these situations, an arbitration scheme takes place on the SDA line while SCL is High. During arbitration, the first of the competing master devices places a 1 (High) on SDA, while another master transmits a 0 (Low), switches off its data output stage and retires until the bus is idle again.

Arbitration can take place over several bits. Its first stage is a comparison of address bits, and if both masters are trying to address the same device, arbitration continues on to the comparison of data bits.

Glitch Suppression in Multi-Master Configuration. When a multi-master configuration is used, the GFE bit in the I2C Master Configuration Register (I2CMCR) can be set to enable glitch suppression on the SCL and SDA lines to assure proper signal values. The filter can be programmed to different filter widths using the GFPW bit in the I2C Master Configuration Register 2 (I2CMCR2). The glitch suppression value is based on the buffered system clocks. Note that all signals will be delayed internally when glitch suppression is applied. For example, if GFPW is set to 0x7, 31 clocks should be added onto the calculation for the expected transaction time.

8.4.6 I2C Module Running Speeds (Clock Rates) and Interrupts

As we mentioned in the introduction section, four I2C modules can operate at four speeds: Standard (100 kbps), Fast (400 kbps), Fast-Mode Plus (1 Mbps), and High Speed (3.33 Mbps). These speeds can be selected by using the I2C Master Timer Period (I2CMTPR) register.

The I2C clock rate is determined by four parameters: CLK_PRD, TIMER_PRD, SCL_LP, and SCL_HP. The definitions for these parameters are as follows:

- CLK_PRD is the system clock period.
- SCL_LP is the low period of SCL (fixed at 6).
- SCL_HP is the high period of SCL (fixed at 4).
- TIMER_PRD is a programmed value in the I2CMTPR register. This value is determined by using the equation below and solving for TIMER_PRD.

The I2C clock period is calculated as follows:

$$SCL\_PERIOD = 2 \times (1 + TIMER\_PRD) \times (SCL\_LP + SCL\_HP) \times CLK\_PRD$$

For example, if CLK_PRD = 50 ns, TIMER_PRD = 1, SCL_LP = 6, and SCL_HP = 4. This yields a SCL period as 2000 ns = 2 μs with a frequency of 1/SCL_PERIOD = 500 kHz.

Table 8.21 shows some examples of the timer periods (TIMER_PRD) that should be used to generate Standard, Fast mode, and Fast mode plus SCL frequencies for various system clocks.

Table 8.21. Examples of I2C master timer period versus speed mode.

System Clock	Period	Standard Mode	Period	Fast Mode	Period	Fast mode Plus
4 MHz	0x01	100 Kbps	—	—	—	—
6 MHz	0x02	100 Kbps	—	—	—	—
12.5 MHz	0x06	89 Kbps	0x01	312 Kbps	—	—
16 MHz	0x07	100 Kbps	0x02	278 Kbps	—	—
20 MHz	0x09	100 Kbps	0x02	333 Kbps	—	—
25 MHz	0x0C	96.2 Kbps	0x03	312 Kbps	—	—
33 MHz	0x10	97.1 Kbps	0x04	330 Kbps	—	—
40 MHz	0x13	100 Kbps	0x04	400 Kbps	0x01	1000 Kbps
50 MHz	0x18	100 Kbps	0x06	357 Kbps	0x02	833 Kbps
80 MHz	0x27	100 Kbps	0x09	400 Kbps	0x03	1000 Kbps

8.4.6.1 I2C Module High-Speed Mode

The TM4C123GH6PM I2C peripheral provides supports for High-speed operation as both a master and a slave. High-Speed mode is configured by setting the HS bit in the I2C Master Control/Status (I2CMCS) register. High-Speed mode transmits data at a high bit rate with a 33.3% duty cycle, but communication and arbitration are done at Standard, Fast mode, or Fast-mode plus speed, depending on which is selected by the user. When the HS bit in the I2CMCS register is set, current mode is enabled.

The clock period can be calculated using the equation below. But in the High-Speed mode, both SCL_LP and SCL_HP are fixed as SCL_LP = 2 and SCL_HP = 1.

$$SCL\_PERIOD = 2 \times (1 + TIMER\_PRD) \times (SCL\_LP + SCL\_HP) \times CLK\_PRD$$

For example: If CLK_PRD = 25 ns and TIMER_PRD = 1, it yields a SCL period as 300 ns with a frequency of 1/T = 3.33 MHz.

Table 8.22 shows some examples of timer period and system clock in High-Speed mode. Note that the HS bit in the I2CMTPR register needs to be set for the TPR value to be used in High-Speed mode.

When working as a master, the master is responsible for sending a master-code-byte in either Standard (100 Kbps) or Fast-mode (400 Kbps) before it begins transferring in High-speed mode.

The master-code byte must contain data in the form of 00001XXX and is used to tell the slave devices to prepare for a High-speed transfer. The master-code byte should never be acknowledged by a slave since it is only used to indicate that the upcoming data is going to be transferred at a higher-speed data rate. To send the master-code byte, software should place the value of the master-code byte into the I2CMSA register and write the I2CMCS register with a value of 0x13. This places the I2C master peripheral in High-speed mode, and all subsequent transfers are carried out at High-speed data rate using the normal I2CMCS command bits, without setting the HS bit in the I2CMCS register. Again, setting the HS bit in the I2CMCS register is only necessary during the master-code byte.

When operating as a High-speed slave, there is no additional software required.

8.4.6.2 I2C Module Interrupts Generation and Processing

The I2C module can generate interrupts when the following conditions are observed:

- Master transaction completed
- Master arbitration lost
- Master transaction error
- Master bus timeout

Table 8.22. Examples of master timer period in High-Speed mode.

System Clock	Period	Transmit Speed
40 MHz	0x01	3.33 Mbps
50 MHz	0x02	2.77 Mbps
80 MHz	0x03	3.33 Mbps

- Slave transaction received
- Slave transaction requested
- Stop condition on bus detected
- Start condition on bus detected

The I2C master and slave modules have separate interrupt signals. While both modules can generate interrupts for multiple conditions, only a single interrupt signal can be sent to the interrupt controller.

8.4.6.2.1 I2C Master Interrupts The I2C master module generates an interrupt when a transaction completes in either transmit or receive mode, when arbitration is lost, or when an error occurs during a transaction. To enable the I2C master interrupt, software must set the IM bit in the I2C Master Interrupt Mask Register (I2CMIMR).

When an interrupt condition is met, software must check the ERROR and ARBLST bits in the I2C Master Control/Status (I2CMCS) register to verify that an error didn't occur during the last transaction and to ensure that arbitration has not been lost. An error condition is asserted if the last transaction was not acknowledged by the slave. If an error is not detected and the master has not lost arbitration, the application can proceed with the transfer. The interrupt is cleared by writing a 1 to the IC bit in the I2C Master Interrupt Clear Register (I2CMICR).

If the application does not need to use interrupts, the raw interrupt status is always visible in the I2C Master Raw Interrupt Status (I2CMRIS) register.

8.4.6.2.2 I2C Slave Interrupts The slave module can generate an interrupt when data has been received or requested. This interrupt is enabled by setting the DATAIM bit in the I2C Slave Interrupt Mask Register (I2CSIMR).

As an interrupt occurs, the software determines whether the module should write (transmit) or read (receive) data from the I2C Slave Data Register (I2CSDR), by checking the RREQ and TREQ bits of the I2C Slave Control/Status Register (I2CSCSR). If the slave module is in receive mode and the first byte of a transfer is received, the FBR bit is set along with the RREQ bit. The interrupt is cleared by setting the DATAIC bit in the I2C Slave Interrupt Clear Register (I2CSICR).

As we mentioned, the slave module can generate an interrupt when a START and a STOP state is detected. These interrupts are enabled by setting the STARTIM and STOPIM bits in the I2C Slave Interrupt Mask Register (I2CSIMR) and cleared by writing a 1 to the STOPIC and STARTIC bits of the I2C Slave Interrupt Clear Register (I2CSICR).

If the application does not need to use any interrupt, the raw interrupt status is always visible via the I2C Slave Raw Interrupt Status (I2CSRIS) register.

8.4.7 I2C Interface Control Signals and GPIO I2C Control Registers

As we know, all peripheral devices used in the TM4C123GH6PM MCU system are interfaced to MCU via related GPIO Ports and pins, and this is also true to I2C modules. Table 8.23 lists the external signals of the I2C interface and related function.

Table 8.23. I2C control signals and GPIO pins distributions.

I2C Pin	GPIO Pin	Pin Type	Buffer Type	Pin Function
I2C0SCL	PB2 (3)	I/O	NON-OD	I2C Module 0 Clock.
I2C0SDA	PB3 (3)	I/O	OD	I2C Module 0 Data.
I2C1SCL	PA6 (3)	I/O	NON-OD	I2C Module 1 Clock.
I2C1SDA	PA7 (3)	I/O	OD	I2C Module 1 Data.
I2C2SCL	PE4 (3)	I/O	NON-OD	I2C Module 2 Clock.
I2C2SDA	PE5 (3)	I/O	OD	I2C Module 2 Data.
I2C3SCL	PD0 (3)	I/O	NON-OD	I2C Module 3 Clock.
I2C3SDA	PD1 (3)	I/O	OD	I2C Module 3 Data.

The I2C interface signals are alternate functions for some GPIO pins and default to be GPIO signals at reset, with the exception of the I2C0SCL and I2CSDA pins which default to the I2C function. The AFSEL bit in the GPIO Alternate Function Select (GPIOAFSEL) register should be set to choose the I2C function. The number (3) in the parentheses is the encoding that must be programmed into the PMCx field in the GPIO Port Control (GPIOPCTL) register to assign the I2C signal to the specified GPIO port pins. Note that the I2CSDA pin should be set to open drain using the GPIO Open Drain Select (GPIOODR) register, but the I2CSCL cannot do that setting.

8.4.8 I2C Module Control Registers and Their Functions

As shown in Figure 8.44, all I2C module components and their control functions are globally illustrated by this block diagram. However, in order to get more details about these components and control signals, we need to discuss them one by one with more details based on each group of registers and their functions.

8.4.8.1 I2C Module Master Control Registers

As we discussed in Section 8.4.2, there are 11 popular control registers in the master control register group and we will discuss them one by one in the following sections.

8.4.8.1.1 I2C Master Slave Address Register (I2CMSA) This is a 32-bit register and only the lower 8 bits are used to contain seven bits address (A6~A0) for the selected slave device and a Receive/Send (R/S) bit, which determines whether the next operation is a Receive (1) or a Transmit (0) (Figure 8.49).

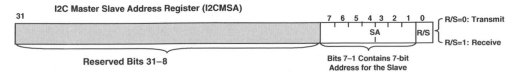

Figure 8.49. The bit field and function for the I2CMSA register.

I2C Master Control/Status Register (I2CMCS) in Reading Status

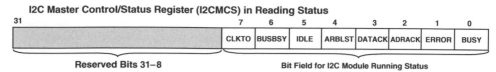

Figure 8.50. The bit configurations in the I2CMCS register (Reading).

8.4.8.1.2 I2C Master Control/Status Register (I2CMCS) This is a 32-bit register and provides double functions for the I2C module to perform either a reading or a writing operation. When reading, this register uses the lower 8-bit to indicate the current running status of the I2C module. When writing, this register uses the lower 5 bits to set up the operational parameters for the next data operation.

Figure 8.50 shows the bit-field configurations in the reading status, and Table 8.24 shows the bit-field values and functions in the reading status.

Figure 8.51 shows the bit field configurations in the writing status, and Table 8.25 shows the bit field values and functions in the writing status.

8.4.8.1.3 I2C Master Data Register (I2CMDR) This is a 32-bit register with lowest 8-bit (byte) used to contain the data to be transmitted when in the Master Transmit state and the data received when in the Master Receive state.

8.4.8.1.4 I2C Master Timer Period Register (I2CMTPR) This register is programmed to set the timer period for the SCL clock and assign the SCL clock to either standard or high-

Table 8.24. Bit-field value and its function for I2CMCS register (Reading Status).

Bit	Name	Reset	Function
31:8	Reserved	0x0	Reserved
7	CLKTO	0x0	Clock Timeout Error. 0: No clock timeout error occurred. 1: A clock timeout error has occurred.
6	BUSBSY	0x0	Bus Busy. 0: The I2C bus is idle. 1: The I2C bus is busy. The bit changes based on the START and STOP conditions.
5	IDLE	0x0	0: The I2C controller is NOT idle. 1: The I2C controller is idle
4	ARBLST	0x0	Arbitration Lost. 0: The I2C controller won arbitration. 1: The I2C controller lost arbitration
3	DATACK	0x0	Acknowledge Data. 0: The transmitted data was acknowledged. 1: The transmitted data was NOT acknowledged.
2	ADRACK	0x0	Acknowledge Address. 0: The transmitted address was acknowledged. 1: The transmitted address was NOT acknowledged.
1	ERROR	0x0	0: No error was detected on the last operation. 1: An error occurred on the last operation.
0	BUSY	0x0	0: The I2C controller is idle. 1: The I2C controller is busy.

I2C Master Control/Status Register (I2CMCS) in Writing Status

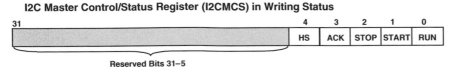

Figure 8.51. The bit configurations in the I2CMCS register (Writing).

speed mode (Figure 8.52). The bits 6:0 store a TPR value (TIMER_PRD) used to calculate the SCL clock period and frequency as we discussed in Section 8.4.6. If HS = 0, the calculated SCL rate is used for Standard, Fast, or Fast Plus mode data operations. If HS = 1, the calculated SCL rate is used for High-Speed data operations. The TPR is the Timer Period register value with a range of 1 to 127. It is exactly equal to TIMER_PRD value.

8.4.8.1.5 I2C Master Configuration Register (I2CMCR) This 32-bit register is used to configure the operational mode (Master or Slave) for the I2C modules, enable the glitch filter, and set the interface for test mode loopback. Figure 8.53 shows the bit configurations for the I2CMCR register.

If GFE = 0, this means that the glitch filter is not applied. Otherwise if GFE = 1, it means that the glitch filter is enabled. The pulse width of this glitch filter can be configured by programming the GFPW bits (bits 6:4) in the `I2C Master Configuration 2 Register (I2CMCR2)`.

If SFE and MFE is 0, this means that both slave mode and the master mode is disabled. Otherwise if SFE = 1 or MFE = 1, which means that the slave mode or master mode is enabled and the I2C module works in either mode.

The bit 0 (LPBK bit) is used to set the I2C module in a loopback mode to test its function when this bit is set to 1.

8.4.8.1.6 I2C Master Clock Low Timeout Count Register (I2CMCLKOCNT) This is a 32-bit register with only the lowest 8 bits used to contain the upper 8 bits of a 12-bit counter that can be used to keep the timeout limit for clock stretching by a remote slave. The lower

Table 8.25. Bit-field value and its function for I2CMCS register (Writing Status).

Bit	Name	Reset	Function
31:5	Reserved	0x0	Reserved
4	HS	0x0	High-Speed Enable. 0: The master operates in Standard, Fast mode, or Fast mode plus as selected by using a value in the I2CMTPR register that results in an SCL frequency of 100 kbps for Standard mode, 400 kbps for Fast mode, or 1 Mpbs for Fast mode plus. 1: The master operates in High-Speed mode with transmission speeds up to 3.33 Mbps.
3	ACK	0x0	Data Acknowledge Enable. 0: The received data byte is not acknowledged automatically by the master. 1: The received data byte is acknowledged automatically by the master.
2	STOP	0x0	0: The controller does not generate the STOP condition. 1: The controller generates the STOP condition.
1	START	0x0	0: The controller does not generate the STOP condition. 1: The controller generates the STOP condition.
0	RUN	0x0	I2C Master Enable. 0: The master is unable to transmit or receive data. 1: The master is able to transmit or receive data.

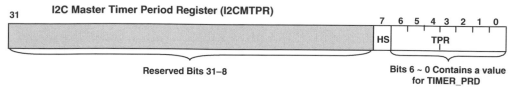

Figure 8.52.   The bit configurations in the I2CMTPR register.

four bits of the counter are not user visible and are always 0x0. The Master Clock Low Timeout counter counts for the entire time when SCL is held Low continuously. If SCL is returned to High at any point, the Master Clock Low Timeout Counter is reloaded with the value in this I2CMCLKOCNT register and begins counting down from this value.

8.4.8.1.7 I2C Master Bus Monitor Register (I2CMBMON)   This is a 32-bit register, but only the lowest 2 bits are used to determine the SCL and SDA signal status. If bit 0 (SCL) = 1, the I2CSCL signal is High; otherwise if this bit is 0, the I2CSCL signal is Low. Similar situation is true to bit 1 (SDA) signal.

8.4.8.1.8 I2C Master Interrupt Mask Register (I2CMIMR)   This is a 32-bit register, but only the lowest 2 bits are used to control whether a raw interrupt is promoted to a controller interrupt. The bit 1 (CLKIM) is used to control whether a clock timeout interrupt that has been set by the CLKRIS bit in the I2CMRIS register can be sent to the NVIC, and bit 0 (IM) is used to control whether a master interrupt that has been set by the RIS bit in the I2CMRIS register can be sent to the interrupt controller. If any of these bits is set to 1, the related interrupt can be sent to the NVIC. Otherwise if any of these bits is 0, the related interrupt cannot be sent to the NVIC.

8.4.8.1.9 I2C Master Raw Interrupt Status Register (I2CMRIS)   This is a 32-bit register, but only the lowest 2 bits are used to specify whether a raw interrupt is pending to be processed. The bit 1 (CLKRIS) is used to indicate whether a clock timeout raw interrupt has been generated and pended in the I2CMRIS register. If this bit is set to 1, a timeout raw interrupt is pending. Otherwise there is no timeout interrupt if this bit is 0. Similarly, the bit 0 (RIS) is to monitor whether a master raw interrupt is pending. If this bit is 1, a master raw interrupt is pending. Otherwise there is no master interrupt.

   This register specifies whether an interrupt is pending or not.

8.4.8.1.10 I2C Master Masked Interrupt Status Register (I2CMMIS)   This is a 32-bit register but only the lowest 2 bits are used to specify whether an interrupt has been sent to the NVIC to be processed. The bit 1 (CLKMIS) is used to indicate whether a clock timeout interrupt has been sent to the interrupt controller to be processed. If this bit is set to 1, a

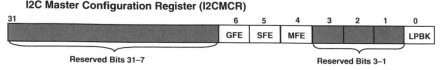

Figure 8.53.   The bit configurations for the I2CMCR register.

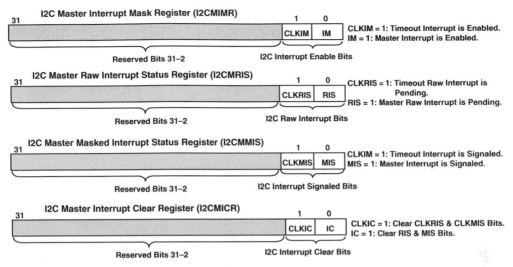

Figure 8.54. Bit functions of four I2C master interrupt registers.

timeout interrupt is signaled and sent to the NVIC. Otherwise no timeout interrupt has been occurred if this bit is 0. Similarly, the bit 0 (MIS) is to monitor whether an I2C interrupt has been sent to the interrupt controller to be processed. If this bit is 1, an I2C interrupt is signaled and sent to the NVIC. Otherwise no I2C interrupt has been occurred.

This register specifies whether an interrupt is signaled and sent to the interrupt controller.

8.4.8.1.11 I2C Master Interrupt Clear Register (I2CMICR)   This is a 32-bit register but only the lowest 2 bits, bit 1 (CLKIC) and bit 0 (IC), are used to clear the raw and masked interrupts. If a 1 is written to the bit CLKIC, both the CLKRIS bit in the I2CMRIS register and the CLKMIS bit in the I2CMMIS register are cleared to 0. Similarly, if a 1 is written to the bit IC, both the RIS bit in the I2CMRIS register and the MIS bit in the I2CMMIS register are cleared to 0. Figure 8.54 shows these four I2C master interrupt registers' bit functions.

8.4.8.2 I2C Module Slave Control Registers

As we discussed in Section 8.4.2, there are nine popular control registers in the slave control register group and we will discuss them one by one in the following sections.

8.4.8.2.1 I2C Slave Own Address Register (I2CSOAR)   This is a 32-bit register, but only the lowest 7 bits (bits 6:0) are used to contain seven address bits that identify the TM4C123GH6PM I2C device on the I2C bus. Exactly these 7 bits contain an I2C Slave Own Address (OAR) field that specifies bits A6 through A0 of the slave address.

8.4.8.2.2 I2C Slave Control Status Register (I2CSCSR)   Similar to the I2C Master Control Status Register (I2CMCSR), this register also provides dual functions for the I2C slave device. When reading, the lowest four bits on this register indicate the current

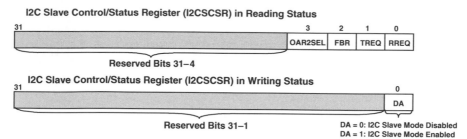

Figure 8.55. Bit-field configurations of the I2CSCS register.

running status of the slave device. When writing, the value of the LSB on this register can be used to configure whether the I2C slave operation is enabled or disabled.

Figures 8.55 shows the bit-field configurations of this register in the reading and writing status. Table 8.26 shows the bit-field values and functions of this register in the reading status.

When working in the writing status, writing 1 to the DA bit in this register is to enable the I2C slave operation, and writing 0 to this bit is to disable the I2C slave operation.

8.4.8.2.3 I2C Slave Data Register (I2CSDR) This is a 32-bit register, but only the lowest 8 bits are used to contain the data to be transmitted when working in the Slave Transmit state, along with the data received when working in the Slave Receive state.

8.4.8.2.4 I2C Slave Own Address 2 Register (I2CSOAR2) This is a 32-bit register, but only the lowest 8 bits are used to enable and provide an alternate address for the I2C data operations. The bit 7 (OAR2EN) is used to enable (OAR2EN = 1) or disable (OAR2EN = 0) the alternate address. The bits 6:0 are used to provide a valid 7-bit alternate address. By using this register, an alternate address can be used for the I2C data operation if the primary address is not matched or not desired.

8.4.8.2.5 I2C Slave ACK Control Register (I2CSACKCTL) This is a 32-bit register, but only the lowest 2 bits are used to enable the I2C slave to NACK for invalid data or command

Table 8.26. Bit-field value and its function for the I2CSCSR register (Reading Status).

Bit	Name	Reset	Function
31:4	Reserved	0x0	Reserved
3	OAR2SEL	0x0	OAR2 Address Matched. 0: Either the address is not matched or the match is in legacy mode. 1: OAR2 address matched and ACKed by the slave.
2	FBR	0x0	First Byte Received. 0: The first byte has not been received. 1: The first byte following the slave's own address has been received.
1	TREQ	0x0	Transmit Request. 0: No transmit request. 1: The I2C controller has been addressed as a slave transmitter and is using clock stretching to delay the master until data has been written to the I2CSDR register.
0	RREQ	0x0	Receive Request. 0: No receive request. 1: The I2C controller has outstanding receive data from the I2C master and is using clock stretching to delay the master until the data has been read from the I2CSDR register.

Table 8.27. Bit-field value and its function for the I2CSACKCTL register.

Bit	Name	Reset	Function
31:2	Reserved	0x0	Reserved
1	ACKOVAL	0x0	I2C Slave ACK Override Value. 0: An ACK is sent indicating valid data or command. 1: A NACK is sent indicating invalid data or command.
0	ACKOEN	0x0	I2C Slave ACK Override Enable. 0: A response is not provided. 1: An ACK or NACK is sent according to the value written to the ACKOVAL bit.

or ACK for valid data or command. The I2C clock is pulled low after the last data bit until this register is written. Table 8.27 shows the bit-field values and functions of this register.

8.4.8.2.6 I2C Slave Interrupt Mask Register (I2CSIMR)   This is a 32-bit register, but only the lowest 3 bits are used to enable or disable three kinds of slave-related raw interrupts to be sent to the interrupt controller or not. These 3 bits are:

- Bit 2 (STOPIM): Set this bit to 1 to enable the STOP interrupt, and 0 to disable it.
- Bit 1 (STARTIM): Set this bit to 1 to enable the START interrupt, and 0 to disable it.
- Bit 0 (DATAIM): Set this bit to 1 to enable the DATA interrupt, and 0 to disable it.

The precondition of using this register is that the related STOPRIS, STARTRIS and DATARIS bits in the I2CSRIS register have been set to indicate that the related raw interrupt is pending.

8.4.8.2.7 I2C Slave Raw Interrupt Status Register (I2CSRIS)   Similar to I2CSIMR, only the lowest three bits are used for this 32-bit register, and they are:

- Bit 2 (STOPRIS): If a STOP condition interrupt occurred, this bit is set to 1 to indicate this.
- Bit 1 (STARTRIS): If a START raw interrupt occurred, this bit is set to 1 to indicate this.
- Bit 0 (DATARIS): If a DATA received or a DATA requested raw interrupt occurred, this bit is set to 1 to indicate this.

8.4.8.2.8 I2C Slave Masked Interrupt Status Register (I2CSMIS)   Similar to I2CSIMR, only the lowest 3 bits are used for this 32-bit register, and they are:

- Bit 2 (STOPMIS): If a STOP condition interrupt is signaled, this bit is set to 1 to indicate this.
- Bit 1 (STARTMIS): If a START raw interrupt is signaled, this bit is set to 1 to indicate this.
- Bit 0 (DATAMIS): If a DATA received or a DATA requested raw interrupt is signaled, this bit is set to 1 to indicate this.

8.4.8.2.9 I2C Slave Interrupt Clear Register (I2CSICR)   This register is used to clear any signaled and responded interrupt.

Similar to I2CSIMR, only the lowest 3 bits are used for this 32-bit register, and they are:

- Bit 2 (STOPIC): Writing a 1 to this bit clears the STOPRIS bit in the I2CSRIS register and the STOPMIS bit in the I2CSMIS register.

- Bit 1 (STARTIC): Writing a 1 to this bit clears the STARTRIS bit in the I2CSRIS register and the STARTMIS bit in the I2CSMIS register.
- Bit 0 (DATAIC): Writing a 1 to this bit clears the DATARIS bit in the I2CSRIS register and the DATAMIS bit in the I2CSMIS register.

At this point, we complete our discussions about control and status registers used in the I2C master and slave operations. Next let's take a look at the initialization and configuration of these registers to make them ready to perform desired I2C data operations.

8.4.9 I2C Module Initializations and Configurations

Before using the I2C module to perform related data operations, all I2C modules must be properly initialized and configured. Depending on the different operational modes, the initialization and configuration procedures may be different. In this section we use an example to illustrate how to initialize and configure one of the most popular operation modes, I2C module to transmit multiple bytes by a master. The system clock is 16 MHz.

This configuration process can be divided into two major parts: (a) the configurations to the I2C-related GPIO Ports and pins and (b) the configurations to the I2C module.

8.4.9.1 Initializations and Configurations for the I2C-Related GPIO Pins

These initializations and configurations include the following operations:

1. Enable the clock to the appropriate GPIO module via the RCGCGPIO register.
2. In the GPIO module, enable the appropriate pins for their alternate function using the GPIOAFSEL register.
3. Configure the PMCx fields in the GPIOPCTL register to assign the I2C signals to the appropriate pins.
4. Enable the I2CSDA pin for open-drain operation using the GPIOODR register.

8.4.9.2 Initializations and Configurations for the I2C Module

These initializations and configurations include the following operations:

1. Initialize the I2C Master by writing the I2CMCR register with a value of 0x0000.0010 to set MFE bit (bit-4) to 1 to enable the master function mode.
2. Set the desired SCL clock speed as 100 Kbps by writing the I2CMTPR register with the correct value. This value represents the number of system clock periods in one SCL clock period. The TPR or TIMER_PRD value is determined by the following equation (see Table 8.21 and section 8.4.6):

$$\text{TPR} = (\text{System Clock}/(2 \times (\text{SCL\_LP} + \text{SCL\_HP}) \times \text{SCL\_CLK})) - 1, \text{which is}$$
$$\text{TPR} = (16\,\text{MHz}/(2 \times (6 + 4) \times 10,0000)) - 1 = 7$$

Write 0x0000.0007 into the I2CMTPR register.

3. Specify the slave address of the master and followed by a Transmit by writing the I2CMSA register with a value of 0x0000.0076. This sets the slave address to 0x3B.

4. Place a desired data byte to be transmitted into the I2CMDR register.

5. Initiate the first byte transmit of the data from Master to Slave by writing the I2CMCS register with a value of 0x0000.0003 (HS:ACK:STOP:START:RUN = 00011).

6. Wait until the transmission completes by polling the I2CMCS register's BUSBSY bit until it has been cleared.

7. Check the ERROR bit in the I2CMCS register to confirm the transmit was acknowledged.

8. Write the next data to be transmitted into the I2CMDR register.

9. Check whether all data have been transmitted.

10. If no, write 0x0000.0001 (HS:ACK:STOP:START:RUN = 00001) to the I2CMCS register to continue transmitting the next data.

11. If yes, write 0x0000.0101 (HS:ACK:STOP:START:RUN = 00101) to the I2CMCS register to send STOP condition to the slave to inform the slave that the data transmission is done.

12. Wait until the transmission completes by polling the I2CMCS register's BUSBSY bit until it has been cleared.

13. Check the ERROR bit in the I2CMCS register to confirm that the transmit is acknowledged.

Now let's build an example project to illustrate how to use the I2C module to perform data transmission job between a master and a slave.

8.4.10 Build an Example I2C Module Project

In the EduBASE ARM® Trainer, a Real Time Clock (RTC) module BQ32000 is installed to work as an I2C device. In this project, we use this device as an I2C salve device to ask it to transmit some real-time data to the TM4C123GH6PM MCU who works as an I2C master device, and display these received data on four LEDs PB3~PB0 via GPIO Port B on the Trainer.

First let's have a closer look at the structures and functions of the RTC BQ32000.

8.4.10.1 The BQ32000 Real Time Clock (RTC)

The BQ32000 is an 8-bit real time clock device that provides accurate real time for most industrial applications. It contains a 32 kHz oscillator input and two-wire I2C interface with IRQ function to allow this RTC to interface to most popular I2C devices via I2C bus, SDA and SCL.

The BQ32000 also provides an automatic backup supply with integrated trickle charger. The backup supply can be implemented using a capacitor or non-rechargeable battery to greatly save the system power.

A functional block diagram of the RTC BQ32000 is shown in Figure 8.56.

The specific features provided by the RTC include:

- I2C interface supports serial clock up to 400 kHz.
- I2C salve address 11010000B for writing commands and salve address 11010001B for reading commands.
- Ten 8-bit normal registers stored the current time, including the seconds, minutes, hours, date, and years. Some other items are calibration and configuration parameters. These registers are addressed from 0x00~0x09. The 0x00 is for SECONDS register, 0x01 is for MINUTES register, and 0x02 is for CENT_HOURS register and so on.
- Three special function registers stored special function keys are addressed from 0x20~0x22.

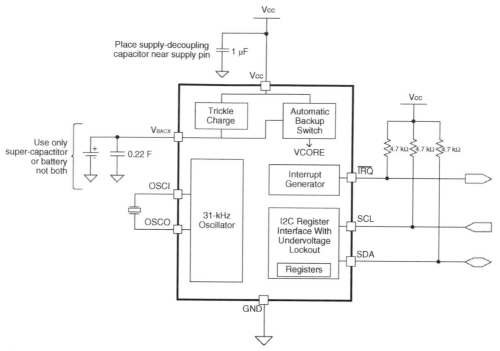

Figure 8.56. The functional block diagram of BQ32000 RTC.

All of these registers can be accessed in terms of their unique addresses.

Each register, either normal or special, is an 8-bit register. Specially for the normal registers containing the time information, such as seconds, minutes and hours, each of them has seven bits (D6~D0) used to store the valid time information, but the MSB (D7) is used to store a function bit that can be used to perform some function to the RTC.

For three time information registers, SECONDS, MUNITES, and CENT_HOURS, the current time information is formatted in the BCD (0~9) coding. An example structure of this kind of register, SECONDS, is shown in Figure 8.57.

The STOP bit D7 is used to force the oscillator to stop oscillating. STOP is set to 0 (normal) on the initial application of power; on all subsequent power cycles, STOP remains unchanged. On the initial power application, STOP can be written to 1 (stop) and then written to 0 to force start the oscillator again.

The 10_SECOND bits (D6~D4) are the BCD representation of the number of tens of seconds on the clock, and the valid values are 0 to 5. The 1_SECOND bits (D3~D0) are also the BCD representation of the number of seconds on the clock with the valid values of 0 to 9.

D7	D6	D5	D4	D3	D2	D1	D0	BIT(S)
STOP	10_SECOND			1_SECOND				Name
r/w	r/w			r/w				Read/Write
0	X	X	X	X	X	X	X	Initial
UC	UC	UC	UC	UC	UC	UC	UC	Cycle

Figure 8.57. The bit field and function of the SECONDS register.

8.4.10.2 *The Interface Between the BQ32000 and EduBASE ARM® Trainer*

A functional block diagram of the interface between the EduBASE Trainer and BQ32000 RTC is shown in Figure 8.58.

The I2C Module 1 is used to interface to the BQ32000 RTC with PA7 as SDA1 and PA6 as SCL1 wires. Both wires are pulled up by two resistors in the RN3 resistor group.

In this example project, we use the TM4C123GH6PM MCU as a master to request data from the slave device BQ32000 (request the time information from the SECONDS register in the BQ32000 RTC via I2C1 module with SDA1 and SCL1 wires). The acquired time information or seconds are in the BCD format and displayed in four LEDs, PB3~PB0 installed in the EduBASE Trainer via PB3~PB0 pins on the GPIO Port B.

To request the data from the slave RTC via I2C1 module, the following operational sequence should be performed:

1. The I2C-related GPIO Ports are enabled, and related pins should first be initialized and configured with the GPIOAFSEL, GPIOPCTL, and GPIOODR registers.

2. The I2C-module-1-related registers should be initialized and configured; these include the I2CMCR and I2CMTPR registers.

3. Write the first 9-bit commands, including a 7-bit slave address ($1101000 = 0x68$), R/S bit (W = 0), and an ACK bit to the I2C1_MSA register.

4. Then write the address of the SECONDS register ($0x00$) in the BQ32000 to the I2C1_MDR register as a data item to be transmitted.

5. Write $0x3$ (HS:ACK:STOP:START:RUN = $00011 = 0x3$) to the I2C1_MCS register to start and send this command to the slave device BQ32000 via the SDA line. The complete command is a combination of steps 3~5, which is START:Slave_Address + Write + ACK: SECONDS_Register_Address + ACK.

6. Check the I2C1_MCS register to make sure that the ACK is received with no error and that the bus is not busy.

7. Then send a 0 as the first data to the slave by placing it into the I2C1_MDR register. Since we do not want to transmit any data to the slave, instead we want to require data (*seconds* in time) from the SECONDS register in the slave RTC, therefore we do not need to send any real data to it.

8. Write $0x5$ (HS:ACK:STOP:START:RUN = $00101 = 0x5$) to the I2C1_MCS register to send this data item following with an ACK to the slave device BQ32000 via the SDA line. This command indicates that the data transfer is done (STOP = 1) after this item is transmitted.

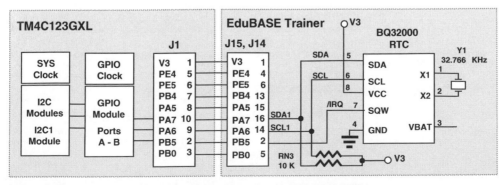

Figure 8.58.   The interface between EduBASE Trainer and BQ32000 RTC.

9. Check the I2C1_MCS register to make sure that the ACK is received with no error and that the bus is not busy.

10. Next we can use an infinitive loop to repeatedly require or read data (*seconds* in time) from the SECONDS register in the slave RTC. In order to this, we need to repeat the jobs we did in steps 3~5 to identify and inform the slave RTC that we want to access the SECONDS register to pick up the current seconds in time from this salve device.

11. Then write a 9-bit command, including 7-bit slave address 0x68, R/S bit = 1 (Read) and an ACK bit to the I2C1_MSA register to inform the slave RTC that the master needs to require data from the slave. The complete command is START:Slave_Address + Read + ACK.

12. Write 0x7 (HS:ACK:STOP:START:RUN = 00111 = 0x7) to the I2C1_MCS register to inform the slave that the master needs to get the current seconds from the slave and stop after this data query operation. This means that we only read a single data item from the slave.

13. Check the I2C1_MCS register to make sure that the ACK is received with no error and that the bus is not busy.

14. Read the received data from the I2C1_MDR register and store it to the desired location.

15. Check the I2C1_MCS register to make sure that the ACK is received with no error and that the bus is not busy.

16. Return to step 10 to read and pick up the next data from the slave RTC.

Ok, now let's create our example project DRAI2C.

8.4.10.3 Create a DRA Model I2C Project DRAI2C

Perform the following operations to create a new project DRAI2C:

1. Open the Windows Explorer window to create a new folder named DRAI2C under the C:\ARM Class Projects\Chapter 8 folder.

2. Open the Keil® ARM-MDK µVersion5 and go to Project|New µVersion Project menu item to create a new µVersion Project. On the opened wizard, browse to our new folder DRAI2C that is created in step 1 above. Enter DRAI2C into the **File name** box and click on the **Save** button to create this project.

3. On the next wizard, you need to select the device (MCU) for this project. Expand three icons, Texas Instruments, Tiva C Series, and TM4C123x Series, and select the target device TM4C123GH6PM from the list by clicking on it. Click on the **OK** to close this wizard.

4. Next the Software Components wizard is opened, and you need to setup the software development environment for your project with this wizard. Expand two icons, CMSIS and Device, and check the CORE and Startup checkboxes in the **Sel.** column, and click on the **OK** button since we need these two components to build our project.

Since this project is relative simple, only a C source file is good enough.

8.4.10.4 Create the Source File DRAI2C

Create a new C source file DRAI2C.c and enter the first part codes shown in Figure 8.59 into this file. Let's have a closer look at this first part codes to see how they works.

1. Four user-defined subroutines are declared in the top of this source file in lines 7~10.

2. In line 11, the address of the slave device BQ32000 RTC is defined. Compare with the RTC addresses discussed in Section 8.4.10.1, two different addresses are used for this slave; the

```
1    //*********************************************************************************************************
2    DRAI2C.c - Main Application File for I2C Module 1 to BQ32000 (First Part Codes)
3    //*********************************************************************************************************
4    #include <stdint.h>
5    #include <stdbool.h>
6    #include "tm4c123gh6pm.h"

7    void delay_ms(int  n);
8    void I2C1_Init(void);
9    uint8_t I2C1_Write(int  sAddr, uint8_t rAddr, uint8_t  data);
10   void I2C1_Read(int  sAddr, uint8_t rAddr);

11   #define SLAVE_ADDR  0x68                    // 1101 000.

12   int main(void)
13   {
14     uint8_t  error;

15     SYSCTL_RCGCGPIO_R |= 0x2|0x20;           // enable clock to GPIOB & GPIOF
16     error = SYSCTL_RCGCGPIO_R;
17     GPIO_PORTB_DIR_R |= 0x0F;                // set PORTB 3-0 as output pins
18     GPIO_PORTB_DEN_R |= 0x0F;                // set PORTB 3-0 as digital pins
19     GPIO_PORTF_DIR_R |= 0x0F;                // set PORTF 3-0 as output pins
20     GPIO_PORTF_DEN_R |= 0x0F;                // set PORTF 3-0 as digital pins

21     I2C1_Init();
22     error = I2C1_Write(SLAVE_ADDR,  0,  0);
23     if (error) {GPIO_PORTF_DATA_R = 0x0F;}
24     I2C1_Read(SLAVE_ADDR,  0);
25   }

26   void I2C1_Init(void)
27   {
28     SYSCTL_RCGCI2C_R |= 0x02;                // enable clock to I2C1
29     SYSCTL_RCGCGPIO_R |= 0x1;                // enable clock to GPIOA
30     GPIO_PORTA_AFSEL_R |= 0xC0;              // PA7 for SDA1, PA6 for SCL1
31     GPIO_PORTA_PCTL_R |= 0x33000000;
32     GPIO_PORTA_DEN_R |= 0xC0;                // PA7 & PA6 as digital pins
33     GPIO_PORTA_ODR_R |= 0x80;                // PA7 as open drain
34     I2C1_MCR_R = 0x10;                       // I2C1 works as master mode
35     I2C1_MTPR_R = 0x7;                       // SCL1 = 100 kHz at system clock = 16 MHz
36   }

37   static int I2C1_Wait_Done(void)
38   {
39     while(I2C1_MCS_R & 1);                   // wait until I2C1 master is not busy
40     return I2C1_MCS_R & 0xE;                 // return I2C1 error code
41   }

42   uint8_t I2C1_Write(int sAddr,  uint8_t rAddr,  uint8_t data)         // Write one byte
43   {
44     uint8_t error;

45     I2C1_MSA_R = sAddr << 1;                 // write: S:(sAddr+W)+ACK+rAddr+ACK+data+ACK+P
46     I2C1_MDR_R = rAddr;
47     I2C1_MCS_R = 0x3;                        // S:(sAddr+W)+ACK+rAddr+ACK

48     error = I2C1_Wait_Done();                // wait until write is complete
49     if (error) { return  error; }
50     I2C1_MDR_R = data;
51     I2C1_MCS_R = 0x5;                        // +data+ACK+P
52     error = I2C1_Wait_Done();                // wait until write is complete
53     while(I2C1_MCS_R & 0x40);                // wait until bus is not busy
54     error = I2C1_MCS_R & 0xE;                // check if any error occurred
55     return  error;
     }
```

Figure 8.59.   The first part codes for the C source file DRAI2C.c.

writing address (11010000B) and the reading address (11010001B). Here we defined the upper 7-bit address 1101000 (0x68) since they are identical for both writing and reading addresses. This address will be further processed to get the writing and the reading address when used inside the different subroutines later.

3. A local 8-bit unsigned integer variable `error` is declared in the main program, and this variable is used to hold the returned error code when calling subroutines later.

4. The codes in lines 15~20 are used to initialize and configure GPIO ports and pins related to the I2C module operations. In line 15, the GPIO Ports B and F are enabled and clocked since we need to use some LEDs to display the running results via these two ports and pins.

5. The code in line 16 has nothing to do except delaying a period of time to make the GPIO Ports B and F initialization process done and both ports are stable.

6. In line 21, the subroutine `I2C1_Init()` is called to initialize and configure the I2C module 1.

7. The subroutine `I2C1_Write()` is executed in line 22 to send commands to the slave RTC to initiate the data communications between the master (MCU) and the slave RTC. The point to be noted is that the second argument is the slave register address and the third argument is the data value to be sent to the slave. Both parameters' values are 0 since the address of the SECONDS register in the BQ32000 is 0x00 (see Section 8.4.10.1) and the first data value is also 0 since we do not want to transmit any data to the slave RTC, but instead we need to get the current seconds in time from the slave.

8. If this subroutine returned an error, the three-color LED connected to the PF3~PF1 is ON to indicate this situation in line 23.

9. In line 24, the `I2C1_Read()` subroutine is called to continuously read the seconds values from the SECONDS register in the slave BQ32000. The first argument of this subroutine is the slave address, and the second argument is the data with a value of 0.

10. The `I2C1_Init()` subroutine starts at line 26, and this subroutine is used to initialize and configure the I2C module 1 and related GPIO Ports and pins.

11. In lines 28 and 29, the I2C module and the GPIO Port A are enabled and clocked since we need to use PA7 and PA6 as alternate function, exactly as I2C function, to work as SDA and SCL wires to transfer data and clock for the I2C module 1.

12. Both PA7 and PA6 pins are set to 1 in the GPIOAFSEL register to indicate that both pins are working as alternate functions in line 30.

13. In line 31, the GPIOPCTL register is configured with 0x33000000 to indicate that both PA7 and PA6 are working as I2C function (refer to Table 8.23). In that table, the number (3) in the parentheses is the encoding that must be programmed into the PMCx field in the GPIO Port Control (GPIOPCTL) register to assign I2C signals to the specified GPIO port pins.

14. Both PA7 and PA6 pins are configured to work as digital function pins in line 32.

15. The PA7 pin is configured as an open drain pin in line 33 since this pin is used to transfer serial data signals via the SDA wire, and it must be configured in this way.

16. In line 34, the I2C module 1 is configured to work as a master device by setting bit 4 (MFE) in the `I2CMCR` register (refer to Figure 8.53).

17. The TPR value in the `I2C Master Timer Period Register (I2CMTPR)` is set to 0x7 to generate a 100 Kbps bit rate for the SCL signal (refer to Section 8.4.6 and Table 8.21) when the system clock is 16 MHz (SCL_PERD $= 2 \times (1 + TPR) \times (6 + 4) \times$ CLK_PERD $= 2 \times 8 \times 10 \times (1/16 \times 10^6) = 10^{-5}$, SCL_FREQ $= 10^5$ Hz $= 100$ Kbps).

18. The subroutine `I2C1_Wait_Done()` starts at line 37. This subroutine is defined as a `static` subroutine, and this means that this is a class level or global subroutine and can be

accessed by any other functions in this project. Also the lifetime of this subroutine is the same as that of this project.

19. In line 39, a `while()` loop is used to check the BUSY bit (bit 0) on the I2CMCS register to wait for the SDA line to be idle (BUSY = 0).

20. When the SDA line is idle, the returned status of the last operation is returned to the main program. This status includes the bit 3 (DATACK), bit 2 (ADRACK), and bit 1 (ERROR) in the I2CMCS register to indicate whether a transmitted data was acknowledged, a transmitted address was acknowledged, or an error has occurred. A 1 on any of these three bits indicates that either a transmitted item was not acknowledged or an error has occurred.

21. The I2C1_Write() subroutine starts at line 42. This subroutine is used to transmit the start or initial commands including the slave address, SECONDS register address, and R/S signal to the slave RTC to make the slave ready to provide request data.

22. In line 45, the slave address (0x68) is shifted left by 1 bit to make it a slave writing command address 11010000B (refer to Section 8.4.10.1) and assigned to the I2C1_MSA register.

23. Then the address of the SECONDS register in the BQ32000, which is rAddr with a value of 0x00, is assigned to the I2C1_MDR register as the first data to be sent to the slave.

24. In line 47, the 0x3 (HS:ACK:STOP:START:RUN) = 00011 is written into the I2C1_MCS register and sent to the slave to ask the latter to respond with ACK signal.

25. The codes in lines 48 and 49 are used to wait for this transmission to be done and return any error if any of them has occurred.

26. Then the first data to be transmitted, which is 0, is written into the I2C1_MDR register in line 50, and a command 0x5 (HS:ACK:STOP:START:RUN) = 00101 is written to the I2C1_MCS register in line 51 to ask the slave to stop any operation after this operation. Since we do not want to transmit any data to the slave, the transmitted data should be 0.

27. The codes in lines 52~54 are used to wait the transactions to be done and check any possible error. If any error has occurred, it is returned to the main program in line 55.

Now let's continue to take care of the second part of the source codes for this project, which is shown in Figure 8.60. The codes in this part contain the I2C1_Read() and delay_ms() two subroutines. The first subroutine is used to continuously read multiple bytes transmitted by the slave, and the second subroutine is used to delay some period of time for the project.

Let's have a closer look at the codes in this part.

1. An infinitive `while()` loop is used to repeatedly get the data from the slave RTC in line 7.

2. As we did in the I2C1_Write() subroutine, the codes in lines 9~13 are used to send commands to the slave to start a data operation. These commands include the slave address, the SECONDS register's address, and a R/S bit (= 0).

3. In line 14, the slave address is shifted left by one 1 bit and a 1 is added into the LSB of this address to get a slave reading command address 11010001B (refer to Section 8.4.10.1) and assigned to the I2C1_MSA register.

4. The parameter 0x7 (HS:ACK:STOP:START:RUN) = 00111 is written into the I2C1_MCS register in line 15 to ask the slave to read the data from the SECONDS register and send it back the master. This command is executed by one time (start, run and stop this operation).

5. The codes in lines 16 and 17 are used to wait for this transmission to be done and return any error if any of them is occurred.

6. The requested data obtained from the slave is stored to the local variable data in line 18.

```
 1   //*********************************************************************
 2   DRAI2C.c - Main Application File for I2C Module 1 to BQ32000 (Second Part Codes)
 3   //*********************************************************************
 4   void I2C1_Read(int sAddr, uint8_t rAddr)          // Read multiple bytes
 5   {
 6     uint8_t error, data;
 7     while (1)
 8     {
 9       I2C1_MSA_R = sAddr << 1;              // read: S:(sAddr+W)+ACK+rAddr+ACK+R+(sAddr+R)+ACK+data+NACK+P
10       I2C1_MDR_R = rAddr;
11       I2C1_MCS_R = 0x3;                     // S:(sAddr+W)+ACK+rAddr+ACK
12       error = I2C1_Wait_Done();
13       if (error) { GPIO_PORTF_DATA_R |= 0x0F; }
14       I2C1_MSA_R = (sAddr << 1) + 1;                     // restart: +R+(sAddr+R)+ACK
15       I2C1_MCS_R = 0x7;                                  // +S+(sAddr+R)+NACK+P
16       error = I2C1_Wait_Done();
17       if (error) { GPIO_PORTF_DATA_R |= 0x0F; }
18       data = I2C1_MDR_R;
19       while(I2C1_MCS_R & 0x40);              // wait until bus is not busy
20       error = I2C1_MCS_R & 0xE;
21       if (error) { GPIO_PORTF_DATA_R |= 0x0F; }
22       GPIO_PORTB_DATA_R = data;              // display received data on LEDs
23       delay_ms(500);
24     }
25   }
26   void delay_ms(int time)                    // delay n milliseconds (16 MHz CPU clock)
27   {
28     int i, j;
29     for(i = 0 ; i < time; i++)
30       for(j = 0; j < 3180; j++){}
     }
```

Figure 8.60.   The second part codes for the C source file DRAI2C.c.

7. The codes in lines 19~21 are used to wait for this operation to be done and return any error if any of them is occurred.

8. The received data is sent to the PB3~PB0 LEDs via GPIO PB3~PB0 pins in line 22.

9. The subroutine `delay_ms()` is called in line 23 to delay a period of time for the project to stabilize the LEDs displaying.

10. The codes in lines 26~30 are the coding body for the `delay_ms()` subroutine.

Now let's set up the environment to build and run our project to test the I2C module function.

8.4.10.5 Set Up the Environment to Build and Run the Project

Before you can build and run the project, make sure that the following two issues have been set up correctly:

- The path of the system header file `tm4c123gh6pm.h` has been included into the project `Include Paths`, which is in the C/C++ tab under the menu item `Project|Options for Target 'Target 1'`. The path is: C:\ti\TivaWare_C_Series-2.0.1.11577\inc.
- The debug adapter used for this project is `Stellaris ICDI`. This adapter can be configured in the Debug tab under the menu item `Project|Options for Target 'Target 1'`.

Now go to the `Project|Build target` menu item to build the project. Then go to the menu item `Flash|Download` to download the project image file into the flash memory. Run the project by going to Debug|Start/Stop Debug Session menu item.

As the project runs, you can find that the 4-bit LEDs installed on the EduBASE ARM® Trainer are periodically displaying BCD codes staring from 0 and ending at 9.

8.4.11 I2C API Functions Provided by TivaWare™ Peripheral Driver Library

In this section, we will introduce another way to access and interface the I2C modules to perform desired I2C serial communication tasks via I2C modules. In the TivaWare™ Peripheral Driver Library, there are more than 50 API functions used to interface to I2C modules. However, in this section we concentrate on some most important and popular master functions to illustrate how to use them to build sophisticated project to efficiently access and interface to I2C modules to fulfill the desired serial data communication tasks.

These I2C API functions can be categorized into the following groups:

- Status and initialization API functions for the I2C modules are I2CMasterInitExpClk(), I2CMasterEnable(), I2CMasterDisable(), I2CMasterBusBusy(), I2CMasterBusy(), I2CMasterErr().
- Sending and receiving data from the I2C modules are handled by I2CMasterSlaveAddrSet(), I2CMasterControl(), I2CMasterDataGet(), I2CMasterDataPut().

We only concentrate on the master device operations in this part.

8.4.11.1 *Master Operations*

When using these APIs to drive the I2C master module, the user must perform the I2C module configurations and data operations in the following sequence:

1. First initialize the I2C master module with a call to I2CMasterInitExpClk(). That function sets the bus speed and enables the master module.

2. After that, the user may transmit or receive data via I2C master module. Data is transferred by first setting the slave address using I2CMasterSlaveAddrSet(). This function is also used to define whether the transfer is a send (a write to the slave from the master) or a receive (a read from the slave by the master).

3. Then, if connected to an I2C bus that has multiple masters, the I2C master must first call I2CMasterBusBusy() before attempting to initiate the desired transaction.

4. After determining that the bus is not busy, if trying to send data, the user must call the I2CMasterDataPut() function.

5. The transaction can then be initiated on the bus by calling the I2CMasterControl() function with any of the following commands:
   - I2C_MASTER_CMD_SINGLE_SEND
   - I2C_MASTER_CMD_SINGLE_RECEIVE
   - I2C_MASTER_CMD_BURST_SEND_START
   - I2C_MASTER_CMD_BURST_RECEIVE_START

   Any of those commands results in the master arbitrating for the bus, driving the start sequence onto the bus, and sending the slave address and direction bit across the bus. The remainder of the transaction can then be driven using either a polling or interrupt-driven method.

6. For the single send and receive cases, the polling method involves looping on the return from `I2CMasterBusy()`. Once that function indicates that the I2C master is not busy, the bus transaction has been completed and can be checked for errors using `I2CMasterErr()`.

7. If there are no errors, then the data has been sent or is ready to be read using `I2CMasterDataGet()`.

8. For the burst send and receive cases, the polling method also involves calling the `I2CMasterControl()` function for each byte transmitted or received (using `I2C_MASTER_CMD_BURST_SEND_CONT` or `I2C_MASTER_CMD_BURST_RECEIVE_CONT` commands) and for the last byte sent or received (using `I2C_MASTER_CMD_BURST_SEND_FINISH` or `I2C_MASTER_CMD_BURST_RECEIVE_FINISH` commands).

9. If any error is detected during the burst transfer, the `I2CMasterControl()` function should be called using the appropriate stop command (`I2C_MASTER_CMD_BURST_SEND_ERROR_STOP` or `I2C_MASTER_CMD_BURST_RECEIVE_ERROR_STOP`).

10. For the interrupt-driven transaction, the user must register an interrupt handler for the I2C devices and enable the I2C master interrupt; the interrupt occurs when the master is no longer busy.

Now let's have a closer look at these API functions.

8.4.11.2 I2C Module Status and Initialization API Functions

Table 8.28 shows some popular and important I2C module status and configuration API functions. The API function `I2CMasterInitExpClk()` is a very important and useful function used to set up and configure the entire I2C module. Only after the I2C module is correctly configured by using this function, it can work properly to provide the normal functions. Before performing any data operations, the I2C master and master bus must be checked to confirm that both are in the idle status by using `I2CMasterBusBusy()` and

Table 8.28. The I2C module status and configuration functions.

API Function	Parameter	Description
void I2CMasterInitExpClk(uint32_t ui32Base, uint32_t ui32I2CClk, bool bFast)	ui32Base is the base address of the I2C Master module. ui32I2CClk is the rate of the clock for the I2C module. bFast set up for fast data transfers.	Initialize operation of the I2C Master block by configuring the bus speed for the master and enabling the I2C Master block. If the parameter bFast is true, then the master block is set up to transfer data at 400 Kbps; otherwise, it is set up to transfer data at 100 Kbps. If Fast Mode Plus (1 Mbps) is desired, software should manually write the I2CMTPR after calling this function. For High Speed (3.4 Mbps) mode, a specific command is used to switch to the faster clocks after the initial communication with the slave is done at either 100 Kbps or 400 Kbps.
void I2CMasterEnable(uint32_t ui32Base)	ui32Base is the base address of the I2C Master module.	This function enables operation of the I2C Master block.
bool I2CMasterBusBusy(uint32_t ui32Base)	ui32Base is the base address of the I2C Master module.	Indicate whether or not the I2C bus is busy. Returns true if the I2C bus is busy; otherwise, returns false
bool I2CMasterBusy(uint32_t ui32Base)	ui32Base is the base address of the I2C Master module.	Indicate whether or not the I2C Master is busy. Returns true if the I2C Master is busy; otherwise, returns false
uint32_t I2CMasterErr(uint32_t ui32Base)	ui32Base is the base address of the I2C Master module.	Get the error status of the I2C Master module. Returns the error status, as one of I2C_MASTER_ERR_NONE, I2C_MASTER_ERR_ADDR_ACK, I2C_MASTER_ERR_DATA_ACK, or I2C_MASTER_ERR_ARB_LOST.

Table 8.29. The I2C module sending and receiving data functions.

API Function	Parameter	Description
void I2CMasterSlaveAddrSet(uint32_t ui32Base, uint8_t ui8SlaveAddr, bool bReceive)	ui32Base is the base address of the I2C Master module. ui8SlaveAddr 7-bit slave address. bReceive flag for the type of communication with the slave.	Configure the address that the I2C Master places on the bus when initiating a transaction. When the bReceive parameter is set to true, the address indicates that the I2C Master is initiating a read from the slave; otherwise the address indicates that the I2C Master is initiating a write to the slave.
void I2CMasterControl(uint32_t ui32Base, uint32_t ui32Cmd)	ui32Base is the base address of the I2C Master module. ui32Cmd is the command to be issued to the I2C Master module.	Control the state of the Master module send and receive data. The ui8Cmd parameter can be one of the following values: I2C_MASTER_CMD_SINGLE_SEND I2C_MASTER_CMD_SINGLE_RECEIVE I2C_MASTER_CMD_BURST_SEND_START I2C_MASTER_CMD_BURST_SEND_CONT I2C_MASTER_CMD_BURST_SEND_FINISH I2C_MASTER_CMD_BURST_SEND_ERROR_STOP I2C_MASTER_CMD_BURST_RECEIVE_START I2C_MASTER_CMD_BURST_RECEIVE_CONT I2C_MASTER_CMD_BURST_RECEIVE_FINISH I2C_MASTER_CMD_BURST_RECEIVE_ERROR_STOP I2C_MASTER_CMD_QUICK_COMMAND I2C_MASTER_CMD_HS_MASTER_CODE_SEND
void I2CMasterDataPut(uint32_t ui32Base, uint8_t ui8Data)	ui32Base is the base address of the I2C Master module. ui8Data is the data to be transmitted from the I2C Master	Place the supplied data into I2C Master Data Register.
uint32_t I2CMasterDataGet(uint32_t ui32Base)	ui32Base is the base address of the I2C Master module.	Read a byte of data from the I2C Master Data Register. Returns the byte received from by the I2C Master, cast as an uint32_t.

I2CMasterBusy() functions. The I2CMasterEnable() function must be called before the master can perform any data operation. The error status can be checked using the I2CMasterErr() function.

8.4.11.3 I2C Module Sending and Receiving Data API Functions

Table 8.29 shows some popular and important I2C module sending and receiving data API functions.

The function I2CMasterSlaveAddSet() is an important function used to initiate a data operation, either transmit or receive between the master and the slave. The second argument is a 7-bit slave address ui8SlaveAddr. The third argument bReceive is a Boolean value and it is used to indicate the address type for the slave device. If this value is true, it means that the slave address ui8SlaveAddr is a reading address and the master initiated a reading operation from the slave. Otherwise if this value is false, this means that the master is issuing a writing or transmitting operation to the slave device with the slave writing address.

The I2CMasterControl() is a multi-purpose API function with more powerful control abilities for the master data operations. The second argument of this function ui32Cmd is a command parameter used to indicate what kind of control function should be applied to the master device. This command can be any one from a collection of commands, exactly from a collection of command macros listed in Table 8.29. For a single data operation, it should be prefixed by I2C_MASTER_CMD_SINGLE; and for burst operations, it can be I2C_MASTER_CMD_BURST.

An I2C project built with these I2C Module API functions can be found from the Lab project Lab8_5, which is a loopback I2C master and slave testing project modified based on an example project provided by TI. This lab belongs to a part of the home works for the readers.

8.5 UNIVERSAL ASYNCHRONOUS RECEIVERS/TRANSMITTERS (UARTs)

The Universal Asynchronous Receivers and Transmitters (UART) provide asynchronous serial data communications for MCU- and UART-compatible devices. The UART is very similar to Synchronous Serial Interface (SSI) in working principle and structure, but the only difference is that the former belongs to the asynchronous communications and the latter is the synchronous serial communication interface.

The UART performs the parallel-to-serial functions in the transmitting mode and serial-to-parallel conversions in the receiving mode. It is very similar in functionality to a popular UART, but is not register-compatible with any UART.

Some of important features of the Tiva™ UART include:

- A 16×12-bit receive FIFO (16×8-bit data with 4 control-bit) and a 16×8-bit transmit FIFO.
- Programmable baud rate generator.
- Automatic generation and stripping of Start, Stop, and Parity bits.
- Line break generation and detection.
- Programmable serial interface with
  - 5, 6, 7, or 8 data bits.
  - Even, Odd, Stick, or no parity bit generation and detection.
  - 1 or 2 stop bits generation.
  - Baud rate generation, from 0 to processor clock/16.
- Modem control/flow control.
- IrDA serial-IR (SIR) encoder/decoder.
- DMA interface and 9-bit operation.

First let's take a look at the asynchronous serial data communication protocols.

8.5.1 Asynchronous Serial Communication Protocols and Data Framing

We have provided detailed discussions about the asynchronous serial data communication protocols and data framing in Section 8.3.1. Unlike SSI, in which both transmitter and receiver use the same clock rate as the data operation timing base to ensure both master and slave to transmit and receive data correctly, in asynchronous serial data communications, the transmitter and receiver use its own clock as the timing base, and therefore the pre-defined data communication protocols and data framing are necessary to make this kind of data transmitting and receiving successful.

As shown in Figure 8.3, each piece of serial data to be transmitted should be configured as follows:

1. A logic High is appeared on the communication line when the transmission line is idle.
2. A High-to-Low transaction starts an asynchronously data communication.
3. The data can be 5, 6, 7, or 8 bits long attached with 0 or 1 parity bit and 1 or 2 stop bits.

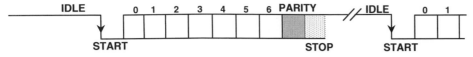

Figure 8.61.   7 Bits + Parity + 1 Stop Bit data framing.

Figure 8.61 shows an example of using 7 data bits with 1 parity and 1 stop bit protocol.

The TM4C123GH6PM MCU system provides eight UART modules (UART0~UART7), and each module can work independently to perform asynchronous serial data communications. Each module can be programmed to transmit (TX) and receive (RX) data by using the different baud rates, and each module can be driven by using the System Clock or the internal Precision Oscillator PIOSC.

The data to be transmitted is first converted from the parallel format to the serial format and is then placed into the transmit FIFO via UARTDR. Then the data can be serially transmitted to the communication line via the transmit logic. When receiving data, the data stream is first converted from the serial to the parallel format and is then placed into the receive FIFO. Then the data can be picked up from the receive FIFO and loaded into the MCU via UARTDR.

The UART can be configured for transmit or receive via the TXE and RXE bits in the UART Control (UARTCTL) register. Transmit and receive are both enabled after a system reset. Before any control registers can be programmed, the UART must be disabled by clearing the UARTEN bit in UARTCTL register. If the UART is disabled during a TX or RX operation, the current transaction is completed prior to the UART stopping.

The UART module also includes a serial IR (SIR) encoder/decoder block that can be connected to an infrared transceiver to implement an IrDA SIR physical layer. The SIR function is programmed using the UARTCTL register.

8.5.2 Asynchronous Serial Interface Architecture and Functional Block Diagram

The functional block diagram for one UART module is shown in Figure 8.62.

Each UART module can be configured and controlled by four groups of registers: the Clock Control and Baud Rate Generation registers, the Control/Status registers (including FIFOs), the Interrupt Control and DMA Control registers, and Identification registers.

The functions and properties of these registers can be described in terms of each group.

1. Clock Control and Baud Rate Generation Register Group:
   - UART Clock Configuration (UARTCC) Register: Configure UART clock source.
   - UART Control (UARTCTL) Register: Control the operations of UART.
   - UART Integer Baud Rate Divisor (UARTIBRD) Register: Provide integer divider.
   - UART Fractional Baud Rate Divisor (UARTFBRD) Register: Provide fraction divider.

2. Control/Status Register Group:
   - UART Control (UARTCTL) Register: Control the operations of UART.
   - UART Line Control Register (UARTLCHR): Setup data framing parameters.
   - UART Data Register (UARTDR): Provide a temporary data storage for FIFO.
   - UART Receive Status/Error Clear Register (UARTRSR/UARTECR): Provide data receive status and clear data framing, break, and overrun errors.

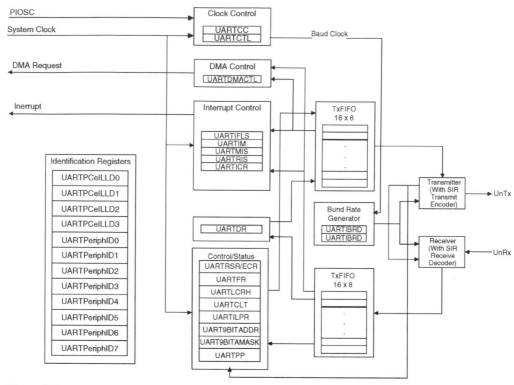

Figure 8.62. The functional block diagram for one UART module. (Reprinted with the permission of the Texas Instruments Incorporated.)

- UART Flag Register (UARTFR): Provide UART working status.
- UART IrDA Low-Power Register (UARTILPR): Store the 8-bit low-power counter divisor value.
- UART 9-Bit Self Address Register (UART9BITADDR): This register is used in conjunction with UART9BITAMASK to form a match for address-byte received.
- UART 9-Bit Self Address Mask (UART9BITAMASK): Enable the address mask for 9-bit mode.
- UART Peripheral Properties (UARTPP) Register: Provide information to indicate whether to support 9-bit operation or smart card operation.
- Transmit FIFO (T_xFIFO): Store 16×8-bit data to be transmitted.
- Receive FIFO (R_xFIFO): Store 16×12-bit data to be received.

3. Interrupt Control and DMA Control Register Group:

- UART Interrupt FIFO Level Select (UARTIFLS) Register: Select the interrupt triggering level based on the FIFO data storage level.
- UART Raw Interrupt Status (UARTRIS) Register: Provide the raw interrupt status.
- UART Interrupt Mask (UARTIM) Register: Control whether the UARTRIS can be sent to the interrupt controller or not.
- UART Masked Interrupt Status (UARTMIS) Register: Provide the current masked interrupt status.
- UART Interrupt Clear Register (UARTICR): Clear any interrupt.
- UART DMA Control (UARTDMACTL) Register: Control the DMA operations.

4. UART Identification Register Group: 12 registers are included in this group to provide software identification functions for each UART module.

Next let's discuss these registers based on their group one by one.

8.5.3 UART Module Operations and Control Registers

In this section we introduce and discuss most popular UART operations and detail popular registers including the bit fields and their functions.

8.5.3.1 Transmit/Receive Logic and Data Transmission and Receiving

As we mentioned, the transmit logic performs parallel-to-serial conversion on the data read from the transmit FIFO. The control logic outputs the serial bit stream beginning with a Start bit (High-to-Low edge) and followed by the data bits with LSB first, parity bit, and the stop bits. The receive logic performs serial-to-parallel conversion on the received data bit stream after a valid Start pulse (Low-to-High) has been detected. The Overrun, parity, frame error checking, and line-break detection are also performed, and their status (4 bits) accompanying the data (8 bits) together are written to the receive FIFO (16×12).

Data received or transmitted are stored in two 16-byte FIFOs; however, the receiving FIFO has an extra four bits per 8-bit data item for status information.

For transmission, data is written into the transmit FIFO. If the UART is enabled, it causes a data frame to start transmitting with the parameters indicated in the UARTLCRH register. Data continues to be transmitted until there is no data left in the transmit FIFO. The BUSY bit in the UART Flag (UARTFR) register is asserted as soon as data is written to the transmit to make the FIFO non-empty and remains asserted as long as data is being transmitted. The BUSY bit is cleared only when the transmit FIFO is empty, and the last character has been transmitted from the shift register, including the Stop bits. The UART can indicate that it is busy even though the UART may no longer be enabled.

When the receiver is idle (the UnRx signal is continuously 1), and the data input detects a High-to-Low transition (a Start bit has been received), the receive counter begins running and data is sampled on the 8th cycle of Baud16 or 4th cycle of Baud8 depending on the setting of the HSE bit (bit 5) in UARTCTL register.

The Start bit is valid and recognized if the UnRx signal is still low on the 8th cycle of Baud16 (HSE = 0) or the 4th cycle of Baud 8 (HSE = 1); otherwise it is ignored. After a valid Start bit is detected, successive data bits are sampled on every 16th cycle of Baud16 or 8th cycle of Baud8 (that is, one bit period later) according to the programmed length of the data and value of the HSE bit in UARTCTL register. The parity bit is then checked if the parity mode is enabled. Data length and parity are defined in the UARTLCRH register.

Lastly, a valid Stop bit is confirmed if the UnRx signal is High; otherwise a framing error has occurred. When a full word is received, the data is stored into the receive FIFO along with any error bits associated with that word.

8.5.3.2 UART Modem Handshake Support

A UART can work as a modem to provide the interface between a computer and a serial asynchronous device. A computer can also be considered to be a UART device when it is

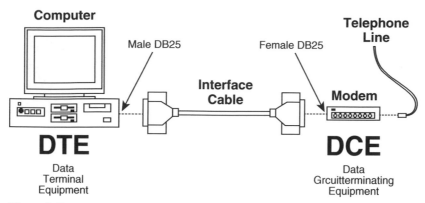

Figure 8.63. The DTE and DCE connections.

connected as Data Terminal Equipment (DTE), and a model can be considered to be Data Communication Equipment (DCE). In general, a modem is a DCE and a computing device that connects to a modem is a DTE. Figure 8.63 shows an illustrating block diagram for these equipments.

In all eight UART modules, only UART1 can be used to work as a modem to provide flow control ability for asynchronous data communications.

When using UART to perform asynchronous data operations, the data communication can be divided into the following four modes based on its functionality: simplex, half-duplex, full-duplex, and multiplex.

- `Simplex`: Serial communication is only taking place in one direction, either from DTE to DCE or vice versa.
- `Half-duplex`: Serial communication can take place in both directions, but the communication can only take place in one direction at a moment. This means that either sender or receiver can send or receive the information in different time, but they cannot send and receive the data simultaneously.
- `Full-duplex`: Allows serial communications to take place in both directions at the same time, which means that both sender and receiver can handle and exchange the data information simultaneously.
- `Multiplex`: Allows multiple serial communications channels to occur over the same serial communication line. Multiplex operations are performed by allocating either separate frequencies or time slice to the individual serial communication channels.

A full group of modem flow control signals used for DTE and DCE is shown in Figure 8.64. In UART module 1, only two signals, U1CTS and U1RTS, are used and they are defined differently based the roles of these signals. When used as a DTE, the modem flow control signals are defined as follows (see Figure 8.64):

- $/\overline{\text{U1CTS}}$ is Clear To Send (CTS).
- $/\overline{\text{U1RTS}}$ is Request To Send (RTS).

When used as a DCE, the modem flow control signals are defined as:

- $/\overline{\text{U1CTS}}$ is Request To Send (RTS).
- $/\overline{\text{U1RTS}}$ is Clear To Send (CTS).

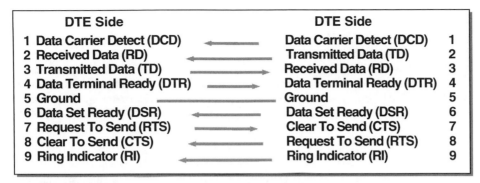

Figure 8.64.   The modem flow control signals used in UART communications.

The flow control can be designed and implemented by either hardware or software. The so-called hardware flow control is to use RTS and CTS lines to get the UART status. The software flow control is to use UART interrupts to get the UART status.

Hardware flow control between two devices is accomplished by connecting the/U1RTS output to the/CTS input on the receiving device and then connecting the/RTS output on the receiving device to the/U1CTS input.

The/U1CTS input controls the transmitter. The transmitter may only transmit data when the/U1CTS input is asserted. The/U1RTS output signal indicates the state of the receive FIFO./U1CTS remains asserted until the preprogrammed watermark level is reached, indicating that the Receive FIFO has no space to store additional characters.

The UARTCTL register bits 15 (CTSEN) and 14 (RTSEN) specify the flow control mode as shown in Table 8.30.

Software flow control between two devices is implemented by using interrupts to indicate the status of the UART. Interrupts may be generated for the/U1CTS signal using bit 1 of the UARTIM register. The raw and masked interrupt status may be checked using the UARTRIS and UARTMIS register. These interrupts may be cleared using the UARTICR register.

8.5.3.3 UART FIFO Operations

The UART has two FIFOs; one for transmit FIFO (16×8) and one for receive FIFO (16×12). Both FIFOs are accessed via two UARTDR registers. Read operations of the UARTDR register return a 12-bit value from the receive FIFO, which is consisting of 8 data bits and 4 error flags while write operations place 8-bit data into the transmit FIFO. Two different UARTDR registers, one for transmit data and the other one for receive data, are used in each UART module although they have the same address.

Table 8.30.   The modem flow control signals used in UART1.

CTSEN	RTSEN	Description
1	1	Both RTS and CTS flow control enabled
1	0	Only CTS flow control enabled
0	1	Only RTS flow control enabled
0	0	Both RTS and CTS flow control disabled

After a system reset, both FIFOs are disabled and act as 1-byte-deep holding registers. Both FIFOs are enabled by setting the FEN bit in UARTLCRH register.

FIFO status can be monitored via the UART Flag Register (UARTFR) and the UART Receive Status Register (UARTRSR). Three FIFO statuses, empty, full, and overrun, are monitored. The UARTFR register contains empty and full flags in TXFE, TXFF, RXFE, and RXFF bits, and the UARTRSR register shows overrun status via the OE bit. If both FIFOs are disabled, the empty and full flags are set based on the status of the 1-byte-deep holding registers.

The trigger points at which the FIFOs generate interrupts is controlled via the UART Interrupt FIFO Level Select (UARTIFLS) register. Both FIFOs can be individually configured to trigger interrupts at different levels, such as 1/8, 1/4, 1/2, 3/4, and 7/8. For example, if the 1/4 option is selected for the receive FIFO, the UART generates a receive interrupt after 4 data bytes are received. After a system reset, both FIFOs are configured to trigger an interrupt at the ½ level.

8.5.3.4 UART Interrupts and DMA Control

An UART interrupt can be generated for many possible reasons and interrupt sources, which include (1) any data operation error such as overrun, break, parity, framing, and receive timeout and (2) either data transmit or data receive complete.

All of these can be considered as interrupt sources and can be combined or ORed together to generate a single interrupt request that can be handled and processed in a single interrupt service routine (ISR) or handler.

The interrupt events that can trigger a controller-level interrupt are defined in the UART Interrupt Mask (UARTIM) register by setting the corresponding IM bits. If interrupts are not used, the raw interrupt status is visible via the UART Raw Interrupt Status (UARTRIS) register.

Any UART interrupt can be cleared by writing 1 to the corresponding bit in the UART Interrupt Clear Register (UARTICR).

A receive timeout interrupt is generated when the receiving FIFO is not empty and no further data is received over a 32-bit period when the HSE bit is clear or over a 64-bit period when the HSE bit is set. This receive timeout interrupt can be cleared either when the FIFO becomes empty through reading all the data or by reading the holding register, or when a 1 is written to the corresponding bit in the UARTICR register.

The receive interrupt changes state when one of the following events occurs:

- If both FIFOs are enabled and the receive FIFO reaches the programmed trigger level, the RXRIS bit is set. The receive interrupt is cleared by reading data from the receive FIFO until it becomes less than the trigger level, or by clearing the interrupt by writing a 1 to the RXIC bit.

- If both FIFOs are disabled and data is received thereby filling the location, the RXRIS bit is set. The receive interrupt is cleared by performing a single read of the receive FIFO or by clearing the interrupt by writing a 1 to the RXIC bit.

The transmit interrupt changes state when one of the following events occurs:

- If both FIFOs are enabled and the transmit FIFO progresses over the programmed trigger level, the TXRIS bit is set. Then the transmit interrupt is generated based on a transition through level, and therefore the FIFO must be written past the programmed trigger level; otherwise no further transmit interrupts will be generated. The transmit interrupt is cleared by writing data to the transmit FIFO until it becomes greater than the trigger level, or by clearing the interrupt by writing a 1 to the TXIC bit.

- If both FIFOs are disabled and there is no data present in the transmitters single location, the TXRIS bit is set. It is cleared by performing a single write to the transmit FIFO, or by clearing the interrupt by writing a 1 to the TXIC bit.

The UART also provides an interface to the μDMA controller with separate channels for data transmit and receive. The DMA operation is enabled via the UART DMA Control (UARTDMACTL) register. When DMA operation is enabled, the UART asserts a DMA request on the receive or transmit channel when the associated FIFO can transfer data.

For the receive channel, a single transfer request is generated whenever any data is in the receive FIFO. A burst transfer request is asserted whenever the amount of data in the receive FIFO is at or above the FIFO trigger level configured in the UARTIFLS register.

For the transmit channel, a single transfer request is generated whenever there is at least one empty location in the transmit FIFO. The burst request is generated whenever the transmit FIFO contains fewer characters than the FIFO trigger level. The single and burst DMA transfer requests are handled automatically by the μDMA controller depending on how the DMA channel is configured.

To enable DMA operation for the receive channel, set the RXDMAE bit of the DMA Control (UARTDMACTL) register. To enable DMA operation for the transmit channel, set the TXDMAE bit of the UARTDMACTL register. The UART can also be configured to stop using DMA for the receive channel if a receive error occurs. If the DMAERR bit of the UARTDMACR register is set and a receive error occurs, the DMA receive requests are automatically disabled. This error condition can be cleared by clearing the appropriate UART error interrupt.

8.5.3.5 UART Serial IR (SIR) Support

The UART peripheral includes an IrDA serial-IR (SIR) encoder/decoder block. The IrDA SIR block provides functionality that converts between an asynchronous UART data stream and a half-duplex serial SIR interface. No analog processing is performed on-chip. The role of the SIR block is to provide a digital encoded output and decoded input to the UART. When enabled, the SIR block uses the UnTx and UnRx pins for the SIR protocol. These signals should be connected to an infrared transceiver to implement an IrDA SIR physical layer link. The SIR block can receive and transmit, but it is only half-duplex so it cannot do both at the same time. Transmission must be stopped before data can be received. The IrDA SIR physical layer specifies a minimum 10 ms delay between transmission and reception.

8.5.3.6 9-Bit UART Mode

The UART provides a 9-bit mode that is enabled with the 9BITEN bit in the UART9-BITADDR register. This feature is useful in a multi-drop configuration of the UART where a single master connected to multiple slaves can communicate with a particular slave through its address or set of addresses along with a qualifier for an address byte. When working in this mode, all the slaves check for the address qualifier in the place of the parity bit and, if set, then compare the byte received with the preprogrammed address. If the address matches, then it receives or sends further data. If the address does not match, it drops the address byte and any subsequent data bytes. If the UART is in 9-bit mode, then the receiver operates with no parity mode. The address can be pre-defined to match with the received byte and it can be configured with the UART9BITADDR register. The matching can be extended to a set of addresses using the address mask in the UART9-BITAMASK register. By default, the UART9BITAMASK is 0xFF, meaning that only the specified address is matched.

When no match can be found, the rest of the data bytes with the 9th bit cleared are dropped. If a match is found, then an interrupt is generated to the NVIC for further action. The subsequent data bytes with the cleared 9th bit are stored in the FIFO. Software can mask this interrupt in case μDMA and/or FIFO operations are enabled for this instance and processor intervention is not required. All the sending transactions with 9-bit mode are data bytes and the 9th bit is cleared. Software can override the 9th bit to be set by overriding the parity settings to sticky parity with odd parity enabled for a particular byte. To match the transmission time with correct parity settings, the address byte can be transmitted as a single and then a burst transfer. The Transmit FIFO does not hold the address/data bit, hence software should take care of enabling the address bit appropriately. Next let's concentrate on these control registers used for these operations.

8.5.3.7 *UART Module Clock Control and Baud Rate Generation Registers*

The registers in this group are used to select the clock source for the UART module and define the baud rate for the data operations. There are four registers in this group and they are:

- UART Clock Configuration (UARTCC) Register.
- UART Control (UARTCTL) Register.
- UART Integer Baud Rate Divisor (UARTIBRD) Register.
- UART Fractional Baud Rate Divisor (UARTFBRD) Register.

The UARTCC is a 32-bit register but only the 4 lowest bits, bits 3~0 or CS bit-field, are used to determine the clock source for the UART module. When CS = 0x0, the System Clock is selected as the clock source. When CS = 0x5, the PIOSC is selected as the clock source.

Only bit 5 (HSE) in the UARTCTL register is used to enable the UART module to use different clock rate by dividing the System Clock with different factors. If the HSE = 0, the System Clock is divided by 16; otherwise if HSE = 1, the System Clock is divided by 8.

Both the UARTIBDR and UARTFBDR registers are 32-bit registers and used to store integer and fractional dividing factors used to calculate the baud rate for the UART module. The lower 16 bits on the UARTIBDR register is used to reserve an integer divisor (BRDI), and the lower 6 bits in the UARTFBDR register is to reserve a fractional divisor (BRDF). The relationship between these divisors and the Baud Rate Divisor (BRD) is

$$BRD = BRDI + BRDF = UARTSysClk /(ClkDiv \times Baud\ Rate)$$

where UARTSysClk is the System Clock frequency. The ClkDiv = 16 if HSE = 0 and ClkDiv = 8 if HSE = 1 in the UARTCTL register. Therefore the Baud Rate for the UART is

Baud Rate = UARTSysClk/(BRDI + BRDF) × ClkDiv

The 6-bit fractional number that is in the DIVFRAC bit field in the UARTFBRD register can be calculated by taking the fractional part of the baud-rate divisor, multiplying it by 64, and adding 0.5 to account for rounding errors:

UARTFBRD[DIVFRAC] = Integer(BRDF∗64 + 0.5)

The reason for using the ClkDiv parameter is because the UART generates an *internal baud-rate reference clock* at 8× or 16× the baud-rate referred to as Baud8 and Baud16, depending on the setting of the HSE bit (bit 5) in UARTCTL. This reference clock must be divided by 8 or 16 to get the transmit clock. This reference clock is used for error detection during receive operations. Note that the state of the HSE bit has no effect on clock generation in ISO 7816 smart card mode.

The UART Line Control Register (UARTLCRH) is combined with the UARTIBRD and UARTFBRD registers together to form an internal 30-bit register (UARTLCRH, Lower 8 bits; UARTIBRD, Lower 16 bits; and UARTFBRD, Lower 6 bits). Only when a writing operation is performed to the UARTLCRH register, this international 30-bit register should be updated. This means that any change to the baud rate divisor (including changes to either UARTIBRD or UARTFBRD register) must be followed by a write operation to the UARTLCRH register for the change to take effect.

8.5.3.8 UART Module Control/Status and FIFO Control Registers

The registers in this group include:

- UART Control (UARTCTL) Register.
- UART Line Control Register (UARTLCHR).
- UART Data Register (UARTDR).
- UART Receive Status/Error Clear Register (UARTRSR/UARTECR).
- UART Flag Register (UARTFR).
- UART IrDA Low-Power Register (UARTILPR).
- UART 9-Bit Self-Address Register (UART9BITADDR).
- UART 9-Bit Self-Address Mask (UART9BITAMASK).
- UART Peripheral Properties (UARTPP) Register.
- Transmit FIFO (T_XFIFO) and Receive FIFO (R_XFIFO).

In this section we only introduce and discuss some important and popular registers. For UART9BITADDR, UART9BITAMASK, and UARTPP registers, refer to related documents to get details.

8.5.3.8.1 UART Control Register (UARTCTL) The bit configuration for the UARTCTL register is shown in Figure 8.65. The bit field and bit function for this register is shown in Table 8.31.

	31	30	29	28	27	26	25	24	23	22	21	20	19	18	17	16
	reserved															
Type	RO	RO	RO	RO	RO	RO	RO	RO	RO	RO	RO	RO	RO	RO	RO	RO
Reset	0	0	0	0	0	0	0	0	0	0	0	0	0	0	0	0

	15	14	13	12	11	10	9	8	7	6	5	4	3	2	1	0
	CTSEN	RTSEN	reserved		RTS	reserved	RXE	TXE	LBE	reserved	HSE	EOT	SMART	SIRLP	SIREN	UARTEN
Type	RW	RW	RO	RO	RW	RO	RW	RW	RW	RO	RO	RO	RO	RO	RO	RO
Reset	0	0	0	0	0	0	1	1	0	0	0	0	0	0	0	0

Figure 8.65. Bit configurations of the UARTCTL register. (Reprinted with the permission of the Texas Instruments Incorporated.)

The UARTCTL register is the control register. All bits are cleared on a system reset except for the `Transmit Enable` (TXE) and `Receive Enable` (RXE) bits, which are set. To enable the UART module, the UARTEN bit must be set. If software requires a configuration change in the module, the UARTEN bit must be cleared to disable the UART before the configuration changes can be written.

A point to be noted is that the UARTCTL register should not be modified while the UART is enabled or else the results are unpredictable. The following sequence is recommended for making changes to the UARTCTL register.

1. Disable the UART.
2. Wait for the end of transmission or reception of the current character.
3. Flush the transmit FIFO by clearing bit 4 (FEN) in the line control register UARTLCRH.

Table 8.31. Bit-field value and its function for UARTCTL register.

Bit	Name	Reset	Function
31:16 13:12 10, 6	Reserved	0x000 0x0 0x0	Reserved
15	CTSEN	0x0	Clear To Send Enable. 0: CTS is disabled. 1: CTS is enabled. Data is only transmitted when the U1CTS signal is asserted.
14	RTSEN	0x0	Request To Send Enable. 0: RTS is disabled. 1: RTS is enabled. Data is only requested when receive FIFO has available entries..
11	RTS	0x0	Request To Send. When RTSEN is clear, the status of this bit is reflected on the U1RTS signal. If RTSEN is set, this bit is ignored on a write and should be ignored on read.
9	RXE	0x0	UART Receive Enable. 0: Receiver is disabled. 1: Receiver is enabled.
8	TXE	0x0	UART Transmit Enable. 0: Transmitter is disabled. 1: Transmitter is enabled.
7	LBE	0x0	UART Loop Back Enable. 0: Normal operation. 1: UnTx is connected to the UnRx to form a loop.
5	HSE	0x0	High-Speed Operation. 0: UART clock = System Clock/16; 1: UART clock = System Clock/8.
4	EOT	0x0	End Of Transmission. 0: The TXRIS bit is set when the transmit FIFO condition specified in UARTIFLS is met. 1: The TXRIS bit is set only after all transmitted data have cleared the serialized.
3	SMART	0x0	Smart Card Support. 0: Normal operation. 1: Smart card mode.
2	SIRLP	0x0	UART SIR Low-Power Mode. 0: Low-level bits are transmitted as an active High pulse with a width of 3/16th of the bit period; 1: SIR low-power mode.
1	SIREN	0x0	UART SIR Enable. 0: Normal operation; 1: The SIR mode.
0	UARTEN	0x0	UART Enable. 0: UART is disabled; 1: UART is enabled.

UARTLCRH Register

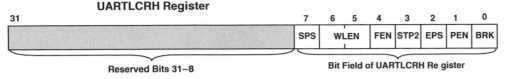

Figure 8.66. Bits configurations for UARTLCRH register.

4. Reprogram to modify the control register.

5. Enable the UART.

8.5.3.8.2 UART Line Control Register (UARTLCRH) The UARTLCRH register is the line control register, and it is used to configure serial data communication parameters such as data length, parity, and stop bit.

When updating the baud-rate divisor (UARTIBRD and/or UARTIFRD), the UARTLCRH register must also be written. The bit configuration for the UARTLCRH register is shown in Figure 8.66. The bit field and bit function for this register are shown in Table 8.32.

8.5.3.8.3 UART Receive Status/Error Clear Register (UARTRSR/UARTECR) The UARTRSR/UARTECR is a 32-bit register, but only the lowest 4/8 bits are used to indicate the data operation status and all of these status bits can be cleared by writing any value to this register. Therefore this register has two functions: When reading, the data operational status and error status are displayed, when writing, all error bits are cleared.

In addition to the UARTDR registers, receive status can also be read from this UARTRSR register. If the status is read from this register, then the status information corresponds to the entry read from UARTDR prior to reading UARTRSR. The status information for overrun is set immediately when an overrun condition occurs.

Table 8.32. Bit-field value and its function for the UARTLCRH register.

Bit	Name	Reset	Function
31:8	Reserved	0x000	Reserved
7	SPS	0x0	UART Stick Parity Select When bits 1, 2, and 7 of UARTLCRH are set, the parity bit is transmitted and checked as a 0. When bits 1 and 7 are set and 2 is cleared, the parity bit is transmitted and checked as a 1. When this bit is cleared, stick parity is disabled.
6:5	WLEN	0x0	UART Word Length The bits indicate the number of data bits transmitted or received in a frame as follows: 0x0: 5 bits (default); 0x1: 6 bits; 0x2: 7 bits; 0x3: 8 bits.
4	FEN	0x0	UART FIFOs Enable. 0: The FIFOs are disabled (Character mode). The FIFOs become 1-byte-deep holding registers. 1: The transmit and receive FIFO buffers are enabled (FIFO mode).
3	STP2	0x0	UART 2 Stop Bits Select. 0: 1 stop bit is used. 1: 2 stop bits are used.
2	EPS	0x0	UART Even Parity Select. 0: Odd parity is selected. 1: Even parity is selected.
1	PEN	0x0	UART Parity Enable. 0: No parity is used. 1: Parity is enabled.
0	BRK	0x0	UART Send Break. 0: Normal operation. 1: A Low level is continually output on the UnTx signal, after completing transmission of the current character. For the proper execution of the break command, software must set this bit for at least two frames (character periods).

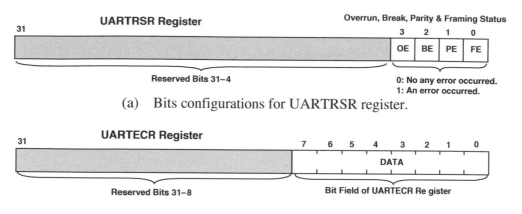

(a) Bits configurations for UARTRSR register.

(b) Bits configurations for UARTECR register.

Figure 8.67. Bits configurations for UARTRSR/ECR register.

The UARTRSR register is a read-only register and it cannot be written. The UARTECR is a write-only register and it cannot be read. The bits configurations for the registers UARTRSR and UARTECR are shown in Figures 8.67a and 8.67b, respectively.

The lower 4 bits on the UARTRSR register are used to monitor four data operational statuses, which include: Overrun, Break, Parity, and Framing statuses. If any kind of error is occurred, the corresponding bit is set to 1.

The lower 8 bits in the UARTECR register allow users to write any data into these fields to clear all errors displayed in the UARTRSR register if any of them occurred. The point to be noted is that the UARTRSR is a read-only register, but the UARTECR is a write-only register.

8.5.3.8.4 UART Data Register (UARTDR) There are two 32-bit UARTDR registers with two different functions for data transmit and receive. In fact, these registers work as a bridge buffer between the MCU and FIFOs to temporarily store data to be transmitted into the transmit FIFO, and store data receiving from the receive FIFO. Physically these two UARTDR registers have no connection between them.

For transmitted data, if the FIFO is enabled, an 8-bit or a byte data written to the transmit UARTDR register is pushed onto the transmit FIFO. If the FIFO is disabled, data is stored in the transmitter holding register (the bottom word of the transmit FIFO). A write to this register initiates a transmission from the UART.

For received data, if the FIFO is enabled, the received data byte and the 4-bit status, break, frame, parity, and overrun are pushed onto the 12-bit wide receiving FIFO. If the FIFO is disabled, the data byte and status are stored in the receiving holding register (the bottom word of the receive FIFO). The received data can be retrieved by reading this receive UARTDR register.

Figure 8.68 shows the bits configurations for the receive UARTDR register.

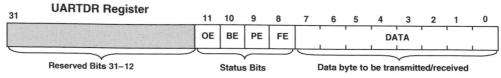

Figure 8.68. Bits configurations for UARTDR register.

Figure 8.69. Bits configurations for UARTFR register.

8.5.3.8.5 UART Flag Register (UARTFR) The UARTFR is a 32-bit flag register used to monitor and display the UART running status. After reset, the TXFF, RXFF, and BUSY bits are 0, and TXFE and RXFE bits are 1. The CTS bit indicates the modem flow control. A point to be noted is that the modem bits are only implemented on UART1 and are reserved on UART0 and UART2.

The bit configuration for the UARTFR register is shown in Figure 8.69. The bit field and bit function for this register is shown in Table 8.33.

It can be found that the function of this register is an addition to the UARTRSR register with more running statuses provided. Most of these statuses are dependent on the FIFOs Enable bit FEN in the UARTLCRH register. The bit 3 (BUSY) is an important status used to indicate whether the UART is currently busy in transmitting data or not.

8.5.3.9 UART Module Interrupt and DMA Control Registers

The registers in this group include:

- UART Interrupt FIFO Level Select (UARTIFLS) Register.
- UART Raw Interrupt Status (UARTRIS) Register.

Table 8.33. Bit-field value and its function for the UARTFR register.

Bit	Name	Reset	Function
31:8	Reserved	0x000	Reserved
7	TXFE	0x0	UART Transmit FIFO Empty. The meaning of this bit depends on the state of the FEN bit in the UARTLCRH register. 0: Transmitter has data to transmit. 1: If the FIFO is disabled (FEN = 0), the transmit holding register is empty. If the FIFO is enabled (FEN = 1), the transmit FIFO is empty.
6	RXFF	0x0	UART Receive FIFO Full. The meaning of this bit depends on the state of the FEN bit in the UARTLCRH register. 0: The receiver can receive data. 1: If the FIFO is disabled (FEN = 0), the receive holding register is full. If the FIFO is enabled (FEN = 1), the receive FIFO is full.
5	TXFF	0x0	UART Transmit FIFO Full. The meaning of this bit depends on the state of the FEN bit in the UARTLCRH register. 0: The transmitter is not full. 1: If the FIFO is disabled (FEN=0), the transmit holding register is full. If the FIFO is enabled (FEN=1), the transmit FIFO is full.
4	RXFE	0x0	UART Receive FIFO Empty. The meaning of this bit depends on the state of the FEN bit in the UARTLCRH register. 0: Receiver is not empty. 1: If the FIFO is disabled (FEN=0), the receive holding register is empty. If the FIFO is enabled (FEN=1), the receive FIFO is empty.
3	BUSY	0x0	UART Busy. 0: UART is not busy. 1: UART is busy transmitting data.
2:1	Reserved	0x0	Reserved
0	CTS	0x0	Clear To Send. 0: The U1CTS signal is not asserted. 1: The U1CTS signal is asserted.

Figure 8.70.   Bits configurations for UARTIFLS register.

- UART Interrupt Mask (UARTIM) Register.
- UART Masked Interrupt Status (UARTMIS) Register.
- UART Interrupt Clear Register (UARTICR).
- UART DMA Control (UARTDMACTL) Register.

Now let's have a closer look at these registers one by one.

8.5.3.9.1 UART Interrupt FIFO Level Select (UARTIFLS) Register   The UARTIFLS register is the interrupt FIFO level select register. This register can be used to define the FIFO level at which the TXRIS and RXRIS bits in the UARTRIS register are triggered.

The interrupts are generated based on a transition through a level rather than being based on the level. This means that the interrupts are generated when the fill level progresses through the trigger level. For example, if the receive trigger level is set to the half-way mark, the interrupt is triggered as the module is receiving the 9th character.

After a system reset, the TXIFLSEL and RXIFLSEL bits are configured so that the FIFOs trigger an interrupt at the half-way mark.

Figure 8.70 shows the bit configurations of the UARTIFLS register, and Table 8.34 shows the bit field and functions for this register.

8.5.3.9.2 UART Raw Interrupt Status (UARTRIS) Register   This is a 32-bit register, but only the lower 9 bits are used to indicate the raw interrupt status for related UART events or errors. If any of these bits is set to 1, it means that a corresponding raw interrupt has occurred. Otherwise if that bit is 0, no related interrupt has occurred. Figure 8.71 shows the bit configurations for this register.

8.5.3.9.3 UART Interrupt Mask (UARTIM) Register   Similar to UARTRIS register, this register is used to enable or disable the related raw interrupt to be sent to the interrupt controller to be further processed. The bit configurations for this register are also shown in Figure 8.71. If a bit is set to 1, the corresponding raw interrupt set in the UARTRIS register is unmasked and can be sent to the NVIC to be further handled. If a bit is 0, the corresponding raw interrupt cannot be sent to the NVIC.

Table 8.34.   Bit-field value and its function for the UARTIFLS register.

Bit	Name	Reset	Function
31:6	Reserved	0x000	Reserved
5:3	RXIFLSEL	0x0	UART Receive Interrupt FIFO Level Select. 0x0: RX FIFO ≥ ⅛ full; 0x1: RX FIFO ≥ ¼ full; 0x2: RX FIFO ≥ ½ full (default) 0x3: RX FIFO ≥ ¾ full; 0x4: RX FIFO ≥ ⅞ full; 0x5–0x7 Reserved.
2:0	TXIFLSEL	0x0	UART Transmit Interrupt FIFO Level Select. 0x0: TX FIFO ≤ ⅞ empty; 0x1: TX FIFO ≤ ¾ empty; 0x2: TX FIFO ≤ ½ empty (default) 0x3: TX FIFO ≤ ¼ empty; 0x4: TX FIFO ≤ ⅛ empty; 0x5-0x7 Reserved.

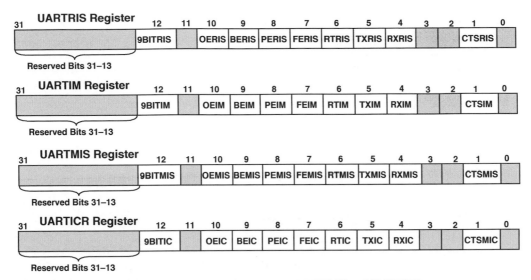

Figure 8.71. Bit configurations for UARTRIS, UARTIM, UARTMIS and UARTICR.

8.5.3.9.4 UART Masked Interrupt Status (UARTMIS) Register The UARTMIS register is the masked interrupt status register. On a read, this register gives the current masked status value of the corresponding interrupt. A write has no effect.

The bit configurations for this register are also shown in Figure 8.71. If a bit is set to 1, the corresponding raw interrupt set in the UARTRIS register has been sent to the NVIC to be further handled. If a bit is 0, the corresponding raw interrupt was not sent to the NVIC.

8.5.3.9.5 UART Interrupt Clear Register (UARTICR) The UARTICR register is the interrupt clear register. When writing a 1, the corresponding interrupt, both raw interrupt and masked interrupt, is cleared. A write of 0 has no effect.

The bit configurations for the UARTICR register are shown in Figure 8.71.

8.5.3.9.6 UART DMA Control (UARTDMACTL) Register This is a 32-bit register, but only the lowest 3 bits are used to control the DMA operations on the UART. The bit configurations of this register are shown in Figure 8.72. The bit field and function are shown in Table 8.35.

Next let's take a look at the UART control signals applied on the related GPIO Ports and GPIO pins.

Figure 8.72. Bit configuration on UARTDAMCTL register.

Table 8.35. Bit-field value and its function for the UARTDMACTL register.

Bit	Name	Reset	Function
31:3	Reserved	0x000	Reserved
2	DMAERR	0x0	DMA Error. 0: μDMA receiving requests are unaffected when a receive error occurs. 1: μDMA receiving requests are automatically disabled when a receive error occurs.
1	TXDMAE	0x0	Transmit DMA Enable. 0: μDMA for the transmit FIFO is disabled. 1: μDMA for the transmit FIFO is enabled.
0	RXDMAE	0x0	Receive DMA Enable. 0: μDMA for the receive FIFO is disabled. 1: μDMA for the receive FIFO is enabled.

8.5.4 UART Module Control Signals and Related GPIO Pins

All eight UART modules in the TM4C123GH6PM MCU system use the related GPIO pins to perform UART functions, such as transmit and receiving operations.

The UART signals are alternate functions for related GPIO signals and default to be GPIO signals at reset, with the exception of the U0Rx and U0Tx pins which default to the UART function.

Table 8.36 lists these GPIO pins when they work as alternate functions. The column in the Table 8.36 titled GPIO Pin lists the possible GPIO pin placements for these UART

Table 8.36. UART control signals and the related GPIO pins distributions.

UART Pin	GPIO Pin	Pin Type	Buffer Type	Pin Function
U0RX	PA0 (1)	I	TTL	UART Module 0 Receive.
U0TX	PA1 (1)	O	TTL	UART Module 0 Transmit.
U1CTS	PC5 (8) PF1 (1)	I	TTL	UART Module 1 Clear To Send.
U1RTS	PC4 (8) PF0 (1)	O	TTL	UART Module 1 Request To Send.
U1RX	PC4 (2) PB0 (1)	I	TTL	UART Module 1 Receive.
U1TX	PC5 (2) PB1 (1)	O	TTL	UART Module 1 Transmit.
U2RX	PD6 (1)	I	TTL	UART Module 2 Receive.
U2TX	PD7 (1)	O	TTL	UART Module 2 Transmit.
U3RX	PC6 (1)	I	TTL	UART Module 3 Receive.
U3TX	PC7 (1)	O	TTL	UART Module 3 Transmit.
U4RX	PC4 (1)	I	TTL	UART Module 4 Receive.
U4TX	PC5 (1)	O	TTL	UART Module 4 Transmit.
U5RX	PE4 (1)	I	TTL	UART Module 5 Receive.
U5TX	PE5 (1)	O	TTL	UART Module 5 Transmit.
U6RX	PD4 (1)	I	TTL	UART Module 6 Receive.
U6TX	PD5 (1)	O	TTL	UART Module 6 Transmit.
U7RX	PE0 (1)	I	TTL	UART Module 7 Receive.
U7TX	PE1 (1)	O	TTL	UART Module 7 Transmit.

signals. The AFSEL bit field in the GPIO Alternate Function Select (GPIOAF-SEL) register should be set to 1 to choose the UART function. The number in parentheses is the encoding that must be programmed into the PMCx field in the GPIO Port Control (GPIOPCTL) register to assign the UART signal to the specified GPIO port pin.

8.5.5 UART Module Initializations and Configurations

Before any UART module can perform any data operations, either transmit or receive, the selected UART module must be initialized and configured properly to enable the module to perform its normal data operations.

This initialization and configuration job can be divided into the following three parts based on their functions on different peripherals:

1. Initialize and configure the UART-related GPIO ports and pins.

2. Initialize and configure the clock source and baud rate for the UART module.

3. Initialize and configure UART module.

Let's use an example to illustrate how to initialize and configure a UART module with an assumption of using a default 16-MHz system clock as the clock source for the UART module 1.

8.5.5.1 Initialize and Configure the UART-Related GPIO Ports and Pins

Perform the following operations to complete the configurations for the UART-related GPIO Ports and GPIO pins:

- Enable and clock the appropriate GPIO module via the RCGCGPIO register. Here since we use UART module 1, enable and clock the GPIO Port B (see Table 8.36).
- Set the AFSEL bits on the GPIOB_AFSEL register for the appropriate pins. Here since we use PB0 and PB1, set 0x03 to this register to select and set PB0 and PB1.
- Configure the PMCx fields in the GPIOPCTL register to assign the UART signals to the appropriate pins. Here since PB1 and PB0 are used for U1TX and U1RX pins, a 0x00000011 should be set to the GPIOB_PCTL register (see number in the parentheses on Table 8.36).
- Set GPIO Port B, exactly PB1 and PB0, as digital function pins.

8.5.5.2 Initialize and Configure Clock Source and Baud Rate for the UART Module

Perform the following operations to complete these configurations:

- Enable the clock for the UART module using the RCGCUART register.
- The following asynchronous communication parameters are selected and used for this UART module 1 operations:
  - 115,200 baud rate.
  - 8-bit data length.
  - One Stop bit.
  - No parity.
  - FIFOs disabled.
  - No interrupts.

- Use the following equation (see Section 8.5.3.7) to calculate the Baud Rate Divisor (BRD):

$$BRD = 16,000,000 \ /(16 \times 115,200) = 8.6806$$

This means that the DIVINT field on the UARTIBRD register should be set to 8 decimal or 0x8. The value to be loaded into the UARTFBRD register is calculated (see Section 8.5.3.7) by the equation:

$$UARTFBRD[DIVFRAC] = Integer(0.6808*64 + 0.5) = 44.$$

This decimal value 44 (0x2C) should be written to the UARTFBDR register as the fractional divisor.

8.5.5.3   Initialize and Configure the UART Module

Perform the following operations to complete this configuration job for this UART module:

- Disable the UART by clearing the UARTEN bit (bit 0) in the UARTCTL register.
- Write the integer portion of the BRD (0x8) to the UARTIBRD register.
- Write the fractional portion of the BRD (0x2C) to the UARTFBRD register.
- Write the desired serial communication parameters to the UARTLCRH register. In this case, a value of 0x0000.0060 should be written into this register.
- Setup 0x00 to the UARTCC register to select the System Clock as the clock source.
- Optionally, configure the μDMA channel and enable the DMA options in the UARTDMACTL register if the DMA operation is used.
- Enable the UART module 1 by setting the UARTEN bit in the UARTCTL register.

Next let's build an example UART project to illustrate how to use this peripheral to communicate a PC to transmit and receive characters asynchronously.

8.5.6   Build an Example UART Module Project

In this section, we build an example UART project to echo each character sent via the UART transmitter. This project can be considered as a self-testing project to check the UART transmit and receive functions.

In order to do this project, we need to perform a loop back testing for the UART Module 1. The hardware setups and software features for this project include the following points:

1. In the EduBASE ARM® Trainer, GPIO PB1 and PB0 work as alternate function pins with PB1 working as the U1TX pin and PB0 as the U1RX pin (refer to Table 8.36), respectively.

2. To make the UART Module 1 to work as a loop back testing mode, we need to connect U1TX (PB1) and U1RX (PB0) pins together with a wire. Make this connection by inserting a jumper wire in the PB1 and PB0 holes in connector J10 in the EduBASE ARM® Trainer. After this connection, the transmit UARTDR is connected with the receive UARTDR and the transmitted data can be fed into the receive UARTDR.

3. In our software code, the FIFOs are disabled and therefore only the single byte data can be sent to the transmit UARTDR and fed into the receive UARTDR because of the connection wire we made in step 2.

4. In order to transmit a byte data, first we must confirm that the transmitter is empty and is ready to accept any data. This can be done by checking the TXFF bit (bit 5) in the UARTFR register. A value of 1 on this bit indicates that the transmitter is full, and a 0 indicates that the transmitter is empty and it can accept a new data item. A while() loop can be used to fulfill this checking job.

5. In order to receive a valid data item, we also need to check whether the receiver is empty or not. This can be done by checking the RXFE bit (bit 4) in the UARTFR register. A value of 0 on this bit means that the receiver is not empty and it contained a valid data item, but a 1 indicates that the receiver is empty with no data item available. A while() loop can also be used to fulfill this checking job.

Keeping all these points in mind, now let's create a new UART project named DRAUART.

8.5.6.1 Create a New UART Module Project DRAUART

Perform the following operations to create a new project DRAUART:

1. Open the Windows Explorer to create a new folder named DRAUART under the C:\ARM Class Projects\Chapter 8 folder.

2. Open the Keil® ARM-MDK µVersion5 and go to Project|New µVersion Project menu item to create a new µVersion Project. On the opened wizard, browse to our new folder DRAUART that is created in step 1 above. Enter DRAUART into the **File name** box and click on the **Save** button to create this project.

3. On the next wizard, you need to select the device (MCU) for this project. Expand three icons, Texas Instruments, Tiva C Series, and TM4C123x Series, and select the target device TM4C123GH6PM from the list by clicking on it. Click on the **OK** to close this wizard.

4. Next the Software Components wizard is opened, and you need to set up the software development environment for your project with this wizard. Expand two icons, CMSIS and Device, check the CORE and Startup checkboxes in the **Sel.** column, and click on the **OK** button since we need these two components to build our project.

Since this project is relatively simple, therefore only a C source file is good enough.

8.5.6.2 Create a New C Source File

Create a new C Source File and name it DRAUART.c in the new created project. Enter the codes shown in Figure 8.73 into the source file.

Let's have a closer look at this piece of codes to see how it works.

1. Three system header files are included in lines 4~6 since we want to use the structure pointers to access related registers in this project.

2. Three user-defined subroutines are declared in lines 7~9. The main program starts at line 10.

3. Some local variables are defined in lines 12~13.

4. In line 14, the UART_Init() subroutine is called to initialize and configure UART Module 1 to make it ready to perform asynchronous serial data self-testing jobs.

```c
1   //**********************************************************************************************************
2   // DRAUART.c - Main Application File for UART Module 1 Self-Loop Test
3   //**********************************************************************************************************
4   #include <stdint.h>
5   #include <stdbool.h>
6   #include "TM4C123GH6PM.h"
7   void UART_Init(void);
8   void UART_Transmit(char sdata);
9   char UART_Receive(void);
10  int main(void)
11  {
12    uint8_t num = 0;
13    char s_data, chr[26];
14    UART_Init();
15    for(s_data = 'A'; s_data <= 'Z'; s_data = s_data + 1)
16    {
17      UART_Transmit(s_data);                      // transmit a byte of data
18      chr[num] = UART_Receive();                  // receive a byte of data
19      num++;
20    }
21    while(1);                                     // keep program running...
22  }
23  void UART_Init(void)
24  {
25    SYSCTL->RCGCGPIO |= 0x02|0x20;                // enable clock to GPIOB & GPIOF
26    SYSCTL->RCGCUART = 0x02;                      // enable clock to UART1
27    GPIOB->AFSEL = 0x03;                          // PB1 & PB0 for U1TX & U1RX
28    GPIOB->PCTL = 0x00000011;
29    GPIOB->DEN = 0x03;                            // PB1 & PB0 as digital pins
30    GPIOF->DEN = 0xF;                             // PF3 ~ PF0 as digital and output pins
31    GPIOF->DIR = 0xF;
32    UART1->CTL &= 0xFFFFFFFE;                     // disable UART1
33    UART1->IBRD = 0x8;                            // set the integer baud rate period (IBRD = 8)
34    UART1->FBRD = 0x2C;                           // set fractional baud rate period (FBRD = 44)
35    UART1->LCRH = 0x60;                           // set baud rate = 115200,8-bit data, 1 stop, no parity
36    UART1->CC = 0x0;                              // set UARTCC as 00 to select System Clock as source
37    UART1->CTL |= 0x1;                            // enable UART1
38  }
39  void UART_Transmit(char sdata)
40  {
41    while ((UART1->FR & 0x20) != 0);
42    UART1->DR = sdata;
43  }
44  char UART_Receive(void)
45  {
46    uint32_t ret;
47    char rdata;
48    while((UART1->FR & 0x10) != 0);
49    ret = UART1->DR;
50    if (ret & 0xF00) { GPIOF->DATA = 0xF;    }    // error occurred...
51    else { rdata = (char)(UART1->DR & 0xFF); }
52    return rdata;
    }
```

Figure 8.73. The codes for the source file DRAUART.c.

5. A `for()` loop is used in line 15 to continuously transmit 26 uppercase letters from A to Z via `UART_Transmit()` subroutine and the U1TX pin.

6. In line 18, the subroutine `UART_Receive()` is executed to receive the uppercase letter from the receive UARTDR register that is connected to the transmit UARTDR register. The received letter is sent to the array `chr[]` to be stored.

7. The index of the array `num` is updated by 1 in line 19.

8. In line 21, an infinitive `while()` loop is executed to keep the project running to enable us to check the received letters via `Call Stack + Locals` windows later.

9. The `UART_Init()` subroutine starts at line 23.

10. In line 25, both GPIOB and GPIOF are enabled and clocked since we need to use PB1 and PB0 as U1TX and U1RX pins to transfer and receive data via this UART Module 1. We also need to use PF3~PF1 to display any possible error if they occurred.

11. The UART Module 1 is enabled and clocked in line 26.

12. The codes in lines 27~29 are used to configure GPIO Ports B, exactly PB1 and PB0, to work as alternate function pins, or U1TX and U1RX pins.

13. The codes in lines 30 and 31 are used to set the PF3~PF1 as digital and output pins.

14. In line 32, the UART Module 1 is disabled first to enable us to configure it. One point to be noted is that after a system reset, both TXE and RXE bits (bits 8 and 9) in the UARTCTL register are set to 1. You cannot assign a 0 to this register to disable it since both TXE and RXE bits would be cleared to 0 to disable both functions if you did that.

15. The codes in lines 33 and 34 are used to configure UARTIBRD and UARTFBRD registers to set up correct Baud Rate Period (BRD) value.

16. In line 35, the UARTLCRH register is configured to setup the desired asynchronous serial data communication parameters and framing for this UART Module 1. Both FIFOs are disabled based on this setting (`0x60`) and both FIFOs now work as a single byte holder.

17. The UARTCC register is configured with `0x00` to select the System Clock as the clock source for this UART Module 1 in line 36.

18. The UART Module 1 is enabled in line 37 by ORing this register with `0x1` to set the UARTEN bit (bit 0) in this register.

19. The codes in lines 39~43 are used to transmit a byte of data to the transmit UARTDR register. First a `while()` loop is used to check whether the transmitter is empty by ANDing the UARTFR register with `0x20` to confirm if the bit TXFF (bit 5) is 0. If this bit is 1, it means that the transmitter is full. This `while()` is used to checking this bit until it becomes to 0.

20. If this bit is 0, the data item `sdata` is sent to the transmit UARTDR in line 42.

21. The subroutine `UART_Receive()` starts at line 44.

22. Since the receive UARTDR is 12 bits long, we need to create a 32-bit local variable `ret` to receive and hold this 12-bit received value in line 46. The local variable `rdata` is used to get and hold the received 8-bit data.

23. In line 48, another `while()` loop is used to check and wait the RXFE bit (bit 4) in the UARTFR register until it becomes 0, which means that the receive UARTDR is not empty and a valid data item is ready to be picked up.

24. If the RXFE bit is 0, the received data with 4 status bits is sent to the local variable `ret` first.

25. Then we need to check whether any error has been occurred by ANDing `0xF00` with the variable ret in line 50. If this ANDing operation result is 1, which means some error occurred, the PF3~PF0 pins are set to light the three-color LED to indicate this situation.

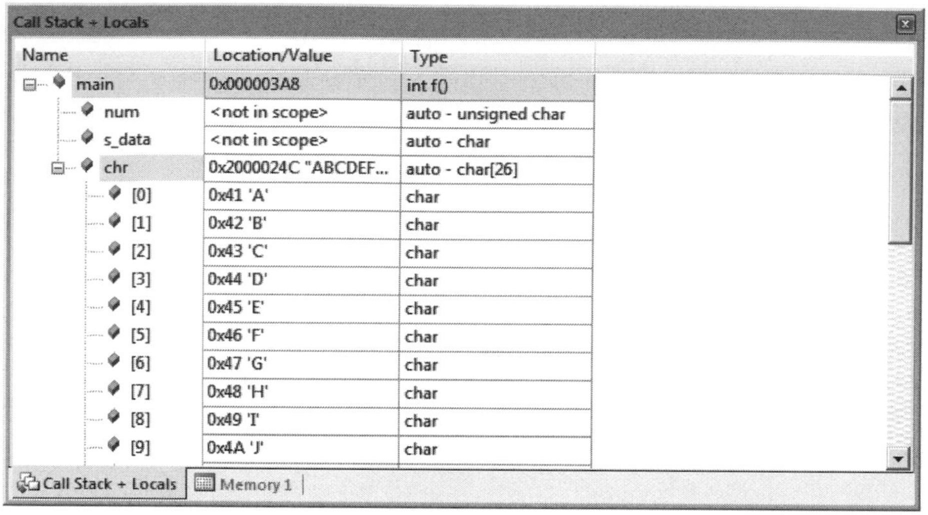

Figure 8.74. Running result of the project DRAUART. (Reproduced with permission from ARM® Limited. Copyright © ARM Limited.)

26. Otherwise if no error, the received data is sent to the local variable rdata and returns to the main program in line 52. A point to be noted is that since this received data is a 12-bit data item with 4 status bits, this value is ANDed with 0xFF to mask the higher 4 bits to get only the lower 8-bit data and is sent to the rdata.

Now let's set up environments to build and run the project.

8.5.6.3 Set Up the Environment to Build and Run the Project

Before the project can be built, make sure that the following issue has been setup correctly:

- The debug adapter used for this project is Stellaris ICDI. This adapter can be configured in the Debug tab under the menu item Project|Options for Target 'Target 1'.

Now go to the Project|Build target menu item to build the project. Then go to the menu item Flash|Download to download the project image file into the flash memory. Run the project by going to Debug|Start/Stop Debug Session and Run menu items.

After the project runs, go to Debug|Stop menu item to stop the project. Then open the Call Stack + Locals windows and expand the chr variable. You can find that all 26 uppercase letters have been transmitted and received as shown in Figure 8.74.

8.5.7 The UART API Functions Provided by the TivaWare™ Peripheral Driver Library

The Universal Asynchronous Receiver/Transmitter (UART) API provides a set of functions for using the Tiva™ UART modules. Functions are provided to configure and control the UART modules, to send and receive data, and to manage interrupts for the UART modules.

There are more than 40 UART API functions provided by this library. In this section we only introduce and discuss some popular and important API functions.

The UART API function set can be divided into four groups of functions: configure and control the UART modules, send and receive data, and deal with interrupt handling.

The clock source for the baud rate generator is handled by

- UARTClockSourceSet()
- UARTClockSourceGet()

Configuring and control the UART can be handled by

- UARTConfigSetExpClk()
- UARTEnable()
- UARTDisable()
- UARTParityModeSet()
- UARTDMAEnable()
- UARTDMADisable()

Sending and receiving data via the UART can be handled by

- UARTCharPut() and UARTCharGet()
- UARTCharPutNonBlocking()
- UARTCharGetNonBlocking()
- UARTCharsAvail()
- UARTSpaceAvail()
- UARTBreakCtl()

Managing the UART interrupts can be handled by

- UARTIntRegister()
- UARTIntUnregister()
- UARTIntEnable()
- UARTIntDisable()
- UARTIntStatus()
- UARTIntClear() and UARTFIFOLevelSet()

Let's have a closer look at these API functions based on their groups.

8.5.7.1 Clock Source for the Baud Rate Generator API Functions

Two API functions are included in this group and Table 8.37 shows the function body and arguments of these two functions. The function UARTClockSourceSet() is used to select the clock source for the selected UART module, either UART_CLOCK_SYSTEM or UART_CLOCK_PIOSC. The UARTClockSourceGet() just performs the opposite function, and it is used to get back the current clock source for the selected UART module. If a default clock source is used, it is unnecessary to use these functions. An optional way is to use the SysCtlClockGet() function to get the clock.

Table 8.37. The clock source for the baud rate generator API functions.

API Function	Parameter	Description
void UARTClockSourceSet(uint32_t ui32Base, uint32_t ui32Source)	ui32Base is the base address of the UART port. ui32Source is the baud clock source for the UART.	Select the baud clock source for the specified UART. Choose the baud clock source for the UART. The possible clock source are the system clock (UART_CLOCK_SYSTEM) or the precision internal oscillator (UART_CLOCK_PIOSC).
uint32_t UARTClockSourceGet(uint32_t ui32Base)	ui32Base is the base address of the UART port.	Get the baud clock source for the specified UART. Return the baud clock source for the specified UART. The baud clock source are the system clock (UART_CLOCK_SYSTEM) or the precision internal oscillator (UART_CLOCK_PIOSC).

8.5.7.2 Configure and Control the UART Modules API Functions

Six popular API functions are involved in this group. Table 8.38 shows these functions.

Most popular and important API functions in this group are UARTConfigSetExpClk() and UARTEnable() since they are directly used to configure and control the UART module.

Table 8.38. The configure and control the UART modules API functions.

API Function	Parameter	Description
void UARTConfigSetExpClk(uint32_t ui32Base, uint32_t ui32UARTClk, uint32_t ui32Baud, uint32_t ui32Config)	ui32Base is the base address of the UART port. ui32UARTClk is the rate of the clock supplied to the UART. ui32Baud is desired baud rate. ui32Config is the data format for the port (number of data bits, number of stop bits, and parity).	Configure the UART for operation in the specified data format. The ui32Config parameter is the logical OR of three values: the number of data bits, the number of stop bits, and the parity. UART_CONFIG_WLEN_8, UART_CONFIG_WLEN_7, UART_CONFIG_WLEN_6, and UART_CONFIG_WLEN_5 select from eight to five data bits per byte. UART_CONFIG_STOP_ONE and UART_CONFIG_STOP_TWO select one or two stop bits. UART_CONFIG_PAR_NONE, UART_CONFIG_PAR_EVEN, UART_CONFIG_PAR_ODD, UART_CONFIG_PAR_ONE, and UART_CONFIG_PAR_ZERO select the parity mode (no parity bit, even parity bit, odd parity bit, parity bit always one, and parity bit always zero. The peripheral clock is the processor clock. The frequency of the system clock is the value returned by SysCtlClockGet(), or it can be explicitly hard coded if it is constant.
void UARTEnable(uint32_t ui32Base)	ui32Base is the base address of the UART port.	Enables the UART and its transmit and receive FIFOs.
void UARTDisable(uint32_t ui32Base)	ui32Base is the base address of the UART port.	Disable the UART, waits for the end of transmission of the current character, and flushes the transmit FIFO.
void UARTParityModeSet(uint32_t ui32Base, uint32_t ui32Parity)	ui32Base is the base address of the UART port. ui32Parity specifies the type of parity to use	Configure the type of parity to use for transmitting and expect when receiving. The ui32Parity parameter must be one of UART_CONFIG_PAR_NONE, UART_CONFIG_PAR_EVEN, UART_CONFIG_PAR_ODD, UART_CONFIG_PAR_ONE, or UART_CONFIG_PAR_ZERO. The last two parameters allow direct control of the parity bit; it is always either one or zero based on the mode.
void UARTDMAEnable(uint32_t ui32Base, uint32_t ui32DMAFlags)	ui32Base is the base address of the UART port. ui32DMAFlags is a bit mask of the DMA features to enable.	The UART can be configured to use DMA for transmit or receive and to disable receive if an error occurs. The ui32DMAFlags parameter is the logical OR of any of the following values: UART_DMA_RX - enable DMA for receive; UART_DMA_TX—enable DMA for transmit; UART_DMA_ERR_RXSTOP—disable DMA receive on UART error.
void UARTDMADisable(uint32_t ui32Base, uint32_t ui32DMAFlags)	ui32Base is the base address of the UART port. ui32DMAFlags is a bit mask of the DMA features to disable.	This function is used to disable UART DMA features that were enabled by UARTDMAEnable(). The specified UART DMA features are disabled. The ui32DMAFlags parameter is the logical OR of any of the following values: UART_DMA_RX - disable DMA for receive; UART_DMA_TX—disable DMA for transmit; UART_DMA_ERR_RXSTOP—do not disable DMA receive on UART error.

8.5.7.3 UART Send and Receive Data API Functions

Seven popular API functions are involved in this group. Table 8.39 shows these functions.

The difference between the UARTCharPut() and UARTCharPutNonBlocking() is that the former will wait for a space on the transmit FIFO to be available and then put the character into the transmit FIFO, but the latter will not do this waiting and just put the character into the transmit FIFO if a space is available, and return to the main program without doing anything if no space is available in the transmit FIFO. Similar case is true to the UARTCharGet() and UARTCharGetNonBlocking() functions.

Regularly, the UARTSpaceAvail() and UARTCharsAvail() functions should be called before sending and receiving data for the selected UART modules.

8.5.7.4 UART Interrupt Handling API Functions

Seven popular API functions are involved in this group. Table 8.40 shows these functions.

Generally the operational sequence of enable and response to an interrupt is as follows:

- Use the UARTIntRegister() function to first register the interrupt's handler.
- Use the UARTFIFOLevelSet() function to setup the level at which the transmit and receive interrupts to be triggered. This function is important and must be correctly configured. To use single byte, either transmit or receive, to trigger an interrupt, the UART_FIFO_TX1_8 and UART_FIFO_RX1_8 should be used.

Table 8.39. The UART send and receive data API functions.

API Function	Parameter	Description
void UARTCharPut(uint32_t ui32Base, unsigned char ucData)	ui32Base is the base address of the UART port. ucData is the character to be transmitted.	Send the character ucData to the transmit FIFO for the specified port. If there is no space available in the transmit FIFO, this function waits until there is space available before returning.
int32_t UARTCharGet(uint32_t ui32Base)	ui32Base is the base address of the UART port.	Get a character from the receive FIFO for the specified port. If there are no characters available, this function waits until a character is received before returning. Return the character read from the port, cast as a int32_t.
bool UARTCharPutNonBlocking(uint32_t ui32Base, unsigned char ucData)	ui32Base is the base address of the UART port. ucData is the character to be transmitted.	Write the character ucData to the transmit FIFO for the specified port. This function does not block, so if there is no space available, then a false is returned and the application must retry the function later. Returns true if the character was successfully placed in the transmit FIFO or false if there was no space available in the transmit FIFO.
int32_t UARTCharGetNonBlocking(uint32_t ui32Base)	ui32Base is the base address of the UART port.	Receive a character from the specified port. Return the character read from the specified port, cast as a int32_t. This function does not block, so if there is no character present in the receive FIFO, then -1 is returned. The function UARTCharsAvail() should be called before attempting to call this function to get data.
bool UARTCharsAvail(uint32_t ui32Base)	ui32Base is the base address of the UART port.	Return a flag indicating whether or not there is data available in the receive FIFO. Returns true if there is data in the receive FIFO or false if there is no data in the receive FIFO.
bool UARTSpaceAvail(uint32_t ui32Base)	ui32Base is the base address of the UART port.	Return a flag indicating whether or not there is space available in the transmit FIFO. Returns true if there is space available in the transmit FIFO or false if no space available in the transmit FIFO.
void UARTBreakCtl(uint32_t ui32Base, bool bBreakState)	ui32Base is the base address of the UART port. bBreakState controls the output level.	Calling this function with bBreakState set to true asserts a break condition on the UART. Calling this function with bBreakState set to false removes the break condition. For proper transmission of a break command, the break must be asserted for at least two complete frames.

Table 8.40. The UART interrupt handling API functions.

API Function	Parameter	Description
void UARTIntRegister(uint32_t ui32Base, void (*pfnHandler)(void))	ui32Base is the base address of the UART port. pfnHandler is a pointer to the interrupt handler.	Register an interrupt handler for a UART interrupt. Enable the global interrupt in the interrupt controller; specific UART interrupts must be enabled via UARTIntEnable(). It is the interrupt handler's duty to clear the interrupt source.
void UARTIntUnregister(uint32_t ui32Base)	ui32Base is the base address of the UART port.	Unregister an interrupt handler for a UART interrupt. Clear the handler to be called when a UART interrupt occurs. This function also masks off the interrupt in the interrupt controller so that the interrupt handler no longer is called.
void UARTIntEnable(uint32_t ui32Base, uint32_t ui32IntFlags)	ui32Base is the base address of the UART port. ui32IntFlags is the bit mask of the interrupt sources to be enabled.	Enables individual UART interrupt sources. The ui32IntFlags is the logical OR of any of the following: UART_INT_9BIT - 9-bit Address Match interrupt. UART_INT_OE - Overrun Error interrupt. UART_INT_BE - Break Error interrupt. UART_INT_PE - Parity Error interrupt. UART_INT_FE - Framing Error interrupt. UART_INT_RT - Receive Timeout interrupt. UART_INT_TX - Transmit interrupt. UART_INT_RX - Receive interrupt. UART_INT_DSR - DSR interrupt. UART_INT_DCD - DCD interrupt. UART_INT_CTS - CTS interrupt. UART_INT_RI - RI interrupt.
void UARTIntDisable(uint32_t ui32Base, uint32_t ui32IntFlags)	ui32Base is the base address of the UART port. ui32IntFlags is the bit mask of the interrupt sources to be disabled.	Disable the indicated UART interrupt sources. Only the sources that are enabled can be reflected to the processor interrupts. The ui32IntFlags parameter has the same definition as the ui32IntFlags parameter to UARTIntEnable().
uint32_t UARTIntStatus(uint32_t ui32Base, bool bMasked)	ui32Base is the base address of the UART port. bMasked is false if the raw interrupt status is required and true if the masked interrupt status is required.	Return the interrupt status for the specified UART. Either the raw interrupt status or the status of interrupts that are allowed to reflect to the processor can be returned. Return the current interrupt status, enumerated as a bit field of values described in UARTIntEnable().
void UARTIntClear(uint32_t ui32Base, uint32_t ui32IntFlags)	ui32Base is the base address of the UART port. ui32IntFlags is bit mask of interrupt to be cleared.	The specified UART interrupt sources are cleared, so that they no longer assert. This function must be called in the interrupt handler to keep the interrupt from being triggered again immediately upon exit. The ui32IntFlags parameter has the same definition as the ui32IntFlags parameter to UARTIntEnable().
void UARTFIFOLevelSet(uint32_t ui32Base, uint32_t ui32TxLevel, uint32_t ui32RxLevel)	ui32Base is the base address of the UART port. ui32TxLevel is the transmit FIFO interrupt level. ui32RxLevel is the receive FIFO interrupt level.	Set the FIFO level at which interrupts are generated. ui32TxLevel is the transmit FIFO interrupt level, specified as one of UART_FIFO_TX1_8, UART_FIFO_TX2_8, UART_FIFO_TX4_8, UART_FIFO_TX6_8, or UART_FIFO_TX7_8. ui32RxLevel is the receive FIFO interrupt level, specified as one of UART_FIFO_RX1_8, UART_FIFO_RX2_8, UART_FIFO_RX4_8, UART_FIFO_RX6_8, or UART_FIFO_RX7_8.

- Use the UARTIntEnable() function to enable the desired UART interrupt sources.
- When any interrupt occurred, use UARTIntStatus() function to check and identify the UART interrupt sources.
- Use the UARTIntClear() function to clear the processed interrupt inside the interrupt handler.

Because of the space limitation, we will discuss a UART loop back project with the receiving interrupt-driven fashion in the project lab Lab8_6, and we leave this as a part of homework.

8.6 Chapter Summary

The main topics discussed in this chapter are about the ARM® Cortex®-M4 MCU serial port programming, which includes the synchronous and asynchronous serial data communications and operations. Because the TM4C123GH6PM MCU contains quite a few peripherals related to serial interface and communications, we only introduced and discussed three major serial peripherals, SSI, I2C, and UART. We leave some other serial peripherals to be introduced in the following chapters, such as USB and CANs.

We started our discussion from the Synchronous Serial Interface (SSI) that is also called Synchronous Peripheral Interface (SPI) in this chapter. Three example projects related to SSI are introduced and discussed with line-by-line illustrations:

- On-Board LCD Interface Programming Project
- On-Board 7 Segment LED Interface Programming Project
- Digital to Analog Converter Programming Project

These projects are built by using the Direct Register Access (DRA) model and method.

Also some important and popular API functions provided by the TivaWare™ Peripheral Driver Library are discussed in Section 8.3.8. An SSI-related project using the API function, SDLCD, is analyzed and discussed with details in that part.

Following the discussions about the SSI, we began our discussion about the I2C bus with a real project to interface the BQ32000 Real Time Clock via the I2C bus.

The I2C API functions provided by TivaWare™ Peripheral Driver Library are discussed in Section 8.4.11. A lab project Lab8_5 is assigned as a part of home work for the readers.

The Universal Asynchronous Receivers and Transmitters (UART) are discussed at Section 8.5. This is an asynchronous serial data communication protocol and widely applied in most data communication implementations. A real project that is about the loop back test for the UART is built with the DRA model.

The API functions provided by TivaWare™ Peripheral Driver Library are discussed in Section 8.5.7. An example UART project developed by using the UART API functions is provided as a lab project Lab8_6, which belongs to a part of homework.

HOMEWORK

I. True/False Selections

_____**1.** In order to enable a GPIO pin to work as an alternate function pin, the related bit on the GPIO Alternate Function Select register (GPIOAFSEL) should be cleared to 0.

_____**2.** The SSI and I2C belong to synchronous serial interface or bus, but the UART is an asynchronous serial data communication system.

_____**3.** Generally, the SCI belongs to the asynchronous serial communication interface and SSI or SPI belongs to the synchronous serial communication interface.

_____**4.** Both full-duplex and half-duplex communication mode use two data lines to transmit and receive data in the serial format.

_____**5.** A basic asynchronous serial data framing is composed of Start signal, number of data bits, number of stop bits, and parity bit.

_____**6.** For the synchronous serial data communications, both master and slave use the same clock source, but for the asynchronous serial operations the transmitter and receiver use the different clock sources.

_____**7.** Three control signals are used in SSI and they are SSInClk, SSInTx, and SSInRx.

_____**8.** Three basic frame types used in the TM4C123GH6PM MCU system are Texas Instruments Synchronous Serial, Freescale SPI, and MICROWIRE.

_____**9.** Each I2C module uses two signals, SCL and SDA, to transmit and receive data between the master and the slave. The SDA pin must be configured as an open-drain signal.

_____**10.** Each UART module has two FIFOs, transmit and receive FIFO. Both FIFOs can be used to hold 16×8 data bytes.

II. Multiple Choices

1. Which of the following modules belong to asynchronous serial data operation modules?

   a. SSI

   b. I2C

   c. SPI

   d. UART

2. To use PB4, PB6, and PB7 to work as `SSI2Clk`, `SSI2Rx`, and `SSI2Tx` pins, the GPIO Port B `GPIOAFSEL` register should be configured as _____.

   a. 0xF0

   b. 0xB0

   c. 0x3C

   d. 0x0F

3. The `Full-duplex` protocol is defined as: _____.

   a. Serial communications can take place in both directions at the same time.

   b. Serial communications are only taking place in one direction.

   c. Serial communications can take place in both directions, but the communication can only take place in one direction at a moment.

   d. Multiple serial communications can occur over the same serial communication line.

4. Both SCI and SSI can use either _____ or _____ mode to perform the data transfers between terminals and peripherals.

   a. Full-duplex, single-duplex

   b. Half-duplex, multi-duplex

   c. Half-duplex, full-duplex

   d. Multi-duplex, single-duplex

5. Each SSI module contains two FIFOs, transmit and receive FIFO, and the transmit FIFO can hold ___ data items, and the receive FIFO can hold _____ data items.

   a. 16×8, 16×12

   b. 16×8, 16×8

   c. 8×16, 16×8

   d. 8×16, 8×16

6. Every transaction on the I2C bus is _____ bits long, cons_____isting of ____ bits and a single acknowledge bit.

    a. 8, 7 data

    b. 9, 8 data

    c. 10, 9 data

    d. 11, 10 data

7. The number of bytes per I2C transfer is defined as the time period between a valid _____ and _____ condition and is unrestricted, but each data byte has to be followed by an acknowledge bit, and data must be transferred _____ first.

    a. START, LSB, STOP

    b. STOP, START, MSB

    c. LSB, START, STOP

    d. START, STOP, MSB

8. In each I2C module, after the START condition, a slave address is first transmitted. This address is _____ bits long followed by a _____ bit.

    a. 8, START

    b. 8, STOP

    c. 7, R/S

    d. 8, R/S

9. If the I2CMCS register is configured as 0x3 (H:ACK:STOP:START:RUN = 00111), this means that this transaction _____.

    a. Performs multiple bytes transmission

    b. Performs a single byte transmission

    c. Performs no byte transmission

    d. None of the above

10. Each UART module contains one _____ transmit FIFO and one _____ receive FIFO.

    a. 16×8, 16×12

    b. 16×8, 16×8

    c. 8×16, 16×8

    d. 8×16, 8×16

III. Exercises

1. Provide a brief description about how to configure the GPIOAFSEL and GPIOPCTL registers to enable related GPIO pins to work as alternate functions for SSI1 module.

2. Provide a brief description about the data transmit and receive operational procedure of one SSI module with the used registers.

3. Provide a brief description about the operational procedure of one I2C module worked in the master transmit mode.

4. Provide a brief discussion about the initialization process for the SSI module 0 (SSI0).

5. Provide a brief discussion about the initialization and configuration process for the I2C module 3 (I2C3)-related GPIO pins.

6. Provide a brief description about the UART modules in the TM4C123GH6PM MCU system.

IV. Practical Laboratory

Laboratory 8: ARM® Cortex®-M4 GPIO Serial Port Programming

8.0 Goals   This laboratory exercise allows students to learn and practice ARM® Cortex®-M4 serial ports programming by developing six labs.

1. Program Lab8_1 lets you build a LCD project to display Tiva on the first line on the LCD panel and ARM LaunchPad on the second line in the LCD panel. The first line starts from the position 06 (DDRAM address) and the second line starts at 41.

2. Program Lab8_2 enables students to use DRA model to build an 7-segment LED project to use SSI2 module to repeatedly display seven segments in a sequence for all four 7-segment LEDs on the EduBASE ARM® Trainer.

3. Program Lab8_3 allows students to use SSI2 module to interface the DAC-MCP4922 to generate sawtooth and sinusoidal waveforms using the API functions provided by the TivaWare™ Peripheral Driver Library.

4. Program Lab8_4 is similar to project Lab8_2. However, this time the students need to build a similar project as Lab8_2 by using the SSI API functions provided by the TivaWare™ Peripheral Driver Library to repeatedly display seven segments in a sequence for all four 7-segment LEDs on the EduBASE ARM® Trainer.

5. Program Lab8_5 enables students to use I2C module 0 (I2C0) to build a master-slave loop back testing project to check the transmit and receive functions of I2C0 module by using the I2C API functions provided by the TivaWare™ Peripheral Driver Library.

6. Program Lab8_6 allows students to use UART module 1 (UART1) to build a transmit-receive loop back testing project to test the asynchronous serial data communication functions by using UART API functions provided by the TivaWare™ Peripheral Driver Library.

After completion of these programs, you should understand the basic architecture and operational procedure for most popular serial related peripheral devices, including the SSI, I2C and UART modules installed in the TM4C123GH6PM MCU system. You should be able to code some sophisticated programs to access the desired peripheral devices to perform desired control operations via serial ports, either synchronously or asynchronously.

8.1 Lab8_1

8.1.1 Goal   In this project, students need to build a LCD project to display Tiva on the first line on the LCD panel and display ARM LaunchPad on the second line in the LCD panel. The first line starts from the position 06 (DDRAM address) and the second line starts at 41.

8.1.2 Data Assignment and Hardware Configuration   No hardware configuration is needed in this project. Refer to Figure 8.18 to get a detailed hardware configuration about this LCD architecture and connection in the Trainer. Refer to Figure 8.30 to get a clear picture about the DDRAM address and LCD letter positions.

8.1.3 Development of the Source Code   Only a C code file is used in this project since it is a simple application without needing any header file. Refer to class project DRALCD to complete this project.

8.1.4 Set up the Environment to Build and Run the Project   To build and run the project, one needs to perform the following operations to set up the environments:

- Select the `Stellaris ICDI` debug driver in the **Debug** tab under the **Project|Options for Target 'Target 1'** menu item.
- Now let's build the project by going to a `Project|Build target` menu item.
- Then go to `Flash|Download` menu item to download the image file of this project into the flash memory in the TM4C123GXL Evaluation Board.
- Now go to `Debug|Start/Stop Debug Session` to ready to run the project.
- Go to Debug|Run menu item to run the project.

8.1.5 Demonstrate Your Program by Checking the Running Result
After the project runs, check the LCD panel to make sure that the required letters are displayed in the desired positions and lines.

8.2 Lab8_2

8.2.1 Goal
This project enables students to use DRA model to build a 7-segment LED project to use SSI module 2 (`SSI2`) to repeatedly display seven segments in a sequence for all four 7-segment LEDs on the EduBASE ARM® Trainer.

8.2.2 Data Assignment and Hardware Configuration
No hardware connections are needed for this project.

Refer to Figure 8.32 to get a detailed hardware configuration about these four 7-segment LEDs architecture and connection in the Trainer. Refer to Table 8.14 to get a clear picture between the output bits of serial shift register 74VHCT595 and a selected LED digit.

8.2.3 Development of the Project
To make this project easy, we used the Direct Register Access (DRA) model with three user-defined functions, LED_Init(), SSI2_Write(), and delay_ms(), to support this project.

Follow the steps below to develop this project. Only a C code source file is used in this project since this project is simple. Create the project and develop the C source file with the following steps:

1. Create a new folder `Lab8_2` under the folder `C:\ARM Lab Projects\`Chapter 8 in the Windows Explorer.
2. Open the Keil® ARM-MDK µVersion5, create a new project named `Lab8_2`, and save this project into the folder `Lab8_2` created in step 1.
3. On the next wizard, you need to select the device (MCU) for this project. Expand three icons, `Texas Instruments`, `Tiva C Series`, and `TM4C123x Series`, and select the target device `TM4C123GH6PM` from the list by clicking on it. Click on the **OK** to close this wizard.
4. Next the Software Components wizard is opened, and you need to set up the software development environment for your project with this wizard. Expand two icons, CMSIS and `Device`, and check the CORE and `Startup` checkboxes in the **Sel.** column, and click on the **OK** button since we need these two components to build our project.

8.2.4 Development of the C Source File

1. In the **Project** pane, expand the `Target` folder and right click on the Source Group 1 folder and select the Add New Item to Group 'Source Group 1'.
2. Select the C File (.c) and enter Lab8_2 into the **Name:** box, and click on the **Add** button to add this source file into the project.

3. Include the following system header files into this source file:

- #include <stdint.h>
- #include <stdbool.h>
- #include "TM4C123GH6PM.h"

4. Declare three user defined functions, LED_Init(void), SSI2_Write(unsigned char data), and delay_ms(int time). All functions return void.

5. Inside the main() program, first declare three uint8_t local variables, uiLoop, uiUpper = 8, and uiDigit = 0xF7. The first variable is used as a loop number, the second works as the upper bound for a for() loop, and the third one is used to provide a digit selection for the selected LED. Refer to Table 8.14 to get a clear picture about the digit of the selected LED.

6. Call the LED_Init() function to initialize and configure the LEDs.

7. Start with an infinitive for() loop or while() loop to repeatedly display all segments for four LEDs in a sequence.

8. Start with a finite for() loop with the uiLoop as the loop number, starting from 0 and ending at uiUpper (8). In this way, we can scan and turn on all 8 segments, including the decimal point segment DP, one by one.

9. Inside the finite for() loop, call the SSI2_Write() function to send the first segment (a) to all four LEDs. The argument of this function should be 1 shifted left by uiLoop bits. In this way, all 7 segments can be turned ON from a, and b, c, ... until g.

10. Call the SSI2_Write() function again to select the desired LED by turning on the related digit of the LEDs. The argument of this function should be the digit number of the desired LED (uiDigit). The first digit, DIGIT3, should be 0xF7 if we prefer to start from DIGIT3.

11. Call delay_ms(500) to delay the project by 500 ms.

12. Outside the finite for() loop, all 8 segments for one LED digit has been done. Now we need to point to the next LED digit by shifting the uiDigit right by 1 bit. However, in order to make sure that the MSB on the above shifted result is 1, the shift result should be ORed with 0xF0.

13. Use an if() selection structure to check whether the uiDigit gets 0xFF, which means that all four LEDs have been completed in one loop. If this is true, we need to re-initialize uiDigit to 0xF7 to continue for the next loop.

The following codes are used for LED_Init() function.

14. Use the SYSCTL pointer structure to point to the RCGRGPIO register and assign appropriate values to this register to enable and clock the GPIO Ports B and C.

15. Use the SYSCTL pointer structure to point to the RCGCSSI register and assign an appropriate value to this register to enable and clock the SSI2 module.

16. Use the GPIOB pointer structure to point to AFSEL register and assign appropriate values to this register to setup PB7 and PB4 as alternate function pins.

17. Use the GPIOB pointer structure to point to PCTL register and assign appropriate values to this register to configure PB7 and PB4 as SSI2 function pins, PB7 for SSI2Tx and PB4 for SSI2Clk.

18. Use the GPIOB pointer structure to point to DEN register and assign an appropriate value to this register to set up PB7 and PB4 as digital function pins.

19. Use the GPIOC pointer structure to point to DATA register and assign an appropriate value to this register to set up PC7 pin idle as High.

20. Use the GPIOC pointer structure to point to DIR register and assign an appropriate value to this register to set up PC7 as output pin.

21. Use the GPIOC pointer structure to point to DEN register and assign an appropriate value to this register to set up PC7 as digital pin.

22. Use the SSI2 pointer structure to point to CR1 register and assign an appropriate value to this register to disable the SSI2 module.

23. Use the SSI2 pointer structure to point to CC register and assign an appropriate value to this register to select the System Clock for the SSI2 module.

24. Use the SSI2 pointer structure to point to CPSR register and assign 16 to this register to divide the system clock by 16 to get 1 MHz bit rate the SSI2 module.

25. Use the SSI2 pointer structure to point to CR0 register and assign an appropriate value to this register to set up the data framing parameters:
   a. Clock rate is divided by 1.
   b. SPO:SPH = 0:0.
   c. freescale mode.
   d. data size = 8.

26. Use the SSI2 pointer structure to point to CR1 register and assign an appropriate value to this register to enable the SSI2 module since the configuration for SSI2 is done.
   The following codes are used for the function SSI2_Write(unsigned char data).

27. Use the GPIOC pointer structure to point to DATA register and assign an appropriate value to this register to select the slave and clear the STCP clock on 74VHCT595 to Low.

28. Use the SSI2 pointer structure to point to DR register and assign the argument data to this register to transmit the data to the LEDs.

29. Use a while() loop to wait for data transmit done by checking the BSY bit in SSISR register. The loop condition should be SSI2 → SR & 0x10.

30. Use the GPIOC pointer structure to point to DATA register and assign an appropriate value to this register to select the slave and set the STCP clock on 74VHCT595 to High. This step is to simulate a Low-to-High edge to trigger a serial-to-parallel conversion on the serial shift register 74VHCT595.

For the delay_me() function, refer to a same function used in the DRALED project.

8.2.5 Set Up the Environment to Build and Run the Project Perform the following operations to make sure that the debugger you are using is the Stellaris ICDI. You can do this checking as follows:

- Go to Project|Options for Target 'Target 1' menu item to open the Options wizard.
- On the opened Options wizard, click on the Debug tab.
- Make sure that the debugger shown in the Use: box is Stellaris ICDI. Otherwise you can click on the dropdown arrow to select this debugger from the list.

8.2.6 Build and Demonstrate Your Program As the project runs, 8 segments for each LED are turned on one by one in a sequence.

Based on these results, try to answer the following questions:

- Can we modify this project to display only 7 segments without the DP segment? If your answer is yes, How can we do that?
- What did you learn from this project?

8.3 Lab8_3

8.3.1 Goal This project allows students to use SSI2 module to interface the DAC-MCP4922 to generate sawtooth and sinusoidal waveforms using the API functions provided by the TivaWare™ Peripheral Driver Library.

8.3.2 Data Assignment and Hardware Configuration Refer to Section 8.3.7 and Figure 8.34 to get a detailed hardware configuration for the interface between the SSI2 module and DAC-MCP4922.

8.3.3 Development of the Project Use the steps below to develop this project. Both a header file and a C source file are used in this project since it is a little complicated. Create a new project with the following steps:

1. Create a new folder Lab8_3 under the folder C:\ARM Lab Projects\Chapter 8 in the Windows Explorer.
2. Create a new ARM-MDK μVersion5 project named Lab8_3 and save this project in the folder Lab8_3 created in step 1.
3. Do the necessary steps to use CMSIS CORE and the Device Startup tools for this project.

8.3.4 Development of the Header File Lab8_3.h

1. Create a new header file and include the following system header files and macros:

```
#include <stdint.h>
#include <stdbool.h>
#include <math.h>
#include "inc/hw_memmap.h"
#include "inc/hw_ssi.h"
#include "driverlib/ssi.h"
#include "driverlib/gpio.h"
#include "driverlib/sysctl.h"
#define GPIO_PB7_SSI2TX                0x00011C02
#define GPIO_PB4_SSI2CLK               0x00011002
void DAC_Init(void);
void DAC_Write(int value, int channel);
```

Two user-defined functions, DAC_Init() and DAC_Write(), are declared in this header file.

Save this header file as Lab8_3.h.

8.3.5 Development of the C Source File

1. Create a new C source file and name it Lab8_3.c.
2. Include the header file "Lab8_3.h" into this source file.

3. Inside the `main` program, declare two local variables, `int idata = 0` and `float fdata`.

4. Call `DAC_Init()` to initialize and configure the DAC module MCP4922.

5. Use an infinitive `while()` loop to repeatedly generate a sawtooth and a sinusoidal signal.

6. Inside the `while()` loop, call `DAC_Write(idata++, 0)` to generate a sawtooth waveform in channel 0 on the DAC module.

7. Inside the `while()` loop, use `fdata = sinf(0.00314159 * idata) * 0x07FF + 0x800;` to get the data for the sinusoidal signal.

8. Inside the `while()` loop, call `DAC_Write((int)fdata, 1)` to generate a sinusoidal waveform in channel 1 on the DAC module.

The following codes are used for function `DAC_Init()` to configure DAC module.

9. Use `SysCtlPeripheralEnable()` API function to enable and clock GPIO Ports B and D since we need to use PB7 as SSI2Tx, PB4 as SSI2Clk and PD6 as CS_DAC control signals.

10. Use `SysCtlPeripheralEnable()` API function to enable and clock the SSI2 module.

11. Use `GPIOPinTypeSSI()` API function to setup PB7 and PB4 as SSI2 function pins.

12. Use `GPIOPinConfigure()` API function to configure PB7 as SSI2Tx pin. The macro defined in the header file, GPIO_PB7_SSI2TX, should be used as the argument for this function.

13. Use `GPIOPinConfigure()` API function to configure PB4 as SSI2Clk pin. The macro defined in the header file, GPIO_PB4_SSI2CLK, should be used as the argument for this function.

14. Use `GPIOPinTypeGPIOOutput()` API function to define the PD6 as an output pin.

15. Use `GPIOPinWrite()` API function to make PD6 pin output a High.

16. Call the `SSIDisable()` API function to disable the SSI2 module before the configuration can be performed for this module.

17. Call the `SSIConfigSetExpClk()` API function to set up the data framing parameters for this module with the following arguments:

    a. SSI2_BASE.
    b. 16000000.
    c. SSI_FRF_MOTO_MODE_0.
    d. SSI_MODE_MASTER.
    e. 1000000.
    f. 16

where $16,000,000 = 16$ MHz system clock, $1,000,000 = 1$ MHz bit rate, $16 = 16$ bits data.

18. Use `SSIEnable()` API function to enable the SSI2 module after it has been configured.

The following codes are used for function `DAC_Write(int value, int channel)`.

19. Create a local integer variable `config`.

20. Check the DAC output channel (DAC0 or DAC1) based on the input argument `channel`. If `channel = 0`, the `config` should be 0x07000 (A/B:BUF:GA:SHDN = 0111; refer to Table 8.15).

21. If `channel = 1`, the `config` should be 0xF000 (A/B:BUF:GA:SHDN = 1111; refer to Table 8.15).

22. Call the GPIOPinWrite() API function to reset PD6 pin to Low to select the DAC module.

23. Use value = (value & 0x0FFF)|config; to combine 4 config bits with 12-bit data together.

24. Call the SSIDataPut() API function to send out value to the DAC module.

25. Use a while() loop to wait for the value to be transmitted by checking the working status of the SSI2 module. The loop condition should be SSIBusy(SSI2_BASE). If this SSIBusy() function returns a true, it means that the SSI2 module is still busy and the value has not been transmitted. Otherwise if this function returns a false, it means that the SSI2 module is idle and the value has been set out.

26. Use GPIOPinWrite() API function to set PD6 pin to High to deselect the DAC module.

8.3.6 Set Up the Environment to Build and Run the Project
This setup contains the following three operations:

1. Include the system header files by adding the include path.

2. Check and configure the correct debugger driver used in the project.

3. Add the TivaWare™ Peripheral Driver Library into the project since we need to use some API functions provided by that library.

Perform the following operations to include the header file path in the project:

- Go to Project|Options for Target 'Target 1' menu item. Then click on the C/C++ tab.
- Go to Include Paths box and browse to the folder where our header files are located, it is C:\ti\TivaWare_C_Series-2.0.1.11577. Select this folder and click on the **OK** button.

Perform the following operations to check the debugger driver:

- Going to Project|Options for Target 'Target 1' menu item to open the Options wizard.
- On the opened Options wizard, click on the Debug tab.
- Make sure that the debugger driver shown in the Use: box is Stellaris ICDI. Otherwise you can click on the dropdown arrow to select this debugger from the list.

Perform the below operations to add the TivaWare™ peripheral driver library into the project:

- Go to the **Project** pane and right click on the **Source Group 1** item, and select the Add Existing Files to Group 'Source Group 1' menu item.
- Browse to the folder where the library file is located, which is C:\ti\TivaWare_C_S-eries-2.0.1.11577\driverlib\rvmdk. Then select the library file driverlib.lib and click on the **Add** button. Click on the **Close** button to finish this step.

8.3.7 Demonstrate Your Program
Perform the following operations to run your program and check the running results:

- Go to Flash|Download menu item to download your program into the flash ROM.
- Go to Debug|Start/Stop Debug Session to begin debugging your program. Click on the **OK** button on the 32KB memory size limitation message box to continue.
- Then go to Debug|Run menu item to run your program.

As the project runs, you can use a two-channel oscilloscope to monitor two DAC outputs, DAC0 and DAC1, via J11-1 and J11-2 connectors on the EduBASE ARM® Trainer. A sawtooth and a sinusoidal signal should be displayed on those two channels.

Based on these results, try to answer the following questions:

- What are the periods and frequencies for these two signals?
- Can we just generate and display one, signal not two? If it is, what is the period and frequency for that signal?
- What did you learn from this project?

8.4 Lab8_4

8.4.1 Goal This project is similar to project Lab8_2. However, this time the students need to build a similar project as Lab8_2 by using the SSI API functions provided by the TivaWare™ Peripheral Driver Library to repeatedly display seven segments in a sequence for all four 7-segment LEDs on the EduBASE ARM® Trainer.

8.4.2 Data Assignment and Hardware Configuration No hardware connections are needed for this project.

Refer to Figure 8.32 to get a detailed hardware configuration about these four 7-segment LEDs architecture and connection in the Trainer. Refer to Table 8.14 to get a clear picture between the output bits of serial shift register 74VHCT595 and the selected LED digit.

8.4.3 Development of the Project and the Header File This project is very similar to Lab8_2, but a header file is added into this project to make the project short. Create a new project with the following steps:

1. Create a new folder Lab8_4 under the folder C:\ARM Lab Projects\Chapter 8 in the Windows Explorer.
2. Create a new ARM-MDK μVersion5 project named Lab8_4 and save this project in the folder Lab8_4 created in step 1.
3. Do the necessary steps to use CMSIS CORE and the Device Startup tools for this project.
4. Create a new header file Lab8_4.h and enter the following codes into this file:

```
#include <stdint.h>
#include <stdbool.h>
#include "inc/hw_memmap.h"
#include "inc/hw_ssi.h"
#include "driverlib/ssi.h"
#include "driverlib/gpio.h"
#include "driverlib/sysctl.h"
#include <math.h>

#define GPIO_PB7_SSI2TX            0x00011C02
#define GPIO_PB4_SSI2CLK           0x00011002

void delay_ms(int time);
void LED_Init(void);
void SSI2_Write(unsigned char data);
```

Three user-defined functions are identical to those used in the Lab8_2 project.

8.4.4 Development of the C Source File   Because the main program and the delay_ms() functions are identical to those used in the Lab8_2 project, we only take care of two other user defined functions, LED_Init() and SSI2_Write() in this project.

1. Create a new C source file named Lab8_4.c.

2. Include the header file #include "Lab8_4.h".

3. Inside the LED_Init() function, use SysCtlPeripheralEnable() API function to enable and clock GPIO Ports B and C since we need to use PB7 as SSI2Tx, PB4 as SSI2Clk, and PC7 as CS_7LED control signals.

4. Use SysCtlPeripheralEnable() API function to enable and clock the SSI2 module.

5. Use GPIOPinTypeSSI() API function to setup PB7 and PB4 as SSI2 function pins.

6. Use GPIOPinConfigure() API function to configure PB7 as SSI2Tx pin. The macro defined in the header file, GPIO_PB7_SSI2TX, should be used as the argument for this function.

7. Use GPIOPinConfigure() API function to configure PB4 as SSI2Clk pin. The macro defined in the header file, GPIO_PB4_SSI2CLK, should be used as the argument for this function.

8. Use GPIOPinTypeGPIOOutput() API function to define the PC7 as an output pin.

9. Use GPIOPinWrite() API function to make PC7 pin output a High.

10. Call the SSIDisable() API function to disable the SSI2 module before the configuration can be performed for this module.

11. Call the SSIConfigSetExpClk() API function to set up the data framing parameters for this module with the following arguments:

   a. SSI2_BASE
   b. 16,000,000
   c. SSI_FRF_MOTO_MODE_0
   d. SSI_MODE_MASTER
   e. 1000000
   f. 8

where 16000000 = 16 MHz system clock, 1000000 = 1 MHz bit rate, 8 = 8 bits data.

12. Use SSIEnable() API function to enable the SSI2 module after it has been configured.

The following codes are used for function SSI2_Write(unsigned char data).

13. Call the GPIOPinWrite() API function to reset PC7 pin to Low for the STCP clock of the 74VHCT595 serial shift register.

14. Call the SSIDataPut() API function to send out data to the LED module via 74VHCT595.

15. Use a while() loop to wait for the data to be transmitted by checking the working status of the SSI2 module. The loop condition should be SSIBusy(SSI2_BASE). If this SSIBusy() function returns a true, which means that the SSI2 module is still busy and the data has not been transmitted. Otherwise if this function returns a false, it means that the SSI2 module is idle and the data has been set out.

16. Use GPIOPinWrite() API function to set PC7 pin to High to trigger a serial-to-parallel conversion on the 74VHCT595 to output the data value to the LED module.

8.4.5 Set Up the Environment to Build and Run the Project   This setup contains the following three operations:

1. Include the system header files by adding the include path.
2. Check and configure the correct debugger driver used in the project.
3. Add the TivaWare™ Peripheral Driver Library into the project since we need to use some API functions provided by that library.

Perform the following operations to include this header file path in your project:

- Go to `Project|Options for Target 'Target 1'` menu item. Then click on the C/C++ tab.
- Go to `Include Paths` box and browse to the folder where our header files are located, it is `C:\ti\TivaWare_C_Series-2.0.1.11577`. Select this folder and click on the **OK** button.

Perform the following operations to make sure that the debugger you are using is the `Stellaris ICDI`. You can do this checking as follows:

- Go to `Project|Options for Target 'Target 1'` menu item to open the Options wizard.
- On the opened Options wizard, click on the `Debug` tab.
- Make sure that the debugger shown in the `Use:` box is `Stellaris ICDI`. Otherwise you can click on the dropdown arrow to select this debugger from the list.

Perform the below operations to add the TivaWare™ peripheral driver library into the project:

- Go to the **Project** pane and right click on the **Source Group 1** item, and select the `Add Existing Files to Group 'Source Group 1'` menu item.
- Browse to the folder where the library file is located, which is `C:\ti\TivaWare_C_Series-2.0.1.11577\driverlib\rvmdk`. Then select the library file `driverlib.lib` and click on the **Add** button. Click on the **Close** button to finish this step.

8.4.6 Demonstrate Your Program Perform the following operations to run your program and check the running results:

- Go to `Flash|Download` menu item to download your program into the flash ROM.
- Go to `Debug|Start/Stop Debug Session` to begin debugging your program. Click on the **OK** button on the 32-KB memory size limitation message box to continue.
- Then go to `Debug|Run` menu item to run your program.

As the project runs, 8 segments for each LED are turned on one by one in a sequence. Based on these results, try to answer the following questions:

- Compare `Lab8_2` and `Lab8_4`. Which one is better in coding process and control performance? Why?
- Explain advantages and disadvantages for both projects.
- What did you learn from this project?

8.5 Lab8_5

8.5.1 Goal This project enables students to use I2C module 0 (`I2C0`) to build a master–slave loop back testing project to check the transmit and receive functions of `I2C0` module by using the I2C API functions provided by the TivaWare™ Peripheral Driver Library.

8.5.2 Data Assignment and Hardware Configuration   No hardware connections are needed for this project.

Refer to Table 8.23 to get details about the I2C control signals and GPIO pins distributions. Based on this table, PB2 works as the I2C0SCL and PB3 works as the I2C0SDA signal pins.

8.5.3 Development of the Project   Create a new project Lab8_5 with the following steps:

1. Create a new folder Lab8_5 under the folder C:\ARM Lab Projects\Chapter 8 in the Windows Explorer.

2. Create a new ARM-MDK μVersion5 project named Lab8_5 and save this project in the folder Lab8_5 created in step 1.

3. Do the necessary steps to use CMSIS CORE and the Device Startup tools for this project.

8.5.4 Development of the C Source File

1. Create a new C source file named Lab8_5.c and add the following system header files and macros into this source file:

```
#include <stdint.h>
#include <stdbool.h>
#include "inc/hw_memmap.h"
#include "inc/hw_i2c.h"
#include "inc/hw_types.h"
#include "driverlib/i2c.h"
#include "driverlib/gpio.h"
#include "driverlib/sysctl.h"
#define SLAVE_ADDRESS            0x3C
#define GPIO_PB2_I2C0SCL         0x00010803
#define GPIO_PB3_I2C0SDA         0x00010C03
```

2. Inside the main function, declare three local variables: char pui32DataTx[3] = {'I', '2', 'C' };, char pui32DataRx[3]; and uint32_t ui32Index; .

3. Use SysCtlPeripheralEnable() API function to enable and clock the I2C0 module.

4. Use SysCtlPeripheralEnable() API function to enable and clock the GPIO Port B.

5. Use GPIOPinTypeI2C() API function to setup PB3 and PB2 as I2C0 function pins.

6. Use GPIOPinConfigure() API function to configure PB3 as I2C0SDA pin. The macro defined above, GPIO_PB3_I2C0SDA, should be used as the argument for this function.

7. Use GPIOPinConfigure() API function to configure PB2 as I2C0SCL pin. The macro defined above, GPIO_PB2_I2C0SCL, should be used as the argument for this function.

8. Use HWREG(I2C0_BASE + I2C_O_MCR) |= 0x01; to set the LPBK bit (bit 0) in the I2C0 MCR register to 1 to enable the I2C0 module to work in the loop back mode. The macro HWREG(x) is a definition used to define a valid address for a register x. The I2C_O_MCR is a numbered offset address 0x00000020 for the I2C0 MCR register, and the I2C0_BASE is the base address for I2C0 module. Therefore this macro is used to convert the complete numbered address of the I2C0 MCR, I2C0_BASE + I2C_O_MCR, to a pointer or a real address.

9. Call the `I2CMasterInitExpClk()` API function to setup the I2C0 module to work as a master with 100-Kbps rate. Three parameters are used for this function. The first is the base address of this mode, `I2C0_BASE`. The second can be directly typed with the real system clock frequency, such as `16000000` (16 MHz) or obtained by calling the system function `SysCtlClockGet()`. The third is a Boolean value and a `false` means that the rate is 100 Kbps.

10. Call the `I2CSlaveEnable()` API function to enable the slave mode of the I2C0.

11. Call the `I2CSlaveInit()` API function to initialize and configure the slave mode of the I2C0. Two parameters are used for this function. The first is the base address of the I2C0 mode, and the second is the slave address, which is defined above SLAVE_ADDRESS (`0x3C`).

12. Use `I2CMasterSlaveAddrSet()` API function to set the slave address to be sent by the master when the transmit or receive starts. Three parameters are used for this function; the first one is the base address of the I2C0 mode, the second is the slave address, and the third one is a Boolean value. If it is `true`, the master initiates a reading operation from the slave, but a `false` means that the master initiates a writing operation to the slave device.

The following codes are used for master sending data to the slave.

13. A `for()` loop is used to allow the master to send three characters, I, 2, and C, to the slave. The local variable `ui32Index` is used as the loop counter.

14. Inside the `for()` loop, call the `I2CMasterDataPut()` API function to put the character to be sent to the master SDA line. Two arguments are used for this function. The first is the `I2C0_BASE`, and the second is the data to be sent, which can be used by the local variable array `pui32DataTx[ui32Index]`.

15. Use the `I2CMasterControl()` API function to define the data sending state. Two parameters are used for this function; the first is the `I2C0_BASE`, and the second is a macro used to indicate the data transmit state, `I2C_MASTER_CMD_SINGLE_SEND`.

16. Use a `while()` loop to monitor and wait for the data to be sent out and has been received by the slave. The loop condition can be an ANDing between the `I2CSlaveStatus` (`I2C0_BASE`) API function and the macro `I2C_SLAVE_ACT_RREQ`. This macro indicates that an I2C0 master has sent data to the I2C0 Slave module. If this ANDing result is `false`, it means that the slave has not received this request from the master; the `while()` loop will keep its waiting until a `true` is obtained from this ANDing, and this means that the slave has received this data sending request from the master.

17. Then the local variable array `pui32DataRx[ui32Index]` can be used to pick up the received character from the slave by calling the `I2CSlaveDataGet()` API function. This function returns a 32-bit data, so a (`char`) converter should be used to convert it to a char data.

18. Use another `while()` loop to wait for the master until it is not busy, and we can send the next character with this `for()` loop. The loop condition is the API function `I2CMasterBusy()`.

The following codes are used for master receiving data from the slave.

19. Use a `for()` loop to initialize the `pui32DataRx[ui32Index]` array to contains three '0'.

20. Use `I2CMasterSlaveAddrSet()` API function to set the slave address to be sent by the master when the transmit or receive starts. Three parameters are used for this function; the first one is the base address of the I2C0 mode, the second is the slave address, and the third one is a Boolean value. If it is `true`, the master initiates a reading operation from the slave.

21. Use the `I2CMasterControl()` API function to define the data receiving state. Two parameters are used for this function; the first is the `I2C0_BASE`, and the second is a macro used to indicate the data receive state, `I2C_MASTER_CMD_SINGLE_RECEIVE`.

22. Use a `while()` loop to monitor and wait for the command to be sent out and has been received by the slave. The loop condition can be an ANDing between the API function `I2CSlaveStatus(I2C0_BASE)` and the macro `I2C_SLAVE_ACT_TREQ`. This macro indicates that an I2C master has requested that the I2C Slave module send data. If this ANDing result is `false`, it means that the slave has not received this request from the master, the `while()` loop will keep its waiting until a `true` is obtained from this ANDing, and this means that the slave has received this data receiving request from the master.

23. Then a `for()` loop can be used to retrieve three characters sending by the slave. The local variable `ui32Index` can be used as the loop counter for this `for()` loop.

24. Inside the `for()` loop, call the `I2CSlaveDataPut()` API function to put the character to be sent to the slave SDA line. Two arguments are used for this function. The first is the `I2C0_BASE`, and the second is the data to be sent, which can be used by the local variable array `pui32DataTx[ui32Index]`.

25. Use the `I2CMasterControl()` API function to define the data receiving state. Two parameters are used for this function; the first is the `I2C0_BASE`, and the second is a macro used to indicate the data receive state, `I2C_MASTER_CMD_SINGLE_RECEIVE`.

26. Use a `while()` loop to monitor and wait for the character that has been received by the master. The loop condition can be an ANDing between the `I2CSlaveStatus (I2C0_BASE)` and the macro `I2C_SLAVE_ACT_TREQ`. This macro indicates that an I2C master has requested that the I2C Slave module send data. If this ANDing result is `false`, it means that the character has not been received by the master, the `while()` loop will keep its waiting until a `true` is obtained from this ANDing, and this means that the character has been received by the master.

27. Then the local variable array `pui32DataRx[ui32Index]` can be used to pick up the received character by calling the `I2CMasterDataGet()` API function. This function returns a 32-bit data, so a `(char)` converter should be used to convert it to a char data.

28. Finally outside of the `for()` loop, leave an infinitive `while()` loop in there to keep the project running to enable us to check the transmitted and received characters via `pui32-DataTx[]` and `pui32DataRx[]` arrays, respectively.

8.5.5 Set Up the Environment to Build and Run the Project This setup contains the following three operations:

1. Include the system header files by adding the include path.
2. Check and configure the correct debugger used in the project.
3. Add the TivaWare™ Peripheral Driver Library into the project.

Perform the following operations to include the header file path in the project:

- Go to `Project|Options for Target 'Target 1'` menu item. Then click on the C/C++ tab.
- Go to `Include Paths` box and browse to the folder where our header files are located, it is `C:\ti\TivaWare_C_Series-2.0.1.11577`. Select this folder and click on the **OK** button.

Perform the following operations to select the correct debugger driver:

- Going to Project|Options for Target 'Target 1' menu item to open the Options wizard.
- On the opened Options wizard, click on the Debug tab.
- Make sure that the debugger shown in the Use: box is Stellaris ICDI. Otherwise you can click on the dropdown arrow to select this debugger from the list.

Perform the following operations to add the TivaWare™ driver library into the project:

- Go to the **Project** pane and right click on the **Source Group 1** item, and select the Add Existing Files to Group 'Source Group 1' menu item.
- Browse to the folder where the library file is located, which is C:\ti\TivaWare_C_S-eries-2.0.1.11577\driverlib\rvmdk. Then select the library file driverlib.lib and click on the **Add** button. Click on the **Close** button to finish this step.

8.5.6 Demonstrate Your Program   Perform the following operations to run your program and check the running results:

- Go to Flash|Download menu item to download your program into the flash ROM.
- Go to Debug|Start/Stop Debug Session to begin debugging your program. Click on the **OK** button on the 32-KB memory size limitation message box to continue.
- Then go to Debug|Run menu item to run your program.
- Go to Debug|Stop menu item to pseudo-stop the project.

Now open the Call Stack + Locals window and expand the receive array pui32DataRx []. You can find that three characters sent by the master, I, 2, and C, have been received by the slave and displayed in this array, which is shown in Figure 8.75.

Based on these results, try to answer the following questions:

- Why we need to use an infinitive while() loop to keep this project running? What will happen without this loop?
- What is the function of the instruction HWREG(I2C0_BASE + I2C_O_MCR) |= 0x01;. Why do we need to use this HWREG() macro? Without this macro, can we access the I2C0 MCR register with only those API functions provided by the TivaWare™ Peripheral Driver Library?
- Is there any other way to access the I2C0 MCR register?
- What did you learn from this project?

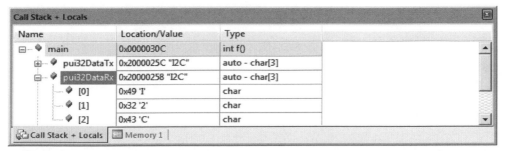

Figure 8.75.   Running result of the project Lab8_5. (Reproduced with permission from ARM® Limited. Copyright © ARM Limited.)

8.6 LAB8_6

8.6.1 Goal This project allows students to use UART module 1 (UART1) to build a transmit–receive loop back testing project to test the asynchronous serial data communication functions by using UART API functions provided by the TivaWare™ Peripheral Driver Library. The UART interrupt mechanism is used in this project to enable received data to be picked up immediately.

8.6.2 Data Assignment and Hardware Configuration Connect PB0 and PB1 pins together with a jumping wire since we need to do a loop back testing for this UART module 1. An easy way to do this connection is to connect PB1 and PB0 on the J11 connector on the EduBASE ARM® Trainer.

Refer to Table 8.36 to get details about the UART1 control signals and related GPIO pins distributions. Based on this table, PB1 works as the U1TX and PB0 works as the U1RX signal pins.

8.6.3 Development of the Project Create a new project Lab8_6 with the following steps:

1. Create a new folder Lab8_6 under the folder C:\ARM Lab Projects\Chapter 8 in the Windows Explorer.
2. Create a new ARM-MDK μVersion5 project named Lab8_6 and save this project in the folder Lab8_6 created in step 1.
3. Do the necessary steps to use CMSIS CORE and the Device Startup tools for this project.

This project is to use UART1 to transmit and receive 26 characters with a loop back running mode. Two GPIO pins, PB1 (U1TX) and PB0 (U1RX), are used to transmit and receive characters asynchronously. The LED connected to PF2 is ON when this testing is complete. The UART1 receiving interrupt mechanism is used to enable the received data to be picked up immediately.

8.6.4 Development of the C Source File

1. Create a new C source file named Lab8_6.c and add the following system header files and macros into this source file:

```
#include <stdint.h>
#include <stdbool.h>
#include "inc/hw_memmap.h"
#include "driverlib/gpio.h"
#include "driverlib/interrupt.h"
#include "driverlib/sysctl.h"
#include "driverlib/uart.h"

#define GPIO_PB0_U1RX          0x00010001
#define GPIO_PB1_U1TX          0x00010401
#define INT_UART1              22

void UARTIntHandler(void);

char rdata[26];
uint8_t rnum=0;
bool intFlag=true;
```

Three global variables are sued for this project, rdata[26], rnum and intFlag.

2. Inside the main function, declare two local variables: char s_data and rcdata[26].
3. Use SysCtlPeripheralEnable() API function to enable and clock the GPIO Port B.

4. Use `SysCtlPeripheralEnable()` API function to enable and clock the GPIO Port F.

5. Use `SysCtlPeripheralEnable()` API function to enable and clock the UART1 module.

6. Use `GPIOPinTypeGPIOOutput()` API function to define PF2 as an output pin.

7. Use `GPIOPinTypeUART()` API function to setup PB1 and PB0 as UART function pins.

8. Use `GPIOPinConfigure()` API function to configure PB1 as U1TX pin. The macro defined above, GPIO_PB1_U1TX, should be used as the argument for this function.

9. Use `GPIOPinConfigure()` API function to configure PB0 as U1RX pin. The macro defined above, GPIO_PB0_U1RX, should be used as the argument for this function.

10. Use `UARTDisable()` to disable the UART1 module since we need to start the initialization and configuration process for this UART module 1.

11. Call the `UARTConfigSetExpClk()` API function to setup the UART1 module to work as a master with a baud rate of 115200. Four parameters are used for this function. The first is the base address of this mode, UART1_BASE. The second can be directly typed with the real system clock frequency, such as 16000000 (16 MHz) or obtained by calling the system function `SysCtlClockGet()`. The third is the baud rate used by this UART1 module, here one can directly type 115200 for this parameter. The fourth is an ORed combination of multiple framing parameters, such as data length, number of stop bits, and parity bits. Here one can use some macros for these parameters and OR them together, such as UART_CONFIG_WLEN_8|UART_CONFIG_STOP_ONE|UART_CONFIG_PAR_NONE.

12. Call the `UARTFIFOLevelSet()` API function to set the interrupt triggering levels for both transmit and receive FIFOs. Three parameters are used for this function. The first is the UART1_BASE, the second and third are the interrupt triggering levels for transmit and receive FIFOs. We prefer to trigger both transmit and receive interrupt levels to 1/8, which means that a transmit or a receive interrupt would be generated if only one character is placed into the transmit FIFO or received from the receive FIFO. Two macros, UART_-FIFO_TX1_8 and UART_FIFO_RX1_8, can be used for these two parameters.

13. Call the `UARTEnable()` API function to enable the UART1 module after this initialization.

14. Use `UARTIntRegister()` API function to register an interrupt handler for either interrupt. Two parameters are used for this function. The first is the UART1_BASE and the second is a pointer point to the interrupt handler. This handler has been declared at the beginning on this source code, `void UARTIntHandler(void);`. So just place the name of this handler `UARTIntHandler` as the second parameter for this function.

15. Call the `IntEnable()` API function with the INT_UART1 as the unique argument to enable the UART1 interrupt sources.

16. Call the `UARTIntEnable()` API function to enable specified UART1 interrupt sources. Here we only take care of data receiving and data receiving timeout, therefore two macros, UART_INT_RX | UART_INT_RT can be ORed together as the second parameter for this function. The first parameter is the UART1_BASE.

17. Call the `IntMasterEnable()` API function to globally enable all maskable interrupts.

18. A `for()` loop is used to continuously transmit 26 English letters, from 'A' to 'Z', to the slave. The local variable `s_data` can be used as the loop counter starting from 'A' and ending at 'Z'.

19. The loop body for the `for()` loop is to call the `UARTCharPut()` API function to write the `s_data` to the transmit FIFO.

20. Use a `while()` loop with the `intFlag` as the loop condition to wait all 26 English letters have been received inside the UART1 interrupt handler. The `intFlag` is a global Boolean variable and has been initialized to `true` at the beginning. It will be changed to `false` when all 26 letters have been received inside the UART1 interrupt handler later.

21. After all 26 letters have been received, another `for()` loop is used to transfer received 26 letters from the global array `rdata[]` to the local array `rcdata[]`. The global variable `rnum` can be used as the loop counter for that `for()` loop and index for both arrays, `rdata[]` and `rcdata[]`, to assist this data transferring. The reason of doing this transfer is because the global array `rdata[]` cannot be inspected and checked after the project is pseudo-stopped.

22. An infinitive `while()` loop should be added here to enable us to check the running result of the project, exactly to check the `rcdata[]` array to confirm that all 26 letters have been successfully received by this loop back test project.

The following codes are used for the UART1 interrupt handler.

23. A local 32-bit integer variable `ui32Status` is declared first inside this interrupt handler.

24. Call the `UARTIntStatus()` API function to get the current UART1 interrupt source status. This function contains two parameters, the `UART1_BASE` and a Boolean value `false`. If the Boolean value is `false`, this function returns all raw interrupt source status. Otherwise it returns all interrupts that have been responded and sent to the NVIC to be processed if it is `true`. In this application, we only take care of the raw interrupt status; therefore a `false` is used for this function. The returned status is assigned to the local variable `ui32Status`.

25. Use the `UARTIntClear()` API function to clear the accepted interrupt sources to enable them to generate interrupts in the future. This step is very important, and no further interrupts could be generated if this step is missed. Two parameters are used for this function, the `UART1_BASE` and the interrupt source to be cleared. One can directly use the `ui32Status` as the interrupt source since it did contain the interrupt source.

26. Use a `while()` loop to monitor and wait for the receiving letter to come and available. Use the `UARTCharsAvail()` API function as the loop condition, and this function returns a `true` if a data item is available in the receive FIFO.

27. If a data item is available in the receive FIFO, call the `UARTCharGet()` API function to pick up the received letter. Since this function returns a 32-bit data item, an `0xFF` should be ANDed with this returned value to make it an 8-bit data. Also a `(char)` converter should be used to convert that 8-bit data to a char, and assign the converted result to the global array `rdata[]`. The `rnum` may work as the index for this array (do not forget to update `rnum` for each loop).

28. Call the `GPIOPinWrite()` API function to turn on the LED via PF2 pin.

29. Outside the `while()` loop, use an `if()` selection structure to check whether `rnum` is greater than 25. If it is, change the global Boolean variable `intFlag` to `false` to inform the main program that all 26 letters have been received and stored.

8.6.5 Set Up the Environment to Build and Run the Project
Refer to Lab8_5 to complete this setup.

8.6.6 Demonstrate Your Program
Perform the following operations to run your program and check the running results:

- Go to `Flash|Download` menu item to download your program into the flash memory.
- Go to `Debug|Start/Stop Debug Session` to begin debugging your program. Click on the **OK** button on the 32-KB memory size limitation message box to continue.

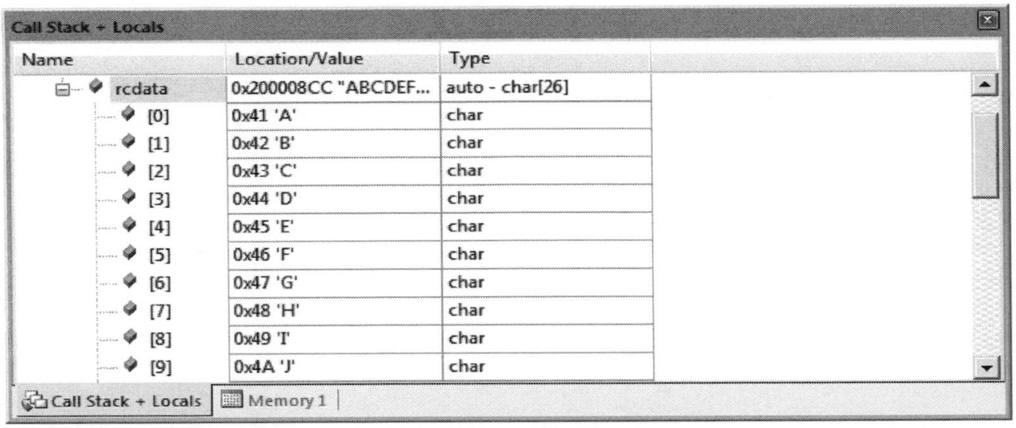

Figure 8.76. Running result of the project Lab8_6. (Reproduced with permission from ARM® Limited. Copyright © ARM Limited.)

- Then go to Debug|Run menu item to run your program.
- Go to Debug|Stop menu item to pseudo-stop the project.

Now open the Call Stack + Locals window and expand the receive array rcdata[]. You can find that all 26 letters sent by the master have been received by the slave and displayed in this array, which is shown in Figure 8.76.

Based on these results, try to answer the following questions:

- Why we can use the local char variable s_data as the loop counter?
- What is the advantage of using the UART1 receiving interrupt mechanism? What is your opinion for using this interrupt in this project?
- What did you learn from this project?

Chapter 9

ARM® Cortex®-M4 Timer and USB Programming

This chapter provides general information about the ARM® Cortex®-M4 Microcontroller General-Purpose Timer programming, including the Watchdog Times programming. Because of the space limitations, we moved the USB programming to this chapter. The discussion also includes the GPIO Ports related to General-Purpose Timers and USB modules used in TM4C123GH6PM MCU system. This discussion concentrates on the architectures and programming interfaces applied on General-Purpose Timers, Watchdog Timers as well as USB modules specially designed for the TM4C123GH6PM MCU system. Special or alternative control functions for different GPIO pins related to different peripherals, including timers and USB modules, are also discussed and introduced with example projects in this chapter.

9.1 OVERVIEW AND INTRODUCTION

As we discussed in Section 2.6.2 in Chapter 2, in the TM4C123GH6PM MCU system the GPIO module provides interfaces for multiple peripherals or I/O devices. Generally, GPIO provides six popular GPIO Ports, Ports A~F, to interface and access most system or on-chip peripherals as well as external peripherals and I/O devices to perform input/output functions.

Each GPIO Port can be mapped to an I/O block, and each block contains 8 bits or 8 pins. Each bit or each pin can be configured as either input or output pin. Also with the help of the GPIO Alternate Function Selection register (GPIOAFSEL), each pin can be configured to perform multiple or different functions, which are called alternate functions.

Most of peripherals, including system, on-chip and interfaces to the external peripherals, are connected and controlled to the GPIO Ports with related GPIO pins. In this chapter, we will concentrate on the following peripherals used in the TM4C123GH6PM MCU system:

- General-Purpose Timers
- Watchdog Timers
- Universal Serial Bus (USB) Controller

Some example projects related to those peripherals are to be developed and built.

Practical Microcontroller Engineering with ARM® Technology, First Edition. Ying Bai.
© 2016 by The Institute of Electrical and Electronics Engineers, Inc. Published 2016 by John Wiley & Sons, Inc.
Companion Website: www.wiley.com/goarmbai

9.2   GENERAL-PURPOSE TIMERS

The timer system is one of the most complex subsystems in the TM4C123GH6PM MCU system since quite a few general-purpose timers and blocks are involved in this system.

The General-Purpose Timer Module (GPTM) contains six 16/32-bit GPTM blocks and six 32/64-bit Wide GPTM blocks. Each 16/32-bit GPTM block can provide two 16-bit (half-width) timers/counters that are referred to as Timer A and Timer B. These timers/counters can be further configured to operate independently as timers or event counters, or concatenated together to operate as one 32-bit (full-width) timer or one 32-bit Real-Time Clock (RTC).

Similarly, each 32/64-bit Wide GPTM block provides two 32-bit timers, also called Timer A and Timer B, and they can be concatenated together to form a 64-bit timer. Timers can also be used to trigger μDMA transfers. All timers have interrupt controls and separate interrupt vectors as well as separate interrupt handlers.

In summary, each of six 16/32-bit GPTM blocks (block0~block5) can:

- Be configured as either two half-width (16-bit) timers/counters called Timer**N**A and Timer**N**B or a full-width (32-bit) timer/counter that can also be called Timer**N**A. When working in the full-width mode, only Timer**N**A control registers are available to control its operations (**N** = 0~5).

- Be set up to run as a one-shot timer or a continuous timer in either half-width or full-width modes. If configured in one-shot mode, the timer stops counting when it reaches zero when counting down or the load value when counting up. If in continuous mode, the timer counts to zero (counting down) or the load value (counting up), then reloads and continues counting. When configured as a full-width timer, the timer can also be configured to operate as an RTC. In this mode, the timer expects to be driven by a 32.768 kHz external clock, which is divided down to produce 1 second clock ticks.

- Be configured for event capture or as a PWM generator when working in the half-width mode. When configured for event capture, the timer acts as a counter. It can be configured to either count the time between events or the events themselves. The type of event being counted can be configured as a positive edge, a negative edge, or both edges. When a timer is configured as a PWM generator, the input signal used to capture events becomes an output signal, and the timer drives an edge-aligned pulse onto that signal.

- Be configured as an interrupt generator. Interrupts can be generated to indicate that an event has been captured, or that a certain number of events have been captured. Interrupts can also be generated when the timer has counted down to zero or when the timer gets or matches a certain value.

- Be synchronized for multiple timer modules. Synchronized counters are useful in PWM and edge time capture modes. In PWM mode, the PWM outputs from multiple timers can be in lock-step by having the same load value and synchronizing the counters (meaning that the counters always have the same value). Similarly, by using the same load value and synchronized counters in edge time capture mode, the absolute time between two input edges can be easily measured.

- Be configured to perform efficient transfers using Micro Direct Memory Access Controller (μDMA) in (1) a Dedicated channel for each timer and (2) a Burst request generated on timer interrupt.

The six 32/64-bit WGPTM blocks provide the similar controls and functions.

9.2.1 The GPTM Architecture and Functional Block Diagram

Figure 9.1 shows the architecture and functional block diagram for one GPTM block. All GPTM blocks have the same function and block diagram for Timer**N**A and Timer**N**B (**N** = 0~5).

Each GPTM block is composed of different control and status registers, and these control and function registers can be divided into six groups based their functions (**N** is ignored):

- Timer A Control Register group.
- Timer B Control Register group.
- Timer A Status Register group.
- Timer B Status Register group.
- Timers A and B Interrupt and Configuration Register group.
- External Controls group.

The registers in the Timer A Control group are used to control and configure Timer A operational functions, such as the prescaler value, matching value, loading value, and corresponding actions when these values are matched in the Timer A timer. Similar functions are performed for those registers in the Timer B Control group.

The registers in the Timer A Status group are used to monitor and report the current running status of the selected timer module. These statuses include the prescale value setup for the timer, the current free-running value, and the output of the comparator for upper/down counter values to indicate whether a matched situation has occurred for the selected timer. Similar functions are performed by the registers in the Timer B Status group.

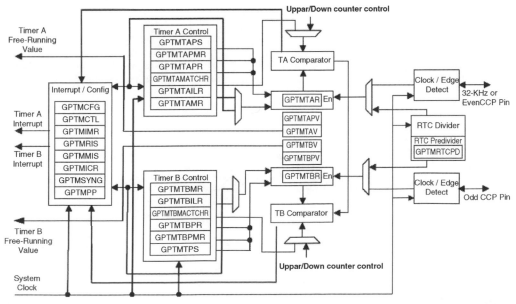

Figure 9.1. The architecture and block diagram of one GPTM block. (Reprinted with the permission of the Texas Instruments Incorporated.)

The registers in the Interrupt and Configuration group are used to configure and set up any timer-related interrupt, including the interrupt source selection, masking, triggering, and responding.

The external control group is used to monitor and direct external events and signals to the appropriate path to enable timers to obtain the desired results based on these inputs.

This architecture and functional block diagram also works for 32/64-bit Wide GPTM blocks.

9.2.2 The General-Purpose Timer Module Components

The cores of each GPTM block are two free-running up/down counters referred to as Timer A and Timer B shown in Figure 9.1, two prescaler registers, two match registers, two prescaler match registers, two shadow registers, and two load/initialization registers and their associated control functions.

The exact functionality of each GPTM is controlled by software and configured through the register interface. Timer A and Timer B can be used individually, in which case they have a 16-bit counting range for the 16/32-bit GPTM blocks and a 32-bit counting range for 32/64-bit Wide GPTM blocks.

In addition, Timer A and Timer B can be concatenated to provide a 32-bit counting range for the 16/32-bit GPTM blocks and a 64-bit counting range for the 32/64-bit Wide GPTM blocks. Note that the prescaler can only be used when the timers are used individually.

The available modes for each GPTM block are shown in Table 9.1. Note that when counting down in one-shot or periodic modes, the prescaler acts as a true prescaler. When counting up in one-shot or periodic modes, the prescaler acts as a timer extension and holds the most-significant bits of the count. In input edge count, input edge time and PWM mode, the prescaler always acts as a timer extension, regardless of the count direction.

Before we can continue to dig deep for each GPTM block, we need to clarify some special terminologies and registers, such as prescaler registers, match registers, and shadow registers.

Table 9.1. Available modes for each GPTM block.

Mode	Timer	Count Mode	Counter Size 16/32-bit GPTM	Counter Size 32/64-bit Wide GPTM	Prescaler Size 16/32-bit GPTM	Prescaler Size 32/64-bit Wide GPTM	Prescaler Function
One-Shot	Individual	Up or Down	16-bit	32-bit	8-bit	16-bit	Timer Extension (Up) Prescaler (Down)
	Concatenated	Up or Down	32-bit	64-bit	—	—	—
Periodic	Individual	Up or Down	16-bit	32-bit	8-bit	16-bit	Timer Extension (Up) Prescaler (Down)
	Concatenated	Up or Down	32-bit	64-bit	—	—	—
RTC	Concatenated	Up	32-bit	64-bit	—	—	—
Edge Count	Individual	Up or Down	16-bit	32-bit	8-bit	16-bit	Timer Extension (Both)
Edge Time	Individual	Up or Down	16-bit	32-bit	8-bit	16-bit	Timer Extension (Both)
PWM	Individual	Down	16-bit	32-bit	8-bit	16-bit	Timer Extension

9.2.2.1 Prescaler Registers

Depending on different operational modes, this prescaler has different functions.

- When working on count down in one-shot or periodic modes, this prescaler works as a true prescaler and the whole start value is divided into two parts; the real start value is loaded into the GPTMTnILR register and the prescale is loaded into the GPTMTnPR register. The prescale value works as a divider to divide the input clock frequency to certain value, and therefore to get a desired working cycle T_0, and this T_0 can be used by the counter as a timing-cycle-base to do the counting-down jobs. The timer period obtained by the countdown is: $(\text{start value}) \times (\text{prescale} + 1) \times T_0$.

- When working on count up in one-shot or periodic modes, the prescaler works as a timer extension and holds the MSB of the counter. When timer gets its upper bound stored in the GPTMTnILR register, the MSB in the GPTMTnPR register is reduced by 1, and the timer continues to count up until a 0 is obtained from the GPTMTnPR register.

9.2.2.2 Match Registers

The GPTM Timer A Match (GPTMTAMATCHR) register can be used to load a match value, and this value can be compared with the current timer value stored in the GPTM Timer A (GPTMTAR) register to trigger a matching interrupt or set a flag to indicate that a time value matching has occurred if both values are equal. The GPTM Timer B has the similar registers and functions.

9.2.2.3 Shadow Registers

The so-called shadow registers are exactly the GPTM Timer A Value (GPTMTAV) register and GPTM Timer B Value (GPTMTBV) register.

In a 16-bit mode, bits 15:0 of the GPTMTAV register contain the value of the current counter and bits 23:16 contain the current, free-running value of the prescaler, which is the upper 8 bits of the count in the Input Edge Count, Input Edge Time, PWM, and one-shot or periodic count-up modes. In one-shot or periodic count-down modes, the prescaler stored in 23:16 is a true prescaler, meaning that bits 23:16 count down before decrementing the value in bits 15:0.

However, the GPTM Timer A Prescale (GPTMTAPR) register is used to store the prescaler value for the Timer A module; therefore the GPTMTAV can be considered as a shadow of the GPTMTAPR register. In fact, bits 23:16 in the GPTMTAV register contain a duplicated value of the prescaler stored in the GPTMTAPR register.

9.2.3 The General-Purpose Timer Module Operational Modes

Each GPTM block can work in one of the following modes:

1. One-Shot Timer Mode.
2. Periodic Timer Mode.
3. Periodic Snapshot Timer Mode.
4. Wait-for-Trigger Mode.
5. Real-Time Clock Timer Mode.

6. Input Edge-Count Mode.

7. Input Edge-Time Mode.

8. PWM Mode.

9. DMA Mode.

10. Synchronizing GP Timer Blocks.

11. Concatenated Modes.

In the following sections we will provide a review and discussion for these modes one by one. We will use Timer A as an example timer to illustrate these modes. Similar modes operations can be obtained for Timer B module.

9.2.3.1 One-Shot and Periodic Timer Mode

The one-shot and periodic timer mode can be illustrated by the operational sequences of Timer A shown in Figures 9.2a and 9.2b.

When the timer is in counting-down mode and starts, (1) the start values in the GPTMTAILR and GPTMTAPR registers are loaded into the Timer A and its Prescaler. (2) Then the timer begins the count-down by first decrementing 1 from the Prescaler. (3) Until the Prescaler is 0, (4) the GPTMTAPR is reloaded to the Prescaler, and (5) the free-running

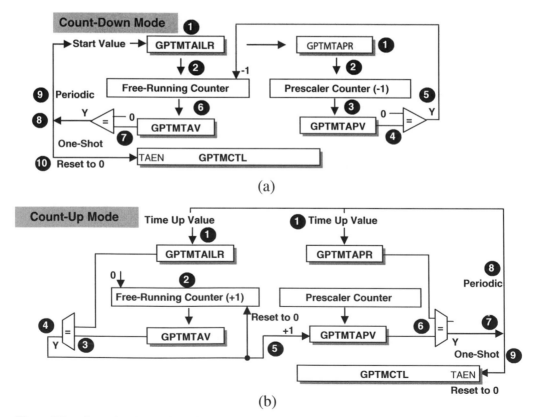

(a)

(b)

Figure 9.2. Operational procedures for one-shot and periodic mode.

counter begins its count-down operation. (6) The current value of the free-running counter can be obtained from the GPTMTAV register, and (7) this value is compared with 0. (8) If it is equals to 0, re-do decrementing 1 from the Prescaler and then free-running counter until the free-running counter gets 0. (9) For a periodic timer, the start values are reloaded from the GPTMTAILR and the GPTMTAPR registers into the timer and continue for the next cycle. (10) For one-shot mode, the TAEN bit in the GPTMCTL register is reset to 0 to stop the timer's operation. Refer to Figure 9.2a for this sequence.

When the timer is in the counting up mode and starts, (1) the time-up values are loaded into the GPTMTAILR and the optional GPTMTAPR registers, and (2) the free-running counter starts its increment by 1 action from 0. The current value of the free-running counter can be obtained from the GPTMTAV register, (3) and this value is compared with a value in the GPTMTAILR register to see whether they are equal. (4) If they are same, (5) a signal is sent to the GPTMTAPV to increment it by 1 and reset the free-running counter to 0 to restart its increment by 1 action. (6) Then the value in the GPTMTAPV register is compared with the value in the GPTMTAPR register (prescaler). (7) If they are equal, it means that the time is up and a flag should be set to report this situation. (8) For periodic count-up mode, the updated or the same time-up values are reloaded into the GPTMTAILR and the optional GPTMTAPR registers to begin the next cycle. (9) For a one-shot mode, the TAEN bit in the GPTMCTL register is reset to 0 to stop the timer's operation. Refer to Figure 9.2b for this operational sequence. An interrupt can also be generated for steps 8 and 7 in Figures 9.2a and 9.2b.

The following registers are important and useful for the timer's operations:

- The GPTMTAILR and the GPTMTAPR registers: These two registers are used to keep the start values (for count-down mode) and time-up values (for count-up mode). The former stores the value used for the free-running counter, and the latter is for the prescaler.
- The GPTMTAV and the GPTMTAPV registers: These two registers store the current values for free-running counter and the prescaler. The software can access these two registers to get the current values for the free-running counter and the current value for the prescaler in real time.

In addition to reloading the count value, the timer can generate interrupts, CCP outputs, and triggers when it reaches the timeout event. When a time-up occurred, the TATORIS bit (bit 0) in the GPTM Raw Interrupt Status (GPTMRIS) register is set to 1, and this value will be held until it is cleared by writing the GPTM Interrupt Clear (GPTMICR) register. If the time-out interrupt is enabled in the GPTM Interrupt Mask (GPTMIMR) register, the GPTM also sets the TATOMIS bit in the GPTM Masked Interrupt Status (GPTMMIS) register.

By setting the TAMIE bit in the GPTMTAMR register, an interrupt condition can also be generated when the Timer value equals the value loaded into the GPTM Timer A Match (GPTMTAMATCHR) and GPTM Timer A Prescale Match (GPTMTAPMR) registers. This interrupt has the same status, masking, and clearing functions as the timeout interrupt, but uses the match interrupt bits instead. For example, the raw interrupt status is monitored via TAMRIS bit in the GPTMRIS register.

A point to be noted is that the interrupt status bits are not updated by the hardware unless the TAMIE bit in the GPTMTAMR register is set, which is different than the behavior for the time-out interrupt. The ADC trigger is enabled by setting the TAOTE bit in GPTMCTL.

Table 9.2. 16-bit Timer with prescaler configurations.

Prescale (8-Bit Value)	Number of Timer Clocks	Max Time	Unit
00000000	1	0.8192	ms
00000001	2	1.6384	ms
00000010	3	2.4576	ms
00000011	4	3.2768	ms
00000100	5	4.0960	Ms
00000101	6	4.9152	Ms
00000110	7	5.7344	Ms
00000111	8	6.5536	ms
—	—	—	—
11111101	254	208.0768	ms
11111110	255	208.8960	ms
11111111	256	209.7152	ms

If software updates the GPTMTAILR or the GPTMTAPR register while the counter is counting down, the counter loads the new value on the next clock cycle and continues counting from the new value if the TAILD bit in the GPTMTAMR register is clear. If the TAILD bit is set, the counter loads the new value after the next timeout. If software updates the GPTMTAILR or the GPTMTAPR register when the counter is counting up, the timeout event is changed on the next cycle to the new value.

If software updates the GPTM Timer A Value (GPTMTAV) register while the counter is counting up or down, the counter loads the new value on the next clock cycle and continues counting from the new value. If software updates the GPTMTAMATCHR or the GPTMTAPMR registers, the new values are reflected on the next clock cycle if the TAMRSU bit in the GPTMTAMR register is clear. If the TAMRSU bit is set, the new value will not take effect until the next timeout.

Table 9.2 shows a group of configurations for a 16-bit free-running timer using the prescaler. All values assume an 80 MHz clock with the clock period $T_c = 12.5$ ns. The prescaler can only be used when a 16/32-bit timer is configured in 16-bit mode and a 32/64-bit timer is configured in 32-bit mode.

9.2.3.2 Periodic Snapshot Timer Mode

The operation principle of the periodic Snapshot mode is very similar to the Periodic mode shown in Figures 9.2a and 9.2b. The only difference is that the start values (for count-down) and the time-up values (for count-up) are not only stored into the GPTMTAILR and the optional GPTMTAPR registers, but also reserved in the GPTM Timer A (GPTMTAR) register and the GPTM Timer A Prescale Snapshot (GPTMTAPS) register. In this way, software can determine the time elapsed from the interrupt generation to the ISR entry by examining the snapshot values and the current value of the free-running timer. Snapshot mode is not available when the timer is configured in one-shot mode.

9.2.3.3 Wait-for-Trigger Mode

When software sets the TAEN bit in the GPTM Control (GPTMCTL) register, the Timer A is enabled and begins counting up from 0 or down from its preloaded value. However, if the TAWOT bit (Timer A Wait-On-Trigger) in the GPTMTAMR register is set to 1, even after the TAEN bit is set, the timer does not start its work, instead it waits for a trigger to begin its counting actions. This operational mode can be used to count the period or the number of times when an external event occurred to trigger the timer.

9.2.3.4 Real-Time Clock Timer Mode

When working in the Real-Time Clock (RTC) mode, both Timer A and Timer B must be concatenated to form a 32-bit count-up timer.

When RTC mode is selected for the first time after a system reset, the counter is loaded with a value of 1. All subsequent load values must be written to the GPTM Timer A Interval Load (GPTMTAILR) registers. If the GPTMTAILR register is loaded with a new value, the counter begins counting at that value until the upper bound value of 0xFFFFFFFF.

The input clock to the RTC is required to be 32.768 kHz in RTC mode. The clock signal is then divided down to a 1 Hz rate and is passed along to the input of the counter.

When software writes the TAEN bit in the GPTMCTL register to enable the RTC, the counter starts counting up from 1. When the current count value matches the preloaded value in the GPTMTAMATCHR registers, the GPTM sets the RTCRIS bit in GPTMRIS register and continues counting until either (a) a hardware reset occurs or (b) it is disabled by software by clearing the TAEN bit. When the timer value reaches the terminal count, the timer rolls over and continues counting up from 0. If the RTC interrupt is enabled in GPTMIMR, the GPTM also sets the RTCMIS bit in GPTMMIS register and generates a controller interrupt. The status flags (RTCMIS bit) are cleared by writing the RTCCINT bit in GPTMICR register.

In this mode, the GPTMTAR and GPTMTAV registers always have the same value.

9.2.3.5 Input Edge-Count Mode

In Edge-Count mode, the timer is configured as a 24-bit or 48-bit up- or down-counter. The optional prescaler with the upper count value stored in the GPTM Timer A Prescale (GPTMTAPR) register and the lower bits in the GPTMTAR register. In this mode, the timer is capable of capturing three types of events: rising edge, falling edge, or both.

To enable the timer to work in the Edge-Count mode, the TACMR bit of the GPTMTAMR register must be cleared. The type of edge that the timer counts is determined by the TAEVENT fields of the GPTMCTL register.

During the initialization for the count-down mode, the GPTMTAMATCHR and GPTMTAPMR registers are configured to enable the difference between the start values stored in the GPTMTAILR and GPTMTAPR registers and the matched values stored in the GPTMTAMATCHR and GPTMTAPMR registers to equal to the number of edge events that must be counted. In the count-up mode, the timer counts from 0 to the value in the GPTMTAMATCHR and GPTMTAPMR registers. Note that when executing a count-up mode, the terminal value stored in the GPTMTAPR and GPTMTAILR registers must be greater than the value of GPTMTAPMR and GPTMTAMATCHR.

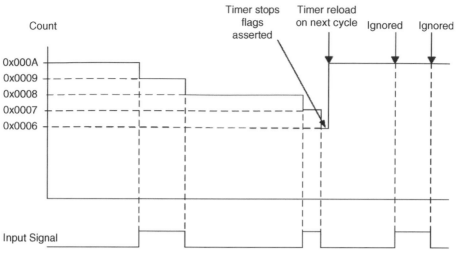

Figure 9.3. An example of using a count-down timer to detect input edge events. (Reprinted with the permission of the Texas Instruments Incorporated.)

When software writes the TAEN bit in the GPTMCTL register, the timer is enabled for event capture. Each input event on the CCP pin decrements or increments the counter by 1 until the event count matches GPTMTnMATCHR and GPTMTnPMR. When the counts match, the GPTM sets the CAMRIS bit in the GPTMRIS register, and holds it until it is cleared by writing the GPTMICR register. If the capture mode match interrupt is enabled in the GPTM Interrupt Mask (GPTMIMR) register, the GPTM also sets the CAMMIS bit in the GPTM Masked Interrupt Status (GPTMMIS) register. In this mode, the GPTMTAR and GPTMTAPS registers hold the count of the input events while the GPTMTAV and GPTMTAPV registers hold the free-running timer value and the free-running prescaler value. In the count-up mode, the current count of input events is held in both the GPTMTAR and GPTMTAV registers.

After the match value is reached in the count-down mode, the counter is then reloaded using the value in GPTMTAILR and GPTMTAPR registers and finally stopped because the GPTM automatically clears the TAEN bit in the GPTMCTL register. Once the event count has been reached, all further events are ignored until TAEN bit is re-enabled by software. In the count-up mode, the timer is reloaded with 0 and continues counting.

Figure 9.3 shows an example of using a count-down timer to perform Input Edge-Count detections. In this example, the timer start value is set to GPTMTAILR = 0x000A and the match value is set to GPTMTAMATCHR = 0x0006 so that four edge events are counted. The counter is configured to detect both edges of the input signal.

Note that the last two edges are not counted because the timer automatically clears the TAEN bit after the current count matches the value in the GPTMTAMATCHR register.

9.2.3.6 Input Edge-Time Mode

This operational mode is similar to the Input Edge-Count mode discussed in the previous section. The difference is that the timer should be configured to the Input Edge-Time mode by setting the TACMR bit in the GPTMTAMR register, and the type of event that the timer captures is determined by the TAEVENT fields of the GPTMCTL register.

At the start, the TAEN bit in the GPTMCTL register is set to 1 and the timer is enabled for event capture and starts its counting. When the selected input event is detected, the current timer counting value is captured in the GPTMTAR and GPTMTAPS register and is available to be read by the microcontroller. The GPTM then sets the CAERIS bit in the GPTMRIS register, and holds it until it is cleared by writing the GPTMICR register. If the capture mode event interrupt is enabled in the GPTMIMR register, the GPTM also sets the CAEMIS bit in the GPTMMIS register.

In this mode, the GPTMTAR and GPTMTAPS registers hold the time at which the selected input event occurred while the GPTMTAV and GPTMTAPV registers hold the free-running timer value and the free-running prescaler value.

After an event has been captured, the timer does not stop counting. It continues to count until the TAEN bit is cleared. When the timer reaches the timeout value, it is reloaded with 0 in the count-up mode and the value from the GPTMTAILR and GPTMTAPR registers in the count-down mode.

Figure 9.4 shows an example of using a count-down mode timer to perform the input edge timing detections. In the diagram, it is assumed that the start value of the timer is the default value of 0xFFFF, and the timer is configured to capture rising edge events.

Each time a rising edge event is detected, the current count value is loaded into the GPTMTAR and GPTMTAPS registers, and is held there until another rising edge is detected. At that point the new count value is loaded into the GPTMTAR and GPTMTAPS registers again.

When operating in Edge-time mode, the counter uses a modulo 2^{24} count if the prescaler is enabled or 2^{16} if the prescaler is not enabled. If there is a possibility that the edge could take longer than the count, then another timer configured in periodic-timer mode can be implemented to ensure detection of the missed edge. The periodic timer should be configured in such a way that:

- The periodic timer cycles at the same rate as the edge-time timer.
- The periodic timer interrupt has a higher interrupt priority than the edge-time timeout interrupt.

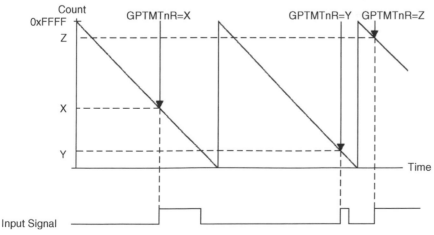

Figure 9.4. An example of using the count-down mode timer to detect the edge time. (Reprinted with the permission of the Texas Instruments Incorporated.)

- If the periodic timer interrupt service routine is entered, software must check if an edge-time interrupt is pending and if it is, the value of the counter must be subtracted by 1 before being used to calculate the snapshot time of the event.

9.2.3.7 PWM Mode

When working in this mode, each timer can be configured as a 24- or 48-bit count-down counter to generate PWM output signals. At start, the timer loads the start values stored in the GPTMTAILR and GPTMTAPR registers (if prescaler is used) and begins its count-down actions. When gets 0, the timer reloads the start value and begin the next cycle.

The period and frequency of the PWM signal is controlled by the start values setup in the GPTMTAILR and GPTMTAPR registers, and the pulse width is controlled by the values set in the GPTMTAMATCHR and GPTMTAPMR registers (if prescaler is used). The PWM pulse is generated (outputs High) when the timer is at its start value and terminated (outputs Low) when the timer equals to the terminate values stored in the GPTMTA-MATCHR and GPTMTAPMR registers.

The timer can generate three types of interrupt: rising edge, falling edge, and both. The event is configured by the TAEVENT field of the GPTMCTL register, and the interrupt is enabled by setting the TAPWMIE bit in the GPTMTAMR register.

In this mode, the GPTMTAR and GPTMTAV registers always have the same value, as do the GPTMTAPS and the GPTMTAPV registers.

The operational sequence of using the Timer A to generate a PWM signal is as follows:

1. The start values are loaded into the GPTMTAILR and GPTMTAPR registers, and the terminate values are loaded into the GPTMTAMATCHR and GPTMTAPMR registers. The period and duty cycle of the PWM signal are determined based on these values.

2. The PWM mode is enabled with the GPTMTAMR register by setting the TAAMS bit to 1, the TACMR bit to 0, and the TAMR field to 0x2.

3. The timer is enabled and starts its count-down operation by setting the TAEN bit in the GPTMCTL register to 1. The counter begins counting down until it reaches the 0 state. Then it reloads the start values and continues for the next cycle until disabled by software clearing the TAEN bit in the GPTMCTL register. Alternatively, if the TAWOT bit is set in the GPTMTAMR register, once the TAEN bit is set, the timer waits for a trigger to begin counting.

4. As the timer starts counting from its start values, the PWM pulse is generated with outputting High. During the counting-down process, when the value in the timer is equal to the terminate values set in the GPTMTAMATCHR and GPTMTAPMR registers, the pulse of the PWM signal is terminated with outputting Low.

5. The output level of the PWM signal can be controlled by the software, it means that the software has the capability of inverting the output PWM signal by setting the TAPWML bit in the GPTMCTL register.

Figure 9.5 shows an example of using Timer A to generate an output PWM with a 1-ms period and a 66% duty cycle (TAPWML = 0) assuming a 50 MHz input clock. The duty cycle could be 33% if the TAPWML = 1. For this example, the start value is GPTMTAILR = 0 xC350 and the match value in GPTMTAMATCHR is 0x411A.

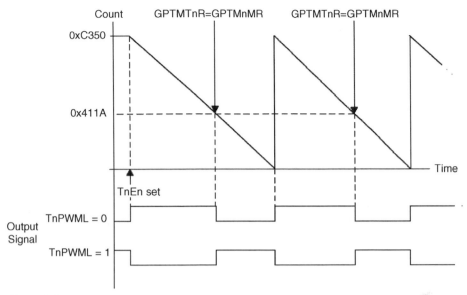

Figure 9.5. An example of using Timer A to generate a PWM signal. (Reprinted with the permission of the Texas Instruments Incorporated.)

9.2.3.8 DMA Mode

Each timer has a µDMA channel and can provide a request signal to the µDMA controller. The request is a burst type and occurs whenever a timer raw interrupt condition occurs. The size of the µDMA transfer should be set to the amount of data that should be transferred whenever a timer event occurs.

For example, to transfer 256 items, 8 items at a time every 10 ms, configure a timer to generate a periodic timeout at 10 ms. Configure the µDMA transfer for a total of 256 items, with a burst size of 8 items. Each time when the timer times out, the µDMA controller transfers 8 items, until all 256 items have been transferred.

No other special steps are needed to enable Timers for µDMA operation.

9.2.3.9 Synchronizing GP Timer Blocks

The GPTM Synchronizer Control (GPTMSYNC) register in the GPTM0 block can be used to synchronize selected timers to begin counting at the same time. Setting a bit in the GPTMSYNC register causes the associated timer to perform the actions of a timeout event. No interrupt is generated when the timers are synchronized. If a timer is being used in concatenated mode, only the bit for Timer A should be set in the GPTMSYNC register.

All timers must use the same clock source for this feature to work correctly.

9.2.3.10 Concatenated Modes

The GPTM can be placed into concatenated mode by writing a 0x0 or a 0x1 to the GPTMCFG bit field in the GPTM Configuration (GPTMCFG) register. In both configurations, certain 16/32-bit GPTM registers are concatenated to form pseudo 32-bit registers.

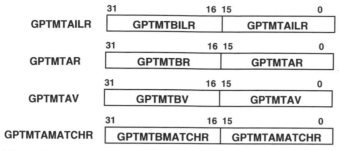

Figure 9.6. The pseudo 32-bit registers.

These pseudo 32-bit registers are made by combining registers used for Timer A and Timer B together, as shown in Figure 9.6.

The resulting 32-bit registers are made by placing 16 bit registers used for Timer B in the upper 16-bit position and 16-bit registers used for Timer A in the lower 16-bit position. The pseudo 32-bit registers are considered and accessed by using the addresses of the related registers used for Timer A.

9.2.4 The General-Purpose Timer Module Registers

As we mentioned in Section 9.2.1, each GPTM block is composed of different control and status registers and these control and function registers can be divided into six groups based their functions. To save time and space, we only discuss those registers used for the Timer A since the same registers are used for the Timer B.

These registers can be divided into the following groups:

- Timer A Control Register group
- Timer A Status Register group
- Timers A and B Interrupt and Configuration Register group
- External Controls group

9.2.4.1 Timer A Control Register Group

Eight registers are used to configure and control the operations of the Timer A:

- GPTM Configuration Register (GPTMCFG)
- GPTM Control Register (GPTMCTL)
- GPTM Timer A Mode Register (GPTMTAMR)
- GPTM Timer A Interval Load Register (GPTMTAILR)
- GPTM Timer A Match Register (GPTMTAMATCHR)
- GPTM Timer A Prescale Register (GPTMTAPR)
- GPTM Timer A Prescale Match Register (GPTMTAPMR)
- GPTM Timer A Prescale Snapshot Register (GPTMTAPS)

Table 9.3. Bit value and its function for GPTMCFG register.

Bit	Name	Reset	Function
31:3	Reserved	0x0	Reserved

2:0	GPTMCFG	0x0	0x0: For a 16/32-bit timer, this value selects the 32-bit timer configuration.
			     For a 32/64-bit wide timer, this value selects the 64-bit timer configuration.
			0x1: For a 16/32-bit timer, this value selects the 32-bit real-time clock (RTC) counter.
			     For a 32/64-bit wide timer, this value selects the 64-bit real-time clock (RTC) counter.
			0x4: For a 16/32-bit timer, this value selects the 16-bit timer configuration.
			     For a 32/64-bit wide timer, this value selects the 32-bit timer configuration.
			     The function is controlled by bits 1:0 of GPTMTAMR and GPTMTBMR.

9.2.4.1.1 GPTM Configuration Register (GPTMCFG)

This is a 32-bit register but only the lowest 3 bits (bits 2~0) are used to configure the global operation of the GPTM module. The value written to this register determines whether the GPTM is in 32- or 64-bit mode (concatenated timers) or in 16- or 32-bit mode (individual, split timers).

Table 9.3 shows the bit field and bit functions for this register.

9.2.4.1.2 GPTM Control Register (GPTMCTL)

This is a 32-bit register but only the lower 12-bit are used to alongside the GPTMCFG and GMTMTAMR registers to fine-tune the timer configuration and to enable other features such as timer stall and the output trigger. The output trigger can be used to initiate transfers on the ADC.

The bit configuration for this register is shown in Figure 9.7. The bit field and functions for this register is shown in Table 9.4.

9.2.4.1.3 GPTM Timer A Mode Register (GPTMTAMR)

This is a 32-bit register but only the lower 12-bit are used to configure the GPTM based on the configuration selected in the GPTMCFG register. This register controls the modes for Timer A when it is used individually. When Timer A and Timer B are concatenated, this register controls the modes for both Timer A and Timer B, and the contents of GPTMTBMR are ignored.

The bit configuration for this register is shown in Figure 9.8. The bit field and functions for this register is shown in Table 9.5.

A point to be noted is that all bits in this register should only be changed when the TAEN bit in the GPTMCTL register is cleared or the Timer A is disabled.

9.2.4.1.4 GPTM Timer A Interval Load Register (GPTMTAILR)

This is a 32-bit register and all 32 bits are used to store either the start value or upper bound value for the count-down or count-up timers. When the timer is counting down, this register is used to load the starting count value into the timer. When the timer is counting up, this register sets the upper bound for the timeout event.

GPTM Control Register (GPTMCTL)

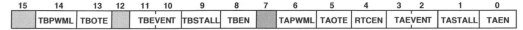

Reserved Bits 31 ~ 15, 12, 7.

Figure 9.7. Bit fields for the GPTMCTL register.

Table 9.4.   Bit value and its function for the GPTMCTL register.

Bit	Name	Reset	Function
31:15	Reserved	0x0	Reserved
14	TBPWML	0x0	GPTM Timer B PWM Output Level: 0: Output is unaffected; 1: Output is inverted.
13	TBOTE	0x0	GPTM Timer B Output Trigger Enable: 0: The output Timer B ADC trigger is disabled; 1: The output Timer B ADC trigger is enabled.
11:10	TBEVENT	0x0	GPTM Timer B Event Mode: 0x0: Positive going edge; 0x1: Negative going edge; 0x3: Both edges; 0x2: Reserved.
9	TBSTALL	0x0	GPTM Timer B Stall Enable: 0: Timer B continues counting while the processor is halted by the debugger. 1: Timer B freezes counting while the processor is halted by the debugger.
8	TBEN	0x0	GPTM Timer B Enable: 0: Timer B is disabled; 1: Timer B is enabled.
6	TAPWML	0x0	GPTM Timer A PWM Output Level: 0: Output is unaffected; 1: Output is inverted.
5	TAOTE	0x0	GPTM Timer A Output Trigger Enable: 0: The output Timer A ADC trigger is disabled; 1: The output Timer A ADC trigger is enabled.
4	RTCEN	0x0	GPTM RTC Stall Enable: 0: RTC counting freezes while the processor is halted by the debugger. 1: RTC counting continues while the processor is halted by the debugger.
3:2	TAEVENT	0x0	GPTM Timer A Event Mode: 0x0: Positive going edge; 0x1: Negative going edge; 0x3: Both edges; 0x2: Reserved.
1	TASTALL	0x0	GPTM Timer A Stall Enable: 0: Timer A continues counting while the processor is halted by the debugger. 1: Timer A freezes counting while the processor is halted by the debugger.
0	TAEN	0x0	GPTM Timer A Enable: 0: Timer A is disabled; 1: Timer A is enabled.

9.2.4.1.5 GPTM Timer A Match Register (GPTMTAMATCHR)   This is a 32-bit register and all 32 bits are used to store a matched value. Interrupts can be generated when the timer value is equal to the value in this register in one-shot or periodic mode.

In Edge-Count mode, this register along with GPTMTAILR determines how many edge events are counted. The total number of edge events counted is equal to the value in GPTMTAILR minus this value. Note that in edge-count mode, when executing an up-count, the value of GPTMTAPR and GPTMTAILR must be greater than the value of GPTMTAPMR and GPTMTAMATCHR.

In PWM mode, this value along with GPTMTAILR determines the duty cycle of the output PWM signal.

GPTM Timer A Mode Register (GPTMTAMR)

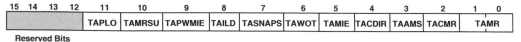

Reserved Bits

Figure 9.8.   Bit fields for the GPTMTAMR register.

Table 9.5. Bit value and its function for the GPTMTAMR register.

Bit	Name	Reset	Function
31:12	Reserved	0x0	Reserved
11	TAPLO	0x0	GPTM Timer A PWM Legacy Operation: 0: CCP pin is driven Low when the GPTMTAILR is reloaded after the timer reaches 0. 1: CCP is driven High when the GPTMTAILR is reloaded after the timer reaches 0.
10	TAMRSU	0x0	GPTM Timer A Match Register Update: 0: Update GPTMTAMATCHR register and GPTMTAPR register, if used, on the next cycle. 1: Update GPTMTAMATCHR register and GPTMTAPR register, if used, on the next timeout.
9	TAPWMIE	0x0	GPTM Timer A PWM Interrupt Enable: 0: Capture event interrupt is disabled; 1: Capture event interrupt is enabled.
8	TAILD	0x0	GPTM Timer A Interval Load Write: 0: Update the GPTMTAR and GPTMTAV registers with the value in the GPTMTAILR register on the next cycle. Also update the GPTMTAPS and GPTMTAPV registers with the value in the GPTMTAPR register on the next cycle. 1: Update the GPTMTAR and GPTMTAV registers with the value in the GPTMTAILR register on the next timeout. Also update the GPTMTAPS and GPTMTAPV registers with the value in the GPTMTAPR register on the next timeout.
7	TASNAPS	0x0	GPTM Timer A Snap-Shot Mode: 0: Snapshot mode is disabled; 1: Snapshot mode is enabled.
6	TAWOT	0x0	GPTM Timer A Wait-on-Trigger: 0: Timer A begins counting as soon as it is enabled. 1: Timer A does not begin counting until it receives a trigger.
5	TAMIE	0x0	GPTM Timer A Match Interrupt Enable: 0: The match interrupt is disabled for match events. 1: An interrupt is generated when the match value in the GPTMTAMATCHR register is reached in the one-shot and periodic modes.
4	TACDIR	0x0	GPTM Timer A Count Direction: 0: The timer counts down; 1: The timer counts up.
3	TAAMS	0x0	GPTM Timer A Alternate Mode Select: 0: Capture or compare mode is enabled. 1: PWM mode is enabled. To enable PWM mode, you must also clear the TACMR bit and configure the TAMR field to 0x1 or 0x2.
2	TACMR	0x0	GPTM Timer A Capture Mode: 0: Edge-Count mode; 1: Edge-Time mode.
1:0	TAMR	0x0	GPTM Timer A Mode: 0x1: One-Shot Timer mode. 0x0: Reserved. 0x2: Periodic Timer mode. 0x3: Capture mode.

9.2.4.1.6 GPTM Timer A Prescale Register (GPTMTAPR)

This is a 32-bit register but only the lower 16 bits are used to store a prescaler value. The value in this register allows software to extend the range of the timers when they are used individually. When working in one-shot or periodic countdown mode, this register acts as a true prescaler for the timer counter. When acting as a true prescaler, the prescaler counts down to 0 before the value in the GPTMTAR and GPTMTAV registers are incremented. In all other individual/split modes, this register is a linear extension of the upper range for the timer counter, taking bits 23:16 in the 16-bit modes of the 16/32-bit GPTM and bits 47:32 in the 32-bit modes of the 32/64-bit Wide GPTM.

Regularly this register is used together with the GPTMTAILR register to get an extended range for a timer, and the start values or upper bound values can be stored into these two registers when a timer starts its works. However, this register is optional, and it is unnecessary to use this register if no any prescaler is needed for an application. In that case, only the GPTMTAILR register can be used to store a start or an upper bound value for the counter. This is true for most applications.

9.2.4.1.7 GPTM Timer A Prescale Match Register (GPTMTAPMR) Similar to the GPTMTAPR register discussed above, only the lower 16 bits are used for this 32-bit register. This lower 16 bits are used to store a matched value used to compare the value in the GPTMTAPR register to try to find a match between them.

In other words, this register allows software to extend the range of the GPTMTA-MATCHR when the timers are used individually. This register holds bits 23:16 in the 16-bit modes of the 16/32-bit GPTM and bits 47:32 in the 32-bit modes of the 32/64-bit Wide GPTM.

The upper byte on this register (bits 15~8) is called the GPTM Timer A Prescale Match High Byte, and the lower byte (bits 7~0) is called the GPTM Timer A Prescale Match Byte.

9.2.4.1.8 GPTM Timer A Prescale Snapshot Register (GPTMTAPS) This is a 32-bit register, but only the lower 16-bit is used to store the prescaler value used to determine the time interval between the generation of a timer-related interrupt and entry to the corresponding interrupt handler.

For the 32/64-bit Wide GPTM, this register shows the current value of the Timer A prescaler in the 32-bit modes. For 16-/32-bit Wide GPTM, this register shows the current value of the Timer A prescaler for periodic snapshot mode.

9.2.4.2 Timer A Status Register Group

Three registers are used to monitor and detect the status of the Timer A:

- GPTM Timer A Register (GPTMTAR)
- GPTM Timer A Value Register (GPTMTAV)
- GPTM Timer A Prescale Value Register (GPTMTAPV).

9.2.4.2.1 GPTM Timer A Register (GPTMTAR) This is a 32-bit register and all 32 bits are used to indicate the current value of the 16-bit free-running counter or the Timer A.

In fact, this register shows the current value of the Timer A counter in all cases except for Input Edge Count and Input Edge Time modes. In the Input Edge Count mode, this register contains the number of edges that have occurred. In the Input Edge Time mode, this register contains the time at which the last edge event took place.

When a 16/32-bit GPTM is configured to one of the 32-bit modes, GPTMTAR works as a 32-bit register with the upper 16 bits corresponding to the contents of the GPTMTBR register. In the16-bit Input Edge Count, Input Edge Time, and PWM modes, bits 15:0

contain the value of the counter and bits 23:16 contain the value of the prescaler, which is the upper 8 bits of the count. Bits 31:24 always read as 0.

To read the value of the prescaler in 16-bit One-Shot and Periodic modes, read bits [23:16] in the GPTMTAV register. To read the value of the prescalar in periodic snapshot mode, read the `Timer A Prescale Snapshot` (GPTMTAPS) register.

9.2.4.2.2 GPTM Timer A Value Register (GPTMTAV) This is a 32-bit read/write register and is used to store the current value of the Timer A free running counter.

When read, this register shows the current, free-running value of Timer A in all modes. Software can use this value to determine the time elapsed between an interrupt and the ISR entry when using the snapshot feature with the periodic operating mode. When written, the value written into this register is loaded into the GPTMTAR register on the next clock cycle.

The difference between the GPTMTAR and GPTMTAV is that the former is a read only register, but the latter is a read/write register. This means that the content of the GPTMTAR register can be modified, and this modification can be accomplished by first writing the updated value into the GPTMTAV register and loaded into the GPTMTAR register in the next clock cycle.

When a 16/32-bit GPTM is configured to one of the 32-bit modes, GPTMTAV works as a 32-bit register with the upper 16-bits corresponding to the contents of the GPTMTBV register. In a 16-bit mode, bits 15:0 contain the value of the counter and bits 23:16 contain the current, free-running value of the prescaler, which is the upper 8 bits of the count in Input Edge Count, Input Edge Time, PWM, and one-shot or periodic up count modes. In one-shot or periodic down count modes, the prescaler stored in 23:16 is a true prescaler, meaning bits 23:16 count down before decrementing the value in bits 15:0. The prescaler in bits 31:24 always reads as 0.

9.2.4.2.3 GPTM Timer A Prescale Value Register (GPTMTAPV) This is a 32-bit read only register, but only the lower 16 bits are used to store the current value of the prescaler for the Timer A.

Usually, this register is used as a 32/64-bit-Wide GPTM register to show the current free-running value of the Timer A prescaler in the 32-bit modes. Software can use this value in conjunction with the GPTMTAV register to determine the time elapsed between an interrupt and the ISR entry.

9.2.4.3 Timers A and B Interrupt and Configuration Register Group

Six registers are used to control and handle interrupts of the Timers A and B:

- GPTM Interrupt Mask Register (GPTMIMR)
- GPTM Raw Interrupt Status Register (GPTMRIS)
- GPTM Masked Interrupt Status Register (GPTMMIS)
- GPTM Interrupt Clear Register (GPTMICR)
- GPTM Synchronize Register (GPTMSYNC)
- GPTM Peripheral Properties Register (GPTMPP)

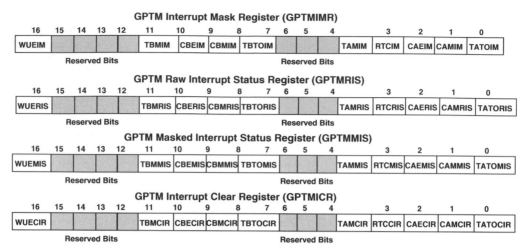

Figure 9.9. Bit fields and functions of GPTM interrupt-related registers.

9.2.4.3.1 GPTM Interrupt Mask Register (GPTMIMR)
This is a 32-bit register, but only the lower 10 bits are used to enable or disable a GPTM-related interrupt to be generated and has received a response. Setting a bit to 1 is to enable the corresponding interrupt, but clearing a bit to 0 is to disable the corresponding interrupt.

The bit configuration for this register is shown in Figure 9.9. The bit field and functions for this register is shown in Table 9.6.

Table 9.6. Bit value and its function for the GPTMIMR register.

Bit	Name	Reset	Function
31:17	Reserved	0x0	Reserved
16	WUEIM	0x0	32/64-Bit Wide GPTM Write Update Error Interrupt Mask: 0 : Interrupt is disabled; 1 : Interrupt is enabled.
11	TBMIM	0x0	GPTM Timer B Match Interrupt Mask: 0 : Interrupt is disabled; 1 : Interrupt is enabled.
10	CBEIM	0x0	GPTM Timer B Capture Mode Event Interrupt Mask: 0 : Interrupt is disabled; 1 : Interrupt is enabled.
9	CBMIM	0x0	GPTM Timer B Capture Mode Match Interrupt Mask: 0 : Interrupt is disabled; 1 : Interrupt is enabled.
8	TBTOIM	0x0	GPTM Timer B Time-Out Interrupt Mask: 0 : Interrupt is disabled; 1 : Interrupt is enabled.
4	TAMIM	0x0	GPTM Timer A Match Interrupt Mask: 0 : Interrupt is disabled; 1 : Interrupt is enabled.
3	RTCIM	0x0	GPTM RTC Interrupt Mask: 0 : Interrupt is disabled; 1 : Interrupt is enabled.
2	CAEIM	0x0	GPTM Timer A Capture Mode Event Interrupt Mask: 0 : Interrupt is disabled; 1 : Interrupt is enabled.
1	CAMIM	0x0	GPTM Timer A Capture Mode Match Interrupt Mask: 0 : Interrupt is disabled; 1 : Interrupt is enabled.
0	TATOIM	0x0	GPTM Timer A Time-Out Interrupt Mask: 0 : Interrupt is disabled; 1 : Interrupt is enabled.

9.2.4.3.2 GPTM Raw Interrupt Status Register (GPTMRIS) Similar to GPTMIMR register, this 32-bit register only used the lower 10 bits to monitor and set a raw or internal interrupt if a GPTM-related raw interrupt occurred. These bits are set whether or not the interrupt is masked in the GPTMIMR register. However, whether these set raw interrupts can be sent to the interrupt controller to be further processed, it depends on whether the corresponding bits on the GPTMIMR register are set (enabled) or not (disabled). Only for those bits that have been set on the GPTMIMR register, they can be sent to the NVIC.

The bit configuration for this register is shown in Figure 9.9. The bit field and functions for this register are similar to those in the GPTMIMR register shown in Table 9.6. If a GPTM-related raw interrupt is generated, the corresponding bit on this register is set to 1. Each bit can be cleared by writing a 1 to its corresponding bit in GPTMICR register.

9.2.4.3.3 GPTM Masked Interrupt Status Register (GPTMMIS) Similar to the GPTMIMR register, this 32-bit register only used the lower 10 bits to monitor and make a responded interrupt if a GPTM related interrupt is occurred and has been responded.

The bit configuration for this register is shown in Figure 9.9. The bit field and functions for this register is similar to those in the GPTMIMR register shown in Table 9.6. A value of 1 on a bit in this register indicates that the corresponding interrupt has occurred and has received a response. All bits are cleared by writing a 1 to the corresponding bit in GPTMICR register.

9.2.4.3.4 GPTM Interrupt Clear Register (GPTMICR) Similar to GPTMIMR register, this 32-bit register only used the lower 10 bits to clear related responded interrupts if the GPTM-related interrupts have received a response and have been processed.

This register is used to clear the status bits in the GPTMRIS and GPTMMIS registers. Writing a 1 to a bit clears the corresponding bit in the GPTMRIS and GPTMMIS registers. All processed or responded interrupts must be cleared by using this register. Otherwise the responded interrupt cannot be generated again in the future if it is not cleared.

The bit configuration for this register is shown in Figure 9.9. The bit field and functions for this register is similar to those in the GPTMIMR register shown in Table 9.6.

9.2.4.3.5 GPTM Synchronize Register (GPTMSYNC) This is a 32-bit register, but only the lower 24 bits are used to provide 12 bit fields, two bits for each field, to configure and set up different synchronizing combinations for different timers. The upper 6-bit fields are used for 32/64-bit timers, from timer 5 to timer 0, and the lower 6 bit fields are used for 16/32-bit timers, timer 5 to timer 0, for any timeout event occurred.

This register is only implemented on GPTM Module 0 and allows software to synchronize a number of timers.

9.2.4.3.6 GPTM Peripheral Properties Register (GPTMPP) The GPTMPP is a 32-bit register, but only the lowest 4 bits, bits 3~0, are used to indicate whether each timer, Timer A and Timer B, is a 16-bit or 32-bit timer. Anyway, this register provides information regarding the properties of the General-Purpose Timer module.

The External Controls group contains one register, the GPTM RTC Predivide (GPTMRTCPD) register, and other event/time-detecting logics. This register provides the current RTC pre-divider value when the timer is operating in RTC mode. Software must perform an atomic access with consecutive reads of the GPTMTAR, GPTMTBR, and GPTMRTCPD registers.

9.2.5 The General-Purpose Timer Module GPIO-Related Control Signals

In the GPTM block diagram shown in Figure 9.1, the specific Capture Compare PWM (CCP) available pins depend on the TM4C123GH6PM MCU. Table 9.7 shows available CCP pins and their timer assignments.

As we mentioned, all peripherals in TM4C123GH6PM MCU system are interfaced to the processor via GPIO Ports and pins, and most GPIO pins can be configured as alternate function pins to perform multiple special digital functions. This is also true to the general-purpose timers. Table 9.8 shows all related GPIO pins used for GPTM functions.

Generally, if the timers are only used for the timing-base or timing-up indications, one does not need to use these CCP pins since these pins are mainly connected to the external signals to detect the number of events that have occurred or the time period events that have been experienced. In most applications, the timer interrupts are used to indicate that the specified time period has passed and the time is up to ask users to handle desired jobs.

Table 9.7. General-Purpose Timers CCP pins distributions.

Timers	Up/Down Counter	Even CCP Pins	Odd CCP Pins
16/32-bit Timer 0	Timer A	T0CCP0	—
	Timer B	—	T0CCP1
16/32-bit Timer 1	Timer A	T1CCP0	—
	Timer B	—	T1CCP1
16/32-bit Timer 2	Timer A	T2CCP0	—
	Timer B	—	T2CCP1
16/32-bit Timer 3	Timer A	T3CCP0	—
	Timer B	—	T3CCP1
16/32-bit Timer 4	Timer A	T4CCP0	—
	Timer B	—	T4CCP1
16/32-bit Timer 5	Timer A	T5CCP0	—
	Timer B	—	T5CCP1
32/64-bit-Wide Timer 0	Timer A	WT0CCP0	—
	Timer B	—	WT0CCP1
32/64-bit-Wide Timer 1	Timer A	WT1CCP0	—
	Timer B	—	WT1CCP1
32/64-bit-Wide Timer 2	Timer A	WT2CCP0	—
	Timer B	—	WT2CCP1
32/64-bit-Wide Timer 3	Timer A	WT3CCP0	—
	Timer B	—	WT3CCP1
32/64-bit-Wide Timer 4	Timer A	WT4CCP0	—
	Timer B	—	WT4CCP1
32/64-bit-Wide Timer 5	Timer A	WT5CCP0	—
	Timer B	—	WT5CCP1

Table 9.8. General-Purpose Timers signals and GPIO pins distributions.

GPTM Pin	GPIO Pin	Pin Type	Pin Function
T0CCP0	PB6 (7) PF0 (7)	I/O	16/32-Bit Timer 0 Capture/Compare/PWM 0.
T0CCP1	PB7 (7) PF1 (7)	I/O	16/32-Bit Timer 0 Capture/Compare/PWM 1.
T1CCP0	PB4 (7) PF2 (7)	I/O	16/32-Bit Timer 1 Capture/Compare/PWM 0.
T1CCP1	PB5 (7) PF3 (7)	I/O	16/32-Bit Timer 1 Capture/Compare/PWM 1.
T2CCP0	PB0 (7) PF4 (7)	I/O	16/32-Bit Timer 2 Capture/Compare/PWM 0.
T2CCP1	PB1 (7)	I/O	16/32-Bit Timer 2 Capture/Compare/PWM 1.
T3CCP0	PB2 (7)	I/O	16/32-Bit Timer 3 Capture/Compare/PWM 0.
T3CCP1	PB3 (7)	I/O	16/32-Bit Timer 3 Capture/Compare/PWM 1.
T4CCP0	PC0 (7)	I/O	16/32-Bit Timer 4 Capture/Compare/PWM 0.
T4CCP1	PC1 (7)	I/O	16/32-Bit Timer 4 Capture/Compare/PWM 1.
T5CCP0	PC2 (7)	I/O	16/32-Bit Timer 5 Capture/Compare/PWM 0.
T5CCP1	PC3 (7)	I/O	16/32-Bit Timer 5 Capture/Compare/PWM 1.
WT0CCP0	PC4 (7)	I/O	32/64-Bit Wide Timer 0 Capture/Compare/PWM 0.
WT0CCP1	PC5 (7)	I/O	32/64-Bit Wide Timer 0 Capture/Compare/PWM 1.
WT1CCP0	PC6 (7)	I/O	32/64-Bit Wide Timer 1 Capture/Compare/PWM 0.
WT1CCP1	PC7 (7)	I/O	32/64-Bit Wide Timer 1 Capture/Compare/PWM 1.
WT2CCP0	PD0 (7)	I/O	32/64-Bit Wide Timer 2 Capture/Compare/PWM 0.
WT2CCP1	PD1 (7)	I/O	32/64-Bit Wide Timer 2 Capture/Compare/PWM 1.
WT3CCP0	PD2 (7)	I/O	32/64-Bit Wide Timer 3 Capture/Compare/PWM 0.
WT3CCP1	PD3 (7)	I/O	32/64-Bit Wide Timer 3 Capture/Compare/PWM 1.
WT4CCP0	PD4 (7)	I/O	32/64-Bit Wide Timer 4 Capture/Compare/PWM 0.
WT4CCP1	PD5 (7)	I/O	32/64-Bit Wide Timer 4 Capture/Compare/PWM 1.
WT5CCP0	PD6 (7)	I/O	32/64-Bit Wide Timer 5 Capture/Compare/PWM 0.
WT5CCP1	PD7 (7)	I/O	32/64-Bit Wide Timer 5 Capture/Compare/PWM 1.

The polling method can also be used to detect the TATORIS bit or TAMRIS bit in the GPTMRIS register to check whether a timeout event or a time match event has been occurred for the Timer A module.

9.2.6 The General-Purpose Timer Module Initializations and Configurations

Before any GPTM block and related timers can start to work, each timer and GPTM block must be properly initialized and configured. To use a GPTM, the appropriate TIMERn bit must be set in the RCGCTIMER or RCGCWTIMER registers to enable and clock the selected timer. If any CCP pin is to be used, the clock to the appropriate GPIO module must be enabled via the RCGCGPIO register.

Depending on the different implementation modes, this initialization and configuration process can be divided into the following five parts:

- One-Shot/Periodic Timer Mode
- Input Edge-Count Mode
- Input Edge-Time Mode
- Real-Time Clock (RTC) Mode
- PWM Mode

9.2.6.1 Initialization and Configuration for One-Shot/Periodic Timer Mode

Perform the following operational steps to complete the initialization and configuration process for this mode ($n = A$ or B):

1. Disable the selected timer by clearing the TnEN bit in the GPTMCTL register.
2. Initialize the GPTMCFG register by writing 0x0 to set up all timers as 32-bit default timers.
3. Configure the TnMR field in the GPTMTnMR register by writing
   - 0x1 for one-shot mode.
   - 0x2 for periodic mode.
4. Optionally configure the TnSNAPS, TnWOT, TnMTE, and TnCDIR bits in the GPTMTnMR register to select whether to capture the value of the free-running timer at timeout, use an external trigger to start counting, configure an additional trigger or interrupt, and count-up or count-down operational mode.
5. Load the start value (time up value) into the GPTMTnILR and the GPTMTnPR (if prescaler is used) registers for the count-down (count-up) operations.
6. If interrupts are required, set the appropriate bits in the GPTMIMR register to enable the selected interrupt source.
7. After these initializations and configurations done, set the TnEN bit in the GPTMCTL register to enable the timer and start counting.
8. If no interrupt is used, one can poll the GPTMRIS register to check the appropriate bits and wait for the time event to occur. If an interrupt is used, put appropriate codes inside the interrupt handler to process the interrupt. In both cases, the status flags are cleared by writing a 1 to the appropriate bit of the GPTMICR register.

In One-Shot mode, the timer stops counting after the timeout event. If the timer is configured as a periodic mode, the timer reloads the start value (time up value) and continues counting after the timeout event.

9.2.6.2 Initialization and Configuration for Input Edge-Count Mode

Perform the following operational steps to complete the initialization and configuration process for this mode ($n = A$ or B):

1. Disable the selected timer by clearing the TnEN bit in the GPTMCTL register.
2. Initialize the GPTMCFG register by writing 0x4 to setup all timers as 16-bit default timers.

3. Configure the TnMR and TnCMR fields in the GPTMTnMR register by writing:
   - TnMR = 0x3 for capture mode.
   - TnCMR = 0x0 for edge count mode.
4. Configure the event type (positive-going, negative-going or both) that the timer captures by writing the TnEVENT field of the GPTMCTL register.
5. Configure the following registers according to count direction:
   - In count-down mode, the GPTMTnMATCHR and GPTMTnPMR registers are configured so that the difference between the value in the GPTMTnILR and GPTMTnPR registers and the GPTMTnMATCHR and GPTMTnPMR registers equals the number of edge events that must be counted. Make sure that the value in the GPTMTnILR and GPTMTnPR registers is greater than the value in the GPTMTnMATCHR and GPTMTnPMR registers.
   - In count-up mode, the timer counts from 0x0 to the value in the GPTMTnMATCHR and GPTMTnPMR registers. Note that when executing a count-up, the value of the GPTMTnPR and GPTMTnILR must be greater than the value of GPTMTnPMR and GPTMTnMATCHR registers.
6. If interrupts are required, set the CnMIM bit in the GPTMIMR register.
7. After these initializations and configurations done, set the TnEN bit in the GPTMCTL register to enable the timer and begin waiting for edge events.
8. If no interrupt is used, one can poll the CnMRIS bit in the GPTMRIS register to wait for the edge event to be occurred. If interrupt is used, put appropriate codes inside the interrupt handler to process the interrupt. In both cases, the status flags are cleared by writing a 1 to the CnMCIR bit on the GPTMICR register.

When counting down in the Input Edge-Count Mode, the timer stops after the programmed number of edge events has been detected. To re-enable the timer, ensure that the TnEN bit is cleared and repeat steps 4 through 8.

9.2.6.3 Initialization and Configuration for Input Edge-Time Mode

Perform the following operational steps to complete the initialization and configuration process for this mode (n = A or B):

1. Disable the selected timer by clearing the TnEN bit in the GPTMCTL register.
2. Initialize the GPTMCFG register by writing 0x4 to setup all timers as 16-bit default timers.
3. Configure the TnMR and TnCMR fields in the GPTMTnMR register by writing:
   - TnMR = 0x3 for capture mode.
   - TnCMR = 0x1 for edge time mode.
   - Select a count direction by programming the TnCDIR bit (0, count-down; 1, count-up).
4. Configure the event type (positive-going, negative-going, or both) that the timer captures by writing the TnEVENT field of the GPTMCTL register.
5. If a prescaler is to be used, write the prescale value to the GPTMTnPR register.
6. Load the timer start value into the GPTMTnILR register.
7. If interrupts are required, set the CnEIM bit in the GPTMIMR register.
8. After these initializations and configurations are done, set the TnEN bit in the GPTMCTL register to enable the timer and begin waiting for edge events.
9. If no interrupt is used, one can poll the CnERIS bit in the GPTMRIS register to wait for the edge event to occur. If interrupt is used, put appropriate codes inside the interrupt handler to

process the interrupt. In both cases, the status flags are cleared by writing a 1 to the CnECIR bit on the GPTMICR register. The time at which the event happened can be obtained by reading the GPTMTnR register.

In the Input Edge Timing mode, the timer continues running after an edge event has been detected, but the timer interval can be changed at any time by writing the GPTMTnILR register and clearing the TnILD bit in the GPTMTnMR register. The change takes effect at the next cycle after the write taking placing.

9.2.6.4 *Initialization and Configuration for Real-Time Clock (RTC) Mode*

To use the RTC mode, the timer must have a 32.768 kHz input signal on an even CCP input. To enable the RTC feature, follow these steps (n = A or B):

1. Disable the selected timer by clearing the TnEN bit in the GPTMCTL register.
2. If the timer has been operating in a different mode prior to this, clear any residual set bits in the GPTMTnMR register before reconfiguring.
3. Initialize the GPTMCFG register by writing 0x1 to select the 32-bit RTC mode.
4. Write the match value to the GPTMTnMATCHR register.
5. Set/clear the RTCEN and TnSTALL bit in the GPTMCTL register as needed.
6. If interrupts are required, set the RTCIM bit in the GPTMIMR register.
7. After these initializations and configurations are done, set the TnEN bit in the GPTMCTL register to enable the timer and begin counting.

When the timer count equals the value in the GPTMTnMATCHR register, the GPTM sets the RTCRIS bit in the GPTMRIS register and continues counting until the timer is disabled or a hardware reset. The interrupt is cleared by writing 1 to the RTCCINT bit in the GPTMICR register. Note that if the GPTMTnILR register is loaded with a new value, the timer begins counting at this new value and continues until it reaches 0xFFFF.FFFF, at which point it rolls over.

9.2.6.5 *Initialization and Configuration for PWM Mode*

Perform the following operational steps to complete the initialization and configuration process for this mode (n = A or B):

1. Disable the selected timer by clearing the TnEN bit in the GPTMCTL register.
2. Initialize the GPTMCFG register by writing 0x4 to se tup all timers as 16-bit default timers.
3. Configure the TnMR, TnAMS, and TnCMR fields in the GPTMTnMR register by writing:
   - TnMR = 0x2 for periodic timer mode.
   - TnCMR = 0x0 for edge count mode.
   - TnAMS = 0x1 for PWM mode
4. Configure the output state of the PWM signal, either inverted or not, in the TnPWML field of the GPTMCTL register.
5. If a prescaler is to be used, write the prescale value to the GPTMTnPR register.
6. If PWM interrupts are used, configure the interrupt condition in the TnEVENT field in the GPTMCTL register and enable the interrupts by setting the TnPWMIE bit in the GPTMTnMR register. Note that edge detect interrupt behavior is reversed when the PWM output is inverted.

7. Load the timer start value into the GPTMTnILR register.

8. Load the GPTMTnMATCHR register with the match value.

9. Set the TnEN bit in the GPTMCTL register to enable the timer and begin generation of the output PWM signal.

In the PWM Time mode, the timer continues running after the PWM signal has been generated. The PWM period can be adjusted at any time by writing the GPTMTnILR register, and the change takes effect at the next cycle after the write.

Next let's build an example GPTM project to illustrate how to use a GPTM Timer to perform a specific control function.

9.2.7 Build an Example General Purpose Timer Project

In this example project, we use GPTM block 0 Timer A (Timer0A) as a 16-bit count-down counter to periodically generate a timeout interrupt to turn on four LEDs, PB3~PB0, via GPIO Port B. The input clock to the timer is the 16 MHz system clock, and the period to be counted in the Timer0A counter is 65.536 ms.

To perform this periodic interrupt for each 65.536 ms, one needs to:

1. Enable and clock the Timer0A for GPTM Block 0.

2. Enable and clock the GPIO Port B.

3. Disable the Timer0A module before any configuration can be performed.

4. Configure the Timer0A to work as a 16-bit count-down periodic counter.

5. Load 65535 (65536 – 1) into the GPTMTAILR register as the start value since we want to get the maximum period of time, which is 65.536 ms, for each period.

6. Load 15 (16 – 1) into the GPTMTAPR register as a prescale value. After this 16 MHz system clock is divided by this prescaler (16), the working clock for this counter is 1 MHz with a 1-μs period.

7. Clear any previous timeout interrupt for Timer0A by writing 1 to an appropriate bit in the GPTMICR register.

8. Enable Timer0A timeout interrupt by writing 1 to an appropriate bit in the GPTMIMR register.

9. Use CMSIS NVIC→IP[] structure and an appropriate value to set the interrupt priority level as 3 for the Timer0A.

10. Use CMSIS NVIC→ISER[] structure and an appropriate value to enable the timeout interrupt for the Timer0A.

11. Enable the Timer0A module after these configuration and the Timer0A begins to count.

12. Use __enable_irq() intrinsic function to globally enable all interrupts.

13. Use an infinitive while() loop to wait for any interrupt coming.

In addition to the main program, one also needs to build the Timer0A interrupt handler:

1. Clear the timeout interrupt for Timer0A by writing 1 to an appropriate bit in the GPTMICR register to enable it to be generated in the future.

2. Turn on the related LED via GPIO Port B.

```
1   //****************************************************************************************************
2   // DRATimerInt.c - Main Application File for Using Timer0A Interrupt to Turn LEDs on
3   //****************************************************************************************************
4   #include <stdint.h>
5   #include <stdbool.h>
6   #include "TM4C123GH6PM.h"

7   uint8_t count = 1;

8   int main(void)
9   {
10      SYSCTL->RCGCTIMER |= 0x01;                      // enable clock to Timer0A
11      SYSCTL->RCGCGPIO |= 0x02;                       // enable clock to GPIOB

12      GPIOB->DEN |= 0x0F;                             // set PB3 ~ PB0 as digital pins
13      GPIOB->DIR |= 0x0F;                             // set PB3 ~ PB0 as output pins

14      TIMER0->CTL &= ~0x01;                           // disable Timer0A during setup
15      TIMER0->CFG = 4;                                // configure as 16-bit timer mode
16      TIMER0->TAMR = 0x02;                            // count-down & periodic mode
17      TIMER0->TAILR = 65535;                          // max period = 65.536 ms, each count is 1 us
18      TIMER0->TAPR = 15;                              // prescaler = 16 (f = 16MHz/16 = 1MHz, T = 1us)
19      TIMER0->ICR = 0x01;                             // clear Timer0A timeout flag
20      TIMER0->IMR |= 0x01;                            // enable Timer0A time out interrupt
21      NVIC->IP[19] = 0x6;                             // bits 31:29 is priority level (011) = priority 3
22      NVIC->ISER[0] = 0x00080000;                     // bit 19 is for Timer0A interrupt
23      TIMER0->CTL |= 0x01;                            // enable Timer0A after setup
24      __enable_irq();

25      while(1) {}
26  }

27  void TIMER0A_Handler(void)
28  {
29      TIMER0->ICR = 0x01;                             // clear Timer0A timeout interrupt
30      GPIOB->DATA = count;
31      count++;
32      if (count > 8)
33          count = 1;
34  }
```

Figure 9.10.   The codes for the example project DRATimerInt.

3. Update the count number to make it point to the next LED.

4. If the count number is greater than 8, reset it to 1.

Figure 9.10 shows the detailed codes for these steps.

For steps 21 and 22, refer to Sections 5.2.3 (Tables 5.5, 5.10), and 5.4.3.4 (Table 5.18) to get more details about these instructions.

Next let's take at closer look for most popular implementations of using the Timer modules.

9.2.8 Popular Implementations on GPTM Modules

Timer system is a complex system with many different components and functions. In this section we only discuss some very popular and important implementations. These include:

- Using timer capture functions to detect the number of the input edges.
- Using timer detecting functions to measure the period for periodic signals.

- Using timer control functions to generate PWM signals to control motors.

First let's start from the timer capture function implementations.

9.2.8.1 Input Edge-Count Implementations

In Section 9.2.3.5, we have provided a detailed discussion about this mode. In this section we try to use two timers, a pseudo 32-bit timer made of `Timer0A` and `Timer0B` and a 16-bit timer, `Timer1A`, to use this input edge count function to measure the number of input edges for an input signal. The input source can be the position switch SW5 installed in the EduBASE ARM® Trainer, which is connected to the PD0 (refer to Figure 4.39).

This implementation includes the following components and methods (Figure 9.11):

- The hardware connection is to connect PD0 to PB4 with a jumping wire at J10 connector in the EduBASE Trainer since the T1CCP0 pin (for `Timer1A` CCP) uses PB4 pin as the input for the edge signal to be detected, and the switch SW5 is connected to the PD0 pin. After this connection, SW5 is connected with PB4 as an input edge detection signal.

- Use `Timer0A` and `Timer0B` to make a 32-bit one-shot count-down timer to generate a fixed time period, such as 10 seconds, via the timeout interrupt.

- Use `Timer1A` to capture and count the number of rising edges for the input signal within the fixed time period generated by the `Timer0A` and `Timer0B` in the above step.

- The `Timer1A` works in the 16-bit capture mode and generates a captured rising edge interrupt when the SW5 is pressed and a rising edge is detected.

- When a rising edge is detected, a `Timer1A` edge-capture interrupt is generated. Inside the interrupt handler, the detected edge is incremented by 1. Also, the PF2 pin connected to the blue LED is toggled to indicate that an edge has been detected.

- When the total time period, such as 10 seconds, is up, a `Timer0A` timeout interrupt occurs. In this interrupt handler, calculate the total number of detected edges, and reset a global flag to `false` to release the infinitive loop in the main program to collect the total number of edges have been detected.

Figure 9.12 shows the detailed codes for this project named `DRAEdgeInt`.

As the project runs, try to press SW5 in any times you want. Each time when you press SW5, the blue LED in PF2 is toggled to indicate that an edge has been detected and counted. When the green LED is on, it means that the time is up and 10 seconds is over. To check the total edges detected, you must set up a break point in line 42 for infinitive

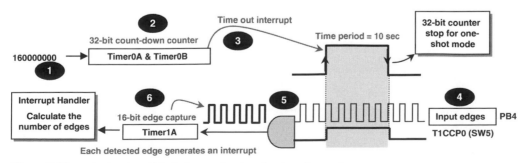

Figure 9.11.   The functional block diagram for the edge detection project.

```c
//**********************************************************************************************************
// DRAEdgeInt.c - Main Application File for Edge Detection - SW5
//**********************************************************************************************************
#include <stdint.h>
#include <stdbool.h>
#include "TM4C123GH6PM.h"

uint8_t  edgeCount = 0;
bool  intFlag = true;

int main(void)
{
   uint8_t count[1];

   SYSCTL->RCGCTIMER |= 0x03;              // enable clock to Timer0 & Timer1
   SYSCTL->RCGCGPIO |= 0x22;               // enable clock to GPIOB & GPIOF

   GPIOF->DEN |= 0x0F;                     // set PF3 – PF0 as digital pins
   GPIOF->DIR |= 0x0F;                     // set PF3 – PF0 as output pins
   GPIOB->DATA = 0;                        // clean all LEDs in Port B
   GPIOB->DEN |= 0x1F;                     // set PB4 – PB0 as digital pins
   GPIOB->DIR |= 0x0F;                     // set PB3 – PB0 as output pins, PB4 as input pin
   GPIOB->AFSEL |= 0x10;                   // enable PB4 as alternate function
   GPIOB->PCTL |= 0x00070000;              // set PB4 as alternate function to Timer1A

   TIMER0->CTL &= ~0x0101;                 // disable Timer0A & Timer0B during setup
   TIMER0->CFG = 0;                        // configure as 32-bit timer mode
   TIMER0->TAMR = 0x01;                    // count-down & one-shot mode
   TIMER0->TAILR = 1600000000;             // max period = 10s, 16 MHz/160000000 = 0.1 Hz
   TIMER0->ICR = 0x01;                     // clear Timer0A timeout flag
   TIMER0->IMR |= 0x01;                    // enable Timer0A time out interrupt
   NVIC->IP[19] = 0x6;                     // bits 31:29 is priority level (011) = priority 3
   NVIC->ISER[0] = 0x00080000;             // bit 19 is for Timer0A interrupt
   TIMER0->CTL |= 0x0101;                  // enable Timer0A & Timer0B after setup

   TIMER1->CTL &= ~0x01;                   // disable Timer1A during setup
   TIMER1->CFG = 4;                        // configure as 16-bit timer mode
   TIMER1->TAMR = 0x07;                    // capture mode
   TIMER1->CTL &= ~(0x000C);               // TAEVENT is rising edge trigger
   TIMER1->ICR = 0x04;                     // clear Timer1A capture mode event interrupt
   TIMER1->IMR |= 0x04;                    // enable Timer1A capture mode event interrupt
   NVIC->IP[21] = 0x4;                     // bits 15:13 is priority level (010) = priority 2
   NVIC->ISER[0] = 0x00200000;             // bit 21 is for Timer1A interrupt
   TIMER1->CTL |= 0x01;                    // enable Timer1A after setup

   __enable_irq();
   while(intFlag) {}                       // wait for all edges to be detected
   count[0] = edgeCount;                   // collect the total edges detected
   while(1) {};                            // this while() is used to check the total edges in count[0]
}

void TIMER1A_Handler(void)                 // Timer1A interrupt handler
{
   TIMER1->ICR = 0x04;                     // clear Timer1A capture interrupt
   edgeCount++;
   GPIOF->DATA ^= 0x4;                     // toggle PF2 blue LED for each SW5 pressing
}

void TIMER0A_Handler(void)                 // Timer0A & Timer0B interrupt handler
{
   TIMER0->ICR = 0x01;                     // clear Timer0A timeout interrupt
   GPIOF->DATA = 0x8;                      // send terminal signal to PF3 green LED
   intFlag = false;                        // release the infinitive while() loop in main program
}
```

Figure 9.12.   The detailed codes for the project DRAEdgeInt.

while(1) loop. Then as the green LED is on, you can expand the variable count[0] from the Call Stack + Locals window.

Because of the hardware vibrations and bouncing, it may generate some wrong pressing times and actions when SW5 is pressed, and the edge numbers may not be the same as the times the SW5 is pressed. This problem can be easily solved if a standard digital signal coming from a logic circuit or a function generator is used.

All codes in this project are straightforward and easy to be understood after those line-by-line explanations.

9.2.8.2 Input Edge-Time Implementations

As we discussed in Section 9.2.3.6, when a timer is configured to work in this mode, it can perform both counting and event detecting functions at the same time.

At start, the TAEN bit in the GPTMCTL register is set to 1 and the timer is enabled for event capture and starts its counting. When the selected input event is detected, the current timer counting value is captured in the GPTMTAR and GPTMTAPS register and is available to be read by the microcontroller.

In this section we try to use Timer2A to work as a 16-bit timer to measure the period of a periodic input signal. The input source can be a function generator.

The working principle of using this Timer2A to measure the period is as follows:

1. The Timer2A is configured as event capture or input edge-time mode with the interrupt mechanism, and it begins to perform the counting-down action as it is enabled.
2. When the first rising edge of a periodic signal is detected, the current count value can be obtained from the GPTMTAR register and stored to a variable.
3. When the second rising edge of a periodic signal is detected, similarly the current count value can also be obtained from the GPTMTAR register. The difference between these two rising edges can be considered as the period of the signal to be detected. This difference can be performed and obtained in the interrupt handler.

Before we can continue to develop the codes for an example project, first let's have a closer look at some properties of the period of a signal to be measured. Two popular parameters for measuring a period are the *resolution* and *range* of the period to be measured.

Generally, the resolution is determined by the clock frequency used by the timer. For example, if the working clock used by a timer is 16 MHz, the period for this clock is 62.5 ns. This is the minimized measurable period unit, and this is can be considered to be the resolution for the period that can be measured by using this clock.

The range of the period is determined by the size or length of the register to be used by the timer. For example, for a 16-bit counter, the maximized range of a period that can be measured is $65536 \times 62.5\,ns = 4.096\,ms$. When an 8-bit prescaler is used, the length of the counter can be expanded to 24-bit. In that case, the maximized measurable period is $16777216 \times 62.5\,ns = 1.0486\,s$. However, for a 32-bit register or counter, the maximized period range can be expanded to $4294967296 \times 62.5\,ns = 268.435\,s$.

There are no significant differences in measuring long or short periods for any periodic signal, therefore in this section we use a 16-bit timer to illustrate this period measurement. If you want to use an optional 8-bit prescaler to get a larger size counter (24-bit) and therefore a longer measured period, you can initialize the `Timer2A TAPR` register by assigning `0xFF` to that register just under the loading the start value to the `Timer2A TAILR` register.

This implementation includes the following components and methods:

- The hardware connection is to connect PB0 to a function generator via J10 connector in the EduBASE Trainer since the T2CCP0 pin (for `Timer2A` CCP) uses PB0 pin as the input for the edge signal to be detected.
- Use `Timer2A` to capture rising edges for a periodic input signal coming from a function generator or an oscilloscope since most modern oscilloscopes have a standard built-in testing signal. Usually this testing signal is a 1 kHz (1-ms period) square waveform.
- The `Timer2A` works in the 16-bit capture mode and generates a captured rising edge interrupt when a rising edge is detected.
- When a rising edge is detected, a `Timer2A` edge-capture interrupt is generated. Inside the interrupt handler, the period can be calculated by two different count values: One is the current count value and the other is the previous count value stored in a user-defined variable. Also, the `PF2` pin connected to the blue LED is toggled to indicate that an edge has been detected.
- When the period is obtained, a global Boolean flag can be reset to `false` to release the infinitive `while()` loop in the main program to enable user to check the period measurement result.

In order to use exactly 16 MHz system clock, we used a header file `DRAPeriodInt.h` to define some system clock definition parameters, which is shown in Figure 9.13. These parameters are `ORed` together to make sure that the system clock used for all Timers is 16 MHz.

Figure 9.14 shows the detailed codes for this project named `DRAPeriodInt`.

One point to be noted is that the codes in lines 14 and 29 are reserved. The code in line 14 can be used to replace the code in line 13 to make the line shorter, and the code in line 29 is used to configure the `Timer2A` to work as a 24-bit counter in the future.

As the project runs, a function generator or an oscilloscope can be connected to the T2CCP0 (PB0) pin as the input for the edge signal to be detected. As soon as the green LED is on, 32 periods have been detected and collected in the user-defined variable `Period[]`. To check this value, a break point can be set in line 38 with the `Call Stack + Locals` window.

For this example, we used an oscilloscope that outputs a standard 1 kHz square waveform as the input signal and connect to PB0. The measured result stored in the `Period[]` is `0x3E7F`, which is equivalent to a decimal value of 15999 $(15999 \times 62.5 \, \text{ns}) = 0.999 \, \text{ms} \approx 1 \, \text{ms}$.

```
1   //********************************************************************************************
2   // DRAPeriodInt.h - Header File for DRAPeriodInt.c.
3   //********************************************************************************************
4   #define SYSCTL_RCC_XTAL_16MHZ        0x00000540        // 16 MHz
5   #define SYSCTL_RCC_PWRDN             0x00002000        // PLL Power Down
6   #define SYSCTL_RCC_BYPASS            0x00000800        // PLL Bypass
7   #define SYSCTL_SYSDIV_1              0x07800000        // Processor clock is osc/pll /1
```

Figure 9.13. The header file for the project DRAPeriodInt.

```
1   //********************************************************************************************************
2   // DRAPeriodInt.c - Main Application File for Period Measurement
3   //********************************************************************************************************
4   #include <stdint.h>
5   #include <stdbool.h>
6   #include "TM4C123GH6PM.h"
7   #include "DRAPeriodInt.h"

8   uint32_t period, edgeCount, count = 0;
9   bool intFlag = true;

10  int main(void)
11  {
12    uint32_t RCC, Period[1];

13    RCC = (SYSCTL_RCC_XTAL_16MHZ|SYSCTL_RCC_PWRDN|SYSCTL_RCC_BYPASS|SYSCTL_SYSDIV_1);
14    // RCC = 0x00802D91;
15    SYSCTL->RCC = RCC;
16    SYSCTL->RCGCTIMER |= 0x04;                      // enable clock to Timer2
17    SYSCTL->RCGCGPIO |= 0x22;                       // enable clock to GPIOB & GPIOF

18    GPIOF->DEN |= 0x0F;                             // set PF3 – PF0 as digital pins
19    GPIOF->DIR |= 0x0F;                             // set PF3 – PF0 as output pins
20    GPIOB->DEN |= 0x0F;                             // set PB3 – PB0 as digital pins
21    GPIOB->DIR |= 0xE;
22    GPIOB->AFSEL |= 0x01;                           // enable PB0 as alternate function
23    GPIOB->PCTL |= 0x00000007;                      // set PB0 as alternate function to Timer1A

24    TIMER2->CTL &= ~0x01;                           // disable Timer2A during setup
25    TIMER2->CFG = 4;                                // configure as 16-bit timer mode
26    TIMER2->TAMR = 0x07;                            // capture mode
27    TIMER2->CTL &= ~(0x000C);                       // TAEVENT is rising edge trigger
28    TIMER2->TAILR = 65535;                          // load 65535 into GPTMTAILR as start value
29    //TIMER2->TAPR = 0xFF;                          // activate prescale, creating 24-bit
30    TIMER2->ICR = 0x04;                             // clear Timer2A capture mode event interrupt
31    TIMER2->IMR |= 0x04;                            // enable Timer2A capture mode event interrupt
32    NVIC->IP[23] = 0x4;                             // bits 31:29 is priority level (010) = priority 2
33    NVIC->ISER[0] = 0x00800000;                     // bit 23 is for Timer2A interrupt
34    TIMER2->CTL |= 0x01;                            // enable Timer2A after setup

35    __enable_irq();
36    while(intFlag) {}                               // wait for the period to be collected
37    Period[0] = period;                             // collect the period value
38    while(1) {};                                    // used for checking the period value
39  }
40  void TIMER2A_Handler(void)
41  {
42    TIMER2->ICR = 0x04;                             // clear Timer2A capture mode interrupt
43    period = (edgeCount - TIMER2->TAR);             // 16 bits, 62.5-ns resolution
44    edgeCount = TIMER2->TAR;                        // setup for next value
45    GPIOF->DATA ^= 0x4;                             // toggle PF2 LED for each detected edge
46    count++;
47    if (count > 0x20)                               // collect 32 periods
48    {
49      intFlag = false;
50      GPIOF->DATA = 0x8;                            // send terminal signal to PF3
51    }
52  }
```

Figure 9.14. The detailed codes for the project DRAPeriodInt.

9.2.8.3 PWM Implementations

As we discussed in Section 9.2.3.7, when the timer works in the PWM mode, the timer can be configured as a 16, 24, 32, or 48 bit count-down counter. The counter outputs High when it starts from its start value loaded into the GPTMTnILR and GPTMTnPR registers and

Low when the current counter value matches the value in the GPTMTnMATCHR and GPTMTnPMR registers. Thus, the start value can be considered to be the period of the PWM signal and the value stored in the GPTMTnMATCHR and GPTMTnPMR registers can be considered as the start point from where the High pulse stops and Low output starts. In other words, the GPTMTnMATCHR and GPTMTnPMR registers store the Low pulse value or the length of the Low pulse for this PWM signal.

If a 16-bit timer is used, the start value is only loaded into the GPTMTnILR register and the match value is loaded into the GPTMTnMATCHR register.

The duty cycle of the PWM signal generated can be calculated by (16-bit counter):

$$\text{DUTY-CYCLE} = \text{High/Period} = (\text{GPTMTnILR-GPTMTnMATCHR})/\text{GPTMTnILR}.$$
$$= 1\text{-}(\text{GPTMTnMATCHR}/\text{GPTMTnILR}).$$

Actual period and duty cycle values depend on the PWM clock source used in the timer. For example, for an 8 MHz PWM clock source, the clock period is 125 ns. To use this clock source to generate a PWM signal with 5 ms as period and 1% duty cycle on Timer3A, the following parameters and registers should be used:

The length of the High pulse = 5 ms × 1% = 0.05 ms, the length of the Low pulse = 4.95 ms.
Timer3A_TAILR = Period = 5 ms/125 ns = 5000000/125 = 40000.
Timer3A_TAMATCHR = Length of Low Pulse = 4.95 ms/125 ns = 4950000/125 = 39600.

When the count-down counter gets 0, it will reload the start value and continue for the next counting operation until the TAEN bit in the GPTMCTL is clear.

For the PWM initialization and configuration process, refer to Section 9.2.3.7. The timer is also able to generate interrupts based on three types of events, and the interrupt is enabled by setting the TnPWMIE bit in the GPTMTnMR register.

The resolution or the minimized period of the PWM signal that can be generated by the timer is determined by the clock source. Still using an 8 MHz clock, the normal minimized PWM signal is 125 ns with 0% duty cycle.

Figure 9.15 shows a functional block diagram for using Timer3A as a 16-bit count-down counter to generate a PWM output signal to control a DC/Servo motor. The T3CCP0 (PB2) pin in the Timer3A module is the PWM signal output pin to transfer PWM signal to the motor driver to control the running speed of the DC/Servo motor.

In the following implementation, we use a 32/64-bit Wide timer2A WTimer2A to make it a 32-bit count-down timer to generate a variable-duty PWM signal, which means that the duty cycle can be changed by software to control the running speed of a DC/Servo motor. No interrupt is used for this project since it is very simple.

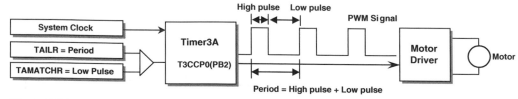

Figure 9.15. The functional block diagram of using Timer3A to generate PWM signals.

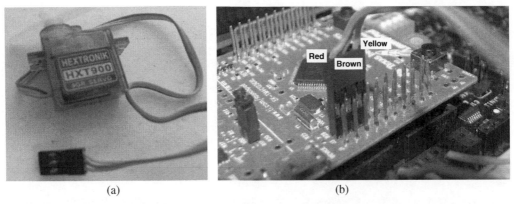

(a)   (b)

Figure 9.16. The HXT900 9GR RC Servo motor and its connection.

This implementation includes the following hardware components and methods:

1. A RC servo motor HXT900 9GR is used in this project as the target motor to be driven. One can buy this motor in any related site, such as HobbyKing.com, with less than $5.00. This is a low-voltage servo motor that can be driven by 3V DC power, as shown in Figure 9.16a. To connect this motor to the circuit, you need to change three pins arrangement to make them as the following order:

   VCC—Red color wire
   GND—Brown color wire
   Signal—Yellow color wire

2. The WT2CCP0 pin works as the PWM output pin for the Wide timer2A WTimer2A via the PD0 pin. The order of these three pins, VCC, GND, and PD0, on the J3 connector in the TM4C123GXL Evaluation Board is exactly same as the order of those three signal pins we just changed above. Therefore it is very easy to directly insert the motor connector to the first three pins, as shown in Figure 9.16b, on the J3 connector.

3. After the hardware connection is configured and completed, you need to take care of the software control and configuration part. For this project, we want to change the duty cycle from 1% to 100% with an 8-MHz clock input. Refer to the calculations we did above: For a 5-ms period, 40000 should be loaded into the WTimer2A_TAILR register as the start value, and 39600 should be loaded into the WTimer2A_TAMATCHR register as the Low pulse value for 1% duty cycle.

4. Refer to Section 9.2.3.7 to complete the PWM mode configuration and initialization to the WTimer2A module.

The complete codes for this implementation DRATimerPWM are shown in Figure 9.17.

All initialization and configuration processes are placed in a subroutine PWM_Init (). Since we use PF2 as an indicator for the modifications of the duty cycle, the GPIO Port F is configured as an output port. The PD0 pin is configured as an alternate function pin to work as a WT2CCP0 to output the PWM signal to the motor.

An infinitive while() is used to tune the duty cycle for this PWM signal. The TAMATCHR register in the WTIMER2A module is updated by subtracting a fixed number of 5 (high) periodically to reduce the Low pulse value and increment the High pulse

```
1   //*********************************************************************************************************
2   // DRATimerPWM.c - Main Application File for Using Timer to Generate PWM - PD0
3   //*********************************************************************************************************
4   #include <stdint.h>
5   #include <stdbool.h>
6   #include "TM4C123GH6PM.h"

7   #define SYSCTL_RCC_XTAL_8MHZ   0x00000380          // 8 MHz
8   #define SYSCTL_RCC_PWRDN       0x00002000          // PLL Power Down
9   #define SYSCTL_RCC_BYPASS      0x00000800          // PLL Bypass
10  #define SYSCTL_SYSDIV_1        0x07800000          // Processor clock is osc/pll /1

11  void PWM_Init(void);
12  void delay_ms(int time);

13  int main(void)
14  {
15      uint32_t  RCC, high = 1;

16      RCC = (SYSCTL_RCC_XTAL_8MHZ|SYSCTL_RCC_PWRDN|SYSCTL_RCC_BYPASS|SYSCTL_SYSDIV_1);
17      SYSCTL->RCC = RCC;
18      SYSCTL->RCGCWTIMER |= 0x04;                      // enable clock to 32-bit WDTimer2 module
19      SYSCTL->RCGCGPIO |= 0x28;                        // enable clock to GPIOD & GPIOF

20      PWM_Init();
21      while(1)
22      {
23          WTIMER2->TAMATCHR = 39600 - high;            // increment the duty cycle
24          high += 5;
25          delay_ms(1);
26          GPIOF->DATA ^= 0x4;                          // toggle blue LED (PF2)
27          if (high >= 39600)
28              high = 1;
29      }
30  }

31  void PWM_Init(void)
32  {
33      GPIOF->DEN |= 0x0F;                              // set PF3 ~ PF0 as digital pins
34      GPIOF->DIR |= 0x0F;                              // set PF3 ~ PF0 as output pins
35      GPIOD->DEN |= 0x01;                              // set PD0 as digital pins
36      GPIOD->AFSEL |= 0x1;                             // enable PD0 as alternate function
37      GPIOD->PCTL |= 0x00000007;                       // set PD0 as alternate function to WDTimer2A

38      WTIMER2->CTL &= ~0x01;                           // disable WDTimer2A during setup
39      WTIMER2->CFG = 4;                                // configure as 32-bit wide timer mode
40      WTIMER2->TAMR = 0xA;                             // PWM mode with periodic count
41      WTIMER2->TAILR = 40000;                          // load 40000 into GPTMTAILR as start value (period)
42      WTIMER2->TAMATCHR = 39600;                       // set the Low pulse value as 39600
43      WTIMER2->CTL |= 0x01;                            // enable WDTimer2A after setup
44  }

45  void delay_ms(int time)
46  {
47      int i, j;
48      for(i = 0 ; i < time; i++)
49          for(j = 0; j < 3200; j++) {}
50  }
```

Figure 9.17.   The complete codes for the project DRATimerPWM.

value since the value stored in the TAMATCHR register is the length of the Low pulse. The smaller this value, the shorter the length of the Low pulse, and therefore the longer the High pulse. As the `high` value becomes higher and higher, the length of the Low pulse becomes shorter and shorter. When this `high` value goes up to 39600, the duty cycle is 100%. Then it is reduced back to 1 (duty cycle is 1%) to continue for the following loops.

9.2.9 The API Functions Used for General-Purpose Timer Module

The TivaWare™ Peripheral Driver Library provides more than 35 API functions to support the project developments by using the GPTM modules. These API functions can be divided into three groups based on their functions:

- GPTM Module Configurations and Controls.
- GPTM Module Contents and Related Operations.
- GPTM Module Interrupts Handling.

9.2.9.1 The API Functions Used for GPTM Module Configurations and Controls

The following API functions are included in this group:

1. `TimerConfigure()` — Perform the high-level setup for the timer module.
2. `TimerEnable()` and `TimerDisable()` — Enable and disable the selected timer module.
3. `TimerControlLevel()` — Control the output level of the PWM.
4. `TimerControlTrigger()` — Control ADC trigger output.
5. `TimerControlEvent()` — Control and select the event type.
6. `TimerRTCEnable()` and `TimerRTCDisable()` — Enable and disable the RTC counting.

Table 9.9 shows these API functions and their parameters as well as available values for those parameters. Because of the similarity between the Enable and Disable functions, only the Enable function is shown in Table 9.9.

The `TimerConfigure()` API function is a complex one with quite a few macros used for control and configure parameters. This function can be used to configure a full-width (32-bit or 64-bit) timer for 16/32-bit and 32/64-bit timer module. It can also be used to configure a pair of half-width (16-bit or 32-bit) timers for 16/32-bit and 32/64-bit timer modules. For the full-width configurations, use TIMER_CFG_ macro prefix; and for the half-width timers, use TIMER_CFG_A_ or TIMER_CFG_B_ prefix, respectively.

The `TimerControlLevel()` API function is used to control the PWM output level, and the `TimerControlTrigger()` function is used to control the ADC trigger signal.

9.2.9.2 The API Functions Used for GPTM Module Contents and Related Operations

The following API functions are included in this group:

1. `TimerLoadSet()` and `TimerLoadGet()` — Set and get the timer load value.
2. `TimerLoadSet64()` and `TimerLoadGet64()` — Set and get the timer load value for 64-bit timer.
3. `TimerPrescaleSet()` and `TimerPrescaleGet()` — Set and get the timer prescale value.
4. `TimerMatchSet()` and `TimerMatchGet()` — Set and get the timer match value.

Table 9.9. The GPTM module configuration and control API functions.

API Function	Parameter	Description
void TimerConfigure(uint32_t ui32Base, uint32_t ui32Config)	ui32Base is the base address of the timer module. ui32Config is the configuration for the timer.	Configure the operating mode of the timer(s). The timer module is disabled before being configured. The timer can be configured to be a single full-width timer by using the TIMER_CFG_ values or a pair of half-width timers using the TIMER_CFG_A_ and TIMER_CFG_B_ values passed in the ui32Config parameter. The ui32Config can be one of the following values: TIMER_CFG_ONE_SHOT - Full-width one-shot timer. TIMER_CFG_ONE_SHOT_UP - Full-width one-shot timer that counts up instead of down (not available on all parts). TIMER_CFG_PERIODIC - Full-width periodic timer. TIMER_CFG_PERIODIC_UP - Full-width periodic timer that counts up instead of down (not available on all parts). TIMER_CFG_RTC - Full-width real time clock timer. TIMER_CFG_SPLIT_PAIR - Two half-width timers. When configured for a pair of half-width timers, each timer is separately configured. The first timer is configured by setting ui32Config to the result of a logical OR operation between one of the following values and ui32Config: TIMER_CFG_A_ONE_SHOT - Half-width one-shot timer. TIMER_CFG_A_ONE_SHOT_UP - Half-width one-shot timer that counts up instead of down (not available on all parts). TIMER_CFG_A_PERIODIC - Half-width periodic timer. TIMER_CFG_A_PERIODIC_UP - Half-width periodic timer that counts up instead of down (not available on all parts). TIMER_CFG_A_CAP_COUNT - Half-width edge count capture TIMER_CFG_A_CAP_COUNT_UP - Half-width edge count capture that counts up (not available on all parts). TIMER_CFG_A_CAP_TIME - Half-width edge time capture. TIMER_CFG_A_CAP_TIME_UP - Half-width edge time capture that counts up (not available on all parts). TIMER_CFG_A_PWM - Half-width PWM output.
void TimerEnable(uint32_t ui32Base, uint32_t ui32Timer)	ui32Base is the base address of the timer module. ui32Timer is the timer(s) to enable; must be one of TIMER_A, TIMER_B, or TIMER_BOTH.	Enable the selected timer module. The timer must be first configured before it can be enabled.
void TimerControlLevel(uint32_t ui32Base, uint32_t ui32Timer, bool bInvert)	ui32Base is the base address of the timer module. ui32Timer is the timer(s) to adjust; must be one of TIMER_A, TIMER_B, or TIMER_BOTH. bInvert is the output level.	Configure the PWM output level for the specified timer. If the bInvert parameter is true, then the timer's output is made active low; otherwise, it is made active high.
void TimerControlTrigger(uint32_t ui32Base, uint32_t ui32Timer, bool bEnable)	ui32Base is the base address of the timer module. ui32Timer is the timer to adjust; must be one of TIMER_A, TIMER_B, or TIMER_BOTH. bEnable is the ADC trigger state.	Control the ADC trigger output for the specified timer. If the bEnable is true, then the timer's ADC output trigger is enabled; otherwise it is disabled.
void TimerControlEvent(uint32_t ui32Base, uint32_t ui32Timer, uint32_t ui32Event)	ui32Base is the base address. ui32Timer is the timer(s) to be adjusted; must be one of TIMER_A, TIMER_B, or TIMER_BOTH. ui32Event is the type of event and must be one of TIMER_EVENT_POS_EDGE, TIMER_EVENT_NEG_EDGE, or TIMER_EVENT_BOTH_EDGES.	Configure the signal edge(s) that triggers the timer when in capture mode.
void TimerRTCEnable(uint32_t ui32Base)	ui32Base is the base address of the timer.	Cause the timer to start counting when in RTC mode. If not configured for RTC mode, this function does nothing.

5. `TimerMatchSet64()` and `TimerMatchGet64()` — Set and get the timer match value for 64-bit timers.
6. `TimerPrescaleMatchSet()` and `TimerPrescaleMatchGet()` — Set and get the timer prescale match value
7. `TimerValueGet()` and `TimerValueGet64()` — Get the current timer value.

Because of the similarity, only the set functions are discussed in this section.

Table 9.10 shows these API functions and their parameters as well as available values for those parameters.

Usually, for `TimerLoadSet()`, `TimerMatchSet()`, and `TimerValueGet()` API functions, these API functions can be used for both full-width (32-bit) and half-width

Table 9.10. The GPTM module contents and related operations API functions.

API Function	Parameter	Description
void `TimerLoadSet(` uint32_t ui32Base, uint32_t ui32Timer, uint32_t ui32Value)	ui32Base is the base address of the timer module. ui32Timer is the timer(s) to adjust; must be one of TIMER_A, TIMER_B, or TIMER_BOTH. Only TIMER_A should be used when the timer is configured for full-width operation. ui32Value is the load value.	Configure the timer load value; if the timer is running then the value is immediately loaded into the timer. This function can be used for both full- and half-width modes of 16/32-bit timers and for half-width modes of 32/64-bit timers. Use `TimerLoadSet64 ()` for full-width modes of 32/64-bit timers.
void `TimerLoadSet64(` uint32_t ui32Base, uint64_t ui64Value)	ui32Base is the base address of the timer module. ui64Value is the load value.	Configure the timer load value for a 64-bit timer; if the timer is running, then the value is immediately loaded into the timer.
void `TimerPrescaleSet(` uint32_t ui32Base, uint32_t ui32Timer, uint32_t ui32Value)	ui32Base is the base address of the timer module. ui32Timer is the timer(s) to adjust; must be one of TIMER_A, TIMER_B, or TIMER_BOTH. ui32Value is the prescale value which must be between 0 and 255 for 16/32-bit timers and between 0 and 65535 for 32/64-bit timers.	Configure the value of the input clock prescaler. The prescaler is only operational when in half-width mode and is used to extend the range of the half-width timer modes. The prescaler provides the least significant bits when counting down in periodic and one-shot modes; in all other modes, the prescaler provides the most significant bits.
void `TimerMatchSet(` uint32_t ui32Base, uint32_t ui32Timer, uint32_t ui32Value)	ui32Base is the base address of the timer module. ui32Timer is the timer(s) to adjust; must be one of TIMER_A, TIMER_B, or TIMER_BOTH. Only TIMER_A should be used when the timer is configured for full-width operation. ui32Value is the match value.	Configure the match value for a timer. This value is used in capture count mode to determine when to interrupt the processor and in PWM mode to determine the duty cycle of the output signal. This function can be used for both full- and half-width modes of 16/32-bit timers and for half-width modes of 32/64-bit timers. Use `TimerMatchSet64()` for full-width modes of 32/64-bit timers.
void `TimerMatchSet64(` uint32_t ui32Base, uint64_t ui64Value)	ui32Base is the base address of the timer module. ui64Value is the match value.	Configure the match value for a timer. This value is used in capture count mode to determine when to interrupt the processor and in PWM mode to determine the duty cycle of the output signal.
void `TimerPrescaleMatchSet(` uint32_t ui32Base, uint32_t ui32Timer, uint32_t ui32Value)	ui32Base is the base address of the timer module. ui32Timer is the timer(s) to adjust; must be one of TIMER_A, TIMER_B, or TIMER_BOTH. ui32Value is the prescale match value which must be between 0 and 255 for 16/32-bit timers and between 0 and 65535 for 32/64-bit timers.	Configure the value of the input clock prescaler match value. When in a half-width mode that uses the counter match and the prescaler, the prescale match effectively extends the range of the match. The prescaler provides the least significant bits when counting down in periodic and one-shot modes; in all other modes, the prescaler provides the most significant bits.
uint32_t `TimerValueGet(` uint32_t ui32Base, uint32_t ui32Timer)	ui32Base is the base address of the timer module. ui32Timer is the timer; must be one of TIMER_A or TIMER_B. Only TIMER_A should be used when the timer is configured for full-width timer.	Read the current value of the specified timer. This function can be used for both full- and half-width modes of 16/32-bit timers and for half-width modes of 32/64-bit timers. Use `TimerValueGet64()` for full-width modes of 32/64-bit timers.
uint64_t `TimerValueGet64(` uint32_t ui32Base)	ui32Base is the base address of the timer module.	This function reads the current value of the specified timer.

(16-bit) modes of 16/32-bit timers and for half-width (32-bit) modes of 32/64-bit timers. To handle full-width (64-bit) modes of 32/64-bit timers, use `TimerLoadSet64()`, `TimerMatch-Set64()` and `TimerValueGet64()` for full-width (64-bit) modes of 32/64-bit timers.

9.2.9.3 The API Functions Used for GPTM Module Interrupt Handling

The following API functions are included in this group:

1. `TimerIntRegister()` and `TimerIntUnregister()` — Register and unregister the timer interrupt handler.
2. `TimerIntEnable()` and `TimerIntDisable()` — Enable and disable the timer interrupt source.
3. `TimerIntStatus()` — Get the current timer interrupt status.
4. `TimerIntClear()` — Clear the responded interrupt source.

Because of the similarity, we only discuss the `TimerIntRegister()` and `TimerIntEnable()` API functions in this section.

Table 9.11 shows these API functions and their parameters as well as available values for those parameters.

When using these API functions to register the interrupt handler and enable interrupt sources for any timer, the operational sequence should be as follows:

1. Use `TimerIntRegister()` function to register a desired and related interrupt handler for the selected interrupt source.

Table 9.11. The GPTM module interrupt handling API functions.

API Function	Parameter	Description
void TimerIntRegister(uint32_t ui32Base, uint32_t ui32Timer, void (*pfnHandler)(void))	ui32Base is the base address of the timer module. ui32Timer is the timer(s); must be one of TIMER_A, TIMER_B, or TIMER_BOTH. pfnHandler is a pointer to the function called when the timer interrupt occurs.	Register the handler to be called when a timer interrupt occurs. In addition, this function enables the global interrupt in the interrupt controller; specific timer interrupts must be enabled via TimerIntEnable(). It is the interrupt handler's responsibility to clear the interrupt source via TimerIntClear().
void TimerIntEnable(uint32_t ui32Base, uint32_t ui32IntFlags)	ui32Base is the base address of the timer module. ui32IntFlags is the bit mask of the interrupt sources to be enabled.	Enable the indicated timer interrupt sources. The ui32IntFlags parameter must be the logical OR of any combination of the following: TIMER_TIMB_DMA - Timer B DMA complete. TIMER_TIMA_DMA - Timer A DMA complete. TIMER_CAPB_EVENT - Capture B event interrupt. TIMER_CAPB_MATCH - Capture B match interrupt. TIMER_TIMB_TIMEOUT - Timer B timeout interrupt. TIMER_RTC_MATCH - RTC interrupt mask. TIMER_CAPA_EVENT - Capture A event interrupt. TIMER_CAPA_MATCH - Capture A match interrupt. TIMER_TIMA_TIMEOUT - Timer A timeout interrupt.
uint32_t TimerIntStatus(uint32_t ui32Base, bool bMasked)	ui32Base is the base address of the timer module. bMasked is false if the raw interrupt status is required and true if the masked interrupt status is required.	Return the interrupt status for the timer module. Either the raw interrupt status or the status of interrupts that are allowed to reflect to the processor can be returned. The current interrupt status, enumerated as a bit field of values described in TimerIntEnable() is returned.
void TimerIntClear(uint32_t ui32Base, uint32_t ui32IntFlags)	ui32Base is the base address of the timer module. ui32IntFlags is a bit mask of the interrupt sources to be cleared.	The specified timer interrupt sources are cleared, so that they no longer assert. This function must be called in the interrupt handler to keep the interrupt from being triggered again immediately upon exit. The ui32IntFlags parameter has the same definition as the ui32IntFlags parameter to TimerIntEnable().

2. Use `TimerIntEnable()` to enable the selected interrupt source.

3. Use `TimerIntStatus()` to check the current interrupt status if it is required. Usually, this step is optional and not necessary.

4. After the interrupt is generated and processed, the `TimerIntClear()` must be called to clear the processed interrupt to enable this interrupt to be occurred in the future.

The `ui32IntFlags` parameter used in the `TimerIntEnable()` and `TimerIntClear()` API functions has the same definition, which can be ORed of a sequence of macros defined for each different interrupt source used in the timer modules.

9.2.9.4 *An Implementation of Using Timer API Functions to Measure PWM Pulses*

In this section we try to use some API functions discussed above to measure the width of a PWM pulse. The principle of pulse width measurement is to generate two interrupts for both rising and falling edge capture events. Each event captures a timer value, and the difference between two timer values is the width of the PWM pulse.

As we discussed in the previous sections, the resolution and the range of the PWM width are determined by the frequency of the clock source and the length of the counter used. For example, when a 24-bit timer with a 16 MHz clock source, the resolution is 62.5 ns and the range is about 1 second.

As we know, for the rising-edge detection, the input signal must be High for at least two system clock periods following the rising edge. Similarly, for the falling edge detection, the input signal must be Low for at least two system clock periods following the falling edge. Therefore, the maximum input frequency for edge detection is 1/4 of the system frequency. For a 16 MHz clock source, the maximized input frequency should be 4 MHz.

If we need to consider the time period spent for interrupt handler to record the current timer count for either the rising or the falling edge, the maximized input frequency should be further lower than 4 MHz. Give some reservations, the maximized input frequency should be about 2~3 MHz.

In this project, we use a 24-bit timer, `Timer3A` with T3CCP0 (PB2) pin to get the input PWM signal and to detect both rising and falling edges for this signal to get the pulse width. The clock source we used is 16 MHz.

Two files are included in this project, the header file, `SDPWMPulse.h`, and the main program file, `SDPWMPulse.c`.

The codes for the header file are shown in Figure 9.18.

Some project-used macros and variables are declared in this header file. All of these macros can be found from the related system header files. To save compiling time and space, we moved those macros into this header file. The interrupt handler, `TIMER3A_Handler()`, is declared in line 18; three global unsigned integer variables, `period`, `edgeCount`, and `count`, as well as one global Boolean variable `intFlag`, are also declared in this file.

The complete C source codes for this project are shown in Figure 9.19.

All of these codes are straightforward and easy to be understood. Some important coding lines are emphasized here:

- Because we want to use a 16 MHz clock source as our timer input clock, we must clearly indicate this with the codes and macros shown in lines 8 and 9.

```
 1  //****************************************************************************************************************
 2  // SDPWMPulse.h - Header File for PWM Pulse Measurement (Timer3A – T3CCP0)
 3  //****************************************************************************************************************
 4  #include <stdint.h>
 5  #include <stdbool.h>
 6  #include "inc/hw_memmap.h"
 7  #include "inc/hw_types.h"
 8  #include "driverlib/interrupt.h"
 9  #include "driverlib/sysctl.h"
10  #include "driverlib/timer.h"
11  #include "driverlib/gpio.h"

12  #define SYSCTL_RCC_XTAL_16MHZ  0x00000540        // 16 MHz
13  #define SYSCTL_RCC_PWRDN       0x00002000        // PLL Power Down
14  #define SYSCTL_RCC_BYPASS      0x00000800        // PLL Bypass
15  #define SYSCTL_SYSDIV_1        0x07800000        // Processor clock is osc/pll /1
16  #define GPIO_PB2_T3CCP0        0x00010807        // PB2 pin for T3CCP0 pin
17  #define INT_TIMER3A            51                // Timer 3A

18  void TIMER3A_Handler(void);

19  uint32_t  period, edgeCount,  count = 0;
20  bool  intFlag = true;
```

Figure 9.18.   The codes for the header file SDPWMPulse.h.

- We did not clearly disable the `Timer3A` before we configure it since all timers are disabled after a system reset. Thus we did not include that step in this program.

- The API function `TimerIntRegister()` is a very important function and step to set up and connect the `Timer3A` interrupt sources with its interrupt handler TIMER3A_Handler(). This function should be called before the `TimerIntEnable()` and `TimerEnable()` functions to make it effect. The third argument of the `TimerIntRegister ()`, which is the name of the interrupt handler, must be identical to the handler used in this program. Also, this handler must be declared first in the header file or at the beginning of this file before it can be used.

- Inside this interrupt handler, the API function `TimerIntClear()` must be called first to clear the current responded interrupt to enable this interrupt source to be generated in the future.

- An infinitive `while()` loop is necessary to enable us to check the measured pulse from the variable `Period[]` via the `Call Stack + Locals` window. A break point should be set on this line 26 to enable us to do this checking.

An oscilloscope with a standard 1-kHz 5-V square waveform output signal is used for this project and the measured pulse result is `Period[0] = 0x001F43`, which is `0.500` ms.

9.3   WATCHDOG TIMERS

Like a general timer module, the core of the watchdog timer module is a 32-bit count-down counter. The purpose of using the watchdog timer is to prevent the processor from hangs by generating some kind of interrupts or reset functions to warn and restart the MCU to resume its operation from some possible errors caused by software or external peripheral mis-operations.

```
1   //********************************************************************************************************************
2   // SDPWMPulse.c - Main Application File - PWM Pulse Measurement (Timer3A – T3CCP0)
3   //********************************************************************************************************************
4   #include "SDPWMPulse.h"
5   int main(void)
6   {
7      uint32_t RCC, Period[1];
8      RCC = (SYSCTL_RCC_XTAL_16MHZ|SYSCTL_RCC_PWRDN|SYSCTL_RCC_BYPASS|SYSCTL_SYSDIV_1);
9      SysCtlClockSet(RCC);
10     SysCtlPeripheralEnable(SYSCTL_PERIPH_TIMER3);              // enable clock to Timer3
11     SysCtlPeripheralEnable(SYSCTL_PERIPH_GPIOB);              // enable clock to GPIOB & GPIOF
12     SysCtlPeripheralEnable(SYSCTL_PERIPH_GPIOF);
13     GPIOPinTypeGPIOOutput(GPIO_  PORTF_BASE, GPIO_PIN_2|GPIO_PIN_3);    // PF2 and PF3 as output pins
14     GPIOPinTypeTimer(GPIO_PORTB_BASE, GPIO_PIN_2);           // set PB2 as alternate function to Timer3A
15     GPIOPinConfigure(GPIO_PB2_T3CCP0);                       // set PB2 as T3CCP0 pin
16     TimerConfigure(TIMER3_BASE, (TIMER_CFG_SPLIT_PAIR|TIMER_CFG_A_CAP_TIME));
17     TimerControlEvent(TIMER3_BASE, TIMER_A, TIMER_EVENT_BOTH_EDGES);
18     TimerLoadSet(TIMER3_BASE, TIMER_A, 65535);
19     TimerPrescaleSet(TIMER3_BASE, TIMER_A, 255);
20     TimerIntRegister(TIMER3_BASE, TIMER_A, TIMER3A_Handler);
21     IntEnable(INT_TIMER3A);
22     TimerIntEnable(TIMER3_BASE, TIMER_CAPA_EVENT);
23     TimerEnable(TIMER3_BASE, TIMER_A);
24     while(intFlag) {}                                        // wait for the period to be collected
25     Period[0] = period & 0xFFFFFF;                           // collect pulse value (24-bit)
26     while(1) {};
27  }
28  void TIMER3A_Handler(void)
29  {
30     TimerIntClear(TIMER3_BASE, TIMER_CAPA_EVENT);            // clear Timer3A capture mode interrupt
31     GPIOPinWrite(GPIO_PORTF_BASE, GPIO_PIN_2, 0x4);          // turn on PF2 LED for each detected edge
32     count++;
33     if (count == 1)
34        edgeCount = TimerValueGet(TIMER3_BASE, TIMER_A);      // 1st edge detected, save the 1st count
35     else                                                     // 2nd edge detected, get period
36     {
37        period = edgeCount - TimerValueGet(TIMER3_BASE, TIMER_A);    // 24 bits, 62.5 ns resolution (1s)
38        TimerDisable(TIMER3_BASE, TIMER_A);                  // disable Timer3A counter
39        GPIOPinWrite(GPIO_  PORTF_BASE, GPIO_PIN_3, 0x8);    // set PF3 LED to indicate the program is done
40        intFlag = false;                                     // release the while() loop in the main() program
41     }
42  }
```

Figure 9.19. The complete codes for the project SDPWMPulse.

When a watchdog timer begins its monitoring work, its counting-down function and interrupt mechanism are enabled. The watchdog module monitors and checks the processor's working status during its count-down period. If no any CPU action had been taken for the entire count-down period and the counter keep 0, a watchdog timeout interrupt (either a normal or a NMI) can be generated to warn the MCU system to resume its normal operations. However, if the second time-out comes before the first timeout interrupt can be cleared, a reset function is executed to restart the MCU's operation from any possible errors.

Two watchdog timer modules are provided by the TC4C123GH6PM MCU system: Watchdog Timer 0 (WDT0) and Watchdog Timer 1 (WDT1). The two modules are exactly identical except the clock source used to drive these two modules. The WDT0 is driven by the system clock but the WDT1 is driven by the PIOSC.

Each watchdog timer module consists of a 32-bit down counter, a programmable load register, interrupt generation logic, and a locking register. Once the watchdog timer has been configured, the lock register can be written to prevent the timer configuration from being inadvertently altered.

9.3.1 The Watchdog Timer Architecture and Functional Block Diagram

Figure 9.20 shows the functional block diagram of the watchdog time modules. Each module has the same architecture and functional block diagram.

As we mentioned, the core of the watchdog timer is a 32-bit count-down counter that can be loaded with a start value with the WDTLOAD register. During the working process, the counter performs a count-down function starting from this start value until it reaches 0. When the timeout happened, depending on the setup on the watchdog timer interrupt mechanism that is determined by the WDTMIS register, a standard interrupt or an NMI can be generated by setting the WDTRIS register. After this interrupt is processed and handled, the interrupt can be cleared by writing 1 to the WDTICR register. All configurations and operations are under the control of the WDTCTL register, and the current value on the watchdog counter can be read from the WDTVALUE register.

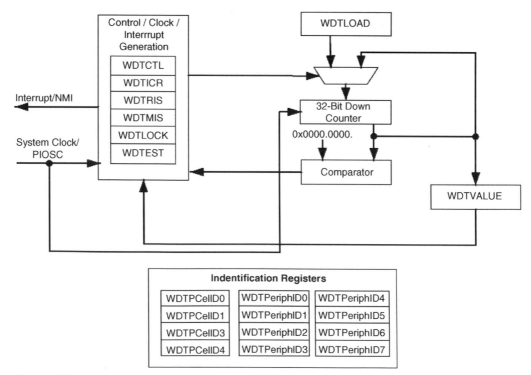

Figure 9.20. The functional block diagram of the watchdog modules. (Reprinted with the permission of the Texas Instruments Incorporated.)

9.3.2 The Watchdog Timer Operational Sequence and Timing Access

Each watchdog module performs the monitoring operation in the following sequence:

1. The INTEN bit in the WDTCTL register is set to enable the watchdog, enable interrupts, and lock the control register.

2. The WDTLOAD register is loaded with the desired start value or the time period during which the processor is to be monitored.

3. Because the WDT1 module uses an independent clocking source, its registers must be written with a timing gap between accesses. Software must guarantee that this delay is inserted between back-to-back writes to WDT1 registers or between a write followed by a read to the registers. The WRC bit in the WDTCTL register for WDT1 indicates whether the required timing gap has elapsed or not. This bit is cleared to 0 on a write operation and set to 1 once the write completes, indicating to software that another write or read may be started. Software should check WDTCTL for WRC = 1 prior to accessing another register. Note that WDT0 does not have this restriction as it runs on the system clock.

4. The Watchdog Timer module can be fully locked by writing any value to the WDTLOCK register. To unlock the Watchdog Timer, write a value of 0x1ACC.E551 to that register.

5. If a timeout occurred at the first time and the INTTYPE bit in the WDTCTL register is cleared to 0, a standard watchdog timeout interrupt is occurred. However, if the INTTYPE bit in the WDTCTL register is set to 1, an NMI is occurred. The NMI interrupt is still treated the same as if it were a standard interrupt, but it must be cleared inside the NMI handler.

6. After the first timeout, the watchdog is reloaded with the start value and continues for the next counting period. During the countdown process, a new start value can be loaded into the WDTLOAD register and the counter starts its counting based on that new value immediately.

7. If after the first timeout occurred and the timeout interrupt, either standard or NMI, has not been cleared, the second timeout comes again. If the RESEN bit in the WDTCTL register is set to 1, a reset function is generated and the whole MCU system is reset to restart its operations.

Unlike other peripheral devices, there are no any GPIO Ports and pins used for the watchdog timer modules as alternate functions.

9.3.3 The Watchdog Timer Registers

Because of the simplicity, the registers used for each watchdog timer module can be divided into two groups: Control and Content register group and Interrupt handling group. First let's take a look at the control and content group registers.

9.3.3.1 The Watchdog Module Control and Content Registers

Five registers are included in this group:

- Watchdog Timer Control Register (WDTCTL)
- Watchdog Timer Load Register (WDTLOAD)
- Watchdog Timer Value Register (WDTVALUE)

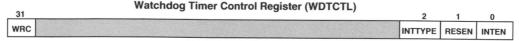

Reserved Bits 31 ~ 3.

Figure 9.21. The bit configurations for WDTCTL register.

- Watchdog Timer Lock Register (WDTLOCK)
- Watchdog Timer Test Register (WDTTEST)

Let's have a closer look at these registers one by one.

9.3.3.1.1 Watchdog Timer Control Register (WDTCTL) The bit configurations for this register are shown in Figure 9.21. The bit field and function of this register are shown in Table 9.12.

One point to be noted is that the WRC bit is a read-only bit and any writing to this bit has no effect to the value on this bit. This bit is specially designed for the WDT1 module. Before accessing to this module, the value on this bit must be checked to make sure that the bit value is 1, which means that the previous writing/reading operation is completed and the next accessing can be performed now.

9.3.3.1.2 Watchdog Timer Load Register (WDTLOAD) This is a 32-bit register used to store the start value for the watchdog timer counter. When this register is written, the value is immediately loaded and the counter restarts counting down from this value. If this register is loaded with 0x0000.0000, a related interrupt, either standard or NMI, is immediately generated.

9.3.3.1.3 Watchdog Timer Value Register (WDTVALUE) This is a 32-bit register used to store the current count value for the watchdog timer counter. This is a read-only register without any writing ability.

9.3.3.1.4 Watchdog Timer Lock Register (WDTLOCK) This is a 32-bit register used to lock all watchdog registers except the WDTTEST register.

Table 9.12. Bit value and its function for WDTCTL register.

Bit	Name	Reset	Function
31	WRC (Read Only)	0x1	Write Complete: 0: A write access to the WDT1 has NOT been completed. 1: A write access to the WDT1 is been completed, and WDT1 register can be read or write.
30:3	Reserved	0x000	Reserved.
2	INTTYPE (R/W)	0x0	Watchdog Interrupt Type: 0: Standard interrupt; 1: Non Maskable Interrupt (NMI)
1	RESEN (R/W)	0x0	Watchdog Reset Enable: 0: Reset is disabled; 1: Reset is enabled.
0	INTEN (R/W)	0x0	Watchdog Interrupt Enable: 0: Interrupt event disabled. If this bit is set, it can only be cleared by a hardware reset or a software reset initiated by setting the appropriate bit in the Watchdog Timer Software Reset (SRWD) register 1: Interrupt event enabled. Once enabled, all writes are ignored. Setting this bit also enables the Watchdog Timer.

When writing 0x1ACC.E551 to this register, all watchdog registers, including the control, contents and interrupt handling registers, are unlocked or enabled to be accessed for writing and modification functions. Writing any other values to this register is to lock all those registers and prevent any of them from being accessed to do any modifications.

Reading the WDTLOCK register returns the lock status rather than the 32-bit value written into this register. Therefore, when all registers are locked and all write accesses are disabled, reading the WDTLOCK register returns 0x0000.0001. Otherwise, if all registers are unlocked, the returned value is 0x0000.0000. This is a Read/Write register.

9.3.3.1.5 Watchdog Timer Test Register (WDTTEST)   This is a 32-bit register but only the STALL bit (bit 8) is used to control whether the watchdog timer can continue to work (STALL = 0) or not (STALL = 1) when the MCU is stopped with a debugger.

9.3.3.2 *The Watchdog Module Interrupt Handling Registers*

Four registers are included in this group:

- Watchdog Raw Interrupt Status Register (WDTRIS)
- Watchdog Masked Interrupt Status Register (WDTMIS)
- Watchdog Interrupt Clear Register (WDTICR)
- Watchdog Timer Software Reset Register (SRWD)

Let's have a closer look at these registers one by one.

9.3.3.2.1 Watchdog Raw Interrupt Status Register (WDTRIS)   This is a 32-bit register but only the lowest bit, WDTRIS bit (bit 0), is used to provide a flag to indicate whether a watchdog raw interrupt has been generated (WDTRIS = 1) or not (WDTRIS = 0). Watchdog interrupt events can be monitored via this register if the controller interrupt is masked. In other words, if the watchdog interrupt is disabled, any watchdog interrupt event can be reflected on this bit. The bits 31~1 are reserved on this register.

This bit can be cleared when writing any value to the Watchdog Interrupt Clear Register (WDTICR).

9.3.3.2.2 Watchdog Masked Interrupt Status Register (WDTMIS)   This is a 32-bit register but only the lowest bit, WDTMIS (bit 0), is used to indicate whether a watchdog interrupt has been responded (WDTMIS = 1) or not (WDTMIS = 0). In fact, the value of the bit WDTMIS on this register is the logical AND of the raw interrupt bit (WDTRIS) in the WDTRIS register and the watchdog interrupt enable bit (INTEN) in the WDTCTL register.

If this bit is set to 1, it also means that a watchdog timeout interrupt is occurred.

9.3.3.2.3 Watchdog Interrupt Clear Register (WDTICR)   This is a 32-bit register used to clear any watchdog interrupt that has been generated and responded. Writing any value to this register is to clear the watchdog interrupt and reload the 32-bit counter from the WDTLOAD register to enable the counter to continue for the next counting operation. After any watchdog interrupt, including the standard and NMI, is occurred and handled, those interrupts must be cleared by writing any value to this register.

Locking the watchdog registers by using the WDTLOCK register does not affect the WDTICR register and allows interrupts to always be serviced. Thus, a write at any time of the WDTICR register clears the WDTMIS and WDTRIS registers and reloads the 32-bit counter from the WDTLOAD register.

9.3.3.2.4 Watchdog Timer Software Reset Register (SRWD)

This is a 32-bit register but only the lowest two bits, R1 and R0 (bits 1 and 0), are used to indicate the reset status for two watchdog modules, WDT1 and WDT0. If the R1 bit is 0, it means that the WDT1 is not reset, and a 1 means that the WDT1 is reset. Same situation is true to R0 and WDT0 module.

The SRWD register provides software the capability to reset the related watchdog modules. This register provides the same capability as the Software Reset Control n (SRCRn) registers specifically for the watchdog modules and has the same bit polarity as the corresponding SRCRn bits.

Any peripheral like watchdog can be reset by software using a simple two-step process:

1. Software first sets a bit (R1 or R0) or bits (R1 and R0) in the SRWD register. While the SRWD bit is 1, the peripheral is held in reset.
2. Software completes the reset process by clearing the SRWD bit.

Now let's take care of the watchdog initialization and configuration process.

9.3.4 The Watchdog Timer Module Initializations and Configurations

To use any watchdog module, it must be first initialized and configured. The Watchdog Timer is configured using the following sequence:

1. The watchdog clock must be enabled by setting the Rn bit in the Watchdog Timer Run Mode Clock Gating Control (RCGCWD) register.
2. Load the WDTLOAD register with the desired time-out load value.
3. If WDT1 is used, wait for the WRC bit in the WDTCTL register to be set.
4. If the watchdog is configured to trigger system resets, set the RESEN bit in the WDTCTL register.
5. If WDT1 is used, wait for the WRC bit in the WDTCTL register to be set.
6. Set the INTEN bit in the WDTCTL register to enable the watchdog, enable interrupts, and lock the control registers.

If software requires that all of the watchdog registers are locked, the Watchdog Timer module can be fully locked by writing any value to the WDTLOCK register. To unlock the Watchdog Timer, write a value of 0x1ACC.E551 to the WDTLOCK register.

If any interrupt, including the standard and NMI, has occurred, the interrupt is directed to the corresponding interrupt handler to be processed. Inside the ISR, the processed interrupt must be cleared by writing any value to the WDTICR to enable the following interrupts to occur again in the future.

When the WDTICR is used to clear any processed interrupt, the watchdog counter is reloaded to the start value from the WDTLOAD register to begin the next cycle.

9.3.5 Build an Example Watchdog Timer Project

In this implementation, we try to build a watchdog timer project named DRAWatchdog to use WDT1 module to periodically generate standard timeout interrupts to send a 400 Hz audio signal to the speaker and the three-color LED to indicate that the interrupts have been occurred.

With a 16 MHz PIOSC as the clock source for the WDT1 module, if we want to the standard interrupt to be generated for each 0.25 s, the start value to be loaded into the WDTLOAD register should be 250 ms/62.5 ns = 4000000.

The complete and detailed codes for this implementation are shown in Figure 9.22.

The codes for this project are straightforward and easy to be understood except for the following points to be noted:

- Unlike the WDT0 module, you must first enable and clock another peripheral before you can enable and clock the WDT1 module. Otherwise the WDT1 module cannot be enabled even if you put the code like line 29 to clearly enable this module. Without the coding line 28, in which the UART0 module is enabled, you cannot enable the WDT1 module and a HardFault error would appear when you run this project since the WDT1 has not been enabled when you want to access it to write commands to it.

- Unlike the WDT0 module, you must use a while() loop to wait for the current writing to be complete before you can perform the next writing to any register in the WDT1 module. This step is necessary since there is a timing gap existing between the adjacent writings to the WDT1 module. This while() loop is used to check and wait for the WRC bit (bit 31) in the WDTCTL register to be set to 1, which means that the current writing operation is complete and the next accessing can be performed to any register in this module. This step is necessary and must be used for any register in the WDT1 module since it used a PIOSC as the clock source. The operation of the WATCHDOG1→CTL & 0x80000000 returns a 0 if the WRC bit is 0, and it returns a 1 if the WRC is set to 1. This is the reason why we used this while() loop in lines 36 and 38 with two times.

- The IRQ number for WDT1 and WDT0 interrupts is 18 (Table 5.10 in Chapter 5), thus the NVIC→IP[18] is used to set up the interrupt priority level to 3 at bits 23:21 segment (Table 5.12 in Chapter 5).

- Another point to be noted is that both WDT0 and WDT1 use the same IRQ number and same interrupt handler WDT0_Handler(). Any standard interrupt generated for either module is directed and transferred into this handler to be processed.

- Finally when we use WATCHDOG1→ICR to clear the processed interrupt, both the bit WDTRIS in the WDTRIS register and the bit WDTMIS in the WDTMIS register are cleared, too. Also the start value is reloaded into the counter to begin the next counting period.

9.3.6 The API Functions Used for Watchdog Timer Modules

Eighteen API functions are provided by the TivaWare™ Peripheral Driver Library to assist users to build and develop watchdog timer-related projects to monitor and detect the MCU running status as well as other implementations. Among these functions, basically they can be divided into two groups based on their functions: the watchdog timer configuration and control functions and interrupt handling functions.

```
1  //*********************************************************************************************************
2  // DRAWatchdog.c - Main Application File for Watchdog Timer 1 (WDT1) Module
3  //*********************************************************************************************************
4  #include <stdint.h>
5  #include <stdbool.h>
6  #include "TM4C123GH6PM.h"

7  #define SYSCTL_RCC_XTAL_16MHZ   0x00000540      // 16 MHz
8  #define SYSCTL_RCC_PWRDN        0x00002000      // PLL Power Down
9  #define SYSCTL_RCC_BYPASS       0x00000800      // PLL Bypass
10 #define SYSCTL_SYSDIV_1         0x07800000      // Processor clock is osc/pll /1

11 void Delay(int  time)
12 {
13    int  i;
14    for(i = 0 ; i < time; i++) {}
15 }

16 void SetSound(int period)
17 {
18    GPIOC->DATA = 0x10;
19    Delay(period);                              // set speaker 400-Hz signal
20    GPIOC->DATA = 0x0;
21    Delay(period);
22 }

23 int main(void)
24 {
25    uint32_t RCC;

26    RCC = (SYSCTL_RCC_XTAL_16MHZ|SYSCTL_RCC_PWRDN|SYSCTL_RCC_BYPASS|SYSCTL_SYSDIV_1);
27    SYSCTL->RCC = RCC;
28    SYSCTL->RCGCUART |= 0x1;                     // useless, but you must do this to enable WDT1
29    SYSCTL->RCGCWD |= 0x02;                      // enable clock to WDT1 module
30    SYSCTL->RCGCGPIO |= 0x24;                    // enable clock to GPIOC & GPIOF

31    GPIOF->DEN |= 0x0F;                          // set PF3 – PF0 as digital pins
32    GPIOF->DIR |= 0x0F;                          // set PF3 – PF0 as output pins
33    GPIOC->DEN |= 0x10;                          // set PC4 as digital pin
34    GPIOC->DIR |= 0x10;                          // enable PC4 as output pin

35    WATCHDOG1->LOAD = 4000000;                   // load 4000000 to set count period = 0.25 second
36    while (!(WATCHDOG1->CTL & 0x80000000));      // wait for WRC bit to be set
37    WATCHDOG1->CTL = 0x1;                        // enable WDT1 interrupt and enable the timer
38    while (!(WATCHDOG1->CTL & 0x80000000));      // wait for timer to be enabled
39    WATCHDOG1->LOCK = 0x4;                       // lock all registers

40    NVIC->IP[18] = 0x6;                          // bits 23:21 is priority level (011) = priority 3
41    NVIC->ISER[0] = 0x00040000;                  // bit 18 is for WDT0 & WDT1 interrupt
42    __enable_irq();

43    while(1);                                    // wait for WDT1 interrupt to be occurred…
44 }

45 void WDT0_Handler(void)                         // WDT0 & WDT1 uses the same handler
46 {
47    WATCHDOG1->ICR = 0x4;                        // clear WDT1 interrupt & reload the start value
48    GPIOF->DATA ^= 0x4;                          // toggle PF2 LED for each interrupt
49    SetSound(25000);                            // set speaker 400-Hz signal
50 }
```

Figure 9.22. The complete codes for the project DRAWatchdog.

9.3.6.1 The API Functions Used to Configure and Control the Watchdog Timers

Twelve API functions are included in this group:

- WatchdogEnable()—Enable the watchdog timers and interrupts.
- WatchdogRunning()—Determine whether the watchdog timer is enabled.

- WatchdogLock()—Lock all watchdog related registers except the WDTTEST.
- WatchdogUnlock()—Unlock all watchdog timers.
- WatchdogLockState()—Check the lock status for all watchdog registers.
- WatchdogReloadSet()—Set the watchdog reload value.
- WatchdogReloadGet()—Get the watchdog reload value.
- WatchdogValueGet()—Get the current watchdog counter value.
- WatchdogResetEnable()—Enable the watchdog reset function.
- WatchdogResetDisable()—Disable the watchdog reset function.
- WatchdogStallEnable()—Enable stalling of the watchdog timer during debug events.
- WatchdogStallDisable()—Disable stalling of the watchdog timer during debug events.

Because of the similarity between the enable and disable functions, we only discuss the enable functions in this section. Table 9.13 shows these API functions and their parameters as well as available values for those parameters.

Table 9.13. The API functions used to configure and control the watchdog timers.

API Function	Parameter	Description
void WatchdogEnable(uint32_t ui32Base)	ui32Base is the base address of the watchdog timer module.	Enable the watchdog timer counter and interrupt. This function has no effect if the watchdog timer has been locked.
bool WatchdogRunning(uint32_t ui32Base)	ui32Base is the base address of the watchdog timer module.	Check to see if the watchdog timer is enabled. Returns true if the watchdog timer is enabled and false if it is not.
void WatchdogLock(uint32_t ui32Base)	ui32Base is the base address of the watchdog timer module.	Lock out write access to the watchdog timer configuration registers.
void WatchdogUnlock(uint32_t ui32Base)	ui32Base is the base address of the watchdog timer module.	Enable write access to the watchdog timer configuration registers.
bool WatchdogLockState(uint32_t ui32Base)	ui32Base is the base address of the watchdog timer module.	Return the lock state of the watchdog timer registers. Returns true if the watchdog timer registers are locked, and false if they are not locked.
void WatchdogReloadSet(uint32_t ui32Base, uint32_t ui32LoadVal)	ui32Base is the base address of the watchdog timer module. ui32LoadVal is the load value for the watchdog timer.	Configure the value to load into the watchdog timer when the count reaches 0 for the first time; if the watchdog timer is running when this function is called, then the value is immediately loaded into the watchdog timer counter. If the ui32LoadVal parameter is 0, then an interrupt is immediately generated.
uint32_t WatchdogReloadGet(uint32_t ui32Base)	ui32Base is the base address of the watchdog timer module.	Get the value that is loaded into the watchdog timer when the count reaches zero for the first time.
uint32_t WatchdogValueGet(uint32_t ui32Base)	ui32Base is the base address of the watchdog timer module.	Read the current value of the watchdog timer.
void WatchdogResetEnable(uint32_t ui32Base)	ui32Base is the base address of the watchdog timer module.	Enable the capability of the watchdog timer to issue a reset to the processor after a second timeout condition.
void WatchdogStallEnable(uint32_t ui32Base)	ui32Base is the base address of the watchdog timer module.	Allow the watchdog timer to stop counting when the processor is stopped by the debugger.
void WatchdogStallDisable(uint32_t ui32Base)	ui32Base is the base address of the watchdog timer module.	Allow the watchdog timer to continue counting when the processor is stopped by the debugger.

The point to be noted is that most of these API functions are effective when the registers are unlocked. However, if the selected register is locked, these API functions have no effect on those registers. These functions include: `WatchdogEnable()`, `WatchdogReloadSet()`, `WatchdogResetEnable()`, and `WatchdogReset-Disable()`.

Another point to be noted is that only `WatchdogEnable()` function is provided without its pair function `WatchdogDisable()` available. The reason for that is because once the watchdog timer is enabled by setting the bit `INTEN` in the `WDTCTL` register, this bit cannot be cleared unless a hardware reset action is taken or a software reset is initiated by setting the appropriate bit in the `Watchdog Timer Software Reset` (SRWD) register.

9.3.6.2 The API Functions Used to Handle Interrupts of the Watchdog Timers

Five API functions are included in this group:

- WatchdogIntRegister()—Register the interrupt handler for the watchdog interrupt source.
- WatchdogIntUnregister()—Unregister the interrupt handler for watchdog interrupt.
- WatchdogIntEnable()—Enable the watchdog interrupt.
- WatchdogIntStatus()—Get the current watchdog interrupt status.
- WatchdogIntClear()—Clear the current watchdog interrupt.

Table 9.14 shows these API functions and their parameters as well as available values for those parameters.

Table 9.14. The API functions used to handle interrupts of the watchdog timers.

API Function	Parameter	Description
void WatchdogIntRegister(uint32_t ui32Base, void (*pfnHandler)(void))	ui32Base is the base address of the watchdog timer module. pfnHandler is a pointer to the function to be called when the watchdog timer interrupt occurs.	This function does the actual registering of the interrupt handler. This function also enables the global interrupt in the interrupt controller; the watchdog timer interrupt must be enabled via `WatchdogEnable()`. It is the interrupt handler's responsibility to clear the interrupt source via `WatchdogIntClear()`.
void WatchdogIntUnregister(uint32_t ui32Base)	ui32Base is the base address of the watchdog timer module.	This function does the actual unregistering of the interrupt handler. It clears the handler to be called when a watchdog timer interrupt occurs. This function also masks off the interrupt in the interrupt controller so that the interrupt handler no longer is called.
void WatchdogIntEnable(uint32_t ui32Base)	ui32Base is the base address of the watchdog timer module.	This function enables the watchdog timer interrupt.
uint32_t WatchdogIntStatus(uint32_t ui32Base, bool bMasked)	ui32Base is the base address of the watchdog timer module. bMasked is `false` if the raw interrupt status is required and `true` if the masked interrupt status is required	Return the interrupt status for the watchdog timer module. Either the raw interrupt status or the status of interrupt that is allowed to reflect to the processor can be returned. Return 1: interrupt is active. 0: not.
void WatchdogIntClear(uint32_t ui32Base)	ui32Base is the base address of the watchdog timer module.	The watchdog timer interrupt source is cleared, so that it no longer asserts.

9.3.6.3 *An Implementation Example of Using API Functions to Control the Watchdog Timer*

In this section we try to use this example project to show readers how to use the watchdog timer API functions to reset the processor after two timeouts for WDT1 module. Because this project is simple, we leave this as a lab project, Lab9_4.

9.4 UNIVERSAL SERIAL BUS (USB) CONTROLLER

Like the RS-232 and RS-422, the Universal Serial Bus (USB) is a protocol or interface designed for serial data communications. In fact, the USB is developed based on RS-422 protocol and is a host-controlled and token-based high-speed network device with three possible running speeds:

- Low speed—1.5 MBits per second
- Full speed—12 MBits per second
- High speed—480 MBits per second

USB is an industry standard developed in the mid-1990s that defines the cable, connector, and communication protocols used in a bus for connection, communication, and power supply between computers and electronic devices.

By using the USB protocol, many different devices such as printer, zip driver, hard disk, scanner, modem, and USB flash memory can be connected together to make a network, as shown in Figure 9.23a. Each device, including the host, can be considered as an endpoint connected together with some four-wire or five-wire cables (Figure 9.23b) to form a network.

When connected in this way, the device or endpoint at one side is called device A or an endpoint at the A side, and the device or endpoint at another side is called device B or an endpoint at the B side. Different connectors are used at different sides, the connector in the A side is called A Type and the connector is the B side is B Type. The hardware connectors can be divided into three types shown in Figure 9.23b:

- Standard Type—A Type; Type A; B Type; Type B (4-connection-pin)
- Mini Type—A Type; Mini-A; B Type; Mini-B (5-connection-pin)
- Micro Type—A Type; Micro-A; B Type; Micro-B (5-connection-pin)

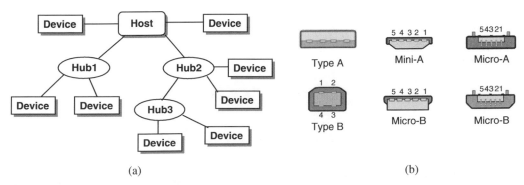

(a)   (b)

Figure 9.23.   A USB network and USB Connectors.

Usually, the A Type connector is connected to a host and the B Type connector is to a device. But the host controls the entire serial communication process, including the power up, transmission parameters, and starting and ending of the communications.

Three types of connectors provide different lifetime capacities or sizes. The standard and mini connectors were designed for less than daily connections, with a design lifetime of 1500 insertion/removal cycles. Microconnectors are designed for the lifetime of the connector and have been improved to 10,000 cycles.

The USB On-The-Go (OTG) is a specification first used in late 2001, which allows USB devices to act as a host and allows other USB devices like a USB flash drive, digital camera, mouse, or keyboard to be attached to them as a device.

Since the USB is a relatively complicated device, we cannot use a single chapter to give a complete introduction about this. One can go to related sites to get more details about this device. In this chapter, we only provide a quick introduction and mainly concentrate on the working principle and protocol as well as hardware interfaces about the USB.

9.4.1 The Hardware Configuration of the USB Devices

As we mentioned, the USB connectors and cables can be categorized to Standard Type, MiniType, and MacroType. The electrical specifications and signals for these USB connector types can be illustrated in Tables 9.15 and 9.16.

In the Standard Type shown in Table 9.15, four shielded wires are used and they are: +5 V power, D−, D+, and Ground. Unlike RS232, in which two wires such as Tx and Rx are used to transmit and receive serial signals separately, the D+ and D− are twisted together to transmit and receive a differential signal. On the transmission side, a differential '1' is transmitted when the D+ is pulling up and over 2.8 V and D- is pulling down and less than 0.3 V, and the difference between the D+ and the D− is >2.5 V. Similarly, a '0' is transmitted when the D− is pulling up and over 2.8 V and the D+ is pulling down and less than 0.3 V. On the receive side, a differential '1' is received if the D+ is 0.2 V greater than D−, and a '0' is received if the D+ is 0.2 V less than the D−.

Table 9.15. USB signals (Standard).

Pin Number	Color	Function
1	Red	VBUS (5V)
2	White	D−
3	Green	D+
4	Black	GND

Table 9.16. USB signals (Mini & Macro).

Pin Number	Color	Function
1	Red	VBUS (5V)
2	White	D−
3	Green	D+
4	Brown	ID
5	Black	GND

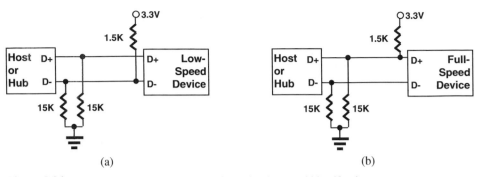

Figure 9.24.   The USB device hardware configuration for speed identification.

The difference between the Standard Type and the Mini or Micro Types shown in Table 9.16 is that a fourth pin, ID, is added into the Mini- and Micro- Type connectors. The main purpose of using this ID is to identify the type of packet sending from the host to the devices.

Both differential and single-end signals can be transferred with the USB devices. The bus states can be indicated by single-ended signals on D+, D−, or both. For a single-ended 0 (SE0), it can be used to identify a device reset action when it held for more than 10 ms. The SE0 can also be generated by holding both D+ and D− to Low.

As we mentioned, the USB devices can operate in one of three speeds, Low speed, Fullspeed, and High speed. A USB device shows its speed by configuring the related resistors in the hardware connection circuits. As shown in Figure 9.24, by pulling either the D+ or D− line to 3.3 V, different speed modes can be identified.

For example, a pull-up resistor attached to the D− means that a Low-speed mode is employing in the USB device and host (Figure 9.24a). However, a pull-up resistor attached to the D+ indicates that a full-speed running mode is used for the USB device and the host (Figure 9.24b).

9.4.2 The USB Components and Operational Sequence

The USB 2.0 specification was released in April 2000 and was ratified by the USB Implementers Forum (USB-IF) at the end of 2001. The USB 3.0 specification was published on 12 November 2008. Its main goals were to increase the data transfer rate to up to 5 Gbit/s, decrease power consumption, increase power output, and be backwards-compatible with USB 2.0.

A physical USB device may consist of several logical sub-devices that are referred to as *device functions*. A single device may provide several functions. This kind of device is called a *composite device*. An alternative to this is *compound device,* in which the host assigns each logical device a distinctive address and all logical devices connect to a built-in hub that connects to the physical USB cable.

The USB device communication is based on *pipes* or logical channels. A pipe is a connection from the host controller to a logical entity, found on a device and named an *endpoint*. Because pipes correspond 1-to-1 to endpoints, the terms are sometimes used interchangeably. A USB device could have up to 32 endpoints (16 IN, 16 OUT). An endpoint is defined and numbered by the device during the initialization period or called enumeration period, and so is relatively permanent, whereas a pipe may be opened and closed.

There are two types of pipe: stream and message. A message pipe is bi-directional and is used for *control* transfers. Message pipes are typically used for short, simple commands to the device, and a status response is used, for example, by the bus control pipe number 0. A stream pipe is a one-directional pipe connected to a one-directional endpoint that transfers data using an *isochronous, interrupt,* or *bulk* transfer:

- *Isochronous transfers*: at some guaranteed data rate but with possible data loss.
- *Interrupt transfers*: devices that need guaranteed quick responses such as pointing devices and keyboards.
- *Bulk transfers*: large sporadic transfers using all remaining available bandwidth, but with no guarantees on bandwidth or latency.

The USB itself is made of several layers of protocols, and it uses different packets to build the foundation to perform its low-level communications. Each USB is composed of three packets:

- Token Packet (data header)
- Data Packet (information)
- Status Packet or Handshake Packet (acknowledge)

The token packet is the first packet to be sent by the host to initiate the communications. Following the token packet, the data packet carrying the information is transferred. The status packet containing the acknowledgment and handshaking signals is transferred in the last.

The general operational sequence of using a USB to perform serial communications is:

1. When a USB device is first connected to a USB host, the USB device enumeration process is started. The enumeration starts by sending a reset signal from the host to the USB device. The data rate of the USB device is determined during the reset signaling.

2. After reset, the USB device's information is read by the host and the device is assigned a unique 7-bit address. If the device is supported by the host, the device drivers are loaded and the device is set to a configured state. If the USB host is restarted, the enumeration process is repeated for all connected devices.

3. All three packets are then sent by the host to the device one by one, however, all packets must start with a `sync` field, which is 8 bits long for the Low- and Full-speed mode or 32-bit long for High-speed mode. The purpose of this sync field is to synchronize the clock of the receiver with the clock in the transmitter side.

4. If the transaction is successful, the status packet or handshaking packet returns an ACK signal to inform the host with the CRC result. This process will continue until an EOP (End Of Packet) is received by the device.

An endpoint of a pipe is addressable with a tuple that includes the *device_address* and the *endpoint_number* as specified in a TOKEN packet that the host sends when it wants to start a data transfer session. If the direction of the data transfer is from the host to the endpoint, an OUT packet indicated in the TOKEN packet having the desired device address and endpoint number is sent by the host. If the direction of the data transfer is from a device to a host, the host receives an IN packet instead. If the destination endpoint is a uni-directional endpoint whose designated direction does not match the TOKEN packet,

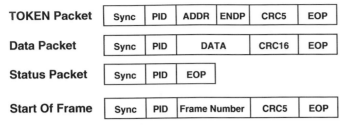

Figure 9.25. the USB packet types.

the TOKEN packet is ignored. Otherwise, it is accepted and the data transaction can start. A bi-directional endpoint accepts both IN and OUT packets.

Endpoints are grouped into interfaces and each interface is associated with a single device function. An exception to this is endpoint zero, which is used for device configuration and is not associated with any interface. A single device function composed of independently controlled interfaces is called a *composite device*. A composite device only has a single device address because the host only assigns a device address to a function.

The host controller directs traffic flow to devices, so no USB device can transfer any data on the bus without an explicit request from the host controller. In USB 2.0, the host controller polls the bus for traffic, usually in a round-robin fashion. The throughput of each USB port is determined by the slower speed of either the USB port or the USB device connected to the port.

9.4.3 The Serial Interface Protocol of the USB Communications

To better understand the USB serial communications, let's have a closer look at the interface protocol used in the USB systems.

Figure 9.25 shows three popular packets and their bit fields and functions. Table 9.17 shows the related PID values and their functions for these packets.

Table 9.17. The USB PID numbers and their functions.

Packet	PID Value	Packet Identifier
TOKEN	0001	OUT Token: Address + Endpoint
	1001	IN Token: Address + Endpoint
	0101	SOF Token: Start-Of-Frame marker and frame number
	1101	SETUP Token: Address + Endpoint
DATA	0011	DATA0
	1011	DATA1
	0111	DATA2 (High-Speed)
	1111	MDATA (High-Speed)
STATUS or HANDSHAKE	0010	ACK Handshake: Receiver accepts error-free data packet
	1010	NAK Handshake: Device cannot accept data or cannot send data
	1110	STALL Handshake: Endpoint is halted or pipe request is not supported
	0110	NYET: No Response Yet from receiver
Special	1100	PREamble: Enable downstream bus traffic to low-speed devices
	1100	ERR: Split transaction error handshake
	1000	Split: High-speed split transaction token
	0100	Ping: High-speed flow control probe for a bulk/control endpoint

As we mentioned, all packets must be started with a sync field to synchronize the serial communications between the host and the endpoint or the device. The PID field contains the type of the packet to be sent, as shown in Table 9.17.

The address field (ADDR) is used to identify the target device. In the USB system, a 7-bit address is used to enable up to 127 devices or endpoints to be employed. All addresses are available except address 0, and any device that is not assigned an valid address must report to the host by responding with a pocket of address 0. This address is an unique identifier for the target device assigned by the host during one data process.

The endpoint (ENDP) is a 4-bit field used to indicate the number of the endpoint.

The Cyclic Redundancy Checks (CRC) field is used to perform a self-test or self-checking for any possible error occurred during the data communications. All token packets use a 5-bit CRC with an exception, which is that the data packet used a 16-bit CRC module.

The End Of Packet (EOP) indicates the end of a packet.

The Start Of Frame (SOF) packet is used to inform all devices to use this frame to perform the data communications. The selected frame is indicated in an 11-bit frame number and this packet is periodically sent out by the host to all devices for every 1 ms on full-speed bus or every 125 µs on high-speed bus.

All data transactions are under the control of the host, not the device or endpoint. If the device or endpoint wants to send data to the host, the data is first written into the endpoint transmit buffer with a request to the host, and the data cannot be transmitted to the bus until the host sends an IN packet to the device requesting the data.

9.4.4 The USB Interface Used in the Embedded System

Usually, two USB implementations are popularly used in the interface to the embedded systems; the serial and parallel interfaces.

For the serial applications, a USB interface is used to interface to the traditional RS-232 port to transfer signals between a PC and an embedded system. In the PC side, a USB-to-Serial converter is used to convert the USB style signals to the COM style signals. However, if you want to speed up the processing between a PC and an embedded system with the USB interface, a USB-to-Parallel converter is available to connect a PC with a parallel port installed in the embedded system. In the latter case, a USB interface is supposed to be available in the PC.

Another implementation of using the USB is to integrate the USB functions into a MCU system. A typical example is the TM4C123GXL Evaluation Board, in which the entire embedded system can be considered as a USB device to be connected to a host computer. As shown in Figure 9.26, the entire TM4C123GXL EVB can be considered as a USB device.

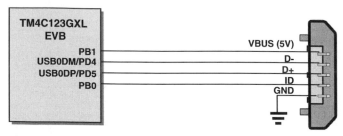

Figure 9.26. The TM4C123GXL EVB as a USB device.

9.4.5 The USB in the TM4C123GH6PM MCU System

The USB controller used in the TM4C123GH6PM provides full OTG negotiation by supporting both the Session Request Protocol (SRP) and the Host Negotiation Protocol (HNP). The session request protocol allows devices on the B side of a cable to request the A side device to turn on VBUS or the power supply to power up the bus. The host negotiation protocol is used after the initial session request protocol has powered the bus and provides a method to determine which end of the cable can act as the Host controller. When the device is connected to non-OTG peripherals or devices, the controller can detect which cable end is used and provides a register to indicate if the controller should act as the Host or the Device controller. This indication and the mode of operation are handled automatically by the USB controller. This auto-detection allows the system to use a single A/B connector instead of having both A and B connectors in the system and supports full OTG negotiations with other OTG devices.

When the USB module is in operation, MOSC must be the clock source, either with or without using the PLL, and the system clock must be at least 20 MHz.

In addition, the USB controller provides support for connecting to non-OTG peripherals or Host controllers. The USB controller can be configured to act as either a dedicated Host or Device, in which case, the USB0VBUS and USB0ID signals can be used as GPIOs or any corresponding alternate functions.

The USB can be used as either a host or a device in the TM4C123GH6PM MCU system. They play different roles when they working at different mode. Therefore we need to discuss these roles based on their functions.

9.4.5.1 USB Working as a Device

Before the USB controller's operating mode is changed from Device to Host or Host to Device, software must reset the USB controller by setting the USB0 bit in the `Software Reset Control 2 (SRCR2)` register.

When in Device mode, both IN and OUT operation is referenced and defined to the host. All IN transactions are inputs to the host and controlled by an endpoint's transmit interface and use the transmit endpoint registers for the given endpoint. OUT transactions are outputs of the host and handled with an endpoint's receive interface and use the receive endpoint registers for the given endpoint.

When configuring the size of the FIFOs for endpoints, take into account the maximum packet size for an endpoint.

- `Bulk`: Bulk endpoints should be the size of the maximum packet (up to 64 bytes) or twice the maximum packet size if double buffering is used.
- `Interrupt`: Interrupt endpoints should be the size of the maximum packet (up to 64 bytes) or twice the maximum packet size if double buffering is used.
- `Isochronous`: Isochronous endpoints are more flexible and can be up to 1023 bytes.
- `Control`: It is also possible to specify a separate control endpoint for a USB Device. However, in most cases the USB Device should use the dedicated control endpoint on the USB controller's endpoint 0.

When operating as a Device, the USB controller provides totally 16 endpoints: one control endpoint IN and one control endpoint OUT, along with 14 configurable endpoints with 7 IN and 7 OUT that can be used for communications with a host controller. The endpoint number and direction associated with an endpoint is directly related to its register designation.

Endpoint 0 is a dedicated control endpoint used for all control transactions to endpoint 0 during enumeration or when any other control requests are made to endpoint 0. Endpoint 0 uses the first 64 bytes of the USB controller's FIFO RAM as a shared memory for both IN and OUT transactions.

The remaining 14 endpoints can be configured as control, bulk, interrupt, or isochronous endpoints. They should be treated as 7 configurable IN and 7 configurable OUT endpoints. The endpoint pairs are not required to have the same type for their IN and OUT endpoint configuration. For example, the OUT portion of an endpoint pair could be a bulk endpoint, while the IN portion of that endpoint pair could be an interrupt endpoint. The address and size of the FIFOs attached to each endpoint can be modified to fit the application's needs.

9.4.5.1.1 IN Transactions as a Device When operating in an IN transaction, the host receives data from the endpoint and the IN data is handled via the device FIFOs attached to the transmit endpoints. The starting address of the FIFOs for the 7 configurable IN endpoints are determined by the USB Transmit FIFO Start Address (USBTXFIFOADD) register. The maximum size of a data packet that may be placed in a transmit endpoint's FIFO is programmable and is determined by the value written to the USB Maximum Transmit Data Endpoint n (USBTXMAXPn) register for that endpoint. The endpoint's FIFO can also be configured to use double-packet or single-packet buffering. When double-packet buffering is enabled, two data packets can be buffered in the FIFO, which also requires that the FIFO be at least two packets in size. When double-packet buffering is disabled, only one packet can be buffered, even if the packet size is less than half the FIFO size.

The maximum packet size set for any endpoint must not exceed the FIFO size. When the FIFO still contains data, the USBTXMAXPn register should not be written to avoid unexpected results to be occurred.

Single-Packet Buffering If the size of the transmit endpoint's FIFO is less than twice the maximum packet size for this IN endpoint, which is set in the USB Transmit Dynamic FIFO Sizing (USBTXFIFOSZ) register, only one packet can be buffered in the FIFO and single-packet buffering is used. When each packet is completely loaded into the transmit FIFO, the TXRDY bit in the USB Transmit Control and Status Endpoint n Low (USBTXCSRLn) register must be set. If the AUTOSET bit in the USB Transmit Control and Status Endpoint n High (USBTXCSRHn) register is set, the TXRDY bit is automatically set when a maximum-sized packet is loaded into the FIFO. For packet sizes less than the maximum, the TXRDY bit must be set manually. When the TXRDY bit is set, the packet is ready to be sent. When the packet has been successfully sent, both TXRDY and FIFONE are cleared, and the appropriate transmit endpoint interrupt signaled. At this point, the next packet can be loaded into the FIFO.

Double-Packet Buffering If the size of the transmit endpoint's FIFO is at least twice the maximum packet size for this IN endpoint, two packets can be buffered in the FIFO and double-packet buffering is allowed. As each packet is loaded into the transmit FIFO, the TXRDY bit in the USBTXCSRLn register must be set. If the AUTOSET bit in the

USBTXCSRHn register is set, the TXRDY bit is automatically set when a maximum-sized packet is loaded into the FIFO. For packet sizes less than the maximum, TXRDY must be set manually. When the TXRDY bit is set, the packet is ready to be sent. After the first packet is loaded, TXRDY is immediately cleared and an interrupt is generated. A second packet can now be loaded into the transmit FIFO and TXRDY set again, either manually or automatically if the packet is the maximum size. At this point, both packets are ready to be sent.

After each packet has been successfully sent, TXRDY is automatically cleared and the appropriate transmit endpoint interrupt signaled to indicate that another packet can now be loaded into the transmit FIFO. The state of the FIFONE bit in the USBTXCSRLn register at this point indicates how many packets may be loaded. If the FIFONE bit is set, then another packet is in the FIFO and only one more packet can be loaded. If the FIFONE bit is clear, then no packets are in the FIFO and two more packets can be loaded.

Double-packet buffering is disabled if an endpoint's corresponding EPn bit is set in the USB Transmit Double Packet Buffer Disable (USBTXDPKTBUFDIS) register. This bit is set by default, so it must be cleared to enable double-packet buffering.

9.4.5.1.2 OUT Transactions as a Device   When operating in the OUT mode, the host transmits the data to the device and all OUT transactions are handled via the USB controller receive FIFOs. The sizes of the receive FIFOs for the 7 configurable OUT endpoints are determined by the USB Receive FIFO Start Address (USBRXFI-FOADD) register. The maximum amount of data received by an endpoint in any packet is determined by the value written to the USB Maximum Receive Data Endpoint n (USBRXMAXPn) register for that endpoint. When double-packet buffering is enabled, two data packets can be buffered in the FIFO. When double-packet buffering is disabled, only one packet can be buffered even if the packet is less than half the FIFO size. In all cases, the maximum packet size must not exceed the FIFO size.

Single-Packet Buffering   If the size of the receive endpoint FIFO is less than twice the maximum packet size for an endpoint, only one data packet can be buffered in the FIFO and single-packet buffering is used. When a packet is received and placed in the receive FIFO, the RXRDY and FULL bits in the USB Receive Control and Status Endpoint n Low (USBRXCSRLn) register are set and the appropriate receive endpoint is signaled, indicating that a packet can now be unloaded from the FIFO. After the packet has been unloaded, the RXRDY bit must be cleared in order to allow further packets to be received. This action also generates the acknowledge signal to the Host controller. If the AUTOCL bit in the USB Receive Control and Status Endpoint n High (USBRXCSRHn) register is set and a maximum-sized packet is unloaded from the FIFO, the RXRDY and FULL bits are cleared automatically. For packet sizes less than the maximum, RXRDY must be cleared manually.

Double-Packet Buffering   If the size of the receive endpoint FIFO is at least twice the maximum packet size for the endpoint, two data packets can be buffered and double-packet buffering can be used. When the first packet is received and loaded into the receive FIFO, the RXRDY bit in the USBRXCSRLn register is set and the appropriate receive endpoint interrupt is signaled to indicate that a packet can now be unloaded from the FIFO.

While the FULL bit in the USBRXCSRLn register is not set when the first packet is received, it is only set if a second packet is received and loaded into the receive FIFO.

After each packet has been unloaded, the RXRDY bit must be cleared to allow further packets to be received. If the AUTOCL bit in the USBRXCSRHn register is set and a maximum-sized packet is unloaded from the FIFO, the RXRDY bit is cleared automatically. For packet sizes less than the maximum, RXRDY must be cleared manually. If the FULL bit is set when RXRDY is cleared, the USB controller first clears the FULL bit and then sets RXRDY again to indicate that there is another packet waiting in the FIFO to be unloaded.

Double-packet buffering is disabled if an endpoint's corresponding EPn bit is set in the USB Receive Double Packet Buffer Disable (USBRXDPKTBUFDIS) register. This bit is set by default, so it must be cleared to enable double-packet buffering.

9.4.5.1.3 Other Device Functions

Stalling Control   When any of the following conditions occurred, the USB controller automatically issues a STALL handshake to terminate a transfer:

- The host sends more data during an OUT data period of a control transfer than was specified in the Device request during the SETUP phase. This condition is detected by the USB controller when the host sends an OUT token after the last OUT packet has been unloaded and the DATAEND bit in the USB Control and Status Endpoint 0 Low (USBCSRL0) register has been set.
- The host requests more data during an IN data period of a control transfer than was specified in the Device request during the SETUP phase. This condition is detected by the USB controller when the host sends an IN token after the CPU has cleared TXRDY and set DATAEND in response to the ACK issued by the host to what should have been the last packet.
- The host sends more than USBRXMAXPn bytes of data with an OUT data token.
- The host sends more than a zero length data packet for the OUT STATUS phase.

A zero-length OUT data packet is to indicate the end of a control transfer. In normal operation, such packets should only be received after the entire length of the device request has been transferred.

However, if the host sends a zero-length OUT data packet before the entire length of device request has been transferred, it is signaling the premature end of the transfer. In this case, the USB controller automatically flushes any IN token ready for the data phase from the FIFO and sets the DATAEND bit in the USBCSRL0 register.

Setting the Device Address   When a host is trying to enumerate the USB device, it requests the device to change its address from zero to some other value. The address is changed by writing the value that the host requested to the USB Device Functional Address (USBFADDR) register. However, it should be careful when writing to the USBFADDR register to avoid changing the address before the transaction is complete. This register should only be set after the SET_ADDRESS command is complete.

Working in the SUSPEND Mode   When no any action has occurred on the USB bus for 3 ms, the USB controller automatically enters SUSPEND mode. If the SUSPEND interrupt has been enabled in the USB Interrupt Enable (USBIE) register, an interrupt is generated at this time. In the SUSPEND mode, the USB physical layer interface (PHY) also goes into SUSPEND mode. When a RESUME signal is detected, the USB controller exits SUSPEND mode and takes the PHY out of SUSPEND. If the RESUME interrupt is enabled, an interrupt is generated. The USB controller can also be forced to exit

SUSPEND mode by setting the RESUME bit in the USB Power (USBPOWER) register. The RESUME bit must be cleared after 10 ms (up to 15 ms) to end RESUME signaling.

Start-of-Frame When the USB controller is operating in the device mode, it receives a Start-Of-Frame (SOF) packet from the host once every 1 ms. When the SOF packet is received, the 11-bit frame number contained in the packet is written into the USB Frame Value (USBFRAME) register, and an SOF interrupt is also signaled and can be handled by the application. Once the USB controller has started to receive SOF packets, it expects one for each 1 ms. If no SOF packet is received after 1.00358 ms, the packet is assumed to have been lost, and the USBFRAME register is not updated. The USB controller continues and resynchronizes these pulses to the received SOF packets when these packets are successfully received again.

USB RESET When the USB controller works in the device mode and a RESET condition is detected on the USB bus, the USB controller automatically performs the following jobs:

1. Clears the USBFADDR register.
2. Clears the USB Endpoint Index (USBEPIDX) register.
3. Flushes all endpoint FIFOs.
4. Clears all control/status registers.
5. Enables all endpoint interrupts.
6. Generates a RESET interrupt.

When the application software driving the USB controller receives a RESET interrupt, any open pipes are closed and the USB controller waits for bus enumeration to begin.

Connect/Disconnect The USB controller can be connected to the USB bus by software. The USB PHY can be switched between normal mode and nondriving mode by setting or clearing the SOFTCONN bit of the USBPOWER register. When the SOFTCONN bit is set to 1, the USB is placed in its normal mode, and the USB0DP/USB0DM lines of the USB bus are enabled. At the same time, the USB controller does not respond to any USB signal except a USB RESET.

When the SOFTCONN bit is cleared, the USB is put into nondriving mode, USB0DP/USB0DM lines are tri-stated, and the USB controller appears to be disconnected. The nondriving mode is the default mode so the USB controller appears disconnected until the SOFTCONN bit is set to 1. The application software can then choose when to set the PHY into its normal mode. Systems with a lengthy initialization procedure may use this to ensure that initialization is complete, and the system is ready to perform enumeration before connecting to the USB bus. Once the SOFTCONN bit is set, the USB controller can be disconnected by clearing this bit.

The point to be noted is that the USB controller does not generate an interrupt when the device is connected to the host. However, an interrupt is generated when the host terminates a session.

In summary, to connect a device to the USB bus, the following operations should be performed before it can be connected to the bus:

- When the device is in its default mode, nondriving mode, perform all necessary initializations and configurations for the selected device.

- Perform all necessary enumeration jobs for all devices.
- Set SOFTCONN bit in the USBPOWER register with software to connect the device to the USB bus and enable it to work in the normal mode.

Next let's take a look at the USB controller when it works as a host.

9.4.5.2 USB Working as a Host

When a USB controller is operating in the host mode, it can either be used for point-to-point communications with another USB device or for communication with multiple devices when a hub is attached. Before the USB controller's operating mode is changed from host to device or device to host, software must reset the USB controller by setting the USB0 bit in the `Software Reset Control 2` (SRCR2) register. Full-speed and low-speed USB devices are supported, both for point-to-point communication and for operation via a hub. The USB controller automatically carries out the necessary transaction translation to allow a low-speed or full-speed device to be used with a USB 2.0 hub. Control, bulk, isochronous, and interrupt transactions are supported.

When in host mode, IN transactions are controlled by an endpoint's receive interface. All IN transactions use the receive endpoint registers and all OUT endpoints use the transmit endpoint registers for a given endpoint. Similar to device mode, the host FIFOs for endpoints should take into account the maximum packet size for an endpoint.

- `Bulk`: Bulk endpoints should be the size of the maximum packet, up to 64 bytes or twice the maximum packet size if double buffering is used.
- `Interrupt`: Interrupt endpoints should be the size of the maximum packet, up to 64 bytes or twice the maximum packet size if double buffering is used.
- `Isochronous`: Isochronous endpoints are more flexible and can be up to 1023 bytes.
- `Control`: It is also possible to specify a separate control endpoint to communicate with a device. However, in most cases the USB controller should use the dedicated control endpoint to communicate with a device's endpoint 0.

The endpoint registers are used to control the USB endpoint interfaces which communicate with connected devices. The endpoints consist of a dedicated control IN endpoint, a dedicated control OUT endpoint, 7 configurable OUT endpoints, and 7 configurable IN endpoints.

The dedicated control interface can only be used for control transactions to endpoint 0 of devices. These control transactions are used during enumeration or other control functions that communicate using endpoint 0 of devices. This control endpoint shares the first 64 bytes of the USB controller's FIFO RAM for IN and OUT transactions. The remaining 7 IN and 7 OUT interfaces can be configured to communicate with control, bulk, interrupt, or isochronous device endpoints.

These USB interfaces can be used to simultaneously schedule as many as 7 independent OUT and 7 independent IN transactions to any endpoints on any device. The IN and OUT controls are paired in three sets of registers. However, they can be configured to communicate with different types of endpoints and different endpoints on devices.

Before accessing any device, whether for point-to-point communications or for communications via a hub, the relevant USB `Receive Functional Address Endpoint n` (USBRXFUNCADDRn) or USB `Transmit Functional Address`

Endpoint n (USBTXFUNCADDRn) registers must be set for each receive or transmit endpoint to record the address of the device being accessed.

9.4.5.2.1 IN Transactions as a Host
When a host is working in the IN mode, all IN transactions are handled in a similar way in which all OUT transactions are handled when the USB controller works in the device mode except that:

1. The transaction must be first initiated by the host by setting the REQPKT bit in the USBCSRL0 register to indicate to the transaction scheduler that there is an active transaction on this endpoint.

2. The transaction scheduler then sends an IN token to the target device.

3. When the packet is received by the device and placed in the receive FIFO, the RXRDY bit in the USBCSRL0 register is set, and the appropriate receive endpoint interrupt is signaled to indicate that a packet can now be unloaded from the FIFO.

4. When the packet has been unloaded by the device, the RXRDY bit must be cleared. The AUTOCL bit in the USBRXCSRHn register can be used to make the RXRDY bit automatically cleared when a maximum-sized packet has been unloaded from the FIFO.

5. The AUTORQ bit in USBRXCSRHn register causes the REQPKT bit to be automatically set when the RXRDY bit is cleared to enable the device to request the next packet. The AUTOCL and AUTORQ bits can be used with μDMA accesses to perform complete bulk transfers without main processor intervention.

6. When the RXRDY bit is cleared, the host controller sends an acknowledgement to the device. When there is a known number of packets to be transferred, the USB Request Packet Count in Block Transfer Endpoint n (USBRQPKTCOUNTn) register associated with the endpoint should be configured to the number of packets to be transferred. The USB controller decrements the value in the USBRQPKTCOUNTn register following each request. When the USBRQPKTCOUNTn value decrements to 0, the AUTORQ bit is cleared to prevent any further transactions being attempted.

7. If the size of the transfer is unknown, USBRQPKTCOUNTn should be cleared. The AUTORQ bit then remains set until cleared by the reception of a short packet, which is less than the MAXLOAD value in the SBRXMAXPn register, such as may occur at the end of a bulk transfer.

8. If the device responds to a bulk or interrupt IN token with a NAK, the USB host controller keeps retrying the transaction until the upper bound number of the NAK has been reached.

9. If the target device responds with a STALL, however, the USB host controller does not retry the transaction but sets the STALLED bit in the USBCSRL0 register.

10. If the target Device does not respond to the IN token within the required time, or the packet contained a CRC or bit-stuff error, the USB host controller retries the transaction. If after three attempts the target device has still not received a response, the USB host controller clears the REQPKT bit and sets the ERROR bit in the USBCSRL0 register.

9.4.5.2.2 OUT Transactions as a Host
When a host is working in the OUT mode, all OUT transactions are handled in a similar way in which all IN transactions are handled when the USB controller works in the device mode.

1. The TXRDY bit in the USBTXCSRLn register must be set when each packet is loaded into the transmit FIFO.

2. Also setting the AUTOSET bit in the USBTXCSRHn register automatically sets TXRDY when a maximum-sized packet has been loaded into the host FIFO. Furthermore, the AUTOSET bit can be used with the μDMA controller to perform complete bulk transfers without software intervention.

3. If the target device responds to the OUT token with a NAK, the USB host controller keeps retrying the transaction until the upper bound number of the NAK is reached.

4. However, if the target device responds with a STALL, the USB controller does not retry the transaction but interrupts the main processor by setting the STALLED bit in the USBTXCSRLn register.

5. If the target device does not respond to the OUT token within the required time, or the packet contained a CRC or bit-stuff error, the USB host controller retries the transaction. If after three attempts the target device has still not received a response, the USB controller flushes the FIFO and sets the ERROR bit in the USBTXCSRLn register.

9.4.5.2.3 Transactions Scheduling

As we mentioned, the scheduling of transactions is handled by the USB host controller. The host controller performs configuration of the endpoint communication scheduling based on the type of endpoint transaction. Interrupt transactions can be scheduled to occur in the range of every frame to every 255 frames with 1 frame increments. Bulk endpoints do not need scheduling parameters, but do need a NAK timeout in the event an endpoint on a device is not responding. Isochronous endpoints can be scheduled from every frame to every 216 frames, in powers of 2.

The USB controller maintains a frame counter. If the target device is a full-speed device, the USB controller automatically sends an SOF packet at the start of each frame and increments the frame counter. If the target device is a low-speed device, a *K* state is transmitted on the bus to act as a *keep-alive* to stop the low-speed device from going into SUSPEND mode.

After the SOF packet has been transmitted, the USB host controller cycles through all the configured endpoints looking for active transactions. An active transaction is defined as a receive endpoint for which the REQPKT bit is set or a transmit endpoint for which the TXRDY bit and/or the FIFONE bit is set.

An isochronous or interrupt transaction is started if the transaction is found on the first scheduler cycle of a frame and if the interval counter for that endpoint has counted down to zero. As a result, only one interrupt or isochronous transaction occurs per endpoint every n frames, where n is the interval set via the USB Host Transmit Interval Endpoint n (USBTXINTERVALn) or USB Host Receive Interval Endpoint n (USBRXINTERVALn) register for that endpoint.

An active bulk transaction starts immediately, if sufficient time is left in the frame to complete the transaction before the next SOF packet is due. If the transaction must be retried, then the transaction is not retried until the transaction scheduler has first checked all the other endpoints for active transactions.

This process ensures that an endpoint that is sending a lot of NAKs does not block other transactions on the bus. The controller also allows the user to specify a limit to the length of time for NAKs to be received from a target device before the endpoint times out.

9.4.5.2.4 Other Host Functions

USB Hubs When a full- or low-speed device is connected to the USB controller via a USB 2.0 hub, details of the hub address and the hub port also must be recorded in the corresponding USB Receive Hub Address Endpoint n (USBRXHUBADDRn) and USB Receive Hub Port Endpoint n (USBRXHUBPORTn) or the USB Transmit Hub Address Endpoint n (USBTXHUBADDRn) and USB Transmit Hub Port Endpoint n (USBTXHUBPORTn) registers. In addition, the speed at which the device operates, full or low, must be recorded in the USB Type Endpoint 0 (USBTYPE0) (endpoint 0), USB Host Configure Transmit Type Endpoint n (USBTXTYPEn), or USB Host Configure Receive Type Endpoint n (USBRXTYPEn) registers for each endpoint that is accessed by the device.

For hub communications, the settings in these registers record the current allocation of the endpoints to the attached USB devices. To maximize the number of devices supported, the USB host controller allows this allocation to be changed dynamically by simply updating the address and speed information recorded in these registers. Any changes in the allocation of endpoints to device functions must be made following the completion of any ongoing transactions on the endpoints affected.

The USB host controller does not start a transaction until the bus has been inactive for at least the minimum inter-packet delay. The controller also does not start a transaction unless it can be finished before the end of the frame. If the bus is still active at the end of a frame, then the USB host controller assumes that the target device has malfunctioned, and the USB controller suspends all transactions and generates a babble interrupt.

Host SUSPEND and USB RESET If the SUSPEND bit in the USBPOWER register is set, the USB host controller completes the current transaction and then stops the transaction scheduler and frame counter. No further transactions are started and no SOF packets are generated and transmitted.

To exit SUSPEND mode, set the RESUME bit and clear the SUSPEND bit. While the RESUME bit is set, the USB host controller generates RESUME signal on the bus. After 20 ms, the RESUME bit must be cleared, at which point the frame counter and transaction scheduler start. The host supports the detection of a remote wake-up.

If the RESET bit in the USBPOWER register is set, the USB host controller generates USB RESET signal on the bus. The RESET bit must be set for at least 20 ms to ensure correct resetting of the target device. After the CPU has cleared the bit, the USB host controller starts its frame counter and transaction scheduler.

Connect/Disconnect A session is started by setting the SESSION bit in the USB Device Control (USBDEVCTL) register, enabling the USB controller to wait for a device to be connected. When a device is detected, a connect interrupt is generated. The device speed can be determined by reading the USBDEVCTL register; the bit FSDEV = 1 is for a full-speed device, and the bit LSDEV = 1 is for a low-speed device. The USB controller must generate a RESET interrupt to the device, and then the USB host controller can begin device enumeration. If the device is disconnected while a session is in progress, a disconnect interrupt is generated.

9.4.5.3 *The OTG Mode*

To conserve power, the USB On-The-Go (OTG) mechanism allows VBUS (5 V) to only be powered up when required and to be off when the bus is not in use. VBUS is always supplied by the A device on the bus.

9.4.5.3.1 Using OTG to Start a Session Starting a session process with the OTG mode can be summarized as below:

1. When the USB OTG controller starts a session, the SESSION bit in the USBDEVCTL register must be set to enable the USB controller to wait for a device to be connected.

2. When a device is detected, a connect interrupt is generated. The device speed is determined by reading the USBDEVCTL register where the FSDEV bit is set for a full-speed device, and the LSDEV bit is set for a low-speed device.

3. Then the USB controller must generate a RESET to the device to initialize the device, and then the USB host controller can begin device enumeration. If the device is disconnected while a session is in progress, a disconnect interrupt is generated.

4. The USB OTG controller then enables ID pin sensing to detect the type of the USB endpoint. The ID input is Low if an A-type connection is detected, or it is High if a B-type connection is detected. The DEV bit in the USBDEVCTL register is also set to indicate whether the USB OTG controller has adopted the role of the A device or the B device.

5. The USB OTG controller also generates an interrupt to indicate that ID pin sensing has completed and the mode value in the USBDEVCTL register is valid.

6. This interrupt is enabled in the USBIDVIM register, and the status can be checked in the USBIDVISC register. As soon as the USB controller has detected that it is on the A side of the cable, it must enable VBUS power within 100 ms or the USB controller reverts to device mode.

7. If the USB OTG controller is the A device, then the USB OTG controller enters the host mode since the A device is always the default host, turns on VBUS, and waits for VBUS to go above the VBUS Valid threshold, as indicated by the VBUS bit in the USBDEVCTL register going to 0x3.

8. The USB OTG controller then waits for a peripheral to be connected. When a peripheral is detected, a Connect interrupt is signaled and the device speed can be determined by the FSDEV or LSDEV bit in the USBDEVCTL register when either of them is set, depending on whether a full-speed or a low-speed peripheral is detected.

9. The USB controller then issues a RESET to the connected device. The SESSION bit in the USBDEVCTL register can be cleared to end a session. The USB OTG controller also automatically ends the session if a babble is detected or if the VBUS drops below the session valid value.

In addition, the USB OTG controller may not remain in Host mode when a device is told that it can start using its active configuration. At this point the device starts drawing more current and can also drop VBUS below VBUS valid.

If the USB OTG controller is the B device, the connection process is as follows:

1. The USB OTG controller requests a session using the session request protocol defined in the USB On-The-Go supplement, which is, it first discharges VBUS. Then when the VBUS bit in the USBDEVCTL register goes to 0x0, it means that the VBUS has gone below the Session End threshold and the line state has been a single-ended zero for more than 2 ms, and the USB OTG controller pulses the data line, and then pulses VBUS.

2. At the end of the session, the SESSION bit is cleared either by the USB OTG controller or by the application software. The USB OTG controller then causes the PHY to switch out the pull-up resistor on D+, signaling the A device to end the session.

9.4.5.3.2 Using OTG to Perform Detecting Activity   When the other device of the OTG setup wishes to start a session, it either raises VBUS above the Session Valid threshold if it is the A device, or it pulses the data line and then pulses VBUS if it is the B device. Depending on which of these actions happens, the USB controller can determine whether it is the A device or the B device in the current setup and act accordingly.

If VBUS is raised above the Session Valid threshold, then the USB controller is the A device. The USB controller sets the SESSION bit in the USBDEVCTL register. When the RESET signal is detected on the bus, a RESET interrupt is signaled, which is the start of a session.

The USB controller in the device mode as the B device is the default mode. At the end of the session, the A device turns off the power to VBUS. When VBUS drops below the Session Valid threshold, the USB controller detects this drop and clears the SESSION bit to indicate that the session has ended, causing a disconnect interrupt to be signaled. If data line and VBUS pulsing is detected, then the USB controller is the B device. The controller generates a SESSION REQUEST interrupt to indicate that the B device is requesting a session. The SESSION bit in the USBDEVCTL register must be set to start a session.

9.4.5.3.3 Using OTG to Perform Host Negotiation   When the USB controller is the A device, its ID is Low, and the controller automatically enters host mode when a session starts. When the USB controller is the B device, its ID is High, and the controller automatically enters device mode when a session starts. However, software can request that the USB controller become the host by setting the HOSTREQ bit in the USBDEVCTL register. This bit can be set either at the same time as requesting a Session Start by setting the SESSION bit in the USBDEVCTL register or at any time after a session has started.

When the USB controller next enters SUSPEND mode and if the HOSTREQ bit remains set, the controller enters host mode and begins host negotiation by causing the PHY to disconnect the pull-up resistor on the D+ line, causing the A device to switch to device mode and connect its own pull-up resistor. When the USB controller detects this, a Connect interrupt is generated and the RESET bit in the USBPOWER register is set to begin resetting the A device. The USB controller begins this reset sequence automatically to ensure that RESET is started as required within 1 ms of the A device connecting its pull-up resistor. The main processor should wait at least 20 ms and then clear the RESET bit and enumerate the A device.

When the USB OTG controller B device has finished using the bus, the USB controller goes into SUSPEND mode by setting the SUSPEND bit in the USBPOWER register. The A device detects this and either terminates the session or reverts to host mode. If the A device is USB OTG controller, it generates a Disconnect interrupt.

9.4.5.4 The USB Module Functional Block Diagram

Figure 9.27 shows the functional block diagram of the USB module used in the TM4C123G MCU system.

The entire USB control function can be divided into the following groups:

- Endpoints Control and Status
- USB Synchronization

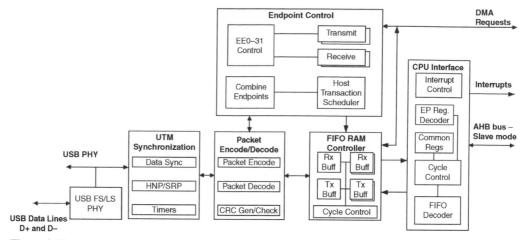

Figure 9.27. Functional block diagram of the USB module. (Reprinted with the permission of the Texas Instruments Incorporated.)

- Packet Encoder/Decoder
- FIFO RAM Controller
- CPU Interface

For Endpoint Control and Status group, nominally 32 endpoints can be accessed but only 16 endpoints are used in the TM4C123GH6PM MCU system, which include 1 dedicated control IN endpoint, 1 dedicated control OUT endpoint, and 14 configurable endpoints (7 configurable IN endpoints and 7 configurable OUT endpoints).

Each endpoint can work in either IN (transmit) or OUT (receive) mode, and these IN and OUT modes are relatively to a host, not a device. If an endpoint works as a host, all transactions are scheduled by the host by using a Transaction Scheduler.

For the USB Synchronization group, it includes the data synchronization by using the SYNC field in each packet. The Session Request Protocol (SRP) and Host Negotiation Protocol (HNP) are also involved in this group to perform host negotiation and session request between the host and the device.

The Packet Encoder/Decoder group is used to pack each packet to certain suitable format to be sent or received by each endpoint.

The FIFO RAM Control group is used to control and manage the FIFO used by the USB endpoints. Both transmit and receive packets can be buffered in this FIFO space.

The CPU Interface group is used to interface the USB endpoints with the processor to make the controls and transactions between the processor and the USB module smooth and effective.

9.4.5.5 The USB Module Control Signals

Table 9.18 lists all external control signals used for USB modules. Some signals are analog signals and can be directly used by the USB endpoints. However, some other signals are shared with the GPIO pins together, and those signals must be configured with the

Table 9.18. USB control signals and GPIO pins distributions.

USB Pin	GPIO Pin	Pin Type	Buffer Type	Pin Function
USB0ID	PB0	I	Analog	Sense the state of the USB ID signal. The USB PHY enables an integrated pull-up, and an external element (USB connector) indicates the initial state of the USB controller (pulled down is the A side and pulled up is the B side).
USB0VBUS	PB1	I/O	Analog	This signal is used during the session request protocol. This signal allows the USB PHY to both sense the voltage level of VBUS, and pull up VBUS momentarily during VBUS pulsing.
USB0DM	PD4	I/O	Analog	Bidirectional differential data pin (D− per USB specification) for USB0.
USB0DP	PD5	I/O	Analog	Bidirectional differential data pin (D+ per USB specification) for USB0.
USB0EPEN	PC6 (8) PD2 (8) PF4 (8)	O	TTL	Optionally used in Host mode to control an external power source to supply power to the USB bus.
USB0PFLT	PC7 (8) PD3 (8)	I	TTL	Optionally used in Host mode by an external power source to indicate an error state by that power source.

appropriate values to make those related GPIO pins to work as alternate functions to perform USB functions.

The AFSEL bit in the GPIOAFSEL register should be set to choose the USB function. The number in parentheses is the encoding that must be programmed into the PMCx field in the GPIOPCTL register to assign the USB signal to the specified GPIO pin. The USB0VBUS and USB0ID signals are configured by clearing the appropriate DEN bit in the GPIODEN register and setting in the AFSEL bits in the GPIOAFSEL register to make those pins to work as analog pins.

It can be found from Table 9.18 that only two USB signal pins, USB0EPEN and USB0PFLT, are working as GPIO alternate function pins and need to be configured with GPIOAFSEL and GPIOPCTL registers. All other four signals, USB0ID, USB0VBUS, USB0DM and USB0DP, are not GPIO alternate function pins and they may not need to be configured with GPIOAFSEL and GPIOPCTL registers. But in fact, they also need to be configured with the GPIOAFSEL and GPIODEN registers to make them as analog function pins. The buffer type TTL is used to indicate that it is a digital signal and the digital function pins can be used to transfer these signals.

9.4.6 The USB Registers

The USB module provides a huge set of registers that are used to access the USB device, host and/or device, or OTG controllers. Therefore these registers can be divided into different groups according to the functionality provided by the USB controller used in the microcontroller. The register groups are presented in the following sequence:

1. USB Host-Related Registers
2. USB Device-Related Registers
3. USB Host/Device-Related Registers
4. USB FIFO-Related Registers
5. USB Interrupt-Related Registers

The registers in the USB Device group are only used with microcontrollers that have a USB device controller. The registers in the USB Host group can only be used with microcontrollers that have a USB host controller. The USB Host/Device related registers are used by microcontrollers with an OTG interface. With USB OTG controllers, once the mode of the USB controller is configured, the device- or host-related registers can be shared. Some of the registers are used for both USB host and USB device controllers. The USB interrupt-related registers are used to configure and access the interrupts while the USBFIFO-related registers are used to configure the size and location of the FIFOs.

In this section we cannot cover all the registers used in the USB module. Thus we only discuss some popular and important registers used for most USB operations.

9.4.6.1 USB Host-Related Registers

The following registers are involved in this group (Figure 9.28):

1. USB Device Control Register (USBDEVCTL)
2. USB Type Endpoint 0 Register (USBTYPE0)
3. USB NAK Limit Register (USBNAKLMT)
4. USB Transmit Functional Address Endpoint 0~7 Registers (USBTXFUNCADDR0~ USBTXFUNCADDR7)
5. USB Receive Functional Address Endpoint 1~7 (USBRXFUNCADDR1~USBRXFUNCADDR7)
6. USB Host Transmit Configure Type Endpoint 1~7 (USBTXTYPE1~USBTXTYPE7) Registers
7. USB Host Configure Receive Type Endpoint 1~7 (USBRXTYPE1~USBRXTYPE7) Registers

All of these registers are 8-bit registers. The bit fields of these registers are shown in Figure 9.28. The bit fields and functions of these registers are shown in Table 9.19. Since the USB Host Configure Receive Type Endpoint 1~7 (USBRXTYPE1~ USBRXTYPE7)

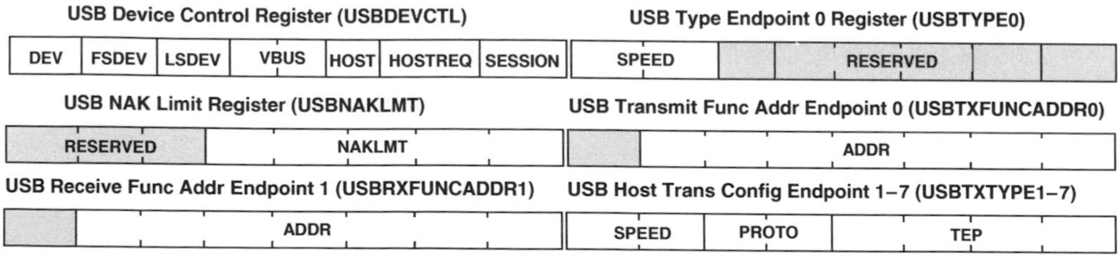

Figure 9.28.   The USB host related registers.

Table 9.19. Bit value and its function for USB host-related registers.

Bit	Name	Reset	Function
	USB Device Control Register (USBDEVCTL)
7	DEV	1	0: The USB controller is operating on the OTG A side of the cable. 1: The USB controller is operating on the OTG B side of the cable.
6	FSDEV	0	0: A full-speed Device has not been detected on the port. 1: A full-speed Device has been detected on the port.
5	LSDEV	0	0: A low-speed Device has not been detected on the port. 1: A low-speed Device has been detected on the port.
4:3	VBUS	0x0	0x0: Below SessionEnd VBUS is detected as under 0.5 V. 0x1: Above SessionEnd, below AValid VBUS is detected as above 0.5 V and under 1.5 V. 0x2: Above AValid, below VBUSValid VBUS is detected as above 1.5 V and below 4.75 V. 0x3: Above VBUSValid VBUS is detected as above 4.75 V.
2	HOST	0	0: The USB controller is acting as a Device. 1: The USB controller is acting as a Host.
1	HOSTREQ	0	0: No effect. 1: Initiates the Host Negotiation when SUSPEND mode is entered.
0	SESSION	0	0: A session is ended. 1: A session is started.
	USB Type Endpoint 0 Register (USBTYPE0)
7:6	SPEED	0x0	0x0 ~ 0x1: Reserved; 0x2: Full-Speed; 0x3: Low-Speed.
	USB NAK Limit Register (USBNAKLMT)
4:0	NAKLMT	0x0	EP0 NAK Limit: This field specifies the number of frames after receiving a stream of NAK responses
	USB Transmit Function Address Endpoint 0~7 Registers (USBTXFUNCADDR0~7)
6:0	ADDR	0x0	Device Address: Specifies the USB bus address for the target Device.
	USB Receive Function Address Endpoint 1~7 Registers (USBRXFUNCADDR1~7)
6:0	ADDR	0x0	Device Address: Specifies the USB bus address for the target Device.
	USB Host Transmit Configure Endpoint Registers 1~7 (USBTXTYPE1~7)
7:6	SPEED	0x0	0x0: The target is using the same connection speed as the USB controller (Default). 0x1: Reserved; 0x2: Full; 0x3: Low.
5:4	PROTO	0x0	0x0: Control; 0x1: Isochronous; 0x2: Bulk; 0x3: Interrupt.
3:0	TEP	0x0	Target Endpoint Number: Software must configure this value to the endpoint number contained in the transmit endpoint descriptor returned to the USB controller during Device enumeration.
	USB Host Configure Receive Endpoint Registers 1~7 (USBRXTYPE1~7)
7:6	SPEED	0x0	0x0: The target is using the same connection speed as the USB controller (Default). 0x1: Reserved; 0x2: Full; 0x3: Low.
5:4	PROTO	0x0	0x0: Control; 0x1: Isochronous; 0x2: Bulk; 0x3: Interrupt.
3:0	TEP	0x0	Target Endpoint Number: Software must set this value to the endpoint number contained in the receive endpoint descriptor returned to the USB controller during Device enumeration.

Registers are similar to those USB Host Transmit Configure Type Endpoint 1~7 (USBTXTYPE1~USBTXTYPE7) Registers, they are not shown in Figure 9.28.

9.4.6.2 USB Device-Related Registers

Only one register, USB Device Functional Address (USBFADDR), is specially designed for the device. This is an 8-bit register but only 7-bit, bits 6:0, or bit field FUNCADDR are used to define the Function Address of device as received through SET_ADDRESS command.

9.4.6.3 USB Host/Device-Related Registers

Quite a few registers are included in this group since these registers can be used by both the host and the device as well as the OTG mode:

- USB Power Register (USBPOWER)
- USB Test Mode Register (USBTEST)
- USB Endpoint Index (USBEPIDX)
- USB Maximum Transmit Data Endpoint 1~7 (USBTXMAXP1~USBTXMAXP7)
- USB Maximum Receive Data Endpoint 1 (USBRXMAXP1~USBRXMAXP7)
- USB Control and Status Endpoint 0 Low (USBCSRL0)
- USB Control and Status Endpoint 0 High (USBCSRH0)
- USB Receive Byte Count Endpoint 0 (USBCOUNT0)
- USB Transmit Control and Status Endpoint 1~7 Low (USBTXCSRL1~USBTXCSRL7)
- USB Transmit Control & Status Endpoint 1~7 High (USBTXCSRH1~USBTXCSRH7)
- USB Maximum Receive Data Endpoint 1~7 (USBRXMAXP1~USBRXMAXP7)
- USB Receive Control and Status Endpoint 1~7 Low (USBRXCSRL1~USBRXCSRL7)
- USB Receive Control and Status Endpoint 1~7 High (USBRXCSRH1~USBRXCSRH7)

Figure 9.29 shows the bit fields of these registers. Most registers in this group are paired, and one is for the OTG A/Host and the other is for the OTG B/Device used. The bit fields and functions of these registers are shown in Table 9.20.

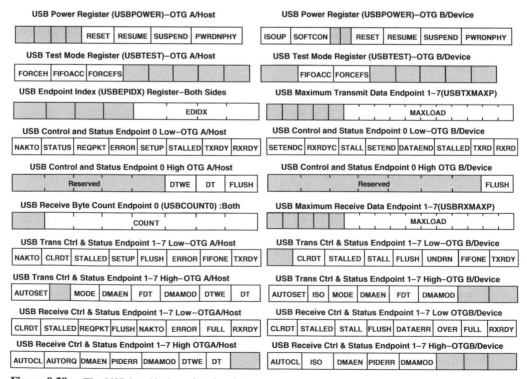

Figure 9.29. The USB host/device-related registers.

Table 9.20a. Bit value and its function for USB host/device-related registers.

Bit	Name	Reset	Function
USB Power Register (USBPOWER) – OTG A/Host			
7:4	Reserved	0x2	Reserved
3	RESET	0	0: Ends RESET signaling on the bus. 1: Enables RESET signaling on the bus.
2	RESUME	0	0: Ends RESUME signaling on the bus. 1: Enables RESUME signaling when the Device is in SUSPEND mode.
1	SUSPEND	0	0: No effect. 1: Enables SUSPEND mode
0	PWRDNPHY	0	Power Down PHY: 0: No effect. 1: Powers down the internal USB PHY

9.4.6.4 USB FIFO-Related Registers

The registers in this group are used to control and manage the operations of the FIFO:

- USB Transmit FIFO Start Address (USBTXFIFOADD) Register
- USB Receive FIFO Start Address (USBRXFIFOADD) Register
- USB Transmit Dynamic FIFO Sizing (USBTXFIFOSZ) Register
- USB Receive Dynamic FIFO Sizing (USBRXFIFOSZ) Register

Figure 9.30 shows the bit fields of these registers. All registers in this group are paired and one is for the OTG A/Host and the other is for the OTG B/Device used. However, the

Table 9.20b. Bit value and its function for USB host/device-related registers.

Bit	Name	Reset	Function
USB Power Register (USBPOWER)–OTG B/Device			
7	ISOUP	0	Isochronous Update: 0: No effect. 1: The USB controller waits for an SOF token from the time the TXRDY bit is set in the USBTXCSRLn register before sending the packet. If an IN token is received before an SOF token, then a zero-length data packet is sent.
6	SOFTCON	0	Soft Connect/Disconnect: 0: The USB D+/D− lines are tri-stated. 1: The USB D+/D− lines are enabled.
5:4	Reserved	0x2	Reserved.
3	RESET	0	0: RESET signaling is not present on the bus; 1: RESET signaling is present on the bus.
2	RESUME	0	0: Ends RESUME signaling on the bus. 1: Enables RESUME signaling when the Device is in SUSPEND mode.
1	SUSPEND	0	0: This bit is cleared when software reads the interrupt register or sets the RESUME bit above. 1: The USB controller is in SUSPEND mode
0	PWRDNPHY	0	Power Down PHY: 0: No effect. 1: Powers down the internal USB PHY
USB Test Mode Register (USBTEST)–OTG A/Host			
7	FORCEH	0	Force Host Mode: 0: No effect. 1: Forces the USB controller to enter Host mode when the SESSION bit is set, regardless of whether the USB controller is connected to any peripheral.
6	FIFOACC	0	FIFO Access: 0: No effect; 1: Transfers the packet in the endpoint 0 transmit FIFO to the endpoint 0 receive FIFO.
5	FORCEFS	0	Force Full-Speed Mode. 0: The USB controller operates at Low Speed; 1: Forces the USB controller into Full-Speed mode upon receiving a USB RESET.

Table 9.20c. Bit value and its function for USB host/device-related registers.

Bit	Name	Reset	Function
	USB Test Mode Register (USBTEST)–OTG B/Device
7	Reserved	0	Reserved.
6	FIFOACC	0	FIFO Access: 0: No effect; 1: Transfers the packet in the endpoint 0 transmit FIFO to the endpoint 0 receive FIFO.
5	FORCEFS	0	Force Full-Speed Mode. 0: The USB controller operates at Low Speed; 1: Forces the USB controller into Full-Speed mode upon receiving a USB RESET.
	USB Endpoint Index (USBEPIDX) Register–Both OTG A/Host and OTG B/Device
7:4	Reserved	0x0	Reserved.
3:0	EPIDX	0x0	Endpoint Index: This bit-field configure which endpoint is accessed when reading or writing to one of the USB controller's indexed registers. A value of 0x0 corresponds to Endpoint 0 and a value of 0x7 corresponds to Endpoint 7.
	USB Maximum Transmit Data Endpoint 1~7(USBTXMAXP1~7) Registers–OTG A/Host & OTG B/Device
15:11	Reserved	0x0	Reserved.
10:0	MAXLOAD	0x000	This field specifies the maximum payload in bytes per transaction.
	USB Maximum Receive Data Endpoint 1~7(USBRXMAXP1~7) Registers–OTG A/Host & OTG B/Device
15:11	Reserved	0x0	Reserved.
10:0	MAXLOAD	0x000	This field specifies the maximum payload in bytes per transaction.
	USB Control and Status Endpoint 0 Low (USBCSRL0) Register–OTG A/Host
7	NAKTO	0	NAK Timeout: 0: No timeout; 1: Indicates that endpoint 0 is halted following the receipt of NAK responses for longer than the time set by the USBNAKLMT register.
6	STATUS	0	STATUS Packet: 0: No transaction; 1: Initiates a STATUS stage transaction. This bit must be set at the same time as the TXRDY or REQPKT bit is set.
5	REQPKT	0	Request Packet: 0: No request; 1: Requests an IN transaction. This bit is cleared when the RXRDY bit is set.
4	ERROR	0	0: No error; 1: Three attempts have been made to perform a transaction with no response from the peripheral. The EP0 bit in the USBTXIS register is also set in this situation.
3	SETUP	0	Setup Packet: 0: Sends an OUT token; 1: Sends a SETUP token instead of an OUT token for the transaction. This bit should be set at the same time as the TXRDY bit is set.
2	STALLED	0	Endpoint Stalled: 0: No handshake has been received; 1: A STALL handshake has been received. Software must clear this bit.
1	TXRDY	0	Transmit Packet Ready: 0: No transmit packet is ready; 1: Software set this bit after loading a data packet into the TX FIFO. The EP0 bit in the USBTXIS register is also set in this situation. If both the TXRDY and SETUP bits are set, a setup packet is sent. If just TXRDY is set, an OUT packet is sent. This bit is cleared automatically when the data packet has been transmitted.
0	RXRDY	0	Receive Packet Ready: 0: No received packet has been received; 1: Indicates that a data packet has been received in the RX FIFO. The EP0 bit in the USBTXIS register is also set in this situation. Software must clear this bit after the packet has been read from the FIFO to acknowledge that the data has been read from the FIFO
	USB Control and Status Endpoint 0 Low (USBCSRL0) Register–OTG B/Device
7	SETENDC	0	Setup End Clear: Writing a 1 to this bit clears the SETEND bit.
6	RXRDYC	0	RXRDY Clear: Writing a 1 to this bit clears the RXRDY bit.
5	STALL	0	Send Stall: 0: No effect; 1: Terminate the current transaction and transmit the STALL handshake.
4	SETEND	0	Setup End: 0: A control transaction has not ended or ended after the DATAEND bit was set. 1: A control transaction has ended before the DATAEND bit has been set. The EP0 bit in the USBTXIS register is also set in this situation.
3	DATAEND	0	Data End: 0: No effect; 1: Set this bit in the following situations: • When setting TXRDY for the last data packet. • When clearing RXRDY after unloading the last data packet. • When setting TXRDY for a zero-length data packet.

Table 9.20c (*Continued*)

Bit	Name	Reset	Function
2	STALLED	0	Endpoint Stalled: 0: No handshake has been transmitted; 1: A STALL handshake has been transmitted. Software must clear this bit.
1	TXRDY	0	Transmit Packet Ready: 0: No transmit packet is ready; 1: Software set this bit after loading an IN data packet into the TX FIFO. The EP0 bit in the USBTXIS register is also set in this situation. This bit is cleared automatically when the data packet has been transmitted.
0	RXRDY	0	Receive Packet Ready: 0: No received packet has been received; 1: Indicates that a data packet has been received in the RX FIFO. The EP0 bit in the USBTXIS register is also set in this situation. Software must clear this bit after the packet has been read from the FIFO to acknowledge that the data has been read from the FIFO. This bit is cleared by writing a 1 to the RXRDYC bit.
	USB Control and Status Endpoint 0 High (USBCSRH0) Register–OTG A/Host		
7:3	Reserved	0x0	Reserved.
2	DTWE	0	Data Toggle Write Enable: 0: The DT bit cannot be written. 1: Enables the current state of the endpoint 0 data toggle to be written (see DT bit).
1	DT	0	Data Toggle: When read, this bit indicates the current state of the endpoint 0 data toggle. If DTWE is set, this bit may be written with the required setting of the data toggle. If DTWE is Low, this bit cannot be written. Care should be taken when writing to this bit as it should only be changed to RESET USB endpoint 0.
0	FLUSH	0	Flush FIFO: 0: No effect; 1: Flushes the next packet to be transmitted/read from the endpoint 0 FIFO. The FIFO pointer is reset and the TXRDY/RXRDY bit is cleared.
	USB Control and Status Endpoint 0 High (USBCSRH0) Register–OTG B/Device		
7:1	Reserved	0x0	Reserved.
0	FLUSH	0	Flush FIFO: 0: No effect; 1: Flushes the next packet to be transmitted/read from the endpoint 0 FIFO. The FIFO pointer is reset and the TXRDY/RXRDY bit is cleared.
	USB Receive Byte Count Endpoint 0 (USBCOUNT0) Register–OTG A/Host and OTG B/Device		
7	Reserved	0	Reserved.
6:0	COUNT	0x0	FIFO Count: COUNT is a read-only value that indicates the number of received data bytes in the endpoint 0 FIFO.
	USB Transmit Control and Status Endpoint 1~7 Low (USBTXCSRL1~7) Registers–OTG A/Host		
7	NAKTO	0	NAK Timeout: 0: No timeout; 1: Indicates that endpoint 0 is halted following the receipt of NAK responses for longer than the time set by the NAKLMT field in the USBTXINTERVALn register. Software must clear this bit to allow the endpoint to continue.
6	CLRDT	0	Clear Data Toggle: Writing a 1 to this bit clears the DT bit in the USBTXCSRHn register.
5	STALLED	0	Endpoint Stalled: 0: No handshake has been received; 1: A STALL handshake has been received. Software must clear this bit.
4	SETUP	0	Setup Packet: 0: No SETUP token is sent; 1: Sends a SETUP token instead of an OUT token for the transaction. This bit should be set at the same time as the TXRDY bit is set.
3	FLUSH	0	Flush FIFO: 0: No effect; 1: Flushes the latest packet from the endpoint transmit FIFO. The FIFO pointer is reset and the TXRDY bit is cleared. The EPn bit in the USBTXIS register is also set.
2	ERROR	0	0: No error; 1: Three attempts have been made to send a packet with no response from the peripheral. The TXRDY bit is cleared, the EPn bit in the USBTXIS register is set, and the FIFO is completely flushed in this situation.
1	FIFONE	0	FIFO Not Empty: 0: The FIFO is empty; 1: At least one packet is in the transmit FIFO.
0	TXRDY	0	Transmit Packet Ready: 0: No transmit packet is ready; 1: Software set this bit after loading a data packet into the TX FIFO. This bit is cleared automatically when a data packet has been transmitted. The EPn bit in the USBTXIS register is also set at this point. TXRDY is also automatically cleared prior to loading a second packet into a double-buffered FIFO.

Table 9.20d. Bit value and its function for USB host/device-related registers.

Bit	Name	Reset	Function
USB Transmit Control and Status Endpoint 1~7 Low (USBTXCSRL1~7) Registers—OTG B/Device			
7	Reserved	0	Reserved.
6	CLRDT	0	Clear Data Toggle: Writing a 1 to this bit clears the DT bit in the USBTXCSRHn register.
5	STALLED	0	Endpoint Stalled: 0: A STALL handshake has not been transmitted; 1: STALL handshake has been transmitted. The FIFO is flushed and the TXRDY bit is cleared. Software must clear this bit.
4	STALL	0	Send STALL: 0: No effect; 1: Issues a STALL handshake to an IN token.
3	FLUSH	0	Flush FIFO: 0: No effect; 1: Flushes the latest packet from the endpoint transmit FIFO. The FIFO pointer is reset and the TXRDY bit is cleared. The EPn bit in the USBTXIS register is also set.
2	UNDRN	0	Underrun: 0: No underrun; 1: An IN token has been received when TXRDY is not set.
1	FIFONE	0	FIFO Not Empty: 0: The FIFO is empty; 1: At least one packet is in the transmit FIFO.
0	TXRDY	0	Transmit Packet Ready: 0: No transmit packet is ready; 1: Software set this bit after loading a data packet into the TX FIFO. This bit is cleared automatically when a data packet has been transmitted. The EPn bit in the USBTXIS register is also set at this point. TXRDY is also automatically cleared prior to loading a second packet into a double-buffered FIFO.
USB Transmit Control and Status Endpoint 1~7 High (USBTXCSRH1~7) Registers—OTG A/Host			
7	AUTOSET	0	Auto Set: 0: The TXRDY bit must be set manually. 1: Enables the TXRDY bit to be automatically set when data of the maximum packet size (value in USBTXMAXPn) is loaded into the transmit FIFO. If a packet of less than the maximum packet size is loaded, then the TXRDY bit must be set manually.
6	Reserved	0	Reserved.
5	MODE	0	Mode: 0: Enables the endpoint direction as RX; 1: Enables the endpoint direction as TX.
4	DMAEN	0	DMA Request Enable: 0: Disables the DMA request for the transmit endpoint. 1: Enables the DMA request for the transmit endpoint.
3	FDT	0	Force Data Toggle: 0: No effect; 1: Forces the endpoint DT bit to switch and the data packet to be cleared from the FIFO, regardless of whether an ACK was received. This bit can be used by interrupt transmit endpoints that are used to communicate rate feedback for isochronous endpoints.
2	DMAMOD	0	DMA Request Mode: 0: An interrupt is generated after every DMA packet transfer. 1: An interrupt is generated only after the entire DMA transfer is complete.
1	DTWE	0	Data Toggle Write Enable: 0: The DT bit cannot be written. 1: Enables the current state of the endpoint 0 data toggle to be written (see DT bit).
0	DT	0	Data Toggle: When read, this bit indicates the current state of the endpoint 0 data toggle. If DTWE is set, this bit may be written with the required setting of the data toggle. If DTWE is Low, this bit cannot be written. Care should be taken when writing to this bit as it should only be changed to RESET USB endpoint 0.
USB Transmit Control and Status Endpoint 1~7 High (USBTXCSRH1~7) Registers—OTG B/Device			
7	AUTOSET	0	Auto Set: 0: The TXRDY bit must be set manually. 1: Enables the TXRDY bit to be automatically set when data of the maximum packet size (value in USBTXMAXPn) is loaded into the transmit FIFO. If a packet of less than the maximum packet size is loaded, then the TXRDY bit must be set manually.
6	ISO	0	Isochronous Transfers: 0: Enables the transmit endpoint for bulk or interrupt transfers. 1: Enables the transmit endpoint for isochronous transfers.
5	MODE	0	Mode: 0: Enables the endpoint direction as RX; 1: Enables the endpoint direction as TX.
4	DMAEN	0	DMA Request Enable: 0: Disables the DMA request for the transmit endpoint. 1: Enables the DMA request for the transmit endpoint.

Table 9.20d (*Continued*)

Bit	Name	Reset	Function
3	FDT	0	Force Data Toggle: 0: No effect; 1: Forces the endpoint DT bit to switch and the data packet to be cleared from the FIFO, regardless of whether an ACK was received. This bit can be used by interrupt transmit endpoints that are used to communicate rate feedback for isochronous endpoints.
2	DMAMOD	0	DMA Request Mode: 0: An interrupt is generated after every DMA packet transfer. 1: An interrupt is generated only after the entire DMA transfer is complete.
1:0	Reserved	0	Reserved.
	USB Receive Control and Status Endpoint 1–7 Low (USBRXCSRL1–7) Registers–OTG A/Host
7	CLRDT	0	Clear Data Toggle: Writing a 1 to this bit clears the DT bit in the USBTXCSRHn register.
6	STALLED	0	Endpoint Stalled: 0: No handshake has been received; 1: A STALL handshake has been received. Software must clear this bit.
5	REQPKT	0	Request Packet: 0: No request; 1: Requests an IN transaction.
4	FLUSH	0	Flush FIFO: 0: No effect; 1: Flushes the latest packet from the endpoint transmit FIFO. The FIFO pointer is reset and the TXRDY bit is cleared. The EPn bit in the USBTXIS register is also set.
3	NAKTO	0	Data Error/NAK Timeout: 0: No timeout; 1: Indicates that endpoint 0 is halted following the receipt of NAK responses for longer than the time set by the NAKLMT field in the USBTXINTERVALn register. Software must clear this bit to allow the endpoint to continue.
2	ERROR	0	0: No error; 1: Three attempts have been made to send a packet with no response from the peripheral. The TXRDY bit is cleared, the EPn bit in the USBTXIS register is set, and the FIFO is completely flushed in this situation.
1	FULL	0	FIFO Full: 0: The receive FIFO is not full; 1: No more packets can be loaded into the receive FIFO.
0	RXRDY	0	Receive Packet Ready: 0: No received packet has been received; 1: Indicates that a data packet has been received in the RX FIFO. The EP0 bit in the USBTXIS register is also set in this situation. Software must clear this bit after the packet has been read from the FIFO to acknowledge that the data has been read from the FIFO. This bit is cleared by writing a 1 to the RXRDYC bit.
	USB Receive Control and Status Endpoint 1–7 Low (USBRXCSRL1–7) Registers–OTG B/Device
7	CLRDT	0	Clear Data Toggle: Writing a 1 to this bit clears the DT bit in the USBTXCSRHn register.
6	STALLED	0	Endpoint Stalled: 0: No handshake has been received; 1: A STALL handshake has been received. Software must clear this bit.
5	STALL	0	Send STALL: 0: No effect; 1: Issues a STALL handshake to an IN token.
4	FLUSH	0	Flush FIFO: 0: No effect; 1: Flushes the latest packet from the endpoint transmit FIFO. The FIFO pointer is reset and the TXRDY bit is cleared. The EPn bit in the USBTXIS register is also set.
3	DATAERR	0	Data Error: 0: Normal operation; 1: Indicates that RXRDY is set and the data packet has a CRC or bit-stuff error.
2	OVER	0	Overrun: 0: No overrun error; 1: Indicates that an OUT packet cannot be loaded into the receive FIFO.
1	FULL	0	FIFO Full: 0: The receive FIFO is not full; 1: No more packets can be loaded into the receive FIFO.
0	RXRDY	0	Receive Packet Ready: 0: No received packet has been received; 1: Indicates that a data packet has been received in the RX FIFO. The EP0 bit in the USBTXIS register is also set in this situation. Software must clear this bit after the packet has been read from the FIFO to acknowledge that the data has been read from the FIFO. This bit is cleared by writing a 1 to the RXRDYC bit.
	USB Receive Control and Status Endpoint 1–7 High (USBRXCSRH1–7) Registers–OTG A/Host
7	AUTOCL	0	Auto Clear: 0: No effect. 1: Enables the RXRDY bit to be automatically cleared when a packet of USBRXMAXPn bytes has been unloaded from the receive FIFO. When packets of less than the maximum packet size are unloaded, RXRDY must be

(*continued*)

Table 9.20d (*Continued*)

Bit	Name	Reset	Function
			cleared manually. Care must be taken when using µDMA to unload the receive FIFO as data is read from the receive FIFO in 4 byte chunks regardless of the value of the MAXLOAD field in the USBRXMAXPn register.
6	AUTORQ	0	Auto Request: 0: No effect; 1: Enable the REQPKT bit to be automatically set when the RXRDY bit is cleared.
5	DMAEN	0	DMA Request Enable: 0: Disables the DMA request for the transmit endpoint. 1: Enables the DMA request for the transmit endpoint.
4	PIDERR	0	PID Error: 0: No error; 1: Indicates a PID error in the received packet of an isochronous transaction.
3	DMAMOD	0	DMA Request Mode: 0: An interrupt is generated after every DMA packet transfer. 1: An interrupt is generated only after the entire DMA transfer is complete.
2	DTWE	0	Data Toggle Write Enable: 0: The DT bit cannot be written. 1: Enables the current state of the endpoint 0 data toggle to be written (see DT bit).
1	DT	0	Data Toggle: When read, this bit indicates the current state of the endpoint 0 data toggle. If DTWE is set, this bit may be written with the required setting of the data toggle. If DTWE is Low, this bit cannot be written. Care should be taken when writing to this bit as it should only be changed to RESET USB endpoint 0.
0	Reserved	0	Receive
			USB Receive Control and Status Endpoint 1~7 High (USBRXCSRH1~7) Registers–OTG B/Device
7	AUTOCL	0	Auto Clear: 0: No effect. 1: Enables the RXRDY bit to be automatically cleared when a packet of USBRXMAXPn bytes has been unloaded from the receive FIFO. When packets of less than the maximum packet size are unloaded, RXRDY must be cleared manually. Care must be taken when using µDMA to unload the receive FIFO as data is read from the receive FIFO in 4 byte chunks regardless of the value of the MAXLOAD field in the USBRXMAXPn register.
6	ISO	0	Isochronous Transfers: 0: Enables the transmit endpoint for bulk or interrupt transfers. 1: Enables the transmit endpoint for isochronous transfers.
5	DMAEN	0	DMA Request Enable: 0: Disables the DMA request for the transmit endpoint. 1: Enables the DMA request for the transmit endpoint.
4	PIDERR	0	Disable NYET/PID Error: 0: No error; 1: Indicates a PID error in the received packet of an isochronous transaction.
3	DMAMOD	0	DMA Request Mode: 0: An interrupt is generated after every DMA packet transfer. 1: An interrupt is generated only after the entire DMA transfer is complete.
2:0	Reserved	0	Reserved.

bit fields and configurations for both mode registers are same, which means that for the OTG A/Host and the OTG B/Device modes, they have the same bit fields and structures with two different registers. The USBTXFIFOADD and the USBRXFIFOADD are both 16-bit registers and used to control the start address of the selected transmitting and receiving endpoint FIFOs.

Figure 9.30. Bit fields for the USB FIFO-related registers.

Table 9.21. Bit value and its function for USB FIFO-related registers.

Bit	Name	Reset	Function
	USB Transmit FIFO Start Address Register (USBTXFIFOADD)—OTG A/Host and OTG B/Device		
15:9	Reserved	0x00	Reserved.
8:0	ADDR	0x00	Transmit/Receive Start Address (Start address of the endpoint FIFO): 0x0: 0; 0x1: 8; 0x2: 16; 0x3: 24; 0x4: 32; 0x5: 40; 0x6: 48; 0x7: 56; 0x8: 64 . . . . . . 0x1FF: 4095
	USB Receive FIFO Start Address Register (USBRXFIFOADD)—OTG A/Host and OTG B/Device		
15:9	Reserved	0x00	Reserved.
8:0	ADDR	0x00	Transmit/Receive Start Address (Start address of the endpoint FIFO): 0x0: 0; 0x1: 8; 0x2: 16; 0x3: 24; 0x4: 32; 0x5: 40; 0x6: 48; 0x7: 56; 0x8: 64 . . . . . . 0x1FF: 4095
	USB Transmit Dynamic FIFO Sizing Register (USBTXFIFOSZ)—OTG A/Host and OTG B/Device		
7:5	Reserved	0x00	Reserved.
4	DPB	0	Double Packet Buffer Support: 0: Only single-packet buffering is supported. 1: Double-packet buffering is supported.
3:0	SIZE	0x0	Max Packet Size (If DPB = 0, the FIFO also is this size; if DPB = 1, the FIFO is twice this size): 0x0: 8; 0x1: 16; 0x2: 32; 0x3: 64; 0x4: 128; 0x5: 256; 0x6: 512; 0x7: 1024; 0x8: 2048; 0x9–0xF: Reserved
	USB Receive Dynamic FIFO Sizing Register (USBRXFIFOSZ)—OTG A/Host and OTG B/Device		
7:5	Reserved	0x00	Reserved.
4	DPB	0	Double Packet Buffer Support: 0: Only single-packet buffering is supported. 1: Double-packet buffering is supported.
3:0	SIZE	0x0	Max Packet Size (If DPB = 0, the FIFO also is this size; if DPB = 1, the FIFO is twice this size): 0x0: 8; 0x1: 16; 0x2: 32; 0x3: 64; 0x4: 128; 0x5: 256; 0x6: 512; 0x7: 1024; 0x8: 2048; 0x9–0xF: Reserved

The USBTXFIFOSZ and the USBRXFIFOSZ are 8-bit registers and they allow the selected TX/RX endpoint FIFOs to be dynamically sized. The USBEPIDX register is used to configure each transmit endpoint's FIFO size.

The bit fields and functions of these registers are shown in Table 9.21.

9.4.6.5 USB-Interrupt-Related Registers

The registers in this group are used to control and manage the USB interrupts:

- USB Interrupt Enable Register (USBIE)
- USB Transmit Interrupt Enable Register (USBTXIE)
- USB Receive Interrupt Enable Register (USBRXIE)
- USB Transmit Interrupt Status Register (USBTXIS)
- USB Receive Interrupt Status Register (USBRXIS)
- USB General Interrupt Status Register (USBIS)

Figure 9.31 shows the bit fields of these registers. All registers in this group are paired and one is for the OTG A/Host and the other is for the OTG B/Device used.

The bit fields and functions of these registers are shown in Table 9.22.

USB Interrupt Enable Register (USBIE) OTG A/Host

VBUSERR	SESREQ	DISCON	CONN	SOF	BABBLE	RESUME	

USB Interrupt Enable Register (USBIE) OTG B/Device

		DISCON		SOF	RESET	RESUME	SUSPEND

USB Transmit Interrupt Enable (USBTXIE) – Both Modes

								EP7	EP6	EP5	EP4	EP3	EP2	EP1	EP0

USB Receive Interrupt Enable (USBRXIE) – Both Modes

								EP7	EP6	EP5	EP4	EP3	EP2	EP1	

USB Transmit Interrupt Status (USBTXIS) – Both Modes

								EP7	EP6	EP5	EP4	EP3	EP2	EP1	EP0

USB Receive Interrupt Status (USBRXIS) – Both Modes

								EP7	EP6	EP5	EP4	EP3	EP2	EP1	

USB General Interrupt Status (USBIS) OTG A/Host

VBUSERR	SESREQ	DISCON	CONN	SOF	BABBLE	RESUME	

USB General Interrupt Status (USBIS) OTG B/Device

		DISCON		SOF	RESET	RESUME	SUSPEND

Figure 9.31.   Bit fields for the USB interrupts related registers.

Table 9.22.   Bit value and its function for USB interrupts related registers.

Bit	Name	Reset	Function
USB Interrupt Enable Register (USBIE)–OTG A/Host			
7	VBUSERR	0	Enable VBUS Error Interrupt: 0: The VBUSERR interrupt is suppressed and not sent to the interrupt controller. 1: An interrupt is sent to interrupt controller when VBUSERR bit in the USBIS register is set.
6	SESREQ	0	Enable Session Request: 0: The SESREQ interrupt is suppressed and not sent to the interrupt controller. 1: An interrupt is sent to interrupt controller when SESREEQ bit in the USBIS register is set.
5	DISCON	0	Enable Disconnect Interrupt: 0: The DISCON interrupt is suppressed and not sent to the interrupt controller. 1: An interrupt is sent to interrupt controller when DISCON bit in the USBIS register is set.
4	CONN	0	Enable Connect Interrupt: 0: The CONN interrupt is suppressed and not sent to the interrupt controller. 1: An interrupt is sent to interrupt controller when the CONN bit in the USBIS register is set.
3	SOF	0	Enable Start-of-Frame Interrupt: 0: The SOF interrupt is suppressed and not sent to the interrupt controller. 1: An interrupt is sent to the interrupt controller when the SOF bit in the USBIS register is set.
2	BABBLE	0	Enable Babble Interrupt: 0: The BABBLE interrupt is suppressed and not sent to the interrupt controller. 1: An interrupt is sent to interrupt controller when the BABBLE bit in the USBIS register is set.
1	RESUME	0	Enable RESUME Interrupt: 0: The RESUME interrupt is suppressed and not sent to the interrupt controller. 1: An interrupt is sent to interrupt controller when the RESUME bit in the USBIS register is set.
0	Reserved	0	Reserved.
USB Interrupt Enable Register (USBIE)–OTG B/Device			
7:6	Reserved	0x0	Reserved.
5	DISCON	0	Enable Disconnect Interrupt: 0: The DISCON interrupt is suppressed and not sent to the interrupt controller. 1: An interrupt is sent to interrupt controller when DISCON bit in the USBIS register is set.
4	Reserved	0x0	Reserved.
3	SOF	0	Enable Start-of-Frame Interrupt: 0: The SOF interrupt is suppressed and not sent to the interrupt controller. 1: An interrupt is sent to the interrupt controller when the SOF bit in the USBIS register is set.
2	RESET	0	Enable RESET Interrupt: 0: The RESET interrupt is suppressed and not sent to the interrupt controller. 1: An interrupt is sent to the interrupt controller when RESET bit in the USBIS register is set.
1	RESUME	0	Enable RESUME Interrupt: 0: The RESUME interrupt is suppressed and not sent to the interrupt controller. 1: An interrupt is sent to interrupt controller when the RESUME bit in the USBIS register is set.
0	SUSPEND	0	Enable SUSPEND Interrupt: 0: The SUSPEND interrupt is suppressed and not sent to the interrupt controller. 1: An interrupt is sent to the interrupt controller when SUSPEND bit in USBIS register is set.

Table 9.22 (*Continued*)

Bit	Name	Reset	Function
	USB Transmit Interrupt Enable (USBTXIE)—OTG A/Host and OTG B/Device		
15:8	Reserved	0x00	Reserved.
7	EP7	0	TX Endpoint 7 Interrupt Enable: 0: The EP7 transmit interrupt is suppressed and not sent to the interrupt controller. 1: An interrupt is sent to the interrupt controller when EP7 bit in the USBTXIS register is set.
6:0	EP6:EP0	0x0	TX Endpoints 6–0 Interrupts Enable. Same definitions as EP7.
	USB Receive Interrupt Enable (USBRXIE)—OTG A/Host and OTG B/Device		
15:8	Reserved	0x00	Reserved.
7	EP7	0	RX Endpoint 7 Interrupt Enable: 0: The EP7 receive interrupt is suppressed and not sent to the interrupt controller. 1: An interrupt is sent to the interrupt controller when EP7 bit in the USBRXIS register is set.
6:0	EP6:EP0	0x0	RX Endpoints 6–0 Interrupts Enable. Same definitions as EP7.
	USB Transmit Interrupt Status (USBTXIS)—OTG A/Host and OTG B/Device		
15:8	Reserved	0x00	Reserved.
7	EP7	0	TX Endpoint 7 Interrupt Status: 0: No interrupt. 1: An endpoint 7 transmit interrupt is generated.
6:0	EP6:EP0	0x0	TX Endpoints 6–0 Interrupts Statuses. Same definitions as EP7.
	USB Receive Interrupt Status (USBRXIS)—OTG A/Host and OTG B/Device		
15:8	Reserved	0x00	Reserved.
7	EP7	0	RX Endpoint 7 Interrupt Status: 0: No interrupt. 1: An endpoint 7 receive interrupt is generated.
6:0	EP6:EP0	0x0	RX Endpoints 6–0 Interrupts Statuses. Same definitions as EP7.
	USB General Interrupt Status (USBIS)—OTG A/Host		
7	VBUSERR	0	VBUS Error Interrupt Status: 0: No interrupt. 1: A VBUS interrupt is generated.
6	SESREQ	0	Session Request Status: 0: No interrupt. 1: A Session Request interrupt is generated.
5	DISCON	0	Disconnect Interrupt Status: 0: No interrupt. 1: A Disconnect interrupt is generated.
4	CONN	0	Connect Interrupt Status: 0: No interrupt. 1: A Connect interrupt is generated.
3	SOF	0	Start-of-Frame Interrupt Status: 0: No interrupt. 1: A SOF interrupt is generated.
2	BABBLE	0	Babble Interrupt Status: 0: No interrupt. 1: A Babble interrupt is generated.
1	RESUME	0	RESUME Interrupt Status: 0: No interrupt. 1: A RESUME interrupt is generated.
0	Reserved	0	Reserved.
	USB General Interrupt Status (USBIS)—OTG B/Device		
7:6	Reserved	0x00	Reserved.
5	DISCON	0	Disconnect Interrupt Status: 0: No interrupt. 1: A Disconnect interrupt is generated and the device has been discounted from the host.
4	Reserved	0	Reserved.
3	SOF	0	Start-of-Frame Interrupt Status: 0: No interrupt; 1: A SOF interrupt is generated and a new frame starts.
2	RESET	0	RESET Signal Detected: 0: No interrupt; 1: A RESET interrupt occurred.
1	RESUME	0	RESUME Interrupt Detected: 0: No interrupt; 1: A RESUME interrupt is detected.
0	SUSPEND	0	SUSPEND Interrupt Detected: 0: No interrupt; 1: A SUSPEND interrupt is detected.

9.4.7 The USB Initializations and Configurations

The USB initializations and configurations process can be divided into three layers:

1. Enable and clock the USB controller and related GPIO Ports and pins
2. USB control pins configurations
3. Endpoint configurations

9.4.7.1 Enable and Clock the USB Controller and Related GPIO Ports and Pins

Perform the following operations to complete this configuration:

- To drive the USB Controller, the clock must be enabled via the RCGCUSB register. In addition, the clock to the appropriate GPIO module must be enabled via the RCGCGPIO register. Configure the PMCx fields in the GPIOPCTL register and AFSEL bits on the GPIOAFSEL register to assign the USB signals to the appropriate pins (refer to Table 9.18).

- The initial configuration also requires that the processor enables the USB controller and USB controller's physical layer interface (PHY) before setting any registers. When the USB module is in operation, MOSC must be the clock source, either with or without using the PLL, and the system clock must be at least 20 MHz.

- The next step is to enable the USB PLL so that the correct clocking is provided to the PHY. To ensure that the voltage is supplied to the bus correctly, the external power control signal, USB0EPEN, should not be driven on start up by configuring the USB0EPEN and USB0PFLT pins to be controlled by the USB controller and not exhibit their default GPIO behavior. This step is optional since the USBEPEN is optionally used in the host mode to control an external power source to supply power to the USB bus.

- When used in the OTG mode, USB0VBUS and USB0ID do not require any configuration as they are dedicated pins for the USB controller and directly connect to the USB connector's VBUS and ID signals.

- If the USB controller is used as either a dedicated host or device, the DEVMODOTG and DEVMOD bits in the USB General-Purpose Control and Status (USBGPCS) register can be used to connect the USB0VBUS and USB0ID inputs to fixed levels internally, allowing the PB0 and PB1 pins for GPIO usage.

- For proper self-powered Device operation, the VBUS value must still be monitored to assure that if the host removes VBUS, the self-powered Device disables the D+/D- pull-up resistors. This function can be accomplished by connecting a standard GPIO to VBUS.

9.4.7.2 USB Control Pins Configurations

When the USB controller is acting as a host, it is controlled by two signals that are attached to an external voltage supply that provides power to VBUS. The host controller uses the USB0EPEN signal to enable or disable the external power to the USB0VBUS pin on the USB connector. An input pin, USB0PFLT, provides feedback when there has been a power fault on VBUS. The USB0PFLT signal can be configured to automatically negate the USB0EPEN signal to disable power, and/or it can generate an interrupt to the interrupt controller to allow software to handle the power fault condition.

Optionally, when using the device controller portion of the USB controller in a system that also provides host functionality, the power to VBUS must be disabled to allow the external Host controller to supply power. Usually, the USB0EPEN signal is used to control the external regulator and should be negated to avoid having two devices driving the USB0VBUS power pin on the USB connector.

The polarity and actions related to both USB0EPEN and USB0PFLT are fully configurable in the USB controller. The controller also provides interrupts on device insertion and removal to allow the host controller code to respond to these external events.

9.4.7.3 Endpoint Configurations

Before starting communications in the host or the device mode, the endpoint registers must first be configured. In the host mode, this configuration establishes a connection between an endpoint register and an endpoint on a device. In the device mode, an endpoint must be configured before enumerating to the host controller:

- In both cases, the endpoint 0 configuration is limited because it is a fixed-function, fixed-FIFO-size endpoint.
- In the device and host modes, the endpoint requires almost no setup but does require a software-based state machine to progress through the setup, data, and status phases of a standard control transaction.
- In the device mode, the configurations for all remaining endpoints must be done before the enumerating process starts.
- In the host mode, the endpoints must be configured to operate as control, bulk, interrupt, or isochronous mode.
- Once the type of endpoint is configured, a FIFO area must be assigned to each endpoint. In the case of bulk, control, and interrupt endpoints, each has a maximum of 64 bytes per transaction. Isochronous endpoints can have packets with up to 1023 bytes per packet. In either mode, the maximum packet size for the given endpoint must be set prior to sending or receiving data.
- Configuring each endpoint's FIFO involves reserving a portion of the overall USB FIFO RAM to each endpoint. The total FIFO RAM available is 2 Kbytes with the first 64 bytes reserved for endpoint 0. The endpoint's FIFO must be at least as large as the maximum packet size. The FIFO can also be configured as a double-buffered FIFO so that interrupts occur at the end of each packet and allow filling the other half of the FIFO.
- If operating as a device, the USB device controller's soft connect must be enabled when the device is ready to start communications, indicating to the host controller that the device is ready to start the enumeration process.
- If operating as a host controller, the device soft connect must be disabled and power must be provided to VBUS via the USB0EPEN signal.

Generally speaking, the USB system is a complicated system including a huge set of registers and control functions with a lot of options and configuration selections, especially for the OTG implementations.

Next let's use an example project to illustrate how to use USB host and device to transmit and receive data via USB bus with host and device endpoints.

9.4.8 A USB Implementation Example Project

In this project, we use the DRA model to build a project to utilize endpoint 1 as a USB device and endpoint 2 as a USB host. Both the host and the device are working in the IN mode.

The design and implementation of this project include the following steps:

1. Create a new USB project named DRAUSBHostDevice.
2. Initialize and configure the USB endpoint 1 as a device working in the IN mode.
3. Initialize and configure the USB endpoint 2 as a host working in the IN mode, too.
4. Initialize and configure the host and device related FIFOs.
5. Make the IN device to place 64 bytes data as a packet to the device transmit FIFO.
6. Transmit that 64 bytes packet to the host via the USB bus.
7. Enable the IN host to receive that 64-byte packet in the host receive FIFO.
8. Pick up the 64-byte packet from the host FIFO.

Both endpoints are working as dedicated host and device without OTG mode and external power being related. Since we can connect the USB0VBUS and USB0ID via the USB General-Purpose Control and Status (USBGPCS) register to the fixed levels internally, we do not need to use the PB1 and PB0 pins and can release them to work as GPIO pins.

The first part codes for this project are shown in Figure 9.32.

The second part codes for this project are shown in Figure 9.33.

```
//*************************************************************************************
// DRAUSBHostDevice.c - Main Application File for USB as a Host and a Device – Both IN Mode
//*************************************************************************************
#include <stdint.h>
#include <stdbool.h>
#include "TM4C123GH6PM.h"
void  USBDevice_Init(void);
void  USBHost_Init(void);
uint32_t  USBDevice_SendData(void);
uint32_t  USBDevice_PutData(uint8_t *pui8Data, uint32_t ui32Size);
void  USBHost_RecvData(uint8_t *pui8Data, uint32_t ui32Size);
int main(void)
{
   uint8_t  ret, SndData[64], RevData[64];
   for (ret = 0; ret < 64; ret++)              // initialize sending data array
     SndData[ret] = ret;
   SYSCTL->RCGCUSB = 0x1;                // enable the USB module
   SYSCTL->RCGCGPIO = 0x20;             // enable GPIO Port F
   GPIOF->DIR = 0xF;                    // set PF3 ~ PF0 as output pins
   GPIOF->DEN = 0xF;                    // set PF3 ~ PF0 as digital function pins
   USBDevice_Init();
   USBHost_Init();
   ret = USBDevice_PutData(SndData, 64);
   if (ret != 0) { return 1;}
   ret = USBDevice_SendData();
   if (ret != 0) { return 1;}
   USB0->DEVCTL = 0x1;                  // start a session
   USBHost_RecvData(RevData, 64);
   while(1);
}
```

Figure 9.32. The first part codes for the project DRAUSBHostDevice.

```
31  void USBDevice_Init(void)                         // the device is endpoint 1 (IN Device)
32  {
33      USB0->EPIDX = 0x1;                             // set endpoint 1
34      USB0->TXMAXP1 = 64;                            // set the max transmit packet size as 64
35      USB0->TXCSRH1 = 0x80;                          // enable AUTOSET in USBTXCSRH1 register (Auto set of TXPKTRDY
36                                                     // when max packet size has been loaded into the FIFO).
37      USB0->TXCSRH1 |= 0x20;                         // set device IN endpoint 1 as TX mode
38      USB0->TXCSRL1 |= 0x40;                         // Reset the Data toggle to zero
39      USB0->TXFIFOSZ = 0x3;                          // set the transmit FIFO size for endpoint 1 (64B)
40      USB0->TXFIFOADD = 0x8;                         // set device IN endpoint 1 FIFO starting at address 64
41      USB0->POWER |= 0x40;                           // set SOFTCONN to connect the device to the USB bus
42  }

43  uint32_t USBDevice_PutData(uint8_t *pui8Data, uint32_t ui32Size)
44  {
45      if (USB0->TXCSRL1 & 0x1)                       // check if TXRDY in TXCSRL1 is already set (FIFO is full)
46          return 1;                                  // if it is, return 1 to indicate this case
47      for (; ui32Size > 0; ui32Size--)
48      {
49          USB0->FIFO1 = *pui8Data++;
50      }
51      return 0;
52  }

53  uint32_t USBDevice_SendData(void)
54  {
55      if (USB0->TXCSRL1 & 0x1)                       // check if TXRDY in TXCSRL1 is already set (FIFO is full)
56          return 1;                                  // if it is, return 1 to indicate this case
57      USB0->TXCSRL1 = 0x1;                           // set TXRDY to begin to transmit data
58      return 0;
59  }

60  void USBHost_Init(void)                            // the host is endpoint 2 (IN Host)
61  {
62      USB0->EPIDX = 0x2;                             // set endpoint 2 as host
63      USB0->RXMAXP2 = 64;                            // set the max receive packet size as 64
64      USB0->RXTYPE2 = 0xA1;                          // full-speed, bulk with  target endpoint 1
65      USB0->RXINTERVAL2 = 0x10;                      // max number of frame as 255
66      USB0->RXCSRH2 = 0xC0;                          // enable auto clear RXRDY bit when a packet is unloaded from host FIFO
67                                                     // and allow auto set REQPKT when RXRDY is cleared to request next packet
68      USB0->RXFIFOADD = 0x8;                         // set host IN endpoint 2 FIFO starting at address 64
69      USB0->GPCS = 0x2;                              // use the internal signal levels to release PB0 & PB1 pins
70      USB0->POWER = 0x8;                             // reset the host
71  }

72  void USBHost_RecvData(uint8_t *pui8Data, uint32_t ui32Size)
73  {
74      GPIOF->DATA = 0x4;                             // set blue color LED on
75      for (; ui32Size > 0; ui32Size--)
76          pui8Data[ui32Size - 1] = USB0->FIFO2;      // pick up data from host endpoint 2 FIFO
77  }
```

Figure 9.33. The second part codes for the project DRAUSBHostDevice.

Now let's have a closer look at these pieces of codes to see how they work.

1. Five user-defined functions are declared in lines 7~11, and these functions are used to access and configure the related USB endpoints and perform associated data operations.

2. In line 14, one local variable `ret` and two data arrays, `Snddata[64]` and `RevData[64]`, are declared and these are used to transmit and receive data packets in different modes.

3. The transmit data array `SndData[]` is initialized by assigning 64 numbers and characters to it in lines 15~16.

4. The USB module and the GPIO Port F are enabled and clocked in lines 17 and 18.

5. The PF3~PF0 pins are configured to work as digital function and output pins in lines 19 and 20. The reason for these configurations is that we need to use some LEDs connected to PF3~PF1 pins later.

6. Both user-defined functions, USBDevice_Init() and USBHost_Init(), are called in lines 21 and 22 to initialize and configure USB endpoint 1 and endpoint 2 as the IN device and IN host, respectively.

7. In lines 23 and 24, another user-defined function USBDevice_PutData() is called to place a 64-byte packet, SndData[], into the device transmit FIFO. The length of this packet is 64 bytes, which is the second argument of this function. If this function is executed successfully, it returns a 0; otherwise a nonzero value is returned if it is failed. Similarly, a nonzero value is returned to the system if anything is wrong for calling this function.

8. Another user-defined function USBDevice_SendData() is called in lines 25 and 26 to transmit this 64-byte packet to the host via the USB bus.

9. In line 27, a session is started by setting the SESSION bit in the USB Device Control Register (DEVCTL).

10. The user-defined function USBHost_RecvData() is called in line 28 to pick up the 64-byte packet data sent by the endpoint 1 device IN. The first argument of this function is the data array RevData[] that is passed as a pointer to this function, and the second argument is the size of the packet.

11. In line 29, an infinitive while() loop is used to hold the project to run and check the this host and device communication result.

12. The codes in lines 31~42 are used for the function USBDevice_Init() to initialize and configure the USB endpoint 1 as an IN device.

13. First the USB Endpoint Index Register (EPIDX) is configured by assigning the EPIDX field as 0x1 to indicate that this endpoint works as the endpoint 1 in line 33.

14. In line 34, the USB Maximum Transmit Data Endpoint 1 Register (TXMAXP1) is configured by assigning the maximum number of bytes as 64 for each packet to be transmitted to the host.

15. The USB Transmit Control and Status Endpoint 1 High Register (TXCSRH1) is configured in line 35 by setting the AUTOSET bit (bit 7) in this register to auto set the bit TXPKTRDY when the max packet size has been loaded into the device transmit FIFO.

16. In line 37, the bit MODE (bit 5) in this TXCSRH1 register is also set to 1 to enable this endpoint to work as a transmit endpoint.

17. The bit CLRDT (bit 6) in the USB Transmit Control and Status Endpoint 1 Low Register (TXCSRL1) is set to 1 to reset the data toggle function to zero in line 38.

18. The USB Transmit Dynamic FIFO Sizing Register (TXFIFOSZ) is configured in line 39 by assigning the SIZE bit-field as 0x3, which means that the maximum size of bytes for a transmitting packet is 64.

19. In line 40, the ADDR bit field in the USB Transmit FIFO Start Address Register (TXFIFOADD) is assigned 0x8 to indicate that the transmit FIFO starting address is 64. The reason for that is because the endpoint 0 occupied the first 64 bytes in either FIFO.

20. The SOFTCONN bit (bit 6) in the USB Power Register (POWER) is set to 1 to connect the device to the USB bus in line 41. A point to be noted is that this register has two modes; one is for the host mode and the other one is for the device mode. One needs to use the device mode to setup this register.

21. The user-defined function USBDevice_PutData() is described by the codes in lines 43~52. The first argument of this function is a pointer pui8Data that is the starting address

of 64 bytes data to be transmitted to the host endpoint, and the second is the size of this packet. The purpose of this function is to place 64 bytes data into the device transmit FIFO before they can be transmitted. Therefore this function should be called before another user-defined function USBDevice_SendData().

22. Before transmitting any packet, one needs to check if the bit TXRDY in the TXCSRL1 register is already set, which means that the device transmit FIFO is full. The bit TXRDY is bit 0 in the TXCSRL1 register, thus a AND with 0x1 can be used to do this checking. If it is full, a 1 is returned to the main program to indicate this situation. The code lines 45 and 46 performed this checking and retuning function.

23. If the FIFO is not full, a for() loop is used to place 64 bytes data into the device transmit FIFO or endpoint 1 FIFO (FIFO1) in lines 47~50.

24. In line 51, a returning 0 indicates that this function is executed successfully.

25. The user-defined function USBDevice_SendData() is described by the codes in lines 53~59. The purpose of this function is to start to transmit 64 bytes data as a packet to the host endpoint 2.

26. In lines 55 and 56, as we did before, first we need to check if the TXRDY has been set. If it is, this means that the packet has been sent and a 1 is returned to the main program.

27. If not, set the bit TXRDY in the TXCSRL1 register to inform the host to start this transmit in line 57.

28. A returning 0 indicates that this function is executed successfully in line 58.

29. The user-defined function USBHost_Init() is described by the codes in lines 60~71. The purpose of this function is to initialize and configure the endpoint 2 as an IN host to receive the packet transmitted by the IN device in endpoint 1.

30. First the USB Endpoint Index Register (EPIDX) is configured by assigning the EPIDX field as 0x2 to indicate that this endpoint works as the endpoint 2 in line 62.

31. In line 63, the USB Maximum Receive Data Endpoint 2 Register (RXMAXP2) is configured by assigning the maximum number of bytes as 64 for each packet to be received by the host.

32. The USB Host Configure Receive Type Endpoint 2 Register (RXTYPE2) is configured in line 64 by assigning 0x2 (full-speed) to the SPEED bit field (bits 7 and 6), 0x2 (Bulk) to the PROTO bit field (bits 5 and 4), and 0x1 (endpoint 1) to the TEP (Target Endpoint Number) bit field (bits 3~0). The resulted assignment value is 0xA1.

33. In line 65, the USB Host Receive Polling Interval Endpoint 2 Register (RXINTERVAL2) is configured to define the number of frames after the endpoint 2 has timeout on receiving a stream of NAK response. Here a value of 0x10 is used to set up this number to 255.

34. The USB Receive Control and Status Endpoint 2 High Register (RXCSRH2) is configured in line 66 by setting the bits AUTOCL (bit 7) and AUTORQ (bit 6) to enable to auto clear the RXRDY bit when a packet is unloaded from the host FIFO and allow to auto set the REQPKT bit when the RXRDY bit is cleared to request the next packet.

35. The USB Receive FIFO Start Address Register (RXFIFOADD) is configured in line 68 to indicate that the receive FIFO starting address is 64. The reason for that is because the endpoint 0 occupied the first 64 bytes in either FIFO.

36. The USB General-Purpose Control and Status Register (GPCS) is configured in line 69 by setting the bit DEVMODOTG (bit 1) and resetting the bit DEVMOD (bit 0) to use the internal ID signals in the host mode to release the PB0 and PB1 pins to enable them to work as general GPIO pins.

37. In line 70, the RESET bit (bit 3) in the USB Power Register (POWER) is set to 1 to generate a Reset function to the entire USB system to start the connect and enumeration process.

38. The user-defined function USBHost_RecvData() is described by the codes in lines 72~77. The first argument of this function is a pointer pui8Data that is the starting address of 64 bytes data to be received by the host endpoint, and the second is the size of this packet. The purpose of this function is to pick up 64 bytes data from the host receive FIFO.

39. First the blue-color LED is turned on by assigning 0x4 to the PF2 pin to indicate that the host picking-up process starts.

40. Then a for() loop is used to get 64 bytes data from the host receive FIFO or endpoint 2 FIFO (FIFO2) in lines 75~76. One point to be noted is that the order of this picking-up process starts from the bottom of the receive FIFO and ends at the top of this FIFO. Therefore the order of the received data stored into the RevData[] array should be opposite to the order of the transmitted data stored in the SndData[] array.

Now let's run this project to test its function.

Build and run the project, and then click on the Debug|Stop menu item to stop the project running. Now check the running result by expanding the RevData[] array from the Call Stack + Locals window, and you can find that the total 64 bytes data have been received and stored in this array in the opposite order. You can compare these 64 bytes data with those stored in the SndData[] array to confirm this order.

9.4.9 The USB API Functions Provided by the TivaWare™ Peripheral Driver Library

A set of USB API functions is provided by the TivaWare™ to assist and help users to build USB-related applications easily and effectively.

These API functions can be divided into different groups based on their functions. The groups are: USBClock, USBMode, USBDev, USBHost, USBOTG, USBEndpoint, USBInterrupt, and USBFIFO.

The USBClock and USBMode API functions are used to globally set up the driving clock and mode for the USB controllers. The APIs in the USBDev group are used with microcontrollers that have a USB device controller. The APIs in the USBHost group can be used with microcontrollers that have a USB host controller. The USBOTG APIs are used by microcontrollers with an OTG interface. With USB OTG controllers, once the mode of the USB controller is configured, the device or host APIs can be used. The remainder of the APIs are used for both USB host and USB device controllers. The USBEndpoint APIs are used to configure and access the endpoints while the USBFIFO APIs are used to configure the size and location of the FIFOs. The USBInterrupt API functions are used to configure and handle USB related interrupts.

In fact, in the TM4C123GH6PM MCU system, all kinds of USB controllers are included.

One important fact is that all endpoints in the USB controller, whether host or device, have two sides to them, allowing each endpoint to both transmit and receive data. An application can use a single endpoint for both IN and OUT transactions. For example: In the device mode, endpoint 1 can be configured to have BULK IN and BULK OUT handled by endpoint 1. It is important to note that the endpoint number used is the endpoint number reported to the host.

For microcontrollers with host controllers, the application can use a single endpoint to communicate with both IN and OUT endpoints of different types as well. For example: Endpoint 2 can be used to communicate with one device's interrupt IN endpoint and another device's bulk OUT endpoint at the same time. This configuration effectively gives the application one dedicated control endpoint for IN or OUT control transactions on endpoint 0, and three, seven, or fifteen IN endpoints and three, seven, or fifteen OUT endpoints, depending on the total number of endpoints on the device.

The USB controller has a global FIFO memory space that can be allocated to endpoints. The overall size of the FIFO RAM is 2048 bytes. It is important to note that the first 64 bytes of this memory are dedicated to endpoint 0 for control transactions.

The remaining 1984 bytes are configurable based on the application requires. The FIFO configuration is usually set up at the beginning of the application and cannot be modified once the USB controller is in use. The FIFO configuration uses the USBFI-FOConfig() API to configure the starting address and the size of the FIFOs that are dedicated to each endpoint.

9.4.9.1 The USBClock and USBMode API Functions

Four API functions are covered by this group:

- USBClockEnable()—Enable the clocking to the USB controller's PHY
- USBClockDisable()—Disable the clocking to the USB controller's PHY
- USBModeConfig()—Change the operating mode of the USB controller
- USBModeGet()—Get the current operating mode of the USB controller

Table 9.23 shows these API functions and their prototypes.

9.4.9.2 The USBDev API Functions

The following API functions are covered by this group:

- USBDevAddrSet()—Set the address in device mode.
- USBDevConnect()—Connect the USB controller to the bus in device mode.
- USBDevEndpointConfigSet()—Set the configuration for a device endpoint.

Table 9.23. The USBClock and USBMode API functions.

API Function	Parameter	Description
void USBClockEnable(uint32_t ui32Base, uint32_t ui32Div, uint32_t ui32Flags)	ui32Base specifies the USB module base address. ui32Div specifies the divider for the input clock. ui32Flags specifies which clock to use for the USB clock.	Configure and enable the USB PHY clock as an input to the USB controller or as output to an externally connect USB PHY. The ui32Flags parameter specifies the clock source with the following values: USB_CLOCK_INTERNAL uses the internal clock for the USB PHY clock source. USB_CLOCK_EXTERNAL specifies that the USB0CLK input pin is used as the USB PHY clock source. The ui32Div is used to specify a divider for the internal clock (480 MHz) if the USB_CLOCK_INTERNAL is specified and is ignored if USB_CLOCK_EXTERNAL is specified. When the USB_CLOCK_INTERNAL is specified, the ui32Div value must be set so that the PLL 480-MHz clock source can be divided into an appropriate value.
void USBClockDisable(uint32_t ui32Base)	ui32Base specifies the USB module base address.	Disable the USB PHY clock input or output.
void USBModeConfig(uint32_t ui32Base, uint32_t ui32Mode)	ui32Base specifies the USB module base address. ui32Mode specifies the operating mode of the USB OTG pins.	Change the operating modes of the USB controller. The ui32Mode value should be one of the following values: USB_MODE_OTG, USB_MODE_HOST, USB_MODE_HOST_VBUS, USB_MODE_DEVICE, USB_MODE_DEVICE_VBUS.
uint32_t USBModeGet(uint32_t ui32Base)	ui32Base specifies the USB module base address.	Return the current operating mode on USB controllers with OTG or Dual mode functionality.

- `USBDevEndpointDataAck()`—Acknowledge that data was read from the given endpoint's FIFO in device mode.
- `USBDevEndpointStatusClear()`—Clear the status bits in this endpoint in device mode.
- `USBDevMode()`—Change the mode of the USB controller to device.
- `USBDevSpeedGet()`—Return the current speed of the USB controller in device mode.

Table 9.24 shows these API functions and their prototypes. All of these API functions must be called in the device mode.

Table 9.24. The USBDev API functions.

API Function	Parameter	Description

void
USBDevAddrSet(
    uint32_t ui32Base,
    uint32_t ui32Address)
	ui32Base specifies the USB module base address.
	ui32Address is the address to use for a device.
		Configure the device address on the USB bus. This address was likely received via a SET ADDRESS command from the host controller. This function must only be called in the device mode.

void USBDevConnect(uint32_t ui32Base)	ui32Base specifies the USB module base address.	Cause the soft connect feature of the USB controller to be enabled. Call USBDevDisconnect() to remove the USB device from the bus.

void
USBDevEndpointConfigSet(
    uint32_t ui32Base,
    uint32_t ui32Endpoint,
    uint32_t ui32MaxPacketSize,
    uint32_t ui32Flags)
	ui32Base specifies the USB module base address.
	ui32Endpoint is the endpoint to access.
	ui32MaxPacketSize is the max packet size for this endpoint.
	ui32Flags are used to configure other endpoint settings.
		Set the basic configuration for an endpoint in device mode. Endpoint 0 does not have a dynamic configuration, so this function must not be called for endpoint 0. The ui32Flags includes some of the configuration as the other parameters provide the rest. The USB_EP_MODE_ flags define what the type is for the given endpoint. USB_EP_MODE_CTRL is a control endpoint. USB_EP_MODE_ISOC is an isochronous endpoint. USB_EP_MODE_BULK is a bulk endpoint. USB_EP_MODE_INT is an interrupt endpoint. When configuring an IN endpoint, the bit USB_EP_AUTO_SET can be specified to cause the automatic transmission of data on the USB bus as soon as ui32MaxPacketSize bytes of data are written into the FIFO for this endpoint. When configuring an OUT endpoint, the bit USB_EP_AUTO_REQUEST is specified to trigger the request for more data once the FIFO has been drained enough to receive ui32MaxPacketSize more bytes of data. Also for OUT endpoints, the USB_EP_AUTO_CLEAR bit can be used to clear the data packet ready flag automatically once the data has been read from the FIFO. If this option is not used, this flag must be manually cleared by USBDevEndpointStatusClear().

void USBDevMode(uint32_t ui32Base)	ui32Base specifies the USB module base address.	Change the mode of the USB controller to device mode. This function must only be called on microcontrollers that support OTG operation and have the DEVMODOTG bit in the USBGPCS register.

void
USBDevEndpointDataAck(
    uint32_t ui32Base,
    uint32_t ui32Endpoint,
    bool bIsLastPacket)
	ui32Base specifies the USB module base address.
	ui32Endpoint is the endpoint to access.
	bIsLastPacket indicates if this packet is the last one.
		Acknowledge that the data was read from the endpoint's FIFO. The bIsLastPacket is set to a true value if this is the last in a series of data packets on endpoint 0. The bIsLastPacket is not used for endpoints other than endpoint 0. This call can be used if processing is required between reading the data and acknowledging that the data has been read.

void
USBDevEndpointStatusClear(
    uint32_t ui32Base,
    uint32_t ui32Endpoint,
    uint32_t ui32Flags)
	ui32Base specifies the USB module base address.
	ui32Endpoint is the endpoint to access.
	ui32Flags are the status bits that are cleared.
		Clear the status of any bits that are passed in the ui32Flags parameter. The ui32Flags can take the value returned from the USBEndpointStatus() call.

uint32_t USBDevSpeedGet(uint32_t ui32Base)	ui32Base specifies the USB module base address.	Return the operating speed of the connection to the USB host controller. This function returns either USB_HIGH_SPEED or USB_FULL_SPEED to indicate the connection speed in device mode.

9.4.9.3 The USBHost API Functions

The following API functions are covered by this group:

- `USBHostAddrSet()` — Set the address in host mode.
- `USBHostEndpointConfig()` — Set the base configuration for a host endpoint.
- `USBHostEndpointDataAck()` — Acknowledge that data was read from the given endpoint's FIFO in host mode.
- `USBHostEndpointStatusClear()` — Clear the status bits in this endpoint in host mode.
- `USBHostMode()` — Change the mode of the USB controller to host.
- `USBHostPwrDisable()` — Disable the external power pin.
- `USBHostRequestIN()` — Schedule a request for an IN transaction on an endpoint in host mode.
- `USBHostRequestINClear()` — Clear a scheduled IN transaction for an endpoint in host mode.
- `USBHostRequestStatus()` — Issue a request for a status IN transaction on endpoint zero.
- `USBHostReset()` — Generate a USB bus reset condition.
- `USBPHYPowerOn()` — Power on the USB PHY.
- `USBPHYPowerOff()` — Power off the USB PHY.

Table 9.25 shows these API functions and their prototypes. All of these API functions must be called in the host mode.

Table 9.25. The USBHost API functions.

API Function	Parameter	Description

void
USBHostAddrSet(
    uint32_t ui32Base,
    uint32_t ui32Endpoint,
    uint32_t ui32Addr,
    uint32_t ui32Flags)
	`ui32Base` specifies the USB module base address. `ui32Endpoint` is the endpoint to access. `ui32Addr` is the functional address for the controller to use for this endpoint. `ui32Flags` determines if this is an IN or an OUT endpoint.	Configure the functional address for a device that is using this endpoint for communication.
		This `ui32Addr` parameter is the address of the target device that this endpoint is communicating with. The `ui32Flags` parameter indicates if the IN or OUT endpoint is set.

void
USBHostEndpointConfig(
    uint32_t ui32Base,
    uint32_t ui32Endpoint,
    uint32_t ui32MaxPayload,
    uint32_t ui32NAKPollInterval,
    uint32_t ui32TargetEndpoint,
    uint32_t ui32Flags)
	`ui32Base` specifies the USB module base address. `ui32Endpoint` is the endpoint to access. `ui32MaxPayload` is the max payload for this endpoint. `ui32NAKPollInterval` is the either the NAK timeout limit or the polling interval, depending on the type of endpoint. `ui32TargetEndpoint` is the endpoint that the host endpoint is targeting. `ui32Flags` are used to configure other endpoint settings.	Set the basic configuration for the transmit or receive portion of an endpoint in host mode. The `ui32Flags` parameter determines some of the configuration while the other parameters provide the rest. The `ui32Flags` parameter determines whether this is an IN endpoint (USB_EP_HOST_IN or USB_EP_DEV_IN) or an OUT endpoint (USB_EP_HOST_OUT or USB_EP_DEV_OUT), whether this is a Full speed (USB_EP_SPEED_FULL) or a Low speed (USB_EP_SPEED_LOW) endpoint.
		The USB_EP_MODE_ flags control the type of the endpoint: USB_EP_MODE_CTRL is a control endpoint. USB_EP_MODE_ISOC is an isochronous endpoint. USB_EP_MODE_BULK is a bulk endpoint. USB_EP_MODE_INT is an interrupt endpoint. There are two special time out values that can be specified when setting the `ui32NAKPollInterval` value. The first is MAX_NAK_LIMIT, which is the maximum value that can be passed in this variable. The other is DISABLE_NAK_LIMIT, which indicates that there is no limit on the number of NAKs. When configuring the OUT portion of an endpoint, the USB_EP_AUTO_SET bit is specified to cause the transmission of

(continued)

Table 9.25 (*Continued*)

API Function	Parameter	Description
		data on the USB bus to start as soon as the number of bytes specified by ui32MaxPayload has been written into the OUT FIFO for this endpoint. When configuring the IN portion of an endpoint, the USB_EP_AUTO_REQUEST bit can be specified to trigger the request for more data once the FIFO has been drained enough to fit ui32MaxPayload bytes. The USB_EP_AUTO_CLEAR bit can be used to clear the data packet ready flag automatically once the data has been read from the FIFO. If this option is not used, this flag must be manually cleared via a call to USBDevEndpointStatusClear() or USBHostEndpointStatusClear().
void USBHostEndpointDataAck(uint32_t ui32Base, uint32_t ui32Endpoint)	ui32Base specifies the USB module base address. ui32Endpoint is the endpoint to access.	Acknowledge that the data was read from the endpoint's FIFO. This call is used if processing is required between reading data & acknowledging the data has been read.
void USBHostEndpointStatusClear(uint32_t ui32Base, uint32_t ui32Endpoint, uint32_t ui32Flags)	ui32Base specifies the USB module base address. ui32Endpoint is the endpoint to access. ui32Flags are the status bits that are cleared.	Clear the status of any bits that are passed in the ui32Flags parameter. The ui32Flags can take the value returned from the USBEndpointStatus() call.
void USBHostMode(uint32_t ui32Base)	ui32Base specifies the USB module base address.	Change the mode of the USB controller to host mode. This function must only be called on microcontrollers that support OTG operation and have the DEVMODOTG bit in the USBGPCS register.
void USBHostPwrDisable(uint32_t ui32Base)	ui32Base specifies the USB module base address.	Disable the USBnEPEN signal, which disables an external power supply in host mode operation. This function must only be called in host mode.
void USBHostRequestIN(uint32_t ui32Base, uint32_t ui32Endpoint)	ui32Base specifies the USB module base address. ui32Endpoint is the endpoint to access.	Schedule a request for an IN transaction. When the USB device being communicated with responds with the data, the data can be retrieved by calling USBEndpointDataGet() or via a DMA transfer.
void USBHostRequestStatus(uint32_t ui32Base)	ui32Base specifies the USB module base address.	Cause a request for a status IN transaction from a device on endpoint 0. This function can only be used with endpoint 0 as that is the only control endpoint.
void USBHostRequestINClear(uint32_t ui32Base, uint32_t ui32Endpoint)	ui32Base specifies the USB module base address. ui32Endpoint is the endpoint to access.	Clear a previously scheduled IN transaction if it is still pending. This function is used to safely disable any scheduled IN transactions if the endpoint specified by ui32Endpoint is reconfigured for communications with other devices.
void USBHostReset(uint32_t ui32Base, bool bStart)	ui32Base specifies the USB module base address. bStart specifies whether to start or stop reset on the USB bus.	When this function is called with the bStart set to true, it causes the start of a reset condition on the USB bus. The caller must then delay at least 20ms before calling this function again with the bStart set to false.
void USBPHYPowerOn(uint32_t ui32Base)	ui32Base specifies the USB module base address.	Power on the USB PHY, enabling it return to normal operation. By default, the PHY is powered on, so this function must only be called if USBPHYPowerOff() has previously been called.
void USBPHYPowerOff(uint32_t ui32Base)	ui32Base specifies the USB module base address.	Power off the USB PHY, reducing the current consumption of the device. While in the powered-off state, the USB controller is unable to operate.

9.4.9.4 The USBEndpoint API Functions

The following API functions are covered by this group:

- USBEndpointDataAvail()—Determine the number of bytes of data available in a given endpoint's FIFO.

- USBEndpointDataGet()—Retrieve data from the given endpoint's FIFO.

- `USBEndpointDataPut()`—Put data into the given endpoint's FIFO.
- `USBEndpointDataSend()`—Start the transfer of data from an endpoint's FIFO.
- `USBEndpointDataToggleClear()`—Sets the data toggle on an endpoint to zero.
- `USBEndpointStatus()`—Return the current status of an endpoint.

Table 9.26 shows these API functions and their prototypes.

Table 9.26. The USBEndpoint API functions.

API Function	Parameter	Description

uint32_t
USBEndpointDataAvail(
  uint32_t ui32Base,
  uint32_t ui32Endpoint)
	ui32Base specifies the USB module base address.
	ui32Endpoint is the endpoint to access.
		Return the number of bytes of data currently available in the FIFO for the given receive (OUT) endpoint. It may be used prior to calling USBEndpointDataGet() to determine the buffer size required to hold the newly-received packet.

int32_t
USBEndpointDataGet(
  uint32_t ui32Base,
  uint32_t ui32Endpoint,
  uint8_t *pui8Data,
  uint32_t *pui32Size)
	ui32Base specifies the USB module base address.
	ui32Endpoint is the endpoint to access.
	pui8Data is a pointer to the data area used to return the data from the FIFO.
	pui32Size is initially the size of the buffer passed into this call via the pui8Data. It is set to the amount of data returned in the buffer.
		Return the data from the FIFO for the given endpoint. The pui32Size indicates the size of the buffer passed in the pui32Data parameter. The data in the pui32Size parameter is changed to match the amount of data returned in the pui8Data parameter. If a 0-byte packet is received, this call does not return an error but instead just returns a 0 in the pui32Size parameter. The only error case occurs when there is no data packet available. This call returns 0, or −1 if no packet was received.

int32_t
USBEndpointDataPut(
  uint32_t ui32Base,
  uint32_t ui32Endpoint,
  uint8_t *pui8Data,
  uint32_t ui32Size)
	pui8Data is a pointer to the data area used as the source for the data to put into the FIFO.
	ui32Size is the amount of data to put into the FIFO.
		Put the data from the pui8Data into the FIFO for this endpoint. If a packet is already pending for transmission, then this call does not put any of the data into the FIFO and returns −1. Care must be taken to not write more data than can fit into the FIFO allocated by the call to USBFIFOConfigSet().

int32_t
USBEndpointDataSend(
  uint32_t ui32Base,
  uint32_t ui32Endpoint,
  uint32_t ui32TransType)
	ui32Base specifies the USB module base address.
	ui32Endpoint is the endpoint to access.
	ui32TransType is set to indicate what type of data is being sent.
		Start the transfer of data from the FIFO for a given endpoint. This function is called if USB_EP_AUTO_SET bit was not enabled for the endpoint. Setting the ui32TransType allows the appropriate signaling on the USB bus for the type of transaction being requested. The ui32TransType must be one of the following: USB_TRANS_OUT for OUT transaction on any endpoint in host mode. USB_TRANS_IN for IN transaction on any endpoint in device mode. USB_TRANS_IN_LAST for the last IN transaction on endpoint 0 in a sequence of IN transactions. USB_TRANS_SETUP for setup transactions on endpoint 0. USB_TRANS_STATUS for status results on endpoint 0. This call returns 0 on success, or −1 if a transmission is already in progress.

void
USBEndpointDataToggleClear(
  uint32_t ui32Base,
  uint32_t ui32Endpoint,
  uint32_t ui32Flags)
	ui32Base specifies the USB module base address.
	ui32Endpoint specifies the endpoint to reset the data toggle.
	ui32Flags specifies whether to access the IN or OUT endpoint.
		Cause the USB controller to clear the data toggle for an endpoint. This call is not valid for endpoint 0 and can be made with host or device controllers. The ui32Flags parameter must be one of: USB_EP_HOST_OUT, USB_EP_HOST_IN, USB_EP_DEV_OUT, or USB_EP_DEV_IN.

uint32_t
USBEndpointStatus(
  uint32_t ui32Base,
  uint32_t ui32Endpoint)
	ui32Base specifies the USB module base address.
	ui32Endpoint is the endpoint to access.
		Return the status of a given endpoint. If any of these status bits must be cleared, then the USBDevEndpointStatusClear() or the USBHostEndpointStatusClear() must be called.

9.4.9.5 The USBFIFO API Functions

The following API functions are covered by this group:

- USBFIFOAddrGet() – Returns the absolute FIFO address for a given endpoint.
- USBFIFOConfigGet() - Returns the FIFO configuration for an endpoint.
- USBFIFOConfigSet() - Sets the FIFO configuration for an endpoint.
- USBFIFOFlush() - Forces a flush of an endpoint's FIFO.
- USBFrameNumberGet() - Get the current frame number.

Table 9.27 shows these API functions and their prototypes.

9.4.9.6 The USBInterrupt API Functions

The following API functions are covered by this group:

- USBIntEnableControl()—Enable control interrupts on a given USB controller.
- USBIntDisableControl()—Disable control interrupts on a given USB controller.
- USBIntEnableEndpoint()—Enable endpoint interrupts on a given USB controller.

Table 9.27. The USBFIFO API functions.

API Function	Parameter	Description
uint32_t USBFIFOAddrGet(uint32_t ui32Base, uint32_t ui32Endpoint)	ui32Base specifies the USB module base address. ui32Endpoint specifies which endpoint's FIFO address to return.	Return the actual physical address of the FIFO. This address is needed when the USB is going to be used with the uDMA controller and the source or destination address must be set to the physical FIFO address for a given endpoint.
void USBFIFOConfigGet(uint32_t ui32Base, uint32_t ui32Endpoint, uint32_t *pui32FIFOAddress, uint32_t *pui32FIFOSize, uint32_t ui32Flags)	ui32Endpoint is the endpoint. pui32FIFOAddress is the starting address for the FIFO. pui32FIFOSize is the size of the FIFO as specified by one of the USB_FIFO_SZ_ values. ui32Flags specifies what information to retrieve from the FIFO configuration.	Return the starting address and size of the FIFO for a given endpoint. Endpoint 0 does not have a dynamically configurable FIFO, so this function must not be called for endpoint 0. The ui32Flags parameter specifies whether the endpoint's OUT or IN FIFO must be read. If in host mode, the ui32Flags must be USB_EP_HOST_OUT or USB_EP_HOST_IN, and if in device mode, the ui32Flags parameter must be either USB_EP_DEV_OUT or USB_EP_DEV_IN.
void USBFIFOConfigSet(uint32_t ui32Base, uint32_t ui32Endpoint, uint32_t ui32FIFOAddress, uint32_t ui32FIFOSize, uint32_t ui32Flags)	ui32Base specifies the USB module base address. ui32Endpoint is the endpoint to access. ui32FIFOAddress is the starting address for the FIFO. ui32FIFOSize is the size of the FIFO specified by one of the USB_FIFO_SZ_ values. ui32Flags specifies what information to set in the FIFO configuration.	Configure the starting FIFO RAM address and size of the FIFO for a given endpoint. Endpoint 0 does not have a dynamically configurable FIFO, so this function must not be called for endpoint 0. The ui32FIFOSize must be one of the values in the USB_FIFO_SZ_ values. The ui32FIFOAddress value must be a multiple of 8 bytes and directly indicates the starting address in the USB controller's FIFO RAM. For example, a value of 64 indicates that the FIFO starts 64 bytes into the USB controller's FIFO memory. The ui32Flags value specifies whether the endpoint's OUT or IN FIFO must be configured. If in host mode, use USB_EP_HOST_OUT or USB_EP_HOST_IN, and if in device mode, use USB_EP_DEV_OUT or USB_EP_DEV_IN.
void USBFIFOFlush(uint32_t ui32Base, uint32_t ui32Endpoint, uint32_t ui32Flags)	ui32Base specifies the USB module base address. ui32Endpoint is the endpoint to access. ui32Flags specifies if the IN or OUT endpoint is accessed.	Force the USB controller to flush out the data in the FIFO. The function can be called with either host or device controllers and requires the ui32Flags parameter be one of: USB_EP_HOST_OUT, USB_EP_HOST_IN, USB_EP_DEV_OUT, or USB_EP_DEV_IN.
uint32_t USBFrameNumberGet(uint32_t ui32Base)	ui32Base specifies the USB module base address.	This function returns the last frame number received.

- `USBIntDisableEndpoint()`—Disable endpoint interrupts on a given USB controller.
- `USBIntRegister()`—Register an interrupt handler for the USB controller.
- `USBIntStatusControl()`—Return the control interrupt status on a given USB controller.
- `USBIntStatusEndpoint()`—Return the endpoint interrupt status on a given USB controller.
- `USBIntUnregister()`—Unregister an interrupt handler for the USB controller.

Table 9.28 shows these API functions and their prototypes. To save space, we only discuss the Enable and Register API functions.

Table 9.28. The USBInterrupt API functions.

API Function	Parameter	Description
void USBIntEnableControl(uint32_t ui32Base, uint32_t ui32Flags)	ui32Base specifies the USB module base address. ui32Flags specifies which control interrupts to enable.	Enable the control interrupts for the USB controller specified by the ui32Base parameter. The ui32Flags specifies which control interrupts to enable. The flags passed in the ui32Flags parameters must be the definitions that start with USB_INTCTRL__ and not any other USB_INT flags.
void USBIntEnableEndpoint(uint32_t ui32Base, uint32_t ui32Flags)	ui32Base specifies the USB module base address. ui32Flags specifies which endpoint interrupts to enable.	Enable endpoint interrupts for the USB controller specified by the ui32Base parameter. The ui32Flags specifies which endpoint interrupts to enable. The flags passed in the ui32Flags parameters must be the definitions that start with USB_INTEP__ and not any other USB_INT flags.
void USBIntRegister(uint32_t ui32Base, void (*pfnHandler)(void))	ui32Base specifies the USB module base address. pfnHandler is a pointer to the function to be called when a USB interrupt occurs.	Register the handler to be called when a USB Interrupt occurs and enables the global USB interrupt in the interrupt controller. The specific desired USB interrupts must be enabled via a separate call to USBIntEnable(). It is the interrupt handler's responsibility to clear the interrupt sources via calls to USBIntStatusControl() and USBIntStatusEndpoint().
uint32_t USBIntStatusControl(uint32_t ui32Base)	ui32Base specifies the USB module base address.	Read control interrupt status for a USB controller. This call returns the current status for control interrupts only, the endpoint interrupt status is retrieved by calling USBIntStatusEndpoint(). The bit values returned are compared against the USB_INTCTRL__ values. This call clears the source of all of the control status interrupts. The following are the meanings of all USB_INCTRL_ flags and the modes for which they are valid. These values apply to any calls to USBIntStatusControl(), USBIntEnableControl(), USBIntDisableControl(). Some of these flags are only valid in the following modes as indicated in the parentheses: Host, Device, and OTG. USB_INTCTRL_ALL—A full mask of all control interrupt sources. USB_INTCTRL_VBUS_ERR—A VBUS error has occurred (Host Only). USB_INTCTRL_SESSION—Session Start Detected on A-side of cable (OTG Only). USB_INTCTRL_SESSION_END—Session End Detected (Device Only) USB_INTCTRL_DISCONNECT—Device Disconnect Detected (Host Only) USB_INTCTRL_CONNECT—Device Connect Detected (Host Only) USB_INTCTRL_SOF—Start of Frame Detected. USB_INTCTRL_BABBLE—USB controller detected a device signaling past the end of a frame (Host Only) USB_INTCTRL_RESET—Reset signaling detected by device (Device Only) USB_INTCTRL_RESUME—Resume signaling detected. USB_INTCTRL_SUSPEND—Suspend signaling detected by device (Device Only) USB_INTCTRL_MODE_DETECT—OTG cable mode detection has completed (OTG Only) USB_INTCTRL_POWER_FAULT—Power Fault detected (Host Only)
uint32_t USBIntStatusEndpoint(uint32_t ui32Base)	ui32Base specifies the USB module base address.	Read endpoint interrupt status for a USB controller. This call returns the current status for endpoint interrupts only, the control interrupt status is retrieved by calling USBIntStatusControl(). The bit values returned are compared against the USB_INTEP__ values. These values are grouped into classes for USB_INTEP_HOST__ and USB_INTEP_DEV__ values to handle both host and device modes with all endpoints. This call clears the source of all of the endpoint interrupts.

Table 9.29. The USBOTG API functions.

API Function	Parameter	Description
void USBOTGMode(uint32_t ui32Base)	ui32Base specifies the USB module base address.	Change the mode of the USB controller to OTG mode. This function is only valid on microcontrollers that have the OTG capabilities.
void USBOTGSessionRequest(uint32_t ui32Base, bool bStart)	ui32Base specifies the USB module base address. bStart specifies if this call starts or ends a session.	This function is used in OTG mode to start a session request or end a session. If the bStart parameter is set to true, then this function starts a session and if it is false it ends a session.

9.4.9.7 The USBOTG API Functions

The following API functions are covered by this group:

- USBOTGMode()—Change the mode of the USB controller to OTG.
- USBOTGSessionRequest()—Start or end an OTG session.

Table 9.29 shows these API functions and their prototypes.

9.4.10 Build a USB Implementation Example Project Using the API Functions

In this section we try to build a USB example project with the USB API functions we discussed above.

In order to build a real USB project with API functions to interface actual USB host or device, it needs a lot of codes and device drivers used for the different platforms, and those are too complicated and beyond the scope of this book. Some real application projects, such as usb_dev_bulk and usb_dev_serial, can be found at the default directory when the TivaWare™ for C Series software is installed, which is ti\TivaWare_C_Series-2.0.1.11577\examples\boards\ek-tm4c123gxl.

In this project, two endpoints are used, the host endpoint 2 and a device endpoint 1, and both endpoints work as the IN mode. A 64-byte data packet is sent from the device IN endpoint 1 to the host IN endpoint 2.

Since this project is relatively easy, we leave this to the students as a lab project, Lab9_5.

9.5 CHAPTER SUMMARY

This chapter provides general information about ARM® Cortex®-M4 Microcontroller General-Purpose Timer programming, including the Watchdog Times programming. Because of the space limitations, we moved the USB programming to this chapter. The discussion also includes the GPIO Ports related to General-Purpose Timers and USB modules used in TM4C123GH6PM MCU system. This discussion concentrates on the architectures and programming interfaces applied on General Purpose Timers, Watchdog Timers as well as USB modules specially designed for the TM4C123GH6PM MCU system. Special or alternative control functions for different GPIO pins related to different peripherals, including timers and USB modules, are also discussed and introduced with example projects in this chapter.

Starting at Section 9.2, the General-Purpose Timers implemented in the TM4C123GXL system are introduced and discussed.

The General-Purpose Timer Module (GPTM) contains:

- Six 16/32-bit GPTM blocks and six 32/64-bit Wide GPTM blocks.
- Each 16/32-bit GPTM block can provide two 16-bit (half-width) timers/counters that are referred to as Timer A and Timer B.
- These timers/counters can be further configured to operate independently as timers or event counters, or concatenated together to operate as one 32-bit (full-width) timer or one 32-bit Real-Time Clock (RTC).
- Similarly, each 32/64-bit Wide GPTM block provides two 32-bit timers, also called Timer A and Timer B, and they can be concatenated together to form a 64-bit timer. Timers can also be used to trigger μDMA transfers. All timers have interrupt controls and separate interrupt vectors as well as separate interrupt handlers.

Following the overview, the functional block diagram and the operational modes of the GPTM blocks are discussed and analyzed in details. These operational modes include:

1. One-Shot Timer Mode
2. Periodic Timer Mode
3. Periodic Snapshot Timer Mode
4. Wait-for-Trigger Mode
5. Real-Time Clock Timer Mode
6. Input Edge-Count Mode
7. Input Edge-Time Mode
8. PWM Mode
9. DMA Mode

The GPTM control and status registers are discussed starting at Section 9.2.4. Because of the similarity between the Timer A and Timer B module, only Timer A module registers are discussed in details.

The GPTM GPIO-related control signals are discussed in Section 9.2.5. This discussion covers the GPIO shared pins and alternate functions for the GPTM modules. The GPTM initialization and configuration process is introduced in Section 9.2.6, and an example project of using the GPTM blocks is provided in Section 9.2.7.

In Section 9.2.8, some popular implementations on GPTM blocks are discussed with three real example projects. These implementations include the Input-Edge-Count, Input-Edge Time, and PWM applications.

The API functions provided by the TivaWare™ Peripheral Driver Library are discussed in Section 9.2.9, and an example project of using those Timer API functions to measure PWM pulses is provided in Section 9.2.9.4.

The Watchdog Timer is introduced at Section 9.3. The introduction and discussion in this section contain the functional block diagram of the Watchdog Timers, control registers implemented in the Watchdog Timers, and Watchdog Timer module initializations and configurations. An example project developed with Direct Register Access (DRA) model is provided in Section 9.3.5. The Watchdog Timer-related API functions are discussed in Section 9.3.6.

Starting at Section 9.4, the Universal Serial Bus (USB) modules are discussed. Following the overview, the hardware configuration of the USB devices and operational sequence of the USB are provided in Sections 9.4.1 and 9.4.2.

The USB used in the TM4C123GH6PM MCU system is discussed in Section 9.4.5. All different operating modes, including the host IN, host OUT, Device IN, OTG and Device OUT, are discussed and analyzed in detail in that section.

The functional block diagram of the USB modules and the GPIO related control signals are discussed in Sections 9.4.5.4 and 9.4.5.5. The USB control registers and initialization and configuration process are discussed in Sections 9.4.6 and 9.4.7. Most important and popular registers used in the USB modules are discussed in detail.

An example project built with the DRA model using the USB host and device endpoints to transmit data packet is provided in Section 9.4.8. The USB-related API functions provided by the TivaWare™ Peripheral Driver Library is discussed in Section 9.4.9.

Another example project built with the Software Driver (SD) model or API functions is introduced as a student lab project in Section 9.4.10.

HOMEWORK

I. True/False Selections

_____**1.** Each of six 16/32-bit GPTM blocks can be configured as either two half-width (16-bit) timers/counters or a full-width (32-bit) timer/counter.

_____**2.** If configured in one-shot mode, the timer continues counting when it reaches zero when counting down or the load value when counting up.

_____**3.** The cores of each GPTM block are two free-running up/down counters referred to as Timer A and Timer B.

_____**4.** When counting down in one-shot or periodic modes, the prescaler acts as a true prescaler. When counting up in one-shot or periodic modes, the prescaler acts as a timer extension and holds the most-significant bits of the count.

_____**5.** The GPTM Timer A Interval Load Register (GPTMTAILR) is the only register used to store the starting or upper bound value for a 16/32-bit counter.

_____**6.** To configure a 16/32-bit timer as a 16-bit timer, the GPTMCFG register should be 0x4.

_____**7.** Like a general timer module, the core of the watchdog timer module is a 32-bit count-down counter.

_____**8.** Because the WDT1 module uses an independent clocking source, its registers can be written without any timing gap between accesses.

_____**9.** Locking the watchdog registers does not affect the WDTICR register and allows interrupts to always be serviced. Thus, a write at any time of the WDTICR register clears the WDTMIS and WDTRIS registers and reloads the 32-bit counter.

_____**10.** In the USB module, different connectors are used at different sides: The connector in the A side is called A Type and the connector is the B side is B Type.

II. Multiple Choices

1. The prescaler can only be used when the timers are _____.

    a. Concatenated to a 32-bit timer

    b. Concatenated to a 64-bit timer

   c. Either concatenated or the used individually

   d. Used individually

2. Before any GPTM block or timers can start their work, they must be initialized and configured properly. In order to do that, the timers must be first ____.

   a. Enabled

   b. Disabled

   c. Either enabled or disabled

   d. Clocked

3. In order to configure a 32/64-bit timer as a 32-bit timer, the GPTMCFG bit field in the GPTM Configuration register must be set to _____.

   a. 0x0.

   b. 0x1.

   c. 0x2.

   d. 0x4.

4. In order to use the GPTM Timer A as an Event Mode to detect rising edges of some evens, the bit field ___ in the _____ register must be set to ____.

   a. TAEVENT, GPTMCFG, 0x0

   b. TBEVENT, GPTMCTL, 0x0

   c. TAEVENT, GPTMCTL, 0x0

   d. TAEVENT, GPTMCFG, 0x1

5. After a timer related interrupt has been responded, inside the interrupt handler, that interrupt must be __ by using the ___ register.

   a. Enabled, GPTMIMR

   b. Disabled, GPTMMIS

   c. Set, GPTMRIS

   d. Cleared, GPTMICR

6. To use the 16/32-bit Timer5A to measure the pulse width of a PWM signal via its CCP pin, the _____ pin should be configured as an alternate function pin.

   a. GPIO PC0

   b. GPIO PC1

   c. GPIO PC2

   d. GPIO PC3

7. If the input clock to the Timer0A is the 16-MHz system clock and the Timer0A works as a 24-bit counter, the maximum period to be measured is ____ ms.

   a. 65.536

   b. 65.535

   c. 1048.575

   d. 1048.576

8. If the INTEN bit in the Watchdog Timer Control (WDTCTL) register is set, this is used to _____.

   a. Enable the watchdog

   b. Enable the Watchdog interrupts

   c. Lock the Watchdog control registers

   d. All of them

9. To access and write any value to the WDT1 module, the bit ____ in the WDT Control register (WDTCTL) must be checked to make sure that the previous operations are done.

   a. WRC

   b. INTEN

   c. INTTYPE

   d. RESEN

10. When a USB transmits information to the target, three packets are involved on each transmission, and they are _____.

   a. Status packet, data packet, and token packet

   b. Data packet, token packet, and handshake packet

   c. Token packet, data packet, and status packet

   d. Token packet, status packet, and data packet

III. Exercises

1. Provide a brief description about the General-Purpose Timer Module Components.

2. Provide a brief description about the prescaler registers.

3. Provide a brief description about the timer's operational procedure of the Input Edge-Time Mode.

4. Provide a brief discussion about the Watchdog timers and the major components.

5. Provide a brief discussion about the endpoints for both IN and OUT modes.

6. Provide a brief description about the packets used in the communications between endpoints.

IV. Practical Laboratory

Laboratory 9: ARM® Cortex®-M4 Timers and USB Programming

9.0 Goals   This laboratory exercise allows students to learn and practice ARM® Cortex®-M4 General Timers, Watchdog Timers, and USB programming by developing five labs.

   1. Program Lab9_1 lets students use the GPTM Timer3B Input-Edge Count mode to detect and count the fixed number of a sequence of edges coming from the switch SW1 that is connected to the PF4 pin in the GPIO Port F. The falling edges will be detected and counted by using the Timer3B module. The number of the edges to be detected is pre-known and it is a fixed number (5).

   2. Program Lab9_2 enables students to use the Input-Edge Time mode to measure the period of two edges coming from the switch SW1 that is connected to the PF4 pin in the GPIO Port F. Two falling edges of SW1 will be detected by using the Timer3A module. The period between two edges is calculated and collected by the Timer3A module.

   3. Program Lab9_3 is similar to Lab9_2, but it uses a wide 32-bit timer to enable students to measure much longer period (up to 268 seconds for a 16 MHz clock).

   4. Program Lab9_4 enables students to build a watchdog timer project to use WDT1 module to generate a reset action after two standard timeout interrupts.

5. Program `Lab9_5` enables students to use two endpoints to build a project to perform data packets transmission functions between a host and a device endpoint. In this project, two endpoints are used, the host endpoint 2 and a device endpoint 1, and both endpoints work as the IN mode. A 64-byte data packet is sent from the device IN endpoint 1 to the host IN endpoint 2.

After completion of these programs, students should understand the basic architecture and operational procedure for most popular GPTM timers, Watchdog timers, and USB modules installed in the TM4C123GH6PM MCU system. They should be able to code some sophisticated programs to access the desired peripheral devices to perform desired control operations via GPTM blocks, Watchdog timers, and USB modules.

9.1 Lab9_1

9.1.1 Goal   In this project, students will use the DRA model with the GPTM `Timer3B` Input-Edge Count mode to detect and count the fixed number of a sequence of edges coming from the switch SW1 that is connected to the PF4 pin in the GPIO Port F. The falling edges will be detected and counted by using the `Timer3B` module. The number of the edges to be detected is pre-known and it is a fixed number (5).

In order to use a count-down timer to perform Input Edge-Count detections, two registers must be used and configured; the timer start value is set to GPTMTBILR = 0 x000A and the match value is set to GPTMTBMATCHR = 0x0005 so that five edge events can be detected and counted.

After five edges have been detected, an event-matched interrupt is generated. Inside the interrupt handler, the blue color LED connected to PF3 is ON to indicate this situation and the global Boolean flag should be reset to false to inform the infinitive `while()` loop in the main program to stop its running and waiting.

9.1.2 Data Assignment and Hardware Configuration   Connect the PF4 pin that is connected to SW1 and the PB3 pin (T3CCP1 for `Timer3B`) together with a jumping wire since we need to use SW1 to generate falling edges to be detected. This connection can be easily done in the J8 connector in the EduBASE ARM® Trainer.

9.1.3 Development of the Source Code   Perform the following operations to complete this project:

1. Create a new project named `Lab9_1` in the folder `C:\ARM Lab Projects\Chapter 9 \Lab9_1` and a new C file named `Lab9_1.c`. Build this C file with the following steps.

2. Include the system structure header file "`TM4C123GH6PM.h`" since we want to use the structure and pointer to access all related registers in this project.

3. Create a global Boolean flag, such as `intFlag`, and initialize it to `true`.

4. Use the SYSCTL structure pointer to access the RCGCTIMER register to enable and clock the `Timer3` module.

5. Similarly, use the SYSCTL structure pointer to access the RCGCGPIO register to enable and clock the GPIO Ports B and F.

6. Use the GPIOF structure pointer to set PF4~PF0 as digital pins, PF3~PF0 as output pins, and PF4 as an input pin.

7. Use the GPIOF structure pointer to access its PUR register to enable pull-up on the PF4 pin since we need to use SW1 to generate falling edges when it is pressed.

8. Use the GPIOB structure pointer to access its DEN register to set PB3~PB0 as digital pins.

9. Similarly, use GPIOB structure pointer to access its AFSEL register to enable the PB3 pin to work as the alternate function.

10. Use the GPIOB structure pointer to access its PCTL register to enable the PB3 pin to work as an alternate function to the Timer3B module.

    Now using the following steps to configure the Timer3B module to enable it to work as an Input Edge Count mode:

11. Use the TIMER3 structure pointer to access its CTL register to disable the Timer3B module.

12. Use the TIMER3 structure pointer to access its CFG register to configure it as a 16-bit timer mode.

13. Use the TIMER3 structure pointer to access its TBMR register to configure it as a capture mode.

14. Use the TIMER3 structure pointer to access its CTL register to configure the TBEVENT bit field as the falling-edge detector.

15. Use the TIMER3 structure pointer to load the start value (10) to its TBILR register.

16. Use the TIMER3 structure pointer to load the end value (5) to its TBMATCHR register.

17. Use the TIMER3 structure pointer to access its ICR register to clear any previous Timer3B capture mode match interrupt.

18. Use the TIMER3 structure pointer to access its IMR register to enable the Timer3B capture mode match interrupt.

19. Use the NVIC structure pointer to access its IP[] register to set up the Timer3B's interrupt priority level as 2 (010). Refer to Table 5.10 to get the IRQ number and Table 5.12 in Chapter 5 to get the bits range and numbers for the Timer3B module.

20. Use the NVIC structure pointer to access its ISER[] register to enable the Timer3B's interrupt. One point to be noted is that ISER[0] controls 32 interrupts whose IRQ is numbered from 0 to 31. For interrupts whose numbers are higher than 31, one needs to use ISER[1]. The bit number in the ISER[] register is equal to the IRQ number of each interrupt source.

21. Use the TIMER3 structure pointer to access its CTL register to enable the Timer3B module after these configurations and the timer begins to work.

22. Use the intrinsic function __enable_irq() to globally enable all interrupt sources.

23. Use a while() loop with the global flag intFlag to wait for all 5 edges to have been detected.

    Use the following steps for the codes inside the interrupt handler TIMER3B_Handler ():

24. After an interrupt occurred, use the TIMER3 structure pointer to access its ICR register to clear this interrupt to enable it to occur in the future.

25. Use the GPIOF structure pointer to access its DATA register to turn on the blue LED that is connected to the PF2 pin to indicate that all 5 edges have been detected and that the counter has stopped its detecting work.

26. Reset the global flag intFlag to false to release the while() loop in the main program to stop the project.

9.1.4 Set Up the Environment to Build and Run the Project To build and run the project, one needs to perform the following operations to set up the environments:

- Select the `Stellaris ICDI` debug driver in the**Debug** tab under the**Project|Options for Target 'Target 1'** menu item.
- Now let's build the project by going to `Project|Build target` menu item.
- Then go to `Flash|Download` menu item to download the image file of this project into the flash memory in the TM4C123GXL Evaluation Board.
- Now go to `Debug|Start/Stop Debug Session` to ready to run the project.
- Go to Debug|Run menu item to run the project.

9.1.5 Demonstrate your program by checking the running result As the project runs, each time the SW1 is pressed, a negative-going edge is generated and the PB3 LED should be flashed at one time. After pressing 5 times, the blue LED should be ON to indicate that all 5 edges have been detected.

Based on the running result, try to answer the following questions:

- Sometimes the blue LED is ON even when the SW1 is pressed less than 5 times. Why did this happen?

9.2 Lab9_2

9.2.1 Goal This project enables students to use the DRA model with the Input-Edge Time mode to measure the period of two edges coming from the switch SW1 that is connected to the PF4 pin in the GPIO Port F. Two falling edges of SW1 will be detected by using the `Timer3A` module. The period between two edges is calculated and collected by the `Timer3A` module.

Since the period measured in this project is a little longer, the prescaler is used for the `Timer3A` module to get a 24-bit counter. In this mode, the maximized measurable period is 4.19 s when a 4 MHz system clock is used.

In order to use a count-down timer to perform Input Edge-Time mode, the PB2 pin that works as the T3CCP0 pin for the `Timer3A` module must be configured as an alternate function to work as an input pin to detect two edges coming from the SW1 switch.

Each time an input edge is detected, a capture interrupt is generated and processed in the interrupt handler `TIMER3A_Handler()`. The blue color LED connected to the PF2 is toggled to indicate this situation. After two input edges have been detected, the green color LED connected to PF3 is ON to indicate this situation and the global Boolean flag should be reset to `false` to inform the infinitive `while()` loop in the main program to stop its running and waiting. Also, an infinitive `while()` loop should be used to enable students to check the detected and calculated period value.

This period value should be a random number since the time when the SW1 is pressed can be at any moment, and this is determined by the student. However, since the maximized measurable period is 4.19 seconds, these two SW1 pressings must be within 4 seconds.

9.2.2 Data Assignment and Hardware Configuration Connect PF4 pin (connected to SW1) and PB2 pin (T3CCP0 for `Timer3A`) together with a jumping wire since we need to use SW1 to generate falling edges to be detected. This connection can be easily done in the J8 connector in the EduBASE ARM® Trainer since they are neighbors.

9.2.3 Development of the Project To make this project easy, we used Direct Register Access (DRA) model.

Create a new project named Lab9_2 in the folder C:\ARM Lab Projects \Chapter 9\Lab9_2 and a new C file named Lab9_2.c. Add the following codes into this C file.

9.2.4 Development of the C Source File Perform the following operations to complete this project:

1. Include the system structure header file "TM4C123GH6PM.h" since we want to use the structure and pointer to access all related registers in this project.

2. Include the following definition macros:

```
#define SYSCTL_RCC_XTAL_4MHZ    0x00000180    // 4MHz
#define SYSCTL_RCC_PWRDN        0x00002000 // PLL Power Down
#define SYSCTL_RCC_BYPASS       0x00000800 // PLL Bypass
#define SYSCTL_SYSDIV_1         0x07800000 // Processor clock is osc/pll/1
```

Since you need to use 4-MHz system clock in this project, do the following:

3. Create a global Boolean flag, such as intFlag, and initialize it to true.

4. Create three global uint32_t variables, period, edgeCount and count = 0.

5. Inside the main() program, create two uint32_t variables, RCC and Period[1].

6. OR all macros defined above together and assign the result to the RCC variable.

7. Assign the RCC variable to the SYSCTL→RCC register to use a 4 MHz system clock.

8. Use SYSCTL structure pointer to access the RCGCTIMER register to enable and clock the Timer3 module.

9. Similar, use the SYSCTL structure pointer to access the RCGCGPIO register to enable and clock the GPIO Ports B and F.

10. Use GPIOF structure pointer to set PF4~PF0 as digital pins, and set PF3~PF0 as output pins and PF4 as an input pin.

11. Use GPIOF structure pointer to access its PUR register to enable pull-up on PF4 pin since we need to use SW1 to generate falling edges when it is pressed.

12. Use GPIOB structure pointer to access its DEN register to set PB3~PB0 as digital pins.

13. Similarly, use GPIOB structure pointer to access its AFSEL register to enable PB2 pin to work as the alternate function.

14. Use GPIOB structure pointer to access its PCTL register to enable PB2 pin to work as an alternate function to Timer3A module.

Now use the following steps to configure the Timer3A module to enable it to work as an Input Edge Time mode:

15. Use TIMER3 structure pointer to access its CTL register to disable the Timer3A module.

16. Use TIMER3 structure pointer to access its CFG register to configure it as a 16-bit timer mode.

17. Use TIMER3 structure pointer to access its TAMR register to configure it as a capture mode.

18. Use TIMER3 structure pointer to access its CTL register to configure the TAEVENT bit-field as the falling-edge detector.

19. Use TIMER3 structure pointer to access its TAILR register to load 65535 as the start value.

20. Use TIMER3 structure pointer to access its TAPR register to load 255 (0xFF) to the prescaler register to extend the Timer3A to a 24-bit counter.

21. Use TIMER3 structure pointer to access its ICR register to clear any previous Timer3A capture mode interrupt.

22. Use TIMER3 structure pointer to access its IMR register to enable Timer3A capture mode interrupt.

23. Use the NVIC structure pointer to access its IP[] register to set up the Timer3A's interrupt priority level as 3 (011). Refer to Table 5.10 to get the IRQ number and Table 5.12 in Chapter 5 to get the bits range and numbers for the Timer3A module.

24. Use NVIC structure pointer to access its ISER[] register to enable the Timer3A's interrupt. One point to be noted is that ISER[0] controls 32 interrupts whose IRQ is numbered from 0 to 31. For interrupts whose numbers are higher than 31, one needs to use ISER[1]. The bit number in the ISER[] register is equal to the IRQ number of each interrupt source. Refer to Table 5.10 to get the IRQ number and bit number for Timer3A module.

25. Use the TIMER3 structure pointer to access its CTL register to enable the Timer3A module after these configurations and the timer begins to work.

26. Use the intrinsic function __enable_irq() to globally enable all interrupt sources.

27. Use a while() loop with the global flag intFlag to wait for two edges have been detected.

28. Assign the period value calculated in the interrupt handler and stored in the global variable period to the local array variable Period[0]. This assignment should be bit-ANDed with 0x00FFFFFF since only 24-bit is a valid period value.

29. Use another infinitive while() loop to enable one to check the calculated period value via the variable Period[0] later.

Use the following steps for the codes inside the interrupt handler TIMER3A_Handler():

30. After an interrupt occurred, use the TIMER3 structure pointer to access its ICR register to clear this interrupt to enable it to be occurred in the future.

31. Use the GPIOF structure pointer to access its DATA register to toggle the blue LED that is connected to the PF2 pin to indicate that an edge has been detected.

32. The global variable count is incremented by 1.

33. Use an if() structure to check whether this is the first edge. If it is, save the current count value stored in the TAR register to the global variable edgeCount. The TAR register can be accessed via the TIMER3 structure pointer.

34. If it is not the first edge, it should be the second edge. Then calculate the period by subtracting the current count value stored in the TAR register from the last count value stored in the global variable edgeCount, and assign the result to the global variable period.

35. Then disable Timer3A module to stop its counting function.

36. Use GPIOF structure pointer to access its DATA register to turn on the green LED that is connected to the PF3 pin to indicate that the period has been collected and the project can be stopped.

37. Reset the global flag intFlag to false to release the while() loop in the main program to stop the project.

9.2.5 Set Up the Environment to Build and Run the Project Make sure that the debugger you are using is the Stellaris ICDI.

9.2.6 Build and Demonstrate Your Program Build and run the project. As the project runs, press SW1 two times within a 4-second period. The blue LED should be ON in the first pressing, and the green LED should be ON in the second pressing.

To check the detected period value, a break point should be set in the infinitive while() loop in the main program. Open the Call Stack + Locals window after the green LED is ON, and expand the Period[] array, and you can find the period value presented in hexadecimal format. Convert it to the decimal value if you want to get the actual period.

Based on these results, try to answer the following questions:

- Because of the counter-bit limitation, for a 24-bit counter, the maximized counting time period is 4 seconds, and this makes this project not convenient.
- Can you modify this project to make the counting time longer? A possible choice is to use a 32/64-bit Wide timer to make it a 32-bit counter, to improve this situation.

9.3 Lab9_3

9.3.1 Goal Program Lab9_3 is similar to Lab9_2 but it uses a wide 32-bit timer to enable students to measure much longer period (up to 268 seconds for 16 MHz clock).

A recommendation is to use Wide Timer3A or WTimer3A. In this way, the counting time can be expanded to:

- 268 seconds for 16 MHz clock source
- 536 seconds for 8 MHz clock source
- 1073 seconds for 4 MHz clock source.

You can use 16 MHz clock source since 268 seconds is good enough for this project.

9.3.2 Data assignment and Hardware Configuration Note that the WT3CCP0 pin is used to receive and detect the input edges via the PD2 pin. You need to use a jumping wire to connect PD2 with PF4 pins together to enable a falling edge to be generated when the SW1 is pressed as the project runs. This connection can be done easily by finding the PD0 pin in the J10 and PF4 pin in the J8 connectors in the EduBASE ARM® Trainer.

9.3.3 Development of the Project Modify the project Lab9_2 by replacing the 24-bit Timer3A with 32/64-bit Wide Timer3A to make it as Lab9_3. The following modifications are needed:

9.3.4 Development and Modification of the C Source File

1. Use SYSCTL_RCC_XTAL_16MHZ to select the 16 MHz clock source.
2. Use SYSCTL→RCGCWTIMER |= 0x08; to enable and clock Wide timer3A.
3. Enable and clock GPIO D and F.

4. Set PD2 as a digital function pin.

5. Enable PD2 pin as an alternate function pin with GPIOD→AFSEL register.

6. Configure PD2 as the WT3CCP0 pin with GPIOD→PCTL register.

7. For all WTimer3A configurations, just prefix W before TIMER3A to make them for Wide Timer3A module.

8. Use NVIC→IP[100] to set up the priority level for WTimer3A as 3 (011) since the IRQ number for the WTIMER3A is 100, and the priority bits should be located at bits 7:5.

9. Use NVIC→ISER[3] to enable the WTIMER3A interrupt. Since the IRQ number of the WTIMER3A is 100, and each ISER[] contains 32 bits interrupt source. Therefore the index for the ISER[] should be 3. You need to figure out what value should be assigned to the ISER[3].

10. For the WTIMER3A interrupt handler, just prefix W before the original handler.

11. Inside the interrupt handler, prefix W before each TIMER3A module to make them as 32-bit wide Timer3a module.

9.3.5 Set Up the Environment to Build and Run the Project
Make sure that the debugger you are using is the Stellaris ICDI.

9.3.6 Demonstrate Your Program
Build and run the project if everything is fine. As the project runs, press SW1 two times within 268-second period. The blue LED should be ON in the first pressing, and the green LED should be ON in the second pressing.

To check the detected period value, a break point should be set in the infinitive while() loop in the main program. Open the Call Stack + Locals window after the green LED is ON, and expand the Period[] array, and you can find the period value presented in the hexadecimal format. Convert it to the decimal value if you want to get the actual period.

Based on these results, try to answer the following questions:

- Is the period between two pressings of the SW1 longer than that in the project Lab9_2?

- What did you learn from this project?

9.4 Lab9_4

9.4.1 Goal
Program Lab9_4 enables students to use the Watchdog related API functions to build a watchdog timer project to use the WDT1 module to generate a reset action after two standard timeout interrupts.

9.4.2 Data Assignment and Hardware Configuration
With a 16 MHz PIOSC as the clock source for the WDT1 module, if one wants to the standard interrupt to be generated for each 1 second, the start value to be loaded into the WDTLOAD register should be 1000 ms/62.5 ns = 16000000.

Each time a WDT1 standard timeout interrupt occurs and is handled by the WDT1 interrupt handler, first the interrupt should be cleared. Then the blue color LED should be ON the first time the interrupt happened, and green LED should be ON the second time the interrupt occurred.

9.4.3 Development of the Project and the Header File
Create a new project named Lab9_4 in the folder C:\ARM Lab Projects\Chapter 9\Lab9_4 and a new C source file Lab9_4.c.

Perform the following operations to complete this project with API functions.

9.4.4 Development of the C source file

1. Declare the following header files and interrupt handler as well as some global variables.

```
#include <stdint.h>
#include <stdbool.h>
#include "inc/hw_memmap.h"
#include "inc/hw_types.h"
#include "driverlib/interrupt.h"
#include "driverlib/sysctl.h"
#include "driverlib/watchdog.h"
#include "driverlib/gpio.h"

#define SYSCTL_RCC_XTAL_16MHZ    0x00000540  //16 MHz
#define SYSCTL_RCC_PWRDN         0x00002000  //PLL Power Down
#define SYSCTL_RCC_BYPASS        0x00000800  //PLL Bypass
#define SYSCTL_SYSDIV_1          0x07800000  //Processor clock is osc/pll/1

void WDT1_Handler(void);                     //WDT1 interrupt handler
uint32_t count = 0;
```

2. Create a local `uint32_t` variable RCC, and assigned it with a sequence of macros to use the 16 MHz PIOSC clock source, like:

RCC = (SYSCTL_RCC_XTAL_16MHZ|SYSCTL_RCC_PWRDN|SYSCTL_RCC_BYPASS|SYSCTL_SYSDIV_1);

3. Use the `SysCtlClockSet()` function with this RCC as an argument to configure the clock source used by this WDT1 module.

4. Use the `SysCtlPeripheralEnable()` functions to enable the UART1, WDT1 and GPIO Port F.

5. Use the `GPIOPinTypeGPIOOutput()` to configure PF2 & PF3 as output pins.

6. Register the watchdog module 1's interrupt handler `WDT1_Handler()`.

7. Use `WatchdogLockState()` to check whether WDT1 related registers are locked.

8. If locked, unlock them.

9. Use `WatchdogReloadSet()` to load start vale 16000000 to the WDT1 counter.

10. Use `WatchdogResetEnable()` to enable the reset function for the WDT1 module to allow a reset action to be occurred after two times WDT1 time-out interrupt occurred.

11. Use `WatchdogIntEnable()` to enable the WDT1 interrupt source.

12. Use `WatchdogEnable()` to enable the WDT1 timer to begin its counting function.

13. Wait for interrupts to be occurred.

Develop the codes for the WDT1 interrupt handler.

14. Use `WatchdogIntClear()` API function to clear standard interrupts.

15. Increment the global variable `count` by 1.

16. Check whether the value of `count` is 1, which means that this is the first time the interrupt occurred if it is equal to 1. If it is, turn on the blue color LED.

17. If not, which means that this is the second time the interrupt occurred, turn on the green color LED.

9.4.5 Set Up the Environment to Build and Run the Project   This setup contains the following three operations:

1. Include the system header files by adding the include path.
2. Check and configure the correct debugger driver used in the project.
3. Add the TivaWare™ Peripheral Driver Library into the project since we need to use some API functions provided by that library.

Perform the following operations to include this header file path in your project:

- Go to the `Project|Options for Target 'Target 1'` menu item. Then click on the C/C++ tab.
- Go to the `Include Paths` box and browse to the folder where our header files are located, which is `C:\ti\TivaWare_C_Series-2.0.1.11577`. Select this folder and click on the **OK** button.

Make sure that the debugger driver you are using is the `Stellaris ICDI`.
Perform the below operations to add the TivaWare™ peripheral driver library into the project:

- Go to the **Project** pane and right click on the **Source Group 1** item, and select the Add `Existing Files to Group 'Source Group 1'` menu item.
- Browse to the folder where the library file is located, which is `C:\ti\TivaWare_C_Series-2.0.1.11577\driverlib\rvmdk`. Then select the library file `driverlib.lib` and click on the **Add** button. Click on the **Close** button to finish this step.

9.4.6 Demonstrate Your Program   Build and run the project if everything is fine. Based on these results, try to answer the following questions:

- The first time the interrupt occurred, the blue LED was on, but the second time the interrupt happened, the color of the LED was not green Why?
- Can you modify your project to turn the green LED on for the interrupt to be generated the second time?
- In this project, you never used the UART1 peripheral. Why do you need to enable this peripheral first in this project? What would happen if you did not enable this peripheral? Why?

9.5 Lab9_5

9.5.1 Goal   This project enables students to use the USB API functions with two endpoints to build a project to perform data packets transmission functions between a host and a device endpoint. In this project, two endpoints are used, the host endpoint 2 and a device endpoint 1, and both endpoints work as the IN mode. A 64-byte data packet is sent from the device IN endpoint 1 to the host IN endpoint 2.

9.5.2 Data Assignment and Hardware Configuration   In this project, two endpoints are used, the host endpoint 2 and a device endpoint 1, and both endpoints work as the IN mode. A 64-byte data packet is sent from the device IN endpoint 1 to the host IN endpoint 2.

9.5.3 Development of the Project   Create a new project Lab9_5 in the folder C:\ARM Lab Projects\Chapter 9\Lab9_5 with a new C source file Lab9_5.c. Follow the steps below to complete the coding process for this project.

9.5.4 Development of the C Source File   Perform the following operations to complete this project with API functions:

1. Declare the following header files and macros as well as user defined functions.

```
#include <stdint.h>
#include <stdbool.h>
#include "inc/hw_memmap.h"
#include "driverlib/gpio.h"
#include "driverlib/sysctl.h"
#include "driverlib/usb.h"

#define USB0_FIFO2_R              (*((volatile uint32_t *)0x40050028))
#define USB0_FIFO1_R              (*((volatile uint32_t *)0x40050024))
#define USB0_TXCSRL1_R            (*((volatile uint8_t *)0x40050112))

void USBDevice_Init(void);
void USBHost_Init(void);
uint32_t USBDevice_PutData(uint8_t *pui8Data, uint32_t ui32Size);
void USBHost_RecvData(uint8_t *pui8Data, uint32_t ui32Size);
```

Three macros are used for the USB registers, and four user-defined functions are used to the initialization and configuration of the USB host and device as well as data packets operations.

2. Inside the `main()` function, create one local variable `ret` and two data arrays, `SndData[64]` and `RevData[64]`, and the data type is `uint8_t` for all of these three items.

3. Initialize `SndData[]` array by assigning 64 bytes data from 0 to 63.

4. Use `SysCtlPeripheralEnable()` to enable and clock the USB0 and the GPIO Port F.

5. Use GPIO API function to set the GPIO Port F pin 2 as an output pin.

6. Call `USBDevice_Init()` user-defined function to initialize IN Device endpoint 1.

7. Call `USBHost_Init()` user-defined function to initialize IN Host endpoint 2.

8. Call `USBDevice_PutData()` user-defined function to place 64-byte data packet into the device endpoint 1 FIFO. The first argument of this function is a pointer `*pui8Data` that is the starting address of this data array and the second argument is the size of this array, which is 64. This function should return a `uint32_t` type value. A returned 0 indicates that this function is executed successfully.

9. Call `USBHost_RecvData()` user-defined function to pick up the 64-byte data packet transmitted to the host endpoint 2 FIFO. The first argument of this function is a pointer `RevData` and the second is the size of this packet, which is 64.

10. Put an infinitive `while()` loop in here to check the transmission result.

11. The `main()` function body is done.
    Following are the codes for the user-defined function `USBDevice_Init()`:

12. Use `USBDevAddrSet()` to setup the device endpoint 1 address.

13. Use `USBDevEndpointConfigSet()` to configure the IN device endpoint 1. The following parameters should be sued for this function:
    - USB base address—USB0_BASE
    - Device endpoint 1—USB_EP_1
    - Packet size—64
    - Setup flags—USB_EP_MODE_BULK|USB_EP_AUTO_CLEAR|USB_EP_DEV_IN

14. Use `USBEndpointDataToggleClear()` to clear the digit toggle. The flag parameter should be USB_EP_DEV_IN.

15. Use `USBFIFOConfigSet()` to configure the FIFO for IN device endpoint 1. The following parameters should be used for this function:

- FIFO address – 64
- FIFO size - USB_FIFO_SZ_64
- Flag - USB_EP_DEV_IN

16. Use `USBDevConnect()` to connect the device endpoint 1 to the USB bus.
Following are the codes for the user-defined function `USBDevice_PutData()`:

17. Check whether the bit TXRDY (bit 0) in the USB0_TXCSRL1_R has been set or not. If this bit is set, it means that the FIFO is full and cannot hold any more data. Return a 1 to the main() program to indicate this case.

18. If the bit TXRDY is not set, use a `for (; ui32Size > 0; ui32Size--)` loop to repeatedly assign 64 bytes of data to the FIFO with: `USB0_FIFO1_R = *pui8Data++;`

19. Return a 0 to indicate that this function is executed successfully.
Following are the codes for the user-defined function `USBHost_Init()`:

20. Use `USBHostAddrSet()` to setup the host address. The following parameters should be sued for this function:

- USB base address—USB0_BASE
- Host endpoint—USB_EP_2
- Target endpoint—USB_EP_1
- Setup flag—USB_EP_HOST_IN

21. Use `USBHostEndpointConfig()` to configure the IN host endpoint 2. The following parameters should be sued for this function:

- USB base address—USB0_BASE
- Host endpoint—USB_EP_2
- The max payload—64
- The NAKPollInterval—255
- Target endpoint—USB_EP_1
- Setup flag—USB_EP_HOST_IN|USB_EP_SPEED_FULL|USB_EP_MODE_BULK| USB_EP_AUTO_SET

22. Use `USBEndpointDataToggleClear()` to clear any digital toggle. The setup flag parameter for this function should be USB_EP_HOST_IN.

23. Use `USBFIFOConfigSet()` to setup the FIFO RAM for this IN Host endpoint 2. The setup flag parameter for this function should be USB_EP_HOST_IN. The FIFO address and size are identical with those used in the `USBFIFOConfigSet()` in the device FIFO configuration.
Following are the codes for the user-defined function `USBHost_RecvData()`:

24. Use `GPIOPinWrite()` API function to set the PF4 pin to turn on the blue-color LED to indicate that the pick-up data packet process starts.

25. Use a `for (; ui32Size > 0; ui32Size--)` loop to repeatedly pick up 64-byte data from the IN Host endpoint 2 FIFO with: `pui8Data[ui32Size-1]=USB0_FIFO2_R;` Two arguments are used for this function, a pointer `pui8Data` and the data-size `ui32Size`.

9.5.5 Set Up the Environment to Build and Run the Project   This setup contains the following three operations:

1. Include the system header files by adding the include path.

2. Check and configure the correct debugger driver used in the project.

3. Add the TivaWare™ Peripheral Driver Library into the project.

Perform the following operations to include the header file path in the project:

- Go to Project|Options for Target 'Target 1' menu item. Then click on the C/C++ tab.
- Go to Include Paths box and browse to the folder where our header files are located, it is C:\ti\TivaWare_C_Series-2.0.1.11577. Select this folder and click on the OK button.

Perform the following operations to select the correct debugger:

- Go to the Project|Options for Target 'Target 1' menu item to open the Options wizard.
- On the opened Options wizard, click on the Debug tab.
- Make sure that the debugger shown in the Use: box is Stellaris ICDI. Otherwise you can click on the dropdown arrow to select this debugger from the list.

Perform the below operations to add the TivaWare™ peripheral driver library into the project:

- Go to the Project pane and right click on the Source Group 1 item, and select the Add Existing Files to Group 'Source Group 1' menu item.
- Browse to the folder where the library file is located, which is C:\ti\TivaWare_C_Series-2.0.1.11577\driverlib\rvmdk. Then select the library file driverlib. lib and click on the Add button. Click on the Close button to finish this step.

9.5.6 Demonstrate Your Program
Build and run the project if everything is fine. Based on these results, try to answer the following questions:

- Why is the USB device sending data function missed? Without this function, how can the data packet be sent to the host endpoint? Is it possible for a data packet that is stored in the device FIFO to be sent to the host endpoint FIFO without the device sending function? If it is, how?
- What did you learn from this project?

Chapter 10

ARM® Cortex®-M4 Other Peripherals Programming

This chapter provides general information about other ARM® Cortex®-M4 MCU related peripherals and their implementations. These peripherals include the Controller Area Network (CAN), Quadrature Encoder Interface (QEI) and Analog Comparators. Because of the space limitations in the previous chapters, we leave the CAN module that is a kind of serial interface to this chapter. The discussion also includes the GPIO Ports and pins related to the CAN, QEI, and Analog Comparators modules used in the TM4C123GH6PM MCU system. This discussion concentrates on the architectures and programming interfaces applied on these three modules specially designed for the TM4C123GH6PM MCU system. Some special control functions for general motors and robots are also discussed and introduced with example projects in this chapter.

10.1 OVERVIEW AND INTRODUCTION

Most of peripherals, including the CAN, QEI, and Analog Comparators, are connected to and controlled by the MCU via the GPIO Ports with related GPIO pins. In this chapter, we will concentrate on the following peripherals used in the TM4C123GH6PM MCU system:

- Controller Area Network (CAN)
- Quadrature Encoder Interface (QEI)
- Analog Comparators (ACMP)

Some example projects related to those peripherals are to be developed and built.

10.2 THE CONTROLLER AREA NETWORK (CAN)

Controller Area Network (CAN) is a serial bus system especially suited to interconnect smart devices to build smart systems or sub systems. CAN was first developed from a Bosch internal project, which was to develop an in-vehicle network, in 1983. In 1987, the first CAN controller chips from Intel and Philips Semiconductors were emerged in the

Practical Microcontroller Engineering with ARM® Technology, First Edition. Ying Bai.
© 2016 by The Institute of Electrical and Electronics Engineers, Inc. Published 2016 by John Wiley & Sons, Inc.
Companion Website: www.wiley.com/go/armbai

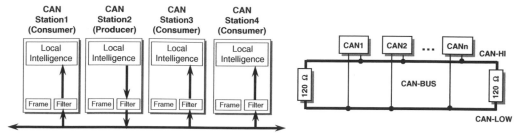

Figure 10.1.   The operational diagram of a CAN System.

market. CAN in Automation (CiA) international users and manufacturers group was established in 1992.

CAN is used as an embedded network for machine control within industries like textile machinery, printing machines, injection molding machinery, or packaging machines. Mainly the protocol CANopen is used for such applications. Other industries for embedded control are building automation, maritime applications, medical applications, and railway applications.

The CAN protocol is an international standard defined in the ISO 11898. Beside the CAN protocol itself, the conformance test for the CAN protocol is defined in the ISO 16845, which guarantees the interchangeability of the CAN chips.

Figure 10.1 shows an operational diagram of a CAN system.

CAN is based on the so-called broadcast communication mechanism. This broadcast communication is achieved by using a message oriented transmission protocol. Thus not defining stations and station addresses, it only defines message. These messages are identified by using a message identifier. Such a message identifier has to be unique within the whole network and it defines not only the content but also the priority of the message. This will be important when several stations compete for bus access.

Transmission and receiving message objects among CAN nodes are performed via the two-wire bus system, CAN-HI and CAN-LOW, as shown in Figure 10.1. As for the CAN connectors, the most common connectors are the 9-pin D-sub-type male connector with the four pin outs: CAN-LOW (CAN_), GND, CAN-HIGH (CAN+), and CAN V+ (Power).

The CAN protocol supports two message frame formats, the only essential difference being in the length of the identifier. The so-called CAN standard frame, also known as CAN 2.0 A, supports a length of 11 bits for the identifier; and the so-called CAN extended frame, also known as CAN 2.0 B, supports a length of 29 bits for the identifier.

10.2.1 CAN Standard Frame

Figure 10.2 shows a typical CAN standard frame format. A message in the CAN standard frame format begins with the start bit called `Start Of Frame` (SOF); this is followed by the `Arbitration field`, which consists of the identifier (11- or 29-bit ID) and the `Remote Transmission Request` (RTR) bit used to distinguish between the data frame and the data request frame called remote frame. The following control field contains the `IDentifier Extension` (IDE) bit to distinguish between the CAN standard frame

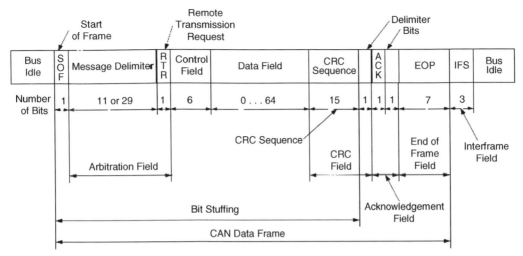

Figure 10.2.   A typical standard CAN frame format. (Reprinted with the permission of the Texas Instruments Incorporated.)

and the CAN extended frame, as well as the `Data Length Code` (DLC) used to indicate the number of following data bytes in the `Data field`.

If the message is used as a remote frame, the DLC contains the number of requested data byte. The `Data field` that follows is able to hold up to 8 data bytes. The integrity of the frame is guaranteed by the following `Cyclic Redundant Check` (CRC) sum. The `ACKnowledge` (ACK) field compromises the ACK slot and the ACK delimiter. The bit in the ACK slot is sent as a recessive bit and is overwritten as a dominant bit by those receivers, which have at this time received the data correctly. Correct messages are acknowledged by the receivers regardless of the result of the acceptance test. The end of the message is indicated by `End Of Frame` (EOF). The `Intermission Frame Space` (IFS) is the minimum number of bits separating consecutive messages. If there is no following bus access by any station, the bus remains idle.

10.2.2 CAN Extended Frame

A message in the CAN extended frame format is likely the same as a message in CAN standard frame format. The difference is the length of the identifier used. The identifier is made up of the existing 11-bit identifier (base identifier) and an 18-bit extension (identifier extension). The distinction between the CAN standard frame format and the CAN extended frame format is made by using the IDE bit, which is transmitted as dominant in the case of a frame in the CAN standard frame format but is transmitted as recessive in the case of a frame in the CAN extended frame format. As the two formats have to co exist on one bus, it is laid down which message has higher priority on the bus in the case of bus access collision with different formats and the same identifier/base identifier: The message in the CAN standard frame format always has priority over the message in the extended format.

CAN controllers that support the messages in CAN extended frame format are also able to send and receive messages in CAN standard frame format. When CAN controllers that only cover the CAN standard frame format are used in one network, then only messages in the CAN standard frame can be transmitted in the entire network. Messages in CAN extended frame format would be misunderstood. However, there are CAN controllers which only support the CAN standard frame format but recognize messages in CAN extended frame format and ignore them, and this is called version 2.0 B passive.

10.2.3 Detecting and Signaling Errors

Unlike other bus systems, the CAN protocol does not use acknowledgment messages but instead signals any errors immediately as they occur. For error detection the CAN protocol implements three mechanisms at the message level:

- `Cyclic Redundancy Check ( CRC)`. The CRC safeguards the information in the frame by adding redundant check bits at the transmission end. At the receiver these bits are re-computed and tested against the received bits. If they do not agree, then there has been a CRC error.

- `Frame Check`. This mechanism verifies the structure of the transmitted frame by checking the bit fields against the fixed format and the frame size. Errors detected by frame checks are designated format errors.

- `ACK Errors`. As already mentioned, frames received are acknowledged by all receivers through positive acknowledgment. If no acknowledgment is received by the transmitter of the message, an ACK error is indicated.

The CAN protocol also implements two mechanisms for error detection at the bit level:

- `Monitoring`. The ability of the transmitter to detect errors is based on the monitoring of bus signals. Each station that transmits also observes the bus level and thus detects differences between the bit sent and the bit received. This permits reliable detection of global errors and errors local to the transmitter.

- `Bit Stuffing`. The coding of the individual bits is tested at bit level. The bit representation used by CAN is `Non Return to Zero` (NRZ) coding, which guarantees maximum efficiency in bit coding. The synchronization edges are generated by means of bit stuffing. This means that after five consecutive equal bits the transmitter inserts into the bit stream a stuff bit with the complementary value, which is removed by the receivers.

If one or more errors are discovered by at least one station using the above mechanisms, the current transmission is aborted by sending an error flag. This prevents other stations accepting the message and thus ensures the consistency of data throughout the network. After transmission of an erroneous message that has been aborted, the sender automatically re-attempts transmission (automatic re-transmission). There may again competition for bus allocation.

However effective and efficient the method described may be, in the event of a defective station, it might lead to all messages (including correct ones) being aborted. If no measures for self-monitoring were taken, the bus system would be blocked by this. The CAN protocol therefore provides a mechanism to distinguish sporadic errors from permanent errors and local failures at the station. This is done by statistical assessment of station error situations with the aim of recognizing a stations own defects and possibly entering an operation mode where the rest of the CAN network is not negatively affected. This may go as far as the station switching itself off to prevent messages erroneously from being recognized as incorrect.

10.2.4 The CAN Functional Block Diagram in the TM4C123GH6PM System

The functional block diagram of the CAN module used in the TM4C123GH6PM MCU system is shown in Figure 10.3.

Two CAN modules are provided in this system, and both have the identical architecture and function. In the TM4C123GH6PM MCU system, the CAN controller provides supports to the CAN protocol version 2.0 (parts A and B).

Like standard or extended CAN frames, each piece of transferred message includes data, remote, error, and overload frames with an 11-bit identifier (standard) or a 29-bit identifier (extended). Transfer rates can be programmed up to 1 Mbps.

The CAN module consists of three major groups:

- CAN global protocol controller and message handler
- Message memory used to store 32 message objects
- CAN interface registers used to interface between the CPU and the message memory

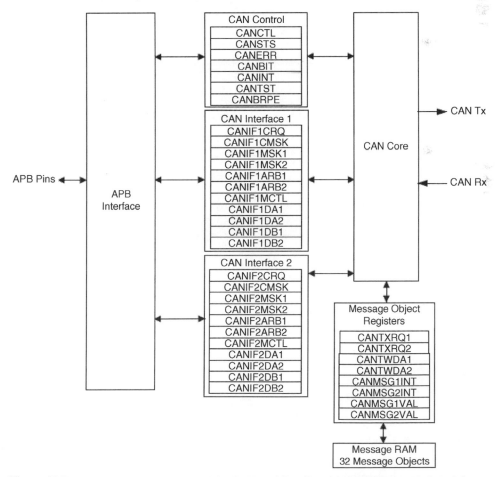

Figure 10.3. Functional block diagram of the CAN modules. (Reprinted with the permission of the Texas Instruments Incorporated.)

A data frame contains data for transmission, whereas a remote frame contains no data and is used to request the transmission of a specific message object.

Each group contains a set of related registers used to perform the associated functions. There are two sets of interface registers, one is for the CAN data transmit and the other is for the CAN data receive function.

10.2.5 The CAN Components and Operational Procedures

Two sets of CAN Interface Registers (CANIF1x and CANIF2x) are used to access the message objects in the Message RAM. The CAN controller coordinates transfers to and from the Message RAM to and from the registers. The two sets are independent and identical and can be used to queue transactions.

Figure 10.4 shows an illustration of the CAN operational procedure for data transfer. The registers in the CAN global control group control and coordinate all CAN operations. The CANERR register is exactly an error counter used to accumulate the total number of errors occurred. The CANSTS register is a global CAN status register used to provide the working status of the CAN module, such as CAN controller working in the bus-on or bus-off status, CAN transmit OK (TXOK), or CAN receive OK (RXOK). The CANINT register is used to hold and indicate the interrupt source via its message object ID.

- In order to enable the CAN module to perform normal functions, the first step is the CAN initialization and configuration process. The bit INIT (bit 0) and bit CCE (bit 6) in the CANCTL register must be set to 1 to start this initialization process. Also, these two bits must be kept in the set status during the entire initialization and configuration process until this process is done. The initialization process includes the setup and configuration of the CAN bit timing and baud rate, along with configuration of the message objects stored in the message memory.

- The basic CAN operation is to transmit or receive information composed as a group or a sequence of message objects in the standard or extend frames via CAN bus. As shown in Figure 10.4, each transmit message object is configured during the initialization process by the CPU via the CAN interface registers.

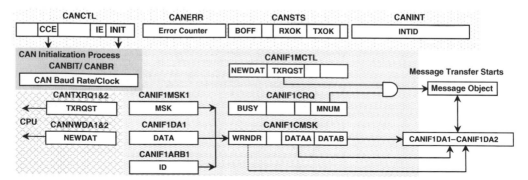

Figure 10.4. CAN Operational procedure.

- The MSK bit field in the CANIF1MSK1 register is used to enable or disable the ID filtering function for the message object to be transmitted. The DATA and the ID bit fields in the CANIF1DA1 and the CANIF1ARB1 registers are used to contain and hold the data to be transmitted and ID for each of 32 message objects to be sent.

- Based on the CANIF1MSK1 register's configuration, the CANIF1CMSK register is used to determine the data transfer direction and data source or target, such as the message object or the interface register. The bit WRNDR (bit 7) is a key bit and it is used to determine the data transfer direction, either a reading (WRNDR = 0) or a writing (WRNDR = 1). When the bit WRNDR is cleared, the data bytes 0~3 in the CANIF1DA1 and CANIF1DA2 registers are sent to the message object, otherwise they are transferred in the opposite way.

- After the message object has been configured and ready to be transmitted, the bit TXRQST (bit 8) in the CANIF1MCTL register is set to 1 to request a data transmit. The bit NEWDAT (bit 15) in this register is also set to 1 to indicate that a new data has been written into the message object. If a valid message number is written into the bit field MNUM in the CANIF1CRQ register, the message object is transmitted immediately.

- Also the bit BUSY (bit 15) in the CANIF1CRQ register is set to 1 to indicate that a data transmit process is started. This bit is cleared to 0 when the message object has been successfully transmitted.

- Two sets of message object registers, CANTXRQ1 and CANTXRQ2, and CANNWDA1 and CANNWDA2, are used to provide the data transmitting and data status of all 32 message objects. The bit fields TXRQST, which are the lower 16 bits on both CANTXRQ1 and CANTXRQ2 registers, contains transmit request pending status for all 32 message objects. A value of 1 on a bit indicates that the corresponding message object has been transmitted, and a 0 indicates that the transmit request is still pending. Also the bit fields NEWDAT in both CANNWDA1 and CANNWDA2 registers indicate whether a new data has been written to the data portion on the related message object.

The CAN message object receive procedure is similar to this transmit procedure. In the following sections, let's have a closer look at these procedures.

10.2.5.1 CAN Initialization and Configuration Process

To initialize the CAN controller, the peripheral clock must be enabled using the RCGC0 register, or the bits CAN0 or CAN1 on the RCGC0 register must be set to 1. In addition, the clock to the appropriate GPIO module must be enabled via the RCGC2 register. Set the GPIO AFSEL bits for the appropriate pins and configure the PMCx fields in the GPIOPCTL register to assign the CAN signals to the appropriate pins.

As we discussed in the previous section, the CAN software initialization is started by setting the INIT bit in the CANCTL register or by going bus-off, which occurs when the transmitter's error counter exceeds a count of 255. When the bit INIT is set, all message transfers to and from the CAN bus are stopped and the CANnTX signal is held High. Doing the initialization does not change the configuration of the CAN controller, the message objects, and the error counters. However, some configuration registers are only accessible while in the initialization state.

The first job in the initialization process is to configure the bit timing or the baud rate by setting the CAN Bit Timing (CANBIT) register and configuring each message object. If a message object is not needed, label it as not valid by clearing the MSGVAL bit in the CAN IFn Arbitration 2 (CANIFnARB2) register. Otherwise, the whole message object must be initialized since some fields of the message object may not have valid information and this may cause unexpected results.

Both the INIT and CCE bits in the CANCTL register must be set in order to access the CANBIT register and the CAN Baud Rate Prescaler Extension (CANBRPE) register to configure the bit timing.

To finish the initialization process and leave the initialization state, the INIT bit must be cleared. Then, the CAN synchronizes itself to the data transfer on the CAN bus by waiting for the occurrence of 11 consecutive recessive bits (bus idle condition) before it takes part in bus activities and starts message transfers. Message object initialization does not require the CAN to be in the initialization state and can be done on the fly. However, message objects should all be configured to particular identifiers or set to not valid before message transfer starts.

To change the configuration of a message object during normal operation, clear the MSGVAL bit in the CANIFnARB2 register to indicate that the message object is not valid during the change. When the configuration is completed, set the MSGVAL bit again to indicate that the message object is once again valid.

10.2.5.2 Transmit Message Objects

The transmission of message objects is under the control of the software that is managing the CAN hardware. Message objects can be used for one-time data transfers or multi-time transfers message objects used to respond in a more periodic manner. At the start of transmission, the appropriate TXRQST bit in the CAN Transmission Request n (CANTXRQn) register and the NEWDAT bit in the CAN New Data n (CANNWDAn) register are set. If several transmit messages are assigned to the same message object as the number of message objects is not sufficient, the whole message object has to be configured before the transmission of this message is requested.

The transmission of any number of message objects may be requested at the same time; they are transmitted according to their internal priority that is based on the message number (MNUM) for the message object, with 1 being the highest priority and 32 being the lowest priority. Messages may be updated or set to not valid any time, even when their requested transmission is still pending.

A message transmission can be automatically started by the reception of a matching remote frame. Set the RMTEN bit in the CAN IFn Message Control (CANIFnMCTL) register to enable this mode. The TXRQST bit is set when a matching received remote frame is detected, and the message object automatically transfers its data or generates an interrupt. The CAN mask registers, CANIFnMSKn, configure which groups of frames are identified as remote frame requests. The UMASK bit in the CANIFnMCTL register enables the MSK bits in the CANIFnMSKn register to filter which frames are identified as a remote frame request. The MXTD bit in the CANIFnMSK2 register should be set if a remote frame request is expected to be triggered by 29-bit extended identifiers.

Usually, a message object is transmitted in the following sequence:

- If the internal transmit shift register of the CAN module is ready for loading, and if a data transfer is not occurring between the CAN Interface Registers and message RAM, the valid message object with the highest priority that has a pending transmission request is loaded into the transmit shift register by the message handler and the transmission is started.

- The message object's NEWDAT bit in the CANNWDAn register is cleared to indicate that there is no any new data in the message object.
- After a successful transmission, and if no new data was written to the message object since the start of the transmission, the TXRQST bit in the CANTXRQn register is cleared.
- If the CAN controller is configured to generate an interrupt on a successful transmission of a message object by setting the TXIE bit in the CAN IFn Message Control (CAN-IFnMCTL) register, the INTPND bit in the CANIFnMCTL register is set after a successful transmission.
- If the CAN module has lost the message object or if an error occurred during the transmission, the number of the errors that have occurred is recorded in the CANERR register and the message is re-transmitted as soon as the CAN bus is free again. If, meanwhile, the transmission of a message with higher priority has been requested, the messages are transmitted in the order of their priority based on their MNUM number.

Before the message object can be transmitted, each of them needs the configuration and setup. The following steps illustrate how to configure a transmit message object:

1. First configure the CAN IFn Command Mask (CANIFnCMSK) Register:
   - Set the WRNRD bit to specify a write to the CANIFnCMSK register, and specify whether to transfer the IDMASK, DIR, and MXTD of the message object into the CAN Interface Registers using the MASK bit (bit 6).
   - Specify whether to transfer the ID, DIR, XTD, and MSGVAL of the message object into the interface registers using the ARB bit (bit 5).
   - Specify whether to transfer the control bits into the interface registers using the CONTROL bit (bit 4).
   - Specify whether to clear the INTPND bit in the CANIFnMCTL register using the CLRINTPND bit (bit 3).
   - Specify whether to clear the NEWDAT bit in the CANNWDAn register using the NEWDAT bit (bit 2).
   - Specify which bits to transfer using the DATAA and DATAB bits (bits 1 and 0).
2. Configure the CANIFnMSK1 register by using the bit field MSK[15:0] bits to specify which of the bits in the 29-bit or 11-bit message identifier are used for acceptance filtering. A point to be noted is that the MSK[15:0] in this register are used for bits [15:0] of the 29-bit message identifier and are not used for an 11-bit identifier. A value of 0x00 in this bit field enables all messages to pass through the acceptance filtering. Also note that in order for these bits to be used for acceptance filtering, they must be enabled by setting the UMASK bit in the CANIFnMCTL register.
3. Configure the CANIFnMSK2 register by using the bit field MSK[12:0] bits to specify which of the bits in the 29-bit or 11-bit message identifier are used for acceptance filtering. A point to be noted is that the MSK[12:0] are used for bits [28:16] of the 29-bit message identifier, but MSK[12:2] are used for bits [10:0] of the 11-bit message identifier. Use the MXTD and MDIR bits to specify whether to use XTD and DIR for acceptance filtering. A value of 0x00 in this bit field enables all messages to pass through the acceptance filtering. Also note that in order for these bits to be used for acceptance filtering, they must be enabled by setting the UMASK bit in the CANIFnMCTL register.
4. Configure the CANIFnARB1 register by configuring ID[15:0] for bits [15:0] for a 29-bit identifier and configuring ID[12:0] in the CANIFnARB2 register for bits [28:16] of the message identifier. Set the XTD bit to indicate an extended identifier and set the DIR bit to indicate transmit, and set the MSGVAL bit to indicate that the message object is valid.

5. For an 11-bit identifier, disregard the CANIFnARB1 register and configure ID[12:2] in the CANIFnARB2 register for bits [10:0] of the message identifier. Clear the XTD bit to indicate a standard identifier and set the DIR bit to indicate transmit, and set the MSGVAL bit to indicate that the message object is valid.

6. Configure the CANIFnMCTL register by:
   - Setting the UMASK bit to enable the mask bits MSK, MXTD, and MDIR specified in the CANIFnMSK1 and CANIFnMSK2 registers for acceptance filtering if the filtering function is used.
   - Setting the TXIE bit to enable the INTPND bit to be set after a successful transmission if the CAN transmit interrupt function is enabled and used.
   - Setting the RMTEN bit to enable the TXRQST bit to be set to begin an automatic message object transmit on the reception of a matching remote frame if the automatic transmission function is enabled and used.
   - Setting the EOB bit for a single message object if only a single message object is transmitted.
   - Configuring the DLC[3:0] field to specify the size of the data frame. Take care during this configuration not to set the NEWDAT, MSGLST, INTPND or TXRQST bits.

7. Load the data to be transmitted into the CANIFnDATn (CANIFnDA1, CANIFnDA2, CANIFnDB1, CANIFnDB2) registers. Byte 0 of the CAN data frame is stored in DATA [7:0] in the CANIFnDA1 register. Each of these registers is a 32-bit register but only the lower 16-bit is used to store data. The CANIFnDA1 register contains data bytes 1 and 0, CANIFnDA2 for data bytes 3 and 2, CANIFnDB1 **for** data bytes 5 and 4, and CANIFnDB2 **for** data bytes 7 and 6, respectively, since each data field contains 64-bit data (refer to Figure 10.2).

8. Determine and program the number of the message object to be transmitted in the MNUM field in the CANIFn Command Request (CANIFnCRQ) register. This is a priority number for the selected message object with 1 being Highest and 32 being Lowest priority levels.

9. After all steps above are properly configured, set the TXRQST bit in the CANIFnMCTL register. Once this bit is set, the message object is available to be transmitted, of course this depends on the priority of the message object (MNUM) and the bus availability. Remember, as we mentioned that setting the RMTEN bit in the CANIFnMCTL register can also start message transmission if a matching remote frame has been received.

A Transmit Message Object (TMO) can be updated or modified at any time by the processor via the CAN Interface Registers. Even if only some of the data bytes are to be updated, all four bytes of the corresponding CANIFnDAn/CANIFnDBn register have to be valid before the content of that register is transferred to the message object. Either the CPU must write all four bytes into the CANIFnDAn/CANIFnDBn register or the message object is transferred to the CANIFnDAn/CANIFnDBn register before the CPU writes the new data bytes.

Regularly, the updating procedure follows the steps listed below:

- Before the updating starts, both the MSGVAL bit in the CANIFnARB2 register and the TXRQST bits in the CANIFnMCTL register must be kept to 1.
- If only the data portion in a message object needs to be updated, the WRNRD, DATAA, and DATAB bits in the CANIFnMSKn register need to be set, followed by writing the updated data into the CANIFnDA1, CANIFnDA2, CANIFnDB1, and CANIFnDB2 registers.
- Then the number of the message object is written to the MNUM field in the CANIFnCRQ register. To begin transmission of the new data as soon as possible, set the TXRQST bit in the CANIFnMSKn register.

- To prevent the clearing of the TXRQST bit in the CANIFnMCTL register at the end of a transmission that may already be in progress while the data is updated, the NEWDAT and TXRQST bits have to be set at the same time in the CANIFnMCTL register. When these bits are set at the same time, NEWDAT is cleared as soon as the new transmission has started.

Next let's take a look at accepting the received message objects.

10.2.5.3 *Receive Message Objects*

The message object receiving process starts from the detecting and receiving a group of CAN parameters, which includes the ID and XTD bits in the CANIFnARB2 register and the RMTEN and DLC[3:0] bits on the CANIFnMCTL register.

The message handling controller then starts scanning the message RAM and tries to find a matching valid message object. To do this scanning process, the controller uses the acceptance filtering programmed through the mask bits in the CANIFnMSKn register and enabled using the UMASK bit in the CANIFnMCTL register. Each valid message object stored in the message RAM, starting with object 1, is compared with the incoming message to locate a matching message object in the message RAM. If a match is found, the scanning process is stopped and the message handler proceeds depending on whether it is a data frame or remote frame that was received.

For a data frame, the message handler stores the message located at the CAN controller receive shift register into the matching message object in the message RAM. All related information for this matching message object, including the data bytes, arbitration bits, and the DLC bits, is stored into the corresponding message object. In this way, the data bytes are connected with the identifier even if arbitration masks are used. The NEWDAT bit in the CANIFnMCTL register is set to inform the processor that new data has been received. The CPU should clear this bit when it reads the message object to inform the controller that the message has been received, and the buffer is free to receive more messages.

When the CAN controller receives a message and the NEWDAT bit is already set, the MSGLST bit in the CANIFnMCTL register is set to indicate that the previous data was lost. If an interrupt on successful reception of a frame is enabled, the RXIE bit in the CANIFnMCTL register should be set. In this case, the INTPND bit in the same register is set to enable the CANINT register to point to the message object that just received a message. The TXRQST bit of this message object should be cleared to prevent the transmission of a remote frame.

For a remote frame, it contains no data, but instead specifies which message objects stored in the message RAM should be transmitted. Three different configurations of the matching message object have to be considered.

1. The TXRQST bit of this message object is set. The entire message object keeps no change, and the controller automatically transfers the data in the message object as soon as possible (DIR = 1, RMTEN = 1, UMASK = 1 or 0).

2. The TXRQST bit of this message object remains unchanged, and the remote frame is ignored. This remote frame is disabled, the data is not transferred, and nothing indicates that the remote frame ever happened (DIR = 1, RMTEN = 0, UMASK = 0).

3. The TXRQST bit of this message object is cleared. The arbitration and control field (ID + XTD + RMTEN + DLC) from the shift register is stored into the message object in the message

RAM, and the NEWDAT bit of this message object is set. The data field of the message object remains unchanged; the remote frame is treated similar to a received data frame. This mode is useful for a remote data request from another CAN device for which the TM4C123GH6PM controller does not have readily available data. The software must fill the data and answer the frame manually (DIR = 1, RMTEN = 0, UMASK = 1).

Before a matching message object can be processed, each of them needs the configuration and setup. The following steps illustrate how to configure a receive message object:

1. First configure the CAN IFn Command Mask (CANIFnCMSK) Register:
   - Set the WRNRD bit to specify a write to the CANIFnCMSK register, and specify whether to transfer the IDMASK, DIR, and MXTD of the message object into the CAN Interface Registers using the MASK bit (bit 6).
   - Specify whether to transfer the ID, DIR, XTD, and MSGVAL of the message object into the interface registers using the ARB bit (bit 5).
   - Specify whether to transfer the control bits into the interface registers using the CONTROL bit (bit 4).
   - Specify whether to clear the INTPND bit in the CANIFnMCTL register using the CLRINTPND bit (bit 3).
   - Specify whether to clear the NEWDAT bit in the CANNWDAn register using the NEWDAT bit (bit 2).
   - Specify which bits to transfer using the DATAA and DATAB bits (bits 1 and 0).

2. Configure the CANIFnMSK1 register by using the bit-field MSK[15:0] bits to specify which of the bits in the 29-bit or 11-bit message identifier are used for acceptance filtering. A point to be noted is that the MSK[15:0] in this register are used for bits [15:0] of the 29-bit message identifier and are not used for an 11-bit identifier. A value of 0x00 in this bit field enables all messages to pass through the acceptance filtering. Also note that in order for these bits to be used for acceptance filtering, they must be enabled by setting the UMASK bit in the CANIFnMCTL register.

3. Configure the CANIFnMSK2 register by using the bit-field MSK[12:0] bits to specify which of the bits in the 29-bit or 11-bit message identifier are used for acceptance filtering. A point to be noted is that the MSK[12:0] are used for bits [28:16] of the 29-bit message identifier, but MSK[12:2] are used for bits [10:0] of the 11-bit message identifier. Use the MXTD and MDIR bits to specify whether to use XTD and DIR for acceptance filtering. A value of 0x00 in this bit field enables all messages to pass through the acceptance filtering. Also note that in order for these bits to be used for acceptance filtering, they must be enabled by setting the UMASK bit in the CANIFnMCTL register.

4. Configure the CANIFnARB1 register by configuring ID[15:0] for bits [15:0] for a 29-bit identifier and configuring ID[12:0] in the CANIFnARB2 register for bits [28:16] of the message identifier. Set the XTD bit to indicate an extended identifier and set the DIR bit to indicate transmit, and set the MSGVAL bit to indicate that the message object is valid.

5. For an 11-bit identifier, disregard the CANIFnARB1 register and configure ID[12:2] in the CANIFnARB2 register for bits [10:0] of the message identifier. Clear the XTD bit to indicate a standard identifier and set the DIR bit to indicate transmit, and set the MSGVAL bit to indicate that the message object is valid.

6. Configure the CANIFnMCTL register by:
   - Setting the UMASK bit to enable the mask bits MSK, MXTD, and MDIR specified in the CANIFnMSK1 and CANIFnMSK2 registers for acceptance filtering.
   - Setting the RXIE bit to enable the INTPND bit to be set after a successful reception.

* Clearing the RMTEN bit to keep the TXRQST bit unchanged.
* Setting the EOB bit for a single message object.
* Configuring the DLC[3:0] field to specify the size of the data frame.

    During this configuration the following bits, such as the NEWDAT, MSGLST, INTPND, or TXRQST, should not be set.

7. Determine and program the number of the message object to be received in the MNUM field in the CANIFnCRQ register. Reception of the message object begins as soon as a matching frame is available on the CAN bus.

After a data frame is received, the message handler stores a data frame into the message object. It stores the received Data Length Code (DLC) and eight data bytes into the CANIFnDA1, CANIFnDA2, CANIFnDB1, and CANIFnDB2 registers. Byte 0 of the CAN data frame is stored in DATA[7:0] in the CANIFnDA1 register. If the DLC is less than 8, the remaining bytes of the message object are filled by unspecified values.

In addition to receiving a single data frame, a group of data frames can be received by a message object by configuring the CAN mask registers CANIFnMSK1 and CAN-IFnMSK2. The MSK bit fields in these registers can be used to configure which groups of frames are received by a message object. The UMASK bit in the CANIFnMCTL register enables the MSK bit fields in the CANIFnMSKn register to filter which frames are received. The MXTD bit in the CANIFnMSK2 register should be set if only 29-bit extended identifiers are expected by this message object.

The CPU may read a received message any time via the CAN Interface registers. Generally, the CPU first writes 0x007F to the CANIFnCMSK register and then writes the number of the message object to the CANIFnCRQ register. That combination transfers the whole received message object from the message RAM into the Message Buffer registers such as CANIFnMSKn, CANIFnARBn, and CANIFnMCTL. Additionally, the NEWDAT and INTPND bits are cleared in the message RAM to acknowledge that the message has been read and clearing the pending interrupt generated by this message object.

If the message object uses masks for acceptance filtering, the CANIFnARBn registers show the full and unmasked ID for the received message. The NEWDAT bit in the CANIFnMCTL register shows whether a new message has been received since the last time this message object was read. The MSGLST bit in the CANIFnMCTL register shows whether more than one message has been received since the last time this message object was read. Since the MSGLST bit cannot not be cleared automatically, it should be cleared by software after reading its status.

When using a remote frame, the CPU may request new data from another CAN node on the CAN bus. Setting the TXRQST bit of a receive object causes the transmission of a remote frame with the receive object's identifier. This remote frame triggers the other CAN node to start the transmission of the matching data frame. If the matching data frame is received before the remote frame could be transmitted, the TXRQST bit is automatically reset. This prevents the possible loss of data when the other device on the CAN bus has already transmitted the data slightly earlier than expected.

10.2.5.4 Handle CAN Module Interrupts

If more than one interrupt are pending, the CAN Interrupt (CANINT) register points to the pending interrupt with the highest priority disregarding their requesting order.

Among the message interrupts, the message object's interrupt with the lowest message number (MNUM) has the highest priority. A message interrupt is cleared by clearing the message object's INTPND bit in the CANIFnMCTL register or by reading the CAN Status (CANSTS) register. The status Interrupt is cleared by reading the CANSTS register.

The interrupt identifier INTID in the CANINT register indicates the source of the interrupt. When no interrupt is pending, the register reads as 0x0000. If the value of the INTID field is different from 0, then an interrupt is pending. If the IE bit is set in the CANCTL register, the interrupt line to the interrupt controller is active. The interrupt line remains active until the INTID field is 0, which means that all interrupt sources have been cleared, or until IE bit is cleared, which disables interrupts from the CAN controller.

The INTID field of the CANINT register contains the number of the message object that created the interrupt, and this number MNUM has the highest interrupt priority. The following bits have the special functions to trigger a related interrupt:

- The SIE bit in the CANCTL register controls whether a change of the RXOK, TXOK.
- The LEC bits in the CANSTS register can cause an interrupt.
- The EIE bit in the CANCTL register controls whether a change of the BOFF and EWARN bits in the CANSTS register can cause an interrupt.
- The IE bit in the CANCTL register controls whether any interrupt from the CAN controller actually generates an interrupt to the interrupt controller. The CANINT register can be updated even when the IE bit in the CANCTL register is clear, but the interrupt is not indicated to the CPU.

A value of 0x8000 in the INTID field of the CANINT register indicates that an interrupt is pending because the CAN module has updated, but not necessarily changed, the CANSTS register, indicating that either an error or status interrupt has been generated. A write access to the CANSTS register can clear the RXOK, TXOK, and LEC bits in that same register; however, the only way to clear the source of a status interrupt is to read the CANSTS register.

The source of an interrupt can be determined in two ways during the interrupt handling:

- Read the INTID bit in the CANINT register to determine the highest priority interrupt that is pending,
- Read the CAN Message Interrupt Pending (CANMSGnINT) register to see all message objects that have pending interrupts.

An interrupt service routine reading the message that is the source of the interrupt may read the message and clear the message object's INTPND bit at the same time by setting the CLRINTPND bit in the CANIFnCMSK register. Once the INTPND bit has been cleared, the CANINT register contains the message number for the next message object with a pending interrupt.

10.2.5.5 CAN Module Operational Modes

The CAN module can work in one of the following six possible modes:

1. Test Mode – Enable various diagnostics to be performed.
2. Silent Mode–Analyze the traffic on a CAN bus without affecting it by the transmission of dominant bits (Acknowledge Bits & Error Frames).

3. Loopback Mode–Used for self-test functions (CANnTX is connected to CANnRX).

4. Loopback Combined with the Silent Mode – Enable the CAN Controller to be tested without affecting a running CAN system connected to the CANnTX and CANnRX signals.

5. Basic Mode–Enable the CAN Controller to be operated without the Message RAM.

6. Normal Mode–Enable the CAN Controller to be operated with the Message RAM.

Let's take a closer look at the silent, loopback, and basic modes.

The Loopback Mode can be used to allow the CAN Controller to perform a self-test without affecting a running CAN system connected to the CANnTX and CANnRX signals. In this mode, the CANnRX signal is disconnected from the CAN Controller and the CANnTX signal is held recessive.

This mode is enabled by setting both the TEST bit in the CANCTL register and the LBACK bit in the CANTST register.

The Silent Mode is similar to the Loopback Mode.

The Basic Mode allows the CAN Controller to be operated without the Message RAM. In Basic Mode, the CANIF1 interface register group is used as the transmit buffer. The operational sequence for this mode is as follows:

- The transmission of the contents of the IF1 registers is requested by setting the BUSY bit of the CANIF1CRQ register.
- When the BUSY bit is set, all CANIF1 registers are locked.
- The BUSY bit indicates that a transmission is pending.
- As soon the CAN bus is idle, the CANIF1 registers are loaded into the shift register of the CAN Controller and transmission is started.
- When the transmission has completed, the BUSY bit is cleared and the locked CANIF1 registers are released.
- A pending transmission can be aborted at any time by clearing the BUSY bit in the CANIF1CRQ register while the CANIF1 registers are locked. If the CPU has cleared the BUSY bit, a possible retransmission in case of lost arbitration or an error is disabled.

The CANIF2 interface registers are used as a receive buffer. After the reception of a message, the contents of the shift register are stored in the CANIF2 registers without any acceptance filtering. Additionally, the actual contents of the shift register can be monitored during the message transfer. The operational sequence for this mode is as follows:

- Each time, a read message object is initiated by setting the BUSY bit in the CANIF2CRQ register.
- The contents of the shift register are stored into the CANIF2 registers.

In Basic Mode, all message-object-related control and status bits and the control bits of the CANIFnCMSK registers are not used. The message number in the CANIFnCRQ registers is also not evaluated. But in the CANIF2MCTL register, the NEWDAT and MSGLST bits retain their function and the DLC[3:0] field shows the received DLC, but all other control bits are cleared.

Basic Mode is enabled by setting the BASIC bit in the CANTST register.

10.2.5.6 CAN Clock and Baud Rate Configuration

In order to successfully transmit and receive message objects via CAN bus, the transmitting and receiving process must be controlled and synchronized to make both

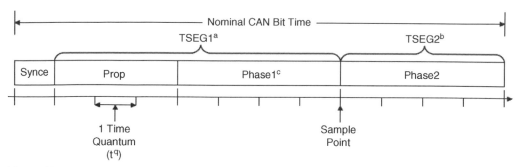

Figure 10.5. A normal CAN bit time configuration. (Reprinted with the permission of the Texas Instruments Incorporated.)

transmitter and receiver work at the same timing base to reduce the possible error to the lowest levels. Therefore the basic transmit and receive timing unit, bit time or bit rate (bit time = 1/(bit rate)), must be evaluated as accurately as possible to make sure that each bit can be transmitted and received in a timing range that can be tolerated by the CAN bus.

The CAN system supports bit rates in the range of lower than 1 Kbps up to 1000 Kbps. Each node of the CAN network has its own clock generator. The timing parameter of the bit time can be configured individually for each CAN node, creating a same bit rate even though the CAN nodes may use different clock rates.

A standard or normal CAN bit time configuration is shown in Figure 10.5.

As shown in Figure 10.5, each bit time period is composed of four segments: the Synchronization Segment (Sync), the Propagation Time Segment (Prop), the Phase Buffer Segment 1 (Phase 1), and the Phase Buffer Segment 2 (Phase 2). Each segment consists of a specific and programmable number of time quanta (tq). The length of the time quantum tq, which is the basic time unit of the bit time, is defined by the CAN controller's input clock frequency (F_{sys}) or period (P_{sys}) and the Baud Rate Prescaler (BRP):

$$tq = BRP \times P_{sys} = BRP/F_{sys}$$

The F_{sys} is the system clock frequency as configured by the RCC or RCC2 registers.

The reason to use these four segments to make the bit time is to automatically adjust the normal bit time by adding or removing some numbers of t_q to make it match to the actual bit time to avoid some timing errors caused by the variations on the temperature and environment. The Sample Point shown in Figure 10.5 is the time moment when the bit transmission or reception has occurred. The purpose of using this kind of bit time structure is to modify the bit time to enable the nominal sample point to approach the actual sample point as closely as possible to make the bit transmit and receive as precisely as possible.

The Synchronization Segment Sync is used to compensate the timing difference or so-called phase errors between the nominal and the actual CAN bus edges to be occurred.

The Propagation Time Segment Prop is intended to compensate for the physical propagation time delay occurred for the entire CAN network.

The Phase Buffer Segments Phase1 and Phase2 surround the Sample Point.

The Re-Synchronization Jump Width (SJW) defines how far a resynchronization may move the Sample Point inside the limits defined by the Phase Buffer Segments to compensate for edge phase errors.

Table 10.1. The minimum programmable ranges of four segments in CANBIT register.

Parameter	Range	Function
BRP	1~64	Defines the length of the time quantum tq. The CANBRPE register can be used to extend the range to 1024.
Sync	1 tq	Fixed length, synchronization of bus input to system clock.
Prop	1~8 tq	Compensates for the physical delay times.
Phase 1	1~8 tq	May be lengthened temporarily by synchronization.
Phase 2	1~8 tq	May be shortened temporarily by synchronization.
SJW	1~4 tq	May not be longer than either Phase Buffer Segment.

In TM4C123GH6PM MCU system, the bit timing configuration can be programmed in lower 15 bits in the CANBIT register. Four bit fields, TSEG2, TSEG1, SJW, and BRP, are mapped to those segments shown in Figure 10.5 and can be programmed to a numerical value that is one less than its functional value. Table 10.1 shows the numerical value range of those segments programmed in the CANBIT register.

Therefore, the length of the bit time in the programmed and function values are:

$(\text{TSEG1} + \text{TSEG2} + 1) \times \text{tq}$ (programmed values)

$(\text{Sync} + \text{Prop} + \text{Phase1} + \text{Phase2}) \times \text{tq}$ (function values)

The value in the CANBIT register is the configuration input of the CAN protocol controller. The baud rate prescaler (BRP field) defines the length of the time quantum, and the bit timing logic configured by TSEG1, TSEG2, and SJW defines the number of time quanta in the bit time.

The information processing time (IPT) is the time after the sample point needed to calculate the next bit to be transmitted on the CAN bus. The IPT includes any of the following time periods: retrieving the next data bit, handling a CRC bit, determining if bit stuffing is required, generating an error flag, or simply going idle.

The IPT is application-specific but may not be longer than 2 tq. The typical CAN's IPT is 0 tq. Its length is the lower limit of the programmed length of Phase2. In case of synchronization, Phase2 may be shortened to a value less than IPT, which does not affect bus timing.

10.2.5.6.1 Calculate the Bit Time Parameters and Configure the CANBIT Register
The calculation of the bit timing configuration starts with a required bit rate or bit time. The resulting bit time must be an integer multiple of the system clock period.

The bit time may consist of 4 to 25 time quanta. Several combinations may lead to the required bit time, allowing iterations of the following steps.

The first part of the bit time to be defined is the propagation time delay Prop. Its length depends on the delay times measured in the system. A maximum bus length as well as a maximum node delay has to be defined for expandable CAN bus systems. The resulting time for Prop is converted into time quanta that is rounded up to the nearest integer multiple of tq.

The Synchronization Segment Sync is fixed at 1 tq long. If the number of remaining tq is even, the Phase Buffer Segments have the same length, that is, Phase2 = Phase1, else Phase2 = Phase1 + 1.

The length of the synchronization jump width SJW is set to the least of 4, `Phase1` or `Phase2`.

CAN nodes with different system clocks require different configurations to come to the same bit rate. The calculation of the propagation time in the CAN network, based on the nodes with the longest delay times, is done once for the whole network.

An example for bit timing at low baud rate is shown in Figure 10.6. In this example, the frequency of the CAN clock is 50 MHz and the bit rate is 100 Kbps.

Since the bit rate is 100 Kbps, the bit time is $1/10^5 = 0.000001$ seconds $= 10\,\mu s$.

1. In line 1, we allow bit time $10\,\mu s = 10 \times tq$ to get $tq = 1\,\mu s$ in line 2.
2. The baud rate prescaler (BRP) can be calculated based on the equations in lines 4 and 5, which is 50.
3. In line 6, the `Sync` is obtained since it is a fixed number with 1 tq value.
4. The calculations in lines 7~9 are for the total CAN system propagation time delay, which is 500 ns or $0.5\,\mu s$. This value is rounded to a nearest integer value of 1 for the `Prop` in line 10.
5. The programmed and function values for these timing parameters are shown in lines 11 and 12.
6. Based on line 12, the `Phase1` and `Phase2` values are calculated in lines 16 and 17, and both of are 4.
7. Starting at line 18, three bit-field values, TSEG1, TSEG2, and SJW, in the CANBIT register are calculated. The results are: BRP = 50, TSEG1 = 5, TSEG2 = 4 and SJW = 4.

However, each of the actual values put into these bit fields in the CANBIT register should be one less than the calculated values shown above since all of them are counted

```
 1 bit time = 10 µs = n * tq = 10 * tq          // n = 10
 2 tq = 1 µs
 3 tq = (Baud Rate Prescaler)/CAN Clock Freq
 4 Baud Rate Prescaler = tq * CAN Clock Freq
 5 Baud Rate Prescaler = 1E-6 * 50E6 = 50
 6 Sync = 1 * tq = 1 µs                         // fixed at 1 time quanta
 7 delay of bus driver 200 ns
 8 delay of receiver circuit 80 ns
 9 delay of bus line (40m) 220 ns
10 Prop 1 µs = 1 * tq                           // 1 µs is next integer multiple of tq
11 bit time = Sync + TSeg1 + TSeg2 = 10 * tq    // programmed values
12 bit time = Sync + Prop + Phase1 + Phase2     // function values
13 Phase1 + Phase2 = bit time - Sync - Prop
14 Phase1 + Phase2 = (10 * tq) - (1 * tq) - (1 * tq)
15 Phase1 + Phase2 = 8 * tq
16 Phase1 = 4 * tq
17 Phase2 = 4 * tq                              // Phase1 = Phase2
18 TSeg1 = Prop + Phase1
19 TSeg1 = (1 * tq) + (4 * tq)
20 TSeg1 = 5 * tq                               // TSeg1 = 5
21 TSeg2 = Phase2
22 TSeg2 = (Information Processing Time + 4) × tq
23 TSeg2 = 4 * tq                               // TSeg2 = 4 (assumes IPT=0)
24 SJW = 4 * tq                                 // SJW = 4 (<= Phase1 or Phase2)
```

Figure 10.6. An example for bit timing calculation at low baud rate.

starting from 0, not 1; therefore the final values put into these bit fields are BRP = 49, TSEG1 = 4, TSEG2 = 3, and SJW = 3. The final value programmed into the CANBIT register is 0x34F1.

During this calculation, the Information Processing Time (IPT) is assumed to be 0 and can be neglected in this case. For the propagation time delay parameter Prop, the maximum possible value is used.

10.2.6 The CAN Module Registers

As we discussed in Section 10.2.4, all CAN-module-related registers can be categorized into three groups: the CAN Global Control and Status Registers, the CAN Interface Registers, and Message Object Registers. Because of the similarity between the CAN Interface 1 Registers and CAN Interface 2 Registers group, we only concentrate on the CAN Interface 1 Registers group.

10.2.6.1 The CAN Global Control and Status Registers

The following registers are involved in this group:

- CANCTL — Interrupt enable, error interrupt enable and initialization enable.
- CANSTS — Bus-On or Bus-Off, error upper bound of the error counter.
- CANERR — Error Counter, accumulate the error numbers.
- CANBIT — Bit time width and amount.
- CANTST – CAN Test function.
- CANBRPE — Prescale Extension.
- CANINT — Indicate the interrupt source (which message object).

10.2.6.1.1 The CAN Global Control Register (CANCTL) The CANCTL is a global control register for all CAN modules and its bit field configuration is shown in Figure 10.7. The bit field and functions are shown in Table 10.2.

This is a 32-bit register but only the lower 7 bits are used to initialize the CAN module and enable test mode and CAN interrupts.

When the initialization process starts, the CAN device is Bus-Off and the INIT bit (bit 0) is set to stop all bus activities to enable the initialization and configuration process to start.

Once the initialization process is complete, the INIT bit is cleared immediately by the processor and the device then waits for 129 occurrences of Bus Idle (129 * 11 consecutive High bits) before resuming normal operations. At the end of the Bus-Off recovery sequence, the Error Management Counters are reset.

During the waiting time after INIT is cleared, each time a sequence of 11 High bits has been monitored, a BITERROR0 code is written to the CANSTS register by setting the LEC

CAN Global Control Register (CANCTL)

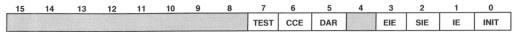

15	14	13	12	11	10	9	8	7	6	5	4	3	2	1	0
								TEST	CCE	DAR		EIE	SIE	IE	INIT

Reserved Bits 31–8, 4.

Figure 10.7. The bit-field configuration of the CANCTL register.

Table 10.2. Bit value and its function for CANCTL register.

Bit	Name	Reset	Function
31:8	Reserved	0x0	Reserved
7	TEST	0	Test Mode Enable: 0: The CAN controller is operating normally; 1: The CAN controller is in test mode.
6	CCE	0	Configuration Change Enable: 0: Write accesses to the CANBIT register are not allowed. 1: Write accesses to the CANBIT register are allowed if the INIT bit is 1.
5	DAR	0	Disable Automatic-Retransmission: 0: Auto-retransmission of disturbed messages is enabled; **1:** Auto-retransmission is disabled.
3	EIE	0	Error Interrupt Enable: 0: No error status interrupt is generated. 1: A change in the BOFF or EWARN bits in the CANSTS register generates an interrupt.
2	SIE	0	Status Interrupt Enable: 0: No status interrupt is generated. 1: An interrupt is generated when a message has successfully been transmitted or received, or a CAN bus error has been detected. A change in the TXOK, RXOK or LEC bits in the CANSTS register generates an interrupt.
1	IE	0	CAN Interrupt Enable: 0: Interrupts disabled; 1: Interrupts enabled.
0	INIT	1	Initialization Enable: 0: Normal operation; 1: Initialization started.

field as 0x5 to enable the CPU to readily check whether the CAN bus is stuck Low or continuously disturbed and to monitor the proceeding of the bus-off recovery sequence.

10.2.6.1.2 The CAN Global Status Register (CANSTS) This is a 32-bit register but only the lower 8 bits are used to contain and hold information for interrupt servicing such as Bus-Off, error count threshold, and error types. The bit-field configuration of this register is shown in Figure 10.8, and bit functions are shown in Table 10.3.

The LEC field holds the code that indicates the type of the last error to occur on the CAN bus. This field is cleared when a message has been transferred or received without error. The unused error code 0x7 may be written by the CPU to manually set this field to an invalid error so that it can be checked for a change later.

An error interrupt is generated by the BOFF and EWARN bits, and a status interrupt is generated by the RXOK, TXOK, and LEC bits if the corresponding enable bits in the CANCTL register are set. A change of the EPASS bit or a write to the RXOK, TXOK, or LEC bits does not generate any interrupt. Three bits, BOFF, EWARN, and EPASS, are read-only bits without writing ability.

A point to be noted is that a reading this register (CANSTS) clears the CAN Interrupt (CANINT) register if any interrupt is pending.

CAN Global Status Register (CANSTS)

Figure 10.8. The bit-field configuration of the CANSTS register.

Table 10.3. Bit value and its function for CANSTS register.

Bit	Name	Reset	Function
31:8	Reserved	0x0	Reserved
7	BOFF	0	Bus-Off Status: 0: The CAN controller is not in Bus-Off state; 1: The CAN controller is in Bus-Off state.
6	EWARN	0	Warning Status: 0: Both error counters are below the error warning limit of 96. 1: At least one of the error counters has reached the error warning limit of 96.
5	EPASS	0	Error Passive: 0: The CAN module is in the Error Active state, it means, the receive or transmit error count is less than or equal to 127. 1: The CAN module is in the Error Passive state, that is, the receive or transmit error count is greater than 127.
4	RXOK	0	Received a Message Successfully: 0: No message has been successfully received. 1: A message is successfully received, independent of the result of the acceptance filtering. This bit must be cleared by writing a 0 to it.
3	TXOK	0	Transmitted a Message Successfully: 0: no message has been successfully transmitted. 1: a message is successfully transmitted error-free and acknowledged by one other node. This bit must be cleared by writing a 0 to it.
2:0	LEC	0x0	Last Error Code: 0x0: No Error; 0x1: Stuff Error—More than 5 equal bits in a sequence have occurred in a part of a received message where this is not allowed. 0x2: Format Error—A fixed format part of the received frame has the wrong format. 0x3: ACK Error—The message transmitted was not acknowledged by another node. 0x4: Bit 1 Error—When a message is transmitted, the CAN controller monitors the data lines to detect any conflicts. When the arbitration field is transmitted, data conflicts are a part of the arbitration protocol. When other frame fields are transmitted, data conflicts are considered errors. A Bit 1 Error indicates that the device wanted to send a High level (logical 1) but the monitored bus value was Low (logical 0). 0x5: Bit 0 Error—A Bit 0 Error indicates that the device wanted to send a Low level, but the monitored bus value was High. During bus-off recovery, this status is set each time a sequence of 11 High bits has been monitored. By checking for this status, software can monitor the proceeding of the bus-off recovery sequence without any disturbances to the bus. 0x6: CRC Error—The CRC checksum was incorrect in the received message, indicating that the calculated value received did not match the calculated CRC of the data. 0x7: No Event—When the LEC bit shows this value, no CAN bus event was detected since this value was written to the LEC field.

10.2.6.1.3 The CAN Error Counter Register (CANERR) This is a 32-bit register but only the lower 16 bits are used to contain and hold the error counter values that can be used to analyze the cause of an error. The bit field configuration of this register is shown in Figure 10.9, and bit functions are shown in Table 10.4.

10.2.6.1.4 The CAN Bit Timing Register (CANBIT) This is a 32-bit register but only the lower 15 bits (bits 14:0) are used to program the bit width and bit quantum utilized for the message

CAN Error Counter Register (CANERR)

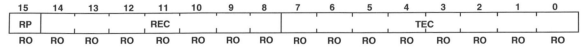

Figure 10.9.   The bit-field configuration of the CANERR register.

Table 10.4. Bit value and its function for CANERR register.

Bit	Name	Reset	Function
31:16	Reserved	0x0	Reserved
15	RP	0	Received Error Passive: 0 : The Receive Error counter is below the Error Passive level (127 or less). 1 : The Receive Error counter has reached the Error Passive level (128 or greater).
14:8	REC	0	Receive Error Counter: This field contains the state of the receiver error counter (0 to 127).
7:0	TEC	0	Transmit Error Counter: This field contains the state of the transmit error counter (0 to 255).

CAN Bit Timing Register (CANBIT)

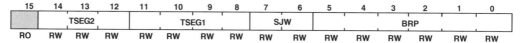

Figure 10.10. The bit field configuration of the CANBIT register.

object bits transfer. Values are programmed based on the system clock period and frequency. This register is write-enabled by setting the CCE and INIT bits in the CANCTL register.

The bit-field configuration of this register is shown in Figure 10.10, and bit functions are shown in Table 10.5.

10.2.6.1.5 The CAN Test Register (CANTST) This is a 32-bit register but only the lower 6 bits, bits 7~2, are used to enable the CAN controller to perform self-testing and external pin access. It is write-enabled by setting the TEST bit in the CANCTL register. Different test functions may be combined, however, CAN transfers are affected if the TX bits in this register are not zero. The bit-field configuration of this register is shown in Figure 10.11, and bit functions are shown in Table 10.6.

10.2.6.1.6 The CAN Baud Rate Prescaler Extension Register (CANBRPE) This is a 32-bit register but only the lower 4 bit-field BRPE (bits 3:0) are used to further divide the bit time set with the BRP bit in the CANBIT register. It is write-enabled by setting the CCE bit in the CANCTL register.

Table 10.5. Bit value and its function for CANBIT register.

Bit	Name	Reset	Function
31:15	Reserved	0x0	Reserved
14:12	TSEG2	0	Time Segment after Sample Point: Refer to Section 10.2.5.6 to determine this value.
11:8	TSEG1	0	Time Segment Before Sample Point: Refer to Section 10.2.5.6 to determine this value.
7:6	SJW	0	(Re)Synchronization Jump Width: Refer to Section 10.2.5.6 to determine this value.
5:0	BRP	0	Baud Rate Prescaler: Refer to Section 10.2.5.6 to determine this value.

CAN Test Register (CANTST)

15	14	13	12	11	10	9	8	7	6	5	4	3	2	1	0
		Reserved Bits 31–8						RX	TX		LBACK	SILENT	BASIC	Reserved	
								RO	RW	RW	RW	RW	RW	RO	RO

Figure 10.11.   The bit-field configuration of the CANTST register.

This 4 bit-field BRPE has a range of 0x00~0x0F, and it is used to extend the BRP bit field in the CANBIT register to values up 1023. Since the baud rate prescaler (BRP) in the CANBIT register occupies 6 bits, plus this 4 bits (BRPE), the total bits can be extended to 10 ($2^{10} = 1024$).

As we mentioned, by using this BRPE value, the total baud rate prescaler (BRP) in the CANBIT register can be extended. In fact, this extension is achieved by dividing the input system clock frequency by the value in the BRPE bit field. For example, if the system clock frequency is 10 MHz and if the BRPE value is 10 (0x0A), the actual operational or driven clock frequency to the CAN module is reduced by 10 times. This is equivalent to pre-divide the system clock to relatively extend the range of the BRP value without touching the original BRP value.

10.2.6.1.7 The CAN Interrupt Register (CANINT)   This is a 32-bit register but only the lower 16 bits (INTID) are used to contain and hold the current highest-priority interrupt source represented as the message object number (MNUM). This is a read-only register without any writing ability.

The interrupt sources contained in this register are divided into two different ranges based on their numbers: 0x0001~0x0020 indicates the number of the message object that had the highest priority level and caused the interrupt; 0x8000 indicates that a status interrupt has been occurred. All other number ranges are reserved.

If several interrupts are pending, this register points to the pending interrupt with the highest priority disregarding the order in which the interrupts occurred. An interrupt remains pending until the CPU has cleared it. If the INTID field is not 0x0000 (the default) and the IE bit in the CANCTL register is set, the interrupt is active. The interrupt line remains active until the INTID field is cleared by reading the CANSTS register or until the IE bit in the CANCTL register is cleared.

Table 10.6.   Bit value and its function for CANTST register.

Bit	Name	Reset	Function
31:8	Reserved	0x0	Reserved
7	RX	0	Receive Observation: 0: The CANnRx pin is low; 1: The CANnRx pin is high.
6:5	TX	0	Transmit Control: 0x0: CAN Module Control, 0x1: Sample Point, 0x2: Driven Low, 0x3: Driven High.
4	LBACK	0	Loopback Mode: 0: Loopback mode is disabled. 1: Loopback mode is enabled. The data from the transmitter is routed into the receiver.
3	SILENT	0	Silent Mode: 0: Silent mode is disabled, 1: Silent mode is enabled.
2	BASIC	0	Basic Mode: 0: Basic mode is disabled, 1: Basic mode is enabled.

CAN IF1 Command Request Register (CANIF1CRQ)

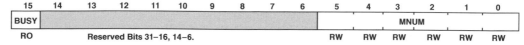

Figure 10.12. The bit-field configuration of the CANIF1CRQ register.

10.2.6.2 The CAN Interface 1 Registers

The following registers are involved in this group:

- CANIF1CRQ–Control the message transfer starting command and transfer status.
- CANIF1CMSK–Provide the mask bits to enable or disable the control commands.
- CANIF1MCTL–Hold the control information of the message object to be sent to the Message RAM.
- CANIF1MSK1–Provide Identifications masks for 29-bit identifier.
- CANIF1MSK2 – Provide Identifications masks for 11-bit identifier.
- CANIF1ARB1 – Hold the ID for 29-bit identifier.
- CANIF1ARB2 – Hold the ID for 11-bit identifier.
- CANIF1DA1, CANIF1DA2, CANIF1DB1, CANIF1DB2–Contain the data to be sent or the data has been received (8-byte).

10.2.6.2.1 CAN IF1 Command Request Register (CANIF1CRQ) This is a 32-bit register but only the bit 15 (bit BUSY) and lower 6 bits, bits MNUM (bits 5:0), are used to hold the number of the current message object and the transfer status of the message object, as shown in Figure 10.12. As soon as a valid message object number is written into the MNUM bit field and the bit TXRQST in the CANIF1MCTL register is set, a message object transfer starts. During this transferring process, the BUSY bit in this register is automatically set to indicate that a transfer between the CAN Interface Registers and the internal message RAM is in progress. This BUSY bit is reset to 0 when the transfer process between the interface registers and the message RAM is complete. A point to be noted is that this BUSY bit is a read-only bit without any writing ability.

The valid value range of the bit-field MNUM is from 0x01 to 0x20, which covered 1~32 message object numbers. The range 0x21~0x3F is reserved and all other numbers are invalid.

10.2.6.2.2 CAN IF1 Command Mask Register (CANIF1CMSK) This is a 32-bit register but only the lowest 8 bits (bits 7:0) are used to either read the command mask status or write the command mask to indicate the transfer direction and data source or data target. The bit-field configuration of this register is shown in Figure 10.13, and bit functions are shown in Table 10.7.

CAN IF1 Command Mask Register (CANIF1CMSK)

Figure 10.13. The bit-field configuration of the CANIF1CMSK register.

Table 10.7. Bit value and its function for CANIF1CMSK register.

Bit	Name	Reset	Function
31:8	Reserved	0x0	Reserved
7	WRNRD	0	Write, Not Read: 0: Transfer the data in the message object specified by the MNUM field in the CANIFnCRQ register into the CANIFn registers. 1: Transfer the data in the CANIFn registers to the message object specified by the MNUM field in the CANIFnCRQ register.
6	MASK	0	Access Mask Bits: 0: Mask bits unchanged. 1: Transfer IDMASK + DIR + MXTD of the message object into the Interface registers.
5	ARB	0	Access Arbitration Bits: 0: Arbitration bits unchanged. 1: Transfer ID + DIR + XTD + MSGVAL of the message object into the Interface registers.
4	CONTRL	0	Access Control Bits: 0: Control bits unchanged. 1: Transfer control bits from the CANIFnMCTL register into the Interface registers.
3	CLINTPND	0	Clear Interrupt Pending Bit: 0: If WRNRD is clear, the interrupt pending status is transferred from the message buffer into the CANIFnMCTL register. If WRNRD is set, the INTPND bit in the message object remains unchanged. 1: If WRNRD is clear, the interrupt pending status is cleared in the message buffer. Note the value of this bit that is transferred to the CANIFnMCTL register always reflects the status of the bits before clearing. If WRNRD is set, the INTPND bit is cleared in the message object.
2	NEWDAT/ TXRQST	0	NEWDAT/TXRQST Bit: 0: If WRNRD is clear, the value of the new data status is transferred from the message buffer into the CANIFnMCTL register. If WRNRD is set, a transmission is not requested. 1: If WRNRD is clear, the new data status is cleared in the message buffer. Note the value of this bit that is transferred to the CANIFnMCTL register always reflects the status of the bits before clearing. If WRNRD is set, a transmission is requested. Note that when this bit is set, the TXRQST bit in the CANIFnMCTL register is ignored.
1	DATAA	0	Access Data Bytes 0–3: 0: Data bytes 0–3 are unchanged. 1: If WRNRD is clear, transfer data bytes 0–3 in CANIFnDA1 and CANIFnDA2 to the message object. If WRNRD is set, transfer data bytes 0–3 in message object to CANIFnDA1 and CANIFnDA2.
0	DATAB	0	Access Data Byte 4 to 7: 0: Data bytes 4–7 are unchanged. 1: If WRNRD is clear, transfer data bytes 4–7 in CANIFnDA1 and CANIFnDA2 to the message object. If WRNRD is set, transfer data bytes 4–7 in message object to CANIFnDA1 and CANIFnDA2.

This register has two functions, reading and writing, and these functions are controlled by the bit 7 (bit WRNRD). If this bit is clear to 0, a reading function is performed and the data is read from the CAN message object specified by the MNUM field in the CANIF1CRQ register and sent into the CANIFn interface registers. If the bit WRNDR is set to 1, a writing function is executed and the data in the CANIFn interface registers is written into the message object specified by the MNUM field in the CANIF1CRQ register.

A point to be noted is that when the WRNRD bit is cleared and a read operation is performed, if the CLRINTPND and/or NEWDAT bits are set, the interrupt pending and/or new data flags in the message object buffer are cleared after this reading operation.

Another point to be noted is that these reading and writing operations are controlled by the CPU. When CPU needs data, a reading is performed and the data is read from the message RAM and sent to the CPU via the interface registers. When CPU sends data, a

CAN IF1 Message Control Register (CANIF1MCTL)

15	14	13	12	11	10	9	8	7	6	5	4	3	2	1	0
NEWDAT	MSGLST	INTPND	UMASK	TXIE	RXIE	RMTEN	TXRQST	EOB	Reserved			DLC			
RW	RW	RW	RW	RW	RW	RW	RW	RW	RO	RO	RO	RW	RW	RW	RW

Figure 10.14. The bit field configuration of the CANIF1MCTL register.

writing is performed and the data is written into the message RAM, exactly to the message object stored in the message RAM, via the interface registers.

10.2.6.2.3 CAN IF1 Message Control Register (CANIF1MCTL) This is a 32-bit register but only the lower 13 bits are used to hold the control information associated with the message object to be sent to the Message RAM. The bit-field configuration of this register is shown in Figure 10.14, and the bit functions are shown in Table 10.8.

Table 10.8. Bit value and its function for CNAIF1MCTL register.

Bit	Name	Reset	Function
31:16	Reserved	0x0	Reserved
15	NEWDAT	0	New Data: 0 : No new data has been written into the data portion of this message object by the message handler since the last time this flag was cleared by the CPU. 1 : The message handler/CPU writes new data into the data portion of this message object.
14	MSGLST	0	Message Lost: 0 : No message was lost since the last time this bit was cleared by the CPU. 1 : The message handler stored a new message into this object when NEWDAT was set; the CPU has lost a message.
13	INTPND	0	Interrupt Pending: 0 : This message object is not the source of an interrupt. 1 : This message object is the source of an interrupt. The interrupt identifier in the CANINT register points to this message object if no another higher priority interrupt source.
12	UMASK	0	Use Acceptance Mask: 0 : Mask is ignored. 1 : Use mask, (MSK, MXTD, and MDIR bits in the CANIFnMSKn registers for acceptance filtering.
11	TXIE	0	Transmit Interrupt Enable: 0 : The INTPND bit in the CANIFnMCTL register is unchanged after a successful transmission. 1 : The INTPND bit in the CANIFnMCTL register is set after a successful transmission.
10	RXIE	0	Receive Interrupt Enable: 0 : The INTPND bit in the CANIFnMCTL register is unchanged after a successful reception. 1 : The INTPND bit in the CANIFnMCTL register is set after a successful reception of a frame.
9	RMTEN	0	Remote Enable: 0 : At the reception of a remote frame, the TXRQST bit in the CANIFnMCTL register is no change. 1 : At the reception of a remote frame, the TXRQST bit in the CANIFnMCTL register is set.
8	TXRQST	0	Transmit Request: 0 : This message object is not waiting for transmission. 1 : The transmission of this message object is requested and is not yet done.
7	EOB	0	End of Buffer: 0 : Message object belongs to a FIFO Buffer and is not the last message object on FIFO Buffer. 1 : Single message object or last message object of a FIFO Buffer.
3:0	DLC	0x0	Data Length Code: **0x0–0x8:** Specifies the number of bytes in the data frame. **0x9–0xF:** Defaults to a data frame with 8 bytes.

CAN IF1 Mask 2 Register (CANIF1MSK2)

15	14	13	12	11	10	9	8	7	6	5	4	3	2	1	0
MXTD	MDIR								MSK						
RW	RW	Reserved	RW	RW	RW	RW	RW	RW	RW	RW	RW	RW	RW	RW	RW

Figure 10.15.   The bit-field configuration of the CANIF1MSK2 register.

10.2.6.2.4 CAN IF1 Mask 1 Register (CANIF1MSK1)   This is a 32-bit register but only the lower 16 bits, MSK bits (bits 15:0), are used to hold the mask bits [15:0] of the ID for a 29-bit identifier to enable or disable the ID filtering function. These 16-bit masks are used with the ID bit in the CANIF1ARB1 register for acceptance filtering. When reset, all of these MSK bits are set to 1 to enable all masks for all ID.

When using a 29-bit identifier, these 16 bits are used for bits [15:0] of the ID of a message object. When a bit in this MSK field is set to 1, this means that the corresponding ID is used for acceptance filtering. Otherwise the related ID is not used for acceptance filtering.

The MSK field in the CANIF1MSK2 register are used for bits [28:16] of the ID of a message object. When using an 11-bit identifier, these 16 mask bits are ignored.

10.2.6.2.5 CAN IF1 Mask 2 Register (CANIF1MSK2)   This register holds extended mask information that accompanies the CANIF1MSK1 register. In fact, the lower 11 bits, MSK bits (bits 12:2), in this register are used for bits [10:0] of the ID when an 11-bit identifier is used. The bit-field configuration of this register is shown in Figure 10.15, and the bit functions are shown in Table 10.9.

When using a 29-bit identifier, these bits are used for bits [28:16] of the ID. The MSK field in the CANIF1MSK1 register are used for bits [15:0] of the ID. When using an 11-bit identifier, MSK[12:2] are used for bits [10:0] of the ID.

10.2.6.2.6 CAN IF1 Arbitration 1 Register (CANIF1ARB1)   This is a 32-bit register but only the lower 16 bits, ID bits (bits 15:0), are used to hold the identifiers for acceptance filtering.

Table 10.9.   Bit value and its function for CNAIF1MSK2 register.

Bit	Name	Reset	Function
31:16	Reserved	0x0	Reserved
15	MXTD	0	Mask Extended Identifier: 0: The extended identifier bit XTD in the CANIF1ARB2 register has no effect on the acceptance filtering. 1: The extended identifier bit XTD is used for acceptance filtering.
14	MDIR	0	Mask Message Direction: 0: The message direction bit DIR in the CANIFnARB2 register has no effect for acceptance filtering. 1: The message direction bit DIR is used for acceptance filtering.
12:0	MSK	0	Identifier Mask: 0: The corresponding identifier field (ID) in the message object is not used. 1: The corresponding identifier field (ID) is used for acceptance filtering.

Figure 10.16. The bit-field configuration of the CANIF1ARB2 register.

This 16-bit ID field is used with another 16-bit ID field in the CANIF1ARB2 register to create 32 message identifiers. When using a 29-bit identifier, bits 15:0 on this register are [15:0] of the ID, while bits 12:0 on the CANIF1ARB2 register are [28:16] of the ID.

When using an 11-bit identifier, these 16 ID bits are not used. The reset value for this ID field is 0x00, which means that no any ID has been used.

10.2.6.2.7 CAN IF1 Arbitration 2 Register (CANIF1ARB2)
This is a 32-bit register but only the lower 16 bits are used to hold information for acceptance filtering and ID for an 11-bit identifier. The bit-field configuration of this register is shown in Figure 10.16, and the bit functions are shown in Table 10.10.

A point to be noted is that all unused message objects should have the MSGVAL bit cleared during initialization and before clearing the INIT bit in the CANCTL register.

The MSGVAL bit must also be cleared before any of the following bits are modified or if the message object is no longer required: the ID fields in the CANIF1ARB1 and CANIF1ARB2 registers, the XTD and DIR bits in the CANIF1ARB2 register, or the DLC field in the CANIF1MCTL register.

10.2.6.2.8 CAN IF1 Data A1, CAN IF1 Data A2, CAN IF1 Data B1, CAN IF1 Data B2 (CANIF1DA1~CANIF1DA2, CANIF1DB1~CANIF1DB2) Registers
These are 32-bit registers but only the lower 16 bits are used for each of them to contain 8 bytes data

Table 10.10. Bit value and its function for CNAIF1ARB2 register.

Bit	Name	Reset	Function
31:16	Reserved	0x0	Reserved
15	MSGVAL	0	Message Valid: 0: The message object is invalid and ignored by the message handler. 1: The message object is configured and ready to be considered by the message handler within the CAN controller.
14	XTD	0	Extended Identifier: 0: An 11-bit Standard Identifier is used for this message object. 1: A 29-bit Extended Identifier is used for this message object.
13	DIR	0	Message Direction: 0: Receive. When the TXRQST bit in the CANIFnMCTL register is set, a remote frame with the identifier of this message object is received. On reception of a data frame with matching identifier, that message is stored in this message object. 1: Transmit. When the TXRQST bit in the CANIFnMCTL register is set, the respective message object is transmitted as a data frame. On reception of a remote frame with matching identifier, the TXRQST bit of this message object is set (if RMTEN = 1).
12:0	ID	0	Message Identifier: This ID bit field is used with the ID field in the CANIFnARB2 register to create the message identifier. When using a 29-bit identifier, ID[15:0] of the CANIFnARB1 register are [15:0] of the ID, while these bits, ID[12:0], are [28:16] of the ID. When using an 11-bit identifier, ID[12:2] are used for bits [10:0] of the ID. The ID field in the CANIFnARB1 register is ignored

to be sent or that has been received. In a CAN data frame, data byte 0 is the first byte to be transmitted or received and data byte 7 is the last byte to be transmitted or received. In CAN's serial bit stream, the MSB of each byte is transmitted first.

The CANIF1DA1 register contains data bytes 1 and 0, and the CANIF1DA2 register for data bytes 3 and 2. The CANIF1DB1 register contains data bytes 5 and 4, and the CANIF1DB2 register contains data bytes 7 and 6.

10.2.6.3 The CAN Message Object Registers

The following registers are involved in this group:

- CANTXRQ1 & CANTXRQ2 – Hold the TXRQST bits of the 32 message objects.
- CANNWDA1 & CANNWDA2 – Hold the NEWDAT bits of the 32 message objects.
- CANMSG1INT & CANMSG2INT – Hold the INTPND bits of the 32 message objects.
- CANMSG1VAL & CANMSG2VAL – Hold the MSGVAL bits of the 32 message objects.

Generally, these registers are used to hold and maintain the running and interrupt pending statuses.

All of these registers are 32-bit registers but only the lower 16 bits are used as related bit field, such as TXRQST, NEWDAT, INTPND, and MSGVAL, to monitor and indicate the running and interrupt pending statuses for 32 message objects.

If a bit on any bit-field in these registers is set to 1, this means that the related property of the corresponding message object is activate. Otherwise if a bit is 0, this means that the related property of the corresponding message object is inactive.

For example, if a bit in the TXRQST bit field in the CANTXRQ1 or CANTXRQ2 registers is set to 1, it indicates that the corresponding message object has a transmission request pending; if a bit in the NEWDAT bit field in the CANNWDA1 or CANNWDA2 register is set to 1, it indicates that the corresponding message object has a new data and its data portion has been updated.

Similarly, if a bit in the INTPND bit-field in the CANMSG1INT or CANMSG2INT register is cleared to 0, it means that the corresponding message object has no interrupt pending. If a bit in the MSGVAL bit field is set to 1, this means that the corresponding message object has been configured and is valid in this CAN bus system.

10.2.7 The CAN Module Interfacing and External Control Signals

As we mentioned in Section 10.2.5.1, all external control and interfacing signals used for the CAN modules are shared with some GPIO pins since the CAN module itself has no real hardware connection with other peripherals in the TM4C123GH6PM MCU system.

The CAN controller signals are applied by using alternate functions for some GPIO signals. Table 10.11 shows these GPIO pins with related CAN external control and signal pins. The column GPIO Pin in the Table 10.11 lists the possible GPIO pin placements for the CAN signals. The AFSEL bit in the GPIOAFSEL register must be set to choose the CAN controller function. The number in parentheses is the encoding that must be programmed into the PMCx field in the GPIOPCTL register to assign the CAN signal to the specified GPIO port pin.

Table 10.11. CAN external control signals and GPIO pins distributions.

CAN Pin	GPIO Pin	Pin Type	Buffer Type	Pin Function
CAN0RX	PF0 (3) PB4 (8) PE4 (8)	I	TTL	CAN Module 0 Receive.
CAN0TX	PF3 (3) PB5 (8) PE5 (8)	O	TTL	CAN Module 0 Transmit.
CAN1RX	PA0 (8)	I	TTL	CAN Module 1 Receive.
CAN1TX	PA1 (8)	O	TTL	CAN Module 1 Transmit.

10.2.8 The CAN API Functions Provided by TivaWare™ Peripheral Driver Library

Since the CAN programming is a little complicated compared with other peripherals, some CAN API functions provided by the TivaWare™ Peripheral Driver Library may be used to combine with the DRA model together to make the program short and easy. We should have a closer look at these API functions before we can build any CAN implementation projects.

Before we can discuss these API functions, first let's take a look at some special and important data structures used in these API functions.

10.2.8.1 Special Data Structures and Enumerations Used in the CAN Programming

Two data structures are popular and widely implemented in the CAN programming:

- tCANBitClkParms
- tCANMsgObject

The first structure is used for encapsulating the values associated with setting up the bit timing for a CAN controller, and the second structure is used for encapsulating all the items associated with a CAN message object in the CAN controller.

Three enumerations are defined and used in the TM4C123GH6PM CAN system:

- tCANIntStsReg–Identify the interrupt status register.
- tCANStsReg–Identify which of several status registers to read.
- tMsgObjType–Determine the type of message object that will be set up.

Table 10.12 shows these data structures and enumerators.

The CAN API functions provide a set of interfacing functions to access two CAN modules. Functions are provided to configure the CAN controllers, configure message objects, and manage CAN interrupts. About 20 API functions are provided by the TivaWare™ Peripheral Driver Library, and these functions can be divided into the three groups based on their functions:

- CAN module initialization and configuration functions.
- CAN module message setting and processing functions.
- CAN module interrupt configuration and handle functions.

Table 10.12. Some data structures and enumerations in CAN controller programming.

Data Structure/Enumerator	Data Member Function
| ```
typedef struct
{
    uint32_t ui32SyncPropPhase1Seg;
    uint32_t ui32Phase2Seg;
    uint32_t ui32SJW;
    uint32_t ui32QuantumPrescaler;
}
tCANBitClkParms
``` | `ui32SyncPropPhase1Seg`: Hold the sum of the Synchronization, Propagation, and Phase Buffer 1 segments, measured in time quanta. The valid values for this setting range from 2 to 16.<br>`ui32Phase2Seg`: Hold the Phase Buffer 2 segment in time quanta. The valid values for this setting range from 1 to 8.<br>`ui32SJW`: Hold the Resynchronization Jump Width in time quanta. The valid values for this setting range from 1 to 4.<br>`ui32QuantumPrescaler`: Holds the CAN_CLK divider used to determine time quanta. The valid values for this setting from 1 to 1023. |
| ```
typedef struct
{
    uint32_t ui32MsgID;
    uint32_t ui32MsgIDMask;
    uint32_t ui32Flags;
    uint32_t ui32MsgLen;
    uint8_t *pui8MsgData;
}
tCANMsgObject
``` | `ui32MsgID`: The CAN message identifier used for 11- or 29-bit identifiers.<br>`ui32MsgIDMask`: The message identifier mask used when identifier filtering is enabled.<br>`ui32Flags`: This value holds various status flags and settings specified by `tCANObjFlags`.<br>`ui32MsgLen`: This value is the number of bytes of data in the message object.<br>`pui8MsgData`: This is a pointer to the message object's data. |
`tCANIntStsReg`	`CAN_INT_STS_CAUSE`: Read the CAN interrupt status information. `CAN_INT_STS_OBJECT`: Read a message object's interrupt status.
`tCANStsReg`	`CAN_STS_CONTROL`: Read the full CAN controller status. `CAN_STS_TXREQUEST`: Read the full 32-bit mask of message objects with a transmit request set. `CAN_STS_NEWDAT`: Read the full 32-bit mask of message objects with new data available. `CAN_STS_MSGVAL`: Read the full 32-bit mask of message objects that are enabled.
`tMsgObjType`	`MSG_OBJ_TYPE_TX`: Transmit message object. `MSG_OBJ_TYPE_TX_REMOTE`: Transmit remote request message object. `MSG_OBJ_TYPE_RX`: Receive message object. `MSG_OBJ_TYPE_RX_REMOTE`: Receive remote request message object. `MSG_OBJ_TYPE_RXTX_REMOTE`: Remote frame receive remote, with auto-transmit message object.

10.2.8.2 CAN Module Initialization and Configuration Functions

Generally, a normal initialization and configuration process for any CAN module includes the following operational sequence:

1. Before any CAN module can be initialized and configured, the selected CAN module must be enabled and clocked by calling the related `SysCtlPeripheralEnable()` functions. Also, the related GPIO pins should be enabled and clocked by using the same function.

2. The CAN module is disabled by default after a reset, so the `CANInit()` function must be called before any other CAN functions can be called. This call initializes the message objects to a safe state prior to enabling the controller on the CAN bus.

3. Then the bit timing values must be programmed prior to enabling the CAN controller. The `CANBitTimingSet()` function should be called with the appropriate bit timing values for the CAN bus. An alternative way to setup the bit timing is to use another API function `CANBitRateSet()` to simplify this process.

4. Once these two functions have been called, a CAN controller is ready to go and can be enabled by using the `CANEnable()` function.

5. The `CANDisable()` function does not reinitialize a CAN controller, so it can be used to temporarily remove a CAN controller from the bus.

Table 10.13.   The CAN module initialization and configuration API functions.

API Function	Parameter	Description
void CANInit(uint32_t ui32Base)	ui32Base is the base address of the CAN controller.	Initialize the CAN controller after reset. After reset, the CAN controller is in the disabled state. However, the memory used for message objects may contain undefined values and must be cleared prior to enabling the CAN controller the first time.
void CANBitTimingSet(uint32_t ui32Base, tCANBitClkParms *psClkParms)	ui32Base is the base address of the CAN controller. psClkParms points to the structure with the clock parameters.	Configure the various timing parameters for the CAN bus bit timing. Refer to Section 10.2.5.6.1 and tCANBitClkParms structure in Table 10.11 to get more details.
uint32_t CANBitRateSet(uint32_t ui32Base, uint32_t ui32SourceClock, uint32_t ui32BitRate)	ui32Base is the base address of the CAN controller. ui32SourceClock is the system clock for the device in Hz. ui32BitRate is the desired bit rate.	Set the CAN bit timing for the bit rate passed in the ui32BitRate parameter based on ui32SourceClock parameter. Because the CAN clock is based off of the system clock, the calling function should pass in the source clock rate either by retrieving it from SysCtlClockGet() or using a specific value in Hz.
void CANEnable(uint32_t ui32Base)	ui32Base is the base address of the CAN controller to enable.	Enable the CAN controller for message processing. Once enabled, the controller automatically transmits any pending frames, and processes any received frames. The controller can be stopped by calling CANDisable(). Prior to calling CANEnable(), CANInit() should have been called to initialize the controller and the CAN bus clock should be configured by calling CANBitTimingSet().
void CANDisable(uint32_t ui32Base)	ui32Base is the base address of the CAN controller to disable.	Disable the CAN controller for message processing. When disabled, the controller no longer automatically processes data on the CAN bus.

Table 10.13 shows these functions with the arguments.

One point to be noted is that if any CAN module interrupt is involved, such as error and status interrupt, transmit or receive interrupt, the configuration and setup processes for those interrupts must be performed before the CAN module can be enabled.

10.2.8.3 CAN Module Message Setting and Processing Functions

Before any message object can be transmitted or received via CAN bus, it must be set up and configured to become appropriate message object with suitable frame and structure. To configure message objects to perform any action, the application must first set up one of the 32 message objects using the API function CANMessageSet(). This function is used to configure a message object to send data, or to configure a message object to receive data. Each message object can be configured to generate interrupts on transmission or reception of CAN messages.

When data is received from the CAN bus, the application can use the CANMessageGet() API function to read the received message. This function can also be used to read a message object that is already configured in order to populate a message structure prior to making changes to the configuration of a message object. Reading the message object using this function also clears any pending interrupt on the message object.

Once a message object has been configured using CANMessageSet(), the message object has been allocated and continues to perform its programmed function unless it is released by a call to the function CANMessageClear(). The application is not required to clear out a message object before setting it with a new configuration because each time the CANMessageSet() function is called, it overwrites any previously programmed configuration.

Table 10.14 shows these functions with the arguments.

Table 10.14. The CAN module message setting and processing functions.

API Function	Parameter	Description
void CANMessageSet(uint32_t ui32Base, uint32_t ui32ObjID, tCANMsgObject *psMsgObject, tMsgObjType eMsgType)	ui32Base is the base address of the CAN controller. ui32ObjID is the object number to configure (1-32). psMsgObject is a pointer to a structure containing message object settings. eMsgType indicates the type of message for this object.	Configure a message object in the CAN controller. The eMsgType must be one of the following values: MSG_OBJ_TYPE_TX — CAN transmit message object. MSG_OBJ_TYPE_TX_REMOTE — CAN transmit remote request message object. MSG_OBJ_TYPE_RX — CAN receive message object. MSG_OBJ_TYPE_RX_REMOTE — CAN receive remote request message object. MSG_OBJ_TYPE_RXTX_REMOTE — CAN remote frame receive remote, then transmit message object. The message object pointed to by psMsgObject must be populated by the caller, as follows: ui32MsgID — contain the message ID, 11 or 29 bits. ui32MsgIDMask — mask of bits from ui32MsgID that must match if identifier filtering is enabled. ui32Flags • Set MSG_OBJ_TX_INT_ENABLE flag to enable interrupt on transmission. • Set MSG_OBJ_RX_INT_ENABLE flag to enable interrupt on receipt. • Set MSG_OBJ_USE_ID_FILTER flag to enable filtering based on the identifier mask specified by ui32MsgIDMask. ui32MsgLen — the number of bytes in the message data. This parameter should be nonzero even for a remote frame; it should match the expected bytes of data in the responding data frame. pui8MsgData — points to a buffer containing up to 8 bytes of data for a data frame.
void CANMessageClear(uint32_t ui32Base, uint32_t ui32ObjID)	ui32Base is the base address of the CAN controller. ui32ObjID is the message object number to disable (1-32).	Free the specified message object from use. Once a message object has been "cleared, " it no longer automatically sends or receives messages, nor does it generate interrupts.
void CANMessageGet(uint32_t ui32Base, uint32_t ui32ObjID, tCANMsgObject *psMsgObject, bool bClrPendingInt)	ui32Base is the base address of the CAN controller. ui32ObjID is the object number to read (1-32). psMsgObject points to a structure containing message object fields. bClrPendingInt indicates whether an associated interrupt should be cleared.	Read the contents of one of the 32 message objects in the CAN controller and return it to the caller. The data returned is stored in the fields of the caller-supplied structure pointed to by psMsgObject. The data consists of all of the parts of a CAN message, plus some control and status information. When using CANMessageGet(), all of the same fields of the structure are populated in the same way as when the CANMessageSet() function is used, with the following exceptions: psMsgObject->ui32Flags: MSG_OBJ_NEW_DATA indicates if this data is new since the last time it was read. MSG_OBJ_DATA_LOST indicates that at least one message was received on this message object and not read by the host before being overwritten.

10.2.8.4 CAN Module Interrupt Configuration and Handle Functions

The CAN controller can generate interrupts on several conditions:

- When any message object transmits a message.
- When any message object receives a message.
- On warning conditions such as an error counter reaching a limit or occurrence of various bus errors.
- On controller status error conditions such as entering the Bus-Off state.

An interrupt handler must be installed in order to process CAN interrupts. If dynamic interrupt configuration is desired, the CANIntRegister() must be used to register the interrupt handler first before it can be used. This function places the vector in a RAM-based vector table. The interrupt must also be enabled on the host processor master interrupt controller using the IntEnable() function. The CAN module interrupts are enabled using the CANIntEnable() function.

Once CAN interrupts are enabled, the handler is invoked whenever a CAN interrupt is triggered. The handler can determine which condition caused the interrupt by using the CANIntStatus() function.

Multiple conditions can be pending when an interrupt occurs, so the handler must be designed to process all pending interrupt conditions before exiting. Each interrupt condition must be cleared before exiting the handler. There are two ways to do this. The CANIntClear() function clears a specific interrupt condition without further action required by the handler. However, the handler can also clear the condition by performing certain actions. If the interrupt is a status interrupt, the interrupt can be cleared by reading the status register with CANStatusGet(). If the interrupt is caused by one of the message objects, then it can be cleared by either reading the message object using CANMessageGet() or calling the CANIntClear() function.

There are several status registers that can be used to help the application manage the controller. Different status registers can be read by using the CANStatusGet() function. There is a controller status register that provides general status information such as error or warning conditions. There are also several status registers that provide information about all of the message objects using a 32-bit map of the status, with one bit representing each message object.

10.2.9 A CAN Module Implementation Example Project

To build a real CAN module application project, it needs some hardware configurations and preparations, such as CAN bus configuration and interface conversions. These include the conversions between the TTL/CMOS levels to the transmission levels for all message bits and hardware connections via specified connectors. The MCP2551 CAN High-Speed Transceiver is a good choice for these conversions and the 9-pin D-sub-type male connector is a good selection for the connector.

A general implementation is to use two TM4C123GXL evaluation boards (EVBs) to work as two CAN controllers to transfer and receive message objects via two CAN modules installed on two evaluation boards. One EVB works as a CAN master and uses PF3 and PF0 as CAN0TX and CAN0RX signal wires to transmit message objects, and the

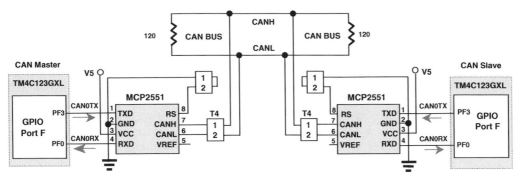

Figure 10.17.   Hardware configuration of the CAN interface MCP2551.

other EVB works as a CAN slave to use PF3 and PF0 to receive these message objects. Both CAN controllers use the CAN Module 0 Transmitter (CAN0TX) and the CAN Module 0 Receiver (CAN0RX).

As we mentioned, a typical CAN transceiver interfacing circuit is MCP2551. Any node connected to the CAN bus needs this interface to transmit and receive message objects from/to another nodes.

A typical hardware configuration with two pieces of TM4C123GXL EVBs and MCP2551 transceivers is shown in Figure 10.17.

In this hardware CAN interface configuration, two pieces of MCP2551 are used and each one is working as an interfacing transceiver to interface to the related CAN controller and external CAN bus to transmit or receive messages via external CAN bus. The two-wire bus operates on a differential signal and allows reliable operation in high Electrical Magnetic Interference (EMI) environments. Inductive spikes or noises will not degrade the signals as they will affect each wire equally, particularly for a twisted pair configuration.

The message is transferred via a differential signal on the CANH (1) and the CANL (2) twisted wires. The resistance between CANH and CANL is about $120\,\Omega$. In this configuration, two TM4C123GXL EVBs are used as two CAN node controllers, and each one controls one node.

Unlike other serial peripheral devices, such as USB, I2C, SSI, and UART, you cannot just cross over two CANH and CANL wires to test the transfer and receive ability of the CAN module. Instead, you must use the MCP2551 transceiver as interfaces to convert the TTL or MOS logic level to the CAN signal level and meet the requirements of the CAN bus impedance $(120\,\Omega)$ since the CAN is not same as any other serial peripheral devices.

Before one can develop the master or salve software on two EVBs, one must set up and connect the hardware components as shown in Figure 10.17. You can use the breadboard provided by the EduBASE ARM® Trainer to make these connections.

Since the CAN project is a little complicated, we left this as a lab project to the readers. In this section we try to build a simple and easy CAN project to perform the self-testing function by using the Loopback mode provided by the CAN controller.

10.2.9.1 Build a Simple CAN Self-Test Project

For the self-testing function, one does not need to do any hardware configuration and connection. By setting the TEST bit in the CANCTL register and the LBACK bit in the

CANTST register, the RX pin is loopback to the TX pin in the CAN module to enable it to work in the self-test mode.

To make this project simple, we will use DRA and SD models together since some CAN initialization and processing functions are complicated and need big volume on the coding process. In this project, we use the transmit interrupts to inform the main program to pick up the message data. After each message object is transmitted, a related TX interrupt is generated and passed to the handler. Inside the handler, a receiving flag is set to inform the main program that a message object has been received, and the data stored in the message object can be picked up. Then the received data can be sent to the PB3~PB0 LEDs to be displayed.

The build processes and steps of this project are listed below:

1. Declare some global variables and flags to be used in this project.
2. Declare some transmit and receive structures discussed in Section 10.2.8.1.
3. Initialize and configure the GPIO pins and CAN0 module. These include:
   - Enable and clock CAN0 module and GPIO Ports B and F.
   - Configure PB4 and PB5 as CAN0RX and CAN0TX pins.
   - Initialize CAN0 module.
   - Set up the bit timing or bit rate for the CAN0 module.
   - Register the CAN0 transmit interrupt handler and enable the CAN0 interrupt.
   - Enable the CAN0 module.
4. Configure TEST bit in the CANCTL register and LBACK bit in the CANTST register to enable the CAN0 module to work in the loopback mode.
5. Set up message object to make it ready to be transmitted.
6. Transmit the message object to the CAN0 module.
7. Receive the message object from the CAN0 module.

Now let's create a new project CANLoopBack in the folder C:\ARM Class Projects\Chapter 10. First let's start from the header file since this project needs to use quite a few macros.

10.2.9.2 Build the Header File for the CAN Project CANLoopBack

Open the Keil® μVersion®5 IDE and create a new header file CANLoopBack.h under the project CANLoopBack we created in the last section. Enter the codes shown in Figure 10.18 into this new created header file.

Let's have a closer look at this piece of codes to see how it works.

1. The codes between lines 4 and 11 are used to include all system header files used in this project.
2. The CAN0 module interrupt number is defined at line 12.
3. Four user-defined functions are declared in lines 13 and 16. These functions are used to simplify the whole project and break the project into different pieces of functions to make project neat.
4. The codes in lines 17 and 19 are used to declare some global variables and flags to be used in the project. These variables and flags include the receiving flag rcFlag that is used to indicate to the main program that a message object has been received and it is ready to be

```
1  //*********************************************************************************************************
2  // CANLoopBack.h - Header File for CANLoopBack.c - Loop Back Test for CAN0
3  //*********************************************************************************************************
4  #include <stdbool.h>
5  #include <stdint.h>
6  #include "inc/hw_can.h"
7  #include "driverlib/can.h"
8  #include "driverlib/gpio.h"
9  #include "driverlib/interrupt.h"
10 #include "driverlib/sysctl.h"
11 #include "TM4C123GH6PM.h"

12 #define INT_CAN0   55          // CAN0 interrupt number

13 void  InitCAN(void);
14 void  SetMsgObj(uint8_t *sdata, tCANMsgObject*sMsg, uint8_t *rdata, tCANMsgObject *rMsg);
15 void  TransMsg(uint8_t *sData, tCANMsgObject *sMsg);
16 void  RecvMsg(uint8_t *rData, tCANMsgObject *rMsg);

17 int  rcFlag = 0;
18 bool  errFlag = 0;
19 uint8_t  rccData[4],  ui8MsgD    ata[4] = {1, 2, 4, 8};

20 void  SimpleDelay(double  seconds)               // delay time function in seconds
21 {
22    SysCtlDelay((seconds * 16000000) / 3);
   }
```

Figure 10.18. The codes for the header file CANLoopBack.h.

picked up. The errFlag is used to indicate whether an error, either a status and bus error, has been detected during the program running process. Two global data array, rccData[] and ui8MsgData[], are used to hold and define the data values to be transmitted.

5. The codes in lines 20 and 22 are used to define a simple time delay function by calling the system function SysCtlDelay(). The input argument seconds is the number of seconds to be delayed by calling this function.

A point to be noted is that the delay function length is represented by the equation (seconds * 16000000)/3. The system clock used in this project is 16 MHz or 16000000 Hz. Each period of this clock is 1/16000000 seconds. Inside the system function SysCtlDelay(), three instructions are used to do this delay. Therefore the total delay time by calling this system function is $T_p = 3 \times$ period of the system clock, which is $T_p = 3 \times (1/16000000) = 3/16000000$ if each instruction takes one clock period to be executed.

Suppose we need to delay 1 second, the total numbers of executing this function N is:

$$N \times T_p = 1 \text{ second}, \quad \text{thus} \quad N = 1/T_p = 1/3/16000000 = 16000000/3$$

If the delay time is 1 ms, this number N will be: $N \times T_p = 0.001$ second, and $N = 16000/3$.

10.2.9.3 Build the Source File for the CAN Project CANLoopBack

Now let's create a new C source file named CANLoopBack.c under this project and enter the first part codes shown in Figure 10.19 into this source file.

```
1  //********************************************************************************************************
2  // CANLoopBack.c - CAN Loop Back Test Program
3  //********************************************************************************************************
4  #include "CANLoopBack.h"
5  void CANInt_Handler(void)
6  {
7    uint32_t ui32Status;

8    ui32Status = CAN0->INT;                          // get the interrupt source
9    if (ui32Status == 0x8000)                        // If a status inte rrupt, get the status
10   {
11       GPIOF->DATA = 0x2;                           // turn on red LED to indicate a status error
12       ui32Status = CAN0->STS;                      // read CANSTS register to clear any interrupt
13       errFlag = 1;                                 // set flag to indicate some errors may have occurred
14   }
15   else if (ui32Status == 1)                        // check if this interrupt is for message object 1
16   {
17       GPIOF->DATA = 0x4;                           // turn on blue LED to indicate an interrupt
18       CAN0->IF1CMSK = 0x08;                        // set CLRINTPND bit in CANIF1CMSK register to clear interrupt
19       CAN0->IF1CRQ |= 1;                           // send clear pending interrupt  command to the CAN controller
20       while (CAN0->IF1CRQ & 0x8000){}              // wait for BUSY bit in CANIF1CRQ register to 0
21       rcFlag = 1;                                  // set the receive flag to enable main program to collect data
22       errFlag = 0;                                 // clear any error flag
23   }
24 }

25 int main(void)
26 {
27   int size;
28   tCANMsgObject  sCANMsg, rCANMsg;
29   uint8_t sMsgData[4], rMsgData[4];

30   SysCtlClockSet(SYSCTL_SYSDIV_1|SYSCTL_USE_OSC|SYSCTL_OSC_MAIN|SYSCTL_XTAL_16MHZ);
31   InitCAN();                                       // Initialize & configure CAN0 and GPIO pins
32   CAN0->CTL |= 0x80;                               // TEST bit in CANCTL register is set to 1 to begin the test mode
33   CAN0->TST|= 0x10;                                // LBACK bit in the CANTST register is set to 1 to do loop back test
34   SetMsgObj(sMsgData, &sCANMsg, rMsgData, &rCANMsg);
35   TransMsg(sMsgData, &sCANMsg);
36   RecvMsg(rMsgData, &rCANMsg);

37   GPIOF->DATA = 0x8;                               // set green LED to indicate the completion
38   for (size = 0; size < rCANMsg.ui32MsgLen; size++)
39   {
40       GPIOB->DATA |= rMsgData[size];               //  send received data to PB3 ~ PB0 LEDs to display them
41       SimpleDelay(0.5);
42   }
43   while(1){}
44 }
```

Figure 10.19.   The codes for the source file CANLoopBack.c (first part).

The entire source file is composed of five parts:

- The main() program and the CAN transmit interrupt handler.
- The CAN module 0 initialization and configuration.
- The CAN module 0 message object setup process.
- The CAN module 0 message object transmit process.
- The CAN module 0 message object receiving process.

Now let's have a closer look at the first part codes for this source file.

1. A local variable ui32Status is first declared inside the CAN transmit interrupt handler CANInt_Handler() in line 7. This variable is used to receive and hold the interrupt and status error for the CAN transmit process.

2. In line 8, the CAN0→INT instruction is used to access the CANINT register to get the interrupt source to this handler and assign the source to the variable ui32Status.

3. If the returned interrupt source is a status interrupt (0x8000), the red color LED connected to the PF1 pin is turned on to indicate this status, and the CAN0→STS instruction is used to perform a reading operation to the CANSTS register to clear this interrupt and all other pending interrupts in the CANINT register. Also, the error flag errFlag is set to 1 to record this error information that can be sued later by the main() program. The codes related to these operations are involved in lines 9 and 14.

4. If this interrupt is caused by the message object 1, which means that a message object has been successfully transmitted and it is ready to be picked up, the blue color LED connected to the PF2 pin is turned on to indicate this situation in line 17.

5. In line 18, the CLRINTPND bit (bit 3) in the CANIF1CMSK register is set to clear this message object 1 interrupt in the message buffer.

6. Also, this interrupt pending clear instruction is sent to the CAN controller with the message object number (1) in line 19.

7. In line 20, a while() loop is used to check the BUSY bit (bit 15) in the CANIF1CRQ register to wait for the clearing instruction in line 19 to be complete.

8. The receiving flag rcFlag is set to 1 to indicate to the main program that a message object is ready to be picked up in line 21, and the error flag errFlag is reset to 0 in line 22.

9. The main() program starts at line 25.

10. Some local variables, data structure, and data arrays are declared first. The sCANMsg and rCANMsg are special CAN data structures tCANMsgObject we discussed in Section 10.2.8.1. The sMsgData[] and rMsgData[] are two data arrays used to reserve the data to be transmitted to and received from the CAN bus.

11. In line 30, the system API function SysCtlClockSet() is called to set up the system clock with 16-MHz frequency.

12. The user-defined function InitCAN() is called in line 31 to initialize and configure the CAN module 0 and related GPIO ports and pins.

13. In lines 32 and 33, the TEST bit (bit 7) in the CANCTL register and the LBACK bit (bit 4) in the CANTST register are set to 1 to begin the test mode and loop back function.

14. The user-defined function SetMsgObj() is called in line 34 to set up the message object to be transmitted to the CAN bus.

15. Another user-defined function TransMsg() is executed in line 35 to transmit the message object out via the CAN bus.

16. In line 36, the RecvMsg() function is called to pick up the transmitted message object.

17. The green color LED connected to the PF3 pin is turned on to indicate that both the transmission and receiving processes have been completed in line 37.

18. The codes between lines 38 and 45 are used to display received data on the PB3~PB0 LEDs in the EduBASE ARM® Trainer. A SimpyDelay() function is executed to place certain time intervals between each data item to be displayed in those LEDs.

19. An infinitive while() loop is executed in line 43 to enable users to check the received data and compare them with the transmitted data via the Call Stack + Locals window as the project runs.

Now let's take a closer look at the second through the fifth part codes for this source file. These parts include the CAN module 0 initialization function InitCAN(), the CAN module 0 message object setup process function SetMsgObj(), the CAN transmit message object function TransMsg(), and the CAN receiving function RecvMsg(). Figure 10.20 shows the detailed codes for these parts.

20. The InitCAN() function starts at line 45.

21. First the SYSCTL→RCGC2 instruction is used to enable and clock the GPIO Ports B and F.

22. In line 48, the SYSCTL→RCGC0 instruction is sued to enable and clock the CAN0 module. Bit 24 in the RCGC0 register is the CAN0 enabled and clock gating control bit.

23. The codes in lines 49 and 50 are used to configure the PF3–PF0 as digital function and output pins.

24. The code in line 51 is used to configure the PB5 and PB4 as alternate function pins.

25. In line 52, the PB5 and PB4 pins are configured as the CAN0TX and CAN0RX pins.

26. The codes in lines 53 and 54 configure the PB5~PB0 as digital function and output pins, but the exception is that the PB4 is configured as an input pin since it is connected to the CAN0RX pin to work as a data receiving pin.

27. In line 55, the system API function CANInit() provided by the TivaWare™ Peripheral Driver Library is called to initialize and configure the CAN0 module.

28. The CAN0 bit rate is configured and set up in line 56 by using the CAN0→BIT instruction to access and set up 0x34CF. Refer to Section 10.2.5.6.1 and a related example to get more details about this setup parameter and its value.

29. The CAN0 interrupt handler CANInt_Handler() is registered in line 57 and the related interrupt sources to CAN0 are also enabled by calling the API function CANIntEnable() in line 58. Three macros, CAN_INT_MASTER, CAN_INT_ERROR, and CAN_INT_STATUS, represent three interrupt sources; the first macro is to enable global interrupt, the second one is to enable all CAN0 error interrupts, and the third one is to enable all CAN0 related status interrupts.

30. The interrupt controller is enabled in line 59, but the code in line 60 is not necessary.

31. After initialization and configuration, the CAN0 module is enabled by calling the API function CANEnable() in line 61 and it is going to start its functions.

32. The user-defined function SetMsgObj() starts at line 63. The purpose of this function is to set up and configure the transmitting and receiving message objects to make them ready to be transmitted and received.

33. The codes in lines 65~69 are used to configure the transmitting message object, which include setting the message object ID and mask in lines 65 and 66, enabling the transmitting message object to generate interrupts in line 67, assigning the data length for each transmitting message object in line 68, and assigning the starting address of the transmitting data array to the transmitting data array in line 69.

34. The codes in lines 70~74 are used to set up the receiving message object, which include the similar configurations to the transmitting message object. The only difference is that the macro MSG_OBJ_USE_ID_FILTER is assigned to the flag item in the receiving data structure to enable the receiver to use the message object ID as a filter to identify the correct transmitted message object.

35. In line 75, the system API function CANMessageSet() is called to set up the configurations for the received message object. The macro MSG_OBJ_TYPE_RX is used to indicate to this function that the message object to be configured is a receiving message object.

36. The user-defined function TransMsg() starts at line 71. The purpose of this function is to transmit the message object.

```
45  void InitCAN(void)
46  {
47    SYSCTL->RCGC2 = 0x22;                                // enable & clock PB & PF
48    SYSCTL->RCGC0 = 0x01000000;                          // enable & clock CAN0 module
49    GPIOF->DEN = 0xF;                                    // PF1 ~ PF3 as digital pins
50    GPIOF->DIR = 0xF;                                    // PF1 ~ PF3 as output pins

51    GPIOB->AFSEL = 0x00000030;                           // set PB4 & PB5 as alternate pins
52    GPIOB->PCTL = 0x00880000;                            // set PB4 & PB5 as CAN0 pins
53    GPIOB->DEN = 0x3F;                                   // PB 5 ~ PB0 as digital pins
54    GPIOB->DIR = 0x2F;                                   // PB5, PB3 ~ PB0 output pins, PB4 input pin

55    CANInit(CAN0_BASE);
56    CAN0->BIT = 0x34CF;                                  // tseg2 = 4-1, tseg1 = 5-1, sjw = 4-1, BRP=16-1
57    CANIntRegister(CAN0_BASE, CANInt_Handler);           // register interrupt handler
58    CANIntEnable(CAN0_BASE, CAN_INT_MASTER|CAN_INT_ERROR|CAN_INT_STATUS);
59    IntEnable(INT_CAN0);
60    IntMasterEnable();
61    CANEnable(CAN0_BASE);
62  }

63  void SetMsgObj(uint8_t *sdata, tCANMsgObject *sMsg, uint8_t *rdata, tCANMsgObject *rMsg)
64  {
65    sMsg->ui32MsgID = 1;
66    sMsg->ui32MsgIDMask = 0;
67    sMsg->ui32Flags = MSG_OBJ_TX_INT_ENABLE;
68    sMsg->ui32MsgLen = sizeof(sdata);
69    sMsg->pui8MsgData = sdata;

70    rMsg->ui32MsgID = 0;                                 // CAN msg ID = 0 for any message object
71    rMsg->ui32MsgIDMask = 0;                             // mask is 0 for any ID
72    rMsg->ui32Flags = MSG_OBJ_USE_ID_FILTER;
73    rMsg->ui32MsgLen = sizeof(rdata);
74    rMsg->pui8MsgData = rdata;

75    CANMessageSet(CAN0_BASE, 2, rMsg, MSG_OBJ_TYPE_RX);
76  }

77  void TransMsg(uint8_t *sData, tCANMsgObject *sMsg)
78  {
79    int index;

80    for (index = 0; index < 4; index++)
81      sData[index] = ui8MsgData[index];

82    CANMessageSet(CAN0_BASE, 1, sMsg, MSG_OBJ_TYPE_TX);
83    SimpleDelay(1);
84    if(errFlag)
85      GPIOF->DATA = 0x6;                                 // set both red & blue LEDs on to indicate this error
86  }

87  void RecvMsg(uint8_t *rData, tCANMsgObject *rMsg)
88  {
89    while(1)
90    {
91      if(rcFlag == 1)
92      {
93        rMsg->pui8MsgData = rData;
94        CANMessageGet(CAN0_BASE, 2, rMsg, 0);
95        rcFlag = 0;

96        if(rMsg->ui32Flags & MSG_OBJ_DATA_LOST)
97          GPIOF->DATA = 0x2;                             // set red LED on to indicate this data lost
98        break;
99      }
    }
  }
```

Figure 10.20. The detailed codes for the second through the fifth parts.

37. A local variable `index` is declared first and it works as a loop counter for a `for` loop to assign the data to be transmitted to the data array in the data structure `sMsg` in lines 80 and 81.

38. The system API function `CANMessageSet()` is called again to transmit the configured message object in line 82.

39. The `SimpleDelay()` function is called in line 83 to delay the system by 1 second.

40. The codes in lines 84 and 85 are sued to turn the blue and green colors LED on if any error is encountered.

41. The user-defined function `RecvMsg()` starts at line 87. Two arguments passed into this function are receiving message object structure `tCANMsgObject` and the starting address of the data array included in this structure.

42. An infinitive `while()` loop is used to check the global receiving flag `rcFlag` that is set by the interrupt handler `CANInt_Handler()` to identify whether a desired message object has been received in line 89.

43. If this flag is set, the starting address of the user-defined receiving data array, `rData`, is assigned to the starting address of the receiving data array in the `tCANMsgObject`, `pui8MsgData` in line 93.

44. The system API function `CANMessageGet()` is executed to pick up the received message object data stored in the message RAM space in line 94. The point to be noted is that the object number used in this function call is 2, which is identical to the object number used in the function `CANMessageSet()` that is to set up the receiving message object in line 75. This object number is not the message object ID used in this project.

45. In line 95, the `rcFlag` is reset to 0 to make it ready to receive the next message object.

46. The codes in lines 96 and 97 are used to check and indicate whether a message object lost error has been occurred. If it is, the red color LED connected to PF1 is on to indicate this error situation.

47. If a message object has been successfully received and picked up, the infinitive `while()` loop is stopped with a `break` instruction in line 98.

Now let's set up the environment to build and run the project to test the CAN function.

10.2.9.4 Set Up the Environment to Build and Run the Project

This setup contains the following three operations:

1. Include the system header files by adding the include path.
2. Check and configure the correct debugger driver used in the project.
3. Add the TivaWare™ Peripheral Driver Library into the project.

Perform the following operations to include the header file path in the project:

- Go to `Project|Options for Target` 'Target 1' menu item. Then click on the C/C++ tab.
- Go to `Include Paths` box and browse to the folder where our header files are located, it is `C:\ti\TivaWare_C_Series-2.0.1.11577`. Select this folder and click on the **OK** button.

Perform the following operations to select the correct debugger:

- Going to `Project|Options for Target` 'Target 1' menu item to open the `Options` wizard.

- On the opened Options wizard, click on the Debug tab.
- Make sure that the debugger shown in the Use: box is Stellaris ICDI. Otherwise you can click on the dropdown arrow to select this debugger from the list.

Perform the following operations to add the TivaWare™ peripheral driver library into the project:

- Go to the **Project** pane and right click on the **Source Group 1** item, and select the Add Existing Files to Group 'Source Group 1' menu item.
- Browse to the folder where the library file is located, which is C:\ti\TivaWare_C_Series-2.0.1.11577\driverlib\rvmdk. Then select the library file driverlib.lib and click on the **Add** button. Click on the **Close** button to finish this step.

Now run the project to test the CAN function. As the project runs, the blue LED is on first and then the green LED is turning on. This sequence means that the transmit interrupt is occurred first and then the receiving process is complete. Four LEDs PB3~PB0 are turned on one by one in a sequence to indicate that all four data values, 1, 2, 4, and 8, have been received.

10.3 THE QUADRATURE ENCODER INTERFACE (QEI)

A quadrature encoder that can also be called a two-phase incremental encoder converts linear displacement into a pulse signal. By monitoring both the number of pulses and the relative phase of the two signals, you can track the position, direction of rotation, and speed. In addition, a third channel, or index (Z-channel) signal, can be used to indicate the absolute start position (position 0) of the rotation and used to reset the position counter.

The TM4C123GH6PM microcontroller includes two quadrature encoder interface (QEI) modules, QEI0 and QEI1. Each QEI module interprets the code produced by a quadrature encoder wheel to integrate position over time and determine direction of rotation. In addition, it can capture a running estimate of the velocity of the encoder wheel.

10.3.1 Introduction to Quadrature Encoder

Typically two types of encoders are very popularly used in most applications: linear and rotary. Linear encoders are used for items moving only in a single dimension or direction, and they convert the linear position into an electronic signal. These often are used in conjunction with actuators. Rotary encoders are used for items moving around an axis, like a motor, and convert the rotary positions or angles into electronic signals. Since the rotary encoders are more popular and widely implemented in the motor-related manufactures, such as automobiles and robots, we concentrate our discussions in this type of encoder in this section.

There are three common types of rotary encoders:

- Absolute Position Encoder
- Incremental Position Encoder
- Incremental Sinusoidal Encoder

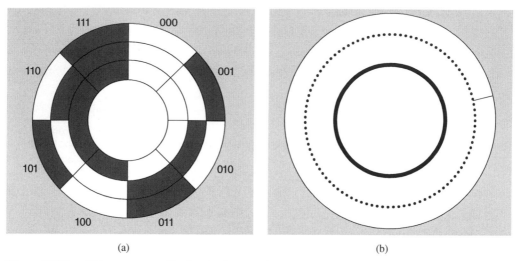

(a)   (b)

Figure 10.21. Disk patterns used in the absolute and the incremental encoders.

One of the most popular rotary encoders is the optical encoder. An optical encoder has a disk with specific patterns mounted to the motor shaft. The patterns on the disk either block light or allow it to pass through. Therefore, a light-emitting transmitter is used along with a photocell receiver. The receiver signal output can be correlated to the motor's rotary position.

For absolute position value rotary encoders, the pattern on the disk is broken up into a very specific format based on its location. As an example, if the absolute position encoder has a 3-bit digital output, it would have eight different patterns, evenly spaced around the center of the disk, as shown in Figure 10.21a. Since this is on a disk and is evenly spaced out, the spacing between each pattern is $360°/8 = 45°$. Now the position of the rotary motor is known to be within 45° for a 3-bit absolute position value rotary encoder.

For the incremental rotary encoder, the pattern on the disk outputs a digital High or Low, which is a TTL signal. As shown in Figure 10.21b, the TTL-output disk pattern is relatively simple compared to the absolute position value rotary encoder because it needs to represent only one digital High or digital Low. In addition to the TTL signal, there also is a reference mark or called index which is essential in determining the motor's base or current rotary position. The reference mark or index can be thought of as a position 0 or angle 0°. Thus, simply counting the digital pulses can determine the exact rotary position of the motor.

Figure 10.21b illustrates multiple periods/lines in one revolution of the motor shaft. Different encoder venders provide various incremental rotary encoders with 50 to 5,000 periods/lines per revolution. As with absolute position value rotary encoders, the output is already in a digital format, and therefore no analog signal converter is required.

For the incremental sinusoidal rotary encoder, the output and disk pattern is quite similar to the incremental rotary encoder. Instead of a digital output, the output is a sinusoidal wave output. Actually, it has both sine and cosine outputs along with the reference mark signal. These outputs are all analog, so an analog signal converter is required.

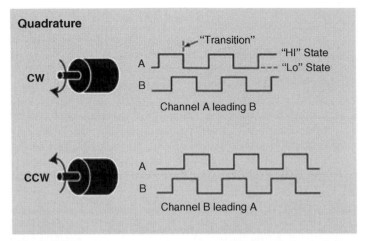

Figure 10.22.   Quadrature encoder rotation direction and phases A and B.

10.3.2 The Working Principle of the Increment Rotary Encoder

As we mentioned in the last section, the incremental rotary encoders provide a specific number of equally spaced pulses per revolution (PPR) or per millimeter of linear motion.

The code disk inside an increment rotary or a quadrature encoder contains two 90-degree installed tracks usually denoted Channel A (Phase A) and Channel B (Phase B). These tracks or channels are coded 90 electrical degrees out of phase, as indicated in Figure 10.22. These channels are the key design elements that will provide the quadrature encoder its functionality.

In applications where direction sensing is required, a controller can determine direction of movement of the motor based on the phase relationship between Phases A and B. As illustrated in Figure 10.22, when the detected Phase A leading Phase B, the quadrature encoder is rotating in a clockwise direction, and the reverse will happen when the quadrature encoder rotates counterclockwise.

When a higher resolution is needed, it is possible for the counter to count the rising and the falling edges of the quadrature encoder's pulse train from one channel, which doubles ($\times2$) the number of pulses per revolution (Figure 10.23). Counting both rising and falling edges of both channels of a quadrature encoder will quadruple ($\times4$) the number of pulses per revolution, as shown in Figure 10.23. As a result, a 2,500 PPR quadrature encoder can create 10,000 pulses per turn with this method. Typically this $4\times$ signal will be accurate to better than ±1 count.

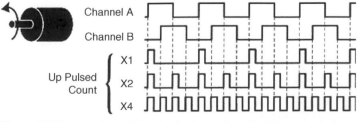

Figure 10.23.   Double and Quadruple the number of pulse per revolution.

10.3.3 The Increment Rotary Encoder Applied in the Closed-Loop Control System

Traditionally the control systems can be divided into open-loop and closed-loop control systems. Figure 10.24 shows an open-loop and a closed-loop control system diagram.

For the open-loop control system shown on the top of Figure 10.24, the desired set point S, either desired position or desired velocity, is directly applied to the controller and the controller output is implemented to the motor driver and motor itself. For this kind of control strategy, the actual motor position and velocity cannot be guaranteed to be the desired value set by the set point. This means that the target motor position or speed may be or may not be equal to the desired setup input value and the output of the system is out-of-control.

However, for the closed-loop control strategy shown on the bottom of Figure 10.24, the output of the motor, either position or velocity, is fed back to the input via the encoder and is compared with the input setup value. The error between the input setup value and the output feedback value works as the net input signal to the controller. The advantages of using a closed-loop control system are as follows:

- The output of the motor, either position or the velocity, can be exactly equal to the input setup value theoretically since the output is fed back to the input.

- Compared with the open-loop control system, the closed-loop control system has the automatic tuning ability to make output to equal to the input and make the error to 0.

- When the output is far away from the input, a greater error is obtained and applied to the input of the controller to obtain bigger control output to the motor. As the output is closed to the input, a smaller error is obtained and applied to the controller to make the control output smaller.

- If the output is exactly equal to the input, the error is 0 and the control output is also 0 until some errors coming.

Generally, the encoder provides a position feedback and a tachometer provides a velocity feedback of the motor for a given voltage applied on the motor. An internal timer can be used to count the number of pulses of either Phase A or Phase B, or both of them to calculate an estimated velocity by dividing that number of pulses by a pre-defined time interval.

The H(s) in Figure 10.24 is a transfer function or a coefficient (scalar factor) used to convert the pulse numbers to the positions of the motor.

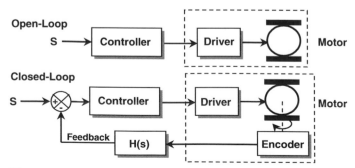

Figure 10.24. The open-loop and the closed-loop control system.

10.3.4 The Increment Rotary Encoder Applied in the TM4C123GH6PM MCU System

A functional block diagram of the QEI modules, QEI0 and QEI1, is shown in Figure 10.25. Since both modules have the same architecture, only one diagram is provided in this section.

The QEI module supports two operation modes: phase mode and clock/direction mode.

In the phase mode, the encoder produces two clocks that are 90 degrees out of phase. The edge relationship is used to determine the direction of rotation. In clock/direction mode, the encoder produces a clock signal to indicate steps and a direction signal to indicate the direction of rotation of the motor.

When in phase mode, edges on the first channel or edges on both channels can be counted; counting edges on both channels provides higher encoder resolution if required. In either mode, the input signals can be swapped before being processed, allowing wiring mistakes to be corrected without modifying the hardware circuit board.

The index pulse can be used to reset the position counter, allowing the position counter to maintain the absolute encoder position. Otherwise, the position counter maintains the relative position and is never reset.

The velocity capture has a timer to measure equal periods of time. The number of encoder pulses over each time period is accumulated as a measure of the encoder velocity. The running total for the current time period and the final count for the previous time period are available to be read. The final count for the previous time period is usually used as the measured velocity.

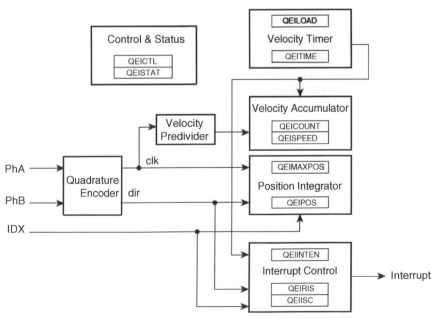

Figure 10.25. Functional block diagram of the QEI Modules. (Reprinted with the permission of the Texas Instruments Incorporated.)

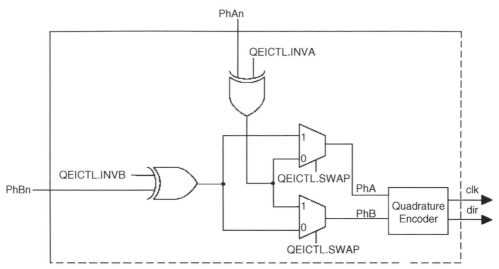

Figure 10.26.   The inversion and swapping logic circuit. (Reprinted with the permission of the Texas Instruments Incorporated.)

The QEI module generates interrupts when the index pulse is detected, when the velocity timer expires, when the encoder direction changes, and when a phase signal error is detected. These interrupt sources can be individually masked so that only the events of interest cause a processor interrupt.

A point to be noted is that both PhA and PhB signals shown in Figure 10.25 are not the external Phase A and Phase B signals coming from the motor encoder, but instead they are the internal PhA and PhB signals that have passed through inversion and swapping logic that is enabled through the QEI Control (QEICTL) register. Figure 10.26 shows this inversion and swapping logic circuit for the external Phase A (PhAn) and Phase B (PhBn) signals.

10.3.5 The QEI Module Registers

Based on Figure 10.25, each QEI module is composed of related registers and these registers can be divided into different groups based on their functions:

- QEI Control and Status Registers–Control and monitor the QEI running status.
- QEI Position Registers–Calculate the positions of the motor based on Phases A and B.
- QEI Velocity Registers–Calculate the motor velocity based on Phases A and B.
- QEI Interrupt Processing Registers–Configure and handle the QEI interrupts.

Now let's have a closer look at these registers.

10.3.5.1 QEI Control and Status Registers

Three registers are included in this group: QEI Control Register (QEICTL), QEI Status Register (QEISTAT), and QEI Run Mode Clock Gating Control Register (RCGCQEI).

QEI Control Register (QEICTL)

19 18 17 16	15 14	13	12	11	10	9	8 7 6	5	4	3	2	1	0
FILTCNT		FILTEN	STALLEN	INVI	INVB	INVA	VELDIV	VELEN	RESMODE	CAPMODE	SIGMODE	SWAP	ENABLE

Reserved

Figure 10.27. The bit-field functions of the QEICTL register.

The bit-field configurations for the QEICTL register are shown in Figure 10.27. The bit function for this register is shown in Table 10.15.

Refer to Figures 10.26 and 10.27 as well as Table 10.15, it can be found that the inversion and swapping logic circuit shown in Figure 10.26 is under the control of the bits INVA, INVB, and SWAP, or bits 10, 9, and 1 in the QEICTL register. When these bits

Table 10.15. Bit value and its function for QEICTL register.

Bit	Name	Reset	Function
31:20	Reserved	0x0	Reserved
19:16	FILTCNT	0x0	Input Filter Prescale Count: This field controls the frequency of the input update. When this field is 0x0, the input is sampled after 2 system clocks. When this field ix 0x1, the input is sampled after 3 system clocks. Similarly, when this field is 0xF, the input is sampled after 17 clocks.
15:14	Reserved	0x0	Reserved
13	FILTEN	0	Enable Input Filter: 0: The QEI inputs are not filtered; 1: Enable the digital noise filter on the QEI input signals.
12	STALLEN	0	Stall QEI: 0: The QEI module does not stall when the microcontroller is stopped by a debugger. 1: The QEI module stalls when the microcontroller is stopped by a debugger.
11	INVI	0	Invert Index Pulse: 0: No effect; 1: Invert the IDX input.
10	INVB	0	Invert PhB: 0: No effect; 1: Invert the PhBn input.
9	INVA	0	Invert PhA: 0: No effect; 1: Invert the PhAn input.
8:6	VELDIV	0x0	Predivide Velocity: This field defines the predivider of the input quadrature pulses before being applied to the QEICOUNT accumulator. 0x0 ÷1; 0x1 ÷2; 0x2 ÷4; 0x3 ÷8; 0x4 ÷16; 0x5 ÷32; 0x6 ÷64; 0x7 ÷128
5	VELEN	0	Capture Velocity: 0: No effect; 1: Enable capture of the velocity of the quadrature encoder.
4	RESMODE	0	Reset Mode: 0: The position counter is reset when it reaches the maximum as defined by the MAXPOS field in the QEIMAXPOS register. 1: The position counter is reset when the index pulse is captured.
3	CAPMODE	0	Capture Mode: 0: Only the PhA edges are counted. 1: The PhA & PhB edges are counted, providing twice the positional resolution but half range. When SIGMODE=1, the CAPMODE setting is not applicable and is reserved.
2	SIGMODE	0	Signal Mode: 0: The internal PhA and PhB signals operate as quadrature phase signals. 1: The internal PhA input operate as the clock (CLK) signal and the internal PhB input operate as the direction (DIR) signal.
1	SWAP	0	Swap Signals: 0: No effect; 1: Swaps the PhAn and PhBn signals. If the INVA or INVB bit are set, the inversion of the signals occur prior to the swap.
0	ENABLE	0	Enable QEI: 0: No effect; 1: Enables the quadrature encoder module. Once the QEI module has been enabled by setting the ENABLE bit, it cannot be disabled. The only way to clear the ENABLE bit is to reset the module using the Quadrature Encoder Interface Software Reset (SRQEI) register.

values are set to 1 s, the corresponding external Phase A (PhAn) and Phase B (PhBn) are inverted and swapped, respectively.

One point to be noted is the VELDIV bit field in this register. The value in this bit field is used to perform a predivider function for the input quadrature pulses before it can be loaded into the QEICOUNT register. The main purpose of this predivider is to extend and enlarge the counting range for the input quadrature pulses.

Another important bit in this register is CAPMODE bit. As we discussed in Section 10.3.2, a 2× resolution can be obtained by only capture the rising and falling edges of the Phase A signal when this CAPMODE is cleared to 0. However, a 4× resolution can be obtained if both Phase A and Phase B rising and falling edges are captured or counted when this CAPMODE bit is set to 1. A point to be noted for this bit is that when SIGMODE bit is set to 1, the setting for the CAPMODE bit and its function is ignored since the Phase A and Phase B will be working as different roles for that setting. This means that when SIGMODE bit is cleared to 0, the internal PhA and PhB signals work together to provide quadrature phase signals as a normal rotary increment encoder did. However, when this SIGMODE bit is set to 1, the internal PhA input operates and provides the clock (CLK) step signal and the internal PhB input operates and provides the direction (DIR) signal for the detected motor. In this way, we do not need to set up any additional hardware component and circuit to interpret and convert the quadrature signals to the position clock steps and direction signal for the detecting motor.

The QEI Status Register (QEISTAT) is used to check and monitor the running status of the QEI modules. This is a 32-bit register but only the lowest two bits, bits 1 and 0, are used to provide the encoder running information and status.

The bit 1, or the DIRECTION bit in this register, provides the rotation direction of the encoder; a value of 0 indicates that the encoder is rotating in a forward (clockwise) direction, and a value of 1 indicates that the encoder is rotating in a reverse (counter clockwise) direction.

The bit 0, or the ERROR bit in this register, provides the running status of the QEI module. A value of 0 means that no error has been detected. But a value of 1 indicates that an error has been detected for the QEI module.

The RCGCQEI is a 32-bit register but only the lowest two bits, bits 1 (R1) and 0 (R0), are used to enable and clock the QEI modules. If the R1 bit is set, the QEI module 1 is enabled and clocked. Similarly, if the R0 bit is set, the QEI module 0 is enabled and clocked.

10.3.5.2 QEI Position Control Registers

Two registers are included in this group: QEI Position Register (QEIPOS) and QEI Maximum Position Register (QEIMAXPOS).

The QEIPOS is a 32-bit register and it contains the current value of the position integrator or position accumulator. The value can be updated by the status of the QEI phase inputs and can be set to a specific value by writing to it.

The QEIMAXPOS is also a 32-bit register containing the maximum value of the position integrator. When moving forward, the position register QEIPOS resets to zero when it increments past this value. When moving in reverse, the position register QEIPOS resets to this value when it decrements to zero.

10.3.5.3 QEI Velocity Control Registers

Four registers are coved in this group and they are:

- QEI Timer Load Register (QEILOAD)
- QEI Timer Register (QEITIME)
- QEI Velocity Counter Register (QEICOUNT)
- QEI Velocity or Speed Register (QEISPEED)

All of these registers are 32-bit registers and are used to store related encoder speed information.

The QEILOAD register contains the loaded value for the velocity timer. Because this value is loaded into the timer in terms of the clock cycle after the timer is zero, this value should be one less than the number of clocks in the desired period. For example, to have 2000 decimal clocks per timer period, this register should contain 1999 decimal.

The QEITIME register contains the current numbers or counts of the clock cycles in this velocity timer. The total counts in the QEICOUNT register will be divided by this numbers of clock cycle to get an estimated encoder speed value.

The QEICOUNT register contains the current running counts of velocity pulses for the current time period stored in the QEITIME register. Because this count is a running total, the time period to which it applies cannot be known accurately, which means that a reading of this register does not necessarily correspond to the time returned by the QEITIME register because there is a small window of time between the two reads and during which either value may have changed. The QEISPEED register should be used to determine the actual encoder velocity. Thus, this register only provides velocity-related information.

The QEISPEED register contains the most recently measured velocity of the quadrature encoder. This value corresponds to the number of velocity pulses (QEICOUNT) counted in the previous velocity timer period (QEITIME).

10.3.5.4 QEI Interrupt Processing Registers

Three registers are included in this group and they are:

- QEI Interrupt Enable Register (QEIINTEN).
- QEI Raw Interrupt Status Register (QEIRIS).
- QEI Interrupt Status and Clear Register (QEIISC).

All of these three registers are 32-bit registers but only the lowest 4 bits, bits 3 – 0, are used to configure, set up and clear four related QEI module operational interrupts:

- Phase Error Interrupt
- Direction Change Interrupt
- Timer Expires Interrupt
- Index Pulse Detected Interrupt

Figure 10.28 shows the bit fields for these registers.

If any of the lowest four bits on these registers is set to 1, which means that the selected interrupt is enabled for the QEIINTEN register, and the corresponding interrupt is

QEI Interrupt Enable Register(QEIINTEN)

31		3	2	1	0
Reserved Bits 31–4.		INTERROR	INTDIR	INTTIMER	INTINDEX

QEI Raw Interrupt Status Register (QEIRIS)

31		3	2	1	0
Reserved Bits 31–4.		INTERROR	INTDIR	INTTIMER	INTINDEX

QEI Interrupt Status and Clear Register (QEIISC)

31		3	2	1	0
Reserved Bits 31–4.		INTERROR	INTDIR	INTTIMER	INTINDEX

Figure 10.28.   QEI interrupt processing registers.

generated for the QEIRIS register, and the related interrupt can be cleared for the QEIISC register.

Otherwise if any bit on these lowest four bits is 0, this means that the selected interrupt is disabled for the QEIINTEN register, and the corresponding interrupt is not generated for the QEIRIS register, and the related interrupt has not been cleared for the QEIISC register if that interrupt has occurred.`

10.3.6 The QEI Interfacing Signals and Related GPIO Pins

Table 10.16 shows the QEI module external signals and related GPIO pin distributions.

Like other peripheral devices, the QEI signals are alternate functions for some related GPIO signals on the associated GPIO pins. The column in the Table 10.16 titled GPIO Pin lists the possible GPIO pin placements for these QEI signals. The AFSEL bits in the GPIOAFSEL register should be set to choose the QEI function. The number in parentheses is the encoding that must be programmed into the PMCx field in the GPIOPCTL register to assign the QEI signal to the specified GPIO port pin.

10.3.7 The QEI Initialization and Configuration Process

Before the rotary encoder can be used in any application, the QEI module should be selected and initialized to make it ready to measure the desired motor rotating position and

Table 10.16.   QEI external control signals and GPIO pin distributions.

QEI Pin	GPIO Pin	Pin Type	Buffer Type	Pin Function
IDX0	PF4 (6) PD3 (6)	I	TTL	QEI Module 0 Index.
IDX1	PC4 (6)	I	TTL	QEI Module 1 Index.
PhA0	PF0 (6) PD6 (6)	I	TTL	QEI Module 0 Phase A.
PhA1	PC5 (6)	I	TTL	QEI Module 1 Phase A.
PhB0	PD7 (6) PF1 (6)	I	TTL	QEI Module 0 Phase B.
PhB1	PC6 (6)	I	TTL	QEI Module 1 Phase B.

speed. Regularly, the initialization and configuration process should include the following operational steps:

1. Enable the clock for the QEI module by configuring the RCGCQEI register.
2. Enable the clock for the appropriate GPIO module via the RCGCGPIO register (refer to Table 10.16).
3. Configure the appropriate GPIO pins by setting the related bits on the GPIOAFSEL register to enable related pins to work as alternate functions (refer to Table 10.16).
4. Configure the appropriate bit field in the GPIOPCTL register to enable selected GPIO pins to work as QEI functions (refer to number inside the parentheses in Table 10.16).
5. Configure the QEI module to capture both rising and falling edges for the PhAn and PhBn signals and maintain an absolute position by resetting on index pulses. For a 1000-line encoder with four edges per line, it can generate 4000 pulses per revolution. Therefore, set the maximum position to 3999 (4000 − 1) since the count is zero-based. Perform the following two writing operations to complete this configuration:
   • Write the QEICTL register with the value of 0x28 to enable the capture mode to capture the velocity of the motor.
   • Write the QEIMAXPOS register with the value of 3999 as the maximum position value.
6. Enable the QEI module by setting bit 0 (ENABLE) of the QEICTL register. The point to be noted is that once the QEI module has been enabled by setting the ENABLE bit in the QEICTL register, it cannot be disabled. The only way to clear the ENABLE bit is to reset the module using the QEI Software Reset (SRQEI) register. A two-step operation is needed to complete this reset operation.
7. Delay a period of time until the encoder position is required.
8. Read the encoder position by reading the QEI Position (QEIPOS) register value. One point to be noted is that if the application requires the QEI module to have a specific initial position, this value must be programmed in the QEIPOS register after the QEI module has been enabled by setting the ENABLE bit in the QEICTL register.
9. Read the velocity of the motor rotation by reading the QEI Velocity (QEISPEED) register value.

Before we can build the real implementation projects with QEI modules, let's become familiar with some popular API functions provided by the TivaWare™ Peripheral Driver Library since we need to build some mixed models projects later.

10.3.8 QEI API Functions Provided by the TivaWare™ Peripheral Driver Library

About 17 QEI-related API functions are provided by the TivaWare™ Peripheral Driver Library. In this section we only concentrate on some popular and important API functions. These functions are used to support users to access, configure, and control the QEI modules in the TM4C123GH6PM MCU system. These API functions can be divided into four groups based on their functions:

1. QEI Configuration and Enable API Functions
2. QEI Position Capture API Functions
3. QEI Velocity Capture API Functions
4. QEI Interrupt Handling API Functions

Table 10.17. The QEI configuration and enable API functions.

API Function	Parameter	Description
void QEIConfigure(uint32_t ui32Base, uint32_t ui32Config, uint32_t ui32MaxPosition)	ui32Base is the base address of the quadrature encoder module. ui32Config is the configuration for the quadrature encoder. ui32MaxPosition specifies the maximum position value.	Configure the operation of the quadrature encoder. The ui32Config parameter provides the configuration of the encoder and is the logical OR of several values: QEI_CONFIG_CAPTURE_A or QEI_CONFIG_CAPTURE_A_B specify if edges on channel A or on both channels A and B should be counted by the position integrator and velocity accumulator. QEI_CONFIG_NO_RESET or QEI_CONFIG_RESET_IDX specify if the position integrator should be reset when the index pulse is detected. QEI_CONFIG_QUADRATURE or QEI_CONFIG_CLOCK_DIR specify if quadrature signals are being provided on ChA and ChB, or if a direction signal and a clock are being provided instead. QEI_CONFIG_NO_SWAP or QEI_CONFIG_SWAP to specify if the signals provided on ChA and ChB should be swapped before being processed. ui32MaxPosition is the maximum value of the position integrator and is the value used to reset the position capture when in index reset mode and moving in the reverse (negative) direction.
void QEIEnable(uint32_t ui32Base)	ui32Base is the base address of the quadrature encoder module.	Enable operation of the QEI module. The module must be configured before it is enabled.
void QEIDisable(uint32_t ui32Base)	ui32Base is the base address of the quadrature encoder module.	Disables operation of the quadrature encoder module.

Let's discuss these functions based on their group one by one in the following sections.

10.3.8.1 QEI Configuration and Enable API Functions

Three API functions are involved in this group, they are

- QEIConfigure()
- QEIEnable()
- QEIDisable()

Table 10.17 shows the prototypes and arguments of these three functions.

One point to be noted is that before any QEI module can be enabled, it must be first configured correctly. Another point is that once the QEI module has been enabled by setting the ENABLE bit, it cannot be disabled. The only way to clear the ENABLE bit is to reset the module using the Quadrature Encoder Interface Software Reset (SRQEI) register.

10.3.8.2 QEI Position Capture API Functions

Two API functions are involved in this group and they are:

- QEIPositionSet()
- QEIPositionGet()

Table 10.18 shows the syntax and argument of these API functions. These functions are used to setup and retrieve back the current position of the encoder.

Table 10.18.   The QEI position capture API functions.

API Function	Parameter	Description
void QEIPositionSet(uint32_t ui32Base, uint32_t ui32Position)	ui32Base is the base address of the quadrature encoder module. ui32Position is the new position for the encoder.	Set the current position of the encoder; the encoder position is then measured relative to this value.
uint32_t QEIPositionGet(uint32_t ui32Base)	ui32Base is the base address of the quadrature encoder module.	Return the current position of the encoder. Depending on the configuration of the encoder, and the incident of an index pulse, this value may or may not contain the expected data (that is, if in reset on index mode, if an index pulse has not been encountered, the position counter is not yet aligned with the index pulse).

10.3.8.3 QEI Velocity Capture API Functions

Four API functions are involved in this group and they are:

- QEIVelocityConfigure()
- QEIVelocityEnable()
- QEIVelocityDisable()
- QEIVelocityGet()

Table 10.19 shows the syntax and argument of these API functions. These functions are used to setup and retrieve back the current velocity of the encoder.

10.3.8.4 QEI Interrupt Handling API Functions

Five API functions are involved in this group and they are

- QEIIntRegister()
- QEIIntEnable()

Table 10.19.   The QEI velocity capture API functions.

API Function	Parameter	Description
void QEIVelocityConfigure(uint32_t ui32Base, uint32_t ui32PreDiv, uint32_t ui32Period)	ui32Base is the base address of the quadrature encoder module. ui32PreDiv specifies the predivider applied to the input QEI signal before it is counted; This value can be one: QEI_VELDIV_N; (N = 1, 2, 4, 8, 16, 32, 64 or 128). ui32Period specifies the number of clock ticks over which to measure the velocity; must be non-zero.	Configure the operation of the velocity capture portion of the quadrature encoder. The position increment signal is predivided as specified by ui32PreDiv before being accumulated by the velocity capture. The divided signal is accumulated over ui32Period system clock before being saved and resetting the accumulator.
void QEIVelocityEnable(uint32_t ui32Base)	ui32Base is the base address of the quadrature encoder module.	Enable the velocity capture in the QEI module. The module must be configured before velocity capture is enabled.
void QEIVelocityDisable(uint32_t ui32Base)	ui32Base is the base address of the quadrature encoder module.	Disable the velocity capture in the QEI module.
uint32_t QEIVelocityGet(uint32_t ui32Base)	ui32Base is the base address of the quadrature encoder module.	Return the current speed of the encoder. The value returned is the number of pulses detected in the specified time period; this number can be multiplied by the number of time periods per second and divided by the number of pulses per revolution to obtain the number of revolutions per second.

Table 10.20.   The QEI interrupt handling API functions.

API Function	Parameter	Description
void QEIIntRegister(uint32_t ui32Base, void (*pfnHandler)(void))	ui32Base is the base address of the quadrature encoder module. pfnHandler is a pointer to the function to be called when the quadrature encoder interrupt occurs.	Register the handler to be called when a quadrature encoder interrupt occurs. This function enables the global interrupt in the interrupt controller; specific quadrature encoder interrupts must be enabled via QEIIntEnable(). It is the interrupt handler's responsibility to clear the interrupt source via QEIIntClear().
void QEIIntEnable(uint32_t ui32Base, uint32_t ui32IntFlags)	ui32Base is the base address of the quadrature encoder module. ui32IntFlags is a bit mask of the interrupt sources to be enabled. Can be any of the values: QEI_INTERROR, QEI_INTDIR, QEI_INTTIMER, or QEI_INTINDEX.	Enable the indicated quadrature encoder interrupt sources. Only the sources that are enabled can be reflected to the processor interrupt; disabled sources have no effect on the processor.
void QEIIntDisable(uint32_t ui32Base, uint32_t ui32IntFlags)	ui32Base is the base address of the quadrature encoder module. ui32IntFlags is a bit mask of the interrupt sources with the same values as QEIIntEnable().	Disable the indicated quadrature encoder interrupt sources. Only the sources that are enabled can be reflected to the processor interrupt; disabled sources have no effect on the processor.
void QEIIntClear(uint32_t ui32Base, uint32_t ui32IntFlags)	ui32Base is the base address of the quadrature encoder module. ui32IntFlags is a bit mask of the interrupt sources to be cleared. This parameter can be any values: of the QEI_INTERROR, QEI_INTDIR, QEI_INTTIMER, or QEI_INTINDEX.	The specified quadrature encoder interrupt sources are cleared, so that they no longer assert. This function must be called in the interrupt handler to keep the interrupt from being triggered again immediately upon exit.
uint32_t QEIIntStatus(uint32_t ui32Base, bool bMasked)	ui32Base is the base address of the quadrature encoder module. bMasked is false if the raw interrupt status is required and true if the masked interrupt status is required.	Return the interrupt status for the quadrature encoder module. Either the raw interrupt status or the status of interrupts that are allowed to reflect to the processor can be returned.

- QEIIntDisable()
- QEIIntClear()
- QEIIntStatus()

Table 10.20 shows the syntax and argument of these API functions. These functions are used to configure and process the interrupts of the encoder.

A point to be noted is that the function QEIIntRegister() should be executed first to set up an interrupt handler to response to the specified QEI interrupt source before any QEI interrupt can be enabled. The second argument of this function is a pointer pointing to the interrupt handler entrance. Inside the interrupt handler, the API function QEIIntClear() must be called first to clear the current interrupt request to enable this interrupt source to send another request in the future or allow other higher-level interrupts to be responded.

Now we are ready to build a real implementation project to use QEI module to detect and receive the position and velocity of a tested motor system via a closed-loop mode.

10.3.9 An Implementation of Using Rotary Encoder for a Closed-Loop Control System

To properly use a QEI module to detect and retrieve the desired position and velocity of a tested motor system, we need to perform the following operational steps:

1. Calibrate the rotary encoder attached on the motor system.
2. Develop and build a floating chart to use rotary encoder as a feedback device to control the motor rotating speed or position via PWM module.
3. Build the closed-loop control program based on the floating chart via the software codes.

Let's start from the first step.

10.3.9.1 *Calibration of the Rotary Encoder*

The purpose of the calibration of the rotary encoder is to get a correct relationship or a mapping between the controller PWM outputs and the encoder outputs that work as feedback to the controller inputs.

In real implementations, this calibration process can be performed by building an implementation program to collect a sequence of encoder speeds in terms of a sequence of PWM output values. Ideally the relationship between the encoder feedback speeds and PWM outputs should be a linear equation and it should be a straight line in a 2D plane, but in practice, it is a nonlinear function with a nonlinear trajectory in a 2-D coordinate system, as shown in Figure 10.29. When the voltage applied on the motor is higher than certain value, the motor speed becomes saturated.

The motor we used is a DC motor, Mitsumi 448 PPR Motor with an optical rotary encoder including a 448 lines/pulses speed disk, as shown in Figure 10.30. This motor can be purchased from some sites such as ebay for about $5.00.

If this 448-line/pulse per revolution rotary encoder is used in this closed-loop control system, a total of 1792 (448×4) pulses per revolution (PPR) can be obtained if both rising and falling edges for Phase A and Phase B inputs are utilized. To calibrate this encoder, a user program can be built to continuously send the PWM outputs to the motor starting from 5% to 100%. Then the user program can collect all related encoder speeds on those PWM output values and store them in a data array.

Then a data fitting method, such as the Least Squares method, can be used to get the actual equation for this relationship ($ES = k \times PWM + b$), where b is the intersection across the vertical axis and k is the slope of this linear equation. The estimated linear function should be a straight line similar to the linear range shown in Figure 10.29.

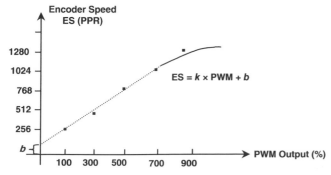

Figure 10.29. Relationship between the encoder speed (ES) and the PWM.

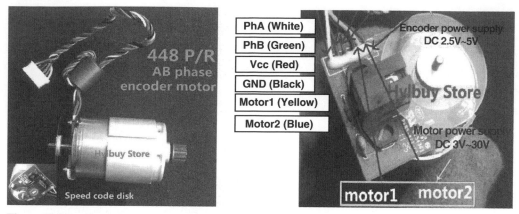

Figure 10.30.   The DC motor: Mitsumi 448 PPR motor with an optical encoder.

In this calibration project, we use the following components to perform this calibration:

- The QEI0 with its PhA0 (PD6) and PhB0 (PD7) as two external phase input signals.
- The PWM1_2B or M1PWM5 pin as PWM output signal to control a DC motor.
- The DC motor is a Mitsumi 448 PPR Motor with an optical rotary encoder including a 448-line/pulse speed disk.

Before the encoder calibration process can be performed, this DC motor and its encoder must be connected to the TM4C123GXL EVB via GPIO Ports B, D, and F to enable this calibration process to be started. The hardware configuration and connection for this DC motor are shown in Figure 10.31.

As shown in Figure 10.31, all components and connections inside the dashed-line box have been done by the TM4C123GXL EVB and the EduBASE ARM® Trainer, and the users do not need to touch these connections. However, the users need to do those connections outside of this dashed-line box. These connections include:

1. DC motor connections via Motor 1 (Yellow wire) and Motor 2 (Blue wire) on the Mitsumi 448 PPR DC motor to the T1 connector in the EduBASE ARM® Trainer.

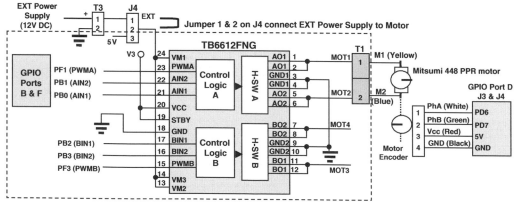

Figure 10.31.   The hardware configuration for the encoder calibration process.

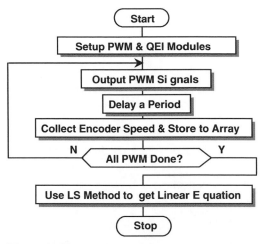

Figure 10.32.   The block diagram of the encoder calibration program.

2. Motor external 12 V DC power connection via connectors 1 and 2 on the T3 connector in the EduBASE ARM® Trainer to provide the external power supply to the motor.

3. Jumper connection by connecting pins 1 and 2 on the J4 connector in the EduBASE ARM® Trainer to enable the motor to use the external power supply.

4. Two encoder phases connections via PhA (White wire) and PhB (Green wire) phase outputs in the Mitsumi 448 PPR DC motor to PD6 and PD7 pins on the J4 connector in the TM4C123GXL EVB since we used PhA0 and PhB0 as two-phase inputs for this project. Refer to Table 10.16 to get the related GPIO pins corresponding to these phases.

5. Encoder power supply connections via Vcc (Red wire) and GND (Black wire) on the Mitsumi 448 PPR DC motor to 5 V and GND pins on the J3 connector in the TM4C123GXL EVB.

The finished hardware connection should be matched to the one that is shown in Figure 10.31. Figure 10.32 shows the block diagram of this user program.

Before we can start building this user program to calibrate the encoder, we should have a clear picture about the relationships between the motor rotating speed, the encoder output phases, and the maximum pulse load value for the QEI velocity timer.

The Mitsumi 448 PPR DC motor has an optical rotary encoder including a 448-line/pulse speed disk, which means that 448 pulses for both PhA and PhB are output for each revolution of the motor rotating. The relationship between the motor rotating speed (`rmp`), the system clock frequency (`clock`), the output pulses per revolution (`ppr`), and the maximum load pulse value for the QEI velocity timer (LOAD) are

$$rpm = (clock \times (2\,\hat{}\,VELDIV) \times SPEED \times 60) \div (LOAD \times ppr \times edges)$$

where the parameter `edges` is 2 or 4, based on the capture mode bit in the QEI Control (`QEICTL`) register (2 for CAPMODE clear and 4 for CAPMODE set). The `VELDIV` is the bit field in the `QEICTL` register to determine the velocity predivider's value.

In this project, we select and set up the following parameters for this encoder calibration:

1. The rotating speed of the Mitsumi 448 PPR DC motor is 8700 revolutions per minute. This result in `rpm`=8700.

2. System clock is 6.67 MHz when the 400 MHz PLL clock source is used and divided by a system divider of 30 (clock = 6.67 MHz).

3. The QEI module velocity pre-divider is set to ÷1 (VELDIV bit is clear).

4. Clock and count on both PhA and PhB edges by setting CAPMODE bit to 1 in the QEICTL register to get edges = 4.

5. The motor running at 8700 rpm and each revolution creates 448 pulses in both PhA and PhB. Thus a total of 1792 pulses can be generated for each revolution since the edges have been set to 4 in step 4 above (4 × 448 = 1792).

6. This result in 259840 pulses per second ((1792 × 8700)/60) since the motor rotates 8700 revolution per minute or 145 revolution per second, or 0.26 pulses per μs.

7. Since the clock frequency is 6.67 MHz with a period of 1.5×10^{-7} seconds, if we select the LOAD value as 2500, it would count 98 pulses per update ($1.5 \times 10^{-7} \times 2500 = 375\,\mu s \times 0.26 = 98$).

Using above equation, we have

$$\text{rpm} = (6.67 \times 10^6 \times 1 \times 98 \times 60) \div (2500 \times 448 \times 4) = 8754$$

As this program is developed and the rotary encoder has been calibrated, the real PWM value matched to any desired encoder speed can be estimated based on the linear equation. In the real control program, this estimated PWM value can be considered as a nominal PWM output value used to control the motor, and it can be adjusted (either increasing or decreasing) based on the actual feedback encoder speed by comparing the PWM value and the encoder feedback speed value in a loop in the control program.

Create a new project CalibEncoder in the folder C:\ARM Class Projects \Chapter10. The detailed codes for this user program are shown in Figures 10.33 and 10.34.

Figure 10.33 shows the first part of this calibration encoder codes, and Figure 10.34 shows the second part of these codes. Let's have a closer look at these codes to see how they work.

1. The codes in lines 4~9 are used to include some system header files to be implemented in this project.

2. The codes in lines 10~14 are used to define some system constants and macros used in this project.

3. Two user-defined functions, InitPWM() and InitQEI(), are declared in lines 15~16 and used to initialize the PWM and QEI modules.

4. The main program starts at line 17. Some uint32_t variables and data array are declared first in the main program and they are used as the PWM output variable pw, loop counter index, and the data array esData[] to save the collected encoder speed values in line 19.

5. In line 21, the system clock used for this QEI module and this project is configured as 6.67-MHz clock (PLL = 400 MHz/2 = 200 MHz divided by SYSDIV_30 = 6.67 MHz).

6. The codes in lines 22~28 are used to enable and clock the PWM module 1 and GPIO Ports B, D, and F.

7. Two initialization functions, InitPWM() and InitQEI(), are called in lines 29 and 30 to configure the PWM1 and QEI0 modules.

8. In lines 31 and 32, the PWM1_2B output and the PWM module 1 is enabled to make it ready to drive the DC motor.

```
1  //**********************************************************************************************
2  // CalibEncoder.c - User Program used to Calibrate Rotary Optical Encoder
3  //**********************************************************************************************
4  #include <stdint.h>
5  #include <stdbool.h>
6  #include "driverlib/sysctl.h"
7  #include "driverlib/gpio.h"
8  #include "driverlib/qei.h"
9  #include "TM4C123GH6PM.h"
10 #define  GPIO_PD6_PHA0        0x00031806
11 #define  GPIO_PD7_PHB0        0x00031C06
12 #define  GPIO_PORTD_BASE      0x40007000
13 #define  GPIO_PORTF_CR_R      (*((volatile uint32_t *)0x40025524))
14 #define  GPIO_PORTD_CR_R      (*((volatile uint32_t *)0x40007524))
15 void InitPWM(void);
16 void InitQEI(void);

17 int main(void)
18 {
19   uint32_t pw, index = 0, esData[20];
20   // Set the clocking to run directly from the crystal with 6.67 MHz clock frequency.
21   SysCtlClockSet(SYSCTL_SYSDIV_30|SYSCTL_USE_PLL|SYSCTL_XTAL_4MHZ|SYSCTL_OSC_MAIN);
22   SYSCTL->RCGC2 = 0x2A;                      // enable & clock GPIO Ports B, D & F
23   GPIOB->DEN = 0xF;                          // enable PB3 ~ PB0 as digital function pins
24   GPIOB->DIR = 0xF;                          // configure PB3 ~ PB0 as output pins
25   GPIOD->DEN = 0xC0;                         // enable PD7 ~ PD6 as digital function pins
26   GPIOD->DIR = ~0xC;                         // configure PD7 ~ PD6 as input pins
27   GPIOF->DEN = 0xF;                          // enable PF3 ~ PF0 as digital function pins
28   GPIOF->DIR = 0xF;                          // configure PF3 ~ PF0 as output pins
29   InitPWM();                                 // configure PWM module 1
30   InitQEI();                                 // configure QEI module 0
31   PWM1->_2_CTL = 0x1;                        // enable PWM1_2B or M1PWM5
32   PWM1->ENABLE = 0x20;
33   for (pw = 100; pw < 3999; pw += 200)       // send PWM signal to motor from 2.5% to 100%
34   {
35     PWM1->_2_CMPB = pw;                      // output the PWM values to the motor
36     SysCtlDelay(1000);
37     esData[index] = QEI0->SPEED;             // collect the encoder speed values
38     index++;
39   }
40   PWM1->_2_CTL = 0x0;                        // disable PWM1_2B or M1PWM5
41   PWM1->ENABLE = ~0x20;
42   while(1);                                  // check and get the encoder speed values array
43 }
```

Figure 10.33.   The first part of the codes for the project CalibEncoder.c.

9. The codes in lines 33~39 provide a fixed number loop operation to continuously send PWM outputs to the target DC motor from 5% to 100% to rotate the motor with different speeds. After each PWM signal is sent out, the `SysCtlDelay()` function is called to delay the program a period of time to make the motor rotation speed stable. Then the encoder speed is collected by reading the `QEISPEED` register and assigning them to the data array `esData[]` to store them into this array.

10. After all encoder speed values are collected, the `PWM1_2B` and the PWM module 1 are disabled in lines 40 and 41.

11. An infinitive `while(1)` loop in line 42 provides a temporary stop state to enable users to check the encoder speed values stored in the `esData[]` array.

```
44  void InitPWM(void)
45  {
46    SYSCTL->RCGCPWM |= 0x2;                          // enable PWM1 with clock
47    while((SYSCTL->PRPWM & 0x2) == 0) {};            // wait for PWM1 ready
48    SYSCTL->RCC |= 0x00100000|0x00000000;            // 20 MHz clock

49    GPIOF->LOCK = 0x4C4F434B;                        // unlock GPTOF commit register
50    GPIO_PORTF_CR_R |= 0x2;                          // enable PF1 to be committed
51    GPIOF->LOCK = 0x0;                               // lock GPIOF commit register

52    // PWM1_2B - PF1 - M1PWM5 pin - Module 1 Generator 2 - pwm2B
53    PWM1->_2_CTL = 0x0;                              // disable PWM1_2B or M1PWM5
54    PWM1->_2_GENB = 0x0000080C;                      // high on LOAD, low on CMPB down
55    PWM1->_2_LOAD = 3999;                            // load = 4000 - 1

56    GPIOF->AFSEL |= 0x2;                             // PF1 - Alternate Function: PWM1-2B
57    GPIOF->PCTL = 0x00000050;                        // M1PWM5 on PF1 = 0x00000050
58    GPIOF->AMSEL &= ~0x02;                           // disable analog function on PF1
59    GPIOB->DATA |= 0x1;                              // enable PB0 for motor CW-rotation
60  }

61  void InitQEI(void)
62  {
63    SYSCTL->RCGCQEI = 0x1;                           // enable and clock QEI0 module

64    GPIOD->LOCK = 0x4C4F434B;                        // unlock GPTOD commit register
65    GPIO_PORTD_CR_R |= 0x80;                         // enable PD7 to be committed
66    GPIOD->LOCK = 0x0;                               // lock GPIOD commit register

67    GPIOPinConfigure(GPIO_PD6_PHA0);                 // set PD6 as PhA0 pin
68    GPIOPinConfigure(GPIO_PD7_PHB0);                 // set PD7 as PhB0 pin
69    GPIOPinTypeQEI(GPIO_PORTD_BASE, GPIO_PIN_6);
70    GPIOPinTypeQEI(GPIO_PORTD_BASE, GPIO_PIN_7);

71    QEI0->CTL = 0x0;                                 // disable QEI0 to enable configuration
72    QEI0->CTL = 0x08;                                // enable QEI0 quadrature A & B mode
73    QEI0->LOAD = 2499;                               // set the max number of clock cycles
74    QEIVelocityEnable(QEI0_BASE);                    // enable the QEI0 velocity mode
75    QEIEnable(QEI0_BASE);                            // enable the quadrature encoder.
76  }
```

Figure 10.34. The second part of the codes for the project CalibEncoder.c.

Now let's have a closer look at the second part of the codes for this encoder calibration project, which is shown in Figure 10.34.

12. The detailed codes for the function InitPWM() start at line 44.

13. The PWM module 1 is clocked and enabled in line 46.

14. A while() loop is used to wait for this clock and enable process to be completed and the PWM module 1 to be stable in line 47.

15. In line 48, the register RCC is configured to enable to use the PWMDIV parameter to make the PWM module-driven clock to be 20 MHz.

16. In lines 49 and 50, the lock register for the Port F is unlocked to enable the PF1 pin to be committed by setting bit 1 in the GPIOCR register to 1. Then in line 51, this register is locked again to prevent it from modifying again in the future.

17. The codes in lines 52~55 are used to configure the related registers in the PWM1 module. First the PWMCTL register is disabled to start this configuration process in line 53.

18. Then the PWMGENB register is configured to output High when loading and output Low when performing compare-down operations in line 54.

19. The PWMLOAD register is loaded with the upper bound value of 3999 in line 55.

20. The codes in lines 56~60 are used to configure PF1 as an alternate function pin, exactly as a PWM output signal pin for PWM1_2B generator.

21. The code in lines 59 is used to enable PB0 pin as an output and digital function pin to control the motor rotation direction.

22. The InitQEI() function starts at line 61.

23. The QEI module 0 is enabled and clocked by configuring the RCGCQEI register in line 63.

24. In lines 64 and 65, the lock register for the Port D is unlocked to enable the PD7 pin to be committed by setting bit 1 in the GPIOCR register to 1. Then in line 66, this register is locked again to prevent it from modifying again in the future.

25. In lines 67 and 70, the GPIO Port D are configured to make PD7 and PD6 as alternate function pins, exactly as two encoder phase input pins, PhB0 and PhA0.

26. In line 71, the QEICTL register is disabled to enable the configuration process to be started.

27. In line 72, the QEI module 0 is configured to enable QEI0 quadrature A & B mode.

28. The LOAD register is configured in line 73 by loading the maximum number of clock cycles (2500 − 1) into the velocity timer register as the upper bound of the timer.

29. After these configurations have been done, the QEI0 velocity capture mode is enabled in line 74 by calling the API function QEIVelocityEnable().

30. The QEI module 0 is enabled in line 75 by calling the API function QEIEnable().

Before one can run this project to calibrate the motor encoder, the following environments need to be set:

- Add the path for all system header files used in this project into the Include Paths box in the C/C++ tab under the Project|Options for Target 'Target 1' menu item. The correct path should be: C:\ti\TivaWare_C_Series-2.0.1.11577.

- Select the correct debug driver Stellaris ICDI in the Debug tab under the Project-|Options for Target 'Target 1' menu item.

- Add the TivaWare™ Peripheral Driver Library driverlib.lib file into the project. This library file is located at: C:\ti\TivaWare_C_Series-2.0.1.11577\driverlib \rvmdk. By right clicking on the Source Group 1 in the Project pane and selecting the Add Existing File . . . item, one can add this library file into the project.

Now run the project to collect the motor encoder speed values based on the given PWM values. The collected encoder speed values should be stored in the esData[] array. After the project runs, go to the Debug|Stop menu item to stop the project. Then open the Call Stack + Locals window, and one can expand the esData[] array and record these speed values to be used later.

Now that the encoder has been calibrated, we are ready to build the entire block diagram for this closed-loop motor control system.

10.3.9.2 *Build the Floating Chart for the Motor Closed-Loop Control System*

To build a closed-loop motor control system, a floating chart is a good tool to enable designers to have a clear and global picture about this control system. Figure 10.35 shows the floating chart of this closed-loop control system.

The PWM and QEI modules are initialized and configured first to make them ready to work for this closed-loop control system.

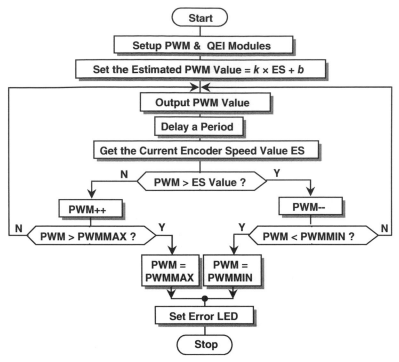

Figure 10.35. The floating chart of the closed-loop motor control system.

The current PWM output control signal is estimated based on the linear equation calculated by using the `CalibEncoder` project in Section 10.3.9.1 and output to the motor control system.

The equation $ES = k \times PWM + b$ can be used to estimate the slope K and b. Based on the running result of the project `CalibEncoder` we developed in the last section, the estimated average value for the slope K is 0.45 and b is about 0. Therefore the speed feedback transfer function is a constant and its value is 0.45. Based on this equation, for a given PWM value, the feedback encoder speed value ES should be $ES = 0.45 \times PWM$.

A time period is delayed to wait for the motor rotating speed stable. Then the current encoder speed is collected by reading the `QEISPEED` register. A comparison between the current PWM value and the feedback encoder speed multiplied by the slope K is performed. If the PWM output value is greater than the encoder speed, the current PWM value is decreased. Otherwise it is increased to try to match or equal to the encoder speed. An error is detected if the PWM value gets its maximum or minimum values and the related LED is ON to indicate this error situation.

If no error is detected, this closed-loop control will be continued to try to make the PWM value equal to the feedback encoder speed or make the speed error between them as small as possible, which is the target of the closed-loop control system.

With this floating chart available, next let's build and develop our real motor closed-loop control system.

10.3.9.3 *Build the Closed-Loop Control Program Based on the Floating Chart*

Open the Keil® µVersion®5 IDE and create a new project named DRAQEI under the C:
\ARM Class Projects\Chapter 10\DRAQEI folder. Then create a new C file
named DRAQEI.c under this project and enter the codes shown in Figure 10.36 into this C
file.

Let's have a closer look at this piece of codes to see how it works.

1. The codes in lines 4~9 are used to declare some system header files used in this project.

2. Some system and user defined macros are declared in lines 10~17. These macros include the
   upper and lower bounds of the PWM values PWMMAX and PWMMIN, the transfer function or
   the slope between the PWM and the feedback encoder speed value HS, and other system
   macros, such as PHA0 and PHB0 phase inputs, GPIO Ports D and F base, and commit
   registers.

3. Two user-defined functions, InitPWM() and InitQEI(), are declared in lines 18 and
   19.

4. The main() program starts at line 20. Two local variables, pw and es, represented the
   PWM and encoder speed value ES, are declared at the beginning of this program in line 22.

5. The system clock is defined in line 23. The GPIO Ports B, D, and F are clocked and enabled
   in line 24.

6. The codes in lines 25~30 are used to configure the related GPIO pins to be digital output or
   input pins to enable them to work as PhA and PhB or LED-driven pins.

7. Both user-defined functions, InitPWM() and InitQEI(), are called to initialize and
   configure the PWM1 and QEI0 modules to make them ready to output desired PWM values
   and receive rotary encoder feedback speed values to perform the closed-loop control
   function.

8. The codes in lines 33 and 34 are used to enable the PWM1_2B PWM output pin and the
   PWM1 module.

9. A selected desired PWM value, which is 12.5%, is assigned to the pw variable that is to be
   sent to the DC motor to make the motor rotate in line 35.

10. To repeatedly send the PWM outputs to the motor to make it rotate, an infinitive while()
    loop is used starting at line 36.

11. The desired PWM value is sent to the motor to make the motor rotate in line 38, and a
    system delay is executed to make the rotating speed of the DC motor stable in line 39.

12. In line 40, the motor encoder feedback speed value is collected and multiplied by the
    transfer function of the feedback path H(s), which is a constant HS = 1/0.45 = 2.22,
    to convert the speed to the corresponding PWM value, and is assigned to the es
    variable.

13. The codes in lines 41~46 are used to compare the encoder feedback speed value with
    the output PWM value to see whether the latter is greater than the former. If this is true,
    the output PWM value will be reduced by 1 to try to match the encoder speed. If
    the reduced PWM value is too small to be less than the lower bound of the PWM,
    PWMMIN, the PB3 LED will be on to indicate this error and the loop is broken to stop the
    program.

14. Similarly, the codes in lines 48~54 are used to compare the encoder feedback speed value
    with the output PWM value to see whether the latter is smaller than the former. If this is
    true, the output PWM value will be increased by 1 to try to match the encoder speed. If the
    increased PWM value is too large to be greater than the upper bound of the PWM,

```
1   //*********************************************************************************************************************
2   // DRAQEI.c - Motor Closed-Loop Control Program - QEI0 (Bounds Control System)
3   //*********************************************************************************************************************
4   #include <stdint.h>
5   #include <stdbool.h>
6   #include "driverlib/sysctl.h"
7   #include "driverlib/gpio.h"
8   #include "driverlib/qei.h"
9   #include "TM4C123GH6PM.h"

10  #define PWMMAX              3999
11  #define PWMMIN              5
12  #define HS                  2.22           // Hs = 1/K = 1/0.45 = 2.22
13  #define GPIO_PD6_PHA0       0x00031806
14  #define GPIO_PD7_PHB0       0x00031C06
15  #define GPIO_PORTD_BASE     0x40007000          // GPIO Port D
16  #define GPIO_PORTF_CR_R     (*((volatile uint32_t *)0x40025524))
17  #define GPIO_PORTD_CR_R     (*((volatile uint32_t *)0x40007524))

18  void InitPWM(void);
19  void InitQEI(void);

20  int main(void)
21  {
22      uint32_t pw, es;

23      SysCtlClockSet(SYSCTL_SYSDIV_30|SYSCTL_USE_PLL|SYSCTL_XTAL_4MHZ|SYSCTL_OSC_MAIN);
24      SYSCTL->RCGC2 = 0x2A;                    // enable & clock GPIO Ports B, D & F
25      GPIOB->DEN = 0xF;                        // enable PB3 – PB0 as digital function pins
26      GPIOB->DIR = 0xF;                        // configure PB3 – PB0 as output pins
27      GPIOD->DEN = 0xC0;                       // enable PD7 – PD6 as digital function pins
28      GPIOD->DIR = ~0xC;                       // configure PD7 – PD6 as input pins
29      GPIOF->DEN = 0xF;                        // enable PF3 – PF0 as digital function pins
30      GPIOF->DIR = 0xF;                        // configure PF3 – PF0 as output pins

31      InitPWM();                               // configure PWM module 1
32      InitQEI();                               // configure QEI module 0

33      PWM1->_2_CTL = 0x1;                      // enable PWM1_2B or M1PWM5
34      PWM1->ENABLE = 0x20;
35      pw = 500;                                // PWM = 500 makes es = 0.45*PWM = 0.45*500 = 225 ppr
                                                 // the 225 ppr can be considered as a setup input velocity

36      while(1)
37      {
38          PWM1->_2_CMPB = pw;
39          SysCtlDelay(5);
40          es = (QEI0->SPEED) * HS;             // get the current encoder speed value -> PWM
41          if (pw >= es) {
42              pw--;
43              if (pw < PWMMIN)
44              {
45                  GPIOB->DATA |= 0x8;   break;          // set PB3 to indicate an error occurred
46              }
47          }
48          else if (pw < es) {
49              pw++;
50              if (pw > PWMMAX)
51              {
52                  GPIOB->DATA |= 0x8;   break;          // set PB3 to indicate an error occurred
53              }
54          }
55      }
56      PWM1->_2_CTL = 0x0;                      // disable PWM1_2B or M1PWM5
57      PWM1->ENABLE = ~0x20;
58  }
```

Figure 10.36. The detailed codes for the project DRAQEI.

PWMMAX, the PB3 LED will be also turned on to indicate this error and the loop is broken to stop the program.

15. Finally the PWM1_2B PWM output pin and the PWM1 module are disabled if any error were encountered.

For the detailed codes of both user-defined functions, `InitPWM()` and `InitQEI ()`, refer to the project `CalibEncoder` built in Section 10.3.9.1 since both of them are identical to those functions defined in that project.

Also refer to Section 10.3.9.1 to set up the environments for this project and to build and run the project if everything is fine. As the project runs, one can find that the motor is rotating between two bounds, the upper and the lower bounds PWMMIN and PWMMAX, as a bound–bound control system did. To improve this control performance, a PID or a fuzzy logic control system should be developed and used.

10.4 THE CONTINUOUS AND DISCRETE PID CLOSED-LOOP CONTROL SYSTEM

The closed-loop motor control system discussed in the last section belongs to a simple closed-loop control system, which is called a bang–bang control system. In that control system, only two limits, the upper bound and the lower bound of the errors, are provided to limit the error between the input and the output of the system in a small range. The control target is to try to make this error as small as possible.

A more professional and traditional closed-loop control system is a so-called Proportional Integral Differential (PID) control system. A block diagram of this kind of PID control system is shown in Figure 10.37.

The following symbols are used in this continuous closed-loop control system:

- E(s) – Laplace transformation of the error signal $e(t) = e(t_2) - e(t_1)$.
- D(s) – Laplace transformation of the PID controller $D(t) = K_p + K_i \int dt + K_d \, d/dt$.
- U(s) – Laplace transformation of the controller output $U(t) = K_p e(t) + K_i \int e(t)dt + K_d \, de(t)/dt$.
- G(s) – Laplace transformation of the physical plant $G(t)$ (including the driver and motor).
- H(s) – Laplace transformation of the feedback system $H(t)$.

The reason we used so many Laplace transformations is that this is a typical method and strategy to analyze and design a PID and other closed-loop control systems, and this

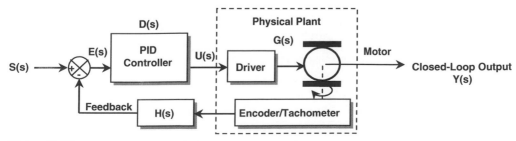

Figure 10.37. The block diagram of PID closed-loop control system.

method can be directly applied in the frequency domain to make all designs and analyses easier. Some complicated calculations in the time domain, such as integrations and differentials, can be replaced by the divisions and multiplications in the frequency domain or in the Laplace domain.

Regularly, three transformations are important to our system design: the $D(s)$, $G(s)$, and $H(s)$.

The $D(s)$ is the Laplace transformation of PID controller $D(t) = K_p + K_i \int dt + K_d \, d/dt$. In the frequency domain, this controller becomes $D(s) = K_p + K_i/s + sK_d$.

The $G(s)$ is the Laplace transformation of the physical plant $G(t)$. Basically most motor systems can be considered or approximated as linear systems and their transformation functions can be represented by the first or the second-order differential equations in the form of $K/(1 + \tau s)$ and τ is the time constant.

In most motor control systems, the feedback transformation function $H(s)$ can be considered as a linear coefficient K_H used to convert the encoder/tachometer position/velocity feedback output to the corresponding input variable.

Based on Figure 10.37, the overall transfer function for the complete closed-loop control system can be derived as

- The error $E(s) = S(s) - H(s)Y(s)$.
- The closed-loop output $Y(s) = D(s)G(s)E(s) = D(s)G(s) \, [S(s) - H(s)Y(s)]$.
- So the $Y(s) = D(s)G(s)S(s) - D(s)G(s)H(s)Y(s)$.

Finally the overall closed-loop transfer function is equal to

$$\frac{Y(s)}{S(s)} = \frac{D(s)G(s)}{1 + D(s)G(s)H(s)} = \frac{sK_0 + K}{s(1 + \tau s)}$$

This is a one-zero and two-pole system with zero $= -K/K_0$ and two poles; $s_1 = 0$ and $s_2 = -1/\tau$. In most actual applications, the plant transfer function $G(s)$ can be simplified to

$$G(s) = \frac{K}{1 + \tau s}$$

The open-loop transfer function $D(s)G(s)H(s)$ is an important function used to design the complete closed-loop control system.

The regular PID control system design method and procedure are as follows:

1. Collect the encoder or tachometer feedback values based on a sequence of PWM outputs applied to a motor system (including the driver and motor) when the motor is working in an open-loop condition (as we did in Section 10.3.8.1).

2. Identify the dynamic model of the plant G(s) based on the collected encoder or tachometer values and the corresponding PWM output values applied on the motor system in step 1 by using the MATLAB® Identification Toolbox™.

3. Based on the identified dynamic model in step 2, use either Ziegler–Nichols method or MATLAB® Control System Toolbox™ to design the desired PID controller.

4. After the PID controller is designed, use the MATLAB® SIMULINK® method to perform simulation to obtain the optimal PID parameters by tuning these control gain parameters.

5. Apply the simulated optimal PID parameters on our real motor control system in the following ways in our control software:
   - First get the position or velocity errors $e(t)$ between the setup values and the encoder or tachometer feedback values via encoder or tachometer.
   - Use the PID equation with three control gain parameters to get the control output $u(t)$ in terms of the input error $e(t)$ obtained from the last step.
   - Output this control output $u(t)$ with a PWM module to the motor system.
   - Loop back to the first step.

Since a computer is a digital electronic device and only the digital or discrete variables and functions can be applied and implemented in a computer, the software control program applied on any computer must also be digital program composed of digital codes. When using the above steps to build the actual PID control software, the following continuous variables must be converted to the discrete variables to match the digital controller:

1. The discrete position error $e(n) = s(n) - h(n)y(n) = s_n - Ky(n) = s - Ky_n$ (if s is a constant and n is an increment discrete number).
2. The discrete velocity error $\Delta e(n)/\Delta n = (e(n) - e(n-1))/[n - (n-1)] \approx e(n) - e(n-1) = e_n - e_{n-1}$.
3. The discrete integration $\Sigma e(t_i) = e(n_1) + e(n_2) + \ldots + e(n_n) = e_1 + e_2 + \ldots + e_n = \Sigma e_i$.
4. The discrete differential is similar to the velocity error, which is $e_n - e_{n-1}$.
5. The controller discrete output $U_n = K_p e_n + K_i \Sigma e_i + K_d(e_n - e_{n-1})$.

In the following sections, we will use these steps and procedures to build our PID controller for this motor control system.

10.4.1 Identify the Dynamic Model for the Motor Plant

Since we have collected the encoder speed values for given PWM outputs in Section 10.3.9.1, we can directly go to step 2 to identify the dynamic model of the physical plant, which includes the motor driver and motor itself.

In order to make our identification process simple and successful, we cannot use all of collected encoder speed output values. Instead, we can select the collected encoder speed values that are in the linear range of the output–input relationship shown in Figure 10.29. In other words, we should not use the encoder speed values closed to the starting point and the point from which the motor speed enters the saturation region. For example, if we collect 10 or 20 encoder speed values based on 10 or 20 PWM outputs, we can use the collected data between 3 and 10 collected encoder speed values or between 5 and 15 collected encoder speed values to this identification process.

As we mentioned, the MATLAB® Identification Toolbox™ is a good tool to identify the dynamic model for this DC motor. In order to do this identification job, the following operational sequence is needed:

1. Collect and format the motor input and output data, or the PWM outputs values that can be considered as the input to the motor and the encoder speed values that can be considered as the output of the motor, to divide them into two data arrays to be in a data file. This step needs to build a MATLAB® script file to complete this format.
2. In the MATLAB® workspace, load this data file into the MATLAB® workspace.

3. Open the MATLAB® Identification Toolbox™ to begin the identification process.

Now let's begin this identification process, and readers need to have MATLAB® and Identification Toolbox™ to fulfill this process.

10.4.1.1 Format the Input and Output Data for the DC Motor

In Section 10.3.9.1 we built an encoder calibration program `CalibEncoder` to collect a group of encoder speed values based on a sequence of PWM values outputs to the DC motor, as well as to save the encoder speed values into a data array `esData[]`. The collected encoder speed values and the corresponding PWM values are shown in Table 10.21.

In order to get the optimal and satisfied identification results, as we mentioned, we cannot use all of these collected data. Instead, we need to select some of these data as shown in Table 10.21. The reason for this is because the data items at the beginning and the data items closed to the ending part belong to very nonlinear data and they are not appropriate to be used to estimated the optimal and true motor plant model. In order to avoid this incorrect identification result based on those nonlinear data, we need to do this kind of selection. The data we have chosen are 8 pieces of them starting from data number 3 and ending at data number 10.

In this section we need to format those PWM and encoder speed values to form another data array to enable the MATLAB® Identification Toolbox™ to use that array to perform identification process.

We need to build a MATLAB® script file `getMData` to do this data array format.

Open MATLAB® and create a new MATLAB® Script file by going to `File|New|-Script` menu item to open a new script file. Enter the codes shown in Figure 10.38 into this script file.

Let's have a closer look at this piece of codes to see how it works.

1. The initial PWM value 500 is assigned to an accumulated variable S in line 2.
2. An 8×1 array u is declared in line 3 and initialized with all zeros. This array is a group of PWM outputs to the motor and it can be considered as the input to the DC motor.

Table 10.21. The collected QEI encoder speed values and the PWM values.

Number	PWM Values (u) %	Encoder Velocity Values (es) PPR	
		Hexadecimal	Decimal
1	100	49	73
2	300	F4	244
3	500	15C	348
4	700	19F	415
5	900	1E0	480
6	1100	1EF	495
7	1300	1FA	506
8	1500	201	513
9	1700	206	518
10	1900	20C	524
12	2100	20D	525
13	2300	20C	524
14	2500	20E	526
15	2700	20E	526

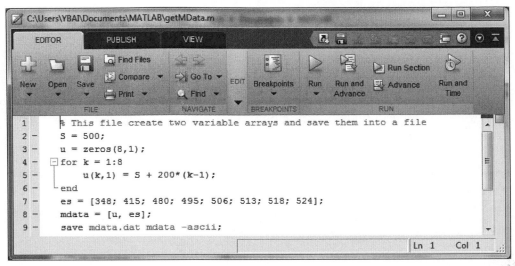

Figure 10.38.   The MATLAB Script file getMData.m. (Reprinted with the permission of MathWorks, Inc.)

3. A `for` loop is used to fill the array u with a sequence of PWM values starting from 500 to 1900 in lines 4~6.

4. The encoder speed values collected in the `CalibEncoder` project are assigned to the data array es in line 7. One has to convert the collected encoder speed values in the array esData[] from the hexadecimal to the decimal and put them in this new data array es. This array can be considered as the output of the DC motor.

5. A new data array mdata used for identification purpose is created in line 8. This array includes two 8×1 vectors or one 8×2 matrix.

6. This new formatted data array mdata is saved to a MATLAB® ASCII file named mdata. dat in line 9.

7. Save this script as `getMData` and run this script file by clicking on the Run arrow on the toolbar to create this new data array and data file mdata.dat.

A new data array file mdata.dat is created and it is located at the MATLAB® default user folder C:\User\User_Name\Documents\MATLAB.

Next let's load this data file into the MATLAB® workspace to enable the Identification Toolbox™ to recognize it and use it.

In the opened MATLAB® Command Window with the *fx>>* cursor ready, type:

load mdata.dat;

and press the Enter key on your keyboard. Then type mdata and press the Enter key on your keyboard again. All data items in this array are displayed in this window, as shown in Figure 10.39. If the Workspace window is opened, you can find that two arrays, u and es, as well as the data array mdata, have been added into the Workspace located at the upper-right corner. You can open this Workspace window by going to Desktop menu and checking the Workspace item.

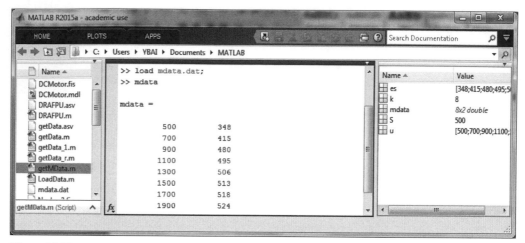

Figure 10.39. Load the data array mdata.dat into the MATLAB Workspace. (Reprinted with the permission of MathWorks, Inc.)

10.4.1.2 Identify the DC Motor Dynamic Model with Identification Toolbox™

Now open the MATLAB® Identification Toolbox™ by typing ident in the MATLAB® Command window after the fx>> cursor and press the Enter key.

The opened Identification Toolbox is shown in Figure 10.40a.

Click on the drop-down arrow on the Import data combo box and select the Time domain data item from this box to open the Import data wizard, as shown in Figure 10.40b.

Now type the following items into the Input, Output, Data name, Starting time, and Sampling interval textboxes:

- Input: u
- Output: es

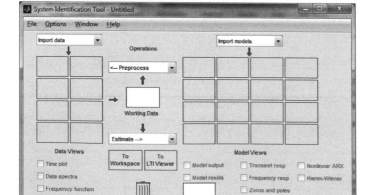
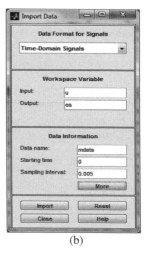

(a)   (b)

Figure 10.40. The opened Identification Toolbox and Import data wizard. (Reprinted with the permission of MathWorks, Inc.)

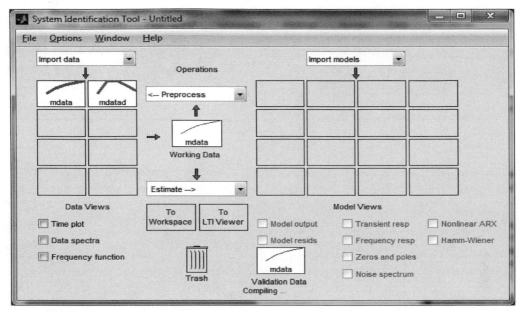

Figure 10.41.   The modified data array mdatad in the identification Toolbox. (Reprinted with the permission of MathWorks, Inc.)

- Data name: `mdata`
- Starting time: 0
- Sampling interval: `0.005`

Then click on the `Import` button to import these items into the Identification Toolbox. Now in the opened Identification Toolbox, perform the following operations to begin this identification process:

1. Click on the drop-down arrow in the `Preprocess` combo box and select `Remove trends` item to remove any possible trend for this data array. The modified data array `mdatad` with removed trends is shown in the second graphic cell, as shown in Figure 10.41.

2. Click on the drop-down arrow in the `Estimate` combo box and select `Process Models` item to identify the desired model.

3. The Process Model wizard now appears, as shown in Figure 10.42. Check the `Delay` checkbox and click on the Estimate button.

4. The identified dynamic model for this DC motor is complete and the identified result is shown in Figure 10.42. The values for the coefficient K and the pole are listed in the K and Tp1 `Value` boxes, respectively. The dynamic model is

$$G(s) = \frac{3.776}{(1 + 0.56s)} e^{-0.09s} \cong \frac{6.74}{(1.79 + s)}$$

5. Now return to the System identification Toolbox, and drag the identified model P1D and place it into the `LTI Viewer` box. The simulated step response of this model is pop up, as shown in Figure 10.43a. The `LTI Viewer` (Linear Time-Invariant Viewer) allows users to view the simulated results for the identified model, such as transient response, model output, model residuals, frequency response, zeros, and poles, as well as noise spectrum.

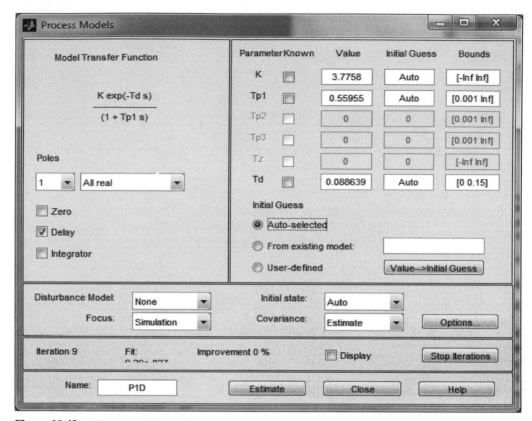

Figure 10.42. The opened Process Models wizard. (Reprinted with the permission of MathWorks, Inc.)

Check the following checkboxes in the System Identification Toolbox™ window to open the related plotting wizards to check the identification result:

- Model output
- Model resids
- Transient resp
- Frequency resp

The related identification results are shown in Figures 10.43b, 10.43c, and 10.43d.

From these analyses and responses, one can find that our identified model is very close to the actual motor system, and it is good for us to continue to build a PID control system to control this DC motor to get the optimal control performances.

10.4.2 Design the PID Controller Using the MATLAB® Control System Toolbox™

It is very easy and convenient to design and tune a practical PID controller for our closed-loop motor control system by using the MATLAB® Control System Toolbox™. In this section we use MATLAB® R2015a to illustrate how to use this tool to design and tune a

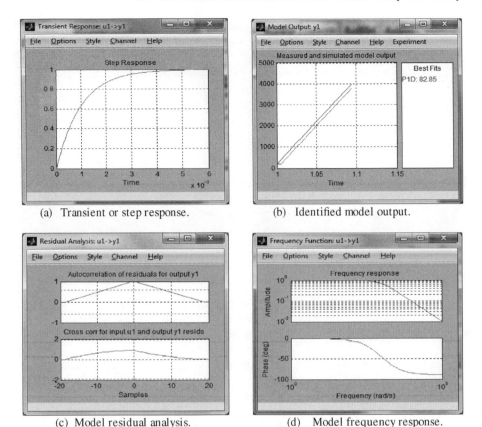

(a) Transient or step response.   (b) Identified model output.

(c) Model residual analysis.   (d) Model frequency response.

Figure 10.43.   The identified model responses and analysis. (Reprinted with the permission of MathWorks, Inc.)

practical PID controller applied in our motor closed-loop control system. The old version of the MATLAB® Control System Toolbox™, such as MATLAB® R2010b, provides similar functionalities.

Open the command window of the MATLAB® R2015a, and type the following commands shown in Figure 10.44 to set up the Laplace variable s and the transfer function sys for our DC motor plant identified from the previous section to open the PID tune wizard.

The opened PID Tuner is shown in Figure 10.45.

Select the PID from the Type combo box located on the top of this Tuner to begin this tuning. The created step response can be used as the starting point for this tuning process. Tune this step response by moving the arrow-mark on the Response time bar on the top of this Tuner to get the optimal step response.

The so-called optimal step response meets the following conditions:

- A short rising and settling time
- A small overshoot (%)
- A big phase margin
- A stable control system

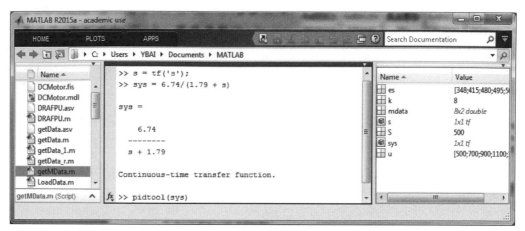

Figure 10.44. Commands used to set transfer function of the DC motor and start PID tuner. (Reprinted with the permission of MathWorks, Inc.)

As shown in Figure 10.45, by moving the arrow-mark on the Response Time bar, we obtained the optimal step response with 0.5 s response time, 0.35 s rise time, 1.36 s settling time, 15% overshoot, and 60° phase margin, and the system is a stable one.

Click on the Show Parameters icon on the upper-right corner of this Tuner, and you can find all of these tuned parameters.

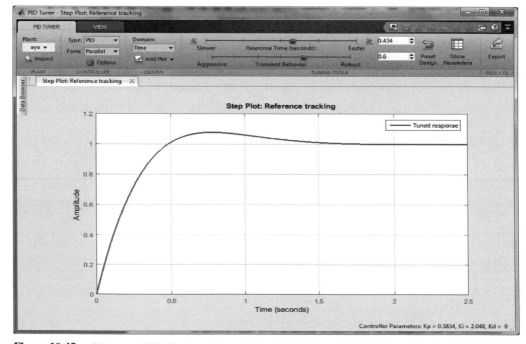

Figure 10.45. The opened PID Tuner and the tuning result. (Reprinted with the permission of MathWorks, Inc.)

The tuned and optimal PID control parameters are

- The proportional gain Kp$=0.5834$
- The integral gain Ki$=2.0484$
- The differential gain Kd$=0$

Now we can close this PID Tuner by clicking on the Close button on this Tuner. Next let's use the MATLAB® SIMULINK® to perform some simulation techniques to obtain the optimal PID parameters with this simulation process.

10.4.3 Simulate the PID Control System Using the MATLAB® SIMULINK®

Open the MATLAB® SIMULINK® by typing simulink after the cursor *fx>>* in the MATLAB® command window, and the opened SIMULINK® window is shown in Figure 10.46.

Create a new SIMULINK® model by going to New Model icon to open the SIMULINK® workspace. Perform the following operations to build this SIMULINK function block:

1. On the left Libraries panel, click on the Sources item to open the Sources library. Drag and place the Step block into the SIMULINK workspace.

2. Click on the Sinks item to open the Sinks library. Drag and place the Scope block into the SIMULINK® workspace.

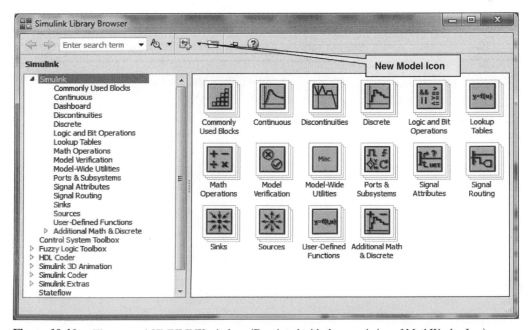

Figure 10.46. The opened SIMULINK window. (Reprinted with the permission of MathWorks, Inc.)

3. Click on the Commonly Used Blocks item to open this library. Drag and place the Sum and the Gain blocks into the SIMULINK® workspace. Rotate the Gain block by 180 degree by going to Format|Flip Block menu item. Double click the Sum block to open its property wizard. Then replace the second + sign with a minus – sign in the List of signs box. Click on the OK button to close this wizard.

4. Click on the Continuous item to open the Continuous library. Drag the PID Controller and Transfer Fcn blocks and place them into the SIMULINK® workspace.

5. Now make connections for each block one by one by dragging the output terminal of each block to the following block input terminal. One point to be noted is that when connecting between the output terminal of the Transfer Fcn and the input terminal of the Scope and the Gain blocks, make sure to do the connection between the Transfer Fcn and the Gain block first. Then drag the input terminal of the Scope block back to the Transfer Fcn block to do this connection.

Your finished SIMULINK® block function connection should match one that is shown in Figure 10.47. Save this SIMULINK® model as DCMotor.mdl to a desired location in your host computer by going to File|Save menu item.

Now let's modify each block's parameters to meet our real system requirements.

1. Double click on the Step block and enter 0 to the Step time and 0.005 to the Sample time textboxes, respectively.

2. Double click on the PID Controller block and enter the tuned PID parameters as we did in the last section into the corresponding box for Kp, Ki, and Kd, which is Kp = 0.5834, Ki = 2.0484, and Kd = 0.

3. Double click on the Transfer Fcn block to enter our identified dynamic model parameters for the DC motor, which is [6.74] for the numerator and [1 1.79] for the denominator.

Now double click on the Scope block to open this scope to monitor our simulation result.

One can tune the PID parameters to try to get the optimal step response for this motor control system. After tuning the PID parameters, the optimal PID parameters are

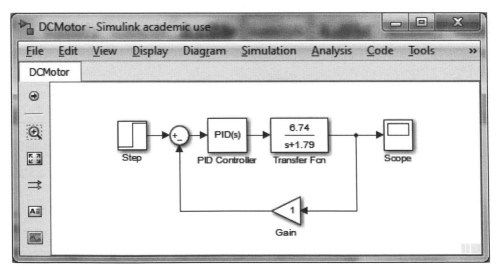

Figure 10.47. The finished SIMULINK bock connections. (Reprinted with the permission of MathWorks, Inc.)

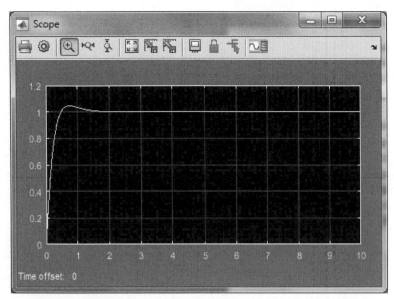

Figure 10.48.   The simulated step response result. (Reprinted with the permission of MathWorks, Inc.)

- $K_p = 0.7500$
- $K_i = 2.0484$
- $K_d = 0.0000$

Start the simulation by going to Simulation|Run menu item. The final optimal simulated result is shown in Figure 10.48.

Next we need to use these simulated control parameters into our control program to complete the closed-loop control to our motor system.

10.4.4 Build the Control Software to Implement the PID Controller

Open the Keil® µVersion®5 IDE to create a new project named PID-Control under the folder C:\ARM Class Projects\Chapter 10 and add a new C source file PID-Control.c into the project.

Enter the first part codes shown in Figure 10.49 into this source file. Let's have a closer look at this piece of codes to see how it works.

1. The codes in lines 4~9 are used to declare some system header files used in this project.

2. Some system and user-defined macros are declared in lines 10~17. These macros include the upper and lower bounds of the PWM values PWMMAX and PWMMIN, the transfer function or the slope between the PWM and the feedback encoder speed value HS, and other system macros, such as PHA0 and PHB0 phase inputs, GPIO Ports D and F base, and commit registers.

3. Two user-defined functions, InitPWM() and InitQEI(), are declared in lines 18 and 19.

4. The main() program starts at line 20. Some local variables, pw and es, represented the output PWM value and encoder speed value ES, upper and motor[] array are used to define the upper bound of the loop and the collected encoder speed values, and these are declared at the beginning of this program in lines 22.

```
1  //***************************************************************************************************************
2  // PID-Control.c - Motor PID Closed-Loop Control Program – QEI0
3  //***************************************************************************************************************
4  #include <stdint.h>
5  #include <stdbool.h>
6  #include "driverlib/sysctl.h"
7  #include "driverlib/gpio.h"
8  #include "driverlib/qei.h"
9  #include "TM4C123GH6PM.h"
10 #define PWMMAX              3999
11 #define PWMMIN              5
12 #define HS                 2.22                          // HS = 1/K = 1/0.45 = 2.22
13 #define GPIO_PD6_PHA0       0x00031806
14 #define GPIO_PD7_PHB0       0x00031C06
15 #define GPIO_PORTD_BASE     0x40007000                   // GPIO Port D
16 #define GPIO_PORTF_CR_R     (*((volatile uint32_t *)0x40025524))
17 #define GPIO_PORTD_CR_R     (*((volatile uint32_t *)0x40007524))
18 void InitPWM(void);
19 void InitQEI(void);
20 int main(void)
21 {
22    uint32_t pw, es, index, upper = 1000, s, n = 0, motor[100];
23    double ie = 0, de, e[2], Kp = 0.75, Ki = 2.118, Kd = 0;
24    SysCtlClockSet(SYSCTL_SYSDIV_25|SYSCTL_USE_PLL|SYSCTL_XTAL_4MHZ|SYSCTL_OSC_MAIN);
25    SYSCTL->RCGC2 = 0x2A;                  // enable & clock GPIO Ports B, D & F
26    GPIOB->DEN = 0xF;                      // enable PB3 – PB0 as digital function pins
27    GPIOB->DIR = 0xF;                      // configure PB3 – PB0 as output pins
28    GPIOD->DEN = 0xC0;                     // enable PD7 – PD6 as digital function pins
29    GPIOD->DIR = ~0xC;                     // configure PD7 – PD6 as input pins
30    GPIOF->DEN = 0xF;                      // enable PF3 – PF0 as digital function pins
31    GPIOF->DIR = 0xF;                      // configure PF3 – PF0 as output pins
32    InitPWM();                             // configure PWM module 1
33    InitQEI();                             // configure QEI module 0
34    while(1)
35    {
36       PWM1->_2_CTL = 0x1;                 // enable PWM1_2B or M1PWM5
37       PWM1->ENABLE = 0x20;
38       s = 1000;                           // s = 1000 makes es = 0.45*PWM = 0.45*1000 = 450 ppr
                                             // the 450 ppr can be considered as a setup input velocity
39       PWM1->_2_CMPB = s;                  // send desired PWM value or 450 ppr to motor
40       e[1] = s;
41       for (index = 0; index < upper; index++)      // output a square wave form to motor
42       {
43          es = QEI0->SPEED;                // get the current encoder speed value
44          e[0] = s - es*HS;                // convert speed to PWM value
45          de = e[1] - e[0];                // get differential error
46          ie = ie + e[0];                  // get integral error
47          pw = (uint32_t)(Kp*e[0] + Ki * ie + Kd * de);   // calculate the PID control value
48          e[1] = e[0];                     // save the next error
49          PWM1->_2_CMPB = pw;              // output the PID control value to the motor
50          SysCtlDelay(5);
51          if (n < 100) { motor[n] = es; }  // collect the first 100 encoder speed values
52          n++;
53       }
54       PWM1->_2_CMPB = 0;                  // 0 to motor to stop motor
55       PWM1->_2_CTL = 0x0;                 // disable PWM1_2B or M1PWM5
56       PWM1->ENABLE &= ~0x20;
57       for (index = 0; index < upper; index++)      // stop the motor for a period of time
58          SysCtlDelay(10);
59    }
60 }
```

Figure 10.49. The first part codes for the project PID-Control.

5. In line 23, the input velocity error `e[]`, error rate `de` and integral error `ie`, as well as PID parameters, `Kp`, `Ki`, and `Kd`, are declared and defined.

6. The system clock is defined in line 24. The GPIO Ports B, D, and F are clocked and enabled in line 25.

7. The codes in lines 26~31 are used to configure the related GPIO pins to be digital output or input pins to enable them to work as `PhA` and `PhB` or LED-driven pins.

8. In lines 32 and 33, both user-defined functions, `InitPWM()` and `InitQEI()`, are called to initialize and configure the `PWM1` and `QEI0` modules to make them ready to output desired PWM values and receive rotary encoder feedback speed values to perform the closed-loop control function.

9. An infinitive `while()` loop is started at line 34 to enable the program to repeatedly output the desired PWM value to drive the motor to rotate in a constant speed.

10. The codes in lines 36 and 37 are used to enable the `PWM1_2B` PWM output pin and the `PWM1` module.

11. A selected desired PWM value, which is 25%, is assigned to the `s` variable that is to be sent to the DC motor to make the motor rotate in line 38. This PWM value `1000` can be considered to be a desired velocity input setup value, 450 PPR, for the target motor rotating velocity since $ES = K \times PWM = 0.45 \times PWM = 0.45 \times 1000 = 450$.

12. The desired PWM value `1000` or the target motor velocity 450 PPR stored in the variable `s` is sent to the motor to make the motor rotate in line 39, and this setup motor velocity is sent to the first velocity error `e[1]` to be reserved in line 40.

13. Starting at line 41, a `for` loop is used to repeatedly send out this desired motor setup velocity value 225 PPR that is equivalent to $PWM = 500$; get the feedback encoder velocity value `es` in line 43, and then compare both values to calculate the velocity error `e[0]` in line 44, error rate `de` in line 45, and integral error `ie` in line 46.

14. In line 44, in order to get the velocity error, the feedback encoder velocity is converted to the corresponding PWM value by multiplying $HS = 1/0.45 = 2.22$ since $es = 0.45 \times PWM$, and $PWM = es/0.45 = es \times 2.22$. The simulated PID control gains `Kp`, `Ki`, and `Kd` are used to estimate the optimal PWM output value in line 47.

15. In line 48, the current velocity error `e[0]` is sent to the next error `e[1]` to be reserved.

16. The calculated optimal PID control out is sent to the motor to try to rotate the motor in a constant setup speed in line 49. Then the system is delayed by some time to make the motor rotating speed stable in line 50.

17. The codes in lines 51 and 52 are used to collect the first 100 motor encoder feedback velocity values and save them into the data array `motor[100]`. These velocity values can be used to analyze the actual motor step response later with the MATLAB® `plot()` function.

18. The codes in lines 54 and 56 are used to enable a Low level applied on the motor driver to stop the DC motor and disable the PWM1 module.

19. Another `for` loop is used to make this Low output with a certain period of time in lines 57 and 58.

The second part codes for this project contain the codes for the `InitPWM()` and `InitQEI()` functions. For the detailed codes about these two functions, refer to the project `CalibEncoder` built in Section 10.3.9.1 since both of them are identical with those functions defined in this project.

```
% plot the PID closed-loop motor step response - 100 samples
t = 1:100;
y = [0; 0; 0; 0; 0; 49; 49; 49; 179; 179; 179; 179; 267; 267; 267; 267; 326; 326; 326; 364; 364; 364; 364;
    388; 388; 388; 388; 405; 405; 405; 418; 418; 418; 418; 426; 426; 426; 426; 432; 432; 432; 435; 435; 435;
    435; 440; 440; 440; 440; 441; 441; 441; 443; 443; 443; 443; 443; 443; 443; 443; 444; 444; 444; 444; 444;
    444; 444; 445; 445; 445; 445; 446; 446; 446; 450; 450; 450; 450; 449; 449; 449; 449; 449; 449; 449; 449;
    447; 447; 447; 448; 448; 448; 448; 447; 447; 447; 447; 447; 447; 447];

plot(t, y);
grid;

xlabel('Numer of Samples');
ylabel('Motor Output Speed (PPR)');
title('PID Closed-Loop Motor Step Response');
```

Figure 10.50.   The codes to plot the motor step response.

Also refer to Section 10.3.9.1 to set up the environments for this project; build and run the project if everything is fine. As the project runs, one can find that the motor is rotating periodically from Low to High and from High to Low.

To confirm the performance of the PID controller applied on this closed-loop motor control system, one can use the 100 collected encoder velocity values stored in the `motor [ ]` data array. One needs to record and convert them from hexadecimal to the decimal values, and then create a MATLAB® script and put these data into a data array or a vector to plot them in the time domain to check its performance.

A piece of example codes is shown in Figure 10.50 and it is saved as a MATLAB® Script file named `PlotMotorPIDStep.m`. When running this MATLAB® script file, the step response of this PID closed-loop motor control system is plotted in the time domain, as shown in Figure 10.51.

Next let's take care of the fuzzy logic controller to improve the control performance to this closed-loop motor control system.

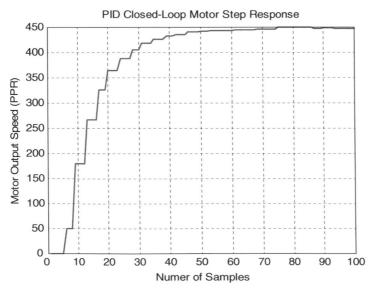

Figure 10.51.   The step response of the actual closed-loop motor control system. (Reprinted with the permission of MathWorks, Inc.)

10.5 THE FUZZY LOGIC CLOSED-LOOP CONTROL SYSTEM

The fuzzy logic controller belongs to a general-purpose controller that can handle both linear and nonlinear control systems. As we know, the PID controller can only handle the linear system or a linear time-invariant (LTI) system. However, all actual systems in our world are nonlinear systems. In order to develop a closely matched controller to control nonlinear systems, the fuzzy logic controller is a good candidate.

The procedure of developing a fuzzy logic controller is as follows:

1. Fuzzification process: Convert crisp variables to the fuzzy variables.
2. Control rule process: Design control rules.
3. Defuzzification process: Convert fuzzy variables back to crisp variables.

Figure 10.52 shows this fuzzy logic controller developing process. To build a fuzzy logic controller (FLC), both input error e and error rate Δe need to be calculated in advance and both work as inputs to the FLC.

10.5.1 The Fuzzification Process

The so-called fuzzification process is to convert the crisp variables to the corresponding fuzzy variables. The converted fuzzy variables are presented by a group of membership functions. Before doing this conversion, the range of the inputs (input error and error rate) and the output of the system should be determined first. In this way, the membership functions for the input error, the error rate, and the output of the system can be defined, respectively.

For the present application, the ranges of the input and the output of the system are given in Table 10.22.

These input velocity errors, error rates, and output motor speeds are calculated based on the data collected from the `CalibEncoder` and the `PID-Control` projects. For example, the minimum input velocity error is $49 - 450 = -401$. The maximum input velocity error rate is $179 - 49 = 130$, and the range of the motor PWM output values are $-2000\sim2000$ (50%). A symmetry data structure is used. Although the -2000 motor

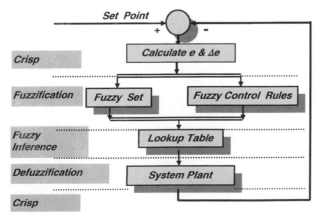

Figure 10.52.   The developing procedure of the fuzzy logic controller.

Table 10.22.   The range of the input error, error rate and the output.

Variable	Range of the Variable	Units
Input Error e	−400 ~ 400	PPR
Input Error Rate Δe	−130 ~ 130	PPR
Motor PWM Value	−2000 ~ 2000	PWM

PWM value can never exist, for the fuzzy system design purpose a symmetry structure is recommended to be considered and applied for the fuzzy controller.

To represent these input and output variables using fuzzy sets, a set of linguistic variables is chosen to represent a 5-*degree* of error, 5-*degree* of error rate, and 5-*degree* of control output. Membership functions are constructed to represent the input and output in which degree belongs to a different membership set or linguistic variable set.

The linguistic variables are defined as follows:

Inputs: LN, Large Negative; LP, Large Positive; SN, Small Negative; SP, Small Positive; ZE, Zero

Output: LN, Large Negative; LP, Large Positive; SN, Small Negative; SP, Small Positive; ZE, Zero

The membership functions of the input error, the error rate and the controller output are shown in Figure 10.53. The units for all of these variables are PPR and PWM value.

The MATLAB® Fuzzy Logic Toolbox™ is used to build and develop this fuzzy controller. Both inputs, error and error rate, used the Gauss waveform as the shape of the membership functions (MFs). But the output PWM values used the triangular form as the shape of its MF.

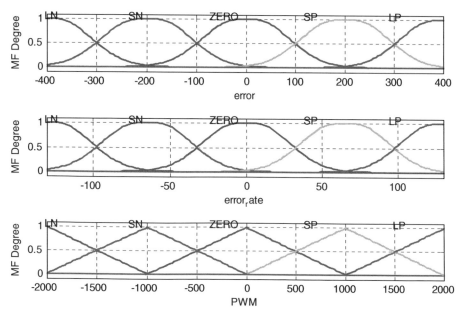

Figure 10.53.   Membership functions for input error, error rate, and output.

10.5.2 Design of Control Rules

Totally 25 control rules are designed for this fuzzy controller, as shown in Figure 10.54.

These control rules are designed based on the common sense for a general control strategy by using the MATLAB® Fuzzy Logic Toolbox™. Go to the Edit|Rules menu to open the control Rule Editor window to build these rules.

10.5.3 The Defuzzification Process

To perform real time control for any control system, a crisp control output is necessary. Therefore the fuzzy outputs must be converted back to the crisp outputs by using the defuzzification process.

The core of the defuzzification process is the so-called Center-Of-Gravity (COG) method. If we assume that u_i is the membership function, U_i the universe of discourse, and m the number of contributions, then the traditional output of the fuzzy inference system can be represented as

$$u = \frac{\sum_{i=1}^{m}(u_i \times U_i)}{\sum_{i=1}^{m} u_i}$$

where u is the current crisp output of the fuzzy inference system and this equation is called the Center-of-Gravity method.

---

1. If (error is LN) and (error_rate is LN) then (PWM is LP) (1)
2. If (error is LN) and (error_rate is SN) then (PWM is LP) (1)
3. If (error is LN) and (error_rate is ZERO) then (PWM is SP) (1)
4. If (error is LN) and (error_rate is SP) then (PWM is SP) (1)
5. If (error is LN) and (error_rate is LP) then (PWM is ZERO) (1)
6. If (error is SN) and (error_rate is LN) then (PWM Is LP) (1)
7. If (error is SN) and (error_rate is SN) then (PWM is SP) (1)
8. If (error is SN) and (error_rate is ZERO) then (PWM is SP) (1)
9. If (error is SN) and (error_rate is SP) then (PWM is ZERO) (1)
10. If (error is SN) and (error_rate is LP) then (PWM is SN) (1)
11. If (error is ZERO) and (error_rate is LN) then (PWM is LP) (1)
12. If (error is ZERO) and (error_rate is SN) then (PWM is SP) (1)
13. If (error is ZERO) and (error_rate is ZERO) then (PWM is ZERO) (1)
14. If (error is ZERO) and (error_rate is SP) then (PWM is SN) (1)
15. If (error is ZERO) and (error_rate is LP) then (PWM is LN) (1)
16. If (error is SP) and (error_rate is LN) then (PWM is LP) (1)
17. If (error is SP) and (error_rate is SN) then (PWM is SP) (1)
18. If (error is SP) and (error_rate is ZERO) then (PWM is SN) (1)
19. If (error is SP) and (error_rate is SP) then (PWM is SN) (1)
20. If (error is SP) and (error_rate is LP) then (PWM is LN) (1)
21. If (error is LP) and (error_rate is LN) then (PWM is ZERO) (1)
22. If (error is LP) and (error_rate is SN) then (PWM is SN) (1)
23. If (error is LP) and (error_rate is ZERO) then (PWM is LN) (1)
24. If (error is LP) and (error_rate is SP) then (PWM is SN) (1)
25. If (error is LP) and (error_rate is LP) then (PWM is LN) (1)

Figure 10.54. Fuzzy control rules.

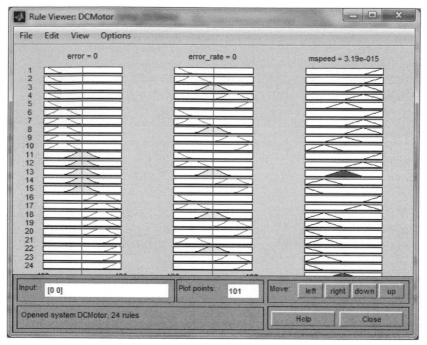

Figure 10.55. Graphic representation of the control rules. (Reprinted with the permission of MathWorks, Inc.)

With the help of the MATLAB® Fuzzy Logic Toolbox™, one can easily view the control rules and their functions based on a graphical output control wizard, as shown in Figure 10.55. In the MATLAB® Fuzzy Logic Toolbox™ window, go to View|Rules menu item to open this graphical view for all control rules built for this fuzzy controller. The entire control output or envelope can also be viewed by going to View|Surface menu item, as shown in Figure 10.56.

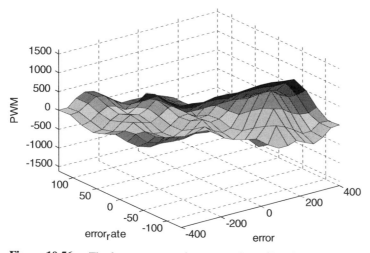

Figure 10.56. The fuzzy output surface or envelope. (Reprinted with the permission of MathWorks, Inc.)

The results of the defuzzification process are the real crisp outputs. The motor encoder speeds in our project can be derived or calculated in two different ways: the off-line and the on-line methods. The so-called off-line method is to build a lookup table before the project runs. In the lookup table, each crisp control output can be uniquely determined based on the current input error and error rate pair. The online method is to calculate the control output in real time based on the current error inputs and the control output in terms of the COG equation.

In this project, we try to use the off-line method to calculate a lookup table to simplify this defuzzification process to obtain the control outputs.

In order to apply these control rules and defuzzification processes in our project, we need to convert them to the C codes with the help of an `if` selection structure.

10.5.4 Apply the Fuzzy Logic Controller to the DC Motor Control System

To use the lookup table to get the desired control output, the `if` selection structure should be used to divide the input errors and the output controls into the different ranges. Based on the different ranges, the control output can be determined from the lookup table. The control outputs in the lookup table are crisp variables.

It can be found from Table 10.23 that the control output PWM value is grouped based on their peak values, not the ranges, and these peak values are corresponded to the U_i values in the COG equation shown above since this is required by the COG method.

Based on control rules shown in Figure 10.54, an input–output relationship table can be developed and shown in Table 10.24. This table can be considered to be a 2-D matrix, and each intersection cell is the control output PWM or `pwm(i, j)`.

Table 10.23. The ranges of the inputs and the output of the DC motor.

Input Velocity Error	< −300	−300 ~ −100	−100 ~ 100	100 ~ 300	> 300
MF	LN	SN	ZE	SP	LP
Input Error Rate	< −100	−100 ~ −50	−50 ~ 50	50 ~ 100	> 100
MF	LN	SN	ZE	SP	LP
Output Velocity	−1500	−1000	0	1000	1500
MF	LN	SN	ZE	SP	LP

Table 10.24. The control rules.

e \ Δe	LN	SN	ZE	SP	LP
LN	LP	LP	SP	SP	ZE
SN	LP	SP	SP	ZE	SN
ZE	LP	SP	ZE	SN	LN
SP	LP	SP	SN	SN	LN
LP	ZE	SN	LN	SN	LN

Table 10.25. The input errors.

e \ Δe	LN	SN	ZE	SP	LP
LN	u(0,0)	u(0,1)	u(0,2)	u(0,3)	u(0,4)
SN	u(1,0)	u(1,1)	u(1,2)	u(1,3)	u(1,4)
ZE	u(2,0)	u(2,1)	u(2,2)	u(2,3)	u(2,4)
SP	u(3,0)	u(3,1)	u(3,2)	u(3,3)	u(3,4)
LP	u(4,0)	u(4,1)	u(4,2)	u(4,3)	u(4,4)

According to the COG equation, each u_i should be the AND or the minimum value selected between the MF_e and MF_Δe pair: u(i, j) = min(MF_e, MF_Δe) if each u_i can be presented by an element in a 2D matrix, as shown in Table 10.24. The MF_e and the MF_Δe are the membership functions of the error e and the error rate Δe. In this way, by using these two tables, we can easily calculate each crisp control output or PWM value based on the COG equation shown above since each cell in these two tables has a one-to-one relationship. For example, u(0,1) in Table 10.25 should be multiplied by the cell LP in the Table 10.24 if e is LN and Δe is SN to get pwm(0,1). Similarly, u(0,2) in the Table 10.25 should be multiplied by the cell SP in the Table 10.24 if e is LN and Δe is ZE to get pwm(0,2). Finally we can get the crisp control output by adding all pwm(i, j) together as the numerator and adding all u(i,j) together as the denominator.

The pseudo codes for these two examples can be presented as follows:

If e = LN and Δe = SN, then the u_1 = u(0, 1) × LP = min(MF_e, MF_Δe) × LP.

If e = LN and Δe = ZE, then the u_2 = u(0, 2) × SP = min(MF_e, MF_Δe) × SP.

Furthermore, these two pseudo instructions can be written as

If e < −300 and −100 < Δe < −50, then u_1 = min(0.5, 0.8) × 1500 = 0.5 × 1500 = pwm(0, 1) = 750.

If e < −300 and −50 < Δe < 50, then u_2 = min(0.5, 1) × 1000 = 0.5 × 1000 = pwm(0, 2) = 500.

Refer to Figure 10.53 to get the values of the membership functions for each error and error rate. Finally the control output can be calculated as

$$u = \frac{u(0,1) \times LP + u(0,2) \times SP}{u(0,0) + u(0,2)} = \frac{0.5 \times 1500 + 0.5 \times 1000}{0.48 + 0.5} = 1276$$

In this example, we used the approximated MF values as the real MF values to simplify this calculation process. To make our project easy and simple, we used MATLAB® Fuzzy Logic Toolbox™ to build our lookup table.

Basically, the core of using a lookup table is to pre-define or pre-calculate all crisp control outputs based on the different ranges of input errors and error rates. In other words, each control output in the lookup table does not correspond to the current error and error rate input value, but instead it is based on a range of the input error and error rate. All input errors and error rates can be divided into different ranges, and each range covered a crisp control output in the lookup table. The smaller the error and the error rate

```
% Calculate the fuzzy lookup table for DC Motor control system – DCMotorLT.m
% Feb 28, 2015
% Y. Bai

MLT = zeros(5, 5);          % lookup table is a 5 by 5 matrix
e  = -400;                  % most negative speed error: range: -400 ~ 400: step 200 (4 steps)
de = -120;                  % most negative speed error rate: range: -120 ~ 120: step: 60 (4 steps)

% the resulted lookup table is a 5 by 5 matrix.
a = readfis('DCMotor'); % get the DCMotor fuzzy inference system – DCMotor.fis

for i = 1:5
  for j = 1:5
  MLT(i, j) = evalfis([(e + (i-1)*200) (de + (j-1)*60)], a);
  end
end

MLT                         % display the resulted lookup table
```

Figure 10.57. The script used to calculate the lookup table.

ranges, the greater the number of accurate control outputs can be obtained from the lookup table. However, more memory space is needed to store those control outputs in a larger lookup table. For example, if both the errors and error rates in our project are divided into 4 ranges, such as $-400 \sim 400$ for errors and $-120 \sim 120$ for error rates with each range for the errors and the error rates being 200 and 60, the control output lookup table would be a 5×5 matrix with 25 elements. In the program, 25 if-then instructions would be used to distinguish these errors and error rates to obtain desired control output from the lookup table.

To make a more accurate lookup table, one can divide the input velocity error e and error rate Δe into more equal segments or ranges. A trade-off needs to be made between the accuracy and space for any control system. In this project, we select to use a 5×5 lookup table to divide the inputs into 4 ranges.

The MATLAB® script used to calculate our lookup table is shown in Figure 10.57. In this script, an MATLAB® function evalfis() in the Fuzzy Logic Toolbox is used to calculate this 5×5 lookup table. The finished lookup table is shown in Figure 10.58.

Table 10.26 shows the relationship between the input errors, error rate ranges and the control outputs in our lookup table. This table can be directly used by our program to determine and identify the desired control outputs based on the velocity error and error rate input ranges with the help of the if-then selection instructions. One point to be

```
MLT =

  1616.5   1573.4    958.2    919.7     76.8
  1513.0    958.2    889.5     30.0    818.5
  1513.0    860.0    0.000   -860.0  -1419.6
  1289.9    809.9   -889.5   -958.2  -1513.0
   -74.6   -889.6  -1364.8  -1002.6  -1513.0
```

Figure 10.58. The finished lookup table.

Table 10.26. The relationship of input errors and control outputs.

e \ Δe	<−120	−120 ~ −60	−60 ~ 0	0 ~ 60	60 ~ 120
< −400	1617	1573	958	920	77
−400 ~ −200	1513	958	890	30	819
−200 ~ 0	1513	860	0	−860	−1420
0 ~ 200	1290	810	−890	−958	−1513
200 ~ 400	−75	−890	−1365	−1003	−1513

noted is that some negative control outputs may never be used since we did not configure the motor to rotate in the CCW direction in our program.

Regularly, you should use the MATLAB® SIMULINK® to perform simulations for this fuzzy controller. Because of the space limitation, we have to skip this step. Now let's build our fuzzy control program Fuzzy-Control to control the DC motor with the fuzzy logic controller.

10.5.5 Build the Fuzzy Logic Control Project Fuzzy-Control

Create a new folder Fuzzy-Control under the folder C:\ARM Class Projects \Chapter 10 and a new Keil® μVersion®5 project named Fuzzy-Control under that folder. Since this project is a little large, thus a header file and a C source file are needed to be developed.

10.5.5.1 Create the Header File Fuzzy-Control.h

Create a new header file Fuzzy-Control.h and add it into the project Fuzzy-Control that is just created above. Enter the codes shown in Figure 10.59 into this header file.

Let's have a closer look at this header file to see how it works.

1. The codes in lines 4~9 are used to declare some system header files to be used in this project.
2. The codes in lines 10~12 are used to define three constants to be used in the project; these are the upper bound and the lower bound of the PWM output values as well as the conversion coefficient HS that is used to convert the feedback speed value to the corresponded PWM value.
3. The mapping addresses for the GPIO Ports D and F as well as QEI0-related GPIO pins are defined in lines 13~17.
4. Three user-defined functions, InitPWM(), InitQEI(), and GetLookup(), are declared in lines 18~20. The GetLookup() function is used to get the crisp control output value from the fuzzy lookup table based on the current input velocity error and the error rate values.
5. The ranges of the fuzzy input velocity errors and error rates are defined in lines 21 and 22. Five points are defined to divide the input errors and error rates into 4 ranges, and these points are obtained from the Table 10.26 directly.

```
1  //*******************************************************************************************************************
2  // Fuzzy-Control.h - Header File for Fuzzy-Control Program
3  //*******************************************************************************************************************
4  #include <stdint.h>
5  #include <stdbool.h>
6  #include "driverlib/sysctl.h"
7  #include "driverlib/gpio.h"
8  #include "driverlib/qei.h"
9  #include "TM4C123GH6PM.h"

10 #define  PWMMAX          3999
11 #define  PWMMIN          5
12 #define  HS              2.22                              // HS = 1/K = 1/0.45 = 2.22

13 #define  GPIO_PD6_PHA0        0x00031806
14 #define  GPIO_PD7_PHB0        0x00031C06
15 #define  GPIO_PORTD_BASE      0x40007000        // GPIO Port D
16 #define  GPIO_PORTF_CR_R      (*((volatile uint32_t *)0x40025524))
17 #define  GPIO_PORTD_CR_R      (*((volatile uint32_t *)0x40007524))

18 void InitPWM(void);
19 void InitQEI(void);
20 int GetLookup(double error, double error_rate);

21 int E_LN = -400, E_SN = -200, E_ZE = 0, E_SP = 200, E_LP = 400;
22 int ER_LN = -120, ER_SN = -60, ER_ZE = 0, ER_SP = 60, ER_LP = 120;

23 static int MLT[5][5] = {{1617, 1573, 958,   920,   77},
24                         {1513, 958,  890,   30,  819},
25                         {1513, 860,  0,   -860, -1420},
26                         {1290, 810, -890, -958, -1513},
27                         {-75, -890, -1365,-1003, -1513}};
```

Figure 10.59.   The header file of the project Fuzzy-Control.

6. The lookup table MLT[ ] is declared in lines 23~27, and it is a 5×5 matrix. The values on this lookup table are also obtained from Table 10.26.

Next let's build the C source file for this project.

10.5.5.2 Create the C Source File Fuzzy-Control.c

The size of this source file is a little large since it contains the codes for the fuzzy inference process. Thus this source file can be divided into three parts; the main() program part, the fuzzy inference process part, and the initialization processes for the PWM1 and QEI0 modules. Because the initialization process functions for the PWM and QEI modules, InitPWM() and InitQEI(), are identical to those functions built for the previous projects, such as CalibEncoder and PID-Control, we will not discuss them in this section. Refer to those projects to get more details about the codes for these two functions.

The first part of this source file is shown in Figure 10.60.

Basically the codes in this part are identical to those in the PID-Control project built in the previous section; therefore we only discuss the codes that are different from those codes in that project. Let's have a closer look at these codes to see how they work.

1. The type of the PWM output variable pw is changed from uint32_t to int in line 9 since both positive and negative PWM output values exist in the fuzzy lookup table.

```
1   //*******************************************************************************************************
2   // Fuzzy-Control.c - Motor Fuzzy Logic Control Program - QEI0
3   //*******************************************************************************************************
4   #include "Fuzzy-Control.h"
5   int main(void)
6   {
7     uint32_t es, index, upper = 1000, s, n = 0, motor[100];
8     double de, e[2];
9     int pw;
10    SysCtlClockSet(SYSCTL_SYSDIV_25|SYSCTL_USE_PLL|SYSCTL_XTAL_4MHZ|SYSCTL_OSC_MAIN);
11    SYSCTL->RCGC2 = 0x2A;                          // enable & clock GPIO Ports B, D & F
12    GPIOB->DEN = 0xF;                              // enable PB3 ~ PB0 as digital function pins
13    GPIOB->DIR = 0xF;                              // configure PB3 ~ PB0 as output pins
14    GPIOD->DEN = 0xC0;                             // enable PD7 ~ PD6 as digital function pins
15    GPIOD->DIR = ~0xC;                             // configure PD7 ~ PD6 as input pins
16    GPIOF->DEN = 0xF;                              // enable PF3 ~ PF0 as digital function pins
17    GPIOF->DIR = 0xF;                              // configure PF3 ~ PF0 as output pins
18    InitPWM();                                     // configure PWM module 1
19    InitQEI();                                     // configure QEI module 0
20    while(1)
21    {
22      PWM1->_2_CTL = 0x1;                          // enable PWM1_2B or M1PWM5
23      PWM1->ENABLE = 0x20;
24      s = 1000;                                    // s = 1000 makes es = 0.45*PWM = 0.45*1000 = 450 ppr
25                                                   // the 450 ppr can be considered as a setup input velocity
26      PWM1->_2_CMPB = s;                           // send desired PWM value or 450 ppr to motor
27      e[1] = s;
28      for (index = 0; index < upper; index++)      // output a square wave form to motor
29      {
30        es = QEI0->SPEED;                          // get the current encoder speed value
31        e[0] = s - es*HS;                          // convert speed to corresponding PWM value
32        de = e[1] - e[0];                          // get differential error
33        pw = GetLookup(e[0], de);                  // get crisp control output from lookup table
34        e[1] = e[0];
35        PWM1->_2_CMPB = pw;                        // with fuzzy logic control
36        SysCtlDelay(5);
37        if (n < 100) { motor[n] = es; }
38        n++;
39      }
40      PWM1->_2_CMPB = 0;                           // 0 to motor to stop motor
41      PWM1->_2_CTL = 0x0;                          // disable PWM1_2B or M1PWM5
42      PWM1->ENABLE &= ~0x20;
43      for (index = 0; index < upper; index++)
44        SysCtlDelay(10);
45    }
46  }
```

Figure 10.60. The first part codes for the project Fuzzy-Control.

2. The code in line 33 is replaced by calling a user defined function GetLookup() to perform the fuzzy inference calculation to get the crisp PWM output from the lookup table, instead of using the PID algorithm to get PID control output values.

All of the rest codes in this part are identical to those built in the PID-Control project. Now let's take a look at the second part codes for this project, which is another user-defined function GetLookup(). The detailed codes for this function are shown in Figure 10.61. Let's have a closer look at the codes inside this function to see how they work.

1. The GetLookup() function starts at line 1 with two arguments, the feedback velocity error and error rate, error and error_rate, and both of them are double data type. The returned variable data type is int.

```
1   int GetLookup(double error, double error_rate)
2   {
3     int u;
4     if (error < E_LN)
5     {
6        if (error_rate < ER_LN) { u = MLT[0][0]; }
7        else if (error_rate < ER_SN && error_rate >= ER_LN) { u = MLT[0][1]; }
8        else if (error_rate < ER_ZE && error_rate >= ER_SN) { u = MLT[0][2]; }
9        else if (error_rate < ER_SP && error_rate >= ER_ZE) { u = MLT[0][3]; }
10       else if (error_rate < ER_LP && error_rate >= ER_SP) { u = MLT[0][4]; }
11    }
12    else if (error < E_SN && error >= E_LN)
13    {
14       if (error_rate < ER_LN) { u = MLT[1][0]; }
15       else if (error_rate < ER_SN && error_rate >= ER_LN) { u = MLT[1][1]; }
16       else if (error_rate < ER_ZE && error_rate >= ER_SN) { u = MLT[1][2]; }
17       else if (error_rate < ER_SP && error_rate >= ER_ZE) { u = MLT[1][3]; }
18       else if (error_rate < ER_LP && error_rate >= ER_SP) { u = MLT[1][4]; }
19    }
20    else if (error < E_ZE && error >= E_SN)
21    {
22       if (error_rate < ER_LN) { u = MLT[2][0]; }
23       else if (error_rate < ER_SN && error_rate >= ER_LN) { u = MLT[2][1]; }
24       else if (error_rate < ER_ZE && error_rate >= ER_SN) { u = MLT[2][2]; }
25       else if (error_rate < ER_SP && error_rate >= ER_ZE) { u = MLT[2][3]; }
26       else if (error_rate < ER_LP && error_rate >= ER_SP) { u = MLT[2][4]; }
27    }
28    else if (error < E_SP && error >= E_ZE)
29    {
30       if (error_rate < ER_LN) { u = MLT[3][0]; }
31       else if (error_rate < ER_SN && error_rate >= ER_LN) { u = MLT[3][1]; }
32       else if (error_rate < ER_ZE && error_rate >= ER_SN) { u = MLT[3][2]; }
33       else if (error_rate < ER_SP && error_rate >= ER_ZE) { u = MLT[3][3]; }
34       else if (error_rate < ER_LP && error_rate >= ER_SP) { u = MLT[3][4]; }
35    }
36    else if (error < E_LP && error >= E_SP)
37    {
38       if (error_rate < ER_LN) { u = MLT[4][0]; }
39       else if (error_rate < ER_SN && error_rate >= ER_LN) { u = MLT[4][1]; }
40       else if (error_rate < ER_ZE && error_rate >= ER_SN) { u = MLT[4][2]; }
41       else if (error_rate < ER_SP && error_rate >= ER_ZE) { u = MLT[4][3]; }
42       else if (error_rate < ER_LP && error_rate >= ER_SP) { u = MLT[4][4]; }
43    }
44    return u;
45  }
```

Figure 10.61. The detailed codes for the function GetLookup().

2. The returned variable u is declared in line 3.

3. Totally we have 25 control outputs located in a 5×5 lookup table. In order to identify and select the desired control output from the lookup table, we need to use the feedback velocity error and error rate as inputs. In other words, we need to do this selection based on the different error and error rate ranges defined in the header file Fuzzy-Control.h, and these ranges are defined based on the error and error rate ranges defined in Table 10.26. Therefore a sequence of if and else if selection structures is used to do this selection job.

4. We do this selection by dividing error ranges into 5 segments, and we perform 5 sub-selections based on the error rate ranges inside each error segment. Starting at line 4, the first error segment is: If the error is less than E_LN, we continue to check 5 error rate ranges, <ER_LN, ER_LN~ER_SN, ER_SN~ER_ZE, ER_ZE~ER_SP, and ER_SP~ER_LP, in lines 6~10. Based on each error rate range, the corresponding control output can be identified

by the related element located at the lookup table MLT[0,n] and assigned to the returned variable u.

5. The second error segment, `error < E_SN && error >= E_LN`, starts at line 12. If the velocity error is in this range, the 5 sub-selections are performed to check 5 error rate ranges that are identical to those inside the last error segment to select the corresponding control output MLT[1,n] from the lookup table in lines 14~18, respectively.

6. In a similar way, the following three error segments and related 5 sub-selections can be performed to select the corresponding control outputs MLT[2,n], MLT[3,n] and MLT [4,n] and assigned them to the returned variable u in lines 22~26, 30~34, and 38~42.

7. Finally the identified control output stored in the returned variable u is returned to the main program in line 44.

One point to be noted is the motor rotation direction and the direction we defined in our program. In this project, we defined the motor positive rotating direction as Clockwise (CW), and the membership functions and control outputs defined in the lookup table are based on this definitions. If you find that the direction is opposite or your simulation result is negative, you need to change the direction in your program to redefine this direction. Also, the membership function input definitions, such as LN, SN, SP, and LP, need to be inverted in polarity.

10.5.5.3 Set Up Environments to Build and Run the Project

Before one can run this project to test the fuzzy logic controller, the following environments need to be set:

- Add the path for all system header files used in this project into the `Include Paths` box in the C/C++ tab under the `Project|Options for Target 'Target 1'` menu item. The correct path should be `C:\ti\TivaWare_C_Series-2.0.1.11577`.

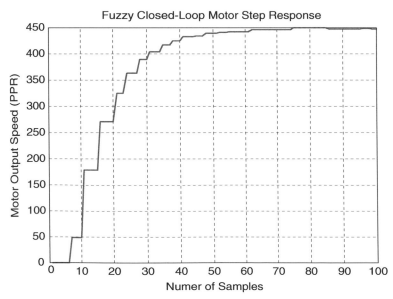

Figure 10.62. The step response of the fuzzy logic control system. (Reprinted with the permission of MathWorks, Inc.)

- Select the correct debugger `Stellaris ICDI` in the Debug tab under the `Project-|Options for Target 'Target 1'` menu item.
- Add the TivaWare™ Peripheral Driver Library `driverlib.lib` file into the project. This library file is located at `C:\ti\TivaWare_C_Series-2.0.1.11577\driverlib\rvmdk`. By right clicking on the `Source Group 1` in the `Project` pane and selecting the `Add Existing File ...` item, one can add this library file into the project.

Now run the project to test the fuzzy logic controller for our DC motor closed-loop control system. You can find that the motor is periodically rotating and stopping. The step response of this fuzzy logic control system is shown in Figure 10.62, which is plotted based on the collected motor output velocity feedback values `motor[]` acquired from the QEI0 module.

10.6 THE ANALOG COMPARATORS

Generally, an analog comparator provides the comparison function for two analog inputs (`Vin+` and `Vin−`) to the comparator. The output of the analog comparator `Vout` is a digital or a logic signal with the following two possible values:

- `Vout` = 1 if `Vin+` > `Vin−`
- `Vout` = 0 if `Vin+` < `Vin−`

In the TM4C123GH6PM MCU system, two Analog Comparator modules, ACMP0 and ACMP1, are provided to enable users to perform the comparison:

- Between one external analog input and another external analog input.
- Between one external analog input with an internal programmable voltage reference.
- Between an external analog input and an individual or a shared external reference voltage.

Since two Analog Comparator modules are provided in the TM4C123GH6PM MCU system, two analog input pairs, `Vin0−` and `Vin0+`, `Vin1−` and `Vin1+`, can be mapped to C0− and C0+, and C1− and C1+, respectively. The corresponding outputs for these two modules are C0o and C1o.

10.6.1 The Analog Comparator Architecture and Functional Block Diagram

Figure 10.63 shows the architecture and functional block diagram of the Analog Comparator (AC) applied in the TM4C123GH6PM MCU system.

It can be found from Figure 10.63 that two Analog Comparator modules, ACMP0 and ACMP1, are identical and they are composed of three major parts; the AC Control/Status, the AC Voltage Reference and the AC Interrupt Control. Each part is composed of the corresponding registers. Let's have a closer look at these registers to see what kind of control functions they can provide for these modules.

10.6.2 The Control Registers Used in the Analog Comparator Modules

Because of the similarity between two modules, let's use the module 0 or ACOMP0 as an example to illustrate these registers.

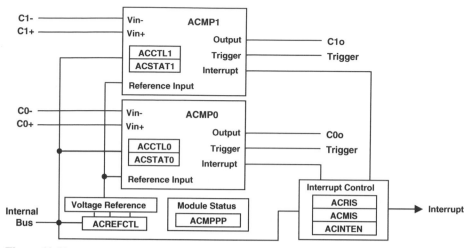

Figure 10.63. Architecture and functional block diagram of the Analog Comparator modules. (Reprinted with the permission of the Texas Instruments Incorporated.)

The Control/Status group contains two registers, the Analog Comparator Control Register (ACCTL0) and the Analog Comparator Status Register (ACSTAT0). The ACCTL0 register is mainly used to configure the inputs and the output of the comparator, and the ACSTAT0 register is used to specify the output value for the comparator.

The bit map and bit fields of the ACCTL0 register is shown in Figure 10.64. The bit function of this register is shown in Table 10.27.

It can be found from Table 10.27 that for both Analog Comparator modules, the negative analog input Vin− is fixed and it is always to be connected to the negative analog input. But the positive analog input, Vin+, can be modified to be connected to the different input sources, such as the C1+, C0+ or the internal voltage reference.

It can also be found from Table 10.27 that most control bits in this register are used to control the ADC-related events, such as bits 11, 7, and 6~5.

The Analog Comparator Status Register (ACSTAT0) is a 32-bit register but only one bit, bit 1 or OVAL bit, is used to specify the output value for the comparator. A value 0 in this bit indicates that the comparison result is Vin− > Vin+. Otherwise if this bit is 1, the comparison result is Vin− < Vin+.

10.6.3 The Voltage Reference Registers Used in the Analog Comparator Modules

The ACMP Voltage Reference group contains only one register, the Analog Comparator Reference Voltage Control Register (ACREFCTL).

Analog Comparator Control 0 Register (ACCTL0)

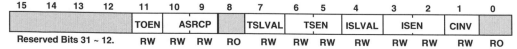

Figure 10.64. The bit map and bit field of the ACCTL0 register.

Table 10.27. Bit value and its function for ACCTL0 register.

Bit	Name	Reset	Function
31:12	Reserved	0x0	Reserved
11	TOEN	0	ADC Trigger Output Enable: 0: ADC events are suppressed and not sent to the ADC. 1: ADC events are sent to the ADC.
10:9	ASRCP	0x0	Analog Source Positive. The ASRCP field specifies the source of input voltage to the Vin+ terminal of the comparator. The encodings for this field are as follows: 0x0: Pin value of C1+; 0x1: Pin value of C0+; 0x2: Internal voltage reference (VIREF) 0x3: Reserved.
8	Reserved	0	Reserved
7	TSLVAL	0	ADC Trigger Sense Level Value. 0: An ADC event is generated if the comparator output is Low. 1: An ADC event is generated if the comparator output is High.
6:5	TSEN	0x0	ADC Trigger Sense: The TSEN field specifies the sense of the comparator output that generates an ADC event. The sense conditioning is as follows: 0x0: Level sense, see TSLVAL; 0x1: Falling edge; 0x2: Rising edge; 0x3: Either edge.
4	ISLVAL	0	Interrupt Sense Level Value: 0: An interrupt is generated if the comparator output is Low. 1: An interrupt is generated if the comparator output is High.
3:2	ISEN	0x0	Interrupt Sense: The ISEN field specifies the sense of the comparator output that generates an interrupt. The sense conditioning is as follows: 0x0: Level sense, see ISLVAL; 0x1: Falling edge; 0x2: Rising edge; 0x3: Either edge.
1	CINV	0	Comparator Output Invert. 0: The output of the comparator is unchanged. 1: The output of the comparator is inverted.
0	Reserved	0	Reserved

This register is used to control the programming operations for the internal reference voltage to provide a flexible and different reference voltage to enable users to select desired reference voltage. This control is realized by dividing the reference voltage into two different ranges, the High and the Low range, which are determined by the value in the bit RNG in this ACREFCTL register. When the bit RNG is 0, the internal reference is in High-range mode, and when RNG is 1, the internal reference is in Low-range mode (Figure 10.65).

Figure 10.65 shows a relationship between the architecture of the internal reference circuit and the Analog Comparator Reference Voltage Control Register (ACREFCTL).

Basically this internal voltage reference circuit provides a ladder or a divider to divide the standard reference voltage into a sequence of different step or threshold voltages. The bit RNG controls the ranges of the reference voltages, either in High or Low, by turning on or off the MOSFET switch to remove or add more ladder resistors. The bit EN is used to enable or disable the connection between the power VDDA and the resistor ladder, furthermore to enable (EN=1) or disable (EN=0) the reference output. The bit-field VREF (bits 3~0 in the ACREFCTL register) is used to select the different voltage step or threshold voltage to be reference output.

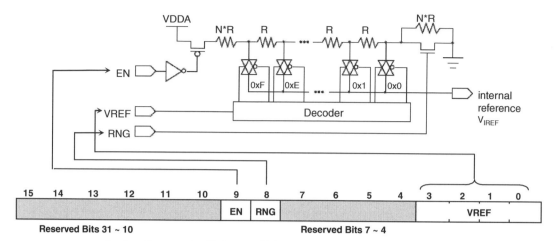

Analog Comparator Reference Voltage Control Register (ACREFCTL)

Figure 10.65. The structure of the internal reference and ACREFCTL register.

For both High and Low ranges, the internal reference V_{IREF} provides 16 preprogrammed thresholds or step values. These 16 threshold or step values can be selected using the VREF bit field in the ACREFCTL register, as shown in Figure 10.65.

When working in the High-range mode, the V_{IREF} threshold voltages start at the ideal high-range starting voltage of VDDA/4.2 and increase in ideal constant voltage steps of VDDA/29.4. In the Low-range mode, the V_{IREF} threshold voltages start at 0V and increase in ideal constant voltage steps of VDDA/22.12.

The following equations provide the relationships between each step reference and bit values in the ACREFCTL register.

For the High range mode:

Ideal V_{IREF}*threshold values* : $V_{IREF}(VREF) = VDDA/4.2 + VREF*(VDDA/29.4)$

when VREF $= 0x0, 0x1, 0x2, 0x3, \dots 0xF$, $EN = 1$, $RNG = 0$

For the Low range mode:

Ideal V_{IREF} *threshold values* : $V_{IREF}(VREF) = 0 + VREF*(VDDA/22.12)$

when VREF $= 0x0, 0x1, 0x2, 0x3, \dots 0xF$, $EN = 1$, $RNG = 1$

Based on the equations above, the maximum reference voltage is $3.3/4.2 + 15 \times 3.3/29.4 = 2.469$ V and the minimum reference voltage is $3.3/4.2 = 0.785$ V for the High-range mode if the VDDA is 3.3 V. The maximum reference voltage is $15 \times 3.3/22.12 = 2.238$ V and the minimum reference voltage is 0 V for the Low-range mode if the VDDA is 3.3 V. The conclusion is that the range of the reference voltages for the High-range mode is $0.785 \sim 2.469$ V, and the range of the reference voltage for the Low-range mode is $0 \sim 2.238$ V.

A point to be noted is that the range values shown above are the ideal reference values of the V_{IREF} step or threshold voltages. These values actually vary between the minimum and the maximum values for each threshold step and they are depending on the process and environment temperatures. The minimum and maximum values for each step are:

- V_{IREF}(VREF) [Min] = Ideal V_{IREF}(VREF) − (Ideal Step voltage − 2 mV)/2
- V_{IREF}(VREF) [Max] = Ideal V_{IREF}(VREF) + (Ideal Step voltage − 2 mV)/2

Next let's have a closer look at the AC Interrupt Process registers.

10.6.4 The Interrupt Processing Registers Used in the Analog Comparator Modules

Three registers are included in this group and they are:

- Analog Comparator Interrupt Enable Register (ACINTEN)
- Analog Comparator Raw Interrupt Status Register (ACRIS)
- Analog Comparator Masked Interrupt Status Register (ACMIS)

All of these three registers are 32-bit registers; however, only the lowest two bits, bit 1 and bit 0, or bits INT1 and INT0, are used to manage the interrupt process for both Analog Comparator modules, ACMP1 and ACMP0.

If the bits INT1 or INT0 in the ACINTEN register are set to 1, the interrupt on AC1 or AC0 is enabled. Otherwise if any of INT1 or INT0 bit is cleared to 0, the interrupt on AC1 or AC0 is disabled.

Similarly, if the bits INT1 or INT0 in the ACRIS register are set to 1, this means that an interrupt on ACMP1 or ACMP0 has been generated. Otherwise if any of these bits is cleared to 0, no interrupt has been created.

If the bit INT1 in the ACMIS register is set to 1, this means that both INT1 bits in the ACINTEN and the ACRIS registers have been set to 1, and an interrupt related to the ACMP1 has been generated and sent to the interrupt controller to be further processed. The same function resulted in the ACMP0 if the bit INT0 in the ACMIS register is set to 1. Otherwise no interrupt has been generated or the selected interrupt has been masked if INT1 and INT0 bits in the ACMIS register are cleared to 0.

To clear the generated interrupt after that interrupt has been handled or processed, write a 1 to the INT1 or INT0 bit in the ACMIS register. This clearing also clears the related INT1 or INT0 bit in the ACRIS register.

10.6.5 The Input and Output Control Signals Used in the Analog Comparators

As we discussed in Section 10.6, each ACMP module has two analog-comparing inputs, Vin− and Vin+, and one logic-comparing output Vout. All of these input and output signals are interfaced to other peripherals via some specified GPIO Ports and GPIO pins. In order to enable selected GPIO pins to work as analog input or output pins, the bit field AFSEL in the GPIOAFSEL register and the corresponding PMCx bit field in the GPIOPCTL register must be configured to allow the GPIO pins to work as alternate function pins.

Table 10.28. ACMP external control signals and GPIO pin distributions.

ACMP Pin	GPIO Pin	Pin Type	Buffer Type	Pin Function
C0+	PC6	I	Analog	Analog comparator 0 positive input (Vin+).
C0−	PC7	I	Analog	Analog comparator 0 negative input (Vin−).
C0o	PF0 (9)	O	TTL	Analog comparator 0 output (Vout0).
C1+	PC5	I	Analog	Analog comparator 1 positive input (Vin+).
C1−	PC4	I	Analog	Analog comparator 1 negative input (Vin−).
C1o	PF1 (9)	O	TTL	Analog comparator 1 output (Vout1).

Table 10.28 shows the related GPIO pins used for two ACMP modules.

The number inside the parentheses indicates the PMCx value in the GPIOPCTL register, and this value must be set to enable the selected GPIO pins to work as alternate function pins.

10.6.6 The Initialization and Configuration Process for the Analog Comparator

Before any ACMP module can be used to perform the analog signal comparison function, it must be properly initialized and configured to enable it to play this kind of role. Generally, the initialization and configuration process can be described in the following sequence:

1. Enable and clock the analog comparator by writing a value of 0x1 to the RCGCACMP register in the System Control module. This value will enable and clock both ACMP modules.

2. Enable the clock to the appropriate GPIO modules via the RCGCGPIO register, particularly the GPIO Ports C and F modules.

3. In the GPIO module, enable the GPIO Port C and related pins (PC4~PC7) to work as analog input pins for the ACMP modules. This can be done by clearing the DEN bit in the GPIO Port C Digital Enable (GPIOCDEN) register.

4. Configure the PMCx bit fields in the GPIOPCTL register to assign the analog comparator output signals to the appropriate pins, particularly to the GPIO PF1 and PF0 pins.

5. Configure the internal voltage reference to the desired value by writing the ACREFCTL register. The desired value can be obtained from two equations shown in Section 10.6.3.

6. Configure the comparator to use the internal voltage reference and *not* to invert the output by writing the ACCTLn (n = 0 or 1) register with the value of 0x400.

7. Delay a period of time, such as 10 μs, to make the ACMP stable.

8. Read the comparator output value by reading the value in the bit OVAL in the ACSTATn (n = 0 or 1) register or by connecting the comparison output **Vout** to a peripheral to check the comparison result.

Now let's build a simple project to test the functions of the ACMP modules.

10.6.7 Build a Project to Test the Functions of the Analog Comparator Module

In this simple project, we try to use ACMP0 module to compare an external voltage coming from the potentiometer VR2 installed in the EduBASE ARM® Trainer with a

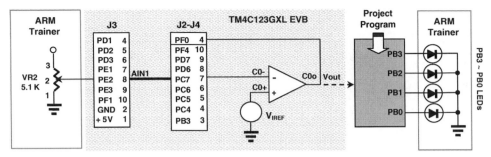

Figure 10.66.   The hardware and software configuration for the ACMP0.

programmable internal reference voltage V_{IREF}. The hardware configuration for this project is shown in Figure 10.66.

One needs to use some jump wires to perform the following connections to finish this hardware and software configuration:

- Connect the potentiometer output that is AIN1 input to the ADC to the C0− on ACMP0 input as an external analog input to the comparator. To do this connection, just connect the PE2 pin on the J3 connector with the PC7 pin on the J4 connector in the TM4C123GXL EVB.

- To monitor and check the comparison result, one needs to build this project to use the software to check the ACSTAT0 register, particularly the bit 1 or the bit OVAL on this register, to see the output of this comparator. If this bit is set to 1, which means that the Vin+ > Vin−, four LEDs PB3~PB0 installed in the ARM® Trainer are turned on. Otherwise if this bit is cleared to 0, this means that the Vin+ < Vin−, four LEDs are off.

The only hardware connection has been highlighted in Figure 10.66. All other connections have been completed by the vendor. Your finished connection should match one that is shown in Figure 10.66.

Now let's build the project ACMP0 to complete this analog comparator function.

Create a new Keil® μVersion®5 project named ACMP0 under the folder C:\ARM Class Projects\Chapter 10. Then create a new C source file ACMP0.c and enter the codes shown in Figure 10.67 into this source file.

Let's have a closer look at this source file to see how it works.

1. The codes in lines 4~9 are used to include all system header files used in this project.

2. The macro of the GPIO Port F Commit Register, GPIO_PORTF_CR_R, is declared in line 10, and this macro is used to access this register to unlock the PF0 pin to enable this pin to be configured as the C0o pin for the ACMP0 module in this project.

3. The user-defined function InitACMP0() is declared in line 11, and it is used to initialize and configure the ACMP0 module.

4. Another user-defined function SimpleDelay() is declared in line 12. This function is used to delay a certain period of time for the program to be executed. A point to be noted is the time delay length represented by the equation (ms * 16000)/3. The system clock used in this project is 16 MHz or 16000000 Hz. Each period of this clock is 1/16000000 second. Inside the system function SysCtlDelay(), three instructions are used to perform this delay. Therefore the total delay time by calling this system function is $T_p = 3 \times$ period of the system clock, which is $T_p = 3 \times (1/16000000) = 3/16000000$ if each instruction takes one clock period to be executed. If we need to delay 1 ms, the total numbers of executing this function N is $N \times T_p = 0.001$ second, thus $N = 1/T_p = 0.001/3/16000000 = 16000/3$.

```
1   //*********************************************************************************************
2   // ACMP0.c - Main Application Program for ACMP0 - Compare with PE2-AIN1-Poteniometer
3   //*********************************************************************************************
4   #include <stdint.h>
5   #include <stdbool.h>
6   #include "driverlib/sysctl.h"
7   #include "driverlib/gpio.h"
8   #include "driverlib/comp.h"
9   #include "TM4C123GH6PM.h"
10  #define GPIO_PORTF_CR_R   (*((volatile uint32_t *)0x40025524))
11  void InitACMP0(void);
12  void SimpleDelay(double ms)
13  {
14     SysCtlDelay((ms * 16000) / 3);
15  }
16  int main(void)
17  {
18     uint32_t status;
19     SYSCTL->RCGC2 = 0x26;                    // enable & clock GPIO Ports B, C & F
20     GPIOB->DEN = 0xF;                        // enable PB3 ~ PB0 as digital function pins
21     GPIOB->DIR = 0xF;                        // configure PB3 ~ PB0 as output pins
22     GPIOC->DEN = ~0xC0;                      // enable PC7 ~ PC6 as analog function pins
23     GPIOC->DIR = ~0xC0;                      // configure PC7 ~ PC6 as input pins
24     GPIOF->DEN = 0xF;                        // enable PF3 ~ PF0 as digital function pins
25     GPIOF->DIR = 0xF;                        // configure PF3 ~ PF0 as output pins
26     InitACMP0();
27     SimpleDelay(0.01);                       // delay 10 us
28     while(1)
29     {
30        status = COMP->ACSTAT0 & 0x2;         // check the
31        if (status == 0x2)
32           GPIOB->DATA = 0xF;
33        else
34           GPIOB->DATA = 0x0;
35     }
36  }
37  void InitACMP0(void)
38  {
39     SYSCTL->RCGCACMP = 0x1;                  // enable and clock the ACMP0
40     GPIOF->LOCK = 0x4C4F434B;                // unlock GPTOF commit register
41     GPIO_PORTF_CR_R |= 0x1;                  // enable PF0 to be committed
42     GPIOF->LOCK = 0x0;                       // lock GPIOF commit register
43     GPIOF->AFSEL |= 0x1;                     // PF0 - Alternate Function: C0o
44     GPIOF->PCTL = 0x00000009;                // C0o on PF0 = 0x00000009
45     COMP->ACCTL0 = 0x400;                    // set VIREF to be connected to VIN+ with no output invert
46     COMP->ACREFCTL = 0x20F;                  // EN = 1, RNG = 0 (High-range) VREF = 1111: Viref = 2.469V
    }
```

Figure 10.67. The detailed codes for the project ACMP0.

5. The `main()` function starts at line 16, and a local `uint32_t` variable `status` is declared. This variable is used to get and hold the running status of the analog comparator module 0 via the ACSTAT0 register later.

6. The codes in lines 19~25 are used to enable, clock and configure GPIO Ports B, C, and F to enable the associate GPIO pins to work as the LED driving pins and the ACMP0 analog signal input pins, particularly to make PB3~PB0 pins work as four LEDs driving pins, make PC7 and PC6 pins work as analog signal input pins, and male the PF0 pin work as the analog comparator output pin.

7. In line 26, the `InitACMP0()` function is called to initialize and configure the ACMP0 module to make it ready to perform analog signals comparison function.

8. The user-defined function `SimpleDelay()` is executed in line 27 to delay the program for about $10\,\mu s$ to wait for the ACMP0 module stable.

9. Starting at line 28, an infinitive `while()` loop is executed to repeatedly check the output status of the ACMP0 module. The codes in lines 30~34 are used to get the running status of the ACMP0, to check whether a High or a Low comparison result is obtained via the OVAL bit (bit 1) in the ACSTAT0 register. If a logic High is obtained, this means that the Vin− is less than the Vin+, four LEDs PB3~PB0 installed in the EduBASE ARM® Trainer are turned on. Otherwise if a logic Low is obtained, this means that the Vin- is greater than the Vin+, four LEDs are off.

10. The user-defined function `InitACMP0()` starts at line 37.

11. First the ACMP0 and ACMP1 modules are clocked and enabled by setting the bit 0 in the RCGCACMP register in line 39. A point to be noted is that the bit 0 in this register controls both ACMP modules.

12. The codes in lines 40~42 are used to unlock the GPIO Port F Commit Register by sending a specified code `0x4C4F434B` to the GPIO Port F Lock register to release the PF0 pin to enable it to be configured as an alternate function pin, particularly to an analog comparator output pin for the ACMP0 module. This step is necessary since the PF0 pin is locked by default. Then the GPIO Port F Commit Register (CR) is set to `0x1` to enable the PF0 pin to be committed in line 41. After the PF0 pin is committed, it is locked again in line 42 to prevent any other pin from being committed.

13. In line 43, the GPIO Port F AFSEL register is set to `0x1` to enable the PF0 pin to work as an alternate function pin.

14. Then in line 44, the PCMx bit value, `0x00000009`, is assigned to the GPIO Port F PCTL register to enable the PF0 pin to work as an output pin for the ACMP0 module.

15. In line 45, the Analog Comparator Control Register 0, ACCTL0, is configured with `0x400` to enable the V_{IREF} to be connected to the Vin+ or C0+ of the ACMP0 module as one of the analog inputs and the output of the comparator remains non-inverted. Refer to Figure 10.64 and Table 10.27 for this code configuration.

16. The ACREFCTL register is configured with `0x20F` in line 46 to enable the power VDDA to be connected to the resistor ladder (EN = 1), enable the ACMP0 to work in the High-range (RNG = 0), and enable the internal reference step to be 2.469 V (VREF = 1111). Refer to Figure 10.65 to get more details for this code configuration.

Next let's set up the environments to build and run this project to test its function.

10.6.8 Set Up the Environments to Build and Run the Project

Before one can run this project to test the analog comparator function, the following environments need to be set:

- Add the path for all system header files used in this project into the `Include Paths` box in the C/C++ tab under the `Project|Options for Target 'Target 1'` menu item. The correct path should be `C:\ti\TivaWare_C_Series-2.0.1.11577`.

- Select the correct debugger `Stellaris ICDI` in the Debug tab under the `Project-|Options for Target 'Target 1'` menu item.

- Add the TivaWare™ Peripheral Driver Library `driverlib.lib` file into the project. This library file is located at `C:\ti\TivaWare_C_Series-2.0.1.11577\driverlib\rvmdk`. By right clicking on the `Source Group 1` in the `Project` pane and selecting the `Add Existing File ...` item, one can add this library file into the project.

Now you can run the project by going to `Debug|Run` menu item. As the project runs, you can rotate the potentiometer VR2 with a small screw driver to change the analog input to the `Vin−` of the ACMP0 module. You can find that all four LEDs, PB3~PB0, become on and off when the input value is changed.

10.7 CHAPTER SUMMARY

This chapter provides general information about other ARM® Cortex®-M4 MCU related peripherals and their implementations; these peripherals include the Controller Area Network (CAN), Quadrature Encoder Interface (QEI), and Analog Comparators.

An introduction and overview about the CAN module and its architecture are given in Section 10.2. The overview and introduction include the CAN standard frame, extended frame, and CAN signal as well as error detections.

A functional block diagram about the CAN modules is provided in Section 10.2.4, and the CAN components and operational principle is discussed in Section 10.2.5. These discussions include:

- CAN Transmitting Message Objects
- CAN Receiving Message Objects
- CAN Module Interrupt Processing
- CAN Operate Modes
- CAN Initialization and Configuration Process
- CAN Clock and Baud Rate Configuration

A detailed discussion about all CAN module registers starts at Section 10.2.6. The CAN API functions provided by TivaWare™ Peripheral Driver Library is discussed in Section 10.2.8. A CAN module implementation example project is introduced in Section 10.2.9.

Starting at Section 10.3, the Quadrature Encoder Interface (QEI) is discussed and introduced. First an introduction and overview are given in Section 10.3.1.

The working principle of the increment rotary encoder and its application in a closed-loop control system are discussed in Sections 10.3.2 and 10.3.3. The discussion about the increment rotary encoder modules applied in the TM4C123GH6PM MCU system is provided in Section 10.3.4. All control registers applied in these QEI modules are introduced in Section 10.3.5.

The QEI API functions provided by the TivaWare™ Peripheral Driver Library are discussed in detail in Section 10.3.8. A real implementation of using a rotary encoder for a closed-loop control system is discussed in Section 10.3.9. This implementation includes:

- Calibration of the rotary encoder with the QEI module.
- Building a closed-loop bang–bang control program by using the rotary encoder with the QEI module.

- Designing a PID motor closed-loop control system with the QEI module and rotary encoder.
- Identifying the dynamic model of the DC motor with the MATLAB® System Identification Toolbox.
- Tuning the PID parameters with the MATLAB® Control System Toolbox™.
- Simulation of the PID closed-loop control system with the MATLAB® SIMULINK®.
- Building a motor control software to implement the PID controller.
- Designing a fuzzy logic controller to control the closed-loop motor control system with the MATLAB® Fuzzy Logic Toolbox™.
- Building a motor control software to implement the fuzzy logic controller.

The Analog Comparator is discussed starting at Section 10.6.

The Analog Comparator architecture and functional block diagram is introduced in Section 10.6.1. Most control registers used in the ACMP modules in the TM4C123GH6PM MCU system are discussed in Section 10.6.2. A special register, Voltage Reference Control Register (ACREFCTL) used in the ACMP modules, is discussed in Section 10.6.3. Some interrupt processing-related registers are introduced in Section 10.6.4.

The important ACMP control signals and related GPIO multiple function pins are discussed in Section 10.6.5. Section 10.6.6 provides the initialization and configuration process for the ACMP modules. A real example implementation project ACMP0 is given in Section 10.6.7.

HOMEWORK

I. True/False Selections

_____**1.** Transmission and receiving message objects among CAN nodes are performed via the two-wire bus system, CAN-HI and CAN-LOW.

_____**2.** The CAN standard frame, also known as CAN 2.0 A, supports a length of 11 bits for the identifier, and the CAN extended frame, also known as CAN 2.0 B, supports a length of 29 bits for the identifier.

_____**3.** Both a data frame and a remote frame contain data for transmission, and they can be used to request the transmission of a specific message object.

_____**4.** The basic CAN operation is to transmit or receive information composed as a group or a sequence of message objects in the standard or extend frames via CAN bus.

_____**5.** The MSK bit field in the CANIF1MSK1 register is used to enable or disable the ID filtering function for the message object to be transmitted. The DATA and the ID bit fields in the CANIF1DA1 and the CANIF1ARB1 registers are used to contain and hold the data to be transmitted and ID for each of 32 message objects to be sent.

_____**6.** Generally, the encoder provides a velocity feedback and a tachometer provides a position feedback of the motor for a given voltage applied on the motor.

_____**7.** Counting both rising and falling edges for two channels of a quadrature encoder will quadruple (×4) the number of pulses per revolution.

_____**8.** The QEISPEED register contains the most recently measured velocity of the quadrature encoder. This value corresponds to the number of velocity pulses (QEICOUNT) counted in the previous velocity timer period (QEITIME).

_____**9.** The point to be noted is that once the QEI module has been enabled by setting the ENABLE bit in the QEICTL register, it can be disabled at any time by software.

_____**10.** For both Analog Comparator modules, the negative analog input Vin− is fixed, and it is always to be connected to the negative analog input. But the positive analog input, Vin+, can be modified to be connected to the different input sources, such as the C1+, C0+ or the internal voltage reference.

II. Multiple Choices

1. The CAN supports two frame formats and the only difference between them is _____.

   a. The size of the message RAM

   b. The length of the message object

   c. The length of the identifier

   d. The transmit/receive speed

2. In a CAN standard frame, the Data field is able to hold up to _____ data bytes.

   a. 4

   b. 8

   c. 16

   d. 32

3. CAN controllers that support the _____ also support the CAN _____.

   a. Standard frame format, extended frame format.

   b. Extended frame format, normal frame format.

   c. Normal frame format, standard frame format.

   d. Extended frame format, standard frame format

4. The CAN module consists of the following major components, they are _____.

   a. CAN global protocol controller and message handler

   b. Message memory used to store 32 message objects

   c. CAN interface registers used to interface between the CPU and the message memory

   d. All of them

5. The bit _____ and bit _____ in the CANCTL register must be set to 1 to start the CAN initialization process. These two bits must be in the set status until this process is done.

   a. EIE (bit 3), SIE (bit 2)

   b. INIT (bit 0), CCE (bit 6)

   c. SIE (bit 2), IE (bit 1)

   d. INIT (bit 0), IE (bit 1)

6. After a message object has been configured and ready to be transmitted, the bit _____ in the CANIF1MCTL register is set to 1 to request a data transmit.

   a. TXIE (bit 11)

   b. NEWDAT (bit 15)

   c. INTPND (bit 13)

   d. TXRQST (bit 8)

7. The MNUM bit field in the CANIFn Command Request (CANIFnCRQ) register is used to _____.

    a. Determine which message object should be transmitted

    b. Determine whether the message object is ready to be transmitted

    c. Determine the message object's position in the message RAM

    d. Determine which message object has the higher priority

8. There are three common types of rotary encoders; they are _____ encoders.

    a. Absolute position, increment position, increment sinusoidal

    b. Relative position, absolute position, absolute velocity

    c. Increment position, decrement position, absolute position

    d. Absolute velocity, relative velocity, increment velocity

9. If both the rising and the falling edges of the quadrature encoder's pulse train is counted from one channel, this creates _____ the number of pulses per revolution (PPR).

    a. 2 times

    b. 4 times

    c. 8 times

    d. 16 times

10. Two Analog Comparator modules, ACMP0 and ACMP1, are provided to enable users to perform the comparison between _____ and _____.

    a. One external analog voltage, one internal analog voltage

    b. One external analog voltage, one internal reference voltage

    c. One external analog voltage, another external analog voltage

    d. One internal analog voltage, another internal analog voltage

III. Exercises

1. Provide a brief description about the CAN operational modes.

2. Provide a brief description about the CAN standard frame.

3. Provide a brief description about the CAN extended frame.

4. Provide a brief discussion about the working principle of the increment rotary encoder.

5. Provide a brief discussion about the closed-loop control system.

6. Provide a brief description about the analog comparators.

IV. Practical Laboratory

Laboratory 10: ARM® Cortex®-M4 Other Peripherals Programming

10.0 Goals This laboratory exercise allows students to learn and practice ARM® Cortex®-M4 CAN modules, QEI modules, and Analog Comparator programming by developing five labs. The first two labs are related to applying CAN modules to transmit and receive message objects via CAN bus by using two TM4C123GXL EVBs, and each one works as a CAN controller.

    1. Program Lab10_1, or the project CANMaster, lets students use one TM4C123GXL EVB to build a CAN transmitter with transmit interrupts to continuously transmit one message object with four bytes data items; 1, 2, 4, and 8. The transmit node used PF0 and PF3 pins as the receiving and transmit pins via MCP2551 transceiver to interface to the CAN bus.

2. Program Lab10_2, or the project CANSlave, enables students to use another TM4C123GXL EVB to build a CAN receiver with receiving interrupts to check and receive one message object with four bytes of data items sent by the CAN master. The receiver also used PF0 and PF3 pins as the receiving and transmitting pins to interface the MCP2551 transceiver to communicate with the CAN master.

3. Program Lab10_3, or the project PIDControl, enables students to build a PID closed-loop control system to control a DC motor with a rotary optical encoder with either position or velocity feedback. The students need to use MATLAB® Toolboxes, such as Identification Toolbox™, PID Control System Toolbox™, and SIMULINK®, to identify the dynamic model for the DC motor, design PID control parameters, and simulate and tune the PID control gains to complete this control system design. The students also need to implement this control strategy in software to build and test the performances of the designed closed-loop control system.

4. Program Lab10_4, or project RobotControl, enables students to design and build a control system to control a simulated robotic system. The students need to use PWM model and ADC module to complete this control system design. A photosensor Q1 (VEMT2520) that is connected to the analog input channel AIN2 via PE1 pin and installed in the EduBASE ARM® Trainer works as an optical signal detector to control the running and stopping of a DC motor that can be considered to be a robotic running motor.

5. Program Lab10_5, or project ACMP1, enables students to design and implement an analog comparator to control and compare a sequence of analog input signals or waveforms with a programmable reference voltage to display the comparison results on a group of LEDs.

After completion of these programs, students should understand the basic architecture and operational procedure for the CAN modules, QEI modules, and analog comparator modules installed in the TM4C123GH6PM MCU system. They should be able to code some sophisticated programs to access the desired CAN nodes to perform communications between those nodes, and they should also be able to use the QEI modules to build closed-loop control system to control and operate robots controlled by the different motors.

10.1 Lab10_1

10.1.1 Goal In this project, students will use the DRA and SD models to build a CAN transmitter with the TM4C123GXL EVB, and this can be considered to be a CAN Master used to transmit message objects to the CAN Slave module.

In order to use a CAN controller installed on each TM4C123GXL EVB to build a CAN transmitter, a special transceiver interface MCP2551 should be used to convert TTL/CMOS logic to the CAN bus level signals. In order to enable the GPIO PF3 and PF0 pins to work as CAN0TX and CAN0RX signal pins, related GPIOAFSEL and GPIOPCTL registers should be configured. In this project, students are encouraged to use some API functions to do these configurations.

10.1.2 Data Assignment and Hardware Configuration Refer to Figure 10.17 to finish the interfacing circuit connection, which includes the CAN bus network that is composed of two 120-ohm resistors and a pair of twisted wires as CANH and CANL lines, two pieces of MCP2551 as transceivers, and two pieces of TM4C123GXL EVBs as CAN controllers. Students can complete this circuit connection on a breadboard provided by the EduBASE ARM® Trainer. A point to be noted is that pin-8 on two MCP2551 should be connected to the ground and two MCP2551 need to use separate 5 V and ground.

A sample circuit connection is shown in Figure 10.68.

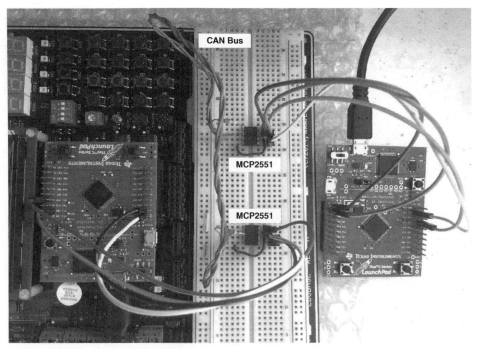

Figure 10.68. A sample CAN interfacing circuit connection. Reproduced with permission from ARM® Limited. Copyright © ARM Limited.

The right-hand side TM4C123GXL EVB in Figure 10.68 works as a CAN transmit controller with four color wires connected to the power (blue), ground (green), and PF0 (orange) as well as PF3 (yellow) pins in that EVB and top MCP2551 transceiver.

The left-hand side TM4C123GXL EVB works as a CAN receiver controller with another set of four-color wires connected to the power (white), ground (black), PF0 (brown), and PF3 (red) pins to that EVB and the lower MCP2551 transceiver.

The pins 2 and 8 in each MCP2551 should be connected together to get the maximum slew rate. Two 120-ohm resistors should be connected to pins 6 and 7 on each MCP2551, and a pair of twisted wires should also be connected to these two pins of two MCP2551 to work as the CAN bus.

For the software development procedure, one point to be noted is that the PF0 pin is a special pin and it is used by the button switch SW2 in the TM4C123GXL EVB by default, and this switch allows the EVB to enter a sleep mode when it is pressed via a Non-Maskable Interrupt (NMI). Therefore usually the PF0 pin is locked after a system reset. In order to configure PF0 pin to enable it to work as a GPIO alternate function pin, or specifically enable it to work as the CAN0RX pin, it must be first unlocked. After this pin is configured, it must be locked again to prevent any possible change for this pin in the future for this project. One needs to use GPIOLOCK and GPIOCR registers to do there unlock and lock functions. As soon as the GPIOCR register is unlocked, the PF0 pin or the GPIO Port F can be configured and modified.

10.1.3 Development of the Header and Source Codes
Perform the following operations to complete this project:

1. Create a new project named CANMaster in the folder C:\ARM Lab Project\ Chapter 10\CANMaster and a new header file CANMaster.h.

2. Place the following system header files and macros into this header file:

```
#include <stdint.h>
#include <stdbool.h>
#include "inc/hw_types.h"
#include "inc/hw_can.h"
#include "TM4C123GH6PM.h"
#include "driverlib/can.h"
#include "driverlib/interrupt.h"
#include "driverlib/sysctl.h"
#include "driverlib/gpio.h"
#include "driverlib/uart.h"
#define INT_CAN0                        55          //CAN0
#define GPIO_PF0_CAN0RX      0x00050003
#define GPIO_PF3_CAN0TX      0x00050C03
#define GPIO_PORTF_BASE      0x40025000   //GPIO Port F
#define GPIO_LOCK_KEY         0x4C4F434B   //unlock key for
                                                           GPIOCR register
#define GPIO_O_LOCK            0x00000520   //GPIO Lock register
#define GPIO_O_CR               0x00000524   //GPIO Commit register
#define HWREG(x) (*((volatile uint32_
  t*)(x)))
bool errFlag = 0;                                   //global error flag
int rcFlag = 0;                                     //global receiving flag
void SimpleDelay(double seconds)          //delay subroutine
{
  SysCtlDelay((seconds * 16000000)/3);
}
```

3. Create a new C file named CANMaster.c. and build this C file with the following steps.

4. Include the user header file "CANMaster.h" created in the last step.

Now using the following steps to build the CAN interrupt handler, do the following:

5. Declare the CAN interrupt handler as void CANInt_Handler(void).

6. Declare a local uint32_t variable ui32Status. This variable is used to get and hold the interrupt status by calling some API functions later.

7. Call an API function CANIntStatus(CAN0_BASE, CAN_INT_STS_CAUSE) to get the interrupt source, and the returned source is assigned to the local variable ui32Status.

8. Then check the interrupt source by using an if() statement to see whether the ui32Status is equal to a macro CAN_INT_INTID_STATUS. If it is, this means that the interrupt is triggered by a status error interrupt.

9. If the interrupt is caused by a status error interrupt, another API function is called to get the actual status via CANStatusGet(CAN0_BASE, CAN_STS_CONTROL). The returned status should also be assigned to the local variable ui32Status.

10. The global error flag errFlag should be set to 1 to indicate this error.

11. If the interrupt is not triggered by the status error, use else if() statement to check whether this interrupt is caused by the message object transmit interrupt by checking if the ui32Status is equal to 1.

12. If the interrupt is triggered by the message object transmit interrupt, call an API function CANIntClear(CAN0_BASE, 1) to clear that interrupt to make it ready for the next interrupt.

13. Set the global receive flag rcFlag to 1 and set the error flag errFlag to 0. This rcFlag is used to inform the main program that a message object has been received and can be picked up.

Now using the following steps to build the main program `int main(void)`, do the following:

14. Declare a local integer variable `index`.
15. Declare a new instance `sCANMsg` based on the CAN data structure `tCANMsgObject`.
16. Use `uint8_t sMsgData[4]`, `ui8MsgData[4] = {1, 2, 4, 8}` to declare two data arrays.
17. Use `SysCtlClockSet()` API function with the arguments SYSCTL_SYS-DIV_1|SYSCTL_USE_OSC |SYSCTL_OSC_MAIN|SYSCTL_XTAL_16MHZ to set up the system clock as 16 MHz.
18. Use SYSCTL- > RCGC2 with appropriate value to clock and enable GPIO Ports B and F.
19. Use SYSCTL- > RCGC0 with appropriate value to clock and enable CAN0 module.
20. Use GPIOB→DEN with appropriate value to set PB3~PB0 as digital function pins.
21. Use GPIOB→DIR with appropriate value to set PB3~PB0 as output pins.
22. Use the following codes to unlock and configure PF0 pin as a CAN0RX pin, and lock the GPIOCR register and configure PF3 pin as a CAN0TX pin:

```
HWREG(GPIO_PORTF_BASE + GPIO_O_LOCK) =        //unlock GPIOCR register
 GPIO_LOCK_KEY;
HWREG(GPIO_PORTF_BASE + GPIO_O_CR) = 0x1;     //enable PF0 to be modified
GPIOPinConfigure(GPIO_PF0_CAN0RX);            //set PF0 as CAN0RX pin
GPIOPinTypeCAN(GPIO_PORTF_BASE,
 GPIO_PIN_0);
HWREG(GPIO_PORTF_BASE + GPIO_O_LOCK) = 0;     //lock GPIOCR register
                                                again
GPIOPinConfigure(GPIO_PF3_CAN0TX);            //set PF3 as CAN0TX pin
GPIOPinTypeCAN(GPIO_PORTF_BASE,
 GPIO_PIN_3);
```

23. Call the API function `CANInit(CAN0_BASE)` to initialize CAN0 module.
24. Set the bit rate as 500 kHz by calling the API function `CANBitRateSet(CAN0_BASE, SysCtlClockGet(), 500000)`.
25. Register the CAN module 0 interrupt handler by calling the `CANIntRegister (CAN0_BASE, CANInt_Handler)` API function.
26. Use `CANIntEnable(CAN0_BASE, CAN_INT_MASTER|CAN_INT_ERROR|CAN_INT_STATUS)` API function to set up the interrupt sources for the CAN module 0.
27. Use the API function `IntEnable(INT_CAN0)` to enable the CAN module 0 interrupt.
28. Call the API function `CANEnable(CAN0_BASE)` to enable the CAN module 0.
29. Use the following codes to setup the message object to be transmitted:

```
sCANMsg.ui32MsgID = 1;                    //set up msg object to be
                                            transmitted
sCANMsg.ui32MsgIDMask = 0;
sCANMsg.ui32Flags =                       //enable transmit interrupts
 MSG_OBJ_TX_INT_ENABLE;
sCANMsg.ui32MsgLen = sizeof(sMsgData);
sCANMsg.pui8MsgData = sMsgData;
for (index = 0; index < 4; index++)       //init the data array
 sMsgData[index] = ui8MsgData[index];
```

30. Use an infinitive `while()` loop to repeatedly transmit 4 bytes of data.

31. Use the API function `CANMessageSet(CAN0_BASE, 1, &sCANMsg, MSG_OBJ_TYPE_TX)` to send out the message object 1.

32. Call the user-defined function `SimpleDelay(1)` to delay 1 second.

33. Check if the `errFlag` is set, which means that an error has been occurred, and set PB3 LED to on to indicate this case.

10.1.4 Set Up the Environment to Build and Run the Project To build and run the project, one needs to perform the following operations to set up the environments:

- Select the `Stellaris ICDI` debugger in the **Debug** tab under the **Project | Options for Target ' Target 1 '** menu item.
- Add the system header files path `C:\ti\TivaWare_C_Series-2.0.1.11577` via the `C/C++` tab in the `Options for Target 'Target 1'` under the `Project` menu item.
- Add the TivaWare™ Peripheral Driver Library file driverlib.lib into the project. The file is located at `C:\ti\TivaWare_C_Series-2.0.1.11577\driverlib\rvmdk`.
- Now you can build and run the project. Usually, this project `CANMaster` should be run first before the `CANSlave` can be run.

10.2 Lab10_2

10.2.1 Goal This project or the project `CANSlave` enables students to use another TM4C123GXL EVB to build a CAN receiver with receiving interrupts to check and receive one message object with four bytes of data items sent by the `CANMaster` project built in `Lab10_1`. The receiver also used PF0 and PF3 pins as the receiving and transmitting pins to interface the MCP2551 transceiver to communicate with the CAN master.

Refer to Figure 10.17 to finish the interfacing circuit connection for this CAN slave project.

10.2.2 Data Assignment and Hardware Configuration A sample circuit connection is shown in Figure 10.68.

Similar to the `CANMaster` project, the PF0 pin is a special pin, and it is used by the button switch SW2 in the TM4C123GXL EVB by default; this switch allows the EVB to enter a sleep mode when it is pressed via a Non-Maskable Interrupt (NMI). Therefore, usually the PF0 pin is locked after a system reset. In order to configure the PF0 pin to enable it to work as a GPIO alternate function pin, or specifically enable it to work as the CAN0RX pin, it must be first unlocked. After this pin is configured, it must be locked again to guard against any possible change for this pin in the future for this project. One needs to use `GPIOLOCK` and `GPIOCR` registers to do this unlock and lock functions. As soon as the `GPIOCR` register is unlocked, the PF0 pin or the GPIO Port F can be configured and modified.

10.2.3 Development of the Project Create a new project named `CANSlave` in the folder `C:\ARM Lab Projects\Chapter 10\CANSlave` and a new header file named `CANSlave.h`.

Add the following codes into this header file:

```
#include <stdint.h>
#include <stdbool.h>
#include "inc/hw_types.h"
#include "inc/hw_can.h"
#include "TM4C123GH6PM.h"
#include "driverlib/can.h"
```

```
#include "driverlib/interrupt.h"
#include "driverlib/sysctl.h"
#include "driverlib/gpio.h"
#define INT_CAN0                          55              //CAN0
#define GPIO_PF0_CAN0RX            0x00050003
#define GPIO_PF3_CAN0TX            0x00050C03
#define GPIO_PORTF_BASE           0x40025000      //GPIO Port F
#define GPIO_LOCK_KEY             0x4C4F434B      //unlocks key for
                                                                    GPIOCR register
#define GPIO_O_LOCK               0x00000520      //GPIO Lock register
#define GPIO_O_CR                 0x00000524      //GPIO Commit register
#define HWREG(x) (*((volatile uint32_
 t*)(x)))
int rcFlag = 0;                                       //global msg receiving flag
int errFlag = 0;                                      //global error flag
void SimpleDelay(double seconds)                      //delay subroutine
{
  SysCtlDelay((seconds*16000000)/3);
}
```

10.2.4 Development of the C Source File   Perform the following operations to complete this project:

1. Create a new C file named CANSlave.c and add it into the project CANSlave.

2. Refer to steps 5~13 in the last project C file CANMaster.c to build the CAN0 interrupt handler CANInt_Handler().

    Now using the following steps to build the main program int main(void):

3. Declare a local integer variable size.

4. Declare a new instance rCANMsg based on the CAN data structure tCANMsgObject.

5. Use uint8_t rMsgData[4] to declare a receiving data array.

6. Use SysCtlClockSet() API function with the arguments SYSCTL_SYS-DIV_1|SYSCTL_USE_OSC |SYSCTL_OSC_MAIN|SYSCTL_XTAL_16MHZ to set up the system clock as 16 MHz.

7. Use SYSCTL→RCGC2 with appropriate value to clock and enable GPIO Ports B and F.

8. Use SYSCTL→RCGC0 with appropriate value to clock and enable CAN0 module.

9. Use GPIOB→DEN with appropriate value to set PB3~PB0 as digital function pins.

10. Use GPIOB→DIR with appropriate value to set PB3~PB0 as output pins.

11. Use GPIOF→DEN with appropriate value to set PF3~PF0 as digital function pins.

12. Use GPIOF→DIR with appropriate value to set PF3~PF1 as output pins.

13. Use the following codes to unlock, configure PF0 pin as CAN0RX pin, lock the GPIOCR register and configure PF3 pin as CAN0TX pin:

```
HWREG(GPIO_PORTF_BASE + GPIO_O_LOCK) =           //unlock GPIOCR register
 GPIO_LOCK_KEY;
HWREG(GPIO_PORTF_BASE + GPIO_O_CR) = 0x1;         //enable PF0 to be
                                                              modified
GPIOPinConfigure(GPIO_PF0_CAN0RX);               //set PF0 as CAN0RX pin
```

```
GPIOPinTypeCAN(GPIO_PORTF_BASE, GPIO_PIN_0);
HWREG(GPIO_PORTF_BASE + GPIO_O_LOCK) = 0;           //lock GPIOCR register
                                                      again
GPIOPinConfigure(GPIO_PF3_CAN0TX);                  //set PF3 as CAN0TX pin
GPIOPinTypeCAN(GPIO_PORTF_BASE, GPIO_PIN_3);
```

14. Call the API function CANInit(CAN0_BASE) to initialize CAN0 module.

15. Set the bit rate as 500 kHz by calling the API function CANBitRateSet(CAN0_BASE, SysCtlClockGet(), 500000).

16. Register the CAN module 0 interrupt handler by calling the CANIntRegister (CAN0_BASE, CANInt_Handler) API function.

17. Use CANIntEnable(CAN0_BASE, CAN_INT_MASTER|CAN_INT_ERROR|CAN_INT_STATUS) API function to set up the interrupt sources for the CAN module 0.

18. Use the API function IntEnable(INT_CAN0) to enable the CAN module 0 interrupt.

19. Call the API function CANEnable(CAN0_BASE) to enable the CAN module 0.

20. Use the following codes to set up the message object to be received:

```
rCANMsg.ui32MsgID = 0;
rCANMsg.ui32MsgIDMask = 0;
rCANMsg.ui32Flags = MSG_OBJ_RX_INT_ENABLE |
 MSG_OBJ_USE_ID_FILTER;
rCANMsg.ui32MsgLen = sizeof(rMsgData);
CANMessageSet(CAN0_BASE, 1, &rCANMsg, MSG_OBJ_TYPE_RX);
```

21. Use an infinitive while() loop to wait for a matched ID occurred.

22. Use an if() statement to check whether the global receiving flag rcFlag has been set. This flag should be set inside the CAN0 interrupt handler if a message object has been transmitted by the CANMaster and received by the CANSlave project.

23. If this rcFlag is set, use rCANMsg.pui8MsgData = rMsgData; to initialize the data array in the receiving message object.

24. Then call the API function CANMessageGet(CAN0_BASE, 1, &rCANMsg, 0) to pick up the received message object.

25. Call the user defined function SimpleDelay(0.005) to delay 5 ms and reset the rcFlag to 0 to make it ready for the next matched message object to be received.

26. Use if(rCANMsg.ui32Flags & MSG_OBJ_DATA_LOST) to check if any data has been missed. If this happened, set PF1 red color LED to on to indicate this case.

27. Use a for() loop to pick up all 4 bytes data and assign them to the PB3~PB0 LEDs to display them (GPIOB→DATA |= rMsgData[size]).

28. Inside the for() loop, call the delay function SimpleDelay(0.5) to delay the program with 0.5 second to enable the data to be displayed on LEDs are stable.

29. Place a break instruction to get out of the while() loop if the data have been received.

30. An infinitive while() loop can be placed here to check the received data array rMsgData[] in the Call Stack + Locals window to confirm our project running result.

10.2.5 Set Up the Environment to Build and Run the Project Refer to Section 10.2.9.4 to complete these environments setups. Now you can build and run the project. However, usually this CANSlave project should be run after the CANMaster runs.

10.2.6 Build and Demonstrate Your Program   Before running the projects, make sure that the hardware connection has been done and that both TM4C123GXL EVBs have been connected to two related MCP2551 transceivers and are ready to go. First you need to run the `CANMaster` project from one host computer that is connected to the master TM4C123GXL EVB, and then run the `CANSlave` project from another host computer connected to the slave TM4C123GXL EVB.

As both projects run, 4 bytes data are transmitted from the CANMaster project and received by the CANSlave project. The received 4 bytes data are displayed in PB3~PB0 LEDs.

To check the received data values, go to the `Debug|Stop` menu to stop the CANSlave project. Then open the `Call Stack + Locals` window, and expand the `rMsgData[]` array, and you can find that four bytes data values, 1, 2, 4, and 8, have been received and stored in this array.

Based on these results, try to answer the following questions:

- Can you modify these projects, `CANMaster` and `CANSlave`, to transmit and receive multiple message objects? If it is possible, what are the key points?
- What did you learn from these projects?

10.3 Lab10_3

10.3.1 Goal   Program `Lab10_3`, or the project `PIDControl` enables students to build a PID closed-loop control system to control a DC motor with a rotary optical encoder with either position or velocity feedback. The students need to use MATLAB® Toolboxes, such as Identification Toolbox™, PID Control System Toolbox™, and SIMULINK®, to identify the dynamic model for the DC motor, design PID control parameters, and simulate and tune the PID control gains to complete this control system design. The students also need to implement this control strategy in software to build and test the performances of the designed closed-loop control system.

Refer to Sections 10.3.8 and 10.4 in Chapter 10 to perform the calibration of the encoder, identification of the dynamic model of the DC motor, design and tuning of the PID parameters, simulation of the PID control system, and building of the control software to complete this lab.

10.3.2 Data Assignment and Hardware Configuration   Refer to Sections 10.3.8 and 10.4 in Chapter 10 for hardware configurations and connections.

10.3.3 Development of the Project   Refer to Section 10.4.4 in Chapter 10 to build this lab project.

10.3.4 Development of the C Source File   Refer to Section 10.4.4 to finish the building of this control software and source codes.

10.3.5 Set Up the Environment to Build and Run the Project   Make sure that the debugger you are using is the `Stellaris ICDI`.

10.3.6 Demonstrate Your Program   Build and run the project if everything is fine. As the project runs, try to use an oscilloscope to monitor the output of the closed-loop control system or the encoder output to confirm that your project works fine.

Based on these results, try to answer the following questions:

- Can you modify this project to perform a motor position control, not a motor velocity control? If it is, how?
- What did you learn from this project?

10.4 Lab10_4

10.4.1 Goal
Program Lab10_4, or project RobotControl, enables students to design and build a control system to control a simulated robotic system. The students need to use PWM model and ADC module to complete this control system design. A photosensor Q1 (VEMT2520) that is connected to the analog input channel AIN2 via PE1 pin and installed in the EduBASE ARM® Trainer works as a optical signal detector to control the running and stopping of a DC motor that can be considered to be a robotic running motor. The DC motor used in this project is a DC motor fan, and it is similar to one used in the project DARPWM built in Chapter 7 (model number: EE80251S2-000U-999). The Module 1 PWM Generator 2 (M1PWM5) generates a PWM signal to control this DC motor via PF1 pin in the GPIO Port F.

The PB0 and PB1 pins are used to provide the rotating direction signal (PB1 : PB0 = 01 → CW and PB1 : PB0 = 10 → CCW) for the motor. In this project, we use the first rotating direction PB1 : PB0 = 01 since the motor can be rotated in a single direction.

10.4.2 Data assignment and Hardware Configuration
Refer to Sections 7.5.6 and 7.6.7 in Chapter 7 to get more details about the hardware configurations and connections for the photo sensor Q1 with ADC module (PE1 pin) and the PWM module with PF1 pin.

10.4.3 Development of the Project
Create a new project named RobotControl in the folder C:\ARM Lab Projects\Chapter 10\RobotControl and a new C source file RobotControl.c.

Perform the following operations to complete this project with the DRA model.

10.4.4 Development of the C Source File

1. Declare the following header files and a macro for the GPIO Port F Commit Register. The reason of defining this macro is that we need to use PF1 pin as a PWM signal output pin to output PWM signal to the DC motor, but the PF1 pin is locked by default after a system reset; therefore we need to unlock the GPIO Port F Commit Register to enable us to configure the PF1 pin to work as a PWM output pin.

```
#include <stdint.h>
#include <stdbool.h>
#include "TM4C123GH6PM.h"

#define GPIO_PORTF_CR_R (*((volatile uint32_t *)0x40025524))
```

2. Declare two user-defined functions used to initialize ADC and PWM modules:

```
void InitADC(void);
void InitPWM(void);
```

3. Build the codes for another two user-defined functions as below:

```
void Delay(uint32_t time)
{
    uint32_t Loop;
    for (Loop = 0; Loop<time; Loop++) {}
}
void SetSound(int period)                          //set speaker 400 Hz signal
```

```
{
   GPIOC->DATA = 0x10;
   Delay(period);
   GPIOC->DATA = 0x0;
   Delay(period);
}
```

The first function is used to simply delay a period of time for the program, and the second function is used to send a 400 Hz audio signal to the speaker.

4. Inside the `main()` program, create two local `uint32_t` variables, pw = 50 and pSensor. The first variable works as a PWM output value to the motor and the second works as a value holder for the collected ADC value from the photosensor Q1.

5. Call two user-defined functions, `InitADC()` and `InitPWM()`, to initialize the ADC and the PWM modules.

6. Use an infinite `while()` loop to repeatedly check the ADC input from the photosensor and send appropriate PWM output values to the DC motor to make motor run or stop.

7. Inside the `while()` loop, use ADC0→PSSI to assign an appropriate value to the PSSI register to initiate the ADC0 Processor Sample Sequencer Initiate (ADCPSSI) Register (refer to Section 7.5.3.2.4 in Chapter 7).

8. Use `while((ADC0→RIS & 2) == 0);` to wait for the ADC0 to complete its conversion.

9. Use `pSensor = ADC0→SSFIFO1;` to get the photosensor input coming from the first sample from SS1 FIFO register.

10. Assign the appropriate value to the ADC0 `ISC` register by using ADC0→ISC to clear the interrupt caused by the completion of the ADC0 conversion.

11. Use the `if` statement to check whether the photosensor input stored in the pSensor variable greater than 0x800 or not.

12. If the photosensor input is greater than 0x800, this means that the photosensor is not covered and the motor should be driven to rotate in the CW direction. Assign an appropriate value to the PWM1 CTL register to enable the PWM1_2B generator by using PWM1→_2_CTL instruction.

13. Assign an appropriate value to the PWM1 ENABLE register to enable the PWM5 output by using the instruction PWM1→ENABLE.

14. Assign the PWM value stored in the variable pw to the DC motor via PWM1_2B CMPB register by using PWM1→_2_CMPB instruction.

15. Turn on the green color LED installed in the TM4C123GXL EVB by assigning an appropriate value to the GPIO Port F DATA register by using the instruction GPIOF→DATA.

16. If the photo sensor input is less than 0x800, which means that the photosensor is covered and the motor should be stop immediately. Assign 0 to the DC motor via PWM1_2B CMPB register by using PWM1→_2_CMPB instruction. Also assign an appropriate value to the PWM1 CTL register to disable the PWM1_2B generator by using PWM1→_2_CTL instruction.

17. Assign an appropriate value to the PWM1 ENABLE register to disable the PWM5 output by using the instruction PWM1→ENABLE.

18. Turn on the blue color LED installed in the TM4C123GXL EVB by assigning an appropriate value to the GPIO Port F DATA register by using the instruction GPIOF→DATA.

19. Call the user-defined function SetSound(2000); to send a 400 Hz audio signal to the speaker to indicate that the motor has been stopped.

The following codes are for the function InitADC() used to initialize the ADC Module.

1. Assign an appropriate value to the RCGC2 register to enable and clock the GPIO Ports B, C, E, and F by using the instruction SYSCTL→RCGC2 =.

2. Assign an appropriate value to the RCGCADC register to enable and clock the ADC0 module by using the instruction SYSCTL→RCGCADC |=.

3. Assign an appropriate value to the GPIO Port E AFSEL register to enable PE5~PE0 pins to work as alternate function pins by using the instruction GPIOE→AFSEL =.

4. Assign an appropriate value to the GPIO Port E DEN register to define PE5~PE0 as analog function pins by using the instruction GPIOE→DEN =.

5. Assign an appropriate value to the GPIO Port E AMSEL register to disable the analog isolation circuit for PE5~PE0 pins by using the instruction GPIOE→AMSEL =.

6. Assign the appropriate values to the GPIO Port B to enable PB3~PB0 as digital function and output pins by using the instructions GPIOB→DEN and GPIOB→DIR.

7. Assign an appropriate value to the GPIO Port C to enable PC4 pin as a digital function and output pin by using the instructions GPIOC→DEN and GPIOC→DIR.

8. Assign the appropriate values to the GPIO Port F to enable PF3~PF0 as digital function and output pins by using the instructions GPIOF→DEN and GPIOF→DIR.

9. Initialize the ADC module 0 (ADC0) to use the default trigger source, processor, by assigning the ADCCTL register with an appropriate value via the GPIOE→ADCCTL instruction.

10. In order to initialize the ADC0 Sample Sequence 1 (SS1)-related registers, first one needs to disable the ADC0 SS1 by assigning an appropriate value to the ADC0 ACTSS register via the instruction ADC0→ACTSS (refer to Section 7.5.3.2.3 in Chapter 7).

11. Select the default trigger source for the SS1 by assigning an appropriate value to the ADC0 EMUX register via the ADC0→EMUX instruction (refer to Section 7.5.3.3.3.1 in Chapter 7).

12. Define the analog input channel 2 (AIN2) that is connected to the photosensor as the first sample in the SS1 by assigning an appropriate value to the ADC0 SSMUX1 register via the instruction ADC0→SSMUX1 |= (refer to Section 7.5.3.2.1 in Chapter 7).

13. Define the SS1 to be ended at the first sample with interrupt by assigning an appropriate value to the ADC0 SSCTL1 register via the instruction ADC0→SSCTL1 |= (refer to Section 7.5.3.2.2 in Chapter 7).

14. Enable the ADC0 SS1 by assigning an appropriate value to the ACTSS register via the instruction ADC0→ACTSS |= (refer to Section 7.5.3.2.3 in Chapter 7).

The following codes are for the function InitPWM() used to initialize the PWM Module.

1. Enable the PWM1 module with the clock by assigning an appropriate value to the RCGCPWM register via the instruction SYSCTL→RCGCPWM |=.

2. Use instruction while((SYSCTL→PRPWM & 0x2) == 0) {}; to wait for the PWM1 module to be stable.

3. Assign the RCC register with an appropriate value to set up a 20 MHz PWM clock to drive the PWM module 1 via the instruction SYSCTL→RCC.

4. Unlock the GPTOF commit register CR by assigning an appropriate value to the GPIO Port F LOCK register via the instruction GPIOF→LOCK.

5. Enable the PF1 pin to be committed by assigning an appropriate value to the GPIO Port F commit register via the instruction GPIO_PORTF_CR_R |=.

6. Lock the GPIOF commit register CR again by assigning an appropriate value to the GPIO Port F LOCK register via the instruction GPIOF→LOCK.

7. Disable the PWM1_2B or M1PWM5 output by assigning an appropriate value to the PWM1 CTL register via the instruction PWM1→_2_CTL to enable this output to be configured.

8. Configure the PWM1 GENB register to generate High on LOAD and Low on CMPB down by assigning an appropriate value to the GENB register via the instruction PWM1→_2_GENB.

9. Load the PWM1 LOAD register with the upper bound value 3999 with the instruction PWM1→_2_LOAD.

10. Configure the PF1 pin as an alternate function pin by assigning an appropriate value to the GPIO Port F AFSEL register via the instruction GPIOF→AFSEL |=.

11. Configure the PF1 pin as the PWM1_2B or M1PWM5 PWM output pin by assigning an appropriate value to the PWM1 PCTL register via the instruction GPIOF→PCTL.

12. Disable the analog function on PF1 pin by assigning an appropriate value to the GPIO Port F AMSEL register via the instruction GPIOF→AMSEL &=.

13. Set up the PB0 pin as 0x1 to enable the motor to rotate in the CW direction.

10.4.5 Set Up the Environment to Build and Run the Project   Make sure that the debugger you are using is the Stellaris ICDI.

10.4.6 Demonstrate Your Program   Build and run the project if everything is fine.

As the project runs, the motor should rotate in the CW direction. Now use your hand and fingers to cover the photosensor Q1 in the EduBASE ARM® Trainer; the motor should stop and the Blue color LED in the TM4C123GXL EVB should be on. Also a 400 Hz audio signal is sent to the speaker to make some noises. The motor will continue to rotate as soon as your hand is removed from the photosensor. This is very similar to a robot controlled by the photosensor to enable it to move or stop.

Based on these results, try to answer the following questions:

- When the photosensor is not covered and the motor is rotating, the Green color LED in the TM4C123GXL EVB should be on. But the color is not green, why?
- When the motor is stopped, it cannot be stopped immediately, why?
- What did you learn from this project?

10.5 Lab10_5

10.5.1 Goal   Program Lab10_5, or project ACMP1 enables students to design and implement the analog comparator module 1 to control and compare a sequence of analog input signals or waveforms with a programmable reference voltage to display the comparison results on a group of LEDs.

10.5.2 Data Assignment and Hardware Configuration   In this project, students need to build a project named ACMP1, which is very similar to the project ACMP0 built in Section 10.6.7 in Chapter 10.

The analog input connected to the Vin– or C1– still comes from the potentiometer VR2 via PE2 pin. But this analog input needs to be connected to the C1- input terminal in this project via the PC4 pin since the ACMP1 module is adopted now. The only modification in the hardware connection is to connect the PE2 pin in the J3 connector to the PC4 pin in the J4 connector in the TM4C123GXL EVB.

Students need to use the PF1 pin, not the PF0 pin, as the analog comparison output pin for the ACMP1 module, and they also need to program the V_{IREF} to make it varied in an increment sequence to make the output varied with that sequence. The varied outputs can be displayed in four LEDs PB3~PB0 in the ARM® Trainer.

10.5.3 Development of the Project
Create a new project ACMP1 in the folder `C:\ARM Lab Projects\Chapter 10\ACMP1` with a new C source file ACMP1.c, and follow the steps below to complete the coding process for this project.

10.5.4 Development of the C Source File
Perform the following operations to complete this project with API functions:

1. Declare the following header files and user-defined functions.

```
#include <stdint.h>
#include <stdbool.h>
#include "driverlib/sysctl.h"
#include "driverlib/gpio.h"
#include "driverlib/comp.h"
#include "TM4C123GH6PM.h"

void InitACMP1(void);
void SimpleDelay(double ms)
{
   SysCtlDelay((ms * 16000)/3);
}
```

Two user-defined functions, `InitACMP1()`, and `SimpleDealy()` are used to initialize the ACMP1 module and delay the program by a certain period of time.

2. Inside the `main()` function, create two local `uint32_t` variables, `status` and `index`. The former is used to get and hold the running status of the ACMP1, and the latter works as a loop counter.

3. Use the SYSCTL→RCGC2 instruction to assign an appropriate value to the RCGC2 register to clock and enable GPIO Ports B, C, and F.

4. Use the GPIOB→DEN and GPIOB→DIR instructions to assign two appropriate values to the GPIO Port B DEN and DIR registers to set the PB3~PB0 pins as digital function and output pins.

5. Use the GPIOC→DEN and GPIOC→DIR instructions to assign two appropriate values to the GPIO Port C DEN and DIR registers to set the PC5 and PC4 pins as analog and input pins.

6. Use the GPIOF→DEN and GPIOF→DIR instructions to assign two appropriate values to the GPIO Port F DEN and DIR registers to set the PF3~PF0 pins as digital function and output pins.

7. Call the `InitACMP1()` user-defined function to initialize and configure the ACMP1 module.

8. Use the COMP→ACREFCTL instruction to assign an appropriate value to the ACREFCTL register to connect the power VDDA to the resistor ladder (EN = 1), enable the V_{IREF} to be in the High-range (RNG = 0), and set V_{IREF} = 0.785 V (VREF = 0000).

9. Call the `SimpleDelay()` user-defined function to delay the program by $10\,\mu s$.

10. Place an infinitive `while()` loop in here to repeatedly check the output status and turn the LEDs PB3~PB0 on and off based on the value on the bit OVAL in the ACSTAT1 register.

11. Use a `for()` loop with the `index` as the loop counter to increment the V_{IREF} from 0.785 V to 2.469 V, and this is equivalent to increasing the `index` from 0 to 0xF (15). This increment equation can be represented as $V_{IREF} = 0.785 + VREF \times 0.112$ or $0.785 + index \times 0.112$.

12. Inside the `for()` loop, use the COMP→ACREFCTL instruction to access the ACREFCTL register and increment the bit field VREF by 1 for each loop.

13. Use the COMP→ACSTAT1 & 0x2 instruction to check the status of the bit OVAL in the ACSTAT1 register to get the output value of the ACMP1 module, and assign this ANDing result to the `status` variable.

14. If the `status` = 0x2 or the bit OVAL is 1, which means that the Vin− < Vin+, use the GPIOB→DATA instruction to assign the DATA register with an appropriate value to turn on four LEDs, PB3~PB0 installed in the ARM® Trainer, to indicate this situation.

15. Otherwise assign another appropriate value to turn off four LEDs, PB3~PB0.

16. After or in the outside of the `for()` loop but inside the `while()` loop, call the `SimpleDelay()` function to delay the program by 50 ms.

Following are the codes for the user-defined function `InitACMP1()`:

17. Use the SYSCTL→RCGCACMP instruction to access and assign an appropriate value to the RCGCACMP register to clock and enable the ACMP1 module.

18. Use the GPIOF→AFSEL instruction to access and assign an appropriate value to the GPIIO Port F AFSEL register to configure the PF1 pin as an alternate function pin.

19. Use the GPIOF→PCTL instruction to access and assign an appropriate value to the GPIO Port F PCTL register to enable the PF1 pin to work as the output pin for the ACMP1 module. Refer to Table 10.28 to get more details about this PMCx coding for the PCTL register.

20. Use the COMP→ACCTL1 instruction to configure the ACCTL1 register to enable the V_{IREF} to be connected to the Vin+ input to the ACMP1 with the output non-inverted.

10.5.5 Setup the Environment to Build and Run the Project This setup contains the following three operations:

1. Include the system header files by adding the include path.
2. Check and configure the correct debugger used in the project.
3. Add the TivaWare™ Peripheral Driver Library into the project.

Perform the following operations to include the header file path in the project:

- Go to the `Project|Options for Target 'Target 1'` menu item. Then click on the C/C++ tab.
- Go to the `Include Paths` box and browse to the folder where our header files are located, it is `C:\ti\TivaWare_C_Series-2.0.1.11577`. Select this folder and click on the **OK** button.

Perform the following operations to select the correct debugger:

- Going to the `Project|Options for Target 'Target 1'` menu item to open the `Options` wizard.

- On the opened Options wizard, click on the `Debug` tab.
- Make sure that the debugger shown in the `Use:` box is `Stellaris ICDI`. Otherwise you can click on the dropdown arrow to select this debugger from the list.

Perform the below operations to add the TivaWare™ peripheral driver library into the project:

- Go to the **Project** pane and right click on the **Source Group 1** item, and select the `Add Existing Files to Group 'Source Group 1'` menu item.
- Browse to the folder where the library file is located, which is `C:\ti\TivaWare_C_Series-2.0.1.11577\driverlib\rvmdk`. Then select the library file `driverlib.lib` and click on the **Add** button. Click on the **Close** button to finish this step.

10.5.6 Demonstrate Your Program   Build and run the project if everything is fine.

As the project runs, one can tune the potentiometer VR2 with a small screw driver. Four LEDs, PB3~PB0, may be flashing periodically. This means that the programmable interval reference voltage is increased step by step, and the comparison result is either High or Low in terms of the analog input coming from the VR2.

Based on the project running results, try to answer the following questions:

- When you tune the potentiometer VR2 in a certain value, four LEDs will be flashing periodically. Why did this happen?
- When you tune the potentiometer VR2 in a certain value, four LEDs will be kept ON permanently. Why did this happen?
- When you tune the potentiometer VR2 in a certain value, four LEDs will be kept OFF permanently. Why did this happen?
- What did you learn from this project?

Chapter 11

ARM® Floating Point Unit (FPU)

As we discussed in Chapter 2, one of the most important differences between the Cortex®-M4 MCU and Cortex®-M3 MCU is that an optional Floating Point Unit (FPU) is added into the Cortex®-M4 Core to enhance the floating point data operations. The Cortex®-M4 FPU implements ARMv7E-M architecture with FPv4-SP extensions. It provides floating-point computation functionality that is compliant with the *ANSI/IEEE Standard 754-2008, IEEE Standard for Binary Floating-Point Arithmetic*. In this chapter, we will concentrate our discussions on this FPU element with more detailed analysis for this unit.

11.1 OVERVIEW AND INTRODUCTION

In the Cortex®-M4 MCU, an optional floating-point unit (FPU) is provided to supply different methods for manipulating the behavior of the floating point data in an easy and convenient way. By default, the FPU is disabled and must be enabled prior to the execution of any floating-point instructions. If a floating-point instruction is executed but the FPU is disabled, a No Co-Processor (NOCP) usage fault is generated.

The Cortex®-M4F FPU fully supports half- and single-precision add, subtract, multiply, divide, multiply and accumulate, and square root operations. It provides conversions between fixed-point and floating-point data formats, as well as floating-point constant instructions. It also supports the half-precision and single-precision floating-point formats to provide different manipulations for the floating-point data with the different lengths and accuracies.

The usage of the FPU in the Cortex®-M4 MCU system can be divided into two categories: (1) in the main thread of the program without using any interrupt and (2) inside an interrupt handler.

When using FPU inside an interrupt handler, the usage of the FPU can still be further divided into the following three categories:

- It can do nothing with the floating-point data.
- It can always save the floating-point data into the stack.
- It can perform a lazy save/restore of the floating-point data.

Practical Microcontroller Engineering with ARM® Technology, First Edition. Ying Bai.
© 2016 by The Institute of Electrical and Electronics Engineers, Inc. Published 2016 by John Wiley & Sons, Inc.
Companion Website: www.wiley.com/go/armbai

The default handling of the floating-point data is to perform a lazy save/restore. When an interrupt is occurred, spaces are reserved on the stack for the floating-point data but the data are not written into the stack. This method reduces the interrupt working load to a minimum because only the integer state is written to the stack. When a floating-point instruction is executed within the interrupt handler, the floating-point data are written to the stack prior to the execution of the floating-point instruction. Finally, upon return from the interrupt, the floating-point data are restored from the stack only if they were written. Using lazy save/restore provides a blend between fast interrupt response and the ability to use floating-point instructions in the interrupt handler.

The FPU can generate an interrupt when one of several exceptions occurs. These exceptions include the underflow, overflow, divide by zero, invalid operation, abnormal input, and inexact exception. The application can optionally choose to enable one or more of these interrupts and use the interrupt handler to decide which action should be taken for each case.

Let's first have a basic idea about different floating-point data.

11.2 THREE TYPES OF THE FLOATING-POINT DATA

Floating-point data allow the MCU to process a much wider data range, from a huge to a very small value in a computer system. Based on the different precision requirements and formats, a floating-point data can be divided into the following three format groups:

- The half-precision floating-point format (16-bit data)
- The single-precision floating-point format (32-bit data)
- The double-precision floating-point format (64-bit data)

One point to be noted is that not all C compilers support the half-precision floating-point format numbers. Both gcc and ARM® C compilers support this kind of half-precision floating-point format. However, they do not support the double-precision floating-point format.

11.2.1 The Half-Precision Floating-Point Data

The half-precision is exactly a binary floating-point computer number format that occupies 16 bits or two bytes in the computer memory.

According to the IEEE 754-2008 definition, a half-precision floating-point number can be represented as three segments as shown in Figure 11.1, which include the Sign bit (bit 15), Exponent field (5 bits, bits 14~10), and Fraction field (10 bits, bits 9~0).

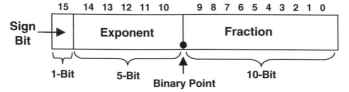

Figure 11.1. IEEE 754 half-precision floating-point format.

When using this half-precision floating-point format to represent a floating-point number, the following points need to be noted:

1. The 1-bit `Sign` field is used to determine the polarity of the floating-point number. A value of 0 on this bit indicates that this floating point number is a positive one, but a value of 1 means that this floating-point number is a negative number.

2. The 5-bit `Exponent` field is a *biased* exponent value and a biased value of 15 must be subtracted from this biased exponent, `Exponent`, to get the real or the true exponent value for the given floating-point number. The reason for using this biased exponent is to enlarge the range of the floating-point numbers.

3. The 10-bit `Fraction` field contains 10-bit binary significant bits (significands) after the decimal point. The key is that between the bit 10 and bit 9, or between the `Exponent` and the `Fraction` fields, a binary point exists and this must be kept in mind when converting this half-precision floating-point number to its real value.

Thus the real or the true value of a floating-point number can be calculated as

$$\text{True Value} = (-1)^{Sign} \times 2^{(\text{Exponent}-15)} \times (1.0 + \textit{Fraction}) \tag{11.1}$$

When using Eq. (11.1) to calculate the true value for a given half-precision floating-point number, the following issues must be considered:

1. If the biased exponent, `Exponent`, is in the range $0 < \text{Exponent} < 0x1F$, the value of the true floating-point number is a normalized value and it can be calculated by using the Eq. (11.1).

2. If the biased exponent, `Exponent`, is 0, the following possible results exist:
   - If the `Fraction` is 0 and the `Sign` bit is 0, then the true value is 0 (+0).
   - If the `Fraction` is 0 but the `Sign` bit is 1, then the true value is also 0 (−0).
   - If the `Fraction` is not 0, then the true value is a subnormal or a denormalized value and its true value should be calculated by using Eq. (11.2):

$$\text{True Value} = (-1)^{Sign} \times 2^{-14} \times (0.0 + \textit{Fraction}) \tag{11.2}$$

3. If the biased exponent, `Exponent`, is equal to $0x1F$ (11111), the following possible results exist:
   - If the `Fraction` is 0 and the `Sign` bit is also 0, then the true value is infinitive (+∞).
   - If the `Fraction` is 0 and the `Sign` bit is 1, then the true value is also infinitive (−∞).
   - If the `Fraction` is not 0, then it is a special code or known as NaN (Not a Number).

A NaN value can be categorized into a signaling NaN or a quiet NaN, and this is defined as

1. If bit-9 of the `Fraction` is 0, it is a signaling NaN.
2. If bit-9 of the `Fraction` is 1, it is a quiet NaN.

Table 11.1 shows a summarization for these possible results.

The IEEE 754 standard specifies a `binary16` as a data type for a half-precision floating-point number.

An example of using the IEEE 754 standard to present a half-precision floating-point number is 1111101101101000. The `Sign` bit is 1, which means that this is a negative

Table 11.1. The possible true value for a given half-precision floating point number.

Exponent	Fraction = 0	Fraction ≠ 0	Calculation Equation
00000	+0, −0	Subnormal Numbers	$(-1)^{Sign} \times 2^{-14} \times (0.0 + Fraction)$
00001~11110	Normalized Numbers		$(-1)^{Sign} \times 2^{(Exponent-15)} \times (1.0 + Fraction)$
11111	±infinitive (±∞)	NaN (Signaling or Quiet)	

floating-point number. The biased exponent, Exponent, is 11110B = 30D, and the Fraction is 1101101000B. Based on Eq. (11.1), the true value of this floating-point number is

$$
\begin{aligned}
\textit{True Value} &= (-1)^1 \times 2^{(30-15)} \times (1.0 + 1 \times 2^{-1} + 1 \times 2^{-2} + 1 \times 2^{-4} + 1 \times 2^{-5} + 1 \times 2^{-7}) \\
&= -(2^{15} \times (1.0 + 0.5 + 0.25 + 0.0625 + 0.03125 + 0.0078125)) \\
&= -(2^{15} \times 1.8515625) = -60672
\end{aligned}
$$

To convert −60672 back to the IEEE 754 standard half-precision floating-point format, perform the following operations:

1. Convert 60672 to hexadecimal or binary number, which is ED00 or 1110110100000000.
2. Convert this binary number to the normalized format, which is 1.1101101×2^{15}. This is equivalent to moving the binary point to the left by 15 bits.
3. Convert the normal exponent 15 to the biased exponent, Exponent, by adding the bias value 15. The biased exponent, Exponent, is 15 + 15 = 30D (11110B).
4. The Fraction is the significant bits after the decimal point, 1101101000. The tailed 3 zeros can be added to make this Fraction become 10 bits.
5. Add the Sign bit 1 to the bit 15 since this is a negative number.
6. The final IEEE 754 standard half-precision floating-point format for this number is
7. Sign-Bit, 1; Exponent, 11110; Fraction, 1101101000. Together it is 1111101101101000.

Next let's take a look at the single-precision floating point format.

11.2.2 The Single-Precision Floating-Point Data

Similar to IEEE 754 half-precision floating point format, the single-precision data is also a binary floating-point computer number that occupies 32 bits or four bytes in the computer memory.

According to the IEEE 754-2008 definition, a single-precision floating-point number can be represented as three segments as shown in Figure 11.2, these include the Sign bit (bit 31), Exponent field (8 bits, bits 30~23), and Fraction field (23 bits, bits 22~0).

Similar to the half-precision format, when using this single-precision floating-point format to represent a floating-point number, the following points need to be noted:

1. The 1-bit Sign field is used to determine the polarity of the floating point number. A value of 0 on this bit indicates that this floating-point number is a positive one, but a value of 1 means that this floating-point number is a negative number.

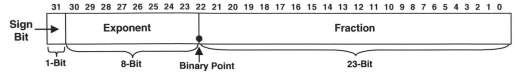

Figure 11.2.   IEEE 754 single-precision floating point format.

2. The 8-bit `Exponent` field is a *biased* exponent value and a biased value of `127` must be subtracted from this biased exponent, `Exponent`, to get the real or the true exponent value for the given floating-point number. The reason for using this biased exponent is to enlarge the range of the floating-point numbers.

3. The 23-bit `Fraction` field contains 23-bit binary significant bits (significands) after the decimal point. The key is that between bit 23 and bit 22, or between the `Exponent` and the `Fraction` fields, a binary point exists and this must be kept in mind when converting this single-precision floating-point number to its real value.

The real or the true value of a single-precision floating point number can be calculated as

$$\text{True Value} = (-1)^{Sign} \times 2^{(\text{Exponent}-127)} \times (1.0 + \textit{Fraction}) \tag{11.3}$$

When using Eq. (11.3) to calculate the true value for a given single-precision floating-point number, the following issues must be considered:

1. If the biased exponent, `Exponent`, is in the range $0 < \text{Exponent} < \text{0xFF}$, the value of the true floating-point number is a normalized value and it can be calculated by using the Eq. (11.3).

2. If the biased exponent, `Exponent`, is 0, the following possible results exist:

- If the `Fraction` is 0 and the `Sign` bit is 0, then the true value is 0 (+0).
- If the `Fraction` is 0 but the `Sign` bit is 1, then the true value is also 0 (−0).
- If the `Fraction` is not 0, then the true value is a subnormal or a denormalized value and its true value should be calculated by using Eq. (11.4):

$$\text{True Value} = (-1)^{Sign} \times 2^{-126} \times (0.0 + \textit{Fraction}) \tag{11.4}$$

3. If the biased exponent, `Exponent`, is equal to `0xFF` (11111111B), the following possible results are existed:

- If the `Fraction` is 0 and the `Sign` bit is also 0, then the true value is infinitive (+∞).
- If the `Fraction` is 0 and the `Sign` bit is 1, then the true value is also infinitive (−∞).
- If the `Fraction` is not 0, then it is a special code or known as NaN (Not a Number).

A NaN value can be categorized into a signaling NaN or a quiet NaN, and this is defined as follows:

1. If bit-22 of the `Fraction` is 0, it is a signaling NaN.

2. If bit-22 of the `Fraction` is 1, it is a quiet NaN.

Table 11.2 shows a summarization for these possible results.

The IEEE 754 standard specifies a `binary32` as a data type for a single-precision floating-point number.

Table 11.2. The possible true value for a given single-precision floating point number.

Exponent	Fraction = 0	Fraction ≠ 0	Calculation Equation
00000000	+0, −0	Subnormal Numbers	$(-1)^{Sign} \times 2^{-126} \times (0.0 + Fraction)$
01H~FEH	Normalized Numbers		$(-1)^{Sign} \times 2^{(Exponent-127)} \times (1.0 + Fraction)$
11111111	±infinitive (±∞)	NaN (Signaling or Quiet)	

An example of using the IEEE 754 standard to present a single-precision floating-point number is 11000001011011010001000000000000. The Sign bit is 1, which means that this is a negative floating-point number. The biased exponent, Exponent, is 10000010B = 130D, and the Fraction is 11011010001000000000000B. Based on Eq. (11.3), the true value of this single precision floating-point number is

$$True\ Value = (-1)^1 \times 2^{(30-127)} \times (1.0 + 1 \times 2^{-1} + 1 \times 2^{-2} + 1 \times 2^{-4} + 1 \times 2^{-5} + 1 \times 2^{-7})$$
$$= -(2^3 \times (1.0 + 0.5 + 0.25 + 0.0625 + 0.03125 + 0.0078125 + 0.00048828125))$$
$$= -(2^3 \times 1.85205078125) = -14.81640625$$

To convert −14.81640625 back to the IEEE 754 standard single-precision floating-point format, perform the following operations:

1. Convert 14.81640625 to hexadecimal or binary number, which is 0xE.D1 or 1110.11010001B.

2. Convert this binary number to the normalized format, which is 1.11011010001 × 2³. This is equivalent to move the binary point to the left by 3 bits.

3. Convert the normal exponent 3 to the biased exponent, Exponent, by adding the bias value 127. The biased exponent, Exponent, is 3 + 127 = 130D (10000010B).

4. The Fraction is the significant bits after the decimal point for the normalized format value, which is 11011010001000000000000. The tailed 12 zeros can be added to make this Fraction to be 23 bits.

5. Add the Sign bit 1 to the bit 31 since this is a negative number.

6. The final IEEE 754 standard single-precision floating-point format for this number is Sign-Bit, 1; Exponent, 10000010; Fraction, 11011010001000000000000. Together it is 11000001011011010001000000000000.

Next let's take a look at the double-precision floating point format.

11.2.3 The Double-Precision Floating-Point Data

Similar to IEEE 754 single-precision floating-point format, the double-precision data is also a binary floating-point computer number that occupies 64 bits or eight bytes in the computer memory.

According to the IEEE 754 definition, a double-precision floating point number can be represented as three segments as shown in Figure 11.3; these include the Sign bit (bit 63), Exponent field (11 bits, bits 62~52), and Fraction field (52 bits, bits 51~0).

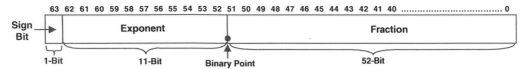

Figure 11.3.   IEEE 754 double-precision floating-point format.

Similar to the single-precision format, when using this double-precision floating-point format to represent a floating-point number, the following points need to be noted:

1. The 1-bit `Sign` field is used to determine the polarity of the floating-point number. A value of 0 on this bit indicates that this floating-point number is a positive one, but a value of 1 means that this floating-point number is a negative number.

2. The 11-bit `Exponent` field is a *biased* exponent value, and a biased value of 1023 must be subtracted from this biased exponent, `Exponent`, to get the real or the true exponent value for the given floating-point number. The reason for using this biased exponent is to enlarge the range of the floating-point numbers.

3. The 52-bit `Fraction` field contains 52-bit binary significant bits (significands) after the decimal point. The key is that between bit 52 and bit 51, or between the `Exponent` and the `Fraction` fields, a binary point exists and this must be kept in mind when convert this double-precision floating-point number to its real value.

The real or the true value of a double-precision floating-point number can be calculated as

$$\text{True Value} = (-1)^{Sign} \times 2^{(\text{Exponent}-1023)} \times (1.0 + Fraction) \tag{11.5}$$

When using Eq. (11.5) to calculate the true value for a given double-precision floating-point number, the following issues must be considered:

1. If the biased exponent, `Exponent`, is in the range $0 < \text{Exponent} < 0x7FF$, the value of the true floating point number is a normalized value and it can be calculated by using Eq. (11.5).

2. If the biased exponent, `Exponent`, is 0, the following possible results are existed:
   - If the `Fraction` is 0 and the `Sign` bit is 0, then the true value is 0 (+0).
   - If the `Fraction` is 0 but the `Sign` bit is 1, then the true value is also 0 (−0).
   - If the `Fraction` is not 0, then the true value is a subnormal or a denormalized value and its true value should be calculated by using Eq. (11.6):

$$\text{True Value} = (-1)^{Sign} \times 2^{-1022} \times (0.0 + Fraction) \tag{11.6}$$

3. If the biased exponent, `Exponent`, is equal to `0x7FF` (011111111111B), the following possible results are existed:
   - If the `Fraction` is 0 and the `Sign` bit is also 0, then the true value is infinitive (+∞).
   - If the `Fraction` is 0 and the `Sign` bit is 1, then the true value is also infinitive (−∞).
   - If the `Fraction` is not 0, then it is a special code or known as NaN (Not a Number).

A NaN value can be categorized into a signaling NaN or a quiet NaN, and this is defined as follows:

1. If bit 51 of the `Fraction` is 0, it is a signaling NaN.
2. If bit 51 of the `Fraction` is 1, it is a quiet NaN.

Table 11.3. The possible true value for a given double-precision floating point number.

Exponent	Fraction = 0	Fraction ≠ 0	Calculation Equation
000H	+0, −0	Subnormal Numbers	$(-1)^{\text{Sign}} \times 2^{-1022} \times (0.0 + \text{Fraction})$
001H~07FEH	Normalized Numbers		$(-1)^{\text{Sign}} \times 2^{(\text{Exponent}-1023)} \times (1.0 + \text{Fraction})$
07FFH	±infinitive (±∞)	NaN (Signaling or Quiet)	

Table 11.3 shows a summarization for these possible results.

The IEEE 754 standard specifies a `binary64` as a data type for a double-precision floating-point number. One point to be noted when dealing with the double-precision floating-point number is that the ARM® Cortex®-M4 MCU does not support this kind of floating-point data.

11.3   THE FPU IN THE CORTEX®-M4 MCU

As we mentioned, the Cortex®-M4F FPU fully supports single-precision floating-point data operations, which include the addition, subtraction, multiplication, division, multiplication and accumulation (MAA), and square root operations. It also provides conversions between fixed-point and floating-point data formats, along with floating-point constant instructions.

Basically the FPU in the Cortex®-M4F system provides the following functions:

- 32-bit instructions for single-precision (C float) data-processing operations.
- Combined multiply and accumulate instructions for increased precision (Fused MAC).
- Hardware support for conversion, addition, subtraction, multiplication with optional accumulate, division, and square-root operation.
- Hardware support for denormals and all IEEE rounding modes.
- 32 dedicated 32-bit single-precision registers, also addressable as 16 double-word registers.
- Decoupled three-stage pipelines.

The Cortex®-M4F floating-point instruction set does not support all operations defined in the IEEE 754-2008 standard. Also the FPU is disabled from a system reset and you must enable it before you can use any floating-point instructions. The processor must be in privileged mode to read from and write to the Coprocessor Access Control (CPAC) register.

11.3.1   The Architecture of the Floating-Point Registers

The Cortex®-M4 MCU provides an optional Floating-Point Unit (FPU). Additional registers are needed to support floating data operations if this FPU is used. These registers include `Floating-Point Data Processing Registers` (FPDPR) and `Floating-Point Status and Control Register` (FPSCR).

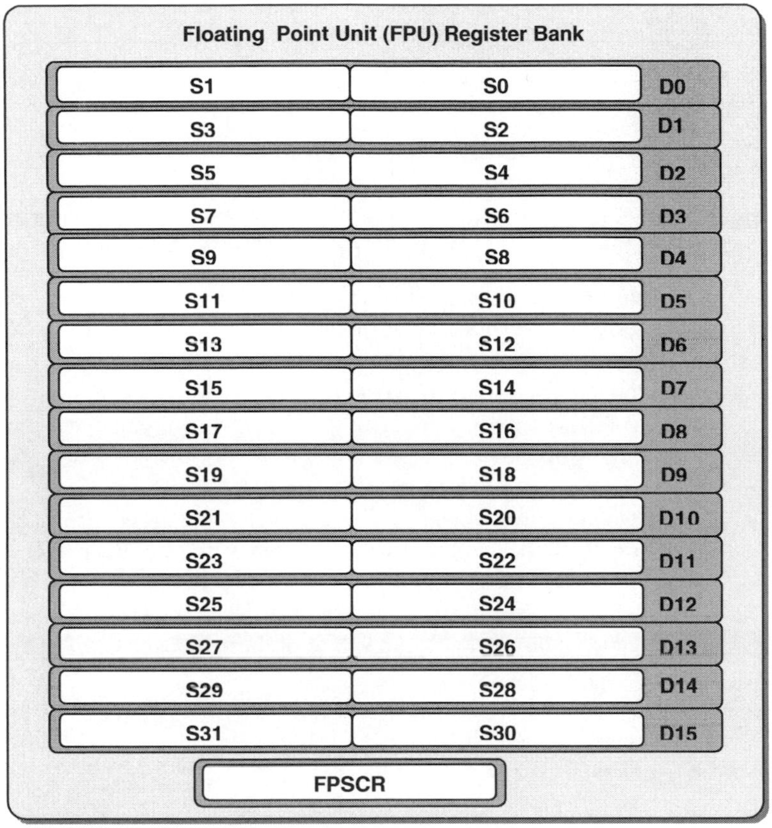

Figure 11.4.   The configuration of the floating-point register bank.

The FPDPR are composed of 32 single-precision registers, S0~S31, or 16 double-precision registers, D0~D15, respectively. Each of the 32-bit single-precision registers S0 to S31 can be accessed using floating point instructions. These registers can also be accessed as a pair or double-precision registers D0 to D15 (64-bit). The configuration of these registers is shown in Figure 11.4. All of these registers make up a so-called floating point register bank.

One point to be noted is that the FPU in the Cortex®-M4 does not support double precision floating-point calculations, but you can still use floating point instructions to transfer double-precision data to the single-precision data via some run-time library functions.

All floating point data calculations are under the control of the `Floating Point Status and Control Register` (FPSCR). This register provides the following control functions:

- Define the floating point operation behaviors.
- Provide status information about the floating-point operation results.

Bits functions on the FPSCR are shown in Figure 11.5.

Bits	31 30 29 28	27	26	25	24	23:22	21:8	7	6.5	4	3	2	1	0
FPSCR	N Z C V		AHP	ND	FZ	RMode		IDC		IXC	UFC	OFC	DZC	IOC

Figure 11.5.   Bit function and structure on FPSCR.

The functions of bits N, Z, C, and V are identical to those in the PSR. The function of each other bit in the FPSCR is (bits 5~6, 8~21 and 27 are reserved) as follows:

- AHP (Bit 26): The value on this bit defines the Alternative Half-Precision format for the floating-point operations. A 0, which is the default value on this bit, is used to define the IEEE half-precision format. A 1 is to define an alternative half-precision format.

- DN (Bit 25): The value on this bit is used to define the default Not a Number (NaN) mode. A 0 means that the NaN operands propagate through to the output of a floating-point operation, and this is the default value. A 1 indicates that any operation including one or more NaNs returns the default NaN.

- FZ (Bit 24): The value on this bit indicates whether the Flush-to-Zero model is enabled or disabled. A value of 0, which is the default value, on this bit means that the FZ model is disabled, otherwise if this bit value is 1, this means that the FZ model is enabled.

- RMode (Bits 23 and 22): These two bits are used to set up the specified rounding mode that is used by all floating-point operational instructions. The values of these bits are:
  - 00—Round to Nearest (RN) mode (default).
  - 01—Round to Plus Infinity (RP) mode.
  - 10—Round to Minus Infinity (RM) mode.
  - 11—Round to Zero (RZ) mode.

- IDC (Bit-7): This bit is used to monitor whether a floating-point exception has occurred or not. A 1 indicated that a floating-point exception has happened, and the result is not within the normalized value range. A 0 means that no floating-point exception occurred. This bit can be cleared by writing 0 to it.

- IXC (Bit-4): This bit is used to detect whether an Inexact Cumulative exception occurred or not. A 1 in this bit indicated that a floating exception has occurred; otherwise a 0 means that no floating-point exception occurred. This bit can be cleared by writing 0 to it.

- UFC (Bit-3): This bit is the Underflow Cumulative exception status bit. A 1 in this bit indicated that an Underflow Cumulative exception has occurred. Otherwise if this bit is 0, this means that no Underflow Cumulative exception has occurred. This bit can be cleared by writing 0 to it.

- OFC (Bit-2): This bit is the Overflow Cumulative exception status bit. A 1 in this bit indicated that an Overflow Cumulative exception has occurred. Otherwise if this bit is 0, which means that no Overflow Cumulative exception has occurred. This bit can be cleared by writing 0 to it.

- DZC (Bit-1): This bit is the Divided by Zero cumulative exception status bit. A 1 in this bit indicated that a Divided by Zero Cumulative exception has occurred. Otherwise if this bit is 0, this means that no Divided by Zero Cumulative exception has occurred. This bit can be cleared by writing 0 to it.

- IOC (Bit-0): This bit is the Invalid Operation cumulative exception status bit. A 1 in this bit indicated that an Invalid Operation Cumulative exception has occurred. Otherwise if this bit is 0, this means that no Invalid Operation Cumulative exception has occurred. This bit can be cleared by writing 0 to it.

In addition to this register bank, some additional registers are provided to support the floating-point data operations, and these registers include:

- Coprocessor Access Control Register (CPACR) in the System Control Block (SCB).
- Floating-Point Context Control Register (FPCCR).
- Floating-Point Context Address Register (FPCAR).
- Floating-Point Default Status Control Register (FPDSCR).
- Media and FP Feature Register 0 (MVFR0).
- Media and FP Feature Register 1 (MVFR1).

In the ARM® Cortex®-M4 system, a set of floating-point instructions are used to perform floating-point operations and floating-point data transfers, instead of using the coprocessor access instructions.

The CPACR register allows the users to enable or disable the FPU by using SCB→CPACR instruction in the CMSIS Core. Since the Cortex®-M4 MCU system does not use any coprocessor-related instruction to access and control the floating-point operations, we will not provide very detailed discussions about these registers in this section. Refer to related documents to get more details for these registers.

Now let's have a closer look at the operation modes of the FPU.

11.3.2 The FPU Operational Modes

In the ARM® Cortex®-M4 MCU system, the FPU is considered as a coprocessor and all operations related to this FPU belong to Coprocessor Data Operations (CDP). This coprocessor provides three operation modes to handle and accommodate a variety of operations.

- `Full-Compliance Mode`: In this operation mode, the FPU processes all operations according to the IEEE 754 standard in hardware.
- `Flush-to-Zero Mode`: Setting the FZ bit of the Floating-Point Status and Control (FPSC) register to enable Flush-to-Zero mode. In this mode, the FPU treats all subnormal input operands of arithmetic CDP operations as zeros in the operation. Exceptions that result from a zero operand are signaled appropriately. Some floating-point operations, such as absolute (VABS), negative (VNEG), and move immediate (VMOV), are not considered arithmetic CDP operations and are not affected by Flush-to-Zero mode. A result that is tiny, as described in the IEEE 754 standard, where the destination precision is smaller in magnitude than the minimum normal value before rounding, is replaced with a zero. The IDC bit in FPSC indicates when an input flush occurs. The UFC bit in FPSC indicates when a result flush occurs.
- `Default NaN Mode`: Setting the DN bit in the FPSC register enables default NaN mode. In this mode, the result of any arithmetic data processing operation that involves an input NaN, or that generates a NaN result, returns the default NaN. Propagation of the fraction bits is maintained only by VABS, VNEG, and VMOV operations. All other CDP operations ignore any information in the fraction bits of an input NaN.

Next let's take care of the implementations of the FPU in the Cortex®-M4 system.

11.4 IMPLEMENTING THE FLOATING-POINT UNIT

In the ARM® Cortex®-M4F MCU system, all FPU-related operations are performed by using a set of floating-point instructions. The Cortex®-M4F floating-point instruction set does not support all operations defined in the IEEE 754-2008 standard. Most unsupported operations include, but are not limited to, the following operations:

- Floating point remainder, such as $z = f\mathrm{mod}(x, y)$
- Round floating-point number to integer-valued floating-point number
- Binary-to-decimal conversions
- Decimal-to-binary conversions
- Direct comparison of single-precision and double-precision values

The Cortex®-M4 FPU supports fused MAC operations as described in the IEEE standard. For complete implementation of the IEEE 754-2008 standard, floating-point functionality must be cooperated with library run-time functions.

11.4.1 Floating-Point Support in CMSIS-Core

The CMSIS-Core provides a set of macros, data structure, and instructions to support the FPU-related operations in the Cortex®-M4 MCU system. Two of often-used macros are:

- __FPU_PRESENT
- __FPU_USED

If the FPU is present in the Cortex®-M4 MCU system, the macro __FPU_PRESENT is set to 1 by the device specific header file. If the __FPU_PRESENT is 0, the __FPU_USED must be also cleared to 0 to indicate that no FPU is presented and used in this Cortex®-M4 system.

All FPU-related data structures are available if __FPU_PRESENT is set to 1. The system initialization function SystemInit() is executed to enable the FPU if the __FPU_USED is set to 1 by writing to the CPACR when a reset is generated and the reset handler is executed.

Some popular FPU-related instructions supported by CMSIS-Core include the SCB→CPACR that is used to access the Coprocessor Access Control Register (CPACR), FPU→FPSCR that is used to access the FPSCR, FPU→FPCCR that is used to access the Floating-Point Context Control Register (FPCCR), FPU→FPCAR that is used to access the Floating-Point Context Address Register (FPCAR), and Floating-Point Default Status Control Register (FPDSCR) and Media and FP Feature Registers (MVFR0 and MVFR1).

By default, the FPU is presented and used in most Cortex®-M4 related IDEs. For example, in Keil® MDK-ARM µVersion5 IDE, the FPU is automatically selected and used as this IDE is opened, as shown in Figure 11.6.

The Use FPU is selected in the Floating-Point Hardware combo box in the Target wizard when the Keil® MDK-ARM µVersion5 IDE is opened.

For the gcc users, you need to type some special command with some options to activate the FPU in that IDE.

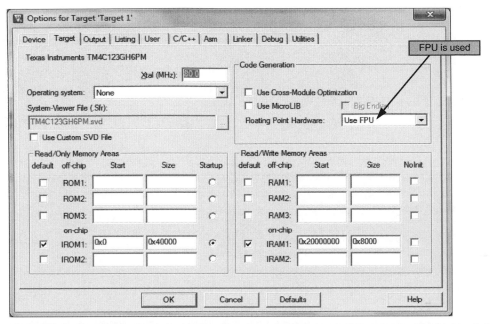

Figure 11.6. The FPU is automatically used in MDK-ARM µVersion5 IDE. Reproduced with permission from ARM® Limited. Copyright © ARM Limited.

11.4.2 Floating-Point Programming in the TM4C123GH6PM MCU System

In TM4C123GH6PM MCU system, several control registers are used to support the FPU operations, and these registers are:

- Coprocessor Access Control Register (CPACR)
- Floating-Point Context Control Register (FPCCR)
- Floating-Point Context Address Register (FPCAR)
- Floating-Point Default Status Control Register (FPDSCR)

After a system reset operation, the FPU is disabled. You must enable it before you can use any floating-point instructions. The processor must be in privileged mode to read from and write to the Coprocessor Access Control (CPAC) register.

Ideally, a total of about 16 coprocessors can be defined in an ARM® MCU system, but the FPU is defined as coprocessor 10 (CP10) and 11 (CP11) in the Cortex®-M4 MCU system by using this CPACR. Since no other coprocessor is available, both CP10 and CP11 are used for the FPU. When programming this register, the coding for CP11 and CP10 must be identical to make sure to select and use the FPU. As we mentioned, one can use SCB→CPACR to access this register.

Let's have a closer look at these registers in the next section.

Coprocessor Access Control Register (CPACR)

31	24 23 22 21 20 19			0
Reserved Bits 31–24	CP11	CP10	Reserved Bits 19–0	

Figure 11.7.   Bit configuration for the CPAC register.

11.4.2.1 FPU in the Direct Register Access Model

The so-called Direct Register Model (DRA) is to access and assign the values to these FPU related control registers directly.

First let's take care of the Coprocessor Access Control Register (CPACR).

Figure 11.7 shows the bit configuration for this register.

Two bit fields, CP11 (bits 23:22) and CP10 (bits 21:20), have the same following bit values and functions:

1. 0x0: Access Denied (no any access to this FPU allowed).
2. 0x1: Privileged Access Only.
3. 0x2: Reserved (equivalent to no access).
4. 0x3: Full Access.

By default the CP11 and CP10 bit fields are zeros after a system reset, and this setting disables the FPU functions to allow lower power dissipations on the MCU. To enable the FPU operations, one can set CP11 and CP10 fields to enable the FPU to be fully accessed as

$$SCB \rightarrow CPACR = 0x00F00000;$$

In this setting, both CP11 and CP10 fields are set to 11 to enable the FPU to be fully accessed.

The bit configuration of the Floating-Point Context Control Register (FPCCR) is shown in Figure 11.8. The bit functions of this register are shown in Table 11.4.

The FPCC register is used to set or return the FPU-related control data. These control data include the top six settings, which contain the Automatic State Preservation Enable to automatically preserve and restore the hardware state for floating-point context on exception and exit, the Lazy State Preservation Enable to allow lazy state to be preserved automatically for floating-point context, the Monitor Ready to enable the Debug Monitor to set the MON_PEND bit when the floating-point stack is allocated, the Bus Fault Ready to set the BusFault bit to pending the BusFault handler as the floating-point stack is allocated, the Memory Management Fault Ready to set the MemManage handler to the pending state as the floating-point stack is allocated, and the Hard Fault Ready to set the HardFault handler to the pending state when the floating-point stack is allocated.

The lower three data are used to show the running status for the FPU operations. These include the Thread Mode that is used to indicate whether the current running mode is the Thread mode or not, the User Privilege Level that is used to indicate whether the user has the privilege level to run the user's program, and the Lazy State

Floating Point Context Control Register (FPCCR)

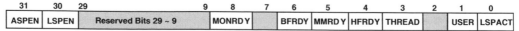

31	30	29	9	8	7	6	5	4	3	2	1	0
ASPEN	LSPEN	Reserved Bits 29 ~ 9		MONRDY		BFRDY	MMRDY	HFRDY	THREAD		USER	LSPACT

Figure 11.8.   Bit configuration for the FPCC register.

Table 11.4. Bit value and its function for FPCC register.

Bit	Name	Reset	Function
31	ASPEN	1	Automatic State Preservation Enable: When set, enables the use of the FRACTV bit in the CONTROL register on execution of a floating-point instruction. This results in automatic hardware state preservation and restoration, for floating-point context, on exception entry and exit.
30	LSPEN	1	Lazy State Preservation Enable: When set, enables automatic lazy state preservation for floating-point context.
29:9	Reserved	0x00	Reserved.
8	MONRDY	0	Monitor Ready: When set, the Debug Monitor is enabled and priority permits setting MON_PEND when the floating-point stack frame was allocated.
7	Reserved	0	Reserved.
6	BFRDY	0	Bus Fault Ready: When set, the BusFault is enabled and priority permitted setting the BusFault handler to the pending state when the floating-point stack frame was allocated.
5	MMRDY	0	Memory Management Fault Ready: When set, the MemManage is enabled and priority permitted setting the MemManage handler to the pending state when the floating-point stack frame was allocated.
4	HFRDY	0	Hard Fault Ready When set, priority permitted setting the HardFault handler to the pending state when the floating-point stack frame was allocated.
3	THREAD	0	Thread Mode: When set, mode was Thread Mode when the floating-point stack frame was allocated.
2	Reserved	0	Reserved.
1	USER	0	User Privilege Level: When set, privilege level was user when the floating-point stack frame was allocated.
0	LSPACT	0	Lazy State Preservation Active: When set, Lazy State preservation is active. Floating-point stack frame has been allocated but saves the state to it has been deferred.

`Preservation Active` that is used to indicate whether the lazy preservation is active or not.

The FPCA register holds the address of the unpopulated floating-point register space allocated on an exception stack frame. This is a 32-bit register, but only the top 29 bits (31:3) are used to hold the address of the unpopulated floating point register space used in the stack space.

The FPDSC register is used to hold the default values for the Floating-Point Status Control (FPSC) register. The bit configuration of the Floating-Point Default Status Control Register (FPDSCR) is shown in Figure 11.9.

For the upper three bits, AHP (bit 26), DN (bit 25), and FZ (bit 24), each bit holds the default value for the corresponding bit, AHP, DN, and FZ, in the Floating-Point Status Control Register (FPSCR). The bit field RMODE (bits 23:22) in this register also hold the

Floating Point Default Status Control Register (FPDSCR)

31	26	25	24	23 22		0
Reserved Bits 31–27	AHP	DN	FZ	RMODE	Reserved Bits 21–0	

Figure 11.9. Bit configuration for the FPDSC register.

default values for the corresponding bit field RMODE in the FPSCR. The available bit values and the function values for this bit field are:

- 0x0: Round to Nearest (RN) mode.
- 0x1: Round towards Plus Infinity (RP) mode.
- 0x2: Round towards Minus Infinity (RM) mode.
- 0x3: Round towards Zero (RZ) mode.

Next let's have a closer look at the FPU-related API functions provided by the TivaWare™ Peripheral Driver Library.

11.4.2.2 FPU in the Software Driver Model

In the TM4C123GH6PM MCU system, the TivaWare™ Peripheral Driver Library provides some API functions for manipulating the behavior of the floating point unit in the Cortex®-M4 microprocessor.

The behavior of the floating-point unit can also be adjusted and specified to the different formats, such as the half-precision and single-precision floating-point values, the handle of NaN values, the flush-to-zero mode that sacrifices the full IEEE 754 compliance for execution speed, and the rounding mode for results.

This driver is contained in C source file fpu.c and the header file fpu.h, and both files are located at the default folder C:\ti\TivaWrae_C_Series-2.0.1.11577 \driverlib.

These FPU API functions can be divided into the following three groups based on their functions:

1. Enable and disable the FPU: FPUEnable() and FPUDisable().
2. Control how the floating-point state is stored on the stack when interrupts occur: FPUStackingEnable(), FPULazyStackingEnable(), and FPUStackingDisable().
3. Adjust the operation of the floating-point unit: FPUHalfPrecisionModeSet(), FPU-NaNModeSet(), FPUFlushToZeroModeSet(), and FPURoundingModeSet().

Table 11.5 shows most of these API functions with the related arguments. All FPU interrupt-related API functions are not provided in this library and therefore they are not supported in this library.

11.4.3 A FPU Example Project Using the Direct Register Access Model

In this section we build an example FPU project to access the FPU-related registers directly to perform some floating-point operations.

Open the Keil® μVersion5 IDE and create a new project named DRAFPU under the folder C:\ARM Class Projects\Chapter 11. Create a new C source file DRAFPU.c and enter the codes shown in Figure 11.10 into the source file.

Table 11.5. The FPU enable and disable API functions.

API Function	Parameter	Description
void FPUEnable(void)	None	Enable the floating-point unit, allowing the floating-point instructions to be executed. This function must be called prior to performing any hardware floating-point operations.
void FPUDisable(void)	None	Disable the floating-point unit, preventing floating-point instructions from executing.
void FPUStackingEnable(void)	None	Enable the stacking of floating-point registers s0–s15 when an interrupt is generated and handled. When enabled, space is reserved on the stack for the floating-point context and the floating-point state is saved into this stack space. Upon return from the interrupt, the floating point context is restored.
void FPULazyStackingEnable (void)	None	Enable the lazy stacking of floating-point registers s0–s15 when an interrupt is handled. When lazy stacking is enabled, space is reserved on the stack for the floating-point context, but the floating-point state is not saved. If a floating-point instruction is executed from within the interrupt context, the floating-point context is first saved into the space reserved on the stack. On completion of the interrupt handler, the floating-point context is only restored if it was saved (as the result of executing a floating-point instruction).
void FPUStackingDisable (void)	None	Disable the stacking of floating-point registers s0–s15 when an interrupt is generated and handled. When floating-point context stacking is disabled, floating-point operations performed in an interrupt handler destroy the floating-point context of the main thread of execution.
void FPUHalfPrecisionModeSet (uint32_t ui32Mode)	ui32Mode is the format for half-precision floating-point value, which is either FPU_HALF_IEEE or FPU_HALF_ALTERNATE.	Select between the IEEE half-precision floating-point representation and the Cortex-M processor alternative representation. The alternative representation has a larger range but does not have a way to encode infinity (positive or negative) or NaN (quiet or signaling). The default setting is the IEEE format.
void FPUNaNModeSet (uint32_t ui32Mode)	ui32Mode is the mode for NaN results; which is either FPU_NAN_PROPAGATE or FPU_NAN_DEFAULT.	Select the handling of NaN results during floating-point computations. NaNs can either propagate (the default), or they can return the default NaN.
void FPUFlushToZeroModeSet (uint32_t ui32Mode)	ui32Mode is the flush-to-zero mode; which is either FPU_FLUSH_TO_ZERO_DIS or FPU_FLUSH_TO_ZERO_EN.	Enable or disables the flush-to-zero mode of the floating-point unit. When disabled (the default), the floating-point unit is fully IEEE compliant. When Enabled, values close to zero are treated as zero, greatly improving the execution speed at the expense of some accuracy (as well as IEEE compliance).
void FPURoundingModeSet (uint32_t ui32Mode)	ui32Mode is the rounding mode.	Select the rounding mode for floating-point results. After a floating point operation, the result is rounded toward the specified value. The default mode is FPU_ROUND_NEAREST. The following rounding modes are available (as specified by ui32Mode): FPU_ROUND_NEAREST—round toward the nearest value. FPU_ROUND_POS_INF—round toward positive infinity. FPU_ROUND_NEG_INF—round toward negative infinity. FPU_ROUND_ZERO—round toward zero.

Let's have a closer look at this piece of codes to see how it works.

1. The codes in lines 4~7 are used to include all necessary system header files to be used in this project. The `<math.h>` header file is specially used for the floating-point function `sinf()`.

2. The codes in lines 8 and 9 are used to declare two user-defined constants, M_PI, and the length of the floating point array gSData[].

3. The `main()` program starts at line 10.

4. Two local variables, `count` and `fRadians`, along with a data array `gSData[]`, are declared in lines 12 and 13. These variables are used as the loop counter and intermediate

```
1  //******************************************************************************************
2  // DRAFPU.c - Main Application File for the DRAFPU Project
3  //******************************************************************************************
4  #include <stdint.h>
5  #include <stdbool.h>
6  #include <math.h>
7  #include "TM4C123GH6PM.h"

8  #define M_PI      3.14159265358979323846
9  #define sLength  100

10 int main(void)
11 {
12    int32_t count = 0;
13    float fRadians,  gSData[sLength];

14    FPU->FPCCR |= 0xC0000000;                    // set ASPEN & LSPEN bits to enable auto HW & Lazy set/restore
15    SCB->CPACR = 0x00F00000;                     // enable FPU
16    fRadians = ((2 * M_PI)/sLength);

17    while(count < sLength)
18    {
19      gSData[count] = sinf(fRadians * count);
20      count++;
21    }

22    while(1){}
23 }
```

Figure 11.10.   The detailed codes for the project DARFPU.

value holder as well as the data collector of the calculated results for the floating-point data.

5. The ASPEN and the LSPEN bits on the FPU Context Control Register (FPCCR) are set to 1 to enable the hardware state and the lazy state to be automatically preserved and restored for the floating-point context in line 14.

6. In line 15, the bit field CP11 and CP10 in the Coprocessor Access Control Register (CPACR) are set to 0xFF to enable the co-processor (FPU) to begin its normal operations.

7. The unit radian degree fRadians is calculated as $2\pi/\text{sLength}$, which is 0.2π, in line 16.

8. A limited while() loop starts at line 17. This loop is to repeatedly update the unit radian degree fRadians by incrementing it by 0.2π, calculate the sinusoidal result for that updated fRadians, and assign them to the data array gSData[] in lines 17~19. Then the loop counter count in updated by 1 in line 20. This loop can be replaced by a for() loop. The difference between the sin() and the sinf() function in the C codes is that the former accepts only a double-precision value and return a double-precision value. However, the latter only accepts the single floating point value and returns a single floating-point value.

9. In line 22, an infinitive while() loop is used to enable users to check the calculation results stored in the data array gSData[] from the Call Stack + Locals window.

Before the project can be run, one needs to set up the environment to build and run the project to check the running results for this project. The only environment set up is to select the correct debugger driver for this project. Perform the following operations to select the correct debugger driver:

- Going to Project|Options for Target 'Target 1' menu item to open the Options wizard.
- On the opened Options wizard, click on the Debug tab.

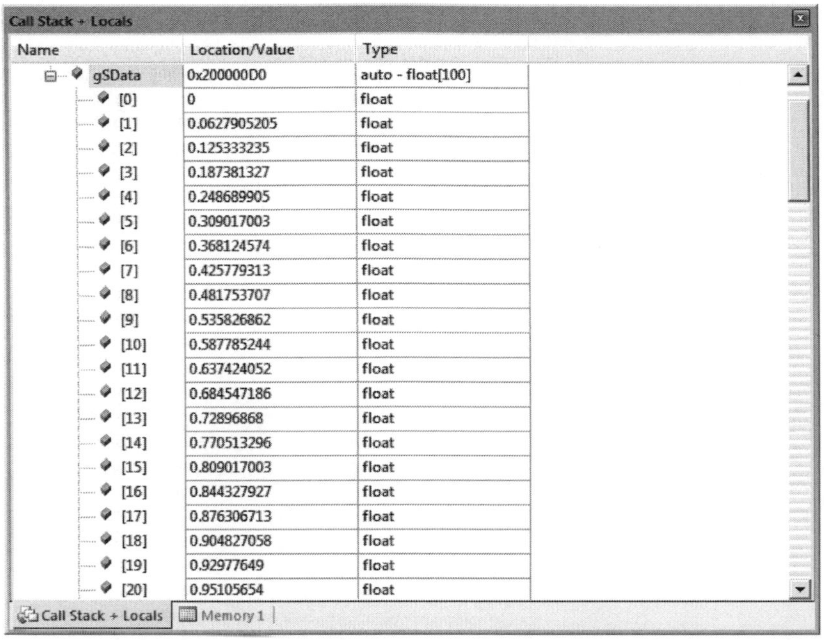

Call Stack + Locals

Name	Location/Value	Type
gSData	0x200000D0	auto - float[100]
[0]	0	float
[1]	0.0627905205	float
[2]	0.125333235	float
[3]	0.187381327	float
[4]	0.248689905	float
[5]	0.309017003	float
[6]	0.368124574	float
[7]	0.425779313	float
[8]	0.481753707	float
[9]	0.535826862	float
[10]	0.587785244	float
[11]	0.637424052	float
[12]	0.684547186	float
[13]	0.72896868	float
[14]	0.770513296	float
[15]	0.809017003	float
[16]	0.844327927	float
[17]	0.876306713	float
[18]	0.904827058	float
[19]	0.92977649	float
[20]	0.95105654	float

Call Stack + Locals | Memory 1

Figure 11.11. The running result of the project DRAFPU. (Reproduced with permission from ARM® Limited. Copyright © ARM Limited.)

- Make sure that the debugger shown in the `Use:` box is `Stellaris ICDI`. Otherwise you can click on the dropdown arrow to select this debugger from the list.

Now run the project by going to `Debug`|`Start/Stop Debug Session` and the `Debug`|Run menu items. In order to check the running result, one needs to go to `Debug`|`Stop` menu item to stop the project. On the opened `Call Stack+Locals` window, expand the data array `gSData[]` and you can find all 100 floating point results, as shown in Figure 11.11.

If plotting the data array `gSData[]`, the graphic result is a sinusoidal signal with one cycle time of 2π, as shown in Figure 11.12.

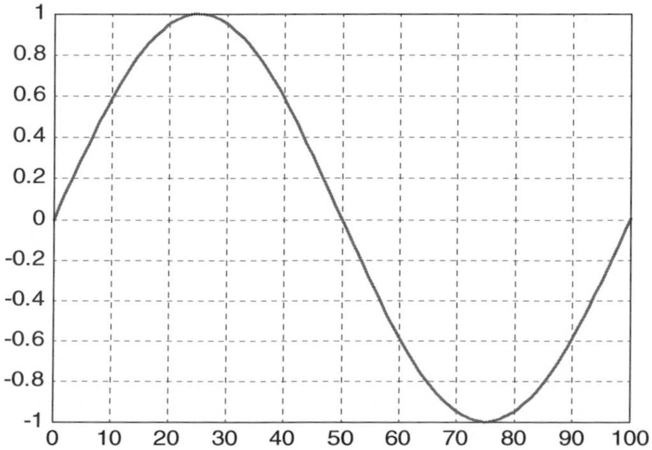

Figure 11.12. The plotting result for the data array gSData[]. (Reprinted with the permission of MathWorks, Inc.)

11.5 CHAPTER SUMMARY

One of the most important differences between the Cortex®-M4 MCU and Cortex®-M3 MCU is that an optional Floating Point Unit (FPU) is added into the Cortex®-M4 Core to enhance the floating-point data operations. The Cortex®-M4 FPU implements the ARMv7E-M architecture with FPv4-SP extensions. It provides floating-point computation functionality that is compliant with the *ANSI/IEEE Standard 754-2008, IEEE Standard for Binary Floating-Point Arithmetic*. In this chapter we concentrated our discussions on this FPU element with a completed and detailed analysis for this unit.

An introduction and overview about the floating point unit are given in Section 11.1. Three types of the floating-point data formats, half-precision, single-precision, and double-precision, are discussed in Section 11.2 with some real examples.

A detailed discussion about the FPU applied in the Cortex®-M4 MCU is provided in Section 11.3. This discussion includes the architecture of most popular FPU-related registers and FPU operational modes. The implementations of the Floating Point Unit are given in Section 11.4. This section contains the Floating-Point support in CMSIS-Core, Floating-Point programming in TM4C123GH6PM MCU system, and a real FPU example project using the Direct Register Access model.

HOMEWORK

I. True/False Selections

_____**1.** One of the most important differences between the Cortex®-M4 MCU and Cortex®-M3 MCU is that an optional FPU is added into the Cortex®-M4 Core to enhance the floating point data operations.

_____**2.** If a floating-point instruction is executed but the FPU is disabled, no fault would be generated.

_____**3.** The Cortex®-M4F FPU fully supports half-precision, single-precision and double-precision floating-point data operations.

_____**4.** The FPU can generate an interrupt when one of several exceptions occurs. These exceptions include the underflow, overflow, divide by zero, invalid operation, abnormal input, and inexact exception.

_____**5.** In the half-precision floating point format, it includes one `Sign` bit (bit 15), 5 `Exponent` bits (bits 14~10) and 10 `Fraction` bits (bits 9~0).

_____**6.** If the biased exponent, `Exponent`, is 0 and if the `Fraction` is not 0, then the true value for a half-precision number is `True Value` = $(-1)^{\text{Sign}} \times 2^{(\text{Exponent-15})} \times (1.0 + \text{Fraction})$.

_____**7.** If the biased exponent, `Exponent`, is equal to `0xFF` (11111111B) and if the `Fraction` is not 0, then it is a special code or known as NaN (Not a Number).

_____**8.** The FPU is disabled from a system reset and you must enable it before you can use any floating-point instructions. The processor must be in privileged mode to read from and write to the Coprocessor Access Control (CPAC) register.

_____**9.** In the Cortex®-M4 MCU system, the FPU is defined as coprocessor 10 (CP10) and 11 (CP11). The coding for CP11 and CP10 bit fields in the CPACR can be different to make sure to select and use the FPU.

_____**10.** For complete implementations of the IEEE 754-2008 standard, the floating-point functionality must be cooperated with some library run-time functions.

II. Multiple Choices

1. Which one of the following statements is true?

   a. An optional FPU in the Cortex®-M4 is to enhance the floating point data operations.

   b. The Cortex®-M4 FPU implements ARMv7E-M architecture with FPv4-SP extensions.

   c. It is compliant with the *ANSI/IEEE Standard 754-2008*.

   d. All of the above.

2. The Cortex®-M4F FPU fully supports _____ .

   a. Half-precision and single-precision floating-point formats

   b. Single-precision and double-precision floating-point formats

   c. Only a

   d. Both a and b

3. The usage of the FPU in the Cortex®-M4 MCU system can be divided into two categories: _____.

   a. Full-Compliance Mode, Flush-to-Zero Mode

   b. Default NaN Mode, Normal Mode

   c. In the main thread of the program, inside an interrupt handler

   d. Inside an interrupt handler, in the Normal Mode

4. The FPU can generate an interrupt when one of several exceptions occurs. These exceptions include: _____.

   a. A NaN result is obtained.

   b. The Exponent is 0.

   c. The Fraction is 0.

   d. An overflow or an underflow occurred.

5. A single-precision floating-point number is composed of _____.

   a. 1 Sign bit, 8 Exponent bits and 10 Fraction bits

   b. 1 Sign bit, 5 Exponent bits and 10 Fraction bits

   c. 1 Sign bit, 8 Exponent bits and 23 Fraction bits

   d. 1 Sign bit, 8 Exponent bits and 52 Fraction bits

6. The true value for a half-precision floating-point number 0011100010010100 is _____.

   a. 0.576256256

   b. 0.572265625

   c. 0.672256256

   d. 0.472256256

7. The half-precision floating-point presentation for the number 15.5 is _____.

   a. 1100101111000000

   b. 0100101111111111

   c. 1100101111111111

   d. 0100101111000000

8. The FPU can perform _ operation modes and they are _____.

   a. 2, Full-Compliance Mode and Flush-to-Zero Mode

   b. 3, Full-Compliance Mode, Default NaN Mode and Flush-to-Zero Mode

   c. 4, Full-Compliance Mode, NaN Mode, Normal Mode and Flush-to-Zero Mode

   d. 5, Full Mode, Default Mode, NaN Mode, Normal Mode and Flush-to-Zero Mode

9. Two often-used macros defined in the Cortex®-M4 FPU are _____.

   a. __FPU_USED, __FPU_PRESENT

   b. __FPU_NOT_USED, __FPU_SHOW

   c. __FPU_WORK, __FPU_ON

   d. __FPU_DONE, __FPU_OK

10. Set CP11 and CP10 bit fields to enable the FPU to be fully accessed as _____.

   a. 0x0

   b. 0x1

   c. 0x2

   d. 0x3

III. Exercises

1. Provide a brief description about the FPU used in the Cortex®-M4 Core.

2. Provide a brief description about the half-precision format.

3. Provide a brief description about the single-precision format.

4. Provide a brief discussion about the FPU operation modes.

5. Provide a brief discussion about the popular control registers used for the FPU.

IV. Practical Laboratory

Laboratory 11: ARM® Cortex®-M4 Floating Point Unit (FPU)

11.0 Goals   This laboratory exercise allows students to learn and practice ARM® Cortex®-M4 floating-point unit (FPU) and related operations. Some FPU-related API functions are used in this lab to enable students to familiar them with these functions.

   1. Program Lab11_1 or SDFPU lets students use some FPU-related API functions to access some FPU registers to perform desired floating-point data operations.

After completion of this program, students should understand the basic architecture and operational procedure for the FPU installed in the TM4C123GH6PM MCU system. They should be able to code some sophisticated programs to perform desired FPU-related operations with specified algorithms.

11.1 Lab11_1

11.1.1 Goal   In this project, students will use the SD model to build a floating-point data program to perform desired floating-point data operations. Some FPU-related API functions are to be used in this lab project to enable students to familiar them with these functions and apply them in the real applications.

The advantage of using these API functions to access and operate the FPU related registers is that some complicated registers structures and bit-field values can be avoided to improve the coding efficiency and coding process seed.

11.1.2 Data Assignment and Hardware Configuration   No data assignment and hardware configuration are needed for this lab project.

11.1.3 Development of the Source Code   Perform the following operations to complete this project:

1. Create a new project named SDFPU in the folder C:\ARM Lab Projects\Chapter 11 \SDFPU and a new C source file SDFPU.c.

2. Place the following system header files and macros into this source file:

```
#include <stdint.h>
#include <stdbool.h>
#include <math.h>
#include "inc/hw_memmap.h"
#include "inc/hw_types.h"
#include "driverlib/fpu.h"
#include "driverlib/sysctl.h"
```

3. Use #define to define M_PI as 3.14159265358979323846.

4. Use #define to define a variable sLength as 100.

5. Inside the main() program, declare one unit32_t variable count and one float variable fRadian. Then declare another float data array gSData[100];.

6. Use the API function FPULazyStackingEnable() to set the ASPEN and LSPEN bits on the FPU Context Control Register (FPCCR) to enable the hardware state and the lazy state to be automatically preserved and restored for the floating point context.

7. Call the API function FPUEnable() to set the bit fields CP11 and CP10 in the Coprocessor Access Control Register (CPACR) to 0xFF to enable the coprocessor (FPU) to begin its normal operations.

8. Use the code line fRadians = ((2 * M_PI)/sLength) to get the unit radian degree.

9. Use a for() loop with the variable count as the loop counter to repeatedly calculate the sinusoidal value for each radian degree unit, and assign them to the data array gSData[].

10. Use an infinitive while() loop to check the running result of this project.

11.1.4 Set Up the Environment to Build and Run the Project   To build and run the project, one needs to perform the following operations to set up the environments:

- Select the Stellaris ICDI debugger in the Debug tab under the Project|Options for Target 'Target 1' menu item.

- Add the system header files path: C:\ti\TivaWare_C_Series-2.0.1.11577 via the C/C++ tab in the Options for Target 'Target 1' under the Project menu item.

- Add the TivaWare™ Peripheral Driver Library file driverlib.lib into the project. The file is located at C:\ti\TivaWare_C_Series-2.0.1.11577\driverlib\rvmdk.

Now you can build and run the project. Then you can check the running result of this project by expanding the gSData[] array from the Call Stack+Locals window.

Chapter 12

ARM® Memory Protection Unit (MPU)

As we discussed in Chapter 2, both Cortex®-M3 and Cortex®-M4 MCU support an optional feature called the Memory Protection Unit (MPU). In fact, the MPU can be considered as a programmable device used to:

- Divide the memory space into several (eight) regions that can be used for the different applications with different access levels.
- Define the memory access permissions to enable different memory regions to be accessed in either privileged level or full access level.
- Define the memory attributes as bufferable or catcheable regions.

Each memory region has its own programmable starting addresses, sizes, and settings. The MPU also supports the background region feature.

One point to be noted is that there is no need to set up the memory regions for the Private Peripheral Bus (PPB) address ranges and the Vector Table, including the System Control Space SCS. Accessing to PPB, which includes the MPU, NVIC, SysTick and ITM, are always allowed in the privileged state and the vector fetches are always permitted by the MPU.

The MPU can make an embedded system more robust and secure by:

- Preventing applications from corrupting stack or data memory used by other tasks.
- Preventing unprivileged tasks from accessing some peripherals that can be critical to the system applications.
- Defining the SRAM or RAM regions as non-executable to prevent code injection attacks.

In summary, the MPU is a programmable security device used to protect the system memory and the user's memory spaces from corrupting and attacking by undesired tasks.

12.1 OVERVIEW AND INTRODUCTION

The Memory Protection Unit (MPU) is an optional component in the ARM® Cortex®-M4 MCU. This component is not used in most applications and can be ignored. The main purpose of using this MCU is to protect memory regions by defining different access

Practical Microcontroller Engineering with ARM® Technology, First Edition. Ying Bai.
© 2016 by The Institute of Electrical and Electronics Engineers, Inc. Published 2016 by John Wiley & Sons, Inc.
Companion Website: www.wiley.com/go/armbai

permissions in privileged and unprivileged access levels for some embedded operating systems (OS).

The MPU is a programmable unit and can be programmed up to eight regions. In some simple applications, the MPU can be programmed to protect certain memory regions only, for example, to make some memory regions read only.

In the Tiva™ for C Series LaunchPad™ evaluation board, TM4C123GXL, the MPU has been defined with the following protection functions:

- The memory attributes affect the behavior of memory accesses to the region. The Cortex®-M4 MPU defines eight separate memory regions, 0~7, and a background region accessible only from privileged mode. The background region has the same memory access attributes as the default memory map.

- When memory regions overlap, a memory access is affected by the attributes of the region with the highest number. For example, if a transfer address is within the address region defined for region 1 and region 4, the region 4 settings will be used.

- Regions of 256 bytes or more are divided into 8 equal-sized subregions.

- MPU definitions for all regions include:
  - Location
  - Size
  - Access permissions
  - Memory attributes

- Accessing a prohibited region causes a memory management fault.

- The Cortex®-M4 MPU memory map is unified, meaning that instruction accesses and data accesses have the same region settings.

- If a program accesses a memory location that is prohibited by the MPU, the processor generates a memory management fault, causing a fault exception and possibly causing termination of the process in an OS environment.

One also needs to define the fault handler for either the HardFault or MemManage (Memory Management) fault. The MemManage exception by default is disabled, and one can enable this by setting the MEMFAULTENA bit in the System Handler Control and State Register (SHCSR) with the CMSIS-Core supported instructions.

The MemManage handler, `void MemManage_Handler(void)`, should be defined in the user's program if the MemManage exception is enabled. Also the HardFault exception handler, `void HardFault_Handler(void)`, should always be defined even if the MemManage exception is enabled.

The MPU needs to be programmed and enabled before it can be used in any application. If the MPU is not enabled or programmed, all MPU regions can be overlapped.

12.2 IMPLEMENTATION OF THE MPU

Depending on the different applications, the MPU can be used in several different ways.

For a system without any embedded OS, the MPU can be configured to have a static feature, and this includes the following functions:

1. Configure a RAM or SRAM region as a read-only region to prevent important program data from attacking or corrupting.

2. Make a part or a portion of a RAM or SRAM region at the bottom of the stack inaccessible to detect stack overflow.

3. Set a SRAM or RAM region as non-executable to prevent code injection attacks.

4. Define the memory attributes that can be used by system level catch or the memory controllers.

For a system with an embedded OS, the MPU can be configured to make each application to have its own MPU settings, which includes:

1. Set memory access permissions to the different levels for the stack operations of all applications to enable each application to access its own stack space to prevent stack corruptions of other stacks if the stack leaking situation occurred.

2. Set memory access permissions to limit any application to only access to a limited number of peripherals to avoid any conflict among peripherals.

3. Set memory access permissions to limit each application to access its own data to prevent any possible data corruption.

The static configuration is not limited to be used by a system without an embedded OS. A system with an embedded OS can also be configured with a static feature.

In order to use MPU to protect a memory system, we need to have the basic knowledge about the memory requirements and properties.

12.2.1 Memory Regions, Types, and Attributes

The memory map and the programming of the TM4C123GH6PM MPU splits the memory map into different regions, as shown in Figure 6.14 and Table 6.11 in Chapter 6. Each region has a defined memory type, and some regions have additional memory attributes. The memory type and attributes determine the behavior of accesses to the region.

In order to correctly and effectively access the desired memory region to perform the selected operations, we need to have a clear and fully picture about the memory requirements and some important memory properties.

We have provided detailed discussions about these memory requirements and properties in Section 6.5 in Chapter 6. Refer to that section to get more details for this issue.

In fact, the MPU is configured and controlled by a set of registers. Let's first have a closer look at these registers and their functions. The MPU registers can only be accessed from the privileged mode.

12.2.2 MPU Configuration and Control Registers

The MPU contains 11 registers, and all of these registers are located at the System Control Space (SCS) with a starting memory address of 0xE000E000 (Figure 6.14 in Chapter 6). In fact, only the top five registers in those 11 registers are important, and the other six registers are only the alias registers used to duplicate some of top five registers.

The top five registers include:

• MPU Type Register (MPUTYPE)—Read-only register
• MPU Control Register (MPUCTRL)

- MPU Region Number Register (MPUNUMBER)
- MPU Region Base Address Register (MPUBASE)
- MPU Region Attribute and Size Register (MPUATTR)

The following six alias registers include:

- MPU Region Base Address Alias 1 Register (MPUBASE1)
- MPU Region Attribute and Size Alias 1 Register (MPUATTR1)
- MPU Region Base Address Alias 2 Register (MPUBASE2)
- MPU Region Attribute and Size Alias 2 Register (MPUATTR2)
- MPU Region Base Address Alias 3 Register (MPUBASE3)
- MPU Region Attribute and Size Alias 3 Register (MPUATTR3)

To use any alias register, such as MPUBASE1, it is appropriate to use the MPUBASE register itself. The reason to use these alias registers is to allow multiple MPU regions to be accessed and programmed in one instruction, such as store-multiple (STM), to save time and speed up the execution of the programs.

12.2.2.1 The MPU Type Register (MPUTYPE)

This is a 32-bit register, but only some bits or bit fields are used to indicate whether the MPU is present and how many regions it supports. The bit fields and bit configurations of this register are shown in Figure 12.1.

The bit field IREGION contains 8 bits (bits 23~16), and this field is used to indicate how many memory regions can be used for the instructions. The default value for this field is 0x00 after a system reset.

The bit field DREGION also contains 8 bits (bits 15~8), and this field is used to indicate how many memory regions can be used for the data. The default value for this field is 0x08 after a system reset.

The bit SEPARATE (bit 0) is used to indicate whether the MPU is unified (0) or separate (1). The default value for this bit is 0 (unified) after a system reset.

One point to be noted for using this register is that this register is a read-only register, and it can be accessed from privileged mode.

12.2.2.2 The MPU Control Register (MPUCTRL)

This is a 32-bit register but only the lowest three bits (bits 2~0) are used to enable the MPU, enable the default memory map background region, and enable use of the MPU when in the hard fault, Non-Maskable Interrupt (NMI), and Fault Mask Register (FAULTMASK) escalated handlers.

MPU Type Register (MPUTYPE)

31 30 29 28 27 26 25 24 23	16 15	8 7	1 0
Reserved Bits 31 ~ 24	IREGION	DREGION	Reserved Bits 7 ~ 1	SEPARATE

Figure 12.1. The bit fields of the MPUTYPE register.

MPU Control Register (MPUCTRL)

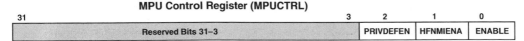

31		3	2	1	0
Reserved Bits 31–3			PRIVDEFEN	HFNMIENA	ENABLE

Figure 12.2. The bit configuration of the MPUCTRL register.

The bit configuration of this register is shown in Figure 12.2. The bit function of this register is shown in Table 12.1. This register can only be accessed from the privileged mode, and these three bits are readable and writable.

When using this register to enable or disable the MPU, the following points should be noted:

- When the ENABLE and the PRIVDEFEN bits are both set:
  - For privileged accesses, the default memory map is as described in Figure 6.14 in Chapter 6. Any access by privileged software that does not address an enabled memory region behaves as defined by the default memory map.
  - Any access by unprivileged software that does not address an enabled memory region causes a memory management fault.
- Execute Never (XN) and Strongly Ordered rules always apply to the System Control Space regardless of the value of the ENABLE bit.
- When the ENABLE bit is set, at least one region of the memory map must be enabled for the system to function unless the PRIVDEFEN bit is set. If the PRIVDEFEN bit is set and no regions are enabled, then only privileged software can operate.
- When the ENABLE bit is clear, the system uses the default memory map, which has the same memory attributes as if the MPU is not implemented. The default memory map applies to accesses from both privileged and unprivileged software.
- When the MPU is enabled, accesses to the System Control Space and vector table are always permitted. Other areas are accessible based on regions and whether PRIVDEFEN is set.

Table 12.1. Bit value and its function for MPUCTRL register.

Bit	Name	Reset	Function
31:3	Reserved	0x00	Reserved.
2	PRIVDEFEN	0	MPU Default Region: This bit enables privileged software to access the default memory map. 0: If the MPU is enabled, this bit disables use of the default memory map. Any memory access to a location not covered by any enabled region causes a fault. 1: If the MPU is enabled, this bit enables use of the default memory map as a background region for privileged software accesses. When this bit is set, the background region acts as if it is region number −1. Any region that is defined and enabled has priority over this default map. If the MPU is disabled, the processor ignores this bit.
1	HFNMIENA	0	MPU Enabled During Faults: This bit controls the operation of the MPU during hard fault, NMI, and FAULTMASK handlers. 0: The MPU is disabled during hard fault, NMI, and FAULTMASK handlers, regardless of the value of the ENABLE bit. 1: The MPU is enabled during hard fault, NMI, and FAULTMASK handlers. When the MPU is disabled and this bit is set, the resulting behavior is unpredictable.
0	ENABLE	0	MPU Enable: 0: The MPU is disabled; 1: The MPU is enabled. When the MPU is disabled and the HFNMIENA bit is set, the behavior is unpredictable.

12.2.2.3 The MPU Region Number Register (MPUNUMBER)

This is a 32-bit register, but only the lowest three bits (bits 2~0) are used to indicate which memory region (0~7) is used currently. In fact, this register is used to select which memory region is referenced by the MPU Region Base Address (MPUBASE) and MPU Region Attribute and Size (MPUATTR) registers. Normally, the required region number should be written to this register before accessing the MPUBASE or the MPUATTR register. However, the region number can be changed by writing to the MPUBASE register with the VALID bit set. This write updates the value of the REGION field in that register.

In the TM4C123GH6PM MCU system, the MPU supports up to 8 (0~7) memory regions.

12.2.2.4 MPU Region Base Address Register (MPUBASE)

This is a 32-bit register used to hold the valid base address of the MPU region selected by the MPU Region Number (MPUNUMBER) register and can update the value stored in the MPUNUMBER register. To change the current region number and update the MPUNUMBER register, write the MPUBASE register with the VALID bit set.

Although the default base address, ADDR bit field, takes 27 bits (bits 31~5), in real applications, this ADDR field takes only bits 31:N on the MPUBASE register. Bits (N−1):5 are reserved. The actual value N is determined by the region size specified by the SIZE field in the MPU Region Attribute and Size (MPUATTR) register as

$$N = Log2(SIZE)$$

If the region size is configured to 4 GB in the MPUATTR register, there is no valid ADDR field. In this case, the region occupies the complete memory map, and the base address is 0x0000.0000. The base address should be aligned to the size of the region. For example, a 64-KB region must be aligned on a multiple of 64 KB, for example, at 0x0001.0000 or 0x0002.0000.

The bit configuration of this register is shown in Figure 12.3.

The bit VALID is used to indicate whether the region number stored in the MPUNUMBER register is updated and equal to the number stored in the REGION bit field in this register or not. If this VALID is 1, the region number in the MPUNUMBER register is updated and equal to the value in the REGION bit field in this register. Otherwise if this VALID is 0, this means that the region number in the MPUNUMBER register is not updated and the processor updates the base address based on the non-updated region number stored in the MPUNUMBER register and ignores the number in the REGION bit field in this register.

The value in the bit field REGION contains the current region number. When writing, this value is written into the MPUNUMBER register; when reading, it returns the current region number stored in the MPUNUMBER register.

MPU Region Base Address Register (MPUBASE)

31		5	4	3	2	1	0
	ADDR		VALID			REGION	

Figure 12.3. The bit configuration of the MPUBASE register.

MPU Region Attribute and Size Register (MPUATTR)

31		28	27	26	25	24	23	22	21	20	19	18	17	16	15			8	7	6	5		1	0
		XN		AP					TEX			S	C	B		SRD					SIZE			ENABLE

Figure 12.4.   The bit configuration of the MPUATTR register.

Three MPU Region Base Address Alias Registers (MPUBASE1~MPUBASE3) have the same bit fields and functions.

12.2.2.5 The MPU Region Attribute and Size Register (MPUATTR)

This is a 32-bit register used to define the region size and memory attributes of the MPU region specified by the MPU Region Number (MPUNUMBER) register and enables that region and any subregions.

The bit configuration of this register is shown in Figure 12.4.

The MPUATTR register is accessible using word or half-word accesses with the most-significant half-word holding the region attributes, and the least-significant half-word holds the region size and the region and subregion enable bits.

The MPU access permission attribute bits, XN, AP, TEX, S, C, and B, are used to control access to the corresponding memory region. If an access is made to an area of memory without the required permissions, then the MPU generates a permission fault. The bit functions of this register are shown in Table 12.2. The MPU access permission

Table 12.2.   Bit value and its function for MPUATTR register.

Bit	Name	Reset	Function
31:29	Reserved	0x00	Reserved.
28	XN	0	Instruction Access Disable: 0 : Instruction fetches are enabled; 1 : Instruction fetches are disabled.
27	Reserved	0	Reserved.
26:24	AP	0x00	Access Privilege: 000 : No access; 001–010 : Access from privileged software only; 011 : Full access. 100 : Reserved; 101 : Reads by privileged software only; 110–111 : Read-only by privileged or unprivileged software.
23:22	Reserved	0x00	Reserved.
21:19	TEX	0	Type Extension Mask. For MPU access permissions, see Table 12.4.
18	S	0	Shareable. For MPU access permissions, see Table 12.4.
17	C	0	Cacheable. For MPU access permissions, see Table 12.4.
16	B	0	Bufferable. For MPU access permissions, see Table 12.4.
15:8	SRD	0x00	Sub-Region Disable Bits. 0 : The corresponding subregion is enabled. 1 : The corresponding subregion is disabled.
7:6	Reserved	0x0	Reserved.
5:1	SIZE	0x00	Region Size Mask: The SIZE field defines the size of the MPU memory region specified by the MPUNUMBER register.
0	ENABLE	0	Region Enable: 0 : The region is disabled; 1 : The region is enabled.

Table 12.3. Some popular SIZE values and related region sizes.

SIZE	Region Size	N	Description
0x4	32B	5	The Min permitted size.
0x9	1 KB	10	
0x13	1 MB	20	
0x1D	1 GB	30	
0x1F	4 GB	No valid ADDR field in MPUBASE; The Max possible size region occupies the complete memory map.	The Max possible size.

attributes bits, XN, AP, TEX, S, C, and B, as well as their functions, are shown in Table 12.4.

The SIZE field defines the size of the MPU memory region specified by the MPUNUMBER register as follows:

$$(\text{Region Size in Bytes}) = 2^{(\text{SIZE}+1)}$$

The smallest permitted region size is 32 bytes, corresponding to a SIZE value of 4. Table 12.3 shows some popular example SIZE values with the corresponding region size and value of N in the MPU Region Base Address (MPUBASE) register.

All encodings shown in Table 12.4 are completeness. However, the current implementation of the Cortex®-M4 does not support the concept of cacheability or shareability.

Table 12.4. The TEX, S, C, and B bit field encoding.

TEX	S	C	B	Memory Type	Shareable	Others
000	X	0	0	Strongly Ordered	Shareable	—
000	X	0	1	Device	Shareable	—
000	0	1	0	Normal	Not Shareable	Outer and inner write-through. No write allocate.
000	1	1	0	Normal	Shareable	
000	0	1	1	Normal	Not Shareable	
000	1	1	1	Normal	Shareable	
001	0	0	0	Normal	Not Shareable	Outer and inner non-cacheable.
001	1	0	0	Normal	Shareable	
001	X	0	1	Reserved Encoding	—	—
001	X	1	0	Reserved Encoding	—	—
001	0	1	1	Normal	Not Shareable	Outer and inner write-back. Write and read allocate.
001	1	1	1	Normal	Shareable	
010	X	0	0	Device	Not Shareable	Not Shareable Device
010	X	0	1	Reserved Encoding	—	—
010	X	1	X	Reserved Encoding	—	—
1BB	0	A	A	Normal	Not Shareable	Cached memory (BB = outer policy, AA = inner policy). See Table 12.5 for the encoding of the AA and BB bits.
1BB	1	A	A	Normal	Shareable	

Table 12.5. The cache policy for memory attribute encoding.

Encoding (AA or BB)	Cache Policy
00	Non-Cacheable.
01	Write back, write and read allocate.
10	Write through, no write allocate.
11	Write back, no write allocate.

Table 12.5 shows the cache policy for memory attribute encodings with a TEX value in the range of 0x4~0x7.

Three MPU Region Attribute and Size Alias Registers (MPUATTR1~MPUATTR3) have the same bit fields and functions.

Now that all MPU-related control and status registers have been discussed, let's take a look at the MPU setups and configurations.

12.3 INITIALIZATION AND CONFIGURATION OF THE MPU

In most real applications, the MPU is not required. By default the MPU is disabled and the MCU system works as if the MPU does not exist. In order to use MPU, one needs to configure out what memory regions the user's program needs to access.

In a simple application, the goal is just to prevent unprivileged tasks from accessing certain memory regions. In that case, the background region feature is a very useful tool since it reduced the memory set up requirements. One only needs to setup the region setting for unprivileged tasks, and the privileged tasks and interrupt handlers have full access abilities to other memory spaces using the background region.

Basically the MPU setup procedure can be completed by the following steps:

1. Check the MPU Type register (MPUTYPE) to see whether the MPU is presented and how many regions are supported.
2. If the MPU exists, disable the MPU before it can be configured and initialized.
3. Select all regions one by one, and program the region base address and configuration. This step can be performed in a loop with n times, and the n is the number of regions to be selected and configured.
4. Select the configured region and disable unused regions. This step can be performed as a loop with 8 − n times, and the n is the number of used regions.
5. Enable the MPU.

One also needs to define the fault handler for either the HardFault or MemManage (Memory Management) fault. The MemManage exception by default is disabled, and one can enable this by setting the MEMFAULTENA bit in the System Handler Control (SCB) and State Register (SHCSR) with the CMSIS-Core supported instruction SCB → SHCSR = 0x00010000 (set bit 16).

The MemManage handler, `void MemManage_Handler(void)`, should be defined in the user's program if the MemManage exception is enabled. Also the HardFault exception handler, `void HardFault_Handler(void)`, should always be defined even if the MemManage exception is enabled.

The MPU interrupt handler should also be registered and enabled before any exception can receive a response and be handled.

Prior to enabling the MPU, at least one region must be set or else it can be set by enabling the default region for privileged mode. Once the MPU is enabled, a memory management fault is generated for memory access violations.

Now let's build a real example MPU project to illustrate how to set up and use the MPU to protect the memory regions from being illegally accessed based on our above discussions.

12.4 BUILDING A PRACTICAL EXAMPLE MPU PROJECT

In this project, we use the Direct Register Access (DRA) model to build a MPU project to divide the entire memory map into three regions with the base addresses and sizes as below:

- Region 1: A 28-KB region of flash from 0x00000000 to 0x00007000. The region is executable and read-only for both privileged and user modes. To set up the region, a 32-KB region (#0) is defined starting at address 0, and then a 4-KB hole is removed at the end by disabling the last subregion. The region is initially enabled.
- Region 2: A 32-KB region (#1) of RAM from 0x20000000 to 0x20008000. The region is not executable, and is read/write accessible for privileged and user modes.
- Region 3: An additional 8-KB region (#2) in RAM from 0x20008000 to 0x2000A000 that is read/write accessible only from privileged mode. This region is initially disabled and it can be enabled later.

In order to test the MPU function, we develop a function WriteFlash() to try to access the flash memory at 0x1000, which has been defined as a read-only region (Region 1), to trigger the MPU to start its protection function. This protection function is performed by calling and executing two handlers, HardFault_Handler() and Mem–Manage_Handler(), respectively.

The unused five regions are also disabled in this project by using a loop function.

12.4.1 Create a New DRA Model MPU Project DRAMPU

Open the Keil™ ARM-MDK μVersion5 to create a new project named DRAMPU in the folder C:\ARM Class Projects\Chapter 12. Add a new C source file named DRAMPU.c into this new project. Then enter the first part codes of this project shown in Figure 12.5 into this C file.

Let's have a closer look at this first part codes to see how they work.

1. The codes in lines 4~8 are used to include all system header files to be used in this project.
2. Two user-defined function, SetupMPU() and WriteFlash(), are declared in lines 9 and 10. These two functions are used to configure the MPU before it can be operated and try to access a read-only region to program some flash RAM units to test the MPU later.
3. In line 11, a data array ui32RegionAddr[] is declared and initialized with three starting base addresses, 0, 0x20000000 and 0x20008000, for three regions to be divided by this project.

```
1    //********************************************************************************************************************
2    // DRAMPU.c - Main Application File for MPU – The First Part Codes
3    //********************************************************************************************************************
4    #include <stdint.h>
5    #include <stdbool.h>
6    #include "TM4C123GH6PM.h"
7    #include "inc\tm4c123gh6pm.h"
8    #include "driverlib\mpu.h"

9    int SetupMPU(void);
10   void WriteFlash(void);

11   uint32_t ui32RegionAddr[3] = {0, 0x20000000, 0x20008000};
12   uint32_t ui32RegionAttr[3] = {(MPU_RGN_SIZE_32K|MPU_RGN_PERM_EXEC|
13                    MPU_RGN_PERM_PRV_RO_USR_RO|MPU_SUB_RGN_DISABLE_7|MPU_RGN_ENABLE),
14                    (MPU_RGN_SIZE_32K|MPU_RGN_PERM_NOEXEC|
15                     MPU_RGN_PERM_PRV_RW_USR_RW|MPU_RGN_ENABLE),
16                    (MPU_RGN_SIZE_8K|MPU_RGN_PERM_NOEXEC|
17                     MPU_RGN_PERM_PRV_RW_USR_NO|MPU_RGN_DISABLE)};
18   int main(void)
19   {
20       SYSCTL->RCGC2 = 0x20;                            // enable & clock port F
21       GPIOF->DEN = 0xF;                                // PF0 ~ PF3 as digital pins
22       GPIOF->DIR = 0xF;                                // PF0 ~ PF3 as output pins

23       if (SetupMPU()){return 1;}                       // setup the MPU. if error, stop program
24       SCB->SHCSR = 0x00010000;                         // enable the MemManage exception
25       WriteFlash();                                    // try to access flash RAM at 0x1000 (read-only region)
26   }

27   int SetupMPU(void)
28   {
29       uint32_t index;

30       if (MPU->TYPE == 0) {return 1;}                  // MPU is not presented & returns an error
31       MPU->CTRL = 0;                                   // disable MPU to setup it
32       for (index = 0; index < 3; index++)              // configure 3 regions (0, 1, 2)
33       {
34           MPU->RNR = index;
35           MPU->RBAR = ui32RegionAddr[index];
36           MPU->RASR = ui32RegionAttr[index];
37       }
38       for (index = 3; index < 8; index++)              // disable unused 5 regions
39       {
40           MPU->RNR = index;
41           MPU->RBAR = 0;
42           MPU->RASR = 0;
43       }
44       MPU->CTRL = 0x1;                                 // enable the MPU
45       return 0;
46   }
```

Figure 12.5.   The first part codes for the project DRAMPU.

4. Similarly in line 12, another data array `ui32RegionAttr[]` is declared and initialized with three groups of configuration data for the corresponding attributes of three regions created above. The reason we use these data arrays is to save the space for the setup of three memory regions. These attributes can be `ORed` together to get the target attributes.

5. The attributes for the first region are defined by the following macros:

- `MPU_RGN_SIZE_32K:` The Initial region size is 32 KB
- `MPU_RGN_PERM_EXEC:` The region is executable
- `MPU_RGN_PERM_PRV_RO_USR_RO:` Read-only for privileged and user modes
- `MPU_SUB_RGN_DISABLE_7:` The last 4-KB hole are removed to get 28 KB
- `MPU_RGN_ENABLE:` This region is initially enabled

6. The attributes for the second region are defined by the following macros:

- MPU_RGN_SIZE_32K: The region size is 32 KB
- MPU_RGN_PERM_NOEXEC: The region is non-executable
- MPU_RGN_PERM_PRV_RW_USR_RW: Read/Write for privileged and user modes
- MPU_RGN_ENABLE: This region is initially enabled

7. The attributes for the third region are defined by the following macros:

- MPU_RGN_SIZE_8K: The region size is 8 KB
- MPU_RGN_PERM_NOEXEC: The region is non-executable
- MPU_RGN_PERM_PRV_RW_USR_NO: Read/Write for privileged mode only
- MPU_RGN_DISABLE: This region is initially disabled

8. The main program starts at line 18.

9. The codes in lines 20~22 are used to clock and enable the GPIO Port F, specifically the Port F lower 4 pins, PF3~PF0, since we need to use these LEDs to indicate the testing results for the MPU if any violation or illegal accessing to the protection memory regions occurred.

10. In line 23, the user-defined function SetupMPU() is called to perform the setup and configuration process for the MPU. A 0 is returned if this function execution is successful. Otherwise a nonzero value is returned if any error is encountered. A 1 is returned to the operating system if any error occurred when executing this function.

11. If the function SetupMPU() is executed successfully, the SCB → SHCSR instruction is executed to set bit MEMFAULTENA (bit 16) on the SHCSR to enable the MemManage exception in line 24.

12. Another user-defined function WriteFlash() is called in line 25 to try to access the flash memory region at addresses starting at 0x1000, which has been defined as a read-only region by the MPU, to write some bytes. The purpose of calling this function is to test the MPU protection function. A HardFault and a MemManage exception should be triggered if this writing occurred, and the handlers for both exceptions should be excited and performed to handle this violation.

13. The first user-defined function SetupMPU() starts at line 27.

14. A local uint32_t variable index is declared first and this variable works as a loop counter.

15. In line 30, the MPU Type register MPUTYPE is checked first to make sure that a MPU is presented in the current system. Otherwise a 1 would be returned to the main program to indicate an MPU non-present error if all bits on the MPUTYPE register are zeros.

16. If an MPU is presented, the MPU Control Register, MPUCTRL, is reset to disable the MPU to enable the setup and configuration of the MPU to start in line 31.

17. A for() loop is used starting at line 32 to repeatedly set up three memory regions by assigning the region numbers (0~2) to the MPU Region Number Register (MPU → RNR) via the index, by assigning three memory starting or base addresses, 0, 0x20000000 and 0x20008000, to the MPU Region Base Address Register (MPU → RBAR) via the data array ui32RegionAddr[], by assigning three memory attributes to the MPU Region Attribute and Size Register (MPU → RASR) via the data array ui32RegionAttr[].

18. Similarly, another for() loop is used for the codes in lines 38~43 to disable the remaining five unused memory regions by assigning the corresponding region numbers to the MPU Region Number Registers and assigning 0 to those MPU Region Base Address Registers and MPU Region Attribute and Size Registers.

19. When the MPU is configured, it is enabled in line 44 by assigning 0x1 to the MPU Control Register (MPU → CTRL).

20. A 0 is returned to the main program if no error is encountered in line 45.

Now let's build the second part codes for this C source file. The second part codes include the function `WriteFlash()` and two memory exception handlers.

Enter the codes shown in Figure 12.6 into this C source file and make them follow the first part codes. Let's have a closer look at this piece of codes to see how it works.

21. The user-defined function `WriteFlash()` starts at line 51.

22. Some local variables are declared and initialized first. These variables include the data counts `ulCount`, flash memory starting address `ulAddress`, data array starting address `*proData`, and data array `Data[]`. All of these variables are initialized with given values.

23. A `while()` loop is used in line 57 to try to continuously write three words of data into the flash memory starting at address `0x1000`.

24. The codes in lines 59~61 are used to perform these words programming or writing operations. The flash memory address register FLASH_FMA_R, data register FLASH_FMD_R and control register FLASH_FMC_R, are initialized with the appropriate values.

25. Another `while()` loop is used in line 63 to wait for the completion of a single-word writing operation.

26. The codes in lines 65~67 are used to update the `ulCount`, `ulAddress` and `proData` to point to the next word to be written into this flash memory region. In fact, this writing operation can never be executed since this flash memory region is a protected region with the read-only accessing protection, and a MemManage and HardFault exception would occur when this writing operation begins.

27. The codes in lines 70~73 and lines 74~77 are two exception handlers. These two handlers must be defined in this project to enable them to be executed. Two LEDs connected to PF1 (red-color) and PF2 (blue-color) are turned on when these handlers are triggered and responded. The execution order of these handlers is as follows: The `MemManage_Handler()` is executed first, and the `HardFault_Handler()` is executed second.

Now let's set up the environment to build and run this project to test the MPU function.

12.4.2 Set Up the Environment to Build and Run the Project

This setup contains the following two steps:

1. Include the system header files by adding the include path.

2. Check and configure the correct debugger driver used in the project.

Perform the following operations to include the header file path in the project:

- Go to `Project|Options for Target 'Target 1'` menu item. Then click on the C/C++ tab.
- Go to `Include Paths` box and browse to the folder where our header files are located, it is `C:\ti\TivaWare_C_Series-2.0.1.11577`. Select this folder and click on the **OK** button.

Perform the following operations to select the correct debugger:

- Going to `Project|Options for Target 'Target 1'` menu item to open the `Options` wizard.

```
47  //*********************************************************************************************
48  // DRAMPU.c - Main Application File for MPU – The Second Part Codes
49  //*********************************************************************************************
50  // try to access a read-only region
51  void WriteFlash(void)
52  {
53    unsigned long ulCount= 3, ulAddress = 0x1000, *proData;
54    unsigned long Data[3] = {0x78563412, 0x8B674523, 0xA3456789};
55    proData = Data;

56    // loop to perform words programming
57    while(ulCount)
58    {
59      FLASH_FMA_R = ulAddress;
60      FLASH_FMD_R = *proData;
61      FLASH_FMC_R = FLAS H_FMC_WRKEY | FLASH_FMC_WRITE;

62      // wait all words programmed
63      while(FLASH_FMC_R & FLASH_FMC_WRITE) {}

64      // Increment to the next word
65      proData++;
66      ulAddress += 4;
67      ulCount--;
68    }
69  }

70  void HardFault_Handler(void)              // this handler must be defined
71  {
72      GPIOF->DATA = 0x2;                    // turn on red LED
73  }

74  void MemManage_Handler(void)              // this handler must be defined
75  {                                         // to trigger the HardFault_Handler()
76      GPIOF->DATA = 0x4;                    // turn on blue LED
77  }
```

Figure 12.6. The second part codes for the project DRAMPU.

- On the opened Options wizard, click on the Debug tab.
- Make sure that the debugger shown in the Use: box is Stellaris ICDI. Otherwise you can click on the dropdown arrow to select this debugger from the list.

Now let's build and run the project if everything is fine. After the project runs, the red-color LED is on to indicate that a memory access violation has occurred and the related exception handlers have been triggered and have responded to handle this error. This indicates that our MPU works fine.

A small question is, Why is only the red-color LED on but the blue-color LED is never on? You can figure out this question and find out the solution yourself easily.

Next let's take care of the API functions provided by the TivaWare™ Peripheral Driver Library. By using these API functions, one can directly call them to avoid direct accessing to those MPU registers to make the program simple and easy.

12.5 THE API FUNCTIONS PROVIDED BY THE TIVAWARE™ PERIPHERAL DRIVER LIBRARY

The TivaWare™ Peripheral Driver Library provides nine MPU-related API functions to configure, enable, set, and get required memory regions for the MPU. The MPU is tightly coupled to the Cortex®-M4 processor core and provides a means to establish access permissions on regions of memory.

The entire memory map can be divided into eight regions, and each region can be configured for read-only access, read/write access, or no access for both privileged and user modes. Access permissions can be used to create an environment where only kernel or system code can access certain hardware registers or sections of code.

The MPU can create eight subregions within each region. Any subregion or combination of subregions can be disabled, allowing creation of holes or complex overlaying regions with different permissions. The subregions can also be used to create an unaligned beginning or ending of a region by disabling one or more of the leading or trailing subregions.

Once the regions are defined and the MPU is enabled, any access violation of a region causes a memory management fault, and the fault handlers, including the `MemManage_Handler()` and `HardFault_Handler()`, are activated.

These nine API functions can be divided into three groups based on their functions and purposes as shown below:

1. The MPU Setup and Status Group

- MPURegionSet()
- MPURegionGet()
- MPURegionCountGet()
- MPURegionEnable()
- MPURegionDisable()

2. The MPU Enable and Disable Group

- MPUEnable()
- MPUDisable()

3. The MPU Interrupt Handler Control Group

- MPUIntRegister()
- MPUIntUnregister()

Let's have a closer look at these API functions one by one based on their groups.

12.5.1 The MPU Set Up and Status API Functions

As we mentioned, the MPU must be setup and configured before it can be enabled. This setup and configuration process includes the memory regions defined (region number, region base address, and region attributes). The regions can be configured by calling the API function `MPURegionSet()` once for each region to be configured.

When each region is set up and configured by the function `MPURegionSet()`, it can be initially enabled or disabled. If a region is not initially enabled, it can be enabled later by calling the API function `MPURegionEnable()`. An enabled region can be disabled by calling another API function `MPURegionDisable()`. When a region is disabled, its configuration is preserved as long as it is not overwritten. In this case, it can be enabled again with `MPURegionEnable()` without the need to reconfigure the region.

After a region has been configured, the attributes of a region can be retrieved and saved using the `MPURegionGet()` function. This function is used to save the attributes in a format that can be used later to reload the region using the `MPURegionSet()` function. Note that the enable state of the region is saved with the attributes and takes effect when the region is reloaded.

The function `MPURegionCountGet()` can be used to get the total number of regions that are supported by the MPU, including regions that are already programmed and configured.

12.5.1.1 The API Function MPURegionSet()

This function is used to set up the protection rules for a region. The region has a base address and a set of attributes including the size. The base address parameter, `ui32Addr`, must be aligned according to the size, and the size must be a power of 2.

The protocol of this function is

void `MPURegionSet`(uint32_t `ui32Region`, uint32_t `ui32Addr`, uint32_t `ui32Flags`)

- `ui32Region` is the region number to set up.
- `ui32Addr` is the base address of the region. It must be aligned according to the size of the
- region specified in `ui32Flags`.
- `ui32Flags` is a set of flags to define the attributes of the region.

The `ui32Flags` parameter is the logical OR of all of the attributes of the region. It is a combination of region size, execute permission, read/write permissions, disabled subregions, and a flag to determine if the region is enabled.

The size flag determines the size of a region and must be one of the following:

`MPU_RGN_SIZE_32B`; `MPU_RGN_SIZE_64B`; `MPU_RGN_SIZE_128B`;

`MPU_RGN_SIZE_256B`; `MPU_RGN_SIZE_512B`; `MPU_RGN_SIZE_1K`;

`MPU_RGN_SIZE_2K`; `MPU_RGN_SIZE_4K`; `MPU_RGN_SIZE_8K`;

`MPU_RGN_SIZE_16K`; `MPU_RGN_SIZE_32K`; `MPU_RGN_SIZE_64K`;

`MPU_RGN_SIZE_128K`; `MPU_RGN_SIZE_256K`; `MPU_RGN_SIZE_512K`;

`MPU_RGN_SIZE_1M`; `MPU_RGN_SIZE_2M`; `MPU_RGN_SIZE_4M`;

`MPU_RGN_SIZE_8M`; `MPU_RGN_SIZE_16M`; `MPU_RGN_SIZE_32M`;

`MPU_RGN_SIZE_64M`; `MPU_RGN_SIZE_128M`; `MPU_RGN_SIZE_256M`;

`MPU_RGN_SIZE_512M`; `MPU_RGN_SIZE_1G`; `MPU_RGN_SIZE_2G`;

`MPU_RGN_SIZE_4G`

The execute permission flag must be one of the following:

`MPU_RGN_PERM_EXEC`:	Enables the region for execution of code.
`MPU_RGN_PERM_NOEXEC`:	Disables the region for execution of code.

The read/write access permissions are applied separately for the privileged and user modes. The read/write access flags must be one of the following:

`MPU_RGN_PERM_PRV_NO_USR_NO`:	No access in privileged or user mode.
`MPU_RGN_PERM_PRV_RW_USR_NO`:	Privileged read/write, user no access.
`MPU_RGN_PERM_PRV_RW_USR_RO`:	Privileged read/write, user read-only.
`MPU_RGN_PERM_PRV_RW_USR_RW`:	Privileged read/write, user read/write.
`MPU_RGN_PERM_PRV_RO_USR_NO`:	Privileged read-only, user no access.
`MPU_RGN_PERM_PRV_RO_USR_RO`:	Privileged read-only, user read-only.

Each region is automatically divided into 8 equally sized subregions by the MPU. Subregions can only be used in regions of size 256 bytes or larger. Any of these 8 subregions can be disabled, allowing for creation of holes in a region which can be left open, or overlaid by another region with different attributes. Any of the 8 subregions can be disabled with a logical OR of any of the following flags:

MPU_SUB_RGN_DISABLE_0

MPU_SUB_RGN_DISABLE_1

MPU_SUB_RGN_DISABLE_2

MPU_SUB_RGN_DISABLE_3

MPU_SUB_RGN_DISABLE_4

MPU_SUB_RGN_DISABLE_5

MPU_SUB_RGN_DISABLE_6

MPU_SUB_RGN_DISABLE_7

Finally, each region can be initially enabled or disabled with one of the following flags:

MPU_RGN_ENABLE

MPU_RGN_DISABLE

Table 12.6 shows all other MPU setup and status API functions.

12.5.2 The MPU Enable and Disable API Functions

After one or more regions are configured, the MPU can be enabled by calling the API function MPUEnable(). This function turns on the MPU and also defines the behavior in

Table 12.6.   The MPU setup and status API functions.

API Function	Parameter	Description
void MPURegionGet(uint32_t ui32Region, uint32_t *pui32Addr, uint32_t *pui32Flags)	ui32Region is the region number to get. pui32Addr points to storage for the base address of the region. pui32Flags points to the attribute flags for the region.	This function retrieves the configuration of a specific region. The meanings and format of the parameters is the same as that of the MPURegionSet() function. This function can be used to save the configuration of a region for later use with the MPURegionSet() function. The region's enable state is preserved in the attributes that are saved.
uint32_t MPURegionCountGet (void)	None	This function is used to get the total number of regions that are supported by the MPU, including regions that are already programmed and configured. The function returns the number of memory protection regions that are available for programming using MPURegionSet().
void MPURegionEnable(uint32_t ui32Region)	ui32Region is the region number to enable.	This function is used to enable a memory protection region. The region should already be configured with the MPURegionSet() function. Once enabled, the memory protection rules of the region are applied and access violations cause a memory management fault.
void MPURegionDisable(uint32_t ui32Region)	ui32Region is the region number to disable.	This function is used to disable a previously enabled memory protection region. The region remains configured if it is not overwritten with another call to MPURegionSet(), and can be enabled again by calling MPURegionEnable().

privileged mode, in the Hard Fault and NMI fault handlers. The MPU can be configured to use the default memory map or the background region when in privileged mode, and no regions are enabled. If this feature is not enabled, then a memory management fault is generated if the MPU is enabled and no regions are configured and enabled.

The MPU can also be set to use a default memory map when in the Hard Fault or NMI handlers, instead of using the configured regions. All of these features can be selected when calling MPUEnable(). When the MPU is enabled, it can be disabled by calling MPUDisable().

The protocol of the MPUEnable() function is

void MPUEnable(uint32_t ui32MPUConfig)

- ui32MPUConfig is the logical OR of the possible configurations.

This function is used to enable the Cortex®-M4 memory protection unit. It also configures the default behavior when in privileged mode and while handling a hard fault or NMI. Before any MPU can be enabled, at least one region must be set by calling the API function MPURegionSet() or by enabling the default region for privileged mode by passing the MPU_CONFIG_PRIV_DEFAULT flag to the API function MPUEnable().

Once the MPU is enabled, a memory management fault is generated for any memory access violations.

The ui32MPUConfig parameter should be the logical OR of any of the following:

- MPU_CONFIG_PRIV_DEFAULT: Enables the default memory map when in privileged mode and when no other regions are defined. If this option is not enabled, there must be at least one valid region that has been already defined when the MPU is enabled.

- MPU_CONFIG_HARDFLT_NMI: Enables the MPU while in a hard fault or NMI exception handler. If this option is not enabled, the MPU would be disabled when one of these exception handlers is triggered and the default memory map is applied.

- MPU_CONFIG_NONE: Chooses none of the above options. In this case, no default memory map is provided in privileged mode, and the MPU is not enabled in the fault handlers.

The protocol of the MPUDisable() function is

void MPUDisable(void)

This function disables the Cortex®-M4 memory protection unit. When the MPU is disabled, the default memory map is used and memory management faults are not generated.

12.5.3 The MPU Interrupt Handler Control API Functions

If the application is using run-time interrupt registration, then the function MPUIntRegister() can be used to set up the fault handler which is called whenever a memory protection violation occurs. This function also enables the hard fault handler. If compile-time interrupt registration is used, then the IntEnable() function with the parameter FAULT_MPU must be used to enable the memory management fault handler. When the memory management fault handler has been installed with MPUIntRegister(), it can be removed by calling MPUIntUnregister() function.

Table 12.7.   The MPU interrupt handler control API functions.

API Function	Parameter	Description
void MPUIntRegister(void (*pfnHandler)(void))	pfnHandler is a pointer to the function to be called when the memory management fault occurs.	This function sets and enables the handler to be called when the MPU generates a memory management fault due to a protection region access violation.
void MPUIntUnregister(void)	None	This function disables and clears the handler to be called when a memory management fault occurs.

Table 12.7 shows these MPU interrupt handler control functions.

At this point, we have completed our discussions about the MPU API functions provided by the TivaWare™ Peripheral Driver Library. We need to build a real MPU project by using these API functions to test the MPU functions. We prefer to leave this as a lab project for the readers to allow readers to do something themselves.

12.6 CHAPTER SUMMARY

The main topic in this chapter is the memory protection unit (MPU) applied in the ARM® Cortex®-M4 MCU system. The purpose of the MCU is to protect the memory regions in the Cortex®-M4 system from illegal accessing by some other programs and devices. This protection is performed by dividing the entire memory map into eight regions, and each region has its own region base address, region size, and related attributes. In fact, the MPU can be considered to be a programmable device used to:

- Divide the memory space into several (eight) regions that can be used for the different applications with different access levels.
- Define the memory access permissions to enable different memory regions to be accessed in either privileged level or full access level.
- Define the memory attributes as bufferable or catchable regions.

An introduction and overview for the MPU applied in the Cortex®-M4 MCU is provided in Section 12.1. Starting in Section 12.2, the implementation of the MPU is discussed in detailed with all aspects of applications of a MPU in real systems and applications. These include the memory regions, types, and attributes and are discussed in Section 12.2.1. The MPU-related configuration and control registers are given in Section 12.2.2.

Some major and useful MPU registers, such as MPU Region Number Register (MPUNUMBER), MPU Type Register (MPUTYPE), MPU Control Register (MPUCTRL), MPU Region Base Address Register (MPUBASE), and MPU Region Attribute and Size Register (MPUATTR), are discussed in this section.

The initialization and configuration of the MPU is provided in Section 12.3. The detailed operational procedure of the setup and configuration of a MPU is discussed. Starting in Section 12.4, a practical example MPU project is provided step by step to illustrate how to use these MPU registers to perform memory regions protection functions.

The API functions provided by the TivaWare™ Peripheral Driver Library are introduced in Section 12.5.

HOMEWORK

I. True/False Selections

____ **1.** Both Cortex®-M3 and Cortex®-M4 MCU support an optional feature called the Memory Protection Unit (MPU).

____ **2.** Each memory region shares a common set of base address, size, and setting.

____ **3.** The MPU is a programmable security device used to protect the system memory and the user's memory spaces from corrupting and attacking by undesired tasks.

____ **4.** Accessing to PPB, which includes the MPU, NVIC, SysTick, and ITM, are always prohibited in the privileged state, and the vector fetches are blocked by the MPU.

____ **5.** The Cortex®-M4 MPU defines eight separate memory regions, 0~7, and a background region accessible only from privileged mode.

____ **6.** If a program accesses a memory location that is prohibited by the MPU, the processor generates a memory management fault, causing a fault exception.

____ **7.** The MPU does not need to be programmed and enabled before it can be used in any application. If the MPU is not enabled or programmed, it still can work.

____ **8.** In order to check whether a MPU is presented in a Cortex®-M4 system, one can use the MPU Control Register (MPUCTRL) to do this checking.

____ **9.** In order to enable or disable a MPU, one needs to use the MPU Control Register (MPUCTRL) to do this job.

____ **10.** The SIZE field in the MPUATTR register defines the size of the MPU memory region specified by the MPUNUMBER register as (Region Size in Bytes) = $2^{(SIZE + 1)}$.

II. Multiple Choices

1. A MPU can be considered as a programmable device used to _____.

    a. Divide the memory space into several regions that can be used for the different applications with different access levels

    b. Define the memory access permissions to enable different memory regions to be accessed in either privileged level or full access level

    c. Define the memory attributes as bufferable or catcheable regions

    d. All of the above

2. You may set up the memory regions for the device _____.

    a. NVIC

    b. ITM

    c. GPIO

    d. SysTick

3. Each memory region has its own programmable ___.

    a. Starting or base address

    b. Size

    c. Attributes

    d. All of the above

4. A MPU region includes all definitions except ____.

    a. Base address

    b. Size

    c. Function

    d. Attributes

5. The HardFault exception handler should always be defined even if the ___ is enabled.

    a. HardFault exception

    b. MemManage exception

    c. NMI exception

    d. MPU

6. To check whether a MPU is presented in a Cortex®-M4 system, one needs to use ____.

    a. MPUATTR

    b. MPUTYPE

    c. MPUNUMBER

    d. MPUCTRL

7. Basically the MPU setup procedure can be completed by _____.

    a. Check MPU, enable MPU, set up used regions, disable unused regions

    b. Check MPU, disable MPU, set up used region, disable unused regions, enable MPU

    c. Disable MPU, check MPU, set up used regions, disable unused regions, enable MPU

    d. Enable MPU, set up used regions, disable unused regions

8. Prior to enabling the MPU, at least __ region(s) must be set or else by enabling the default region for privileged mode. Once the MPU is enabled, a ___ fault is generated for memory access violations.

    a. 1, Memory Management

    b. 2, Hard Fault exception

    c. 3, NMI exception

    d. 4, Memory Overlapping exception

9. Each region is automatically divided into __ equally sized subregions by the MPU. Subregions can only be used in regions of size ____ bytes or larger.

    a. 2, 64

    b. 4, 128

    c. 8, 256

    d. 16, 512

10. In the `MPURegionSet()` API function, the base address parameter, `ui32Addr`, must be aligned according to the __, and the size must be a power of ___.

    a. Starting address, 4

    b. Region number, 8

    c. IREGION, 16

    d. Size, 2

III. Exercises

1. Provide a brief description about the MPU used in the Cortex®-M4 MCU.

2. Provide a brief description about the HardFault and MemManage exceptions and how to define both handlers to handle these exceptions.

3. Provide a brief description about the configuration for a MPU without embedded OS.

4. Provide a brief discussion about the MPU setup procedure.

IV. Practical Laboratory

Laboratory 12: ARM® Cortex®-M4 Memory Protection Unit (MPU)

12.0 Goals This laboratory exercise allows students to learn and practice the ARM® Cortex®-M4 memory protection unit (MPU) and related operations. Some MPU-related API functions are used in this lab to enable students to familiar them with these functions.

> **1.** Program Lab12_1 or SDMPU lets students use some MPU-related API functions to configure and set up an entire memory map with 8 memory regions. Furthermore, it enables students to use MPU to set up a protection mechanism to limit other programs or devices to access the protected memory regions.

After completion of this program, students should understand the basic architecture and operational procedure for the MPU installed in the TM4C123GH6PM MCU system. They should be able to code some sophisticated programs to perform desired MPU protection functions with specified memory regions.

12.1 Lab12_1

12.1.1 Goal In this project, students will use the SD model with MPU-related API functions to build a MPU program to perform desired memory regions protection operations. Some popular MPU-related API functions are to be used in this lab project to enable students to familiarize them with these functions and apply them in the real applications.

The advantage of using these API functions to access and operate the MPU-related registers is that some complicated registers structures and bit-field values can be avoided to improve the coding efficiency and coding process seed.

12.1.2 Data Assignment and Hardware Configuration No data assignment and hardware configuration are needed for this lab project.

In this project, the entire memory map is divided into 8 different regions. The first three regions with region numbers 0~2 have the base addresses as 0x00000000, 0x20000000, and 0x20008000 and have the following sizes and attributes:

> **1.** A 32-KB region of flash from 0x00000000 to 0x00008000 is set up. The region is executable and read-only for both privileged and user modes. To set up this region, a 32-KB region (#0) is defined starting at address 0 and the region is initially enabled.

> **2.** Another 32-KB region (#1) of RAM from 0x20000000 to 0x20008000 is configured. The region is not executable and is read/write access for both privileged and user modes.

3. An additional 8-KB region (#2) in RAM from 0x20008000 to 0x2000A000 is defined and this region is read/write accessible only from privileged mode. This region is initially disabled, and can be enabled later.

To setup and configure the MPU with the above requirements and attributes, you need to use two data structures, `ui32RegionAddr[]` and `ui32RegionAttr[]`, to store these base addresses and attributes.

This project needs a header file and a source file.

12.1.3 Development of the Header File   Perform the following operations to build this header file:

1. Create a new project named SDMPU in the folder C:\ARM Lab Projects\Chapter 12 \SDMPU and a new header file SDMPU.h.

2. Place the following system header files and macros into this header file:

```
#include <stdint.h>
#include <stdbool.h>
#include "inc\tm4c123gh6pm.h"
#include "driverlib\mpu.h"
#include "inc\hw_memmap.h"
#include "inc\hw_types.h"
#include "driverlib\sysctl.h"
#include "driverlib\gpio.h"
#include "driverlib\interrupt.h"

#define FAULT_MPU 4                 //MPU fault
int SetupMPU(void);
void WriteFlash(void);
uint32_t ui32RegionAddr[3]         = {0, 0x20000000, 0x20008000};
uint32_t ui32RegionAttr[3]         = {(MPU_RGN_SIZE_32K|MPU_RGN_PERM_EXEC
                                    |MPU_RGN_PERM_PRV_RO_USR_RO
                                    |MPU_RGN_ENABLE),(MPU_RGN_SIZE_32K
                                    |MPU_RGN_PERM_NOEXEC
                                    |MPU_RGN_PERM_PRV_RW_USR_RW
                                    |MPU_RGN_ENABLE),(MPU_RGN_SIZE_8K
                                    |MPU_RGN_PERM_NOEXEC
                                    |MPU_RGN_PERM_PRV_RW_USR_NO
                                    |MPU_RGN_DISABLE)};
```

Now let's build the source file SDMPU.c.

12.1.4 Development of the Source File   Perform the following operations to complete this project:

1. Create a new C source file SDMPU.c and add it into the project.

2. Place the following system header files and macros into this source file:
   #include "SDMPU.h"

3. Start the `main()` program and the main program needs to return an integer variable.

4. Use `SysCtlPeripheralEnable()` to enable the GPIO Port F.

5. Use `GPIOPinTypeGPIOOutput()` to set PF2 and PF1 as output pins.

6. Call the `SetupMPU()` function to set up and configure the MPU. A 1 is returned to the operating system if this function calling encountered any error.

7. Use MPURegionEnable() to enable the second memory region.

8. Use IntEnable(FAULT_MPU) to enable the MPU fault exception.

9. Call the function WriteFlash() to try to access a read-only region starting at 0x1000. This access would generate a memory fault exception to trigger the HardFault_Handler() and the MemManage_Handler() to handle this exception.

The following codes are for the user-defined function SetupMPU():

10. Declare a uint32_t local variable index.

11. Call the API function MPUDisable() to disable the MPU to enable it to be configured.

12. Use a for() loop to call the API function MPURegionSet() three times to configure three memory regions. Three arguments of this function are: index, ui32RegionAddr[index] and ui32RegionAttr[index], which have been defined in the header file.

13. Still use another for() loop to call the API function MPURegionSet() five times to disable the remaining five memory regions with index starting from 3 but less than 8.

14. Use the API function MPUEnable(MPU_CONFIG_NONE) to enable the MPU.

15. Return a 0 to the main program to indicate that this function is executed successfully.

The codes for the function WriteFlash() are identical to those codes in the class project DRAMPU. Refer to that section and that project to complete the coding for this function. The following codes are for two exception handlers, HardFault_Handler() and the MemManage_Handler():

16. Inside the HardFault_Handler(), use GPIOPinWrite() to turn on the red-color LED.

17. Inside the MemManage_Handler(), use GPIOPinWrite() to turn on the blue-color LED.

12.1.5 Set Up the Environment to Build and Run the Project To build and run the project, one needs to perform the following operations to set up the environments:

- Select the Stellaris ICDI debugger in the Debug tab under theProject|Options for Target 'Target 1' menu item.
- Add the system header files path: C:\ti\TivaWare_C_Series-2.0.1.11577 via the C/C++ tab in the Options for Target 'Target 1' under the Project menu item.
- Add the TivaWare™ Peripheral Driver Library file driverlib.lib into the project. The file is located at C:\ti\TivaWare_C_Series-2.0.1.11577\driverlib\rvmdk.

Now you can build and run the project. Then you can check the MPU protection function by monitoring the red-color LED.

Index

__FPU_PRESENT, 938, 948
__FPU_USED, 938, 948
9-Bit UART Mode, 649
16/32-bit GPTM blocks, 692, 694, 789–790
32/64-bit Wide GPTM blocks, 40, 694, 789

A

A Type, 743–744, 790
Absolute Position Encoder, 847
ACK errors, 635, 638, 808
Acknowledgement (ACK) signal, 552, 614, 807
ADC Active Sample Sequencer (ADCACTSS)
    register, 447, 458
ADC Clock Configuration (ADCCC) register,
    447, 462, 527
ADC Conversion Resolution, 471–472
ADC Event Multiplexer Select (ADCEMUX)
    Register, 467
ADC Interrupt Mask (ADCIM) Register, 463,
    465, 483
ADC Interrupt Status and Clear (ADCISC)
    Register, 463, 466, 483
ADC Module Initialization, 474
ADC modules, 446–447, 449, 459–463, 470,
    472–473, 480, 484, 527, 529
ADC Peripheral Property (ADCPP)
    register, 448
ADC Processor Sample Sequencer Initiate
    (ADCPSSI) Register, 458–459
ADC Raw Interrupt Status (ADCRIS)
    Register, 463–464, 483
ADC Related GPIO Ports Initialization, 473
ADC Run Mode Clock Gating Control
    (RCGCADC) register, 463
ADC Sample Sequencer Control
    (ADCSSCTLn) Register, 454, 483
ADC Sample Sequencer Input Multiplexer
    Select (ADCSSMUXn) Register, 452
ADC Sample Sequencer Result FIFO
    (ADCSSFIFOn) Register, 458, 460

ADCIntClear(), 483, 486
ADCIntEnable(), 481, 483–484
ADCIntRegister(), 481, 483
ADCIntStatus(), 481, 483, 486
ADCProcessorTrigger(), 481–482
ADCSequenceConfigure(), 480–481, 486
ADCSequenceDataGet(), 481, 486
ADCSequenceDisable(), 480
ADCSequenceEnable(), 480, 486
ADCSequenceStepConfigure(), 480–481
ADC-TLC548, 596, 598–600, 602–603
Address Bus, 2, 27, 37, 49, 230, 270, 333
Address counter (AC), 575–577, 579
Advanced Encryption Standard (AES), 41,
    196–197, 224, 351
Advanced High-performance Bus (AHB), 80,
    334–335, 422
Advanced Microcontroller Bus Architecture
    (AMBA), 4, 16
Analog Comparator, 283, 287–288, 469,
    899–904, 907, 909–911
Analog Comparator Control Register
    (ACCTL0), 900
Analog Comparator Interrupt Enable Register
    (ACINTEN), 903
Analog Comparator Masked Interrupt Status
    Register (ACMIS), 903
Analog Comparator Raw Interrupt Status
    Register (ACRIS), 903
Analog Comparator Reference Voltage
    Control Register (ACREFCTL), 902
Analog Comparator Status Register
    (ACSTAT0), 900
Analog Comparators (ACMP), 805
Application Interrupt and Reset Control
    Register (APINT), 71
Application Program Status Register (APSR),
    22, 188, 199, 204
Arbitration, 619, 624, 806, 811, 829, 831–832
Arithmetic Instructions, 158, 174

ARM architecture, 18
ARMv7E-M architecture, 18, 927, 946–947
Automatic State Preservation Enable, 940–941
Auxiliary Control Register (ACTLR), 70

B

B Type, 743–744, 790
Base Priority (BASEPRI) register, 23, 262
Baud Rate Prescaler (BRP), 820, 822, 827
Big endian, 28, 334, 373–375
Binary64, 934
Bit stuffing, 808, 821
Bit-band addresses, 365–366
Bit-band alias, 29, 43, 363, 365, 368–369
Bit-band alias region, 361–362, 364–370,
  422–423
Bit-band region, 361–362, 364–365, 367–370,
  422–423, 430–431
Bit-Field Processing Instructions, 158, 182
Boot Configuration (BOOTCFG) register, 41,
  60, 351
BQ32000 Real Time Clock (RTC), 631
Break Signal, 554
Bulk transfers, 746, 755–756
Bus Fault Address Register (FAULTADDR),
  71
Busy Flag (BF), 575, 5777
BYPASS, 45–46, 65–66, 72, 722–723, 726,
  732–733, 740, 796, 800

C

Calibration of the Rotary Encoder, 861
CAN API Functions, 834, 908
CAN Baud Rate Prescaler Extension Register
  (CANBRPE), 826
CAN Bit Timing Register (CANBIT),
  825–826
CAN Clock and Baud Rate Configuration, 819,
  908
CAN Error Counter Register (CANERR), 825
CAN Extended Frame, 806–808, 909, 911
CAN external control signals, 834
CAN Functional Block Diagram, 809
CAN Global Control Register (CANCTL), 823
CAN Global Status Register (CANSTS), 824
CAN IF1 Arbitration 1 Register
  (CANIF1ARB1), 831
CAN IF1 Arbitration 2 Register
  (CANIF1ARB2), 832
CAN IF1 Command Mask Register
  (CANIF1CMSK), 828

CAN IF1 Command Request Register
  (CANIF1CRQ), 828
CAN IF1 Mask 1 Register (CANIF1MSK1),
  831
CAN IF1 Mask 2 Register (CANIF1MSK2),
  831–832
CAN IF1 Message Control Register
  (CANIF1MCTL), 830
CAN Initialization, 810–811, 840, 908, 910
CAN Interface 1 Registers, 823, 828
CAN Interrupt Register (CANINT), 827
CAN Message Object Registers, 833
CAN Module 0 Receiver (CAN0RX), 839
CAN Module 0 Transmitter (CAN0TX), 839
CAN Module Interrupts, 817, 838
CAN Standard Frame, 806–808, 908–911
CAN Test Register (CANTST), 826–827
CANBitRateSet(), 835
CANBitTimingSet(), 835–836
CANDisable(), 835–836
CANEnable(), 835–836, 844
CANH, 189, 839, 912
CAN-HIGH (CAN+), 806
CANInit(), 835–836, 844
CANIntClear(), 838
CANIntEnable(), 838
CANIntRegister(), 838
CANIntStatus(), 838
CANL, 839–842, 912
CAN-LOW (CAN-), 806, 909
CANMessageClear(), 837
CANMessageGet(), 836–838, 846
CANMessageSet(), 836–837, 844, 846
CANStatusGet(), 838
Center-Of-Gravity (COG) method, 889
Channel A (Phase A), 849
Channel B (Phase B), 849
Character Generator RAM (CGRAM),
  574–576
Character Generator ROM (CGROM), 576
Clear To Send (CTS), 646–647
Clock Low Timeout (CLTO), 619
Closed-loop control system, 850, 860–861,
  867–868, 871–873, 875, 877, 879, 881–883,
  885, 887, 889–897, 908–912, 919
CMSIS Core Functions, 314
CMSIS Core Intrinsic Functions, 198
CMSIS Core Package (CMSISCP), 286, 295,
  316–319
CMSIS-CORE, 87–88, 90
CMSIS-DSP, 87–88

CMSIS-RTOS, 87–88, 115
CODE region, 27, 333
Compare and Test Instructions, 158, 186
Composite device, 745, 747
Configurable Fault Status Register
   (FAULTSTAT), 71
Configuration and Control Register
   (CFGCTRL), 70
Control Area Network (CAN), 40
Control Bus, 2, 19
CONTROL Register, 21, 24–25
Control rule process, 887
Control rules, 887, 890–891
Controller Area Network (CAN), 224, 805,
   807, 809, 811–845
Coprocessor Access Control (CPAC)
   register, 934, 939, 946
Coprocessor Data Operations (CDP), 937
Count-Down mode, 488, 492, 494, 514
Count-Up/Down mode, 488–489, 492, 494
CPU ID Register (CPUID), 70
Cyclic Redundant Check (CRC), 807

D
Data Bus, 2, 27
Data Communication Equipment (DCE), 646
Data Control Register (GPIODATA), 49
Data Conversion Instructions, 158, 179,
   246
Data Direction Register (GPIODIR), 49
Data framing, 552–553, 642–643, 669, 675,
   677, 680
Data Length Code (DLC), 807, 817
Data Moving Instructions, 158, 172–174
Data Packet, 746–747
Data RAM (DDRAM), 574–575
DATA region, 27, 333
Data Terminal Equipment (DTE), 646
Data Watchpoint and Trace (DWT), 19,
   42–43, 363, 433
DCode Bus, 28, 333, 335, 422
Dead-Band Generator, 490–491
Debug Access Port (DAP), 16, 19,
   78, 130
Debug Adapter, 38, 96, 129–131
Debug State, 33
Default NaN Mode, 937, 947
Defuzzification process, 887
Device functions, 745, 752, 757
Differential Input Mode, 471
Direct Memory Access (DMA), 470

Direct Register Access (DRA) model, 213–214,
   238, 243–244, 285, 318, 322, 534, 584, 592,
   599, 669, 673, 789, 796, 960
Direct Register Model (DRA), 213–214
Display Data RAM (DDRAM), 574–575
DMA Mode, 48, 437, 696, 703, 789
Double-Packet Buffering, 750–751
Double-Precision Floating Point Data, 932, 946
Dual Address, 619

E
EEPROM Current Block Register
   (EEBLOCK), 357
EEPROM Current Offset Register
   (EEOFFSET), 357
EEPROM Done Status (EEDONE) Register,
   65, 355–356, 402
EEPROM Interrupt (EEINT) register, 356,
   401, 415–416, 418
EEPROM Protection Register (EEPROT),
   357, 359
EEPROM Read-Write Register (EERDWR),
   360, 401–402
EEPROM Run Mode Clock Gating Control
   (RCGCEEPROM) register, 356, 402, 407,
   411
EEPROM Support Control and Status Register
   (EESUPP), 357, 359
EEPROMInit(), 380, 411, 427, 429
EEPROMIntClear(), 378, 380
EEPROMIntEnable(), 380
EEPROMMassErase(), 378
EEPROMProgram(), 378, 380, 428–429
EEPROMRead(), 380, 411, 428–429
Embedded Trace Buffer (ETB), 128, 135
Embedded Trace Macrocell (ETM), 16, 20, 38,
   43, 78, 132, 363
End Of Frame (EOF), 807
End Of Packet (EOP), 748
Endpoint (ENDP), 748
Endpoint Configurations, 774–775
EPROM, 1–3, 371
Exception Related Instructions, 158, 193
Execution Program Status Register (EPSR), 22
Execution-Only Protection, 351
Exponent field, 928–933

F
Fault Mask (FAULTMASK) register, 23
Flash Controller Interrupt Mask Register
   (FCIM), 346, 381, 388

Flash Controller Masked Interrupt Status and Clear Register (FCMISC), 345–346, 381, 384, 389

Flash Controller Raw Interrupt Status Register (FCRIS), 344, 381, 388

Flash Memory Address Register (FMA), 341, 381, 385–386, 399

Flash Memory Control 2 Register (FMC2), 342, 381, 399

Flash Memory Control Register (FMC), 342, 381, 385

Flash Memory Data Register (FMD), 342, 381, 386

Flash Patch and Breakpoint (FPB), 19, 42–43, 363, 433

Flash Write Buffer n Registers (FWBn), 349, 397

Flash Write Buffer Valid Register (FWBVAL), 343, 381, 399

FLASH_Handler(), 403, 415, 417–418, 420

FlashErase(), 376, 391, 394, 396, 424–425

FlashIntClear(), 376

FlashIntEnable(), 376

FlashIntRegister(), 376

FLASHM_Handler(), 391–392, 395

FlashProgram(), 376, 424–425

Floating Point Context Address Register (FPCAR), 937–939

Floating Point Context Control Register (FPCCR), 937–940

Floating Point Data Processing Registers (FPDPR), 25, 934

Floating Point Default Status Control Register (FPDSCR), 937–939, 941–942

Floating Point Status and Control Register (FPSCR), 25, 934–935

Floating Point Unit (FPU), 927–928, 930, 932, 934–936, 938, 942–948

Floating-Point Status and Control (FPSC) register, 937

Flush-to-Zero Mode, 937, 947–948

FPU Operational Modes, 937, 946

FPUDisable(), 942

FPUEnable(), 942, 949

FPUFlushToZeroModeSet(), 942

FPUHalfPrecisionModeSet(), 942

FPULazyStackingEnable(), 942, 949

FPUNaNModeSet(), 942

FPURoundingModeSet(), 942

FPUStackingDisable(), 942

FPUStackingEnable(), 942

FPv4-SP extensions, 18, 927, 946–947

Fraction field, 928–933

Frame check, 808

Freescale SPI, 551, 555, 557–559, 563, 571–572, 670

FTDI Drivers, 145, 147–149

Full-Compliance Mode, 937, 947–948

Full-duplex, 646, 670

Full-duplex communication mode, 551

Fuzzification process, 887

Fuzzy Logic Closed-Loop Control System, 887, 889, 891, 893, 895, 897

Fuzzy logic controller (FLC), 887

Fuzzy sets, 888

G

General Purpose Timer Module Initializations, 713

General Purpose Timers CCP pins, 712

General Purpose Timers signals, 713

General-Purpose Timer Module (GPTM), 692, 789

Glitch Suppression in Multi-Master Configuration, 620

GPIO ADC Control (GPIOADCCTL) Register, 467, 469, 474

GPIO Alternate Function Select Register (GPIOAFSEL), 54, 435, 548

GPIO Analog Mode Select (GPIOAMSEL) Register, 449, 451, 473, 561, 571

GPIO Architecture, 47, 434, 548

GPIO Commit Register (GPIOCR), 51, 218, 519

GPIO Digital Enable (GPIODEN) Register, 449–450, 473, 561, 570

GPIO DMA Control Register (GPIODMACTL), 49

GPIO High-Performance Bus Control (GPIOHBCTL), 56, 215

GPIO Interrupt Both Edges Register (GPIOIBE), 51, 273

GPIO Interrupt Clear Register (GPIOICR), 52, 274

GPIO Interrupt Event Register (GPIOIEV), 51, 274

GPIO Interrupt Mask Register (GPIOIM), 51, 274

GPIO Interrupt Sense Register (GPIOIS), 51, 319

GPIO Lock Register (GPIOLOCK), 51

GPIO Masked Interrupt Status Register (GPIOMIS), 52, 274

GPIO Open Drain Select Register
(GPIOODR), 52
GPIO Raw Interrupt Status Register
(GPIORIS), 52, 274
GPIO Run Mode Clock Gating Control
Register (RCGCGPIO), 67
GPIOPinConfigure(), 523, 543, 609, 677, 680,
682, 687
GPIOPinRead(), 229–231, 312, 543
GPIOPinTypeGPIOInput(), 231, 251,
254, 543
GPIOPinTypeGPIOOutput(), 232, 235, 240,
251, 254, 310, 427, 609, 677, 680, 687,
800, 973
GPIOPinTypePWM(), 521, 543
GPIOPinTypeSSI(), 609, 677, 680
GPIOPinWrite(), 229–230, 235, 241, 312, 354,
427–428, 543–544, 609, 611, 677–678, 680,
688, 803, 974
GPTM Architecture, 693
GPTM Configuration Register (GPTMCFG),
704–705
GPTM Control Register (GPTMCTL),
704–705
GPTM Interrupt Clear Register (GPTMICR),
709–711
GPTM Interrupt Mask Register (GPTMIMR),
709–710
GPTM Masked Interrupt Status Register
(GPTMMIS), 709–711
GPTM Peripheral Properties Register
(GPTMPP), 709, 711
GPTM Raw Interrupt Status Register
(GPTMRIS), 709–711
GPTM Synchronize Register (GPTMSYNC),
709, 711
GPTM Timer A Interval Load Register
(GPTMTAILR), 704–705, 790
GPTM Timer A Match Register
(GPTMTAMATCHR), 704
GPTM Timer A Mode Register
(GPTMTAMR), 704–706
GPTM Timer A Prescale Match Register
(GPTMTAPMR), 704, 708
GPTM Timer A Prescale Register
(GPTMTAPR), 704, 707
GPTM Timer A Prescale Snapshot Register
(GPTMTAPS), 704, 708
GPTM Timer A Prescale Value Register
(GPTMTAPV), 708–709
GPTM Timer A Register (GPTMTAR), 708

GPTM Timer A Value Register (GPTMTAV),
708–709

H
Half-duplex, 551, 557–558, 646, 649, 669–670
Half-duplex communication mode, 551, 669
Half-Precision Floating Point Data, 928
Handler Mode, 21, 25, 32–33, 79
Handshake Packet, 746, 792
Hard Fault Status Register (HFAULTSTAT),
71
HardFault exception handler, 952,959, 971
Hibernate RTC Oscillator (RTCOSC), 71,
80, 226
High-range mode, 901–902
Host Negotiation Protocol (HNP), 749, 760
HWREG(x), 398–399, 406, 409, 416, 430, 682,
914, 917

I
I2C Interface Control Signals, 622
I2C Master Bus Monitor (I2CMBMON)
Register, 619
I2C Master Clock Low Timeout Count
Register (I2CMCLKOCNT), 625
I2C Master Configuration Register (I2CMCR),
613, 625–626
I2C Master Control/Status (I2CMCS) Register,
619, 621–622
I2C Master Data Register (I2CMDR),
613, 624
I2C Master Interrupt Clear Register
(I2CMICR), 622, 627
I2C Master Interrupt Mask Register
(I2CMIMR), 622, 626–627
I2C Master Masked Interrupt Status Register
(I2CMMIS), 626–627
I2C Master Raw Interrupt Status (I2CMRIS)
Register, 619, 622
I2C Master Slave Address Register (I2CMSA),
613, 623
I2C Master Timer Period Register
(I2CMTPR), 624, 626
I2C Module Architecture, 613
I2C Module Bus Configuration, 612
I2C Module High Speed Mode, 621
I2C Module Initializations, 630
I2C Slave ACK Control Register
(I2CSACKCTL), 613, 628
I2C Slave Control Status Register (I2CSCSR),
613, 622, 627–628

I2C Slave Data Register (I2CSDR), 613, 622, 628

I2C Slave Interrupt Clear Register (I2CSICR), 622, 629

I2C Slave Interrupt Mask Register (I2CSIMR), 622, 629

I2C Slave Masked Interrupt Status Register (I2CSMIS), 629

I2C Slave Own Address 2 Register (I2CSOAR2), 628

I2C Slave Own Address Register (I2CSOAR), 613, 627

I2C Slave Raw Interrupt Status Register (I2CSRIS), 629

I2CMasterBusBusy(), 639–640

I2CMasterBusy(), 639–641, 683

I2CMasterControl(), 639–641, 683–684

I2CMasterDataGet(), 639–640, 684

I2CMasterDataPut(), 639, 683

I2CMasterEnable(), 639, 641

I2CMasterErr(), 639–641

I2CMasterInitExpClk(), 639–640, 683

I2CMasterSlaveAddSet(), 641

I2CSCL, 612, 623, 626

I2CSDA, 612, 623, 630

ICode Bus, 28, 333, 335, 422

ICode interface, 19

IDentifier Extension (IDE), 806

Identify the DC Motor Dynamic Model, 876

Idiom Recognition, 198, 205–207, 243

Increment Rotary Encoder, 849–851, 908, 911

Incremental Position Encoder, 847

Incremental Sinusoidal Encoder, 847

Inline Assembler, 204, 243

Input Edge-Count Implementations, 719

Input Edge-Count Mode, 696, 699, 714–715, 789

Input Edge-Time Implementations, 721

Input Edge-Time Mode, 696, 700, 714–715, 789, 792

Instrumentation Trace Macrocell (ITM), 16, 19, 42–43, 78, 136, 363, 433

IntEnable(), 267, 306–307, 378, 536, 687, 838, 968

Inter-Integrated Circuit (I2C), 548, 611, 613–641

Intermission Frame Space (IFS), 807

Internal Read Only Memory (ROM), 351

Internal Temperature Sensor, 446, 456, 472, 479–480, 482

Interrupt Control and State Register (INTCTRL), 71

Interrupt Priority-Level Registers, 276

Interrupt Processing Unit (IPU), 34, 263

Interrupt Program Status Register (IPSR), 22

Interrupt Set Enable Registers, 269, 276–277, 280, 303, 313

Interrupt transfers, 746

Intrinsic Functions, 91, 198, 200–202, 243

IQMath Library, 145, 147–149

Isochronous transfers, 746, 768, 770

L

Lazy save/restore, 927–928

Lazy State Preservation Active, 941

Lazy State Preservation Enable, 941

LCD Controller SPLC780, 573–575, 580, 583

LCD Initialization Process, 578, 581

LCD Module TC1602A, 574

Linear encoders, 847

Linguistic variables, 888

Little endian, 334, 373–374, 387, 396, 401, 421

LM45 temperature sensor, 476

LMFlash Programmer, 144–145, 147–149

Load-Store Architecture, 20

Logic Instructions, 158, 176

Lookup table, 887, 891–898

Low Frequency Internal Oscillator (LFIOSC), 45, 65, 71, 226

Low-range mode, 901–902

M

Main Oscillator (MOSC), 45–46, 63, 65, 71, 80, 226

Main Oscillator Control (MOSCCTL) Register, 63

Main Stack Pointer (MSP), 21, 25, 33, 270

Mark and Space, 554

MCP2551 CAN High-Speed Transceiver, 838

MCP4922 DAC, 595–598, 602

MDK Core, 86–87, 90–91, 103, 153, 197, 221, 244

Media and FP Feature Register 0 (MVFR0), 937

Media and FP Feature Register 1 (MVFR1), 937

Membership functions, 887–888, 892, 898

MemManage exception, 952, 959, 961–962, 971–972

MemManage handler, 940–941, 952, 959

Memory access attributes, 333, 371–373, 952

Memory attributes, 34, 373, 952
Memory Barrier Instructions, 158, 194
Memory endianness, 333, 371, 373
Memory Management Fault Address Register
   (MMADDR), 71
Memory Management Fault Ready, 940–941
Memory Protection Unit (MPU), 951–952,
   954–974
Memory Regions, Types and Attributes, 953,
   969
Message pipe, 746
Micro Type, 743, 745
Micro-A, 72, 197, 743
Micro-B, 146, 743
Microcontroller Unit (MCU), 13, 39, 132, 152
MICROWIRE, 551, 555, 557, 559, 563, 566,
   571, 670
Mini Type, 743
Mini-A, 743, 745
Mini-B, 743
Miscellaneous Instructions, 158, 195, 201
Mitsumi 448 PPR Motor, 861–862
Modems, 554
MPU Control Register (MPUCTRL), 953–955,
   969–970
MPU Region Attribute and Size Alias
   Registers, 959
MPU Region Attribute and Size Register
   (MPUATTR), 954, 957, 969
MPU Region Base Address Register
   (MPUBASE), 954, 956, 969
MPU Region Number Register
   (MPUNUMBER), 954, 956, 969
MPU setup procedure, 959, 971–972
MPU Type Register (MPUTYPE), 953–954,
   959, 969
MPUDisable(), 965, 968, 974
MPUEnable(), 965, 967–968
MPUIntRegister(), 965, 968
MPUIntUnregister(), 965, 968
MPURegionCountGet(), 965–966
MPURegionDisable(), 965
MPURegionEnable(), 965, 967, 974
MPURegionGet(), 965
MPURegionSet(), 965–968, 971, 974
Multiplex, 646

N
Named Register Variables, 203
NaN value, 929, 931, 933
Negative acknowledgement (NAK) signal, 552

Nested Vectored Interrupt Controller (NVIC),
   16, 18, 34–35, 78–79, 263
Non Return to Zero (NRZ), 553, 808
Non-Maskable Interrupt (NMI), 35–36, 62,
   263, 913, 916, 954
NVIC Clear Enable Registers, 280
NVIC→IP[], 279, 321, 331, 717
NVIC→ISER[], 277, 717

O
One-Shot Timer Mode, 695, 707, 789
Open Source RTOS, 142–143, 353
Open Source Stacks, 142–143, 353
Open-loop control system, 850
Open-loop transfer function, 872
OTG Mode, 757–758, 764, 774, 776, 788

P
Pack Installer, 87, 97, 113–115, 153
Pad Control Registers, 52, 531
PendSV, 71, 264, 266, 271, 273, 278–279,
   283, 298
Periodic Timer Mode, 695–696, 714, 789
Peripheral Bus Bridge, 335
Phase Buffer Segment 1 (Phase 1), 820
Phase Buffer Segment 2 (Phase 2), 820
Phase Locked Loop (PLL), 45–46, 71, 80, 226
PID Closed-Loop Control System, 871, 873,
   875, 877–885
PID Tuner, 879–881
Port Control Register (GPIOPCTL), 49, 54, 79,
   218, 435, 548
Potentiometer VR2, 446, 475–476, 480, 486,
   533, 904, 908, 923, 926
Power-On Reset (POR), 59–60, 63
Precision Internal Oscillator (PIOSC), 69,
   80, 555
Primary Interrupt Mask (PRIMASK)
   Register, 262
Primary Mask (PRIMASK) Register, 23
Private Peripheral Bus (PPB), 6, 19, 29, 41,
   362, 951
Process Model, 877–878
Process Stack Pointer (PSP), 21, 25, 33
Program Flow Control Instructions, 158, 187
PROM, 2
Propagation Time Segment (Prop), 820
Pseudo assembly instructions, 160, 243
Pulse Width Modulator (PWM), 224
Pulses per revolution (PPR), 849, 861, 863, 911
PWM Comparators, 488

PWM Counter, 488, 493

PWM Enable Update Register (PWMENUPD), 505, 507

PWM Fault Condition Value Register (PWMFAULTVAL), 505

PWM Fault Source n Register (PWMFLTSRCn), 501

PWM Generator A Register (PWMnGENA), 494

PWM Generator B Register (PWMnGENB), 495

PWM generator block, 487–494, 498, 504–505, 509, 512, 515, 522, 526, 528

PWM Generator Block Comparator A Register (PWMnCMPA), 493

PWM Generator Block Comparator B Register (PWMnCMPB), 494

PWM Generator Block Control Register (PWMnCTL), 491

PWM Generator Block Count Register (PWMnCOUNT), 493

PWM Generator Block Load Register (PWMnLOAD), 493

PWM Generator Dead-Band Control Register (PWMnDBCTL), 496

PWM Generator Dead-Band Falling-Edge Delay Register (PWMnDBFALL), 497

PWM Generator Dead-Band Rising-Edge Delay Register (PWMnDBRISE), 497

PWM Implementations, 723

PWM Interrupt and Trigger Enable Register (PWMnINTEN), 498

PWM Interrupt Enable Register (PWMINTEN), 507–509

PWM Interrupt Status and Clear Register (PWMISC), 507, 509

PWM Master Control Register (PWMCTL), 503–504

PWM Mode, 696, 702, 714, 716, 789

PWM Module Architecture, 490, 502, 515

PWM Module Initialization, 513

PWM Output Enable Register (PWMENABLE), 505

PWM Output Fault Register (PWMFAULT), 505–506

PWM Output Inversion Register (PWMINVERT), 505–506

PWM Output Signals Generator, 489

PWM Peripheral Properties Register (PWMPP), 503, 505

PWM Principle, 487

PWM Raw Interrupt Status Register (PWMRIS), 507, 509

PWM related control signals, 510

PWM Run Mode Clock Gating Control (RCGCPWM) Register, 513

PWM Status Register (PWMSTATUS), 503, 505

PWM Timer Base Synchronous Register (PWMSYNC), 503–504

PWMDeadBandDisable(), 523

PWMDeadBandEnable(), 523

PWMGenConfigure(), 521, 543

PWMGenDisable(), 521

PWMGenEnable(), 521, 543

PWMGenIntClear(), 523

PWMGenIntRegister(), 523, 525

PWMGenIntTrigDisable(), 525

PWMGenIntTrigEnable(), 523, 525–526

PWMGenPeriodSet(), 521, 543

PWMIntDisable(), 525

PWMIntEnable(), 525–526

PWMOutputInvert(), 523

PWMOutputState(), 523–524, 543

PWMOutputUpdateMode(), 523

PWMPulseWidthSet(), 521, 543–544

Q

QEI Control Register (QEICTL), 852–853

QEI Initialization, 856

QEI Interfacing Signals, 856

QEI Interrupt Enable Register (QEIINTEN), 855

QEI Interrupt Status and Clear Register (QEIISC), 855

QEI Maximum, 854

QEI Maximum Position Register (QEIMAXPOS), 854

QEI Position Register (QEIPOS), 854

QEI Raw Interrupt Status Register (QEIRIS), 855

QEI Run Mode Clock Gating Control Register (RCGCQEI), 852

QEI Software Reset Register (SRQEI), 857

QEI Status Register (QEISTAT), 852, 854

QEI Timer Load Register (QEILOAD), 855

QEI Timer Register (QEITIME), 855

QEI Velocity Counter Register (QEICOUNT), 855

QEI Velocity or Speed Register (QEISPEED), 855

QEI velocity timer, 863

QEIConfigure(), 858
QEIDisable(), 858
QEIEnable(), 858, 867
QEIIntClear(), 860
QEIIntDisable(), 860
QEIIntEnable(), 859–860
QEIIntRegister(), 859–860
QEIIntStatus(), 860
QEIPositionGet(), 858
QEIPositionSet(), 858
QEIVelocityConfigure(), 859
QEIVelocityDisable(), 859
QEIVelocityEnable(), 859, 867
QEIVelocityGet(), 859
Quadrature Encoder Interface (QEI), 805,
    847, 849–869, 908

R
RC servo motor HXT900–9GR, 725
RCGCACMP register, 904, 907, 925
Read-Only Protection, 350–351
Real-Time Clock Timer Mode, 695, 699, 789
Receive FIFO (RxFIFO), 555, 564, 566,
    644, 651
Receive Message Objects, 815, 819,
    838–839, 911
Reduced Instruction Set Computing
    (RISC), 4, 15
Remote Transmission Request (RTR), 806
Repeated Start, 613–614, 618–619
Request To Send (RTS), 646–647
Response Time, 267, 306, 879–880
ROM Control Register (RMCTL), 354, 381
ROM Software Map Register (ROMSWMAP),
    354, 381
Rotary encoders, 847–849, 911
Run-Mode Clock Configuration (RCC)
    Register, 46, 68, 503–504, 513, 539
Run-Mode Clock Configuration 2 (RCC2)
    Register, 46

S
Sample Sequencers Initialization, 474
Saturation Instructions, 158, 191–192
Sensor Hub Library, 41, 142, 145, 196–197,
    286–287, 335, 351
Serial Communication Interface (SCI), 551
Serial Peripheral Interface (SPI), 40, 87, 551
Serial Shift Register 74VHCT595, 573,
    580–581, 586, 611, 673, 675, 679
Serial Wire Viewer (SWV), 16, 38, 129, 136

Session Request Protocol (SRP), 749, 760
Shift and Rotate Instructions, 158, 178
Sign field, 929–930, 933
Signed byte, 162, 164–165
Signed halfword, 162, 164, 166
Simplex, 646
Single-Packet Buffering, 750–751, 771
Single-Precision Floating Point Data, 930, 934
Sleep Mode Instructions, 158, 194
Software Driver (SD) Model, 213, 224, 238,
    243, 790
Software Packs, 86–88, 97, 103, 113–115, 153
Software Reset, 60–62, 356, 402, 407–411, 493,
    736–738, 742, 749, 754, 853, 858
Specific Intrinsic Functions, 198, 200, 202, 243
SSI Clock Configure Register (SSICC), 555
SSI Clock Prescale Register (SSICPSR), 555
SSI Control 0 Register (SSICR0), 555, 564
SSI Control 1 Register (SSICR1), 555, 564
SSI Control Signals, 560–562
SSI Data Register (SSIDR), 555, 564–565
SSI DMA Control Register (SSIDMACTL),
    556, 567, 569
SSI Interrupt Mask Register (SSIIM), 555,
    567–568
SSI Module Transmit/Receive Logic
    Control, 570
SSI Modules Initialization, 570
SSI Raw Interrupt Status Register (SSIRIS),
    555, 567, 569
SSI Status Register (SSISR), 555, 564–565, 567
SSIBusy(), 604–606, 611, 678, 680
SSIClockSourceGet(), 604
SSIClockSourceSet(), 604
SSIConfigSetExpClk(), 604, 606, 609, 677, 680
SSIDataGet(), 604, 606
SSIDataPut(), 604, 606, 611, 678, 680
SSIDataPutNonBlocking(), 604, 606
SSIDisable(), 604–605, 609, 677, 680
SSIEnable(), 604–605, 609, 677, 680
SSIIntClear(), 604, 607
SSIIntDisable(), 604, 607
SSIIntEnable(), 604, 607
SSIIntRegister(), 604, 607
SSIIntStatus(), 604, 607
SSInClk, 556–560, 562–563, 567, 570–572, 670
Stack Pointer Register (SPR), 21
Stalling Control, 752
Standard Type, 743–745
Start Of Frame (SOF), 734, 794
Status Packet, 746–747, 766, 792

Stellaris In-Circuit Debug Interface (ICDI), 5
Stream pipe, 746
SVCall, 36, 71, 266, 273, 283, 298
Symbolic definitions, 218
Synchronization Segment (Sync), 820
Synchronizing GP Timer Blocks, 696, 703
Synchronous Serial Interface (SSI), 224, 548,
    551–609, 642, 669
Synchronous Serial Interface Run Mode Clock
    Gating Control (RCGCSSI) Register, 566
SysCtlClockSet(), 226, 235, 240, 250, 254, 800,
    843, 915, 917
SysCtlDelay(), 226, 229, 235, 241, 865
SysCtlPeripheralEnable(), 226–227, 235, 309,
    379, 542–543, 609, 677, 680, 682, 686–687,
    800, 802, 835, 973
SysCtlPWMClockSet(), 521, 542
System Control Block (SCB), 6, 19, 67, 70,
    265, 937
System Control Register (SYSCTRL), 70
System Control Space (SCS), 19, 29, 35, 41, 70,
    268, 362, 953
System Handler Control and State Register
    (SHCSR), 952
System Handler Control and State Register
    (SYSHNDCTRL), 70
System Timer SysTick, 6, 18, 69
SysTick Control and Status (STCTRL)
    Register, 69
SysTick Current Value (STCURRENT)
    Register, 69
SysTick Reload Value (STRELOAD)
    Register, 69

T
TB6612FNG driver, 516
tCANBitClkParms, 834–836
tCANIntStsReg, 834–835
tCANMsgObject, 834–835, 837, 841–843,
    845–846, 915, 917
tCANStsReg, 834–835
Texas Instruments Synchronous Serial, 563, 670
Thread Mode, 21, 25, 32–33, 70, 79, 940–941
Thumb instruction set, 156, 160, 196
Thumb State, 23, 33, 37, 156, 270
Thumb-2 technology, 156, 196, 204, 244
Timer A Control group, 693
Timer A Status group, 693
Timer B Control group, 693
Timer B Status group, 693
TimerConfigure(), 727

TimerControlEvent(), 727
TimerControlLevel(), 727
TimerControlTrigger(), 727
TimerEnable(), 727, 732
TimerIntClear(), 730–732
TimerIntEnable(), 730–732
TimerIntRegister(), 730, 732
TimerIntStatus(), 730–731
TimerLoadGet(), 727
TimerLoadGet64(), 727
TimerLoadSet(), 727, 729
TimerLoadSet64(), 727, 730
TimerMatchGet(), 727
TimerMatchGet64(), 729
TimerMatchSet(), 727, 729
TimerMatchSet64(), 729
TimerPrescaleGet(), 727
TimerPrescaleMatchGet(), 729
TimerPrescaleMatchSet(), 729
TimerPrescaleSet(), 727
TimerRTCEnable(), 727
TimerValueGet(), 729
TimerValueGet64(), 729–730
TivaWare™ Boot Loader, 41, 80, 196–197,
    351, 363
TivaWare™ Driver Libraries, 362
TivaWare for C Series suite, 142
TivaWare Software Package (TWSP), 297,
    306, 313–314, 316, 318–321, 403
tMsgObjType, 834–835, 837
Token Packet, 746–748, 792
Trace Port Interface Unit (TPIU), 20, 42–43,
    130, 135, 363, 433
Transmit FIFO (TxFIFO), 555, 564, 566,
    644, 651
Transmit Message Objects, 812, 838, 912

U
UART API functions, 664, 665, 669, 672,
    686
UART Clock Configuration (UARTCC)
    Register, 643, 650
UART Control Register (UARTCTL), 651
UART Data Register (UARTDR), 643,
    651, 654
UART DMA Control (UARTDMACTL)
    Register, 644, 649, 656–657
UART Flag Register (UARTFR), 644, 648,
    651, 655
UART Fractional Baud Rate Divisor
    (UARTFBRD) Register, 643, 650

UART Integer Baud Rate Divisor (UARTIBRD) Register, 643, 650

UART Interrupt Clear Register (UARTICR), 644, 648, 656–657

UART Interrupt FIFO Level Select (UARTIFLS) Register, 644, 648, 655–656

UART Interrupt Mask (UARTIM) Register, 644, 648, 656

UART Line Control Register (UARTLCRH), 651, 653

UART Masked Interrupt Status (UARTMIS) Register, 644, 656–657

UART Module Control Signals, 658

UART Module Initializations, 659

UART Raw Interrupt Status (UARTRIS) Register, 644, 648, 655–656

UART Receive Status/Error Clear Register (UARTRSR/UARTECR), 643, 651, 653

UART Serial IR (SIR) Support, 649

UARTBreakCtl(), 665

UARTCharGet(), 665, 667, 688

UARTCharGetNonBlocking(), 665, 667

UARTCharPut(), 665, 667, 687

UARTCharPutNonBlocking(), 665

UARTCharsAvail(), 665, 667, 688

UARTClockSourceGet(), 665

UARTClockSourceSet(), 665

UARTConfigSetExpClk(), 665–666, 687

UARTDisable(), 665, 687

UARTDMAEnable(), 665–666

UARTEnable(), 665–666, 687

UARTFIFOLevelSet(), 665, 667, 687

UARTIntClear(), 665, 668, 688

UARTIntDisable(), 665

UARTIntEnable(), 665, 668, 687

UARTIntRegister(), 665, 667, 687

UARTIntStatus(), 665, 668, 688

UARTParityModeSet(), 665

UARTSpaceAvail(), 665, 667

Unified Assembly Language (UAL), 160

UniFlash, 145, 147–149

Universal Asynchronous Receivers/ Transmitters (UARTs), 548, 643, 645–667

Universal Serial Bus (USB) Controller, 691, 743, 745, 747–787

Unsigned byte, 162–165, 245

Unsigned halfword, 162, 164, 166

USB API Functions, 780, 788, 801

USB Control Pins Configurations, 774

USB Device Related Registers, 762–763

USB FIFO Related Registers, 762, 765, 770–771

USB Host Related Registers, 762–763

USB Host/Device Related Registers, 762, 764–766, 768

USB Hubs, 756

USB Implementers Forum (USB-IF), 745

USB initializations, 774

USB Interrupt Related Registers, 762, 771

USB Module Control Signals, 760

USB On-The-Go (OTG), 744, 757

USB physical layer interface (PHY), 752

USB PID numbers, 747

USB RESET, 753, 757, 765–766

USB0EPEN signal, 774–775

USB0PFLT signal, 774

USBClockDisable(), 781

USBClockEnable(), 781

USBDevAddrSet(), 781, 802

USBDevConnect(), 781, 803

USBDevEndpointConfigSet(), 781, 802

USBDevEndpointDataAck(), 782

USBDevEndpointStatusClear(), 782, 784–785

USBDevMode(), 782

USBDevSpeedGet(), 782

USBEndpointDataAvail(), 784

USBEndpointDataGet(), 784–785

USBEndpointDataPut(), 785

USBEndpointDataSend(), 785

USBEndpointDataToggleClear(), 785, 802–803

USBEndpointStatus(), 782, 784–785

USBFIFOAddrGet(), 786

USBFIFOConfigGet(), 786

USBFIFOConfigSet(), 785–786, 803

USBFIFOFlush(), 786

USBFrameNumberGet(), 786

USBHostAddrSet(), 783, 803

USBHostEndpointConfig(), 783, 803

USBHostEndpointDataAck(), 783

USBHostEndpointStatusClear(), 783–785

USBHostMode(), 783

USBHostPwrDisable(), 783

USBHostRequestIN(), 783

USBHostRequestINClear(), 783

USBHostRequestStatus(), 783

USBHostReset(), 783

USBIntEnableControl(), 786–787

USBIntEnableEndpoint(), 786

USBIntRegister(), 787

USBIntStatusControl(), 787

USBIntStatusEndpoint(), 787

USBModeConfig(), 781
USBModeGet(), 781
USBOTGMode(), 788
USBOTGSessionRequest(), 788
USBPHYPowerOff(), 783–784
USBPHYPowerOn(), 783

V
Vector Table, 19, 34, 37, 43, 70–71, 263, 269–270, 277, 282, 295, 362–363, 951
Vector Table Offset Register (VTOR), 19, 270
Velocity capture, 851, 857, 859, 867
Virtual COM Ports, 75
Voltage Reference Negative (VREFN), 471
Voltage Reference Positive (VREFP), 471

W
Wait-for-Trigger Mode, 695, 699, 789
Watchdog Interrupt Clear Register (WDTICR), 737
Watchdog Masked Interrupt Status Register (WDTMIS), 737
Watchdog Raw Interrupt Status Register (WDTRIS), 737
Watchdog Timer 0 (WDT0), 60, 733
Watchdog Timer 1 (WDT1), 60, 733, 740
Watchdog Timer Architecture, 734
Watchdog Timer Control Register (WDTCTL), 735–736
Watchdog Timer Load Register (WDTLOAD), 735–736

Watchdog Timer Lock Register (WDTLOCK), 736
Watchdog Timer Module Initializations, 738, 789
Watchdog Timer Run Mode Clock Gating Control (RCGCWD) Register, 738
Watchdog Timer Test Register (WDTTEST), 736–737
Watchdog Timer Value Register (WDTVALUE), 735–736
WatchdogEnable(), 740, 742, 800
WatchdogIntClear(), 742, 800
WatchdogIntEnable(), 742, 800
WatchdogIntRegister(), 742
WatchdogIntStatus(), 742
WatchdogLock(), 741
WatchdogLockState(), 741, 800
WatchdogReloadGet(), 741
WatchdogReloadSet(), 741–742, 800
WatchdogResetEnable(),741–742, 800
WatchdogRunning(), 740
WatchdogStallEnable(), 741
WatchdogUnlock(), 741
WatchdogValueGet(), 741
Write Key, 342–344, 385–386

X–Z
XOFF signal, 552
XON signal, 552
Z-channel, 847
Zero-Length OUT data packet, 752